International Directory of
COMPANY
HISTORIES

International Directory of

COMPANY HISTORIES

VOLUME 120

Editor

Tina Grant

ST. JAMES PRESS
A part of Gale, Cengage Learning

GALE
CENGAGE Learning

Detroit • New York • San Francisco • New Haven, Conn • Waterville, Maine • London

International Directory of Company Histories, Volume 120

Tina Grant, Editor

Project Editor: Miranda H. Ferrara

Editorial: Virgil Burton, Donna Craft, Peggy Geeseman, Julie Gough, Hillary Hentschel, Sonya Hill, Keith Jones, Matthew Miskelly, Lynn Pearce, Laura Peterson, Paul Schummer, Holly Selden

Production Technology Specialist: Mike Weaver

Imaging and Multimedia: John Watkins

Composition and Electronic Prepress: Gary Leach, Evi Seoud

Manufacturing: Rhonda Dover

Product Manager: Jenai Drouillard

For product information and technology assistance, contact us at
Gale Customer Support, 1-800-877-4253.
For permission to use material from this text or product,
submit all requests online at **www.cengage.com/permissions.**
Further permissions questions can be emailed to
permissionrequest@cengage.com

Gale
27500 Drake Rd.
Farmington Hills, MI, 48331-3535

LIBRARY OF CONGRESS CATALOG NUMBER 89-190943
ISBN-13: 978-1-55862-787-1
ISBN-10: 1-55862-787-1

This title is also available as an e-book
ISBN-13: 978-1-55862-802-1   ISBN-10: 1-55862-802-9
Contact your Gale, a part of Cengage Learning sales representative for ordering information.

BRITISH LIBRARY CATALOGUING IN PUBLICATION DATA
International directory of company histories, Vol. 120
Tina Grant
33.87409

Printed in Mexico
1 2 3 4 5 6 7 14 13 12 11

Contents

Preface

The St. James Press series *The International Directory of Company Histories* (*IDCH*) is intended for reference use by students, business people, librarians, historians, economists, investors, job candidates, and others who seek to learn more about the historical development of the world's most important companies. To date, *IDCH* has profiled more than 11,320 companies in 120 volumes.

INCLUSION CRITERIA

Most companies chosen for inclusion in *IDCH* have achieved a minimum of US$25 million in annual sales and are leading influences in their industries or geographical locations. Companies may be publicly held, private, or nonprofit. State-owned companies that are important in their industries and that may operate much like public or private companies also are included. Wholly owned subsidiaries and divisions are profiled if they meet the requirements for inclusion. Entries on companies that have had major changes since they were last profiled may be selected for updating.

The *IDCH* series highlights 25% private and nonprofit companies, and features updated entries on approximately 35 companies per volume.

ENTRY FORMAT

Each entry begins with the company's legal name; the address of its headquarters; its telephone, toll-free, and fax numbers; and its web site. A statement of public, private, state, or parent ownership follows. A company with a legal name in both English and the language of its headquarters country is listed by the English name, with the native-language name in parentheses.

The company's founding or earliest incorporation date, the number of employees, and the most recent available sales figures follow. Sales figures are given in local currencies with equivalents in U.S. dollars. For some private companies, sales figures are estimates and indicated by the abbreviation *est*. The entry lists the exchanges on which the company's stock is traded and its ticker symbol, as well as the company's NAICS codes.

Entries generally contain a *Company Perspectives* box which provides a short summary of the company's mission, goals, and ideals; a *Key Dates* box highlighting milestones in the company's history; lists of *Principal Subsidiaries, Principal Divisions, Principal Operating Units, Principal Competitors*; and articles for *Further Reading*.

American spelling is used throughout *IDCH*, and the word "billion" is used in its U.S. sense of one thousand million.

SOURCES

Entries have been compiled from publicly accessible sources both in print and on the Internet such as general and academic periodicals, books, and annual reports, as well as material supplied by the companies themselves.

CUMULATIVE INDEXES

IDCH contains three indexes: the **Cumulative Index to Companies**, which provides an alphabetical index to companies profiled in the *IDCH* series, the **Index to Industries**, which allows researchers to locate companies by their principal industry, and the **Geographic Index**, which lists companies alphabetically by the country of their headquarters. The indexes are cumulative and specific instructions for using them are found immediately preceding each index.

SPECIAL TO THIS VOLUME

This volume of *IDCH* contains entries on Ron Jon Surf Shop, the world's largest supplier to surfing enthusiasts, and BCP Imports LLC, maker of Silly Bandz.

SUGGESTIONS WELCOME

Comments and suggestions from users of *IDCH* on any aspect of the product as well as suggestions for companies to be included or updated are cordially invited. Please write:

The Editor
International Directory of Company Histories
St. James Press
Gale, Cengage Learning
27500 Drake Rd.
Farmington Hills, Michigan 48331-3535

St. James Press does not endorse any of the companies or products mentioned in this series. Companies appearing in the *International Directory of Company Histories* were selected without reference to their wishes and have in no way endorsed their entries.

Notes on Contributors

Gerald E. Brennan
Writer and musician based in Germany.

M. L. Cohen
Novelist, business writer, and researcher living in Paris.

Ed Dinger
Writer and editor based in Bronx, New York.

Paul R. Greenland
Illinois-based writer and researcher; author of three books and former senior editor of a national business magazine; contributor to *The Encyclopedia of Chicago History*, *The Encyclopedia of Religion*, and the *Encyclopedia of American Industries*.

Robert Halasz
Former editor in chief of *World Progress* and *Funk & Wagnalls New Encyclopedia Yearbook*; author, *The U.S. Marines* (Millbrook Press, 1993).

Evelyn Hauser
Researcher, writer and marketing specialist based in Germany.

Frederick C. Ingram
Writer based in South Carolina.

Christina M. Stansell
Writer and editor based in Louisville, Kentucky.

Frank Uhle
Ann Arbor-based writer, movie projectionist, disc jockey, and staff member of *Psychotronic Video* magazine.

Ellen D. Wernick
Writer and editor based in Florida.

List of Abbreviations

€ European euro
¥ Japanese yen
£ United Kingdom pound
$ United States dollar

A

AB Aktiebolag (Finland, Sweden)
AB Oy Aktiebolag Osakeyhtiot (Finland)
A.E. Anonimos Eteria (Greece)
AED Emirati dirham
AG Aktiengesellschaft (Austria, Germany, Switzerland, Liechtenstein)
aG auf Gegenseitigkeit (Austria, Germany)
A.m.b.a. Andelsselskab med begraenset ansvar (Denmark)
A.O. Anonim Ortaklari/Ortakligi (Turkey)
ApS Amparteselskab (Denmark)
ARS Argentine peso
A.S. Anonim Sirketi (Turkey)
A/S Aksjeselskap (Norway)
A/S Aktieselskab (Denmark, Sweden)
Ay Avoinyhtio (Finland)
ATS Austrian shilling
AUD Australian dollar
Ay Avoinyhtio (Finland)

B

B.A. Buttengewone Aansprakeiijkheid (Netherlands)
BEF Belgian franc

BHD Bahraini dinar
Bhd. Berhad (Malaysia, Brunei)
BND Brunei dollar
BRL Brazilian real
B.V. Besloten Vennootschap (Belgium, Netherlands)
BWP Botswana pula

C

C. de R.L. Compania de Responsabilidad Limitada (Spain)
C. por A. Compania por Acciones (Dominican Republic)
C.A. Compania Anonima (Ecuador, Venezuela)
C.V. Commanditaire Vennootschap (Netherlands, Belgium)
CAD Canadian dollar
CEO Chief Executive Officer
CFO Chief Financial Officer
CHF Swiss franc
Cia. Compagnia (Italy)
Cia. Companhia (Brazil, Portugal)
Cia. Compania (Latin America [except Brazil], Spain)
Cie. Compagnie (Belgium, France, Luxembourg, Netherlands)
CIO Chief Information Officer
CLP Chilean peso
CNY Chinese yuan
Co. Company
COO Chief Operating Officer
Coop. Cooperative

COP Colombian peso
Corp. Corporation
CPT Cuideachta Phoibi Theoranta (Republic of Ireland)
CRL Companhia a Responsabilidao Limitida (Portugal, Spain)
CZK Czech koruna

D

D&B Dunn & Bradstreet
DEM German deutsche mark (W. Germany to 1990; unified Germany to 2002)
Div. Division (United States)
DKK Danish krone
DZD Algerian dinar

E

E.P.E. Etema Pemorismenis Evthynis (Greece)
EBIDTA Earnings before interest, taxes, depreciation, and amortization
EC Exempt Company (Arab countries)
Edms. Bpk. Eiendoms Beperk (South Africa)
EEK Estonian Kroon
eG eingetragene Genossenschaft (Germany)
EGMBH Eingetragene Genossenschaft mit beschraenkter Haftung (Austria, Germany)
EGP Egyptian pound

Ek For Ekonomisk Forening (Sweden)
EP Empresa Portuguesa (Portugal)
ESOP Employee Stock Options and Ownership
ESP Spanish peseta
Et(s). Etablissement(s) (Belgium, France, Luxembourg)
eV eingetragener Verein (Germany)
EUR European euro

F

FIM Finnish markka
FRF French franc

G

G.I.E. Groupement d'Interet Economique (France)
gGmbH gemeinnutzige Gesellschaft mit beschraenkter Haftung (Austria, Germany, Switzerland)
GmbH Gesellschaft mit beschraenkter Haftung (Austria, Germany, Switzerland)
GRD Greek drachma
GWA Gewerbte Amt (Austria, Germany)

H

HB Handelsbolag (Sweden)
HF Hlutafelag (Iceland)
HKD Hong Kong dollar
HUF Hungarian forint

I

IDR Indonesian rupiah
IEP Irish pound
ILS Israeli shekel (new)
Inc. Incorporated (United States, Canada)
INR Indian rupee
IPO Initial Public Offering
I/S Interesentselskap (Norway)
I/S Interessentselskab (Denmark)
ISK Icelandic krona
ITL Italian lira

J

JMD Jamaican dollar
JOD Jordanian dinar

K

KB Kommanditbolag (Sweden)
KES Kenyan schilling

Kft Korlatolt Felelossegu Tarsasag (Hungary)
KG Kommanditgesellschaft (Austria, Germany, Switzerland)
KGaA Kommanditgesellschaft auf Aktien (Austria, Germany, Switzerland)
KK Kabushiki Kaisha (Japan)
KPW North Korean won
KRW South Korean won
K/S Kommanditselskab (Denmark)
K/S Kommandittselskap (Norway)
KWD Kuwaiti dinar
Ky Kommandiitiyhtio (Finland)

L

L.L.C. Limited Liability Company (Arab countries, Egypt, Greece, United States)
L.L.P. Limited Liability Partnership (United States)
L.P. Limited Partnership (Canada, South Africa, United Kingdom, United States)
LBO Leveraged Buyout
Lda. Limitada (Spain)
Ltd. Limited
Ltda. Limitada (Brazil, Portugal)
Ltee. Limitee (Canada, France)
LUF Luxembourg franc
LYD Libyan dinar

M

mbH mit beschraenkter Haftung (Austria, Germany)
Mij. Maatschappij (Netherlands)
MUR Mauritian rupee
MXN Mexican peso
MYR Malaysian ringgit

N

N.A. National Association (United States)
N.V. Naamloze Vennootschap (Belgium, Netherlands)
NGN Nigerian naira
NLG Netherlands guilder
NOK Norwegian krone
NZD New Zealand dollar

O

OAO Otkrytoe Aktsionernoe Obshchestve (Russia)
OHG Offene Handelsgesellschaft

(Austria, Germany, Switzerland)
OMR Omani rial
OOO Obschestvo s Ogranichennoi Otvetstvennostiu (Russia)
OOUR Osnova Organizacija Udruzenog Rada (Yugoslavia)
Oy Osakeyhtiö (Finland)

P

P.C. Private Corp. (United States)
P.L.L.C. Professional Limited Liability Corporation (United States)
P.T. Perusahaan/Perseroan Terbatas (Indonesia)
PEN Peruvian Nuevo Sol
PHP Philippine peso
PKR Pakistani rupee
P/L Part Lag (Norway)
PLC Public Limited Co. (United Kingdom, Ireland)
PLN Polish zloty
PTE Portuguese escudo
Pte. Private (Singapore)
Pty. Proprietary (Australia, South Africa, United Kingdom)
Pvt. Private (India, Zimbabwe)
PVBA Personen Vennootschap met Beperkte Aansprakelijkheid (Belgium)
PYG Paraguay guarani

Q

QAR Qatar riyal

R

REIT Real Estate Investment Trust
RMB Chinese renminbi
Rt Reszvenytarsasag (Hungary)
RUB Russian ruble

S

S.A. Sociedad Anónima (Latin America [except Brazil], Spain, Mexico)
S.A. Sociedades Anônimas (Brazil, Portugal)
S.A. Société Anonyme (Arab countries, Belgium, France, Jordan, Luxembourg, Switzerland)
S.A. de C.V. Sociedad Anonima de Capital Variable (Mexico)
S.A.B. de C.V. Sociedad Anónima Bursátil de Capital Variable (Mexico)

S.A.C. Sociedad Anonima Comercial (Latin America [except Brazil])

S.A.C.I. Sociedad Anonima Comercial e Industrial (Latin America [except Brazil])

S.A.C.I.y.F. Sociedad Anonima Comercial e Industrial y Financiera (Latin America [except Brazil])

S.A.R.L. Sociedade Anonima de Responsabilidade Limitada (Brazil, Portugal)

S.A.R.L. Société à Responsabilité Limitée (France, Belgium, Luxembourg)

S.A.S. Societe Anonyme Syrienne (Arab countries)

S.A.S. Societá in Accomandita Semplice (Italy)

S.C. Societe en Commandite (Belgium, France, Luxembourg)

S.C.A. Societe Cooperativa Agricole (France, Italy, Luxembourg)

S.C.I. Sociedad Cooperativa Ilimitada (Spain)

S.C.L. Sociedad Cooperativa Limitada (Spain)

S.C.R.L. Societe Cooperative a Responsabilite Limitee (Belgium)

S.E. Societas Europaea (European Union Member states

S.L. Sociedad Limitada (Latin America [except Brazil], Portugal, Spain)

S.N.C. Société en Nom Collectif (France)

S.p.A. Società per Azioni (Italy)

S.R.L. Sociedad de Responsabilidad Limitada (Spain, Mexico, Latin America [except Brazil])

S.R.L. Società a Responsabilità Limitata (Italy)

S.R.O. Spolecnost s Rucenim Omezenym (Czechoslovakia

S.S.K. Sherkate Sahami Khass (Iran)

S.V. Samemwerkende Vennootschap (Belgium)

S.Z.R.L. Societe Zairoise a Responsabilite Limitee (Zaire)

SAA Societe Anonyme Arabienne (Arab countries)

SAK Societe Anonyme Kuweitienne (Arab countries)

SAL Societe Anonyme Libanaise (Arab countries)

SAO Societe Anonyme Omanienne (Arab countries)

SAQ Societe Anonyme Qatarienne (Arab countries)

SAR Saudi riyal

Sdn. Bhd. Sendirian Berhad (Malaysia)

SEK Swedish krona

SGD Singapore dollar

S/T Salgslag (Norway)

Soc. Sociedad (Latin America [except Brazil], Spain)

Soc. Sociedade (Brazil, Portugal)

Soc. Societa (Italy)

Sp. z.o.o. Spólka z ograniczona odpowiedzialnoscia (Poland)

Ste. Societe (France, Belgium, Luxembourg, Switzerland)

Ste. Cve. Societe Cooperative (Belgium)

T

THB Thai baht

TND Tunisian dinar

TRL Turkish lira

TTD Trinidad and Tobago dollar

TWD Taiwan dollar (new)

U

U.A. Uitgesloten Aansporakeiijkheid (Netherlands)

u.p.a. utan personligt ansvar (Sweden)

V

V.O.f. Vennootschap onder firma (Netherlands)

VAG Verein der Arbeitgeber (Austria, Germany)

VEB Venezuelan bolivar

VERTR Vertriebs (Austria, Germany)

VND Vietnamese dong

VVAG Versicherungsverein auf Gegenseitigkeit (Austria, Germany)

W – Z

WA Wettelika Aansprakalikhaed (Netherlands)

WLL With Limited Liability (Bahrain, Kuwait, Qatar, Saudi Arabia)

YK Yugen Kaisha (Japan)

ZAO Zakrytoe Aktsionernoe Obshchestve (Russia)

ZAR South African rand

ZMK Zambian kwacha

ZWD Zimbabwean dollar

84 Lumber Company

1019 Route 519
Eighty Four, Pennsylvania 15330-2813
U.S.A.
Telephone: (724) 222-8600
Fax: (724) 222-1078
Web site: http://www.84lumber.com

Private Company
Incorporated: 1956
Employees: 4,500
Sales: $1.35 billion (2009)
NAICS: 444110 Home Centers; 444190 Other Building
    Materials Dealers

■■■

84 Lumber Company is a family-run company that provides building materials and services to professional contractors. The company operates over 280 stores across the United States that sell a variety of building materials including lumber, plywood, insulation, trim, flooring, siding, drywall, decks, roofing, skylights, doors and windows, and items for kitchen and bath construction. 84 Lumber's sales, which topped out at $3.92 billion in 2006 have fallen dramatically as a result of the housing and mortgage crisis in the United States. The company has closed stores in response to the weak housing market. Maggie Hardy Magerko, daughter of founder Joseph A. Hardy III, remains president of 84 Lumber.

COMPANY ORIGINS

The history of 84 Lumber is primarily the story of entrepreneur Joseph A. Hardy III. After military service in World War II and earning a degree in industrial engineering at the University of Pittsburgh, Hardy went to work for the family jewelry company, Hardy & Hayes. Although proving to be a top salesman, at the age of 31 he left to start his own business, entering the building materials supply business at the suggestion of a friend. In 1952 he started Green Hills Lumber, which fared so well that by 1956 Hardy partnered with his two younger brothers and a friend to build a new cash-and-carry lumberyard at a location that would be convenient to home builders in the tri-state area of Pennsylvania, West Virginia, and Ohio.

The property on which Hardy settled was located near a small town 20 miles south of Pittsburgh called Eighty Four. The town, at least according to the most likely of many competing legends, was named in honor of Grover Cleveland's presidential election in 1884. In any case, Hardy liked the sound and decided to name his new lumberyard after the small town. The number 84 would provide the basis for the company's marketing and graphics for the next 50 years.

Hardy's business philosophy consisted primarily of keeping things simple. He soon became renowned for his frugal approach to sales and management. As he built more stores, he continued to pay cash for land and facilities that, typically, had no heating or air conditioning systems since that would have increased overhead costs. Hardy's example sent a message to company employees, whom he preferred to call "associates" in order to foster a sense of family working toward a common goal. The plain, no-frills stores conveyed the company's commitment to keeping costs down for its target market of skilled do-it-yourselfers and small contractors.

Hardy continued as owner and president of 84 Lumber for almost 30 years, working in the lumberyards, visiting each store, and talking with the associates. Although he strove to maintain his image as a small town, small business owner, his interests were diversifying during this time. He acquired real estate in several states and began collecting artwork, including paintings by Norman Rockwell, Pablo Picasso, and Andy Warhol. In 1983 Hardy spent $170,000 to purchase an English lord's title and an additional $58.1 million to acquire and renovate Nemacolin, a 550-acre retreat in southeastern Pennsylvania. Hardy's daughter Maggie took charge of the resort, which soon featured a spa, five restaurants, and a golf course.

EXPANDING AND DIVERSIFYING: 1980–90

While Hardy focused on new interests and enterprises, the character of 84 Lumber changed as the stores began to stock nonlumber items in order to compete with such home improvement superstores as Home Depot, which were taking market share away from lumberyards. The company also ordered a 200-store expansion. Rapid expansion and diversification of products, however, resulted in a drop in earnings from $52 million in 1987 to less than half of that two years later.

Hardy responded by slowing his expansion plans and even closing some stores. Furthermore, Hardy's oldest son, Joe Hardy Jr., who had served as executive vice president and had run the company for several years, was found to be in the early stages of multiple sclerosis. When his father decided that his son was not up to the task of running the company, Joe Jr. left in anger to run

his own real estate development company. A rapid succession of top executives at 84 Lumber ensued, and the company continued to lose its focus, targeting "yuppie" consumers rather than its traditional market of contractors and do-it-yourselfers.

In 1990 chief operating officer Jerry Smith joined 84 Lumber. In an effort to refocus the company, he drafted a mission statement clarifying the goals and values of the company and communicating its character to associates, vendors, and consumers. The mission statement said, in part, that "84 Lumber is dedicated to being the low-cost provider of lumber and building products to residential builders, residential remodelers, and dedicated do-it-yourselfers, while adding value to our products through trained, knowledgeable and motivated associates." The company further hoped to gain an edge through personalized service, inventory maintenance and competitive prices, and growth and strong leadership. Associates began carrying laminated business card-sized copies of the mission statement in their pockets, and messages posted throughout company buildings and in an employee newsletter reminded associates of company goals and plans.

MODERNIZING: 1990–92

In 1991 Hardy reclaimed a more active role as head of the company and designated his daughter Maggie Magerko as his heir-apparent to the company presidency. He halted the expansion plans and recommitted the company's merchandising efforts to the lumber business. However, the increasing number of home improvement superstores was still an impediment to 84 Lumber's growth. Hardy's response was to diversify into do-it-yourself home and kitchen design centers. In 1991, 84 Lumber opened 24 new kitchen design centers, which featured state-of-the-art computer technology for designing kitchens and baths.

In its approach to materials purchasing, 84 Lumber opted to switch to a centralized system for its hundreds of lumberyards during this time. The company had tried unsuccessfully to implement such a system in the mid-1970s, but had quickly returned to regional and store purchasing. Regional buying had allowed more market awareness since inventory could be tailored to the specific store in response to customer demand and new markets. This splintered purchasing structure, however, also meant loss of bulk-buying power. Furthermore, the lack of coordination with company headquarters also meant dead inventory in stores and wide discrepancies in prices each region or store paid for its products.

When company management decided to institute centralized purchasing, it also moved operations, ac-

KEY DATES

1956: Company is founded.
1964: Company expands to 15 stores.
1992: Maggie Hardy Magerko is named president.
1994: Company reaches $2 billion in annual sales.
1998: International Sales Division is added.
1999: 84 Plus store format is introduced.
2000: Company opens 35 new stores and revamps 50 existing stores to meet its new 84 Plus format.
2006: Sales reach $3.92 billion.
2009: Company continues to shutter stores; sales fall to $1.35 billion.

counts payable, and sales from the store and regional levels and centralized them at company headquarters. A team of purchasing managers was formed from former store managers familiar with operations at the store level. Purchasing managers developed expertise in specific product categories. Vendors had not been in the habit of making site visits to 84 Lumber stores, but with the new arrangement, they were encouraged to train 84 Lumber sales associates and aid them in merchandising. Stores adopted vendor suggestions for improving efficiency.

The company also invested in new computer technology to upgrade communications and information management, so that each night, daily sales data from each store could be sent to the company headquarters by telephone modem. This daily information became the basis for purchasing. The operations department could now keep in close communication with each store through biweekly bulletins and telephone calls twice a day. The company made communication with store managers a priority, making sure that they were kept up-to-date on any changes or additions to product lines. Despite the centralization of many functions, company executives maintained that store managers and associates still had significant input into product and promotion decisions.

The company continued to purchase wood in the United States and in Canada. About one-third of its stores were served by railroad, some with direct rail service right to the yard. Other 84 Lumber stores were supplied through reload centers, where freight from a rail car was loaded onto trucks or further rerouted by rail. This latter practice allowed the company to reduce inventory at a single 84 yard by splitting railcar loads among several yards rather than sending an entire carload to one yard. The reload centers also allowed the company to send both lumber and plywood to its lumberyards. A reload center in Aurora, Illinois, served 84 Lumber lumberyards as far east as Ohio and as far south as St. Louis, Missouri; Charleston, West Virginia; and Charlotte, North Carolina.

In 1992, 84 Lumber launched a new concept titled 84 Affordable Homes Across America, a line of do-it-yourself homebuilding kits. Hardy was willing to double the company's long-term debt to $80 million to back the new enterprise, which consisted of 30 home models in a price range of $39,900 to $59,900 (not including the cost of the lot). Included in the price were all the supplies necessary for the structure itself as well as the costs of excavation, plumbing, wiring, and heating.

SUCCESS UNDER MAGERKO'S LEADERSHIP: 1992–99

In 1991 Hardy turned over 40 percent of the 84 Lumber stock to Magerko. She was named president the following year. At 27 years old, she faced a tough challenge replacing her father. She had no college degree and her only management experience was at the Nemacolin Woodlands Golf, Spa, and Conference Center. Hardy maintained, however, that Magerko, the youngest of his five children, displayed more of an aptitude and interest in business than her older siblings. In fact, since the age of five she had spent time with her father on the job and over the years accompanied Hardy at new store openings and on-site inspections. She worked for a time in her early 20s at the Bridgeville, Pennsylvania, store to become familiar with everyday operations at 84 Lumber.

Magerko was not afraid to wield her power. She terminated a number of managers that her father had brought in to run the company. She had been unhappy with their buttoned-down look and attitude, which conflicted with the traditional 84 Lumber shirts everyone else wore at headquarters. The following year, the 84 Lumber Company pursued an extensive training and development program, requiring every associate to attend the "84 University" program to learn about new products and sharpen their sales skills. In 1992, 84 Lumber opened a new management training center and dormitory in Eighty Four, Pennsylvania, and throughout the year store managers and other employees from all over the country attended three-day training sessions.

Under Magerko, 84 Lumber reached the $1 billion plateau in annual sales. Much of the success was due to a renewed commitment to contractor sales, which at 25 percent of the company's business would climb over the ensuing five years to account for 75 percent. The purchasing executives also anticipated a shortage of materials in 1993 and took steps to make sure that 84 Lumber had inventory. Many of its competitors were left short. Building on this success, Magerko would lead 84 Lumber to record-breaking sales for the next six years, topping $1.8 billion in 1999.

In 1998, 84 Lumber established an International Sales Division to export building materials, including complete home packages. Shipping primarily from the Port of Baltimore, the company supplied nine countries located in Europe, Asia, and South America. In the first year, the company totaled $300,000 in sales. The following year saw even better results, as international sales reached $2.7 million, or a 900 percent increase over the previous year.

In 1999 the company also took major steps to increase its domestic business. 84 Lumber introduced a new design center called Maggie's Building Suggestions Showroom, a 17,000-square-foot facility located in Pittsburgh. The interactive center, geared toward homeowners, builders, designers, and architects, featured a showroom with hundreds of home products and decor, as well architectural consulting services, multimedia conference rooms, and staff designers.

In 1999, 84 Lumber opened two Installed Sales Centers and announced plans to open several more. The centers would then support outlets on a regional basis. Builders would be able to leave blueprints, materials list, sketches, or just ideas at a local 84 Lumber Store, which would then forward the information to the Installed Sales Center, which would estimate the materials and cost. Within 48 hours a delivery could be made to a contractor's site. The company also instituted a 30-day price guarantee that allowed builders to lock in a price and take delivery as needed without incurring any extra charges.

Perhaps the biggest change was the introduction of its new "84 Plus" store, which was a radical departure from the company's traditional warehouse approach. The 20,000-square-foot, consumer-friendly units devoted half of their space to a hardware store that offered an expanded line of supplies and a showroom that showcased kitchen, bath, door, and window displays.

Growth continued to be at the forefront of 84 Lumber's strategy during the early years of the new millennium. During 2000 the company opened 35 new stores and revamped 50 existing stores to meet its new 84 Plus format. In addition, two new component plants opened that assembled roof and floor trusses as well as wall panels. The two facilities served the Nashville, Tennessee, and Kings Mountain, North Carolina, regions.

The company expanded in 2001 and 2002 through store openings in new markets including Oklahoma. It also purchased some of the assets of bankrupt competitor Payless Cashways Inc., allowing it to enter new markets. In addition, the company bolstered its sales force to keep pace with expanding business. On April 3, 2002, the company opened 20 new stores. Company sales surpassed the $2 billion mark that year.

By refocusing its efforts on professional builders and contractors as well as expansion in the western United States, 84 Lumber had secured a position as the fifth-largest home improvement company in the United States by 2004. Its store count continued to increase at a steady pace and sales surpassed $3 billion that year. 84 Lumber's dramatic growth continued in 2005 when sales climbed to $3.92 billion. The company opened 40 new stores and five component plants that year including its 500th store, which was located in Chandler, Arizona.

50TH ANNIVERSARY IN 2006

The company celebrated its 50th anniversary in 2006 and set forth a strategy that included achieving $10 billion in sales by 2009 by opening new stores and component factories, growing its sales force, and targeting larger-scale customers. It also began closing underperforming stores and backed out of hosting a Professional Golfers' Association tournament. The six-year contract would have cost 84 Lumber $100 million and company management believed the cash would be better suited to fund its expansion efforts.

During the latter half of 2006, 84 Lumber began to experience and slowdown in sales growth brought on by a decline in the U.S. housing market. Most of its sales came from professional builders and as new home and existing home sales began to plummet, the company found itself needing to retool its strategy. Sales fell dramatically from 2006 through 2009, dropping by nearly 60 percent. During the crisis, 84 Lumber closed approximately 100 stores and also left the Idaho and Wisconsin markets during 2010. The company was also forced to trim its workforce.

Much of the decline during this period was due to the bursting of what analysts called the housing bubble. Home prices in the United States had increased dramatically between 2000 and 2006 and mortgage requirements became less stringent. Homebuyers were offered subprime mortgage loans and adjustable rate mortgages with low introductory interest rates. This practice, however, left many homebuyers unable to pay their mortgages when interest rates were raised and home values began to fall. The number of foreclosures began to skyrocket and the housing market found itself in crisis.

The ensuing economic recession in the United States was felt across the globe. Unemployment rates rose and consumer confidence waned. The U.S. government launched the Federal Housing Tax Credit for first-time homebuyers in 2009 in an attempt to bolster home sales. Meanwhile, 84 Lumber was left scrambling to shore up profits. Most of its sales stemmed from new home construction. During 2009 there were 553,800 new housing starts. In comparison, there had been 2.4 million new residential homes under construction in 2005.

The company's revenues were hit hard during the downturn. Sales in 2009 were $1.35 billion, down from $2.1 billion secured in 2008. While 84 Lumber continued to close underperforming stores and trim costs, president Maggie Hardy Magerko believed the company was positioned for success in the years to come as the housing market rebounded. Indeed, even though its aggressive expansion plans were shelved, the company remained the largest privately held building material retailer in the United States.

Wendy J. Stein
Updated, Ed Dinger; Christina M. Stansell

PRINCIPAL COMPETITORS

HD Supply Inc.; Lowe's Companies Inc.; Stock Building Supply Inc.

FURTHER READING

Aeppel, Timothy. "The Favorite." *Wall Street Journal*, April 24, 1997, p. A1.

"Business Brisk at 84 Lumber Co.'s New Convenience Store Prototype." *Do-It-Yourself Retailing*, April 1999, p. 23.

Carlo, Andrew M. "A Family of Thousands." *Home Channel News*, January 1, 2006.

Grant, Tim. "84 Lumber Closes 10 Stores in 10 States." *Pittsburgh Post-Gazette*, March 18, 2010.

———. "84 Lumber's 2009 Sales Plunge." *Pittsburgh Post-Gazette*, February 5, 2010.

Johnson, Walter F. "Life at 84 Lumber." *Do-It-Yourself Retailing*, February 1992.

Lindeman, Teresa F. "84 Lumber Explains Blueprint for Future." *Pittsburgh Post-Gazette*, May 10, 2006.

———, "Loans Give 84 Lumber Breathing Room." *Pittsburgh Post-Gazette*, April 22, 2008.

Schlesinger, Allison. "84 Lumber Builds Upon Success by Changing with Times." *Patriot-News*, April 4, 2004.

Actes Sud S.A.

BP 90038
Arles, F-13633 Cedex
France
Telephone: (+33 04) 90 49 86 91
Fax: (+33 04) 90 96 95 25
Web site: http://www.actes-sud.fr

Private Company
Incorporated: 1978 as Actes Sud SARL
Employees: 150
Sales: EUR 70 million ($89 million) (2008)
NAICS: 511130 Book Publishers

■ ■ ■

Actes Sud S.A. is one of France's most respected independent publishing houses. Based in Arles in the south of France, Actes Sud has built up an impressive catalog of best-selling titles, and a world-class stable of French and international authors. The company publishes more than 400 books per year, including fiction and literature, nonfiction, children's books, photography, and comic books.

In addition to the Actes Sud imprint, the company's holdings include Babel, a publisher of high-quality pocketbooks; Sindbad, specializing in Arabic literature and subjects; children's books specialists Actes Sud Junior and Thierry Magnier; Photo Poche, an innovative series of photography books in pocketbook format; Actes Sud BD, an award-winning comic books publisher; nonfiction publisher Solin; and Gaïa, specializing in Scandinavian literature.

Hubert Nyssen, founder of Actes Sud, remains the company's chairman. His daughter Françoise Nyssen, together with her husband Jean-Paul Capitani, and longtime family friend Bertrand Py, provide the company's day-to-day direction. Together they control more than 60 percent of Actes Sud through a holding company. French publishing giant Flammarion holds 27 percent of the group's capital. In 2008 Actes Sud reported sales of $89 million.

FROM MAPS TO BOOKS IN 1978

Belgian-born Hubert Nyssen built a highly successful career in advertising before realizing his dream to move to the south of France in 1969. Nyssen moved into a converted sheep barn in Paradou, a small village located in the Baux Valley near Arles. Nyssen initially set out to write novels. He had at the same time made the acquaintance of young geographer Jean-Philippe Gautier. In 1969 the pair established their own map-making studio, called ACTES, for Atelier de cartographie thématique et statistique.

Nyssen published his first novel in 1973, and went on to an impressive career as a novelist and poet. Nyssen's exposure to the publishing industry quickly inspired him to a new ambition to found his own publishing house. In 1977 Nyssen, then approaching 50, decided that the time had come to realize this ambition, telling *Le Nouvel Observateur*: "It was my last chance."

Nyssen turned over operation of the cartography company to Gautier and created Actes Sud. The new publishing house initially focused on nonfiction, and in

KEY DATES

1969: Hubert Nyssen and Jean-Philippe Gautier establish ACTES, a mapmaking company.

1977: Nyssen creates Actes Sud in order to launch publishing operations.

1978: Actes Sud incorporates as an independent company.

1985: Actes Sud signs Paul Auster and Nina Berberova.

1987: Actes Sud makes its first acquisition, of Éditions Papiers; the company opens its capital to outside investors.

1995: Actes Sud launches a youth imprint, Actes Sud Junior.

2006: Actes Sud publishes the first novel in Stieg Larsson's Millennium Trilogy.

2009: Actes Sud's total sales volume surpasses 1.3 million books.

1978 succeeded in publishing its first work, *La Campagne Inventée*, by Michel Marié and Jean Viard. Soon after, Nyssen incorporated the company as Actes Sud SARL. The publishing house then became a separate business from the original ACTES cartography firm.

Actes Sud initially met with skepticism, and even outright hostility, from the extremely Paris-centric French publishing world. Nyssen persevered, however, overcoming obstacles such as the distribution of his books by handling this operation himself. Future books were financed on the basis of cash generated by published work, enabling the young business to avoid debt.

MOVING TO ARLES IN 1983

Nyssen was soon joined by the trio that was to help him build Actes Sud into one of France's most respected publishing houses. Nyssen's daughter, Françoise, who had studied microbiology before pursuing a career as a city planner in Paris, moved to Arles to join Actes Sud in 1979. There she met Jean-Paul Capitani, a local businessman with interests in sheep farming and wine growing. Capitani, who later married Nyssen, became Actes Sud's financial manager. Around this time Bertrand Py, then preparing a master's thesis in literature, joined the company as well, becoming its editorial director.

By this time Actes Sud had branched out into literature, publishing its first fiction title in 1980. The

novel, *Pierre pour mémoire*, by Anne-Marie Roy, benefited from Nyssen's background in advertising. Instead of adopting the standard format and plain covers traditionally used by the French publishing industry, Actes Sud adopted its own format, of 10 centimeters by 19 centimeters. The novel also featured artwork on the cover, a rarity at the time. As a result, the release caught the attention of France's media, and particularly of *Le Nouvel Observateur*. With a positive review in that magazine, the novel became an early success for the company.

By the end of 1980 Actes Sud had added another direction that was to become a company hallmark. That year the company published its first translation of a foreign novel, by the German writer Stig Dagerman. Seeking out relatively unknown and otherwise neglected international writers became a passion for Nyssen, who traveled widely in search of new talent.

BREAKTHROUGH IN 1985

Actes Sud moved into the city of Arles itself in 1983, after Capitani proposed that the company convert one of his family's properties into its headquarters. The site, called Le Méjan, developed into a cultural center in its own right, with its own cinema, and the opening of the company's first bookstore. The company continued developing its catalog, in 1984 celebrating the release of its 100th book, a novel by German writer Günter Grass.

The young publishing house's breakthrough came in 1985 with the signing of two previously unknown authors, Nina Berberova and Paul Auster. The success of both established Actes Sud not only as a force to be reckoned with in the French industry, but one with an increasingly international profile as well. As Françoise Nyssen told *Le Nouvel Observateur*: "Things took off like a rocket with them. Actes Sud was no longer simply an adventure, but a company." Their success also convinced France's major book distributors to handle the company's catalog.

With its novels selling briskly, Actes Sud took the next step in developing a foundation for a lasting business. The company then became determined to broaden its publishing business, expanding its range beyond literature. In 1987 the company acquired a struggling Paris-based publisher, Éditions Papiers, which specialized in publishing theatrical works. Actes Sud also opened a Paris press office that year. The company continued to serve as a pioneer in France, becoming one of the first in the country to adopt computer-based publishing technology. The company also brought its own lithography in-house during this time.

In order to fund these investments and to provide for its future financial stability, Actes Sud decided to open its capital to outside investors in 1987. For this the company created a holding company representing the interests of the Nyssens, Capitani, and Py, which guaranteed the company's independence with a 60 percent stake. The company then brought in a number of investors, including major French publisher Flammarion, which acquired a 27 percent stake in the company.

IN-HOUSE DISTRIBUTION IN 1991

By 1988 Actes Sud's catalog had topped its 500th title. The company branched out into the pocketbook market the following year, launching its own imprint, Babel. The new collection took a unique approach to the format, adopting a distinctive, high-quality design. Also in 1989, the company acquired a stake in Solin, a Paris-based publishing house established in 1984. Actes Sud later acquired full control of Solin, noteworthy for the often militant content of its catalog.

In 1991 Actes Sud broke with its distributor and instead installed its own in-house distribution team to handle its growing book list. This effort was eased by several new successes in the early 1990s, including Auster's *Leviathan*, awarded the Medici Prize for a foreign novel in 1993. The production of a film based on Berberova's novel *L'Accompagnatrice* and directed by Claude Miller further helped stimulate the company's sales.

Hubert Nyssen retired from an active role with the company in order to focus on writing. While Nyssen remained the company's chairman, Jean-Paul Capitani became the major force in deciding the company's further expansion. Capitani then led Actes Sud into a new diversification of its editorial policies, adding works focusing on photography and contemporary art, as well as other works on a diverse range of subjects, such as botany, landscaping, and others.

Actes Sud also added to its lineup of imprints through the middle of the 1990s. In 1995 the company launched its first youth titles, forming Actes Sud Junior. The company also acquired Arabic culture specialist Sindbad, founded by Pierre Bernard in 1972.

WINNING AWARDS IN THE NEW CENTURY

With more than 3,000 titles in its catalog, Actes Sud celebrated its 20th anniversary as one of France's leading independent publishers. The company had also been instrumental in breaking the Paris-centric nature of the publishing business, becoming the largest of a growing

number of publishing houses established throughout the country. Actes Sud itself moved beyond its Arles and Paris bases in 1998, buying up the Maupetit bookstore, the oldest in Marseille, located on that city's famed Canebière.

The Marseille store was followed by the acquisition of the Errance bookstore on Paris's Île St. Louis in 2000. The company added a second Paris bookstore, in the Théâtre du Rond Point, soon after. Actes Sud added a number of other imprints at the same time, including a stake in Éditions Jacqueline Chambon, in partnership with Le Rouergue, a Rodez-based publisher, in 2001. Both Le Rouergue and Jacqueline Chambon became wholly owned by Actes Sud in 2004. The company also added another imprint that year, Éditions Bleu de Chine.

The company celebrated a number of new successes in the new century. In 2002 Hungarian writer Imre Kertész, introduced to France by Actes Sud, was awarded the Nobel Prize for Literature. Just two years later, Elfriede Jelinek, discovered by Jacqueline Chambon, also won the Nobel Prize. Also that year, another Actes Sud author, Laurent Gaudé, won France's highest literary prize, the Priz Goncourt. The award, for Gaudé's *Le Soleil des Scorta*, propelled the novel to sales of more than 400,000 copies. This helped boost the company's total revenues to $35 million in 2005.

MILLENNIUM SUCCESS IN 2007

Actes Sud filled a major gap in its portfolio of imprints in 2005 with the launch of Actes Sud BD, specializing in the publishing of comic books and graphic novels. The imprint experienced quick success when its first title, *Une Histoire de Guerre*, by Gipi, won first prize at the annual Festival du BD in Angoulême that year. The company then reinforced its youth publishing operations with the purchase of Éditions Thierry Magnier. Also in 2005, the company acquired Les Éditions de l'Imprimerie Nationale, founded in 1973 as a successor to a publishing house originally established by royal decree under King François I.

Particularly significant for Actes Sud was the 2005 acquisition of a stake in Éditions Gaïä, a company focused on publishing Scandinavian literature. The purchase placed Actes Sud in position to negotiate the rights to a series of novels in the process of being edited in Sweden. Written by Stieg Larsson and known as the Millennium Trilogy, the three novels in the series became an instant international success.

Actes Sud, which published the first volume in 2006, shared strongly in that success. In 2009 the Millennium series claimed three spots among France's top 10 best sellers. In that year alone, the company sold more than 880,000 copies of the Larsson novels, boosting its total sales volume past 1.3 million books. While still a relatively small company, Actes Sud succeeded in capturing seven spots in the top 50 that year.

The company remained on the lookout for new expansion opportunities. In 2007 the company opened its third bookstore in Paris, in the Grande Hall de la Villette. This was followed by the addition of a bookstore in Calais, opened in 2009. Actes Sud also expanded its list of imprints that year, acquiring stakes in Éditions Texuel, Éditions Les Liens qui Libèrent, and Éditions André Versaille. In just over 30 years, Actes Sud had built up a catalog of more than 3,000 titles, including many of the world's most noteworthy authors. Under the direction of founders Françoise Nyssen, Jean-Paul Capitani, and Bertrand Py, Actes Sud looked forward to discovering new literary horizons in the future.

M. L. Cohen

PRINCIPAL DIVISIONS

Publishing; Distribution; Bookstores.

PRINCIPAL OPERATING UNITS

Actes Sud-Papiers; Babel; Solin; Sindbad; Actes Sud Junior; Photo Poche; Imprimerie Nationale; Actes Sud BD; Editions Thierry Magnier; Gaïa; André Versaille.

PRINCIPAL COMPETITORS

Editions Albin Michel S.A.; Editions Gallimard S.A.; Glenat Editions S.A.; Hachette Livre S.A.; La Martiniere Groupe S.A.; Les Editions Hatier S.N.C.; Vivendi S.A.

FURTHER READING

Casassus, Barbara. "French Publishers Help Rival." *Bookseller*, October 5, 2001, p. 10.

"Ces Éditeurs Abonnés aux Best-Sellers." *L'Expansion*, January 18, 2010.

Crignon, Anne. "Tel Père, Telle Fille." *Le Nouvel Observateur*, February 21, 2008.

Froumenty, Carole. "Les Éditions Actes Sud Éditeur de Laurent Gaudé, Paul Auster." *Suite101*, March 12, 2010.

Hennebelle, Isabelle. "Actes Sud: Le Livre en Toute Liberté." *L'Entreprise*, October 31, 2003.

Leménager, Grégoire. "La Saga Nyssen." *Le Nouvel Observateur*, February 21, 2008.

Lottman, Herbert. "Publishing without Paris." *Publishers Weekly*, September 14, 1992, p. 45.

———. "Route to Top Began with Maps." *Bookseller*, February 17, 2006, p. 16.

Riding, Alan. "From the Outside, a French Publisher Thrives." *New York Times*, April 23, 2005.

Aisin Seiki Co., Ltd.

2-1, Asahi-machi
Aichi
Kariya, 448-8560
Japan
Telephone: (81 566) 24-8239
Fax: (81 566) 24-8003
Web site: http://www.aisin.com

Public Company
Incorporated: 1943 as Tokai Aircraft Co., Ltd.
Employees: 73,213
Sales: ¥2,054.4 billion ($21.96 billion) (2010)
Stock Exchanges: Tokyo
Ticker Symbol: 7259
NAICS: 336312 Gasoline Engine and Engine Parts Manufacturing; 336322 Other Motor Vehicle Electrical and Electronic Equipment Manufacturing; 336330 Motor Vehicle Steering and Suspension Components (Except Spring) Manufacturing; 336340 Motor Vehicle Brake System Manufacturing; 336350 Motor Vehicle Transmission and Power Train Parts Manufacturing; 336399 All Other Motor Vehicle Parts Manufacturing; 337910 Mattress Manufacturing; 332321 Metal Window and Door Manufacturing; 333298 Sewing Machines (Including Household-Type) Manufacturing; 339113 Surgical Appliance and Supplies Manufacturing; 333415 Air Purification Equipment Manufacturing

■■■

Aisin Seiki Co., Ltd., is a leading international manufacturer and supplier of engine-related products, drivetrain-related products, brake and chassis-related products, and various other automotive parts. The company also manufactures laser technology, environmentally friendly vacuum pumps, and industrial cooling systems. Through its Creative Lifestyle Products division, Aisin sells beds, furniture, fabrics, medical instruments, gas-engine-driven heat-pump air conditioners, and housing equipment such as microcomputer controlled shutters and high-tech toilet seats. Overall, the company has over 150 subsidiaries that operate in North and South America, Europe, Asia, and Oceania. Aisin's automotive segment accounts for nearly 95 percent of company sales, while its creative lifestyle and energy and environment products make up the rest. It is the largest of the six companies making up the Aisin Group. Toyota Motor Corporation and Toyota Industries Corporation together own 30 percent of the firm.

FROM AIRPLANE ENGINES TO AUTO DRIVETRAINS: 1943–79

Aisin was founded in 1943 as Tokai Aircraft Company by Kiichiro Toyoda, the founder of the Toyota Group. Tokai Aircraft was founded to manufacture engine parts for World War II aircraft. In 1945, at the close of the war, Tokai Aircraft switched its production to sewing machines and automotive parts, both products that had been in short supply during the war.

After World War II, the Japanese economy grew steadily. The increase in individual consumption brought about a sharp rise in domestic demand, and business expanded. Aisin answered the increased demand for consumer production and worked consistently to improve efficiency in its factories, increase sales, and cut costs through rationalization. In 1949 Tokai Aircraft Company changed its name to Aichi Kogyo Company. In the 1950s and 1960s, Aisin's operations were confined to Japan. As part of the Toyota Group, Aisin grew steadily, supplying parts to its parent automotive company and continuing to produce sewing machines. This company then merged with Shinkawa Kogyo Co. Ltd. in 1965 to form Aisin Seiki Co. Ltd.

During 1969 and throughout the 1970s, the company pursued aggressive international growth. In 1969 Aisin reached a technical agreement for power steering gears with Zahnradfabrik Friedrichshafen of West Germany. Aisin-Warner Limited was also established as a joint venture in 1969.

Aisin U.S.A. was formed in 1970, and in 1971 Aisin Europe was established in Belgium. A technical agreement for bumper shock isolators was concluded with Menasco Manufacturing Company in the United States in 1972. The formation of Aisin (U.K.) Ltd. and Aisin (Australia) Pty. Ltd. also took place in 1972. The Liberty Mexicana subsidiary was formed in Mexico in 1973, and Aisin do Brasil was established in Brazil in 1974. The year 1977 saw the formation of Aisin Asia in Singapore, and in 1978 Aisin Deutschland was established in West Germany. In 1979 the Elite Sewing Machine Manufacturing Company was established in Taiwan as a joint venture.

CONTINUED GLOBAL GROWTH: 1980–95

Aisin U.S.A. was established to import aftermarket auto parts for imported cars, primarily Toyotas, in the United States, and also to import specially prepared aftermarket parts for U.S.-made automobiles. During 1988 Aisin made efforts to strengthen project development in the United States by separating the manufacturing division from Aisin U.S.A. and creating a new subsidiary, Aisin U.S.A. Manufacturing Company. Aisin America, Inc., was also established to control jointly both the manufacturing and sales divisions.

Managers of the automotive sector worked during the late 1980s to increase sales of automotive body products such as seat components, sunroofs, and electronic-control equipment for automatic transmissions. This increase contributed to an almost 10 percent sales growth in 1989. At that time, automotive body products were the largest single group of products Aisin Seiki offered, constituting about 25 percent of sales.

In 1990 Aisin U.S.A. imported twice as many parts for U.S. cars as for imported cars. At the same time, Aisin Seiki Company supplied a wide range of products worldwide through its network of 14 overseas subsidiaries and its branches in North America, Europe, Southeast Asia, and throughout the Pacific. In 1989 only 5 percent of Aisin's sales had been to export markets.

By 1990 Aisin's home and industrial and new business sectors were still very small in scale but growing rapidly. Through expanded sales of gas heat-pump air conditioners and beds, sales increased 14.2 percent in 1989. In the 1990s intensive research and development continued for new products such as cryocoolers, Stirling engines, and a supplemental drive unit for artificial human hearts.

Aisin continued its growth strategy throughout most of the 1990s, and expanded internationally as it had during the previous decade. Subsidiaries were created in Indonesia and Mexico, along with a brake system research and development center. In 1992 Aisin U.S.A. was merged with Aisin America to form Aisin World Corp. of America.

A FIRE AND ECONOMIC DISTRESS IN JAPAN: 1997–2000

A near disaster struck in 1997 when a fire destroyed an Aisin brake factory in Japan. The plant supplied Toyota with almost 90 percent of its major brake parts that were used in nearly all Toyota models. It was the only source for the tiny proportioning valve used in all Toyota cars. Overall, the fire cost Toyota $195 million and forced the carmaker to shut its 18 assembly factories in Japan for almost a week due to lack of parts.

The fire also threatened Aisin's supplier relationship with Toyota. In the case of Aisin, Toyota had been going against its policy of double-sourcing materials, in which the firm typically chose two suppliers to split orders evenly. In the long run, the fire did not change the company's alliance and Aisin proved its commitment to safety and quality when later that year its plants became QS9000 and ISO9001 certified.

During this same period, the economy in Japan was faltering, decreasing demand in Aisin's home country.

KEY DATES

1943: Kiichiro Toyoda establishes the Tokai Aircraft Company.

1945: Tokai begins manufacturing sewing machines and automotive parts.

1949: The firm changes its name to Aichi Kogyo Company.

1965: The company merges with Shinkawa Kogyo Co. Ltd. to form Aisin Seiki Co., Ltd.

1970: Aisin U.S.A. is formed.

1979: The Elite Sewing Machine Manufacturing Company is established in Taiwan.

1992: Aisin America merges with Aisin U.S.A. to create Aisin World Corp. of America.

1997: Fire destroys Aisin brake plant in Japan.

2001: Advics Co. Ltd. is established to oversee worldwide brake systems sales.

2006: Aisin introduces world's first front-wheel-drive eight-speed automatic transmission.

Domestic sales in 1999 fell to ¥747 billion, down from ¥766 billion in 1998. Aisin responded by cutting costs, restructuring various operations, and expanding into growth markets. By 2000 Aisin's domestic sales rebounded, growing to ¥847 billion and to ¥904 billion in 2001. Global net sales climbed to ¥1,128 billion in 2001.

Despite some improvement, the economy continued to be weak, and troubled Japanese banks needed to prop up their balance sheets. Many sold their shares in various companies within the Toyota Group. Toyota Motor Company bought up more shares of its four major suppliers, including Aisin Seiki. As a result, its stake in Aisin rose 2 percent to 24 percent. This tightened control occurred as General Motors and Ford were spinning off suppliers and other Japanese carmakers were selling the shares they held in their major suppliers.

JOINT VENTURES AND NEW INVESTMENTS: 2001–04

In 2001 Aisin created a joint venture with Toyota Motor Corp. along with Sumitomo Electric Industries Ltd. and Denso Corp. to form Advics Co. Ltd. Aisin owned 40 percent of the company and each of the other partners owned 20 percent. The new company was positioned to become the second-largest supplier of brake systems in the industry behind Robert Bosch GmbH. Advics'

projected global sales would reach $2 billion by 2005. Toyota was the new firm's largest customer.

This was a significant move for Toyota, which for years had opposed the industry trend toward less-expensive component systems. In the move toward modules and systems, Japanese automakers were helping their large suppliers merge into new entities, with the automakers selling their equity in the original suppliers. Toyota, seeing this as giving the suppliers too much control over the modules, decided to encourage its large suppliers to form joint ventures while keeping its equity stakes in its suppliers (and a small stake in the new ventures).

Meanwhile, Aisin management was strengthening its auto parts business. In 2001 it announced it would supply Ford Motor Co. with gas-electric hybrid systems. Aisin AW Co., owned jointly by Aisin Seiki and Toyota Motor Company, would produce the units. That same year, Nissan Motor sold Aisin Seiki its 23.4 percent stake in clutch manufacturer Exedy Corp. The purchase increased Aisin's share of the global original equipment market for clutches from 6 percent to 16 percent.

INCREASING GLOBAL PRODUCTION

Strategically, Aisin Seiki was also exploring ways to increase its global production efforts. During 2002 alone, the company made three investments to this end. One was a 50-50 joint venture with the Dutch firm Van Doorne Transmission to build CVT (continuous variable transmission) belts in Japan. Another was to have its European subsidiary, Aisin Europe SA, build a new factory in the Czech Republic to make water and oil pumps for car engines. A third was the announcement by Aisin World Corp. of America of a new plant to be built in Ontario, Canada, to produce windshield trim and belt moldings.

Such expansion continued over the next several years. Aisin doubled the size of its Thailand subsidiary to supply parts to Hino Motors Ltd., Isuzu Motors Ltd., and Mitsubishi Motors Corp. It expanded the plant in the Czech Republic to six times its original size and built a factory in Turkey. This brought Aisin's European auto facilities to four, with sites in Belgium and the United Kingdom. Aisin also built a plant in Mexico to produce doorframes for the Nissan Sentra and opened several more factories in China.

The company announced it would be supplying manual transmissions to Porsche for its newest 911 models as well as manufacturing the glass roof section of Toyota's Scion tC. In the fiscal year ending March 31, 2004, Aisin reported automotive parts sales of $15.5

billion. Toyota represented 66 percent of Aisin's sales, down from 73 percent the year before. *Automotive News* ranked Aisin No. 8 on its list of the top 100 global suppliers of original equipment auto parts sales for 2004. In 2005 Aisin acquired the ANSCO brand and began marketing its aftermarket merchandise under the Aisin name.

STRONG FOCUS ON RESEARCH AND DEVELOPMENT

Aisin Seiki's global expansion did not reduce its research and development efforts, in either automotive or other areas. In 2003 the company demonstrated a solar module comprising dye-sensitized solar cells. According to an article in *Forbes* in November of that year, the module was "more efficient than the best silicon versions and [could] be made for one-tenth the cost." By 2007 Aisin, working with Toyota, was exploring how to generate electricity by attaching the thin, lightweight panels to roofs of cars and houses.

Laser technology was another area of interest. Aisin's subsidiary IMRA America Inc., which was founded in 1990, specialized in ultrafast lasers. These were used for precision cutting in automotive manufacturing and medicine. By replacing individual components with fiber-optic cables, IMRA America brought laser costs down and reduced operational problems. In 2007 its technology was incorporated in the VisuMax eye surgery system.

On the purely automotive side, Aisin and its subsidiaries developed various innovative products, including an automatic parking system, rear-wheel-drive hybrid system, electronic stability control, an electric parking brake, and map-on-demand systems. In 2006 the company introduced the world's first front-wheel-drive (FWD) eight-speed automatic transmission. That year Aisin's research and development budget was $814 million. In 2007 the company spent $888 million for research and development.

By mid-decade Aisin's North American sales reached $2.4 billion, with over $1 billion of that from automakers other than Toyota. In fiscal year 2007, North American sales increased 12.5 percent, to $3.6 billion. Nevertheless, Asia was still Aisin's primary market, accounting for 73 percent of its total revenues of $20.6 billion. Early in 2007 Toyota became the world's largest carmaker.

A GLOBAL RECESSION AND TOYOTA RECALLS

In 2008 the global financial crisis and resulting credit freeze and increasing unemployment cut deeply into U.S. car sales. Over the next two years, Aisin worked to broaden its business base while cutting costs. Sales to Volkswagen AG increased 13 percent and the company introduced a lighter, more fuel-efficient FWD six-speed automatic transmission for small cars. Aisin also sold some of its brake business to Advics. On the nonautomotive side, Aisin's natural gas heat pump began selling in the United States under the name NextAire. Aisin saw annual global revenues reach $30.69 billion with an operating profit of $125 million.

By July 2009 two of the Big Three U.S. automakers (General Motors and Chrysler) had filed for bankruptcy and were being reorganized. Toyota's production in North America fell 45 percent through mid-2009 and Japanese exports and sales disintegrated. Aisin's annual revenue dropped 18 percent from the previous year, with an operating loss of $34.9 million.

In early 2010 Toyota recalled millions of cars for safety reasons and stopped producing certain models. These actions led to plant closings and layoffs among it suppliers, including Aisin Seiki. For fiscal year 2010, reported in March 2010, revenue was down 7.2 percent from 2009. Aisin continued to focus on expanding its auto parts business. This was especially true in Asia with the announcement that its Chinese affiliate would be adding lines to produce more manual clutches. A factory in Shanghai was preparing to double its production of an automatic transmission systems part. Structural reform was also announced within the Aisin Group. Looking to globalization and technological developments as key to its future success, Aisin attempted to weather the severe economic environment and maintain its strong position in the automotive sector.

Joan Harpham
Updated, Christina M. Stansell; Ellen D. Wernick

PRINCIPAL SUBSIDIARIES

Aisin Holdings of America Inc. (USA); Aisin World Corp. of America (USA); Aisin U.S.A. Mfg. Inc.; Aisin Electronics Inc. (USA); Aisin Drivetrain Inc. (USA); Aisin Automotive Casting Inc. (USA); IMRA America Inc. (USA); Intat Precision Inc. (USA); AW North Carolina Inc. (USA); Liberty Mexicana S.A. de C.V.; Aisin do Brasil Ltda.; Aisin Europe S.A. (Belgium); Aisin Asia Pte. Ltd. (Singapore); Siam Aisin Co. Ltd. (Thailand); Aisin Hongda Automobile Parts Co. Ltd. (China); Elite Sewing Machine Mfg. Co. Ltd. (Taiwan); Aisin Takaoka Co. Ltd.; Aisin Chemical Co. Ltd.; Aisin AW Co. Ltd.; Aisin Development Co. Ltd. Advics Co. Ltd.

Aisin Seiki Co., Ltd.

PRINCIPAL COMPETITORS

Continental AG; Delphi Automotive, LLP; Denso Corporation; Robert Bosch GmbH; TRW Automotive Holdings Corp.

FURTHER READING

"Aisin Seiki Co., Ltd, SWOT Analysis." *Datamonitor*, July 4, 2008.

Corcoran, Elizabeth, and Benjamin Fulford. "Bright Ideas." *Forbes*, November 24, 2003.

Ohnsman, Alan, et al. "The Humbling of Toyota." *Business-Week*, March 22, 2010.

Treece, James B. "Just Too Much Single-Sourcing Spurs Toyota Purchasing Review." *Automotive News*, March 3, 1997.

———. "Toyota Joins March toward Modules." *Automotive News*, February 18, 2002.

Wilson, Amy. "Japan Venture's Goal: Big 3 Brake Systems." *Automotive News*, March 18, 2002.

Allgemeine Baugesellschaft – A. Porr AG

Absberggasse 47
Vienna, A-1100
Austria
Telephone: (+43 50) 626-0
Fax: (+43 50) 626-1111
Web site: http://www.porr.at

Public Company
Founded: 1869 as Allgemeine österreichische Baugesell-
    schaft AG
Employees: 11,880
Sales: EUR 2.4 billion ($3.4 billion) (2009)
Stock Exchanges: Vienna
Ticker Symbol: POS
NAICS: 234110 Highway and Street Construction;
    233310 Manufacturing and Industrial Building
    Construction; Water, Sewer, and Pipeline Construc-
    tion; 234120 Bridge and Tunnel Construction;
    234930 Industrial Nonbuilding Structure Construc-
    tion; 234990 All Other Heavy Construction;
    233320 Commercial and Institutional Building
    Construction; 233220 Multifamily Housing
    Construction; 235990 All Other Special Trade
    Contractors; 562910 Remediation Services

■ ■ ■

Allgemeine Baugesellschaft – A. Porr AG (Porr) is one of
Austria's largest construction companies. Porr provides a
broad variety of construction and construction-related
services, including general contracting, civil engineering,
building, road and tunnel construction, environmental
technology, and renovation. The various specialized
services are performed by Porr's subsidiaries Porr Technobau und Umwelt AG (PTU), Porr Projekt und Hochbau AG (PPH), Teerag-Asdag AG (T-A), and Porr Solutions Immobilien- und Infrastrukturprojekte GmbH
(PS).

Headquartered in Vienna, the company has
branches in each of Austria's nine federal states. It also
serves markets in central and Eastern Europe, including
Germany, Poland, Switzerland, the Czech Republic,
Hungary, Slovakia, Romania, Croatia, Serbia, and other
states. In 2009 projects in Austria accounted for roughly
60 percent of Porr's revenues, projects in other countries
for approximately 40 percent. Austrian industrialist
Klaus Ortner holds a controlling interest in the
company. The Turkish Renaissance Group owns about
10 percent of Porr AG's ordinary shares.

RESHAPING VIENNA AND TRANSPORTATION INFRASTRUCTURE IN THE 19TH CENTURY

Porr's history began with the foundation of Allgemeine
österreichische Baugesellschaft AG (the General Austrian
Construction Corporation) in Vienna in March 1869.
Ten years earlier the Vienna city council had decided to
tear down the medieval walls and fortifications and the
glacis, an artificial slope of earth that surrounded the
city. The destruction created a large empty space in the
city center. However, large sums of capital were needed
to erect new buildings.

COMPANY PERSPECTIVES

The future is our tradition! It doesn't matter how demanding the technical challenges may be, how difficult the terrain or how complex the construction project, Porr infrastructure solutions are tailor-made to fit what people really need. It is only when a new motorway has made a journey faster and easier, when a residential site has provided security and comfort, when an office tower has contributed to a company's success, or when a power plant has ensured energy supply for thousands of people that Porr has really done its job. This is how the Porr Group has been building infrastructure for a better life for over 140 years. New directions, intelligent solutions and innovative ideas—that's Porr.

In 1869 Niederösterreichische Escomptegesellschaft, a private bank, initiated the establishment of Austria's first construction corporation. With the purpose of carrying out large construction projects that needed significant capital investment, the company had to be a joint stock corporation. After receiving a concession to establish the new entity, Niederösterreichische Escomptegesellschaft prepared the initial public offering and took on the role of the house bank for the construction company, which was named Allgemeine österreichische Baugesellschaft AG. On April 8, 1869, the shares for Allgemeine österreichische Baugesellschaft (AöB) were listed on the Vienna Stock Exchange. Among the first 120 or so shareholders were the city's prominent businesspeople and leading industrialists.

In the following decades AöB built several buildings on Vienna's new inner city circular boulevard which was named Ringstrasse, and 28 large apartment buildings. In 1870 AöB started upgrading the almost 100-mile-long horse-drawn railway line, between Linz and Ceske Budejovice in the Czech part of Austria-Hungary, to a steam locomotive driven railway. One year later, the company got involved in its first large infrastructure project, the regulation of the Danube River near Budapest. The project required a significant investment in special construction equipment.

The next major event that stirred a multitude of construction activities was the World Exposition in Vienna in 1873. AöB built seven exhibition pavilions, the hotel Britannia, and several other hotels, commercial, and residential buildings. The stock market crash of 1873, only a few days after the opening of the World

Exposition, caused a severe economic depression. However, despite many difficulties and critical situations, the company survived the dry spell.

AöB won many major contracts, including general construction as well as infrastructure projects. The company continued to build many structures in Vienna's city center, and participated in the construction of the city's metropolitan railway system. AöB also got involved in railway construction projects in the southern regions of the Austro-Hungarian Empire. In Croatia the company was engaged in building a new railway line connecting the two cities Rijeka and Karlovac. In the county of South Tyrol AöB built the Vintschgau railway line from Meran to Mals.

1907–27: DIVERSIFICATION, ACQUISITIONS, AND MERGER

In 1907 AöB established A. Porr Betonbau-Unternehmung Gesellschaft m.b.H., a subsidiary that specialized in innovative construction methods using reinforced concrete, a new technology at the time. Under the direction of construction engineer Arthur Porr, the company developed "Porr floors," which were built into several structures such as the War Ministry in Vienna. A second innovation of A. Porr Betonbau was the use of patented conical concrete piles instead of the usual wooden ones in the foundations of buildings.

In 1912 AöB bought a majority stake in Union-Baumaterialien-Gesellschaft (UBM), a manufacturer of construction materials. Two years later World War I broke out, and most civil construction projects were put on hold. One of the few exceptions was the construction of a new building for the National Bank in Vienna, which was finished by AöB in 1916. During the war UBM sold its brick manufacturing subsidiary and focused solely on real estate dealings. AöB built ammunition depots, aircraft hangars, barracks, and other structures for the military. One of the company's main projects was a large machinery hall for AEG in Vienna. Arthur Porr died in 1915 at age 43.

When the number of incoming contracts went down in the mid-1920s, AöB came under pressure to cut costs and to streamline the business. In the preceding years A. Porr Betonbau had grown significantly and the two companies had worked closely together on many construction projects. Consequently, the two companies were merged to form the new Allgemeine Baugesellschaft – A. Porr AG in 1927. In the same year Allgemeine Strassenbau-AG, a new road construction subsidiary, was established.

KEY DATES

1869: Allgemeine österreichische Baugesellschaft AG is founded and listed at the Vienna Stock Exchange.

1873: The company builds exhibition pavilions and hotels for the World Exposition in Vienna.

1908: Concrete construction subsidiary A. Porr Betonbau-Unternehmung Gesellschaft m.b.H. is founded.

1912: The company takes over construction materials manufacturer Union-Baumaterialien-Gesellschaft.

1927: Allgemeine österreichische Baugesellschaft is merged with A. Porr Betonbau and renamed Allgemeine Baugesellschaft – A. Porr AG.

1958: Porr commences work on a large dam construction project in Iran.

1984: The new subsidiary Porr International AG is founded.

2002: Industrial leadership is decentralized and transferred to the company's major subsidiaries.

2009: The Turkish Renaissance Group acquires a 10 percent stake in Porr AG.

CONTINUED GROWTH BEFORE AND DURING WORLD WAR II

In the 1930s Allgemeine Baugesellschaft – A. Porr, or Porr for short, became involved in a number of major infrastructure projects. The company participated in Austria's national road construction program, including the southern section of the Packer Strasse, a national highway near Klagenfurt, and the Carinthian section of the famous Alpine road Großglockner Hochalpenstraße. In connection with road construction, Porr also built bridges such as the Seebach Bridge near Villach, and another railway line connecting Feldbach and Bad Gleichenberg in Styria. Furthermore, the company got involved in hydroelectric power plant and industrial construction projects, and continued to build many structures in the country's capital.

After the occupation of Austria by German troops in 1938, Adolf Hitler, a native of Austria, declared its reunification with Germany, and the country was integrated into the Third Reich. The Nazis' massive investments in infrastructure development, housing programs, rearmament, and defense projects in Ostmark, as Austria was now called, prompted Porr's revenues to soar; the company's orders intake grew roughly fivefold between 1937 and 1939. The incoming cash flow, combined with special tax write-offs for new equipment purchases, meant the company was able to modernize its machinery.

However, Jewish Austrians, including major Porr shareholders Ottokar Stern and Siegfried Pick, were forced to give up their shares and to leave the company, while top management positions were filled with Nazi sympathizers. Immediately before and during World War II Porr was mainly involved in war-relevant industrial construction and infrastructure projects. For example, the company was involved in the construction of large manufacturing halls and airport structures, as well as in building or extending major highways, bridges, harbor installations, and waterways.

While the majority of the company's activities were carried out in Austria, Porr also established a subsidiary in German-occupied Slovakia, and it built roads, railways, industrial structures and defense installations in Yugoslavia, Italy, and France. Porr's workforce grew from roughly 700 in 1938 to 4,400 on average in 1941, and peaked at over 7,300 in August 1944, including over 2,300 foreign workers and about 3,900 prisoners of war who were assigned to the company by the German authorities. As the war went on, the shortage of qualified personnel, raw materials, and gasoline made it increasingly difficult to complete construction projects. On the other hand, the company lost a significant amount of machinery during the war. In the last days of World War II, Porr's central storage area in Vienna was heavily damaged.

After the end of the war, Porr came under Soviet control until the victorious Allied forces withdrew from Austria in 1953. Meanwhile, new legal entities had been established in Salzburg and in the Western district of Vienna to continue the company's work there. However, after the foreign troops left the country, Porr was reunited with the former parent company.

During the 1950s Porr benefited from the postwar reconstruction boom that swept over the country. In Vienna, the company rebuilt the State Opera House and Parliament structures that had been damaged or destroyed during the war. In the Alps, Porr was engaged in the construction of several hydroelectric power installations such as two dams at the foot of the Grossglockner, Austria's highest mountain. The company also participated in the extension of the Danube River. Most importantly, Porr got involved in several tunnel and gallery construction projects and was a driving force in developing cutting-edge technologies in that area.

In the 1960s and 1970s Porr continued to participate in many tunnel and hydropower construction projects in the Alps, which contributed an increasing share to the company's total revenues. Other infrastructure projects remained an important activity for Porr. The company had a leading role in building Austria's freeways and the Vienna Metro subway. During the same period the company began to take on larger projects as a general contractor. Porr erected several high rise office buildings in Vienna such as the Ring Tower at the Danube Canal, the Intercontinental Hotel facing the City Park, and the Vienna International Center where the United Nations had their Vienna office, as well as numerous other commercial and residential structures.

INTERNATIONAL EXPANSION
BEGINS 1958

The year 1958 marked the beginning of Porr's international activities after World War II. In that year the company received its first contract from the Iranian government for the construction of a large dam near Hamadan. In the following two decades, Porr built many more dams, railways, and bridges in Iran. With the Iranian Revolution of 1979 the company's activities in the country came to a sudden halt. However, during the 1960s and 1970s Porr had grown by leaps and bounds. In 1971 the company's annual sales exceeded ATS 1 billion for the first time.

To replace the lost business in Iran, Porr turned its sights back to Europe in the 1980s. The company built industrial structures in East Germany, the Austrian embassy, and the Oberhavel South Bridge in Berlin, as well as numerous tunnels in West Germany. In Hungary Porr set up a new airport building and a number of hotels in Budapest. More hotels were built by the company in Warsaw, Prague, Moscow, and St. Petersburg. After the dissolution of the socialist Eastern Bloc, Porr became particularly active in Poland.

Aside from these projects in Eastern Europe, Porr got involved in the construction of a new railway line in Algeria, and built a television center in Jordan in the 1980s. In 1990 the company took over a majority stake in the German construction firm Radmer Bau AG based in Munich, which was later transformed into the company's German subsidiary Porr Deutschland, and became also active in Switzerland. One of the most noteworthy projects in Austria was the construction of the Florido Tower, a circular office high rise in Vienna. Between 1987 and 1992 Porr's annual sales doubled, reaching ATS 10 million at the end of that period.

CONTINUING REORGANIZATION
AFTER 1980

In the 1980s Porr began to redesign its organization to better manage the company's various activities. In 1984 the company founded Porr International AG, a subsidiary for its business abroad. Five years later two additional subsidiaries were created: Porr Technobau AG for civil engineering and specialty construction, including tunnel, bridge, power plant, railway, and pipeline construction; and Porr Umwelttechnik AG which focused on environmental construction and engineering as well as remediation services. UBM focused increasingly on project and real estate development.

As the liberalization and globalization of the world economy progressed in the 1990s, and with Austria's joining of the European Union in 1995, Porr had to hold its ground against an increasing number of competitors. To further increase the flexibility of the company's organization, Porr strengthened its business units by decentralizing the operational management. In 2002 the power of decision making was transferred to the company's main subsidiaries while the parent company took on a management holding function.

A modified corporate structure was approved with specialty and environmental construction united in the new Porr Technobau und Umwelt AG (PTU), general and project construction carried out by Porr Projekt und Hochbau AG (PPH), and real estate development and management led by UBM Realitätenentwicklung AG (UBM). After Porr had acquired a controlling stake in Teerag-Asdag AG, a leading Austrian road and construction and civil engineering firm, in 2000, its own road construction division was united with Teerag-Asdag's and reorganized in the new subsidiary Teerag-Asdag (T-A).

A new subsidiary for the development of real estate and infrastructure projects, Porr Solutions Immobilien-und Infrastrukturprojekte GmbH (PS) was created in 2003. In the following year Porr AG gave up its controlling interest in UBM and lowered its stake in the company below 50 percent. Finally, Porr GmbH, a subsidiary established in 2005, handled all domestic construction projects, working closely together with the company's other divisions.

NEW PROJECTS AND A
STRATEGIC PARTNER

By 2005 Porr had become one of Austria's largest construction firms and was grossing over two billion euros annually. The company was active in 15 countries where more than one-fourth of total sales were generated. In 2005 the company received its first contract in Romania. Porr continued to secure large national and international contracts, with Eastern Europe driving the company's continued growth, and revenues from abroad reaching about 40 percent of total sales by 2009.

Major projects carried out by Porr in the second half of the decade included a new three-story terminal at Vienna Airport and the extension of the capital's U2 subway line; high-rise office buildings, such as the 80-meter-high Zagreb Tower in Croatia; major highway construction projects in Hungary; the 282-meter-long and 50-meter-high Nasenbachtal Bridge in the Eastern German Ore Mountains; the Wienerwald and Tauern tunnels in Austria; the Finne tunnel near Jena for the German railway; and sports stadiums in Klagenfurt and Salzburg. To secure the necessary financing, the company frequently issued corporate bonds. However, in the aftermath of the global financial crisis of 2008, Porr's sales and profits declined.

In 2009 Porr announced that it had entered a strategic partnership with the Ankara-based Renaissance Construction group. One year later Turkey's second-largest construction company (which was also active in Russia, Ukraine, Turkmenistan, Libya, Saudi Arabia, and other countries) acquired a 10.22 percent stake in Porr AG as part of a capital increase. Together with the new shareholder, Porr was hoping to gain access to new geographic markets in the Middle East and North Africa as a major step toward sustained future growth. In June 2010 the Austrian Ortner Beteiligungsverwaltung announced that it had acquired a controlling interest in Porr after Ortner had sealed a syndicate agreement with Porr shareholder B & C Baubeteiligungs GmbH following the exit of longtime Porr shareholder Vienna Insurance.

Evelyn Hauser

PRINCIPAL SUBSIDIARIES

Porr Technobau und Umwelt AG (PTU); Porr Projekt und Hochbau AG (PPH); Teerag-Asdag AG (T-A) (52.52%); Porr Solutions Immobilien- und Infrastrukturprojekte GmbH (PS); Porr GmbH; Porr Deutschland GmbH (Germany; 93.94%); Allgemeine Straßenbau GmbH (52.2%); Porr International GmbH; Wibeba Holding GmbH; Schotter- und Betonwerk Karl Schwarzl Betriebsgesellschaft m.b.H; Porr (Česko) a.s. (Czech Republic); Pražské silnicní a vodohospodárské stavby, a.s. (Czech Republic); Porr Épitési Kft. (Hungary); Porr (POLSKA) Spólka Akcyjna; Porr Suisse AG (Switzerland); Porr Construct S.R.L. (Romania); Porr Construction Holding GmbH (50%); UBM Realitätenentwicklung AG (UBM) (41.33%).

PRINCIPAL COMPETITORS

Bilfinger Berger AG; Hochtief AG; Skanska AB; Strabag Societas Europaea; Vinci S.A.

FURTHER READING

"Austria: Porr Looking for New Shareholders." *Presse*, June 18, 1999, p. 17.

"Austrian Porr Says Renaissance's Stake Not Increased." *M&A Navigator*, July 1, 2010.

Matis, Herbert, and Dieter Stiefel, *Mit der vereinigten Kraft des Capitals, des Credits und der Technik … Die Geschichte des österreichischen Bauwesens am Beispiel der Allgemeinen Baugesellschaft – A. Porr Aktiengesellschaft*. Vienna, Austria: Böhlau Verlag Gesellschaft m.b.H. und Co. KG, 1994.

"Ortner Holds 61 Percent in Porr after VIG's Exit." *APA Economic News Service*, June 11, 2010.

"Ownership Changes at Austrian Porr Continue." *ADPnews Austria*, June 11, 2010.

"Porr Boss in the Running for Siemens Top Job." *Austria Today*, June 14, 2010.

"Porr Reports Environmental Turnover up 38%." *Haznews*, August 1999.

"Porr with Lower Sales and Profits in 2009." *APA Economic News Service*, April 30, 2010.

Austevoll Seafood ASA

Alfabygget
Storebø, N-5392
Norway
Telephone: (+47 56) 18 10 00
Fax: (+47 56) 18 10 03
Web site: http://www.auss.no

Public Company
Founded: 1981 as Austevoll Havfiske AS
Employees: 6,250
Sales: $1.74 billion (2009)
Stock Exchanges: Oslo
Ticker Symbol: AUSS
NAICS: 112511 Finfish Farming and Fish Hatcheries;
    114111 Finfish Fishing; 311711 Seafood Canning;
    311712 Fresh and Frozen Seafood Processing

■ ■ ■

Austevoll Seafood ASA is an international pelagic fishery and seafood company based in Storebø, Norway. Pelagic fish live in the main waters of oceans or lakes, in contrast to fish that forage at sea bottoms or in coral reefs. Typical pelagic fish range from herrings, anchovies, blue whiting, and sardines to larger fish such as mackerel, bluefin tuna, and billfish. Austevoll has operations in Europe and South America. Its four main areas of activity are pelagic fishing; fish meal and fish oil production; the production of fish for human consumption, in particular canned and frozen fish; and salmon farming. Austevoll also has companies engaged in the sale and distribution of fish products.

The company's facilities for production of fish products for human consumption are based in Peru and Chile, the top two pelagic fishing nations in the world. The South American subsidiaries, FoodCorp S.A. in Chile and Austral Group S.A.A. in Peru, produce canned and frozen fish, primarily for sale in the Chilean and Peruvian domestic markets, but also in the United States, the European Union, Bolivia, Jamaica, and Africa. Austevoll's most important canned fish products are horse mackerel, sardines, tuna fish, salmon, and mussels. A relatively new segment of Austevoll's human consumption segment is the production of high-concentrate omega-3 oil by its subsidiary Epax AS in Norway.

Austevoll's fish meal and fish oil production, manufactured primarily as animal feed, is carried out by Welcon AS in Norway, the Austral Group in Peru, and FoodCorp in Chile. The firm's salmon farming operations are located in Norway and are performed by its subsidiary Veststar AS. Austevoll Seafood is committed to environmentally responsible fishing practices and has been honored with awards for its efforts in this area. The main shareholder in Austevoll Seafood is Laco AS, owned by Norway's Møgster family.

ORIGINS IN THE NORWEGIAN ARCHIPELAGO

Alf Møgster and his sons Ole Rasmus and Helge founded Austevoll Seafood ASA. The Møgsters, a family from the Austevoll Islands south of the Norwegian city of Bergen, had fished for generations in the North Sea. In 1981 they set up Austevoll Havfiske AS, a pelagic fishery and salmon farming operation. The business was a small one at first, confined to a single ship. The Møgster family was extremely entrepreneurial, however. They also established DOF ASA at the same time, which like Austevoll went on to become one of the leaders in its sector, supplying equipment for offshore and subsea oil production. The brothers split responsibility for the two companies. Helge Møgster took over the leadership of DOF while Ole Rasmus ran Austevoll.

Austevoll started its expansion to become one of the world's important pelagic fisheries in 1991 when it acquired a second fishing license and a second ship. Its catch was made up primarily of herring, mackerel, blue whiting, and capelin. That same year the Norwegian firm Cermaq ASA approached Laco AS, the Møgster family's holding company, and asked it to take over and run the Cermaq fishing fleet in Chile. The offer was an attractive one.

Chile, along with Norway, was one of the world's top five pelagic fishing nations. Austevoll Havfiske took over Cermaq's licenses and established Pacific Fisheries in Coronel, a seaport town in central Chile. Like Austevoll, Pacific Fisheries grew steadily during the 1990s, engaging in fishing, fish oil production, fish canning, and fish freezing.

Austevoll began to accelerate its rate of growth in the early years of the 21st century, systematically expanding the breadth of its core competencies. For example, in 2000 it enlarged both its fishing and farm-ing capacities by acquiring a 35 percent share in the Norwegian firm Br. Birkeland AS, a company that had two vessels fishing in the seas around Norway at the time. One year later, it purchased an additional 6.5 commercial fishing licenses for Norwegian waters. In 2001 it acquired Veststar AS. That company brought Austevoll increased salmon farming capacity with 27 new licenses.

INCREASED PRESENCE IN SOUTH AMERICA

Austevoll greatly solidified its presence on the Pacific coast of South America in 2002 when it acquired the Chilean company FoodCorp S.A., one of the largest pelagic fisheries in Chile. This acquisition soon gave Austevoll control of over 9 percent of Chile's southern horse mackerel fishing quotas. FoodCorp was operating five fishing vessels and two fish meal and fish oil factories at that time. A factory for frozen fish products was later added.

Two years later Austevoll set its sights on Chile's northern neighbor, Peru, the world leader in pelagic fishing. In 2004 Austevoll purchased the Peruvian firm Austral S.A.A. with two partners. It was a fairly large operation at the time, with 34 ships and six factories for the production of fish meal and fish oil, as well as a plant for processing frozen fish. Austevoll's share was approximately 28 percent.

In June 2006, after Austral had increased its production capacity with the addition of two canning facilities and another freezing plant, the Laco holding company bought out the partners in Austral, bringing its holdings to nearly 90 percent. Laco then transferred the company to Austevoll. The firm ultimately had control of 8 percent of the cargo hold capacity in Peru. Austevoll was also constantly working to acquire ad-ditional commercial fishing licenses in Chile.

ACQUISITIONS IN NORWAY

Austevoll and its affiliated companies undertook an extensive and complicated reorganization of the Norwegian fishing activities in the middle of the decade. In 2004, through the Møgster family's Laco group of holding companies, the Austevoll Havfiske AS subsidiary obtained a 31 percent holding in Welcon AS. The lead-ing producer of fish meal and fish oil in Norway, Wel-con had a history that extended back more than 120 years.

This marked Austevoll's entry into fish meal production in Norway. At the time of the acquisition Welcon was operating four large fish meal production facilities, with approximately a 60 percent share of the total Norwegian fish meal market. Austevoll took over Welcon completely in 2006, making it a wholly owned subsidiary.

In 2005 Austevoll acquired another company, Rong Laks. This acquisition increased Austevoll's salmon farming activities, bringing it 27 additional licenses, which were in turn taken over by the Veststar AS subsidiary. The growth was reflected in Austevoll's books at the end of 2006. Revenues reached a record high that year, climbing by 42 percent from 2004, from NOK 1.15 billion to NOK 2.72 billion. Austevoll produced some 58,000 tons of canned and frozen fish in 2006.

NEW LEADERSHIP AND A NEW FIRM

Austevoll underwent an important change in leadership in 2006, when another member of the Møgster family, Helge's 31-year-old son Arne, was named the company's CEO. Although young, Arne Møgster had spent nearly a decade working in various subsidiaries of the holding company Laco AS, learning the fishery, offshore supply, and shipbuilding sectors. He came to the new position from the Brazil office of Norskan AS, where he had worked since 2003. He took over the CEO post from his uncle, Ole Rasmus Møgster.

After the acquisitions of Welcon and Austral were completed in 2006, a new corporate entity was established, Austevoll Seafood ASA. A number of the various fishing companies were subsumed in the new company. Later that same year Austevoll Seafood was listed on the Oslo Stock Exchange. One of the first actions of the new firm after its creation was a letter of intent to take over 100 percent ownership of Epax AS, an acquisition that was completed a few months later in 2007.

Epax, based in Aalesund, Norway, was the world's leading supplier of ultra-pure, highly concentrated, marine-based omega-3 EPA/DHA fatty acids, a biological product that the body requires but is not able to make itself. The acquisition of Epax was Austevoll's first venture into the omega-3 sector.

Austevoll in 2007 initiated a gradual reorganization of its salmon farming. In March the company sold its operations to another tradition-rich Norwegian fishing company, Lerøy Seafood Group ASA. Lerøy paid for the acquisition with approximately 25 percent of its shares. Austevoll continued to buy Lerøy shares, acquiring some 4.46 million during the rest of 2007. Another large block purchased in October brought its total holdings up to about 75 percent.

Austevoll expanded its presence in Peru significantly at the end of 2007 with the partial acquisition of Corporation del Mar (CORMAR). The deal brought Austevoll six new fishing ships along with their licenses. CORMAR also operated a fish meal facility in the town of Chicama and factories in two other Peruvian towns. As 2008 began Austevoll could report another significant increase in revenues, to NOK 3.47 billion for 2007, up some 21 percent over 2006.

CONTINUED GOOD PERFORMANCE

Austevoll and the seafood sector in general performed relatively well toward the end of the first decade of the 21st century, despite the world financial crisis in 2008. The Austevoll group reported the best operating results in its history to date, with an EBITDA (earnings before interest, taxes, depreciation, and amortization) for 2009 of NOK 1.93 billion, well more than twice the NOK 788 million reported for 2008. One reason was a significant rise in salmon prices due to lower catches overall. Low industry yields for other pelagic fish also resulted in good prices for canned and frozen fish. The company's first months in the omega-3 oil market were also successful and Austevoll anticipated boosting its market share in that sector in the coming years.

By 2009 Austevoll had become Europe's largest producer of fish meal and fish oil, partly as the result of a joint venture with Origin Enterprises plc, an Irish producer of food. Origin spun off its fish meal operation United Fish Industries in a 50-50 cooperative venture with Austevoll. This offered Origin the convenience and efficiency of its operations in Norway, which were close to the catch, as well as Austevoll's logistics infrastructure.

The cofounder and chairman of the board of Austevoll Seafood, Ole Rasmus Møgster, died suddenly at the age of 51 in February 2010. Møgster had been a guiding force in the rise of Austevoll to Norway's most important pelagic fishery. However, the company remained in the good hands of his nephew Arne, who as CEO had guided the firm through four of the most successful years in its history. Despite the unexpected loss, the future continued to look bright for Austevoll Seafood.

Gerald E. Brennan

PRINCIPAL SUBSIDIARIES

A-Fish AS; Atlantic Pelagic AS; Aurmur AS; Austevoll Eiendorn AS; Austevoll Fisk AS; Epax Holding AS; Inversiones Pacfish Ltda. (Chile); Laco IV AS; Lerøy Seafood Group ASA (74.93%); Welcon AS.

PRINCIPAL COMPETITORS

AZ Pelagic Fisheries B.V.; Domstein ASA; Kyokuyo Co., Ltd.; Liao Ning Pelagic Fisheries Co.; Nippon Suisan Kaisha, Ltd.; Norway Pelagic ASA; Oceana Group Limited; Pelagic Fisheries, Inc.; SalMar ASA.

FURTHER READING

"Austevoll Seafood ASA and Origin Enterprises plc Combine Fishmeal and Fish Oil Operations in Norway, Ireland, and the UK." *Nordic Business Report*, February 4, 2009.

"Austevoll Seafood ASA Completes Acquisition of Omega-3 Oils Producer Epax AS." *Nordic Business Report*, January 24, 2007.

"Austevoll Seafood ASA Completes Sale of Salmon Business to Leroy Seafood Group ASA." *Nordic Business Report*, March 21, 2007.

Benz, Adam, and John Lyman. "Chile's Marginalized Small Fishermen: The Secret Weapons of a Disaster-Struck Nation." *Foreign Policy Digest*, March 2010.

"Horse Mackerel Shortage in South Worries Many." *El Diario* (Chile), September 1, 2009.

"Norway's Austevoll Seafood ASA and Ireland's Origin Enterprise plc in Talks to Merge European Fishmeal and Fish Oil Operations." *Nordic Business Report*, January 22, 2008.

"Peru: Exalmar, Austral to Buy Corporacion del Mar." *Gestion*, September 1, 2009.

Australia and New Zealand Banking Group Ltd.

ANZ Centre Level 9
833 Collins Street, Docklands
Melbourne, Victoria 3008
Australia
Telephone: (81 03) 9273-4991
Fax: (81 03) 9273-4875
Web site: http://www.anz.com.au

Public Company
Incorporated: 1835 as Bank of Australasia
Employees: 37,687
Total Assets: AUD 476.99 billion ($418.21 billion) (2010)
Stock Exchanges: Australia New Zealand
Ticker Symbol: ANZ
NAICS: 522110 Commercial Banking; 522210 Credit Card Issuing; 522291 Consumer Lending; 522292 Real Estate Credit; 522293 International Trade Financing; 523110 Investment Banking and Securities Dealing; 523930 Investment Advice; 524113 Direct Life Insurance Carriers; 525910 Open-End Investment Funds; 551111 Offices of Bank Holding Companies

■ ■ ■

Australia and New Zealand Banking Group Ltd. (ANZ) is one of the Big Four banks in Australia and the largest bank in New Zealand. Worldwide, ANZ ranks as one of the top 50 banking and financial services firms. The group offers a full range of retail banking services and serves nearly 5.7 million customers with operations in more than 32 countries. Other products and services include mortgage financing; consumer financing; vehicle and equipment financing and rental services; wealth management; corporate banking for small, medium-sized, and large companies; investment banking; and foreign exchange and commodity trading. ANZ was formed when the Australia and New Zealand Bank Limited (ANZ Bank) merged with the English, Scottish and Australian Bank Limited (ES&A) in 1970. ANZ Bank was the result of a merger in 1951 between the Bank of Australasia and the Union Bank of Australia.

19TH-CENTURY ORIGINS OF THE MAJOR PREDECESSOR BANKS

The Bank of Australasia (the Asia) is believed to have been the idea of Thomas Potter Macqueen, a wealthy colonist who proposed a joint bank and whaling enterprise to some London investors. They liked his idea well enough to become the bank's first provisional directors. Macqueen, however, was caught promoting the rival Commercial Banking Company of Sydney behind the directors' backs, and the Bank of Australasia opened in 1835 without him.

The Union Bank of Australia (the Union) was founded in a similar fashion. This time a struggling Australian bank, the Tamar Bank in Tasmania, went to London in search of capital and found a group of investors prepared to back a bank in the colony. They founded the Union, which took over the Tamar Bank and opened for business in 1837.

These two groups of investors based their hopes for the Asia and the Union on Australia's potential to meet

COMPANY PERSPECTIVES

We aim to become a super-regional bank. Our growth targets are based on four core capabilities. Customer focus: continuing our focus on simplicity, convenience and responsibility. Marketing and sales: shifting our thinking from selling commodity products and being more customer focused in the way we market ourselves and serve our customers. Technology: improving technology to the levels used by banks globally. Performance: out-performing at every level—financial out-performance, out-performance in customer service and in our work ethic.

the large demand for wool by English textile mills. Although some colonial banks already existed, none of these local institutions could match the financial resources of London-based private trading banks such as the Asia or the Union.

Moreover, because these colonial banks were unable to tap the British capital market for another 30 years (except for the Commercial Banking Company of Sydney, which did give the British banks some competition), not one of them survived five years. In contrast, the Asia and the Union were immediately successful. The Asia quadrupled its loans between 1836 and the end of the decade.

In 1838 the New Zealand Company, a colonizing enterprise, approached both the Asia and the Union about opening a branch in the firm's new settlement. The Asia hesitated because it had reservations about the New Zealand Company. The Union agreed, however, and became the first bank to do business in New Zealand.

EARLY GROWTH

Between 1838 and 1841 the Australian sheep-farming boom reached new and feverish heights. During this period both the Asia and the Union consolidated their positions and built up businesses secure enough to withstand the severe depression that began in late 1841. Both banks had the financial strength to take advantage of colonial banks decimated by the depression. In 1840 the Union absorbed the Bathurst Bank, in 1841 the Asia acquired the Bank of Western Australia, and in 1844, at the height of the depression, the Union merged with Archers Gilles & Company.

With the discovery of copper and lead deposits north of Adelaide in 1844, the colonies began moving out of the depression. The discovery of gold near Bathurst, New South Wales, in 1851 soon produced a general boom. In these new economic circumstances, gold and foreign exchange dealing became significant banking services, and branch banking programs flourished with the influx of new mining customers eager for mortgages.

During the "golden decade" of the 1850s, new banks formed to challenge the foreign exchange primacy of the Asia and the Union, among them the English, Scottish and Australian Bank (ES&A), which was founded in 1852. Although the ES&A's presence concerned the Asia and the Union, an even greater threat came from the new colonial banks that burgeoned in the country at mid-century. To better compete with English banks, these colonial institutions established London offices of their own, while they also acquired enough colonial investment resources, mainly gold, to provide their own international banking. Thus, from this time on, the Asia and the Union had to share their international role both with new London-controlled banks and with strong colonial competitors.

SURVIVING THE LATE 19TH-CENTURY BANK CRASH

Between 1860 and 1890 Australia saw prolonged and rapid economic development. However, the conservative Asia and Union banks began in the late 1880s to prepare for the inevitable downturn. Both the Asia and the Union had steadily built cash reserves up to 20 percent of all liabilities to the public. Moreover, both banks had large floating advances to the money market and extensive and varied holdings of gilt-edged stocks from which they could draw in an emergency. Beyond this, they also had many informal connections with other financial institutions. Thus, during the great bank crash of 1893, both the Asia and the Union had a number of sources to turn to for help, including the Bank of England.

With the passing of the banking crisis, both the Asia and the Union attempted to increase their lowered earnings. Salaries were reduced and marginal branch banks were closed, except in western Australia, where gold discoveries promised great opportunities. However, more important than branch policy, both banks tried to restrain the unprofitable accumulation of deposits by cutting interest rates, which they believed would decrease the cost of funds and earn the banks more fees through the marketing of less expensive loans to customers. In 1895 both banks agreed to cut interest

KEY DATES

1835: The Bank of Australasia (the Asia) is founded in London.

1837: The Union Bank of Australia (the Union) is founded in London.

1852: The English, Scottish and Australian Bank (ES&A) is founded.

1951: The Asia and the Union merge to form the Australia and New Zealand Bank Limited (ANZ Bank).

1970: ANZ Bank and ES&A merge to form Australia's third-largest bank, Australia and New Zealand Banking Group Limited (ANZ).

1976: ANZ changes its domicile from London to Melbourne.

1989: ANZ acquires PostBank of New Zealand, becoming the largest banking group in that nation.

1997: John McFarlane takes over as CEO and launches a thorough restructuring.

2003: ANZ purchases National Bank of New Zealand from Lloyds TSB Group plc.

2007: Mike Smith takes over as CEO.

2009: Company completes acquisition of Royal Bank of Scotland's retail, commercial, and private banking operations in Asia; ANZ purchases full ownership of ING Australia.

rates everywhere in the colonies to 3 percent, even though other banks did not follow.

Despite these measures to preserve profits, the Asia and the Union realized losses in loans to customers who had been devastated in the banking crisis. Although neither bank had missed a dividend payment at any time in its history, stockholders voiced concerns when rates of return fell markedly short of their expectations. Although these dividend results were similar for both banks, the Asia's board maintained confidence in Superintendent John Sawers and his staff, while the Union's board resolved that General Manager David Finlayson should retire.

EXPANDING IN THE EARLY 20TH CENTURY

By 1900 the Asia held 12.7 percent of all deposits and 9.3 percent of all advances, and the Union held 12.1 percent of all deposits and 10.6 percent of all advances in Australia, and both were members of Australia's Big Four banks (the Bank of New South Wales and the Commercial Banking Company of Sydney were the other two). The other 17 banks in the country were substantially smaller and confined to one or two colonies. Thus, at the beginning of the 20th century, the Asia and the Union enjoyed relative strength and prestige throughout the Australian Commonwealth.

In the first decade of the new century, a stable economy prompted both the Asia and the Union to pursue policies of "complacent growth" through branch bank expansion. Between 1900 and the outbreak of World War I, the Asia opened 73 branches and the Union opened 100. Their competitors, still suffering from the banking crash and the depression, had to worry about reconstruction obligations; their relatively small and weak condition dictated a strategy of mergers and absorption rather than branch banking in the battle for market share.

One major issue for both the Asia and the Union in the early 1900s was their relationship with their head offices in London. Better communications and new personalities in London caused a marked shift in formal executive authority from Australia to Britain. London executives began demanding more intimate details and more informed advice than the general commentaries from Melbourne that they had drawn on for broad policy directives during the 19th century. Melbourne executives resented their newly subordinate positions. In the end, total executive power was transferred to the London offices, and a new policy was implemented of elevating older, more conservative executives to the top ranks in Melbourne.

With the inauguration of Australia as a commonwealth in January 1901, pressure intensified for a government bank. After much debate and discussion, the Commonwealth Bank opened in January 1913. It offered savings accounts, government banking, public debt management, and rural credit, but it could not issue notes and did not have central bank control. Top executives at both the Asia and the Union were highly critical of and hostile to the Commonwealth Bank. Executives in London took a more balanced view, however, and both boards refused to contribute to campaigns against the government's bank, although several colonial banks had done so. Furthermore, they directed their chief executives to accept the situation and cultivate amicable relations with the Commonwealth's president.

POST-WORLD WAR I COMPETITION LEADS TO MERGERS

World War I crystallized the banking structures existing in 1914. After the war, however, rivals of the Asia and the Union began to merge to make themselves more competitive. In 1917 the Royal Bank of Queensland and the Bank of New Queensland merged to form the Bank of Queensland. By 1932, when the Bank of New South Wales absorbed the Australian Bank of Commerce, 11 amalgamations had occurred, reducing the number of Australian trading banks from 20 to nine. During this period the ES&A merged with three other banks: the Commercial Bank of Tasmania and the London Chartered Bank of Australia, both in 1921, and the Royal Bank of Australia in 1927.

The Asia and the Union continued to expand their branch banking in an attempt to offset their competitors' growing advantages. Between 1918 and 1929 the Asia opened 49 new branches and the Union opened 41. Although both banks could have benefited from mergers with banks in areas such as Tasmania where they were not strong, both kept to the conservative policies that had been in place since the beginning of the 20th century until well into the 1920s.

In London, executives of both the Asia and the Union were aware that their banks had to change strategy if they wanted to rise in rank. However, between the Great Depression and World War II, immediate problems took precedence over long-term rebuilding. There was some discussion about a merger between the Asia and the Union during the 1930s, but it was not until 1943 that serious interest in the project revived. At that time, both the Asia and the Union were approached by other Australian banks as possible partners. However, each thought of the other as the most natural candidate for a merger.

MERGER OF THE ASIA AND THE UNION, FORMING ANZ BANK: 1951

On its own, each bank was less than half the size of the Bank of New South Wales, the largest bank in the country. They both agreed that a merger would make them more competitive, and also would restore lost stature and prestige. Moreover, if they did not act, it seemed likely that they would be left behind as their smaller competitors did merge.

In addition, both were English corporations, with London head offices and a majority of English shareholders, and their scales and styles of business were quite similar. The Union's strength in pastoral business complemented the commercial and industrial emphasis of the Asia. Only 70 out of 420 branches overlapped. Friendly cooperation within competition had characterized the relationship between the two banks for more than a century.

In 1946 lawyers began work on the details of a merger in which the Asia took over the business of the Union. However, while a government threat to nationalize nongovernment banks delayed any action, it was decided that the original merger proposal was too costly. In addition, a group of key Union executives, feeling that the banks were equals and should join accordingly, began to resist being absorbed by the Asia. The solution was to create a new company, the Australia and New Zealand Bank Limited, to subsume both the Asia and the Union. ANZ Bank began business on October 1, 1951.

The merger of the Asia and Union catapulted ANZ Bank to the top tier of banks in Australia and New Zealand. However, being bigger failed to make ANZ Bank more profitable. A tight government liquidity requirement forced the bank to cut lending in order to build liquid assets to the prescribed level. To offset the lost loan business, ANZ Bank began looking for new programs to raise profits and reduce expenses. A savings bank subsidiary, which could use existing skills and facilities and be funded within the government's constraints, was established in 1955. ANZ Bank proved very successful.

While ANZ Bank's administrative hierarchy became more efficient in the early 1960s, General Manager Sir Roger Darval decided that emphasizing the bank's domestic business would boost profits. He began an accelerated expansion of branch banking. ANZ Bank opened 127 branches in six years. Most of these were in central business districts, signaling ANZ Bank's intent to move away from rural business.

MERGER OF ANZ BANK AND ES&A CREATES ANZ: 1970

ANZ Bank had wooed the English, Scottish and Australian Bank four times since 1955. ES&A's conservative controls over lending and liquidity, its highly successful hire-purchase subsidiary, Esanda, and its profit-oriented administration all appealed strongly to the board of ANZ Bank. Furthermore, ES&A came from the same private trade banking tradition as both the Asia and Union. Most of all, the directors thought that a larger bank would command more resources than either organization could raise alone. In addition, some feared that foreign banks would move in on ANZ Bank's corporate and international business, possibly by using ES&A as a host for entry.

In 1970 the merger finally took place. The resulting Australia and New Zealand Banking Group Limited (ANZ) became the third-largest bank in the commonwealth, double the size of the bank in fourth position. Nevertheless, despite its expanded presence in the marketplace, ANZ saw its profits fall and its expenses rise during its first years, primarily because of a lax administration and unexpectedly high merger costs.

The staffs of both ES&A and ANZ Bank had opposed the merger, each side fearing it would lose out on the distribution of the higher posts in the new bank. Angered by this situation, the board hired a U.S. management consultant firm in 1973 to help its executives redesign the ANZ Banking Group's organizational structure. A modern formalized planning system specifying long- and short-range goals emerged, eventually creating an effective and efficient environment. At the same time, the consultants replaced traditional profit goals with goals tied to rates of return on assets.

The group's executives felt that this change immediately required a large amount of capital. When London objected to the exportation of British capital, the group's board realized it would be in the best interests of the bank to change its domicile. After 141 years, the headquarters of ANZ was transferred from London to Melbourne on February 2, 1976. Two years later ANZ moved into the newly constructed ANZ Tower, a symbol of the total transformation in structure, philosophy, and character the bank had undergone.

INTERNATIONAL ACQUISITIONS: 1980–89

During the early 1980s monetary authorities in Australia and New Zealand gradually began to relax the controls that had limited banking operations since the 1950s. This, together with a strenuous program of cost cutting, led to a substantial increase in profits. However, deregulation of the industry also opened Australia and New Zealand to foreign banking. In response to this foreign competition, as well as increased domestic competition, ANZ decided to try to buy strength and diversity.

In 1979 ANZ merged with the Bank of Adelaide. In 1981 ANZ talked to the Commercial Banking Company of Sydney and then the Commercial Bank of Australia about merging, but neither deal was completed. In 1983 and 1984 the group did succeed in acquiring or buying half equity in the Development Finance Corporation; the Trustees, Executors and Agency Company Ltd.; McCaughan Dyson and Company, a stockbroker; and Grindlays Bank plc, of England.

The 1984 acquisition of Grindlays, with representation in 40 countries, greatly strengthened ANZ's international operations, compelling it to redesign its organizational structure. The bank's hierarchical arrangement of authority was replaced with a horizontal structure of more than 50 business units worldwide. These independent business units brought an entrepreneurial spirit of creativity and ambition as well as increased profits.

The bank's 1980s acquisitions, including the 1989 purchase of New Zealand's PostBank, which made ANZ the largest banking group in New Zealand, made it a major international financial player. Nevertheless, the group was still, in large part, a regional organization. In 1989, 77 percent of its profits came from operations in Australia and New Zealand.

FAILED MERGERS AND TOUGH ECONOMIC TIMES: 1989–93

During 1989 ANZ and National Australia Bank, one of the other Big Four Australian banks, entered into serious discussions about a merger, going so far as buying small stakes in each other. However, the Labor government, worried about Australians' increasing concern about the power of the big banks in the run-up to a general election to be held in March 1990, blocked the deal.

Almost immediately after Labor's victory in the election, ANZ announced plans to purchase majority control of National Mutual Life Association, the number two insurance company in Australia. At AUD 3.8 billion ($2.87 billion), it was valued as the largest merger in Australian history. The merger promised to rock the nation's banking sector by forming its largest financial services outfit, which was to be called ANZ-NM Banking and Insurance Group. However, the Labor government once again blocked the deal. Treasurer Paul Keating reasoned that allowing the merger would lead to a series of further mergers within the Australian financial services industries, which as a whole would undermine competition.

ANZ was allowed to acquire National Mutual Royal Bank Limited, a joint banking venture between National Mutual and the Royal Bank of Canada that was formed in 1986 and had assets of AUD 4.5 billion. Also acquired in 1990 were Perth-based Town and Country Building Society, Lloyds Bank plc's operation in Papua New Guinea, and the Bank of Zealand Fiji unit.

Moving beyond the failed mergers of 1989 and 1990, ANZ struggled through the difficult economic environment of the early 1990s. A deep recession in Australia included high unemployment (peaking at 11 percent) and high inflation and interest rates as well.

The stagnation led to an explosion in nonperforming loans, forcing ANZ and other Australian banks to take huge provisions against bad debts. The nadir for ANZ came in the year ending in September 1992 when provisions of AUD 1.9 billion ($1.3 billion) led to a net loss for the year of AUD 579 million ($399.3 million).

ANZ also made staffing reductions during the recession, announcing the elimination of 5,500 jobs in late 1991. During 1992, a new management team was put in charge of turning around the group's fortunes. John Gough took over as chairman from Milton Bridgland, and Don Mercer succeeded Will Bailey as chief executive. Gough was chairman and former managing director of the Australian conglomerate Pacific Dunlop Limited, while Mercer had joined ANZ in 1984 and had most recently served as head of Australian retail banking.

OVERSEAS EXPANSION: 1993–95

As the economy slowly recovered and ANZ returned to profitability, ANZ restarted its overseas expansion, concentrating primarily on East Asia. In 1993 the group gained a presence in Indonesia by purchasing an 85 percent interest in a joint venture bank that was later renamed PT ANZ Panin Bank. That year also saw ANZ become the first bank from an English-speaking country to be allowed into the Vietnamese market, opening a branch in Hanoi and a representative office in Ho Chi Minh City. Similarly, the bank entered China by opening a branch in Shanghai and offices in Beijing and Guangzhou.

By 1994 ANZ was the largest foreign bank in South Asia, and 10 percent of the bank's total profits were being generated through its Asia-Pacific network. Late in 1995 ANZ expanded into the Philippines by opening a commercial banking branch in Manila. Another change to its overseas network came in 1996 when the domicile of Grindlays Bank was moved from England to Australia, and the subsidiary was renamed ANZ Grindlays Bank Limited. Meanwhile, in August 1995, Charles Goode, who was also chairman of Woodside Petroleum Ltd, replaced Gough as chairman.

MAJOR RESTRUCTURING UNDER MCFARLANE: 1997–2000

Just after the Asian economic crisis began to unfold in mid-1997, ANZ made another management change. Board dissatisfaction with the slow pace of cost containment efforts led to Mercer's retirement. Hired as his replacement was a U.S.-trained Scottish banker, John McFarlane. The new CEO had 18 years of experience at Citibank on his resume, followed by four years at

Standard Chartered plc, a leading international bank based in the United Kingdom, where he managed much of the bank's overseas operations, including those in South Asia.

McFarlane led a thorough restructuring of ANZ's operations. Under his leadership, the group began reducing its exposure to certain volatile foreign markets that were hit hard by the economic crisis and its aftereffects. In 1998 ANZ closed its London-based capital markets division and emerging markets business following heavy losses on emerging market debt trading. Reflecting a pullback from both international markets and investment banking, the group's investment banking arm was relocated from London to Sydney.

McFarlane also worked to strengthen the bank's position domestically by accelerating the cost-cutting program and cutting staff. The workforce was slashed by more than 5,000 from 1997 to 1998. Further changes centered on the mix of domestic operations. Traditionally, ANZ had been more of a commercial/corporate bank, and McFarlane began to bolster the bank's domestic retail banking activities to create more of a retail/commercial bank. By early 1999 conditions in Asian markets had improved enough to permit a cautious return to expansion, and ANZ Panin Bank bought the credit card operations of PT Papan Sejahtera, an Indonesian bank that had fallen into receivership.

During 2000 McFarlane further reduced ANZ's exposure to risky foreign markets by selling ANZ Grindlays and its banking network in the Middle East and South Asia to Standard Chartered for AUD 3.1 billion. ANZ also began laying the foundation for a takeover of St. George Bank Ltd. by buying a nearly 10 percent stake in the New South Wales-based regional bank. This bid for domestic growth was scuttled in early 2001 after it became clear that it would not be possible to complete a friendly takeover at a reasonable price.

ANZ then continued with an organic growth model, centered on a reorganization that McFarlane announced in July 2000. ANZ divided itself up into 21 highly autonomous units (later reduced to 16), each of which would have to establish its own competitive position and develop its own growth strategy, as well as develop a mix of Internet and branch-based distribution. The units focused, for example, on personal banking in Australia, mortgages, wealth management, small to medium-sized businesses, institutional banking, and global foreign exchange.

EXPANSION RESUMES: 2001–07

This decentralized structure ran counter to the prevailing model in the financial services that emphasized cross-selling opportunities through integrated operations. McFarlane felt, however, that the future of financial services lay in specialist players rather than generalists. The new ANZ structure also held the advantage of making it easier to shut down or sell off underperforming operations, as well as take successful units public or set them up within joint ventures with other companies.

ANZ did not completely abandon acquisitions but instead sought smaller deals. For example, in late in 2001 the bank bolstered its Asia-Pacific retail banking unit through the purchase of the Bank of Hawaii's operations in Papua New Guinea, Vanuatu, and Fiji for about AUD 100 million. Then in May 2002 came the first major joint venture deal to follow the new growth formula. ANZ combined its Australian and New Zealand funds management operations with ING Group's funds management and life insurance businesses in Australia and New Zealand, forming ING Australia Limited.

The new venture was 51 percent owned by Netherlands-based financial services giant ING and 49 percent by ANZ, but the two owners were to have equal say in the management. ING Australia instantly became the fourth-largest retail funds manager in Australia, with AUD 38.4 billion of funds under management, and the number five life insurer. The main point of logic behind the deal was that it would bring together ING's funds management experience with the power of ANZ's bank distribution channels.

Through 2002 McFarlane's thorough restructuring efforts were paying off. ANZ reported record net profits that year of AUD 2.32 billion ($1.26 billion), a 16 percent increase over the preceding year. Out of the group's 16 specialized units, 14 of them showed an increase in profits for the year. Seeking to continue this growth trend, ANZ looked to strengthen its domestic positions in several areas, including personal banking, mortgages, small to medium-sized businesses, and wealth management.

During 2003 ANZ purchased National Bank of New Zealand from Lloyds TSB Group plc. The deal, estimated to be worth $3.44 billion, secured ANZ's position as the largest bank in New Zealand. The following year the company launched a joint venture bank in Cambodia. With profits rising, ANZ was named Bank of the Year by *Personal Investor* magazine for the fifth consecutive year in 2004.

ANZ continued its international expansion in 2005, forming alliances in Vietnam and opening a new office in Noumea, New Caledonia. It purchased a 20 percent stake in Tianjin City Commercial Bank in 2006. During 2007 the company invested in Malaysia's AMMB Holdings Berhad, Shanghai Rural Commercial

Bank, Vietnam-based Saigon Securities Inc., and ANZ Vientiane Commercial Bank in Laos. ETRADE Australia Limited was also purchased that year.

NEW LEADERSHIP IN 2007

Mike Smith took the helm of ANZ in 2007. The new CEO faced challenges in the first years of his tenure that were brought on by a financial and credit crisis, which was followed by a global economic downturn. During 2008 the company's profits fell by 23 percent over the previous year. Provisions made for bad loans caused the company to post the worst drop in profits in nearly 20 years. Part of the company's problems were related to its lending involvement with brokers Opes Prime Group Ltd., Primebroker Securities Ltd., and Tricom Equities Ltd. Opes Prime and Primebroker declared bankruptcy during the crisis, while Tricom nearly failed. Tricom's name was eventually changed to StoneBridge Securities Ltd. ANZ continued to face litigation related to its involvement in the failed brokerages well into 2009.

While ANZ battled lawsuits related to claims that it had failed to perform due diligence before investing in the brokers, it worked to regain sound financial footing in a changing marketplace. During 2009 leading Wall Street investment banks in the United States had collapsed and many had to accept funds from the U.S. government's Troubled Asset Relief Program (TARP). By this time, the financial woes of U.S. banking, credit, and mortgage companies led to an economic recession that was felt across the globe.

Australia's banks did not fare as poorly as banks in the United States and the company was quick to rebound. It looked to expansion in Asia as a means for future growth. During 2009 the company opened its first branch in rural China. The company also acquired full ownership of ING Australia, giving it a stronger foothold in the wealth management market.

During this time ANZ also purchased Royal Bank of Scotland's commercial, retail, and institutional banking operations in Taiwan, Singapore, Indonesia, Hong Kong, Vietnam, and the Philippines. This was part of Smith's plan to generate at least 20 percent of ANZ's earnings from its Asia-Pacific operations by 2012. As a result of the deal, ANZ gained 49 branches, 1.6 million customers, and $6.5 billion in customer deposits. While global financial markets entered a period of slow recovery, ANZ was expecting its expansion in Asian markets to pay off in the years to come.

Updated, David E. Salamie; Christina M. Stansell

PRINCIPAL SUBSIDIARIES

Amerika Samoa Bank (American Samoa); ANZ Bank (Vietnam) Limited; ANZ Capel Court Limited; ANZ

Capital Hedging Pty Ltd.; ANZ Commodity Trading Pty Ltd.; ANZcover Insurance Pty Ltd.; ANZ Trustees Limited; ANZ Fund Pty Ltd.; ANZ Bank (Europe) Limited (UK); ANZ Bank (Kiribati) Limited; ANZ Bank (Samoa) Limited; ANZ Holdings (New Zealand) Limited; ANZ National Bank Limited (New Zealand); ANZ Investment Services (New Zealand) Limited; ANZ National (Int'l) Limited; Arawata Finance Limited (New Zealand); Arawata Trust (New Zealand); Arawata Holdings Limited (New Zealand); Harcourt Corporation Limited (New Zealand); Endeavor Finance Limited (New Zealand); Tui Endeavor Limited (New Zealand); Private Nominees Limited (New Zealand); UDC Finance Limited (New Zealand); ANZ International (Hong Kong) Limited; ANZ Asia Limited (Hong Kong); ANZ Bank (Vanuatu) Limited; ANZ International Private Limited (Singapore); ANZ Singapore Limited; ANZ Royal Bank (Cambodia) Limited; LFD Limited; Minerva Holdings Limited (UK); Upspring Limited (UK); Votraint No. 1103 Pty Ltd.; ANZ Lenders Mortgage Insurance Pty Ltd.; ANZ Nominees Limited; ANZ Orchard Investments Pty Ltd.; Australia and New Zealand Banking Group (PNG) Limited; Chongqing Liangping ANZ Rural Bank Company Limited (China); Citizens Bancorp Inc. (Guam); Citizens Security Bank (Guam) Inc.; Esanda Finance Corporation Limited; ETRADE Australia Limited; Omeros II Trust; PT ANZ Panin Bank (Indonesia); ANZ Vientiane Commercial Bank Limited (Laos).

PRINCIPAL DIVISIONS

Australia; New Zealand; Institutional; Global Services and Operations; Technology; Asia, Pacific, Europe, and America.

PRINCIPAL COMPETITORS

Commonwealth Bank of Australia; National Australia Bank Limited; Westpac Banking Corporation.

FURTHER READING

"ANZ Buys Rest of ING Australia, NZ for US$1.b BLN." *Asia Pulse*, September 25, 2009.

Bartholomeusz, Stephen. "ANZ at Last Makes an Idiosyncratic Entrance into Funds Management." *Age* (Melbourne), April 11, 2002, p. 3.

———. "ANZ Beats a Smart Retreat to Follow a Different Drum." *Age* (Melbourne), March 9, 2001, p. 3.

———. "ANZ to Play a Risky Hand." *Age* (Melbourne), April 29, 2000, p. 1.

Boreham, Tim. "ANZ Loses the Urge to Merge: Bank Strategy to Divide Not Conquer." *Australian*, July 29, 2000, p. 21.

Butlin, S. J. *Australia and New Zealand Bank.* London: Longmans, 1961.

John, Danny. "ANZ Plugs Gap with $1.86bn ING Buy." *Age* (Melbourne), September 26, 2009.

Johnston, Eric. "ANZ Profit Slumps 23%." *Age* (Melbourne), October 24, 2008.

———. "Worst Is Behind Bank, but ANZ Boss Fears Aftershocks." *Sydney Morning Herald*, April 30, 2010.

Kavanagh, John. "ANZ Lifts Its Game in a Hot Sector." *Business Review Weekly*, February 7, 2002.

Merrett, David Tolmie. *ANZ Bank: A History of Australia and New Zealand Banking Group Limited and Its Constituents.* Sydney: Allen & Unwin Australia, 1985.

Santini, Laura. "Failed Broker Haunts Australian Bank." *Wall Street Journal*, July 24, 2008.

Smith, Peter, and Tom Mitchell. "RBS Morsels Whet ANZ's Appetite." *Financial Times*, August 6, 2009.

Baker Book House Company

6030 East Fulton Road
Ada, Michigan 49301
U.S.A.
Telephone: (616) 676-9185
Toll Free: (800) 877-2665
Fax: (616) 676-9573
Web site: http://www.bakerpublishinggroup.com

Private Company
Incorporated: 1939
Employees: 215
Sales: $55 million (2010 est.)
NAICS: 511130 Book Publishers; 451211 Book Stores

■ ■ ■

Baker Book House Company is the parent of Baker Publishing Group, a leading publisher of Christian books. The firm's offerings range from popular fiction and self-help titles to serious academic works and Bibles, with top-selling books including the novels of Beverly Lewis, Don Piper's inspirational memoir *90 Minutes in Heaven*, and the modern-language *God's Word* Bible translation. Baker Publishing's six divisions include imprints Bethany House, Revell, Chosen, Brazos Press, Baker Books, and Baker Academic, and the firm is also the exclusive North American distributor of the Cambridge University Press Bible. Originally founded as a bookstore, Baker Book House continues to operate a sales outlet in the Grand Rapids, Michigan, area. The family-owned firm is headed by Dwight Baker, the

grandson of founder Herman Baker, and other family members also hold key positions.

BEGINNINGS

Baker Book House was founded in 1939 by Herman Baker, a Dutch immigrant who had settled in Grand Rapids, Michigan, in 1925 at the age of 14. Soon after his arrival Baker began working in his uncle's bookstore, where he came to specialize in selling used religious books. This was a popular category at the store, as Western Michigan was home to many Dutch immigrants who belonged to one of two branches of the Reformed Church, a Christian Protestant sect that had been founded in the Netherlands.

In 1932 Baker married, and in 1939 he decided to open a bookstore of his own in Grand Rapids, starting with a small stock of 500 titles from his personal library that he displayed on handmade shelves. The small business began to grow with help from mail-order sales, and in 1940 Baker branched out into publishing with *More Than Conquerors*, by Calvin Theological Seminary professor William Hendriksen. Over the next several years other titles followed, all in a similar scholarly, religious vein. Although still focused on selling used books, Baker also began to consider reprinting classic titles that had become hard to get, especially with European sources having dried up during World War II.

In 1948 the firm's publishing efforts were expanded with the hiring of an editor, Cornelius Zylstra, and in 1949 Baker launched an ambitious program to reprint *Barnes' Notes on the Old and New Testaments*, which had been out of print for many years. The $30,000 needed

COMPANY PERSPECTIVES

Baker Publishing Group publishes high-quality writings that represent historic Christianity and serve the diverse interests and concerns of evangelical readers.

to print and bind 2,000 copies of the 11-volume set was beyond his means, but Baker hit upon the idea of publishing one book per month at the retail price of $3 per volume. The cost would thus be spread out, with sales of the early volumes paying for the later ones. The set sold out, and this subscription plan established a pattern for future multivolume editions such as the *New Schaff-Herzog Encyclopedia of Religious Knowledge* and successor *The Twentieth Century Encyclopedia of Religious Knowledge*.

In 1953 the company's Wealthy Street store was remodeled and expanded to include additional office and warehouse space. Demand for religious publications was increasing as the number of Bible colleges and seminaries grew following World War II, and by the end of its second decade Baker had nearly 150 titles available, the majority of them reprints. Although scholarly books remained the primary focus, the subject area had been expanded to include religious approaches to science, archaeology, education, and counseling. Original titles included the *Baker Bible Atlas* and *Baker Dictionary of Theology*.

NEW FACILITY OPENS IN 1966

The company's publication schedule grew rapidly in the early 1960s, and in 1966 a new 25,000-square-foot office and distribution center was opened in nearby Ada, Michigan. As it had done from the beginning, Baker continued to delegate printing and binding work to outside contractors.

In 1968 the firm bought the W.A. Wilde Company of Massachusetts, a 100-year-old publisher of educational materials for churches, and also opened a retail store in Holland, Michigan, some 40 miles away. By the end of its third decade, Baker had nearly 750 titles in its catalog.

In 1971 the company began seeking a more mainstream audience with *Fruit of the Spirit* by evangelist Ron Hembree, which sold 25,000 copies. Other so-called trade publications followed, including books on psychology, sex, and divorce, which were seeing growing demand in the Christian market. Popular

titles included Dr. Frank Minirth and Dr. Paul Meier's *Happiness Is a Choice* (1978), which sold 250,000 copies over several editions.

In 1975 Baker acquired a second publishing house, Canon Press, which had been launched by the magazine *Christianity Today*, and in 1980 the company's flagship retail store moved to a larger location in the suburb of Kentwood. The firm was now increasingly focused on publishing original content, and was seeking out prominent theological writers and developing new titles of its own. Although its retail division grew during the decade to a peak of eight stores (including several general-interest outlets and the child-centric Pooh Corner), in the late 1980s it began shrinking due to changing market conditions, in particular the growth of superstore chains Borders and Barnes & Noble.

HERMAN BAKER STEPS DOWN IN 1987

In 1987 Herman Baker stepped back from running the company to become publisher at large, with his son Richard taking the title of president. Herman's other son, Peter, also served as vice president of sales, while daughter Ellen Larsen managed a bookstore and Richard Baker's son Dwight served as art director. In early 1991 Herman Baker died at the age of 79.

In the late 1980s the company found success with a series of Christian storybooks for children called *Precious Moments*, which were marketed to both religious and general booksellers. The initial title sold more than 500,000 copies, and the many follow-ups also did well.

Baker had by now evolved past its reputation as a reprint house, with original titles constituting some 80 percent of the 1,300 that were in print by 1989. The firm was publishing about 125 new books per year, of which 50 were academic. The latter were featured in a semiannual catalog that was mailed to scholars, and Baker was recognized as one of the top names in this field. Recent titles included the *Baker Encyclopedia of the Bible*, edited by Walter Elwell, which was published to coincide with the firm's 50th anniversary.

The company promoted its wares to retailers at Christian-centric book expositions, as well as at the publishing industry's annual World Book Fair in Frankfurt, Germany. Mass-marketers such as Wal-Mart, B. Dalton, and Waldenbooks were the largest volume buyers of Baker books, although focusing only on the most popular titles, while the broader range was available from religious stores or by mail. Foreign sales had grown to comprise 10 percent of the total, and the firm had sales representatives in the United Kingdom, Canada, South Africa, and the Far East.

REVELL PURCHASED IN 1992

In 1990 Baker signed an agreement to become the North American distributor for Cambridge University Press's acclaimed line of Bibles, and in 1992 acquired Gleneida Publishing Group from evangelist Norman Vincent Peale's nonprofit Guideposts Associates, Inc. Gleneida was home to imprints Fleming H. Revell, Chosen Books, Triumph Books, and Wynwood Press. The largest of these was Revell, which had been founded in 1870 by its namesake in Chicago, and had grown from focusing on evangelical Christian titles into a religious trade book publisher. Its roster boasted such well-known writers as Peale, Robert Schuller, Dale Evans Rogers, and Helen Steiner Rice. Revell and sister imprint Chosen were relocated to Baker's headquarters in Ada, while the small Triumph operation was sold and the secular Wynwood imprint (which had published hit author John Grisham's first novel) was mothballed. The acquisition added 800 titles to Baker's catalog, and nearly doubled the company's sales.

During the early 1990s the firm branched out into more new areas, adding a line of mystery books and in 1995 creating a unit called Baker Bytes to develop CD-ROM versions of select titles. In 1997 Richard Baker was named chairman of the board and his son Dwight took the title of company president, having served as executive vice president since 1991. That same year the firm's last remaining general-interest bookstore was closed, although it continued to operate two Pooh Corner locations and two Christian bookstores in Holland and Grand Rapids.

In 1999 Baker created a new imprint called Brazos Press, which would publish titles for an ecumenical Christian audience rather than from a strictly evangelical or mainstream Protestant viewpoint. It was founded by three former employees of InterVarsity Press, who had approached the company with the idea.

BETHANY HOUSE PURCHASED IN 2003

In 2003 Baker again expanded dramatically with the acquisition of Bethany House, America's second-largest publisher of Christian fiction. The 47-year-old imprint offered 2,600 titles, including those of such best-selling authors as Beverly Lewis and Janette Oke. Bethany's staff of 50 would remain in Bloomington, Minnesota, while six new employees were added in Ada to handle the warehousing, payment, sales, and customer service functions that were shifted to Michigan. The company also opened a new warehouse in Ada to accommodate the increased business, as well as consolidating the distribution needs of all its units. The addition of Bethany was expected to again double Baker's sales.

Christian books were now big business, with Rick Warren's *Purpose Driven Life* from rival Zondervan selling 26 million copies and topping the list of U.S. best sellers for two consecutive years, and the "apocalyptic fiction" *Left Behind* series by Tim LaHaye and Jerry B. Jenkins selling a total of more than 63 million books for Tynedale House. Baker's top titles at this time included Don Piper's memoir *90 Minutes in Heaven*, which sold 4 million copies, and the novels of Beverly Lewis, whose combined sales would reach 12 million by the end of the decade. The company's books, although still explicitly Christian in viewpoint, covered a wide range of topics, including business, health, cooking, and pets. In addition to independent Christian publishing houses, Baker's competitors now included giants such as HarperCollins and Simon & Schuster, which had purchased or created their own Christian imprints.

In the spring of 2004 Baker Book House Co. created a new unit called Baker Publishing Group to give its publishing business a unified identity that was separate from the much smaller retail operation. The latter was continuing to struggle, with the Pooh Corner store in Holland sold to its employees in 2003 and the Baker Book House there disposed of in a similar manner in 2008, leaving only the flagship store in the Grand Rapids suburb of Kentwood.

GOD'S WORD BIBLE ACQUIRED IN 2008

In 2008 Baker obtained the exclusive rights to the "clear, natural English" Bible translation called *God's Word,* which had been created by a group of scholars of various denominations working for the God's Word to the Nations Bible Mission Society, and first published in 1995. Although used by many mainstream Protestant churches, it was was also marketed to a younger generation via rock concerts and displays at amusement parks.

The publishing industry was now experiencing a sales slump as the declining number of bookstores, growing uncertainty about the future of paper books, and the ailing U.S. economy all took their toll. For its part Baker was trying new tactics such as working to increase its presence in the African-American market by sending authors in this category on speaking tours, soliciting feedback from booksellers, and trying to generate word of mouth. In 2009 the company's efforts were rewarded with a number five ranking on the *Essence* magazine list of best sellers for *The Someday List* by Stacy Hawkins Adams, from Revell.

Baker had also recently begun testing the waters of the e-book market, although sales were generally tiny compared to print. In early 2010 the firm launched a more aggressive promotional campaign in which free electronic copies of select titles were offered for a limited time. In February 100,000 copies of Julie Klassen's *The Apothecary's Daughter* were downloaded, and although only about 300 digital copies had been sold the year before, 7,000 were purchased in April alone, and the title's print sales also jumped. The marketing campaign was intended to spark interest in individual authors, with the hope that once a free book was read, copies of a writer's other titles would be purchased. Although the retail market remained difficult, Baker took comfort in the fact that sales of Bibles, scholarly texts, study aids, and other academic materials accounted for about half of sales, and the shift to digital formats was much slower in these areas.

During 2010 Baker also purchased 300 academic titles from Hendriksen Publishers and joined Zondervan to promote a Web site to Christian authors whose manuscripts it had rejected. Authonomy.com, which had been created by Zondervan parent HarperCollins, would allow unpublished manuscripts to be posted online for comment or possible discovery by other publishers.

Baker was now publishing 250 new titles per year, with 80 reprints or repackaged versions of older books adding up to an annual total of about 330. Recent popular titles included Beverly Lewis's Seasons of Grace series, whose third and last entry debuted on the *New York Times* paperback trade fiction best-seller list at number six in April 2010. About a third of Baker's books now fell into this category, which made up half of Bethany House and Revell's output.

The firm's flagship retail outlet was also holding its own, generating some $2 million in sales with offerings that included Christian fiction, an extensive collection of academic and scholarly titles (some available in "print-on-demand" format), a stock of 60,000 used books, plus music recordings and gift items. The Kentwood store was a destination for theologians and churchgoers from around the Midwest, with a recently upgraded Web site also helping facilitate online sales.

Now in its eighth decade, Baker Book House Co. had evolved into one of the leading Christian publishers in North America, while still operating a successful retail store in the Grand Rapids, Michigan, area. The firm's Baker Publishing Group was home to the popular Bethany House and Revell imprints, as well as other scholarly and academic names, and although the publishing industry was undergoing turmoil as the digital revolution advanced, the firm served a loyal audience and had an experienced management team that appeared capable of surviving whatever challenges lay ahead.

Frank Uhle

PRINCIPAL DIVISIONS

Baker Publishing Group.

PRINCIPAL COMPETITORS

Barbour Publishing, Inc.; David C. Cook; Hachette Book Group; Harvest House Publishers; Howard Books; Kregel Publications; Moody Publishers; NavPress; Thomas Nelson, Inc.; Tynedale House Publishers, Inc.; WaterBrook Multnomah Publishing Group; William B. Eerdmans Publishing Company; Zondervan.

FURTHER READING

"Baker Book House Opened 70 Years Ago as Small, Theological Business in Grand Rapids." *Grand Rapids Press*, August 2, 2009.

The Baker Book House Story: 1939–89. Grand Rapids: Baker, 1989.

"Herman Baker, Founder of Book Publishing-Marketing Firm, Dies." *Grand Rapids Press*, February 12, 1991, p. B1.

Kirkbride, Rob. "Baker Strengthens Its Foothold in Marketing Christian Fiction." *Grand Rapids Press*, January 24, 2003, p. A6.

———, "Baker Turns Page." *Grand Rapids Press*, April 9, 2004, p. A8.

MacDonald, G. Jeffrey. "Digital Publishing: Adapt, Proceed." *Publishers Weekly*, August 16, 2010, p. 60.

Sher, Joanne M. "Independent Bows to Mega-Bookstores." *Grand Rapids Press*, July 3, 1997, p. A12.

Van Dam, George. "Baker Makes Mark in Publishing." *Grand Rapids Business Journal*, November 6, 1989, p. 9.

Veverka, Amber. "Big-Name Authors Give Baker More Clout—

Acquisition Is New Chapter in Company's Story." *Grand Rapids Press*, July 4, 1993, p. E1.

Winston, Kimberly. "New Division at Baker Book." *Publishers Weekly*, October 11, 1999, p. 20.

Bayer Hispania S.L.

Av. Baix Llobregat 3
Sant Joan Despí, E-08970
Spain
Telephone: (+34 93) 228 40 00
Fax: (+34 93) 217 44 23
Web site: http://www.bayer.es

Wholly Owned Subsidiary of Bayer AG
Founded: 1899 as Federico Bayer y Cía
Employees: 2,500
Sales: EUR 917 million ($1.28 billion) (2009 est.)
NAICS: 551112 Holding Companies

■ ■ ■

Bayer Hispania S.L. serves as the holding company for parent company Bayer AG's operation in Spain. The Sant Joan Despí-based company's operations follow Bayer's own structure of three primary, independently operating, divisions: Bayer HealthCare; Bayer CropScience; and Bayer MaterialScience.

The Bayer HealthCare division includes Química Farmacéutica Bayer, Berlimed, Indendis Farma, Bayhealth, and Schering Spain. Among this division's operations is its factory in La Felguera, in Asturias, which produces 80 percent of Bayer's supply of acetylsalicylic acid, the active ingredient in aspirin. The HealthCare division also operates a major pharmaceuticals production facility in Madrid.

The MaterialScience division also plays a prominent role in parent Bayer AG's global manufacturing network. This division oversees Bayer's largest production plant in southern Europe, a 150,000-metric-ton-per-day factory in Tarragona producing polyurethane component MDI. Bayer Hispania is also a major producer of components for Bayer's wood coating systems range, with a factory in Barcelona's Zona Franca.

Bayer Hispania employs more than 2,500 people and generated revenues of EUR 917 million ($1.28 billion) in 2009. The company also forms the major part of Bayer Iberica, formed in 1997 with the addition of Bayer's smaller Portuguese operations. Frank Bertram is president of Bayer Hispania.

DYESTUFFS ORIGINS: 1899

Friedrich Bayer and Johan Friedrich Weskott founded Bayer AG in 1863 as a dyestuffs factory in Barmen, Germany. Bayer became a multinational company almost from the start, acquiring its first overseas business in 1865, a coal-tar dye factory in the United States. By the end of the 1880s the company had also added factories in Russia and France, as well as throughout Germany, setting the stage for Bayer's later extension into Spain.

The arrival of Carl Duisberg at the head of the company sparked Bayer's diversification into other areas of chemical production, as well as an entry into the nascent pharmaceuticals industry. In the meantime, Bayer's growth into the world's leading producer of chemical dyestuffs had encouraged international expansion, both of its industrial network and in support of its marketing and sales. Bayer's entry into Spain came as part of this latter effort. In 1899 Bayer created Federico Bayer y Cía as its dyestuffs sales subsidiary for the Spanish market.

That year marked another significant milestone for Bayer itself. In 1899 the German chemicals giant patented the process for synthesizing acetylsalicylic acid, a potent analgesic. Bayer began marketing this product under the brand name Aspirin. One of the first commercially available pain relievers, Aspirin was considered by many to be one of the wonder drugs of the 20th century. Bayer's Spanish operations ultimately became a major producer of acetylsalicylic acid for the company.

ADDING CHEMICALS

Bayer's Spanish operations remained focused on sales and marketing for the region through the years of World War I and into the 1920s. Bayer entered the Spanish manufacturing sector in 1925, backing the creation of two companies, La Química Comercial y Farmacéutica S.A., and the Spanish subsidiary of photographic chemicals producer Agfa Photo S.A. The following year, after Bayer itself was absorbed into German chemicals monolith I.G. Farben, the company added a major stake in dyestuffs producer Fabricación Nacional de Colorantes S.A., founded in 1922.

Bayer's operations in Spain remained somewhat limited, in part because of the political turbulence in the country resulting in the outbreak of the Spanish Civil War. The start of World War II also restricted the group's international growth, despite the relationship between Nazi Germany and the Franco regime. Nevertheless, many of the key components of the future Bayer Hispania came into place during the first half of the 20th century.

Among the earliest of these was a dyestuffs company called Lluch y Cía, founded in 1911. Lluch merged with Unión Química Comercial S.A. in 1922, becoming Unión Química Lluch S.A. Colorantes y Productos Químicos. The company then developed its own brand name, Unicolor. In 1939 the company changed its name again, to Unicolor S.A. Colorantes y Productos Químicos. Bayer later acquired Unicolor, which became

part of Bayer Hispania Comercial S.A in 1968. Also that year Bayer's Spanish operations, which had taken on the name Bayer Hispania S.A. in 1966, became known as Bayer Hispania Industrial S.A. (BHI).

NEW COMPONENTS

BHI served as the holding company for another major Spanish chemicals company, PESA. That company had been founded as Productos Electrolíticos S.A. in 1935. PESA expanded in 1946, becoming the first company to build a factory in the newly created industrial zone, Zona Franca, outside of Barcelona. Bayer, through Bayer Foreign Investment, also known as Bayforin, acquired a stake in PESA in 1964. Two years later Bayer Hispania added a new company, buying up Jerez, Cadiz-based Instituto Behring de Terapéutica Experimental, a company founded in 1938. As part of Bayer, this company changed its name to Instituto Bayer de Terapéutica Experimental S.A (IBTE).

The breakup of I.G. Farben following World War II gave Bayer control of the Agfa photographic supplies group. That company merged with rival Gevaert in 1966, creating Agfa-Gevaert. As a result, Agfa's Spanish operation was also renamed, as Agfa-Gevaert S.A. This unit grew shortly after, buying up Manufacturas Fotográficas Españolas S.A., a company founded in 1949.

Bayer Hispania began to take on a more strategic role within the Bayer group as a whole during the 1960s. The lower wages in Spain encouraged Bayer to expand its manufacturing operations there, leading to the establishment of its own chemicals complex in the Zona Franca in 1967. That factory became home to the company's production of chemicals for wood coating systems. Bayer's IBTE subsidiary also expanded, adding a new factory in Gualba that year.

PHARMACEUTICALS

Bayer stepped up its Spanish dyestuffs holdings in 1970, when it acquired majority control of Fabricación Nacional de Colorantes. Also that year, Bayer bought up a stake in fluoride producer Derivados del Flúor S.A. (DdF), a company that had originated as a factory in Lejona-Lehioa, in the Vizcaya region, founded in 1947. DdF grew quickly as part of Bayer, opening a new factory in Onton in 1971.

Chemicals remained the major part of Bayer Hispania's operations, especially following the opening of a new factory in Tarragona in 1971. This facility grew into Bayer's largest production facility in southern Europe and a major producer of polyurethane components. Also that year, Bayer Hispania opened a

KEY DATES

1899: Bayer opens a dyestuffs sales office in Spain, forming Federico Bayer y Cía.
1925: Bayer helps found La Química Comercial y Farmacéutica.
1968: The company incorporates as Bayer Hispania Industrial (BHI).
1981: BHI acquires full control of La Química Comercial y Farmacéutica.
1986: BHI takes control of all Bayer operations in Spain.
1997: BHI becomes part of Bayer Iberica.
1998: Bayer's Spanish subsidiary changes its name to Bayer Hispania.
2002: Bayer Hispania acquires Spanish operations of Aventis CropScience.
2010: Bayer Hispania reports sales of EUR 917 million ($1.28 billion) for the year.

production facility in Quart de Poblet, in the Valencia region.

Along with this chemicals growth, Bayer Hispania also expanded into the pharmaceuticals sector during the 1970s. In 1972 the company gained control of La Química Comercial y Farmacéutica S.A, which became known as Química Farmacéutica Bayer S.A. By 1981 Bayer had completed the takeover of that company, which formed the foundation for the group's pharmaceuticals and health care production.

CONSOLIDATING IN 1986

Bayer Hispania participated in a number of joint ventures, including the establishment of Bayer Rickmann Hispania, with a factory in Vitoria-Gasteiz, in 1972. In 1975 the company, through Bayforin, took a 50 percent stake in the creation of a new company, Alavesa de Productos Químicos Bayquisa, located in Salcedo, in the Alava region.

In the second half of the 1970s Bayer also began the process of restructuring its growing Spanish holdings. The company closed its Gualba factory, part of IBTE, in 1977. The following year IBTE itself was regrouped under Química Farmacéutica Bayer, moving its operations to that company's head office in Barcelona. In 1980 Bayforin increased its share of PESA to 75 percent, formally incorporating that business as a group subsidiary.

The restructuring of Bayer's Spanish interests continued through the first half of the 1980s. The company acquired full control of Química Farmacéutica Bayer S.A. in 1981. Bayer also took full control of Agfa-Gevaert's Spanish operation at this time. Bayer Hispania then acquired Viladecans-based Unisol in 1984. This purchase provided a new home for IBTE, which was then regrouped under Unisol, transferring its own operations to Viladecans that year. In 1986 Bayer restructured all of its Spanish operations, transferring Bayforin's holdings in Spain to BHI. Further restructuring at Bayer, which went public in 1991, resulted in Bayer Hispania becoming a 100 percent subsidiary of Berlin-based Bayer Gesellschaft für Beteiligungen GmbH.

BAYER IBERIA IN 1997

Bayer Hispania continued to grow through the 1990s. The company acquired Technicon España in 1991, combining it with the Spanish subsidiary of another Bayer operation, Miles España, to form Bayer Diagnósticos S.A. This company then merged into Química Farmacéutica Bayer in 1993. The company also expanded its Agfa Gevaert business, taking over Manufacturas Fotográficas Españolas S.A. in 1991. In the meantime, the growth of Bayer's chemicals and pharmaceuticals operations in Spain led it to exit the dyestuffs business. The company shut down its Unicolor operations in 1991.

Other BHI operations took shape during this period. In 1995 the company merged the animal health operations of IBTE and Química Farmacéutica Bayer to form a dedicated Animal Health division. BHI had also become a key part of Bayer AG's parapharmaceuticals operations, with the creation of a factory producing acetylsalicylic acid in La Felguera, in the Asturias region. In 1995 Bayer nearly doubled the capacity of the factory, to 3,500 metric tons per day. As a result, the La Felguera facility became responsible for some 80 percent of Bayer's total supply of acetylsalicylic acid.

BHI had also been part of Bayer's attempt to diversify into other areas, including sugar substitutes and ingredients for the cosmetics industry. However, in 1996 these businesses were sold off to Sara Lee Corporation of the United States. The following year Bayer AG created a new holding company, Bayer Iberica, in order to regroup its Spanish and Portuguese operations.

Bayer's presence in Portugal stemmed from 1909, with the creation of a sales subsidiary for its dyestuffs business. In the 1920s Bayer acquired a stake in Sociedade de Anilinas Lda, based in Lisbon. Bayer also added a pharmaceuticals subsidiary in Portugal in 1955, Bayer Pharma Company Limited, and later acquired chemicals and dyestuffs producer Quimicor SARL, founded in 1953. In 1967 Bayer merged its Portuguese operations together into Bayer SARL, establishing a factory, part of the future Bayer CropScience, in Cacém in 1968.

KEY BAYER REGION IN THE 21ST CENTURY

Bayer's Spanish subsidiary changed its name to Bayer Hispania in 1998. The company's position within the Bayer group had by then been reinforced by Bayer's decision to consolidate its active ingredients production at the La Felguera factory. This unit then became responsible for supplying much of Bayer's international operations, including in Germany, the United States, Australia, and South America.

Bayer Hispania's role as a key component of Bayer's international organization was underscored by other developments at the dawn of the 21st century. The first of these was the appointment of its general manager, Werning Wenning, as chairman of Bayer AG itself. Frank Bertram then filled Wenning's position at Bayer Hispania. Additionally, Bayer Hispania became responsible for Bayer's trade and investment operations in Argentina and Brazil. Both countries represented major markets for Bayer, generating annual revenues of $200 million and $300 million respectively. In 2001 Bayer Hispania became the primary services provider for Bayer's European operations, overseeing a new subsidiary, Euroservices Bayer S.L., based in Sant Joan Despí.

Starting in 2002, Bayer Hispania followed the restructuring of its German parent, adopting its three-part organization based around Bayer CropScience, Bayer HealthCare, and Bayer MaterialScience. Bayer Hispania took over the Spanish operations of Aventis CropScience following its acquisition by Bayer in 2002. Soon after, the company sold off two of its businesses, Lanxess, a sales company, and a factory in Cheste, part of its CropScience division.

Bayer Hispania also continued to invest in expanding its industrial holdings. For example, in 2001 the company launched production at a new styrene plant in Tarragona. The new EUR 50 million facility included a 145,000-metric-ton-per-year ABS thermoplastic unit, becoming one of Bayer AG's largest European factories. Some two-thirds of the production of the new Tarragona plant supported Bayer's international operations.

Bayer's acquisition of Schering Pharma, for $19.6 billion, expanded Bayer Hispania's own operations in

2007. Following that acquisition, Bayer Hispania absorbed Schering Pharma España S.A., which was placed under Química Farmacéutica Bayer's pharmaceuticals division. Bayer acquired full control of Schering in 2008, creating Bayer Schering Pharma as part of its HealthCare business unit in 2009.

Bayer Hispania's revenues topped EUR 900 billion ($1.2 billion) by 2010, making it a key component of Bayer's overall operations. It was then the largest part of Bayer Iberica, which reported EUR 1.1 billion in revenues for the year. Bayer Hispania had grown from a Bayer sales office into one of Spain's leading industrial companies spanning the pharmaceuticals and chemicals industries.

M. L. Cohen

PRINCIPAL SUBSIDIARIES

Bayer CropScience S.L.; Bayer MaterialScience S.L.; Bayer Schering Pharma Medical S.L.; Bayhealth S.L.; Berlimed S.A.; Intendis Farma S.A.; Nunhems Spain S.A.; Química Farmacéutica Bayer S.L.; Schering Spain S.A.

PRINCIPAL DIVISIONS

Bayer CropScience; Bayer HealthCare; Bayer Material-Science.

PRINCIPAL COMPETITORS

Aragonesas Industrias y Energias SAU; Arkema Química S.A.; Basell Polioefinas Iberica S.L.; BASF Espanola S.A.; CEPSA; Dow Chemical Iberica S.L.; La Seda de Barcelona S.A.; Repsol Química S.A.; Uralita S.A.

FURTHER READING

"Bayer Hispania Reports Sales in Brazil and Argentina." *Pharma Marketletter*, May 16, 2005.

"Bayer Launches New Chemical Group in Spain." *Asia Africa Intelligence Wire*, December 9, 2002.

"Bayer Officially Opens Styrene Plant." *Chemical Business Newsbase*, April 24, 2001.

"Bayer Opens Styrenics Plant in Tarragona." *Chemical Business Newsbase*, June 6, 2001.

"Reaffirming the Present and Preparing for the Future: Interview with Bayer Hispania SA's Vice-President." *Chemical Business Newsbase*, March 31, 2006.

BCP Imports, LLC

148 Main Street
Toledo, Ohio 43605-2067
U.S.A.
Telephone: (419) 693-5302
Toll Free: (800) 921-8661
Fax: (419) 697-8324
Web site: http://www.brainchildproducts.com

Private Company
Incorporated: 2005 as Brainchild Products, LLC
Employees: 35
Sales: $100 million (2010 est.)
NAICS: 424310 Piece Goods, Notions, and Other Dry
      Goods Merchant Wholesalers

■ ■ ■

BCP Imports, LLC, doing business as Brainchild Products, is a developer and marketer of promotional and other unique products, mostly sourced from the Far East. The Toledo, Ohio-based private company is best known for its Silly Bandz brand of rubber bands shaped like animals and other objects and worn like bracelets that became a sensation in the United States in 2009 and 2010. In addition, BCP markets apparel, including fleecewear, outerwear, T-shirts and polo shirts, and hats and visors. Other products include printable silicon bracelets, dog tag and custom key chains, lanyards, thunder sticks, mouse pads, coffee and travel mugs, bottle and can coolies, and "fan rollers," recoiling posters that can serve as a messaging medium for sporting events, rallies, and other gatherings. In addition to its

Ohio headquarters, BCP maintains an office in Hong Kong. The company is owned by its chief executive, Robert Croak.

CONCERT PROMOTER ORIGINS

Born and raised in East Toledo, Ohio, Robert Croak, who said he grew up wanting to be a baseball player or an inventor, was initially a bar owner and concert promoter. After graduating from high school in 1982, he earned a degree in marketing from the Owens Community College in Toledo. In 1987 he took over an area restaurant, Frankie's, owned and operated by his grandmother. After her death, the building was slated to be auctioned off, but with the help of his mother Croak was able to secure a bank loan to purchase the property. He then spent several months adding a second room, capable of holding 100 people, and installed a stage for rock concerts.

Croak claimed that he decided to become a concert promoter simply because he wanted to see good bands. He told the *Toledo Blade*, "I was tired of going to clubs that were boring and I decided I was going to do something about it." While renovations were being made to Frankie's, Croak traveled around the Midwest scouting for bands to hire. On Valentine's Day in 1988 Croak held the first concert in his new room, known as Frankie's Inner-City Lounge. Despite a storm that left eight inches of snow on the ground, the show drew a capacity crowd, marking Croak's successful debut as an impresario.

Croak enjoyed enough success with Frankie's that in 1993 he opened a second club across the street.

Called the Main Event, it featured a main concert room that could hold 500 people. Other clubs along the same stretch of Toledo would follow in the 1990s, including Croakie's and Club BPM. Croak emerged as one of Toledo's top three concert promoters, but it was a far from secure career. Not only was competition stiff, Croak had to contend with citations for underage drinking at his clubs that jeopardized his liquor license.

Croak was arrested for underage alcohol sales but never convicted. He faced other legal problems as well. In 2002 he was convicted of one count of forgery for signing a check for a business associate. He was placed on probation, the terms of which banned him from owning or operating a bar. As a result, he told *Businessweek*, "I chose to pursue bigger and better things."

BRAINCHILD PRODUCTS FORMED: 2005

Croak formed Brainchild Products, LLC, in 2005 (replaced in 2009 by BCP Imports, LLC). Setting up shop on Main Street in East Toledo, he began to import promotional products and other items from the Far East and serve as a wholesaler. One of the company's early successes was an iPod plastic sleeve called the iJacket that could be customized with a logo, photographs, text, or other graphics. Another important product was a custom silicon bracelet, made popular by cyclist and cancer survivor Lance Armstrong, whose foundation used the yellow LIVESTRONG rubber wristband as a fundraising product. BCP took advantage of the success of the LIVESTRONG program, becoming the first to market the LIVESTRONG bracelet as a custom product. It also became the sole customer of a Chinese factory for the product.

According to a *Businessweek* profile, around 2007 Croak and the manager of the Chinese factory that furnished BCP with silicon bracelets visited a trade show in China "where the manager spotted stretch animal shapes that were sold in Japan as rubber bands." These animal rubber bands had been around for some time. In fact, the Japanese creator had won a national design award for the product, which had been designed as a way to make office supplies fun in Japan. The rubber bands had been available on a limited basis in the United States since 2002. Most notably, the rubber bands were carried by the Museum of Modern Art Design Store.

FIRST SILLY BANDZ SOLD: 2008

Croak liked the item but thought if the bands were thicker and larger they could be worn as bracelets like the silicon bands the company already carried. He asked his Chinese manufacturer to produce a line of animal-shaped rubber bands but in greater variety to promote collecting and trading. Croak received his first shipment of the bands in 2008 and late in the year began selling them online as Silly Bandz. He spent no money to promote the brand, relying instead on social media platforms and viral marketing. In a matter of months he found himself at the center of a Silly Bandz craze.

Croak was not alone in claiming credit for the Silly Bandz sensation. In nearby Sylvania, Ohio, Gary and Molly Fitzpatrick, owners of three Learning Express stores, told the *Toledo Blade* that they encountered the Japanese animal-shaped rubber bands as well. They thought the item was too expensive, and only after the vendor moved production to China to lower costs did the Fitzpatricks purchase the rubber bands. The manager at one of their stores began giving the bands away to students, who created a local fad in the summer of 2008.

The Fitzpatricks told other Learning Express franchises about the rubber bands, and a number of them ordered supplies. The items were especially popular in Birmingham, Alabama, generally considered the birthplace of the fad. Croak conceded to the *Blade* that Birmingham was an early hotbed for animal-shaped rubber bands. Early in 2009 a Learning Express store in Birmingham became the first retailer to carry Silly Bandz, using them to introduce young children to shapes. Nevertheless, Croak insisted, "We created the craze and we marketed it nationally."

FAD TAKES SHAPE: 2009

Silly Bandz nevertheless was the brand that became synonymous with the animal-shaped rubber bands. The fad took root in the South in mid-2009, spreading to the East Coast and from there to other parts of the United States. Children began wearing them to school and trading them. The popularity of the product coincided with a downturn in the economy. The item was inexpensive and parents could indulge their children with a package of Silly Bandz rather than spend money on a more costly item.

KEY DATES

1988: Robert Croak begins career as concert promoter.
2005: Croak incorporates Brainchild Products, LLC.
2007: Croak is introduced to Japanese animal-shaped rubber bands.
2008: Croak begins selling Silly Bandz.
2009: BCP Imports, LLC, is formed.

By early 2010 the Silly Bandz craze was in full force and BCP struggled to keep up with orders, forcing Croak to hire more people. Given the poor state of the economy, there was no lack of job applicants. The day after the *Blade* ran a story on BCP and Silly Bandz, the company was besieged by job seekers, forcing Croak to lock the doors and turn people away. Faced with an unexpected deadline one evening, Croak sought extra help through a Facebook posting and in a matter of minutes 20 people arrived.

To fill orders and continue to fan the flames of the fad, Croak was willing to pay to fly in supplies rather than wait for regular shipping. Instead of four weeks the delivery time from the factory was cut to four days. He also faced no shortage of competition. Birmingham entrepreneur James Howard introduced Zanybandz, and soon the market was inundated with Rubba Bandz and Logo Bandz as well. Nevertheless, it was Silly Bandz that became the generic name for the item, which put BCP in an enviable position as the competition actually stimulated the market rather than cut into BCP's sales. By June 2010 Silly Bandz were carried in about 18,000 stores in 25 states and each day BCP was shipping some 1,500 boxes of the product.

NEW SHAPES, NEW DEALS

To spur trading and sales Silly Bandz introduced a wide variety of new shapes, moving beyond animals. Included were dinosaurs, princesses, Wild West, baseball, cars, alphabet, fantasy shapes, and miscellaneous "fun" shapes. Additionally, there were tie-dye, glow in the dark, and glitter bands. There were also licensing deals to pursue. Although Disney and Major League Baseball signed with a competitor, there was no shortage of possible partners for Silly Bandz. Deals were struck with television properties SpongeBob, Dora the Explorer, and iCarly, as well as Marvel Comics and teen pop star Justin Bieber. Croak also sought to extend the Silly Bandz brand by introducing Silly Necklaces and Silly Buttons.

While Silly Bandz were just gaining traction in some parts of the United States, areas where they were already popular experienced a backlash. A number of schools banned Silly Bandz, and children were told to leave their collections at home. According to *Time*, "Students fiddle with them during class and arrange swaps—trading say, a bracelet with a mermaid for one with a dragon—when they should be concentrating on schoolwork, teachers say. Sometimes a trade goes bad—kids get buyer's remorse too—and hard feelings, maybe even scuffles, ensue." There were also some health concerns, because children who wore too many of the bands on their arms curtailed their circulation.

As the school year came to an end, many children indulged in their passion for Silly Bandz at summer camp, where the Bandz were more accepted. Children were not the only ones who embraced Silly Bandz. Teenagers began wearing them, as did some young adults. Moreover, celebrities were also spotted wearing Silly Bandz, including actresses Sarah Jessica Parker and Mary-Kate Olsen, model Agyness Deyn, food writer and TV host Anthony Bourdain, and Kelly Ripa of *Live with Regis and Kelly*.

QUIZNOS ALLIANCE: 2010

By the fall of 2010, the excitement among schoolchildren over Silly Bandz in the areas of the country that had initiated the phenomenon had waned. Other parts of the country, primarily the Midwest and West Coast, were just beginning to embrace the product. BCP was also doing what it could to fan the flames, hiring children to serve as Silly Bandz consultants to keep the brand current. The company also continued to find willing partners. Hello Kitty signed a licensing deal, and in September 2010 the Quiznos sandwich chain began giving out Silly Bandz with their Kids Meals. While schoolchildren and teens grew tired of Silly Bandz in some markets, young adults were finding a new use for the product. According to press reports, women were giving Silly Bandz to men in bars and clubs as a way to indicate their interest.

Sales of Silly Bandz would likely trail off in time, but in addition to the United States there were other parts of the world for Silly Bandz to exploit. As was the case with other fad products, there was a good chance that a small but steady market for the product would continue but that replicating the original success would prove difficult. Nevertheless, BCP forged ties with countless retailers and distributors through Silly Bandz, relationships that were likely to prove beneficial to the company in the years ahead.

Ed Dinger

PRINCIPAL SUBSIDIARIES
Brainchild Products, LLC.

PRINCIPAL COMPETITORS
Forever Collectibles; Zanybandz.com.

FURTHER READING

Berfield, Susan. "The Man behind the Bandz." *Businessweek*, June 14, 2010, p. 64.

Horovitz, Bruce. "Silly Bandz Mania Takes Shape." *USA Today*, July 1, 2010, p. 1B.

Lane, Tahree. "Snappy! Toledo Company Makes Stretchy Bracelets that Kids Everywhere Want." *Toledo Blade*, May 16, 2010.

Maltby, Emily. "Silly Bandz Seek to Stretch Popularity." *Wall Street Journal Eastern Edition*, July 8, 2010, p. B4.

"Robert Croak, CEO, BCP Imports." *Bloomberg Daily Programming*. August 13, 2010.

Rochman, Bonnie. "Silly Bandz Banned—What's a Schoolkid to Do?" *Time*, May 25, 2010.

Yonke, David. "Toledo's Nightclub Impresarios." *Toledo Blade*, July 23, 2000, p. D1.

Boston Whaler, Inc.

———————————■———————————

100 Whaler Way
Edgewater, Florida 32141-7213
U.S.A.
Telephone: (386) 428-0057
Toll Free: (800) 942-5379; (877) 294-5645
Fax: (386) 423-8589
Web site: http://www.whaler.com

Wholly Owned Subsidiary of Brunswick Corporation
Incorporated: 1958
Employees: 250
Sales: $58 million (2009 est.)
NAICS: 336612 Boat Building

■ ■ ■

Known as the maker of unsinkable boats, Boston Whaler, Inc., is an Edgewater, Florida-based unit of Brunswick Corporation that manufactures several lines of pleasure motorboats as well as boats modified by others for military and law enforcement uses. The Sport and Tender models are small boats designed for watersports, fishing, and other casual uses. Also on the small end, the Montauk series feature shallow draft hulls and smaller fuel-efficient engines.

More powerful and slighter larger is the Dauntless line, which includes a center console design. Also featuring a center console is the more rugged Outrage line, which includes a hard-top windshield system for weather protection. Finally, Boston Whaler offers the Conquest cabin boat line that provides overnight sleep-ing accommodations. Boston Whaler boats are sold around the world through a network of dealers.

ORIGINS OF THE UNSINKABLE BOAT: 1943

The man behind the founding of Boston Whaler was Dick Fisher. A Harvard University graduate with a degree in philosophy, Fisher had grown up around boating but began his business career in the electronics industry, specializing in photo-controls, sensitive electromagnetic relays, and other equipment used in traffic light systems. In 1943 he developed the idea of using balsa wood to design a lightweight yet strong rowboat. Because balsa wood was so easily dented, it was not a practical concept, but Fisher did not abandon the goal of constructing a sturdy, lightweight boat.

Ten years later he learned about new resins that could fill a mold as foam and then harden in place. This new material, which would take the trade name Styrofoam, was in Fisher's mind a kind of "plastic balsa." Having sailed for the first time during this time, on the then-popular Alcort Sailfish, Fisher began to consider the possibility of using Styrofoam to develop a small unsinkable sailboat.

With the help of a friend, Fisher created a boat hull by covering Styrofoam with an epoxy glass resin. Another friend, naval architect C. Raymond Hunt, urged him to add an outdoor motor to tap into a larger market. Fisher complied, and the result was the 13-foot Boston Whaler. To anyone with a sense of maritime history, the name made little sense, given that Boston had never been a whaling port, but the seaworthy nature of the boat itself was akin to the double-end whaleboats that harpooned whales and were often pulled vigorously through the waves by the wounded beasts on what was known as a "Nantucket sleigh ride." Moreover, Boston Whaler was a catchy name from a marketing point of view. The craft made its debut at the 1958 New York Boat Show, where it was well received.

FIRST PRODUCTION FACILITY
OPENS: 1958

With orders in hand, Fisher established a production facility for Boston Whaler in 1958 in Braintree, Massachusetts, and the first model, The Cox'n, was built. It was followed by the Standard model, and in 1961 a 16-foot model was added to the line. In the development of the larger hull, Fisher toyed with a center console design rather the traditional starboard-side location for the helm. It was roomier, offered better steering, an even keel, and provided an excellent arrangement for fishing. Boston Whaler became the first production boat to offer a center console as a standard feature.

Boston Whaler gained national prominence in 1961 when it the boat featured in a photo spread in *Life* magazine. Dressed in business attire, Fisher was seen motoring away in the back half of a whaler after it had been sawed in half, thus giving birth to the legend that the Boston Whaler was an unsinkable boat. To keep pace with demand, production was soon moved to a new facility in Rockland, Massachusetts.

In 1972 Fisher decided to sell Boston Whaler to CML Group, a Massachusetts marketing company the initials of which stood for Consumer Marketing Lifestyles. In essence a conglomerate, CML would eventually acquire NordicTrack, but Boston Whaler was the company's first major acquisition. Despite the loss of Fisher, Boston Whaler was able to carry on with little difficulty because Bob Dougherty, who had been with the company since 1960, continued as the head of design and development. Under CML's ownership, Boston Whaler enjoyed strong sales. The company introduced cabin models to become involved in the family cruiser sector. In addition to the pleasure boat market, Boston Whaler adapted some of its models for commercial fishing as well as such military and law enforcement applications as safety patrols and rescue operations.

To keep pace with demand, Boston Whaler began in the mid-1980s to search for a place to build a new manufacturing facility. After considering several states the company settled on Florida. The Florida Division of Economic Development was then instrumental in finding a suitable site: a shuttered boatbuilding facility about 20 miles south of Daytona Beach in Edgewater, Florida, that provided ample room for future expansion. In 1987 Boston Whaler acquired the property and began production there. The company also outgrew its corporate headquarters, and in 1988 relocated its administrative offices to Rockland, Massachusetts.

REEBOK BUYS COMPANY: 1983

Boston Whaler performed well as a part of CML but in 1989 CML became the object of corporate raider Irwin Jacobs, who acquired a stake of about 15 percent in the publicly traded company. Over the years Jacobs had acquired several boat manufacturers, which in 1986 he brought together to form Genmar Industries Inc. To many observers, Jacobs was more interested in acquiring Boston Whaler than he was CML. It was a charge that he denied and indeed he did not make an offer for the property. Squeezed for money, CML elected to restructure its operations to fend off Jacobs, and as part of the effort sold Boston Whaler for $43 million in cash in 1989 to Reebok International Ltd., an athletic footwear and apparel company.

Buying Boston Whaler was a curious decision for Reebok. Not only was Reebok unfamiliar with the boating business, it was not the best of times to enter the market due to a downturn in the economy. In fiscal 1988 Boston Whaler posted sales of $66 million, an amount that decreased 10 percent to $60 million a year later, and $45 million in fiscal 1990. In was also in 1990 that the U.S. Congress imposed a 10 percent federal luxury tax that covered new boats costing more than $100,000. The tax was intended to make the rich pay their fair share, but the assumption was that wealthy individuals would continue to buy expensive boats proved wrong. Instead, people stopped buying new boats, and many boatbuilders and companies that depended upon them were driven out of business before the tax was repealed. Boston Whaler fared better than most, but was still forced to layoff a large portion of its workforce.

To matters worse for Boston Whaler, the company introduced new styles in 1991 and neglected the classic boats that had been at the heart of the company for

KEY DATES

1958: Dick Fisher founds Boston Whaler.
1972: CML Group acquires Boston Whaler.
1987: The Edgewater, Florida, production facility is acquired.
1989: Company is sold to Reebok International Ltd.
1996: Brunswick Corporation acquires Boston Whaler.

decades. Sales fell to $38 million in fiscal 1991 and improved to $45 million a year later, due in part to one of those new products, The Rage, which was a mix between a Whaler and a Jet Ski that found a market with younger buyers. Despite the improvement in sales, Reebok was ready to exit the boat business after just three years. In July 1993, Reebok sold Boston Whaler to MacAndrews & Forbes Holdings Inc., a diversified holding company controlled by Revlon Inc. Chairman Ronald Perlman. The purchase price was $20 million, or $25 million less than what Reebok had paid for the property just three years earlier.

Boston Whaler now became part of MacAndrews & Forbes' Meridian Sports, whose boat brands also included Mastercraft. The new owners wasted little time in severing Boston Whaler's New England roots. The decision was made to close the Rockland plant and move all manufacturing operations as well as the corporate headquarters to the larger Edgewater site. Given that many boatbuilders were already calling Florida home because of the favorable climate and a large pool of inexpensive labor, it was an understandable step. The move was completed in 1994.

BRUNSWICK ACQUIRES COMPANY: 1996

Under Meridian, Boston Whaler rebuilt annual sales to the $50 million range, due in large part to its Commercial Products Division, which produced high-margin, custom-built versions of Whalers for military, law enforcement, and commercial customers. Overall, Boston Whaler was not performing well enough for Meridian to keep, and in the spring of 1996 Meridian agreed to sell Boston Whaler to Brunswick Corporation. According to Securities and Exchange Commission filings, Brunswick paid $27.4 million in cash and the assumption of liabilities for the business.

One of America's oldest recreation and leisure-time products manufacturers, Brunswick was launched in Cincinnati, Ohio, in 1845 as a carriage shop. Founder John Moses Brunswick soon took advantage of his woodworking capabilities to produce billiard tables. The company became further involved in the recreational field in the 1880s when it began manufacturing bowling pins and bowling balls. In 1960 Brunswick turned its attention to boating and began acquiring such builders as Owens Yacht Company and Larson Boats. Brunswick deepened its commitment to the sector in the 1980s with the addition of Bayliner Marine Corporation, the Sea Ray line, MonArk Boat Company, Marine Group, Inc., Starcraft Powers Boats, and others. Given that Sea Ray had cost Brunswick $425 million a decade earlier, the purchase of Boston Whaler for less than $30 million was a shrewd deal for a company that was already well entrenched in the boating business.

Boston Whaler was folded into the Sea Ray Division of Brunswick's Marine segment and continued to divide its business between the recreation and commercial division. As the economy improved in the second half of the 1990s, sales of recreation boats increased. As a result, Boston Whaler decided in 2000 to cease producing the small patrol and rescue boats that had been a mainstay for a number of years in order to devote more of its 250,000-square-foot Edgewater facility to the production of recreation boats. Rather, another Brunswick unit converted Whalers for the Navy, Coast Guard, and law enforcement agencies.

LAYOFFS: 2008

A major advantage of being part of the Brunswick family was that Boston Whaler gained access to the engines produced by sister company Mercury Marine. Starting in 2001 Whalers were delivered with Mercury engines as part of the package. Because boats offered thin profits while engines provided hefty margins, the combination of boat and engine served the greater interests of Brunswick and kept Boston Whaler a viable unit. Nevertheless, the boating industry remained cyclical, dependent on the strength of the economy.

By 2008 conditions were poor, resulting in a steep decline in boat sales that impacted all of Brunswick's marine holdings. Boston Whaler was forced to furlough 250 workers, or about half its Edgewater workforce. Sales continued to dwindled in 2009, and the company limited production as a way to allow dealers to reduce their inventory. Nevertheless, Boston Whaler retained its strong brand identity, still known as the maker of unsinkable boats, and its long-term prospects remained promising.

Ed Dinger

PRINCIPAL COMPETITORS

Lowe Boats, Inc.; Tracker Marine Group; Viking Marine Group.

FURTHER READING

Carton, Barbara. "Reebok Pays $43M for Boston Whaler." *Boston Globe*, August 8, 1989, p. 37.

Kelly, R. J. "Boat Maker to Cut Back Commercial Production." *Daytona Beach News-Journal*, November 10, 2000, p. 12A.

Kentouris, Chris. "Reebok International Buys Boston Whaler, Boat Builder." *WWD*, August 9, 1989, p. 27.

Koprowski, Gene. "Reebok Pays $42M, Jogs Off with Boston Whaler." *Metalworking News*, August 14, 1989, p. 4.

Perlmutter, Walter. "The Unsinkable Legend." *Sarasota Herald-Tribune*, September 4, 1999, p. 3E.

Robinson, Bill. "Whaler's Silver." *Yachting*, December 1983, p. 80.

Witters, Jim. "Boston Whaler, Brunswick Struggle amid Economic Woes." *Daytona Beach News-Journal*, May 1, 2009, p. 11A.

Yenkin, Jonathan. "Boston Whaler to Move, Close Massachusetts Plant." *Associated Press*, August 3, 1993.

Brauerei C. & A. Veltins GmbH & Co. KG

An der Streue
Meschede-Grevenstein, 59872
Germany
Telephone: (49 2934) 959-0
Fax: (49 2934) 959-493
Web site: http://www.veltins.de

Private Company
Founded: 1824 as Grevensteiner Brauerei
Incorporated: 1893 as C. & A. Veltins oHG
Employees: 1,380
Sales: EUR 642 million ($892 million) (2009)
NAICS: 312120 Breweries; 312111 Soft Drink
   Manufacturing

■ ■ ■

Brauerei C. & A. Veltins GmbH & Co. KG is one of Germany's largest privately owned breweries. The company's flagship product, Frisches Veltins, is one of the country's most popular premium pilsner brands. Frisches Veltins is also available as a low-calorie and low-alcohol light; in a nonalcoholic version; as a Radler (a combination of beer and lemon-flavored soda pop); and as a nonalcoholic malt variety. With its core market in North Rhine-Westphalia, Frisches Veltins is distributed nationally and exported to 25 countries. C. & A. Veltins also produces a range of mixed beer-and-soda-pop drinks under the Veltins V+ brand. The company owns beverage retail chain Dursty and the wholesale beverage distributors Westdeutsche Getränkelogistik and Westfälische Gastronomie-Service. Based in Grevenstein in the Sauerland region, C. & A. Veltins is owned and managed by a fifth-generation member of the founding Veltins family.

INNKEEPER FOUNDS BREWERY IN 1824

In the 1820s, when innkeeper Franz Kramer started selling his beer to other local inns in Grevenstein, a small town in the western German Sauerland region, it was still commonplace for innkeepers to serve their home-brew only to their own guests. However, the demand for Kramer's beer grew continuously. In 1824 Kramer established the brewery Grevensteiner Brauerei, and within only a few years it became the preferred supplier of beer to other innkeepers as well as to major local events such as the *Schützenfest*, annual marksmen's festival where large amounts of the popular beverage were consumed.

In 1852 Clemens Veltins, who had immigrated to the United States in the early 1840s and returned to his home region about a decade later, acquired the Grevensteiner brewery. The 30-year-old learned the trade in Milwaukee, Wisconsin, an area with a long beer brewing tradition, and he led the brewery through a period of rapid growth in the second half of the 19th century. After remaining steady at production of about 150 hectoliters of beer per year in the 1850s, demand increased constantly in the two decades that followed. By the early 1880s Veltins ran out of production capacity at the old brew house, and a brand-new brewery was built at the outskirts of Grevenstein in 1883.

Brauerei C. & A. Veltins GmbH & Co. KG

COMPANY PERSPECTIVES

The innovations of the past decade have proven that foresight and entrepreneurial action do pay off. With the new reusable crate generation, we send an important signal to the market, particularly in times of economic crises, that we will participate in shaping the premium segment in the future as well.

The two sons of Clemens Veltins, Carl and Anton, followed in their father's footsteps. Carl Veltins attended brewing trade school in Augsburg and worked at different breweries in the Rhineland and in Bavaria. His twin brother Anton worked at two large breweries in Paderborn and Westheim, Bavaria, for several years before he joined the family business. Clemens Veltins retired in 1893, and his two sons founded the general partnership C. & A. Veltins oHG to jointly managed the brewery. Anton Veltins oversaw the production, while Carl Veltins took care of the administrative side of the business. The rapidly advancing industrialization in the late 19th century enabled the Veltins family to increase productivity. The brewery was equipped with a large steam engine, an artificial ice machine, and an electric power generator.

MODERNIZATION, FOCUS ON PILSNER AFTER WORLD WAR I

After Clemens Veltins's death in 1905, Carl and Anton Veltins ran the family brewery together until 1913 when Carl Veltins died. One year later, World War I broke out, and Anton Veltins steered the company through the difficult war years. Despite the scarcity of the necessary raw materials, and the limited purchasing power of the German population, Veltins managed to carry on the business through the war at a decreased rate of production. After the end of the war, Anton Veltins's nephew Carl, who returned from the battlefield in 1918, joined the family business. One year later, the first delivery truck was purchased for the brewery.

Anton Veltins retired in the early 1920s, and his nephew Carl took over the brewery. Carl Veltins immediately invested in the modernization and expansion of the existing production capacity. In 1923 the brewery's cellar area was enlarged, and new refrigeration equipment was installed. One year later, a state-of-the-art brew house with a much higher output capacity was built in Grevenstein.

A second major goal of Carl Veltins was to continue improving the quality of the company's beer. Analyses of the spring water used by the brewery in Grevenstein revealed that it was particularly soft water, good for brewing a light-yellow top-fermented beer called pilsner. When Carl Veltins decided to focus on brewing pilsner beer in 1926, he was taking a big risk. At the time, pilsner had an estimated market share of about 2 to 3 percent. Veltins experimented with different recipes, reduced the hops content, and intensified the fermentation process, until the right formula was found. The resulting pilsner became the basis of the brewery's sustained success.

GROWTH DURING GREAT DEPRESSION, STAGNATION DURING WORLD WAR II

C. & A. Veltins was one of the first German breweries to focus on pilsner beer. Despite the hardship brought on by the Great Depression in the early 1930s, the demand for Veltins Pilsner increased continuously. Carl Veltins pursued a premium strategy right from the beginning. In addition to focusing on the high quality of the beer, he was also very selective in choosing his customers: well-kept inns and bars where only properly cooled Veltins Pilsner would be served. In 1935 the brewery's annual output reached 5,000 hectoliters.

The outbreak of World War II in September 1939 caused a sudden shortage of hops and malt, the distribution of which was controlled by the Nazi government. It became more and more difficult to purchase fuel, electricity, and spare parts. With no ingredients to brew a true beer, the brewery produced a whey-based beverage called *Fliegerbier*, or pilot's beer, during the war years. Many brewery staff, including the owner and his son, were drafted to the military, while production continued in Grevenstein.

Carl Veltins returned from the battlefield unharmed. However, his son and designated heir, Carl Clemens Veltins, was killed in action. Due to restrictions imposed on German breweries by the Allied forces military administration, C. & A. Veltins put out a hybrid version of *Fliegerbier* combined with traditional beer during the immediate postwar years until the restrictions were lifted in the late 1940s.

POSTWAR BOOM DRIVES RAPID EXPANSION

The currency reform of 1948 in western Germany and the foundation of the Federal Republic of Germany the following year laid the foundation for the so-called Ger-

KEY DATES

1824: Innkeeper Franz Kramer starts selling home-brewed beer to other local inns.

1852: Clemens Veltins takes over Grevensteiner brewery.

1893: Carl and Anton Veltins found the general partnership C. & A. Veltins OHG.

1926: Carl Veltins Jr. decides to focus on brewing pilsner beer using selected local spring water.

1974: Rosemarie Veltins takes over company management.

1994: Susanne Veltins succeeds her mother as CEO.

2001: Mixed beer-and-soda-pop range Veltins V+ is launched.

2009: A newly designed reusable Veltins crate generation is introduced.

man economic miracle. Carl Veltins immediately got to work to modernize and expand the brewery. The first filling machine was installed, pouring beer into half-liter bottles from 200-liter beer kegs. A new commercial ice generator was purchased as were the company's first three diesel trucks. Most importantly, in an attempt to secure the necessary water supplies in the long run, Veltins tapped a second spring only three miles away from the brewery.

With the postwar boom in full swing in the mid-1950s, the brewery's output began growing at a rate of 25 percent per year on average. To keep up with the increased demand, a new and much larger brew house was added in 1957. Distribution of Veltins Pilsener was further expanded into western and northern Germany, and the modernization and enlargement of production capacity continued in the 1960s. By 1964, the year when Carl Veltins died, the brewery's output had grown to nine times that of 10 years earlier, reaching more than 100,000 hectoliters.

CONTINUED INVESTMENT, CONTINUED GROWTH AFTER 1964

Carl Veltins's daughter Rosemarie Veltins took over the company in 1964 at age 26 and became CEO in 1974, leading the brewery through another period of rapid growth. With pilsner gaining enormously in popularity among German beer drinkers in the 1970s, Veltins evolved as one of the country's fastest-growing breweries. To build a lasting foundation for the

company's future growth, Rosemarie Veltins acquired the land surrounding the springs to have as much control over the quality of the water used for beer brewing as possible. She also purchased real estate next to the brewery for its further expansion and even decided to have a part of the mountain carved out at the foothills of which the brewery was located to create additional space.

Throughout the 1970s and 1980s C. & A. Veltins invested in the continuous expansion of the brewery's output capacity and in setting up state-of-the-art facilities and equipment. In the 1970s the company added cellar space for filtering, filling, and storing steel kegs, and built a fully automated brew house, two new bottling plants, and a high-rise warehouse for a total of DEM 80 million. Veltins' investment program continued on an even higher level in the 1980s. The company spent roughly DEM 350 million on additional facilities, including 29 large, 57-feet-high, stainless-steel fermentation tanks, automation, and computer controlled processing of the production cycle, and the modernization of the company's own wastewater treatment plant and power generation facilities with a special focus on environmentally friendly technology.

The resulting growth in a generally stagnating beer market was impressive. In 1974, the brewery's 150th anniversary year, Veltins reported an output of more than 500,000 hectoliters. By the end of the decade the company's annual output had grown to 650,000 hectoliters. In 1984 the company's production volume passed the one million hectoliter mark for the first time. Five years later the company's output reached more than 1.8 million hectoliters, making Veltins Germany's fourth-largest privately owned brewery. The heavy investment in the latest technologies also resulted in a productivity level about three times above the industry average.

EXPANDING MARKETING AND DISTRIBUTION AFTER 1984

Until the mid-1980s Veltins had successfully managed to sustain significant growth in the slowly, but steadily shrinking German beer market. To continue on that path, however, the brewery had to respond to fundamentally changing market conditions, including changing consumer tastes, the increasing importance of large retail chains as a distribution channel, the declining popularity of traditional-style bars, and the growing competitive pressure in the beer market.

Beginning in the second half of the 1980s, Veltins significantly increased its investment in marketing measures. The company ran advertising campaigns in national print titles and on national television. In the mid-1990s Veltins modernized its brand image, moving away from traditional-style hospitality, to appeal to a younger, more agile and pleasure-oriented consumer generation. Later in the decade the brewery added sports sponsoring to its marketing mix and started supporting Schalke 04, a national soccer league team based in the Ruhr, and BMW's Formula One team.

After the death of Rosemarie Veltins in 1994, her daughter Susanne Veltins took over as CEO. Under her leadership, the company continued to invest significantly in state-of-the-art technologies and facilities, as well as in marketing. To strengthen its market position in its traditional core market, Veltins set up a key account management for major customers in the hospitality industry and in retail trade in 1999. In addition, the company took steps to gain direct access to important distribution channels.

Export operations, which began in 1992 when the first barrels of Fresh Veltins were shipped to Austria, was greatly expanded in the second half of the 1990s. While some of the Germans' preferred vacation destinations, such as Italy and Spain, accounted for a large part of exports, Veltins was also shipped to other countries, including the United Kingdom, France, Poland, Hungary, Cyprus, the Canary Islands, the United States, and Canada. However, Germany, and the western and northern German regions in particular, remained Veltins' core market.

ADDING NEW PRODUCTS, DISTRIBUTION CHANNELS

As a reaction to changing consumer tastes, the brewery had taken the first step in expanding its product range in 1992, when it launched the low-calorie and low-alcohol pilsner variety Veltins Light. In 1999 the company introduced the nonalcoholic Veltins Alkoholfrei. In the new millennium the company began to tap the rapidly growing market for mixed beer-and-soda-pop beverages. In 2001 the brewery launched the mixed beer-and-soda-pop range V+ with two flavors, V+Lemon and V+Cola, under the Veltins brand.

Veltins Radler, a combination of beer and lemon-flavored soda pop, and Veltins Malz, a malt-based nonalcoholic beverage, were introduced in 2005. Later in the decade the company added several flavors to the V+ range. As a result of the diversification strategy, decreasing beer sales were set off by increasing revenues from the mixed beer-and-soda-pop range.

In an effort to gain direct access to important distribution channels, the company ventured into the retail trade in 2000 when it acquired the beverage retail chain Dursty with 200 outlets in North Rhine-Westphalia, the Rhineland, and Hesse. In the same year Veltins acquired beer wholesaler Bier Schneider, and took over Getränke Janke, a Westphalian beverage wholesaler for the hospitality industry, in 2002. The company's beverage wholesale, retail and distribution activities were reorganized in three subsidiaries, including Westfälische Gastronomie-Service, Dursty GmbH, and Westfälische Getränkelogistik, a shipping company for beverages sold in reusable bottles and crates, serving food retailers in North Rhine-Westphalia. In the middle of the decade the company began to cooperate with additional beverage wholesalers in western and southern Germany.

A visible sign of the brewery's commitment to its premium segment strategy and to multiuse bottles and crates, the company introduced a newly designed reusable crate with a highly visible plastic-molded multicolored relief of the Veltins logo in 2009. In that year, Veltins' total output reached 2.46 million hectoliters. The brewery supplied some 15,000 customers in the hospitality industry, almost double as many as in the late 1980s. Determined to remain an independent player in the increasingly consolidating and competitive German brewery industry, the company announced in 2010 that it was planning to launch a brand-new product generation that year.

Evelyn Hauser

PRINCIPAL SUBSIDIARIES

Veltins Beteiligungen KG; Dursty GmbH; Westdeutsche Getränkelogistik GmbH & Co. KG; Westfälische Gastronomie-Service GmbH & Co. KG.

PRINCIPAL COMPETITORS

Anheuser-Busch InBev; Bitburger Braugruppe GmbH; Brau Holding International GmbH & Co. KGaA; Carlsberg A/S; Haus Cramer Holding KG; Karlsberg Brauerei KG Weber; Krombacher Brauerei Bernhard Schadeberg GmbH & Co. KG; Radeberger Gruppe KG.

FURTHER READING

Geschichte und Gegenwart: 175 Jahre Brauerei Veltins. Meschede-Grevenstein, Germany: Brauerei C. & A. Veltins GmbH & Co., 1999.

"Veltins Defies Negative Trend." *Europe Intelligence Wire,* February 12, 2004.

"Veltins: Einkaufstour auslandischer Brauriesen geht weiter." *DPA–AFX,* February 26, 2003.

"Veltins Increases Turnover in 2003." *Europe Intelligence Wire,* February 12, 2004.

"Veltins Interested in Takeover of Frankenheim." *Europe Intelligence Wire,* February 17, 2005.

Buddy Squirrel, LLC

1801 East Bolivar Avenue
Saint Francis, Wisconsin 53235-5312
U.S.A.
Telephone: (414) 483-4500
Toll Free: (800) 972-2658
Fax: (414) 483-4137
Web site: http://www.qcbs.com

Private Company
Founded: 1916 as Quality Candy Kitchen
Employees: 200
Sales: $48 million (2009 est.)
NAICS: 311330 Confectionery Manufacturing from
   Purchased Chocolate

■ ■ ■

Buddy Squirrel, LLC, is a privately owned Milwaukee, Wisconsin-area chocolate and nut company, the result of a 2010 bankruptcy sale and reorganization of Quality Candy Shoppes Inc. Both Buddy Squirrel and Quality Candy remain major brands for the company. The former is applied to a variety of nuts, nut mixes, and gourmet popcorns, while the latter is found on assorted milk and dark chocolates, peanut brittle, butter almond toffee, and pecan caramel tads. A third brand, Joseph and Lottie, named in honor of the company's founders, offers a variety of confections, including gift boxes and single-serve counter display items. Buddy Squirrel sells its products through three retail stores in southeastern Wisconsin and its Web site, fundraising and corporate gift programs, as well as a wholesale operation. The

company is owned by a group of Milwaukee-area investors led by businessman Richard Koenings and venture capitalist Trevor D'Souza.

COMPANY FOUNDED: 1916

Quality Candy Shoppes was founded in 1916 by Joseph Helminiak and his wife Lottie. As a teenager Helminiak emigrated from Poland to the United States and started a grocery business before getting married. Helminiak and his wife then opened a shop to sell quality candy. In keeping with that idea, they named the shop Quality Candy Kitchen. Located on the 600 block of West Mitchell Street in Milwaukee, the shop was open long hours seven days a week. Helminiak specialized in hand-crafted chocolates but over the years added hard candies and taffy apples. When the shop relocated to a larger site on West Mitchell Street, he added an ice cream parlor as well.

The Heminiaks' children, Edward, Leonard, Raymond, and Alice, helped at the shop. The sons each pursued different majors at the University of Wisconsin but in the end decided to work in the family business. Edward majored in commerce, Leonard in English, and Raymond in economics. They gradually took charge of the company after World War II, when the business boomed, due in large part to the war and the rationing of certain goods. While many candy makers used substitute ingredients and as a result produced inferior products, Joseph Helminiak refused to deviate from his recipes.

Helminiak instead made as much candy as possible with his limited ingredients, closing the shop after his stock ran out, usually around 1:00 p.m. Milwaukee residents took note and traveled to his shop from all over the city. After the war they continued to support Quality Candy. Wartime privations, however, forced the Helminiak family to cease offering ice cream products. These were never reintroduced, and candy became the sole focus of the business.

NEW KITCHEN OPENS: 1952

With Raymond Helminiak in charge of sales, Leonard serving as production manager, and Edward as buyer and accountant, Quality Candy opened 10 Milwaukee-area stores under the Quality Candy Shoppes banner during the postwar era. To support growing demand, the company opened a larger kitchen in 1952 on South Fifth Street in Milwaukee. Eventually their father retired and in 1955 the elder Helminiaks moved to Tucson, Arizona, a climate more suited to their crippling arthritis and where their daughter Alice also resided.

In 1960 the Helminiak brothers expanded the business by acquiring three Buddy Squirrel nut shops and a roasting facility in Milwaukee. The Buddy Squirrel chain had originally been launched by Seattle-based nut wholesaler Continental Nut Company in the late 1920s. The family kept the two businesses separated, with a company called Quality Candy Shoppes, Inc., formed in 1961. Leonard Helminiak served as Buddy Squirrel's president as well as vice president of Quality Candy. Over the next 20 years, 10 more Buddy Squirrel stores were opened in Wisconsin and two in Illinois. In addition to quality nuts, the stores offered gourmet popcorn and snack mixes.

Both Quality Candy and Buddy Squirrel thrived and outgrew their operations. In 1977 Buddy Squirrel moved its production operation to a 5,000-square-foot site. Just five years later the facility was expanded to 15,000 square feet. Soon Quality Candy required larger accommodations as well, and the Helminiak family elected to bring together the Quality Candy and Buddy Squirrel operations under one roof. In 1985 a 45,000-

square-foot facility opened on East Bolivar Avenue in Milwaukee to accomplish that goal.

THIRD GENERATION JOINS BUSINESS

As Quality Candy and Buddy Squirrel approached the end of the 20th century, it became time for a new generation to assume leadership. Edward Helminiak died in 1972 and Raymond Helminiak had retired. Of the three brothers who had grown the family business, by 1990 only Leonard Helminiak remained, and he was well past retirement age. Leonard Helminiak turned to his three daughters to carry on the family tradition. Only one, Margaret Gile, agreed to join Quality Candy and Buddy Squirrel, at least to determine if it was a good fit. She had worked in the cosmetics and fragrance industries and had not lived in Wisconsin for 24 years, having spent most of the intervening time in California and New York.

Gile learned the business during the 1990s. She started out in the Quality Candy retail division and eventually assumed marketing and advertising responsibilities. She then spent time learning the Buddy Squirrel side of the business, again starting out in the retail division. As her father's health began to fail, she was ready to assume the presidency in 1998. Leonard Helminiak would eventually die in 2004 at the age of 83.

Gile quickly placed her mark on the family business by upgrading the image of both the Quality Candy and Buddy Squirrel shops. For the latter, that meant a new look for the Buddy Squirrel character. "Some people thought he looked like a cartoon skunk, and others weren't sure what kind of animal he was," she explained to the *Business Journal of Milwaukee*. In addition to a revised logo, the packaging colors were upgraded.

The stores were also updated because both the Quality Candy and Buddy Squirrel stores failed to reflect the upscale nature of their products. Instead, the stores presented a discount look, with the high prices often confusing customers. New looks were developed for the two chains to eliminate the confusion. For example, Buddy Squirrel stores eliminated fluorescent lighting and replaced bare beige walls with an outdoor motif that featured painted trees and squirrel footprints as well as ceilings that looked like the sky.

SISTER COMPANIES MERGE: 1999

Gile also took steps to bring the sister companies closer together. In 1998 a new store opened that combined Quality Candy and Buddy Squirrel and served as a prototype for future stores. The co-branded store performed well, leading to the opening of other combination stores in 1999 and 2000. Gile also took steps to merge the companies, which had long maintained separate operations despite sharing a facility. In the summer of 1999 the companies were formally merged, creating a legal entity called Quality Candy/Buddy Squirrel of Wisconsin, Inc. The two units could then improve efficiencies by combining their accounting and payrolls. Manufacturing employees could also work for both operations.

Quality Candy expanded its footprint in the new century by developing a broker network that expanded from a single broker to nine, allowing the company to distribute its products to 21 states. In order to better serve its new accounts as well as prepare for future growth, Quality Candy opened a new 15,000-square-foot distribution center in a nearby building in 2001.

A new national approach also brought changes to Quality Candy's traditional packaging. For more than four decades the company had relied on a simple white box and a red company logo. While this look held positive connotations for local retail customers, it did not play well in new markets. Thus, a new gift box was developed in conjunction with a Milwaukee marketing company and was unveiled in September 2002.

In addition to better positioning Quality Candy as an upscale brand, the new packaging also increased interest from wholesale customers. Wholesale business was especially important because it helped to balance out the seasonality of the retail operation, which achieved the vast majority of its sales from the Christmas holiday season through Mother's Day.

By 2006 wholesale customers would make up half the business. They included major department store chains such as Bloomingdale's, Dillard's, Neiman Marcus, and Macy's, as well as gift shops and other retailers. Many of these wholesale customers sold the products under their own labels. The company also developed an online business for both the Quality Candy and Buddy Squirrel brands.

COMPANY FILES FOR BANKRUPTCY

Despite the changes Gile made to the Quality Candy and Buddy Squirrel operations, the business did not perform as expected, due in part to a number of underperforming stores. Although the company claimed to be profitable, opening a new store in the summer of 2009, it found itself lacking the necessary capital to continue business. Later in 2009 Quality Candy was forced to seek forbearance from Harris Bank in order to conduct business during the key Christmas holiday season. To secure needed funding to cover payroll for this period, Gile had to use certificates of deposit and a brokerage account as collateral and agreed to assume personal liability to the bank in the event the company was unable to repay the payroll advances.

Although Quality Candy kept its doors open through 2009, early the following year it filed for protection from creditors under Chapter 11 of the Federal Bankruptcy Code, listing debts of $3.4 million and assets of $4.4 million, which included real estate holdings. Of that $3.4 million, $2.9 million was secured debt owed to Harris Bank. At the same time as the filing, the company announced the closing of the store it had opened just seven months earlier.

Because it was imperative that Quality Candy continue to operate during the ensuing holidays of Valentine's Day and Easter, the bankruptcy court in Milwaukee allowed the company to continue using cash collateral to stay in business. In the meantime, it was required to provide weekly cash collateral statements to Harris Bank and provide the court with a business plan by March 5, 2010.

Well before that deadline, Quality Candy asked the bankruptcy court for permission to sell all of its assets in an auction, a proposal that called for a minimum bid of $2.5 million. There was no shortage of interested suitors. About 20 parties took a close look at the company in the early weeks of 2010 and four buyers emerged by mid-April.

NEW OWNERS: 2010

The court agreed to the plan but Quality Candy did not receive its minimum bid. A group of local investors led by attorney and businessman Richard Koenings and venture capitalist Trevor D'Souza submitted a winning bid of $2.2 million. The new owners took over the company during the summer of 2010, and soon made a number of changes. Most of the retail stores were closed and a greater emphasis was placed on the wholesale operation, with the goal of targeting major retailers. The corporate name was also changed to Buddy Squirrel LLC. What remained the same was a commitment to producing quality products.

Because a number of upscale chocolate sellers had gone out of business during the recent economic downturn, Buddy Squirrel was well positioned for the future. Not only did Quality Candy retain its brand value, the company possessed a manufacturing operation that could easily double its capacity. While there were fewer retail outlets for the company's candies and nuts, there was every reason to expect that wholesale would become the backbone of the company in the years to come.

Ed Dinger

PRINCIPAL OPERATING UNITS
Buddy Squirrel; Joseph & Lottie; Quality Candy.

PRINCIPAL COMPETITORS
Ghirardelli Chocolate Company; Godiva Chocolatier, Inc.; Nestlé S.A.

FURTHER READING

Davis, Stacy Vogel. "New Buddy Squirrel Owners to Expand Wholesale Operations." *Business Journal of Milwaukee*, June 21, 2010.

Fuhrman, Elizabeth. "New Look Takes Shape." *Candy Industry*, March 2003, p. 34.

Hajewski, Doris. "Quality Candy/Buddy Squirrel Files for Bankruptcy Protection." *Milwaukee Journal Sentinel*, January 25, 2010.

———. "Quality Candy Put on Auction Block." *Milwaukee Journal Sentinel*, April 18, 2010, p. 6.

Hoeschen, Brad. "Corporate Images Get a Makeover." *Business Journal of Milwaukee*, April 16, 1999.

Spice, Linda. "Helminiak Sweetened Lives of All He Knew." *Milwaukee Journal Sentinel*, August 1, 2004, p. B1.

CarMax, Inc.

12800 Tuckahoe Creek Parkway
Richmond, Virginia 23238
U.S.A.
Telephone: (804) 747-0422
Fax: (804) 217-6819
Web site: http://www.carmax.com

Public Company
Incorporated: 1993 as CarMax Group
Employees: 13,439
Sales: $7.47 billion (2010)
Stock Exchanges: New York
Ticker Symbol: KMX
NAICS: 441120 Used Car Dealers

■■■

CarMax, Inc., operates as the largest used car retailer in the United States. Known as the pioneer of the used car superstore concept, CarMax stores typically offer roughly 350 to 550 used cars no more than six model years old. The prices of the vehicles are fixed in an effort to create a more relaxed sales atmosphere. CarMax operates 100 used car superstores and five new car franchises. The company has sold over two million cars since its inception in 1993.

ORIGINS

The creation of the CarMax concept was the work of Richard Sharp and W. Austin Ligon. The corporate entity behind the formation of CarMax was Circuit City Stores, Inc. A 375-store, consumer electronics chain with $7 billion in sales during the early 1990s, Circuit City was led by Sharp. Ligon worked under Sharp, serving as Circuit City's senior vice president of corporate planning. Together the pair developed the CarMax concept, a business approach that drew its inspiration from the sprawling Circuit City chain and its "big-box" retail approach.

The story of CarMax's development began with a survey conducted in 1991. "We asked people who bought used and new cars about their shopping experience," Sharp explained in an October 23, 1995, interview with *Forbes*. "Not surprisingly, there were more dislikes than likes." Sharp looked at the $150 billion used car market and saw three qualities that convinced him the Circuit City approach to retailing could be grafted onto the used car market. First, the supply of used cars was abundant. Second, the demand for used cars was consistent. Finally, and perhaps most importantly, the management practices employed within the fragmented industry were unsophisticated.

Sharp and Ligon worked for two years on fine-tuning their concept, devoting much of their time to developing a process to monitor inventory and pricing. The two Circuit City executives concentrated on ways to determine precisely which make, model, and color of vehicles to stock on their proposed chain of lots, and when and how much to adjust prices. The strategy, like that of a Circuit City store, centered on a broad selection of merchandise, a high-volume business, economies of scale, and sharply honed management methods. "We can apply our expertise in electronics retailing to auto retailing," Sharp informed *Discount Store News* in a November 4, 1996, interview.

THE FIRST CARMAX DEBUTS: 1993

Sharp and Ligon were ready by 1993 to put their theories to the test. Using money from Circuit City to finance the start-up, Sharp and Ligon opened their first superstore, a lot operating under the banner "CarMax: The Auto Superstore," in October 1993. The showroom, located in Richmond, Virginia, represented the first unit of the newly created CarMax Group, a wholly owned subsidiary of Circuit City. The Richmond lot served as the prototype for the other used car superstores that would follow in its wake: 500 cars were on display, each no more than five model years old, and each with no more than 70,000 miles on its odometer.

Inside, the Richmond CarMax store contained a service shop and salespeople offering a refreshing approach to used car sales. Prices on the vehicles were fixed, obviating the need for customers to negotiate the price of a prospective purchase. CarMax's "no haggling" policy and the less adversarial atmosphere it created between salespeople and customers was complemented by computer kiosks delineating the lot's inventory and particular details about each vehicle.

As Sharp and Ligon pressed forward with their plan to apply the superstore concept to used car retailing, they did not expect immediate success. Neither executive anticipated the enterprise would generate a profit for several years, and perhaps not until the end of the 1990s. In the interim, substantial sums of money would be needed to establish a network of CarMax superstores and to bring the company to the point of critical mass where economies of scale and its sophisticated management practices would give the concept the advantages of a retail superstore.

When Sharp and Ligon set out, the United States had 42,000 used car dealers and 22,000 new car dealers who sold used cars received as trade-ins. Among this field, the average used car dealer generated $2 million a year, a total deemed too small to achieve economies of scale or to benefit from modern management methods.

OVERCOMING FINANCIAL CHALLENGES: 1995–97

By October 1995, two years after the first CarMax opened, the company had yet to generate a profit, recording $77 million in sales for the previous fiscal year. New superstore openings had lifted CarMax's unit count to four lots, with two superstores in Atlanta and one in Raleigh, North Carolina, having joined the fold. A fifth lot was expected to open in Charlotte, North Carolina, in early 1996, but Sharp had yet to decide whether to turn CarMax into a national chain. A final decision was expected to be made within 18 months on the matter of going national.

As CarMax pressed forward during the critical phase of its development, the company's progress was defined by escalating sales and mounting losses. By the end of the company's 1995 fiscal year, sales had increased substantially, soaring from $77 million to $304 million, which exceeded analysts' estimates of between $200 million and $278 million. However, CarMax's robust sales growth was marred by a $7 million loss for the year, perpetuating speculation that the mass-merchandising approach to used car sales was not a sound business model. Few industry observers doubted whether CarMax could sell cars, but many pundits doubted whether the company could sell cars profitably.

The one glaring problem with the chain, according to the business press, was its inability to secure volume discounts on the purchase of its used cars, an ability intrinsic to the success of the Circuit City chain. CarMax purchased its vehicles at the same auctions attended by independent dealers and paid roughly the same price an independent dealer paid. Without the benefits of volume purchasing, CarMax faced a difficult road to profitability.

The solution to CarMax's cash flow problem, as proposed by Sharp and Ligon, was the physical expansion of the chain. The company opened its fifth and sixth lots in 1996 and announced ambitious expansion plans. In 1997 Sharp and Ligon planned to open between 8 and 10 lots, with new openings of between 15 and 20 stores for each year thereafter. The markets slated for expansion included Miami, Tampa, Dallas, Houston, Washington, D.C., Baltimore, Chicago, Los Angeles, San Francisco, and Tidewater, Virginia. The company projected a chain of 80 to 90 units by 2001.

By the mid-1990s CarMax's expansion strategy added a new facet to the company's business. The company acquired its first new car franchise in 1996, a Chrysler-Plymouth-Jeep store located in Atlanta. CarMax had plans to open between 15 and 25 new car dealerships by 2002, stores that were to operate alongside the company's used car dealerships.

KEY DATES

1993:	The first CarMax used car lot opens in Richmond, Virginia.
1996:	CarMax acquires its first new car franchise.
1997:	A portion of CarMax is sold to the public.
2000:	CarMax records its first annual profit.
2002:	CarMax is spun off from Circuit City Stores.
2003:	Company sells its one-millionth used vehicle.
2005:	Sales for the fiscal year surpass $5 billion; company headquarters moved to Richmond.
2006:	CEO Ligon retires; Tom Folliard is named his replacement.
2007:	Company sells its two millionth used vehicle.
2009:	CarMax marks the opening of its 100th store.

EXPANSION LEADS TO PROFITS: 1997–99

The financial constraints of expanding in the face of persistent losses presented formidable obstacles to Sharp and Ligon. Although Circuit City had contributed to CarMax's start-up, the company's financial assistance to CarMax essentially ended there. The arrangement kept Circuit City's financial health from being drained by CarMax's costly expansion program, forcing Sharp and Ligon to find other ways to secure capital.

At the end of 1996 the pair proposed a new method of securing financing, announcing that Circuit City would sell a portion of the CarMax subsidiary to the public. The initial proposal called for offering between 15 and 20 percent of CarMax to the public, a stake that was expected to raise as much as $300 million. The offering was completed in February 1997, providing CarMax with fresh resources to finance its expansion and to repay its rising debt.

The proceeds gained from CarMax's public offering enabled the company to accelerate its expansion program. At the time of the offering the company had seven superstores in operation, which generated nearly $450 million in revenues. By mid-1998, there were 23 superstores in operation, enabling the company to record $1.47 billion in sales for fiscal 1998. Despite the impressive gain in sales, the company continued to be hobbled by annual losses. CarMax lost $23.5 million in fiscal 1998, enough of a loss to prompt Sharp and Ligon to scale back expansion plans for 1999. Instead of opening between 15 and 20 stores in 1999, as originally planned, the company announced it would open 10 stores that year.

"We've had to learn as we go along," Ligon explained in a July 12, 1999, interview with *Automotive News.* "We're going to hit about $2 billion in sales this year, which is about the critical mass we need to get to make a profit." Roughly six months later, when the financial results for fiscal 2000 were announced, something unprecedented in the history of CarMax occurred. For the year, the company generated $2.01 billion in revenues and a profit of $1.1 million, the first time CarMax ended a fiscal year in the black. The profit total was meager, but it suggested there was financial viability in the big-box used car retailing concept. CarMax's progress in the coming years underscored the success of 2000, prompting critics to alter their assessment of the company's business strategy.

PROFITS AND INDEPENDENCE IN THE 21ST CENTURY

Buoyed by the first annual profit in the company's history, Ligon focused on plans for the future. A national rollout of CarMax superstores remained the company's long-term objective, a goal that was expected to require between 20 and 25 years to achieve. "You can't do it any faster than that," Ligon informed *Automotive News* in a July 10, 2000, interview. More immediate plans called for a measured pace of expansion, as the company sought to add to the 40 new car franchises and used car superstores in operation at the beginning of the century. Despite the eventual goal of national expansion, initially the company planned to open new locations in markets where it already maintained a presence, focusing on markets with populations ranging between one million and two million residents.

As CarMax's 10th anniversary approached, sales in fiscal 2001 leaped to $2.5 billion. Furthermore, CarMax's profit total by far eclipsed the symbolic $1.1 million recorded in 2000. Ligon expected to post between $40 million and $43 million in net income in 2001, but the company did better, posting $45.6 million in profits. In 2002 the results were equally as positive, as revenues swelled 28 percent to $3.2 billion and net income nearly doubled, jumping to $90.8 million.

Against this backdrop of vigorous financial growth, a new era at CarMax began. In the spring of 2002 Circuit City announced it intended to spin off its CarMax subsidiary into a separate, publicly traded company, part of the consumer electronics chain's plan to focus on its core business. The spin-off, completed in October 2002, created CarMax, Inc., a corporate entity distinct from Circuit City with Ligon serving as its CEO, a title he gained at the time of the spin-off.

SUCCESS CONTINUES: 2003–08

CarMax prospered as a public entity. During 2003 the company sold its one-millionth used vehicle. With sales and net earnings on the rise, CarMax made its debut on the *Fortune* 500 in 2004, ranking 435 on the list. By that time, the company operated 49 used car superstores in 23 markets and 12 new car franchises. CarMax sold 224,099 used vehicles during fiscal 2004.

Sales during fiscal 2005 surpassed the $5 billion mark one year ahead of schedule. That year the company set a goal of achieving at least $10 billion in sales by 2010. Also in 2005, the company moved into new company headquarters in Richmond, Virginia.

CEO Austin Ligon retired from his post in 2006, leaving Thomas J. Folliard at the helm. Under Ligon's tenure, CarMax had grown from a single store in 1993 to 71 used car superstores in 34 markets by the time of his departure. Under the new leadership, CarMax continued its expansion plan and opened 10 new locations in fiscal 2007. Sales grew to $7.46 billion that year while net income increased by 48 percent over the previous year to $198.6 million. The company celebrated the sale of its two millionth used vehicle in January 2007. Cofounder Richard Sharp stepped down as chairman that year.

The company continued its aggressive growth plans during most of 2008 despite a drop in consumer demand and a slowdown in the U.S. economy. The company's finance arm, CarMax Auto Finance, experienced a drop in profits as the credit market in the United States faltered. Nevertheless, the company opened 12 stores during the fiscal year, expanding into new markets including Tucson, Milwaukee, Omaha, and San Diego.

OVERCOMING FINANCIAL CHALLENGES: 2009 AND BEYOND

By December 2008 it became apparent that CarMax would not remain immune to volatile economic conditions. CarMax was forced to halt its growth plans as sales and profits fell dramatically. During fiscal 2009, which included the period from February 2008 through February 2009, comparable store sales fell by 16 percent while net income dropped to $59.2 million from $182 million secured in fiscal 2008. Given the turbulent economy, CarMax was forced to revamp its strategy and cut costs, including laying off 600 employees, as consumer demand plunged. Despite the decision to put its growth plans on hold, the company marked the opening of its 100th store in February 2009.

The company fell short of meeting its goal of $10 billion in annual sales by 2010, but its financial results during the year proved the company's strategy was paying off. During the fiscal year, sales climbed to $7.47 billion, and net earnings grew over the previous year to $281.7 million. The company believed its sound business model, strict cost-cutting measures, and waste reduction program were crucial to its success in such a challenging business environment. While used car sales had yet to rebound to 2008 levels, the company sold 357,129 used vehicles during fiscal 2010 and grew its market share by over 10 percent as competitors were forced out of the marketplace.

The company's solid performance led it to resume a much slower pace of growth during the remainder of 2010. CarMax opened a store in Augusta, Georgia, as well as two in Ohio during the year. The company planned for future growth but expected a full recovery in the auto sales market would take some time. The Associated Press published comments made by Folliard at the company's annual meeting in June 2010 regarding the recovery. "It's coming back slow," remarked the CEO. "I still think we're in for a little bit of a rough road. Although we see some positive signs in the economy, I personally feel it's going to be a slow burn." Despite his cautious outlook, Folliard was confident that CarMax was well positioned for continued success in the years to come.

Jeffrey L. Covell
Updated, Christina M. Stansell

PRINCIPAL SUBSIDIARIES

CarMax Auto Superstores, Inc.; CarMax Auto Superstores West Coast, Inc.; CarMax Auto Superstores California, LLC; CarMax Auto Superstores Services, Inc.; CarMax Business Services, LLC; Glen Allen Insurance, LTD.

PRINCIPAL COMPETITORS

AutoNation, Inc.; Hendrick Automotive Group; Penske Automotive Group, Inc.

FURTHER READING

"Circuit City to Spin Off CarMax, Chain Will Focus on Electronics." *Chain Store Age Executive Fax*, March 1, 2002, p. 1.

Felberbaum, Michael. "Used Car Chain CarMax CEO Folliard Expects Slow Recovery in Automotive Market." *Associated Press Newswires*, June 28, 2010.

Gillian, Gregory J. "In High Gear, CarMax Chief Bows Out." *Richmond Times-Dispatch*, June 18, 2006.

Llovio, Louis. "CarMax CEO Optimistic About Future." *Richmond Times-Dispatch*, June 24, 2009.

McLean, Bethany. "Squeaky Wheels." *Fortune*, March 17, 1997, p. 202.

Rubinstein, Ed. "Sharp Touts Potential of CarMax." *Discount Store News*, November 4, 1996, p. 6.

Rudnitsky, Howard. "Would You Buy a Used Car from This Man?" *Forbes*, October 23, 1995, p. 52.

Sawyers, Arlena. "CarMax Sticks to Growth Plans Despite Slowing Sales." *Automotive News*, February 4, 2008, p. 56.

————. "CarMax's Ligon: Shoppers Are Happy, Profits Are Near." *Automotive News*, July 12, 1999, p. 32.

————. "Though in the Black, CarMax Has No Expansion Plans." *Automotive News*, July 10, 2000, p. 34.

Clondalkin Group PLC

Dolcain House
Monastery Road
Clondalkin, Dublin 22
Ireland
Telephone: (+353 01) 459 1559
Fax: (+353 01) 459 1550
Web site: http://www.clondalkin-group.com

Private Company
Incorporated: 1986 as Clondalkin Group
Employees: 4,000
Sales: EUR 789.9 million ($1.11 billion) (2009)
NAICS: 322221 Coated and Laminated Packaging Paper and Plastics Film Manufacturing; 323110 Commercial Lithographic Printing; 323111 Commercial Gravure Printing; 424130 Industrial and Personal Service Paper Merchant Wholesalers

■ ■ ■

Clondalkin Group PLC is a leading Dublin, Ireland-based packaging group, acting as a holding company for subsidiaries in Ireland, the United Kingdom, Canada, Germany, Switzerland, the Netherlands, Spain, Poland, and the United States. Altogether, the company' operations include 45 production facilities, and more than 4,000 employees, generating annual revenues of EUR 789.9 million ($1.11 billion) in 2009. Europe accounts for 70 percent of the company's sales, with the North American market filling in the rest.

Clondalkin operates two primary divisions: Flexible Packaging and Specialist Packaging. The Flexible Packaging division is the group's largest, generating 70 percent of the group's revenues. This division's businesses include Chadwicks of Bury, AP Burt & Sons, Swiftbrook, and CB Packaging in the United Kingdom and Ireland; Direct Plastics in Canada; and Fortune Plastics, Accutech Films, and Spiralkote in the United States. In the Netherlands, the group holds Cats, Vaassen, Van der Windt, and LPF, complemented by Wentus Kunststof, Haensel, and Nyco in Switzerland.

The smaller Specialist Packaging division operates through the Boxes Group in the United Kingdom, which also operates in Poland. Other operations include Cahill Printers in Dublin; Cartonplex, in Barcelona, Spain; Harlands Labels in the United Kingdom and Poland; Keller Crescent in the United States; Linde Vouwkartonnage and Nimax in the Netherlands; and Ritchie, in Scotland. Clondalkin Group is a privately held company; U.S. investment firm Warburg Pincus is the company's largest shareholder. Norbert McDermott serves as the group's chief executive officer.

IRISH PAPER MILL ORIGINS

Clondalkin Group originated in the Dublin region's once-flourishing paper industry. Clondalkin, a village near Dublin, was the site of a paper mill established in the early 19th century by Thomas Seery. The mill became a major part of life in the village, providing employment for many generations, even as it changed ownership several times through the 19th and into the 20th century. In 1914, a new company was formed, called Irish Paper Mills Co. Ltd., which took over the Clondalkin mill. With the outbreak of World War I and

COMPANY PERSPECTIVES

Our focus is the foundation of everything we do. It has got us to where we are today. Our focus on our customers' requirements drives us forward. Just as microscopes and telescopes have made many of science's greatest discoveries by focusing well beyond what is immediately visible to discover and expand knowledge, our vision and dedication are informed by going well beyond the obvious to imagine and create new packaging opportunities and possibilities for our customers. Focus differentiates how we organise our processes, how we interface with our customers, how we invest and deploy our resources, how we create new packaging solutions and how we differentiate our products and services. Our focused attention on all aspects of what we do is our customers' assurance of the integrity, efficiency and functionality of our packaging solutions. Focus has allowed us to create market leading packaging businesses with well invested facilities, producing customised and complex products of unparalleled quality. Focus empowers our management and our employees. Focus means we are successful. Our focus sets us apart.

the conversion of the United Kingdom's paper production for the war effort, demand for Irish Paper's own output soared. As a result, the company invested strongly in expanding its operations, boosting its capacity from just 30 tons per week to 220 tons per week by the beginning of the 1920s.

By then, new owners had taken over Irish Paper Mills. Charles Marsden and Sons, a prominent producer of paper bags and other packaging materials founded in the 1830s, had become part of the Becker Company, a major pulp producer. Through Marsden, Becker took over Irish Paper Mills in 1917. Marsden, which also owned a number of other mills and packaging factories in the United Kingdom, subsequently went public in 1919. One year later, Marsden listed Irish Paper Mills as well.

The end of World War I and the subsequent return of the British paper industry to civilian production ended Marsden's, and Irish Paper Mills' growth. Into the early 1920s, the companies faltered, and by 1922 the Clondalkin mill had been shut down. Marsden went bankrupt, completing its liquidation proceedings in 1924. The Clondalkin mill remained dormant for more

than a decade. In 1936, however, the mill started up operations again, now under the name of Clondalkin Paper Mill (CPM).

FIRST PACKAGING ACQUISITIONS

CPM remained a going concern through World War II and into the 1970s. The company once again grew into the most prominent employer in the village of Clondalkin, which itself became slowly absorbed into Dublin, as that city spread during the second half of the 20th century. Led by Bert Cusack, who remained the company's chief executive until the end of the 1970s, this period represented a time of relative stability for the paper mill.

Nonetheless, the company had begun to explore a diversification beyond paper production and into the fast-growing packaging sector. The rise of supermarkets in particular helped stimulate the packaging industry, creating a demand for new and more varied packaging types. Among CPM's first investments in the sector was a stake in Dublin-based CP Paper Sacks, held in partnership with the Dickinson Robinson Group. When that company sold its stake in 1973, CPM became CP Paper Sacks' majority shareholder, with 66 percent of its shares.

In 1976 CPM expanded its small packaging business with the addition of Dublin-based printing company Cahill Printers Ltd. That company traced its own origins to 1866; its prominence in the Irish capital's printing industry was underscored by its appointment to print the records for Ireland's first parliamentary sessions, following the creation of the independent state in 1922. Two other companies joined the growing Clondalkin group by the end of the 1970s, Bailey Gibson and Guys of Cork.

FOCUSING ON PACKAGING

By the end of the 1970s, Ireland's paper industry had all but disappeared. Like many of the country's traditional industries, such as mining, the Irish paper industry found itself hit hard by international competition, while lacking the scale and the capital to invest in modernizing production. The Clondalkin mill remained a holdout through the decade, in part through the efforts of its workers. In 1964 the mill suffered a strike lasting more than 20 weeks; the mill's workers struck again, in 1974, for 11 weeks.

Despite these efforts, the Clondalkin mill too faced efforts to rationalize Ireland's paper, pulp and packaging industries into the late 1970s. The appointment of Henry Lund as the company's second managing director

KEY DATES

1914: Irish Paper Mills is incorporated to take over a paper mill established in the early 19th century.

1936: Clondalkin Paper Mills (CPM) is formed to revive the Clondalkin paper mill.

1973: CPM enters packaging production with purchase of a stake in CP Paper Sacks.

1979: CPM makes its first overseas acquisition, of AP Burt in the United Kingdom.

1986: Clondalkin Group acquires Fortune Plastics in the United States; the Clondalkin paper mill ends operations.

2004: Warburg Pincus acquires a majority stake in Clondalkin.

in 1978 introduced the next phase in the development of the Clondalkin group. Into the early 1980s, Lund began trimming the mill's employees, shedding 80 jobs in 1980. By 1982 Lund attempted to place the Clondalkin Mill in liquidation altogether. The mill's workers struck again, staging a sit-in that lasted for several years. In the end, however, Lund got his way, and the Clondalkin mill closed down in 1986.

The closure of the mill allowed the company, now the Clondalkin Group, to refocus itself as an international packaging company. Clondalkin had already completed its first acquisition outside of London, buying up AP Burt & Sons in 1979. Based near Bristol, AP Burt was a major producer of paper and plastic bags.

Clondalkin also established a subsidiary in the United States. That company's operations took off with the acquisition of flexible packaging producer Fortune Plastics Inc. Fortune had been founded in 1955 and had expanded to included factories in Arizona, Connecticut, Florida, and Illinois.

GROWTH THROUGH ACQUISITIONS

Acquisitions remained a key component to Clondalkin's growth through the 1990s. They also enabled the company to continue to pursue its internationalization strategy. In 1994, for example, the company acquired Switzerland's NYCO Flexible Packaging GmbH, a company specialized in the production of printed lids and bottle sleeves.

Most of Clondalkin's acquisitions consisted of small, specialized companies. In 1996 the company completed its largest acquisition to that point, buying up the Netherlands' Van der Windt. Founded in 1969, Windt originally supplied the Westland horticultural industry, before branching out to become a major packaging supplier to a variety of industries. Windt had also established a strong international presence, with an international sales and distribution network reaching Belgium, the United Kingdom, and Denmark, as well as Ireland. Clondalkin paid £58 million for Windt.

Clondalkin promised new acquisitions following the Windt purchase. The company quickly delivered, buying up Chadwicks of Bury Ltd. Founded in 1953, Chadwicks had originally supplied foil tops for milk bottles for the local dairy farming community in Bury, before branching out in the 1960s to produce a full range of lids for yogurt and other products.

Lund retired to the chairman's position in 1998, appointing Norbert McDermott as managing director. By then, the company had completed more than £200 million in acquisitions over the previous decade, including specialist packaging company Boxes Group, based in Watford. McDermott immediately promised more acquisitions to come, suggesting the group's interest in a large-scale acquisition into the turn of the century.

MBO IN 1999

In the meantime, Lund and McDermott completed a management buyout (MBO) of the company, backed by investment firm Candover. The MBO was prompted in part by an ongoing slump in Clondalkin's share price, which had been suffering from the Ireland's entry into the Euro zone and the resulting investor interest in international stocks. The MBO was completed in October 1999, for a total price of £303 million. Both Lund and McDermott became major shareholders in the group, alongside Candover.

The newly private company continued its acquisition strategy into the new decade. In 2001, the company bought Dutch rival European Packaging Holding Group–Frievaart Holdings BV. The company then acquired another Netherlands packaging specialist, LPF Flexible Packaging. The following year, Clondalkin expanded its U.S. presence, buying Florida-based Spiralkote Flexible Packaging, a company founded in 1977. This purchase helped boost Clondalkin into the ranks of the world's leading flexible packaging companies.

While acquisitions formed an important part of Clondalkin's growth through the decade, the company also pursued a number of organic growth opportunities. In 2003, for example, the company's Boxes Group entered the Polish market, setting up a production facility in Lublin. The following year, the company added a sales office in Warsaw as well. In 2005 another Clondalkin subsidiary, Harland Lables, opened its own production facility in Lublin on the site beside the Boxes operation.

NEW ACQUISITIONS THROUGH 2010

Clondalkin changed hands again in 2004, when Warburg Pincus bought out Candover, paying £440 million to become the company's major shareholder. Warburg Pincus' share stood at 84 percent, with the remainder shared among 60 company managers, including Lund and McDermott.

Warburg Pincus backed the company's continued expansion through the second half of the decade. The company spent more than £160 million expanding its existing facilities. Clondalkin also continued its acquisition drive, adding U.S.-based Pharmagraphics Inc. in 2006 and Keller Crescent in 2007. The company entered Canada the following year, buying Direct Plastics. Also in 2007, Clondalkin moved into the Spanish market, acquiring Barcelona-based Cartonplex, while expanding its Irish holdings with the purchase of Kenilworth Products.

Through 2009 Clondalkin added to its U.S. operations, buying Accutech Films Inc., founded in Coldwater, Ohio, in 1997, in 2008, and Ohio-based Cleveland Plastic Films in 2009. These purchases were followed by the company's extension into Puerto Rico, where Clondalkin, through Keller-Crescent, added Juncos-based Lehigh Press. By then, Clondalkin had grown into a company with 45 production facilities in 10 countries, generating annual sales of nearly EUR 790 million ($1.1 billion). Clondalkin promised to continue its expansion as it took its place among the world's leading specialist packaging groups at the beginning of the 21st century.

M. L. Cohen

PRINCIPAL SUBSIDIARIES

Accutech Films, Inc. (USA); AP Burt & Sons Limited; Better Business Forms, Inc (USA); Boxes GH PLC (UK); Boxes Prestige Poland Sp.; Cats Flexible Packaging BV (Netherlands); CB Packaging Ltd.; Chadwicks of Bury Ltd.; Cleveland Plastic Films (USA); Direct Plastics Limited; Fortune Plastics, Inc. (USA); Haensel Flexible Packaging GmbH (Germany); Harland Labels PLC (UK); Harlands Labels Poland; Keller Crescent Inc; LPF Flexible Packaging BV (Netherlands); NYCO Flexible Packaging GmbH (Germany); Pharmagraphics Guy Limited; Ritchie (UK) Ltd.; Spiralkote Flexible Packaging Inc. (USA); Swiftbrook Ltd.; Vaassen Flexible Packaging BV (Netherlands); Van der Windt Group (Netherlands); Velsen Flexoplast Group; Wentus Kunststoff GmbH (Germany).

PRINCIPAL DIVISIONS

Flexible Packaging; Specialist Packaging.

PRINCIPAL COMPETITORS

Amcor Flexibles Healthcare; Avery Dennison Corp.; BOC Ltd.; International Paper Co.; Jim Pattison Group; Linpac Group Ltd.; MeadWestvaco Corp.; Mondi PLC; REXAM PLC.

FURTHER READING

Aughney, Jim. "Clondalkin Acquires Share Capital of European Rival." *Irish Independent*, April 11, 2001.

Carson, Gordon. "Packaging from Cork to Carolina." *Packaging News*, October 1, 2007.

Derwin, Des. "Trouble at T'Mill: The Clondalkin Sit-Ins 1982–87." *Red Banner*, May and November 1999.

Weston, Charlie. "US Group Pays €630m for a Majority Stake in Clondalkin." *Irish Independent*, February 2, 2004.

Coflusa S.A.

—■—

Poligono Industrial Inca s/n
Inca, E-07300
Spain
Telephone: (+34 971) 50 70 00
Fax: (+34 971) 50 71 16
Web site: http://www.camper.es

Private Company
Incorporated: 1981
Employees: 217
Sales: EUR 135 million ($190 million) (2009 est.)
NAICS: 448210 Shoe Stores; 424340 Footwear
  Merchant Wholesalers

■ ■ ■

Coflusa S.A. is the family-owned, Majorca-based holding company for three businesses: shoe companies Camper and Lottusse, and the Viajes Iberia travel company. Camper is Coflusa's largest operation, operating more than 240 stores throughout the world. Each year Camper creates over 250 shoe designs, focused largely on the high-end casual shoe segment, selling more than three million pairs of shoes per year. Camper does not manufacture its own shoes but instead contracts with manufacturers in China.

Lottusse is the company's oldest shoe business, stemming from the Fluxa family's entry into shoemaking in the late 19th century. Lottusse maintains its own production network centered on Inca, Majorca. The company also owns a growing chain of retail stores,

counting more than 30 stores, including 20 in China by the end of 2010.

In addition to its small travel agency business, Viajes Iberia, Coflusa has also extended the Camper brand into the hospitality sector, opening the Camper Hotel in Barcelona in 2005. Coflusa is controlled by the Fluxa family, led by Lorenzo Fluxa, founder of the Camper brand, and his sons, Lorenzo and Miguel. In 2009 the company's annual sales were reported at EUR 135 million ($190 million).

BRINGING SHOEMAKING TO MAJORCA IN 1887

Majorca native Antonio Fluxa traveled to England in 1870 in order to train as a shoemaker. Fluxa remained in England for the next seven years. When he returned to Majorca in 1877, he brought with him the new footwear techniques being developed in the United Kingdom during the years of the industrial revolution, such as the Goodyear method of sewing soles. Fluxa also introduced the first production machinery to Majorca.

An island located on the Mediterranean Sea some 150 miles off the Spanish coast, Majorca's economy traditionally focused on agriculture. The island nevertheless boasted a large number of skilled leather craftsmen. In 1877 Fluxa gathered a number of the island's best craftsmen and founded his own shoemaking workshop. Fluxa named the company Lottusse, after one of the shoemaking machines brought back from England. Starting with a men's dress shoe, the company grew quickly, supplying shoe shops on the Spanish mainland.

Fluxa expanded the workshop into a full-fledged factory, and also founded a training school in order to ensure the company's supply of skilled workers. A major breakthrough for the company came when it received an order to supply boots to the French army. By 1891 Lottusse's Inca factory boasted 11 workshops.

SECOND GENERATION IN 1929

Fluxa had also proved an inspiration for other craftsmen on the island. By the dawn of the 20th century Majorca boasted more than 100 shoemakers and had become a major supplier of footwear to the Spanish mainland. Fluxa had also established a leather factory in order to ensure his footwear company's supply of raw materials. Fluxa thus became responsible for establishing a second industry in Majorca. By the beginning of the new century, five leather factories supplied Lottusse and other shoemakers on the island.

Antonio Fluxa died in 1917, leaving the company in disarray for more than a decade. In 1929 Fluxa's son Lorenzo took over the company and began rebuilding its fortunes. Lorenzo Fluxa had been born in the family's shoe factory and quickly displayed a flair for the business. By 1931 Fluxa had led the company in a new direction, focusing on classic men's footwear.

Among the company's products introduced during this time was its popular Camaléon work shoe. This shoe was based on a type of handmade footwear, using worn tire tread for the sole and tire canvas for the upper, that had been common among farmers on Majorca. Fluxa redeveloped the shoe, using a softer and stronger type of canvas, and adding leather tips on the toe and heel in 1931. The design, then transformed into a casual men's shoe, helped the company survive the difficult years of the Spanish Civil War.

Lottusse remained a small but successful company, focused on classic men's dress shoes, through the early decades of the Franco dictatorship. While the Franco regime maintained an isolationist stance, Fluxa did not, and made it a point of sending his sons abroad for summer trips. Fluxa had also begun to recognize Majorca's potential as a tourist destination, as the first tourists arrived from Spain in the mid-1950s. This led the family to acquire its own travel business, Viajes Iberia, in 1957.

NEW DIRECTIONS

Footwear nevertheless remained at the core of the Fluxa family's operations as the next generation entered the business. Fluxa's son, also named Lorenzo, took over running the family's factory by the early 1970s, while in his mid-20s. Lorenzo Fluxa's contact with tourists arriving on Majorca from Spain, as well as a trip he took to the United States at the age of 18, provided him with inspiration to move in a new direction. While the company continued to produce classic shoe designs, Fluxa himself often wore the type of slip-on shoe that had inspired the company's Camaléon shoe years earlier. Fluxa's friends from the mainland began asking him where they could purchase these shoes for themselves.

Fluxa spotted an opportunity to launch a new type of casual shoe that departed from the company's traditional production. Fluxa sought to create a comfortable shoe with a new design aesthetic in keeping with the more casual spirit of the times. Fluxa approached his father for funding to launch a new company dedicated to casual footwear designs. The elder Fluxa resisted, calling the idea the "prostitution of the family business" in the March 2001 edition of *Fast Company*.

Fluxa's father's resistance came from another aspect of the business plan. During his travels to the United States in the mid-1960s, Fluxa had come into contact with Nike and several other shoe and clothing companies that had established themselves as brand marketing companies, rather than as traditional manufacturers. The younger Fluxa decided to focus his new company solely on the design and marketing of footwear, turning to other manufacturers to produce the product. His father was reluctant to agree to the product, in part because it represented abandoning nearly 100 years of the family's own manufacturing tradition. The elder Fluxa also raised quality control issues in objection to the idea.

CAMPER REVOLUTION IN 1975

A crisis in the Majorcan footwear industry, which had remained centered on the town of Inca, helped Fluxa

KEY DATES

1877: Antonio Fluxa returns from England and launches Majorca's footwear manufacturing industry.

1891: Fluxa's company, Lottusse, operates 11 workshops and five leather factories.

1929: Fluxa's son Lorenzo takes over as head of the company.

1975: Third-generation Lorenzo Fluxa launches the Camper casual shoe brand.

1981: Coflusa is incorporated as the holding company for Camper and Lottusse and other family holdings; Camper opens its first store in Barcelona.

1992: Camper opens its first international shoe stores in Paris, Milan, London, and Cologne.

2000: Camper opens stores in the United States, Taiwan, Japan, and South Africa.

2004: Lottusse opens its first retail stores in China.

2009: The company acquires a majority stake in the Camper stores in Turkey owned by Unitim.

prevail. The town's shoemakers had been supplying shoe companies in France and England. When these markets suddenly dried up in the mid-1970s, Fluxa found himself with access to a large, highly skilled, and local pool of workers. Fluxa's father at last agreed to bankroll the new company.

Fluxa launched the company in April 1975 and set out to develop its first design. Fluxa returned to the family's earlier success with the Camaléon model, developing a new shoe with the same name. The new Camaléon inherited the tradition behind the shoe that had inspired its predecessor, and was initially fabricated using production scraps as well as recycled tires for the soles. In order to establish a link to Majorca's cultural traditions, Fluxa named the company Camper, derived from *camperas*, the Catalan word for "farmer."

Fluxa at first found it difficult to place its shoes with Spain's traditionally stodgy shoe retailers. Many of the family's longtime customers refused to even stock the shoes. As Fluxa told *Fast Company*: "I told them of my plan to make casual unisex shoes, and I got two letters back from people who said that they would never sell these 'dirty shoes.' They had never even heard the word 'unisex'! They confused it with 'casual sex.'"

RETAILER IN 1981

Camper's break finally came following Franco's death in November 1975. With the restoration of the Spanish monarchy and the introduction of a new democratic government, Spain ended its years of isolation and embraced the youth culture that had swept through Western Europe. As more and more stores began to stock jeans and other casual clothing, Camper, as one of the only producers of casual shoes in Spain, found its shoe designs in strong demand. The company's unisex shoe, Camaléon, remained a strong seller for the company. In 1977 Camper also launched its first design specifically for the women's footwear market, called Bogart.

The company helped build this demand with the intentionally cheeky advertising that became another company hallmark. Two of the company's earliest advertising slogans exemplified Camper's playful spirit: "Wear shoes. It's more comfortable," said one, while a second declared: "Camper: a mixture of Lamborghini and Kawasaki, with a bit of Kamasutra."

Camper initially distributed its shoes to third-party retailers. In the early 1980s, however, the company prepared to take its branded concept to a new level, opening its own retail store. Determined to develop its own retail concept, the company launched a study of the traditional Spanish footwear retail market. The company then decided to break with the traditional footwear retail format in which customers chose a shoe design that sales personnel then retrieved from a storeroom. Instead, Camper decided to display shoes in the full range of sizes, enabling customers to pick shoes right off the shelf.

The company's first store opened in Barcelona in 1981. The self-service format proved highly popular, and the company quickly opened two more stores, in Madrid and Seville. In order to stock its shelves, the company launched a number of successful new footwear designs, including the Semanarista (Old Bachelor) in 1982, the Kenboot in 1984, and the Brutus and the Palmera in 1985. By the end of the 1980s, the company had established a national chain of 20 shoe stores. Camper had also continued to extend its third-party distributor network, becoming the leading casual shoe brand in Spain.

FACING COMPETITION

The Fluxa family restructured its businesses, incorporating a new company, Coflusa S.A., in 1982 as the holding company for Camper, Lottusse, and the Viajes Iberia travel operations. Camper became the fastest growing and most visible of Coflusa's operations. By the end of the 1980s, however, Camper faced rising competition for the Spanish casual shoe market. The company was then competing against a number of new Spanish companies. Spain's blossoming economy and the run-up to its entry into the European Union had also attracted the attention of many international and global brands.

Camper responded by stepping up its own design efforts, adding new annual collections every year, while also updating its existing shoe lines. The company remained true to its reputation for high-quality shoes that were quirky yet comfortable. This was exemplified with the introduction of its hugely successful TWS (or Twins) line in 1988. Described as "asymmetrical yet complementary," the shoes in a Twins pair were not identical, but instead presented differences in color, pattern, and design. The Twins line became a company mainstay through the dawn of the 21st century.

In a further effort to head off its growing competition, Camper continued to add new stores through the end of the decade, consolidating its presence as a national retailer. The company often placed the stores in upscale shopping districts, allowing the company to position itself among the growing number of designer label and luxury brands, while remaining a relatively inexpensive alternative. In the late 1980s the company also experimented with franchising, which allowed it to expand its network more quickly. However, the company shut down the franchise network in the mid-1990s.

INTERNATIONAL EMPHASIS

The company recognized in the 1990s that securing its future meant developing an international presence. The company had made an earlier effort to go international, setting up a booth at a trade fair in Düsseldorf, Germany. The company was unable to attract international orders, in part because of a stigma still attached to the Spanish export industry at the time.

However, by 1992 Spain had entered the European Union and had successfully hosted the Olympic Games in Barcelona, helping to raise its profile as one of Europe's most buoyant cultural and economic centers. The time was then right for Camper to pursue its international ambitions. That year the company opened its first four foreign showrooms, choosing the cities of London, Paris, Milan, and Cologne.

The Cologne store failed to attract customers and was shut down after only one year. The other stores proved more successful, however, and also helped to drive up interest from third-party retailers for the company's shoe fashions. The London and Paris stores became especially important for the company, serving as a showcase to introduce the company's designs to the rest of the world.

The company's major breakthrough came in 1996, when a Japanese buyer placed an order for Camper's Brothers model for two major Japanese retailers. The Japanese market responded rapidly to Camper's quirky aesthetic, and by the end of that year the company had sold 100,000 pairs of shoes in Japan alone. The company's sales rose past $40 million in 1996.

Success in Japan provided the company with the confidence and cash flow to step up its marketing effort in Europe as well. In 1997 the company launched a new footwear design for the European market. Called Pelotas, the new design had a decidedly retro look, and was often described as a cross between a golf shoe and a bowling shoe. The design became another hit for the company, attracting a growing number of high-profile international celebrities. The company's sales skyrocketed, topping $150 million by the beginning of the new century.

GLOBAL NETWORK IN THE 21ST CENTURY

Camper had also begun distributing its shoes in other international markets during the 1990s. After experiencing difficulties with its U.S. distributor, Camper decided to establish control of its sales there, opening its first retail stores in several cities, including New York, Los Angeles, and Chicago, while taking over the distribution of its shoes to third-party retailers. Camper also launched operations in a number of other international markets during the decade, opening its own stores in Japan, Taiwan, South Africa, and the Middle East. In 2009 the company also acquired a majority stake in a network of Camper stores set up in Turkey by Unitim Holding. The company had adapted its outsourcing model to the realities of the global footwear market by then, shifting nearly all of its manufacturing contracts to China.

At the beginning of the 21st century Lorenzo Fluxa was joined by his sons, Miguel and Lorenzo, ensuring the company's continuation into the fourth generation of family ownership. While the younger Camper brand had become the most widely recognized face of Coflusa, the holding company remained linked to its past through the growing success of the Lottusse brand. Lottusse had also gone international in the new century, building up a network of 30 stores across Europe and the Middle East. The Lottusse brand had been especially successful in the German and Norwegian markets.

However, China became Lottusse's strongest market. The company entered the Chinese market in

2004, and rapidly built up a network of 20 stores there. By the beginning of the next decade, China represented half of Lottusse's total sales. Coflusa represented more than 130 years of Majorca's footwear tradition, while stepping into the 21st century with two strong and complementary footwear brands.

M. L. Cohen

PRINCIPAL SUBSIDIARIES

Camper S.A.; Lottusse SA; Viajes Iberia S.A.

PRINCIPAL OPERATING UNITS

Camper; Lottusse.

PRINCIPAL COMPETITORS

Bata Ltd.; Brown Shoe Company Inc.; C&J Clark International Ltd.; ECCO Sko A/S; Eram S.A.; Industria de Diseno Textil S.A.; Nike Inc.; Paqueta Calcados Ltda.; Vivarte S.A.S.

FURTHER READING

"Casa Camper, Barcelona, Spain." *Independent*, November 15, 2008, p. 12.

Compton, Laura, and Sylvia Rubin. "Spain's Camper Walks Its Way to San Francisco." *San Francisco Chronicle*, January 27, 2002, p. E7.

"Footwear Expertise the Mediterranean Way, by Lottusse." *Fashionfromspain.com*, May 3, 2010.

Lawless, John. "Carry on Camper." *Independent on Sunday*, March 13, 2005, p. 30.

Leiber, Ron. "The Shoes in Spain." *Fast Company*, March 31, 2001.

Lipke, David. "Branquinho Does Shoes for Camper." *WWD*, December 1, 2009, p. 5.

Mitchell, Jordan. *Camper: Imagination Is Not Expensive*. IESE Business School Case Study, University of Navarra, February 2007.

"Spanish Footwear Label Shrinks by Request." *Australasian Business Intelligence*, June 5, 2007.

Vienne, Véronique. "Growing Up Camper." *Metropolis Mag*, October 17, 2007.

Corporación Alimentaria Peñasanta S.A.

—————— ■ ——————

Lugar La Sierra Granda s/n
Siero, E-33199
Spain
Telephone: (+34 98) 510 11 00
Fax: (+34 98) 510 11 22
Web site: http://www.capsa.es

Non-Quoted Public Company
Founded: 1967 as Central Lechera Asturiana (CLAS)
Employees: 1,286
Sales: EUR 723.62 million ($1.01 billion) (2009)
NAICS: 311512 Creamery Butter Manufacturing;
311511 Fluid Milk Manufacturing; 311514 Dry,
Condensed, and Evaporated Dairy Product
Manufacturing

■ ■ ■

Corporación Alimentaria Peñasanta S.A. (CAPSA) is
Spain's leading producer of dairy products. The
company is the marketing arm for dairy cooperative
Central Lechera Asturiana S.A.T (CLAS), which owns
56.39 percent of CAPSA. The Asturias-based company
markets its products under three primary brands,
Central Lechera Asturiana, Ato, and Larsa. Central
Lechera Asturiana is Spain's leading producer of bottled
milk, controlling 44 percent of the national market. The
company is also the largest branded supplier of butter
and cream, with market shares of 11.5 percent and 15.8
percent, respectively. With regional brand leaders Ato
(in Cataluna) and Larsa (in Galicia), the company is

also a major producer of yogurt, cheese, soy milk, and
other products.

The company's Food Service division is also a leading supplier to the institutional, restaurant and catering,
and industrial sectors. CAPSA supports its sales with a
network of eight factories, including three in the Asturias region, two in Galicia, one in Cataluna, one in
Madrid, and one on the island of Baleares. Altogether,
CAPSA's share of the total fluid milk market in Spain is
14.5 percent. Compagnie Laitière Européenne, part of
France's Bongrain group, is CAPSA's other major
shareholder, with a 27 percent stake. Pedro Astals is
CAPSA's chairman. In 2009 the company posted total
revenues of nearly EUR 724 million ($1.01 billion).

MID-20TH-CENTURY CHANGES IN SPAIN'S DAIRY INDUSTRY

Spain's dairy farmers found themselves under growing
pressure in the 1960s. Demographics shifted as large
parts of the country's highly rural population moved
into cities. Where farmers had traditionally served a local clientele, and often directly from their farms, the
changes in demographics forced them to invest in new
methods of transporting and distributing their milk and
other dairy products. Demand for these products also
rose steadily, with the growth of a larger, more affluent
urban population. This demand in turn placed additional pressures on dairy farmers. In order to satisfy
the demand, as well as to ensure the quality and safety
of their dairy products, farmers were faced with new
requirements to invest in modern production
equipment.

The industrialization of Spain's dairy industry achieved significant gains in productivity. However, this productivity came at the cost of the farmers' own livelihood. The surge in volume resulted in the collapse of dairy prices. Under the totalitarian Franco regime, farmers were left with little recourse. In the 1960s some compared their situation to enslavement.

The adoption of a new milk regime, setting still lower milk prices, in 1966 led to widespread protests by dairy farmers throughout Spain. In Asturias, one of the country's main dairy regions, farmers dumped their milk as part of their protest. These events convinced Jesús Sáenz de Miera y Zapico of the need for the region's farmers to group together in order to ensure their survival. Born in 1920, Sáenz de Miera had initially pursued a career as a police officer under the pre-Franco government, before earning a law degree at the University of Oveido.

Following Franco's arrival to power, Sáenz de Miera became a political activist, backing the workers' strikes in Asturias and elsewhere during the 1950s. These strikes led to the passage of the Trade Union Act of 1958. This legislation permitted the creation of workers' unions, and established the possibility of collective bargaining.

CLAS FOUNDED IN 1967

Following the dairy protests of 1966, Sáenz de Miera set to work persuading farmers to join together to form a cooperative to defend their own interests. The path toward this goal proved slow going, however. By 1967 Sáenz de Miera had persuaded a number of Asturias region farmers to come together to found a modern, central dairy production facility, called Central Lechera Asturiana (CLAS). Sáenz de Miera spoke at hundreds of meetings over the next three years, persuading the region's dairy farmers to join the project. By 1970 Sáenz de Miera had persuaded 3,500 farmers to join.

In the meantime, Sáenz de Miera had been studying large-scale dairy operations elsewhere in Europe. This effort enabled Sáenz de Miera to draw up a list of features required by the new company in order to ensure its success. The first of these was scale, ensuring that the Asturias dairy processed sufficient volumes of milk to supply not only the Spanish market but the export market as well. The company also needed to build up its distribution and transport infrastructure, as well as the capacity to develop ancillary products that were less perishable and therefore easier to ship to a larger market. Finally, the company needed capital in order to invest in the production machinery, including its own bottling operations, necessary to meet its objectives.

The company turned to a number of financial backers, notably Caja de Ahorros de Asturias and Caja Rurales, each of whom were given the right to place members on CLAS's board of directors. The new partners helped to arrange a loan of ESP 170 million, and established a financing facility for the group's future expansion. The CLAS dairy launched production in 1970, with an initial production of 200,000 liters per day.

With Sáenz de Miera at the head of the company, CLAS grew strongly through the decade. By 1972 the company had launched an expansion of its production capacity. One year later, having completed a new expansion of its operations, CLAS was among Europe's largest dairy processors. CLAS also took steps to ensure both the quantity and quality of its supply, establishing its own milk collection fleet in 1971 and launching a feed mill in 1972. These investments were soon followed by the installation of a refrigerator facility, enabling the company to further increase its production volumes.

UHT IN 1980

CLAS initially focused on producing and distributing fresh milk in bottles, which it marketed under the Central Lechera Asturiana brand name. CLAS quickly expanded its product range to include a number of other fresh dairy products, including butter, yogurt, and cheese. The success of the Central Lechera Asturiana brand name also helped the cooperative attract a growing number of dairy farmers. By 1976 CLAS counted more than 12,000 farmer-members.

The growing success of this brand enabled the company to put into place the next step in its strategy to develop less perishable, easier-to-transport products. The first of these came in 1980, when the company launched production of UHT (ultra-high-temperature) milk. Packed in specially developed packaging called "bricks" because of their rectangular shape, UHT milk

KEY DATES

1967: Jesús Sáenz de Miera y Zapico leads the creation of Asturias region dairy cooperative Central Lechera Asturiana (CLAS).

1970: CLAS opens its milk processing and bottling facility.

1980: CLAS launches production of UHT (ultra-high-temperature) milk.

1997: Corporación Alimentaria Peñasanta SA (CAPSA) is formed from the merger of the Central Lechera Asturiana, Ato, and Larsa brands.

2010: CAPSA fails in its attempt to acquire Spanish dairy rival Puleva Foods.

presented the advantage of a longer shelf life, of up to three months. The cardboard-based bricks were also easier to stack and less vulnerable to breakage during transport.

The success of the group's UHT products helped propel CLAS to become Spain's largest dairy group. By 1982, with total sales of ESP 11.3 billion, CLAS had also become one of Spain's top 50 largest companies, and among the top 25 companies focused on the Spanish market. By the early 1980s the company's daily production levels had expanded to more than 250,000 liters per day, or more than 100 million liters per year.

CAPSA FOUNDED IN 1997

Continued increases in production volumes enabled CLAS to expand beyond the Spanish market in the mid-1980s. In 1986 the company began supplying the export market, targeting Eastern Europe as well as the Middle East. The company also began supplying countries within the European Union.

In the 1990s CLAS began to restructure its operations, in part in anticipation of Spain's entry into the European Union. This process had begun in the early 1980s, when CLAS converted its status from cooperative to that of an Agrarian Transformation Society (SAT). Similar to a cooperative, the SAT provided a more flexible, corporate-like structure. The conversion to SAT also enabled Sáenz de Miera to strengthen his position as the head of the company.

Spain's entry into the European Union also promised to expose CLAS to new competition in the 1990s. Bracing itself for this competition, particularly

from the major European dairy groups, CLAS in 1993 adopted a new strategy calling for the company to transform itself into a large-scale food corporation in its own right. CLAS adopted a new corporate image and structure in 1994. The company made a number of acquisitions at the same time, including Cantabria-based milk collector CRLC, and cheese producer Quegalsa Ferool, as well as a two-thirds stake in Asturias-based Galeastur.

CLAS next began seeking a partner in order to allow it to achieve the size needed to compete on the European level. This search brought the company to Lechera Iberlat, another major Spanish dairy products group. Iberlat served as the holding company for two main businesses, Larsa in Galicia, and Ato in Cataluna. In 1997 CLAS and Iberlat agreed to merge their dairy products production units into a new company, Corporación Alimentaria Peñasanta SA, or CAPSA. CLAS remained CAPSA's majority shareholder, with more than 56 percent of its shares. French dairy and cheese giant Bongrain, through its subsidiary Compagnie Laitière Européenne, became the company's other major shareholder, with a 27 percent stake.

EXPANDING IN THE 21ST CENTURY

CAPSA then became the clear leader in the Spanish dairy market, with eight factories in Asturias, Cataluna, and Galicia, as well as in Madrid and on the island of Baleares. The company then began a new round of investments, adding a state-of-the-art filling plant in 2000, and then building a new yogurt and dairy dessert production plant, launched in 2001. The company also added a new cheese factory in Galicia that started production in 2002. Other investments included the modernization of a packaging plant in Lugo, and the expansion of the group's warehouse network in Oviedo and Lugo.

CLAS and CAPSA also faced disappointment in the new century, however, when CLAS failed in its attempt to merge with rival Leche Pascual, the two sides unable to agree on terms for the merger. CAPSA instead went in search of acquisitions on its own. In 2001 the company acquired 96 percent of Yogures Andaluces, also known as Yogan. The addition of that company strengthened CAPSA's reach into the Andalusian, Badajoz, Melilla, and Ceuta markets, while adding EUR 30 million to CAPSA's total revenues.

CAPSA announced plans to continue seeking new acquisitions through the middle of the decade, while also continuing to develop new product lines. For example, in 2004 the company introduced a new line of

Naturlinea brand dairy products, incorporating such additives as omega-3, royal jelly, and aloe vera. CAPSA was also developing its range of products for the institutional, restaurant and catering, and industrial sectors. In 2006 the company bundled these operations into a new division, CAPSA Food Service.

Also that year, CAPSA found itself the unwilling target of a takeover bid. In January 2006 Spanish consumer goods group Agrolimen offered to acquire the company for EUR 300 million. CAPSA turned down the offer, reaffirming its intention to remain an independent company. Instead, amid the difficult economic climate at the end of the decade, CAPSA once again went in search of its own takeover targets. This led the company to launch an offer in March 2010 to buy up Puleva Foods, the dairy products division of Ebro Puleva.

The deal would have boosted CAPSA's total share of the Spanish market to nearly 19 percent. However, CAPSA's bid came in too low, and Puleva was instead acquired by French dairy group Lactalis in May 2010. CAPSA, which remained the clear leader in Spain's dairy market, instead looked forward to new expansion opportunities in the future.

M. L. Cohen

PRINCIPAL SUBSIDIARIES

Biòpolis, S.L. (25%); Cueva del Molín, S.L.; Galeastur, S.A.; Iniciativas Astur Balear, S.L. (51%); Lácteos Zarzalejo, S.L.; Llet Ato, S.L. (40%); Menorca Llet, S.L. (25%); Porlac Comercializao de Lacticinios, L.D.A. (Portugal); Sociedad Asturiana de Servicios Agropecuarios, S.L. (44%); Vidreres Llet, S.L. (40%).

PRINCIPAL DIVISIONS

Dairy; Retail; CAPSA Food Service.

PRINCIPAL OPERATING UNITS

Central Lechera Asturiana; Ato; Larsa.

PRINCIPAL COMPETITORS

Acorex, S.C.L.; Industrias Lacteas Asturianas S.A.; Leche Pascual S.A.; Mantequerias Arias S.A.; Nestlé Espana S.A.; Teodoro Garcia S.A.

FURTHER READING

"Capsa Acquires Yoghurt Producer." *Expansion*, September 22, 2001.

"Capsa Is Looking for Takeover Targets." *Europe Intelligence Wire*, August 29, 2004.

"Capsa out of Ebro Puleva Dairy Unit Acquisition Race." *ADP News Spain*, March 3, 2010.

"Capsa Profits Quadruple after Merger." *Dairy Markets Weekly*, May 18, 2000, p. 11.

Castano, Ivan. "Dairy Firm Capsa Rejects Eur300m Agrolimen Bid." *just-food.com*, January 24, 2006.

Hofmann, Olivier. "Spanish Manufacturers Innovate in Health and Wellness Food." *Euromonitor*, March 6, 2007.

"Pascual, Clas Drop Merger after Failure to Agree on Terms." *Dairy Markets Weekly*, February 24, 2000, p. 9.

"Spanish Capsa Bids for Ebro Puleva's Dairy Arm." *M&A Navigator*, February 26, 2010.

Corporación de Radio y Televisión Española S.A.

Edif. Prado del Rey
Avda. Radio Television 4
Pozuelo de Alarcon, E-28223
Spain
Telephone: (+34 91) 581 70 00
Fax: (+34 91) 581 58 79
Web site: http://www.rtve.es

State-Owned Company
Founded: 1956
Employees: 9,000
Sales: EUR 1.3 billion ($1.7 billion) (2010)
NAICS: 515120 Television Broadcasting; 515112 Radio
   Stations

■ ■ ■

Corporación de Radio y Televisión Española S.A. (RTVE) is the state-owned body overseeing Spain's public radio and television broadcasting services. RTVE's television broadcast operations are conducted by Televisión Española (TVE) and include Spain's original television channels TVE 1 and La 2, as well as the 24-hour news broadcaster 24h, youth-oriented Clan TV, Teledeporte, and international Spanish-language broadcaster TVE Internacional. Until 2010 TVE financed its programming both through government subsidies and commercial advertising. However, in 2010 TVE went commercial-free, backed by an annual budget of EUR 1.3 billion ($1.7 billion).

This budget is also used to support RTVE's radio broadcasting unit, Radio Nacional de España (RNE),

which has always been commercial-free and includes the stations Radio Nacional, Radio Clásica, Radio 3, Radio 4, Radio 5, Todo Noticias, and Radio Exterior. Other operations included under RTVE are the Orquesta Sinfónica y Coro de RTVE, Instituto Radio Televisión Española, and Web site Tienda RTVE.es. Alberto Oliart took over as the company's chairman in 2010.

RADIO ORIGINS

The first radio stations in Spain appeared in the 1920s. Limited by technological, financial, and political regions, the early broadcasters tended to remain small, local operations. Movement toward a national radio broadcasting network occurred in the early 1930s, as the Republican government recognized the radio's potential for influencing public opinion. With the outbreak of the Spanish Civil War, both the Republican and Nationalist forces set up their own radio networks for broadcasting propaganda.

The Nationalist victory under Francisco Franco determined the course of the future national radio broadcasting body. The capture of the Castilla region by the Nationalist forces gave it control of its first radio broadcaster, Radio Castilla de Burgos. In January 1937 the Delegación de Estado para Prensa y Propaganda, the body charged by Franco to control the party's propaganda machine, began broadcasting from a new radio station in Palacio de Anaya, in Salamanca, using a transmitter donated by the German Nazi government. This station became known as Radio Nacional de España (RNE).

COMPANY PERSPECTIVES

In the exercise of its public service function, among the obligations of the RTVE Corporation are: Promote dissemination and awareness of constitutional principles and civic values. Guarantee the objectivity and truthfulness of the information provided, while ensuring that a broad range of views is presented. Facilitate democratic debate and the free expression of opinion. Promote the territorial cohesion and linguistic and cultural diversity of Spain. Offer access to different genres of programming and to the institutional, social, cultural, and sporting events that are of interest to all sectors of the audience, paying attention to those topics that are of special interest to the public. To serve the widest audience, ensuring maximum continuity and geographical and social coverage, with a commitment to quality, diversity, innovation, and high ethical standards.

RNE became the official broadcast body of the Franco dictatorship at the end of the Spanish Civil War in 1939. While other privately held radio stations, funded largely through advertisements, continued to broadcast, the RNE asserted itself as the sole provider of news broadcasts. The other radio stations, which were also subject to heavy censorship, were required to transmit the RNE news programming. RNE's broadcasts also supported the Axis powers, broadcasting Spanish-language versions of Italian and German news content.

Following World War II, the RNE installed a new, more powerful transmitter in Arganda del Rey, near Madrid, and began directing shortwave broadcasts to foreign markets in several languages. This activity, and the dictatorial and isolationist policies of the Franco government, led the European Broadcasting Union to refuse to admit RNE as a member until 1955.

NATIONAL TELEVISION NETWORK IN 1956

By then, the Franco government had begun testing its first television broadcasts, under the direction of a new body, Televisión Española (TVE), which was given the monopoly over all television broadcasts in Spain. TVE launched its first official broadcast in October 1956 with a single channel, TVE 1. From the beginning, TVE 1 operated as a commercial television station, while also serving the propagandist directives of the Spanish government.

TVE initially operated from a single studio in Madrid. In 1959 the company added a second studio, Miramar, in Barcelona. However, both studios remained under the control of the authoritarian regime. TVE also began developing a second television channel, UHT, later more popularly known as La 2, which began broadcasting in 1962. Like TVE 1, La 2 was also self-financed through advertising, while remaining under the firm control of the Franco government.

The 1960s also saw the expansion of RNE's network. Unlike TVE, RNE remained state-supported, with no advertisements in its broadcasts. However, in the 1960s RNE launched a new commercial radio station, called Radio Peninsular. The RNE also invested in new broadcasting technologies, setting up a regional broadcasting network with still more powerful transmitters capable of covering all of Spain (and much of Europe as well). The regional broadcasters, established in 1964, combined RNE's national programming with local and regional news content. This regional network became Radio 1.

RNE also installed FM transmitters during this time, which permitted higher-quality, stereo broadcasts. The company then launched a new radio station focusing largely on musical broadcasts, called Radio 2. Early in the 1970s RNE developed an international shortwave broadcast format, featuring localized versions of Spanish propaganda broadcasts targeted at the Soviet Bloc. This service, which became Radio Exterior, switched to Spanish-language programming in 1975, becoming a highly popular broadcaster in Latin America and elsewhere, as well as in Spain.

CREATING RTVE IN 1973

TVE and RNE remained separate operations until the early 1970s. However, in 1973 the Franco government combined the two broadcast bodies, creating Servicio Público Centralizado Radiotelevisión Española (RTVE Centralized Public Service). TVE had gained a measure of respect in the international television broadcast market by then, after a loosening of censorship policies in the mid-1960s. For example, in 1968 TVE won the Golden Rose award at the Montreaux Festival for its series *Historias de la frivolidad* (*Tales of Frivolity*). TVE also received international recognition for *Juan Soldado* (*Soldier John*), and *La Cabina* (*The Cabin*), winning an Emmy award for the latter in 1973. Spanish audiences, however, were presented only with heavily censored versions of these programs.

TVE began broadcasting in color at the beginning of the 1970s. It also developed a number of popular

KEY DATES

1937: Radio Nacional de España (RNE) begins broadcasting in support of the Nationalist civil war effort.

1956: Television Española (TVE) begins television broadcasting in Spain.

1973: RNE and TVE are combined under Servicio Público Centralizado Radiotelevisión Española (RTVE).

1980: RTVE is restructured as Ente Público Radiotelevisión Española.

1990: TVE loses its monopoly on Spain's television broadcasting market.

2007: RTVE is given a new legal framework as Corporación Radio Televisión Española.

2010: TVE begins commercial-free broadcasting.

series for the Spanish market, and notably a number of quiz and game shows, including *Un millon para el mejor* (*A Million for the Best*) and *La union hace la fuerza* (*Strength through Unity*). Another hit game show introduced at the time, *Un, dos, tres* (*One, Two, Three*), remained a Spanish television staple into the 1990s.

Despite these successes, RTVE remained hampered by its position as the broadcast monopoly of the Franco dictatorship. Through the cronyism that marked much of the regime, the company's workforce became bloated with more than 10,000 employees at TVE alone. Many of these employees had no training or background in broadcasting. As a result, RTVE struggled to keep up with evolving broadcasting technologies. For example, for much of its early existence La 2 reached only half of the Spanish population.

TVE had also been given the monopoly for cable television. The body launched plans to build a cable television network, in partnership with the Spanish telephone monopoly, which began cabling Spain's cities in 1973. However, TVE never pursued the implementation of cable television, effectively making Spain one of the few European markets to have had no cable television operations at the time.

POST-FRANCO EVOLUTION

Franco's death in 1975 and the institution of a democratic government in Spain resulted in a number of changes for RTVE. In 1977 the newly elected Spanish government established RTVE as an autonomous body

under governmental control. RTVE nevertheless remained open to charges, notably from the opposition, that it served as a mouthpiece for the Spanish government. This led to the creation of a new framework for RTVE, establishing RTVE as separate, although state-owned, company, called Ente Público Radiotelevisión Española in 1980.

TVE retained its monopoly over Spain's television broadcasting network. RNE, however, lost its right to impose its news content on the country's many private radio stations soon after the end of the Franco regime. RNE remained free of advertisements, and its costs were not borne by TVE, which developed a unique hybrid system of government subsidies, provided for by a television tax, and commercial advertisements.

RNE began restructuring its network of radio stations, which included a number of quasi-official stations operated by other organizations under the previous regime. These included such bodies as the Trade Union movement, the national Youth Organization, and others. In 1981 RNE regrouped these stations and their transmitters into a new channel, Radio Cadena Espanola. RNE also responded to popular demand by expanding its range of radio broadcast formats, including the launch of youth-oriented pop and rock programming, as well as broadcasts in Catalan. In 1989 RNE restructured all of its stations into a group of six radio stations, Radio Nacional, which took over from Radio 1, Radio Clásica, the former Radio 2, the youth-oriented Radio 3, Catalan broadcaster Radio 4, a 24-hour news station, Radio 5, and international broadcaster Radio Exterior.

LOSING THE MONOPOLY IN 1990

TVE also marked a number of milestones during the 1980s. In 1982, in support of Spain's hosting of that year's World Cup, the company built a new transmission tower, the Torrespana, which at 213 meters ranked among the world's 10 tallest television towers at that time. The Torrespana complex also housed a new 50,000-square-foot broadcast news facility. The completion of the Torrespana tower allowed the entire population of Spain to receive La 2. TVE also added new production studios in Barcelona and on the Canary Islands, as well as a network of smaller regional production studios, in addition to its main Madrid site. TVE also succeeded in trimming its employee base, shedding some 4,000 jobs through the 1980s.

Pressure began building for the Spanish government to open up the Spanish television market toward the end of the 1980s. In 1990 the government finally ended TVE's television monopoly. Within months three new privately held commercial broadcasters had appeared, including Telecinco, Canal Plus, and Antena 3. By 1991 the country also counted six regional broadcasters. The new competition quickly began draining both audiences and advertising revenues from TVE.

TVE gained widespread respect for its 24-hour coverage of the Persian Gulf War, despite the heavy toll the operation took on its finances. Similarly, TVE gained a significant bump in audience share during its coverage of the Barcelona Olympics. The cost of this coverage, at $10 billion, left a major new hole in the company's finances. In the meantime, while TVE 1 managed to maintain its lead in terms of viewers, by 1994 La 2 had slipped back into fifth place.

TVE's advertising revenues continued to slip through the decade, while the group's debt rose dramatically, topping EUR 6 billion by decade's end. The company also lost its lead to the private broadcasters, especially Antena 3. TVE nevertheless continued to expand its broadcast offering, rolling out new satellite-based television stations including a 24-hour news channel, and a youth-oriented channel called Clan TV. TVE also struck deals with a number of European satellite television operators, including BSkyB in the United Kingdom and Canal Satellite in France, to carry its broadcasts. TVE also reached broadcast deals in the United States and Mexico.

AD-FREE IN 2010

In the new century RTVE came under increasing attack from the private broadcasters, which did not benefit from the government subsidies supplied to TVE. At the same time, RTVE, despite its supposed autonomy from the government, continued to serve as a de facto government mouthpiece. This situation came to a head following the terrorist attacks in Madrid in March 2004, when RTVE's broadcasts sparked a revolt against the Aznar government, leading to its downfall in the next election. In the meantime, TVE faced other criticism based on its content, which *Daily Variety* labeled as "crassly commercial."

The arrival to power of a new Socialist government led to promises to achieve a true separation of RTVE from government influence. RTVE, which remained crippled by debt, also began slashing its payroll, announcing in 2006 plans to trim its total staff from more than 10,000 back to 6,500. The government then agreed to contribute EUR 3.2 billion ($4 billion) to RTVE in order to help reduce its debt load. By then, RTVE's total debts had risen past EUR 9 billion.

The Spanish government restructured RTVE itself in 2007, creating a new legal framework for the company, which then became known as Corporación Radio Televisión Española. The new mandate also took a step toward placating the private broadcasters by reducing RTVE's total available advertising time by 25 percent. RTVE continued to seek out new sources of revenues as well. For example, in 2008 the company teamed up with Spanish telecom giant Telefonica to provide content for its Internet-based television service. The two companies also agreed to develop other digital and interactive television services.

The government remained under pressure to eliminate RTVE's hybrid revenue structure. In 2009, following a similar move by the French government, the Spanish government announced that TVE would go commercial-free at the beginning of 2010. In place of advertising revenues, RTVE received a dedicated budget of EUR 1.3 billion ($1.7 billion). While TVE was expected to continue to lose market share, particularly with the proliferation of new satellite and Internet-based television channels, the company's newly ad-free films received a notable boost in audience viewers. Freed from a commercial imperative, RTVE was expected to play a major role in developing Spain's cultural identity in the 21st century.

M. L. Cohen

PRINCIPAL SUBSIDIARIES

Española Internacional; Instituto Oficial de Radio y Televisión; Orquesta Sinfónica y Coro.; Radio Nacional de España; Televisión Española Temática; Televisión Española Televisión.

PRINCIPAL DIVISIONS

Televisión Española; RTVE Comercial; Radio Nacional de España.

PRINCIPAL COMPETITORS

Antena 3 de Television S.A.; Corporacio Catalana de Mitjans Audiovisuals; Gestevision-Telecinco S.A.; Promotora de Informaciones S.A.; Sociedad Espanola de Radiodifusion S.A.; Sogecable S.A.; Vocento S.A.

FURTHER READING

De Pablos, Emiliano. "Gov't to Bail Out RTVE." *Daily Variety*, October 17, 2006, p. 10.

Herms, Josep Maria Baget. "The Legacy of Franco's Television." *Formats*, Vol. 3, 2001.

Hopewell, John. "RTVE Backs Local Films." *Daily Variety*, March 25, 2010, p. 4.

————. "RTVE Partners with Telefonica on Digital," *Daily Variety*, February 19, 2008, p. 46.

————. "RTVE Topper's Exit Raises Questions." *Variety*, November 23, 2009, p. 14.

————. "Spain B'cast Reign Ending." *Daily Variety*, August 20, 2009, p. 5.

————. "Spain Codified RTVE Budget." *Daily Variety*, July 20, 2009, p. 7.

Mayorga, Emilio. "Exec Ferrada Ankles TVE." *Daily Variety*, June 8, 2010, p. 15.

Mayorga, Emilio, and John Hopewell. "Labor Pain in Spain." *Daily Variety*, July 14, 2006, p. 6.

Rolfe, Pamela. "GM of Spanish Pubcaster Cuts Top Executives by Half; Measures Part of Cost-Cutting Plan." *Hollywood Reporter*, May 4, 2004, p. 54.

————. "New Mandate for Spain's RTVE." *Hollywood Reporter*, August 10, 2007, p. 8.

Corporación Venezolana de Guayana

Avenida Guayana con Carrera Cuchivero
Edificio Sede CVG
Altavista
Puerto Ordaz, Bolívar
Venezuela
Telephone: (58 286) 966-1930
Fax: (58 286) 961-4161
Web site: http://www.cvg.com

State-Owned Company
Incorporated: 1960
Employees: 18,000
NAICS: 551114 Holding Companies

■ ■ ■

The Corporación Venezolana de Guayana (CVG) is a government development agency that through its 14 subsidiaries dominates the economy of the southern half of Venezuela. The most economically important subsidiaries mine and transport iron ore for conversion into steel, and mine aluminum ore (bauxite) for conversion into alumina and aluminum. CVG also promotes industry, agriculture, fisheries, and forestry in the region, and is engaged in housing and social and urban development.

The Guayana region has 85 percent of Venezuela's known mineral reserves, including diamonds, gold, and manganese, as well as iron ore and bauxite. Moreover, the major deposits lie just a few dozen miles south of the Orinoco River, a year-round direct shipping route to the Atlantic Ocean. The region also includes the Coroní River, which contains natural falls and rapids harnessed to provide vast amounts of hydroelectric power. However, Guayana is far from the nation's population centers and is sparsely settled. Even more remote is Amazonas, in the far south of Venezuela, which was added to CVG's mandate in 1980 and was a territory rather than a state until 1992.

ELECTRICITY, IRON ORE, AND STEEL: 1960–95

The industrial development of Guayana began in 1951, when the government decided to establish a steel mill and hydroelectric power station on the Coroní River. The CVG was established at the close of 1960. An autonomous public agency reporting only to the president of Venezuela, it was charged with promoting physical, economic, and social development in the region. Its mandate included creating a planned city, Ciudad Guayana, at the intersection of the Orinoco and Coroní rivers, building roads, and managing the region's forestry and agricultural enterprises through means such as technical assistance and applied research. The CVG had at its command huge sums of money from Venezuela's oil earnings and also the right to reinvest any profits of its own.

All industrial plans rested on plentiful, inexpensive power. CVG Electrificación del Coroní C.A. (EDELCA) was accordingly established in 1963, when work began on the Guri Dam and an accompanying hydroelectric plant closer to the juncture of the Coroní and Orinoco rivers. The first phase of the Guri Dam was completed in 1968. An expansion project, with as many as 10,400 workers employed at one time, began in 1978. Completed in 1986 at a cost of $5 billion, it immediately made the Guri power station the world's largest electricity producer at that time. The concrete dam itself was one of the five largest in the world in volume.

CVG Ferrominera Orinoco C.A. was the subsidiary chosen in 1976 to administer the two recently nationalized iron ore mines that had been operated since the early 1950s by the two largest U.S. steel companies, U.S. Steel Corp. and Bethlehem Steel Corp. The ore was transported by river to a processing plant, and later to facilities to convert it into pellets and briquets for use in steelmaking.

A steel mill began production in 1962, using imported coke and scrap iron for the open-hearth furnace process. Siderúrgica del Orinoco C.A. (SIDOR) was established as CVG's steel company in 1964. Expansion from 1979 to 1982 almost quadrupled the mill's capacity to produce molten steel that was then turned into ingots, sheets, and bars. The process chosen was direct reduction of unwanted oxygen from the iron ore, which after treatment was fed into electric arc furnaces. Accessory plants manufactured other products. In 1977 Venezolana de Ferrosilicio (Fesilven), with French majority participation, began manufacturing ferrosilicon, an alloy used in steel production.

Ferrominera's attempts to manufacture usable direct-reduced iron (DRI) followed a difficult path. A joint venture with U.S. Steel became operational in 1973, but the plant accumulated $93 million in losses before closing in 1981. That year's production of 200,000 tons could not be sold. This facility was updated during 1988–89 in partnership with the subsidiary of a Japanese company. By the mid-1990s there were several more DRI plants in Venezuela and the country was producing more of this iron than any other country in the world. In 1994 a new $381 million pellet plant for Ferrominera went into production.

ALUMINUM-RELATED ACTIVITIES: 1967–95

The Guayana region's bauxite (aluminum ore) deposits were first extracted in 1977 by CVG Bauxita Venezolana C.A. (Bauxiven). Bauxite was converted to alumina (aluminum oxide), an intermediate product, by CVG Interamericana de Alúmina (Interalúmina), a company established in 1983 in partnership with a Swiss company. The bauxite came at first from Caribbean countries. By 1993 Bauxiven was able to provide Interalúmina with an adequate supply of bauxite, which was shipped by rail and barge to Ciudad Guayana. The two companies merged in 1994 to form CVG Bauxilum.

CVG Aluminio del Coroní S.A. (Alcasa) was founded in 1960 and opened the first aluminum smelter in Venezuela in 1967, with Reynolds Metals Company's subsidiary Reynolds International Inc. as its partner. In addition to sheets, smaller Alcasa plants produced rolled aluminum products, aluminum foil, and other products.

CVG Indústria de Aluminio C.A. (Venalum) was founded in 1973 to produce primary aluminum in diverse forms for export. A Japanese consortium provided most of the initial capital but soon reduced its stake in the enterprise to 20 percent. Venalum's manufacturing plant, the largest aluminum-producing facility in the Western Hemisphere at that time, began production in 1978 at Ciudad Guayana.

CVG Carbones del Orinoco C.A. (Carbonorca) was founded in 1987 to manufacture carbon anodes, an essential material, mostly for use by Alcasa and Venalum, which owned it. CVG Aluminios Nacionales S.A. (Alunasa) was established after CVG purchased a stake in a manufacturer of laminated aluminum products in Costa Rica. Founded in 1976 and fully acquired by Alunasa in 1990, this facility was the only one of its kind in Central America. Conductores de Aluminio del Coroní C.A. (Cabelum) was founded in 1976 to produce aluminum electrical wires and conductors. It became a CVG subsidiary in 2004.

UPS AND DOWNS: 1968–95

CVG Compañía General de Minería de Venezuela S.A. (Minerven) was founded in 1970 as a joint venture, fully nationalized in 1974, to extract gold in Guayana, where Sir Walter Raleigh had sought the legendary treasure of El Dorado centuries earlier. Production began in 1981 and had increased sevenfold by 1993. In 1991 Minerven and the Canadian mining company Placer Dome Inc. formed a joint venture to mine gold deposits at a site named Las Cristinas.

CVG Productos Forestales de Oriente (Profarca) began plantings of Caribbean pines in 1968. Nearly 30

```
┌──────────────────────────────────────────┐
│                                          │
│            KEY DATES                     │
│              ■                           │
│  ────────────────────────────────────    │
│                                          │
│  1960:  Corporación Venezolana de Guayana (CVG)  │
│         is founded.                      │
│  1962:  Steel production begins.         │
│  1978:  Largest aluminum-producing plant in the  │
│         Western Hemisphere opens.        │
│  1986:  Guri Dam is completed, providing vast    │
│         amounts of electrical power.     │
│  1995:  CVG has 18 subsidiaries and stakes in about  │
│         30 other companies.              │
│  2007:  Electrical subsidiary is detached from CVG to  │
│         become part of newly created national utility.  │
│                                          │
└──────────────────────────────────────────┘
```

years later the company owned the largest collection of pine plantations in the world, covering 855,200 hectares (over two million acres). Profarca also owned sawmills and board processing plants.

Between 1979 and 1983 CVG's revenues came to $8.4 billion, but the agency lost $876 million. This was attributed in part to lack of skilled personnel, bureaucratic incompetence, and corruption, but it was also the result of the government's hiring of thousands more workers than could be justified purely on economic grounds. In addition, this period was marked by a world recession that affected CVG's level of export earnings. Venalum and Alcasa lost money in three of these five years. Fesilven and Minerven also operated in the red. SIDOR suffered heavy losses in every year.

The outlook improved in the ensuing years. Between 1984 and 1991 revenues came to $13 billion, and a net profit of $1.77 billion was recorded. Employment, which reached 37,908 in 1990, fell to 31,942 in 1993.

OPERATING IN THE RED IN 1995

After 35 years in existence, CVG in 1995 had 18 subsidiaries and stakes in 30 other companies. EDELCA had the capacity to supply at least 60 percent of national demand for electricity. The industrial plants met all national demands for steel and aluminum and exported much of their production. CVG was garnering more than $2 billion a year in foreign currency. Combined annual sales of CVG holdings were about $4 billion.

Ciudad Guayana had grown in size to more than half a million people. The corporation, although directed from Caracas, the capital, was said to be the

true government of southern Venezuela. During the 1980s it assumed the roles of maintaining sewers and aqueducts, distributing drinking water, collecting urban garbage, and even managing soccer teams.

Nevertheless, after total expenditures of more than $30 billion over more than three decades, the regional corporation had fallen deeply into the red. According to one accounting, the 36 companies entirely or partly under CVG control had a combined debt of $4.6 billion. The CVG subsidiaries engaged in the aluminum industry were the worst offenders.

EDELCA's vast low-cost power was supposed to make Venezuela's aluminum the least expensive in the world. However, Alcasa owed at least $650 million in 1995 and could not even pay for the alumina received from Bauxilum, whose plant was reportedly constructed at a cost 11 times the original estimate. Production from Alcasa's lamination plant, inaugurated in 1991, was reported to be unacceptable for export. Venalum was described as better run, but like Alcasa was reporting annual losses.

The iron and steel sector had a mixed record. Despite a total government investment of about $6 billion, Ferrominera was $800 million in debt. SIDOR in 1993 was relieved by the government of more than half of its debt of about $900 million. Fesilven, the ferrosilicate company, was said to be bankrupt.

The brightest star was EDELCA, which in 1993 on paper had garnered about $150 million in profits. EDELCA was at work on the second of two hydropower complexes on the lower Coroní River closer to the industrial facilities at Ciudad Guayana, at a cost of nearly $1 billion. By the mid-1990s the government had mandated a privatization process aimed at the transfer to the private sector of a majority stake in the aluminum and steel industries, and the transfer of public services to state and local governments.

MOUNTING DEBT

A consortium of Latin American steel companies purchased 70 percent of SIDOR in 1997 for $1.2 billion and the assumption of about $600 million in debt. The company at that time was the third-largest steel producer in Latin America. It was renationalized in 2008 but was not reintegrated into CVG.

Ferrominera remained under the CVG banner. Its sales came to $779.4 million in 2006. In that year the company set a new record of 22.1 million metric tons of iron ore produced. The company was involved in making Venezuela the chief source of hot briqueted iron in the world. A Spanish company acquired 80 percent of Fesilven in 1998.

Bauxilum signed a pact with French-based Pechiney S.A. in 2002 to raise the capacity of its alumina plant, reduce costs, improve operating conditions, and resolve environmental problems. The company's difficulties did not ease, however. It failed to reach previous annual production of more than two million metric tons of alumina after 2003 and could no longer guarantee regular supplies to Alcasa and Venalum. Bauxilum's sales came to $610.6 million in 2006.

CVG's two aluminum companies accounted for some 5 percent of the world's aluminum supply in 1995. Primary aluminum, in the form of ingots, was used to make such products as rolls and sheets, wires, tubes, profiles, roofs, cans, pots, and foil. However, although supported by ample and cheap energy and raw materials, plus access by sea to foreign countries, the output of the two companies was uncompetitive in world markets. Collectively in debt by at least $1.2 billion, they found no bidders at auction and remained in state hands. Venalum's sales came to $1.08 billion in 2007 and slightly more than $1 billion in 2008.

STRIPPED-DOWN CORPORATION

EDELCA completed its third hydroelectric complex on the Coroní River in 2003. Its sales came to $1.24 billion in 2006. The company was detached from CVG in 2007 to become part of a newly created national electricity corporation.

Minerven assumed all rights to exploit the Las Cristinas gold deposits after Placer Dome assigned its stake in the operation to another Canadian corporation in 2002. This action was still being disputed in 2010. Meanwhile, thousands of wildcat prospectors had invaded the site. Elsewhere, Minerven was operating several gold mines but was not an important world producer of the metal.

Profarca's holdings in 2010 included the largest plantation of Caribbean pine in the world, occupying more than 400,000 hectares (about a million acres), or about the size of Rhode Island. The goal of using the pine for pulp and paper or to build housing made little headway, however, for the trees had previously been described as past maturity and poorly maintained. CVG Ferrocasa had built several hundred houses with Profarca's wood and roofs from CVG's aluminum. Ferrocasa had also developed a few small commercial centers.

Observers believed that Ferrominera, Bauxilum, and the two aluminum companies would, like SIDOR and EDELCA, be detached from CVG and placed into newly created national bodies. The stripped-down corporation would continue as a regional development agency with perhaps only a half-dozen subsidiaries remaining.

Robert Halasz

PRINCIPAL SUBSIDIARIES

CVG Aluminio del Coroní S.A.; CVG Bauxilum C.A.; CVG Ferrominera Orinoco C.A.; CVG Indústria Venezolana de Aluminio C.A.; CVG Minerven Compañia General de Minería de Venezuela S.A.

FURTHER READING

Bellone, Amy. "Natural Resources Growth Poles and Frontier Urbanization in Latin America." *Studies in Comparative International Development*, Vol. 39, Fall 2004, pp. 63–70.

Ceaser, Mike. "Lots of Gold, No Rush." *Latin Trade*, May 2004, pp. 22–23.

Colitt, Raymond. "Venezuela in Fresh Approach to Aluminium Privatisation." *Financial Times*, November 2, 1999, p. 44.

Coronel, Gustavo. *Una perspective gerencial de la Corporación Venezolana de Guayana*. Sabana del Medio, Carabobo, Venezuela: Editorial Melvin, 1995.

Enright, Michael J., et al. *Venezuela: The Challenge of Competitiveness*. New York: St. Martin's Press, 1996.

Mendes de Paula, Germano. "Crisis Hits Confidence in Venezuelan Iron and Steel." *Steel Times International*, February/March 2003, p. 40.

Thula Rangel, Benjamín. *Guayana en el desarrollo nacional y global: 1993–2000*. Caracas: Central University of Venezuela, 1994.

Crowley Holdings, Inc.

———— ■ ————

9487 Regency Square Boulevard
Jacksonville, Florida 32225
U.S.A.
Telephone: (904) 727-2200
Fax: (904) 727-2501
Web site: http://www.crowley.com

Private Company
Incorporated: 1906 as Crowley Launch and Tugboat
    Company
Employees: 4,300
Sales: $1.96 billion (2008 est.)
NAICS: 483111 Deep Sea Freight Transportation;
    483113 Coastal and Great Lakes Freight
    Transportation; 488310 Port and Harbor Opera-
    tions; 488330 Navigational Services to Shipping;
    48411 General Freight Trucking, Local; 484121
    General Freight Trucking, Long Distance,
    Truckload; 493110 General Warehousing and Stor-
    age; 336611 Ship Building and Repairing

■ ■ ■

Crowley Holdings, Inc., the holding company for Crowley Maritime Corporation, provides diversified
transportation services with a fleet of more than 210
vessels consisting of roll-on/roll-off (RO/RO) vessels,
lift-on/lift-off vessels, tankers, tugs, and barges. Crowley
is the leading ocean cargo carrier between the United
States and Puerto Rico, the Caribbean, the Bahamas,
Central America, the Dominican Republic, Haiti, and
Cuba.

The company provides liner services, logistics,
energy support, project management services, ocean
towing and transportation, petroleum and chemical
transportation, fuel sales and distribution, ship assist and
escort, salvage and emergency response, vessel construction and naval architecture, and ship management. The
company is owned by members of the Crowley family
and employees.

FOUNDED IN 1892

Thomas Crowley was 17 years old when he founded the
business in 1892. Crowley purchased an 18-foot Whitehall boat for $80 and began a water taxi service,
transporting supplies, passengers, and crew members to
and from ships that were anchored in the San Francisco
Bay. By 1900 Crowley was running 36-foot and 45-foot
gasoline-powered launches and a few years later he
began to acquire gasoline- and steam-powered tugboats.
With the motto "Anything, Anywhere, Anytime, on
Water," the Crowley Launch and Tugboat Company was
legally incorporated in 1906.

Over the next decade or so, Crowley continued to
acquire more and larger vessels, adapting his equipment
to meet the needs of his customers. In 1912 a shipyard,
later known as the Pacific Dry Dock and Repair Co.,
was built in Oakland for repairing Crowley vessels. In
addition, Crowley began operating San Francisco harbor
tours on double-deck passenger boats he had built for
the 1915 Exposition. Crowley also bought a 25 percent
share of Shipowners and Merchants Tugboat Company,
owner of the Red Stack tugs, in 1918. This investment
was increased over the years until Crowley fully owned
the company.

The Crowley fleet continued to expand after World War I, initiating tug and barge operations in Puget Sound and tugboat service in Los Angeles Harbor in the 1920s. Crowley purchased stock in two companies, Drummond Lighterage and the Cary-Davis Tug and Barge Company, and soon acquired a controlling interest in Drummond. In 1929 these two companies merged with two others, Pacific Towboat and Gilkey Bros., to form a new corporation, Puget Sound Tug and Barge Company, with 48 barges and 27 tugs. Puget Sound later became fully owned by Crowley.

BULK BARGE BREAKTHROUGH IN 1948

Crowley's growth and diversification continued through the 1930s. The company's launch and tug services reached all major ports on the West Coast, having expanded its harbor services to Long Beach and San Diego Harbors. In 1935 Crowley purchased the Bay Cities Transportation Company, expanding the company's capability in common carrier freight service, a business it had entered a few years earlier.

Also in 1935, Harbor Tug and Barge Co. became a wholly owned Crowley company. Crowley added bulk petroleum transportation to its list of services in 1939. By the onset of World War II the company had purchased the entire petroleum barge fleet of Shell Oil Company in San Francisco and was delivering petroleum to Shell storage facilities throughout the Bay Area.

In the 1940s Crowley began ocean transportation of lumber along the West Coast using tugs and barges. Crowley achieved a major breakthrough in bulk barge transportation in 1948, when Crowley's United Transportation Co. began operating the first oceangoing bulk petroleum barge service on the Pacific Coast. The shipments, which were made in a brand new barge with a 14,000-barrel capacity, traveled between San Francisco and Coos Bay in North Bend, Oregon.

A second Oakland repair facility was acquired in 1953. The facility, the Martinolich Ship Repair Co. (later renamed the Merritt Shipyards), helped meet the increasing repair needs of Crowley's growing fleet. It was later merged into the Pacific Dry Dock and Repair Co.

MOVING INTO ALASKA: 1956–69

In the mid-1950s Crowley began to establish services in the Arctic. In 1956 United Transportation Co. started shipping large amounts of asphalt between Portland, Oregon, and Anchorage, Alaska. The barges that made this trip were capable of carrying 12,000 barrels of asphalt. In 1958 Crowley began its long-standing relationship with the Military Sealift Command when it participated in the commercial resupply of the U.S. government's Distant Early Warning (DEW) Line installations. The DEW Line installations, part of a radar and defense communication system, were located in remote areas along the Alaskan coastline, in the Bering Sea and the Aleutian Chain.

Within the next few years common carrier service to Alaska was added to Crowley's line. Puget Sound Alaska Van Lines was formed in 1960, providing container and roll-on cargo service to Alaska. This company was the predecessor of Alaska Hydro-Train, which began operating in 1963. Alaska Hydro-Train connected the railroad system of Alaska to that of the lower 48 states with container and RO/RO railcar barge service between Seattle, Washington, and Whittier, Alaska.

During the remainder of the 1960s, Crowley played a major role in support of oil industry activities in Alaska. As oil drilling in the Arctic increased rapidly following the discovery of oil on Alaska's North Slope, so did Crowley's Arctic involvement. In 1966, in order to provide supply and crew boat services to oil companies attempting to set up offshore drilling operations in Cook Inlet, the Rig Tenders Company was organized in Kenai, Alaska.

In 1968 Crowley successfully managed the first of its annual Arctic sealifts to Prudhoe Bay, located on the North Slope of Alaska, a voyage of close to 4,000 miles north from Seattle around Alaska's perimeter. The sealifts were made on 400-foot flat-deck barges and carried oil industry cargo and plant modules, some of which were the size of an 11-story building. Crowley's 1970 sealift of 187,000 tons of cargo to Prudhoe Bay was the largest commercial sealift in the history of such endeavors to that date.

KEY DATES

1892: Thomas Crowley launches a water taxi service in the San Francisco Bay area.

1906: Crowley Launch and Tugboat Company is incorporated.

1948: Crowley's United Transportation Co. begins operating the first oceangoing bulk petroleum barge service on the Pacific Coast.

1970: Crowley's sealift of 187,000 tons of cargo to Prudhoe Bay is the largest commercial sealift in history at this time.

1974: Trailer Marine Transport is acquired.

1986: Company buys Coordinated Caribbean Transport.

1987: Crowley creates American Transport Lines.

1989: Company is the primary contractor for the provision of cleanup support equipment and personnel for the *Exxon Valdez* oil spill.

2000: Marine Transport Corp. is purchased.

GROWTH AND DIVERSIFICATION

Tom Crowley died in 1970 at the age of 95. His son, Thomas B. Crowley, Sr., had been running the company, gradually assuming responsibilities since the 1940s. The 1970s were a decade of tremendous growth and diversification for Crowley. The company started its Marine Oil Pickup Service (MOPS) in 1970. MOPS was designed to clean up oil spills in Puget Sound. That same year, the company began passenger service between Southern California and Santa Catalina Island with its Catalina Cruises.

In 1971 Crowley created Gulf Caribbean Marine Lines, which was organized to carry cargo in warehouse barges from U.S. ports on the Gulf of Mexico to various locations in the Caribbean Sea. The company also began to focus on expansion into Southeast Asia, establishing a company based in Singapore that provided offshore support services in that part of the world. In 1973 Crowley acquired an Alaskan trucking firm, Mukluk Freight Lines. Mukluk was the largest carrier of the 48-inch pipe used in constructing the 800-mile Trans-Alaska Pipeline.

An important development in 1974 was the acquisition of Trailer Marine Transport (TMT). TMT was a small tug and barge common carrier that had been operating since 1954. Crowley proceeded to transform TMT into the largest RO/RO barge operation in the world, ultimately using triple-deck barges that could carry more than 500 semitrailers. Also in 1974 came further involvement in Southeast Asia, including an Indonesia-based joint venture tending drilling rigs and a second joint venture in offshore drilling services.

BROAD RANGE OF SERVICES

In 1975 Crowley Environmental Service evolved out of the earlier Puget Sound environmental operation, offering a broader range of services with offices all along the West Coast and Alaska. Upon the acquisition of the floating equipment of Pacific Inland Navigation Company, common carrier service extended to Hawaii.

Crowley All Terrain Corporation (CATCO), a company that specialized in transporting supplies and personnel in the Arctic through all sorts of weather and over all sorts of terrain, was also organized in 1975. That year the Prudhoe Bay sealift flotilla faced the worst ice conditions of the century to that date, freezing in a number of the barges.

Two additional Crowley companies were formed in 1975, Crowley Maritime Salvage and Global Transport Organization (GTO). GTO, formed jointly with two Canadian companies, was designed to perform tug and barge transportation services internationally, and was particularly active in the Arabian Gulf during Saudi Arabia's large-scale push toward industrialization.

In 1976 Crowley introduced a seasonal common carrier service to western Alaska from Seattle with the creation of Pacific Alaska Line-West. The following year, tanker assist and escort services were initiated at the southern end of the Trans-Alaska Pipeline at Valdez, Alaska. In the late 1970s Crowley added to its fleet an icebreaker barge, the *Arctic Challenger*, followed by the salvage vessel *Arctic Salvor*, built through a vessel conversion in 1980. Also during the 1970s, Crowley developed the "float-on" loading technique, in which a barge is submerged in a controlled manner and cargo is floated into place.

EXPANSION CONTINUES: 1980–85

Crowley's rapid expansion and emphasis on a more international focus continued through the 1980s. In 1981, in order to help meet the heavy lifting and hauling needs of its Alaskan land operations, Crowley acquired Shaughnessy and Company, based in Auburn, Washington. The company purchased Delta Lines from Holiday Inns Inc. in 1982. Delta, which operated 24 ships on five trade routes between the United States and South America, Central America, the Caribbean, and West Africa, was sold again just two years later. *American Shipper* estimated that in 1982 the company earned $42.5 million profit on revenues of $550 million.

However, profits were cut in half in 1983, largely due to a severe drop-off in South American trade that caused Delta Lines alone to lose $20 million. Crowley continued to expand nevertheless. In 1984 TMT's Caribbean business benefited from the lengthening of five of its specially built triple-deck barges. These barges, formerly 400 feet long, were enlarged to 730 feet by the insertion of 330-foot sections into the middle of their bodies.

Crowley controlled 35 percent of the barge business between ports on the Gulf of Mexico and Puerto Rico by 1984. At that time the company had about 500 vessels, and brought in about 70 percent of its sales revenues through its barge and tug operations. In 1985 Crowley established Pacific Alaska Fuel Services to serve western Alaska with the transportation and sale of petroleum products, through tank facilities located in Nome, Kotzebue, and Captain's Bay.

FOCUS ON GLOBAL OPERATIONS: 1986–87

Further expansion took place over the next few years, as two major developments stretched Crowley's service area to include northern Europe, the entire Caribbean, and both coasts of South America. The first of these was the acquisition in 1986 of Coordinated Caribbean Transport, soon renamed Crowley Caribbean Transport (CCT). CCT had been in operation since 1961, when it consisted of two converted Navy landing vessels. CCT's main role was to carry agricultural products north from the Caribbean and head south loaded with industrial equipment. Among the stops included on the route were Costa Rica, Panama, Jamaica, Haiti, the Dominican Republic, Ecuador, and Peru.

In 1987 Crowley created American Transport Lines (AmTrans). AmTrans, organized as two separate ocean liner services to South America and Europe, quickly became the predominant American carrier to South America's east coast. By the early 1990s AmTrans was carrying over 50 percent of the containerized cargo between the United States and Argentina, Brazil, and Venezuela. The company's Sea Wolf class containerships were equipped with their own cranes and were capable of carrying heavy-lift, RO/RO, and oversized cargoes. Crowley's revenues in 1987 were estimated to be between $700 million and $850 million. Crowley consisted of about 40 separate companies with approximately 4,000 employees at that time.

By 1988 Crowley's share of the West Coast-Alaska market was about 18 percent. The company suffered through the worst financial year in its history to date, however, losing $30 million. Half of this loss was due to a Far East line, purchased from Pacific-Atlantic Navigation, which proved to be unprofitable. Catalina Landing, an unsuccessful real estate venture, and a strike by the Inland Boatmen's Union also contributed to the loss.

RESPONDING TO CRISES: 1989–91

A remarkable turnaround occurred for Crowley in 1989, thanks in part to the $40 million the company grossed from the rescue of the *Exxon Valdez*, the oil tanker that ran aground in Alaska, spilling its cargo in Prince William Sound. Crowley was the primary contractor for the provision of cleanup support equipment and personnel. Also in 1989, Crowley designed, built, and operated the *Responder*, the first barge in the world specifically geared for oil spill contingencies for use in exploratory drilling operations.

Crowley involved itself in other disasters that year as well, sometimes for profit, and other times without financial gain. The Red and White Fleet transported 15,000 stranded commuters, at no charge, following the San Francisco earthquake. In addition, rebuilding projects following Hurricane Hugo, a destructive hurricane that struck in September of the 1989 Atlantic hurricane season, increased cargo traffic, although the company also suffered damages from the storm.

In 1990 Crowley moved its headquarters from San Francisco, which had been its base of operations for 98 years, to Oakland, California. By the beginning of the 1990s the company had outposts throughout the world, with offices in over 100 major cities. During the crisis in the Persian Gulf, including both Operation Desert Shield and Operation Desert Storm, Crowley chartered several vessels to the U.S. Military Sealift Command. These ships, which supported the United Nations forces with transportation of personnel and supplies, included three RO/RO containerships, a tug, and a barge.

After the conflict, the government of Saudi Arabia selected Crowley as primary contractor for the cleanup of oil spills covering 450 kilometers of Saudi Arabian coastline, brought about by the demolition of Kuwaiti oil tankers and facilities during the war. These various government contracts helped raise Crowley's 1991 revenues to an estimated $1.1 billion.

REORGANIZATION: 1992–99

In 1992 Crowley underwent a legal reorganization. The 45 companies owned by Crowley were divided into two corporations based on the types of services they performed. Crowley American Transport, Inc. (CAT), was created to encompass all companies that carried cargo on ocean liners or performed related services. The remainder of the companies, primarily those that provided marine contract services such as tugboat operations, were organized as Crowley Marine Services, Inc. The privately held Crowley Maritime Corporation served as a holding company maintaining full ownership of both corporations.

In mid-1994 the top leadership of Crowley Maritime changed for only the second time in company history. At age 28, Thomas B. Crowley, Jr., was elected chairman, president, and CEO following the death of his father from prostate cancer. Also in 1994, Crowley American Transport began scheduled service to the Bahamas from Port Everglades, Florida. Crowley Marine Services formed two joint ventures, Marine Response Alliance (established in 1994) and Clean Pacific (1995) to provide emergency service in accordance with the Oil Pollution Act of 1990.

In 1995 the San Francisco local of the International Longshore and Warehouse Union refused to allow Crowley Maritime to reduce crew sizes by one, prompting the company to pull its tugboats and ships out of its home port, after 100 years operating there. Crowley moved the vessels to Seattle and Los Angeles.

Around this same time an exhaustive study, dubbed Focus 2000, led to the identification of core activities for Crowley Marine Services: oil transportation, contract barge and towing services, marine fuel sales and distribution in western Alaska and Puerto Rico, docking and emergency response services for tankers, vessel salvage and spill cleanup services, western Alaska deck cargo services, and all-terrain transportation services. The study resulted in the divestment of several noncore operations, including the Red and White Fleet ferrying service as well as Catalina Cruises, both of which were sold in 1997.

In 1996 and 1997 CAT greatly expanded its Central American operations, adding vessels and weekly fixed-day sailings. Crowley Maritime created a new subsidiary called Vessel Management Services, Inc., in 1996 to be responsible for the design, engineering, construction, and ownership maintenance of new company vessels. The following year another new subsidiary, Crowley Petroleum Transport, Inc., was inaugurated with the purchase of two double-bottom oil tankers that would provide bulk oil transportation in the U.S. tanker trades. Also in 1997, CAT expanded geographically, adding Chile to its U.S. East Coast-West Coast South America service.

Estimated 1997 revenues for Crowley Maritime were in excess of $1.1 billion, and the company had about 5,000 employees that year. A downturn in the container market coupled with the Asian financial crisis led Crowley to make additional changes to its operating structure during the late 1990s. CAT was sold and the Caribbean and Central American operations were reorganized under Crowley Liner Services.

STREAMLINING FOR THE 21ST CENTURY

Crowley entered the 21st century with streamlined operations. The company's reorganization proved successful and left it positioned for new growth. In December 2000 the company announced its purchase of Marine Transport Corp. (MTC), which gave it access to MTC's chemicals transportation and crude lightering businesses. Crowley then made history in 2001 when it delivered nearly $30 million of containerized frozen poultry and dry food products directly to Cuba. It was the first U.S. shipment to the island since trade sanctions were set in 1959.

The company made several acquisitions at this time to bolster its Logistics business. Miami-based Speed Cargo Service was purchased in 2002. Apparel Transportation Inc. was acquired the following year. The company also launched Crowley Far East Services in April 2003. The newly created subsidiary offered marine and shoreside logistics and transportation services in Russia.

The company returned to San Francisco Bay during 2004, marking its return to its founding waters by placing two tugboats in the Port of Oakland that were used to guide container ships into the harbor. The company's next big move came in 2005 when it purchased Titan Maritime LLC, an international salvage specialist. Titan had been involved in over 200 salvage and wreck removal projects over the course of 25 years. Titan at that time had contracts in Banda Aceh, Indonesia, which had been devastated by a tsunami that struck in December 2004, as well as in New Orleans, where it aided in the relaunch of barges that were displaced during Hurricane Katrina.

NEW EQUIPMENT AND SERVICES AND HEADQUARTERS

During 2007 the company introduced three heavy-lift 455 series barges that supported deepwater exploration projects in the offshore petroleum industry in the Gulf of Mexico. It also began to take delivery of over 900 new 40-foot refrigerated (reefer) containers as well as additional equipment that would be used to meet growing demand in its Latin America, Caribbean, and Puerto

Rico markets. It also took part in the tug-and-barge transportation and discharge and delivery of oversized cargo across a remote beach in Cabinda Province of Angola, West Africa. The delivery, made to Cabinda Gas Plant, was done in partnership with Chicago Bridge and Iron and Cabinda Gulf Oil Company and took nearly 40 days at sea to complete.

Also during this time, the company officially moved its headquarters to Jacksonville, Florida. Over the past several years, operations had been gradually shifting from New Jersey and Miami to Jacksonville, a location central to many of the company's customers. While most of the company's upper level management moved to Jacksonville in 2007, Thomas B. Crowley, Jr., chairman, president, and CEO, remained based in Oakland, although he traveled frequently to Jacksonville. "My office is a laptop and a cell phone," he told the *Florida Times-Union* in September 2009. Under Crowley's leadership, the company remained focused on designing new vessels as well as providing a diverse array of transportation and logistics services.

In addition, it was dedicated to responding quickly to natural disasters. Crowley was among the first to respond after the devastating January 2010 earthquake wreaked havoc on the Caribbean country of Haiti. The company reestablished direct container shipments to Port-au-Prince and vessels delivered relief supplies as well as emergency housing units from Steel Elements International LLC.

With well over 100 years of experience under its belt, Crowley would no doubt be involved in future humanitarian efforts as well as profit-seeking ones in both international and domestic waters for years to come.

Robert R. Jacobson
Updated, David E. Salamie; Christina M. Stansell

PRINCIPAL SUBSIDIARIES

Titan Maritime LLC; Jensen Maritime Consultants, Inc.

PRINCIPAL OPERATING UNITS

Puerto Rico/Caribbean Liner Services; Latin America Liner Services; Logistics; Marine Services; Petroleum Services; Technical Services.

PRINCIPAL COMPETITORS

APL Limited; A.P. Møller-Mærsk A/S; Horizon Lines, Inc.

FURTHER READING

Bauerlein, David. "Crowley Maritime's Headquarters in Jacksonville Fights through the Recession." *Florida Times-Union*, September 20, 2009.

"Crowley Completes Discharge of Gas Plant Modules and Equipment across Beach in Angola, West Africa." *Business Wire*, January 22, 2008.

"Crowley Maritime Corporation: A Century of Service, 1892–1992." *Pacific Maritime*, May 1992.

"Crowley Receives Second of Three New Barges." *Gulf Shipper*, August 20, 2007.

"Crowley Selling Passenger, Ferry Units." *American Shipper*, February 1995, p. 87.

Davies, John. "Crowley Maritime: A Study in Diversity." *Journal of Commerce*, March 6, 1987.

Knee, Richard. "Crowley's Next Generation." *American Shipper*, July 1994, p. 20.

———. "Rebound for Crowley Maritime." *American Shipper*, November 1989.

"Leo Collar." *American Shipper*, October 1987.

"Thomas B. Crowley." *American Shipper*, January 1984.

Detyens Shipyards, Inc.

1670 Drydock Avenue
Building 236, Suite 200
North Charleston, South Carolina 29405-2121
U.S.A.
Telephone: (843) 308-8000
Fax: (843) 308-8059
Web site: http://www.detyens.com

Private Company
Incorporated: 1982 as Interim Investors, Inc.
Employees: 800
Sales: $367 million (2009 est.)
NAICS: 336611 Ship Building and Repairing

■ ■ ■

Detyens Shipyards, Inc. (DSI), is the leading ship repair business in Charleston, South Carolina. It performs emergency and planned repairs for commercial and government customers. Once primarily concerned with smaller naval vessels, the company has seen the bulk of its business shift to cruise liners, tankers, and other commercial ships since moving its main operations to a facility at Charleston's former U.S. Navy base in 1995. It continues to operate a smaller site on the Wando River in nearby Mount Pleasant. Among the company's strategic advantages are low labor rates, a convenient location, and one of the largest marine-oriented machine shops on the East Coast.

ORIGINS

According to his listing in the South Carolina Business Hall of Fame publication *Legacy of Leadership*, company founder William J. Detyens, the son of a carpenter, was born in Georgetown, South Carolina, in 1917. Three years later the family moved south to Charleston. Detyens left school at an early age and joined the U.S. Merchant Marine, where he eventually rose to chief engineer. Detyens left the Merchant Marine in 1950 and spent a year working for U.S. Pipe and Foundry Corporation in Chattanooga, Tennessee. When he returned to Charleston, he operated his own marine surveying business and owned a bar on the Isle of Palms called the Lighthouse.

After launching a successful ship repair business in Charleston in 1957, Detyens opened a larger facility on nearby Beresford Creek. This was outgrown within three years. Detyens then leased a dock on Calhoun Street from the city for about a year before acquiring a site in Mount Pleasant on the Wando River in 1962. His firm then had 200 employees.

An enthusiastic entrepreneur, Detyens also formed a related equipment-leasing business, Berkeley Industries, Inc., around the same time. Other diverse ventures followed. Detyens started a cemetery in Mount Pleasant and was a partner in a condominium developer.

The shipyard specialized in mending smaller vessels. The U.S. Navy came to account for most of its trade. In the 1980s a surge of low-cost foreign competition, primarily from Japan, led to the closure of dozens of repair facilities in the United States, but Detyens survived, although it remained reliant on military work.

COMPANY PERSPECTIVES

Located in the historic city of Charleston, South Carolina, Detyens Shipyards Inc. is busy building a tradition of quality workmanship at a reasonable price. As the largest commercial shipyard on the East Coast, our focus on safety and our exceptional drydock capacity ensure your visit to our one-stop facility will be exceptional. Detyens Shipyards understands the unique challenges with ship refurbishment. With our central location on the United States East Coast, shipping lanes and the easy access into and out of our yards, ships are in and out quickly with either planned or emergency repairs. We offer extensive crane services and shops, flexible work environment including cross-craft policies, three graving docks and six piers. Ship owners who are looking for work to be done in a timely, efficient manner should take a closer look at Detyens Shipyards, Inc.

NEW OWNERSHIP IN 1983

The shipyard was incorporated as Interim Investors, Inc., in March 1982; the name was changed to Detyens Shipyards, Inc., a few weeks later. Upon retirement that year, the founder sold the company to a group led by his son-in-law, D. Loy Stewart, who had worked for him since signing up as a machinist's helper in 1971. Revenues were $24 million in 1983, when the firm had 450 employees.

For about 10 years the company operated a second site, with a dry dock, on Shipyard Creek with space leased from Metal Trades Inc., another ship repair shop. According to figures cited in the *Post & Courier*, Detyens became the largest defense contractor in the Charleston area, with Navy revenues alone of $23.6 million in 1994. It then had 400 employees.

In 1995 Detyens completed an unusual project, the construction of a 145-foot, four-masted schooner called the *Windy*. After years of repairing vessels, this was the first complete ship it had constructed. A sailing ship, the *Windy* was destined to take tourists and students in the Chicago area on tours of Lake Michigan.

The decade was a time of great transition. After years of being dependent on government work, the company was placing increasing emphasis on commercial ships due to the military slowdown following the end of the Cold War. The cutbacks eliminated more than three-quarters of the yard's revenues. The shipyard

until this time had been limited to working on smaller vessels.

CMMC AND THE CHARLESTON NAVAL SHIPYARD

North Charleston had long been home to the Charleston Naval Shipyard (CNS), a massive Navy shipyard spanning 106 acres. It dated back to 1902, when President Theodore Roosevelt authorized construction, and opened seven years later. During World War II employment peaked at 25,000 workers.

When the base was slated for closure in 1993, Detyens joined Metal Trades in studying options for its future. They formed a coalition called Charleston Marine Manufacturing Corp. (CMMC) with Richard K. Gregory, a retired manager of a local General Dynamics Corp. plant, leading it as president. As part of CMMC, Detyens began its first five-year lease of part of the base in October 1995. This included three dry docks, including one 751 feet long, which greatly increased the size of jobs Detyens could handle.

The first vessel to be serviced by private crews at the base was the 9,000-ton combat stores ship *Sirius*. The larger facilities also strengthened the company's bids for foreign military sales (FMS) work, in which decommissioned frigates and destroyers from the U.S. fleet were renovated for sale to allied countries such as Taiwan, Portugal, Bahrain, Turkey, Saudi Arabia, and Egypt.

Nevertheless, it was the commercial side of the business that grew the fastest after the move to the Navy base. The company could take on massive civil jobs such as the 2000 conversion of the long-mothballed tanker *Galleoma*, being fitted to carry liquefied natural gas, which was described as the firm's largest commercial contract to date. At 950 feet the ship was the largest ever to be repaired in Charleston, and 200 feet too long to be put in a local dry dock. (It had previously visited a Baltimore shipyard for that.)

When the Navy base officially closed on April 1, 1996, it employed 6,000 civilians. Within the next few years a variety of large manufacturers began using the base warehouses. The base had more than 4,000 employees by 2001, about one-quarter of them working for various government agencies or the military. With 600 employees on site, Detyens was the largest civilian employer on the old naval base.

LOCATION AND OTHER ADVANTAGES

Charleston was ranked the fourth-largest container port in the United States. Its strategic location midway

KEY DATES

1957: William Detyens launches a ship repair business in Charleston, South Carolina.

1962: The business is moved to nearby Mount Pleasant, on the Wando River.

1982: Detyens retires, sells business to group led by son-in-law D. Loy Stewart.

1995: Detyens, as part of Charleston Marine Manufacturing Corp. (CMMC), begins leasing facilities at the massive U.S. Navy base in North Charleston.

2004: D. Loy Stewart, Jr., succeeds his father as company president.

2005: CMMC buys dry docks and other facilities it had been leasing at Charleston Naval Shipyard.

2006: Detyens opens its own medical center and free clinic.

between New England and Caribbean ports of call made it a convenient maintenance stop for cruise ships. A non-union shop, Detyens offered some of the lowest labor rates among U.S. shipyards. The potential cost savings were great enough for the company to market to ship owners in Scandinavia, noted the trade journal *Lloyd's List International* in 1999.

Detyens boasted some technological advantages, being the only facility on the U.S. East Coast to use hydro-blasting exclusively. The company cleaned ship hulls with a robotic system developed by Remote Tools Inc. of Aiken, South Carolina. This simplified preparation and cleanup and was superior to traditional sandblasting in other ways.

In addition to its sites at the former naval shipyard and on the Wando River, Detyens was also doing some work from a third location in Jacksonville, Florida. The main shipyard became accessible to taller vessels when two bridges connecting Charleston to Mount Pleasant were replaced with a single one 40 feet higher in 2005.

TRANSITIONS IN 2002 AND 2004

Company founder William Detyens died in June 2002. In addition to being considered a leading area entrepreneur and the father of the ship repair industry in Charleston, he was known for his philanthropy. An eighth-grade dropout himself, he helped establish the Trident Academy for children with learning disabilities

in 1972 and contributed to other local schools, churches, and hospitals. Charleston Southern University (originally Baptist College of Charleston), which he cofounded, conferred upon him an honorary doctorate in 1982. Detyens was also an avid sportsman, and enjoyed sailing and traveling. He was inducted into the South Carolina Business Hall of Fame in 1995.

In October 2004 D. Loy Stewart, Jr., became president of the shipyard, succeeding his father, who remained chairman. The transition was a matter of succession planning made more urgent by the elder Stewart's diagnosis of Amyotrophic Lateral Sclerosis (ALS or Lou Gehrig's disease). The younger Stewart had joined the company in 1991 after studying at the Merchant Marine Academy in Kings Point, New York, and became executive vice president in 2003.

CNS SITE ACQUIRED IN 2005

In August 2005, after a decade of paying as much as $1.4 million per year in rent and spending $25 million in improvements such as upgrading its floating dock, CMMC bought its site on the former naval base for $9 million. The property was first transferred to the city of North Charleston, and the Navy's cranes were not included in the purchase.

The FMS program had brought Detyens one of its largest jobs, which was completed in 2006. It involved the refurbishment of four destroyers for Taiwan (they were originally built in 1978 for the shah of Iran). The project, controversial due to U.S. relations with Mainland China, brought 1,500 Taiwanese sailors to Charleston to work on the vessels during the three-year project.

Detyens sometimes sent much smaller contingents of its own personnel to foreign countries to service such vessels. Contractors for cruise ships also brought their own crews to Detyens, sometimes numbering hundreds of people. In September 2006 Carnival brought 400 subcontractors to refurbish the interior of its liner *Fascination*. Detyens typically hired its own subcontractors for specific tasks.

The work could be dangerous and difficult. Detyens in mid-2006 opened its own medical center, and free community clinic, in a vacant three-story building at the front of its main site. The company reported benefits for its bottom line and the well-being of its employees, many of whom would have had a difficult time paying for medical care otherwise.

ON THE HORIZON

In 2010 the shipyard repaired the World War II destroyer *Laffey*, nicknamed "The Ship That Would Not

Die," which weathered numerous kamikaze attacks. The client for the $9 million project, the naval museum at nearby Patriots Point, also offered the prospect of future repairs for the *Yorktown*, an aircraft carrier. This was a much larger job estimated to be worth $100 million.

One source estimated revenues for the privately held company at $367 million in 2009. Although the company had grown in the 50 years since it was launched, it was still small enough to qualify for government assistance. In 2010 Detyens won a nearly $1 million grant to install new cranes and hydro-blast units from the U.S. Maritime Administration's Assistance to Small Shipyards program.

Frederick C. Ingram

PRINCIPAL DIVISIONS

Main Yard; Wando Yard; Detyens Medical Center.

PRINCIPAL OPERATING UNITS

Foreign Military Sales.

PRINCIPAL COMPETITORS

BAE Systems Norfolk Ship Repair Inc.; Braswell Services Group, Inc.; Colonna's Ship Yard, Incorporated; Newport News Shipbuilding and Dry Dock Company; Signal International, LLC; Tecnico Corp.

FURTHER READING

Bartelme, Tony. "Grace Vessel Built at Detyens; Ship Ahoy: The Four-Masted *Windy* Will Carry Tourists and Students on Lake Michigan at Chicago." *Post & Courier*, April 26, 1995, p. A13.

Braswell, Tommy. "Detyens Left Behind a Large Legacy." *Post & Courier*, August 8, 2004.

Burton, Adam. "Faith + Work = Success." *Aiken Standard*, April 14, 2000, p. 1C.

Fennell, Edward C., and Terry Joyce. "Detyens Shipyard Founder Dies." *Post & Courier*, June 7, 2002, p. 4B.

Hall, John. "Closing Bases Doesn't Mean They Can't Have Value." *Richmond Times-Dispatch*, November 25, 2001, p. B2.

Joshi, Rajesh. "US Yard Begins Scandinavia Business Drive." *Lloyd's List*, August 19, 1999.

Joyce, Terry. "Detyens' Business Is Shipshape." *Post & Courier*, February 25, 1996, p. I24.

———. "Detyens to Fix 950-Foot Ship." *Post & Courier*, January 20, 2000.

———. "Firms Ready to Set Up Shop at Shipyard; Babcock & Wilcox of Lynchburg, Va., and Charleston Marine Manufacturing Corp. Were the Top Bidders for Sites at the Charleston Naval Shipyard." *Post & Courier*, June 7, 1995, p. A1.

———. "Private Firm Starts Work at Shipyard; The *Sirius* Docks Here for an Historic Overhaul." *Post & Courier*, October 27, 1995, p. A19.

Lunan, Bert. *Legacy of Leadership*. Columbia: S.C. Business Hall of Fame, 1999.

McDermott, John P. "Company's Ship Comes In: Tenant CMMC Buys Former Navy Shipyard for $9 Million." *Post & Courier*, August 26, 2005, p. 7B.

———. "Shipyard President to Step Down: Loy Stewart Passes Control of Detyens to His Son." *Post & Courier*, October 16, 2004, p. 7B.

Parker, Adam. "Shipyard Medical Clinic for Workers and Families." *Post & Courier*, November 15, 2009.

Williams, Charles. "Workers See Retraining as the Road to a Secure Future." *Post & Courier*, October 14, 1996, p. D10.

The Dress Barn, Inc.

30 Dunnigan Drive
Suffern, New York 10901-4101
U.S.A.
Telephone: (845) 369-4500
Toll Free: (800) 373-4625
Fax: (845) 369-4829
Web site: http://www.dressbarn.com

Public Company
Incorporated: 1966
Employees: 30,000
Sales: $1.5 billion (2009)
Stock Exchanges: NASDAQ
Ticker Symbol: DBRN
NAICS: 448120 Apparel Stores, Women's and Girls'
Clothing

■ ■ ■

The Dress Barn, Inc., is a Suffern, New York-based operator of women's and girls' apparel specialty stores. The flagship unit is the Dress Barn chain, which focuses on 35- to 55-year-old women, sizes 4 to 24. The chain includes 120 dressbarn stores, about 30 Dress Barn Woman stores, and nearly 700 stores that combine the two brands. Serving a younger demographic is the Maurices chain of about 720 stores, mostly found in small markets with populations of less than 100,000. The stores offer moderately priced apparel to 17- to 34-year-old women in sizes 4 to 24 under the Maurices and Studio Y brands. Finally, the Justice chain of about 900 stores serves 7- to 14-year-old girls. Dress Barn is a

public company, but is still operated by the founding Jaffe family.

ORIGINS

The beginnings of The Dress Barn can be traced to 1962, when Elliot Jaffe was working as a merchandising manager for Macy's Department Store in Connecticut. He approached his wife, Roslyn, with an idea for a women's discounted apparel store, and the two decided to begin planning a test store. Knowing that they needed a reliable source of income to support their children, Jaffe retained his job at Macy's while he and Roslyn worked after-hours to open the first Dress Barn store later that year in Stamford, Connecticut.

The first store was marked by numerous retail errors, such as the lack of convenient parking nearby, the lack of dressing rooms for customers, and the existence of stairs that customers had to climb in order to access the store. However, the new store was an immediate success despite these shortcomings. Less than a year after its grand opening, Jaffe was able to leave his job at Macy's to focus solely on the operations of the new enterprise. Meanwhile, Roslyn Jaffe had begun planning the preparation and introduction of a second store nearby. The second store unit was opened in March 1963, and The Dress Barn store chain was born.

INCORPORATED IN 1966

Increased sales demands at the two Dress Barn stores soon prompted the Jaffes to begin searching for another store location and a new warehouse in the Stamford

COMPANY PERSPECTIVES

■

While society and its priorities continually change, dressbarn is poised to respond to these evolutionary trends.

area. Previously, The Dress Barn's warehousing, receiving, and distribution operations had been done from the first store's basement, which could be accessed only by using a narrow flight of stairs. After searching the area for a new location that would lend itself to more efficient operations, the Jaffes chose an old barn in Stamford, a choice well suited to the company's name. This barn was renovated to become the company's third store as well as its distribution center.

In mid-1966 the company's holdings were incorporated as Dress Barn, Inc. Throughout the rest of the decade, the company experienced calculated and planned growth under the watchful eye of Jaffe and his expanding management team. They made sure that the business was not expanded too quickly, in order to maintain available capital and avoid sinking all resources into the company at once. Meanwhile, stores were added to the chain sporadically at a rate consistent with the company's increase in earnings.

By the 1970s, after almost a decade of steady growth and expansion, The Dress Barn, Inc., comprised almost 20 store units. The company was large enough to have the buying power to bring in products from big-name designers such as Liz Claiborne, Calvin Klein, and Jones New York. Dress Barn continued to focus on selling this apparel to career oriented women at discounted prices, usually 20 to 50 percent lower than those of its department store competition. Meanwhile, the chain continued to expand through the opening of new stores and the acquisition of other chains, such as Pants Corral and Off the Rax.

TAKEN PUBLIC: 1983

On May 3, 1983, Dress Barn went public, offering its stock for $23 per share. Half of the shares were sold publicly, while management insiders retained the other half. The public offering gave Dress Barn added capital with which to expand and grow, while also incurring added responsibility for the company to perform well for all of its new owners. By July 1984 Dress Barn owned and operated 100 stores throughout the United States, holdings that marked a 30 percent increase from the previous year. By the end of 1984 the company had

157 stores, after the acquisition of 46 Off the Rax stores, eight stores from The Gap, and the addition of three new Dress Barn stores.

The company began to earn national recognition in 1985, when *Forbes* magazine ranked Dress Barn number 42 on its list of the Top 200 Small Companies in the United States. The following year, *Business Week* listed Dress Barn as number 26 among the country's Top 200 Hot Growth Companies. By that time, the company was operating over 200 stores throughout the United States, with high concentrations in the Atlantic northeast, the Midwest, and California. Two years later, Dress Barn's store count had increased almost 50 percent to 307, spread throughout 26 states.

The company, clearly achieving success in the discount women's apparel niche it had created for itself, decided to build on that success by entering the market for plus-sized women's clothing. Dress Barn Woman was introduced in 1989, targeting plus-sized women from the same basic demographic segment as the original Dress Barn stores. Most new Dress Barn Woman store units were placed in areas near existing Dress Barn stores to capitalize on Dress Barn's name recognition factor.

STRUGGLE AND SUCCESS

Dress Barn received further recognition for its achievements in the retail market in 1990, when it was awarded the High-Performance Retailer Award from Management Horizons, a division of Price Waterhouse. The award was based on four consecutive years of performance highs for the company. Also in 1990, Dress Barn purchased JRL Consulting Corporation for $2.56 million. The 1990s saw the company continue to enter new markets in the United States through the opening of new stores and the acquisition of existing chains. In 1993 Dress Barn added 21 new women's apparel stores purchased from Country Miss. The company was then operating hundreds of Dress Barn and Dress Barn Woman stores, as well as numerous combination units.

Dress Barn, which had traditionally marketed its women's apparel at discounted prices, suffered a hit to its earnings potential in the early 1990s when many department stores began to introduce their own moderately priced, private-label clothing lines. Dress Barn's sales advantage was diminished by this trend, which was reflected by the company's annual profit margins. Another detriment to Dress Barn's sales potential was the fact that a few of its own suppliers, such as Jones Apparel Group, also moved into the discounted apparel market through the introduction of their own factory outlet stores.

MOVE TO SUFFERN: 1994

Despite its hardships, however, Dress Barn continued to achieve increased sales figures each year in the first half of the 1990s. Its continued growth prompted the company to begin searching for a larger and more advanced headquarters and distribution location. In 1994 the company moved into a new facility in Suffern, New York. The state-of-the-art facility handled all distribution and warehousing needs, while also housing the company's executive offices. Also in 1994, Dress Barn issued its own credit card to the public, and soon thereafter over half a million cards were in circulation.

From 1995 through 1996 the company opened 136 new stores. Most new stores being introduced were combination Dress Barn/Dress Barn Woman stores, a decision that allowed the company to reach both target groups while using less space and capital. The chain eventually peaked at some 775 stores. This number had dropped to 680 by mid-1998 due to closures of poorly performing stores. The retrenchment paid off when Dress Barn earned a record $40.2 million on sales of $598.2 million in 1998.

NEW STRATEGY FOR THE 21ST CENTURY

At the dawn of the 21st century Dress Barn was facing an ominous trend. While the chain had long focused on career wear, including suits, dresses, and blazers, the influence of "casual Fridays" was being felt throughout the workweek. The shift impacted Dress Barn's bottom line in 1999, when sales increased 3 percent to $616 million but net income fell 17.1 percent to $33.3 million.

The company created a comprehensive plan to reverse its slide in profitability for 2000. One key component of the repositioning was an increase in private-label clothing, which promised higher profit margins. Over the next two years, Dress Barn's in-house

brand grew from 40 percent of its offerings to 100 percent. During this period the company also expanded its lines to include shoe and petites departments as well as jewelry and casual wear. As stated in its 2002 10-K financial report, Dress Barn "shifted its focus from structured, career looks to softer outfit dressings and assortments."

Sportswear accounted for about 65 percent of sales by the end of 2002. The company hoped that this mix of clothing for both workdays and weekend wear would make its stores "one-stop shopping" destinations for working women. New store openings featured a combination format, including both Dress Barn and Dress Barn Woman merchandise. Although the company continued to open additional locations, it also shuttered poorly performing stores.

A new marketing campaign encompassed a brand makeover, an advertising push, and a foray into cataloging. The company launched its first catalog in September 1999. Dress Barn hoped to put 10 million catalogs in the hands of existing and potential customers over the course of 2000. However, losses in both the catalog and e-commerce divisions brought an end to those outlets in November 2001.

Dress Barn also hoped to shift its appeal to a younger customer in part by refining the name to "dressbarn," a format that subtly reflected a more casual image. As Elliot Jaffe told *WWD* in November 2000, "We intend to promote Dress Barn as a brand and a lifestyle, not just a label, to differentiate ourselves from our competition."

NEW GENERATION TAKES CHARGE: 2002

In 2002 David Jaffe succeeded his father as CEO, with the elder Jaffe remaining as chairman. The Jaffes were cautiously optimistic about Dress Barn's future, setting a goal of $1 billion in sales. In order to reach that target, the company looked to possible acquisitions, a strategy made possible by an excellent cash position that not only allowed the company to buy back stock but to bank at least $200 million.

The pursuit of an appropriate acquisition was a careful process, due in part to legal entanglements that resulted from an earlier effort to acquire the Bedford Fair Industries catalog business. Bedford Fair was on the verge of filing for Chapter 11 bankruptcy protection when Dress Barn withdrew its bid. In 2000 Dress Barn was sued in the Connecticut courts for breach of contract and unfair trade practices. In 2003 a jury returned a verdict of $32 million in compensatory damages, but two years later the Connecticut Supreme

Court reversed the judgment. As a result, Dress Barn was cautious in its approach to acquisitions.

In late 2004 Dress Barn finally settled on a suitable company to purchase, agreeing to pay about $325 million for Duluth, Minnesota-based Maurices Inc. The chain was founded in Duluth in 1931 by E. Maurice Labovitz as a small women's fashion shop. It had since grown into a 500-store specialty chain that served a younger customer than Dress Barn, offering young adult and teen apparel to both men and women.

While Dress Barn was not interested in selling men's apparel, it had been attracted to the chain because of the diversities it offered. Not only was a younger range of customer added, but Maurices was Midwest-centered while Dress Barn was mostly represented on the East Coast. Moreover, Dress Barn offered apparel that was conservative in style, while Maurices was trendier. It was also a chain with growth potential. To bring the chain more in line with the Dress Barn focus, menswear was phased out and plus-size women's apparel was added to the mix at Maurices.

TWEEN BRANDS, INC., ACQUIRED: 2009

The addition of Maurices helped Dress Barn to increase revenues to the $1 billion mark in fiscal year 2005 (ending July 30). With a full-year contribution from Maurices and additional store openings, the company increased that total to $1.3 billion in fiscal year 2006. Dress Barn planned to open as many as 50 new dress-barn stores and 60 Maurices a year, but it also remained interested in further acquisitions of retail chains. David Jaffe made it clear, however, that any target would have to be a non-mall chain and a healthy operation. "We are not seeking something that has problems," he told *WWD*.

Jaffe's comments notwithstanding, in 2009 Dress Barn agreed to pay $157 million in stock to acquire Tween Brands Inc. and its 908 Justice stores. The chain served a third demographic, catering to 7- to 14-year-old girls. Dress Barn could then sell to three generations of shoppers. However, Tween held $165 million in bank debt, and Dress Barn was assuming a large number of leases and other liabilities. The younger market concept had also been underperforming in recent years. Nevertheless, Dress Barn was comfortable with the valu-

ation of the property and expressed confidence that the potential benefits far outweighed the risks.

Dress Barn recorded net sales of $1.5 billion in fiscal year 2009, while in 2008 Tween Brands boasted net sales of nearly $1 billion. By combining the businesses, Dress Barn had more than doubled its sales target established at the start of the decade. In 2010 the company also began making plans to expand the Maurices and Justice chains to Canada. The dressbarn chain, in the meantime, was busy remodeling stores and seeking to replace strip center sites with mall locations. The company appeared to be well positioned to enjoy even greater growth in the years to come.

Laura E. Whiteley
Updated, April D. Gasbarre; Ed Dinger

PRINCIPAL SUBSIDIARIES

Maurices Incorporated; Tween Brands, Inc.

PRINCIPAL COMPETITORS

J.C. Penney Corporation, Inc.; Kohl's Corporation; Lane Bryant, Inc.

FURTHER READING

Clark, Evan. "Dress Barn, Tween in $157M Stock Deal." *WWD*, June 26, 2009, p. 13.

Duff, Mike. "Dress Barn Spells Out Plan for 2000." *Discount Store News*, January 24, 2000, p. 3.

———. "Dress Barn Tailors 2002 Growth Plan to Include Entry into California Market." *DSN Retailing Today*, January 7, 2002, p. 6.

"Jaffe Rises at Dress Barn." *WWD*, September 5, 2001, p. 12.

Moin, David. "Dress Barn Formula Finds Its Moment." *WWD*, May 6, 2010, p. 12.

———. "Dress Barn Secure in Its Niche." *WWD*, November 30, 2005, p. 11.

Power, Denise. "Dress Barn's Dramatic Upgrade." *WWD*, December 22, 1999, p. 16.

Riell, Howard. "Barn Raising." *Retail Merchandiser*, November 2005, p. 25.

Seaton, Jay. "Brand Recognition Is a Springboard." *Communications News*, July 2000, p. 66.

Weitzman, Jennifer. "Specialty Stores Ride a Strong Profit Wave." *WWD*, November 17, 2000, p. 2.

Duro Felguera S.A.

Marques de Santa Cruz 14
Oviedo, E-33007
Spain
Telephone: (+34 98) 522 97 00
Fax: (+34 98) 521 93 39
Web site: http://www.durofelguera.com

Public Company
Incorporated: 1858 as Duro y Compañia
Employees: 2,113
Sales: EUR 927.7 million ($1.26 billion) (2009)
Stock Exchanges: Madrid
Ticker Symbol: MDF
NAICS: 331511 Iron Foundries; 331512 Steel Investment Foundries; 331513 Steel Foundries (Except Investment); 331521 Aluminum Die-Castings; 331524 Aluminum Foundries; 333120 Construction Machinery Manufacturing; 333131 Mining Machinery and Equipment Manufacturing; 333611 Turbine and Turbine Generator Set Unit Manufacturing; 333618 Other Engine Equipment Manufacturing; 333922 Conveyor and Conveying Equipment Manufacturing; 333999 All Other General Purpose Machinery Manufacturing; 336510 Railroad Rolling Stock Manufacturing

■ ■ ■

Duro Felguera S.A. is a major Spanish industrial company operating in four main areas: Power Systems, Industrial Plants, Manufacturing, and Specialized Services. The Power Systems division is the group's largest, accounting for nearly 50 percent of its EUR 928 million ($1.26 billion) in revenues in 2009. This division supplies turnkey power plant installations throughout the world. The company's projects include single-cycle and combined-cycle gas turbine power plants, thermal power plants, and desulfurization and denitrification components for coal-fired power plants. In 2010 the company also began constructing its first solar power plant.

The Industrial Plants division, which adds nearly 20 percent to group sales, specializes in turnkey projects such as storage yards, port terminals, mineral processing facilities, cement handling facilities, and other installations for the mining, steel, petrochemicals, and other industries. The Specialized Services division operates through a group of subsidiaries including Felguera Montajes y Mantenimiento, Feresa, Mompresa, Opemasa, Montajes Eléctricos Industriales (MEI), and Felguera T.I. This division constructs fuel storage facilities, provides building services, and a range of maintenance services for the industrial sector. This division generates nearly 23 percent of group sales.

The Manufacturing division produces a range of components, systems, and installations for the chemical, petrochemicals, and other industries, including vacuum columns, reactors, exchangers, desalinators, separators, storage tanks, converters, steelworks, power systems, and offshore equipment. The Manufacturing division added 10.8 percent to the group's sales in 2009.

Duro Felguera is one of Spain's oldest industrial companies. The company is listed on the Madrid Stock Exchange and is led by Chairman and CEO Juan Carlos Torres Inclán.

COMPANY PERSPECTIVES

Mission, Vision, Values. Vision. A company specialized in the execution of turnkey projects for industrial, energy generation and fuel storage facilities, and in the manufacture of industrial equipment. Dedicated to customer service with internationally oriented activities. Mission. Customer satisfaction through the rigorous fulfilment of our contractual obligations within the time and with the quality foreseen. Commitment to our shareholders, ensuring them an adequate return on their investments.

Sustained growth through technological development and internationalisation. Reinvestment in assets and technological development so as to guarantee our continued competitiveness.

Contribution to the professional and personal development of our employees. Loyalty to our partners and collaborators. Integration in the Community and in the social context where we carry out our work.

Strict compliance with the legislation in all countries where we operate. Respect for the environment, occupational health and safety.

SPAIN STEEL PIONEER IN 1858

Duro Felguera was founded by Pedro Duro Benito in 1858. Born in 1810 in Spain's Rioja region, Duro had already established himself as a prominent business figure. The arrival of industrialization to Spain had caused a sharp rise in the demand for iron and steel in the mid-19th century. At the time, however, the few Spanish steel producers in operation tended to be held by foreign interests, notably in France and Belgium. Duro set out to found a Spanish iron and steel company and began searching the country for the right location.

Duro's choice ultimately fell on Langreo, a town in the Asturias region. This region offered a number of distinct advantages. For one, the region was an important mining center in Spain, with a ready supply of both iron ore and coal. Situated on the northwestern coast of Spain, the region also served as a major port center for the country. Duro, joined by brother Julian and a number of other prominent financial backers, set up a new company called the Sociedad Metalúrgica de Langreo in 1857. That company then acquired land in an area outside of Langreo known as La Felguera. The company launched construction of an iron and steelworks and in 1858 incorporated the works as Duro y Compañia, marking the official start of the future Duro Felguera.

The Felguera works launched production in 1860 and by 1862 had reached a capacity of 9,000 tons of cast iron and 3,000 tons of steel. By 1864 these numbers had climbed to 11,000 tons and 6,000 tons, respectively. The proximity of the Felguera site to the region's large coal and iron ore reserves enabled the company to avoid the heavy transportation costs of its competitors. The Felguera site's access to the waterways of Asturias also enabled the company to ship its finished products less expensively. The company also benefited from the extension of the Spanish railroad into the region, receiving orders to produce rails starting in 1868.

CRISIS IN 1881

Duro y Cia flourished during its early years, profiting in part from the military conflicts of the period, which limited the supply of imported steel to Spain. By 1875 the company accounted for more than one-third of Spain's total steel production. Duro y Cia's operations were also credited with stimulating the industrialization of the Asturias region itself, which became one of Spain's major industrial centers at the time.

With its forge producing at full capacity, the company launched an ambitious expansion of the Felguera site in 1880. The expansion effort came too late, however, as the company entered a period of financial difficulty. By 1881 the Spanish steel market faced a situation of oversupply, in part because of the arrival of large quantities of lower-cost foreign steel. At the same time, the exploitation of vast iron ore reserves in the Biscay region, along with the implementation of more modern and efficient production methods there, made that region, and specifically Viscaya, the new center of the Spanish steel industry.

Duro struggled to adapt. By 1885 the company had clearly lost its position as Spain's steel leader, and its production had dropped to just 50 percent of capacity. The company also faced the loss of its founder, with the death of Pedro Duro in 1886. The company's leadership was then taken over by Antonio Velázquez Duro and Matías F. Bayo. In the meantime, the crisis at the Felguera plant had spread throughout the Asturias region, underscoring the importance of the company to the local economy.

KEY DATES

1858: Pedro Duro Benito incorporates Duro y Compañia and begins building an iron and steel works in Felguera, Spain.

1902: The company goes public as Sociedad Metalúrgica Duro Felguera S.A.

1920: Duro Felguera is Spain's largest steel and mining company.

1961: Duro Felguera merges its steel operations into Unión de Siderúrgicas Asturianas (UNINSA).

1967: Duro Felguera's mining operations are absorbed by Empresa Nacional Hulleras del Norte.

1973: UNINSA is taken over by the state-owned ENSIDESA.

1980s: Duro Felguera focuses on turnkey power plant installations.

2001: The company changes its name to Duro Felguera S.A.

2010: Duro Felguera adds contracts in India and Belarus.

IRON AND STEEL LEADER BY 1900

A number of factors played a role in Duro's survival. The creation of Unión Hullera y Metalúrgica (UHM) in 1886 regrouped the Asturias region's coal mines. UHM introduced modern mining methods, thereby lowering coal prices and allowing Duro and other steelworks in the region to produce iron and steel more cheaply. UHM lost its price advantage by shipping its coal outside of the region, encouraging the company to back the continued expansion of the region's steel industry. Duro and the other steel producers soon accounted for 75 percent of UHM's coal sales.

The conversion of Spain's navy to steel ships provided a new opportunity for Duro, which received the first of a number of major orders for steel sheets in 1887. The revenues from these orders also enabled the company to carry out a major modernization program. Furthermore, the creation of a protective tariff system helped reduce the competitiveness of imported steel, allowing the Spanish steelmakers to claim the major share of the domestic market. Duro grew more strongly than the others, and by the dawn of the 20th century had become Spain's leading iron and steel producer.

Duro y Cia changed its name in 1900, becoming Sociedad Metalúrgica Duro Felguera S.A. Duro Felguera went public two years later, listing on the Madrid Stock Exchange. The public offering led to a new phase of expansion and of diversification for the company. Duro Felguera and UHM began strengthening their relationship soon after Duro Felguera's public offering, and in 1906 the two companies merged together. Duro Felguera then became not only Spain's leading steelmaker, but also one of its largest mining concerns. Luis Adaro, founder and head of UHM, took over as Duro Felguera's director general.

GROWTH BEFORE THE SPANISH CIVIL WAR

Duro Felguera benefited from a new tariff system instituted in 1906, adding further protection for the domestic industry. The company expanded both its coal production and iron and steel production, helping to stimulate industrial growth across the region. As a result, Asturias became an important center for a number of industries, including brick making, ceramics, chemicals, power generation, and a variety of steel products, such as pipes and screws. Duro Felguera itself began producing a range of steel and iron products through the acquisition of local manufacturers. These acquisitions helped form the basis for the company's future Manufacturing division.

Duro Felguera had grown into Spain's leading coal producer by 1920. The company also remained one of Spain's largest iron and steel producers, along with the Viscaya works. The company profited from the revitalization of the Spanish railway system, starting in 1924, as well as the launch of a series of large-scale public works projects by the Spanish government under Primo de Rivera.

EXITING STEEL AND MINING

Duro Felguera also profited during the decades of Spanish autarky under the Franco dictatorship following the end of the Spanish Civil War. The company's position as a leading coal and steel producer made it an essential component in the country's effort to maintain its economic and industrial autonomy. Duro Felguera's operations had swelled to more than 25,000 employees by the end of the 1950s.

The end of autarky in 1959 brought dramatic consequences to the Spanish mining and steel industries in general, and to Duro Felguera in particular. While Duro Felguera had benefited from the closed market, it had not kept pace with new production technologies developed by the international steel and mining industries in the postwar period. As Spain reopened its market to foreign steel imports, the company found itself competing against larger, more efficient steel producers capable of producing higher-quality steel more efficiently. At the same time, the company's coal mining operations were also hard hit by the development of new generations of thermal power stations using petroleum and natural gas, both of which produced energy at a lower cost and with less pollution than coal.

Duro Felguera at first attempted to meet this competition by joining forces with two other Asturias-region steel producers, Fábrica de Mieres and Fábrica de la Sociedad Industrial Asturiana, creating Unión de Siderúrgicas Asturianas (Asturian Iron and Steel Union, or UNINSA) in 1961. In 1966 UNINSA launched a major expansion program, investing heavily in the construction of a modern steel complex in Veriña. This investment, however, proved to be UNINSA's undoing.

The international steel market experienced a major crisis at the beginning of the 1970s, as an oversupply of steel caused prices to drop sharply. As a result, UNINSA was taken over by Spain's state-run industrial company, Instituto Nacional de Industria (INI), which also controlled the country's other major steel firm, ENSIDESA. UNINSA was then merged into ENSIDESA in 1973. By then, Duro Felguera had abandoned its failing coal mining operations as well, transferring these to another INI company, Empresa Nacional Hulleras del Norte (HUNOSA) in 1967.

REFOCUSING

The loss of both of its activities left Duro Felguera in search of new areas of operations. The company's focus turned more firmly to its small manufacturing operations, which then began producing major industrial components and systems for the steel and mining industries, as well as for the petrochemicals and chemical industries, the offshore industry, and others.

Among the group's companies was Felguera Caldereria Pesada, which operated a 76,000-square-meter workshop and Felguera Construcciones Mecanicas, with a combined workshop and storage yard of some 60,000 square meters. This business produced equipment for the steel industry, as well as turbines, generators, cranes, power systems, and construction equipment and machinery, such as tunnel boring machines, for the public works sector. Other equipment produced by Felguera and its subsidiaries, Felguera Melt and Felguera Rail, included components for iron and steel foundries, and railway track materials, including those for high-speed and underground railways.

Duro Felguera also began developing its Specialized Services division during this time, including the launch

of erection services in 1968. Over the next decades the company's services operations expanded to include a full range of services, including turnkey construction, erection, operation, and maintenance services for a variety of industrial plants and installations.

By the 1980s Duro Felguera had developed a new focus, offering turnkey engineering and construction services for both the industrial and power generation sector. "Turnkey" referred to a company providing all services and operations required to bring a project to full completion.

POWER PLANTS

In the 1990s Duro Felguera expanded its turnkey operations beyond the Spanish market, becoming an increasingly prominent contractor in a number of markets, particularly in Latin America. The company entered a number of partnerships for this, such as with Mexico's Empresas ICA Sociedad Controladora S.A. de C.V. in 1993. The company also developed a strategic relationship with Westinghouse, and later with Siemens in the region. These partnerships helped Duro Felguera to compete successfully for more than 14 power plant projects in Mexico, starting with the delivery of a 150 megawatt (MW) plant for Westinghouse in 1998. By then the company had delivered three power plants generating a total of 400 MW in Colombia, also for Westinghouse.

Duro Felguera changed its name to Grupo Duro Felguera SA in 1991, before shortening its name to Duro Felguera in 2001. The company added several more Latin American markets through the decade, including Peru, Argentina, Chile, and Venezuela. Spain remained a major market for the company, however. Between 2002 and 2010 the company delivered 16 power plants generating a total of 8,000 MW, with a 17th slated for completion in 2011. In the meantime, in 2005 the company had completed an 80 MW plant for Endesa in Italy, its first in the Eurozone.

Duro Felguera's operations also achieved strong international expansion through this period, particularly in South America, which came to represent more than 61 percent of group revenues. The company's range of international operations continued to grow at the end of the decade. For example, in 2009 the group won a contract to build the boilers and turbines for the Staythorpe Power Station in Newark, Nottinghamshire, in England. In 2010 the company's Manufacturing division added a contract to supply coal unloading equipment for the Krishnapatnam port terminal in India. Also that year, the group's Industrial Plant division entered Belarus, with a contract to expand an oil refinery complex for that country's OJSC Naftan.

Duro Felguera's revenues neared EUR 928 million ($1.26 billion) by this time. The company had successfully reinvented itself as a major provider of turnkey installations, with the combined operations of the group's Power Plant and Industrial Plant divisions representing 70 percent of its total revenues. The company's Specialized Services division had become a major part of the group's operations as well, accounting for 23 percent of sales. Meanwhile, Duro Felguera remained linked to its past as a major Spanish steel company through its Manufacturing division. As one of Spain's steel pioneers, Duro Felguera represented the continuation of more than 150 years of Spanish industrial history.

M. L. Cohen

PRINCIPAL SUBSIDIARIES

Duro Felguera Plantas Industriales, S.A.; Duro Felguera, S.A., Energía; Felguera Calderería Pesada, S.A.; Felguera Contrucciones Mecánicas, S.A.; Felguera IHI, S.A.; Felguera Melt, S.A.; Felguera Montajes y Mantenimiento, S.A.; Felguera Rail, S.A.; Felguera Revestimientos, S.A.; Felguera Tecnologías de la Información, S.A.; Montajes de Maquinaria de Precisión, S.A. (MOMPRESA); Montajes Eléctricos Industriales, S.L.U. (MEI); Operación y Mantenimiento, S.A. (OPEMASA); Técnicas de Entibación, S.A. (TEDESA).

PRINCIPAL DIVISIONS

Industrial Plants; Manufacturing; Power Systems; Specialized Services.

PRINCIPAL COMPETITORS

Babcock Power Espana S.A.; Ficosa International S.A.; Imasa, Ingenieria, Montajes y Construcciones S.A.; Istobal S.A.; ITW Espana S.A.; MP Productividad S.A.

FURTHER READING

"De Corrupción y Cuentas en Suiza." *Epoca*, May 28, 2000, p. 21.

"Duro Busca 'Cuellos Blancos.'" *El Pais*, January 11, 2004.

"Duro Felguera Leads Risers on Continuous Market at Monday Close." *ADP News Spain*, September 21, 2010.

"Duro Felguera Sets Foot in Belarus." *ADP News Spain*, July 21, 2010.

"Duro Felguera to Build Eur 140m Solar Thermal Plant in Granada." *ADP Renewable Energy Track*, January 21, 2010.

"Duro Felguera Wins USD 25m Deal in India." *ADP News Spain*, February 9, 2010.

Lyons, Rick. "Now It's War." *Daily Star*, February 1, 2009.

"Venezuela Awards $2.1bn Power Project." *Latin American Power Watch*, June 10, 2009.

Eastern Mountain Sports, Inc.

---

1 Vose Farm Road
Peterborough, New Hampshire 03458
U.S.A.
Telephone: (603) 924-9571
Fax: (603) 924-9138
Web site: http://www.ems.com

Private Company
Incorporated: 1967
Employees: 400
Sales: $200 million (2009 est.)
NAICS: 451110 Sporting Goods Stores

■ ■ ■

Eastern Mountain Sports, Inc. (EMS), is a privately owned outdoor equipment and apparel retailer based in Peterborough, New Hampshire. In addition to its Web site, the company operates about 65 stores in 12 states along the East Coast, stretching from Maine to Virginia. EMS carries such major brands as Columbia, North Face, Patagonia, and Teva, as well as its own less-expensive EMS private label. Products include camping and hiking gear, climbing equipment, mountain and road bikes and accessories, kayaks, skiing gear, outdoor sports-related travel equipment, apparel and footwear for adults and children, and a wide variety of miscellaneous merchandise, such as GPS products and other electronic products, first-aid kits, dog gear, sunglasses, swim gear, and power kites.

EMS stores offer outdoor skills clinics, and for the more serious outdoor enthusiasts, the company runs a climbing school in North Conway, New Hampshire, in the heart of the White Mountains, and about 20 other locations. Backcountry skiing, mountain biking, and kayaking are also taught and guided trips are offered as well. EMS is owned by its management team, led by Chief Executive Officer William Manzer, and Connecticut private-equity firm J.H. Whitney & Co., LLC.

COMPANY FOUNDED: 1967

Eastern Mountain Sports was founded in 1967 in Wellesley, Massachusetts, by a pair of transplanted Coloradans, Alan T. McDonough and Roger C. Furst. McDonough had been the manager of a Denver hotel while pursuing an interest in rock climbing. Furst, an attorney who practiced in Denver, shared an interest in outdoor activities with McDonough, who was not only his trout fishing partner but also a client. Weary of long walks back and forth to their cars after fishing, they became backpackers in order to sleep overnight in the outdoors and cook their fish fresh over a campfire. They were already experienced campers and skiers. McDonough was inspired to start a mountaineering business after taking note of the successful mountain shop that rented space in the hotel he managed. In addition, McDonough was a rock climber and had long harbored an ambition to start his own rock climbing school.

McDonough and Furst decided to go into business together but were reluctant to attempt to break into a highly competitive market. McDonough explained to *Backpacker* in 1974, "With limited capital, we chose an area where there were very few real mountaineering shops. At that time Denver, California, and Seattle already had their share." Instead, Furst and McDonough moved their families to the Boston area, a short distance from the White Mountains and the Berkshires. It was there in Wellesley in 1967 that they opened a small shop under the Eastern Mountain Sports name that offered hard-to-find climbing gear and a selection of trustworthy camping equipment.

MANUFACTURING ADDED: 1971

Not only did EMS find a ready market for its climbing and camping gear, it stimulated demand by starting a climbing school, which opened less than a year later. Located in North Conway, New Hampshire, at the foot of Mount Washington, the highest peak in the Northeast, Eastern Mountain Sports Climbing School became the first climbing school in the East. Then in 1971 EMS became involved in manufacturing. It opened a small plant in Boston to produce tents and parkas, and also contracted with other manufacturers to make other EMS-designed products using materials the company supplied.

EMS grew sales on a pair of fronts in the early 1970s. It opened additional retail locations, including a 100,000-square-foot flagship store in Boston, where a closeout store was also operated. By 1974 EMS was operating 10 stores, three with 20,000 square feet of selling space, and five with 10,000 to 12,000 square feet. Locations included Amherst and Cambridge, Massachusetts; Ardsley and Buffalo, New York; North Conway and Intervale, New Hampshire; Burlington, Vermont; and St. Paul, Minnesota.

EMS also launched a catalog operation that enjoyed strong success. The catalog soon expanded to 200 pages, including 50 pages of technical advice, and in 1974 became available at newsstands across the country. According to *Backpacker*, EMS was posting $10 million in annual sales by 1974. Of that amount, nearly $2 million was generated by catalog sales. Moreover, about 40 percent of the products sold were manufactured by EMS.

MOVE TO PETERBOROUGH: 1977

In 1977 EMS moved its headquarters to Peterborough, New Hampshire. The location, although remote, suited EMS well because Peterborough was two hours from both Boston and the White Mountains, and not far from the Berkshires. The growth of the Manchester Airport in New Hampshire would in time also provide access to a major airport. Furthermore, Peterborough placed EMS in the heart of the type of country its customers visited and allowed EMS to easily test equipment in real-life settings. Moose, black bears, and wild turkeys were not strangers to the company's new neighborhood.

By the summer of 1979 EMS was operating 18 retail stores and sales had increased to $23.5 million. In order to grow the business further, McDonough and Furst decided to sell a controlling interest in the business to the Franklin Mint Corporation, a company launched 15 years earlier by Joseph M. Segel. Segel had started a promotional products business while attending business school, and in the early 1960s he decided to issue a series of sterling silver medals commemorating famous Americans. His new company, the National Commemorative Society, introduced other coin series and was renamed the Franklin Mint in 1965.

The Franklin Mint expanded into other collectibles, such as commemorative ingots, Christmas plates, and fine art plaques, and took advantage of the emerging collectibles industry. Sales grew to $113 million in 1973, when Segel sold the Franklin Mint to pursue other ventures, which would include founding the QVC television shopping channel. His longtime president, Charles Lovett Andes, took over the Franklin Mint and expanded its lines of collectibles. Franklin Mint enjoyed considerable success during the 1976 Bicentennial celebration, which was responsible for a surge in revenues to $307 million. Revenues then began to dip, prompting Andes to branch out into new directions. The addition of Eastern Mountain Sports was part of this new strategy and became Franklin Mint's first major acquisition.

EMS SOLD: 1988

The Franklin Mint was in turn sold to Warner Communications Inc. in early 1981. Like the sale of EMS to the Franklin Mint, it was a move made to support further growth through the deeper pockets of a corporate parent. The relationship did not work out as hoped, however. The Franklin Mint soon experienced a sales slump and Warner experienced its own cash problems, due in large part to the poor performance of the Atari game company it acquired, followed by the

KEY DATES

1967: Eastern Mountain Sports (EMS) launched as single store in Wellesley, Massachusetts.
1968: Climbing school opens in North Conway, New Hampshire.
1979: Founders sell company to Franklin Mint.
1985: EMS is sold to Amcena Corp.
2004: Management team acquires EMS.

market collapse in the early 1980s. In danger of falling prey to a hostile takeover, Warner divested Atari in 1984, and then sold the Franklin Mint as well. Warner elected to retain EMS, but just a year later Warner sold the business to Amcena Corp., the U.S. holding company for the Dutch Brenninkmeyer family, who were among the giants of European retail.

Amcena had become involved in the outdoor sporting goods field in the United States in March 1984 when it acquired the small camping and backpacking chain Kreeger & Sons. Amcena believed that EMS held more potential, possibly national in scope, and acquired the 17-store chain. Kreeger & Sons was relegated to secondary status, and although the stores continued to operate under the old name for a while, their inventory was quickly replaced by EMS merchandise.

Over the next decade EMS enjoyed steady growth under the ownership of Amcena, which in 1994 changed its name to American Retail Group, Inc. (ARG). EMS opened stores throughout the Northeast but also operated a few stores in Minnesota and Colorado. The number of total units reached 53 in 1994. The catalog business, in the meantime, was closed. Nevertheless, EMS continued to rely on mass mailings to drive business to its stores, creating a highly focused mailing list that had been trimmed from one million names to less than 300,000. Because the more customers shopped at EMS the more mailings they received, the list proved highly effective. Another key to the chain's success was the development of value-priced hiking footwear and boots available only at EMS stores.

By the end of the 1990s the number of EMS stores approached 80. It was also at the dawn of the new century that EMS launched a campaign to update the signage of the stores and present a consistent image. The company's image had changed over the years, as EMS became better known for its apparel than its outdoor

gear. According to *Fast Company*, the chain had "moved away from selling technical gear" and "began courting older, mainstream customers with such soft stuff as fleece jackets and cotton sweaters." However, while apparel sales were growing, total revenues were tailing off.

NEW CEO: 2003

The shift in the EMS business model was instantly recognized by its new chief executive officer, William Manzer, the former Perry Ellis president who took the reins in 2003 and declared in a 2005 *Fast Company* article that "EMS had become a Gap with climbing ropes." One of the steps Manzer took to return EMS to its roots and reconnect with its core market of outdoor enthusiasts was to gain independence from ARG. With financial backing from private-equity firm J.H. Whitney & Co., Manzer and his management team bought EMS in October 2004.

In order to become a true outdoor outfitter EMS began adding plasma screen and informational kiosks in stores to provide outdoor education and reinforce the chain's dedication to its core customer. The Web site was also reworked, and other, popular new outdoor sports were embraced. Mountain bikes were tested and after receiving positive reviews from customers were introduced to most of the stores over the next two years. Moreover, the stores began to emphasize the products, not the price, placing a premium on expertise over discounts. A good deal of attention was also paid to marketing to female athletes.

EMS began opening new prototype stores in the fall of 2006. At 15,000 square feet, they were twice the size of older stores. Rather than mall locations, the new stores were freestanding units. Smaller, underperforming stores were gradually replaced by the new format. Six stores opened in 2007, followed by eight in 2008. On-line sales, in the meantime, also enjoyed a steady increase.

EMS opened a slightly larger new store, about 18,000 square feet in size, in New York City in the spring of 2009, located in Manhattan's trendy Soho district. It replaced a store that was just one-third the size. EMS did not scrimp on it new flagship store. The company added an advanced integrated audio and video system to match the changing demographics of the store during it operating hours. EMS considered 2009 to be a transformative year. The number of units had been winnowed down to 64 as many of the older, smaller stores were shuttered. The company also enjoyed healthy profits, and had successfully returned to its original focus, both indicators that bode well for the long-term prospects for EMS.

Ed Dinger

PRINCIPAL SUBSIDIARIES

Eastern Mountain Sports Schools.

PRINCIPAL COMPETITORS

Dick's Sporting Goods, Inc.; L.L. Bean, Inc.; Recreation Equipment, Inc.

FURTHER READING

Carofano, Jennifer. "Extreme Makeover." *Footwear News*, January 24, 2005, p. 14.

Conley, Lucas. "Climbing Back Up the Mountain." *Fast Company*, April 2005, p. 84.

"Eastern Mountain Sports." *Backpacker*, Spring 1974, p. 34.

"EMS Stores Going Back to Basics." *New Hampshire Union Leader*, September 8, 2004, p. B3.

Kepple, Benjamin. "EMS: Big Plans for Bigger Stores." *New Hampshire Union Leader*, July 30, 2007, p. C1.

Leighton, Brad. "Peterborough, N.H.-Based Outdoor Sporting Good Retailer Finds Natural Habitat." *Telegraph* (Nashua, N.H.), June 11, 2002.

Lloyd, Brenda. "EMS Celebrates a Milestone Birthday." *Daily News Record*, December 17, 2007, p. 10.

———. "EMS Climbing Back to the Top." *Daily News Record*, November 13, 2006, p. 10.

Education Management Corporation

---

210 6th Avenue, 33rd Floor
Pittsburgh, Pennsylvania 15222-2598
U.S.A.
Telephone: (412) 562-0900
Fax: (412) 562-0598
Web site: http://www.edmc.edu

Public Company
Incorporated: 1962
Employees: 11,300
Sales: $2.01 billion (2009)
Stock Exchanges: NASDAQ
Ticker Symbol: EDMC
NAICS: 511519 Other Technical and Trade Schools;
611210 Junior Colleges; 611310 Colleges, Universi-
ties, and Professional Schools; 611410 Business and
Secretarial Schools; 611430 Professional and
Management Development Training

■ ■ ■

The Education Management Corporation (EDMC)
owns and operates 101 postsecondary schools, providing
career education to more than 136,000 students in 31
states and in Canada. Argosy University, The Art
Institutes, Brown Mackie College, and South University
offer certificate level as well as associate's, bachelor's,
master's, and doctoral degrees in a variety of academic
programs including creative and applied arts, behavioral
sciences, education, health sciences, and business. ED-
MC's Western State University College of Law, the oldest law school in Orange County, California, is fully ac-

credited by the American Bar Association. A consortium
of investors took EDMC private in 2006. The company
went public for the second time in its history in
October 2009.

ORIGINS

EDMC was founded in 1962, offering professional
development education in Pennsylvania. The company's
scope and focus then shifted with the 1970 acquisition
of the Art Institute of Pittsburgh, founded in 1921. As a
postsecondary art school under the parentage of
EDMC, the Art Institute of Pittsburgh offered
certificate programs in graphic design, interior design,
and photography.

Robert B. Knutson joined EDMC in 1969 and
became president of the company in 1971. Knutson
oversaw a period of expansion through acquisition. Over
the next 15 years EDMC added to its higher education
holdings with eight acquisitions, seven of which would
involve commercial arts schools in Denver, Fort
Lauderdale, Atlanta, Philadelphia, Dallas, Houston, and
Seattle. The company grouped these as "The Art
Institutes" in a national marketing campaign. The
eighth acquisition, of the National Center for Paralegal
Training, offered certificates in legal studies.

Another driving force behind EDMC's expansion
was Miryam L. Drucker, who joined the company in
1984 as president of The Art Institute of Dallas. She
became president of The Art Institute of Fort
Lauderdale before heading up The Art Institutes
umbrella organization in 1988. Drucker and Knutson
were married during this time.

Under Knutson, who became EDMC's chairman and CEO in 1986, and Miryam Knutson, who in 1989 was named president and COO, the company upgraded and expanded the educational capacities of its schools by improving student services, updating the curriculum, upgrading facilities and equipment, and increasing the quality and quantity of faculty members.

Also during this time, the company gave increased attention to implementing technology in the classroom, embarking on a multimillion-dollar investment in classroom technology to provide vocational training in computer animation, video production, and desktop publishing. EDMC instituted new programs and restructured several existing programs in order to improve the proportion of students who completed the programs.

Some of the schools offering associate's degrees in interior design, industrial design, and graphic design built those programs into four-year bachelor of arts degrees in 1993. EDMC also initiated career and employment programs to assist graduates in finding quality entry-level positions with higher starting salaries.

PURSUING GROWTH: 1990–95

In the early 1990s EDMC began developing a culinary arts program, launching its School of Culinary Arts at the Colorado Institute of Art. Beginning in late 1993, that school offered an associate of applied science degree, an 18-month to two-year program for the instruction of fine food preparation and fine dining restaurant operation.

In March 1995 EDMC opened Assignments restaurant, a fully operational 71-seat restaurant that provided an on-the-job training experience to students. On a rotating five-week schedule, students experienced all facets of restaurant operations, including table service, bar service, preliminary food preparation, and final food preparation for the customer. The facility featured a kitchen modeled after the one at New York's Waldorf Astoria Hotel, with more than four times the space of an average restaurant kitchen.

EDMC pursued growth through the introduction of new schools and the acquisition of existing schools. In 1995 EDMC purchased two schools from the Ray College of Design for $1.1 million and the assumption of debt, renaming the schools the Illinois Institute of Art at Chicago and the Illinois Institute of Art at Schaumburg. EDMC also made the culinary arts program, with an associate of applied science degree, an integral part of The Art Institute of Phoenix, where classes commenced in January 1996. The following August the company acquired the New York Restaurant School for $9.5 million. EDMC also began to offer certificate programs for legal health care specialists and legal administrative assistants at the National Center for Paralegal Training in Atlanta.

GOING PUBLIC: 1996

EDMC funded further growth with an initial public offering of stock in October 1996. The company offered 5.4 million shares at $15 per share on the NASDAQ and garnered approximately $45 million. The proceeds funded debt reduction and working capital as well as acquisitions and new schools. EDMC added Lowthian College in Minneapolis to its chain in January 1997, renaming it The Art Institutes International Minnesota.

At the Colorado Institute of Art, EDMC expanded the associate's degree programs in interior design, industrial design, and graphic design into bachelor of science degree programs. The school also introduced an 18-month certificate program in Web site administration, which involved existing multimedia and design classes as well as new programming classes staffed by three new faculty members. The Art Institute of Los Angeles opened for classes in October 1997.

For the fiscal year ending June 30, 1997, EDMC reported revenues of $182.8 million, an increase of 23 percent, while income reached $10 million, an increase of 46 percent. The company attributed the rise in income and revenues to increased enrollment and a 5.5 percent tuition increase during the fall 1996 quarter. Student enrollment had increased nearly 20 percent overall, averaging 14,490 students per quarter, while same-school enrollment at schools owned by EDMC for two or more years increased approximately 14 percent.

A secondary offering of stock in November 1997 raised $79.8 million for growth and improvement. Two acquisitions followed closely after the stock offering, the

KEY DATES

1962: Education Management Corporation (EDMC) is founded.
1970: Company acquires Art Institute of Pittsburgh.
1971: Company begins a series of eight acquisitions.
1993: EDMC initiates four-year degree programs.
1996: Initial public offering of stock is made.
1997: Average enrollment reaches 14,490 students per quarter.
1999: Company launches The Art Institute Online.
2000: EDMC opens The Art Institute of Washington, D.C.
2006: A consortium of investors takes EDMC private.
2009: Company goes public for the second time.

Louise Salinger Academy of Fashion in San Francisco and Bassist College in Portland, Oregon. These were renamed The Art Institutes International at San Francisco and The Art Institutes International at Portland, respectively. The Portland school offered associate's and bachelor's degrees in apparel design, merchandising management, and interior design, and a bachelor's degree in business administration. EDMC expected its associate's degree recipients at The Art Institute of Seattle to consider Portland as an option for completion of a bachelor's degree.

In consultation with professionals in computer design technology, EDMC began to formulate new educational programs, launching three new degree programs for Internet marketing and design in June 1999. The company offered a bachelor of science degree in online media and marketing, which involved classes on business strategy and online advertising. EDMC launched the program at the Colorado Institute of Art and planned to extend the programs to several other schools after government approval.

The Art Institute of Phoenix offered a bachelor's degree in game art and design, including character animation and complex mapping and modeling. An associate's degree in multimedia and Web design involved interactive design and technical elements such as audio, video animation, still pictures, text, and data.

EXPANSION CONTINUES: 1999

Revenues at EDMC reached $260.8 million for the fiscal year ending June 30, 1999. Federal funding for student grants and loans constituted approximately 66

percent of revenues. Average quarterly enrollment reached 19,325 students, compared to 17,002 students in fiscal year 1998. Moreover, the company's stock, initially offered at $15 a share, had more than doubled to trade around $33 per share in early 1999. EDMC attributed growth in the student body to new educational programs, expanded degree programs, and more evening degree programs.

Approximately 25 percent of the increase in enrollment stemmed from evening classes. Tuition increased 6 percent in 1999, while net income increased 30.9 percent, to $18.8 million. EDMC also reported that 91 percent of 1998 graduates found employment in their areas of study within six months of graduation. Starting salaries averaged $24,200 per year, a 7.2 percent increase over 1997 graduates' starting salaries.

Culinary arts education continued to be a major focus of growth, with three new programs initiated during the fiscal year. In January 1999 EDMC introduced a new culinary arts school at the Philadelphia Art Institute. Facilities included Suburban Soup, a take-out restaurant at the Suburban Station transit center. EDMC also initiated plans for a culinary arts program at The Art Institute of Chicago, which began in January 2000.

EDMC's strategy for further growth involved the addition of two new schools per year. In August 1999 EDMC acquired the American Business and Fashion Institute in Charlotte, North Carolina. With 135 students, degree programs included interior design, fashion merchandising, and retail management. EDMC renamed the North Carolina school The Art Institute of Charlotte. A second acquisition involved the Massachusetts Communications College in Boston, with 450 students. The school offered Internet communications and technology, multimedia technology, and recording arts and broadcasting programs.

EDMC continued to improve educational programs at existing schools. In October 1999 the state of Pennsylvania approved EDMC to offer bachelor of arts degrees in computer animation, interior design, and industrial design technology at The Art Institutes in Pittsburgh and Philadelphia, and a graphic design program at Pittsburgh. The new curriculum added management classes and other field-related courses.

The New York Restaurant School, renamed The Art Institute of New York City, received approval to offer an associate of occupational studies degree in art and design technology. EDMC also planned to expand the culinary arts program there. The Art Institute of Phoenix initiated a bachelor of science degree program in online media and marketing.

PLANNING FOR ADDITIONAL GROWTH

In the fall of 1999 EDMC introduced The Art Institute Online, which offered 12 courses in graphic design. The pilot project was introduced through The Art Institute of Phoenix and The Art Institute of Fort Lauderdale. The company intended the online courses as a precursor to an online bachelor of arts degree in graphic design, the first of its kind. The Socrates Distance Learning Technologies Group of Phoenix, acquired by EDMC in 1998, designed the courses.

EDMC established corporate partnerships to enrich student education with access to Internet infrastructure and functions. First Regional Telecom (FRT) and Tut Systems, Inc., provided students at The Art Institute of Philadelphia with e-mail services, intranet, and access to the company's private label Web Neighborhood port. While FRT designed the port specifically for The Art Institute students, allowing for interactive capabilities and possibilities for e-commerce, Tut Systems provided the infrastructure for high-speed access. MarketingCentral.com offered Web-based capabilities for collaboration and management of creative projects to students at The Art Institute of Atlanta.

Growth in student enrollment required EDMC to relocate some schools to new facilities. In May 1999 the Colorado Institute of Art, renamed The Art Institute of Colorado, completed a move to a 100,000-square-foot, 10-story building near the site of the original school. The move allowed the school to consolidate offices and classrooms into one building, while adding more student-teacher conference rooms and a larger library. New technology involved the addition of a digital darkroom to the traditional photographer's darkroom, and fully networked computer labs.

ENHANCEMENTS AND UPGRADES

The Art Institute of Pittsburgh, renamed The Design Alliance, moved to a new facility in the summer of 2000. The $20 million project involved internal demolition of a historic landmark downtown. Renovation of the 170,000-square-foot building included updated electrical wiring and fiber optics, providing the infrastructure for 15 state-of-the-industry computer labs with 400 computers and Internet access for faculty and students. New technological capabilities included a digital darkroom, an industrial design technology shop, and video production and postproduction facilities. EDMC projected enrollment at The Design Alliance to increase 30 to 40 percent during the 2000–01 school year.

EDMC received approval by an accrediting organization to offer several new degree programs at The

Art Institute International of Minnesota. With 700 students, the school offered associate of applied science and bachelor of science degrees in graphic design, interior design, media arts and animation, and Internet marketing and advertising. Associate degrees were also available in culinary arts, as well as in multimedia and Web design. Also, the National Center for Paralegal Training received approval from the state of Georgia to offer an associate of arts in legal studies.

EDMC expanded into new markets with its 21st and 22nd schools. Classes commenced at The Art Institute of Washington, D.C., in Roslyn, Virginia, in the summer of 2000. The Art Institute of Los Angeles-Orange County, where classes began in July 2000, offered bachelor of science programs in media arts and animation and in Internet marketing and advertising. Associate degree programs included graphic design and multimedia design. A culinary arts program was offered as well.

21ST-CENTURY SUCCESSES

EDMC continued to grow in the early years of the new millennium. While revenues grew through rising enrollment and increasing tuition rates, the company bolstered its holdings by making key acquisitions. During 2001 EDMC purchased Argosy Education Group Inc. After the deal, the company's holdings included 42 schools and enrollment of nearly 40,000 students. It also made smaller acquisitions that year including the International Fine Arts College, which was located in Miami, as well as various Canadian assets of ITI Education Corporation.

With 25 consecutive years of revenue growth behind it, EDMC's expansion efforts in 2002 included the purchase of Canada's Center for Digital Imaging and Sound and the Institute of Digital Arts, as well as the California Design College based in Los Angeles. Additional acquisitions followed in 2003, including the June purchase of American Education Centers based in Cincinnati, Ohio. American Education changed its name to Brown Mackie College the following year.

Sales surpassed $1 billion in 2005, while net income was approximately $100 million. By this time, the company's solid financial performance and its position as one of the largest postsecondary providers of education in North America made it an attractive target for investors. A consortium including Providence Equity Partners Inc., Goldman Sachs Capital Partners, and Leeds Equity Partners purchased EDMC in 2006 for $3.4 billion. The move returned EDMC to private ownership and was the first buyout of a publicly traded higher education company in the United States. The U.S. Department of Education as well as regional academic accrediting institutions approved the deal and EDMC was delisted from the NASDAQ in June of that year.

For the next several years, EDMC focused on bolstering its online class offerings, adding new programs at its existing colleges, increasing enrollment by using marketing campaigns, and opening new campuses. In May 2007 its Brown Mackie College school locations in Indiana began offering bachelor of science degree programs in legal studies, criminal justice, and business administration. Argosy University launched its first four-year bachelor degree programs in July of that year.

During the same period, the culinary programs offered at The Art Institutes were renamed The International Culinary Schools at The Art Institutes. Tucson Design College and Chaparral College were acquired and renamed The Art Institute of Tucson and Brown Mackie College-Tucson, respectively.

GOING PUBLIC AGAIN: 2009

In July 2008 South University created two new colleges, the College of Nursing and the College of Arts and Sciences. Art Institutes were launched in Lenexa, Kansas, and in Raleigh, North Carolina. Argosy University opened its 19th campus in Draper, Utah, in September 2008. Brown Mackie College-Boise opened its doors, marking EDMC's entry into Idaho. Brown Mackie College-Tulsa became the college's 20th location in October of that year.

EDMC kept expansion at the forefront of its strategy and continued to prosper even as the economy in the United States began to falter. Historically, educational institutions often remained shielded from problems during economic downturns as many unemployed or downsized workers sought vocational certification or postsecondary degrees to bolster resumes. With enrollment climbing, EDMC returned to public trading in October 2009, listing once again on the NASDAQ.

While EDMC had prospered during the first decade of the new millennium, it faced potential problems when a report issued by the U.S. Government Accountability Office (GAO) in August 2010 claimed the company and its peers had encouraged prospective

students to lie on government loan forms, and that the for-profit companies had made misleading statements about cost and length of academic programs as well as earnings potential after graduation. Despite the bad press garnered by the report, EDMC remained focused on helping students achieve their educational goals. The effects these claims would have on student enrollment and the company's bottom line remained to be seen, however.

Mary Tradii
Updated, Christina M. Stansell

PRINCIPAL DIVISIONS

Argosy University; The Art Institutes; Brown Mackie College; South University; Western State University College of Law.

PRINCIPAL COMPETITORS

Apollo Group, Inc.; Career Education Corporation; Laureate Education, Inc.

FURTHER READING

Boselovic, Len. "Education Management Teaches Investors Lessons in Takeovers, Returns." *Pittsburgh Post-Gazette*, December 24, 2001.

Cowan, Lynn. "Going Public: Education Management's Economic Immunity." *Dow Jones News Service*, January 16, 2008.

"Education Management Corporation Named to *Forbes* 200 Best Small Companies List." *PR Newswire*, October 25, 1999.

Gannon, Joyce. "He Found a Career by Chance after Training to Work Internationally." *Pittsburgh Post-Gazette*, August 1, 1999, p. F5.

"GAO Singles Out Schools in Report." *Investor's Business Daily*, August 5, 2010.

Selingo, Jeffrey. "2 Companies Plan to Buy a Chain of For-Profit Colleges for $3.4-Billion." *Chronicle of Higher Education*, March 17, 2006.

Tarquinio, J. Alex. "A Class Act." *Kiplinger's Personal Finance Magazine*, March 1, 2006.

Tascarella, Patty. "Art Schools' Degree OK'd." *Pittsburgh Business Times*, October 22, 1999, p. 3.

"Work Begins at New Site for Art Institute." *Pittsburgh Post-Gazette*, September 11, 1999, p. C12.

Feeding America

---

35 East Wacker Drive, Suite 2000
Chicago, Illinois 60601
U.S.A.
Telephone: (312) 263-2303
Toll Free: (800) 771-2303
Fax: (312) 263-5626
Web site: http://www.feedingamerica.org

Nonprofit Organization
Incorporated: 1979 as Second Harvest
Employees: 170
Public Support and Revenues: $618.74 million (2009 est.)
NAICS: 624210 Food Banks

■ ■ ■

Feeding America is the largest nonprofit domestic hunger-relief organization in the United States. The organization provides food to people who are unable to purchase it themselves by raising money for and distributing food and other grocery products through an extensive and comprehensive network of food banks. In addition, the organization sees its mission as partly educational in raising the public's level of awareness about the nature of hunger in the United States.

Feeding America works closely with more than 63,000 local hunger-relief agencies and organizations, including soup kitchens, day care centers, grassroots youth programs in urban areas, senior centers, homeless shelters, women's shelters, and food pantries. The organization has arranged to secure surplus food from food growers, distributors, retail grocery stores, and food processors, including such corporate giants as General Mills, Kraft, Nabisco, Pillsbury, Procter & Gamble, and Kellogg.

Approximately 35 million people were assisted by the Feeding America food network in 2009, including households with working individuals, women, children, and the elderly. More than one billion pounds of food and grocery products were distributed through its network during the same year. Feeding America distributes 20 pounds of food and grocery products for every dollar that it receives as a donation. Formerly known as America's Second Harvest, the group changed its name in 2008 to make it more effective in television sound bites.

EARLY HISTORY

The creation of Feeding America, originally known as Second Harvest, arose out of an idea put into practice by John Van Hengel. A successful businessman who lived and worked most of his life in Phoenix, Arizona, Van Hengel wanted to give something back to the community after he decided to retire. Not quite sure what to devote his energy to, he volunteered at a local soup kitchen operating in one of the poorer areas of Phoenix.

Van Hengel soon noticed that the soup kitchen was not only overcrowded, but that there was a need for much larger quantities of food and produce. Having been well connected in the Phoenix business community for years, Van Hengel began to solicit food donations from many of the businesspeople he had come to know. Initially, much of the food that he solicited would have otherwise gone to waste, but within a short time the soup kitchen was overwhelmed with food and grocery product donations.

Van Hengel established a warehouse facility where he began to stock the donations and then distribute them to charitable agencies and organizations throughout the Phoenix area that were feeding needy people. Thus the first food bank was developed by Van Hengel during the late 1960s, a concept that was subsequently refined and replicated across the United States.

During the early 1970s, people from around the nation heard about Van Hengel's charitable work in Phoenix, and began to take notice of the food bank concept. Within a few years, food banks modeled on Van Hengel's warehouse facility were started in larger cities throughout the country, including New York, Los Angeles, Denver, Chicago, Atlanta, Minneapolis, Boston, Philadelphia, and San Francisco. All of these provided similar services to the community, relying primarily on the corporate sector and retail groceries in the local area to donate food products so that disadvantaged people could eat more nutritious and well-balanced meals.

1976 TAX REFORM ACT PROVIDES IMPETUS

In 1976 the food bank concept was given the added impetus to make it a national program. The 1976 Tax Reform Act significantly altered the tax structure for most for-profit corporations by making it financially advantageous for large and small companies alike to donate their products to charities. The Tax Reform Act especially affected the pharmaceutical industry, since companies that manufactured drugs were then able to donate large quantities of recently expired items (their

effectiveness still intact) in accordance with rules established by the Food and Drug Administration.

Food processors and food product companies were also able to contribute large amounts of food for charitable causes and take a tax deduction. The result of the 1976 Tax Reform Act was far-reaching, therefore, since food banks such as the one Van Hengel had started were then able to procure donated food products much more easily.

Van Hengel also received a large grant from the federal government to establish a comprehensive network of food banks throughout the country. For nearly 10 years, Van Hengel had worked assiduously to develop an efficient and effective food bank facility in Phoenix. By the late 1970s, his work had not only been replicated by other groups across the nation, but state and federal government representatives had noticed Van Hengel's ability to provide a genuine service that assisted people who were themselves unable to purchase enough food to eat.

As Van Hengel laid the foundation for a national network of food banks, and began to devise a strategic plan for expanding his activities, many of the people who were working closely with him suggested that he form his own nonprofit charitable organization to develop the food bank concept. The federal government agreed, providing additional funding to build the capacities of a new organization devoted to eradicating hunger in the United States.

Second Harvest was formally incorporated in 1979 as a charitable organization, and rapidly developed into a clearinghouse for food and grocery product contributions from national and multinational corporations based in the United States. Van Hengel developed and quickly implemented a comprehensive list of standards that he thought all food banks should follow, including detailed recommendations for quality control, the establishment of storage facilities, and the responsibilities of management. This list of recommendations was enthusiastically received by almost everyone associated with the food bank concept, and served as the national guideline for those groups who wanted to establish a food bank.

FIGHTING HUNGER IN THE REAGAN ERA

By the end of 1982, the large source of funding that had been previously provided by the federal government was discontinued. Representatives of the government had fulfilled their pledge to help the food bank concept expand across the United States, and that goal had been attained by the time federal funding for the program

KEY DATES

1960s: Phoenix businessman John Van Hengel launches first food bank.
1976: Tax Reform Act rewards corporations for charitable contributions.
1979: Second Harvest is incorporated in Phoenix.
1984: Headquarters is relocated to Chicago.
1998: Second Harvest distributes more than one billion pounds of grocery products to more than 26 million people.
1999: Name is changed to America's Second Harvest (A2H).
2000: A2H merges with Foodchain, based in Kansas City, Missouri.
2005: Hurricane Katrina prompts more decentralized response to disasters.
2008: A2H is renamed Feeding America.

was curtailed. As a result, Second Harvest, like other food bank programs, was forced to search for funding from alternative sources. Management at the nonprofit organization decided to pursue the corporate sector as a possibility for funding Second Harvest programs, and began to look for a firm within the food products industry.

The people at Second Harvest were able to persuade Pillsbury Corporation to help them implement the vision of food for the poor in the United States. Pillsbury was one of the nation's leading producers of grocery items, including Green Giant frozen foods, Pillsbury brand-name refrigerated dough products, Hungry Jack canned and frozen meat products, Progresso soup, and many other types of products for the international consumer market, as well as a major supplier of baking goods to the foodservice and commercial baking industries.

During the early 1980s, Second Harvest and Pillsbury Corporation formed a unique partnership to support the Production Alliance, a revolutionary program in which Pillsbury agreed to be the first firm among the top food products companies to produce high-quality food items exclusively for donation to Second Harvest and its network of food banks that fed hungry people. Up until that time, food banks throughout the country, including Second Harvest, had been forced to rely upon surplus, slightly damaged, or discontinued food products as the primary source of contributions for their food supply to the hungry.

In a groundbreaking agreement, Pillsbury agreed to use a philanthropic budget and its available production capacity to make high-quality, top-of-the-line food products for donation to Second Harvest and the organizations and agencies working within its food bank network. In just a short time, Pillsbury's participation as the initial corporate partner in support of the Production Alliance spurred numerous other major firms in the food industry to follow suit.

SHIFT IN FOCUS

By the time Second Harvest relocated its headquarters from Phoenix, Arizona, to Chicago, Illinois, in 1984, there were food banks in almost every major city across the United States, many of which were providing very good services to the hungry due to the Production Alliance program and the growing number of corporate partnerships that resulted in larger and larger high-quality food donations. Because food banks were sprouting up throughout the country, the network expansion that Second Harvest had achieved on its own began to slow down, and management decided to shift its focus to improving the organization's programs that were then operating.

Along with this shift in focus, management also implemented a comprehensive internal evaluation process that led to an increased efficiency in the activities of the Second Harvest food bank network, and that ultimately resulted in greater amounts of food distributed through the network to people in need. As the decade of the 1980s drew to a close, Second Harvest had transformed itself from a largely untrained volunteer organization to a sophisticated, highly professional agency whose reputation continued to grow as it was able to collect and distribute ever-increasing amounts of donated food products to feed the hungry.

THE SECOND GENERATION

When Second Harvest was established in 1979, the people working as volunteers sorting the canned goods at food banks or serving meals at the local soup kitchens felt that their services would not be needed when the U.S. economy improved. However, this did not prove to be the case. Even though the economy expanded during the 1980s and 1990s, unemployment rates continued to increase, with over 13 percent of the U.S. population living at or below the poverty line. According to statistics collected by the Census Bureau, poverty was on the increase due to the reduction of government-sponsored support programs and safety nets, and the new economy that did not welcome unskilled workers.

The people who founded Second Harvest and those from a second generation who worked there took it upon themselves to address the growing problem of hunger in the United States. One of their most successful partnerships was with corporations in the dairy industry. In the mid-1990s, the company formed a partnership with Dean Foods, with the corporation becoming one of the first private-label donors to the Second Harvest food bank network.

Another high-profile firm that agreed to a partnership was Land O'Lakes. That company soon began making ongoing donations that included everything from financial support to sour cream to butter. Kraft joined in partnership as well, making a $200,000 donation in order to ship fresh foods to organizations working within the Second Harvest food bank network. Other large corporate donations during the mid-1990s arrived from General Mills, Borden, and Nabisco.

At the end of the 20th century, Second Harvest had developed into the largest charitable hunger-relief organization in the United States. The organization distributed over one billion pounds of grocery products and other kinds of donated foods in 1998 through a network of more than 200 food banks. That year, more than 26 million men, women, and children in the United States, were being provided with food through Second Harvest.

NEW CHALLENGES, TECHNIQUES IN THE 21ST CENTURY

The organization's name was changed to America's Second Harvest (A2H) in 1999 and five years later further extended to America's Second Harvest–The Nation's Food Bank Network. A2H ended the 1990s with about 70 employees. A2H merged with Foodchain, based in Kansas City, Missouri, in 2000. Foodchain was much smaller but boasted superior capabilities in distributing hot prepared foods.

The number of active donors increased from 35,000 in 1990 to 175,000 in 2000, when A2H received $6 million in contributions from individuals, as noted in *Chronicle of Philanthropy*. Direct-mail campaigns prompted two-thirds of the total. The organization raised a total of $471.8 million in the fiscal year 1999/2000, most of it from donations of food.

Glen Crawford, a vice president at Pillsbury Co., succeeded David Nasby as chairman for A2H in June 2000. Nasby was vice president at the General Mills Foundation. Robert H. Forney, former head of the Chicago Stock Exchange, was named president and CEO of A2H in June 2001.

America's Second Harvest saw corporate donations shrink as food companies applied just-in-time manufacturing techniques and other methods to minimize surplus. The organization learned to use similar tools to maximize the efficiency of its own operations, such as an online database in which to match local food banks with donations. At the same time, there was increasing competition from dollar stores and other off-price retailers for the salvage merchandise that remained available.

Demand increased threefold after the September 11, 2001, terrorist attacks on the United States. A lackluster economy cut back philanthropic donations from corporations and individuals, while rising energy costs competed with food budgets, particularly in the winter. A2H launched National Hunger Awareness Day in 2002.

There was an increasing range of corporate donations as the organization increased its visibility through cause marketing tie-ins with companies and consumer products. In June 2001 Newman's Own and Ford Motor Company teamed up to donate 14 trucks to help distribute aid to rural areas. Two years later, CarMax, Inc., celebrated its one-millionth vehicle sold by covering distribution costs for a million meals. Transportation remained a leading expense. In 2004 pallet supplier CHEP added A2H to its pool, greatly simplifying shipping procedures for A2H's corporate donors.

Forney told *Supermarket News* that fresh produce was easy to come by, since so much of it went unharvested. In 2004 the organization received 300 million pounds of produce. The organization estimated that 29 billion pounds of potentially usable food was wasted each year in the United States. A2H also launched new salvage initiatives with the grocery and seafood industries.

NEW TECHNIQUES AFTER KATRINA

The scale of devastation along the U.S. Gulf Coast after Hurricane Katrina in 2005 forced the organization to improvise new strategies for delivering massive amounts of food quickly to thousands of displaced people. (It had been responding to disasters since Hurricane Hugo in 1989.) With local food banks flooded and volunteers missing, A2H scrambled to forge alternative pathways, leading to decentralization of its relief distribution and communications networks in preparation for future disasters.

A2H had immediate help from Wal-Mart Stores, Inc., which opened its vacant buildings for use as emergency warehouses, and corporations with plants in the area, such as Kraft Foods and Tyson Foods. In the first few weeks after Katrina, A2H brought 650,000 pounds of supplies to the region and raised $20 million. Nearly two-thirds of its disbursements in September 2005 went to Katrina relief.

Vicki Escarra, a marketing and customer services executive with 30 years at Delta Airlines, Inc., was hired as CEO in 2006. America's Second Harvest was renamed Feeding America two years later as part of an extensive rebranding exercise. The organization remained as relevant as ever due to rapid increases in the price of food and a declining economy. It was feeding 35 million people a year, most of them working or unable to work. The national organization had 170 employees in Washington, D.C., and Chicago; it received about $600 million in public support and revenues annually.

Thomas Derdak
Updated, Frederick C. Ingram

PRINCIPAL COMPETITORS

Food Not Bombs; The Salvation Army USA; The Society of St. Andrews; United Way of America.

FURTHER READING

Balu, Rekha. "Food Industry's Efficiency Poses Dilemma for Charity." *Wall Street Journal*, December 18, 1998, p. B4.

"The Dairy Industry Delivers." *Dairy Foods*, February 1998, p. 22.

Gattuso, Greg. "Attack on Hunger: America's Second Harvest Pulls Out All the Stops in Reversing Rising Rates of Hunger." *Supermarket News*, January 17, 2002, p. 22.

Harper, Roseanne. "Gooding's Chefs' Demo Is Recipe for Aid to Poor." *Supermarket News*, February 28, 1998, p. 13.

Lewis, Nicole. "America's Second Harvest: Attacking Hunger Through the Mail." *Chronicle of Philanthropy*, November 2, 2000.

McCormick, John. "Moving Food Far and Fast to Fight Hunger." *Chicago Tribune*, December 24, 2006.

McDonald, Barbara. "Kraft, Chains Aid Second Harvest for Hungry." *Supermarket News*, December 21, 1998, p. 31.

Parsons, Heidi. "Processors Answer the Clarion Call." *Food Processing*, October 2005, pp. 11–12.

"Second Harvest Recognizes Burger King as Special Donor." *Nation's Restaurant News*, October 12, 1998, p. 90.

Seligman, Dan. "Is Philanthropy Irrational?" *Forbes*, June 1, 1998, p. 94.

Sheehan, Charles. "Katrina Brought Change to Hunger-Relief Groups' Response Tactics." *Chicago Tribune*, October 7, 2005.

Stark, Ellen. "Which Charities Merit Your Money." *Money*, November 1996, p. 100.

York, Emily Bryson. "How Feeding America Became the Go-To Cause for Marketers." *Advertising Age*, May 3, 2010.

"Your Money Goes Far at These A+ Charities." *Money*, December 15, 1997, p. 27.

Fiat S.p.A.

250 Via Nizza
Turin, 10126
Italy
Telephone: (+39 011) 006-1111
Fax: (+39 011) 006-3798
Web site: http://www.fiatgroup.com

Public Company
Incorporated: 1906 as Società Anonima Fabbrica Italiana di Automobili
Employees: 190,014
Sales: EUR 50.1 billion ($71.81 billion) (2009)
Stock Exchanges: Italian
Ticker Symbol: F
NAICS: 336111 Automobile Manufacturing; 336211 Motor Vehicle Body Manufacturing; 333111 Farm Machinery and Equipment Manufacturing; 551112 Offices of Other Holding Companies

■ ■ ■

Fiat S.p.A., Europe's largest industrial group, is perhaps best known as a manufacturer of automobiles. The company has over 180 plants across the globe and its customers can be found in over 190 countries. Fiat's automobile brands include its namesake as well as Alfa Romeo, Lancia, Abarth, Fiat Professional, Maserati, and Ferrari. The company also produces agricultural and construction equipment, trucks and commercial vehicles, and components and production systems. The company, which was near bankruptcy in 2004, regained its financial footing under the leadership of CEO Sergio Marchionne. Fiat launched a strategic partnership with U.S. automaker Chrysler Group LLC in 2009. In order to focus on its automotive business, Fiat planned to spin off its industrial arm in January 2011. The founding Agnelli family owns nearly 30 percent of Fiat through its Exor S.p.A. holding company.

FIAT'S TURIN BECOMES "ITALY'S LITTLE DETROIT"

Fiat was founded in 1899 by Giovanni Agnelli, an ex-cavalry officer, and a few other Turin businesspeople. The city of Turin, often known as "Italy's Little Detroit," was developed with Fiat money. In the 1990s, half of its population, either directly or indirectly, remained dependent on Fiat for its livelihood.

The company (Fabbrica Italiana Automobili Torino) began manufacturing automobiles and engine parts for the automotive industry early in the 20th century. With the advent of World War I, however, Fiat significantly expanded its production line, and as the years passed, the company became a conglomeration of various manufacturing enterprises. By the early postwar years, Fiat was manufacturing so many products that Giovanni Agnelli felt it was time to improve central administration.

To help him in his reorganization efforts, Giovanni Agnelli hired Vittorio Valletta, a university professor and former consulting engineer, in 1921. Their aim was to control all of the manufacturing processes as completely as possible, thus reducing their dependence on foreign

COMPANY PERSPECTIVES

Innovation has an important place among the Fiat Group's core values and beliefs. Because the only way to meet the challenges of the future is to be innovative: innovative everywhere and in every way. And being innovative is more than bringing out new products and manufacturing processes. It's finding new ways to work, a more efficient organizational model, and a different market stance. To renew the product range, but above all to create a fresh vision of mobility on a human scale—not just sustainable, but livable, too—Fiat's aim is to strike a balance between experience, creativity and technology, in the conviction that a truly innovative business model, capable of generating stakeholder value and improving the Group's competitiveness over the long haul, can spring only from the synergies between all Group sectors.

suppliers. Soon the company became more diverse by pouring its own steel and producing its own plastics and paints. In a further reorganization, Agnelli formed a holding company, the IFI (Industrial Fiduciary Institute), in 1927. IFI was merged with another holding company to form Exor S.p.A. in late 2008. Exor was set up to control the Agnelli family's assets.

FIAT'S EARLY AUTOMOBILES

In its first two decades, Fiat produced only two types of automobile: the basic, limited options model and the deluxe model. The company had little incentive to offer other models since it was protected by the Italian government's high-tariff policy (known as "kept capitalism"). As a result, imported cars were far beyond the reach of the average Italian. Indeed, more than 80 percent of all the cars sold in Italy were Fiats, and much of the remaining 20 percent of the country's car sales consisted of expensive Italian-made Lancias and Alfa Romeos.

Finally sensitive to Italian complaints that Fiat's "cheap" car was too expensive, the company developed the Topolino, or Little Mouse, a four-cylinder, 16-horsepower two-seater that averaged 47 miles per gallon. It was an immediate success and accounted for 60 percent of the Fiats sold in Italy up until the mid-1950s.

FIAT'S PLANTS TARGETED BY ALLIED FORCES

Fiat flourished in World War II as it had in World War I, and profits increased significantly under Benito Mussolini's much heralded modernization program. However, the company's production of planes, cars, trucks, and armored vehicles for the European and African campaigns of the Axis forces made its plants prime targets for Allied bombing raids.

Fiat faced the postwar era with war-torn plants and antiquated production facilities, and at the height of its disarray, in 1945, Giovanni Agnelli died. Valletta was named president and managing director and immediately set about reviving the company's fortunes, aided by Agnelli's grandson, Giovanni Agnelli II, who became a senior vice president.

Once the Allied effort to rebuild postwar Europe was under way, Valletta applied to the U.S. government for a loan to renovate and modernize company facilities. He reasoned that Fiat was crucial to Italy's recovery and should therefore be entitled to special help. Well aware of the political benefits of a strong Italy, the Americans granted Fiat a $10 million, six-month revolving loan. Other loans soon followed, and the company was back in business, gearing up for full production ahead of most of its West European competitors. By 1948, Fiat's holdings represented 6 percent of Italy's industrial capital.

Fewer people were able to buy cars than before the war, and Fiat, like other car manufacturers, felt the effects of a smaller market. In response, to reduce its production costs substantially, Fiat built a plant for its 600 and 1300 models in Yugoslavia that was able to produce about 40,000 automobiles yearly. Other foreign expansion followed rapidly.

Additionally, the company managed to secure a lucrative manufacturing contract from NATO. Fiat's foreign forays were a mixed blessing; its Italian workers began to fear for their jobs and worker agitation became a severe problem. On a few occasions Valletta was held prisoner in Communist-led worker uprisings in Turin. The political situation did not cease until the mid-1950s when the U.S. government tied an anticommunist clause to its $50 million offshore procurement contracts with Fiat. This resulted in the firing, relocation, and political reeducation of many Fiat employees, as well as improvements in the company's already elaborate (by U.S. standards) social welfare program. The Italian workers formed three unions, the largest of which cooperated closely with company management.

Valletta spent $800 million in expansion and modernization in the 15 years following World War II

KEY DATES

1899: Fabbrica Italiana Automobili Torino (FIAT) is founded in Turin, Italy, by Giovanni Agnelli and a few other Turin businesspeople.

1906: Fiat is incorporated as Società Anonima Fabbrica Italiana di Automobili.

1917: The company's steel manufacturing and railroad industry begins.

1922: Europe's first automobile manufacturing plant designed for mass production is established; Fiat produces the world's first electric diesel locomotive.

1927: The holding company IFI (Industrial Fiduciary Institute) is formed.

1969: Fiat acquires Ferrari and Lancia.

1986: Alfa Romeo is purchased.

1993: Fiat acquires Maserati and introduces the Punto.

2009: Company forms a strategic partnership with Chrysler Group LLC.

2010: Fiat announces plans to separate its automotive and industrial businesses.

and built the most impressive steelworks in Italy. By 1959 Fiat sales reached $644 million, representing one-third of its country's mechanical production and one-tenth of its total industrial output. The price of Fiat's stock quintupled between 1958 and 1960. Even so, Fiat did not reduce the relative price of its cars.

FIAT JOINS EEC

Still running the company in 1960 at the age of 76, Valletta was a keen supporter of Italy's membership in the European Economic Community (EEC). He was sure that Italian companies were strong enough to survive direct competition from the other five members. Fiat itself had the advantage of a highly trained staff, the swiftest production lines in Europe, and listed assets of $1.25 billion. However, Italy's organization of manufacturers, Confindustria, opposed EEC membership, believing that France and Germany would quickly dominate the market. Nevertheless, by the end of the first year of membership, Italian companies made 283 deals with companies in other EEC countries. The only deal involving the giant Fiat was a sales arrangement with the French automaker Simca.

Valletta's confidence in his company's competitiveness within the EEC was seriously questioned when, in 1961, intra-community tariffs were lowered and import quotas were dropped. At the same time, U.S. automakers such as General Motors, Ford, and Chrysler were significantly expanding their European operations. It quickly became apparent that Fiat had underestimated the potential sales of foreign-made cars in Italy. Unwilling to wait months for delivery of a Fiat, or simply tired of its models, Italians were more than ready to consider the increasing array of foreign vehicles. Moreover, Fiat misjudged its domestic market and failed to introduce a model that might appeal to the many Italians moving from the lower- to the middle-income bracket. In three years, from 1960 to 1963, Fiat's domestic sales dropped 20 percent, from 83 to 63 percent.

The company filled the gap in its product line with its 850 sedan, and by 1965, Italian car imports had dropped to 11 percent. However, part of the revival in Fiat's domestic sales was affected by less positive means. The company launched a vigorous campaign against car imports enlisting the aid of its newspaper, *La Stampa*. This campaign was aided and abetted by the Italian government, which angered car-exporting countries by imposing a supposedly nondiscriminatory anti-inflation tax on automobiles.

Meanwhile, Fiat's exports improved and sales to underdeveloped nations flourished. In addition to its assembly plants in Germany and Austria, the company built plants in numerous other countries, including India, Morocco, Egypt, South Africa, Spain, and Argentina. Fiat also signed an agreement with the Soviet Union in 1965 for a facility capable of producing 600,000 units a year by 1970.

GIOVANNI AGNELLI SUCCEEDS VALLETTA

After running Fiat for 21 years, Vittorio Valletta was succeeded in 1966 by Giovanni Agnelli II, the founder's grandson. Under Agnelli's leadership, the company's annual sales came close to $2 billion by 1968, and for a short time Fiat edged out Volkswagen as the world's fourth-largest automaker. At that time, Fiat's cooperative arrangement with the French carmaker Citroën made it the world's sixth-largest non-U.S. firm. The company operated 30 plants and employed 150,000 workers. Giovanni Agnelli II candidly credited Fiat's success to the company's near monopoly of its domestic market for half a century, but he warned that more sophisticated production methods were required if Fiat was to survive in the international market. He imposed a schedule for new models of two years from drawing board to assembly line and standardized many car parts to allow more interchange between models.

Giovanni Agnelli II also sought to further diversify Fiat's products to lessen its dependence on autos and trucks, which accounted for 86 percent of its revenue. At the same time, he set about improving the company's flagging sales performance in underdeveloped countries, and in 1969 he made two notable acquisitions. Fiat took full control of the Italian car manufacturer Lancia and announced a merger with Ferrari, the famous Italian racing car company. When Ferrari's problems had surfaced in 1962, owner Enzo Ferrari had turned down the Ford Motor Company, but accepted financial backing from Fiat. Further losses forced Ferrari to sell, and his company was reconstructed as Fiat's Racing Car division.

While the Ferrari and Lancia acquisitions were good for Fiat's image both at home and abroad, its domestic situation worsened. The company had to contend with Italy's 7.3 percent inflation rate and a series of strikes. Production in 1972 production fell short by 200,000 vehicles. For the first time in its history, Fiat failed to show a profit or pay an interim dividend. Fortunately, news from abroad was good. Agnelli's younger brother, Umberto Agnelli, who had doubled sales at Fiat France in 1965 to 1970 and constructed successful plants in Argentina and Poland, had gone on to direct U.S. sales. The number of Fiats sold there doubled between 1970 and 1972 and Fiat cars became the fourth-largest-selling import in the United States. Umberto returned to Italy as second-in-command to help his brother with the pressing problems at home.

FIAT THRIVES IN FOREIGN MARKETS

Fiat's domestic fortunes deteriorated to the point where the company seemed a likely candidate for partial state ownership. In 1973, Fiat slipped $30 million into the red, and after a three-month strike in 1974, Italy's Socialist Labor minister granted the union a monthly pay increase significantly higher than Fiat's final offer. Amidst Fiat's loud protests, the government also imposed ceilings on the prices the company could charge for its automobiles. To make matters worse, sales were down 45 percent because of worldwide apprehension over the energy crisis. Finally, it seemed, the days of government protection for Fiat were over. The politicians now had to listen to their constituents, many of whom, at that time, viewed the industrial bosses as enemies of the people. Fiat's case was not helped by the Agnelli brothers' refusal to reveal the value of IFI, the family-owned holding company whose funds, which were in Swiss banks, were beyond Italian government scrutiny.

Fiat's foreign holdings continued to offset its severe troubles on the home front and the company thrived in the less saturated markets of Eastern Europe, Turkey, and South America. Its largest overseas investment was an $86 million plant in Brazil, which became operational in 1976. Other foreign ventures included a project with the American Allis Chalmers company, an important manufacturer of earth-moving equipment with units in the United States, Italy, and Brazil, and under an arrangement with Moammar Khadafi in 1976, Libya acquired a 10 percent interest in Fiat. This purchase cost Colonel Khadafi $415 million, and Fiat shares immediately rocketed on the Milan exchange. Since Libya paid almost three times the market price, serious questions were raised about Khadafi's long-term motives. However, Fiat had no such qualms. Khadafi's purchase eased its cash flow at a time when the company earned less than $200,000 on sales of about $4 million and had dipped into reserves in order to pay shareholders.

OVERCOMING DOMESTIC PROBLEMS: 1974–89

Meanwhile, the company's domestic woes continued. In 1974, with a heavy backlog of unsold cars to keep it going, Fiat fired all of its Italian workers with violent records. A year later, the company laid off a massive 15 percent of its Italian workforce and was able to weather the ensuing strike.

Fiat's management was convinced that it could beat its powerful competitors by producing cars at the lowest-possible price. Through its subsidiary Comau, a leader in the automation field, Fiat retooled and partially robotized its factories and standardized more Fiat car parts. The assembly robots provided the company with much greater flexibility on production lines, since the machines could easily be programmed to perform a variety of tasks on a variety of models. Further worker layoffs were justified by Fiat by the rise in production rates. The annual output per worker in 1979 was 14.8 units. In 1983 the output was up to 25 units per worker.

Fiat's bold and successful moves to modernize were matched by major changes abroad. The company entirely removed itself from the U.S. market, choosing not to compete against General Motors, Ford, Chrysler, and Japanese imports. In South America, the company closed operations in Uruguay, Chile, Colombia, and Argentina, retaining only its facility in Brazil. Fiat's international operations were also brought under the aegis of a new holding company, the Fiat Group.

Although it had retreated from several large international markets, conceding in part its role as an export-oriented company, Fiat had led the way in Europe toward factory automation during the early 1980s, a move that several of Europe's other volume carmakers, which included Volkswagen, General Motors, Renault, and Peugeot, copied. In 1986 Fiat purchased Alfa Romeo, paying state-owned Finmeccanica $1.75 billion to acquire the luxury car manufacturer.

The following year, the first Alfa Romeo car, the 164, to appear under Fiat ownership made its debut, selling strongly in Italy but recording disappointing sales elsewhere. The dismal sales performance of the 164 was the first of many difficulties Fiat would experience with Alfa Romeo, as sales and production volume dipped throughout the remainder of the 1980s and into the early 1990s. By 1993, the number of cars manufactured under the Alfa Romeo name had slipped to slightly over 100,000, roughly the same number produced in 1970 and considerably less than the number of cars manufactured before Fiat's takeover.

FIAT ACQUIRES MASERATI

In 1989 Fiat acquired part of another luxury car manufacturer, paying $120 million for a 49 percent interest in Maserati SpA, then four years later purchased the remaining 51 percent from De Tomaso Industries for $51.2 million. The addition of Alfa Romeo and Maserati to Fiat's automobile operations broadened the company's collection of automobile lines, bringing two luxury brand names to the company's established Ferrari, Innocenti, and Lancia-Autobianchi models. Despite the less-than-robust sales performance of Fiat's Alfa Romeo unit, annual sales grew prodigiously throughout the latter half of the 1980s, more than doubling between 1985, a year in which merger discussions with Ford Motor Company collapsed, and 1990.

Fiat's ability to generate additional income from the increase in its revenues also met with considerable success, providing resounding evidence that the company had recovered from the financial malaise that characterized its operations during the early 1980s. In 1981 Fiat's income as a percentage of sales was 0.4 percent. By 1986 the company was realizing 7.2 percent of its annual sales as profit and its pioneering move into factory automation appeared to be paying dividends.

In 1990, however, Fiat's growth came to a stop. A global recession that crippled the economies of many countries hit the European car market particularly hard, exacerbating the traditional problems of high labor costs and industry overcapacity that plagued European carmakers. Fiat's profits plummeted 51 percent in 1990, and its income as a percentage of sales slipped to 2.8 percent. The recession continued to hamper sales

throughout the early 1990s as Fiat struggled to withstand the debilitative effects of the dwindling demand for automobiles. By the mid-1990s, the European car market was showing some signs of recovery but continued to be stifled by depressed economic conditions, inhibiting Fiat's ability to reap the rewards that, under more favorable conditions, would be derived from its enviable share of the European car market.

In an effort to expand its global productivity, Fiat developed new automobile models designed for a broader and more competitive market. The result of this strategy was the introduction in 1993 of the Punto, an intermediate car designed specifically to meet the needs of European drivers. In 2000, Fiat entered into an alliance with General Motors, which created joint ventures in purchasing and power-train production. Following this agreement, Fiat Auto Holdings BV was created and became Fiat's main automotive sector, including automobile and light commercial vehicles, with the exception of Ferrari and Maserati.

In further attempts toward diversification, Fiat continued to make their other products more marketable. Agricultural and construction products made way for aviation equipment, commercial vehicles and production systems. Innovations in the mass transit area produced light transport vans and quarry and construction vehicles, as well as long-distance highway trucks. Although active in the railroad industry from its early beginnings, in 2000, Fiat sold its railroad activities to Alstom.

FIAT'S OPERATING SECTORS AT THE START OF THE 21ST CENTURY

The year 2000 witnessed the development of 10 operating sectors: Automobiles, Agricultural and Construction, Machinery, Commercial Vehicles, Metallurgical Products, Components, Production Systems, Aviation Publishing and Communications, Insurance, and Services. The Agricultural sector, under the auspices of CNH Global in 1999, acquired New Holland NV and American Case Corporation, and excelled in the production of tractors, harvesting and baling equipment, and loaders. Growth in this sector remained positive in 2001 due to a favorable dollar conversion rate and strong demand for farm equipment in North America.

Iveco (Industrial Vehicles Corporation), the Commercial Vehicles sector of Fiat, came about in 1974 as the result of an agreement between Fiat and Germany's Klockner-Humboldt-Deutz. This sector was active in the transport industry, producing light to heavy commercial vehicles. Assisting in the developing momentum in this sector, the EuroCargo Tector (intermediate vehicle) was introduced in September 2000. In the following year Iveco acquired a 50 percent share in Irisbus from Renault and began establishing markets in South America, Eastern Europe, and Asia.

Teksid headed up the Metallurgical Products sector with headquarters in Avigliana, near Turin. This sector specialized in the production of metal components for the automotive industry, including cast iron, aluminum and magnesium, and established Fiat as the world leader in the production of engine blocks (cast iron), cylinder heads (aluminum), and instrument panels (magnesium). New plants during 2001 were in various stages of development in Sylacauga, Alabama, in the United States; Hua Dong, China; Mexico; and Strathroy, Canada. Magneti Marelli, created in 1919, designed, developed, and produced high-tech automotive components, systems and modules. In 2000 this sector established itself as the world leader in the field of car lights, second in Europe for instrument panels, and third for petrol injections systems.

The Production Systems sector, or Comau, began machine tool production in 1935, and continued to expand its product range. In 1999, Fiat acquired Pico (U.S. bodyworks systems) and Renault Automation and Sciaky, strengthening its position as a major supplier. New branches were established in Australia, China, Romania, and Germany.

FiatAvio, the Aviation sector, began in 1908 and continued in 2001 to develop, produce, and distribute components and systems for airplanes and helicopter engines, as well as assemble turbines for marine propulsion. It produced propulsion systems for launchers and satellites in space operations, and was the world leader in power transmission technology for aircraft engines. It participated in programs with General Electric, Pratt & Whitney, and Rolls-Royce. This unit was sold in 2003 as part of ongoing restructuring.

The Fiat Group created Editrice La Stampa in 1926 to publish Turin's daily newspaper, *La Stampa Itedi*. Italiana Edizioni SpA was created in 1980 to further develop Fiat's Publishing and Communications sectors through a single entity. In 1999 an Internet portal was created in partnership with CiaoWeb.

In 1998 the Fiat Group created Toro Targa Assicurazioni as part of a joint venture with Targa Services to distribute insurance products through the Fiat car dealer network. Toro Assicurazioni, created in 1833, remained one of the largest insurance groups in Italy. This unit however, was sold in 2003.

The Business Solutions sector was created in 2000 and grouped together service companies operating in the field of shared services for businesses, especially information technology. Global Value was launched in 2001, the result of a joint venture with IBM to manage technological infrastructure and software applications.

OVERCOMING CHALLENGES: 2003–06

While Fiat had restructured its business in 2000, weak financial results forced the company to rethink its strategy. In fact, with losses mounting in its automotive unit Fiat found itself in a precarious financial position. Losses in 2003 were nearly EUR 2 billion and approximately EUR 1.6 billion in 2004. At the same time, the company experienced upheaval at the management level. Giovanni Agnelli died in early 2003, leaving brother Umberto at the helm for a short time until his death in 2004. Sergio Marchionne was named CEO in June 2004 and was tapped to reverse the company's fortunes.

Marchionne quickly revamped the company's management structure, cut debt, and used a special option structured into its General Motors alliance, which was formed in 2000, to raise cash. The provision allowed Fiat to sell its automotive business to General Motors. The U.S. automaker, which would soon face its own bankruptcy, declined the sale and was forced to pay nearly $2 billion to exit the joint venture.

By trimming the company's management team, making Fiat's manufacturing facilities more efficient, and refocusing on new product development, Marchionne was able to return the company to profitability in 2005. That year, Fiat posted a net income of EUR 1.4 billion. The company's Fiat Auto arm also secured profits after 17 consecutive quarters of losses. The company's strategy, which also included the formation of global industrial alliances and a company-wide reorganization of business operations, was crucial in its success. Fiat's improvement continued in 2006 and the company was able to distribute a dividend to shareholders for the first time in five years.

FOCUSING ON AUTOMOTIVE GROWTH: 2007 AND BEYOND

The company continued to strengthen its foothold in growth markets including Russia, India, and China. With sales and profits continuing to rise in 2007, Fiat's industrial businesses were debt free and in sound financial position. The company relaunched its Abarth automobile that year. Success continued in the first part of 2008 but with the U.S. economy in a free fall and market conditions deteriorating rapidly, Fiat found itself operating in very harsh conditions. Demand was falling and prices of raw materials were rising. The U.S. auto industry was in a steep decline and both General Motors and Chrysler found themselves in bankruptcy and accepting government loans to stay afloat.

Chrysler, which received $12.5 billion from the U.S. government, filed for bankruptcy protection in early 2009. Fiat secured a 20 percent stake in Chrysler Group LLC upon its emergence. The deal made evident Fiat's determination to build its automotive business as well as its plans to relaunch its brands in the U.S. market. Chrysler stood to benefit from Fiat's small car and energy efficient manufacturing know-how while Fiat would gain access to Chrysler's large distribution network.

Marchionne set ambitious goals for both Fiat and Chrysler, claiming that by 2014 production would reach six million vehicles per year. As Marchionne told shareholders in his 2009 annual letter, "The commitment we have taken on with Chrysler will serve not only in restructuring the U.S. automaker, but it also provides the best guarantee of a solid future for Fiat."

With Chrysler under its belt, Fiat began developing plans to secure its future as a leading automotive firm. During 2010, the company announced that by early the next year it would spin off its non-automotive businesses including Iveco, Case New Holland, and part of its powertrain technologies division as Fiat Industrial S.p.A. With demerger plans in place, it appeared as though Fiat's future was slated to be focused on rebuilding the Chrysler brand while penetrating the United States and other global markets.

Updated, Jeffrey L. Covell;
Carol D. Beavers; Christina M. Stansell

PRINCIPAL SUBSIDIARIES

Fiat Group Automobiles S.p.A; Ferrari S.p.A (85%); Maserati S.p.A.; Fiat Netherlands Holding N.V.; Iveco S.p.A.; Fiat Powertrain Technologies S.p.A.; Magneti Marelli S.p.A.; Teksid S.p.A. (84.79%); Teksid Aluminum S.r.l.; Comau S.p.A.; Fiat Partecipazioni S.p.A.; Fiat Finance S.p.A.; Business Solutions S.p.A.; Italiana Edizioni S.p.A.; Fiat Group International S.A. (Switzerland); Fiat Finance North America Inc.; Fiat U.S.A. Inc.; Isvor Fiat Società consortile di sviluppo e addestramento Industriale per Azioni; Elasis-Società Consortile per Azioni; Fiat-Revisione Interna S.c.r.l.; Fiat Servizi per l'Industria S.c.p.A.; Orione S.c.p.A.-Società Industriale per la Sicurezza e la Vigilanza Consortile per Azioni; Sicurezza Industriale Società consortile per Azioni; CNH Global N.V.

PRINCIPAL COMPETITORS

PSA Peugeot Citroën S.A.; Renault; Volkswagen AG.

FURTHER READING

Biagi, Enzo. *Signor Fiat: Una biografia*, Milan: Rizzoli, 1976.

Castronovo, Valerio. *Giovanni Agnelli: La Fiat dal 1899 al 1945*, Turin: Einaudii, 1977.

Gorse, Mathieu. "Fiat Takes Major Step towards Global Megagroup." *Agence France Presse*, July 21, 2010.

"Honorary Chairman Says Fiat Betting on Growth of Auto Sector." *Xinhua News Agency*, April 29, 2002, p. 1008119.

Ingrassia, Paul. "Resurrecting Chrysler." *Wall Street Journal*, July 3, 2010.

Kahn, Gabriel, and Stephen Power. "Steering Clear: Auto Outsider Gets Fiat Going by Flouting Industry Traditions." *Wall Street Journal*, October 26, 2006.

Kapner, Fred. "Umberto Agnelli Takes Centre Stage at Fiat." *Financial Times*, January 26, 2003.

Kurylko, Diane T. "Mercedes, Fiat Discuss Joint Venture." *Automotive News*, April 18, 1994, p. 45.

Vlasic, Bill, and Nick Bunkley. "Party's Over: A New Tone for Chrysler." *New York Times*, November 5, 2009.

"Who'll Take Over from the Patriarchs?" *Business Week*, May 13, 2002, p. 60.

Wielgat, Andrea. "Fiat Optimistic about Sales." *Automotive Industries*, April 2002, Vol. 182, p. 4.

Family Owned Since 1939

Foster Poultry Farms Inc.

1000 Davis Street
Livingston, California 95334
U.S.A.
Telephone: (209) 357-1121
Toll Free: (800) 255-7227
Fax: (209) 394-6342
Web site: http://www.fosterfarms.com

Private Company
Incorporated: 1939
Employees: 10,000
Sales: $1.38 million (2009 est.)
NAICS: 311615 Poultry Processing; 112320 Broilers
and Other Meat-Type Chicken Production; 112340
Poultry Hatcheries; 311119 Other Animal Food
Manufacturing; 484121 General Freight Trucking,
Long-Distance, Truckload

■■■

Headquartered in Livingston, California, Foster Poultry Farms Inc. is one of the nation's leading poultry processors. The company's operations span the states of California, Oregon, Washington, and Alabama, and employs more than 10,000 people. In 2010 Foster Poultry Farms continued to be a family-led organization, headed by CEO Ron Foster.

LAUNCHING A FAMILY BUSINESS

Foster Farms was founded in 1939 when Max and Verda Foster borrowed $1,000 against their life insurance policy to buy a repossessed 80-acre farm near Modesto, California. While Max continued to work as a reporter and the city editor at the *Modesto Bee*, Verda concentrated on raising turkeys. By 1942 the couple's venture had succeeded to the point that Max was able to quit his job at the paper and commit himself to the family business full time.

Although Foster Farms concentrated solely on turkeys during its early years, the company had expanded into chickens and dairy cattle by the late 1940s. After buying a second farm, the company acquired a feed mill in 1950. With the addition of this feed mill, Foster Farms would no longer depend on an outside supplier to feed its chickens. At the time, the Fosters were not the only poultry producer striving for vertical integration of the different aspects of their business; the entire poultry industry was in the midst of a massive reorganization. Fueled by monumental changes both in the technology of food production and in how Americans obtained their food, poultry producers increasingly came to see themselves less as family farms and more as automated factories.

A CHANGING INDUSTRY

Like other agricultural sectors, poultry production was revolutionized by the rise of large supermarkets. Consumers had once bought their meat from local butchers (as well as their produce from local growers and their bread from local bakeries). Beginning in the 1950s, large supermarket chains, which sold all of these items and more under one roof, began to alter the country's patterns of food shopping and supply. As these

COMPANY PERSPECTIVES

We work with great people. They're family to us, and we all strive to give our best every day. The hope is that our commitment to excellence, honesty, quality, service, and our people will shine through in everything we do.

chains encompassed ever-larger geographical areas, they turned to major regional suppliers for their poultry, vegetables, and other perishable goods.

The new interstate highway system made it cheaper and easier to move products over land, and the development of refrigeration technology meant that perishable items could be trucked for some distance without spoiling. The result of these changes for poultry producers was that supermarket chains favored larger operations that provided processed chicken at high volume. The poultry industry, once consisting of thousands of small operations, was increasingly integrated and automated.

EXPANSION IN CALIFORNIA

Foster Farms embraced this trend in 1959 when it bought a processing plant in Livingston, California. Live birds were trucked to the facility, slaughtered, processed, and packaged. Staffed by workers who repeatedly performed one part of the whole operation (much like auto workers on an assembly line), the Livingston plant also incorporated new technology that sped up the tasks. A fire destroyed the original Livingston processing plant in the early 1960s, but Foster Farms quickly rebuilt it on a nearby site. In the 1960s the company moved its corporate headquarters from the original family farm to Livingston.

Although Max and Verda Foster remained at the helm of Foster Farms, their eldest son, Paul, was the dominant force in the company's rapid expansion. While Max concentrated on the fledgling dairy operations, Paul oversaw the burgeoning poultry production arm. In 1969 Paul officially took the company's reins and was named president. Under his guidance Foster Farms acquired a distribution and sales center in El Monte, California, in 1973. This new facility allowed the company to act as a major distributor of poultry products in Southern California. Paul died suddenly of a heart attack in 1977, and was succeeded by his brother, Thomas.

Following in his brother's footsteps, Tom Foster led the family business into new territory. In 1982 the company purchased the assets of the Grange Company and its subsidiary, Valchris Poultry. This deal provided two particular benefits to Foster Farms: It enabled the company to reenter the turkey processing business after a long hiatus, and it also let the company enter a new segment of the poultry industry. Grange produced packaged deli products, especially luncheon meats, and after the acquisition it continued to do so, but under the Foster Farms name. By the mid-1980s Foster Farms offered a number of new products, including poultry franks, bologna, and luncheon meats.

INDUSTRY LEADER

The company's pace of growth was brisk, with sales tripling between 1975 and 1988. By 1987 Foster Farms was the largest chicken producer in California, turning out some 140 million chickens per year. The company's success was due in part to its total vertical integration. "Our production pipeline goes from egg to package," said a company spokesperson in the September 29, 1988, edition of the *San Francisco Chronicle*.

The operations of Foster Farms were a model of industrial efficiency. Chickens were conceived on one of 12 breeder farms within 35 miles of the processing plant in Livingston. After the hens laid their eggs (a total of approximately 2.2 million a week), the eggs were trucked to hatcheries, where they were kept in controlled conditions in an incubator for 18 days. When the newborn chicks hatched, they were taken to one of several ranches, where they remained for about 52 days. During that time the chickens had constant access to the company's own corn and soybean meal feed. "They are pampered," a Foster Farms spokesperson explained to the *San Francisco Chronicle* on June 2, 1987. "Good chicken is good business."

After their time at the ranches, the birds were trucked to the Livingston processing plant. Workers hung the chickens by the ankles upside down on a metal conveyor line. The chickens were then shocked with an electric current to stun them before an automated blade cut their throats. Still on the conveyor line, the bodies were scalded with hot water, had their feathers removed by plucking machines, and were eviscerated by other machines.

Next, some 500 workers cut and packaged the birds: Some bagged whole chickens, others removed breasts and boxed them, and still others cleaved off legs and packaged the parts. At the end of the assembly lines, the packages were mechanically sealed with cellophane, and promptly shipped to supermarkets and foodservice vendors via the company's own fleet of refrigerated trucks. The entire process illustrated the observation of *Southern California Business* that "the conversion of poultry raising from a handicraft into a mass production basis" had occurred.

OPERATIONAL EXPANSION

Sales for Foster Farms had risen so rapidly in the mid-1980s that the company announced plans to substantially increase its poultry producing capacity in 1988. That year, Foster Farms constructed a new fryer ranch with one million square feet of poultry housing in Merced County, California, and upgraded its feed mill in Ceres, California. It also built a new 85,000-square-foot distribution facility in Livingston and a sales office for northern California.

In addition, the company erected a plant to process chicken by-products. Foster Farms also acquired a turkey processing plant in Fresno, California, from Roxford Foods in November 1989. Foster Farms immediately converted the facility to a chicken processing plant, by adding new equipment and making structural additions. The Fresno plant was slated to process an additional 80 million chickens each year.

Booming sales at Foster Farms were driven by a number of factors, foremost of which was the growing popularity of chicken in the United States. With the discovery that saturated fat intake was linked to heart disease, Americans began to consume less red meat, which was often fattier than poultry and contained more cholesterol. In place of meats such as steak, roast beef, and pork, Americans increasingly opted for chicken, which typically contained less saturated fat. According to the March 5, 1996, *USA Today*, poultry's

share of the meat market rose from 24 percent in 1976 to 41 percent in 1996, and per capita poultry consumption rose from 40.6 pounds in 1970 to about 72 pounds in 1996. In 1987 per capita poultry consumption surpassed beef for the first time in history.

POULTRY EVOLUTION

Chicken's more prominent role in the U.S. diet was attributed not only to its lower fat content. Innovations made by the poultry industry itself also spurred demand for the fowl. For most of their history, poultry processors had offered whole chickens and little else. A new trend hit the market in the early 1980s, however.

As the September 17, 1987, *Wall Street Journal* explained, the fast-food chain McDonald's had greatly influenced the poultry industry. In 1982 McDonald's introduced a new product, nuggets of boneless, deep-fried chicken that came with a dipping sauce. These McNuggets sold briskly at McDonald's and also inspired a bevy of knockoffs.

A huge previously untapped market was discovered for prepackaged and embellished chicken products. To capitalize, leading poultry producers, including Foster Farms, quickly released a variety of value-added products. These included boneless, skinless chicken breasts; chicken tenders; and marinated chicken strips.

SAFETY FOCUS

Poultry's meteoric rise up the U.S. food chain was slowed in 1987 by a report broadcast on the television news magazine show *60 Minutes* which claimed that a high percentage of chicken was infected with salmonella. This bacteria, a naturally occurring organism that tainted meats and vegetables, could cause illness ranging from flu-like symptoms to death. Because the bacteria could be spread between birds in fecal matter and blood, the close proximity of so many birds (both on the ranches and in the processing plants) made it more prevalent as the poultry industry became more automated. Poultry prices dropped precipitously in the wake of these revelations as consumer demand slackened.

Foster Farms emerged from the salmonella crisis unscathed, however. The company, notorious for its aversion to publicity, took the uncharacteristic step of inviting members of the media into its processing operations to witness its state-of-the-art anti-contamination measures. The positive coverage generated by this effort boosted public confidence in the company's products. Moreover, Foster Farms was able to rely on its strong brand image to assuage consumers' concerns. A company spokesperson told the *San Francisco Chronicle* on September 29, 1988, "The salmonella scare indirectly boosted Foster sales, because consumers became pickier about the chickens they bought."

In the aftermath of the salmonella scare, other poultry producers realized the importance of branding as well. Brand-name birds could reportedly command an extra 10 cents a pound over their generic counterparts in the supermarket. One of the Foster Farms company's major competitors, Perdue Farms Incorporated, had been advertising since 1967, but stepped up its branding efforts in the late 1980s.

Perdue aired a series of commercials featuring the company's eponymous chairman, Frank Perdue, proclaiming, "It takes a tough man to make a tender chicken." Recognizing the need to defend its position, Foster Farms also increased its television marketing presence in 1988. One spot, portraying a woman showing her daughter-in-law how to prepare chicken, received a prestigious Clio Award that year. Foster Farms subsequently launched a sales promotion aimed at Hispanic people in 1990.

EXPANSION INTO OREGON AND WASHINGTON

Along with its ongoing branding efforts, Foster Farms in the late 1980s decided to expand its geographical presence. Already the undisputed market leader in California, the company eyed the rest of the West Coast as possible territory for expansion. Foster Farms had first ventured into the Northwest in 1987, when it acquired Fircrest Farms. Located in Creswell, Oregon, Fircrest was one of the leading poultry producers in Oregon, and had a firmly ensconced regional brand. In 1994 Foster Farms made a more aggressive move into the markets of the Northwest when it purchased Lynden, Washington-based Lynden Farms for an estimated $8.2 million. Foster Farms shipped the chickens from both Fircrest and Lynden to its Livingston and Fresno plants to be processed.

Although the Foster family continued to play an active role in managing the company, brothers George and Tom had relinquished the roles of president and chief executive to Robert Fox (a nonfamily member) in 1992, while the brothers continued to serve on the board of Foster Farms. The company's growth continued throughout the early and mid-1990s. Although the privately held operation was tightlipped about its sales figures, Foster Farms announced that its 1996 sales topped $900 million.

By this time the company had become the largest poultry producer on the entire West Coast. In addition,

it was the eighth-largest producer in the nation, ranking 231st among all *Fortune* 500 companies. Moreover, the Livingston plant was the largest slaughterhouse in the world, processing 480,000 chickens each day.

ACQUISITION OF PEDERSON'S

The company wanted to keep growing, however. In 1997 Foster Farms spent roughly $7 million to buy the leading poultry producer in the state of Washington, Pederson's Fryer Farms. Pederson's offered Foster Farms a unique opportunity to gain control of most Western markets. As Bob Fox told the *Daily News* on September 2, 1997, "Washington ... is the second-most populated state in the western United States. We believe it's an extension of our California-area business."

Even with the purchase of Pederson's, however, Foster Farms continued to truck its Pacific Northwest-grown birds back to California for processing. This arrangement was both inconvenient and expensive. To remedy the situation, Foster Farms constructed a $45 million processing facility in South Kelso, Washington.

"It's a very major step for us," Fox noted to the *Daily News* on May 15, 1997. "It's the biggest single from-the-ground investment we've made." After opening in 1998, the Kelso facility added over 500 workers to the Foster Farms fold. The company closed Pederson's processing operations in Tacoma, Washington (although it kept the brand name), and shifted processing over to the Kelso site. By the close of 1998, Foster Farms processed about 130 million pounds of poultry at its northwest facilities.

SUCCESSFUL STRATEGIES

As it continued to expand its poultry empire, Foster Farms did not lose sight of the strategies that had helped establish the company. Marketing the Foster Farms brand remained an important aspect of business. During the 1998 Super Bowl, for example, the company launched a major advertising campaign that brought Foster Farms the accolades of both media critics and consumers. The spots, which featured straggly, junk food eating chickens that tried to masquerade as Foster Farms chickens, boosted the company's brand image as a producer of high-quality, carefully vetted chicken. The campaign continued through 1999.

The company continued to grow through acquisition, as well. In 1999 Foster Farms acquired Butterball Turkey Co.'s turkey processing plant and feed mill in Turlock, California, along with a hatchery in Fresno. That same year, Foster Farms also purchased Griffith Foods, an Alabama-based producer of corn dogs.

Although Tom Foster died in 1999, at the age of 49, brother George remained active in the company, as did CEO Bob Fox. Foster Farms produced more than 750 million pounds of fresh poultry in 1999, and was the second-largest corn dog producer in the United States. As the *Modesto Bee* noted on October 28, 1999, "Foster Farms' presence in the industry and the West has been increasing in recent years."

ENTERING THE 21ST CENTURY

Foster Farms ushered in the new millennium by implementing new technology. In early 2000 the company introduced onboard computers from XATA Corporation throughout its fleet of 91 vehicles. Several months later Foster Farms implemented category management technology from Kenosia to enhance its marketing efforts. The software allowed the company to more effectively analyze and sort data, and develop more accurate presentations.

Several leadership changes took place late in the year. Paul Carter was chosen as the company's new president and CEO, succeeding Bob Fox, who announced his retirement. Carter became the second non-family member to lead the company. Although Fox was not a Foster family member, at this time the family continued to influence the company's values and philosophy by serving on its board of directors. Another leadership change took place around this time when Donald Jackson was named president of the poultry division of Foster Farms. By this time the company's revenues exceeded $1 billion.

ACQUISITION OF ZACKY FARMS

In early 2001 Foster Farms agreed to acquire the chicken operations of family-owned Zacky Farms. The deal, which expanded the operations of Foster Farms to Southern California, included 35 live production ranches, a distribution center in Los Angeles, as well as a plant, feed mill, and hatchery near Fresno. Finalized in October, the deal included the addition of roughly 1,500 employees, expanding the company's workforce to 10,600 people.

By early 2002 Foster Farms was processing approximately 21 million pounds of chicken per week. However, international changes posed a threat to the company's operations. At this time Russia imposed a ban on poultry from the United States, citing concerns of antibiotic use and unsanitary industry conditions. Although Foster Farms sold only 1 percent of its output to Russia, the country represented approximately 30 percent of sales for industry giants such as Tyson Foods

and ConAgra Poultry. Foster Farms expressed concerns over heightened competition in the western United States from these industry heavyweights in the absence of a Russian export market.

Foster Farms acknowledged the importance of the Hispanic market to the company's long-term growth strategy. In the summer of 2002 the company chose Anita Santiago Advertising Inc. to serve as its Hispanic agency of record. At that time the company developed a television advertising campaign targeting Hispanic consumers. On the operational front, Foster Farms contracted with an outside company to administer benefits for its workforce of 11,000 employees, including medical, health, vision, and retirement programs.

IMPROVEMENTS AND ENHANCEMENTS

A major branding opportunity unfolded in early 2003. At that time Foster Farms entered into a $1 million partnership with California State University to become the exclusive corporate sponsor of the Save Mart Center sports and entertainment complex in Fresno. Specifically, Foster Farms gained naming rights for the facility's food court and also became its exclusive poultry provider.

Improvements and enhancements also took place on the product front in 2003. That year the company introduced individually wrapped, prewashed, boneless, skinless chicken breasts and thighs under the Fresh & Easy name. In addition, the company redesigned its packaging and made efforts to emphasize the fresh and locally grown attributes of its chicken. Packaging was also enhanced to include easy-to-read product descriptions and recipes.

In 2004 Foster Farms constructed a new distribution center and introduced new operations software. Early the following year the company revealed plans to hire nearly 100 workers at its Porterville cooked chicken plant, following heightened demand for ready-to-eat chicken products. Plans were made to increase capacity by 80 percent at the 100,000-square-foot facility.

CHALLENGING TIMES

Foster Farms faced a number of challenges mid-decade. In late 2005 San Francisco-based East Bay Animal Advocates raised allegations of animal cruelty at the company. When the company failed to participate in a review of humane treatment claims, the National Advertising Division, an industry watchdog group, requested an investigation by the Federal Trade Commission. Then in late 2006, the company was sued by a residents' group alleging that its operations in Fresno County were violating the Clean Air Act.

In December 2008 Don Jackson, president of the poultry division, left Foster Farms to become president and COO of competitor Pilgrim's Pride, which had filed for Chapter 11 bankruptcy. In mid-2009 Foster Farms agreed to acquire Pilgrim's Pride's chicken complex in Farmersville, Louisiana, for $72.3 million. The operations included two hatcheries, a feed mill, a protein conversion plant, a cook plant, and a processing facility. Around the same time the company agreed to acquire the Fernando's and El Extremo Mexican food labels from ConAgra Foods Inc.

By 2010 the Foster family was once again involved in the company's daily operations. Ron Foster, grandson of cofounders Max and Verda, was then serving as the company's president and CEO. Following seven decades of growth and expansion, Foster Farms appeared well positioned for continued success during the second decade of the 21st century.

Rebecca Stanfel
Updated, Paul R. Greenland

PRINCIPAL COMPETITORS

Pilgrim's Pride Corporation; Sanderson Farms, Inc.; Tyson Foods, Inc.

FURTHER READING

Beckett, Jamie. "Foster Feathering Nest." *San Francisco Chronicle*, September 29, 1988.

Bizjak, Tony. "Where 22,000 Chickens Watch B-52s and Think Big." *San Francisco Chronicle*, June 2, 1987.

Britton, Charles. "Zacky Farms ... Is No Turkey." *Southern California Business*, November 1, 1987.

Estrada, Richard. "Livingston, California-Based Poultry Farm Goes Online." *Modesto Bee*, October 28, 1999.

"Foster Farms Names Paul Carter President and Chief Executive Officer." *PR Newswire*, December 4, 2000.

"Foster Farms to Acquire Fernando's and El Extremo Foodservice Brands from ConAgra Foods; Deal in Brief." *Datamonitor Financial Deals Tracker*, June 9, 2009.

Hallman, Tom. "The Chicken Name Becomes an All-Out War." *Atlanta Journal-Constitution*, April 25, 1988.

LaBeck, Paula. "550 Jobs Coming Home to Roost in Kelso." *Daily News*, May 15, 1997.

Lamb, Jonah Owen. "Foster Farms Executive Leaves for Rival Company: Texas-Based Pilgrim's Pride Is in the Midst of Bankruptcy." *Merced Sun-Star*, December 23, 2008.

"Pilgrim's Pride Sells Farmerville Chicken Complex to Foster Farms; Deal in Brief." *Datamonitor Financial Deals Tracker*, May 25, 2009.

Smith, Timothy. "Changing Tastes: By End of This Year Poultry Will Surpass Beef in the U.S. Diet." *Wall Street Journal*, September 17, 1987.

Tyson, Rae. "Beef Industry Hits Hard Times." *USA Today*, March 5, 1996.

Fox Head, Inc.

—————————■—————————

18400 Sutter Boulevard
Morgan Hill, California 95037
U.S.A.
Telephone: (408) 776-8633
Fax: (408) 776-8610
Web site: http://www.foxhead.com

Private Company
Incorporated: 1974 as Moto-X Fox
Employees: 462
Sales: $216 million (2009 est.)
NAICS: 315000 Apparel Manufacturing

■ ■ ■

Fox Head, Inc., doing business as Fox Racing, is a sports apparel and accessories company, catering to both men and women. The core of the company is its motocross apparel, including pants, jerseys, helmets, gloves, and boots. Fox also offers BMX (bicycle motocross) and mountain bike apparel and surfwear, as well as a variety of T-shirts, hoodies, pants, shorts, swimwear, outerwear, headwear, footwear, and eyewear. Products are available at five company-owned stores, sporting goods stores, cycle shops, and surf shops, as well as online and through catalogs. Products are also available in more than 50 other countries, sold through a network of distributors and partners.

A major part of Fox's marketing efforts is the sponsorship of teams involved in motocross, BMX, MTB (mountain bicycling), surfing, and wakeboarding. Fox maintains its headquarters in Morgan Hill, California, and branch offices in Irvine, California, and Newcastle, England. The flagship store is located in the Westfield Valley Fair mall in Santa Clara, California. The company is owned by the Fox family. The four children of founder and board member Geoff Fox run the business on a day-to-day basis. Son Peter Fox serves as chairman and CEO.

ORIGINS

Geoff Fox became familiar with motocross in 1965 and became a racer and passionate follower of the sport. Four years later, with a PhD in physics, he moved his family from Wisconsin to teach physics at the University of California at Santa Clara. There he continued to participate in motocross and made friends with the manager of the parts department at a local motorcycle dealership, Grand Prix Cycles. Several months later, Fox bought a stake in the business, which began providing aftermarket parts for CZ, Maico, and Suzuki motorcycles. Spotting an opportunity, Fox disassembled a CZ, a Czechoslovakian motorcycle, photographed all the parts, and self-published an English-language service manual that became a best seller.

Because Fox was interested in expanding the mail-order business of Grand Prix Cycles and his partners wanted to open more dealerships, Fox sold his stake in the dealership in 1973 and struck out on his own. In February 1974 he launched Moto-X Fox. Operating out of a 1,500-square-foot machine shop in Campbell, California, Moto-X Fox began distributing parts and accessories for European motocross bikes, selling to dealers across the United States. The company became profit-

COMPANY PERSPECTIVES

The Fox brand is the most recognized and best selling brand of motocross apparel in the world today.

able in its second month in business. One of Fox's first major products was a rebuild kit for Koni shock absorbers. The shock absorber business looked so appealing
that Fox decided to become directly involved in the sector.

FOX FACTORY SPUN OFF: 1977

Fox's brother, Bob Fox, also a motocross enthusiast and a physicist by training, who had been riding with his own suspension designs, joined forces with Steve Simons to design an air shock absorber for professional motocross racing. The shock absorber became available on the market in 1975 and gained prominence a year later when racer Kent Howerton won the AMA 500cc MX championship using Fox AirShox. Bob Fox and Simons then spun off this Moto-X Fox division in 1977 as a separate company called Fox Factory. It became a leading player in the suspension business and eventually branched into the Indy car, off-road truck, quad, dune buggy, and snowmobile markets.

In addition to distributing his brother's suspension products, Geoff Fox began producing engine components for professional motocross riders. To better promote the products, he spent $300 in 1975 on a logo, a Fox head that became all but synonymous with motocross. He also formed his own motocross team in 1977 to compete against the factory teams, in particular the powerhouse Japanese teams, to prove the superiority of Moto-X Fox products. Team Moto-X Fox quickly established itself as the best non-factory team in the AMA 125cc National Championship series.

Fox's entry into racing also opened up a new line of business. The company provided its team riders with handmade racing outfits, designed by Geoff Fox to stand out from the rest of the field. The bright red, yellow, and orange kit caught the attention of race fans, who soon began calling the shop to find out if the clothing was available for sale. Moto-X Fox then began selling apparel, which became such an important facet of the business that the Team Moto-X Fox riders in 1978 and 1979 promoted the clothing more than they did the bike parts.

COMPANY REORGANIZED: 1980

Apparel sales proved to be critical to the success of Moto-X Fox when the aftermarket shock business, which had been at the core of the company, was virtually eliminated in 1980 when manufacturers finally began shipping new bikes with better suspensions. Clothing sales were able to pick up the slack for Moto-X Fox. In keeping with this change in focus, the company was reorganized in 1980 as Fox Racing. Spurring growth in the motocross apparel field was the success of one of its team riders, American Mark Barnett, who won Fox Racing's first national championship in 1980. Other top riders would also wear the Fox Racing colors, bringing further prestige to the brand. In 1982 Brad Lackey became the first Fox Racing-sponsored rider to win a World Motocross Championship. Over the next 20 years Fox Racing riders would win more than 40 National Motocross and Supercross Championships.

Geoff Fox's sons, Greg and Peter, shared their father's passion for motocross and became involved in the business. Greg Fox first aspired to become a professional motocross rider, but during his days at the University of California at Santa Barbara became involved in surfing, an interest that would help drive Fox Racing into the surf market. The company would begin advertising in surf magazines, sponsor high school and college surf teams, and hold surf contests. Peter Fox, on the other hand, never attended college, preferring instead to work in the family business and maintain close ties to the motocross circuit.

By the mid-1990s the Fox brothers gained day-to-day control of Fox Racing, albeit informally. Although they were still in their 20s, their age was not considered a handicap. "My brother and I bring to the table a passion for the product, and we're willing to take a lot more risks than my dad was," Peter Fox told *Entrepreneur* in 1999. "It helps that we're closer to the age of our customers, who are between 15 and 30. We know what they like." In addition to keeping up to date on trends in motocross fashion, the Fox brothers moved Fox Racing into new categories, such as sweatshirts, T-shirts, socks, and mountain bike apparel. As they came of age, two other siblings, Anna and John, would join the company as well.

X GAMES LAUNCH SPURS GROWTH: 1995

While interest in motocross was high in the 1970s, it fell off in the 1980s before regaining momentum in the 1990s. Fox Racing benefited greatly from the growing popularity of extreme sports, which gained a wide following with the launch of the X Games by the ESPN

```
┌─────────────────────────────────────────────┐
│                                             │
│              KEY DATES                      │
│                   ■                         │
│ ─────────────────────────────────────────── │
│  1974:  Geoff Fox launches Moto-X Fox to    │
│         distribute parts and accessories    │
│         for European motocross bikes.       │
│  1977:  Company forms a motocross team to   │
│         promote its brand.                  │
│  1980:  Moto-X Fox is reorganized as Fox    │
│         Racing, Inc.                        │
│  2003:  Irvine, California, office opens to │
│         launch surf and casual apparel line.│
│  2006:  Company is renamed Fox Head, Inc.   │
│                                             │
└─────────────────────────────────────────────┘
```

cable sports network in 1995. Motocross in particular enjoyed a surge in popularity that extended into the new century.

The television exposure of the X Games, as well as the Gravity games televised by the NBC network, helped to build the Fox Racing brand. While Fox Racing apparel remained popular with motocross and mountain bike racers, it also achieved a good deal of cachet with a young demographic, especially board enthusiasts, who were more interested in the logo and look than the motocross roots of the company.

By the dawn of the 21st century, Fox Racing apparel could be found at a variety of motorcycle, bicycle, and surf shops, as well as such chains as Pacific Sunwear and Gadzooks. Moreover, the company distributed 1.2 million catalogs. Fox Racing found itself in a category with similar brands such as No Fear and Billabong, but aspired to challenge mainstream brands such as Nike and Tommy Hilfiger. In keeping with this goal, the Fox Head logo was put to use in new markets. The company worked with wakeboard company Tige to produce a Fox Signature Edition board. It also worked with General Motors in 2000 to produce a Fox Edition Chevy Silverado concept pickup truck.

Fox Racing reached $100 million in annual sales in the early years of the new century and continued to extend its brand to new markets. In 2003 it opened a 4,5000-square-foot office in Irvine, California, to launch a surf and casual apparel line. A year later the company launched a street wear division under the Fox Riders Co. name, a fashion forward line targeted at both teenage and young adult men and women interested in an action sports lifestyle.

Fox Racing branded sunglasses were added in 2005, produced under a license by Foothill, California-based Oakley Inc. Snowboarding and motocross goggles were added a year later. These new lines helped to drive annual sales to the $150 million level in 2005. To keep pace with growth the company doubled the size of its Irvine site in 2005 and acquired a pair of Newport Beach offices that brought 15,000 square feet in combined space and housed the company's marketing and women's design teams.

FOX HEAD NAME ADOPTED: 2006

In keeping with the broadened appeal of its brand and in homage to the iconic appeal of its logo, Fox Racing changed its name in the fall of 2006 to Fox Head, Inc. The goal, according to the *Orange County Business Journal*, was to "sell more T-shirts, hats, and other gear to surfers, skateboarders, snowboarders, and others who live for action sports." The company gained appeal with other types of customers as well.

In 2006 Fox Head introduced a fake-leather handbag that sold for about $40 under the Gold Digga name. The boxy tote was intended as a beach accessory but received little interest from surf and action sports store buyers. It found a market instead with fashion-conscious juniors, who embraced the bag. As a result, Gold Digga became Fox Head's best-selling product across all categories in 2006. Other styles were added, as was a limited-edition $100 handbag.

The second generation of the Fox family had played pivotal roles in the success of Fox Head for some time. In the spring of 2008 Geoff Fox stepped down as CEO, turning over the reins to Peter Fox, the former chief creative officer. The elder Fox stayed on as chairman of the board. Greg Fox remained vice president of sales and a member of the board of directors.

Action sports continued to remain popular and the field became more lucrative for companies like Fox Head as retailers such as Macy's, Buckle, and Pacific Sunwear phased out urban wear and turned to action sports apparel as a way to fill the void. In 2009 Fox Head introduced a women's swimwear line that was sold exclusively through Pacific Sunwear before being offered to other retailers a year later. In addition to store channels, Fox Head was enjoying strong growth from its Web site sales, prompting an overhaul of its e-commerce platform in 2010. With the transition to second-generation management successfully completed, the prospects for Fox Head looked bright for many years to come.

Ed Dinger

PRINCIPAL SUBSIDIARIES

Fox Racing Inc.

PRINCIPAL COMPETITORS

Billabong International Limited; Pacific Sunwear of California, Inc.; Quicksilver, Inc.

FURTHER READING

Bellantonio, Jennifer. "Fox Racing Set to Tweak Name." *Orange County Business Journal*, July 10, 2006.

———. "Surfwear Makers Riding Wave of Motocross Popularity." *Los Angeles Business Journal*, March 3, 2003.

"Big Thinker: Marketeer—Geoff Fox." *Motocross Action Magazine*, November 3, 2006.

Estess, Patricia Schiff. "New Blood." *Entrepreneur*, June 1999, p. 83.

Nauman, Matt. "Motocross Firm Builds on Its Brand." *San Jose Mercury News*, December 5, 2001.

Tran, Khanh T. L. "Action Sports Labels Pick Up Speed." *WWD*, May 28, 2008, p. 13.

Zeveloff, Julie. "From Active to Contemporary." *WWD*, August 19, 2004, p. 19.

Fruité Entreprises S.A.

BP 60267, 2 rue du Lac
Annecy, F-74007 Cedex
France
Telephone: (+33 04) 50 33 19 00
Fax: (+33 04) 50 51 42 63
Web site: http://www.fruite.fr

Wholly Owned Subsidiary of Britvic plc
Incorporated: 2000
Employees: 600
Sales: EUR 256.3 million ($358.8 million) (2009)
NAICS: 311421 Fruit and Vegetable Canning

■ ■ ■

Fruité Entreprises SA is one of the leading producers of fruit juices and fruit-based drinks in France. The company's flagship brand is its Fruité line of fruit-based soft drinks, featuring such flavors as grenadine, raspberry/litchi, strawberry, mango/papaya, and lemon/lime. The Fruité brand has also been extended to include a line of yogurt-based drinks called Fruité P'tit Yaourt. The company produces more than 25 million liters per year under the Fruité brand, and claims a 3 percent share of the French fruit drinks market. Fruité Entreprises also controls Teisseire SAS, the world's leading producer of fruit-based syrups and cordials, and Pressade, a leading producer of organic and nonorganic pure fruit juices. In 2009 the company reported revenues of EUR 256.3 million ($358.8 million). In May 2010 Fruité Entreprises became a 100 percent subsidiary of Britvic plc.

APPLE COOPERATIVE ORIGINS

Fruité Entreprises originated as part of a small cooperative of apple growers in France's Savoie region. In 1985 these growers joined together to launch a business to convert their surplus apple harvests into fruit juice. Vergers de Savoie, as the new company was called, launched its line of apple juice under this name.

Vergers de Savoie struggled to get off the ground. According to *LSA*, this was partly because the small company lacked the tools to market its product properly. By the end of the decade, despite building a sales volume of FRF 17 million (approximately $2.75 million) per year, Vergers de Savoie was forced into bankruptcy.

In 1990 a local family purchased control of the company and its equipment. Philippe Meunier, then in his mid-20s, was placed in charge of rebuilding the company's business. Despite his youth, Meunier brought extensive experience in France's grocery and supermarket industry. Meunier was the son of Michel Meunier, longtime head of Francap, a leading supplier of central purchasing services to the supermarket sector. Francap had been part of the Casino supermarket group before becoming an independent company serving the independent grocery channel in the late 1980s.

PACKAGING SUCCESS

By the early 1990s the supermarket industry dominated France's grocery distribution industry. Also by this time, the sector was dominated by a relatively few large-scale supermarket companies. With their greater purchasing

KEY DATES

1963: Evian launches the Fruité brand of fruit-flavored sparkling soft drinks.
1985: A group of Savoie apple farmers form Vergers de Savoie to market apple juice.
1990: Philippe Meunier takes over as head of Vergers de Savoie.
1994: Vergers de Savoie acquires the Fruité brand.
2000: The company changes its name to Fruité Entreprises; acquires Bric Fruit, including the Pressade brand.
2005: Fruité Entreprises acquires Teisseire, the leading syrups producer in France.
2010: Britvic plc acquires Fruité Entreprises for EUR 237 million ($332 million).

volumes, these companies exerted an enormous influence over food and beverage suppliers such as Vergers de Savoie. The rise of the supermarket groups also led the country's independent grocers to join together to form their own purchasing partnerships, such as Francap.

This trend presented both opportunities and challenges to food and beverage producers. Placing their products on supermarket shelves became all-important for a company's survival. At the same time, the greater volumes and wider distribution demanded by the purchasing operations of the supermarket sector represented a major growth opportunity for small companies such as Vergers de Savoie.

Philippe Meunier recognized that packaging played a major role in the supermarket sector, particularly in terms of attracting consumers to purchase a product. Toward this end, Meunier led Vergers de Savoie to invest in developing new packaging for its apple juices. The company also sought to expand its range in order to establish Vergers de Savoie as a full-fledged fruit juice brand. At the same time, Meunier positioned the company as a supplier of fruit juices for the supermarkets' private-label brands. The company's efforts paid off, and by the middle of the decade it had succeeded in raising its sales past FRF 65 million.

FRUITÉ ACQUIRED: 1994

In 1994 Meunier spotted a new opportunity to develop its branded business, buying up the then-dormant soft drink brand Fruité. Evian, the mineral water company, had launched this brand in 1963 as a line of carbonated

fruit-flavored water. Packaging played an early role in the brand's success, especially with the launch of a six-pack bottle format in 1966. Fruité became a stand-alone brand, and then a separate subsidiary under BSN, the future Danone foods empire. In 1974 Fruité scored a major marketing success with its new slogan "Fruité c'est plus musclé." The brand and slogan proved a hit, particularly with France's youth market, gaining national recognition.

Backed by such French celebrities as Michel Platini and Bernard Hinault, Fruité remained a strong seller through much of the 1980s. By the next decade, however, the Fruité brand was running out of steam. Sales dropped off sharply, and by the early 1990s the company was essentially dormant. By 1992 the Fruité brand had disappeared from French supermarket shelves.

According to market research carried out by Vergers de Savoie, the Fruité brand nevertheless maintained a strong recognition rate among French consumers. This was especially true for the over-35 segment, among whom the Fruité brand enjoyed a recognition rate of 95 percent. Overall, more than half of French consumers still recognized the brand, ranking it at number three among soft drink brands in France.

CHEERPACK IN 1996

Encouraged by these scores, Meunier set out to rebuild the Fruité brand. The company relaunched the brand's popular "Fruité c'est plus musclé" slogan, backed by a redesigned label. Vergers de Savoie rolled out a new line of trendier flavors, including mandarin, pink grapefruit, and apple-cassis. At the same time, Vergers de Savoie extended the Fruité range beyond its original carbonated beverages to include a line of pure fruit juices and another of fruit-based nectars. The company also captured attention with the launch of new packaging concepts. These included a highly popular single-serving Tetra Pak brick format, including a drink straw.

In 1995 Vergers de Savoie acquired the rights and equipment for a new packaging technology known as Cheerpack. A flexible, collapsible pouch, Cheerpack offered a number of advantages over traditional aluminum cans. For one, consumers were not required to drink the entire contents at once, since the Cheerpack featured a resealable cap. At the same time, because of the package's flexibility, the Cheerpack took up less room as the drink was consumed, making it an ideal format for children's schoolbags.

Vergers de Savoie backed up the launch of the extended Fruité brand and its new packaging types with a strong marketing effort. This also led the company to form its first sports partnerships, including with the

Nancy soccer team, the Paris Marathon, and auto-racing driver Gilles Panizzi.

The effort paid off quickly, and by 1996 the company's sales had climbed past FRF 100 million. One year later, Vergers de Savoie posted sales of more than FRF 165 million, and then topped FRF 200 million by the end of 1998. The company complemented its brand range with a number of new brand launches, including Velours and Soif de Foot.

Meunier, who gained full control of the company in 1996, also brought in new financial partners, selling a 40 percent stake in the company to SPEC, part of Banques Populaires, and Alliance Entreprendre, part of Caisse d'Epargne. This backing enabled the company to expand its production and sales range. By 2000 the company's annual sales neared FRF 250 million ($30 million).

ACQUISITION DRIVE STARTS IN 2000

Vergers de Savoie changed its name in 2000, becoming Fruité Entreprises, as Meunier launched the company on a new expansion drive. Fruité made its first move in November of that same year, when it agreed to acquire dairy cooperative Lactalis's fruit juice business, Bric Fruit. Based near Nantes, Bric Fruit helped strengthen Fruité's presence in France's western regions, while nearly doubling its total sales. The addition of Bric Fruit also added a number of new brands to Fruité's portfolio. These included Sambo, Recré, and Pressade, one of the country's leading producers of organic fruit juices.

Fruité boosted its fruit juice operations again the following year with the purchase of Unisource. The addition of Unisource, previously held by syrups specialist Teisseire, allowed Fruité to claim the position as France's leading independent fruit juice producer.

Strengthening Fruité's market position played a major part in Meunier's stated ambition to take the company public as early 2002. The company also invested in raising its profile in other areas, notably in its marketing effort. Toward this end the company launched a new series of investments, raising its advertising budget at the beginning of the decade. This also led the company to the development of its first television advertising campaign for Fruité, marking the brand's return to the airwaves after a 20-year absence. The campaign relaunched the "Fruité c'est plus musclé" slogan, while focusing on the group's line of Cheerpack packaged drinks.

YOGURT DRINKS INTRODUCED: 2003

The rising popularity of fruit-based dairy drinks encouraged Fruité Entreprises to explore this market as well. In 2003 the company acquired Savoie Yaourt, jump-starting its own entry into the yogurt drink category. By the beginning of 2004 the company had completed the launch of its first yogurt drink, under the Fruité brand. Called Fruité P'tit Yaourt, the new brand distinguished itself through its packaging, becoming the first yogurt drink available in a flexible pouch.

Packaging remained a key component in the company's expansion elsewhere as well. In 2004 the company launched a new line of fruit juices in small-pack brick containers, called Mini Fruité. The new packs, marketed to children, featured both a drinking straw and a screw cap. Also during 2004, Fruité Entreprises began developing its Internet presence. This resulted in the launch of a Web site dedicated to the Fruité brand in 2004.

TEISSEIRE TAKEOVER: 2004

Fruité's expansion drive enabled the company's total revenues to top EUR 150 million ($180 million) by the end of 2003. The company continued to seek new expansion opportunities through 2004. When Teisseire, a leading producer of syrups and cordials, came up for sale, Fruité jumped at the chance to acquire the company. The deal enabled Fruité Entreprises to double in size once again.

Teisseire traced its own origins to the early 18th century, when Mathieu Teisseire started a business distilling fruit- and plant-based drinks in Grenoble. Among Teisseire's most popular products was the cherry-based Ratafia. The Teisseire name achieved national recognition after the launch of its first fruit-based syrups in 1927.

By the early 1970s Teisseire, buoyed by the rapid growth of the supermarket sector, had become one of France's leading syrups producers. The company expanded again in 1971, building a new factory in Crolles, outside of Grenoble. In the 1990s Teisseire added a second brand name when it acquired Moulin de Valdonne, a producer of organic and other syrups, based in Peypin in the Bouches-du-Rhône region.

At the dawn of the 21st century Teisseire remained a family-owned company, controlled by brothers Eric and Dominique Reynaud. However, in the new decade a dispute broke out between the brothers following a disagreement over the company's future. Despite its success in maintaining its leadership position in the syrups category, Teisseire remained a relatively small company. This also left it highly vulnerable in the event that one of its larger soft drinks competitors should decide to launch its own line of syrups. Such a move could be seen as a natural extension for a soft drinks manufacturer, since colas and other soft drinks are themselves syrup-based drinks.

Teisseire was confronted at the same time with rising competition from the private-label sector, as the supermarket groups launched their own syrup lines. In the face of shrinking market share and increasing vulnerability, Eric Reynaud sought to place Teisseire under the umbrella of a larger company. By 2002 Reynaud had succeeded in ousting his brother, then Teisseire's chairman.

NEW OWNER IN 2010

Fruité Entreprises brought in a new majority shareholder, Al Munajem, a large Saudi Arabian foods company, to provide the financial backing for its bid to acquire Teisseire. As a result, Philippe Meunier reduced his own stake in the company to 25 percent. By November 2004 the company had succeeded in acquiring nearly 72 percent of Teisseire for EUR 90 million ($130 million). By January of the following year, Fruité had completed the Teisseire acquisition. The company, which then became the world's leading manufacturer of fruit-based syrups, reorganized its new business. This involved shutting down the Moulin de Valdonne factory in Peypin, transferring its operations to the larger syrups facility in Crolles.

Fruité Entreprises then became France's largest independent fruit juice and fruit-based drinks company, with annual sales of nearly EUR 270 million ($340 million), and more than 600 employees. The company refocused its brand portfolio largely around three core brands, Fruité, Teisseire, and Pressade.

Teisseire proved the main engine for the company's growth through the second half of the decade. Guided by new CEO Jean-Luc Tivolle, the company set out to rejuvenate the Teisseire range and recapture market share. The company then commenced to expand the brand, launching a new sugar-free syrups line in 2007, as well as a single-serving package, called Teissi. In 2009 the Teisseire brand expanded to include a sports drink line, and again in 2010 with an all-natural line called Fraîcheur de Fruits.

By this time Teisseire had grown to represent approximately half of Fruité's total sales of EUR 256 million ($359 million) in 2009. Teisseire had also become the company's primary profit center, accounting for 70 percent of its profits. Despite its success, Fruité

nevertheless remained a minor player in the increasingly international, and rapidly consolidating, soft drinks sector. Most of the company's competitors in France belonged to larger companies, and many, including chief rivals Rea and Joker, had been acquired by large-scale international companies.

By 2010 Fruité Entreprises itself recognized the need to become part of a larger, more international operation. This led the group to agree to a buyout offer from a leading U.K.-based soft drinks company, Britvic. In May 2010 Britvic paid EUR 237 million ($332 million) to acquire 100 percent control of Fruité Entreprises. The purchase signified the exit from the company of Philippe Meunier. At the same time, Britvic announced plans to introduce a number of its own brands into the French market. With three strong brand families, Fruité Entreprises played an important role in Britvic's determination to become an international soft drinks player in the 21st century.

M. L. Cohen

PRINCIPAL SUBSIDIARIES

Fruité SAS; Teisseire SAS; Unisource SAS.

PRINCIPAL DIVISIONS

Fruit Juices; Syrups; Yogurt Drinks.

PRINCIPAL OPERATING UNITS

Fruité; Teisseire; Pressade; Moulin de Valdonne.

PRINCIPAL COMPETITORS

Cidou SA; EMIG France SAS; Fruival; JFA Pampryl SA; Joker SA; Tropicana; Les Vergers d'Alsace SA.

FURTHER READING

"Britvic Acquires Fruité Entreprises." *Datamonitor Financial Deals Tracker*, May 31, 2010.

Chauvot, Myriam, and Laurent Flallo. "Fruité s'Apprête à Prendre le Contrôle des Sirops Teisseire." *Les Echos*, November 23, 2004, p. 25.

"Des PME Peuvent Apporter de la Marge." *LSA*, May 14, 1998.

"Fruité Entreprises Acquiert Teisseire avec l'Aide d'un Partenaire Saoudien." *Les Echos*, November 26, 2004, p. 19.

"Fruité Entreprises Ferme l'Usine des Sirops Moulin de Valdonne à Peypin." *Les Echos*, October 11, 2005, p. 24.

Fruité Entreprises S.A.

"Fruité Prépare Sa Relance avec l'Agence Paname." *Strategies*, May 3, 2004.

Letessier, Ivan. "Fruité et Teisseire Passent sous Pavillon Anglais." *Le Figaro*, May 19, 2010.

"Success Stories à la Française: Rhône Alpes: Philippe Meunier." *L'Expansion*, May 1, 2007.

Gilster-Mary Lee
Corporation

—■—

1037 State Street
Chester, Illinois 62233-1657
U.S.A.
Telephone: (616) 826-2361
Fax: (618) 826-2973
Web site: http://www.gilstermarylee.com

Private Company
Incorporated: 1897 as Gilster Milling Company
Employees: 3,000
Sales: $926 million (2009 est.)
NAICS: 311423 Dried and Dehydrated Food
Manufacturing

■ ■ ■

Gilster-Mary Lee Corporation is one of the leading private-label manufacturers of breakfast cereal, baking mixes, macaroni and cheese, pastas and add-meat dinners, popcorn, pudding and gelatin mixes, and drink mixes in the United States. The company also sells some products under its own Hospitality label as well as Mother's Joy, a line of organic and natural food products. Based in Chester, Illinois, the family-owned company operates a baking mix plant and a shredded wheat plant in Chester, along with a dozen other plants. A baking mix and macaroni and cheese plant, as well as a pasta plant, are located in Steeleville, Illinois. Also in Illinois, a cocoa plant is operated in Momence and a baking mix plant in Centralia.

Several plants are located in Missouri, including in McBride, where popcorn and cereal plants are operated,

as well as a corrugated sheet plant that produces shipping cases for the other Gilster units. Baking mix and cereal plants are found in Perryville, Missouri; a popcorn plant in Jasper, Missouri; and a cereal plant in Joplin, Missouri. In addition, a plant in Wilson, Arkansas, produces drink, gelatin, and pudding mixes. All told, Gilster produces over 8,000 items sold under more than 500 different private labels. The company is majority owned by its employees.

COMPANY FOUNDED: 1897

Gilster-Mary Lee was founded by the Gilster family in 1897. The patriarch of the family, Henry Gilster, was born in Germany and immigrated to the United States in 1856. He settled in Chester, Illinois, where he became a merchant and banker, and raised a family with his wife Eva. One of their sons, Albert Henry Gilster, was born in 1872 and became a teacher at a Lutheran school.

Albert had to quit the teaching profession in 1897 because of failing eyesight, and his father bought a flour mill in Steeleville, Illinois, to provide him with a livelihood. Originally founded in 1859 as the Steeleville Milling Company, the mill then became known as the Gilster Milling Co., and Albert Gilster served as president of the concern. Some of his siblings also found employment there.

Gilster Milling initially focused on the production of flour, produced from wheat that was delivered to the mill by wagon. The company sold its products under several brand names, including Gilster's Best, Featherlite, and Mother's Joy. Gilster Milling enjoyed excellent success throughout the South, especially in Alabama and Mississippi, and sales reached $1 million by the dawn of the 20th century.

REACHING A TURNING POINT:
1958

Albert Gilster remained president of the company until his death in 1946. However, he did not grow the business beyond the $1 million mark during the last 40 years of his life. Gilster Milling would not resume growth until Don Welge, whose mother was a Gilster, joined the company in 1957. It was a pivotal time for the family business because during the post-World War II years small independent mills like Gilster were being squeezed out of the market by larger concerns like General Mills.

Moreover, Gilster had always depended on the sale of what was known as "family flour," a staple of scratch baking, which was also waning in popularity as people became more pressed for time. Welge recognized that people had less time for baking, and as a result of his influence, Gilster produced its first private-label dry cake mix in 1958. It was a turning point in the history of the company.

Other products soon followed, including potato products and drink mixes, leading to an expansion to Chester, Illinois. While Welge was devoted to growing the business further, other family members were eager to cash in their interests. Short of capital, Welge in 1961 merged the company with Martha White Mills, a major southern marketer of flour and baking mixes.

As Gilster-Martha White Corporation, the company continued to expand, in large part the result of acquisitions. In 1962 the Trenton Milling Company of Illinois and its cake mix business was added. Newark, New Jersey-based Duff Mixes followed in 1965, and in 1968 Chicago-based Kitchen Art Foods was purchased. However, not everyone was pleased with how Martha White was operating the company from its headquarters in Nashville, especially since Gilster-Martha White was losing money. The result of the discontent was a split in 1969. At that time, more than a dozen members of the

top Gilster-Martha White management team, including Don Welge, left to form a competing firm under the name Mary Lee Packaging Co., based in Perryville, Illinois.

GILSTER-MARY LEE FORMED:
1971

For the next two years Gilster-Martha White and Mary Lee Packaging were fierce rivals, but in November 1971 the two sides came to an accommodation and Mary Lee Packaging acquired Gilster-Martha White, with stockholders of the former owning most the combined business, which took the name Gilster-Mary Lee Corporation. Don Welge served as president and general manager and employees from both companies were retained. Gilster continued to produce cake mixes under the Martha White label as well as private supermarket labels.

The larger Gilster enterprise was then a major player in its field. To keep pace with demand, it was operating three plants around the clock six days a week. By 1974 it was supplying 80 companies located in 43 states with a wide variety of dry food mixes in addition to cake mixes, including brownies, hot rolls, corn bread, coffee cake, waffles, pancakes, biscuits, puddings, mashed potatoes, and spaghetti seasonings. The company either used a customer-provided formula or made use of one of its own recipes.

Gilster continued to add new products as well. In 1975 a macaroni and cheese production line was added. The product proved so popular that a second line was added in 1977 and a third line one year later. Also in 1978 the company forged a partnership with Denver, Colorado-based Rustco Corporation to enter the ready-to-spread frosting business and opened a plant in Wilson, Arkansas, to serve as a contract packer for the Pillsbury Company.

The 1980s were a time of further growth. In 1983 the company became involved in the private-label cold breakfast cereal market, which in time would become a core product offering. Cereal production was expanded twice during the decade. Macaroni and cheese production increased as well and a full line of pastas was added. In 1985 Gilster turned its attention to microwave popcorn, becoming the first private-label packager of the increasingly popular product.

C.H.B. FOODS ACQUIRED: 1985

In addition to organic growth, the company pursued acquisitions. In 1985 Gilster acquired the dry cake mix business of Los Angeles-based C.H.B. Foods Inc., which

KEY DATES

1897: Company founded as Gilster Milling Company.
1958: First private-label cake mix offered.
1961: Company combines with Martha White Mills.
1971: Merger results in Gilster-Mary Lee Corporation.
1983: Gilster becomes involved in private-label cold breakfast cereal business.
1999: Gilster acquires Jasper Foods, becoming the country's largest private-label popcorn manufacturer.
2009: Mother's Joy label reintroduced for organic products.

included the Cinch brand as well as private labels. Next, Gilster acquired the dehydrated potato business of the Basic American Company and the baking mix business of Wilkins Roger Company. In 1988 Marshalltown, Iowa-based Party Pac Corporation was acquired, adding the pre-popped holiday tin popcorn business to the mix. Other new categories were added with the acquisition of the KoPac plants in Momence and Watseka, Illinois, which produced instant chocolate and hot cocoa mixes and chocolate syrup.

Changes were made to the Gilster operation in the early 1990s to improve efficiency. In 1992 a corrugated box plant was built in McBride, Missouri, to produce shipping cases and add some vertical integration to the operation. A new distribution center was also added in McBride to provided better coordination of shipments among the company's far-flung network of plants.

Both of these new facilities were impacted by the flooding of the Mississippi River that occurred in the summer of 1993 when a nearby levee was breached. The Gilster facilities were flooded by 18 feet of water, a blow that could have destroyed the company. However, the forbearance of customers and extra effort by employees allowed the company to survive the crisis.

EXPANDING OPERATIONS

Gilster Mary-Lee continued to expand its operations during the balance of the 1990s. In 1995 a new plant to produce shredded wheat cereal was opened in Chester to take advantage of a private-label opportunity. The new plant allowed the company to become the first private-label cereal manufacturer to offer supermarket chains a bite-size shredded wheat product. In the late 1990s the company opened a 200,000-square-foot plant in Centralia, Illinois, to pack Duncan Hines cake mixes, and added capabilities at one of its Chester plants to become involved in the private-label marshmallow business. As a result, revenues increased to $483 million in 1998.

In 1999 Gilster added $60 million in revenue through the acquisition of Joplin, Missouri-based Jasper Foods, a major manufacturer of private-label microwave popcorn as well as private-label cereal. The move made Gilster the country's largest private-label popcorn manufacturer. The Jasper popcorn plant also achieved notoriety when a condition that became known as "popcorn worker's lung" was first discovered there in eight workers in 1999. The cause, according to a subsequent investigation, was likely linked to the chemicals used in the product's butter flavoring.

POOR ECONOMY BOOSTS 21ST-CENTURY SALES

The new century brought difficult economic conditions for most of the first decade, but unlike many companies these conditions favored Gilster. Consumers looking to save money turned to the kind of private-label products the company manufactured rather than to more expensive brand name products. Gilster took further advantage of the trend by adding new lines, such as graham cracker pie shells. As a result, revenues improved to $725 million in 2006. On the other hand, Gilster had to contend with sharp increases in the price of commodities, which made margins tight.

A credit crunch in 2008 precipitated another downturn in the economy that also played to Gilster's strengths. Revenues improved to $800 million in 2008. The company enjoyed especially good results from its cereal business, which was growing at a rate of 15 to 20 percent. Rather than retrench like companies in other industries, Gilster looked to make capital investments to take full advantage of its opportunities. Additional cereal-making equipment was purchased in 2009, and a new warehouse and finished goods truck garage were constructed in Perryville, Missouri.

Sales increased 15.8 percent to $926 million in 2009. While private-label products, in particular breakfast cereals, remained the core business, Gilster was also interested in pursuing branded products while also returning to its roots. Although many consumers bought private-label products for their value, others were still willing to pay a premium for natural and organic products. Gilster sought to tap into this market by reintroducing its Mother's Joy label. Out of commission for many years, Mother's Joy was then applied to a new organic macaroni and cheese product as well as an organic white cheddar and shells product. Whether the label would be extended to other product categories remained to be seen, but the key to the company's future prosperity would likely remain its private-label business.

Ed Dinger

PRINCIPAL COMPETITORS

General Mills, Inc.; Kellogg Company; Ralcorp Holdings, Inc.

FURTHER READING

Berry, DeMaris. "Chester Firm One of Nation's Big Mix Makers." *Southern Illinoisan*, October 7, 1973, p. 1.

"Chester Firm Sold." *Southern Illinoisan*, October 21, 1971, p. 1.

"Gilster-Mary Lee Corp." *St Louis Business Journal*, March 23, 2007.

"Gilster-Mary Lee Corp." *St Louis Business Journal*, March 26, 2010.

Mathis, Christi. "News." *Southern Illinoisan*, September 30, 2005, p. 6F.

Vespereny, Cynthia. "Gilster Pops for $60 Million Firm." *St. Louis Business Journal*, March 1, 1999, p. 1.

Globus SB-Warenhaus Holding GmbH & Co. KG

Leipziger Strasse 8
St. Wendel, 66606
Germany
Telephone: (49 6851) 909-0
Fax: (49 6851) 909-600
Web site: http://www.globus.de

Private Company
Incorporated: 1949 as Franz Bruch Lebensmittel-Großhandlung Gesellschaft mit beschränkter Haftung
Employees: 30,000
Sales: EUR 5.7 billion ($7.9 billion) (2009)
NAICS: 452112 Discount Department Stores; 445110 Grocery Stores; 444110 Home Centers; 444220 Nursery and Garden Centers

■ ■ ■

The operator of a chain of self-service department stores, building centers, and electronics specialty stores in Germany, the Czech Republic, Russia, and Luxembourg, Globus SB-Warenhaus Holding GmbH & Co. KG is one of the largest independent retail groups in central Europe. In Germany, where the firm has its main presence, it ranks number nine among the country's largest food retailers.

The company operates 40 Globus self-service department stores, 53 Globus home improvement stores, 27 Hela professional building centers, and nine Alpha-Tecc. electronics specialty stores in Germany. The company's second-largest market is the Czech Republic, where it operates 14 hypermarket shopping centers. In addition, Globus has five locations in and around Moscow in Russia. Roughly half of the company's 30,000 employees work at the Globus self-department stores which account for about 50 percent of the company's total sales. The company is privately owned and managed in fifth generation by the Bruch family.

1828–1913: FROM RETAIL TO WHOLESALE

On April 15, 1828, the merchant Franz Bruch announced in a local newspaper the opening of his food products and colonial goods store, Handlungshaus Franz Bruch, in St. Wendel, a city in the German Saar region. Before he started his own business, Bruch had worked as an employee at a local retail store for more than seven years, and he knew the trade from the inside out. Centrally located in the city center, across the street from the dome, the store in the basement of Bruch's residence thrived. In addition, Bruch delivered his goods to customers in the neighboring villages by horse-drawn carriage.

After the company founder's death in 1865, his son Joseph Adam Bruch took over the store. Registered as Franz-Bruch Lebensmittel-Futtermittel-Großhandlung, a wholesale partnership, he developed the business and expanded his activities to the wholesale trade of food products and animal feed. Bruch's colonial goods store offered a broad selection of such everyday items as salt, flour, and cooking oil, as well as specialties such as Swiss cheese and lard from the United States, deli items, and spirits.

COMPANY PERSPECTIVES

■

For more than two centuries Globus has competed successfully in the most diverse trade distribution formats. The willingness to adapt the enterprise to permanently changing needs, the continuous commitment to customers as well as employees, who deal on their own responsibility: these success factors run like a red thread through the company's history. They have made Globus into what it is today: one of the few large, independent family-owned companies that tackles things differently than its competitors. And it succeeds constantly anew in satisfying the changing taste of customers.

When the house on St. Wendel's marketplace proved too small for the growing wholesale operation, Bruch acquired a larger property from the city and built a large warehouse as well as stables for the horses there in 1904. In addition to his retail and wholesale activities, Joseph Adam Bruch also lent money to credit seekers during this time, accumulating significant wealth from his enterprise. After he died in 1905, his wife carried on the retail store for several years while the couple's only remaining son, Joseph Karl Bruch, inherited the wholesale business.

CONTINUOUS GROWTH UNTIL WORLD WAR I

Before taking over the business, Joseph Karl Bruch had been educated in Switzerland and had worked in a German wholesale company and in an oil import firm in the Netherlands. Bruch set about transforming the business into a thriving wholesale operation.

The company's salesmen traveled to their customers by bicycle or by train, and the orders they brought in were filled within two days. The first delivery truck was purchased in 1911 and allowed the company to reach additional customers. By that time, Bruch's enterprise was grossing almost one million reichsmarks per year and employed a staff of 14. When World War I broke out, Burch's wife and mother carried on the business while he served in the military.

The Treaty of Versailles in 1918 gave the victorious French hegemony over the Saar. With the new border going right through St. Wendel County, the company lost about one-third of its customers, who remained in German territory while Joseph Bruch's company came under French control. To retain at least some of his clientele beyond the border, Bruch together with three other wholesalers founded Vereinigte Lebensmittel Großhandlung, the united food wholesalers, a distribution company based in the German part of the Saar, in 1920.

SEPARATION, INFLATION, RECOVERY, AND WORLD WAR II

By the early 1920s the company's workforce had grown to 30. From 1920 on, trade between the French dominated Saar and Germany was toll-free until the Saar was integrated into the French customs zone in 1925. Although the introduction of the franc as the dominating currency saved Bruch's enterprise from the devastating effects of the galloping inflation in Germany, all inventory had to be reevaluated and prices recalculated. In the mid-1920s, however, the franc began to weaken as well, losing about 30 percent of its value, and Franz Bruch's prices had to be adjusted on a regular basis.

In the early 1930s the company's product range had outgrown its warehouse capacity. The number of brand name products was on the rise, as was the number of product choices for each variety. For example, there were 10 different kinds of sugar for sale. Consequently, part of the company's inventory was stored in rented spaces. On January 13, 1935, the population of the Saar voted in a referendum for rejoining Germany. With the reintegration into the German Reich in the same year, again, all prices and the company's balance sheet had to be reevaluated. Contacts to Franz Bruch's former suppliers were reactivated and, after persistent efforts by Joseph Bruch, many of the old German customers were won back as well.

Driven by rising incomes resulting from the Nazi government's infrastructure and rearmament programs, the company was able to significantly expand its warehouse capacity and to add more vehicles to its fleet. The beginning of World War II in 1939, however, suddenly ended the short recovery period in the second half of the decade in which sales jumped from roughly two million reichsmark in 1936 to more than three million in 1939.

As more and more products once again became scarce, due to import stoppages and government control, and as an increasing number of Franz Bruch's employees served in the military, less qualified personnel were hired to carry on the business. Moreover, the shortage of gasoline required the company to equip its delivery trucks with wood-based gas generators. As the war returned to Germany in the 1940s, the company's

KEY DATES
■

1828: Food products and colonial goods store Handlungshaus Franz Bruch is founded.

1905: Joseph Karl Bruch takes over the business and transforms it into a wholesale company.

1949: Brothers Walter and Franz Josef Bruch become CEOs.

1966: The first large self-service department retail store is opened in Homburg-Einöd.

1970: The retail company Globus Handelshof St. Wendel is founded.

1980: Walter Bruch's son Thomas Bruch becomes an executive director.

1986: The first stand-alone Globus building center is opened.

1994: The company establishes the first Alpha Tecc. electronics specialty store.

2006: The first Hyperglobus market in Russia is opened near Moscow.

premises, which were located directly next to the railway, were frequently targeted in bombings, but were not as badly damaged as other businesses.

In March 1945 U.S.-Allied troops confiscated several of the company's vehicles, but gave way to the French Allied forces four months later. Following a car accident in December 1945, Joseph Bruch was unable to run the business, and his sons Walter and Franz Josef, who had just returned from the battlefield, took over company management. Once again, the French occupied the Saar in 1946 and integrated it into their country, with all the known problems for the wholesale firm Franz Bruch. Joseph Bruch died three years later, and his sons jointly took over the company.

EMBRACING SELF-SERVICE AFTER 1950

The emergence of the self-service concept in the 1950s revolutionized the retail trade in the following decades. Eager to try their luck with the new trend, the Bruch brothers, both of whom had received an education in commerce and had worked at other wholesale companies, remodeled the old company headquarters into a self-service food store which was named A. Backhaus KG to avoid the association with their wholesale business. It opened in December 1953. However, this venture as well as several other loss-producing retail store experiments launched over the next 10 years were shut down again after a short time.

After the Saar was reintegrated into Germany in the late 1950s, another new concept changed the retail landscape as several food retail cooperatives established a national network of "free store chains." The chains combined their purchasing power and were thereby able to buy and sell their goods at comparatively lower prices. In addition, they rewarded their members with end-of-year refunds depending on the volume of their purchases.

To keep up with the competition, the Bruchs and other independent regional wholesalers established the joint association Fachring, which cooperated in purchasing, advertising, and distribution. Franz Bruch expanded its product range to include fresh produce and built a new and much larger warehouse and store at the outskirts of St. Wendel in 1962. A cash-and-carry market (C & C) for retail customers and small business owners, a fresh fruit and vegetable market, a gas station, and a cafeteria were opened in the same year.

1965–78: FROM WHOLESALE BACK TO RETAIL

In addition to the usual selection of food items, Bruch's C & C market carried a much expanded selection of nonfood items, including household goods, textiles, electric supplies, and toys. Following the success of a joint promotion with a local nearby furniture store, wherein C & C customers received rebate cards for their furniture shopping, the furniture store owner, Werner Martin, visited the C & C store to thank the store manager. By coincidence, Walter Bruch joined the conversation, and the two men soon began discussing a new retail store format that each had noticed, Martin at Ikea in Sweden and Bruch in the United States: the large-area self-service discount department store. The two entrepreneurs decided to start a similar venture. In 1965 the new C & C market was opened in Homburg-Einöd.

With a focus on food and fresh produce, some of which, including baked goods and fresh meat products, were prepared right there at the market, the Globus stores also carried a growing range of nonfood products, including clothing and shoes. The store became so popular that it sometimes had to be shut down because it became too crowded. Three years after the opening of the first self-service department retail store in Homburg-Einöd in 1966, two more stores were opened in the Saar region, followed by a fourth outlet in 1970. They were the first stores that carried the Globus brand name, which Joseph Bruch had registered in the 1930s. In the same year the Globus logo, the word *Globus* within a stylized globe, was introduced.

Franz Bruch's wholesale business, on the other hand, stagnated in the second half of the 1960s. Consequently, the Bruchs made the strategic decision to give up wholesale and focus solely on the new retail stores. Franz Bruch's former customers, retailers themselves, were invited to become silent partners in the newly founded Globus Handelshof St. Wendel GmbH & Co. KG, established in 1970, or to accept employment at one of the new stores. After the wholesale operation was shut down, the Franz Bruch business became a shareholder in Globus Handelshof.

DIVERSIFICATION AND COOPERATION AFTER 1980

In 1978 Walter Bruch's son, Thomas Bruch, joined the company. When he took over his father's shares in the business and the executive management position two years later, the number of Globus superstores had grown to 11. Franz Josef Bruch retired from company management in 1983. Thomas Bruch continued his father's and uncle's work, but also launched new ventures. The successful self-service department store format was copied at a fast pace, with new outlets opening in many southwestern German cities. After the fall of the Berlin Wall in 1989, the company immediately began to expand its presence into the new east German states where the first Globus superstore was opened in 1992, followed by additional 12 outlets in later years.

At the same time, Globus ventured into new retail formats. Until the mid-1980s the company's department stores carried home improvement products as well. However, in 1986 the company opened its first stand-alone Globus home improvement center in Zweibrücken, which, with an area of over 10,000 square meters, was Germany's largest building center. After two more such centers proved successful in the late 1980s, the company continued to open as many as eight new home improvement stores per year in the early to mid-1990s.

In 1994 Globus again entered a new market segment when it opened the first Alpha-Tecc.-Elektrofachmarkt, a large electronics specialty store, in Losheim, Saar. Eight additional Alpha-Tecc. stores were set up in Germany in the following years. However, it took many years of refining the concept and organization to make them profitable. The company's expansion into new markets resulted in substantial growth with two-digit growth rates during the late 1980s to mid-1990s.

Nevertheless, the increasing competition between German retailers put continuous pressure on prices, with the consequence of shrinking profit margins. Around the turn of the 21st century, Globus slipped into the red, according to *Lebensmittel Zeitung* on December 20, 2002. To cut costs on the purchasing side, Globus entered a purchasing alliance with Edeka, one of Germany's largest retail groups, which became effective in 2003. Edeka took over a 10 percent stake in Globus as a silent partner while Thomas Bruch held a stake in Edeka subsidiary AVA, the operator of Marktkauf self-service department stores.

NATIONAL AND INTERNATIONAL EXPANSION

The opening of the first so-called hypermarket in Brno in the Czech Republic in 1996 marked the company's first step toward international expansion. In the following years Globus set up 13 additional hypermarkets with integrated home improvement stores in the Czech Republic. In 2006 the first Hyperglobus market opened its doors in Scholkovo near Moscow in Russia. Four more Hyperglobus superstores were added in the greater Moscow region within three years. At the end of the decade, the company announced that its Russian stores had broken even financially. However, due to the weakening Russian ruble late in the decade, and because of the high investment required, Globus put further expansion plans in the country on hold.

In 2007 Globus acquired 30 Hela home improvement stores, 28 in Germany and 2 in Luxembourg, from competitor Distributa. However, the stores were struggling with decreasing sales and, in 2009, were still producing losses. In the same year the company took over 15 self-service department stores with 3,000 employees and about EUR 435 million in annual sales in western and southwestern Germany from competitor Real SB-Warenhaus GmbH and started transforming them into Globus stores.

In Germany, the company was planning to open two additional Globus self-service department stores in Bavaria. In the Czech Republic, Globus installed the group's first self-service checkout boots at a hypermarket in Prague, where customers scanned their merchandise and paid for it without the assistance of a cashier. To secure the company's independence, all major shareholdings in Globus were transferred to the nonprofit foundation Globus-Stiftung and to the family trust Familie-Bruch-Stiftung, in 2005. A result of the company's employee ownership program, many Globus employees also owned a stake in the company. To successfully compete in the increasingly consolidating German retail market, Globus was focusing on providing outstanding customer service and on addressing special consumer needs such as health-oriented products and services.

Evelyn Hauser

PRINCIPAL SUBSIDIARIES

Globus Holding GmbH & Co. KG; Globus Fachmärkte GmbH & Co. KG; Globus Logistik GmbH & Co. KG; Alpha-Tecc. Elektrofachmärkte GmbH & Co. KG.

PRINCIPAL COMPETITORS

Aldi Group; Edeka Group; Hellweg Die Profi-Baumärkte GmbH & Co. KG; Hornbach Holding AG; Lidl Stiftung & Co. KG; Metro AG; Rewe Group; Tengelmann Warenhandelsgesellschaft KG.

FURTHER READING

Bruch, Franz Josef. *Die Geschichte der Firma Franz Bruch St. Wendel.* St. Wendel, Germany: SWD St. Wendeler Druckerei und Verlag, 1995.

Bruch, Thomas, ed. *Unser Weg: Tradition, Innovation, Zukunft.* St. Wendel, Germany: Globus Holding, 2009.

"Glückwunsch … Thomas Bruch." *Lebensmittel Zeitung*, April 23, 2010, p. 77.

Wessel, Andrea. "Globus weiter krisenfest." *Lebensmittel Zeitung*, March 5, 2010, p. 10.

———. "Währungsverluste bremsen Globus." *Lebensmittel Zeitung*, August 28, 2009, p.4.

Golfsmith International Holdings, Inc.

11000 North IH-35
Austin, Texas 78753
U.S.A.
Telephone: (512) 837-8810
Toll Free: (800) 813-6897
Web site: http://www.golfsmith.com

Public Company
Incorporated: 1966 as Custom Golf Clubs Inc.
Employees: 1,599
Sales: $338 million (2009)
Stock Exchanges: NASDAQ
Ticker Symbol: GOLF
NAICS: 451111 Sporting Goods Stores

■ ■ ■

Golfsmith International Holdings, Inc., is an Austin, Texas-based retailer of golf and tennis equipment, apparel, and accessories. Although the company added tennis products in 2005, its core business remains golf. The company maintains more than 70 superstores in about 20 states and also sells its wares through catalogs and an Internet site. Golfsmith provides custom fitting and repair services for clubs (and rackets), instructs golfers on the process of assembling their own clubs, and operates the Harvey Penick Golf Academy in Austin as well as GolfTec Learning Centers in most of its stores.

In addition to selling major branded golf clubs, Golfsmith offers club components under several proprietary labels, including Clubmaker, Golfsmith, J.G. Hickory, Killer Bee, Profinity, Snake Eyes, and Zevo.

Additionally, the company caters to golfers and tennis players by selling tickets to major events; books tee times for hundreds of golf courses across the United States; and arranges for golfing vacations. Golfsmith also offers Hole-in-One insurance, providing sponsors of golf events with a complete program that offers prizes for hole-in-one contests. A NASDAQ-listed company, Golfsmith maintains subsidiaries in Canada and Europe.

ORIGINS: 1966

Golfsmith was founded by Texas native Carl Paul and his wife Barbara. A civil engineer by training, Carl Paul was working in New York City for the Environmental Protection Agency (EPA) in the mid-1960s when, at the age of 27, he was introduced to the game of golf by a neighbor. Although Paul played his first game with a set of borrowed women's clubs, he enjoyed the experience so much that later in the evening he paid $20 for a set of discount store clubs. He became a regular at driving ranges and a few weeks later invested in brand-name clubs.

Paul's skills did not improve at the pace he expected, however. Unwilling to accept complete blame for his errant shots, he used his skills as an engineer to begin making alterations to his clubs, such as filing the club face, changing the position of the weight, and shaving the clubhead to make it more aerodynamic. In effect, he was becoming a self-taught golf club repairman and maker of customized equipment.

Paul and his wife had always wanted to start their own business, and one day he suggested that they move their baby into their room in their two-bedroom apart-

COMPANY PERSPECTIVES

The company's mission is to establish Golfsmith as the premier golf and tennis retailer in the country providing exceptional guest services and solutions.

ment in order to free up space for a golf business. In 1966 Paul and his wife thus converted their Plainfield, New Jersey, apartment into a golf club repair shop. It was clearly a makeshift affair, more a labor of love than a business. Paul continued to hold his job with the EPA, leaving the management of the company to his wife during the day. She took the orders that he filled at night and on weekends.

The company's first tool, an electric drill, was acquired by trading in the Green Stamp books collected by Barbara Paul. Nevertheless, the business took hold, leading the Pauls to move to a house, where an assembly workshop was set up in the basement and shafts and clubheads were stored in the attic. The company was incorporated as Custom Golf Clubs Inc. and did business under the Golfsmith name.

Soon after he went into business, Paul began to design and produce golf clubheads, followed by other components, which he sold to golf repair shops to create custom-fitted clubs. The operation became more sophisticated over time, as Carl Paul made use of his mechanical talents to design machinery specifically to produce wooden clubheads. For iron clubheads, he relied on a forging company that used Paul's designs and specifications.

MOVE TO TEXAS: 1973

Sales reached $365,000 by 1973 and the Pauls began looking for a more suitable location for the business. After considering a move to Florida, the couple decided to return to his native Texas, settling on Austin because of its mild weather and central location, essentially equally distant from each coast. There in 1973 a 6,000-square-foot former army barracks was converted to provide the company with its first showroom and retail outlet. His brother Frank, a trained civil engineer working for the Army Corps of Engineers, as well as an accomplished amateur golfer, joined Carl in the business.

The Pauls grew Golfsmith into a viable concern despite their lack of commercial experience. They were so ill-prepared to do business, Carl Paul recalled in a 1992 interview with *Austin Business Journal*, that they

were not sure how to create an invoice: "We had no financial background, we had no knowledge of just a lot of common sense type of things." What they had was a clearly defined, and up to that point neglected, niche, providing components for players who wanted custom-fitted clubs rather than the standardized fare offered by the major manufacturers.

To expand the business further, the Paul brothers compiled a two-page mailing list using the Yellow Pages telephone directories from major cities to locate golf-related businesses. The list was then used in 1975 for the mailing of the first Golfsmith Store accessory catalog. It was a rudimentary affair, just two pages typed by Barbara Paul that featured hand-drawn illustrations by her husband. The catalog proved highly successful, however. Golfsmith topped $1 million in sales in 1976.

GOLF BOOM DRIVES BUSINESS

The catalog expanded steadily, as did revenues for Golfsmith. To spur further growth the company in 1980 launched the Golf Clubmakers Association, which provided support to the growing ranks of custom clubmakers. They, along with repair shops and hobbyists, were major purchasers of Golfsmith components. Golfsmith was then established well enough to take advantage of an international golf boom during the 1980s that spurred rapid growth for the company, which expanded its facilities to 90,000 square feet in 1990. Annual sales reached $32 million, 90 percent of which came from catalog sales, and continued to increase at an accelerated rate.

Some bureaucratic difficulties in obtaining building permits to expand its facilities prompted Golfsmith to consider constructing a new and larger manufacturing facility in Round Rock, Texas, in the early 1990s. The city of Austin was eager to retain the company and the hundreds of jobs it provided, and in June 1991 offered a package of incentives valued at nearly $340,000. With these concessions in hand, Golfsmith agreed to stay in Austin, acquired additional land, and in the spring of 1992 broke ground on a two-phase $12 million expansion of its facilities. Once completed, Golfsmith's 40-acre campus included a 200,000-square-foot manufacturing facility, a 240,000-square-foot shipping and distribution center, administrative offices, a 30,000-square-foot Golfsmith superstore, and a practice range.

Later in 1992, Golfsmith established a European division, opening an office in Cambridgeshire in the United Kingdom. Sales reached an estimated $60 million in 1992. The following year Golfsmith branched out further with the opening of the Harvey Penick Golf Academy, which employed the principles taught by famed golf swing instructor, Harvey Penick.

```
┌─────────────────────────────────────────┐
│                                          │
│              KEY DATES                   │
│         ────────────■────────────        │
│                                          │
│   1966:  Carl Paul begins offering golf  │
│          club repair services at his     │
│          New Jersey home.                │
│   1973:  Golfsmith moves to Austin,      │
│          Texas.                          │
│   1975:  Catalog operations launched.    │
│   2002:  First Atlantic Capital acquires │
│          controlling interest.           │
│   2006:  Company is taken public.        │
│                                          │
└─────────────────────────────────────────┘
```

HOUSTON STORE OPENS: 1995

Golfsmith had three retail locations in Austin, but it was not until 1995 that the company expanded to a new market. In that year it opened a new 17,000-square-foot Golfsmith store in Houston. Later in 1995 a store opened in Dallas and the first out-of-state store opened in Denver. Over the next five years another two-dozen stores opened across the country, some of them in the 25,000- to 30,000-square-foot range. This superstore approach worked well for a while, helping to drive sales to $257 million in 1998. That year, however, the golf industry experienced a slump that prompted the company to reconsider its "larger-is-better" strategy. Subsequent stores would make use of a smaller, more efficient footprint.

Despite difficult conditions in the late 1990s, Golfsmith fared well. The company had considered going public and reincorporated in Delaware in 1998, but then shelved its plan to make an initial public offering of stock. Instead, the company raised $30 million in a private placement of stock that supported further growth. Not only was the cash used to open another 10 stores by the end of the decade, it allowed Golfsmith to take advantage of lean times to achieve growth through external means. In late 1998 Golfsmith paid $11.3 million to acquire clubmakers Lynx Golf Inc., Snake Eyes Golf Club Inc., and Black Rock Golf Corp., maker of Killer Bee golf clubs.

Another major development in the final months of 1998 was the launch of an online business. Golfsmith, unlike other golf-related Internet retail operations, already had the necessary brick-and-mortar infrastructure in place, as well as an established brand in the marketplace. Less than a year later, Golfsmith's Internet sales exceeded those achieved by any single Golfsmith retail outlet, including the flagship site. Moreover, the company's catalog operation, which mailed 33 million catalogs a year and had been the backbone of the business for a quarter-century, then fed customers to the Internet site.

MAJORITY INTEREST SOLD: 2002

Annual sales climbed to about $285 million by the end of the 1990s. The golf retail industry experienced another slump at the dawn of the new century, leading to a dip in sales to $250 million by 2002. The Pauls had continued to consider the possibility of taking Golfsmith public, but instead decided to sell a controlling stake in the company. After reviewing some possible financial partners, they agreed in October 2002 to sell a majority interest to First Atlantic Capital for about $120 million.

Although Carl Paul remained a board member, he turned over operational control to a new chief executive, Jim Thompson, who soon put his own stamp on the company. In 2003 Golfsmith expanded into tennis for the first time with the acquisition of San Francisco-based Don Sherwood Golf and Tennis World, a six-store Bay Area chain. The Golfsmith Internet site also began carrying tennis merchandise. A year later the company's retail locations installed in-store kiosks to make all of the company's golf and tennis merchandise available to local shoppers. In 2005 Golfsmith furthered its commitment to tennis by initiating an effort to add tennis merchandise to 60 percent of its Golfsmith locations, which would be rebranded Golfsmith Golf & Tennis stores.

In 2006 the company was taken public as Golfsmith International Holdings Inc. First Atlantic Capital had hoped the stock offering would bring $96 million, but market conditions were poor and the firm had to settle for $69 million. After posting sales of $388.2 million in fiscal 2007, Golfsmith faced deteriorating economic conditions that led to a decline in sales to $378.8 million in fiscal 2008 and prompted the company to slow its new store program. Although sales continued to slide, dipping to $338 million the following year, the company instituted new growth-oriented initiatives that bode well for the future when better economic conditions returned.

The company opened the first of its Golfsmith Xtreme stores, as large as 40,000 square feet in size, which included larger hitting bays than previous stores offered, as well as interactive features for both golfers and tennis players. Many of the Golfsmith retail locations also added GolfTec Learning Centers to provide precision club fitting and PGA of America-certified golf instruction. As a result, Golfsmith was well prepared for ongoing growth.

Ed Dinger

PRINCIPAL SUBSIDIARIES

Golfsmith Canada, LLC; Golfsmith Europe LLC.

PRINCIPAL COMPETITORS

Bridgestone Golf, Inc.; Edwin Watts Golf, LLC; Golf Galaxy, Inc.

FURTHER READING

Alm, Richard. "Golfsmith Remains Profitable with New Business Approach." *Dallas Morning News,* January 26, 2000, p. 1D.

Breyer, R. Michelle. "Green and Acres." *Austin American-Statesman,* July 21, 1996, p. E1.

———. "N.Y. Firm Buys Majority Stake in Golfsmith." *Austin American-Statesman,* October 17, 2002.

McCann, Bill. "Golfsmith to Stay in Austin." *Austin Business Journal,* July 22, 1991, p. 1.

"One Round of Golf Led Man into $120 Million Business." *Fort Worth Star-Telegram,* September 15, 1996, p. 1.

Pletz, John. "On the Ball." *Austin American-Statesman,* January 16, 2000, p. J1.

Smith, Amy. "Carl Paul Keeps Golfsmith in the Green." *Austin Business Journal,* October 19, 1992, p. 3.

Windle, Rickie. "Golfsmith International: Austin Clubmaker Leads the Field." *Austin Business Journal,* March 30, 1992, p. S4.

The Hain Celestial Group, Inc.

58 South Service Road
Melville, New York 11747-2342
U.S.A.
Telephone: (631) 730-2200
Toll Free: (800) 434-HAIN
Web site: http://www.hain-celestial.com

Public Company
Incorporated: 1926 as Hain Pure Foods Co.
Employees: 2,059
Sales: $917.34 million (2010)
Stock Exchanges: NASDAQ
Ticker Symbol: HAIN
NAICS: 311920 Coffee and Tea Manufacturing; 311411 Frozen Fruit, Juice, and Vegetable Manufacturing; 311412 Frozen Specialty Food Manufacturing; 311423 Dried and Dehydrated Food Manufacturing; 311812 Commercial Bakeries; 311821 Cookie and Cracker Manufacturing; 311823 Dry Pasta Manufacturing; 311830 Tortilla Manufacturing; 311919 Other Snack Food Manufacturing; 311999 All Other Miscellaneous Food Manufacturing

∎∎∎

The Hain Celestial Group, Inc., manufactures, markets, distributes and sells natural, organic, medically directed (sugar-free and low-salt), snack, and weight management food products, most of which are at the top in their categories. Among the company's many well-known brands are: Arrowhead Mills (grains), DeBoles (pasta), Estee (diabetic foods), Hain Pure Foods (rice cakes and cooking oils), Health Valley (natural soups, snacks, chili, cereal, and baked goods), Kineret (frozen kosher foods), Westsoy (soy-based drinks), Terra Chips (vegetable snacks), and most notably, Celestial Seasonings (specialty teas). The company branched into personal care products with the acquisition of a number of brands beginning in 2004. It also sells Martha Stewart-branded household cleaning solutions under license.

A little more than half of the company's revenues are derived from products manufactured at independent co-packers. The company has ten of its own plants in North America and five in Europe. Hain Celestial's products are distributed in more than 50 countries. In Europe, the company produces fresh prepared foods at facilities in England and Belgium.

FROM CARROTS TO OILS AND BEYOND: 1926–94

Hain Pure Food Company was founded in 1926 in Stockton, California, by Harold Hain, who was originally interested in marketing carrot juice. The company grew well beyond its humble beverage beginnings to become one of North America's most prominent natural food businesses, known for selling a range of foods that are minimally processed, mostly or completely free of artificial ingredients, preservatives, and other non-naturally-occurring chemicals, and are as near to their whole natural state as possible. In 1955 the company introduced its Hollywood line of vegetable cooking oils. With the debut of Hain Yogurt Chips in the early 1970s, Hain began developing diet and health snacks. By 1983 the company was offering more than

300 natural and health food items. The company's products found their place all over: in supermarkets, health food stores, and specialty shops throughout the United States and abroad in countries such as Austria, England, Germany, and Japan.

The small but promising natural food company was bought and sold through many larger companies throughout the 1980s and into the early 1990s before it could develop and grow significantly. Hain Pure Food was acquired by Ogden Corp. in 1981 and was again sold in 1986 to IC Industries Inc., which assigned Hain Pure Food to its Pet, Inc., specialty foods subsidiary. In 1991 the former IC Industries, which had become Whitman Corp., spun off Pet, which became an independent company. Pet sold Hain in 1993 to focus on its core businesses. The buyer, in April 1994, was Kineret Acquisition Corp., a specialty-foods company based in Jericho, New York, that paid $22 million in cash and stock for the operation.

At last, Hain's latest parent company would prove to be loyal, under the steady leadership of Irwin Simon, a former career executive in the food industry whose mission was to buy specialty food companies that were mismanaged or not realizing their potential, including those selling natural, low-fat, or ethnic foods. At this time, Hain was marketing even more natural food products, including the Hollywood line of specialty cooking oils, carrot juice, mayonnaise, and margarine, and had sales of about $50 million a year.

FLOURISHING UNDER STRONG LEADERSHIP: 1994–97

The Hain acquisition put Kineret in a leading position in the natural food industry. Simon immediately began to focus on one of Hain's most successful product lines, its all-natural rice cakes, which accounted for about 40 percent of Hain's sales. Simon repackaged the line in brightly colored, resealable cardboard cartons, introduced rice cake snack bars, and marketed Mini Munchies, a new line of bite-size rice cakes in several flavors, including strawberry cheesecake. Although Quaker Oats dominated this market, Simon did not let the food giant faze him. "People always ask me, 'Doesn't Quaker frighten you?'" he told a *Forbes* reporter in 1996, adding "But every time I see Quaker ads on TV I just shout, 'Yeah!' They're growing the category."

Simon moved his company to Uniondale in August 1994 and changed its name to Hain Food Group four months later. In fiscal 1994, the company reported a loss of $502,000 on sales of $15 million. However, it also came up with 24 new products to market. With the completion of the Hain acquisition, revenues rose to $58.1 million in fiscal 1995. The company moved into the black that year, with $2.4 million in net income. Hain raised $7.6 million in 1994 from the conversion of warrants to common stock in connection with the company's initial public offering. The funds were used to retire a $7.9 million loan.

In late 1995 Hain Food Group purchased Estee Corp., a deficit-ridden producer of sugar-free and low-sodium products for persons on medically directed diets, including diabetics and other health-conscious consumers, for $11.3 million. Simon immediately closed the company's New Jersey plant, dismissing 180 employees and contracting production to a Canadian firm. Hain's acquisitions continued in 1996, when Simon purchased Growing Healthy Inc., a fledgling baby food company, and Harry's Premium Snacks, a potato chip and pretzel maker.

In March 1997, Hain reached an agreement to manufacture, market, and sell soups, snacks, and other food products of Weight Watchers Gourmet Food Co., a subsidiary of H.J. Heinz Co., with the products to continue to be sold under the Weight Watchers name. Under the five-year agreement, Weight Watchers would receive royalties and a share of the profits. This transaction made Hain, according to one of its executives, the nation's leading marketer of foods sold to dieters and other consumers with special medical needs.

Hain Food Group's next major acquisition, in October 1997, was that of soy milk manufacturer Westbrae Natural, Inc. The purchase allowed Hain to strengthen its presence in natural food stores, where Westbrae averaged 250 to 300 stock-keeping units (SKUs). Following the transaction, Hain's product line reached 1,000 SKUs spanning 13 brand lines. Other 1997 acquisitions included Alba Foods, a Heinz line of dry milk products, and Boston Popcorn Co., a snack food firm.

```
┌─────────────────────────────────────────────┐
│                                               │
│               KEY DATES                       │
│                    ■                          │
│  ─────────────────────────────────────────    │
│  1926:  Hain Pure Food Company is founded.    │
│  1955:  Company introduces Hollywood vegetable│
│         oils.                                 │
│  1994:  Hain is acquired by Kineret Acquisition│
│         Corp.                                 │
│  1998:  Company begins alliance with Heinz.   │
│  2000:  Company acquires Celestial Seasonings and│
│         becomes The Hain Celestial Group.     │
│  2004:  Acquisition of Jason brand brings company│
│         into personal-care products market.   │
│  2008:  Revenues exceed $1 billion.           │
│                                               │
└─────────────────────────────────────────────┘
```

GOING PUBLIC AND MATURING: 1997–99

Hain Food Group made a new public offering of 2.5 million shares of common stock at $9 a share in December 1997. The proceeds of about $21 million were used to pay down debt. In April 1998, Hain Food Group announced that it had agreed to acquire a group of four natural foods businesses: Arrowhead Mills Inc., DeBoles Nutritional Foods Inc., Dana Alexander Inc., and Garden of Eatin' Inc. The acquisition was completed in July 1998.

In addition to its Hain and Westbrae lines of natural food products, Hain Food Group's products, in mid-1998, consisted of the Hollywood Foods line, the Estee and Featherweight lines of sugar-free and low-sodium products, kosher frozen foods under the Kineret and Kosherific labels, the licensed Weight Watchers products, and about 40 snack food items under the Boston Popcorn and Harry's Original names. The additions from the July 1998 acquisitions consisted of 360 ready-to-eat grains, nut butters, and nutritional oils produced by Arrowhead Mills and DeBoles, about 48 natural food vegetable chip items by Terra Chips, and a variety of tortilla chip products from Garden of Eatin'. Nondairy drinks accounted for about 19 percent of Hain's fiscal 1998 net sales.

Also by June 1998, Hain had entered into a license agreement with food giant Heinz to market and sell its Earth's Best baby food products to natural food stores. The venture did so well that, by the end of 1999, Hain had purchased the trademarks for the product line and secured the option to grow the product line itself. That same year, Heinz moved to tap into the growing natural foods market, by making a $100 million investment in Hain, which represented a 19.5 percent stake. During this fruitful time with Heinz, Hain continued to make strategic acquisitions and join company with another food giant: In December, 1998, Hain bought Nile Spice soup and meal cup from The Quaker Oats Company, and, in May 1999, Hain acquired NNG (Natural Nutrition Group, Inc.), an organic food manufacturer that marketed its products under the Health Valley, Breadshop's, and Sahara brands. Sales for fiscal 1998 grew 97.5 percent, as the company continued to flourish.

MERGING WITH CELESTIAL SEASONINGS

In May 2000 Hain acquired Celestial Seasonings, the largest manufacturer and marketer of herbal teas in the United States, which had introduced roughly 50 tea varieties throughout the world. Chiefly responsible for creating the herbal tea industry in the United States, Celestial Seasonings had been founded by Mo Siegel and Wyck Hay, who introduced the country's consumers to colorfully packaged, decaffeinated herbal teas that offered "soothing teas for a nervous world."

During the mid-1990s, Celestial Seasonings controlled an estimated 51 percent of the herbal tea market. By the time of the acquisition by Hain, Celestial Seasonings had reached $109.8 million in revenue for 1999. Together, Hain and Celestial Seasonings became the largest natural foods company in the United States, The Hain Celestial Group. In fiscal 2000, sales reached $404 million, and promised to be even greater in the future with Celestial Seasonings in the mix.

In 2001 Hain Celestial sought to grow its international markets by engaging in key acquisitions and ventures, to help grow its brand presence and distributions channels abroad. It bought Netherlands-based Fruit Chips, maker of Gaston's fruit, vegetable, and potato chips, and then changed its name to Terra Chips to grow the Terra brand in Europe. In June of that same year, the company acquired Vancouver, Canada-based Yves Veggie Cuisine, Inc., a manufacturer and distributor of meat-and cheese-alternative food products made with soy protein. Hain Celestial could take advantage of the Canadian company's extensive and established infrastructure, sales force, and distribution network. Soon after that acquisition, Hain Celestial announced a joint venture with Grupo Siro, Spain's largest snack company, to further expand its distribution channels in Europe.

NEW HQ IN 2002

In 2002 Hain Celestial moved to a larger headquarters on Long Island. It also built a 65,000-square-foot plant in Moonachie, New Jersey, specifically designed to produce Terra Chips, whose vacuum frying process required specialized proprietary equipment.

The natural foods industry was growing quickly amid concerns about the obesity epidemic in the United States. Mainstream marketers such as Frito-Lay and Gerber were offering new formulations of their established mass market products, while some such as Kellogg and Dean Foods were snapping up such natural foods brands as Kashi cereal and Silk soy milk, respectively.

Hain Celestial had 1,400 employees; half of its production was handled by independent co-packers. The group had total revenues of nearly $500 million and had a long-term goal of doubling that. The company offered 600 products and continued to develop dozens more every year. The group added the lower priced Hain Pure Snax line in October 2002 for more mainstream appeal.

The group was expanding on several fronts. In 2002 it acquired Belgium's Lima NV for $20 million. Lima included Biomarché, a distributor of organic produce and salads; the two businesses had combined annual sales of about $20 million. Grains Noirs NV, a maker of prepared food such as sandwiches, was acquired in May 2003.

Hain Celestial bought Imagine Foods, Inc., in February 2003, which added leading Rice Dream and Soy Dream brands of nondairy beverages. In June 2003 it acquired ACIRCA, a maker of juice beverages under the Walnut Acres Certified Organic and Mountain Sun brands that had been established in 1946. It had annual sales of about $20 million.

In 2004 the company introduced its CarbFit sub-brand to designate low-carbohydrate versions of its various products. Expanding its market base, it brought out a line of fortified fruit juices for toddlers. The company acquired natural-diapers distributor TenderCare International in December 2007 for $3.4 million.

Hain Celestial benefited from the rising popularity of natural foods retailers such as Whole Foods while also increasing distribution into mainstream supermarkets. At the same time, McDonald's was test marketing a sandwich made with Yves veggie burgers.

Hain acquired two more frozen food lines from H.J. Heinz in 2004: Ethnic Gourmet and Rosetto, adding $50 million a year to annual sales. It bought the Linda McCartney brand of vegetarian frozen foods from Heinz in August 2006. A few months later it acquired a 100-year-old British manufacturer, Haldane Foods, from Archer Daniels Midland Company. Haldane had annual revenues of £10 million. The group's revenues were $739 million in the 2005/06 fiscal year.

Hain Celestial added Alba Botanica and Avalon Organics, two of the largest natural care brands, in January 2007, paying North Castle Partners $120 million. The purchase added $40 million to Hain's sales in the fast-growing category, which had totaled $125 million and included such brands as Zia Natural Skincare and Queen Helene. It had bought Jeffrey Light's Jason brand in 2004.

Nut butter brands MaraNatha and SunSpire were acquired from American Capital Strategies Ltd. in March 2008. The two were manufactured at a plant in Ashland, Oregon, and had combined sales of about $40 million a year.

REVENUES REACH $1 BILLION IN 2008

Total group sales exceeded $1 billion in fiscal 2008 and peaked at $1.12 billion in 2009 before falling to $917.34 million in 2010. International revenues accounted for a little more than one-fifth total sales.

The group was losing money in Europe, experiencing a significant setback after Marks and Spencer canceled its sandwiches account. It added Churchill Food Products Ltd. of the United Kingdom in June 2010.

In June 2010 the company acquired World Gourmet Marketing, L.L.C., which sold vegetable and fruit "straws" and other snacks. The next month it bought 3 Greek Gods LLC, a manufacturer of specialty yogurt. It had with annual sales of $10 million in the fastest-growing segment of the yogurt market.

Robert Halasz; Jeffrey L. Covell
Updated, Heidi Wrightsman; Frederick C. Ingram

PRINCIPAL SUBSIDIARIES

Acirca, Inc.; AMI Operating, Inc.; Arrowhead Mills, Inc.; Avalon Holding Corporation; Avalon Natural Products, Inc.; Botalia Pharmaceutical, Inc.; Celestial Beverages, Inc.; Celestial Seasonings, Inc.; Celestial Trading B.V. (Netherlands); Churchill Food Products Ltd. (UK); Daily Bread Ltd. (UK); Dana Alexander, Inc.; De Boles Nutritional Foods, Inc.; ENV Lebensmittel GMBH (Germany); General Therapeutics, Inc.; Grains Noirs SA (Belgium); HC Holding BVBA (Belgium); Hain-Celestial Canada, ULC; Hain Celestial Europe B.V. (Netherlands); Hain Celestial UK Ltd.; Hain Europe NV (Belgium); Hain Frozen Foods UK Ltd.; Hain Gourmet, Inc.; Hain Holdings UK Ltd.; Hain Pure Food Co., Inc.; Hain Refrigerated Foods Inc.; Hain Yves, Inc.; Health Valley Company; Jason

Natural Products, Inc.; Kineret Foods Corporation; Lima S.A.R.L. (France); Lima SA/NV (Belgium); Little Bear Organic Foods; Natumi AG (Germany); Natural Nutrition Group, Inc.; nSpired Holdings, Inc.; nSpired Natural Foods, Inc.; Queen Personal Care, Inc.; Sleep Right, Inc.; Spectrum Organic Products, LLC; Tender-Care International, Inc.; Terra Chips, B.V. (Netherlands); W.S.L. NV (Belgium); Westbrae Natural Foods, Inc.; Westbrae Natural, Inc.; Yves Fine Foods Inc.; Zia Cosmetics, Inc.

PRINCIPAL DIVISIONS

Celestial Seasonings; Grocery, Snacks, Refrigerated and Personal Care; Hain Celestial Canada; Hain Celestial Europe; Hain Celestial United Kingdom.

PRINCIPAL COMPETITORS

The B. Manischewitz Company; Campbell Soup Company; ConAgra Foods, Inc.; Dean Foods Company; General Mills, Inc.; Kellogg Company; PepsiCo, Inc.; Unilever PLC.

FURTHER READING

Ain, Stewart. "A Dynamo in the Food Marketing Arena." *New York Times*, April 12, 1998, Sec. 14 (*Long Island Weekly*), p. 2.

Anderson, Duncan Maxwell. "Free at Last." *Success*, July/August 1995, p. 14.

Dwyer, Steve. "Hain's 'Natural' High." *Prepared Foods*, April 1998, pp. 12–13, 15–16.

Edgar, Michelle. "Hain Celestial's Natural Growth." *WWD*, March 2, 2007, p. 13.

Eisenberg, Daniel. "Can Granola Grow Up? Irwin Simon Has Built Hain Celestial into an Organic-Foods Giant." *Time*, January 24, 2005, p. B17.

"Hain Celestial Group Enjoys Record Year." *Nutraceuticals International*, September 1, 2006.

"The Hain Celestial Group Gets Daily Bread." *Food and Beverage Close-Up*, April 9, 2008.

Kestin, Hesh. "The Apprenticeship of Irwin Simon." *Inc.*, March 1, 2002.

Locke, Tom. "A Taste for Success: Mo Siegel Trusts His Tastebuds in Running Celestial Seasonings." *Denver Business Journal*, July 30, 1993, p. 3A.

Nagle, Claire. "It's High Time for Tea Tours." *Colorado Business Magazine*, March 1994, p. 66.

"Natural Foods Superpower Emerges from Hain Food-Celestial Merger." *Boulder County Business Report*, March 2000.

Plank, Dave. "Hain and Celestial Merger Goes 1, 2, 3." *Boulder County Business Report*, April 2000.

Popp, Jamie. "Leading in a Healthy Direction." *Beverage Industry*, December 2004, pp. 22–30.

Strzelecki, Molly. "Terra-In' It Up." *Snack Food & Wholesale Bakery*, January 2003, pp. 24–29.

Sugarman, Carole. "Magic Bullets." *Washington Post*, October 21, 1998, p. E1.

Waters, Jennifer. "Growing Healthy Leftovers for Sale." *Minneapolis-St. Paul City Business*, May 3, 1996, p. 1.

Wolf, Chris. "Celestial Merger Brings Enterprise Clout, Consolidation, Responsibility." *Boulder County Business Report*, April 2000.

Woods, Bob. "Healthy Appetite." *Food & Beverage Marketing*, May 1998, p. 8.

Wooley, Scott. "The Slipstream Strategy." *Forbes*, October 7, 1996, pp. 78, 80.

Hawaiian Electric
Industries, Inc.

■

900 Richards Street
Honolulu, Hawaii 96813
U.S.A.
Telephone: (808) 543-5662
Fax: (808) 543-7966
Web site: http://www.hei.com

Public Company
Incorporated: 1891 as Hawaiian Electric Company
Employees: 3,451
Sales: $2.31 billion (2009)
Stock Exchanges: New York
Ticker Symbol: HE
NAICS: 221110 Electric Power Generation; 522110
   Commercial Banking; 551112 Offices of Other
   Holding Companies

■ ■ ■

Hawaiian Electric Industries (HEI), founded in 1983, is
the holding company for Hawaiian Electric Company,
Inc. (HECO), and the American Savings Bank F.S.B.
(ASB). HECO, in turn, oversees Hawaii Electric Light
Company, Inc., and Maui Electric Company, Ltd.
HECO and its subsidiaries provide power to 95 percent
of the state's total population. HEI also controls ASB,
which is one of the largest banks in Hawaii.

EARLY HISTORY

Hawaiian Electric Company was incorporated in
Honolulu on the island of Oahu during the reign of the
republic's last monarch, Queen Liliuokalani, in 1891.
Her predecessor, King David Kalakaua, had been
instrumental in the introduction of electricity to the
island in the 1880s. Kalakaua was a progressive leader
who had learned of Thomas Edison's revolutionary
electrical experiments and visited the inventor at his
Menlo Park, New Jersey, laboratory in 1881.

By the time HECO was created, there were several
private electrical generators in operation on Oahu,
including one at the monarchy's Iolani Palace that
provided light for the streets of downtown Honolulu
and almost 800 private residences. Jonathan Austin, a
community leader and the driving force behind the
founding of HECO, formed the joint stock company in
1891 to supply light and power to Honolulu. The
company was incorporated with William W. Hall as
president and Austin as treasurer. At that time, HECO
customers were charged a flat rate of 50 cents per light
per month and 20 cents per 1,000 watts per month.

In 1891 King Kalakaua died of a stroke, and agitation for union with the United States intensified after
Queen Liliuokalani ascended to the throne. Pro-
annexation forces deposed the queen and formed a
provisional government in 1893. By 1895 Hawaii had
become a territory of the United States.

In 1893 HECO was awarded an exclusive 10-year
franchise, wherein HECO paid the government 2.5
percent of its gross earnings from all electric light and
power furnished to consumers and agreed to bring
power to everyone in the district of Honolulu who
requested service. Austin died in 1893. He was replaced

as treasurer by William Hall, and Hall's vacant presidency was filled by William G. Irwin.

LATE 19TH-CENTURY EXPANSION

The company expanded rapidly during the remaining years before the dawn of the twentieth century, focusing on adding services and augmenting its customer base. HECO purchased the generator at Iolani Palace and moved it into a larger powerhouse. The new, coal-fired plant was equipped with a 150-horsepower Ball engine and generator and two 45-kilowatt Edison dynamos. Before the advent of the electric refrigerator, the company used its excess capacity to manufacture ice, beginning in 1894. HECO extended light and power service to Waikiki in 1897 and used the proceeds from additional stock offers to buy a 2,000-volt generator. That year, HECO was also able to pay its first dividend, which amounted to 5 percent of the company's $350,000 capitalization.

Just before the turn of the century, HECO president Irwin and another manager resigned, prompting a reorganization of the company's upper level management positions. From that time until 1943, HECO's day-to-day affairs were directed by a general manager, while the president's responsibilities resembled those of a board chairman. Alonzo Gartley was selected as the new general manager, and Frederick Macfarlane became president.

HECO opened the 20th century with the acquisition of the People's Ice and Refrigeration Company, its largest competitor in that industry, for $75,000. The merger increased the company's capitalization to $500,000, but fostered a monolithic image of HECO in the eyes of the press and the general public. The acquisition of People's Ice brought more management changes in 1902, when John A. McCandless, a partner in the ice company, succeeded Frederick Macfarlane as president of HECO. By this time, the company's flat rates for electric power had been increased to $1 for each 16-candle power lamp in use until midnight, and $1.25 for those who kept their lights on after 12:00 a.m.

When HECO's franchise from the provisional government ran out in 1904, the company requested a new contract from the U.S. government. Congress traded rate reductions for a perpetual franchise. By 1906 HECO had registered over 2,500 customers, who used 500,000 kilowatts of electricity annually. Use had grown with the invention of electric fans and irons, the expansion of government offices after annexation, and the construction of the island's first major hotel, the Moana. HECO responded to the increased demand by switching from coal to oil as a fuel source, which saved the company $17,000 annually. The company increased its capacity with the installation of Hawaii's first steam-driven turbine, a 750-kilowatt steam turbo generator, in 1908. The new generator was augmented with a 1,500-kilowatt unit in 1910 and a 2,500-kilowatt unit in 1913.

In 1910 Gartley left the post of general manager and was replaced by President McCandless's son-in-law, Harry M. Hepburn. The company continued to extend its electric network to residential districts in outlying areas of Oahu.

CREATING A PUBLIC UTILITIES COMMISSION: 1913

At the same time, however, momentum was building to bring the increasing powerful utility under public regulation. Led by W. R. Castle (who, not coincidentally, was an executive of the Honolulu Gas Company), anti-HECO forces accused the electric company of charging exorbitant rates. General manager Hepburn responded to the accusations by noting two recent rate cuts. The utility's opponents introduced a bill to the territorial legislature that called for the creation of a Public Utilities Commission (PUC) and an end to HECO's government-sponsored monopoly on electric power.

The legislature passed the bill, but when Hawaii's governor vetoed it, the bill was returned to the legislature, where anti-HECO representatives won out in 1913. HECO president McCandless and his two brothers sold their controlling interest in the company for over $500,000 and resigned their posts. Their shares were purchased by Richard and Clarence Cooke, who became president and secretary, respectively, and Frank C. Atherton, who became HECO's treasurer. Frank E. Blake succeeded Hepburn as general manager. Ironically, this forced change brought increased prosperity to HECO. Cooke and Blake, who would stay with the company for 28 and 14 years, respectively, immediately slashed rates and ended the flat rate payment schedule. The lower rates brought a large influx of new customers and revenues.

KEY DATES

1891: Hawaiian Electric Company (HECO) is incorporated to supply light and power to Honolulu.
1913: Hawaii's Public Utilities Commission is created.
1941: The Hawaiian Electric Union is formed.
1965: HECO goes public.
1968: Maui Electric Company is acquired.
1970: Company purchases Hilo Electric Light Company.
1983: Holding company Hawaiian Electric Industries (HEI) is formed.
1988: American Savings Bank is acquired.
1991: A power outage leaves all of Oahu without power for nearly 12 hours.
2008: HEI signs Hawaii Clean Energy Initiative.

This increased demand led HECO to develop a network of substations in 1914 that facilitated the distribution of power from the main plant to Honolulu's burgeoning suburbs. In 1915 the company also opened a merchandising department that sold electric appliances, such as the newly introduced refrigerator. Within five years, this division's profits topped $60,000.

EXPANSION AND MODERNIZATION: 1920–39

In 1922 HECO added a 10,000-kilowatt generating unit, continuing the expansion of electrification to more isolated regions in the mountains of Oahu. However in 1923, just as these new customers became accustomed to the modern convenience, a severe storm struck. Heavy rain and high winds uprooted trees and downed power lines, causing $100,000 damage to the island, $10,000 of which was borne by HECO. Nonetheless, repairs were accomplished quickly, and the company was even able to bring another 10,000-kilowatt Westinghouse condensing turbo-generator on line that year.

The company's next major project helped beautify Honolulu through the development of an underground conduit system. HECO further enhanced Hawaii's capital when it constructed a new headquarters in 1927. The Spanish Colonial-style building was later nominated to the National Register of Historic Places as one of the most elegant buildings in the state.

HECO was insulated from the stock market crash of 1929 that defined the decade of the 1930s for most of the rest of the world. By 1931 the company claimed 40,650 residential customers and profits nearing $100,000. HECO had also just made a capital investments of $1.5 million for a new plant that was equipped with a 20,000-kilowatt turbo generator. The 1930s saw the modernization of several of HECO's older generators with the installation of more efficient "topping turbines." These units significantly increased the pressure exerted by HECO's existing boilers, which simultaneously increased efficiency and generating capacity. These and other improvements brought the company's total capital investments to almost $3 million in the early 1930s.

General Manager Blake retired in the middle of the decade and was replaced by his son-in-law, Leslie H. Hicks. Hicks continued to expand capacity with a new 7,500-kilowatt turbo-generator on the shores of Pearl Harbor. A second unit with 15,000 kilowatts of capacity was built in 1940. The power plants helped HECO meet the increasing needs of U.S. military establishments and growing sugar and pineapple plantations. Richard Cooke's presidency ended with his passing at the age of 57. He was succeeded by older brother and HECO secretary, Clarence.

THE WAR YEARS

World War II landed the territory in the middle of the Pacific theater. After Pearl Harbor came under surprise attack on December 7, 1941, Honolulu was placed under a strict blackout and the government spent over $300,000 to reinforce HECO's primary power plants against further air attacks. But even the total blackout did not lessen the need for electric energy. With U.S. troops working around the clock on the island, the company built two 44,000-volt lines to service primary military bases. HECO power plants furnished more than one million kilowatt hours of electricity each day at the height of the war effort.

The outbreak of war coincided with the first attempts at unionization at HECO. In 1941 HECO employees John Hall, John Hendrick, and Walters Eli established the Hawaiian Electric Union to lobby for higher wages, sick leave, and paid vacations and holidays. Later that year, the National Labor Relations Board certified the International Brotherhood of Electrical Workers (IBEW) to represent HECO's trades and crafts personnel. The first labor agreement was drafted in 1942, but it was not until 1943 that trades and crafts employees began to join the IBEW. The early years of the management-union relationship were marred by hostile negotiations. Talks grew so rancorous that union leaders petitioned for municipal ownership of the utility in 1943. The movement was soon quelled, however, and management-labor relations were soon normalized.

The year 1943 also saw the end of HECO leadership by the Cookes and the Athertons when Clarence Cooke died after a 32-year association with the company and Frank Atherton retired from the board after 36 years of service. Leslie Hicks was named president, and the corporate hierarchy was reorganized so that the position was made responsible for daily operations.

The wartime blackout was lifted in May 1944 and martial law ended that fall. Over the course of the war, HECO's kilowatt-hour sales had grown from less than two million to more than 12.5 million kilowatt hours. Income for the same period had climbed from $5.3 million to $9.3 million, and generating capacity had jumped from 82,500 kilowatts to 117,500 kilowatts. Pressure on the system was relieved with the 1944 construction of a 42,000-kilowatt unit at the Honolulu power plant and a 50,000-kilowatt unit at the Waiau plant in 1945.

POSTWAR EXPANSION

Although many of the troops left Hawaii at the end of the war, the territory's economy had been transformed. Beginning with the postwar era, Hawaii's economy was dominated by military spending, tourism, and construction. Construction of the $30 million Ala Moana Shopping Center, for example, took over a decade, from 1952 to 1966. It was soon recognized as one of HECO's biggest projects. Indeed, the shopping center was larger than downtown Honolulu and cables had to be run underground in reclaimed swampland.

HECO also undertook two expansion projects in the 1950s. The company built a new power plant on the Honolulu waterfront in 1954. The 116,000-kilowatt plant was named after HECO's president, Leslie Hicks. New technologies, such as a high-capacity (138-kilovolt) line and hydraulic-powered booms that did the heavy work of placing utility poles, helped HECO expand its service area to the relatively undeveloped northeast side of Oahu, across the Koolau mountain range.

These three large projects spanned from 1959 to 1963 and cost HECO $56.8 million. Hawaii became the 50th state of the United States in 1959. The political change helped bring HECO to the attention of the investment community. Hicks retired that year, and was succeeded by Ralph Johnson.

After seven years of research into population growth and residential and industrial expansion, HECO started construction of a new power plant at Kane Point in

West Oahu. Kahe was powered by the state's first reheat steam turbine generator, which cost $16 million. The plant was brought on line with a generating capacity of 86,000 kilowatts, and a second unit with the same capacity was started up in 1964. By the early 1990s, the Kahe plant had six units with a total generating capacity of 648,000 kilowatts and a total cost of $184 million. The expansion helped HECO keep up with demand, which more than doubled during the 1960s.

GOING PUBLIC: 1965

HECO sold a subsidiary, the Honolulu Electric Supply Company, for $3.79 million in the early 1960s and reinvested the proceeds in technical improvements. In 1964 the company initiated a microwave communications system and an automatic dispatch system for control and efficiency. In 1966 Russell Hassler succeeded Ralph Johnson as president when Johnson died unexpectedly. With plans for more expansion underway, HECO made its first public stock offering of $90 million in 1965, then invested the proceeds in its physical plant. The first stage of HECO's 138-kilovolt Halawa Valley station, which would become the utility's largest transmission station, was in operation by 1967.

Acquisition also helped HECO grow in the 1960s. In 1968 the company purchased Maui Electric Company in a friendly takeover, and in 1970 it acquired Hilo Electric Light Company (later known as Hawaii Electric Company), which produced electricity for the "Big Island" of Hawaii. That year, HECO converted its two oldest plants, at Honolulu and Waiau, to low sulfur oil. Although the fuel was more expensive, it reduced air emissions. After three years as president, Russell Hassler died and was succeeded by Lewis W. Lengnick. Lengnick remained president for four years, when he retired and was replaced by Carl H. Williams in 1973.

OVERCOMING HARDSHIPS: 1970–81

The early 1970s were marked by the oil crisis, when the cost of fuel oil increased almost one-third from 1970 to 1971. HECO filed for its first rate increase in 17 years in 1971, and despite widespread public opposition, the PUC permitted a 5.9 percent increase the following year. The cost of fuel oil continued to increase throughout the decade, from under $2.50 per barrel in 1970 to $42 per barrel in 1981. HECO's only labor strike occurred in 1973 and lasted two weeks.

In 1980 Carl Williams retired and C. Dudley Pratt Jr. took over. The following year, the islands of Kauai and Oahu were battered by Hurricane Iwa. Ninety-seven percent of HECO's customers lost power at the height of the storm and it took the company two weeks to restore the entire system. The utility used "rolling blackouts," wherein customers had electricity cut off for an hour every two hours for five to six days, to manage demand while customers were brought back on line. Much of the physical plant was rebuilt to withstand hurricane-force winds. Two other island-wide blackouts in the 1980s left the island without power for half-days. The first, triggered by a fire, occurred in 1983, and another resulted from a transformer explosion the following year.

CREATING HEI: 1983

Following an industry trend, HECO applied to the PUC to form a holding company as a vehicle to diversify the electric company's interests, which would help the company weather periods of low utility profits yet shelter it from bad investments. The reorganization was approved in 1983, and HECO became a subsidiary of Hawaiian Electric Industries, Inc. (HEI).

The ensuing years saw the creation and/or purchase of several endeavors: HEI Investment Corp. (1984); Hawaiian Electric Renewable Systems (a wind farm; 1985); Malama Pacific Corporation (real estate); Hawaiian Tug & Barge (inter-island freight; 1986); Hawaiian Insurance Group (1987); and American Savings Bank's (ASB) Hawaii branches (1988). By far HEI's largest acquisition, ASB soon provided one-fourth of the holding company's annual income. Pratt was replaced by Harwood D. Williamson as president and CEO of HECO in 1990, and Robert F. Clarke was appointed president of HEI.

OVERCOMING CRISES: 1991–93

HEI's rapid growth was halted by two events. First, electricity demand increased dramatically in the final years of the 1980s, soaring 5.6 percent in 1988 alone. Having invested in diversification for most of the decade, HEI was unprepared for the pressure on its electrical systems. The company scrambled to purchase power from independents as customers, politicians, and regulators complained of rotating blackouts, restricted use, and frequent outages. In 1991, for example, the entire island of Oahu was totally blacked out during routine maintenance. The blackout lasted 12 hours, but the backlash raged on during the early 1990s. HEI planned for a five-year, $1 billion capital improvements program in 1992. The program intended to add capacity and transmission and distribution capabilities throughout the service area.

Then, on September 11, 1992, Hurricane Iniki's 160-mile-per-hour winds devastated the island of Kauai.

Although it was the only island to which HEI did not supply power, HEI's Hawaiian Insurance Group (HIG) had sold many islanders hurricane insurance, and 98 percent of HIG's policyholders filed claims, which totaled $300 million. The claims bankrupted HIG, leaving the insurer with a negative net worth of $80 million. HEI abandoned the company, leaving it to a guaranty fund supported by the insurance industry. It was one of the largest insurance insolvencies in the state's history. Early in 1993, Hawaii's insurance regulators brought suit against the holding company, charging breach of fiduciary duty, misrepresentation, and negligence.

HEI's planned $1 billion capital improvements campaign was halted by the news of HIG's insolvency. In the last quarter of 1992, HEI's stock fell 10 percent, and Standard & Poor's floated the idea of downgrading both HEI's and HECO's ratings. HEI put off a stock offer planned for early 1993 that would have furnished funds to start the capital improvements program. The company reported its first annual loss in fiscal 1992.

PREPARING FOR THE NEXT CENTURY: 1993–99

HEI returned to profitability in 1993, securing a net income of $48.7 million. It settled its lawsuits related to the HIG bankruptcy scandal and began working to improve and expand its utilities network. Hawaii's PUC began investigating energy deregulation in 1996 as many states throughout the nation began developing restructuring plans to open up their energy markets to competition. The PUC continued with its investigation in 1997 but did little to change the electricity market on the islands. Deregulation plans remained at a standstill well into the new millennium.

Meanwhile, HEI formed HEI Power in 1995 and was hoping to cash in on international power ventures. The independent power producer was formed to develop and operate electric power facilities throughout the Asia Pacific region. By 2000 HEI Power operated a plant in Guam and owned stakes development projects in China and in the Philippines. Profits from HEI Power failed to materialize and by 2001 the company set plans in motion to shutter its international operations and sell HEI Power in order to focus on its core business in Hawaii.

FOCUSING ON CORE OPERATIONS

HEI spent the early years of the new millennium selling businesses and focusing on its electricity and banking subsidiaries. Most of its real estate and marine businesses, including Hawaiian Tug & Barge Corp., were sold off and the proceeds were used to fund expansion projects. After significant delays brought on by residents complaining of future high levels of pollution and noise, the Keahole power plant expansion project on the island of Hawaii resumed construction in November 2003. HEI also filed a request with the PUC for development of the East Oahu Transmission Project, which would create a major transmission grid on the island of Oahu.

Meanwhile, ASB had grown by making strategic acquisitions as well as expanding internally. By 2003, the bank had $6.5 billion in assets and net income of $56 million. ASB had focused on becoming a full service community bank and served both individuals and business customers. Net income continued to grow as ASB shifted its focus from single-family home mortgages to high-yield, short-term consumer, business, and commercial real estate loans.

From 2000 through 2006, Hawaii's economy was strong due to increased tourism, the strength of the housing market, increases in military spending, and growth in the construction markets. HECO worked to keep pace with demand and to provide reliable electricity to its consumers. Clarke retired in 2006 leaving Constance H. Lau at the helm of HEI.

After years of growth, Hawaii's economy began to feel the effects of the financial, credit, and housing crisis taking place on the U.S. mainland. HEI was forced to cut costs and curb capital spending as electricity demand slowed and revenues faltered. ASB sold its private issue mortgage-related securities portfolio to stem future losses in 2009.

PROMOTING RENEWABLE ENERGY: 2008 AND BEYOND

Amid the economic slowdown, HEI remained committed to promoting renewable energy. HECO had formed Renewable Hawaii Inc. in 2002 to develop renewable energy projects and using renewable energy remained at the forefront of Hawaii's energy strategy for the future. During 2008 HEI signed the Hawaii Clean Energy Initiative, which stipulated that 70 percent of the state's energy needs would come from renewable sources by 2030.

The initiative would no doubt bring changes to HEI's business model in the years to come. The plan required that 40 percent of electric power come from renewable sources while 30 percent of clean energy would stem from consuming less and improved efficiency. Under the terms of the initiative, HECO agreed not to build new coal plants while converting existing fossil fuel generators to use biofuels.

While the Clean Energy Initiative appeared ambitious, Hawaii's Senator Daniel Inouye provided the Associated Press with a rationale in October 2008: "It's not going to be easy, but we must do it, because of all the 50 states in the union, our state is the most vulnerable." Inouye went on to state, "We have no fossil fuels, so we have to manufacture our own energy." Indeed, while HEI and its subsidiaries faced a long road ahead in making the plan a reality, completion of the initiative would alleviate concerns about fluctuating and volatile oil prices that Hawaii had been subject to in its past.

April S. Dougal
Updated, Christina M. Stansell

PRINCIPAL SUBSIDIARIES

Hawaiian Electric Company, Inc.; American Savings Holdings, Inc.; Pacific Energy Conservation Services, Inc.; HEI Properties, Inc.; The Old Oahu Tug Service, Inc.

PRINCIPAL COMPETITORS

The AES Corporation; BancWest Corporation; Constellation Energy Group Inc.

FURTHER READING

"Hawaiian Electric Light Company Files 2010 Rate Request." *Investment Weekly News*, January 2, 2010.

"Hawaiian Electric Will Sell Off Its Unregulated HEI Power Unit." *Global Power Report*, November 9, 2001.

"Insurance Regulators Sue Hawaiian Electric Over Former Unit." *Wall Street Journal*, April 13, 1993, p. A8.

Myatt, Carl. *Hawaii: The Electric Century*. Honolulu: Signature Publications, 1991.

Niesse, Mark. "Hawaii and Its Largest Public Utility Sign Agreement for Using More Renewable Power." *Associated Press Newswires*, October 21, 2008.

"Power Plant Construction Halted for Kona, Oahu Plans Also on Hold." *Associated Press Newswires*, September 24, 2002.

Rose, Frederick. "Hawaiian Electric Drops Insurance Unit as Claims from Hurricane Iniki Mount." *Wall Street Journal*, December 7, 1992, p. B2.

Taketa, Mari. "Coming Out of the Dark." *Hawaii Business*, April 1, 1992.

Torres-Kitamura, Maria. "A Battle for Independents." *Hawaii Business*, August 1, 1997.

Heartland Express, Inc.

———— ■ ————

901 North Kansas Avenue
North Liberty, Iowa 52317
U.S.A.
Telephone: (319) 626-3600
Toll Free: (800) 441-4953
Web site: http://www.heartlandexpress.com

Public Company
Founded: 1955 as Scott's Transportation Services, Inc.
Employees: 2,781
Sales: $459.54 million (2009)
Stock Exchanges: NASDAQ
Ticker Symbol: HTLD
NAICS: 484110 General Freight Trucking, Local;
    484121 General Freight Trucking, Long-Distance,
    Truckload

■ ■ ■

Heartland Express, Inc., is one of the leading trucking companies serving the short-to-medium-haul truckload market in the United States. Based near Liberty, Iowa, Heartland's operations are primarily concentrated within the region east of the Rockies. The company focuses especially on the Midwest and southeast regions. It also offers limited but expanding service to the West and East Coast regions and serves all 48 states in the contiguous United States.

Heartland owns and operates one of the youngest fleets in its industry. Although owner-operators once supplied more than half its tractors, by 2006 the number of independent drivers had slipped below 10

percent. The average haul of a Heartland Express truck covered 513 miles in 2009.

In addition to its headquarters facility in Liberty, Iowa, the company operates 11 regional distribution facilities in Fort Smith, Arkansas; O'Fallon, Missouri; Atlanta, Georgia; Columbus, Ohio; Jacksonville, Florida; Kingsport, Tennessee; Olive Branch, Mississippi; Chester, Virginia; Carlisle, Pennsylvania; Phoenix, Arizona; and Seagoville, Texas. Service from these regional centers focuses on short haul freight runs for major customers in each region.

Heartland boasts high employee retention rates in an industry beset with high driver turnover. The company encourages driver loyalty by maintaining short-distance runs and regularly scheduling drivers to return home; Heartland drivers tend to return home weekly, compared with industry-wide returns of up to six weeks. Heartland drivers, almost all of whom are nonunion, are also compensated for "deadhead" or empty miles. In addition, the company provides college scholarships to the children of all of its employees based on their length of service with the company.

ORIGINS

The origins of Heartland Express can be traced to 1955, when Scott's Transportation Services of Cedar Rapid, Iowa, began as a hauler for the recently launched Whirlpool line of washing machines. The company remained small for the next two decades, growing to a fleet of 16 trucks by the late 1970s. In 1978 Russell A. Gerdin bought the company, renamed it, and relocated it to Coralville, Iowa. By then, Gerdin, whose father had

COMPANY PERSPECTIVES

Our financial strength, approach to customer service, and the winning attitudes of our employees will help us remain in the forefront of our industry. Our focus remains on customer service and the continued improvement of our organization.

owned a small trucking company, had more than a dozen years of experience in the trucking industry.

Gerdin graduated from Moorhead State University in Minnesota in 1965 and went to work for his father's company. However, Gerdin and his father could not agree on the best way to run the family's business. Their conflict centered especially on the best way to increase the company's fleet of trucks. As Gerdin later told *Investor's Business Daily* in 1996, "I watched Dad work on those trucks and pay interest all his life. As soon as he got a dollar, he would buy a new one and take on more interest. I said: 'I'll buy one truck and, when I get that paid off, I'll buy another one'—exactly different from Dad."

Gerdin and his father were unable to resolve their different visions for the company. Gerdin left his father's business after only six months to go into business for himself. He bought his own trucking line in 1966, Great Plains Transportation, a small company based in Nebraska. Over the next decade, Gerdin would own or partly own five more trucking companies, all of which were based in the Midwest.

At that time, however, federal regulations severely restricted the routes available to trucking companies. Because most routes were already controlled by larger, established trucking companies, newer and smaller trucking companies found it difficult, if not impossible, to achieve any real internal expansion. Union control over the trucking industry was also a factor in limiting companies' growth.

DEREGULATION OPENS NEW OPPORTUNITIES

Gerdin moved to Iowa toward the end of the 1970s, and together with several others bought the assets of Scott's Transportation Services, renaming it Heartland Express, in 1978. Gerdin was named chairman, chief executive officer, president, and secretary of the company. In 1979 the trucking industry was deregulated, opening new opportunities for the smaller companies in the industry.

Gerdin set to work building the company's fleet, following his own ideas and adding one truck at a time. Another company policy set early in Heartland's history was that of maintaining a relatively young fleet, thereby limiting costly maintenance, while improving the company's dependability for its customers. The relative youth of its fleet also allowed Heartland to maintain a low service employee to tractor ratio of one employee for every seven tractors, compared with the industry average of one to 3.5.

Heartland quickly established a reputation for reliable service among the industry. While keeping early major customers such as Whirlpool and Amana, Heartland added others, including Sears and Kellogg, which would also maintain long-term relationships with the company. By 1982 the company was bringing in nearly $11 million in annual sales, and, by keeping its costs low, the company managed to achieve net income of more than $1 million.

A PUBLIC COMPANY IN 1986

The company continued to grow slowly but steadily through the first half of the 1980s, despite the nationwide recession of the period. Actually, the new realities of doing business during this time actually helped Heartland grow. More and more manufacturers began to automate production and turn to "just in time" inventory systems, supplying production lines with materials and parts only at the time they were actually needed, which enabled manufacturers to decrease their reliance on costly warehousing. In turn, the manufacturers became more reliant on short-haul shippers to meet their inventory needs.

With reliability more than ever a critical factor in a manufacturer's shipping needs, Heartland's reputation for dependability helped the company secure its growing position in the trucking industry. Another factor in Heartland's success was its high trailer to tractor ratio. By maintaining on average twice as many trailers as tractors, Heartland was able to station some of its trailers at its customers' plants. This had two benefits. Trailers could be loaded and unloaded by the manufacturers, cutting down on time between shipments. Meanwhile, Heartland's tractors were free to haul other loads.

Heartland had doubled its revenues by 1986, to nearly $22 million. The company's string of profits also continued, reaching $3 million that year. By November 1986 Heartland was prepared to step up its expansion. Gerdin took the company public, selling 1.5 million shares at $10 per share. Most of the shares sold were Gerdin's, reducing his control of the company to about 65 percent. Portions of the proceeds from its initial

KEY DATES

1955: Scott's Transportation Services is established as a hauler for Whirlpool washing machines.
1978: Russell A. Gerdin acquires Scott's, renames it Heartland Express.
1986: Gerdin takes the company public with a listing on the NASDAQ.
1989: Assets of Tennessee-based PDQ Transportation Inc. are acquired, extending Heartland into the Southeast.
1992: Short-haul subsidiary Heartland Distribution Services is launched.
1994: Acquisition of Munson Transportation of Illinois doubles size of company, expands it to a national trucking line.
1997: Tennessee-based A&M Express Inc. is acquired.
2002: Virginia-based Great Coastal Express Inc. is acquired.
2009: Dallas terminal begins operations.

public offering (IPO) went to expanding the company's fleet.

By 1987, after posting profits of $3.5 million on revenues of $26 million, the company's fleet had reached 126 company-owned tractors and 125 owner-operator tractors. After purchasing 59 drop deck dry vans from a Missouri-based trucking company, Heartland's fleet included more than 600 trailers, more than half of which were less than a year old. The new acquisition led Heartland to expand its operations as well, as the company added a service center in LaMonte, Missouri, to support the new additions to its fleet.

In 1988, with a tractor fleet numbering more than 300, almost half of which were company owned, and the number of trailers at 715, Heartland posted a net income of more than $5 million on $34.6 million in sales. The following year, Heartland stepped up its expansion, purchasing the assets (including 120 dry van trailers) from PDQ Transportation Inc., a Tennessee-based trucking line. This move enabled Heartland to extend its trucking services beyond the Midwest region into the Southeast. Taking over PDQ's customers proved to be a challenge for the company, however. After a drop in earnings early in 1989, the company moved to shed the less profitable of its new customers. Late that year, Heartland opened a second regional

service facility in Dyersburg, Tennessee, and committed to expanding its service in the southeast region.

PROFITING FROM RECESSION

By late 1989 the economy was in a downturn as the country entered the recession that stretched into the early 1990s. Under Gerdin's guidance, Heartland had consistently avoided taking on long-term debt as the company claimed that it still had not spent all of the money raised in its IPO. As Gerdin told *Forbes*, "In good times, maybe we don't look so smart. But now we do." Gerdin's conservative leadership paid off as Heartland moved to take up business from competitors struggling to survive in the poor economic climate.

Gerdin made a new move in 1989 to solidify the company's standing when it began converting its entire fleet to new 53-foot trailers, the first in the industry to do so. The new trailers, longer than the typical 48-foot trailer, provided the company, and its customers, with 11 percent more freight space, with little difference in operating costs. Heartland also moved to convert its company-owned tractor fleet to the more fuel-efficient cab-over design.

The conversion of the company's nearly 1,500 trailers was completed in 1990. The company's fleet had grown to 525 tractors by that year, including 235 new cab-over tractors, an increase of nearly 100 over the previous year. Despite the conversion of the fleet, Heartland stayed true to Gerdin's original conviction and managed to remain debt free. "Not only do we have no debt, but we are dealing from a base of business decisions, rather than on whether we have enough cash flow," John Cosaert, Heartland's CFO and cofounder told *Investor's Daily*. "A lot of people are putting themselves in a bad position because of leverage." By the end of 1990 the company's fleet had grown to nearly 300 company-owned tractors. Revenues grew to $63 million, providing a net income of more than $7.3 million.

SOUTHEAST EXPANSION

Early in 1991 Gerdin reduced his control of the company, putting up 650,000 of his own shares in a secondary offering, leaving him with 51 percent of the company's stock. By the end of that year, Heartland doubled the size of its company-owned tractor fleet as it continued to expand, especially in the Southeast. To further expansion in that region, in 1992 Heartland started up Heartland Distribution Services (HDS), a subsidiary concentrating on short-haul traffic, and opened a distribution center in Atlanta, Georgia, to service the new subsidiary. HDS outgrew that facility by the end of that year, and the company bought a new, larger center in Atlanta.

Also in 1992, Heartland combined its LaMonte, Missouri, and Dyersburg, Tennessee, centers into a new terminal located in St. Louis, Missouri, designed to accommodate the company's short-haul growth in the region. Meanwhile, the company's trailer fleet underwent a new conversion, to aluminum plate trailers. The new trailers were wider than conventional trailers by more than three inches, further increasing load capacity. The aluminum plate was also stronger, lowering maintenance costs, and the new trailers were expected to last 10 years instead of the seven years that conventional trailers usually lasted.

ACQUISITION DOUBLES SIZE IN 1994

By 1993 Heartland revenues had jumped to $115 million. The following year, Heartland moved to double the size of the company by acquiring Munson Transportation Inc., a struggling trucking company based in Monmouth, Illinois. Under the conditions of the acquisition, Munson received shares of Heartland stock, then worth $73 million, while Heartland assumed Munson's $55 million debt. In addition to acquiring Munson's aging fleet and facilities, Heartland gained access to Munson's northeast and West Coast markets, expanding Heartland to a national trucking line.

After attempting to merge Munson's operation into the company, Heartland finally consolidated both companies, closing Munson's Illinois facilities and moving its operations to Heartland's Coralville, Iowa, headquarters. The company also sold off most of Munson's aging, diversified trailer fleet, returning the company to its uniform, 53-foot aluminum plate fleet of trailers.

A booming year for trucking in 1994 helped Heartland overcome the challenges of the Munson acquisition. By the end of 1995, Heartland had wiped out its entire debt. As a company posting nearly $200 million in sales, with a net income of more than $20.5 million, Heartland had taken its place as one of the top 10 truckload carriers in the United States.

The trucking boom extended into the late 1990s and led to a driver shortage. At this time about 60 percent of the company's drivers owned their own rigs. Mechanics were also scarce. A&M Express Inc. of Kingsport, Tennessee, was acquired in July 1997. It had annual revenues of $28 million.

Heartland's revenues were $275 million in 2000. The company posted net income of $34 million. It was debt free, with more than $150 million in cash. There were more than 3,000 employees. The company had nine terminals: Atlanta, Georgia; Carlisle, Pennsylvania; Columbus, Ohio; Decatur, Illinois; Fort Smith, Arkansas; Jacksonville, Florida; Kingsport, Tennessee; Rochester, New York; and St. Louis, Missouri.

About half of its roughly 2,000 tractors were company owned. Heartland was beginning to use new composite trailers. It continued to operate a standardized fleet of relatively new Freightliner tractors, trading them in at three years or 350,000 miles.

A 2001 profile in the *Wall Street Journal* detailed the unglamorous yet effective working methods of company head Russell Gerdin. The key was a weekly spreadsheet of thousands of routes run and associated revenues and other statistics. The company continued to focus on short, routine hauls for large customers that could be handled by single drivers rather than teams.

Virginia-based Great Coastal Express Inc. was acquired in June 2002. In 2005 Heartland expanded to the West by adding a leased regional base near Phoenix, Arizona. It built its own facility there, which opened two years later.

PREPARING FOR LEADERSHIP TRANSITION

Russell Gerdin's son Michael became president of the holding company in May 2006. Michael Gerdin had been working for the company since 1983 and most recently had been vice president of regional operations. His father, who remained chairman and CEO, had survived a heart attack in 2000 and was being treated for liver cancer.

The publicity-shy Russell Gerdin was named to the Iowa Business Hall of Fame in 2006. In addition to starting the company's own tuition program for children of employees 20 years earlier, he and his wife Ann had donated millions to Iowa State University and the University of Iowa.

Net income reached $87.2 million in 2006 on revenues of $571.9 million. By this time only 7 percent of the company's drivers were owner-operators. Michael Gerdin told *Traffic World* that owning a rig had become much less popular over the preceding several years as engine and truck prices escalated.

In May 2007 Heartland paid out more than half of its $365 million in cash reserves to shareholders in a special $2 per share dividend. The Gerdin family then owned a little more than 40 percent of the firm's common stock. The company relocated its headquarters from Iowa City to a new facility on I-380 near North Liberty, Iowa, in July 2007. In August 2008 Heartland bought a terminal in Seagoville, Texas, near Dallas. This, its 10th regional facility, became operational in January 2009.

The company had 2009 revenues of $459.5 million, down from $625.6 million the previous year. Heartland Express was able to maintain its margins in an enduring economic slowdown, although net income fell from $70 million to $57 million. There were about 2,800 employees at year-end, 500 fewer than the year before.

The introduction of new federal standards, the Comprehensive Safety Analysis 2010, or CSA2010, in July 2010 was expected to weed out weaker operators. The company had one of the youngest fleets in the industry, having bought 2,175 new trucks over the previous two years.

M. L. Cohen
Updated, Frederick C. Ingram

PRINCIPAL SUBSIDIARIES

A&M Express, Inc.; Heartland Express, Inc., of Iowa; Heartland Express Maintenance Services, Inc.; Heartland Express Services, Inc.

PRINCIPAL OPERATING UNITS

North Liberty, Iowa; Fort Smith, Arkansas; O'Fallon, Missouri; Atlanta, Georgia; Columbus, Ohio; Jacksonville, Florida; Kingsport, Tennessee; Olive Branch, Mississippi; Chester, Virginia; Carlisle, Pennsylvania; Phoenix, Arizona; Seagoville, Texas.

PRINCIPAL COMPETITORS

Celadon Group Inc.; Covenant Transportation Group Inc.; J.B. Hunt Transport Services Inc.; Knight Transportation Inc.; Old Dominion Freight Line Inc.; Swift Transportation Co.; Werner Enterprises Inc.

FURTHER READING

Bailey, Jeff. "For One Trucking Entrepreneur, Success Is in the Details." *Wall Street Journal*, November 27, 2001, p. B4.

Bennett, Stephen. "Powerhouse." *Truck Fleet Management*, April 2000, p. 18.

Carey, Bill. "Heartland Changing Drivers: Truckload Carrier's Path to Stay Steady as Leadership Transitions from Father to Son." *Traffic World*, May 29, 2006, p. 31.

DeWitte, Dave. "Fame Awaits Heartland Express Founder." *Gazette* (Cedar Rapids, Iowa), December 1, 2006, p. 9B.

Jones, John A. "Heartland Express Back on Track after Major Overhaul." *Investor's Business Daily*, February 15, 1996, p. B12.

———. "Heartland Express Focuses Growth on Regional Markets." *Investor's Business Daily*, December 18, 1992, p. 30.

Lawless, Jim. "Obscure Heartland Rockets into Limelight." *Des Moines Register*, June 21, 1993, p. 7.

Lazo, Shirley A. "A Truckload of Bucks; Heartland Express Adds a $2 Special Payout." *Barron's*, May 21, 2007, p. B46.

Meeks, Fleming. "Bring on the Flood." *Forbes*, November 12, 1990.

Padley, Karen. "Heartland Express Grows with Service to Big Companies." *Investor's Business Daily*, December 16, 1991, p. 34.

Petroski, William. "Powerful Acceleration." *Des Moines Register*, February 4, 1996.

Rogers, Doug. "Heartland Express Stays in Center of Nation's Road Map." *Investor's Business Daily*, February 13, 1991, p. 32.

Holiday Companies

—■—

4567 American Boulevard West
Bloomington, Minnesota 55437
U.S.A.
Telephone: (952) 830-8700
Fax: (952) 830-8864
Web site: http://www.holidaystationstores.com

Private Company
Founded: 1928
Employees: 4,600
Sales: $2 billion (2008 est.)
NAICS: 447110 Gasoline Stations with Convenience
Stores

■ ■ ■

Based in Bloomington, Minnesota, Holiday Companies is a private company that operates about 400 Holiday Stationstore convenience stores in 10 states: Alaska, Idaho, Michigan, Montana, Minnesota, North Dakota, South Dakota, Washington, Wisconsin, and Wyoming. More than 300 of the units are company-owned, and the rest are franchise operations. They sell the low-sulfur Blue Planet private brand of gasoline, and many of the stores include adjacent car washes. Inside, Holiday Stationstores offer a variety of hot foods and snack foods, including the Holiday Pantry line of sandwiches and salads, but the focus is on national name brands. Locations are concentrated along major highways and interstates. In addition to serving the needs of general customers, the stores provide fleet fueling services.

Holiday Companies is owned and managed by the Erickson family.

COMPANY ORIGINS: 1928

Holiday Companies was founded by the seven Erickson brothers, born to Swedish immigrants: Alfred, Arthur, Elmer, Godfrey, Herman, Ivar, and Joseph. In 1928 Alfred and Arthur Erickson opened a general store in western Wisconsin. According to the 1997 obituary of Alfred Erickson in the *St. Paul Pioneer Press*, they "quickly decided that pumping gasoline for their customers' cars would give them an edge over the competition. They called their innovation the 'stationstore.'" The brothers greatly expanded their business holdings in the late 1930s when they, along with their five other brothers, acquired a bankrupt oil refinery in Texas in 1939 for $75,000. It was dismantled and relocated to St. Paul Park, Minnesota, where it became operational as Northwestern Refining Company. It was a modest affair, employing just 24 people at the start and producing 1,000 barrels a day, but the refinery was the key to the family's improving fortunes.

During the 1940s the refinery was supplied with crude oil delivered by rail from Montana and Wisconsin. Barge shipments were also supplied by Ashland Oil Inc., delivered to a new Mississippi River barge terminal the Ericksons opened in 1946. Pipeline deliveries from North Dakota and Canada began in the 1950s and five large tanks were constructed to store the crude. While the refinery expanded with the steady addition of towers and vessels, increasing capacity to 26,000 barrels a day, the Erickson brothers were active on other fronts

COMPANY PERSPECTIVES

■

With over 400 locations in 10 states, Holiday is a leader in the convenience store industry. We are committed to providing high quality fuel along with an extensive product selection, great value, and friendly, helpful service. Satisfying your needs everyday, wherever you're going.

as well. They cobbled together a chain of service stations through Erickson Petroleum Corporation as an outlet for the gasoline produced by Northwestern Refining. According to an obituary of Arthur Erickson published in October 1955, Erickson Petroleum was operating 135 service stations at the time of his death.

TRAX OIL ACQUIRED: 1962

In 1956 the number of service stations increased further with the acquisition of the Oskey Brothers Company and its North Star gasoline stations. In 1962 Trax Oil Company was acquired, adding 17 gas stations in three states. In 1960 the Ericksons also began opening gas stations under the SuperAmerica banner. The first unit, located in St. Paul, Minnesota, included a car wash. Also in the early 1960s the family opened a food and general merchandise store in a former gas station distribution center under the Holiday Plus name. It was a concept that allowed the company to later claim to be a pioneer of the U.S. hypermarket. Northwestern also invested in an oil well in North Dakota in 1961 to provide a source of crude for the refinery. In 1965 Northwestern drilled its first Canadian oil well.

A significant turning point for the Erickson family occurred in 1970 when Ashland Oil acquired Northwestern Refining and the North Star, Super-America, Trax, and Webb brands. Through merger, Ashland eventually became Marathon Oil Company. Although the Ericksons no longer owned a refinery and had cast off many of their service station brands, they remained committed to the retailing side of the business and continued to operate Erickson Petroleum to supply gasoline to the Holiday Stationstores.

Like the Holiday Plus stores, these units carried a lot of general merchandise not normally associated with a convenience store, such as bicycles, wheelbarrows, and hunting and fishing gear. Over the years, as Wal-Mart and Target stores became more prevalent in the market, the Ericksons phased out the general merchandise and

Holiday Stationstores assumed a more traditional convenience store format.

PETROLEUM OPERATION SPUN OFF: 1981

Growth stagnated in the 1970s, prompting a restructuring in 1981 when the family decided to spin off the petroleum operations from the parent company, which at the time was Erickson Diversified. Erickson Oil then developed the Freedom Valu Centers convenience store chain, while the grocery operations of Erickson Diversified became the Holiday Companies. They would include convenience stores, hypermarkets, and conventional supermarkets under the Holiday Foods name, and superwarehouse markets. The warehouse stores were added in 1984 when Holiday acquired eight Food 4 Less stores in Iowa. To supply the stores with groceries, a wholesaler, Fairway Foods, was acquired in 1980. Four years later Fairway acquired a wholesaler in Ankeny, Iowa, and in 1986 acquired Carpenter Cook, a wholesale operation based in Menominee, Michigan. In addition, Holiday became a major sporting goods retailer in its market during the 1980s.

Although the Ericksons were circumspect about their business interests, in 1987 the family provided *Forbes* magazine with a revenue figure, $1.2 billion, for use in the compilation of the magazine's list of the largest privately held companies. Holiday was less forthcoming in subsequent years. *Progressive Grocer* estimated that Holiday with its 35 corporate stores and some 250 convenience stores, as well as other interests, generated annual sales of $1.3 billion to $1.4 billion in 1988.

Holiday added to its convenience store holdings in 1992 with the purchase of 26 SuperAmerica stores, adding a presence in Montana, Washington, and Wyoming. As a result, Holiday's convenience store holdings reached 248. All told, the company then generated an estimated $1.6 billion in annual sales, which included contributions from four Holiday Plus hypermarkets, 20 Holiday Foods grocery stores, 20 Food 4 Less units, the Fairway wholesale operation, and the sporting goods business.

Holiday added to its sporting goods holdings in June 1995 by acquiring Burger Brothers Outdoor Outfitters, a family-owned chain of Minnesota upscale sporting goods stores. A year later Holiday strengthened the business further with the $19.5 million acquisition of Wilmot, Wisconsin-based Gander Mountain Inc., a struggling retailer that had recently sought Chapter 11 bankruptcy protection in order to reorganize its finances. Holiday picked up Gander Mountain's remaining 12 outdoor sporting goods and apparel stores. All

KEY DATES

1928: Brothers Alfred and Arthur Erickson open general store in western Wisconsin.
1939: Northwestern Refining Company is acquired.
1970: Refining company is sold.
1981: Petroleum and grocery operations split.
1999: Holiday Stationstores introduce Blue Planet gasoline at its Twin Cities locations.
2004: Gander Mountain subsidiary is spun off in a public stock offering.

told, Holiday then operated 27 sporting goods stores in Indiana, Michigan, Minnesota, and Wisconsin.

LAST OF ORIGINAL BROTHERS DIES: 1997

The last of the seven Erickson brothers behind the growth of the Holiday Companies, 90-year-old Alfred Erickson, died in August 1997. He had remained actively involved in the business almost until the end of his life, when illness forced him to step away. By the time of his death, business conditions had changed significantly in the retail business, with the rise of Wal-Mart and other big-box retailers in general merchandise, as well as consolidation in the supermarket field.

Holiday was consequently forced to begin focusing on its Holiday Stationstore chain. In 1998 the company sold its four Holiday Food stores in the Twin Cities area. On the wholesale side, Fairway Foods also faced stiff competition and in late 1999 the decision was made to shut down two of the three distribution operations in Northfield, Minnesota, and Fargo, North Dakota.

As the decade came to a close, the 265 company-owned and 35 franchised Holiday Stationstores in 11 states generated a reported $800 million in sales, $500 million of which was the result of gasoline sales and $300 million in merchandise. Another $7 million was generated from other sources. In 1999 the company began to place greater emphasis on car-wash operations, which began to make an ever-increasing contribution to the balance sheet.

It was also in 1999 that Holiday Stationstores introduced Blue Planet gasoline to its Twin Cities locations. The cleaner gasoline helped to reduce emissions as much as 20 percent without the loss of power or mileage. As a result, the chain became one of the first

gasoline retailers outside of tightly regulated California to offer a cleaner fuel in all grades of gasoline. Given a growing awareness of environmental concerns, Blue Planet provided Holiday Stationstores with a competitive advantage that it hoped would increase in time.

Further changes to the business mix continued for Holiday in the new century. The company found that it was no longer economically viable to maintain its own merchandise distribution network to supply the Holiday Stationstore chain. In 2002 the distribution operation was closed and the company entered into an agreement with the grocery distribution arm of McLane Company. A Texas-based subsidiary of Berkshire Hathaway, Inc., McLane was a major supplier to the convenience store sector, as well as to mass retailers, drug stores, restaurant chains, and military bases.

GANDER MOUNTAIN TAKEN PUBLIC: 2004

Holiday remained involved in sporting goods and devoted a good deal of attention to build its Gander Mountain chain. In September 2002 former Home Depot executive Mark Baker was hired as CEO, and he initiated a program of opening big-box format stores, 50,000 to 100,000 square feet in size. By the spring of 2004 the chain was operating 65 stores in nine midwestern and northeastern states.

Baker was eager to grow Gander Mountain into a regional and perhaps national competitor. In order to pursue that vision, Holiday spun off Gander Mountain in a public stock offering that in April 2004 raised $96.2 million for the company, of which $9.8 million was used to pay a debt to Holiday Companies. The balance helped to reduce Gander Mountain's credit facility. Holiday remained a major shareholder, however.

What remained of the active businesses of the Holiday Companies was the Holiday Stationstore chain. In late 2003, several months before the Gander Mountain spin-off, the chain expanded far beyond its home market by acquiring 26 Williams Express locations in Alaska from Tulsa, Oklahoma-based Williams Cos. The transaction closed in the early months of 2004. Holiday then spent millions of dollars to upgrade the stores and convert them to the Holiday Stationstore format, signage, and colors. The chain added more units in February 2006 when it acquired six stores from the Oasis Markets chain. All told, the Holiday chain grew by 60 stores in less than two years.

The years ahead were not without challenge for the Holiday Stationstores chain. In 2010 the company elected to exit Nebraska and Iowa. In April of that year Holiday sold all 10 of its convenience stores in these states to another regional player, Ankeny, Iowa-based Casey's General Stores Inc. Nevertheless, Holiday Stationstores appeared to be well positioned in its core markets, and in late 2009 renewed its supply contract with McLane Company. There was also every reason to believe that the company would remain in the hands of the Erickson family for many years to come.

Ed Dinger

PRINCIPAL COMPETITORS

Alimentation Couche-Tard Inc.; Casey's General Stores, Inc.; Kum & Go, L.C.

FURTHER READING

Apgar, Sally. "Holiday Affiliate to Buy Burger Brothers Stores." *Minneapolis Star Tribune*, June 6, 1995, p. 1D.

Busse, Drey. "Marathon Announces Plans to Sell St. Paul Refinery." *Woodbury Bulletin*, May 19, 2010.

Dwyer, Steve. "Erickson Oil Seeks Right 'Chemistry' for Market." *National Petroleum News*, June 1994, p. 34.

Kahn, Aron. "A. Erickson of Holiday Cos. Dies." *St. Paul Pioneer Press*, August 23, 1997, p. 5C.

Levy, Melissa. "Angling for Growth." *Minneapolis Star Tribune*, March 7, 2004, p. 1D.

Rockwood, Harvey T. "Holiday Cos. to Drop Distribution Network, Lay Off 70." *Sun Newspapers* (St. Paul, Minn.), June 26, 2002.

"Services Set for Erickson President." *Austin Daily Herald*, October 26, 1955, p. 17.

Weinstein, Steve. "A Diverse Holiday Mix." *Progressive Grocer*, May 1989, p. 107.

Wieffering, Eric J. "Holiday Companies: Riding the Express." *Corporate Report–Minnesota*, May 1993, p. 48.

Horry Telephone Cooperative, Inc.

3480 Highway 701 North
Conway, South Carolina 29526
U.S.A.
Telephone: (843) 365-2154
Toll Free: (800) 824-6779
Fax: (843) 365-1111
Web site: http://www.htcinc.net

Nonprofit Organization
Incorporated: 1952
Employees: 772
Operating Revenues: $160 million (2008)
NAICS: 517110 Wired Telecommunications Carriers;
513322 Cellular and Other Wireless Telecommunications; 517911 Telecommunications Resellers;
515210 Cable and Other Subscription Programming; 514191 On-Line Information Services

■■■

Horry Telephone Cooperative, Inc. (HTC), is one of the
20 largest phone companies, and the largest telephone
cooperative, in the United States. HTC began in the
mid 1950s by providing the first telephone service to
rural parts of Horry County (pronounced o-ree), to the
west of Myrtle Beach, and Georgetown, further south
on the South Carolina coast. It has more than 60,000
members and 98,000 access lines. In addition to local
telephone service, HTC provides long-distance, cable
television, Internet, and mobile phone service (it is a reseller of AT&T Wireless). Its HTC E2IT unit offers
information technology (IT) support for businesses.

RURAL ORIGINS

As late as the 1950s, much of rural Horry County, to
the west of Myrtle Beach, did not have telephone
service. In addition to complicating access for what little
emergency services were available at the time, this made
ordering supplies difficult for farmers. Neighboring
phone companies did not want to invest in the
infrastructure to connect these areas, which were thinly
populated at the time.

In January 1951 a committee was formed to address
the problem. Horry Telephone Cooperative, Inc.
(HTC), was incorporated in the spring of 1952. The
group selected Henry G. McNeill, a farmer, to be its
president, a position he would hold until his death in
January 2007.

The group unsuccessfully tried to persuade seven
independent telephone companies to extend their lines
into rural coastal areas. Finally in December 1952, HTC
borrowed a million dollars from the Rural Electrification
Administration (REA), contingent on reaching a
membership level that was met within the year.
Memberships originally cost $50, then a considerable
amount for many in the chiefly agrarian community.
The fee was reduced to $10 within a few years and
eliminated altogether in 2005.

The Horry Electric Cooperative (HEC) provided
office space to the new phone company for two years, as
well as other support. (McNeill served on HEC's board
as well.) McNeill also credited the National Rural
Electric Cooperative Association with helping the
fledgling cooperative, which joined with seven others to

form the National Telephone Cooperative Association in 1954. This tiny group later helped defeat the threatened cancellation of low-interest REA loans in 1972.

In January 1953 HTC acquired some phone lines just outside Conway, the seat of Horry County, from Continental Telephone Company. It soon began building its own lines as well, including some in Murrells Inlet, which was part of neighboring Georgetown County. In 1954 HTC acquired Coastal Telephone Company, a Loris, South Carolina-based carrier that had been placed on the market two years earlier.

Hurricane Hazel, one of the most destructive Atlantic storms of the 20th century, undid much of the fledgling cooperative's work. By the end of 1954, however, the cooperative was in business. It had eight employees, 421 subscribers, and revenues of $14,523. Three years later, there were 1,500 subscribers, and a permanent headquarters was constructed on Conway's North Main Street. A new headquarters was built in 1986.

ON TOP OF TECHNOLOGY:
1968–96

In spite of its provincial origins, HTC stayed on top of industry trends. After a disastrous ice storm in 1968, HTC began laying its phone lines underground rather than stringing them on telephone poles. After years of open wire and eight-party lines, in 1972 HTC became one of the first in the Southeast to transition to all private lines. HTC then had 10,000 lines in all.

HTC's array of offerings grew. In 1983 HTC established a cable television company, Horry Telephone Cable Vision (later HTC Digital Cable). It launched a long-distance subsidiary in 1991. HTC began offering mobile phone service in July 1995. It also started offering Internet access in 1995, signing up 1,600 subscribers within the first year.

HEIGHTENED COMPETITION
AFTER 1996
TELECOMMUNICATIONS ACT

The Telecommunications Act of 1996 opened new markets, but also allowed competitors to flood the Grand Strand area along the coast of South Carolina. In addition, the act forced HTC and other local carriers to reduce the fees they charged long-distance carriers to access their lines.

At the same time, the Grand Strand was experiencing a growth boom that extended inland to Conway and other once-sleepy farm towns. This attracted competitors who rewarded developers for installing their networks in new subdivisions, a game that HTC had to quickly master, noted trade journal *Rural Telecommunications*.

In a typical deal, in exchange for discounting wiring costs, HTC received contact information for the new residents. However, it found that many of the transient summer residents simply stayed with their national mobile carriers rather than set up local landline service. In addition, the large cable and mobile phone companies could take orders from relocating residents before they even moved. At the end of 1997, HTC had more than 67,000 customers, up more than 10 percent in one year.

The Telecommunications Act of 1996 allowed HTC to break the monopoly GTE held on local phone service in the Grand Strand's cities. In 1998 HTC Communications, Inc., was established as a competitive local exchange carrier. Within two years it was serving Conway, Myrtle Beach, and other densely populated areas along the Grand Strand from North Myrtle Beach to Pawley's Island.

In November 1999 HTC Communications formed a joint venture with Internet service provider Interactive Frontiers Group (IFG) called Intellistrand, LLC, to market Internet services to local businesses. IFG had been in business since 1995.

By this time there were about five major companies supplying mobile phone service in HTC's territory. In 2001 HTC became a reseller of Cingular Wireless (later AT&T Wireless). The co-op began offering a data recovery service for small to medium-sized businesses in 2007 through its E2IT unit. This unit also provided other IT-related services, such as network design.

50TH ANNIVERSARY IN 2002

By the time of its 50th anniversary on June 16, 2002, HTC counted more than 97,000 customers in all. It was spending millions of dollars both to keep up with technological advances and to connect the new subdivi-

KEY DATES

1954: Horry Telephone Cooperative, Inc. (HTC), introduces telephone service to rural Horry County and other thinly populated areas in coastal South Carolina.

1968: Massive ice storm prompts HTC to start laying most of its cables underground.

1972: HTC is among the first phone companies in the Southeast to switch from party lines to private lines.

1983: HTC establishes a cable television company.

1991: HTC forms its own long-distance company.

1995: HTC begins providing Internet and mobile phone service.

1996: Telecommunications Act of 1996 changes competitive landscape.

2008: HTC is named Official Communications Provider for U.S. presidential debates in Myrtle Beach.

sions that were springing up in the area's growth boom.

While HTC was investing in acquiring new technologies and installing infrastructure in new subdivisions, the 1996 Telecommunications Act had resulted in less revenue from long-distance access fees, prompting the cooperative to raise its rates. The membership fee, however, was eliminated in 2005. As a nonprofit organization, HTC disbursed capital credits, eventually worth a few million dollars per year, to its members.

In its marketing, HTC paid special attention to teenagers, who, noted a 2004 *Rural Telecommunications* survey, were much more likely than their parents to have mobile phones from national carriers rather than through their hometown telephone companies. HTC hosted a telecommunications technology summer camp for select seventh graders and sponsored local schools with proceeds from mobile phone sign-ups and phonebook recycling programs. HTC signed up as the official wireless provider for Coastal Carolina University Athletics in 2004. Other community outreach programs included providing toys to local emergency rooms and an annual canned food drive.

ENHANCED PRODUCT OFFERINGS

HTC had long been proud of the fiber optics in its network. In 2000 it announced its new very-high-speed

digital subscriber line (VDSL) service to connect phone, Internet, and television through a single 25-megabit fiber-optic gateway, rather than separate coaxial cable and copper wire hookups. This was branded a few years later as HTC Bluewave.

HTC continued to enhance its product offerings as new technologies became available. Around 2003 the cooperative began storing live coverage of local sports events for viewing on the Internet. By the end of the following year it rolled out new features for cable television service, such as high-definition broadcasts and a digital video recorder feature.

HTC began upgrading its wireless network to third-generation (3G) broadband in October 2007. By the end of 2008 most of its wired Internet connections were broadband and more than two-thirds of its mobile phone sites were up to the 3G standard.

In January 2008 HTC was Official Communications Provider for the presidential debates at the Myrtle Beach Convention Center. Among the assets it deployed to the location was the Cell Site on Wheels unit it had acquired five years earlier to relieve mobile phone congestion.

REGULATORY DISPUTE

Converging technologies occasioned new disputes. For example, in 2005 HTC complained to the Federal Communications Commission (FCC) when a local Fox affiliate withheld its high-definition feed in favor of rival Time Warner Cable (TWC), but this dispute was soon settled privately.

The rise of voice-over-Internet-protocol (VoIP) technology sparked a long-running regulatory dispute between TWC and six rural local exchange carriers (RLECs), including HTC, beginning around 2003. Cable companies such as TWC could not connect calls to the rural carriers' customers without assistance from the RLECs. South Carolina's Public Service Commission (PSC) at first sided with the rural incumbent carriers, who initially refused TWC's requests to connect to their customers' home phones.

In 2009, two years after a decisive FCC ruling, the PSC finally formalized connection rights for VoIP providers. TWC had argued that the RLECs' unregulated ancillary activities, such as cable TV and Internet service, offset their potential for lost revenues from new competition for local telephone service. In this ruling, the PSC defined TWC's VoIP offering as a telecommunications service subject to regulation.

Henry McNeill, the cooperative's president for nearly 55 years, passed away on January 3, 2007, at the age of 87. Ken Summerall, HTC's treasurer since 2003 and a board member since 1971, succeeded him as board president. HTC then had 718 employees (including part-time workers).

In January 2010 HTC named Michael Hagg as CEO, following the retirement of Curley P. Huggins, who had been with the company since 1972 and served as CEO since the 1980s. Hagg, formerly HTC's chief operating officer, had joined the company in 1994 after working at rival cable company Cox Communications Inc. for 10 years. HTC had become the largest telephone cooperative in the United States and the country's 18th-largest telephone company. It counted 98,000 access lines and more than 60,000 members.

Frederick C. Ingram

PRINCIPAL SUBSIDIARIES

IITC Communications, Inc.; Horry Telephone Long Distance, Inc.; Intellistrand, LLC (51%).

PRINCIPAL DIVISIONS

HTC Internet; HTC Horizon; HTC E2IT.

PRINCIPAL COMPETITORS

AT&T; Cellco Partnership d/b/a Verizon Wireless; Cox Communications Inc.; Time Warner Cable Information Services, LLC; T-Mobile USA.

FURTHER READING

Arellano, Jonah. "Henry G. McNeill: A Life of Leadership." *Exchange,* April 1, 2007.

Brown, Rachel. "Learning from Big Business: Strategies for Any Size Company." *Rural Telecommunications,* July 1, 2006, p. 32.

Bryant, Dawn. "Telephone Cooperative in South Carolina Actively Develops Urban Clientele." *Knight-Ridder/Tribune Business News,* March 14, 2000.

Burns, Jenny. "HTC Picks President, Chairman of the Board." *Sun News,* January 23, 2007.

Davidson, Paul. "Rural Phone Competition on Horizon? VoIP Providers Challenge Rules Protecting Carriers." *USA Today,* April 24, 2006, p. 6B.

Dayton, Kathleen Vereen. "Advanced Communications Is Coming to Homes in Myrtle Beach, S.C." *Knight-Ridder/Tribune Business News,* November 2, 2000.

———. "Horry County, S.C.-Area Phone Company Seeks Rate Increase." *Sun News,* July 30, 2001.

McNeill, Henry G. "Reflecting Back on the Early Years." *Rural Telecommunications,* November 1, 2001.

Platis, Athena. "Rural Telcos See Future in Young Customers." *Rural Telecommunications,* September 1, 2004, p. 14.

Shields, Tennille. "Going Local." *Rural Telecommunications,* July 1, 2008, p. 14.

Slafky, Aaryn. "Henry McNeill and Horry Telephone Cooperative: 45 Years and Counting." *Rural Telecommunications,* January 1, 1998, p. 44.

Huffy Corporation

———■———

6551 Centerville Business Parkway
Centerville, Ohio 45459
U.S.A.
Telephone: (937) 865-2800
Toll Free: (800) 872-2453
Fax: (937) 865-5470
Web site: http://www.huffy.com

Private Company
Incorporated: 1928 as Huffman Manufacturing
    Company
Employees: 106
Sales: $438 million (2009 est.)
NAICS: 336991 Motorcycles, Bicycles, and Parts
    Manufacturing; 339920 Sporting and Athletic
    Good Manufacturing

■ ■ ■

Huffy Corporation is a leading private manufacturer of bicycles. The company's products range from tricycles, children's bikes, and scooters, to mountain, cruiser, BMX (bike motocross), and commuter bikes. Huffy markets the majority of its products via leading mass merchandisers, including Wal-Mart and Target. In addition to its own line of bikes, the company offers licensed products from names such as Disney and other popular brands.

ORIGINS

Huffy grew out of the Huffman Manufacturing Company, which was founded in 1924. Founder Horace M. Huffman, Sr., learned the manufacturing business from his father, George P. Huffman, who owned the Davis Sewing Machine Company from 1887 to 1925. Taking advantage of the growing automotive industry, Horace Huffman's young company made equipment that could be used in service stations.

Working out of a factory on Gilbert Avenue in a noisy section of Dayton, Ohio, near the Pennsylvania Railroad tracks, the first Huffman employees were credited with inventing a rigid spout that could be used to dispense motor oil from 50-gallon drums. The company grew quickly through the 1920s and 1930s and its line of service station equipment expanded. When it incorporated in 1928, the company posted earnings of $3,000.

In 1934 Horace Huffman announced plans to manufacture bicycles, speculating that they would become a popular mode of transportation during the Great Depression. Initially, production rates hovered at 12 bikes per day. Within two years this rate increased to 200 daily. However, the company was still not producing fast enough to keep pace with its competition. Huffman suffered several setbacks in the beginning. The Firestone Tire and Rubber Company was a primary bike customer, but in 1938 Huffman lost a major portion of the account because it could not match Firestone's demand.

PRODUCTION IMPROVEMENTS

Horace Huffman, Jr., who was known by the diminutive "Huff," had joined the company on a full-time basis in 1936. After short stints as service manager and sales manager, he became works manager and converted the production process to a straight-line conveyorized assembly line.

This proved to be just the edge the company needed. By 1940 bicycle production doubled and sales figures were nearing the $1.5 million mark. Huffman's improved production rate caught the eye of the Western Auto Company, which became a major customer, and also brought Firestone back into the fold.

The outbreak of World War II necessitated a shift in production. The company joined the thousands of other businesses that were vying for government contracts, and was able to secure an order for primers, an artillery shell part. The increased business brought Huffman's sales to nearly $2.8 million in 1942.

The following year, the federal government placed an order for 4,000 bicycles. At this point much of the work was being done by women who were filling the void left by the vast numbers of men who had been inducted into the armed forces. The later years of the war proved to be difficult as the production of consumer products in all industries virtually ceased. Huffman, Sr., suffered a fatal heart attack in 1945.

POSTWAR GROWTH AND DIVERSIFICATION

The younger Huffman was elected president and immediately had to face the challenge of sustaining production in the postwar period with limited supplies. He knew that the government's allocation program would not provide enough materials to allow the company to compete at its prewar levels. After attending a seminar on "Work Simplification," Huff taught the procedure to his managers and then held a similar workshop for the company's major suppliers.

Huffman was thus able to help suppliers increase their own output and to raise production levels. For two years, the company was able to run two shifts a day without experiencing the traditional slowdown during the winter months. Sales for each of the two years exceeded $10 million.

In 1949 the company ran into the postwar recession. However, two developments allowed the company to survive. First, the Huffy convertible bicycle, a children's bicycle with training wheels, was introduced and was instantly popular. The bike also brought the name Huffy to the forefront of the bicycle industry. The second development occurred as a result of the company's search for a product that could be manufactured during the winter months. The decision to produce lawnmowers was announced in December 1949.

As a result, the company quickly outgrew its physical plants, and in the early 1950s Huffman acquired a building in Delphos, Ohio, and moved the Automotive Service Equipment division to that location. New facilities were built in Celina, Ohio, to house the bicycle and lawnmower divisions. The Dayton manufacturing plant on Gilbert Avenue was closed and the general offices were moved to Davis Avenue. In 1959 Huffman opened its bicycle plant in Azusa, California.

RAPID CHANGE

By 1960 Huffman was the third-largest bike manufacturer in the United States. In 1962 Horace Huffman, Jr., was named chairman and Frederick C. Smith became president and CEO. Smith had been materials manager during the crucial postwar period and was credited with strengthening the company's relationship with its suppliers.

In 1964 Huffman expanded its Outdoor Power Equipment division with the acquisition of Diele & McGuire Manufacturing. It was not an entirely successful expansion, however, and the division continued to lose money over the next decade. That same year the Huffman corporate offices were moved to Miamisburg, Ohio.

Huffman went public with its listing on the American Stock Exchange in 1968 and sales reached $42 million the following year. Stuart Northrup, a former Singer Sewing Machine executive, replaced Smith as president in 1972. By 1973 Huffman employed 2,500 workers at five locations.

Throughout the 1960s and early 1970s, Huffman enjoyed continued growth as the market for adult bicycles grew. More and more adults were turning to bikes for exercise and as a means to cut energy costs. Until the end of the 1960s, nearly half of all bicycles in the United States were sold through small independent bike shops that offered personal customer service.

KEY DATES

1924: The Huffman Manufacturing Company is founded.
1934: Huffman announces plans to manufacture bicycles.
1949: Decision to produce lawnmowers is announced.
1968: Huffman goes public and is listed on the American Stock Exchange.
1977: The company changes its name to Huffy Corporation.
1999: Steep price competition from Chinese manufacturers forces Huffy to cease domestic bicycle production.
2004: Huffy files for bankruptcy.
2005: The company emerges from bankruptcy as a privately held company; Chinese suppliers hold approximately 30 percent of the organization's stock.

In the 1970s the introduction of mass merchandise retail chains that stocked large quantities of consumer goods and sold them at discount prices opened up a new market for bike sales. Because British-owned Raleigh Cycle was firmly entrenched as the leading supplier to the independent shop owner, Huffman set its sights on the retail chains and developed a 10-speed that required the bare minimum of assembly and service.

WEATHERING THE STORM

The company's growth trend hit a snag in 1974, however, as a new recessionary period brought on an industry-wide slump. From a peak in 1973, bicycle sales dropped 50 percent by 1975. Huffman was forced to close its Celina plant for two months and lay off 25 percent of its workers.

Prior to the recession, foreign competition was also putting pressure on U.S. bike makers. In 1972 foreign imports accounted for 37 percent of the U.S. market. The devalued U.S. dollar, however, cut this share to 15 percent by the end of the 1970s. New federal regulations setting safety standards for bicycles also cut into the sale of foreign models.

As the industry revived toward the end of the 1970s, Huffman decided to take an aggressive marketing stance. Children again became the primary focus of the bike industry and Huffman introduced a new, flashy,

motocross-style bike called Thunder Trail. Designed to look like a motorcycle with waffle handle-grips, knobby tires, and racing-like number plates on the front, the new models also sported bright, jazzy colors and decals.

The company held focus groups in shopping centers to determine which features were the most popular. In addition, a greater portion of advertising dollars was spent on television commercials, particularly during the hours when children's programs aired.

INDUSTRY LEADER

The popularity of the Thunder Trail bike made Huffman the number one producer of bicycles in the United States by 1977 and all of the laid-off workers were called back. Net sales for 1977 were $130 million. This marked a 21 percent increase from the previous year.

Although Huffman was still the leading producer of gasoline cans, oil can spouts, oil filters, and jack stands, the Automotive Equipment Division was only accounting for 10 percent of the company's sales. Bikes and bike accessories accounted for 90 percent.

The Outdoor Power Equipment division, which had been struggling for years in the lawnmower market, was finally sold in 1975. The sale brought in $10 million in much-needed cash. Recognizing the need to diversify, Huffman acquired Frabill Manufacturing, a maker of fishing and basketball equipment, in 1977.

Until then, half of Huffman's bicycles were sold under private labels. By the end of the 1970s, however, the company decided to devote more energy to promoting its own brand name. Part of this effort included the decision in 1977 to change the company name to Huffy Corporation. During this period Huffy's management also opted not to enter the moped manufacturing field because of doubts about the motorized bike's potential in the United States. Instead, $5 million was spent to expand existing production facilities.

In 1980 Huffy posted its fifth straight year of record earnings and announced plans to open a third plant in Ponca City, Oklahoma. However, despite its strong financial position, Huffy was not immune to the problems that most U.S. businesses experienced in the 1980s. For one thing, production costs were rapidly increasing.

RESTRUCTURING

In 1982 Harry A. Shaw III was named CEO and immediately embarked on the unpopular path of plant closings and layoffs. Shaw spearheaded the consolidation of all bike manufacturing operations into the Celina plant and sold the Automotive Products Division for cash. Huffy then invested more than $15 million in advanced robotics and new production equipment. The changes resulted in an increase in production capacity by 5,000 bikes a day and a 14 percent cut in production costs. Another $15 million was earmarked to improve computer-generated manufacturing in the bike plant by 1991.

A licensing, sales, and manufacturing agreement with Raleigh Cycle was also cemented in 1982. This gave the company the opportunity to tap the high-specification bike market. The venture did not prove to be an asset, however, and Huffy sold its rights in 1988.

With bike sales still accounting for 90 percent of the company's sales, the need to diversify was as evident as ever. In 1982 Huffy acquired Gerico, a maker of infant car seats and strollers, and YLC Enterprises, a provider of product assembly services for retail consumer purchases. The former was organized as Gerry Baby Products and the latter as Huffy Service First.

Washington Inventory Service, a nationwide inventory taking service, was acquired in 1988. In 1990 Huffy acquired Black & Decker's stake in True Temper Hardware and capital stock in True Temper Ltd. in Ireland for $55 million. A manufacturer of garden and lawn tools, the company claimed approximately 30 percent of that market.

FOREIGN COMPETITION

Buoyed by the completion of its diversification campaign, Huffy entered the 1990s with renewed confidence. As the decade began, the company was collecting nearly half its earnings and sales from its disparate, non-bike businesses, which were beginning to develop their own momentum. Huffy Service First, for instance, had begun to expand its services by assembling, in addition to bikes, gas grills, lawnmowers, and patio furniture for mass retailers.

Diversification engendered its own problems, however. This was especially the case with the newest addition to the Huffy portfolio, True Temper. In an effort to gain market share, Huffy management reduced prices for True Temper lawn and garden equipment, which resulted in a $5 million loss for the division in 1992.

Huffy experienced other difficulties during the early 1990s as well. The company misfired in its attempt to take advantage of the popularity of mountain bikes. Huffy introduced a cross-trainer bike in 1992 that represented a hybrid of a road bike and mountain bike, but following an expensive promotion campaign, sales of the cross-trainer were lackluster.

The problems with True Temper and the unsuccessful introduction of a cross-trainer paled in comparison to Huffy's overriding concern during the 1990s, however, and that was contending with Asian competitors. Benefiting from production costs that were lower than their U.S. counterparts, Asian manufacturers enjoyed significant success in the U.S. market during the 1990s. This caused considerable havoc for domestic bike producers.

HARD TIMES

Huffy, holding a 30 percent share of the $1.5 billion U.S. market, bore the brunt of the damage stemming from the incursion of Asian producers, and saw its profitability sag. The worst period for Huffy to date arrived in 1995, when the company recorded a crippling $10.5 million loss. For the remainder of the decade Huffy management devoted itself to curing the ills that led to the devastating loss and implementing measures to ensure that it would not happen again.

In the wake of 1995's loss, a rebuilding process began that saw the company reduce its size in some departments and expand into new business areas. Management cut workers' wages, considered new product lines to stimulate profits, and looked to divest underperforming businesses. In 1997 Huffy sold Gerry Baby Products Co., gaining $73 million from the divestiture, and purchased Royce Union Bicycle Co., a Hauppauge, New York-based maker of high-end bikes. The company also acquired bankrupt Sure Shot International, a manufacturer and distributor of basketball goods, organizing the $1.5 million purchase into its Huffy Sports Co. subsidiary.

As these transactions were being completed, the company entered a new segment in the bike market. The first Huffy BMX model was introduced in 1997. At the time of Huffy's entry into that market segment, BMX models represented the only segment in the bike industry recording sales growth.

UNION WOES

By the end of 1997 the company's financial results revealed the influence of the changes implemented during the previous two years. The news was encouraging. After posting a $10.5 million loss in 1995, Huffy recorded $10.4 million in net income in 1997.

Although Huffy management had directed a remarkable turnaround between 1995 and 1997, the executives still had to contend with the aftereffects of the mid-1990s crisis. One contentious issue stemming from the $10.5 million loss involved Huffy workers at the Celina, Ohio, bicycle plant. When the losses had mounted in 1995, the workers agreed to a 20 percent wage cut to keep production from moving to Huffy's bike plant in Farmington, Missouri.

In April 1998 the workers' union met with Huffy management, demanding a 20 percent wage increase and additional raises to compensate for the benefits and wages lost since 1995. The negotiations stalled, with Huffy offering less than the workers demanded. In July hope for a settlement disappeared entirely when Huffy announced it was closing the Celina plant and laying off all of the facility's 1,000 employees, representing 25 percent of the company's total workforce. Although unpopular in Celina, Huffy management was determined to make the company's bike operations profitable in the long term.

INVENTORY BUSINESS EXPANDS

As Huffy exited the 1990s it continued to pursue the strategy of paring away assets, acquiring new properties, and entering new business areas. In 1998 the company's Washington Inventory Service subsidiary (the second-largest inventory counter in the nation) acquired Denver, Colorado-based Inventory Auditors, Inc. The deal resulted in the addition of an operation that had 42 offices operating in 23 states.

The acquisition greatly strengthened Washington Inventory Service's position in its industry, since Inventory Auditors ranked third in the industry. The addition of Inventory Auditors, combined with the company's divestitures and efforts to reduce production capacity and increase efficiency, impressed Wall Street. During the last six months of 1998 Huffy's stock value increased 25 percent.

In 1999 the company experienced further significant changes, none more dramatic than the announcement that it was selling True Temper Hardware Co. In February 1999 Huffy sold its garden tools and wheelbarrow business to U.S. Industries, Inc., for $100 million, stripping the company of $123 million in sales. With the proceeds from the divestiture, Huffy planned to reduce its short-term debt and to finance the company's ongoing program of buying back its shares.

GLOBAL COMPETITION INTENSIFIES

The last year of the decade also saw Huffy introduce an electric scooter. Named Buzz, the scooter was rechargeable from a standard 110-volt outlet. To strengthen its foray into the electric scooter segment, Huffy reached an agreement in June 1999 with zapworld.com to sell the company's stand-up version of an electric scooter, called Zappy, through Huffy's distribution channels.

Statistics in the 1990s pointed to a fiercely competitive global market for bike manufacturers in the 21st century. Between 1994 and 1998, comparable retail bike prices dropped 25 percent in the United States, largely because of the wave of foreign imports, plunging 10 percent in 1997 alone. In 1997 foreign manufacturers produced nearly 60 percent of the bikes purchased in the United States.

To combat eroding profit margins, Huffy planned to further reduce costs and to eliminate excess production capacity. In addition, the company was focused on developing a more competitive mix of domestic and nondomestic products. Ultimately, steep price reductions from Chinese bicycle manufacturers forced Huffy to cease domestic bicycle production in September 1999.

ENTERING THE 21ST CENTURY

By mid-2000 Huffy was in the process of relocating its engineering and research staff from the company's Miamisburg, Ohio, headquarters to its technology center in Springboro. The company entered into agreements for the sale of the 50,000-square-foot Miamisburg building, as well as a facility in Farmington, Missouri, and also terminated a long-term lease for its South Haven, Mississippi, plant.

In September Huffy agreed to sell its Washington Inventory Service operation to Westport, Connecticut-based Sterling Investment Partners LP. The $84.75 million deal was completed in November. The following month, Huffy completed the sale of its Miamisburg facility, generating $2.75 million.

A major opportunity emerged in mid-2001 when Huffy agreed to acquire the cycling division of Schwinn/GT Corp. in a deal estimated at more than $60 million. However, Huffy withdrew its offer in September when bidding for Schwinn/GT's assets exceeded what Huffy was willing to spend. Another opportunity presented itself in mid-2002 when Huffy acquired, for $19 million, the Canadian company Gen-X Sports Inc., which manufactured equipment in the snowboarding, golf, skiing, hockey, and inline categories.

SHEDDING ASSETS

Huffy began shedding assets mid-decade. In early 2004 the company agreed to sell its high-end ski brand, Volant, to Atomic AG, the Winter Sports Division of Amer

Group plc. In April Huffy revealed plans to sell its Huffy Service Solutions and Creative Retail Services units. Another sale took place during the summer, when the company agreed to sell its Huffy Sports unit to Russell Corp. in a deal worth $30 million.

Facing liquidity problems, Huffy ultimately hired the firm Lazard Frères & Co. LLC to explore selling the entire company. Over the course of two years, Huffy had seen its stock price decline approximately 96 percent. In August 2004 trading of the company's shares was suspended on the New York Stock Exchange when Huffy's market value reached $4.3 million, down from $50 million two years before.

Huffy filed for bankruptcy in October 2004. John A. Muskovich succeeded Paul R. D'Aloia as president and CEO. After securing $50 million in financing, the company emerged from bankruptcy in October 2005 as a privately held company. Huffy's Chinese suppliers held approximately 30 percent of the company's stock. Zhidong Liang, executive vice president of China Export & Credit Insurance Corp., was named chairman.

RETURN TO STRENGTH

After weathering difficult times, Huffy continued to rank as one of the nation's leading bike brands. In 2006 the company sold its 100 millionth bicycle. The following year, Huffy established an agreement with Hilco Consumer Capital LLC and Crystal Capital for the sale of its Tommy Armour, Ram, Teardrop, and Zebra brand golf lines. Also in 2007, Huffy entered the swing set market and began selling Huffy Playcenters.

By October 2007 Huffy employed 90 people. At that time, plans were made to relocate the company's headquarters to a facility formerly occupied by IKON in Centerville, Ohio. In addition, Huffy experienced more leadership changes. During the latter years of the decade Chicago-based consultant Michael Buenzow served as Huffy's president. However, COO Bill Smith was named president and CEO in May 2010.

Smith brought 25 years of industry experience. His tenure with Huffy began in 1993, when he joined the company as director of marketing. After being promoted to COO in 2008, Smith provided the company with leadership during its emergence from bankruptcy. With expertise in areas ranging from merchandising and marketing to long-range strategic planning, he was well suited to lead the company into the second decade of the 21st century.

Mary McNulty
Updated, Jeffrey L. Covell; Paul R. Greenland

PRINCIPAL COMPETITORS

Dorel Industries Inc.; Giant Manufacturing Co., Ltd.; Trek Bicycle Corporation.

FURTHER READING

"Expansive Huffy Buys Multi-branded Gen-X. Sports." *Brandweek*, June 24, 2002, p. 12.

"Fifty Years of Growth Took Teamwork." *Huffman Highlights*. Miamisburg, Ohio: The Huffman Manufacturing Company, 1973.

"Huffy Corp. Riding High." *America's Intelligence Wire*, May 18, 2010.

"Huffy Goes Private after Bankruptcy; Company Will Stay in Miamisburg." *Dayton Daily News*, October 15, 2005, p. D1.

"Huffy Pedals out of Bankruptcy." *Sporting Goods Business*, November 2005, p. 10.

Ryan, Thomas J. "Huffy Goes up for Sale." *Sporting Goods Business*, June 2004, p. 16.

"Sterling Investment Partners Completes Acquisition of Washington Inventory Service from Huffy Corporation." *PR Newswire*, November 6, 2000.

Ullmer, Katherine. "Huffy Moving Its Headquarters." *Dayton Daily News*, October 16, 2007.

Hy-Vee, Inc.

———————— ■ ————————

5820 Westown Parkway
West Des Moines, Iowa 50266
U.S.A.
Telephone: (515) 267-2800
Toll Free: (800) 289-8343
Fax: (515) 267-2817
Web site: http://www.hy-vee.com

Private Company
Incorporated: 1938 as Hyde & Vredenburg
Employees: 55,000
Sales: $6.4 billion (2009 est.)
NAICS: 445110 Supermarkets and Other Grocery
(Except Convenience) Stores; 446110 Pharmacies
and Drug Stores

■ ■ ■

West Des Moines, Iowa-based Hy-Vee, Inc., is one of
the nation's top 30 supermarket chains. In 2009 the
company generated $6.4 billion in annual sales. At that
time Hy-Vee's operations included a workforce of approximately 56,000 employees who worked at 228 retail
stores in eight midwestern states, as well as a 1.5
million-square-foot distribution facility in Chariton,
Iowa, and a 650,000-square-foot distribution center in
Cherokee, Iowa.

ORIGINS DURING THE GREAT DEPRESSION

In 1930 two Iowa businessmen formed a grocery store
partnership. Charles Hyde and David Vredenburg had
separately owned or managed several stores in Iowa and
Missouri before starting their partnership's first store, a
general retail store in Beaconsfield, Iowa, that sold
groceries and dry goods such as clothing.

For a few years both founders continued to run
separate stores and stores with other partners, while also
running some stores together. However, in 1934 these
general stores with such names as The Supply Stores,
Hyde Service Store, and Vredenburg Grocery began selling only groceries.

In 1938 the original partnership was dissolved when
Hyde & Vredenburg was incorporated. The new operation, with 15 stores in Iowa and Missouri, was owned
by 16 store managers who traded ownership in local
stores for corporate stock. Thus began the company's
heritage of being an employee-owned organization. The
new corporation, headquartered in Lamoni, Iowa, chose
Dwight Vredenburg, a son of the cofounder, as its
president. Its 1938 annual sales were about $1.5 million.

In 1940 Hy-Vee found its customers were reluctant
to start using "baskets on wheels," or grocery carts, said
Dwight Vredenburg in the February 20, 2000, *Des
Moines Register*. First introduced in its Centerville, Iowa,
store, the carts reminded women of baby buggies, and
men felt the carts were "for sissies whose arms weren't
strong enough to carry a few groceries." However, free
candy bars in each new cart soon persuaded customers
to try the new contraptions.

EARLY EXPANSION

After World War II ended, many in the military
returned to civilian life, and the postwar economy saw

increased demands for housing and food as a large segment of younger families began having children. To help meet these demands, Hy-Vee expanded for several years, mainly in Iowa. In 1945 the company moved from Lamoni to Chariton, Iowa, after purchasing the Chariton Wholesale Grocery Company. In 1948 Hy-Vee built its first warehouse/office complex, a 72,000-square-foot facility in Chariton. At the end of 1949 the growing company owned 29 stores that brought in $9.2 million in annual sales.

In the 1950s the company added new warehouse facilities, retail stores, and a new name. In 1952 an employee contest resulted in three employees suggesting that the stores be renamed "Hy-Vee," combining the last names of the two founders. Although the company's name remained Hyde & Vredenburg, in 1953 the Fairfield, Iowa, store was the first to bear the new name of Hy-Vee. Ten years later, in 1963, the corporate name became Hy-Vee Food Stores, Inc.

Company "firsts" in the 1950s included the 1956 introduction of Hy-Vee's first private-label brand and the 1959 opening of a store in the Des Moines suburb of Johnson, the first Hy-Vee in a major urban area. In the 1950s the company also started its data processing department and added 28,000 feet to its Chariton warehouse for storing produce and frozen foods. At the end of fiscal year 1959 the company's annual sales stood at almost $36 million from its chain of 37 stores that employed 1,186 people.

OPERATIONAL EXPANSION

The 1960s brought even more rapid growth in Hy-Vee's operations. The firm expanded its headquarters in Chariton, including a 107,000-square-foot addition to its grocery warehouse in 1960; a new corporate headquarters finished in 1963; a 1965 addition of 93,000 square feet to the warehouse; a 12,000-square-foot addition to the warehouse for its Regal Stamp program started in 1956; and a new addition to its warehouse for truck maintenance and cleaning.

The Hy-Vee Employees Trust Fund in 1963 purchased the locally based National Bank & Trust Company of Chariton, and the same year the company

broadcast its first television commercial. It opened its first Minnesota store in 1969, one of the 12 gained from a merger with Swanson Stores based in Cherokee, Iowa.

Hy-Vee owned 66 stores, including its Drug Town stores acquired in the 1960s, at the end of fiscal 1969. At that time annual sales stood at $130 million. With the company doing so well, it decided to start the Hy-Vee Foundation in 1968 to provide college scholarships.

In the 1970s Hy-Vee continued to grow by opening new stores, building more warehouse space, and adding new technology. A 1971 addition of 78,000 square feet brought the total capacity of the Chariton warehouse to 430,000 square feet. In addition, in 1976 the company built a secondary warehouse/office complex in Cherokee, Iowa.

CONTINUED GROWTH

Hy-Vee started stores in three additional states during the decade: South Dakota in 1975, Nebraska in 1977, and Illinois in 1979. Another company milestone during the decade included the opening of its 100th store, in Keokuk, Iowa. This location was the first to use electronic cash registers. In 1978 annual sales surpassed $500 million for the first time.

In the 1980s Hy-Vee added acquisitions, new stores, and new leadership. In 1982 the company purchased 12 former Safeway stores in western Iowa and eastern Nebraska, including seven stores in Omaha and two in the state capital of Lincoln. In 1988 Hy-Vee opened its first store in Kansas, in Overland Park. To meet the needs of its growing chain, Hy-Vee in 1982 organized Perishable Distributors of Iowa (PDI), an affiliated firm that later became a subsidiary.

In 1983 Ron Pearson replaced Dwight Vredenburg as Hy-Vee's president. Vredenburg remained the chairman and CEO. However, in 1989 Pearson became CEO and chairman when Vredenburg finally retired. At the end of fiscal 1989 Hy-Vee employed 22,778 individuals at 172 stores, up from 9,591 employees at 124 stores in fiscal 1979. Its annual sales increased from $680.3 million in 1979 to $1.8 billion in 1989. Even greater growth was coming in the decade ahead.

The 1990s began with several acquisitions. Hy-Vee purchased Lomar Distributing in 1990, Sunrise Dairy in 1991, D & D Salads and Florist Distributing in 1992, and the Meyocks & Priebe advertising firm in 1994. In 1995 the firm moved its corporate headquarters to West Des Moines and changed its name to Hy-Vee, Inc.

KEY DATES

■

1930: Charles Hyde and David Vredenburg form a partnership and open a small general retail store in Beaconsfield, Iowa.

1938: Hyde & Vredenburg, Inc., is incorporated.

1963: Company changes its name to Hy-Vee Food Stores, Inc.

1982: Hy-Vee organizes Perishable Distributors of Iowa (PDI) to meet the needs of the growing chain.

1995: The firm moves its corporate headquarters to West Des Moines, Iowa; Hy-Vee, Inc., becomes the new corporate name.

2001: Ric Jurgens succeeds Ron Pearson as president; Pearson remains chairman and CEO, and is named COO.

2004: Jurgens is promoted to CEO.

2006: Jurgens is named chairman.

2009: Randy Edeker is named president and Jurgens remains chairman and CEO.

65TH ANNIVERSARY

When Hy-Vee celebrated its 65th anniversary in 1995, Ron Pearson, president, CEO, and chairman, realized the company should do something to preserve and use its history. Inspired by the Coca-Cola History Center in Atlanta, Pearson persuaded the board of directors to spend $1 million on a 4,000-square-foot History Center located next to the company's headquarters in West Des Moines. Marilyn C. Gahm, a professional librarian with about 20 years of experience in corporate libraries, served as the center's coordinator.

With a low unemployment rate in a booming economy, most stores, including Hy-Vee, scrambled to gain and keep good employees. Hy-Vee was a business that made a concerted effort to hire senior citizens. In the April 13, 2000, *Journal Star*, Vice President Steve Meyer said that at Hy-Vee, "recruitment and retention of older workers becomes an imperative as well as a desire and goal." Hy-Vee used flexible scheduling to attract older workers, offering jobs for three seasons so seniors could spend winters in warmer climates.

Hy-Vee, like numerous other supermarkets, began offering more vitamins and natural foods as more consumers tried to improve their health through supplements and organic foods. Hy-Vee called its in-store sections with such products Health Marts. These competed with such huge natural food stores as Wild Oats and

numerous multilevel marketing companies that sold supplements.

In the 1990s Hy-Vee began offering more ethnic foods. Chinese Express was introduced in the Independence, Missouri, store in 1992. In 1994 the Des Moines Store Number 3 became the first one in the chain to offer Mexican Express takeout items.

CONTINUED INDUSTRY CHANGE

Meanwhile, Hy-Vee ended some of its operations. On January 22, 1999, the company sold Heartland Pantry, its chain of 42 Iowa convenience stores, to Kraus Gentle Corporation. By April 1999 all of those stores had been converted to the Kum & Go name. In February 1999 Hy-Vee sold its partnership in Iowa Beverage Manufacturers, Inc.

Another challenge for all retail industries was the booming electronic commerce trend. Shoppers in the 1990s gained the option to buy thousands of items, including food, on the Internet by using a credit card. Although still in its early stages, Internet shopping offered customers a way to save time as they ordered from the convenience of their homes.

Hy-Vee's Rochester Number 3 store in 1998 was the first in the chain to offer optional telephone or Internet shopping. In June 2000 Hy-Vee organized its newest subsidiary, electricfood.com, which began offering gourmet foods for purchase. In a related move, in 2000 Hy-Vee responded to customer requests by adding two new ways to get discount coupons from its Web site at www.hy-vee.com. Hy-Vee also was part of ICS Food One, run by Internet Commerce Systems of Norcross, Georgia, which focused on exchanging information on brands and promotions among farmers, food manufacturers and distributors, and retailers.

In the late 1990s several entities recognized or honored Hy-Vee's achievements and growth. In 1997 *Consumer Reports* ranked the Iowa-based company as the fifth-best U.S. supermarket chain. The Better Business Bureau in 1998 honored Hy-Vee with its "Integrity Award." Finally, in 1999 *Forbes* ranked Hy-Vee as the nation's 32nd-largest private company. Hy-Vee's annual sales reached an all-time high to date of $3.5 billion at the end of fiscal 1999. At that time it employed 42,776 persons at 208 stores.

ENTERING THE 21ST CENTURY

At the start of the new millennium, Hy-Vee and other supermarkets faced competition from the growing strength of Wal-Mart and such warehouse clubs as Sam's Club and Costco. However, strong regional chains continued to receive praise from retail analysts. On the competitive front, one of the company's differentials was to continue focusing on healthy lifestyles. In addition, Hy-Vee spent $160 million on capital improvements for its stores during the 2000 fiscal year.

In mid-2000 Hy-Vee began offering health and lifestyle-related programming and advertisements in its drugstores via RMS Network's PharmaSee TV satellite television network. In addition, the company introduced its HealthMarket private-label line of products in 2001 and began providing customers with access to in-store dietitians.

A number of leadership changes took place during the early years of the new century. In 2001 Ric Jurgens succeeded Ron Pearson as president, becoming the third person to hold the title in Hy-Vee's 72-year history. Jurgens also continued to serve as chief administrative officer. Pearson remained chairman and CEO, and also filled the newly created role of COO.

PHARMACY EXPANSION

In 2001 Hy-Vee expanded its operations by acquiring a mix of 39 independent and chain-owned pharmacies. The company acquired more than 30 additional pharmacies in 2002, including several locations from Kmart Corp. By early 2003 Hy-Vee employed 46,000 people at more than 200 stores in seven states. Annual sales exceeded $3.8 billion.

In 2003 Hy-Vee was named *Progressive Grocer*'s Retailer of the Year. In addition, the company modernized its supply chain operations by implementing technology from Vialink. Specifically, new data synchronization services enabled Hy-Vee to share product-related information with its suppliers.

Additional leadership changes took place early the following year when Ric Jurgens was promoted to CEO. That year, the company unveiled a fourth generation of its logo, which featured red letters on a white background. In addition, a new convention and event center named Hy-Vee Hall, which was part of the Iowa Events Center, was established in downtown Des Moines, Iowa.

Hy-Vee celebrated 75 years of operation in 2005. A new employee intranet named Hy-VeeNet was introduced, along with a redesigned Web site offering a variety of online shopping options for customers. In addition, the company rebranded its 26 Drug Town stores under the Hy-Vee Drugstores name.

TECHNOLOGY AND SERVICE ENHANCEMENTS

Hy-Vee continued to introduce new services for its customers in 2006. That year, the company introduced

gift cards, as well as online imaging services (photo prints) via an arrangement with PhotoChannel Networks. In addition, Hy-Vee was the first retailer in the United States to install a next-generation self-checkout system from IBM. Another leadership change took place that year when Ric Jurgens was named chairman.

Technology enhancements continued at Hy-Vee in 2007, when the company moved forward with plans to install remote check deposit scanners from Dayton, Ohio-based NCR Corp. at all 224 of its stores. By this time Hy-Vee's sales exceeded $5.2 billion. Also that year, the company's first store, located in Beaconsfield, Iowa, was added to the National Register of Historic Places.

For the first time in 20 years, Hy-Vee announced plans to establish operations in a new state in late 2007. A new 90,000-square-foot supermarket was slated to open in Madison, Wisconsin, on the site of a former Kmart. Hy-Vee rounded out the year by announcing plans to offer loose meat beef sandwiches from the regional Maid-Rite chain in its 96 convenience stores.

In 2008 Hy-Vee opened its largest store to date. Located in Des Moines, the store spanned more than 91,000 square feet. In addition, the company unveiled a small-store format under the Heartland Pantry name that offered basic items such as canned goods, meat, and fresh produce.

HEALTH FOCUS

In 2008 Hy-Vee expanded its medical focus with the addition of a new durable medical equipment division called Hy-Vee Home Medical. In addition, the company made a new educational tool available to its customers, as part of an effort to help them make optimum nutritional choices. The tool provided details regarding the nutritional value of approximately 50,000 food items.

In December 2009 Randy Edeker was named president of Hy-Vee. Ric Jurgens remained with the company as chairman and CEO. In addition, Ron Pearson served as chairman emeritus.

In mid-2010 Hy-Vee joined forces with the U.S. Environmental Protection Agency's GreenChill program, in an effort to reduce refrigerant emissions. By following earth-friendly practices ranging from energy conservation and waste reduction efforts to the design and construction of energy-efficient stores, Hy-Vee sought to help combat climate change.

Hy-Vee approached the second decade of the 21st century as the second-largest employee-owned company in the nation. With a workforce of 55,000 employees, the company generated sales of more than $6.3 billion on the strength of approximately 228 stores. Looking to the future, Hy-Vee appeared to have excellent prospects for continued success.

David M. Walden
Updated, Paul R. Greenland

PRINCIPAL SUBSIDIARIES

D & D Foods, Inc.; Florist Distributing, Inc.; Hy-Vee Weitz Construction; Lomar Distributing, Inc.; Midwest Heritage Bank, FSB; Perishable Distributors of Iowa, Ltd.

PRINCIPAL COMPETITORS

Fareway Stores, Inc.; Kroger Co.; Wal-Mart Stores, Inc.

FURTHER READING

Fritz, E. Mae. *The Family of Hy-Vee: A History of Hy-Vee Food Stores.* West Des Moines, Iowa: Hy-Vee Food Stores, Inc., 1989.

"Hy-Vee Center Aisles Stocked with Memories; Hy-Vee Center Features Memories in Every Aisle." *Des Moines Register,* February 20, 2000, p. 1.

"Hy-Vee Partners with EPA GreenChill." *Refrigerated Transporter,* June 9, 2010.

"Hy-Vee Plans to Change the Name of the Company's 26-Store Drug Store Chain from Drug Town to Hy-Vee Drugstores." *Chain Store Age,* August 2005, p. 22.

"Jurgens Named Hy-Vee CEO." *MMR,* January 12, 2004, p. 76.

Love, Alice Ann. "Congress' Goal: Help Workers Keep Working—Lawmakers Look for More Ways for Older Employees to Stay on the Job Longer." *Journal Star* (Peoria), April 13, 2000.

Lovell, Michael. "New Hy-Vee Chief to Focus on Medical Services." *Business Record* (Des Moines), December 31, 2001, p. 1.

Ryberg, William. "Ron Pearson Brings High Energy to Hy-Vee." *Des Moines Register,* April 23, 2000, p. 1.

Weinstein, Steve. "Death of a Salesman?" *Progressive Grocer,* June 2000, p. 33.

J.F. Shea Co., Inc.

———— ■ ————

655 Brea Canyon Road
Walnut, California 91789
U.S.A.
Telephone: (909) 594-9500
Fax: (909) 594-0917
Web site: http://www.jfshea.com

Private Company
Founded: 1881 as John F. Shea Plumbing Company
Employees: 2,300
Sales: $2.88 billion (2006 est.)
NAICS: 237210 Land Subdivision; 233210 Single Family Housing Construction

■ ■ ■

J.F. Shea Co., Inc., is one of the largest privately held construction companies in the United States. J.F. Shea comprises a collection of companies and divisions, including Shea Mortgage, Shea Properties, the Venture Capital Division, J.F. Shea Construction Inc., the Redding Division, Reed Manufacturing, and Shea Homes. Through Shea Homes, J.F. Shea develops master planned communities in California, Arizona, Colorado, North Carolina, Florida, and Nevada.

ORIGINS

J.F. Shea traces its corporate roots to the John F. Shea Plumbing Company, a plumbing contractor and wholesale supplier of plumbing equipment. The company was founded in Portland, Oregon, in 1881, by

its namesake. With the establishment of his plumbing company, John Shea created a family business that would draw upon the talents of four generations of Shea family members (a legacy spanning more than a century). However, the enduring strength of the company stemmed neither from the plumbing business nor did it emanate from Portland.

Instead, J.F. Shea's success and reputation were achieved in the construction industry, specifically in assisting in the construction of major civil engineering projects. The transformation from a plumbing business into a heavy construction business also included the company's relocation from the Pacific Northwest to northern California, the hub of J.F. Shea's operations for much of the 20th century.

J.F. Shea entered the construction business as an offshoot of its plumbing activities. During the 1910s, John Shea and his son Charlie formed the J.F. Shea Company, the abbreviated corporate title signaling the company's entrance into sewer construction. Not long after the company entered the sewer construction field, John Shea's other sons, Gilbert and Edmund, joined the family business.

LARGE-SCALE PROJECTS

One of the company's first large-scale projects was completed during the 1920s. During the decade, J.F. Shea constructed the Portland Seawall on the Willamette River. The company's connection to northern California was established during the decade as well, brought about through the construction of the Mokelumne Pipeline, which transported water across central

COMPANY PERSPECTIVES

One of the oldest and largest privately held operations in the country, the J.F. Shea Co., Inc., has earned a prominent position among construction companies. Built on a solid foundation, J. F. Shea Co., Inc., has inherited the family commitment to hard work and pride in a job well done. Today, the company upholds the ethics and principles established by John Shea more than a century ago.

California to cities such as Oakland and Berkeley. The construction of the Mokelumne Pipeline helped establish the company's reputation outside the Pacific Northwest, leading to its involvement in several of the largest civil engineering projects of the 20th century.

During the 1930s J.F. Shea built the foundation piers for the Golden Gate Bridge in San Francisco and assisted in the construction of the San Francisco–Oakland Bay Bridge. The company also served as the construction manager for the Hoover Dam, which ranked as the tallest dam in the United States when it was completed in 1936.

J.F. Shea's involvement in the massive construction projects of the 1930s gave the business a secure place within the heavy construction industry, but the company's promising new role in civil engineering was put on hold for much of the 1940s. The outbreak of World War II diverted the attention of nearly all types of businesses, forcing them to respond to the different conditions and demands of a country at war. J.F. Shea spent the war years building Liberty ships and shipyards. Construction activity of the type the company had become used to during the 1930s slowed, prompting management to invest in new industries, such as aluminum, magnesium, and cement.

POST-WORLD WAR II GROWTH

The 1950s brought the third generation of leaders into the company, John Shea and cousins Peter and Edmund. The three Sheas took command of the company's heavy construction operations during the 1950s, beginning the diversification and expansion that eventually created the multifaceted collection of business interests that described the company's operations at the dawn of the 21st century. In 1957 the establishment of the Shea Sand and Gravel Plant marked the beginning of what became known as the J.F. Shea Redding Divi-

sion, a supplier of aggregate materials to contractors and government agencies.

As it matured, the Redding Division's business scope increased to embrace highway and bridge construction and repair work in northern California. Through a collection of gravel, asphalt, and concrete plants and quarries, the Redding Division produced construction materials and contracted for construction projects in northern California. During the 1950s, J.F. Shea also established Shasta Electric, a full-service electrical contractor offering services for commercial and industrial construction customers.

The diversification begun during the 1950s continued in earnest during the 1960s, as J.F. Shea followed the prevailing corporate trend of the era. Many companies sought to achieve financial consistency and stability by entering a range of businesses, thereby reducing dependence on a single line of business. In 1968, J.F. Shea established Shea Homes (known until 1974 as PBS Corp.), moving the company into residential housing construction, a business of vital importance to the company's financial well-being at the end of the 20th century.

The company also divested its interests in the "smokestack" industries it had invested in during the 1940s. The money subsequently was diverted to high technology investments, leading to the establishment in 1968 of the J.F. Shea Venture Capital Division. Through Venture Capital, J.F. Shea began investing in private start-up companies. Among the list of fledgling concerns aided by J.F. Shea were Compaq Computer Corporation, Brocade Corp., Exodus Corp., and Altera Corp.

BROADENED BUSINESS SCOPE

Although the 1960s marked J.F. Shea's transformation into a diversified concern, the company continued to be a heavy construction firm at its core. The decade that saw the company delve into the venture capital business and into residential construction also included several major construction projects. J.F. Shea constructed tunnels and stations for the San Francisco Bay Area Rapid Transit System, more commonly known as BART. J.F. Shea's contributions to BART helped the company secure another high-profile project during the 1970s, when it assisted in the construction of the Metro, the subway system in Washington, D.C.

The decade also saw the company broaden its business scope further. J.F. Shea established Shea Properties, the commercial and residential investment and management arm of the family business. Through Shea Properties the company invested in and managed apartment buildings and commercial real estate, at first in

KEY DATES

1881: John F. Shea Plumbing Company is founded.

1910s: Business is renamed J.F. Shea Company.

1968: Shea Homes formed as PBS Corp.

1989: Knoell Homes is acquired, moving J.F. Shea into the Arizona residential construction market.

1996: Shea Homes enters the Colorado homebuilding market.

1997: Mission Viejo Co. is acquired, greatly expanding homebuilding assets in Colorado and California.

1998: UDC Homes is purchased, giving Shea Homes the largest homebuilder in Phoenix.

2007: Shea Homes enters Florida market.

2008: Poor economic conditions lead Shea Homes to suspend construction on two California housing developments.

2010: Shea Construction joint venture wins $1 billion subway tunneling contract in New York.

California and then in Colorado. J.F. Shea also completed an acquisition during the 1970s, purchasing Reed Manufacturing, a producer of concrete guns and pumps used in civil, residential, and commercial construction projects.

During the 1980s Shea Homes came to the fore, its growth fanned by the rapidly expanding real estate industry in California. Shea Homes began developing master planned communities throughout California, registering enough success to warrant the establishment of a division in Arizona at the end of the decade. Meanwhile, aided by the same robust real estate market, Shea Properties substantially expanded its portfolio of retail and commercial properties.

GEOGRAPHIC EXPANSION

During the 1990s J.F. Shea's fourth generation of family management, led by COO John Jr., Ed, and Gil, spearheaded the company's geographic expansion. The company's residential construction business led the way during the decade, as Shea Homes developed into one of the largest privately held developers of residential communities in the United States. Before 1989 J.F. Shea's involvement in residential construction was limited to California markets, but an acquisition completed in the last year of the decade pushed the company beyond that state's borders.

In 1989 the company purchased Knoell Homes, a large-volume construction company that had built roughly 800 homes in Phoenix, Arizona, two years before its acquisition by J.F. Shea. The acquisition gave Shea Homes its Phoenix-based Arizona Division, an enterprise that served as a springboard for further geographic expansion. Initially, the Arizona Division fared poorly. By 1991 the number of sale closings in the Phoenix market had fallen to 324 homes, down substantially from the 800 closings recorded four years earlier.

Other homebuilders in the Phoenix area shared the troubles faced by the Phoenix-based executives of Shea Homes. The total number of new housing permits had fallen from 18,000 in the mid-1980s to 10,000 by the beginning of the 1990s, signaling the onset of a recessive real estate market. At this moment of vulnerability, the management team of Shea Homes showed its mettle, turning the company's troubled condition into a position of strength.

LAND-PURCHASING PROGRAM LAUNCHED

Instead of retreating in the face of a contracting market, Shea Homes restructured its Arizona Division and launched an aggressive land-purchasing program in 1991. Land prices offered exceptional values, spurring management to purchase as much land as possible. The Arizona Division quickly put the purchased land to use. In a May 1994 interview with *Professional Builder and Remodeler*, a Shea Homes executive remarked, "We also put houses in the ground as quickly as possible with new plans. The timing was just right. The market was turning around." Thanks to the aggressive stance, the Arizona Division recorded a substantial surge in business, closing 1,337 homes in 1993. Between 1991 and 1993, the operation's market share in Phoenix increased from 2.7 percent to 7.4 percent.

As J.F. Shea entered the latter half of the 1990s, the actions of Shea Homes accounted for the major successes of the period. There were two important developments outside residential construction: Shea Mortgage, the home financing arm of the family enterprise, was established, and J.F. Shea Construction, the heavy construction arm, completed an acquisition of a Southern California construction company. However, the biggest news revolved around the acquisitions and expansion completed by Shea Homes.

Shea Homes expanded its operating territory to include residential construction in Colorado, where the company entered the Denver market in 1996, and to North Carolina, where housing communities were developed in Charlotte. By the end of 1996, the company recorded $600 million in home sales, enough to make it the 23rd-largest homebuilder in the United States. During the ensuing two years, the company's stature would increase substantially, as Shea Homes completed two pivotal acquisitions that increased its presence in California, Colorado, and Arizona.

MAJOR ACQUISITIONS

In 1997 Shea Homes gave its fledgling Colorado home-building business a tremendous boost. The company reportedly paid $480 million for Mission Viejo Co., an acquisition that included two developments in Southern California (Mission Viejo and Aliso Viejo) and a sprawling community in Colorado dubbed Highlands Ranch. The properties in Southern California comprised 900 acres, while the Highlands Ranch property measured 22,000 acres, or seven square miles.

Highlands Ranch, the prize asset of the acquisition, contained 14,800 homes. At the time of the acquisition 3,600 acres remained to be developed, enough to build an additional 16,000 homes. With the addition of Mission Viejo Co., Shea Homes was able to sell more than 3,000 homes in 1997, generating more than $1 billion in residential construction revenue.

The acquisition of Mission Viejo Co. was followed by another large purchase. In mid-1998 Shea Homes agreed to acquire UDC Homes, the largest homebuilder in Phoenix and one of the major developers of housing for seniors. Additionally, UDC owned lots for nearly 1,600 new homes in Southern California. The acquisition of UDC drew praise from industry observers. One real estate analyst, in a July 11, 1998, interview with Jesus Sanchez in the *Los Angeles Times*, remarked: "Shea came through the tough [recessionary] times very strong, and they have been pursuing a brilliant strategy of expanding strategically into Colorado and Orange County. They've been able to go into these [new markets] and create more value than was previously there through intelligent planning, development, and marketing."

CHANGE IN LEADERSHIP

Combined, the acquisitions of Mission Viejo and UDC represented a transaction value of nearly $1 billion. The magnitude of the acquisitions left J.F. Shea primarily focused on the development of master planned communities, although the company continued to operate as a heavy construction contractor. In the years after the two signal acquisitions, J.F. Shea attempted to acquire Del Webb Corp., a Phoenix-based builder of retirement homes. Against the wishes of Del Webb's management, J.F. Shea launched a $690 million bid for the Phoenix company, but the deal lapsed in November 2000. John F. Shea, the company's chairman and CEO, expressed a desire to resume what he termed "further constructive dialogue," but no definitive agreement was reached.

In 2002 Shea Homes, the main engine driving J.F. Shea's growth, gained a new leader. Roy Humphreys announced his retirement in January, ending his 27-year tenure at the company. Humphreys joined Shea Homes in 1974 as an offsite coordinator for the Southern California division before being appointed president of Shea Homes in 1980. Humphreys was replaced by Bert Selva, who joined Shea Homes in 1996 to head the company's Colorado operations. Selva was named president and CEO in February 2002.

RESIDENTIAL MARKET BOOMS

In 2001 Shea Homes launched a branding initiative around the theme "Caring since 1881," harmonizing the activities of its several home divisions. Shea's largest residential market was Phoenix, accounting for 2,007 of the 5,438 homes it closed in 2002. Arizona was also an important operational base. Both Shea Homes and the company's Active Adult division were based in Scottsdale. In 2003 Shea Homes formed a division dedicated to California's "Inland Empire," San Bernardino and Riverside counties.

Revenues for Shea Homes approached $2.8 billion in 2004, when it closed on more than 6,400 homes. It was the 12th-largest homebuilder in the United States, and the largest privately owned homebuilder. J.F. Shea's total group revenues exceeded $3 billion. The group had approximately 2,500 employees. During the year the company launched investment unit Shea Ventures as well as Shea Properties, which owned more than 5,000 apartments and two million square feet of commercial space in California and Colorado.

Shea Homes opened a development near Raleigh, North Carolina, in 2004. This was not the company's first foray into the state. *Triangle Business Journal* noted that Shea had been in Charlotte since 1994 and sold 437 homes there in 2004, compared to 31 in its first full year in that city.

BOOM TURNS TO BUST

By 2006 California's booming real estate market was showing signs of a bust. Shea Homes benefited from its name recognition when some buyers left the California market to look for housing in Arizona. However, the slowdown soon spread throughout the Southwest. In the midst of this, *Professional Builder* named Shea Homes its Builder of the Year for 2007. It was still the largest private builder in the country, with 2006 revenues of $2.88 billion.

The company entered the Florida market in 2007, buying into a St. Joe Company development. Shea began sales on 705 homes in Victoria Gardens in De-land, Florida, in January 2008, billing them as ecologically friendly. The homes incorporated sensors throughout to keep utilities costs down, and included sustainable materials in their construction. Buyers were willing to pay a 3 percent or greater premium for more efficient houses.

The dismal state of the economy in the wake of the mortgage crisis prompted Shea Homes to take the unusual step of suspending construction on two town-house developments, both former industrial complexes, in Santa Clara and Mountain View, California, in February 2008. The 6.6-acre Santa Clara site, once a research facility for Underwriters Laboratories, reportedly cost Shea more than $20 million.

Shea resumed construction on the sites after about a year, when the market showed signs of recovery and financing became more available, an official told the *Silicon Valley/San Jose Business Journal*. The company felt obliged to discount prices on the units by about 25 percent, however. In San Diego, Shea's new home sales were one-third of their 2000 peak. The era of quickly built large-scale suburban homes appeared to be at an end, with fewer purchasers specifying grand entrances and stairwells.

SURVIVING THE ECONOMIC SLOWDOWN

Shea's heavy construction unit benefited from federal stimulus funding following the mortgage crisis. As part of the S3II Tunnel Constructors joint venture with Schiavone Construction and Skanska USA Civil (Shea had a 30 percent share), in 2009 the company was awarded contracts for $400 million worth of subway projects in New York City alone, including New Jersey's Palisades Tunnel, part of the Trans-Hudson Express Project. These were put on hold, however, when New Jersey Governor Chris Christie canceled the Access to the Region's Core project in October 2010.

S3II had earlier won a rare $1.1 billion tunneling contract, funded by New York City, to extend the No. 7 subway line. Shea Construction was also kept busy in its home territory of California, which landed more Recovery Act funding than any other state.

Shea Properties divested a reported $200 million in holdings, including Acacia on Santa Rosa Creek for $39 million. Nevertheless, Shea Homes used lower prices as an opportunity to bring its Active Adult business into Las Vegas. In April 2010 it bought the 532-lot Ardient planned community from Centex Corp., which was leaving the market.

J.F. Shea Co.'s range of activities and geographic spread helped it ride out one of the worst economic slowdowns in history. Still family owned after 130 years, the company's heritage provided continuity of leadership and respite from the quarterly pressures that faced its publicly traded rivals.

Jeffrey L. Covell
Updated, Frederick C. Ingram

PRINCIPAL SUBSIDIARIES

Shasta Electric LP; J.F. Shea Heavy Civil Engineering; Partners Insurance Co. Inc.

PRINCIPAL DIVISIONS

Shea Homes; Shea Properties; Shea Ventures; J.F. Shea Construction; Redding; Reed Manufacturing; Shea Mortgage; Blue Star Resort & Golf.

PRINCIPAL COMPETITORS

Centex Corp.; Del Webb Corp.; Granite Construction Incorporated; Irvine Co.; Lennar Corp.; Pulte Homes, Inc.; Standard Pacific Corp; Traylor Bros., Inc.

FURTHER READING

Benderoff, Eric. "How to Position Product for Profit." *Professional Builder and Remodeler,* May 1994, p. 78.

Berton, Brad. "Shea Homes Halts Development in Santa Clara, Mountain View." *Silicon Valley/San Jose Business Journal,* February 22, 2008.

Biddle, RiShawn. "Master Planner." *Forbes,* November 25, 2002, p. 171.

Burke, Erica. "All in the Family." *US Business Review,* January/February 2005, pp. 112–116.

Conrad, Katherine. "Shea Homes Is Back in the Fray." *Silicon Valley/San Jose Business Journal,* April 3, 2009.

Mariani, Michele. "Expansion Team: Shea Homes Leverages More than 120 Years of Success in Construction to Extend its Brand across the United States." *Builder* 28.1 (2005): 318+.

Nilsen, Kim. "Hot Triangle Home Market Lures West Coast Firm." *Triangle Business Journal* (N.C.), August 13, 2004.

Power, Matthew. "Lasting Legacy." *Professional Builder (1993),* December 1, 2006, p. 42.

Rodengen, Jeffrey L., and Richard F. Hubbard. *The History of J.F. Shea Co.* Fort Lauderdale: Write Stuff Enterprises, Inc., 2004.

Sanchez, Jesus. "J.F. Shea Unit Plans to Acquire UDC Homes of Ariz." *Los Angeles Times*, July 11, 1998, p. 4.

Scalzitti, James. "J.F. Shea Covers It All." *Construction Today* 3.8 (2005): 204+.

Volpe, Michael. "Shea Focuses on Technology to Market to Homebuyers." *Orange County Business Journal*, December 7, 2009, p. 44.

Wood, Debra. "Tunnel-Boring Machines Are on the Move in New York City." *Engineering News Record*, June 7, 2010, p. 12.

Kagome Company Ltd.

3-14-15 Nishiki
Naka-ku
Nagoya, 460-0003
Japan
Telephone: (+81 052) 951-3571
Fax: (+81 03) 5623-2334
Web site: http://www.kagome.co.jp

Public Company
Incorporated: 1949 as Aichi Tomato Co., Ltd.
Employees: 2,031
Sales: ¥171.94 billion ($1.7 billion) (2009)
Stock Exchanges: Tokyo
Ticker Symbol: 2811
NAICS: 311421 Fruit and Vegetable Canning

■■■

Kagome Company Ltd. is Japan's leading producer of tomato and vegetable-based beverages, condiments, and sauces. The company also produces microwavable meals, soups, and other tomato-based food products for both the consumer and institutional food sectors. Kagome has also developed its own Japan-based fresh vegetables business, with four tomato-growing facilities in Japan. Through subsidiary Kagome Labio Co., Kagome has also launched production of a line of lactic acid bacteria-based probiotic drinks. Kagome is present in the U.S. market, with subsidiaries in California and Arkansas. The company has also established manufacturing and sales operations in China, Taiwan, Italy, Turkey, and Australia. Altogether the company's operations generate nearly ¥172 billion ($1.7 billion) in revenues per year. The company is listed on the Tokyo Stock Exchange and is led by President Hidenori Nishi and Chairman Koji Kioka.

JAPAN'S TOMATO PIONEER IN 1899

In the late 19th century a number of Western food manufacturers began to take inspiration from Far Eastern recipes. Among the best known of these was ketchup, the ubiquitous condiment that had most likely originated in China. At the same time, a number of Far Eastern markets had begun to develop an interest in Western foods, especially such exotic Western fruits and vegetables as tomatoes and carrots.

A growing number of people in Japan became interested in the potential health benefits of these vegetables, especially tomatoes. Among them was Ichitaro Kanie, who, according to Kagome Company, in 1899 was the first to successfully grow tomatoes in Japan. Before long, Kanie's crop had grown sufficiently for him to begin selling his tomatoes, which he gathered in a wicker basket known as a *kagome*.

In 1903 Ichitaro introduced his first processed tomato product, a tomato puree. This was followed in 1908 by the launch of production of tomato ketchup and Worcestershire sauce. As sales grew Ichitaro began developing his own brand name, and officially registered the Kagome brand in 1917. The company achieved new success with the introduction of its first tomato juice drinks in 1933.

BECOMING KAGOME IN 1963

The next phase in the development of the future Kagome Company came after World War II. In 1949 a new company was created, combining several Aichi-based food producers, including Aichi Tomato Manufacturing Co., Aichi Canned Products Co., Aichi Trading Co., Aichi Marine Industries Co., and Shiga Canned Products Co. The new company then took on the name of Aichi Tomato Co., Ltd. Despite the change in organization, Kagome remained the company's flagship brand.

The fast growth of the packaged foods sector in postwar Japan served to underscore the importance of the Kagome brand for the company. By 1963 the company had decided to change its name again, adopting its famous brand as its own and becoming Kagome Company, Ltd. At that time the company introduced its new logo, suggesting the form of a tomato.

Kagome remained a leading producer of tomato-based drinks and other foods in Japan. In 1966 the company also raised its international profile, becoming the first in the world to package its ketchup in plastic tubes. The packaging quickly became popular not only in Japan but around the world.

GOING PUBLIC IN 1978

Strong growth through the 1960s and into the 1970s encouraged Kagome to reinforce its position as a major national foods company. The company opened its new headquarters in Tokyo in 1972. In 1978 Kagome went public, listing on the Tokyo Stock Exchange's First Section. Kagome's growth remained strong over the next decade, allowing the company to top the ¥100 billion sales mark by 1988.

By this time, Kagome had taken its first steps outside of Japan. In 1988 the company set up its first U.S. subsidiary, in Los Banos, California. The company then began construction of a new manufacturing plant, which launched production in 1990. Rather than attempting to enter the U.S. consumer market directly, however, Kagome instead chose to pursue the institutional and restaurant sectors. Kagome then established a reputation for providing customized food development services for the U.S. market. The company's U.S. subsidiary also began to supply the foodservice industry elsewhere in the world, including in Central and South America, Australia, the Middle East, and parts of Asia.

In the next decade Kagome adopted a new dual head office structure, adding a new Nagoya head office to its office in Tokyo. The company continued to seek out new product lines, and especially began developing an interest in extending its operations beyond its core tomato-based products. This effort led to the launch in 1995 of one of Kagome's most successful products, a vegetable drink called Yasai Seikatsu 100.

FRESH TOMATO PRODUCTION IN 1999

For most of its history Kagome had focused its production on processed foods, rather than fresh food products. This changed in 1998, when Kagome was approached by an executive of one of its major supermarket customers, who asked that the company supply it with fresh tomatoes. The company agreed, encouraged by the rapidly rising demand for healthful foods in Japan at the end of the 20th century. Kagome established a new fresh vegetables business unit.

Kagome then developed its own varieties of tomatoes specifically for the Japanese market, including the Kagome Kokumi tomato and the Kagome Delica tomato. While some varieties were meant to appeal to the consumer market, others were developed according to the needs of the foodservice industry. At first, Kagome contracted with a number of Japanese farmers to grow its tomatoes.

When these farmers proved unable to ensure the company with a stable supply of tomatoes, Kagome decided to take matters into its own hands. Over the next year, company representatives traveled around the world visiting other tomato growers. By 1999 the company had built its own model tomato farm in Minori. The success of this venture led the company to roll out two full-scale tomato production operations, the five-hectare Kada Farmland and the eight-hectare Hibikinada Farmland.

Both facilities were organized more as industrial factories than as farms, providing enhanced productivity and year-round growing conditions. Rather than taking up scarce Japanese farmlands, the new facilities were established in more urban surroundings. For example, the company constructed the Kada complex in an industrial park. The Hibikinada farm, on the other, made use of reclaimed land from an industrial site.

KEY DATES

■

1899: Ichitaro Kanie begins growing tomatoes in Japan.

1903: Ichitaro begins sales of tomato puree, his first tomato-based product.

1917: The company introduces the Kagome brand name.

1963: The company changes its name to Kagome Company.

1978: Kagome goes public on the Tokyo Stock Exchange.

1988: Kagome establishes a subsidiary in the United States.

1999: Kagome launches production and sale of fresh tomatoes.

2003: Kagome begins operations in Taiwan.

2007: Kagome acquires a subsidiary in Arkansas.

2010: Kagome acquires leading Australian tomato processor Cedenco.

PROBIOTICS IN 2002

Kagome continued to increase its commitment to the fresh tomatoes market, forming two new industrial farm subsidiaries. These included Iwaki Onahama Greenfarm, which at 10 hectares became Japan's largest organic farming complex. Construction of the farm began in 2003, with the first shipments of fresh tomatoes beginning in 2005.

Kagome also continued to expand its presence in the Japanese condiments sector. The company's expansion included an agreement with U.S. ketchup leader H.J. Heinz Co. to acquire a 51 percent stake in Heinz's Japanese operations, forming a new joint venture company, Heinz Japan Company. As part of the agreement, Heinz acquired a 5 percent stake in Kagome. Following this deal, Kagome's share of the total Japanese ketchup market rose past 50 percent.

Japan's soaring interest in health foods and nutraceuticals (foods with purported health benefits) encouraged Kagome to move into this field as well. The company targeted the promising market for probiotics, and specifically lactic acid bacteria. These naturally occurring bacteria, already present in the human digestive system, were said to provide a wide range of health benefits. Kagome's entry into this category came in 2002 with the acquisition of Snow Brand Labio Co. This company was consolidated into Kagome itself soon after, and renamed Kagome Labio Co., Ltd.

The company then began marketing a number of lactic acid bacteria-based probiotic drinks, such as its Bifidus & Collagen Yogurt Drink, launched in 2005, and Labre, launched in 2006. Kagome also developed a line of "color-coded" mixed vegetable drinks, with names such as Purple Roots and Fruits, and Golden Peach Garden. Each color, derived from the vegetables themselves, was associated with a specific health benefit.

At the same time, Kagome backed research studies exploring the health benefits of vegetables, and tomatoes in particular. For example, in 2006 a study conducted in collaboration with Juntendo University School of Medicine and published in the *American Journal of Physiology: Lung Cellular and Molecular Physiology* showed that tomato juice provided protective benefits against emphysema caused by cigarette smoking.

INTERNATIONAL EXPANSION FROM 2003

Kagome's revenues climbed to ¥146 billion in 2003, and past ¥171 billion by the end of 2009. Part of this growth was attributed to the company's push to develop the international scope of its operations. The strong performance of its U.S. subsidiary encouraged the company to establish a presence in the European market. To this end, in 2003 the company set up a new subsidiary in Italy, one of Europe's largest tomato-growing markets. Called Vegitalia, this company launched production of frozen tomato-based food products for the institutional foodservice sector.

In 2006 Kagome expanded its European presence with the purchase of a 43 percent stake in Holding da Industria Transformadora do Tomate, SGPS S.A., or HIT. That company had been formed through the merger of two of Portugal's leading tomato processors, Italagro and F.I.T., and targeted the institutional foodservice market. Kagome also invested in a 29 percent stake in Turkish seed distributor Tat Tohumculuk.

Closer to home, Kagome had also been establishing a presence in other Asian markets. In 2003 the company entered Taiwan, acquiring a 50.4 percent stake in a tomato-based food products operation there. The company then targeted an entry into the Chinese mainland, establishing Inner Mongolia Kagome Food Inc. in 2005. Held at 55 percent by Kagome, this company produced tomato sauce for the Chinese market. Kagome added a second Chinese subsidiary in Hangzhou the following year, this time to produce and distribute its tomato- and vegetable-based drinks to China.

ENTERING AUSTRALIA IN 2010

Kagome's success in the United States led to the expansion of its Los Banos factory in 2007. Also that year, Kagome acquired Arkansas-based Creative Foods LLC out of bankruptcy. The purchase enabled Kagome to strengthen its supply capacity to the East Coast markets.

Kagome's primary focus nevertheless remained on its core Japanese market. In the second half of the decade the company began seeking out new partnerships in order to expand its product lines and reach new market segments. This led the company to team up with Japanese beer and drinks leader Asahi Breweries to develop lines of vegetable-based alcoholic beverages. The partnership resulted in the launch of three new low-alcohol beverages, Asahi Vegesh, featuring 21 types of vegetables and five types of fruit; Vegete, a fruit- and vegetable-based cocktail; and the strong-selling tomato-based Tomate.

Following the success of its partnership with Asahi, Kagome sought out new prospective partners. This resulted in a deal with Starbucks Japan to develop a new line of vegetable drinks exclusively for the coffee chain. The company unveiled the new drinks line, called Be Juicy!, in 2008.

With demand rising strongly in Japan, Kagome set out both to ensure its tomato supply and to continue its international expansion. Kagome achieved both of these objectives simultaneously in July 2010, when it reached an agreement to acquire Cedenco JV Australia Pty Ltd. This purchase, for AUD 91 million ($70 million), gave Kagome control of Australia's largest tomato processor, as well as its own Victoria-based tomato farm operations, SS Farms Pty Ltd. From a small vegetable garden in 1899, Kagome had grown into a leading Japanese food company with operations throughout the world.

M. L. Cohen

PRINCIPAL SUBSIDIARIES

Hibikinada Greenfarm Co., Ltd. (66%); Holding da Industria Transformadora do Tomate, SGPS S.A. (Portugal; 43%); Inner Mongolia Kagome Food Inc. (55%); Iwaki Onahama Greenfarm Ltd. (49%); Kada Greenfarm Co., Ltd. (70%); Kagome (Hangzhou) Food Co., Ltd. (USA; 61%); Kagome Creative Foods, Inc. (USA); Kagome Inc. (USA); Sera Greenfarm Co., Ltd. (47.06%); Taiwan Kagome Co., Ltd. (50.40%); Tat Tohumculuk A.S. (Turkey; 29%); Vegitalia S.p.A (Italy).

PRINCIPAL DIVISIONS

Beverage Products Business; Food Products Business; Institutional and Industrial Products Business; Overseas Business.

PRINCIPAL COMPETITORS

Hagoromo Foods Corp.; Kenko Mayonnaise Company Ltd.; Kewpie Corp.; Kikkoman Corp.; Morinaga Milk Industry Company Ltd.; Tokan Company Ltd.

FURTHER READING

"Coarse Texture Tomato Ketchup." *Cosmetics & Toiletries & Household Products Marketing News in Japan*, August 25, 2008.

Friedman, Mark. "Creative Foods Bought by Japanese Company." *Arkansas Business*, May 7, 2007, p. 12.

Gianatasio, David. "Kagome Readies U.S. Juice Intro." *Adweek*, May 1, 2007.

"Heinz to Expand Alliance with Japanese Ketchup Producer, Sales Up." *Food Institute Report*, December 17, 2001, p. 2.

"Japanese Buyer Hopes to Get Tomato Plant out of the Red." *ABC Rural*, June 30, 2010.

"Kagome to Acquire Australia's Biggest Tomato Processor." *Japan Today*, July 23, 2010.

"New Starbucks/Kagome Juice Drink." *Innovative New Packaging in Japan*, September 25, 2007.

Knights of Columbus

1 Columbus Plaza
New Haven, Connecticut 06510
U.S.A.
Telephone: (203) 752-4000
Fax: (203) 752-4100
Web site: http://www.kofc.org

Nonprofit Organization
Incorporated: 1882
Employees: 2,800
Sales: $1.7 billion (2008 est.)
NAICS: 813410 Civic and Social Organizations

∎∎∎

Based in New Haven, Connecticut, the Knights of Columbus is the world's largest Catholic fraternal service organization with 1.8 million members divided among 15,000 councils. Heading the organization is the Supreme Knight, in effect the CEO. The Supreme Council comprises 75 state council organizations, which are in turn divided into districts, followed by local councils. The Knights directly supports charitable causes with financial donations, more than $150 million each year, and also creates opportunities for members to engage in charitable work and community service. Additionally, the organization lobbies the government on behalf of socially conservative issues.

Since its inception, the organization has been involved in the life insurance business. What was once a service primarily for poor immigrants has become a modern professional enterprise, offering permanent and term life insurance, long-term care insurance, and annuities. The organization has about $75 billion of life insurance policies in force. The funds are invested widely, but are also used to support the ChurchLoan mortgage program that allows the Knights to provide financing to local parishes and parochial schools for construction and renovation. Each local council is assigned a certified insurance agent, who is also a member of the Knights.

19TH-CENTURY ORIGINS

The man who was inspired to establish the Knights of Columbus was Father Michael Joseph McGivney, born in Waterbury, Connecticut, in 1852 to Irish immigrant parents. He chose to enter the Catholic priesthood, and after he was ordained he joined St. Mary's Church in New Haven, Connecticut, in 1877 as curate. It was a time of challenge for immigrant families and McGivney was dismayed by the plight of the working poor. They had barely enough money for food and shelter, and should the father die the surviving family was all too often left destitute. Although McGivney had parish responsibilities, including raising funds to pay off the considerable building debts of St. Mary's, he began to envision a way to provide low-cost life insurance for the Catholic poor.

McGivney believed that a Catholic fraternal society could provide life insurance and help alleviate the suffering of the poor. The Catholic hierarchy was not receptive to the concept of fraternal societies, however. Many immigrants, farmers or craftsmen in their former countries, became factory workers who felt displaced

COMPANY PERSPECTIVES

Members of the Knights of Columbus, be they Americans, Canadians, Mexicans, Cubans, Poles, or Dominicans, are patriotic citizens. We are proud of our devotion to God and country, and believe in standing up for both. Whether it's in public or private, the Knights remind the world that Catholics support their nations and are amongst the greatest citizens.

and joined secret fraternal societies, such as the Moose and Elks, to provide comradeship and mutual support. Because these groups used rituals that were considered anti-Catholic, the church was less than receptive to McGivney's proposal for a Catholic fraternal society.

McGivney was not easily discouraged. As he politely pressed his case, he did what he could to serve the needs of the poor in his parish, and in time his charitable work and persistence won over church authorities. Given approval to proceed, McGivney recruited local leaders to form an organizing committee while also studying the structure of other societies. McGivney wanted to name the new organization the Sons of Columbus, honoring the Italian explorer who was regarded as the man who discovered America, but committee member James T. Mullen suggested Knights of Columbus, a name that gained general support.

KNIGHTS FORMED: 1882

In February 1882 the Knights of Columbus was founded and a month later incorporated under the laws of Connecticut. According to its charter, the purposes of the organization were threefold: to furnish insurance to members and financial aid to families of deceased members; to develop practical Catholicity among members; and to promote Catholic education and charity. To eliminate concerns that the Knights of Columbus was a secret society, the bylaws entitled church officials admission on all occasions, and all priests were allowed to join the order without examination, although they were required to pay their dues like all other members. Moreover, any male member of the Catholic Church over 16 years of age was allowed to join.

The order established its first headquarters in a single room located in a building near New Haven's City Hall. Mullen served as the first Supreme Knight, a

post he would hold for four years, while McGivney was secretary of the Supreme Council. McGivney was also the order's biggest booster, promoting it at every opportunity and making regular mailings to churches in his diocese to tout the benefits of membership. The key benefit was life insurance. Under the plan originally conceived by McGivney, the widow of a deceased Knight received a $1,000 death benefit, paid for by special member assessments.

MCGIVNEY DIES: 1890

McGivney's efforts bore fruit and soon the membership ranks swelled. In 1884 he chose not to seek reelection as secretary, instead returning his focus to his parish responsibilities, although he remained an ardent supporter. McGivney's efforts on behalf of his parishioners and the Knights reportedly took their toll on his health, however. Already weakened by pneumonia, he fell victim to a flu epidemic. Although he survived the flu, his constitution was weakened and he gradually wasted away. He died in 1890 shortly after his 38th birthday.

At the time of McGivney's death the order numbered 6,000 members. In 1893 the National Council spurred further growth with the addition of the Associate Members class, which would include members unable to pass the physical examination for life insurance or who simply did not desire life insurance. Some 20 years later the Associate Members class, numbering 220,000, was twice as large as the insurance class. The increased ranks played a key role in the ability of the Knights to perform charitable work.

There were other important developments as the 19th century came to a close. In 1895 the Vatican first acknowledged the Knights and gave the organization its blessing, alleviating any lingering concerns about the order being an anti-Catholic secret society. In the late 1890s ladies' auxiliaries also began to take shape, and Canada's first council was established. Additionally, the insurance program was modernized to include the accepted practices of commercial insurers.

The Knights pursued a number of notable causes in the early decades of the new century. During World War I, for example, the Knights established and sponsored service centers, called K. of C. Huts, in military training camps around the country. Despite the organization's increasing presence in the United States, the Knights had to contend with an anti-Catholic bias in many parts of the country. In 1914 an inflammatory counterfeit oath of the order was circulated. It pledged "relentless war, secretly and openly, against all heretics, Protestants and Masons" and to "hang, burn, waste, boil, flay,

KEY DATES

■

1882: Father Michael McGivney spearheads founding of the Knights of Columbus.

1893: Associate Members class added.

1895: Vatican recognizes order.

1937: The Knights meet with President Franklin Roosevelt to ease tensions between the Mexican government and the Catholic Church.

1947: The Knights begin sponsoring radio programs promulgating the dangers of Communism and the need to preserve American ideals.

1971: The organization has $2 billion of insurance in force.

1985: The organization agrees to underwrite restoration of the façade of St. Peter's Basilica.

1997: Process begins to canonize McGivney.

2006: Order expands to Poland.

strangle, and bury alive those infamous heretics." As a result, the Knights launched a lecture series and other education programs to combat such anti-Catholic slurs. Nevertheless, the so-called bogus oath would resurface over the years, in particular when Catholics ran for president of the United States: Alfred E. Smith in 1928 and John F. Kennedy in 1960.

KNIGHTS BECOME POLITICALLY ACTIVE

Following World War I, the Knights established educational, vocational, and employment programs for veterans, including a correspondence school. The order also became more politically active. Attacks on the Catholic Church in Mexico also prompted the order to establish a $1 million fund to publicize the problem and influence U.S. public opinion. These efforts would pay off in 1937 after the Knights met with President Franklin Roosevelt and through his intervention tensions eased between the Mexican government and the Catholic Church.

The Knights made contributions on a number of fronts during World War II and the years that followed. As in the previous war, the organization developed outreach programs to soldiers. The order also created a trust fund for the education for the children of members who died in the war. In the postwar years, when the United States faced a new challenge in the Soviet Union, the Knights published pamphlets that spoke of

the dangers of Communism and the need to preserve American ideals. In 1947 the Knights began sponsoring radio programs with a similar message. The mix of patriotic and religious fervor also led to the order playing a key role in the government adding the words "under God" to the U.S. Pledge of Allegiance in the early 1950s.

The Knights had to respond to sweeping changes in the Catholic Church and the world in general in the 1960s. For the first time in U.S. history, a Catholic, and Fourth Degree Knight, John F. Kennedy, was elected president of the United States. During this time the church took steps to keep pace with political and social developments through the Second Ecumenical Council of the Vatican, or Vatican II. The Knights were also forced to adapt to this call for renewal and reform. Domestically, the order met at the White House with other religious organization to discuss civil rights, an issue that came to the forefront during this period.

INSURANCE OPERATION GROWS

In the meantime, the order's insurance operation continued to grow. In 1971 it reached the $2 billion mark of insurance in force. On other fronts during the 1970s, the Knights funded satellite transmissions for telecasts originating from the Vatican, and in 1979 the order worked with the U.S. Bishops to underwrite the filming of Pope John II's first pastoral visit to the United States. Two years later, the order established a fund for the pope's personal charities.

The Knights funded a number of other endeavors in the 1980s. It established a fund in McGivney's name to finance programs that advanced Catholic schools. In 1982 the organization created a series of funds to finance the studies of priests and seminaries at pontifical colleges in Rome. In 1985 the Knights provided the Vatican Television Center with a mobile television production unit and in that same year agreed to underwrite the restoration of the façade of St. Peter's Basilica, which had not been cleaned in over 350 years. The Knights in 1988 provided the funding for the opening of a Washington, D.C., branch of the Pontifical John Paul II Institute for Studies on Marriage and Family.

MOVE TO CANONIZE MCGIVNEY: 1997

The 1990s were marked by the start of an effort to have Father McGivney canonized, the cause officially opened in December 1997 by the Archdiocese of Hartford. Only two native-born Americans had ever become saints: Elizabeth Anne Seton, founder of the American Sisters of Charity, and Katharine Drexel, who founded a religious order dedicated to helping impoverished Native Americans and African Americans. The process of canonization was long and unpredictable, but there was no lack of support for McGivney's case. In 2007 the Vatican's second-ranking official declared he would work to have McGivney declared a saint, and a year later Pope Benedict XVI recognized the "heroic virtues" of McGivney, an important next step in the canonization process.

Whether Father McGivney will ever be canonized is uncertain, but the organization he founded remained a fixture in life in the United States and the Catholic Church. It was not free of controversy, however. In the mid-1990s the *Boston Globe* took the order to task in a series of articles that called into question the high salaries and perquisites paid to top executives, as well as the organization's reputation for stifling internal criticism. The Knights and its insurance operation were also sued for deceptive sales practices. In the first decade of the 21st century the Knights received notoriety in some quarters, and support in others, for opposing same sex marriages.

Aware that many Catholics, and the public in general, did not fully understand its mission, the order in 2002 hired a marketing firm to create a national branding campaign to encourage involvement in charitable endeavors. The organization continued to find opportunities to remain relevant, establishing a fund for the families of police officers, firefighters, and emergency medical personnel who lost their lives during the terrorist attacks of September 11, 2001, and rebuilding

Catholic churches and schools damaged by Hurricane Katrina in 2005. The Knights also looked to expand to new countries. In 2006 the order chartered its first councils in Poland, its first international foray in 100 years. There was ample reason to believe the order would continue to find relevance in its second century of existence.

Ed Dinger

PRINCIPAL SUBSIDIARIES

Knights of Columbus Insurance.

PRINCIPAL COMPETITORS

Massachusetts Mutual Life Insurance Company; MetLife, Inc.; New York Life Insurance Company.

FURTHER READING

Brinkley, Douglas, and Julie M. Fenster. *Parish Priest*. New York: William Morrow, 2006.

Hogan, Neil. "K of C Founder Began Work Here 100 Years Ago." *New Haven Register*, September 16, 1990.

Knight, Thomas C. *Knights of Columbus Illustrated*. Chicago: Ezra A. Cook, 1920.

"Knight's Charity Said to Begin at Home." *National Catholic Reporter*, April 14, 1995, p. 7.

Lang, Joel. "Making a Case for Sainthood." *Hartford Courant*, March 12, 2006, p. 4.

Schleier, Curt. "One Man's Vision for Change." *Investor's Business Daily*, February 16, 2006, p. A3.

Schmitt, Frederick. "Knights of Columbus Sued over Sales Practices." *National Underwriter Life*, September 2, 1996, p. 4.

Korbitec

———— ■ ————

Great Westerford
240 Main Road
Rondebosch, Cape Town 7700
South Africa
Telephone: (272 21) 658 9700
Fax: (272 21) 658 9701
Web site: http://www.korbitec.com

Private Company
Founded: 1976 as Compustat
Employees: 267
Sales: $457 million (2005 est.)
NAICS: 511210 Software Publishers

■ ■ ■

Korbitec is one of South Africa's leading software developers, and one of the world's top specialists in software for document assembly and management for the legal, real estate, banking, insurance, and other document-intensive professions. The company's product lineup includes GhostConvey, providing document assembly and correspondence capabilities for the real estate and mortgage banking sectors; GhostPractice, which focuses on legal accounting and practice management; and WinDeed, providing a variety of services, including deed searching, property database management, and credit checking. Korbitec's Financial Services arm develops a range of products linking the financial and legal sectors, including securing transmission of mortgage information between lenders and attorneys.

In addition to its Cape Town, South Africa, headquarters, Korbitec has also established a subsidiary in Ontario, Canada, which focuses on providing software for the legal profession there. Korbitec is a privately held company, and last reported revenues of $457 million in 2005. The company is led by CEO and cofounder, Mendel Karpul.

SOFTWARE START-UP: 1976

In 1976 a group of University of Cape Town graduates joined together to found Compustat, one of South Africa's pioneering computer and software companies. Among the company's founders were Mendel Karpul, Rolland Bryan, and Mark Todes, all of whom would remain key figures in the company, later known as Korbitec, into the 21st century. Karpul provided the company's leadership, while Todes and Bryan played instrumental roles in the company's early marketing and product development.

Compustat focused on developing software for the nascent computer industry in South Africa, initially writing code for the then industry standard microcomputers. In the early 1980s the company achieved a breakthrough, developing one of the earliest word-processing systems, called GhostWriter. The DOS-based program, developed under Bryan's direction, quickly became the standard word-processing software for South Africa's legal sector.

Compustat helped boost GhostWriter's popularity through the decade with the addition of a number of add-on programs. In the middle of the decade the company began developing the GhostWriter family as a full-fledged application suite, much like its rivals overseas, which then included Microsoft Word and WordPerfect. Compustat introduced its Mortgage Bond Program, which made use of the newly invented laser printer systems to extend GhostWriter's capabilities into document assembly and other areas required by the legal market.

EXPANDING OPERATIONS

Compustat continued to develop other applications and services for the legal community through the 1980s. In 1988 the company formed a joint venture, Jutastat, with Juta & Co., a major South African legal publisher, which became the first in the world to enter the CD-ROM publishing market. Jutastat's first product provided full-text search capabilities to Juta's legal content. Over the next decade Jutastat expanded its CD-ROM publishing operations to include a number of electronic databases focused on the South African legal sector, as well as for the general reference market.

Compustat was forced in the 1990s to adapt to new market conditions, as the computer sector itself shifted to a focus on the IBM PC standard, especially the Microsoft Windows operating system. By then, Microsoft Word had grown to become a major player, and ultimately a global standard, in word processing. As a result, Compustat redeveloped its core GhostWriter product family into a suite of add-on software designed to extend the capabilities of Microsoft Word. This system, called GhostFill, provided a range of document automation features, including template building and form-filling capabilities. The success of GhostFill soon spread beyond South Africa, achieving particular success in the legal sector in the United States.

By the middle of the decade the company had rolled out two other applications. The first, called Adam, provided network-based document management and organization capacity. The second, QuikFind, functioned as a computer-based card system, enabling users to input and then easily recall important information.

Compustat also emerged as a major computer systems and software distributor during this period, selling such computer brands as Acer, Compaq, Fujitech, Hewlett-Packard, and IBM, and software from Microsoft, Corel, Lotus, and Novell. Compustat extended this business at the beginning of the 1990s with the opening of a branch in Johannesburg.

During the first half of the 1990s Compustat became one of the most well-respected players in the South African software and computer industry. The company grew to include more than 160 employees, posting total revenues of more than ZAR 50 million by mid-decade. Compustat also received a number of awards during this period. For example, in 1992 the Western Province Chapter of the Computer Society of South Africa named Mendel Karpul as IT Personality of the Year. The company itself was included in Arthur Andersen's list of Top 20 Non-listed Companies in South Africa. Compustat's products also won a number of awards.

INTERNET PIONEER: 1994

Compustat could also lay claim to helping pioneer South Africa's Internet market in the early 1990s. Although introduced in South Africa in the early 1980s, Internet usage initially remained almost entirely restricted to the university and research communities. This began to change when Chris Pinkham, who had been exposed to the Internet during a visit to the United States, returned to South Africa to establish the country's first nonacademic Internet access service, called The Internetworking Company of South Africa (TICSA).

TICSA, which functioned as a nonprofit cooperative, established its own Internet hub in Cape Town, which connected via subsea cable to the Alternet network in Virginia, in the United States. TICSA did not provide Internet access to end users, but instead provided a live Internet connection to South Africa's first commercial Internet service providers (ISPs). Compustat immediately recognized the potential of the Internet, and became one of TICSA's first two customers, setting up its own ISP, called iaccess. Compustat's ISP focused on the business market, especially the legal sector.

Another company, Aztec, which provided TICSA with space in its own headquarters, developed its own consumer-oriented ISP. However, in 1994 Aztec decided to establish its own Internet connection. Short of funding, TICSA turned to Compustat, which agreed to

KEY DATES

1976: Mendel Karpul, Rolland Bryan, Mark Todes, and others found Compustat to develop software in South Africa.

1960s: Compustat develops GhostWriter, one of the earliest word-processing systems.

1994: Compustat partners with The Internetworking Company of South Africa (TICSA) to form Internet Africa.

1996: Compustat is acquired by Datatec; Internet Africa is merged with UUNet Technologies, forming UUNet Internet Africa.

1999: Karpul, Bryan, and Todes lead a management buyout of Datatec's software development arm, which is renamed Korbitec.

2001: Korbitec acquires WinDeed.

2006: Korbitec North America acquires Xenex Media.

2010: Korbitec merges with Property24.com.

invest in the company. TICSA moved to Compustat's Cape Town headquarters, and the partners established a new ISP, called Internet Africa.

KORBITEC IN 1999

The first boom in South Africa's Internet market came in 1995, when subscriber rates soared by more than 500 percent. Internet Africa, which continued to focus primarily on the corporate market, emerged as a leader of the sector, even as the number of ISPs in the country grew. By 1996 Internet Africa had attracted the attention of Datatec, another fast-growing South African technology group. Datatec approached Compustat with a takeover offer, and Compustat agreed.

Jens Montanana founded Datatec in 1986 with a focus on the young networking sector. Datatec went public in 1995, listing on the Johannesburg Stock Exchange. The stock offering raised ZAR 9 million for the company, which had recognized the potential for extending its own operations into the Internet market. Following the takeover of Compustat, Datatec agreed to merge Internet Africa with another fast-growing Internet group, UUNet Technologies, forming UUNet Internet Africa. As a result, Compustat's operations were divided into its software development and Internet arms. Datatec retained a 76 percent stake in UUNet Internet Africa, which later changed its name to UUNet SA.

In 1997 Datatec launched a new international expansion strategy, moving into the United Kingdom and Europe, and then into the U.S. market in 1998. Datatec's focus, however, remained on the networking and communications sector, especially after its acquisition of U.K.-based Mason Communications in 1999. As a result, the original Compustat operations, while continuing to perform strongly, had become increasingly marginal to Datatec's strategy.

Datatec launched a reorganization of its operations toward the end of the decade, and began preparing an exit from its noncore operations, particularly the South African businesses that no longer fit in with its core area of focus. The group's software development businesses were among the first to be spun off by Datatec. In 1999 Karpul, Bryan, and Todes led a management buyout of much of the original Compustat line of software products, particularly its highly successful GhostFill. More than 100 former Compustat employees also joined the new company, which took the name Korbitec. UUNet itself was broken up, and its corporate ISP operations, Internet Africa, were sold to M-Web that year. In 2001 Datatec sold off UUNet as well, to WorldCom for $140 million.

NEW PRODUCTS

The Korbitec team had continued to develop its product family, especially GhostFill, launching GhostFill 2.0 in 1998. In 2000, after working in collaboration with Microsoft, the company launched an intermediate upgrade of its popular software, GhostFill 2.5, which was fully integrated into Microsoft Office. However, this launch was quickly followed with the debut of the next generation of GhostFill, called GhostFill 2001, released in December 2000.

Korbitec then eyed its own international expansion. In 2000 the company opened its first overseas offices, in Toronto, London, and Pittsburgh. Korbitec also moved into new headquarters, in Cape Town's Newlands area, as its payroll grew to more than 190 employees. The Canadian office soon grew into a full-fledged subsidiary, Korbitec North America.

Korbitec set out to expand its software development operations into new areas in the new decade. The property market was a natural extension to the group's long experience with the legal sector. Korbitec entered this market in 2001 with the acquisition of WinDeed, which had developed as an online title-deed search service in cooperation with the South African Deeds Office. The WinDeed purchase formed the basis of a new company business unit, Korbitec Search Business.

Korbitec's international ambitions met with success at the beginning of the decade as well. In 2002 the company was selected to develop the contract document handling software for the American Institute of Architects. The new software, based on the GhostFill platform, was launched in 2003 and became a standard in the North American architectural field, with more than 30,000 users.

By this time, Korbitec had also expanded its range of services bridging the legal and property sectors. In 2003 the company launched a publishing arm, GhostDigest, which provided property and conveyance information for the legal market. At the same time, the Korbitec Search Business unit had expanded to include CIPRO (Companies and Intellectual Property Registration Office) and ITC information.

NEW OWNERS IN 2010

Korbitec remained committed to expanding its Ghost family of products through the middle of the decade. The company launched GhostConvey in 2004, described as its new flagship product. The company extended this software family two years later through the launch of GhostPractice, which provided legal practice management and accounting.

Korbitec also scored new successes in the North American market. In 2004 the Thomson West Corporation chose Korbitec to develop document assembly software providing drafting wills and trust agreements. This software, once again based on the GhostFill platform, was then marketed under Thomson West's name.

GhostFill also played a role in the growth of Korbitec's Canadian subsidiary in the second half of the decade. Korbitec North America had teamed up with Xenex Media, based in Ontario, which had developed Automated Civil Litigation (ACL). The two companies teamed up to develop the second generation of the ACL software, which provided automated document creation, assembly, and handling services for court documents. The collaboration proved highly successful, and in 2006 Korbitec North America moved to acquire Xenex outright. This led to the launch of ACL3 by the end of the decade.

Korbitec soon found itself under new ownership. Toward the end of the decade, Korbitec had begun talks with Property24.com, one of South Africa's leading online property search services. Property24 was owned by media group Naspers, operator of MultiChoice, the leading fee-based television service in South Africa. The Naspers group's international holdings included stakes in pay television and Internet businesses in other African markets, as well as Eastern Europe, South America, and China.

In October 2009 Naspers paid ZAR 158 million to acquire a 51 percent stake in Korbitec. Korbitec and Property24 then began integrating their operations, a process completed in April 2010. Dawie Verryne, who had previously served as Korbitec's general manager of financial services, was named the company's new CEO. In this way, Korbitec carried its heritage as one of South Africa's software pioneers into the new century.

M. L. Cohen

PRINCIPAL SUBSIDIARIES

Korbitec Inc. (Canada).

PRINCIPAL DIVISIONS

Financial Services; Korbitec Search Business.

PRINCIPAL OPERATING UNITS

Attorney Gateway; GhostFill; GhostPractice; GhostWare; Korbitec Gateway; WinDeed.

PRINCIPAL COMPETITORS

Bytes Technology Group Proprietary Ltd.; Control Instruments Group Ltd.; FrontRange Solutions Proprietary Ltd.; Microsoft South Africa Proprietary Ltd.; Peresys Proprietary Ltd.; SecureData Holdings Ltd.; Softline Proprietary Ltd.; UCS Group Ltd.

FURTHER READING

"Korbitec and Property24.com Come Together." *Cape Business News*, April 16, 2010.

"Korbitec Launches GhostFill 2.5." *Business Day*, May 17, 2000.

Marrs, Dave. "Korbitec Set to Take on World." *Business Day*, September 8, 2000.

"Property24 Set for Full Service." *Star*, April 29, 2010, p. 3.

Laurel Grocery Company, LLC

———————■———————

129 Barbourville Road
London, Kentucky 40744-9301
U.S.A.
Telephone: (606) 878-6601
Toll Free: (800) 467-6601
Fax: (606) 864-5693
Web site: http://www.laurelgrocery.com

Private Company
Incorporated: 1922
Employees: 411
Sales: $350 million (2009 est.)
NAICS: 424410 General Line Grocery Merchant
   Wholesalers

■ ■ ■

Laurel Grocery Company, LLC, is a London, Kentucky-based full-service grocery wholesaler serving more than 420 independent retail locations, both supermarkets and convenience stores, in Kentucky, Georgia, Illinois, Indiana, Ohio, Pennsylvania, and Tennessee. Laurel is the only full-service wholesaler in Kentucky. It supplies meat, produce, dairy products, eggs, bakery goods, and cigarettes, 23,000 items in all, including brand-name and private-label products. Field support services include retail consultation, and specialists in meat, bakery and deli, nonfoods, specialty foods, and technology. Laurel also offers merchandising and advertising programs, retail development and engineering services, a retail accounting program, and insurance and financial services. Laurel is owned by the Chesnut and Griffin families,

with third-generation family members now involved in the management of the company.

COMPANY FOUNDED: 1922

Laurel Grocery was founded in 1922 in East Bernstadt, Laurel County, Kentucky, by George W. Griffin and W. J. Chesnut, and partners George Pennington and White Sharp. Griffin was employed by L&N Railroad, while Chesnut was a teller at a Laurel County Bank. At the time, the partners realized that area grocers needed a more efficient distribution system than was available at the time.

Their idea was to store goods shipped in via rail in local warehouses where grocers could pick up or have Laurel Grocery make deliveries to them. The partners set up a warehouse in an old railroad station they rented in East Bernstadt. The first order was hardly the typical grocery item, although it was still much needed in rural Kentucky: axle grease for horse-drawn wagons. Because Griffin and Chesnut still kept their jobs at the railroad and the bank, they had to deliver the grease to customers throughout the countryside at night to be back in time for work in the morning.

Griffin and Chesnut worked nights and weekends and developed a distribution network among the independent grocery stores that dotted the mountains of eastern Kentucky. In 1924 Sharp sold his interest in the business to Monroe Pennington, who a year later sold it back to the three remaining partners. In 1927 Pennington was bought out, and from that time forward Laurel Grocery was wholly owned by Griffin and Chesnut, who were finally able to quit their day jobs.

Laurel Grocery enjoyed steady growth for the next dozen years. In addition to grocery stores, the company expanded its range of customers to restaurants, schools, and other institutional customers. In time, the latter customers would be served by a sister company, Institutional Distributors. By the end of the 1930s, annual sales reached the $1 million mark, making Laurel Grocery the first company in Laurel County to reach that level.

POSTWAR TRANSITION TO SECOND GENERATION

In the 1940s, ownership began shifting to the next generation of the Chesnut and Griffin families. In 1946 Chesnut transferred a one-quarter interest of the business to his son William Jennings Chesnut, and two years later Griffin provided a one-sixth interest to his son, George W. Griffin, Jr. Next, in 1950, the young men were admitted into the partnership and were each allowed to purchase a one-sixth interest based on the book value of the company.

The elder Chesnut remained actively involved with the company until 1971 when he retired at the age of 80. (He would live until 1988, dying at the age of 96.) It was at that time that George W. Griffin, Jr., took over as president and began a 34-year-tenure at the helm that would see Laurel Grocery into a major regional wholesaler. The company would not be error-free, however. It attempted at one point to expand into retail, buying or opening a dozen stores. In short order management realized it had made a mistake, divested the stores, and returned its focus to distribution and serving retail customers. Laurel Grocery also bought a distribution center in Cincinnati but soon realized that it was not ready to move into such a major market and closed that operation as well.

To keep pace with changes in the industry, Laurel Grocery upgraded it systems in 1994 with the addition of an enterprise resource planning program to take care of all of the company's accounting and financial functions. Also it 1994 the company beefed up its management ranks, creating the post of chief operating officer. At the time, the company was serving more than 200 supermarkets and 120 convenience stores in Kentucky, Indiana, Ohio, Tennessee, and West Virginia. Annual sales were in the $115 million range.

In 1997 George W. Griffin, Jr., retired but not before overseeing a succession plan that put third-generation members of the Griffin and Chesnut families in positions of responsibility. Bruce Chesnut, who had been serving as CEO and president since 1985, now became chairman and chief executive officer, while Griffin's son, Winston Griffin, became vice chairman and in-house counsel. Bruce Chesnut then supplemented the management team in 1999 by hiring James Buchanan as president and chief operating officer. Buchanan was an industry veteran who had been an operating group president with the Fleming Cos., as well as holding positions with Nash Finch.

Sales topped $200 million at the turn of the new century. In order to achieve further growth, the company made further information technology investments. In 2000 Laurel Grocery unveiled a new management system that covered all aspects of the company's two London, Kentucky warehouses, including receiving, stocking inventory control, date rotation, and picking. These improved capabilities set the stage for one of the most important developments in the history of the company.

IGA ALLIANCE: 2000

In the spring of 2000 Laurel Grocery became the 25th distributor for IGA, Inc. Formerly known as Independent Grocers Alliance, IGA was the world's largest voluntary supermarket network, joint-owned by a large number of global distribution companies. The focus of IGA had always been on small-town independent grocers, which in recent years had been sorely challenged by industry consolidation that resulted in massive supermarket chains. As a result, the ranks of independent stores thinned and the bulk of IGA's growth now came from overseas. Because IGA and Laurel Grocery faced the same challenges, it was not surprising that they would forge an alliance. In truth, it was a matter of survival for both Laurel Grocery and its customers.

Laurel Grocery quickly began to convert many of its customers to the IGA banner, starting with 30 stores by mid-summer 2000, including 19 Food World stores. They now gained access to 3,000 IGA private-label products. The first IGA store was served in November 2000. All of the converted stores enjoyed sales increases over the next year. A second-wave of IGA stores followed in 2001, and by the end of the year about 65 Laurel Grocery customers were operating under the IGA banner. In recognition of the company's success, IGA named Laurel Grocery its 2002 Distributor of the year.

KEY DATES

■

1922: Company is founded.
1927: Griffin and Chesnut families buy out partners.
1950: Second generation is admitted to partnership.
2000: Laurel Grocery becomes IGA distributor.
2007: Tusco Grocers is acquired.

The relationship with IGA helped Laurel Grocery to increase revenues at a steady rate, reaching $250 million in 2002. The company also made money by providing education, training, and administrative services to its customers that helped them to grow their businesses and in turn created more demand for the groceries and goods distributed by Laurel Grocery. The company helped customers to set up new stores, make improvements to existing stores, and convert stores to the IGA banner. Laurel Grocery was also capable of handling bookkeeping, payroll, and inventory, as well as taking charge of promotions and advertising.

Moreover, as a family-owned company with no layers of bureaucracy, Laurel Company was comfortable with allowing many decisions to be made at the local level, allowing the company to better meet the needs of its customers. Sales improved to $285 million in 2003. To meet increasing demand, Laurel Grocery expanded one of its two warehouses to 300,000 square feet in 2004. The $3.5 million project doubled the amount of perishables space and added 100,000 square feet of dry food space.

HALL OF FAME RECOGNITION: 2005

In 2005 the contributions of George W. Griffin, Jr., were recognized when he became the first inductee into the Kentucky Grocers Hall of Fame by the Kentucky Grocers Association. The company did not have the luxury of dwelling on past accomplishments, however. More than half of the stores it served were now impacted directly by Wal-Mart Supercenters, and it was only a matter of time before all of its customers faced the challenge of the giant retailer. Laurel Grocery continued to add to the services its offered customers. It forged banking relationships to help them secure the funding needed to renovate their stores to remain competitive. Point-of-sale specialists were hired to help customers with both their front-end and back-door systems. Additionally, Laurel Grocery established a task

force to develop a program to successfully compete against Wal-Mart.

In the fall of 2005 the company launched what it called a Strategic Marketing Initiative to aid its bid to stave off Wal-Mart. Initially tested in three stores, the program sought to increase sales-per-customers transactions by pricing some 4,000 items within 5 percent to 10 percent of Wal-Mart prices. In-store signage brought the low prices to the attention of shoppers and also promoted high-quality perishables, which provided an edge for local supermarkets over Wal-Mart. Another effort Laurel Grocery launched to help customers better compete with discounters was to make 150 of the fastest-moving items in its Valu Time discount food line available to retail customers if they agreed to sell them at a low price. In some cases, Laurel Grocery sold the product below its own cost as a way to help customers maintain a competitive edge. Laurel also kept tabs on the prices of these products at Wal-Mart, chain supermarkets, and other discounters such as Dollar General.

At the start of 2006 the 62-year-old Bruce Chesnut turned over day-to-day control of Laurel Grocery to James Buchanan, who now became president and CEO. Chesnut remained chairman. No radical changes were in store for the wholesaler, which continued to adapt to changing business conditions. Later in 2006 it unveiled a new limited assortment format store called Sav-U-Mor, building on its success in earlier efforts. Unlike other limited assortment stores that carried 1,900 stock-keeping units (SKUs), Sav-U-Mor stores carried 4,000 to 5,000 SKUs. To attracted mid-income shoppers, the stores offered a more upscale environment and emphasized high-quality perishables as well as in-store butchers and self-serve bakeries.

OHIO WAREHOUSE ACQUIRED: 2007

In 2007 Laurel Grocery positioned itself for further growth with the acquisition of Dennison, Ohio-based Tusco Grocers, adding a 275,000-square-foot full-line wholesale distribution center. The operation now became known as Laurel Grocery Co., Northeast Division and allowed the parent company to broaden its market reach. A year later the company was able to sign up a new customer in Lancaster, Ohio-based Carnival Foods, which operated three large-volume stores in the area. The purchase of the new warehouse was one of the most significant steps ever taken by Laurel Foods and demonstrated that the company was eager to remain vital in an industry that promised to become only more competitive in the years to come.

Ed Dinger

PRINCIPAL DIVISIONS

Laurel Grocery Co., Northeast Division.

PRINCIPAL COMPETITORS

C&S Wholesale Grocers, Inc.; Nash-Finch Company; S. Abraham & Sons, Inc.

FURTHER READING

Brim, Risa. "Living Legacy: Founders' Grandsons Keep Laurel Grocery Co. Thriving." *Lexington Herald-Leader*, April 8, 2003, p. C1.

Burke, Erica. "Grocery Go-Getter." *U.S. Business Review*, May 1, 2005, p. 167.

"Businessman W. J. Chesnut Des at 96." *Lexington Herald-Leader*, August 30, 1988, p. A9.

Hicks, Brad. "Laurel Grocery Looks to Expand." *Times-Tribune* (Corbin, Ky.), January 24, 2008.

"Laurel to Become IGA Distributor." *Supermarket News*, May 29, 2000, p. 14.

Morrison, Lee. "Tusco Grocers to Merge with Kentucky Company." *Times Reporter* (New Philadelphia, Ohio), February 17, 2007.

Moses, Lucia. "Laurel Tries Out Low-Price Program." *Supermarket News*, October 17, 2005, p. 71.

Leder & Schuh AG

Lastenstrasse 11-13
Graz, A-8021
Austria
Telephone: (+43 0316) 78 44 0
Fax: (+43 0316) 78 44 12322
Web site: http://www.leder-schuh-ag.com

Private Company
Founded: 1872 as D.H. Pollak
Employees: 3,670
Sales: EUR 496.4 million ($694.96 million) (2009)
NAICS: 448210 Shoe Stores

■ ■ ■

Leder & Schuh AG is Austria's largest footwear retailer and a leader in the Central European market. The Graz-based company operates five retail brands: Humanic, Corti, Jello, Shoe 4 You, and Dominici. Altogether the company's retail network encompasses 340 stores in Austria, Bulgaria, Croatia, Czech Republic, Germany, Hungary, Romania, Slovakia, Slovenia, and Switzerland. The company employs nearly 3,700 people and generated revenues of EUR 496 million ($695 million) in 2009. Leder & Schuh AG is a private company led by CEO Gottfried Maresch.

19TH-CENTURY ORIGINS

Leder & Schuh's legacy stretches back to the footwear empire founded by David Heinrich Pollak in Austria in the mid-19th century. By the 1860s Pollak's Vienna-based factory was the largest shoe manufacturer in Austria. In 1872 Pollak added a new subsidiary in Graz in order to supply his main Vienna plant. This subsidiary became the forerunner to the future Leder & Schuh.

In 1882 Pollak regrouped his various shoe businesses under a single company, D.H. Pollak and Co., based in Vienna. Pollak also brought in new partners, including Alfred Frankl and Julius and Theodor Reitlinger. Pollak and Frankl withdrew from the partnership in 1888, leaving the Reitlingers in sole control. D.H. Pollak & Co. had by then expanded beyond Austria to include much of the Austrian-Hungarian Empire and beyond.

The company not only opened new factories, but also established an international network of shoe stores. By the dawn of the 20th century, D.H. Pollak & Co. was turning out more than 20,000 pairs of shoes each week, and had stores in Budapest, Ljubljana, Meran, Prague, Temesvar, and Trieste. The company also established a growing trade serving the export market, shipping its footwear to North America, Australia, India, and Africa.

The company changed ownership again in 1904, when it was taken over by Karl Rieckh, a Graz-based leather producer. Rieckh moved the company's headquarters that year. In 1909 Rieckh brought son-in-law Felix Alexander Mayer into the company as a partner, and continued its expansion, setting up stores in Constantinople (later Istanbul), Philippopolis (later Plovdiv, in Bulgaria), as well as Berlin and Sofia. By the beginning of World War I, the company's factories employed more than 600 people and its store network had grown to 100 locations.

POST-WORLD WAR I RECOVERY

D.H. Pollak & Co. lost all of its operations outside of Austria as war engulfed Europe. Felix Mayer, who by then had taken over the company's direction, joined together with Poschl Falkensammer, another major Austrian leather producer, to form Heeresausrustungsges.mbH. That company then began supplying equipment for the Austrian-Hungarian army. The joint venture also set about acquiring a number of other Austrian footwear companies during the war period. These included Vienna-based Allgemeine Österreichische Schuh AG, Iglauer Schuhfabrik Anton Lowenstein, and Brunner Schuhfabrik Ferdinand Heinisch.

The addition of Allgemeine Österreichische Schuh AG was of particular significance. That company had been created through the merger of two other Austrian companies, Vienna-based Schuhwarenfabrik Anton Capiek & Co. Ges.m.b.H, which also operated in Iglau, and Verkaufsgesellschaft Humanic Ltd., based in Iglau. Humanic appeared to have had an earlier connection with D.H. Pollak. According to Leder & Schuh's Web site, the Graz-based company had acquired Humanic, originally a U.S. company, in 1904, and set up a company called American Shoe House Humanic. This company then opened its first two stores in Vienna. As part of Allgemeine Österreichische Schuh AG, Humanic had grown into one of Austria's largest shoe store chains.

The end of World War I resulted not only in the breakup of the Austrian-Hungarian Empire, but the disintegration of D.H. Pollak as well. The group's foreign operations and parts of its domestic businesses were broken up into a number of smaller production and retail companies. However, by 1920 Felix Mayer had begun to pick up the pieces. That year Mayer merged the Humanic shoe chain with the remains of D.H. Pollak, forming a new company, Humanic Leder & Schuh AG, with headquarters in Vienna.

FOCUS ON AUSTRIA

Two other companies were also brought under the Humanic umbrella. These were Vienna-based Schuhfabrik Karl Ahorner, and a leather factory, Österreichisch-Amerikanischen Lederwerke Rudolf Low-Beer, based in Vienna-Stadlau. Humanic sold off the latter company just two years later, however.

Humanic set to work on rebuilding its battered footwear empire through the 1920s. Rather than attempt a new international expansion, the company instead focused on developing itself as a purely Austrian company. This strategy proved successful, and by the end of the decade Humanic boasted 60 stores throughout Austria. In addition to opening its own stores, the company made a number of acquisitions of existing retail shops. Humanic also expanded its production capacity during this period, buying up two shoe factories in Vienna and a third in Graz. In 1929 the company moved its headquarters back to Graz.

Other acquisitions made by the company during the 1920s and 1930s enabled it to become an almost fully vertically operated company. These included a factory in Vienna producing shoe lasts, a leather producer in Wels, a paper mill in Frohnleiten, and a factory producing punch knives in Vienna. Despite these acquisitions, the Depression Era proved a difficult period for the company. By the late 1930s the company's store network had dropped back to 57 stores, while its payroll, which had reached 1,000 workers in the early 1920s, fell to 425.

REBUILDING AFTER WORLD WAR II

The *Anschluss*, the German annexation of Austria, brought new difficulties for the company. While the Mayer-Rieckh family managed to maintain control of the company, placing their shares into a new vehicle, Humanic Heinisch & Mayer-Rieckh KG, the company's operations suffered severe losses. By 1943 the company had been forced to shutter many of its shoe stores, and its workforce dropped to just 120 people. Furthermore, the proximity of the company's main production facility and headquarters to Graz's main railroad station left it vulnerable to Allied bombing raids. By the end of the war, the factory lay in ruins.

The company quickly rebuilt the Graz factory, expanding the original location to become a vertically operated facility in its own right. In addition to footwear production, the facility then produced nearly all of the company's needs, including shoe lasts and punch knives, as well as its own shoeboxes. With demand for shoes building strongly in the postwar years,

KEY DATES

Mid-19th century: David Heinrich Pollak establishes a footwear factory in Vienna, Austria.

1872: Pollak establishes a subsidiary shoe factory in Graz.

1882: Pollak regroups his operations as a single company, D.H. Pollak & Co.

1914–18: D.H. Pollak forms the Heeresausrustungsges.mbH. partnership and acquires Allgemeine Österreichische Schuh AG, including the Humanic retail chain.

1920: Humanic Leder & Schuh AG is created through the merger of Allgemeine Österreichische Schuh and D.H. Pollak.

1955: Humanic acquires Schuhfabrik Strakosch in Vienna.

1977: Humanic launches its multibrand strategy with creation of Top Schuh retail chain.

1990: The holding company Leder & Schuh AG is established.

1991: Leder & Schuh launches first international operations in Hungary.

1994: The company exits footwear manufacturing and refocuses as a retail company.

2009: Leder & Schuh launches its e-commerce Web site, www.shoemanic.com.

the company rebuilt its workforce, which once again reached 1,000 people by 1950.

Just as it had following World War I, the company at first concentrated on rebuilding its retail operations in the Austrian market. In addition to sales of shoes produced in its own factories, Humanic also developed relationships with a number of noted European companies of the time, including Italy's leading shoe producer, Calzaturificio di Varese, and French designer Charles Jourdan. In order to expand its production capacity the company bought up another Austrian footwear producer, Schuhfabrik Strakosch, based in Vienna, in 1955.

INTERNATIONAL EXPORTS

The creation of the European Community and the subsequent European Free Trade Association brought new opportunities for Humanic. The company returned to the international market for the first time since the end of World War I, and by the beginning of the 1960s

had developed an export network reaching across much of northern Europe, including Scandinavia, the Benelux markets, Switzerland, and Germany. In order to meet its rising export orders, the company increased its workforce, which topped 2,000 people in 1960.

Humanic grew into a leading European footwear supplier during the 1960s, delivering to more than 3,000 shoe stores. The company's export reach had by then moved as far afield as the Soviet Union and parts of Asia. Humanic rebuilt its own Austria-based retail network at the same time, which once again topped 50 stores.

During the 1960s the company created a new subsidiary, Leder & Schuh AG, and then launched the expansion of its production network. In 1962 the company built a new factory in Deutschlandsberg dedicated to the production of children's footwear. The company added a stitching facility in Eibiswald in 1966, and then transferred the former Strakosch factory in Vienna to a new and larger plant in Feldbach in 1969.

MULTIBRAND STRATEGY

Humanic's expansion continued in the 1970s. The company had added a second stitching subsidiary in Radkersburg, and this site was expanded and converted to produce men's footwear. In 1971 the company also launched production of ski shoes at a new factory in Graz-St. Martin. The company later sold this operation to ski producer Fischer. In the meantime, Humanic established an international reputation for its often avant-garde and controversial television and print advertisements.

The continued growth of the company's export business led Humanic to establish its first foreign sales and distribution subsidiaries. These included sales and distribution subsidiaries in West Germany, Norway, and Spain, and a wholesale company in Munich. During this period, the company restructured all of its operations into a single company, Humanic Schuh AG, which then became the holding company for one of Europe's leading footwear companies.

Throughout most of the 20th century, Humanic had remained focused on this single company. In 1977 the company took its first step toward developing its multibrand retail strategy, launching its first new retail format, Top Schuh. The new format enabled the company to take advantage of the opportunities presented by the fast-developing suburban commercial shopping zones, which had become increasingly popular in Austria and throughout Europe. The addition of the new brand allowed Humanic to differentiate its product line from the traditionally urban Humanic stores.

LEDER & SCHUH IN 1990

Humanic added two new retail formats at the end of the 1980s. The first of these, Dominici, allowed the company to enter the booming market for high-end designer footwear fashions. This chain focused largely on the Vienna and Graz markets, opening its first shops in 1988.

The following year Humanic targeted the opposite end of the consumer spectrum with the launch of a discount footwear concept, Jello Schuhpark. Described by the company as a "price aggressive concept for retail parks," the Jello Schuhpark stores targeted the family footwear consumer segment, and functioned as an extension of the name brand oriented Top Schuh store format. Humanic later completed its retail lineup with the launch of Corti, a chain of shoe stores specifically targeting the youth market.

The successful development of Humanic's multi-brand strategy led the company to carry out a new restructuring. This included the 1990 creation of a new holding company, Leder & Schuh AG, which not only provided administrative support services to its subsidiary operations, but also coordinated the group's sales and distribution strategies both in Austria and internationally.

RETAIL FOCUS

The collapse of the Soviet Union and the introduction of a free market economy into the former Eastern bloc nations provided new opportunities for Leder & Schuh's expansion. Rather than pursue these markets on a purely export basis, Leder & Schuh became determined to expand its own retail operations beyond tiny Austria into its potentially larger neighbors.

Leder & Schuh first targeted Hungary, acquiring Budapest-based SZIVçRVçNY Rt. in 1991 in order to establish a foothold there. The company then began rolling out the Humanic retail brand to the Hungarian market, marking the brand's return to that country for the first time since World War I. The company later rolled out the Jello store brand to the Hungarian market, and grew to become that country's second-largest footwear retailer.

Leder & Schuh entered the Czech Republic in 1992, focusing on the Humanic brand for that market. Starting with a single store in Brno, the Humanic brand grew into the Czech Republic's third-largest retail footwear chain. In 1994 the company made a move into reunified Germany. The company created a new retail format for this, called Shoe 4 You.

The international footwear market in the meantime had undergone a major transformation. The rise of China as the global footwear manufacturing center had placed European footwear producers under extreme pressure. Unable to compete against the low-wage manufacturers in China and elsewhere, many companies had chosen to abandon their own production divisions and instead redevelop their operations around building their brands and/or retail business. Leder & Schuh joined this trend in 1994, shutting down both its manufacturing and wholesale operations in order to concentrate solely on its fast-growing retail division.

NEW MARKETS IN THE 21ST CENTURY

Leder & Schuh continued to target new markets at the dawn of the new century. The company established its first operations in Slovenia in 2000, opening stores under the Humanic and Jello brands. Leder & Schuh rapidly grew to become the market leader in that country.

The success of the Shoe 4 You brand encouraged the company to extend its operations in Germany. This led to the launch of its first Humanic store, in Regensburg, Germany, in 2002. Leder & Schuh also entered the Slovakian market that year, opening two stores in Bratislava.

Poland became the company's next market, with the opening of its first stores there in 2005. The company revamped its brand portfolio in the second half of the decade, discontinuing the Top Schuh brand in favor of the Shoe 4 You format in 2007. The following year saw the company's entry into two new foreign markets, Romania and Switzerland. The company also targeted the Balkan region, starting in Croatia with the opening of both the Jello and Humanic formats there in 2009. Also that year, the company set out to capture a share of the booming e-commerce sector, launching its own retail Web site, www.shoemanic.com, initially targeting the Austrian and German markets.

Leder & Schuh showed no signs of slowing down its expansion in 2010, despite the ongoing economic recession. In March 2010 the company identified its next expansion target, opening a store in Sofia. The company also announced plans to open a second store in the Bulgarian capital, as well as a store in Varna, on the Black Sea, before the end of the year. Leder & Schuh's network by this time extended to 11 countries, with more than 340 stores. With sales of nearly EUR 500 million ($695 million), Leder & Schuh's retail empire placed it among Europe's retail footwear leaders at the beginning of the 21st century.

M. L. Cohen

PRINCIPAL SUBSIDIARIES

Corti Schuhhandels Gmbh; Dominici Schuhhandelsges. M.B.H.; Humanic Cz Spol. S R.O. (Czech Republic); Humanic Eood (Bulgaria); Humanic Ges.M.B.H.; Humanic Sk S.R.O. (Slovakia); Humanic Sp. Z O.O. (Poland); Jello Handelsgesellschaft M.B.H.; L&S Deutschland Schuhhandels Gmbh (Germany); Leather & Shoe International D.O.O. (Slovenia); Leather & Shoe Srl (Romania); Leder & Schuh Ag; Leder & Schuh Ag, Grabs (Switzerland); Leder & Schuh D.O.O. (Croatia); Leder & Schuh Kereskedelmi Kft. (Hungary); Shoe 4 You Handels Gmbh.

PRINCIPAL DIVISIONS

Corti; Dominici; Humanic; Jello; Shoe 4 You.

PRINCIPAL COMPETITORS

Dosenbach-Ochsner AG; Goertz GmbH; Heinrich Deichmann-Schuhe GmbH and Company; Magazine Zum Globus Ag; Marko Footwear Enterprise Ltd.; NG2 S.A.; Schuhhof GmbH; Stiefelkoenig Schuhhandels Gesellschaft mbH; Top Schuh Gesellschaft mbH; Vertriebs KG.

FURTHER READING

"Austrian Footwear Retailer Leder & Schuh Enters Bulgaria." *SeeNews—The Corporate Wire*, March 10, 2010.

"Austrian Shoe Company Humanic Expanding into Croatia." *Croatian Times*, April 23, 2009.

"German, Austrian Shoe Retailers Storm Bulgaria Market." *Sofia News Agency*, March 5, 2010.

Mathis, Franz. "Big Business in Osterreich." *Osterreichische Grossunternehmen in Kurzdarstellungen*. Munich: Oldenbourg, 1987, pp. 156–158.

LoJack Corporation

———■———

200 Lowder Brook Drive, Suite 1000
Westwood, Massachusetts 02090
U.S.A.
Telephone: (781) 251-4700
Toll Free: (800) 456-5225
Fax: (781) 251-4649
Web site: http://www.lojack.com

Public Company
Incorporated: 1978
Employees: 700
Sales: $135 million (2009)
Stock Exchanges: NASDAQ
Ticker Symbol: LOJN
NAICS: 334290 Other Communications Equipment Manufacturing; 336399 All Other Motor Vehicle Parts Manufacturing; 533110 Lessors of Nonfinancial Intangible Assets (Except Copyrighted Works); 561621 Security Systems Services (Except Locksmiths)

■ ■ ■

LoJack Corporation is the recognized world leader in vehicle tracking and recovery systems. Having invented the market for recovery of stolen cars, the company's technologies now include recovering other mobile assets such as construction equipment, commercial fleets, motorcycles, and laptop computers. It has a 90 percent successful recovery rate for stolen cars and trucks since becoming available to consumers in 1986. The LoJack System is based on signals between a small radio transmitter hidden in a vehicle and a receiver located in police cars or helicopters.

The company's primary technology is a high-frequency radio network, which it can combine with cellular and Global Positioning System (GPS) equipment. Building on this technology and the company's unique relationship with law enforcement and public safety agencies LoJack has diversified its business and expanded internationally. In addition to vehicle recovery it also offers systems to protect cargo and to locate people at risk of wandering off, such as individuals with dementia. The company offers systems in 28 states and the District of Columbia, and in more than 30 countries in Europe, Africa, Asia, and the Western Hemisphere.

NURTURING AN IDEA: 1976–81

William R. Reagan served as a naval aviator with the rank of lieutenant and then held various executive positions at AVCO Corporation before he founded W.R. Reagan Associates, Inc., an investment banking firm. From 1976 to 1981, he also served as a selectman and part-time police commissioner of Medfield, a town in the greater Boston area. During this time, Reagan became preoccupied with the growth of car thefts throughout the nation in general and the greater Boston area in particular. He was particularly concerned about police being killed by car thieves during routine traffic stops.

Stealing cars was a lucrative business. The parts were more valuable than the whole car. For example, a 1984 compact costing $8,885 yielded $32,548 worth of parts. Furthermore, over and above being costly for the consumer and insurance companies and dangerous work for police officers, car thefts were often part of other crimes, such as armed robbery, rape, and murder. On a nationwide basis, theft was the largest single factor impacting the cost of insurance coverage.

Hoping to find a way to recover stolen cars while reducing the danger for police, Reagan came up with the idea to hide a small radio transmitter in a car that could be tracked by the police. He gathered a group of engineers and technicians to work with him and the police to bring his inspiration into reality.

By studying the Federal Bureau of Investigation's profiles of professional motor vehicle thieves, the research group identified the characteristics of car thieves and their way of operating. They found that car thieves were often drug addicts and that they could bypass theft-preventive devices and start cars in a matter of seconds. The research group also found that to avoid being followed by the police, a thief typically drove the car a short distance for a few minutes and then parked it. If the car were still there after about eight hours, the thief drove the car to a chop shop. The chop shop then used or introduced the dismantled parts into the used-part stream. The best way to combat the thieves, the research group concluded, was to work with the police whose mission it was to recover stolen property.

Reagan and his associates spent nine years developing designs and performing tests to create a prototype system for rapid recovery of stolen vehicles. In 1978 Reagan received a patent for what became the LoJack System. The patent became the property of W.R. Reagan Associates, and that entity licensed it to the LoJack Corporation, a company Reagan had established earlier. In 1981 a new LoJack Corporation was formed by the merger of W.R. Reagan Associates and the LoJack Corporation.

Reagan coined the term *LoJack* as the antithesis of hijack. The LoJack System was not an alarm to prevent theft. Rather, it was meant to assist in the recovery of stolen vehicles. The only responsibility resting on the owner of a stolen car equipped with a LoJack Unit was

to report the theft to the local police. There were no switches, buttons, or codes for the car operator to activate. The basic goal of the company was to make optimum use of professional law enforcement officers to recover stolen cars with as little damage as possible and to eliminate false alarms.

DEVELOPING AND TESTING THE LOJACK SYSTEM: 1980–86

The LoJack System consisted of four components. The LoJack Unit was a high-frequency transmitter and receiver package, about the size of a pack of cigarettes, randomly hidden in a car. The Police Tracking Computer was rented to police departments for installation in police patrol cars, helicopters, and other tracking vehicles. The Sector Activation System (SAS) was used by law enforcement agencies to maintain vehicle codes. The Registration System was a proprietary method of assigning digital codes for transmission and reception by LoJack Units. It allowed unique activation codes to be permanently correlated with the unique vehicle identification number the manufacturer had assigned to the car in which the LoJack Unit was located.

When the owner of a stolen car equipped with a LoJack Unit reported the theft to the police, the law enforcement computer and communications network linked to LoJack's SAS emitted a radio-frequency signal to activate the LoJack Unit in the stolen car. Then, this unit broadcasted a silent, coded tracking signal to the LoJack Police Tracking Computer in the patrol cars. It received the signal, homed in, and displayed the stolen vehicle's make, year, distance from the police cruiser, and other pertinent data, while flashing directional signals leading to the stolen car.

To raise funds for the further development of the recovery system, LoJack Corporation completed an initial public offering in 1983 and was traded on NASDAQ under the symbol LOJN. Reagan, who billed himself to his friends as "Kojak from LoJack" and sported a Telly Savalas hairdo, requested his home state of Massachusetts test a prototype of the LoJack System. At the time, this commonwealth had the highest rate of car thefts in the country: 864.8 motor vehicle thefts per 100,000 population.

Massachusetts pledged substantial resources of police vehicles, helicopters, transmission facilities, and technical personnel for the four-month experiment. At the conclusion of the demonstration, all LoJack equipment was to be donated to the state and become the property of Massachusetts, thus constituting the basis for the first operational LoJack system in the country. For the demonstration, 20 vehicles outfitted with the

LoJack Unit were reported as stolen, and then traced. After four months of demonstrations and more than 550 simulations, Massachusetts Governor Michael Dukakis said the state police had located each "stolen" car within 11 minutes of the report of its theft.

In October 1985 Motorola, Inc., was contracted as principal vendor for volume production of the LoJack System. Beginning in December 1985, the LoJack System was distributed to the Massachusetts police. Next, this system was introduced statewide to automobile dealerships and to the public for installation by LoJack's two Massachusetts distribution centers opened in Danvers and in West Roxbury. The LoJack System cost $495, a price that included entering registration of the vehicle and information about the owner in both the LoJack computers and those of the police, as well as installation, warranty, and all hardware. In 1986 Massachusetts became the first state to adopt the LoJack System. Now that his invention was on the market, Bill Reagan resigned from presidency of the Lo-Jack Corporation and was succeeded by C. Michael Daley, who had been a director of the company since 1981.

TRYING TO BUILD A MARKET: 1988–90

In December 1988 LoJack Corporation received federal clearance to sell its system outside Massachusetts. The company expanded into Florida, the number four state in the nation for stolen cars. In September 1989, in answer to a petition filed by the LoJack Corporation, the Federal Communications Commission (FCC) allocated a police radio band of 173.075 megahertz for the Stolen Vehicle Recovery Network. LoJack President Daley commented that the FCC action paved the way for LoJack's nationwide expansion. By year-end 1989, LoJack had "installed 35,000 systems in Massachusetts and south Florida ... and recovered over 900 cars for clients, a 95 percent recovery rate," Jacalyn Carfagno reported in the July 9, 1990, issue of *Money* magazine.

About 38 percent of the cars were recovered within an hour and 75 percent within 12 hours. If the car was not recovered within 24 hours after the theft was reported, the company refunded the cost of the LoJack Unit. In March 1989 Los Angeles signed a contract to establish a Stolen Vehicle Recovery Network in Los Angeles. The states of Michigan, Illinois, and New Jersey soon followed suit. The company's strategy was to expand into areas where the combination of population density, new car sales, and vehicle theft was high.

In spite of a 27 percent increase in revenues for 1991, LoJack Corporation's stock shrank from $100 million to less than $33 million. In a 1992 commentary in *Forbes*, analyst Norm Alster commented, "The company had not yet built a large enough installed base to cover its heavy capital and marketing expenses." One example of its marketing expenses was that LoJack would gain the cooperation of a police department by donating the $1,750 Tracking Units for the police cruisers.

In Los Angeles alone, the bill for outfitting 450 cruisers approached $1 million. LoJack also installed and serviced the police units. Moreover, the company invested heavily in advertising for new customers. Faced with a 1991 net loss of $6.26 million, President Daley and Chief Financial Officer Joseph F. Abely "persuaded holders of convertible debentures to swap their bonds for a convertible preferred that would not pay a dividend until the company could afford it. ... The swap succeeded because Michael Hobert, president of Benefit Capital Management Corp., an investment company with $10 million of the bonds, went along," Alster wrote.

TURNAROUND, GROWTH, INTERNATIONAL EXPANSION: 1994–99

By the middle of the decade, LoJack was installing its system in New York State, Georgia, Rhode Island, and Virginia. Washington, D.C., and Connecticut soon followed. In 1994, revenues increased to $30.23 million, compared with $14.1 million in 1991. Net income reached $1.23 million, the first positive income result posted since 1989. In January 1996, Joseph Abely was promoted to president and chief operating officer. Chairman Daley remained chief executive officer.

To expand beyond the United States, the company licensed the use of its LoJack technology to selected international markets and developed the CarSearch Stolen Vehicle Recovery System. Unlike the LoJack System operational in the United States, CarSearch had the flexibility of operating independently of existing law enforcement communication networks. By the end of 1996, the company had licensees using LoJack's technology in six European countries, four countries in South America, as well as in Hong Kong and Trinidad and Tobago.

The company reported that by June 1997 LoJack had been installed in more than 14 percent of all new cars in Massachusetts. More than 10 percent of new car owners in New York, California, and Florida also bought LoJack Units. The company estimated that stolen cars with installed LoJack Units were recovered more quickly and suffered less damage: about $500 per vehicle, compared with an average loss of several thousand dollars for cars with no LoJack Units. Furthermore, some insurance companies offered discounts of up to 35 percent to the policyholder who had a LoJack Unit in their car.

By 1997 the country's annual vehicle theft had escalated to an estimated cost of $8 billion. In a joint effort to stem the illegal export of stolen cars, an activity that contributed significantly to this escalated car theft, LoJack Corporation and Liberty Mutual Insurance Co. partnered to donate a LoJack Stolen Vehicle Recovery System to the U.S. Customs Service at the Port of Miami.

In 1998 the company introduced a more rugged version of the LoJack Retrieval System specifically designed to meet the needs of the construction and heavy equipment industry. LoJack reported recoveries of a $300,000 Caterpillar front-end loader, a Cat combination front-end loader/backhoe and, for one company, a 580L backhoe, trailer, and a flatbed truck. On the lighter side, the one millionth unit of the LoJack System was installed in the Batmobile, the television vehicle owned by George Barris, the legendary "Kustom Kar King," who had designed the Batmobile for the 1980s series of *Batman*.

MOVING INTO NEW ARENAS: 2000–04

The company began to develop an optional enhancement for cars equipped with the LoJack unit. The LoJack Early Warning System could notify car owners that their car had been moved so that they could immediately report the theft. By reducing the time between theft and notification, this improvement also reduced the amount of time for recovery. Following a waiver from the FCC in 2000, LoJack soon launched this new technology.

In January 2001 Motorola shipped its two millionth LoJack Unit to LoJack Corporation. The first million LoJack Units were shipped over a 10-year period; the second million were shipped over a three-year period. International sales, in large part fueled by collaboration with the insurance industry in foreign countries, increased by 93 percent, a growth due mostly to South African and South American licensees. The LoJack Corporation was doing business in 20 states and the District of Columbia in the United States, and it had licensees in 20 foreign countries.

At the end of 2001, Chairman/CEO Daley retired from the company. That year, LoJack Corporation reported revenues of $95.85 million, down from revenues of over $500 million when he first assumed the presidency. Daley was succeeded by Ronald J. Rossi, who had held senior executive positions at Gillette for 35 years before retiring as president of Oral-B Worldwide.

One of Rossi's first changes was to shift the installation of LoJack units to the car dealers who sold them. A dealer could clear $400 profit with each unit sold, and LoJack could cut down on the expense of sending its own people out to put in the transmitters.

The company was also exploring telematics technology. Using GPS, the emerging technology could locate a vehicle via satellites. Several companies were developing such systems and some analysts were concerned that they might put LoJack out of business. Nonetheless, while telemetric systems could give a car Internet access and provide many services, such as automatic collision notification, roadside assistance, medical alert, and starter disable, the recovery aspect was easy to foil. The system required a direct line of sight. Thieves could simply hide a car in a building.

This period also saw a change in LoJack's approach to international operations. Up until 2004, the company always licensed its technology to local partners in other countries. That year, LoJack began creating wholly owned subsidiaries, not just licensing partners. The company opened its first office in Italy, in Milan. LoJack Italia SRL, a wholly owned subsidiary with LoJack employees was created to operate it.

That August, LoJack Corporation bought the Canadian company, Boomerang Tracking Inc. for about

$49 million (CAD 64 million). Founded in 1995 and based in Montreal, the new wholly owned subsidiary marketed both the LoJack and Boomerang brand tracking systems in Canada.

MORE NEW PRODUCTS AND MARKETS

The year 2005 was a busy one for LoJack. The company introduced the latest version of its product, with the capability to be modified to use either cellular phone frequencies or GPS technology. It also rolled out LoJack for Motorcycles, first in Massachusetts and then Florida. In addition, it established a licensing agreement with Absolute Software to develop and market LoJack for Laptops.

In February an Ingersoll-Rand loader became the 1,000th construction equipment recovery. It was tracked down in 15 minutes. Along with the loader and flatbed trailer, police also found a backhoe and trailer, an excavator and trailer, and a compressor, worth some $500,000. None of this equipment had LoJack installed.

In December, the FCC granted LoJack a temporary waiver to expand the use of its radio frequency beyond recovering stolen vehicles. The waiver permitted the tracking and recovery of cargo and hazardous materials. The company began looking for ways to move into these markets.

During the first half of the decade, company growth and the move to dealership installation contributed to LoJack increasing its market penetration from 4 percent of all cars sold in the United States in 2001 to over 6 percent in 2005. Annual revenues rose 65 percent since 2001 to $191 million in 2005. Profits were up 10-fold to $18.4 million, according to the *Quincy (Massachusetts) Patriot Ledger.*

During the second half of the decade, growth in the vehicle end of the business continued to be helped by incentives offered by insurance companies. Then, in 2008, two significant investments further diversified LoJack's recovery markets. In April the company acquired Locator Systems Corporation. This purchase provided the technology to find and rescue missing people through the LoJack Safety Net. Initial targets were individuals with cognitive disorders, including Alzheimer's, Down syndrome, and autism.

The LoJack SafetyNet consisted of a small transmitter worn by the individual on a wrist or ankle, a receiver for law enforcement, a database of pertinent information about the client, and 24-hour emergency caregiver support. It was available in the United States and Canada.

In August 2008 LoJack increased its ownership in four-year-old Supply Chain Integrity to 60 percent. The new subsidiary changed its name to LoJack Supply Chain Integrity. It offered protection of in-transit cargo using a combination of GPS, cellular, and radio-frequency technology. The portable LoJack InTransit tracking devices monitored the location and/or the temperature of a shipment such as designer clothes, electronics, or pharmaceuticals. LoJack also introduced a self-powered recovery system for hybrid and electric cars.

In September, the FCC issued a final ruling that made earlier waivers permanent and allowed increased mobile output power and digital emissions. LoJack was now able to permanently use the nationwide high frequency for tracking and recovering more than stolen vehicles. With a single national network, it could work more easily with law enforcement agencies to track and recover stolen cargo, hazardous material, and missing people. The ruling also facilitated the transition of LoJack's network from wideband to narrowband. That move was to be completed by 2019.

LoJack's revenues for 2009 reflected the high unemployment during the recession that began in 2007, the tight credit market, and the drop in automobile sales of the U.S. automakers. Corporate sales declined 32 percent to $135 million. During 2010 the company laid off workers at headquarters and in field sales and restructured operations. Despite the economic situation, LoJack continued to look for new ways to deter and recover a theft and locate a missing person.

Gloria A. Lemieux
Updated, Ellen D. Wernick

PRINCIPAL SUBSIDIARIES

Boomerang Tracking Inc. (Canada); LoJack Equipment Ireland Ltd. (Ireland); LoJack Italia SRL (Italy); SC-Integrity, Inc. (60%).

PRINCIPAL COMPETITORS

Lexus Enform; Mercedes Benz TeleAid; MobileIQ (Pty) Ltd.; OnStar Corporation; Toyota Safety Connect; Zoombak LLC.

FURTHER READING

Adams, Steve, "LoJack: Stronger Signals." *Quincy (MA) Patriot Ledger*, March 4, 2006.

Alster, Norm, "A Car Thief's Nemesis." *Forbes*, May 11, 1992, p. 124.

Carfango, Jacalyn, "Auto-Recovery Firms Targeting Hot Wheels." *USA Today*, July 9, 1990, p. B5.

Chesto, Jon, "LoJack Is Tracking People Now, Too." *Quincy (MA) Patriot Ledger*, February 11, 2009.

"Equipment Theft Finding Solutions to a Billion Dollar Problem." *Heavy Equipment News*, June 1999.

Greenwood, Tom, "LoJack Helps Police Recover Stolen Vehicles." *Detroit News*, November 17, 2000.

Hindo, Brian, "LoJack's Stronger Signal." *BusinessWeek*, January 16, 2006, p. 50.

"LoJack Laptop Recovery Software Tracks Notebooks." *Twice*, September 19, 2005, p. 46.

"LoJack Stolen Vehicle Tracking System at Milestone with TV 'Batmobile' the One Millionth Installation." *Insurance Advocate*, August 28, 1999, p. 24.

"LoJack's 'Hottest' Stolen Vehicle Recoveries of the Summer." *PR Newswire*, August 24, 2010.

"Motorola Reaches LoJack Record." *Illinois Daily Herald*, January 2001.

Pham, Alex, "LoJack Corp. Car-Theft Fighter Locks in Success." *Boston Globe*, May 20, 1997, p. C27.

Macintosh Retail Group N.V.

Postbus 5770, Parkweg 20
Maastricht, NL-6202 MH
Netherlands
Telephone: (+31 043) 328 07 80
Fax: (+31 043) 325 70 30
Web site: http://www.macintosh.nl

Public Company
Founded: 1949 as Chas Macintosh Confectie NV
Employees: 6,820
Sales: EUR 1.12 billion ($1.52 billion) (2009)
Stock Exchanges: Euronext Amsterdam
Ticker Symbol: MACIN
NAICS: 448140 Family Clothing Stores; 442110
Furniture Stores; 442299 All Other Home Furnishings Stores; 448150 Clothing Accessories Stores;
448210 Shoe Stores; 452990 All Other General
Merchandise Stores; 453998 All Other Miscellaneous Store Retailers (Except Tobacco Stores)

■ ■ ■

Macintosh Retail Group N.V. is a Netherlands-based
holding company focused on the nonfood retail sector.
The company operates more than 1,250 stores in the
Netherlands, Belgium, Luxembourg, the United
Kingdom, and France. Macintosh operates through
three main divisions: Fashion, Living, and Automotive
and Telecom. The Fashion division is the company's
largest, accounting for 52 percent of group sales of EUR
1.12 billion ($1.52 billion) in 2009. The Fashion division focuses primarily on the footwear market, and to a
lesser extent on handbags and accessories. This division
includes retail brands such as Dolcis, Manfield, Invito,
and Pro (under subsidiary Hoogenbosch Retail Group);
Scapino, a discount footwear chain; and Brantano, with
operations in Belgium and the United Kingdom.

The Living division contributes 22 percent to group
revenues, and includes more than 100 Kwantum
discount home furnishing stores in the Netherlands, as
well as nine stores in Belgium; and GP Decors, a
France-based home furnishing chain with 38 stores. Macintosh's Automotive and Telecom operations include
Halfords, which combines bicycles and car parts and accessories in 157 stores in the Netherlands, as well as
seven stores in Belgium. The Telecom wing of this division focuses on the sale of mobile telephones through
174 BelCompany stores and 24 Telefoonkopen stores, as
well as the telefoonkopen.nl Web site. Macintosh Retail
Group is listed on the Euronext Amsterdam Stock
Exchange and is led by CEO Frank de Moor.

POSTWAR ORIGINS

Macintosh Retail Group traces its origins to the immediate postwar period in the Netherlands. In 1945 the
Dunlop Rubber Company, owner of Scottish raincoat
maker Charles Macintosh, began working with a pair of
Limburg region textiles workshops to produce its garments for the Netherlands market. The textiles
workshops, in operation since 1932, had originally been
established by the state-owned mining operation of the
Netherlands in order to provide additional employment
for the families of mine workers.

By 1949 Dunlop and the Limburg workshops had strengthened their relationship, creating a new company called Chas Macintosh Confectie NV. That company's evolution into the future Mackintosh Retail Group owed its start to the arrival of J. P. Beijer as its head. Beijer, then 38 years old, was head of his own textiles manufacturing company, Beijer Confectie Ateliers. Beijer merged his company into Chas Macintosh Confectie in 1953 and began expanding that business into what soon became Europe's largest textiles company.

Macintosh initially focused on supplying clothing to the Netherlands market. The company also maintained its production in the Netherlands, as wages remained low through the 1950s. By the 1960s Macintosh had grown into a major textiles producer in the Netherlands, a position underscored by its successful listing on the Amsterdam Stock Exchange in 1962.

SHIFT TO RETAIL

Rising wages and a severe labor shortage in the Netherlands forced Macintosh to expand its production to other markets in the 1960s. The company first moved into Belgium, while also subcontracting with manufacturers in Eastern Europe. As the economies of the Netherlands and Belgium continued to improve during the decade, the company turned to other lower-cost markets. Through the end of the 1960s and in the 1970s the company launched or acquired a number of factories in Tunisia, Brazil, and Portugal. The company's Portuguese factory, operating under the Maconde name, grew into that country's largest textiles producer. Macintosh itself by that time had become Europe's largest clothing manufacturer.

The 1970s represented a major turning point for the global textiles industry. Wages had continued to rise steadily with the growing affluence of the Western economies. This growth was cut short, however, with the oil crisis and subsequent dramatic rise in fuel prices at the beginning of the decade. Furthermore, a number of new low-cost manufacturing markets had begun to appear in Japan, South Korea, Taiwan, and other Asian markets. By the end of the decade, these countries had placed Western textiles manufacturers under extreme pressure. Unable to compete against the Asian manufacturers, where wages were many times lower than in the West, many clothing companies converted their operations to focus on brand marketing and retail sales.

Macintosh chose the latter approach, adding its own retail clothing chain, called Superconfex, in 1971. This chain grew strongly in the Netherlands, and Macintosh soon began exporting this business as well. In 1974 the company added Superconfex stores in Portugal, followed by the launch of the retail brand in Spain in 1977.

ACQUISITION STRATEGY

The company's conversion to retail gained momentum after J. P. Beijer's son, G. J. Beijer, took over as head of the company in 1978. By 1980 the company had adopted a new strategic orientation focused on reinventing itself as a nonfood retailer. The company began selling off most of its manufacturing operations at this time. Macintosh's exit from manufacturing was finally completed a decade later, with the sale of the Maconde operations in Portugal in 1993.

Macintosh initially remained focused on the retail clothing market and its Superconfex operations. In the mid-1980s Macintosh, which took on the name of Macintosh Retail Group, revised its retail strategy in order to expand its retail business. Instead of developing its own retail brands, the company decided to pursue a series of acquisitions that would also enable it to move beyond clothing retail.

Macintosh's first retail acquisition came in 1986, when the company acquired Kwantum, a leading discount home furnishing chain in the Netherlands. That company had been founded by Joop Steenbergen, who originally sold herring, a popular snack in the Netherlands, from a food cart in Amsterdam. Steenbergen decided to change careers at the end of the 1960s. After identifying the do-it-yourself (DIY) market as an underdeveloped segment in the Netherlands, Steenbergen launched a wholesale business selling vinyl floor coverings. In the mid-1970s Steenbergen decided to extend this business into a larger DIY retail concept.

The first Kwantum Hallen store opened in Woudenberg in 1976, helping to pioneer the discount DIY market in the Netherlands. Steenbergen quickly expanded the chain, adding locations throughout the country. By 1980 the company had opened more than 20 stores. However, Kwantum began to struggle in the 1980s, in part because of its inability to adapt to the increasingly sophisticated demands of Dutch consumers.

KEY DATES

1949: Chas Macintosh Confectie NV. is founded to produce raincoats and other textiles for the Netherlands market.

1953: J. P. Beijer merges his company with Chas Macintosh and takes over as head of the company.

1979: Beijer's son G. J. Beijer takes over as head of the company and refocuses it on the retail sector.

1986: Macintosh acquires home furnishings chain Kwantum.

1997: Macintosh acquires retail footwear group Hoogenbosch.

2006: Macintosh acquires discount footwear chain Scapino.

2008: Macintosh acquires Brantano in Belgium.

2010: Macintosh announces plans to seek new acquisition opportunities.

This led to Steenbergen's decision to sell the company to Macintosh.

The new owners then set to work revitalizing the Kwantum chain. The company dropped the "Hallen" from its name and revamped the Kwantum retail format, adapting a new look and focusing more on home furnishings. This new formula proved successful, and through the next decade Macintosh expanded Kwantum into a chain of more than 80 stores.

BUILDING BRANDS

Macintosh soon added a third retail brand, and a new category, with the addition of Halfords, the leading automotive accessories and bicycle retailer in the Netherlands. Halfords joined Macintosh's retail family in 1987 and grew into a chain of 160 stores, including several stores in Belgium. By the beginning of the 1990s, Macintosh had added a second home furnishings chain, Piet Klerkx. The company then formed its home furnishing division, acquiring Wooninrichtingen Pot in 1992.

The company added a new acquisition in 1993, buying up Belgian carpet specialist Tonton Tapis. Macintosh also announced in 1993 that it hoped to pursue the further internationalization of its retail operations, opening test stores in Germany, France, and Denmark. The company made a full entry into the French market

by the end of 1993, buying up 50.1 percent of home furnishings chain GP Decors and its 48 stores. GP Decors, formerly known as Galeries du Papier Peint, specialized in wallpaper, paint, and curtains and other wall hangings. Macintosh acquired full control of GP Decors in 1994.

With revenues topping NLG 900 million (approximately $450 million), Macintosh stepped up its ambitions in the middle of the decade. In May 1995 the company entered the men's clothing field, acquiring a concession for France's Celio brand for the Netherlands market. By October 1995 the company had also acquired Crusoë, a Belgium-based furniture chain. Macintosh then formed a joint venture with Pons Holdings to launch a new retail format dedicated to the small but promising market for mobile telephones. The new chain became known as BelCompany, and quickly grew into the leading mobile telephone retailer in the Netherlands.

Macintosh's textiles operations began to slip in the second half of the decade, however, as consumer demand dropped sharply. Macintosh focused its growth instead on new areas, notably the footwear sector. In 1997 the company acquired 50 percent of Hoogenbosch Retail Group, one of the leading retail footwear specialists in the Netherlands. Hoogenbosch's brand family included the Dolcis, Manfield, Invito, and Olympus Sport/Pro Sport chains. Macintosh acquired full control of Hoogenbosch in 1999, adding NLG 320 million ($160 million) to its annual revenues.

SLIMMING DOWN AT THE DAWN OF THE 21ST CENTURY

Macintosh maintained its expansion drive to the end of the decade. The company made its move into Germany, targeting that market's automotive accessories and bicycles sector. The company established its presence there in 1997, acquiring two existing chains, ASZ, based in Berlin, and BAV, in Koblenz. The company also announced plans to roll out the Halfords brand there by the end of the decade, and to expand across Germany through the development of a franchise network.

Back at home, Macintosh moved into the Internet access market, joining the rush to offer free Internet access services with its own Internet service provider, MyWeb. Macintosh attracted users by offering discounts in the company's more than 550 retail stores. By the beginning of the next decade, the company had succeeded in signing on 320,000 subscribers.

Macintosh's clothing operations continued to give it problems in the new decade, dragging down its profits. The company, which sold off Superconfex's Belgian stores at the beginning of the decade, announced plans to sell off Superconfex entirely. By 2001, with no buyers stepping forward, the company decided to shut down that business and exit the clothing sector. In 2002 Macintosh also ended its Internet access experiment, in large part because of the investment required to keep up with developments in the sector, most notably the arrival of high-speed Internet access.

Founder J. P. Beijer died in 2003 at the age of 88. One month later G. J. Beijer, having built the company into one of the leading retail groups in the Netherlands with annual sales of EUR 770 million ($600 million), decided to retire from the company. Belgium-born Frank de Moor was then brought in to take the company's CEO spot. Soon after, the company sold off its Piet Klerkx furniture chain, and exited the German market.

FOCUS ON FOOTWEAR

Macintosh's strategy for the second half of the decade refocused the company's operations around three main divisions: Fashion, especially footwear; Living, grouping the Kwantum and GP Decors chains; and Automotive and Telecom, combining the company's Halfords automotive and bicycle chain with its mobile telephone retail operations.

Footwear appeared to receive the largest share of Macintosh's attention, however. In 2006 the company expanded its footwear business into the discount footwear segment, acquiring Scapino, the Dutch leader, with 184 stores. Scapino also operated 25 stores in Belgium and seven outlet stores in Germany. The new acquisition added EUR 220 million, boosting the company's total revenues past EUR 920 million by 2007.

Macintosh stepped up its footwear operations again in 2008, acquiring Brantano NV. The purchase, for EUR 158 million, made Macintosh the leader in the Belgian footwear market, adding 125 stores to its existing business there. Furthermore, the addition of Brantano brought Macintosh into the United Kingdom, where the company had built a network of 150 stores, and into Luxembourg, with five stores.

The acquisition of Brantano helped Macintosh withstand the worst effects of the global economic collapse at the end of the decade. The company's sales rose to EUR 1.15 billion in 2008, and slipped only slightly in 2009, to EUR 1.12 billion. The company's profit also remained strong, in part following the sale of the group's money-losing BelCompany operations in Belgium in 2009.

As the worst of the recession appeared to be over in 2010, Macintosh announced plans to pursue new acquisitions. The company targeted further expansion of its Fashion division. The company also sought to boost its Living division, which had suffered the most during the economic downturn. Macintosh Retail Group remained one of the largest and most focused retail empires in the Netherlands.

M. L. Cohen

PRINCIPAL SUBSIDIARIES

Retail BV; Brantano Asia Ltd. (China); Brantano Beheer BV; Brantano NV (Belgium); Brantano UK Ltd.; Deco Holding BV; Dolcis BV; GP Decors SNC (France); Halfords België NV; Halfords Nederland BV; Hoogenbosch Retail Group BV; Izet BV; Kwantum België BV; Kwantum Nederland BV; Macintosh Hong Kong Ltd.; Macintosh International BV; Muys NV (Belgium); Nea International BV; Perla NV (Belgium); Pro Sport BV; Shoe City Ltd. (UK).

PRINCIPAL DIVISIONS

Living; Fashion; Automotive and Telecom; Services.

PRINCIPAL OPERATING UNITS

Kwantum; GP Decors; Brantano; Manfield, Scapino; Halfords; BelCompany; Telefoonkopen.nl.

PRINCIPAL COMPETITORS

Delhaize Group; Financiere Pinault S.C.A.; Grospart AG; Groupe Auchan S.A.; Kaufland Stiftung and Company Kg.; Metro AG; Musgrave Group plc.

FURTHER READING

"Beijer Weg." *Trouw*, February 4, 2003.

"Dutch Macintosh Sees Takeover Opportunities in 2010." *M&A Navigator*, March 12, 2010.

"Dutch Macintosh to Dispose of Belcompany Chain in Belgium for Eur6m." *M&A Navigator*, June 26, 2009.

"Dutch Macintosh to Explore Acquisitions for Living, Fashion Divisions." *ADP News*, March 11, 2010.

Koch, Hans. "Schoenengigant Macintosh Verduurzaamt." *Trouw*, March 24, 2010.

"Macintosh Bestormt de Belgische Schoenenmarkt." *Trouw*, October 30, 2007.

"Macintosh Boekt Omzetdaling." *Trouw*, October 20, 2009.

"Macintosh Heeft Wind in de Zeilen en Breidt uit." *Trouw*, March 6, 1998.

"Macintosh Lines up Brantano Bid." *just-style.com*, October 29, 2007.

"Macintosh Takes up 100% of Brantano." *just-style.com*, January 29, 2008.

Smit, Hans, "Oprichter Macintosh Overleden." *ANP*, February 22, 2003.

Mahindra & Mahindra Ltd.

———————————————■———————————————

Gateway Building, Apollo Bunder
Mumbai, 400 001
India
Telephone: (+91 022) 2202 1031
Fax: (+91 022) 2287 5485
Web site: http://www.mahindra.com

Public Company
Incorporated: 1947
Employees: 16,094
Sales: $3.22 billion (2009)
Stock Exchanges: Mumbai
Ticker Symbol: 500520
NAICS: 336111 Automobile Manufacturing; 336399
All Other Motor Vehicle Parts Manufacturing

■ ■ ■

Mahindra & Mahindra Ltd. (M&M) is India's leading manufacturer of farm tractors and one of the country's leading automobile manufacturers. M&M, which originated as a Jeep assembler, continues to focus its automotive production on the multi-utility vehicle (MUV) market, spearheaded by its highly acclaimed Scorpio model. Other popular models include the Bolero and the Xylo, introduced in 2009. M&M is also a leading producer of three-wheeled vehicles and light commercial vehicles, and in 2010 began manufacturing motorcycles of its own design. M&M also produces low-priced automobiles under the Dacia Logan brand for the Indian market in a joint venture partnership with France's Renault.

MUVs represent nearly 70 percent of the more than 220,000 vehicles M&M sold in 2009. This division is also the company's largest, generating nearly 56.5 percent of its total sales of $3.22 billion that year. The Farm Equipment division, which accounts for 43.2 percent of group sales, produced nearly 120,000 tractors and more than 53,000 tractor engines, primarily for the domestic market.

M&M has also launched a global strategy, with sales reaching the United States, South Africa, Europe, and other markets. The company is also present in China, through its 2004 acquisition of Jiangling Tractor Company. In 2010 the company reached an agreement to acquire South Korea's Ssangyong Motor Company. In addition to its core Farm Equipment and Automotive operations, M&M has developed a diversified portfolio of businesses, including in the hospitality, technology, infrastructure, defense systems, and other industries. M&M is listed on the Mumbai (Bombay) Stock Exchange and is led by Chairman Anand G. Mahindra, grandson of one of the company's founders.

ORIGINS IN 1945

The inspiration for the creation of the company that was to become Mahindra & Mahindra came during a visit by K. C. Mahindra to the United States as the leader of the Indian Supply Mission in 1945. Mahindra was introduced to Delmar "Barney" Roos, who had developed the engine for the legendary Willys Jeep for Willys Overland Corporation. The vehicle, renowned for its sturdiness and reliability, had played a significant part in the Allied victory in World War II. Mahindra recognized the Jeep's potential as a civilian vehicle capable of handling India's rudimentary road system.

Mahindra obtained the license to assemble and sell the Willys Jeep in India. Upon his return home, in 1945, he teamed up with his brother, J. C. Mahindra, and a partner, Ghulam Mohammed, founding Mahindra & Mohammed. Mahindra's intuition had been correct, and the company's early entry enabled it to gain control of India's soon-to-boom MUV market. India's independence in 1947 provided a new boost for the company's fortunes. At the same time, Mohammed left the country and moved to the newly established Pakistan, becoming its first finance minister. The company changed its name that year to Mahindra & Mahindra.

M&M grew rapidly in the early years of Indian independence, in part by securing a series of international partnerships. For example, in 1950 the company developed a partnership with Japan's Mitsubishi Corporation. The company also strengthened its ties with Willys, developing a new technical and financial partnership in 1954. M&M showed an early willingness to branch out from Jeep assembly, adding the production of railroad wagons by 1950, and acquiring the Indian franchise from the Otis Elevator Company in 1953.

By 1956 M&M had completed an initial public offering, listing its shares on the Bombay Stock Exchange. The company also developed new joint ventures with international partners, including Dr. Beck & Co. of Germany in 1956 and Rubery Owen & Co. of the United Kingdom in 1957.

MANUFACTURING ADDED

By the end of the 1950s M&M had moved beyond its roots as an assembler to become a full-scale manufacturer. The group added a Machine Tools division in 1958, and teamed up with GKN Group of the United Kingdom to form a sintered products joint venture. In 1962 the company added its own dedicated steel business in a joint venture with France's Ugine Kuhlmann, thus ensuring its steel supply.

That supply became all the more important as M&M prepared to add what was to become one of its largest operations, the production of tractors for the fast-growing Indian agricultural sector. For this M&M teamed up with U.S.-based International Harvester to found International Tractor Company of India in 1963. M&M, which continued to produce Jeeps and other MUVs, also explored other areas of the automotive sector. In 1965 the company launched the production of light commercial vehicles. The company continued to expand its automotive production capacity through the end of the decade. This permitted M&M to add its first international sales of vehicles and spare parts beginning in 1969. M&M emerged at the same time as a major manufacturer of three-wheeled vehicles, one of the largest motor vehicle categories in India.

International Harvester pulled out of International Tractor Company of India in 1971, leaving M&M in sole control of what was rapidly growing into India's largest tractor manufacturer. The company scored one of its first major engineering successes in 1975, when it developed its own fuel-efficient diesel engine. In 1977 the company restructured International Tractor, which was then merged into M&M, becoming its Tractor Division.

The company expanded its engine technology soon after, acquiring the license to build engines based on the Peugeot XDP 4.90 diesel engine. By 1982 M&M was ready to launch its own tractor brand, Mahindra, based on the company's own designs developed specifically for the Indian market. These tractors provided lower horsepower than their western counterparts, taking into account the far smaller size of most Indian farms in comparison to farms in the United States, Europe, and other parts of the world. The smaller size of the Mahindra tractors also permitted the company to export its tractors for sale to the smaller "hobbyist" farmer sector. The Mahindra in the meantime was immediately popular in India, and by 1983 the company claimed the lead in the domestic tractor market.

KEY DATES

1945: Brothers K. C. and J. C. Mahindra, together with partner Ghulam Mohammed, establish a Willys Jeep assembly franchise in India.

1947: The company becomes Mahindra & Mahindra (M&M).

1956: M&M goes public on the Bombay Stock Exchange.

1965: M&M launches production of light utility vehicles.

1982: The company introduces the Mahindra brand of tractors.

1994: M&M establishes U.S. tractor distribution subsidiary.

1999: The company acquires Gujarat Tractors.

2002: M&M launches the Scorpio SUV.

2004: M&M enters China with acquisition of Jiangling Motor Co.'s tractor division.

2010: M&M acquires South Korea's Ssangyong Motor Company.

EXPANSION AND DIVERSIFICATION

M&M continued in its quest both to expand its existing business and to diversify into new areas. The company formed a joint venture in Greece in 1984 for the assembly of light utility vehicles for the European market. In 1986 M&M teamed up with British Telecom to enter the information technology (IT) sector, creating the Mahindra British Telecom (later Tech Mahindra) joint venture. The company completed a number of acquisitions through the end of the decade, buying up International Instruments Limited in 1987, and also acquiring GKN's Automotive Pressing Unit. This latter acquisition was added to the company's Mahindra Ugine steel joint venture.

This subsidiary also provided an important training ground for the next generation of the Mahindra family, as Anand Mahindra, grandson of J. C. Mahindra, became its general manager. By 1991 Anand Mahindra had been appointed deputy managing director of Mahindra & Mahindra itself. The younger Mahindra, who had completed an MBA at Harvard Business School, quickly took charge of modernizing the company in order to position it to meet the new competitive challenges in India in the early 1990s. During this time the Indian government, in order to stabilize the country's long-fragile economy, set into motion a series of reforms. These not only loosened many of the restrictions that had formerly reined in the country's entrepreneurial efforts, but also lowered the barriers for foreign companies to enter the Indian market.

Among other changes, Mahindra pushed through the conversion of the company's bonus system, establishing a new performance-based system. The company also invested in upgrading its production processes through the decade. These efforts quickly paid off, as the company's productivity improved dramatically. M&M also focused its attention on expanding its range of automobiles, launching new models including the Commander in 1991 and the Armada in 1993.

ENTERING THE UNITED STATES IN 1994

The company also expanded into the United States, setting up Mahindra USA Inc. in 1994 in order to begin distributing its tractor line there. At home, M&M formed a joint venture with the Ford Motor Company to produce passenger vehicles for the Indian market, starting in 1996. Other partnerships created during the decade included a steel service center with Japan's Mitsubishi and Nissho Iwai Corporation; an engineering consultancy joint venture with Canada's Acres International Ltd.; and EAC Graphics (India) Ltd., formed in partnership with the East Asiatic Company of Denmark.

Also in 1994, M&M carried out a restructuring of its diverse operations, developing an organization based on six business units, led by its Automotive and Farm Equipment divisions. This new organization did not prevent the company from exploring new business areas, however. For example, in 1996 the company established two new businesses, Mahindra Holidays and Resorts, and Mahindra Consulting, later known as Bristlecone. The following year, after establishing its own university, M&M also expanded into property development, launching Mahindra World City Developers Ltd.

SCORPIO DEBUTS IN 2002

Motor vehicles nevertheless remained M&M's core operation. The company boosted its three-wheeled lineup with the introduction of the battery-powered Bijlee in 1999. This was followed by the launch in 2001 of a diesel-powered three-wheeler, the Champion. M&M expanded its tractor operations as well, buying up a controlling stake in Gujarat Tractors in 1999. That company then became Mahindra Gujarat Tractors. In 2000 the company further expanded the Farm Equipment division's production capacity with the opening of a new factory in Rudrapur. The company also launched the Arjun 605 DI that year, featuring the first of a new series of higher horsepower engines.

However, much of M&M's rapid growth at the dawn of the 21st century came from its Automotive division. The company scored several new successes at the beginning of the decade, notably in 2000 with the Bolero GLX, a sport-utility vehicle (SUV) targeting the urban market, and in 2001 with the MaXX, an MUV.

M&M marked a new milestone in 2002 when it debuted its first world-class SUV, the Scorpio. The development of the Scorpio represented a break from traditional automobile development models in use elsewhere in the industry. Rather than committing its resources to the highly costly process of fully developing a new vehicle in-house, M&M outsourced nearly all of the Scorpio's development to its network of suppliers.

While M&M provided the overall design and specifications for the new SUV, suppliers took the lead in developing its component systems. This led to a major cost savings, both for M&M and for its suppliers, which were able to develop the Scorpio's equipment based on their existing production. As a result, M&M brought the Scorpio to the market far more quickly and for a much lower cost, an estimated $120 million, as opposed to as much as $1 billion using traditional design and development procedures.

The Scorpio helped pave the way for M&M's entry into the international and even global automotive market. As the most expensive vehicle in M&M's automotive lineup, the Scorpio, which represented as much as one-fifth of the division's total sales by the middle of the decade, also became one of its most profitable.

INTERNATIONAL ACQUISITIONS

M&M completed a series of acquisitions through the middle of the decade as it leveraged the success of both its tractor line and the Scorpio SUV into a position among the world's fastest-growing automotive companies. The company's U.S. operations grew strongly, with its dealership network expanding to more than 270 locations, backed by assembly plants in Georgia and Texas.

The company then targeted the Chinese market, acquiring the tractor production unit of Jiangling Motor in 2005. M&M's global ambitions led to further acquisitions around the world, including U.K.-based automotive forging leader Stokes Group in 2006, along with its German counterpart, Jeco Holding. Other

expansion moves included the acquisition of SAR Transmission Private Ltd., a producer of transmission shafts and gears. In 2005 M&M set up a truck and bus manufacturing joint venture for the India market with International Truck and Engine Corporation.

M&M continued to develop the Scorpio lineup as it rolled out the vehicle's global launch. The company introduced a hybrid version of the Scorpio in 2006, and then extended the range with the introduction of a pickup model that year. In order to underscore its ambition to become a global automotive brand, the launch of the new Scorpio (also known as the Goa in international markets) was held in South Africa.

By the end of 2009 M&M had raised its total revenues past $3.22 billion, earning the company a position in the global top 25. The company had moved to fill a major gap in its motor vehicle portfolio, launching its first line of two-wheeled scooters in 2008. The addition of a two-wheeled vehicle lineup was especially important in India, where, despite the growing demand for automobiles, two-wheeled vehicles continued to outsell their four-wheeled counterparts. The success of the scooter line encouraged M&M to expand this range. In July 2010 the company announced plans to launch its first full-scale motorcycles, possibly by the end of the year.

M&M in the meantime continued to develop its expansion strategies both at home and abroad. In August 2010 the company announced plans to build a new tractor factory, its fifth, in order to meet rising demand. M&M announced at the same time that it had signed a memorandum of agreement to acquire struggling South Korean automaker Ssangyong Motor Company. From a small Jeep assembler, M&M had grown into a viable contender in the global automotive market.

M. L. Cohen

PRINCIPAL SUBSIDIARIES

Bristlecone Ltd.; CanvasM (Americas) Inc.; Gesenkschmiede Schneider GmbH (Germany); Jensand Ltd.; Mahindra & Mahindra South Africa (Proprietary) Ltd.; Mahindra (China) Tractor Company Ltd.; Mahindra Engineering and Chemical Products Ltd.; Mahindra Engineering Services (Europe) Ltd. (UK); Mahindra Engineering Services Ltd.; Mahindra Europe s.r.l. (Italy); Mahindra First Choice Wheels Ltd.; Mahindra Forgings Europe AG (Austria); Mahindra Gujarat Tractor Ltd.; Mahindra Renault Private Ltd.; Mahindra Ugine Steel Company Ltd.; Mahindra USA Inc.; NBS International Ltd.; Plexion Technologies GmbH (Germany); PT Tech Mahindra Indonesia; Stokes Forgings Ltd. (UK); Stokes Group Ltd. (UK); Tech Mahindra Ltd.

PRINCIPAL DIVISIONS

Aftermarket; Automotive; Defense Systems; Farm Equipment; Financial Services; Hospitality; Information Technology; Infrastructure Development; Mahindra 2 Wheelers; Mahindra Partners; Mahindra Systech.

PRINCIPAL OPERATING UNITS

Bristlecone; Mahindra Agribusiness; Mahindra Australia; Mahindra China Tractors; Mahindra Defense Systems; Mahindra First Choice Wheels Ltd.; Mahindra Forgings Limited; Mahindra Gujarat Tractor; Mahindra Holidays and Resorts; Mahindra Navistar Automotives Limited; Mahindra Powerol; Mahindra Renault Private Limited; Mahindra USA; Tech Mahindra.

PRINCIPAL COMPETITORS

Ford Motor Co.; General Motors Co.; Honda Motor Company Ltd.; Hyundai Motor Co.; John Deere Company; Maruti Suzuki Ltd.; Shanghai Automotive Industry Corp.; Tata Motors Ltd.; Toyota Motor Corp.

FURTHER READING

Bursa, Mark. "Mahindra's Quiet but Steady Expansion." *Just-auto.com*, November 1, 2006.

"Mahindra to Add First Motorcycles, Challenging Honda." *Business Week*, July 21, 2010.

"M&M to Invest Rs 4,500 Crore for New Tractor Facility in South India." *Accord Fintech*, August 26, 2010.

"M&M to Launch First Motorcycle." *Auto Business News*, August 26, 2010.

Raghunathan, Anuradha. "Putt-Putt Tractors, Revved-Up Goals." *Forbes Global*, April 24, 2006.

"What's Going on with Mahindra?" *Truck Trend*, September–October 2010, p. 16.

Wielgat, Andrea. "Manufacturing the Mahindra Way." *Automotive Industries*, October 2002, p. 34.

MBI Inc.

———■———

47 Richards Avenue
Norwalk, Connecticut 06857
U.S.A.
Telephone: (203) 853-2000
Fax: (203) 831-9661
Web site: http://www.mbi-inc.com

Private Company
Incorporated: 1973
Employees: 600
Sales: $400 million (2009)
NAICS: 327112 Vitreous China, Fine Earthenware, and Other Pottery Product Manufacturing; 339911 Jewelry (Including Precious Metal) Manufacturing; 339914 Costume Jewelry and Novelty Manufacturing

■ ■ ■

MBI Inc. is a Norwalk, Connecticut-based consumer products company comprising four operating divisions. The flagship unit is the Danbury Mint, a maker of a wide variety of collectibles, including plates, bells, jewelry, and sculptures, and especially known for its die-cast models of classic cars and trucks. Danbury also produces sports figurines and other sports memorabilia. It is a major licensee of the National Football League, and also maintains relationships with Major League Baseball, the National Basketball Association, NASCAR (stock car racing), WWE (professional wrestling), and major college athletic programs.

MBI UK, based in London, markets many of the Danbury Mint products, but also caters to a British sensibility. The unit maintains licenses and working partnerships with Baccarat, maker of crystal, jewelry, and other luxury gifts; Royal Doulton, maker of tableware and collectibles; and Wedgwood, the venerable producer of china, table linens, and jewelry. MBI UK also offers die-cast models of Jaguar and Rolls-Royce vehicles, and works with such major English soccer teams as Chelsea, Liverpool, and Manchester United.

Another MBI division is PCS Stamps & Coins, which the company claims is the world's largest philatelic organization. In addition to domestic and international stamps, PCS offers collections of vintage coins, rare currency, and foreign coins, some of which are of ancient origin, and albums. Finally, Easton Press is MBI's publishing unit, specializing in collectible books, many of them signed by their authors. Easton focuses on classic literature but also the works of celebrated authors, U.S. presidents and other world leaders, and celebrity books. The unit produces leather-bound volumes, either individual titles or in sets, featuring fine printing and 22kt gold accents. Clothbound classics are sold under the First Editions Library banner. MBI is owned by its longtime chief executive and chairman, Theodore Stanley.

A PIONEER IN PROMOTIONAL PRODUCTS

MBI grew out of the business endeavors of Ralph O. Glendinning, born in 1923, the son of a New Jersey locksmith. A celebrated Marine carrier fighter during World War II, he completed his education at Princeton

University before launching a business career in 1948 at Procter & Gamble. He was involved in branding and promotions, ultimately becoming the head of the promotion development group. In 1960 Glendinning went into business for himself. Operating out of a cottage overlooking the Saugatuck River in Westport, Connecticut, Glendinning provided marketing and consulting services, specializing in direct response and sweepstakes promotions, serving more than 250 major companies, including Coca-Cola, Ford, General Foods, Heinz, Nabisco, Pepsi, Shell Oil, Warner Lambert, and Volkswagen.

One of Glendinning's most popular promotional efforts during the 1960s was gas station scratch-off games offering instant cash prizes. His first was Win-A-Check for Tidewater. It was the success of a competing promotion, however, that led to the creation of MBI Inc., perhaps as much out of spite as for profit. The man who would become Glendinning's nemesis was Joseph M. Segel, a Philadelphia, Pennsylvania, native who got his start in developing promotional items while still attending the University of Pennsylvania's Wharton School of Business in the late 1940s.

Segel later compiled the *Advertising Specialty Directory* listing all providers of promotional products and serving as the flagship for his company, the Advertising Specialty Institute. After selling the company in the early 1960s, Siegel was inspired to market a series of limited edition sterling silver medals commemorating famous people. His new venture was called the National Commemorative Society and in 1965 became known as the Franklin Mint.

Among the Franklin Mint products were various series of commemorative aluminum coins, such as the series that included the likeness of all 36 U.S. presidents to that date. Segel was able to persuade oil companies to give away his coins as sales incentives rather than Glendinning's scratch-off cards. Customers liked to collect the coins and showed a preference for them over disposable cards and a remote chance of winning some cash. They also had more incentive to return to the gas stations of the same oil company in an effort to collect all of the coins in a series.

DANBURY MINT FORMED: 1969

In 1969 Glendinning formed a subsidiary that was little more than an imitation of the Franklin Mint. He called it the Danbury Mint. Selected to run the business was Theodore Stanley, one of Glendinning's longtime lieutenants, who would eventually become MBI's owner. The purpose of the Danbury Mint was hardly subtle. The Danbury Mint sold knockoffs of the collectibles offered by the Franklin Mint.

If the Franklin Mint thought a product was worth issuing, the Danbury Mint soon offered a less-expensive version. In essence, the Danbury Mint allowed the Franklin Mint to pay for the market research for both companies, and the money it saved on overhead allowed the Danbury Mint to undercut the Franklin Mint on price. Moreover, while the Franklin Mint invested in its own manufacturing operations, the Danbury Mint outsourced everything, gaining a further pricing advantage.

The Danbury Mint's first product was a series of 21 medals commemorating the 1969 moon landing. Other products along the lines of Franklin Mint offerings would include die-cast automobiles, jewelry, and sports collectibles. A year after MBI was formed, a second subsidiary was added in 1970, the Postal Commemorative Society. It started out offering U.S. First Day of Issue Covers and steadily expanded its stamp offerings so that by the start of the 1980s MBI was claiming that it was the world's largest philatelic company. The division also added coins to its offerings, prompting a change in name to PCS Stamps & Coins.

The Danbury Mint and PCS Stamps & Coins were combined in 1973, with MBI Inc. as the holding company, generating sales of $10 million that year. It was an amount that would increase steadily to about $25 million by the mid-1970s, according to *Forbes*. MBI remained a subsidiary of Glendinning Companies until late 1975 when it was spun off as an independent company. As he retired, Glendinning sold control of the business to Stanley during this period.

EASTON PRESS ESTABLISHED: 1975

MBI maintained its strong growth under Stanley's ownership and continued to follow the lead of the Franklin Mint. In answer to its rival's library division, MBI launched the Easton Press in 1975. The Franklin Library division began selling a leather-bound series of literary classics called One Hundred Greatest Masterpieces. Easton Press countered with The 100 Greatest Books Ever Written. MBI also looked overseas to spur further growth. In 1976 it established an office in London to serve as the home of the European

```
┌─────────────────────────────────────────────┐
│                                               │
│             KEY DATES                         │
│                  ■                            │
│  ─────────────────────────────────────────    │
│                                               │
│  1969:  The Danbury Mint is established as Glendin-│
│         ning Companies unit.                  │
│  1973:  MBI Inc. formed as parent company for │
│         Danbury Mint.                         │
│  1975:  MBI spun off as independent company.  │
│  1976:  European division established.        │
│  1977:  Domestic operations consolidated in Nor-│
│         walk, Connecticut.                    │
│  1989:  Annual sales top $200 million.        │
│  2003:  New $10 million distribution center opens in│
│         Torrington, Connecticut.              │
│                                               │
└─────────────────────────────────────────────┘
```

division. This division eventually became MBI UK.

Over the years the MBI operations occupied several Westport locations. PCS had also opened satellite operations in other Connecticut sites. In 1977 MBI consolidated its domestic operations by moving to a larger facility in Norwalk, Connecticut. Annual sales reached $50 million by the end of the decade, and the company continued to grow at a steady pace, leading to the opening of additional facilities in western Connecticut.

A major factor in MBI's ongoing success remained its unabashed willingness to imitate. "MBI copies everyone and their neighbor," the director of product development for a rival firm told *Forbes* in a 1992 profile of MBI. "They do it better than anybody else, they do it quicker, and they do it cheaper." Furthermore, MBI was able to obtain new customers at little expense and then sell them subsequent products. It was on these later purchases that MBI realized the bulk of its profits.

Unlike its rivals, however, MBI was not willing to add a first-time customer to its mailing by taking a loss on the first purchase. Rather, it insisted on achieving a profit from the outset, a goal more easily achieved because it continued to allow the Franklin Mint to shoulder the product development and market research costs. MBI was also willing to allow program managers to invest speculatively on new products. Rather than spend money on testing, the company simply brought a product to market and was quick to cut its losses if necessary.

TOP SCHOOLS PROVIDE TALENT

MBI's willingness to grant greater autonomy to junior-level employees, along with its proximity to Ivy League universities, was another important factor in the company's success. MBI recruiters were able to hire from elite schools because they were willing to offer immediate and significant managerial responsibility. However, while a young program manager would have the opportunity to bring a new product to market, there were no illusions that the company would support a product that did not gain instant traction. "The minute the numbers don't add up anymore, the product is canned. I mean the morning after, it is gone," one artists' agent told *Forbes*. Nevertheless, MBI was more than willing to spend heavily to support products that found an audience.

After 20 years in business, MBI increased annual sales to more than $200 million in 1989. Sales topped $300 million by the end of the century. The Danbury Mint continued to monitor its customers, as well as keeping tabs on what the Franklin Mint had to offer. When actor Tom Cruise enjoyed success in the movie *Top Gun*, the Danbury Mint enjoyed success with replicas of World War II leather flight jackets. The company also enjoyed notable success with the sale of Princess Diana dolls. The taste of MBI offerings was sometimes questioned, however. After the terrorist attacks of September 11, 2001, the company came under criticism from some quarters for its products associated with that event.

NEW DISTRIBUTION CENTER OPENS: 2003

To support its continued growth, MBI in 2002 considered building a much-needed new distribution center for the Danbury Mint outside Connecticut. Consultants advised the company to consider sites in Pennsylvania or Kentucky, and the company was almost ready to abandon Connecticut when Norwalk city and state officials made a concerted effort to keep the operations. An incentive package that included tax abatements and a low-interest loan won the day, and MBI agreed to build its new distribution center in Torrington, Connecticut. In July 2002 MBI acquired a 35.5-acre site for $1.2 million and the following year opened a $10 million, 200,000-square-foot facility.

Over the years, many buyers of MBI and Franklin Mint collectibles had come to believe they were making investments in heirlooms that would steadily increase in value. With the rise of the Internet and auction sites like eBay, however, this merchandise became readily available. Without scarcity to drive prices, even limited-edition collectibles became available at steep discounts. Nevertheless, MBI and its divisions continued to prosper in the new century. Sales reached $400 million by the time the company celebrated its 40th anniversary in 2009. Its mailing list had also expanded to more than 10 million customers, which bode well for the company's ability to sell more commemorative medals, plates, die-cast models, leather-bound books, and other collectibles in the years to come.

Ed Dinger

PRINCIPAL DIVISIONS

Danbury Mint; Easton Press; MBI UK; PCS Stamps & Coins.

PRINCIPAL COMPETITORS

eBay, Inc.; Franklin Mint, LLC; Lenox, Incorporated.

FURTHER READING

Berman, Phyllis, with R. Lee Sullivan. "Getting Even." *Forbes*, August 31, 1992, p. 54.

Dougherty, Philip H. "Consultant for Some 'Smart Companies.'" *New York Times*, July 21, 1968.

"MBI Commemorates 40 Years of Marking History." *Fairfield County Business Journal*, April 13, 2009, p. 11.

Smith, David A. "Torrington, Conn., Aims to Entice Direct Marketer, 100 Jobs." *Waterbury Republican-American*, October 23, 2002.

McCarthy Building Companies, Inc.

—■—

1341 North Rock Hill Road
St. Louis, Missouri 63124
U.S.A.
Telephone: (314) 968-3300
Fax: (314) 968-4642
Web site: http://www.mccarthy.com

Private Company
Incorporated: 1907 as McCarthy Lumber and Construction Company
Employees: 2,300
Sales: $3 billion (2009 est.)
NAICS: 236210 Industrial Building Construction; 236220 Commercial and Institutional Building Construction; 237310 Highway, Street, and Bridge Construction

■ ■ ■

In business since the 1860s, McCarthy Building Companies, Inc., is one of the oldest and largest commercial construction firms in the United States. The St. Louis, Missouri-based, employee-owned company is the 11th-largest general contractor in the country and among the top 20 in individual sectors, including a number two ranking in the construction of health-care facilities and a ranking as third in the construction of correctional facilities. Other project types include office buildings, research and laboratory, educational, biopharmaceutical, nanotechnology, hotels, parking structures, entertainment, bridges and highways, airport terminals, retail, mixed-use, and treatment plants. Branch offices are located in Atlanta, Dallas, Houston, Las Vegas, New Mexico, Newport Beach, Phoenix, Sacramento, Salt Lake City, San Diego, and San Francisco.

19TH-CENTURY ORIGINS

McCarthy traces its roots to 1864, when Irish immigrant Timothy McCarthy founded a lumber company in Ann Arbor, Michigan. The small concern built farmhouses and barns around the Ann Arbor area for the next four decades, later also building some public and commercial structures. During this time McCarthy trained his sons John W. and Timothy, Jr., as carpenters, while their brother Charles became a skilled bricklayer. In 1905 John W. McCarthy decided to move to Farmington, Missouri, to be near a woman he loved. Intent on carrying on the family line of business, he persuaded his brothers to move down and join him. The siblings incorporated the transplanted company in 1907 under the name McCarthy Lumber and Construction Company, with John W. McCarthy named to the post of president. Following the incorporation, the firm began to branch out into a wider range of construction, including commercial projects and post offices.

Business grew beyond the Farmington area over the next decade, and in 1917 the company moved to the larger city of St. Louis, where it was renamed McCarthy Brothers Construction Co. The firm was now well established in its new home state, having been chosen to build the Missouri Building at the San Francisco World's fair in 1916, with the construction crew traveling there by train. Many other projects were built in St. Louis and throughout Missouri during the 1920s and

1930s, including the court house in Farmington, completed in 1926. In 1934 the growing company moved its operations to a larger headquarters in St. Louis. A major contract of the decade was the post office and courthouse built in far-off Anchorage, Alaska, one of many federally generated projects that helped the company weather the Great Depression.

The years of World War II saw McCarthy's government work continue with construction of Army and Navy lock and canal projects in the Panama Canal Zone, as well as an air base at Coco Solo. Following the war the company continued to grow, taking on more out-of-state work in the 1950s. A major project of this decade was the Army Corps of Engineers' Publications Center in St. Louis. In 1952 McCarthy also bought the Rock Hill Quarries Company, which provided a lucrative sideline for the firm. An unusual project in 1961 brought McCarthy notice as a builder that could handle difficult projects and come up with creative solutions to the challenges they presented. The Priory Chapel, in St. Louis, featured two levels of interlocking curved concrete half-ovals, arrayed like petals of a flower, a difficult design that the company successfully executed. Other important jobs of the 1960s included the Queeny Tower and Barnes Hospital.

SUBSIDIARY FORMED: 1972

During this period the company was taking on considerably more work in the health-care area, as well as beginning to design and build parking structures starting in 1969. In 1972 McCarthy formed a subsidiary called McBro to perform health-care construction management. The firm was a pioneer in the development of the new concept of construction management, a team-based approach in which the builder served as an advocate for the owner when working with the architects and consultants, acting to ensure that a project was built to strict standards. The 1970s saw the firm become the national leader in health care and parking structure construction, with a separate parking structure design/build group formed to facilitate work in the latter category. McCarthy's Rock Hill Quar-

ries business was successfully converted into a landfill operation during the decade as well.

After more than a century in operation, McCarthy remained in the hands of its founding family. Melvin McCarthy had served as president during many of the postwar years, with a number of other family members including Merryl McCarthy, Timothy R. McCarthy, John E. McCarthy, and Francis F. McCarthy having also taken roles at the firm during the period. When Melvin died in 1976, his son Michael M. McCarthy took over as president.

As work around the country became more a part of McCarthy's business, setting up offices in other cities became a necessity. The first of these was opened in Phoenix, Arizona, in 1979, and more followed in other major cities including Washington, D.C., Boston, Tampa, Houston, Seattle, San Francisco, Dallas, Houston, Las Vegas, and Kansas City. In the 1980s the company began to take on new areas of work, beginning with bridge and civil construction jobs, and then, starting in 1985, high-tech and industrial projects. A milestone was achieved in 1986 when McCarthy did a billion dollars worth of business for the fist time. The firm was now operating with its first non-McCarthy family president, Roger H. Burnet, who took over the job from Michael M. McCarthy in 1984, although the latter remained CEO and board chairman.

EMPLOYEE OWNERSHIP: 1996

The company's stock, which had been held by the McCarthy family since its founding, was opened to the firm's employees in 1996. Michael McCarthy, who was the only family member to retain a stake in the firm, held on to about 45 percent of the company. Commenting on his motivation for the move, McCarthy later told the *St. Louis Dispatch*, in an article dated June 17, 2001, "When employees have a significant amount of stock, the business becomes much more fun for them and they get a much more visceral feeling about their participation and the possibility of their being able to make a real contribution ... we set a goal to be the best builder in America, which is a very serious goal for us. If we have any chance (to accomplish that goal), we have to have all of our people staying with us and be well trained and all focused on the same goals. Ownership is a part of that."

By this time the company's out-of-state offices included several full-service divisions which themselves were growing into leading building companies in their states. These included McCarthy's Phoenix, Seattle, Dallas, and Irvine, California, locations. In 1991 the company bought SDL, a Bellevue, Washington,

KEY DATES

1864: Timothy McCarthy founds Michigan lumber company.

1907: Business is incorporated as McCarthy Lumber and Construction Company.

1934: Company moves to St. Louis.

1979: First branch office opens in Phoenix.

2002: Company becomes employee owned.

contracting firm that was later named SDL McCarthy. The late 1980s and early 1990s also saw McCarthy's areas of expertise growing again to include semiconductor, biopharmaceutical, educational, research and development, and general manufacturing construction projects. During this period the company merged its health-care, parking, and bridge divisions with the full-service regional offices. Noteworthy projects of the era included the $24 million Salk Institute for Biological Studies in La Jolla, California, and the David Axelrod Laboratory, a $45 million research facility in Albany, New York.

Another change of leadership took place in 1995 when Roger Burnet retired and Michael D. Hurst was named president and chief operating officer. Hurst had worked for McCarthy for 24 years. In the late 1990s the company also began looking at other areas of building to develop specializations in. A study of current trends revealed that the demand for construction of kindergarten through 12th-grade schools was almost triple the size of the health-care market. In 1999 McCarthy executives decided to form a new division, the Educational Services Group, to seek work in this area. Initially accounting for only about 2 percent of McCarthy's revenues, the company projected that K-12 projects could reach one-fifth to one-quarter of its business in less than a decade.

The same year that this division was created, Michael McCarthy turned over the CEO duties to Michael D. Bolen, retaining the role of board chairman. The first non-McCarthy family member to lead the company, Bolen had started as a carpenter at the firm in 1978, later moving up to supervisory positions and then serving as vice president of operations and president of the firm's Pacific Division. He had a degree in engineering from the U.S. Air Force Academy and a graduate degree in guidance and counseling from the University of Northern Colorado.

CONCRETE PAVERS ACQUIRED: 2000

In 2000 the firm's Texas division acquired the assets and contracts of the Houston office of Concrete Pavers, Inc., of Evansville, Indiana. The move was expected to give McCarthy the ability to offer lower bids on civil transportation contracts, which had previously required subcontracting of the paving work. The shrinking U.S. economy was causing a drop in construction projects, and the company made the decision to close its money-losing Bellevue and Portland offices in late 2001.

McCarthy continued to work on many important projects as it celebrated its fifth year of employee ownership. Completed work included the $615 million Hollywood & Highland entertainment/retail complex in Hollywood, which incorporated a new theater that would house the Academy Awards; a $110 million correctional facility in Bonne Terre, Missouri; a $57 million corporate laboratory and learning center in St. Louis; a $44 million psychology center at the University of Texas; and numerous hospitals, parking structures, and building expansions in California, Arizona, New York, Illinois, and other states.

The company also had many projects still on the drawing board including a $100 million office building and a $92 million jail in Phoenix; a $60 million biotechnology studies building at Rensselaer Polytechnic Institute in Troy, New York; an $80 million mixed-use development project in Beaverton, Oregon; a $132 million infectious diseases laboratory for the Centers for Disease Control and Prevention in Atlanta; a $90 million Hornet jet fighter manufacturing plant for the Boeing Company in St. Louis; and many others around the country. McCarthy did not focus solely on large projects; some were budgeted at less than $500,000, including a modernization of a K-12 school in Long Beach, California, expected to cost $350,000, and a $181,000 office tenant improvement in Kirkland, Washington.

LAST OF MCCARTHY FAMILY INTEREST SOLD: 2002

With a proud history of more than 138 years behind it, McCarthy continued to grow and add to its legacy. The firm's reputation for quality and its multiple fields of specialization, including the latest high-tech, biotech, and education facilities, were keeping its schedule full with no end in sight. In 2002 the last remaining family interest in McCarthy, held by Chairman Michael McCarthy, was sold back to the company, which now became the nation's oldest, 100 percent employee-owned construction firm. Michael McCarthy would step into the role of chairman emeritus, while Mike Bolen, McCarthy's CEO, retained that position and took on the role of chairman of the board as well.

Although McCarthy had to contend with challenging economic conditions in 2003, it enjoyed a strong year in 2003. With more than $1.4 billion in revenues the company was ranked as the 16th largest general building contractor in the United States, according to *Engineering News-Record.* A key to McCarthy's continued success was the diversity of the projects it pursued.

Important contracts during this period included the $132 million Emerging Infectious Diseases Laboratory the company built for the Centers for Disease Control and Prevention in Atlanta; a $70 million heart hospital in Creve Coeur, Missouri, which was an addition to St. John's Mercy Hospital; and a $494 million Los Angeles County and University of Southern California Medical Center replacement facility. The firm was also heavily involved in new high-technology projects. McCarthy constructed a $50 million state-of-the-art nanotechnology research and teaching facility for Cornell University, as well as a nanofabrication/cleanroom lab facility for Rice University and a nanofabrication facility at the University of California, Berkeley.

The early 2000s also brought further distance from the company's family roots. In 2006 Francis McCarthy, who retired from the firm in 1994, died at the age of 82. In 2008 his 83-year-old brother, Timothy McCarthy, passed away as well. He had devoted 45 years of his life to the company, and included stints as president and vice chairman, before retiring in 1996 and moving to Scottsdale, Arizona.

The employee-owned company continued to plot its own course. In 2005 it formed an independent company called MC Industrial. The unit focused on industrial construction projects in such market sectors as aerospace, automotive, environmental, manufacturing, power, and preengineered buildings. Business was so strong during this period that McCarthy had to drop out of the running for a significant project in its own backyard, the rebuilding of Highway 40 (Interstate 64). McCarthy was a 30 percent partner in one of the two teams vying for the project, but in March 2006, a year into the process, McCarthy had to withdraw before its team made a formal bid because in the meantime it had won so many significant projects that it lacked the resources needed to participate in the highway job.

McCarthy increased revenues to $2.9 billion in 2007. A year later the firm reorganized itself to improve the efficiency of its operations. With Midwest Division president Karl Kloster set to retire, the massive division, which stretched from the East Coast to the Rocky Mountains, was divided into two operational entities, effective January 1, 2009. A Central Division, using St. Louis as its headquarters, was formed to oversee operations in a several states east of the Rockies along with the health care, science and technology, and St. Louis business units. Based in Atlanta, the new Southeast Division was responsible for operations in Georgia, Alabama, Florida, North Carolina, South Carolina, and Tennessee. Also in early 2009, the company's longtime chief financial officer, George Scherer, retired after 26 years with the company.

McCarthy posted revenues of $3.48 billion in 2008 but a credit crunch caused many private projects to be shelved in 2009. Because of its geographic as well as market diversity, McCarthy was better able to weather the lean times than most construction firms. It was also well positioned to bid successfully on projects funded by the government. The firm won a pair of out-of-state projects in 2009: a $525 million National Bio and Agro-Defense facility in Kansas funded by the U.S. Department of Homeland Security, and a $750 million hospital replacement project in New Orleans for the Veterans Administration.

McCarthy was well positioned to enjoy continued growth in the United States. In particular, there were opportunities in the health care sector, which was expected to expand as the baby boom generation aged. The increasing demand for green buildings also played to McCarthy's strengths. On the other hand, the firm was more dependent on the United States than many of its competitors, who spread their risk by expanding into other parts of the world. Whether McCarthy would continue to focus on the domestic market or would begin to look to foreign markets for sustained growth remained to be seen.

Ed Dinger

PRINCIPAL SUBSIDIARIES

McCarthy Holdings, Inc.; McCarthy Building Companies, Inc.; McCarthy Properties, LLC.

PRINCIPAL COMPETITORS

Bechtel Group, Inc.; Parsons Brinckerhoff Inc.; Foster Wheeler Ltd.

FURTHER READING

Curley, John. "McCarthy Leaders See Future Nailed Down." *St. Louis Post-Dispatch,* June 17, 2001, p. E1.
"Francis F. 'Paddy' McCarthy Executive at McCarthy Building." *St. Louis Post-Dispatch,* April 5, 2006, p. D11.

Jones, Alan. "Cleanroom Construction." *Texas Contractor,* October 18, 2004, p. 10.

"McCarthy Building Military Project." *Northwest Construction,* January 2001, p. 10

"McCarthy Starts 2 Projects." *California Construction Link,* December 2000, p. 90.

Napolitano, Paul. "McCarthy Adds Cedars-Sinai to Impressive Portfolio." *California Construction Link,* September 2001, p. 4.

Stone, Adam. "Builders Get Boost from Work Elsewhere, Stimulus." *St. Louis Business Journal,* October 23, 2009.

"Timothy R. McCarthy Retired President of Building Company." *St. Louis Post-Dispatch,* October 16, 2008, p. D5.

Medipal Holdings Corporation

2-7-15 Yaesu
Chuo-ku
Tokyo, 104-8461
Japan
Telephone: (+81 03) 3517 5800
Fax: (+81 03) 3517 5811
Web site: http://www.mediceo.co.jp

Public Company
Founded: 2004 as Mediceo Holdings Co. Ltd.
Employees: 11,391
Sales: ¥2.46 trillion ($27.37 billion) (2009)
Stock Exchanges: Tokyo
Ticker Symbol: 7459
NAICS: 424210 Drugs and Druggists' Sundries
    Merchant Wholesalers

■■■

Medipal Holdings Corporation is the holding company for Japan's largest pharmaceuticals wholesale group. Altogether Medipal controls more than 24 percent of the prescription pharmaceuticals market in Japan. The company is also Japan's only full-scale pharmacy products wholesaler, adding over-the-counter (OTC) medicines, health and beauty aids, cosmetics, and other pharmacy and drugstore products. Medipal operates through two primary divisions: Prescription Pharmaceutical Wholesale Business; and Cosmetics, Daily Necessities, and OTC Pharmaceutical Wholesale Business.

The Prescription Pharmaceutical Wholesale Business division is the company's largest, generating 71 percent of its revenues. Major subsidiaries in this division include Mediceo Medical, Kuraya Sanseido, and Atol Co. The Cosmetic, Daily Necessities, and OTC division adds 28 percent to company sales and operates through subsidiary Paltac Corporations. Medipal also operates a third Related Business division, trading in fertilizers, chemicals for drug preparation, and food additives, as well as medical consulting services, and cleaning services, among others.

Medipal Holdings has taken a leading role in the ongoing consolidation of Japan's pharmaceuticals wholesale sector, and is the result of the merger of companies including Kuraya, Sanseido, Tokyo Pharmaceuticals, and Paltac. Medipal generated revenues of ¥2.46 trillion ($27.37 billion) in 2009. The company is listed on the Tokyo Stock Exchange and is led by CEO and President Sadatake Kumakura.

ORIGINS IN FRAGMENTED PHARMACEUTICAL WHOLESALE MARKET

Throughout most of the 20th century an array of primarily small-scale companies, generally focused on local or regional markets, carried out distribution of Japan's pharmaceutical and medical supplies. A number of the features of Japan's government-backed health-care system, which had extended universal coverage to the entire population in the 1960s, stimulated the growth of the drug distribution sector. For example, physicians and hospitals generally dispensed medicines directly to

COMPANY PERSPECTIVES

●

In Japan, which is facing a further decline in its birthrate and aging of its population, people's health needs have been growing. At the same time, health-related markets are broadening from "health cures" (treatment) to areas such as health care (health management) and wellness (health promotion). Medipal Holdings is seeking to respond appropriately to these changes and the new needs they create by forming a new type of distribution company that transcends the conventional framework of separation by type of industry. We are a group of distribution specialists in medical care, health and beauty. While taking full advantage of the wealth of experience we have accumulated, we want to provide distribution services with the safety and stable value that meet our stakeholders' various expectations, always maintaining a customer-oriented perspective and awareness. We sincerely hope the continued evolution of Medipal Holdings meets your expectations.

their patients, selling them for prices set according to the health-care system's generous fee schedule.

This in turn encouraged physicians to purchase from wholesalers at discounted prices and then make a profit from the sale of pharmaceuticals to their patients. As a result, per capita pharmaceutical consumption in Japan rose to become the highest among industrialized nations. While the country's health-care system remained relatively inexpensive, by the early 1980s pharmaceutical costs had grown to represent nearly 40 percent of total health-care spending.

This situation also resulted in the large number of wholesalers operating in Japan in the 1990s. By then, there were more than 500 pharmaceutical wholesale companies in the country. In addition to the independent wholesalers, many of the country's pharmaceuticals producers also operated their own wholesale and distribution subsidiaries, or worked closely with affiliated companies.

PHARMACEUTICAL MARKET CHALLENGES

Despite the inherent inefficiencies of a heavily fragmented market, Japan's soaring economic growth during the second half of the 20th century enabled this system to remain in place. The government attempted to rein in soaring drug prices in the early 1980s, instituting a series of drastic price reductions across most drug categories. These price cuts succeeded in limiting spending somewhat, reducing the pharmaceuticals' share of health-care spending to 25 percent in the early 1990s.

These price cuts were applicable only to drugs already on the market, however. The pharmaceutical companies seized on this loophole, launching a series of new formulations of the same molecules, thereby skirting the price limits. The drugmakers focused their research and development efforts on these formulations, rather than on developing entirely new drugs. The prospect of future price cuts, which would make it difficult for companies to recoup their investment, further hampered new drug discoveries.

By the dawn of the new century, amid the absence of new "blockbuster" drugs (often defined as medicines achieving sales of more than $1 billion), the pharmaceutical sector relied more and more on a limited pool of drugs. Many of these drugs were approaching the expiration of their patents and would soon face new competition from much lower-priced generic versions of the same preparations.

FACING HEALTH-CARE REFORM

The dramatic growth that characterized Japan's economy for much of the second half of the 20th century came to a sudden halt at the beginning of the 1990s. Japan's economy continued to falter throughout the decade. As the dawn of the new century neared, evidence was mounting that this stagnation would remain a fixture of the country's economy for some time to come.

The pharmaceutical wholesale sector was among the hardest hit by the downturn. The sector's difficulties were further exacerbated by Japan's changing demographic. With one of the lowest birthrates among the industrialized nations, Japan faced the problems associated with a rapidly aging population. The government increasingly found itself under pressure to enact a more thorough reform of the country's health-care system in order to accommodate this population and ensure the survival of the health-care system itself.

The pharmaceuticals sector was among the earliest and most prominent targets for reform. For example, in 1997 the Japanese government tightened its requirements for new drug launches. As a result, the number of new drugs, which generally commanded the highest prices, dropped sharply. At the end of the decade other reform proposals sought to eliminate the profit incentive encouraged by the country's direct-dispensing model.

KEY DATES

■

1923: Sanseido Co. is founded.

1946: Kuraya Corporation is founded.

1947: Tokyo Pharmaceutical Co. is founded.

1990: Kuraya acquires Institute of Biological Research and Development (IBRD) in the United States.

1995: Sanseido lists on the Tokyo Stock Exchange.

2000: Sanseido, Kuraya, and Tokyo Pharmaceutical merge to become Kuraya Sanseido.

2004: The company adopts a holding company structure as Mediceo Holdings.

2005: Mediceo acquires Paltac Corporation and becomes Mediceo Paltac.

2009: Mediceo Paltac completes a new restructuring, becoming Medipal Holdings Corporation.

2010: Medipal acquires 14 percent interest in China's Sinopharm Group.

Under these proposals physicians would be reimbursed for only their actual purchase price of a given drug. These in turn were fixed to a reference price, so that patients would be required to pay the amount over the established price limit.

KURAYA SANSEIDO: 2000

These proposals and other factors put a damper on the pharmaceutical wholesale sector through the 1990s. Wholesale companies found themselves increasingly squeezed between the pharmaceutical manufacturers and their physician and health-care provider customers. The sector's high fragmentation meant that very few companies were able to achieve the sales volumes needed to counteract the effects of falling prices. Furthermore, the small size of the companies left them unable to carry out the investments, notably in the development of their technological infrastructure, needed to achieve more efficient operations.

Consolidation of the market therefore became imperative to the sector's survival. During the 1990s Japan's pharmaceutical sector experienced a wave of mergers and acquisitions. By the end of the decade, the number of companies in operation had been reduced to 200. Most of these remained quite small. Nevertheless, the consolidation had resulted in the emergence of a growing number of large-scale regional, and soon national, champions.

Among these was Kuraya Sanseido, created in 2000 by the merger of three of the leading wholesalers, Kuraya Corporation, Sanseido Co. Ltd., and Tokyo Pharmaceutical Co. Ltd. Kuraya, founded in 1946 and incorporated in 1949, was the largest of the three. By the beginning of the 1990s Kuraya ranked as Japan's second-largest wholesaler. The company was also one of a number of Japanese companies to attempt to enter the U.S. market. This was accomplished through the 1990 acquisition of the Institute of Biological Research and Development (IBRD), based in Irvine, California. IBRD was then renamed Kuraya USA Corporation.

Sanseido, founded in 1923, provided the leadership for the merger. In 1995 Sanseido listed its shares on the Tokyo Stock Exchange's Second Section. This listing was transferred to the exchange's First Section in 1997. As a result, the merged company retained Sanseido's listing, becoming Kuraya Sanseido. The smaller Tokyo Pharmaceutical Co., founded in 1947, provided the company with increased access to Japan's largest single market.

ACQUISITIONS DRIVE GROWTH

All three companies had been affiliated with Japan's largest pharmaceutical manufacturer, Takeda Corporation. Takeda owned nearly 72 percent of Tokyo Pharmaceutical, and had built up a 22.5 percent stake in Sanseido. While Takeda's holding in Kuraya represented less than 3 percent of the company, the drugmaker had been Kuraya's largest supplier.

Kuraya Sanseido started out with combined revenues of ¥918 billion ($7.6 billion), commanding an 18 percent share of the total Japanese market. This share rose to 35 percent in Kita Kanto, nearly 34 percent in Kansai, and nearly 31 percent in Tokyo. Led by former Sanseido CEO Takashi Yamada, Kuraya Sanseido immediately established its objective to position itself as Japan's wholesale leader. As Sadatake Kumakura, former Kuraya chief and vice president of Kuraya Sanseido, announced to *Comline*: "This is not the last stage. What we have done is to create a company as a nucleus to start from."

Kuraya Sanseido started off by establishing new productivity objectives, initially targeting sales of ¥150 million ($1.25 million) per employee. The company also sought to expand its presence to a national level, setting up a network of subsidiaries and partnerships throughout much of Japan.

Mergers and acquisitions quickly became the major driver of the company's growth. In 2000 the company acquired a 50 percent stake in Ibaraki-based Ushioda Sangokudo Yakuhin Co., a company founded in 1949.

The company also acquired a stake in Senshu Yakuhin, which had been founded in 2001 to cover the Akita market. Other companies regrouped into Kuraya Sanseido during this time included stakes in Heisei Yakuhin Co., in Gifu, founded in 1929; and Chiba-based Chiyaku Co., founded in 1953. In this way, Kuraya Sanseido's revenues topped ¥1.1 trillion by 2002.

MEDICEO HOLDINGS: 2004

Kuraya Sanseido acquired full control of Ushioda Sangokudo Yakuhin and Heisei Yakuhin in 2003, and took over Kyoto-based Izutsu Pharmaceutical Co. that year as well. The company founded two new business alliances in 2004, with Kagawa-based Yonyaku Co., and Kochi-based Nakazawa Ujike Pharmaceutical Co. Also that year, the company, which had operated alliances with two other wholesalers, Everlth Co. in Hiroshima and Atol Co. in Fukuoaka, announced that it had taken over both of these companies. These acquisitions were followed by the takeover of Nakagawa Seikodo Co. in Tokyo in September 2004.

By this time, Kuraya Sanseido had announced plans to carry out its reorganization into a holding company structure. As part of this process, completed in October 2004, the company regrouped its prescription pharmaceutical businesses into a single subsidiary, which was then placed under the new holding company, Mediceo Holdings Co. Ltd.

Mediceo continued to grow through the middle of the decade, gaining full control of Chiyaku Co. in April 2005, and a stake in Shikoku Yakugyo in July 2005. The next major acquisition came in October 2005, when the company acquired Paltac Corporation, becoming Mediceo Paltac Corporation. The addition of Paltac brought the company a new business range as one of Japan's largest wholesale suppliers of cosmetics, health and beauty aids, and OTC drugs. By the end of 2006 Mediceo Paltac's total revenues had climbed to ¥1.9 trillion ($16.4 billion).

ALFRESA MERGER FAILS: 2008

Mediceo Paltac succeeded in securing the leadership of Japan's wholesale pharmaceutical market. The sector's consolidation had resulted in a dramatic transformation of the market. By the end of the decade, the top five wholesalers accounted for more than 80 percent of the total market. This compared favorably with the U.S. market, where the top three wholesale groups controlled 90 percent of the market, and with Europe, where three major companies accounted for 65 percent of the market.

With future growth prospects running out, Mediceo began eyeing the fast-growing, yet heavily fragmented, Chinese market. The company formed a partnership with Mitsubishi Corporation in 2005. This led to the partners' decision to enter the Chinese market by offering drug management services to Beijing region hospitals starting in 2008.

Meanwhile, back in Japan, Mediceo made a new attempt to secure its dominance of the domestic market. The company also sought to alleviate its growing difficulties amid the transformation of the Japanese drug market. This transformation was driven particularly by the consumer market, which increasingly chose generic drugs over the higher-priced brand-name drugs. In order to compensate for these shrinking revenues, Mediceo sought to take the consolidation of the Japanese market to the next level. This led the company to announce in 2008 that it had reached an agreement to acquire its next-largest rival, Alfresa Corporation, for ¥200 billion ($2 billion).

The deal quickly ran into a major hurdle, however. The projected company, which would control more than 50 percent of the total Japanese market, faced a compulsory review by the Japanese Fair Trade Commission (FTC). This review would place a major delay on the company's merger schedule, making it economically unfeasible. Amid the growing economic crisis at the end of the decade, the companies were forced to call off the deal.

PARTNERSHIPS IN 2010

Instead, Mediceo Paltac completed a new restructuring during 2009, adopting a holding structure under a new company, called Medipal Holdings Corporation. The company also proceeded with its move into the Chinese market. In October 2009 the company and its partner Mitsubishi announced that they had reached a strategic alliance with Sinopharm Group Co., one of the largest in China, to develop drug distribution and wholesale operations there. The deal, completed in 2010, called for Mitsubishi to acquire 25 percent of Sinopharm, with Medipal taking another 14 percent.

Medipal also continued to seek out partnerships. This led the company to form a new alliance in Japan in April 2010. Medipal joined with the Growell drugstore chain, and with Quall, which operated a network of pharmacies, to develop a new drugstore format that would develop its own branded line of products. The move not only provided Medipal with an outlet for its range of pharmaceutical and non-pharmaceutical goods, it also gave it an entry into the Japanese retail sector. After leading the consolidation of Japan's wholesale pharmaceutical industry, Medipal was successfully developing new outlets for its future growth.

M. L. Cohen

PRINCIPAL SUBSIDIARIES

Atol Co., Ltd.; Atol Naha Yakuhin Co., Ltd.; Everlth Co., Ltd.; Heisei Yakuhin Co., Ltd.; Izutsu Kuraya Sanseido Inc.; Kuraya (USA) Corporation; Kuraya Kasei, Inc.; Kuraya Sanseido Inc.; Mediceo Corporation; Mediceo Medical Co., Ltd.; Paltac Corporation; Senshu Yakuhin Co., Ltd.; Ushioda Kuraya Sanseido Inc.; Yamahiro Kuraya Sanseido Inc.

PRINCIPAL DIVISIONS

Prescription Pharmaceutical Wholesale Business; Cosmetics, Daily Necessities, and OTC Pharmaceutical Wholesale Business; Related Business.

PRINCIPAL OPERATING UNITS

Mediceo; Paltac.

PRINCIPAL COMPETITORS

Alfresa Holdings Corp.; Daiichi Sankyo Company Ltd.; Kanematsu Corp.; Marubeni Corp.; Mitsubishi Chemical Holdings Corp.; Otsuka Holdings Company Ltd.; Suzuken Company Ltd.; Toho Holdings Company Ltd.

FURTHER READING

"Alfresa Deal Collapse Not Good for Japan's Majors." *Corporate Financing Week*, January 19, 2009, p. 8.

"Growell, Quall and Medipal Form Business Alliances." *TendersInfo*, April 13, 2010.

"Japan's Mediceo Paltac Seeks Early Retirement of 1,000 Employees." *AsiaPulse News*, May 18, 2009.

"Mediceo Paltac Holdings to Build Customer-Oriented Distribution Business Model." *Chemical Business Newsbase*, August 15, 2005.

"Mediceo Paltac to Switch to Pure Holding Company System from 1 Oct 2009." *Chemical Business Newsbase*, February 16, 2009.

Soble, Jonathan. "Mediceo Paltac in $2bn Bid for Rival." *Financial Times*, October 11, 2008, p. 14.

"Three Major Drug Wholesalers Merge." *Comline—Emerging Markets of Japan and Eastern Asia: Health Care & Biotechnology*, June 1999.

"Top 2 Drug Wholesalers Scrap Merger, Saying FTC Move Could Delay Plan." *Kyodo News International*, January 9, 2009.

"Two Japan Drug Wholesalers Setting up China JVS with Local Firms." *AsiaPulse News*, February 21, 2008.

MetoKote Corporation

—■—

1340 Neubrecht Road
Lima, Ohio 45801
U.S.A.
Telephone: (419) 996-7800
Fax: (419) 996-7801
Web site: http://www.metokote.com

Private Company
Incorporated: 1969 as MetoKote Precision, Inc.
Employees: 2,000
Sales: $200 million (2008 est.)
NAICS: 332810 Coating, Engraving, Heat Treating, and
Allied Activities

■ ■ ■

MetoKote Corporation is a global provider of protective coating services for parts used in a wide variety of industries. Markets include agriculture, appliance, automotive, computer, construction equipment, consumer products, electronics, furniture, industrial equipment, lawn and garden, recreation, and truck and bus. The Lima, Ohio-based private company offers three lines of coating technologies: electrocoating, which uses electrical means to deposit paint; powder coating, an environmentally friendly method that uses heat to transform a fine powder into a continuous film; and liquid paint, which is more versatile than the other two methods, especially in terms of quick color changes.

MetoKote also offers pretreatment metal finishing services and such value-added services as subassembly, testing, the packaging of coated parts, labeling, ship-ping, and inventory tracking to keeps tabs on parts through all stages of the coating process. The company operates nine plants in the United States, three plants in Mexico, and single units in Canada, Brazil, the United Kingdom, and Germany. Additionally, MetoKote provides on-site operations for many of its customers.

All told, MetoKote operates more than 100 coating lines around the world. The company also maintains an equipment division to custom design and construct on-site coating systems as well as racks, carriers, parts pallets, coating racks, shipping pallets, and containers. Equity investment firm JPMorgan Partners, a unit of JP-Morgan Chase & Co, owns MetoKote.

COMPANY FOUNDED: 1969

MetoKote was founded as MetoKote Precision, Inc., in 1969 in Mount Cory, Ohio, by James C. Blankemeyer and two brothers, who set up shop in their father's garage. Using refurbished secondhand equipment they built their first powder coating system to start a powder coating business. Within two years MetoKote had attracted such major customers as the Ford Motor Company and 3M. The company enjoyed steady growth and over the next 15 years opened a pair of plants in the Lima, Ohio, area, as well as a facility in Elyria, Ohio.

During the late 1970s MetoKote introduced a number of new coating technologies that spurred accelerated growth. A key was providing customers with an environmentally sound coating method. MetoKote was one of the first in the industry to coat automotive parts with water-based paints and avoid releasing chemicals in the air through spraying. Instead, parts were cleaned and pretreated in a 14-tank process and eventually placed in ovens where the paint was baked on.

Annual sales reached $7 million in 1983. A year later, to keep pace with demand, the company broke ground on a new $4.7 million coatings plant in North Ridgeville, Ohio, to replace the Elyria plant. MetoKote became the largest tenant in the Taylor Woods Industrial Park. However, five years later a new contract with Ford and a package of tax abatements led MetoKote to leave the park in favor of a new 90,000-square-foot plant in Sheffield Village. The larger plant was needed to support the new business with Ford. In addition to Ford, MetoKote would do business with General Motors Corporation and Honda of America Manufacturing Inc. By the early 1990s, 60 percent of MetoKote's business came from the automotive industry.

DOUBLE-DIGIT GROWTH

MetoKote opened other new plants in the early 1990s. To better serve customers in Illinois, MetoKote built a $10 million, 65,000-square-foot plant in Peru, Illinois. A plant was also opened Cedar Falls, Iowa. Located in the heart of the Midwest farming belt, it was the farthest west of MetoKote's facilities. In addition to serving the agriculture industry it provided coating services to the construction, appliance, and automotive industries.

MetoKote expanded into the Dayton, Ohio, area in 1993 after securing a contract with Springfield, Ohio-based truck manufacturer Navistar International Corp. Navistar turned over coating to MetoKote as part of a decision to discontinue a number of operations at its plant. Coating techniques had become so sophisticated that Navistar, like many companies, found that it was more economical to outsource the operation. This trend would only grow more prevalent, helping MetoKote to enjoy double-digit growth throughout the 1990s.

To take advantage of outsourcing, MetoKote developed the InSite program, which assumed responsibility for all aspects of a customer's coating system,

including design, fabrication, installation, ramp up, certification, and operation. A major in-house system was developed for John Deere's compact utility tractor plant in Augusta, Georgia, in 1991. It was so successful that Deere contracted with MetoKote to provide custom in-house coating systems at more than a dozen commercial and consumer equipment, agricultural, and construction manufacturing facilities in North America. By the early years of the 21st century, MetoKote maintained 14 in-plant operations for Deere and other customers.

In addition to strong organic growth, MetoKote also expanded through external means in the 1990s. The company acquired the operating assets of Industrial Finishing, Inc., including a coating facility in Jeffersontown, Kentucky. With its ability to provide wet paint services, the plant expanded MetoKote's capabilities. The new plant also provided powder coating. It was the 16th facility MetoKote had operated over the previous 35 years. In addition to Kentucky, MetoKote was then doing business in Ohio, Illinois, Iowa, Michigan, South Carolina, and Tennessee.

COMPANY SOLD: 1997

MetoKote changed hands in 1997 when JPMorgan Partners acquired the company. A private-equity investment arm of JPMorgan Chase & Co. founded in 1984, JPMorgan Partners was very active in buying out chemical companies in the late 1990s. Better Minerals and Aggregates was acquired in 1996, followed a year later by enamel and ceramics products company Pemco International, along with MetoKote. The deep pockets of its new corporate parent allowed MetoKote to grow into an international player.

In 1997 MetoKote acquired Pegasus Phosprime, Ltd., a Daventry, England provider of coating for auto parts manufacturers and other industrial customers. Pegasus was subsequently renamed MetoKote UK, Ltd. MetoKote also grew its domestic operations as the decade came to a close. In March 1999 the company paid $4.65 million for four paint and coatings plants from Wesley International Inc., a company that several months earlier had been forced to file for Chapter 11 bankruptcy protection. The only company to make a bid, MetoKote received plants in Fraser, Flint, and Grand Blanc, Michigan, and Kitchener, Ontario.

In 2000 MetoKote acquired the assets of Camtron Coating Company to add a plant in Lapeer, Michigan, and the Hopkinsville, Kentucky, plant of the Hopkinsville Coating Corporation. Aside from adding facilities to better serve its customers, MetoKote continued to invest in the development of new technologies. In 2000

KEY DATES

1969: MetoKote Precision, Inc., is established as powder coating business.
1983: Sales reach $7 million.
1991: First John Deere on-site facility is established.
1997: U.K. operation is established.
2010: Plant in Germany opens.

the Engineered Coatings Division introduced a process dubbed MicroKote to coat extremely small parts, from 0.25 inches to 50 microns in size. The new technique allowed the company to serve the powder metallurgy industry.

On another front, MetoKote expanded its Canadian operations to better serve the major U.S. automakers doing business there, including Ford, Chrysler, and General Motors. The plant was built in the city of Cambridge, Ontario. At 150,000 square feet it was one of MetoKote's largest plants, and it also housed the headquarters for MetoKote Canada.

The automotive industry accounted for about 80 percent of MetoKote's business at the dawn of the new century. Reliance on the automotive industry became a concern, however, as the economy stalled. MetoKote made a concerted effort to diversify its business, and by 2003 the auto industry accounted for 60 percent of the company's $200 million in annual sales.

FURTHER DIVERSITY: 2005

In 2005 the company initiated a program to further increase its range of customers, as well as to improve efficiency. To pursue this strategy, MetoKote sought to coat smaller parts and serve smaller customers. As a result, the company broadened its customer base and became less dependent on the automotive industry, supplying coatings to the architectural, energy, health, and military markets. Some of the facilities also established storefront operations to provide electrocoating, zinc plating, and powder coating for individual consumers on a walk-up basis.

MetoKote took steps to maintain a competitive edge. In 2005 MetoKote sold seven of its plants, including operations in Canada and Mexico, as well as plants in Dayton, Cleveland, and Nashville, to investment firm W.P. Carey & Co. LLL. MetoKote then leased back the facilities from W.P. Carey portfolio company Corporate Property Associates 12 Global Incorporated. MetoKote thus freed up capital for more productive uses.

Reshaping the business took on increasing importance through the decade. In early 2006 Ford announced that it would be closing 14 plants and eliminating 30,000 jobs. Although not directly related to the Ford decision, MetoKote responded to a general downturn in the automotive industry by closing a plant in Grand Rapids, Michigan, and laying off some employees at its Lima plant. Nevertheless, MetoKote had been well served by lessening its dependence on the coating of auto parts.

MetoKote made a change at the top ranks of management in July 2006. DeWayne Pinkstaff became the new president and CEO. He had joined the company in 2002 from TRW Corporation and had served as vice president of MetoKote's General Purpose Business Group. He continued the diversification approach undertaken by his predecessor, and MetoKote's business with the three major U.S. automakers was soon reduced to about 20 percent. MetoKote was not completely immune from a further deterioration in the automotive industry, but neither was it pushed to the verge of bankruptcy like other companies that served the industry.

GERMAN PLANT OPENS: 2010

Instead of retrenching, MetoKote continued to expand. In 2008 the company opened its eighth facility in Mexico. Five of them were on-site facilities while three were stand-alone operations. In 2010 MetoKote expanded to continental Europe. In June of that year the company opened a new $9.5 million regional coating center located near Mannheim, Germany, and John Deere's European headquarters and tractor assembly plant. The move was part of a larger effort to grow in global markets where its larger customers operated.

After 40 years in business MetoKote was embarking on a new phase in its history as it grew into a global company seeking to enter any number of emerging markets. China was an obvious strategic choice, but MetoKote was in no hurry to establish an operation there. "It's easy enough to start a business in China right now," Pinkstaff told *Lima News* in 2009, "but we don't want to do it just to say we're in China. We want to do it right."

In addition to entering new regions of the world, MetoKote anticipated new industries to serve. Looking especially inviting were new green technology markets, which the company anticipated would become major customers. Wind energy and solar power would make use of countless parts, all of which would be subject to the elements and require the kind of protective coatings in which MetoKote specialized. There was every reason to believe that MetoKote would embrace these new opportunities in the years to come.

Ed Dinger

PRINCIPAL COMPETITORS

Nippon Paint Co., Ltd.; PPG Industries, Inc.; Rust-Oleum Corporation.

FURTHER READING

Casey, Mike. "Putting Environment First Pays Off in Paint Process." *Dayton Daily News*, July 15, 1993, p. 4B.

Fogarty, Steve. "Ridgeville Gets $4.7 Million Plant." *Chronicle-Telegram* (Elyria, Ohio), May 16, 1984, p. 1.

McKinnon, Julie M. "Lima, Ohio-Based Equipment Coating Company Continues to Prosper." *Blade* (Toledo, Ohio), March 2, 2003.

Mills, Bart. "Around the World in 40 Years." *Lima News*, April 5, 2009.

Sabin, Jim. "MetoKote." *Lima News*, March 3, 2002, p. E17.

Milk Specialties Company

260 South Washington Street
Carpentersville, Illinois 60110-2627
U.S.A.
Telephone: (847) 426-3411
Toll Free: (800) 323-4274
Fax: (847) 426-4121
Web site: http://www.milkspecialties.com

Private Company
Founded: 1953
Employees: 250
NAICS: 311514 Dry, Condensed, and Evaporated Dairy
 Product Manufacturing

■ ■ ■

A private company based in Dundee, Illinois, Milk Specialties Company, doing business as Milk Specialties Global, develops and manufactures protein and fat products, dividing its business among three units. The Animal Nutrition unit is the largest U.S. supplier of milk replacement ingredients for calves, as well as nutritional supplements for baby pigs, kids, lambs, puppies, and kittens. The unit is also one of the world's leading providers of energy supplements for dairy, swine, and horses, and offers other equine products, such as snacks, hoof aid, probiotic paste, and sweat replacer. Manufacturing is conducted at plants in Adell, Boscobel, New Holstein, and Whitehall, Wisconsin, and Norfolk, Nebraska.

The Food Solutions unit manufactures a wide range of value-added whey protein isolates, hydrolysates,

and concentrates used in weight loss and sports nutrition products at its Mountain Lake, Minnesota, plant. Finally, the International Group exports the products of its sister units to customers around the world.

COMPANY FOUNDED: 1953

Established in Dundee, Illinois, in 1953, Milk Specialties was a pioneer in the development of a milk substitute for calves, allowing them to be separated from their mothers, which could then continue to supply milk for dairy production. In 1964 the business was acquired by Cudahy Packing Company, a family company that had been involved in meatpacking since the late 1800s. By the 1920s Cudahy had emerged as a major food company, boasting sales of more than $200 million. After World War II, Cudahy moved its headquarters from Chicago to Omaha, and because its operations migrated further west of the Mississippi River, the family decided in 1965 to relocate company headquarters to Phoenix, Arizona.

The move to Phoenix resulted in other changes in 1965 as well. Cudahy Packing became Cudahy Co., and Milk Specialties was merged with another Dundee-based, Cudahy-owned subsidiary, Midwest Dried Milk Company. The combined operation continued to do business under the Milk Specialties name. Also of note in 1965, the subsidiary introduced crude lactose, which after refining was used in baby food and as a carrier for drugs.

GENERAL HOST ACQUIRES COMPANY: 1971

Milk Specialties received a new corporate parent in 1971 when conglomerate General Host Corporation acquired Cudahy. General Host had been established in 1911 as General Baking Co. when about 20 baking concerns around the country were brought together. The bulk of the company's business was the baking of Bond Bread until the mid-1960s, when control of General Baking passed to an investment-minded mining company, Goldfield Corp., led by its chairman, Richard C. Pistell. Under his direction, General Baking acquired interests in motels and camps, and in 1967 changed its name to General Host Corp. Other acquisitions soon followed, including a chain of convenience stores and a controlling interest in diversified meat processor Armour & Co. Pistell's replacement then acquired Cudahy to add to Host's holdings in the meat processing sector.

Milk Specialties spent 15 years under the ownership of Host. In 1976 the company added its New Holstein, Wisconsin, plant when it was merged with another Cudahy operation, National Northwood Co., Inc., which also produced milk replacers and food for minks and foxes. (In 1970 Cudahy and Milk Specialties had acquired Northwood Mink Farms Inc. of Cary, Illinois, a major mink farm.) By bringing National Northwood into the fold, Milk Specialties was able to enjoy the consolidated benefits of the two companies' research, production, and marketing operations. Also during Host's ownership, Milk Specialties added a new plant in Huntley, Illinois, the construction of which was completed in 1981.

MANAGEMENT BUYOUT: 1986

General Host's holdings became unwieldy, and in the early 1980s management elected to build upon its acquisition of Frank's Nursery & Crafts Inc. to create a national chain of garden nursery and craft centers. As a result, noncore assets were divested. In 1981 Cudahy was bought by its management team to create Bar-S Foods, but Milk Specialties was not included in the deal and remained with General Host for several more years.

A senior management group at Milk Specialties then made a bid to acquire the business from General Host in 1986. With backing from Citicorp Capital Investors, the group paid $35 million in cash and assumed $3 million in long-term debt. George Gill, former General Host treasurer, was named chairman and CEO. Vincent W. Nielsen, president and COO of Milk Specialties, remained in place.

As an independent company, Milk Specialties was slow to recognize significant changes that were taking place in its industry, including consolidation and the introduction of new technology. It did, however, acquire Pet-Ag Inc. in 1991 to strengthen its animal nutrition business. It also became involved in important research to develop a bacterial mix, CF3, to combat salmonella in chickens, and in 1996 initiated plans to build a plant to commercialize that technology. Additionally, the company forged a deal with a Japanese firm to make use of its food safety technology in Japan. By 1996 sales were in the $80 million range and the company's products were available in more than 50 countries. Milk Specialties was nevertheless on shaky ground. Debt was high and the company's future was far from certain.

TURNAROUND BEGINS: 1996

In 1996 a new president, Dr. Trevor Tomkins, was installed to lead a turnaround of the company. Raised and educated in the United Kingdom, with a PhD in animal production/nutrition, Tomkins had been with Milk Specialties since 1985, when he was named vice president of research and quality assurance. One of his first acts as president was to close the company's plant in Huntley, Illinois, in 1997. Production was then consolidated in Wisconsin, where plans had been made to triple the size of the Madison plant to accommodate the production of CF3. Because the plant in Boscobel, Wisconsin, was the easiest of the facilities to be upgraded, Tomkins elected to invest $1.3 million in that facility and fold in the Huntley operations. The result was reduced overhead and a state-of-the-art milk replacement plant.

In 1998 Milk Specialties received U.S. Food and Drug Administration (FDA) approval and the ability to market its drug to control salmonella in chickens, but the company was looking to narrow its focus to the nutrition and health of young animals, especially calves, pigs, and chickens. Milk Specialties was still overburdened with debt and other obligations, however. That situation had to be addressed before the company could enjoy sustained growth. In late 1999 a transaction was completed that not only resulted in new ownership but also recapitalized the corporation. Along with the its

1953: Milk Specialties is founded to develop a milk substitute for calves.
1964: Company is sold to Cudahy Packing Company.
1971: General Host Corporation acquires Cudahy, providing a new corporate parent for Milk Specialties.
1986: Management team acquires Milk Specialties.
1999: Company recapitalized.
2003: Adell Corporation, specializing in liquid milk by-products, acquired.
2008: Milk Specialties announces the creation of a food business unit.

senior lender, the CIT Group, Tomkins and his senior managers worked with a Midwest financial firm to pay off the debts while supplying an infusion of cash.

ADELL CORPORATION ACQUIRED: 2003

With its finances finally in order, Milk Specialties was positioned to enjoy steady growth in the new century, through organic as well as external means. Not every move bore fruit, however. In 2003 the company acquired Dalton, Ohio-based Buckeye Nutrition. Buckeye was a major manufacturer and marketer of nutrition products for companion animals that management believed complemented the offerings of Milk Specialties. Additionally, Buckeye manufactured some of its products in Europe, a factor that Milk Specialties hoped to leverage in its pursuit of international growth.

Buckeye's tenure with Milk Specialties lasted little more than two years. In October 2005 Milk Specialties sold the business to Mars Inc., which was interested in building its position in the global equine nutrition market. Milk Specialties, on the other hand, again realized the importance of keeping its focus narrow. For the previous five years the company had enjoyed annual double-digit growth in the production animal industries, and management believed its resources were better served building on this success rather than developing a companion animal business.

A more lasting acquisition that was also completed in 2003 was the purchase of Adell Corporation, which had filed for bankruptcy a year earlier. Emphasizing liquid milk by-products, the Adell, Wisconsin-based company manufactured lactose, whey, and whey permeates. The deal provided Milk Specialties with a second spray drying plant, complementing the operation in Boscobel while providing new product opportunities. Furthermore, the Adell operation offered a supply of raw whey that could be used for other purposes. Over the next five years Milk Specialties invested in the plant, tripling its output.

PROTIENT PLANT ACQUIRED: 2008

Milk Specialties completed further acquisitions and announced a shift in strategy in 2008. First, in the spring, it bought the Mountain Lake-based food-grade whey processing plant from St. Paul, Minnesota-based Protient Inc., adding to the Nutritional Ingredients business of Milk Specialties. A short time later Milk Specialties announced the creation of a food business unit, headed by Protient Inc.'s cofounder and president, David Lenzmeier. The new unit was structured around the human food products manufactured at Mountain Lake as well as the ready supply of raw whey provided by the Adell plant.

As a result, Milk Specialties was well positioned to take advantage of the growing global demand for milk proteins and milk carbohydrates for both the animal feed and human food markets. Later in 2008 Milk Specialties acquired a feed grade spray dry plant in Whitehall, Wisconsin, that processed pet food flavors and ingredients. The plan was to use the plant to spray dry ingredients for the animal feed produced in Adell and the whey protein and other products produced in Mountain Lake, Minnesota.

Milk Specialties looked to add to its operations in 2009 when it leased the state-of-the-art Protient Dairy Processing Facility located in Norfolk, Nebraska, that had been shuttered since October 2008. The plant was capable of producing lactose, whey proteins, milk proteins, hydrolysates, and other specialty milk products. Milk Specialties took a three-month lease with an option to buy the plant, and only a few days later a fire damaged the facility. Nevertheless, Milk Specialties opted in the spring of 2010 to purchase the plant.

While production capacity was an important element of the success of Milk Specialties, product development remained critical for the company's future. In 2010 the company introduced a pair of new products. The Food Solutions Group unveiled a new clear whey protein concentrate that was well suited for the ready-to-drink energy, recovery, and weight management beverage market. It was a growing category and an important addition to the company's portfolio of whey proteins. The Food Solutions Group also introduced a new goat whey concentrate in the fall of 2010, offering an alternative to the bovine whey protein concentrates that dominated the nutritional beverage market.

There was every reason to believe that Milk Specialties would remain a major supplier of milk replacement products for young animals. Nevertheless, the company was also clearly committed to expanding its offering to the fast-growing sports nutrition and weight-loss beverage business. Whether the two divergent businesses could coexist on a long-term basis, however, remained to be seen.

Ed Dinger

PRINCIPAL OPERATING UNITS

Foods Solutions; Animal Nutrition; International.

PRINCIPAL COMPETITORS

ADM Alliance Nutrition, Inc.; Dairy Manufacturers, Inc.; Land O'Lakes, Inc.

FURTHER READING

"General Host to Sell Milk Specialties Unit." *Wall Street Journal*, May 5, 1986.

Howie, Michael. "Milk Specialties Acquires Adell." *Feedstuffs*, May 5, 2001, p. 9.

"Milk Specialties Agrees to Buy Buckeye Nutrition." *Feedstuffs*, March 17, 2003, p. 6.

"Milk Specialties Announces Buyout by Management." *Feedstuffs*, January 3, 2000, p. 6.

"MSC Acquires Whey Processing Facility." *Feedstuffs*, April 21, 2008, p. 19.

Muirhead, Sarah. "MSC Forms Food Unit." *Feedstuffs*, June 23, 2008, p. 6.

Warneke, Kent. "New Lease on Protient Plant Began Just Days Ago." *Omaha World-Herald*, December 11, 2009, p. 2B.

Mitsubishi Heavy Industries, Ltd.

———■———

16-5, Konan 2-chome
Minato-ku
Tokyo, 108-8215
Japan
Telephone: (+81 3) 6716 3111
Fax: (+81 3) 6716 5800
Web site: http://www.mhi.co.jp

Public Company
Incorporated: 1964
Employees: 39,366
Sales: ¥2.94 trillion ($31.61 billion) (2010)
Stock Exchanges: Tokyo Osaka Nagoya Fukuoka Sapporo
Ticker Symbol: 7011
NAICS: 336611 Ship Building and Repairing; 336411 Aircraft Manufacturing; 235950 Bridge and Tunnel Construction; 221113 Nuclear Electric Power Generation; 333120 Construction Machinery Manufacturing; 333291 Paper Industry Machinery Manufacturing; 333611 Turbine and Turbine Generator Set Units Manufacturing

■ ■ ■

Mitsubishi Heavy Industries, Ltd., Japan's largest shipbuilding and machinery maker, is a mammoth company involved in a wide variety of industries. With nearly 235 subsidiaries, Mitsubishi Heavy Industries (MHI) operates six main business segments including Shipbuilding & Ocean Development, Power Systems, Machinery & Steel Structures, Aerospace, Mass and Medium-Lot Manufactured Machinery, as well as an Others segment. The company produces everything from cruise ships and oil tankers, to construction machinery, air conditioners, turbines, airplanes, and gear-cutting machines.

MHI traces its history back to the latter part of the 19th century, and has demonstrated its ability to withstand periodic downturns in the Japanese economy. These economic vagaries have prodded the company to shift its focus among various sectors over the years. Shipbuilding, for example, was once the heart of MHI, but the company has concentrated more recently on infrastructure projects in developing countries and alternative energy as demand for its large ships waned. The company's Power Systems unit contributed over 36 percent of net sales in fiscal 2010 while its Shipbuilding & Ocean Development division shored up just 7.8 percent of net sales.

MHI'S ORIGINS: THE 19TH CENTURY

Since the 1880s the diversified collection of industrial manufacturers now known as MHI has constituted the heart of the vast Mitsubishi group. Essentially all of Mitsubishi's many industrial offspring were developed as adjuncts to its shipbuilding business, begun in 1884. The Mitsubishi interest in shipping and shipbuilding extends back to the group's founding in 19th-century Japan.

Yataro Iwasaki, born in 1834 to a rural samurai family, early in his life became an official with the Kaiseken, the agency responsible for regulating trade in his native Tosa domain, on the island of Shikoku. By adroitly straddling the roles of public official and private entrepreneur, Iwasaki was able to start a small shipping company in the late 1860s. In 1875 the Japanese government gave Iwasaki the 13 steamships that he had operated on its behalf during a brief military engagement with Formosa, making his newly named Mitsubishi Shokai the dominant shipping agent in Japan. The company's name, Mitsubishi Shokai, stood for Three-Diamond Company. The three diamonds continued to be part of the firm's logo well into the 21st century.

With extensive mining interests and a talent for currency speculation, Iwasaki became so successful that the government created a rival shipping firm, the KUK, to foster competitive pricing. After a short fare war that threatened the ruin of both firms, Mitsubishi's shipping assets were merged with those of the KUK in 1885 to form a single, state-sponsored company. Mitsubishi retained a small amount of stock and exercised some control in the new firm, but its interest shifted to land-based industries, in particular mining and shipbuilding. In 1884, unable to make a go of shipbuilding, the Japanese government had lent and then transferred outright its two leading shipyards to the private sector. Mitsubishi took control of the best of these, located in Nagasaki, and became Japan's premier builder of ships and the only one capable of competing in the international marketplace.

Japan's shipbuilding industry was still relatively primitive, however, and remained so until the 1896 Shipbuilding Promotion Law combined with the Sino-Japanese War to spur domestic demand. Mitsubishi, by this time known as Mitsubishi Goshi Kaisha, became the favorite supplier of large oceangoing vessels to the state shipping company NYK, building 43 percent of all ships ordered between 1896 and World War I. Despite the close ties between the two companies, it appears that Mitsubishi did not receive preferential treatment. Indeed, although Mitsubishi gained fame in 1898 as the supplier of Japan's first oceangoing steamship, which

was the 6,000-ton *Hitachi Maru*, its delivery was so tardy that the NYK awarded a second, similar contract to a British firm.

From 1896 through 1904, the eight years between Japan's wars with China and Russia, Mitsubishi's shipbuilding business increased by nearly 300 percent. In 1905 it acquired a second dockyard, in Kobe, and by 1911 employed some 11,000 workers at Nagasaki alone. Mitsubishi's shipbuilding division was not especially profitable. A disproportionate amount of the parent company's profits still came from mining and stock dividends but it soon gave rise to a panoply of subordinate industries that supplied the yards with raw materials and parts.

For example, in 1905 the Kobe yard spawned what would eventually become Mitsubishi Electric Corporation, a leading manufacturer of generators and electric appliances. Other shipbuilding divisions grew into power plants and independent producers of airplanes, automobiles, and heavy equipment. Bolstered by its highly profitable mining interests, Mitsubishi was able to afford the vast sums of money and years of work required to transform its subsidiaries into world leaders.

THE EARLY 20TH CENTURY AND WORLD WAR I

When World War I began in 1914, Japanese shipping lines were unable to procure a sufficient number of foreign ships to maintain their booming business, and so turned to local manufacturers such as Mitsubishi. Japanese production increased more than tenfold between 1914 and 1919, with Mitsubishi leading the field. So great was the surge in business that the Iwasaki family, still in control of holding company Mitsubishi Goshi Kaisha decided to spin off a number of its leading divisions into separate, publicly held companies, thereby gaining access to outside capital without substantially weakening the company's dominant position. In 1917 the Mitsubishi Shipbuilding Company (MSC) was created, along with Mitsubishi Bank, Ltd., Mitsubishi Iron Works, and a trading company for the entire group, now called Mitsubishi Corporation. The major components of the Mitsubishi *zaibatsu*, or conglomerate, were thus in place by 1920, although the ensuing years would bring many modifications to its structure.

As is generally the case, the wartime buildup in ship orders was followed by a severe depression. As business declined below prewar levels many shipbuilders were bankrupted and all were forced to impose drastic layoffs. The slump continued throughout the 1920s, merging into the Great Depression. Mitsubishi's lack of shipbuilding contracts continued until the beginning of World War II.

KEY DATES

1875: Yataro Iwasaki's company, Mitsubishi Shokai, becomes the largest shipping company in Japan.
1917: Mitsubishi Shipping Company is created.
1934: Mitsubishi Shipping merges with Mitsubishi aircraft and automobile operations to form Mitsubishi Heavy Industries (MHI).
1950: Allies divide MHI into three separate firms.
1956: Suez Canal crisis boosts global tanker market.
1964: MHI is reunified.
1970: Mitsubishi Motor Company is spun off.
2000: MHI reports its first annual loss.
2002: Company returns to profitability.
2004: Development of the wing section for Boeing Co.'s 787 Dreamliner begins.

In the meantime, however, MSC was actively pursuing a number of other technological developments, most notably the airplane and the automobile. Having made its first airplane in 1916 and first automobile in the following year, MSC grouped these products under the name Mitsubishi Internal Combustion Engine Manufacturing Company in 1920. This offshoot went through several changes before taking the name of Mitsubishi Aircraft Company in 1928, at which time it was one of Japan's leading manufacturers of military aircraft. After six years of independence, however, the aircraft and automobile facilities were once again united with MSC to form Mitsubishi Heavy Industries (MHI) in 1934. It is not clear why this strategy was adopted, but the imminent prospect of war with China may have suggested the need for a more unified industrial force.

WORLD WAR II

To stimulate the moribund shipping industry, the Japanese government instituted the Scrap and Build Scheme in 1932. This policy called for shipowners, aided by government subsidies, to replace their older vessels with a smaller number of new, more efficient ships. In this way Japan's excess capacity could be reduced while simultaneously modernizing its fleet and promoting new shipbuilding technology. As the leading Japanese builder, MHI greatly benefited from this program, and even more so from the program's successor, the 1937 Superior Shipbuilding Promotion Scheme. This campaign was clearly prompted by Japan's preparations for war, as it subsidized the construction of large

cargo ships with an eye to their eventual use for the transportation of troops and supplies. In the years following, government intervention in shipbuilding escalated to outright control, as the Imperial Navy placed all dockyard facilities under its direct command in 1942.

The MHI yards at Nagasaki and Kobe produced a wide range of government warships, including the world's largest battleship, the *Musashi*. In addition, MHI used its aircraft experience to build 4,000 bombers and some 14,000 of the famous Zero fighters, widely recognized as the finest flying machine in the Pacific during the war's early years. The Zero provided an early example of the cost efficiency and quality that marked Japanese industrial design. A lightweight machine, the Zero could be produced quickly and economically, yet it boasted superior aerobatic abilities and heavy firing power. The Zero made Mitsubishi infamous in the West, discouraging postwar marketers of other Mitsubishi products from highlighting the company name in advertising.

At the end of the war in 1945, an estimated 80 percent of Japan's shipyards were still in usable condition. Mitsubishi's main yard at Nagasaki, however, did not escape the effects of the world's second atomic explosion. At war's end the occupying Allied forces halted all shipbuilding activity, restricting the heart of Japan's industrial economy. During the two years in which this ban remained in effect, MHI kept busy by repairing damaged vessels and even using its massive plants for the manufacture of furniture and kitchen utensils.

CHALLENGES AFTER WORLD WAR II

With the growing realization that Japan could be a strategic asset in the postwar battle against Asian communism, the Allies relaxed the more stringent limitations, and many Japanese companies resumed production. For MHI, occupation forces waited until 1950 to chop its mighty assets into three distinct and geographically separated firms: West Japan Heavy Industries, Central Japan Heavy Industries, and East Japan Heavy Industries. Part of an effort to destroy the Mitsubishi *zaibatsu* as a recognizable entity, the division of MHI was intended to force the three companies to compete against each other for contracts, thus hindering their growth.

The rest of the Mitsubishi group was similarly fragmented, and although it gradually reassumed its former shape, the Iwasaki family no longer controlled the various subsidiaries by means of a single holding company. Instead, each of the major Mitsubishi companies acquired stock in its fellow companies, and a triumvirate composed of the former MHI companies, Mitsubishi Bank, and the group's trading company became the unofficial head of what remained a voluntary economic entity. It is remarkable that this loosely connected portfolio of war-ravaged corporations should then have proceeded to outperform its global competitors over the next few decades. The three heavy-industry companies, in particular, faced an almost impossible situation. Forced to compete with one another, forbidden from pursuing the military contracts that had formerly provided a huge portion of its business, and confronted by international competitors whose technological progress had not been interrupted by the war, the new MHI trio appeared destined for failure.

Several factors combined to help MHI get past this critical period. The 1947 Programmed Shipbuilding Scheme provided low-interest government loans to the shipping companies that needed but could not afford new vessels. In effect, the government decided which ships should be built and helped pay for them, injecting the capital needed to restart a business cycle that had nearly ground to a halt. Secondly, the three companies were able to use some of their idle aircraft facilities in the manufacture of motor scooters and automobiles. Under the direction of the head designer of the Zero, Kubo Tomyo, the rejuvenated auto division sold about 500,000 scooters before the government asked it to resume making small autos in 1959. Thirdly, Japan's shipbuilders realized that the Japanese economy depended on ships and their manufacture, and that if Japanese ship producers could not compete in the postwar international market the entire nation would suffer.

Driven by such a threat to its existence, the former MHI companies hired an increasing number of highly competent engineering graduates from Japan's leading universities and set them to work emulating the advanced technology of the United States and Western European countries. Able to rely on trade unions that were loyal and flexible in the extreme, they were soon producing oceangoing vessels equal in quality to but less expensive than anything made in the West. The Korean War of 1951–53 triggered a huge increase in orders and, after surviving the short depression following the war, the companies were able to exploit the rapidly developing worldwide demand for oil tankers. The tanker market was in turn given a tremendous jolt by the Suez Canal crisis of 1956 because the canal closing sparked a surge of orders for larger, more efficient ships able to complete the long journey around Africa. Between 1954 and 1956 total orders at Japanese builders more than

tripled to 2.9 million gross tons, of which at least two-thirds were placed by foreign shipping companies.

GROWTH: 1958–74

The post-Suez depression in shipbuilding was severe enough to prompt fresh diversification at MHI. Increased research financing was devoted to civil engineering, plant construction, and automobiles, all of which years of experience in heavy industry had well prepared it to undertake. In 1958, in cooperation with 23 other Mitsubishi Group corporations, MHI created Mitsubishi Atomic Power Industries. Since then, MHI continued to dominate contemporary Japanese production of atomic power. Automobile production rose steadily, if not as quickly as at rivals Toyota and Nissan, and by 1964 the Nagoya plants were manufacturing 4,000 cars per month. Even aircraft production had been resumed by the early 1960s.

With the world increasingly dependent on imported oil and Japan's construction skills honed to perfection, Mitsubishi was hit by an avalanche of orders for tankers during the 1960s and early 1970s. To accommodate this extraordinary boom, the three parts of MHI were once again united, resulting in the 1964 rebirth of Mitsubishi Heavy Industries. This giant's 77,000 employees and $700 million in sales were spread among a handful of the most important heavy industries, but shipbuilding commanded the bulk of MHI's resources. A new dock with 300,000-gross-ton capacity was built at Nagasaki in 1965, followed by the 1972 completion of a mammoth one-million-gross-ton supertanker facility at the same yard. This ultra-efficient dock enjoyed only a short life, however. The oil crisis of 1973 and 1974 soon brought tanker orders to a near standstill, permanently crippling the entire Japanese shipbuilding industry.

ECONOMIC DOWNTURN: 1975–85

The economic downturn was devastating. By 1975, the last of the peak tanker years, 40 percent of MHI sales and one-third of its workers were involved in shipbuilding. By 1985 those numbers had plummeted to 15 percent and 17 percent, respectively. However, MHI managed to shift its assets quickly enough to survive. Having already spun off its automobile division to form Mitsubishi Motors Corporation in 1970, MHI aggressively pursued clients in the power-plant and factory-design fields.

The company also reclaimed its position as the top supplier of military hardware to Japan's growing defense force. At the same time, MHI streamlined its production facilities by shifting employees from older industries such as shipbuilding to newer ones such as machinery and power-plant production, and simultaneously allowed natural attrition to shrink its overall labor bill. Thanks in no small part to this diversification, MHI emerged successfully from the disastrous downturn of the shipbuilding industry, and became an industrial leader in other areas as well.

The early 1990s brought a fresh set of challenges to MHI. A weakening of the global economy and the post-Gulf War oil shock caused a downturn in the company's sales. Moreover, the strength of the Japanese yen made it difficult for MHI's ships and heavy equipment to compete in the global market against equipment produced in countries with weaker currencies, especially South Korea. To compensate, MHI's shipbuilding division embarked on a program of heavy cost-cutting in 1992. However, the situation took a toll, and the company's other division continued to account for greater percentages of MHI's total sales.

INCREASED DEMAND AND DIVERSIFICATION LEADS TO SUCCESS: 1995–97

By the mid-1990s it looked as if MHI had weathered the storm to become an even stronger force. Its construction and power sectors flourished as the company won a number of lucrative contracts. In February 1996, for example, MHI was selected to build six gas turbine thermal power plants for Dubai Electricity and Water Authority in the United Arab Emirates. Two months later, MHI received an order to construct a fertilizer plant for R.P.G. Industries of India, and also teamed up with two Chinese companies (Baoshan Iron & Steel Corp. and Changzhou Metallurgical Equipment Corp.) to produce steelmaking parts and equipment in China.

The resurgence of Japan's shipbuilding industry in the mid-1990s seemed to complete MHI's revival. The yen had at last begun to weaken, making it easier for Japanese companies such as MHI to compete effectively against their Korean rivals. In addition, global demand for tankers and ships boomed because the world's commercial fleets had aged. By 1996, roughly 41 percent of all tankers were more than 20 years old and approaching the end of their useful life span. In this new environment, MHI's shipbuilding division benefited from the company's cost-cutting measures of the early 1990s, as well as from more recent advances in computer-aided design that maximized efficiency.

MHI did not abandon its efforts to emphasize its other divisions despite the renaissance in the shipbuilding sector. MHI not only looked to new sectors in Japan

to drive its recovery, it also sought out new markets abroad for its equipment and services. Southeast Asia and the Middle East sorely needed new power sources, and as the global economy boomed, the private and public sector undertook major construction projects, all which drove demand for MHI's equipment. Late in 1996, MHI won a $1.1 billion contract to install a 2,400-megawatt power plant for the Saudi Consolidated Electric Co., as well as a contract worth about $127.8 million to supply generators for Taiwan Power Co.'s new nuclear power plant. MHI continued to boom in 1997. After winning a contract to build a fertilizer ammonia plant for Indonesia's PT Kaltim Pasifik Amoniak, MHI was selected by Saudi Yanbu Petrochemical Co. to build polyethylene and ethylene glycol plants.

OVERCOMING CHALLENGES: 1998–2000

The year 1998, however, saw a dramatic reversal of this positive trend. Dragged down by the repercussions of the currency crisis that rocked Thailand and other developing countries, Japan's economy slumped along with the rest of Asia. MHI's sales slowed as its key customers cut back on construction and infrastructure projects in response to the growing "Asian economic crisis."

By October 1998, it was clear that MHI could not blame its problems entirely on outside economic forces. MHI had counted on foreign markets to make up for sluggish sales at home through the first part of the 1990s. In an effort to boost its profits even more, MHI had outsourced much of its foreign production to subcontractors without ensuring appropriate supervision. The result was that some of the massive construction and power projects MHI had undertaken in Southeast Asia and the Middle East were hindered by poor quality. These quality control issues severely undercut the profitability of MHI's foreign operations. Eventually, the company had to redo some of the work itself which hurt its earnings.

The company's sales and profits dropped further in 1999, as Japan remained mired in the Asian economic crisis. Nobuyuki Masuda stepped down as MHI's president to become chairman of the board. In his place, Takashi Nishioka was appointed president. Nishioka had won the admiration of shareholders during his tenure as head of MHI's aerospace operations, playing an essential role in moving that division away from its long-standing reliance on defense contracts. Instead, Nishioka had looked to the private sector for business, focusing particularly on bolstering MHI's business ties with Boeing.

Upon taking the helm, Nishioka announced a massive restructuring program, involving 7,000 job cuts, a reorganization of the company's engine and motor operations, and an expansion of its aerospace division. Perhaps more importantly, Nishioka promised to end MHI's policy of "matrix management," in which the company's branch offices competed among themselves and with the division headquarters. In place of this inefficient system, Nishioka pledged to unify management functions.

These changes would take time to implement. In 2000, with Japan's domestic economy still in the doldrums, MHI reported its first net loss since the company had been reunified in 1964. Despite this significant setback, Nishioka remained optimistic that MHI would recover from its latest problems.

REBOUNDING IN THE 21ST CENTURY

While Japan's economy remained in a recession during the early years of the new millennium, MHI continued to secure new orders and forge key partnerships. During fiscal 2001, the company landed contracts to build four new liquefied natural gas carriers, a gas turbine combined cycle thermal power plant, a high-speed train system in Taiwan, and an order for F-2 support fighters from Japan's Defense Agency. Despite the increase in orders and overall revenue, the company posted a net loss of $164 million in fiscal 2001 due in part to investments made in Mitsubishi Motors Corp., the faltering automotive company plagued by a vehicle-defects cover-up scandal.

While economic conditions continued to deteriorate in 2002, MHI secured $198 million in net income for the year. During fiscal 2002, the company established Mitsubishi Power Systems, Inc., in the United States to bolster its international power plant business. It also opened a Mexican facility to construct fiberglass reinforced plastic blades that were used in wind turbines. MHI's Aerospace division began testing the SH-60JKAI next-generation patrol helicopter and landed a contract to manufacturer components for Bombardier Inc.'s business jets.

The company's return to profitability in 2002 occurred despite two major events that threatened the company's bottom line. In October of that year, a fire aboard a cruise ship under construction at Nagasaki Shipyard & Machinery Works caused extraordinary losses and forced the revamping of safety measures at its facilities. At the same time, MHI discovered that electrical cables on its F-4 fighter planes had been cut on-site, prompting the company to strengthen security at its manufacturing plants.

During 2003 Kazuo Tsukuda was named president while Nishioka took over as chairman. The company again achieved profitability that fiscal year due to cost-cutting measures and by landing several key contracts, including a bulk order for 10 gas turbines in China through a partnership with Dongfang Electric Corporation of China. The company also received the first orders for its Diamondstar, the world's fastest sheet-fed offset press used for newspaper printing.

MHI continued to pull out a profit in fiscal 2004 despite an overall drop in revenues. One of the company's major projects during the year was the development of the wing section for Boeing Co.'s 787 Dreamliner. The aircraft was the first to be made using composite materials and its wing section was manufactured using carbon fiber. The Dreamliner made its maiden flight in 2009 and was slated for additional testing in 2010.

FOCUSING ON GLOBAL EXPANSION: 2006 AND BEYOND

Even as raw material costs began to rise in fiscal 2005 and 2006, MHI posted positive financial results. Bboth net sales and net income continued to rise steadily from 2006 through 2008. By securing lucrative contracts, upgrading facilities in its Power Systems division, establishing a new manufacturing facility for its Mass and Medium-Lot Manufactured division in Europe, and increasing its international business, MHI was able to offset rising costs while successfully battling intensifying competition. Net income grew from $414 million in 2006 to $612 million in 2008. Hideaki Omiya was named president of MHI in 2008 while Tsukuda became chairman.

The new leadership team faced challenges as the economic crisis in the United States began to trickle across the globe. Indeed, MHI saw a 12 percent decline in its orders during fiscal 2009. At this time, the company began to focus on its products in the energy and environmental sectors. It also looked to infrastructure projects in Brazil, Russia, India, and China to fuel future growth. Approximately 36 percent of its contracts came from outside of its home country and MHI planned to increase that percentage significantly in the coming years.

Some of its international partnerships at this time included a joint venture with India's Larsen & Toubro Ltd. to manufacture turbines for thermal power plants in India and a licensing agreement with Anupam Industries, an Indian heavy machinery manufacturer. The company also teamed up with the AREVA Group in France to develop and market nuclear reactors. At the same time, MHI teamed up with an Australian government research firm to test what was deemed the world's first solar thermal power system that did not use water. While only time would tell if MHI's international strategy would pay off, it appeared as though the company was well positioned to overcome any future challenges that might come its way.

Jonathan Martin
Updated, Sina Dubovoj; Rebecca Stanfel;
Christina Stansell Weaver

PRINCIPAL DIVISIONS

Shipbuilding & Ocean Development; Power Systems; Machinery & Steel Structures; Aerospace; Mass and Medium-Lot Manufactured Machinery; Others.

PRINCIPAL COMPETITORS

Bouygues S.A.; Hitachi Ltd.; IHI Corporation.

FURTHER READING

Hayashi, Yuka. "Asia Powers Japan's Growth Spurt." *Asian Wall Street Journal*, May 21, 2010.

"Japan Firms Still Tops in Energy, EVs, Robotics." *Nikkei Report*, August 22, 2010.

"Japan MHI to Name Hideaki Omiya President." *Japanese News Digest*, January 29, 2008.

Kanabayashi, Masayoshi. "Ship Firms that Diversify Win Favor of Analysts." *Asian Wall Street Journal*, June 6, 1995.

Lamke, Kenneth. "Miller Park Is Just One of Mitsubishi's Problems." *Milwaukee Journal Sentinel*, October 30, 1999.

"Mitsubishi Heavy Dumps Tradition." *Nikkei Weekly*, March 31, 2003.

"Mitsubishi Heavy Flies on B7E7 Main Wing." *Nikkei Weekly*, January 19, 2004.

"Mitsubishi Heavy Now Expects Deeper FY Group Net Loss." *Dow Jones International News*, March 28, 2001.

"Mitsubishi: The Diamonds Lose Their Sparkle." *Economist*, May 9, 1998.

Wray, William D. *Mitsubishi and the N.Y.K., 1870–1914: Business Strategy in the Japanese Shipping Industry.* Cambridge: Harvard University Press, 1984.

Excellence. Nothing Less.

MXL Industries, Inc.

———————————•———————————

1764 Rohrerstown Road
Lancaster, Pennsylvania 17601
U.S.A.
Telephone: (717) 569-8711
Toll Free: (800) 233-0159
Fax: (717) 569-8716
Web site: http://www.mxl-industries.com

Private Company
Incorporated: 1972 as National Hydron Inc.
Employees: 110
Sales: $9.2 million (2007)
NAICS: 332810 Coating, Engraving, Heat Treating, and
    Allied Activities

■ ■ ■

A private company based in Lancaster, Pennsylvania, MXL Industries, Inc., specializes in the manufacturer of high-quality, optically correct polycarbonate and acrylics parts, serving a variety of markets. A longtime supplier to the motor sports sector, MXL offers a wide range of helmet shields, including such variants as clear, tinted, high-definition, anti-fog, and anti-scratch. For many years the company has also served the industrial safety market, offering chemically resistant respirator lenses used by firefighters and first responders as well as people involved in the civilian protection industries. This product has also found a use in the military market as part of sophisticated pilot visors that combine beam-splitter and anti-reflective coatings with heads-up displays. Another major industry served by MXL is

security. MXL offers zero-distortion, abrasion-resistant camera domes for closed-circuit television security systems.

In addition, MXL manufactures custom optical plastic products, making available to customers an array of capabilities that include optical molding design and construction, optical resin selection and injection molding, anti-fog and anti-abrasion coating technology, vacuum deposition coating assets, as well as assembly operations and international shipping logistics. MXL serves customers around the world, including Yamaha, Rockwell Collins, Sundstrom Safety AB, Honeywell Video Systems, Tyco Fire and Security, and Pitney Bowes. CEO James A. Eberle and other senior members of the management team own MXL.

COMPANY FOUNDED: 1968

MXL began its existence in 1968 as a joint venture between Lititz, Pennsylvania-based Woodstream Corporation and National Patent Development Corporation (NPDC), a New York City-based company that was founded in 1959 to acquire patents and license them to other companies, essentially serving as a middleman. The company's first major success was the licensing of a plastic compound to Bausch & Lomb that was then used to produce soft contact lenses, at a time when hard plastic lenses were the norm.

The goal of the joint venture with Woodstream was to take advantage of a hydrophilic polymer owned by NPDC. A coating was developed from the material that was intended for use on fishing lures, serving as a way to delay the release of a bait scent. Researchers soon found that the polymer also enjoyed anti-fog properties. The coating substance that resulted was used initially on ski goggles but was soon used in numerous other anti-fog applications.

In 1972 NPDC bought out its joint venture partner and formed a new company called National Hydron Inc. to pursue further the optics coating business. The focus was on the safety eyewear industry, but during the 1970s the company also pursued the recreation sports market, developing anti-fog, scratch-resistant goggles for skiing, snowmobiling, and motorcycling. The lenses were available in clear, smoke, amber, and mirror versions. These lines were marketed under the MXL Products banner. To meet increasing demand, National Hydron opened a 34,000-square-foot facility in Lancaster, Pennsylvania, in 1978.

While National Hydron enjoyed some initial success, by the end of the 1970s the company was struggling in some of its key markets. The number of motorcyclists tailed off as baby boomers started families, and a lack of significant snow for several years resulted in a severe downturn in the sale of skiing and snowmobiling equipment. National Hydron attempted to make up for lost revenue by introducing more fashionable sun wear products, but sales were poor.

MXL NAME ADOPTED: 1983

By 1983 National Hydron was on the verge of collapse when the company's production manager, Steve Cliff, took over as president and led a turnaround. The company was renamed MXL Industries, Inc., and the focus was returned to the industrial market that had been long neglected. MXL found ready customers for safety goggle lenses as well as military gas mask eyepieces and automotive instrument covers. With those sales as a base, MXL was ready to expand.

MXL's management team recognized a need in the marketplace for an advanced full-service company that could accommodate the tooling, injection molding, and finishing of optical plastic parts. After a year of planning

and construction, the company opened a new climate-controlled clean room with optical quality injection molding capabilities in 1985. In the meantime, MXL's marketing people took advantage of the upgraded facility to land a number of important new contracts, and soon the plant was running three shifts around the clock to fill the growing number of orders.

WOODLAND MOLD & TOOL ACQUIRED: 1987

To keep up with demand as well as to add mold design and other capabilities, MXL acquired Chicago-based Woodland Mold & Tool in 1987. The operation was subsequently moved to a new 12,600-square-foot facility in Westmont, Illinois, where it operated as the Woodland Mold & Tool Division of MXL Industries, Inc. The unit's design and mold building skills became valuable assets, allowing MXL to create molds that were optically correct and distortion free for projects that proved too difficult for other companies. MXL's annual revenues approached $7 million by the end of the 1980s.

Demand for MXL products was not as strong during the early 1990s, as the U.S. economy struggled and was slow to resume growth. The optical market was also mostly mature, limiting the company's growth potential. Furthermore, MXL was dependent on a single customer that accounted for about 40 percent of all sales. Revenues increased from $7.8 million in 1993 to nearly $9.3 million a year later because of increased orders from this customer, and grew to $10.9 million in 1995.

However, when that customer cut orders the following year due to changes in product line, MXL experienced a drop in sales to $8.9 million. The company made efforts to secure new customers and become less reliant on a single account. MXL enjoyed some success in this regard in 1996, as sales rebounded to $10.4 million, due primarily to new customers.

In 1997 MXL expanded its Lancaster plant to 50,000 square feet to better serve its new and existing customers. To expand sales further the company also looked to its Chicago-area operation to grow its custom molding business beyond such products as computer keyboard wrist supports, compact disc case holders, printer stands, and small appliance components. As a result, Woodland moved to a larger facility in Downers Grove, Illinois, where new molding equipment was installed. Additionally, the Woodland name was phased out and MXL was applied to the Chicago location.

EXPANDED CAPABILITIES

MXL closed the 1990s by posting sales of $10.4 million. Annual revenues climbed to $11.2 million in

KEY DATES

1968: Company begins as joint venture.
1972: National Patent Development Corporation buys out joint venture partner, incorporates business as National Hydron Inc.
1983: Renamed MXL Industries, Inc., company focuses on industrial market.
1987: Woodland Mold & Tool acquired.
2008: Management-led investor group takes MXL independent.

2001 before declining to $8.6 million in 2003 due to the discontinuance of a product line. To expand its capabilities further, MXL acquired the laser eye protection manufacturing equipment of Southbridge, Massachusetts-based AOtec, LLC, for $1.1 million in cash and notes. These assets also included vacuum deposition equipment to provide beam-splitter and anti-reflective coatings, technologies that were needed to fill the orders from the military for precision pilot visors used in next generation fighter and attack aircraft.

In 1998 NPDC changed its name to GP Strategies, Inc., part of an effort to emphasize the importance of its General Physics Corporation subsidiary. Further changes followed in the new century. In November 2004 GP spun off National Patent Development Corporation, which included MXL and an interest in Five Star Products, Inc., and other noncore assets. A manufacturer of non-shrink grout, structural repair products, and chemically resistant coatings for the industrial, infrastructure, commercial, and marine markets, Five Star was an especially good fit with MXL. MXL posted sales of $9 million in 2006 and $9.2 million a year later. Also in 2007, MXL discontinued its Chicago-area operation.

MANAGEMENT BUYOUT: 2008

MXL then sought its independence from NPDC. In June 2008 the company was sold for $5.2 million to an investment group that included the company's senior management team led by James A. Eberle, president and CEO. A graduate of the University of Pennsylvania's Wharton School of Business, Eberle had served as vice president of operations at General Physics. He then joined MXL in 2004 as president and COO. Other members of MXL's management ownership group included Bryan Bess, vice president, finance and administration; Sean Bitts, vice president, manufactur-

ing; Jude Krady, vice president, employee services; Manny Rodriguez, vice president, major accounts; and Larry Swonger, vice president, development and engineering. NPDC also retained about 20 percent of MXL.

There were a number of apparent advantages for MXL in pursuing an independent course. No longer part of a large holding company, MXL could take advantage of government contracts as well as funding for job training programs reserved for small businesses. The company also saved money because it was free of the cost of complying with the reporting requirements imposed upon a publicly traded corporate parent.

MXL wasted little time in taking steps to prepare for future growth, including a preliminary plan to build a new 100,000-square-foot plant, although the company maintained that this was under consideration even if MXL had remained a part of NPDC. If warranted, the proposed facility could be expanded to 150,000 square feet. Management also indicated that the company would remain in the Lancaster area, the retention of its trained workforce outweighing any benefits to a change in locale.

NEW CAPABILITIES

Poor economic conditions and a credit crunch created conditions that were not conducive to such a major expansion. Nevertheless, MXL went forward in the fall of 2008 with a $750,000 investment to install a new automated flow-coat line and high-volume vacuum deposition chamber. The new line included a pair of six-axis robots that could position parts with such great precision that repeatable coating was possible. As a result, MXL then possessed the ability to apply different coatings to different sides of a part. For example, respirator lenses for firefighters could have an anti-fog coating on one side and a hard coating on the other, thus fulfilling the requirements of the National Fire Protection Agency.

In a similar vein, visors used in football and hockey helmets could offer anti-fog properties on the inside and an abrasion-resistant coating on the outside. The new coating capabilities also allowed MXL to meet the rigorous anti-fog performance requirements in Europe. In short order, the new line generated $2 million in new business for MXL.

Although then 40 years old, MXL in many ways was just beginning to emerge as a global niche optical coating company. Moreover, it was no longer dependent on a handful of customers. Rather, it had diversified into a wide range of markets that offered the kind of stability the company lacked in its early years. There was every reason to believe that MXL would enjoy steady growth in the years to come.

Ed Dinger

PRINCIPAL COMPETITORS

Lund International, Inc.; Plaskolite, Inc.; SABIC Innovative Plastics US LLC.

FURTHER READING

Bucher, Dave. "MXL Industries: A World-Class Contender." *Lancaster-Reading Business Digest*, February 1, 1987.

Knight, Jerry. "National Patent Looks to Leaner, Greener Times." *Washington Post*, September 22, 1997, p. F31.

Mekeel, Tim. "MXL Industries Becomes Independent." *Lancaster New Era*, July 10, 2008, p. B6.

———. "New Coating System Adds Jobs at MXL." *Lancaster New Era*, September 5, 2008.

Toloken, Steve. "MXL Expands Its Chicago Plant." *Plastic News*, February 1, 1999.

New Horizons Worldwide, Inc.

———————————————■———————————————

1 West Elm Street, Suite 125
Conshohocken, Pennsylvania 19428
U.S.A.
Telephone: (484) 567-3000
Fax: (484) 567-3002
Web site: http://www.newhorizons.com

Public Company
Founded: 1982
Employees: 215
Sales: $33.98 million (2009)
Stock Exchanges: Over the Counter
Ticker Symbol: NWRZ.PK (Common)
NAICS: 611410 Business and Secretarial Schools

■ ■ ■

Through its New Horizons Computer Learning Centers subsidiary, New Horizons Worldwide, Inc., bills itself as the world's largest independent information technology (IT) training company. New Horizons offers hundreds of courses both for individuals and for businesses. In addition to technical classes and certification packages, the company offers training for everything from simple desktop productivity software to complex business applications.

FORMATIVE YEARS

New Horizons traces its roots to 1982, when Mike Brinda founded the company, setting up a one-room training center in Laguna Hills, California. By the early 1990s New Horizons had decided to pursue growth via franchising arrangements with training companies and resellers. In addition to a fee that ranged from $20,000 to $50,000, franchisees were required to have $200,000 in capital for training center development purposes. In exchange, franchise owners received exclusive territories, along with 10-year agreements.

According to the May 17, 1993, issue of the *San Diego Business Journal*, New Horizons did not initially plan to rely upon franchising for its growth. The publication recapped a December 7, 1992, interview from the *Los Angeles Times* in which Brinda explained: "Franchising wasn't part of the original plan at all. The business evolved. If you want to keep quality people, you have to grow. I saw an exodus in the early years of quality people. Through franchising we opened up new jobs, and we've had several people leave to begin their own company."

In the same article, Brinda revealed a key bit of philosophy behind the establishment of New Horizons. "What I do is a necessity that software publishers don't care to acknowledge," he explained. "Their stated goal is to eliminate the need for training in their products and to create something so user-friendly and intuitive that you don't need training. I'm not here to say that day will never come. I'm here to say it ain't here now. To move the level of productivity up, training is the key. If software publishers would be more forthright in stating that education is an integral part of buying a PC, we would have many more satisfied computer owners."

By the end of 1992 New Horizons had licensed 20 training franchises, 13 of which were in operation. That

---

COMPANY PERSPECTIVES

■

The success of our customers is realized through training classes, but the foundation of New Horizons is
based on inspiring students and companies to become
more productive and successful in their daily activities.

---

year the company saw its workforce grow from 80
employees to approximately 125. Plans were made to
increase franchises to more than 60 locations in 1993.
The company's first international location was
established in 1993 in Mexico City, Mexico. Locations
were established in Asia Pacific, the Middle East, and
Africa the following year.

RAPID GROWTH

By mid-1994 New Horizons was one of the nation's
fastest-growing training businesses. Franchises had
grown to 58, and the company had plans to establish 30
new franchises by 1995. In addition to franchises, the
company marketed coursework to businesses, schools,
and universities. It also published approximately 10 new
training books per month.

In 1994 Brinda sold New Horizons to Handex
Corp. in a $12 million deal. Revenues exceeded $140
million the following year. By 1996 New Horizons
operated approximately 145 training centers throughout
the world. That year, the company established a partnership with Ingram Micro via its new Major Accounts
Program, which provided customers who needed to offer
multi-site training with a one-stop solution for billing,
administration, and centralized scheduling.

As of early 1997 New Horizons Computer Learning
Centers Inc. was operating as a wholly owned subsidiary
of publicly traded Morganville, New Jersey-based New
Horizons Worldwide Inc. Thomas J. Bresnan served as
president of the parent company, and Chuck Kinch was
president of New Horizons Computer Learning Centers.
The company provided more than 1.5 million students
with training courses each year. Operations spanned 28
countries, where training was provided through some
200 centers.

POWERFUL PARTNERSHIPS

In 1997 New Horizons teamed up with Novell as part
of the latter company's Teach for Tomorrow grant
program. Working together, the two organizations

provided technical training to teachers in North
American high schools and colleges. During the late
1990s New Horizons offered training for the latest applications from leading technology companies, including
Microsoft Corp., and provided training to employees of
leading corporations such as Xerox.

In late 1998 New Horizons began looking to the
Internet as a channel for providing training services.
This was made possible via a partnership with online
course developer DigitalThink Inc., which the
companies announced at an annual conference called
Tech Learn. By this time, Chuck Kinch was serving as
president and chief operating officer of New Horizons.
New Horizons began 1999 on a strong note when the
company established a software training alliance with
EDS, a $15 billion global information services company.
Through the alliance New Horizons would provide
software training to clients of EDS.

Midway through the year, New Horizons Computer
Learning Centers of Michigan received a global contract
from General Motors Corp. to provide annual computer
training to more than 20,000 employees. In October
1999 the company held a ribbon-cutting ceremony to
celebrate the establishment of its Long Beach,
California, office, which had opened seven months
before. The location provided services to companies
such as Boeing Co.

RESTRUCTURING

It was also in October 1999 that major organizational
changes were implemented at New Horizons. At that
time the company consolidated its two main operating
segments, combining New Horizons Computer Learning Centers (NHCLC) (franchising) with its company-
owned Center Division (wholly owned training centers).
Following the consolidation, NHCLC became New
Horizons Worldwide's primary operating company, and
the parent organization ceased to have a separate division for company-owned locations. Charles Kinch
stepped down as president of NHCLC and was succeeded by New Horizons Worldwide CEO Thomas
Bresnan.

New Horizons ended 1999 with revenues of $435
million, up $78 million from the previous year. Heading
into the new century the company provided customers
such as Pitney Bowes with a Web-based student registration, scheduling, and reporting system called Reggie.
Around the same time, the company's Federal Systems
Division secured two technical training contracts, totaling $1.8 million, from Unisys Federal Systems and the
U.S. Navy Space and Warfare Command, SS
Charleston, Norfolk, Virginia, Technology Branch.

KEY DATES

∎

1982: The company is founded by Mike Brinda.
1993: New Horizons establishes its first international location in Mexico City, Mexico.
1994: Brinda sells New Horizons to Handex Corp. in a $12 million deal.
1999: The company consolidates its two main operating segments.
2001: New Horizons establishes its 100th international location, in Frankfurt, Germany.
2007: The company celebrates its 25th anniversary.
2010: New Horizons reveals plans to enter the Scandinavian market.

New customer additions continued in 2000 as New Horizons added companies such as Honeywell International and Home Depot to its client roster. For the second year in a row, the company was ranked as the largest computer training provider in the world in a study conducted by Simba Information. New Horizons offered the largest library of computer courseware, with approximately 1,400 selections in 14 languages.

Midway through the year New Horizons earned contracts valued at approximately $1 million to train 23,000 employees for the Missouri Department of Elementary and Secondary Education, as well as the Missouri Department of Natural Resources. In addition, a renewable annual contract, valued at approximately $80,000, was received from St. Louis County. Around this time the company named Jess Hartmann as vice president and chief information officer.

INTERNATIONAL GROWTH

New Horizons furthered its growth via the acquisition of Savio Chan's Technology Training Solutions operations in Long Island, New York. In December the company established a location in the Al-Ahsaa region of Saudi Arabia, in keeping with a strategy to open new locations throughout the area. New Horizons ended 2000 on a high note, having been ranked as one of the 100 Fastest-Growing Companies in America by *Fortune* magazine, one of the 200 Best Small Companies in America by *Forbes* magazine, and cracking *Success* magazine's Franchise Gold 200 ranking.

New Horizons started off 2001 by naming Paula Moreira as vice president of eLearning. Around the same

time, the company opened its 100th international location, in Frankfurt, Germany. Following the establishment of 38 international locations in 2000, including sites in Colombia, Israel, Jamaica, Pakistan, and Qatar, plans were made to continue global expansion in 2001 by opening locations in Honduras, Greece, Ecuador, Oman, Bangladesh, and the Dominican Republic.

In mid-2001 New Horizons was named to *BusinessWeek*'s 100 Hot Growth Companies in America listing. Late in the year the company introduced an online resource center called Your IT Future.com, which offered resources related to IT training. Around the same time New Horizons began offering information security training through a partnership with Ascendant Learning.

New Horizons began 2002 by establishing a new training center in Honolulu, Hawaii. In August the company unveiled a major franchising initiative in India, which was home to an IT training market valued at approximately $400 million. In partnership with Shriram Global Technologies and Education, the company indicated it would form a joint venture called New Horizons India that would open 100 new centers throughout the country, beginning with a location in New Delhi in October. A total of 10 training centers were expected to be in operation by the year's end.

IMPORTANCE OF ONLINE LEARNING

By late 2002 online learning accounted for approximately 7 percent of the company's business. However, strong growth was anticipated moving forward. According to data from the research firm IDC, the e-learning market was expected to grow from $2.9 billion in 2002 to $5.6 billion by 2004.

By mid-2003 New Horizons offered 270 classrooms in 54 countries worldwide. In July the company was chosen by American Airlines to offer current and former employees with both classroom and online-based training that would allow them to advance in their current job, or prepare for a new career. At this time Martin Bean served as COO for New Horizons.

During the middle years of the decade New Horizons continued to offer cutting-edge IT courses, including a security class called Ethical Hacker. In mid-2005 the company was recognized in Training Outsourcing.com's annual ranking of the training outsourcing industry's top 20 companies. By this time New Horizons employed 2,400 instructors and 2,100 account executives. Training was offered in 50 countries, where the organization operated roughly 2,100 classrooms at approximately 250 centers.

New Horizons ended 2005 with revenues of $106.4 million, down from $119.9 million in 2004. By mid-

2006 the company was pursuing a strategy to franchise its owned locations. A new CEO was found in Mark Miller. In addition, New Horizons secured $4 million in financing from several investors, including George Rich, Camden Partners, and Al Khaleej Training and Education Corporation, to be used mainly as working capital.

SILVER ANNIVERSARY

Operations continued to expand in 2006, growing to 280 locations in 56 countries. In November New Horizons announced that it was the training provider to all *Fortune* 100 companies, and more than half of all Global 100 firms. The company celebrated its 25th anniversary in 2007. That year, new centers were established in Romania and Bulgaria, and operations expanded to 300 centers in 60 countries.

In April 2008 the company's stock moved to the Over the Counter (OTC) Bulletin Board. One year later the company terminated existing franchise agreements in England and Scotland and announced plans to reopen its U.K. locations under company ownership. Following a successful pilot in Colorado with National American University, which allowed students to obtain technology training/certifications along with a college degree, New Horizons revealed it would expand the program to the Indianapolis, Indiana, area.

New Horizons established a flagship training center in London in October 2009. Of particular significance was the fact that the center was the organization's first company-owned international operation. International growth continued in early 2010, when New Horizons revealed plans to enter the Scandinavian market, where franchise locations were slated to open in the cities of Stockholm, Malmö, and Göteborg. Around the same time New Horizons Malaysia held a grand opening celebration for its new flagship center, which was part of an 11-branch operation.

After more than a quarter-century of operations, New Horizons enjoyed a position of leadership within the IT training industry. The franchise model adopted by the company during its formative years had enabled it to extend its reach across the globe. New Horizons appeared to be positioned for continued success during the second decade of the 21st century.

Paul R. Greenland

PRINCIPAL SUBSIDIARIES

New Horizons Education Corporation; New Horizons Computer Learning Center of Albuquerque, Inc.; NH-CLC of San Antonio, Inc.; New Horizons Computer Learning Center of Hartford, Inc.; New Horizons Computer Learning Center of Denver, Inc.; New Horizons Computer Learning Center of Charlotte, Inc.; New Horizons Computer Learning Center of Sacramento, Inc.; New Horizons Computer Learning Center of Cleveland, Ltd., LLC Inc.; New Horizons Computer Learning Center of Indianapolis, Inc.; New Horizons Computer Learning Center of Indianapolis, LLC; New Horizons Computer Learning Center of Memphis, Inc.; New Horizons Computer Learning Center of Santa Ana, Inc.; New Horizons Computer Learning Centers, Inc.; New Horizons Computer Learning Centers, Asia-Pacific Pte. Ltd. (Singapore); Computer Training Associates of Chicago, Inc.; New Horizons Computer Learning Center of Nashville, Inc.; New Horizons Computer Learning Center of Metropolitan New York, Inc.; NH Mexico Inc.; New Horizons Computer Learning Center of Atlanta, Inc.; New Horizons Franchising Group, Inc.; New Horizons Computer Learning Centers EMEA, LLC Inc.; New Horizons Computer Learning Centers APAC, LLC Inc.; Nova Vista, LLC; New Horizons Computer Learning Center of London Limited (UK); New Horizons Computer Learning Center of Seattle, Inc.; New Horizons Computer Learning Center of Portland, Inc.; New Horizons Career Learning Centers, Inc.

PRINCIPAL COMPETITORS

Learning Tree International, Inc.; NIIT Limited; SkillSoft Public Limited Company.

FURTHER READING

"New Horizons Celebrates Its 25th Anniversary as the World Leader in the IT Training Industry." *Business Wire*, January 17, 2007.

"New Horizons Extends Collaboration with National American University." *Health & Beauty Close-Up*, September 15, 2009.

"New Horizons Recognized as One of the Top 20 Companies in Training Outsourcing Industry." *Business Wire*, June 14, 2005.

"New Horizons Worldwide Announces Consolidation; Plan Aimed to Realize Operating Benefits between Company-Owned and Franchise Locations." *Business Wire*, October 14, 1999.

"Training People to Use Today's Information." *San Diego Business Journal*, May 17, 1993, p. A3.

Newell Rubbermaid Inc.

3 Glenlake Parkway
Atlanta, Georgia 30328
U.S.A.
Telephone: (770) 418-7000
Fax: (770) 407-3970
Web site: http://www.newellrubbermaid.com

Public Company
Incorporated: 1902 as W.F. Linton Company; 1920 as
    The Wooster Rubber Company
Employees: 19,500
Sales: $5.6 billion (2009)
Stock Exchanges: New York
Ticker Symbol: NWL
NAICS: 551112 Holding Companies

■ ■ ■

Newell Rubbermaid Inc. is a diversified manufacturer and marketer of a variety of brand-name consumer and commercial products. The firm is organized into three business groups including Home & Family; Office Products; and Tools, Hardware & Commercial Products. The company's products range from Rubbermaid brand storage containers and Graco brand infant products, to Sharpie brand writing instruments and Levolor brand window blinds. These brands are sold primarily through mass merchandisers, including discount, variety, chain, and hardware stores, as well as warehouse clubs, hardware and houseware distributors, home improvement centers, office product superstores, and grocery and drugstores. Newell Rubbermaid's products can be found in over 90 percent of U.S. households and are sold in 90 countries across the globe. The two main strands of Newell Rubbermaid's history came together in March 1999 when Newell Co. acquired Rubbermaid Incorporated.

NEWELL'S CURTAIN ROD ROOTS

Newell Co. traces its roots to the short-lived W.F. Linton Company, an Ogdensburg, New York, firm incorporated in 1902 to make brass curtain rods. The Linton Company received $1,000 to move the company from Providence, Rhode Island, to Ogdensburg from the Ogdensburg Board of Trade, with the board's president, Edgar A. Newell, signing off on the loan. In 1903 the company went bankrupt and Newell took control of its operations, renaming the firm Newell Manufacturing Company, Inc.

Although he was familiar with sales, Newell had no understanding of manufacturing and, as a result, hired and subsequently fired several general managers between 1903 and 1907. Edgar Newell then hired his son Allan to run Newell Manufacturing and started a new company, Newell Manufacturing Company Ltd. (Newell Ltd.), in Prescott, Canada. Established to capitalize on Ogdensburg's location, which made shipments south costly and left Canadian distribution channels more financially attractive, Newell Ltd. purchased a small dockside building in Prescott.

Newell Manufacturing's initial product line was composed exclusively of brass curtain rods, created through a method of tube making that used a water-wheel; Newell's was powered by the nearby Oswegatchie

River. In 1908 Newell began producing a greater variety of curtain rod shapes after adopting a new, faster, and more adaptable manufacturing process that used roll forming machines. By the end of the decade the Newell companies were employing about 20 people and generating annual sales of about $50,000.

NEWELL'S EARLY DIVERSIFICATION: 1912–17

Although Ogdensburg operations were sailing smoothly, by 1912 Newell Ltd. found that curtain rods were not enough to keep its operations afloat. A new manager, Lawrence "Ben" Ferguson Cuthbert, was given a chance to bail out the Canadian plant in return for a 20 percent cut of its gross profits. Between 1912 and 1913 Newell Ltd. acquired the factory it had been leasing and expanded its plating department to produce a variety of products, including towel racks, stair nosings, ice picks, and other items requiring a finish of brass, zinc, or nickel. The expanded product line spurred additional sales, and Newell Ltd. soon became profitable.

As war spread across the globe, the cost of brass rose, and Newell hired the Baker Varnish Company to devise a new metal-coating method tailored to Newell's roll forming manufacturing process. By 1917 Newell's curtain rods were being coated with a nontarnishable lacquer. Not only were the new rods less expensive to produce than brass rods, but because they would not tarnish they were better suited to lace and ruffle curtains.

With its new curtain rod Newell courted and won the business of Woolworth stores, after agreeing to buy out Woolworth's on-hand stock of curtain rods. Newell's first buyback deal soon paid dividends, boosting sales and helping to establish the company's first long-term relationship with a major national retailer.

In 1920 Edgar A. Newell died and, for the first time, stockholder changes were made at the company. Cuthbert called in his profit-stake from running Newell Ltd., and, after some subsequent legal jousting, the company's stock ownership was resolved. Allan Newell received a 64 percent share in Newell Ltd., and Cuth-

bert received 33 percent of Newell Manufacturing and 20 percent of Newell Ltd. Albert Newell, Edgar's other son, who had been helping with sales, received 66 percent of Newell Manufacturing and 16 percent of Newell Ltd. Allan Newell was named chairman and president of Newell Manufacturing but bowed out of active affairs with the company, opting for a political life that eventually led him to the New York State Assembly. Albert Newell was also reluctant to be involved with the family business, and management of both companies passed to Cuthbert, who moved to Ogdensburg.

FORMATION OF WESTERN NEWELL IN 1921

In 1921 Cuthbert, the Newell brothers, and a former Ogdensburg employee named Harry Barnwell each put up $5,000 to start a new curtain rod factory in Freeport, Illinois. The new business, Western Newell Manufacturing Company, was designed to take advantage of local railroad transportation and serve as a western branch of Newell Manufacturing. Barnwell served a brief stint as Western Newell's president before selling his 25 percent stake in the operations to Cuthbert's cousin, Leonard Ferguson, who was recruited to manage the fledgling company. Like Newell Manufacturing, Western Newell began operations with 10 employees and initially produced curtain rods in a red brick factory it rented. The company quickly became profitable, and in 1925 a new factory was erected. By 1928 Western Newell's sales had grown to $485,000, more than twice that of Newell Ltd. and about half that of Newell Manufacturing. At the time of the stock market crash in October 1929, Western Newell was producing a wide variety of drapery hardware, including extension curtain rods, ornamental drapery rods, and pinless curtain stretchers.

Despite a dramatic slide in sales that forced the companies to lay off workers and reduce workdays, the Newell companies made it through the Great Depression without dipping into red ink. The bottom of the Depression's well for Newell Manufacturing came in 1933 when that company logged only about one-half of its 1929 level of sales, or $425,000. With a small operational base and modest salaries, Western Newell fared the best of the two U.S. companies during the Depression, and by 1933 the 12-year-old Western Newell, with sales figures 25 percent lower than Newell Manufacturing, had a net income 30 percent greater than the original company.

In 1933 Western Newell earned $61,000 on sales of $320,000, whereas Newell Manufacturing earned $47,000 on sales of $425,000. By 1937 Western Newell, under the leadership of Ferguson, had surpassed Newell

KEY DATES

1902: Ogdensburg, New York-based W.F. Linton Company is incorporated to make brass curtain rods.

1903: Linton goes bankrupt; Edgar A. Newell takes control of the firm, renaming it Newell Manufacturing Company, Inc.

1920: The Wooster Rubber Company is formed in Wooster, Ohio, to make toy balloons.

1933: James R. Caldwell forms an enterprise called Rubbermaid, whose first product is a red rubber dustpan.

1934: Wooster Rubber and Rubbermaid merge, retaining the former's corporate name and headquarters and the latter's brand name.

1957: Wooster Rubber changes its name to Rubbermaid Inc.

1966: The Newell companies are consolidated into Newell Manufacturing Company, which is based in Freeport.

1970: Newell Manufacturing is reincorporated in Delaware as Newell Companies, Inc.

1985: Newell Companies is renamed Newell Co.

1999: Newell acquires Rubbermaid for $6 billion; Newell changes its name to Newell Rubbermaid Inc.

Manufacturing in both revenues and income, earning $126,000 on sales of $553,000, whereas Newell Manufacturing earned $70,000 on sales of $511,000. At Cuthbert's suggestion, in the late 1930s the Newell brothers agreed to give Ferguson a small stake in Newell Manufacturing, effectively taking the founding company out of the hands of the Newell family, although the brothers retained rights to voting control through the late 1940s.

Between 1938 and 1939 Newell Manufacturing established a third domestic factory in Los Angeles. It also made its first acquisition, Drapery Hardware Ltd. (DRACO) of Monrovia, California, a maker of wooden and heavy iron drapery fixtures that eventually was sold to S.H. Kress and other smaller customers. Before the 1930s drew to a close a number of officer changes were made: Cuthbert was named to succeed Allan Newell as president of Newell Manufacturing and Ferguson was named president of Western Newell, although Allan Newell remained president of Newell Ltd. and chairman of all three companies.

During World War II the Freeport factory won a coveted Army/Navy "E" Award for excellence in wartime production, churning out more than 230 million metallic belt links for machine guns within a two-year period. During the postwar decade the Newell companies enjoyed steady growth, although no new manufacturing plants were started or acquired. In 1954 the Newell family ceded further power over its namesake companies as complete operational control was given to Leonard Ferguson, who became president of all three Newell companies.

CONSOLIDATING THE NEWELL COMPANIES AND GOING PUBLIC: 1960–79

During the early 1960s Newell acquired the rights to additional drapery hardware brands and names, including Angevine and Silent Gliss. In 1963 Ferguson was named chairman and chief executive of the three Newell companies and two years later his son, Daniel C. Ferguson, became president of the companies. Under the leadership of the father-and-son team, in 1966 all Newell companies were consolidated into one Illinois corporation, Newell Manufacturing Company, with headquarters in Freeport. Under the guidance of Daniel Ferguson, the $14 million family business turned its focus from its products to its customers and initiated a multiproduct strategy designed to boost sales to its existing buyers.

During the 1970s Newell continued to acquire other companies, greatly expanding its product line in the process. In 1968 Newell purchased a majority interest in Mirra-Cote Industries, a manufacturer of plastic bath accessories. In 1969 Newell acquired Dorfile Manufacturing Company, a maker of household shelving, and E.H. Tate Company, which brought the Bulldog line of picture hanging hardware into the Newell line of products. During the late 1960s DRACO began phasing out of manufacturing operations and finally closed its doors in the early 1970s. In 1970 the company was reincorporated in Delaware as Newell Companies, Inc. The following year Newell added sewing and knitting accessories to its product line when it acquired The Boye Needle Company, a Chicago-based world leader in knitting needles and crochet hooks, and Novel Ideas, Inc., another maker of do-it-yourself sewing materials.

In April 1972 Newell went public as an over-the-counter stock and that same year initiated an acquisition strategy that would later be replayed in various forms. Newell made an offer to buy EZ Paintr Corporation, a paint and sundries company in which Newell already had a 25 percent stake, and EZ Paintr in turn filed a pair of lawsuits to fight back against a possible takeover. However, in February 1973 Newell gained majority control of EZ Paintr after its president and cofounder agreed to sell his family's interest in the paint supply company, a move opposed by EZ Paintr's management. By March 1973 Newell had ousted the EZ Paintr board and Daniel Ferguson had become president of the company, which yielded complete control of its stock to Newell six months later. In 1974 Newell completed another drawn-out acquisition and purchased complete control of Mirra-Cote.

In 1975 Leonard Ferguson died and a descendant of Ben Cuthbert, William R. Cuthbert, was later named chairman. Between 1976 and 1978 Newell expanded its shelving, paint, and sundries offerings and acquired Royal Oak Industries, Inc., Baker Brush Company, and Dixon Red Devil Ltd. (later renamed Dixon Applicators). During the same period the company sold some of its knitting products businesses, including Novel Ideas. In May 1978 Newell acquired 24 percent of the financially troubled BernzOmatic Corporation, a manufacturer of propane torches and other do-it-yourself hand tools. In February 1979 Newell gained operational control over BernzOmatic after its president, who had earlier sold convertible debentures to Newell, yielded his position to Ferguson and Newell had taken control of the smaller firm's board.

In June 1979, after coming off of its first $100 million sales year, Newell began trading on the New York Stock Exchange. About the same time Newell began targeting emerging mass merchandisers such as Kmart in order to piggyback on the increasing popularity of such stores.

ACCELERATING THE PACE OF ACQUISITION AND THE NEWELLIZATION PROCESS: 1980–89

Newell entered the 1980s riding on the growth of mass merchandisers while continuing to expand and complement its product line through acquisitions. Between 1980 and 1981 Newell acquired the drapery hardware division of The Stanley Works and Brearley Co., a manufacturer of bathroom scales. In April 1982 Newell acquired complete control of BernzOmatic and in December of that year entered into a $60 million financing and stock purchase agreement with Western Savings & Loan Association, with the S&L paying $18.4 million for a 20 percent stake in Newell, which it gradually sold off to private investors during the next five years.

Through two separate stock deals worth more than $42 million, in 1983 Newell acquired Mirro Corpora-

tion, a maker of aluminum cookware and baking dishes. In May 1984 Newell increased its number of common stock shares from 14 million to 50 million and later that year through a stock swap acquired Foley-ASC, Inc., a maker of cookware and kitchen accessories. In May 1985 the company changed its name to Newell Co. In June 1985 Newell acquired a 20 percent stake in William E. Wright Company from a group dissenting from the majority, including three board members and the grandson of Wright Company's founder. A few months later Newell raised its stake in Wright, a maker of sewing notions, and by the end of the year Newell had obtained majority control of the company and ousted Wright's board and top officers.

By 1987 Newell had acquired complete control of Wright, which was added to a list of about 30 acquisitions the company had logged since Ferguson had become president. In July 1987 Newell paid $330 million to acquire control of Anchor Hocking Corporation and its targeted glassware operations. At the time of the acquisition Anchor, with $758 million in sales, had nearly double the annual revenues of Newell and provided its new parent with brand-name tabletop glassware, decorative cabinet hardware, and microwave cookware, with each product line holding a number one or two position in its respective market.

Within a week after the takeover Newell began employing its usual post-acquisition strategy on a large scale, dismissing 110 Anchor employees and closing its West Virginia plant. Through this strategy, which became known as "Newellization," Newell aimed to boost the profitability of acquired companies by improving customer service and partnerships, reducing overhead costs by centralizing administrative functions, abandoning underperforming product lines, and reducing inventory. Acquired companies continued to be "Newellized" into the early 21st century.

Newell closed its books on the 1980s having achieved a number of significant financial accomplishments. Between 1987 and 1989 the company's income rose more than $48 million, while during the course of the entire decade sales spiraled from $138 million to $1.12 billion as income ballooned from $7.8 million to $85.3 million. Newell also was listed number 22 on the *Forbes* list of the best stocks of the 1980s, having provided a total return to stockholders that averaged 39.5 percent per year.

NEWELL'S EXPANDS INTO OFFICE PRODUCTS AND PICTURE FRAMES: 1990–93

Newell entered the 1990s as a market leader in electronic data interchange, a computer-to-computer system that allowed Newell customers to place orders electronically. Attempting to once again piggyback on a growing mass merchandiser market, Newell entered the office products business in 1991 by acquiring two small firms, Keene Manufacturing, Inc., and W.T. Rogers Company.

In 1992 Newell became a major force in the office products market. It acquired both Sanford Corporation, a leading producer of felt-tipped pens, plastic desk accessories, storage boxes, and other office and school supplies, and Stuart Hall Company, Inc., a well-known stationery and school supply business, in two stock swaps totaling more than $600 million. The two businesses combined brought Newell's annual office products sales to $350 million. The year 1992 also saw Newell acquire Intercraft Industries, Inc., the largest supplier of picture frames in the United States.

In a 1992 changing-of-the-guard, Daniel Ferguson bowed out of active management to move up to chairman, replacing the retiring William Cuthbert, and Thomas A. Ferguson (no relation to Daniel and Leonard Ferguson) was named president. William P. Sovey was named to succeed Daniel Ferguson as vice chairman and chief executive. Although the company had another Ferguson in line to run Newell, by 1992 stock dilution had reduced insider control of the company to 15 percent. Nevertheless, four members of the 11-person board were members of the Ferguson, Cuthbert, or Newell families.

1993–98: NEWELL ACQUISITION SPREE OF NEARLY $2 BILLION

Having completed more than 50 acquisitions from the late 1960s through 1992, Newell completed a dizzying series of deals from 1993 through 1998. The company spent about $1.9 billion on acquisitions during this period, completing 18 major acquisitions that added about $2.6 billion in annual revenues to Newell's coffers.

Three key deals were consummated in 1993. In April, Sunnyvale, California-based Levolor Corp. was acquired for $72.5 million, giving Newell a leading maker of window blinds that had 1992 sales of $180 million. Then in September Newell bought Lee/Rowan Co., based in St. Louis, Missouri, for $73.5 million, gaining a leading manufacturer of wire storage and organization products with $100 million in 1992 revenues. Two months later Newell spent $147.1 million for Goody Products Inc., which was based in Kearny, New Jersey.

Rounding out its window treatments portfolio, Newell in August 1994 acquired Home Fashions Inc.,

based in Westminster, California. The company's office products operations were bolstered through the October 1994 purchase of Faber-Castell Corporation, which specialized in pencils and rolling-ball pens under the Eberhard Faber and UniBall names. One month later, Newell spent $86 million to acquire Corning Incorporated's European consumer products business, which had 1993 revenues of $130 million. This deal included manufacturing facilities in England, France, and Germany; the trademark rights and product lines for Corning's Pyrex, Pyroflam, and Visions cookware brands in Europe, the Middle East, and Africa; and Corning's consumer distribution network in these areas. Newell also became the distributor of Corning's U.S.-made cookware and dinnerware products, including the Revere Ware and Corelle brands, in these same regions. This acquisition gave Newell its first major overseas foothold.

Newell gained a virtual stranglehold on the picture frame market with the acquisitions of Decorel Incorporated in October 1995 and Holson Burnes Group, Inc., in January 1996. Newell also gained a stronger position in writing instruments by purchasing Berol Corporation in November 1995. Among Berol's products were graphite and coloring pencils, and its 1994 sales exceeded $200 million.

Concluding its heaviest one-year spending spree to that date, Newell spent $563.5 million to complete four major deals during 1997. Office products were the subject of two of the acquisitions, the March purchase of the Rolodex brand from Insilco Corporation and the June buyout of the office products business of Rubbermaid.

In May 1997 Newell bought the Kirsch brand from Cooper Industries, Inc., thereby gaining the leading producer of decorative window hardware in the country, with annual sales in excess of $250 million. Then in August 1997 Newell acquired two subsidiaries of American Greetings Corporation: Acme Frame Products, Inc., producer of picture frames, and Wilhold Inc., maker of hair care accessory products. With the exception of the May acquisition of gourmet cookware maker Calphalon Corporation, all of the major 1998 acquisitions served to strengthen Newell's position outside the United States.

At the end of 1997 Sovey retired from active management, and he became Newell's chairman, replacing Daniel Ferguson. Taking over Sovey's former position of vice chairman and CEO was John J. McDonough, who had been a senior vice president of finance at Newell in the early 1980s and had served on the board of directors since 1992. Continuing as president and COO was Thomas Ferguson.

The steady stream of acquisitions paid off for Newell in the form of record earnings of $396.2 million and record revenues of $3.72 billion for 1998. The earnings figure was more than four and a half times the level of 1989, while sales had more than tripled during the same period. For the 10-year period ending in 1998, Newell's compound annual growth rates for sales and earnings per share were 13 percent and 16 percent, respectively. Starting with the 1994 purchase of the European consumer products unit of Corning, Newell had made a concerted overseas push; as a result, sales outside the United States increased from 8 percent of total sales in 1992 to 22 percent in 1998. It was from this position of strength that Newell announced in October 1998 by far its largest acquisition ever: the $6 billion purchase of Rubbermaid that would be consummated in March 1999.

RUBBERMAID BEGINNINGS: TOY BALLOONS AND A BETTER DUSTPAN

The Wooster Rubber Company got its start in May 1920, when nine Wooster, Ohio, investors pooled $26,800 to form a company to manufacture toy balloons, sold under the Sunshine brand name. Wooster Rubber, contained in one building in Wooster (a small town about 50 miles south of Cleveland), was sold to Horatio B. Ebert and Errett M. Grable, two Aluminum Company of America executives, in 1927. Grable and Ebert retained the firm's management. By the late 1920s, a new factory and office building had been constructed to house the prosperous business, but the fortunes of Wooster Rubber fell during the Great Depression. In 1934 Ebert spotted Rubbermaid products in a New England department store, and worked out a merger between the two firms.

Rubbermaid got its start in 1933, when a New England man named James R. Caldwell, who had first entered the rubber business as an employee of the Seamless Rubber Company in New Haven, Connecticut, looked around his kitchen during the depths of the Great Depression to see what he could improve. Caldwell and his wife conceived 29 products, among them a red rubber dustpan. Although the rubber dustpan, designed and manufactured by Caldwell and his wife, cost $1.00, which was much more than the 39-cent metal pans then available in stores, Caldwell "rang ten doorbells and sold nine dustpans," as he recalled in an interview published in the *New York Times* on May 19, 1974. Convinced there was a market for his products, Caldwell gave his enterprise the Rubbermaid name and expanded his line to include a soap dish, a sink plug, and a drainboard mat, selling these products in department stores throughout New England.

In July 1934 Caldwell's fledgling enterprise merged with Wooster Rubber. Still called The Wooster Rubber Company, the new group began to produce rubber household goods under the Rubbermaid brand name. With the merger, under Caldwell's leadership, Wooster Rubber had a happy reversal in fortunes, and sales rose from $80,000 in 1935 to $450,000 in 1941. Of the 29 new products Caldwell and his wife had thought up in their kitchen in 1933, the company had marketed 27 of them by 1941.

In 1942, however, U.S. involvement in World War II caused the government to cut back civilian use of rubber, so that raw materials would be available for products necessary to the war effort. This eliminated Rubbermaid's housewares business, but the company was able to convert to military manufacturing. Beginning with rubber parts for a self-sealing fuel tank for warplanes, and moving on to other products such as life jackets and rubber tourniquets, the company manufactured military goods through the end of the war, in 1945. In 1944 Wooster Rubber introduced an employee profit-sharing plan.

Following the advent of peace, Wooster Rubber picked up its prewar activities where it had left off, and resumed production of rubber housewares. Because wartime shortages had not been completely redressed, however, no coloring agents were available, and all Rubbermaid products were manufactured in black for several months. In 1947 the company introduced a line of rubber automotive accessories, including rubber floormats and cupholders.

The company's first international operations commenced in 1950, when Wooster Rubber began producing vinyl-coated wire goods at a plant in Ontario, Canada. By 1956 the plant was producing a complete line of Rubbermaid products.

RUBBERMAID MOVES INTO PLASTIC: 1955–56

In 1955 Wooster Rubber went public, offering stock on the over-the-counter market. This capital infusion allowed the company to branch into plastic products, and in 1956 a plastic dishpan was introduced. This switch required significant retooling from the manufacture of exclusively rubber goods.

In 1957 Wooster Rubber changed its name to Rubbermaid Incorporated to increase its association with its well-known brand name. The following year, the company began its first expansion beyond its traditional focus on household goods by broadening its targeted market to include restaurants, hotels, and other institutions. Rubbermaid initially produced bathtub mats and doormats for these customers. By 1974 industrial and commercial products provided 25 percent of the company's sales.

After James Caldwell's retirement and a one-year stint as president by Forrest B. Shaw, the company presidency was taken over by Donald E. Noble in 1959. Noble had joined Wooster Rubber as a "temporary" associate in 1941. Also during 1959, Rubbermaid stock was sold for the first time on the New York Stock Exchange. The following year, Rubbermaid's management set a goal of doubling the company's earnings every six years, a goal that was consistently met throughout Noble's tenure. Noble also placed a heavy emphasis on new product development, evidenced by the objective he set in 1968 that aimed to have 30 percent of total annual sales come from products introduced over the preceding five years.

In 1965 Rubbermaid made its first move outside North America, purchasing Dupol, a West German manufacturer of plastic housewares, whose products and operations were similar to Rubbermaid's U.S. operations. In 1969 Rubbermaid added the sales party to its traditional marketing efforts, a sales technique first popularized by Tupperware. The party division had its own line of slightly more elaborate merchandise, accounting for around 10 percent of Rubbermaid's sales within five years. Nevertheless, the party plan was not profitable until 1976.

RUBBERMAID'S DIFFICULT YEARS: 1970–79

In the early 1970s Rubbermaid marketed a line of recreational goods such as motorboats and snow sleds, but the company lacked the necessary distribution to support the products and abandoned the effort. "We bombed," the company's vice president of marketing told a *Wall Street Journal* reporter on June 9, 1982.

Rubbermaid continued to grow in the early 1970s, but the combination of government controls on prices and the shortage of petrochemical raw materials caused by the energy crisis of the early 1970s kept a lid on earnings. In 1971 Rubbermaid began to market its products through direct supermarket retail distribution. Although initially profitable, this practice resulted in the company running afoul of the Federal Trade Commission (FTC) in 1973. The FTC challenged the company's pricing policies in connection with its role as distributor, charging Rubbermaid with illegal price-fixing and violations of antitrust laws. The complaint alleged that Rubbermaid engaged in price-fixing between

wholesalers because it sold its products directly to some retailers and also allowed other wholesalers to sell its products, while stipulating the price for the products.

Rubbermaid discontinued its minimum price agreements with wholesalers and retailers in 1975, citing pending legislation and negative public opinion. In 1976 the FTC ruled unanimously that Rubbermaid had violated antitrust laws and issued a cease-and-desist order to prevent the company from renewing these practices.

As part of its continued growth, Rubbermaid opened a new plant in La Grange, Georgia, in 1974, to relieve demand on its main Ohio plant and to supply the automotive products division. Despite rising earnings since 1968, a sharp increase in the price of raw materials, combined with a change in accounting practices, caused a large drop in Rubbermaid profits in 1974. By this time, Rubbermaid was selling 240 different items, of which about one-tenth were products introduced that year.

The company experienced labor unrest in 1976, when 1,100 members of the United Rubber Workers called a strike at Rubbermaid's only unionized plant, in Wooster, Ohio, after rejecting a proposed contract. Although the strike eventually was settled amicably, traditionally the company had sought to minimize union activity by building plants outside union strongholds, in places such as Arizona, where it began construction of a plant near Phoenix in 1987 to serve its western markets. In 1985 the company successfully negotiated a contract with its Ohio workers, providing a three-year wage freeze in return for guarantees against massive layoffs.

RUBBERMAID STREAMLINES

Noble retired in 1980, and Stanley C. Gault took over as chairman. Gault, a former General Electric Company executive and a son of one of Wooster Rubber's founders, had grown up in Wooster and worked his way through college in a Rubbermaid plant. Despite the company's record of steady growth throughout the 1970s, caused in part by Rubbermaid's expansion from old-line department stores into discount and grocery stores, Gault felt that the company had become somewhat stodgy and complacent. In 1980 he set out to quadruple its sales (about $350 million in 1981) and earnings (about $25.6 million in 1982) by 1990. Anticipating a recession, Gault streamlined operations and introduced bold new products, such as the "Fun Functional" line of brightly colored containers. Gault's stress on growth through the introduction of new products was exemplified by his continuance of the company's campaign to reap 30 percent of each year's sales from products introduced during the last five years.

By 1983 Gault had eliminated four of Rubbermaid's eight divisions: the unstable party-plan business and the automotive division were each sold at a loss, and the European industrial operations centered in the Netherlands and the manufacture of containers for large-scale garbage hauling also were eliminated. The remaining divisions were combined into two areas: home products (accounting for about 70 percent of the company's sales) and commercial products.

RUBBERMAID GROWS THROUGH ACQUISITIONS

In 1981 Rubbermaid had made its first outright acquisition, buying privately held Carian, owner of the Con-Tact plastic coverings brand name. In the 1980s Rubbermaid was able to move successfully beyond housewares and institutional customers, entering new industries through the strategic purchase of other companies. The company entered the toy industry in 1984 by buying the Little Tikes Company; went into the booming computer field in 1986, with Microcomputer Accessories; into floor care products with Seco Industries in the same year; and into the brush industry with a Canadian company, Viking Brush, in 1987.

Following these and other acquisitions, Rubbermaid created additional divisions to accommodate its new product lines. In 1987 a seasonal products division was formed to produce and sell lawn and garden products, sporting goods, and automotive accessories. A year later the company created an office products division, which included Microcomputer Accessories and Eldon Industries, which was acquired in 1990. Little Tikes became the core of a juvenile products division. The three new divisions gave the company five divisions, with the preexisting home products and commercial products divisions.

MAJOR ACQUISITIONS, TWO RESTRUCTURINGS, DECLINING FORTUNES

Throughout the early and mid-1990s Rubbermaid continued to pump out new products at an amazing rate of about 400 annually, which along with several major acquisitions pushed sales higher every year. Net earnings grew as well, until a major restructuring in 1995–97 cut company profits.

In 1992 the company acquired Iron Mountain Forge Corporation, a U.S. maker of commercial playground systems. Two years later Ausplay, the leader

in commercial play structures in Australia, was purchased. Both Iron Mountain and Ausplay became part of the juvenile products division. Also brought into the Rubbermaid fold in 1994 were Empire Brushes, a leading U.S. maker of brooms, mops, and brushes; and Carex Inc., which made products for the burgeoning home health-care market. Carex was placed in the company's commercial products division.

As of 1993, Rubbermaid generated only 11 percent of its sales outside the United States, and almost all of that went to Canada. Company management aimed to increase nondomestic sales to 25 percent by 2000 (later, this goal was boosted to 30 percent) and began to seek out acquisition and joint venture opportunities to help reach this goal. In 1994 the company entered into a joint venture with Richell Corporation, a leader of housewares in Japan, to form Rubbermaid Japan Inc.

After abandoning its stake in Curver-Rubbermaid, a partnership that ended up being noncompatible, Rubbermaid reentered the European housewares market in 1995 when it bought Injectaplastic S.A., a French plastics manufacturer of such items as home and food storage products, camping articles, bathroom accessories, and garden products. Also in 1995 the company bought 75 percent of Dom-Plast S.A., the leading maker of plastic household products in Poland. By 1996 foreign sales were up to 16 percent of overall sales, a rate of increase that, if continued, would mean the company would fall well short of its 30 percent goal. Nevertheless, in early 1997 Rubbermaid announced that it had entered into a strategic alliance with Amway Corporation to develop and market in Japan a line of cobranded premium Rubbermaid products.

In addition to slow overseas growth, a number of other factors forced Rubbermaid to embark in the mid-1990s on its first major restructuring. In the spring of 1994 the prices of resins, used in nearly all of the company's products, began to rise and eventually doubled, increasing manufacturing costs. Rubbermaid also faced increasing competition in the 1990s as other housewares makers improved their products but kept their prices lower than Rubbermaid's premium prices, leading to customer defections and retailer dissatisfaction with the company's pricing policies.

In response to these difficulties, Rubbermaid began a two-year restructuring effort in late 1995. The company streamlined its product lines, by eliminating 45 percent of its stock-keeping units, which when combined generated only 10 percent of overall sales. The company also added a new infant product division to its organizational chart with its 1996 acquisition of Graco Children's Products Inc., maker of strollers, play yards, and infant swings, for $320 million. Rubbermaid also divested its office products division by selling it to Newell for $246.5 million in May 1997. By now, Rubbermaid was left with four divisions: home products, commercial products, juvenile products, and infant products.

The company significantly increased its overseas sales in January 1998 when it acquired its onetime partner, the Curver Group, for $143 million. Curver was the leading maker of plastic housewares in Europe, with 1996 sales of about $222 million. Amid another restructuring Rubbermaid divested three of its businesses, including its decorative coverings unit, which included the ConTact brand, and had launched the largest consumer advertising campaign in company history. Rubbermaid also completed one more acquisition in 1998, which was its last as an independent company. It purchased Century Products Company from Wingate Partners for $77.5 million. Fitting in nicely alongside the Graco line, Century produced car seats, strollers, and infant carriers.

FORMATION OF NEWELL RUBBERMAID INC.

Newell and Rubbermaid had discussed a merger in mid-1997, but the talks broke down when the two sides could not agree on who would run the company and where it would be headquartered. By late 1998, however, Rubbermaid's position had deteriorated to the point where it gave in on these points and agreed to be bought by Newell for $6 billion in stock. To the credit of the Rubbermaid managers, the price represented a hefty 49 percent premium over the company's stock price. John McDonough, Newell's vice chairman and CEO, continued in these same positions for the newly named Newell Rubbermaid Inc.

Upon completion of the deal in March 1999, Rubbermaid Chairman and CEO Wolfgang R. Schmitt became vice chairman of the company, and William Sovey remained chairman. McDonough was hoping that the usual Newellization process could revitalize Rubbermaid, and he also anticipated that Rubbermaid's renowned ability to develop new products might be spread to the Newell product lines. One of the biggest challenges for McDonough was in improving Rubbermaid's abysmal customer service and its troubled distribution system. Restructuring costs totaled $241.6 million in 1999, dragging profits down to $95.4 million; revenues for the first year of the new Newell Rubbermaid amounted to $6.41 billion.

While the Rubbermaid operations were being overhauled Newell Rubbermaid continued making acquisitions, with a particular emphasis on Europe. In April 1999 the company bought Ateliers 28, a French maker of drapery hardware. In October of that same year the company acquired Reynolds S.A., a manufacturer of writing instruments based in Valence, France. That same month, Newell Rubbermaid purchased McKechnie plc's consumer products division. The largest acquisition during this period, however, was of a U.S. business: the stationery products division of Gillette Company, acquired in December 2000. Newell Rubbermaid gained a rich stable of brands, including Paper Mate, Parker, and Waterman writing instruments and Liquid Paper correction products. The Gillette division had posted revenues of $743 million in 1999.

The challenging integration of Rubbermaid led to inconsistent earnings and a slumping stock price. Late in 2000 the stock fell to its lowest level since 1994. Soon after, at the beginning of November 2000, McDonough resigned from the company. Sovey, his predecessor, temporarily took the reins as CEO, before Joseph Galli Jr. was brought onboard as president and CEO in January 2001, with Sovey returning to the chairman's post. Galli had previously spent 19 years at Black & Decker, where he rose to the number two position before leaving in 1999. He then had short stints with Amazon.com, Inc., and VerticalNet Inc. before accepting the Newell Rubbermaid post.

RESTRUCTURING EFFORTS BEGIN IN 2001

Galli launched a thorough restructuring in a turnaround attempt. In May 2001 the company announced that it would eliminate 3,000 positions from its workforce over a three-year period, a reduction of 6 percent. The plan also involved the consolidation of manufacturing facilities as the company aimed to cut operating costs by $100 million per year. During 2001 alone, 14 facilities were shuttered. The company also sought to shift some manufacturing to lower-cost locations in Mexico, China, Poland, and Hungary. Another key objective was to pare back the company's heavy debt load, which had been incurred during its 1990s acquisition spree. One method to do this was to divest underperforming operations.

As he attempted to turn around Newell Rubbermaid, Galli stayed away from acquisitions, and no major deals were completed in 2001. In April 2002, however, the company took full control of American Tool Companies, Inc., a Hoffman Estates, Illinois, firm in which Newell Rubbermaid already held a 49.5 percent stake. The deal was valued at $419 million and brought into the company fold a line of branded hand tools, including Vise-Grip pliers and Quik-Grip clamps, and a line of power tool accessories, such as Irwin wood-boring bits and Hanson drill bits.

The acquisition of American Tool perhaps signaled a return to the Newell tradition of growth through acquisition, and the optimistic Galli told *Forbes* in October 2001 that he was aiming to grow the company into a $50-billion-in-sales behemoth. Despite Galli's ambitious plans, sales and profits were being hampered by the difficult economic environment of the early 21st century.

OVERCOMING CHALLENGES: 2004 AND BEYOND

During 2004 the company sold its picture frames business in Europe as well as the Anchor Hocking Glass, Burnes Picture Frame, and Mirro Cookware divisions. Mark Ketchum was named president and CEO in 2005 upon Galli's departure from the company. Under new leadership, Newell Rubbermaid embarked on a significant restructuring effort and adopted a new "Brands that Matter" tagline. As part of the company's new strategy, it focused on developing and marketing its brands while divesting noncore and unprofitable businesses.

During this period, a global economic downturn and high raw material costs were forcing the company to shutter facilities and lay off employees. Company offices were consolidated and moved to a new location in Atlanta, Georgia.

The company sold off its Little Tikes line in 2006. By 2010 the company had sold off nearly $3 billion in revenue of what it deemed unprofitable and low-growth businesses. Meanwhile, it continued to make strategic acquisitions that fit in with its brand-focused strategy. During 2005 it had purchased Dymo, an on-demand labeling manufacturer, in a $730 million deal. Three years later it added Japan's Aprica Kassai Inc., a manufacturer of strollers, car seats, and various infant and children's products. It also purchased Technical Concepts Holdings LLC, a restroom hygiene systems manufacturer, in 2008.

By now, Newell Rubbermaid was structured with three main business divisions. Its Home & Family division's major brands included Rubbermaid, Calphalon, Goody, Graco, Levolor, and Aprica. Its Office Products division secured over 50 percent of sales from international operations and included the Sharpie, Paper Mate, Dymo, Waterman, and Expo brands. The company's Tools, Hardware & Commercial Products group included the Irwin, Lenox, Rubbermaid, TC, BernzOmatic, and Shur-Line brands.

With sales of $5.6 billion and net income of $285.5 million in 2009, Newell Rubbermaid appeared to have emerged from its restructuring efforts a more streamlined and financially stable company despite the challenging economic environment. As CEO Ketchum told the *Akron Beacon Journal* in May 2010, "Our strategic transformation is virtually complete and today we are a new Newell Rubbermaid." He went on to claim, "Our biggest opportunities are still ahead as we continue to invest behind our brands to drive sales, grow margins, expand geographically and build best-in-class capabilities."

Roger W. Rouland; Elizabeth Rourke
Updated, David E. Salamie; Christina M. Stansell

PRINCIPAL OPERATING UNITS

Office Products Group; Home and Family Group; Tools, Hardware & Commercial Products Group.

PRINCIPAL COMPETITORS

Avery Dennison Corporation; Cooper Industries plc; Fortune Brands, Inc.; WKI Holding Company, Inc.

FURTHER READING

Christensen, Jean. "How Rubbermaid Invites Profits." *New York Times*, May 19, 1974.

Cimperman, Jennifer Scott. "Rubbermaid Endures Newellization." *Cleveland Plain Dealer*, June 29, 2000, p. 1C.

Cuthbert, William R. *Newell Companies—A Corporate History: The First 40 Years*, Freeport, Ill.: Newell Co., 1983.

Degross, Renee. "Newell Rubbermaid Names Ketchum CEO." *Atlanta Journal-Constitution*, February 14, 2006, p. C1.

Hallinan, Joseph T. "Newell CEO Tries to Shake Up Concern with Little Success." *Wall Street Journal*, January 14, 2002, p. B3.

"Newell Rubbermaid Completes Acquisition of Aprica." *PR Newswire*, April 1, 2008.

"Newell Rubbermaid Expects Growth in 2010 Product Sales." *Akron Beacon Journal*, May 29, 2010.

"Newell Rubbermaid Inc. Announces Definitive Agreement to Acquire Technical Concepts Holdings, LLC." *Reuters Significant Developments*, February 27, 2008.

Noble, Donald E. *Like Only Yesterday: The Memoirs of Donald E. Noble*. Wooster, Ohio: Wooster Book Co., 1996.

Peralte, Paul C. "Rubbermaid to Cut Jobs, Lines." *Atlanta Journal*, July 16, 2008.

Tisch, Carol, and Lisa Vincenti. "Rubbermaid Bounces Back." *HFN—The Weekly Newspaper for the Home Furnishing Network*, January 17, 2000, p. 90.

Upbin, Bruce. "Rebirth of a Sales Man." *Forbes*, October 1, 2001, pp. 94–96+.

Yao, Margaret. "Rubbermaid Reaches for Greater Glamour in World beyond Dustpans and Drainers." *Wall Street Journal*, June 9, 1982.

NG2 S.A.

———■———

ul. Strefowa 6
Polkowice, 59-101
Poland
Telephone: (+48 76) 845 8400
Fax: (+48 76) 845 8431
Web site: http://www.ng2.pl

Public Company
Incorporated: 1999 as CCC Sp. z.o.o.
Employees: 5,613
Sales: PLN 922 million ($312.2 million) (2009)
Stock Exchanges: Warsaw
Ticker Symbol: CCC
NAICS: 316213 Men's Footwear (Except Athletic) Manufacturing; 316214 Women's Footwear (Except Athletic) Manufacturing; 424340 Footwear Merchant Wholesalers; 448210 Shoe Stores

■ ■ ■

NG2 (New Gate Group) S.A. is Poland's leading footwear retailer and manufacturer. The company operates over 700 stores in three primary formats. The largest is the CCC chain, the company's flagship, with 262 company-owned stores and 61 franchised stores in Poland and 40 stores in the Czech Republic. The CCC brand targets the low to medium price segments, with shoe prices ranging from $6 to $100.

The Boti brand features discount footwear with prices ranging up to $60. The company has opened nearly 300 Boti shoe stores since 2006, including 223 company-owned and 65 franchised stores. NG2 has also moved into the higher-end segment with the launch of the Quazi boutique format. The company has opened nearly 50 Quazi stores, featuring higher quality shoes in the mid- to upper price segments, with prices ranging up to $300.

NG2 stocks its stores with its own array of more than 60 brand names. The company develops more than 2,500 shoe designs each year. Its manufacturing facility in Polkowice focuses on its higher-end styles, representing 10 percent of its total volume. The bulk of the group's shoes are produced in partnership with manufacturers in China and India. NG2 is listed on the Warsaw Stock Exchange and is led by founder Dariuz Milek. The company posted total sales of PLN 922 million ($312.2 million) in 2009.

FROM CYCLING CHAMP TO SHOE SALES IN 1991

A graduate of one of Poland's mining schools, Dariuz Milek at first appeared set to pursue a career in professional sports. Milek established himself as Poland's national cycling champion during the 1980s. With the collapse of Communism in 1989, however, Milek joined the throngs of would-be entrepreneurs eager to participate in Poland's newly emerging free market economy. Milek targeted the retail sector, which remained largely undeveloped after decades of Communist rule. In 1991 Milek established his first business in Lubin, in the copper mining region of Lower Silesia, selling a variety of goods from a camp bed set up at one

COMPANY PERSPECTIVES

Development strategy. The strategy of NG2 Group is based on following pillars: 1. Strengthening the market rating—through renting attractive retail spaces in new built business centers and branches expanding branches in places where they are less recognized. Both classic advertising media campaigns, sport sponsoring and unification of internal arrangement and outdoor advertising are the manners of market rating straightening. 2. Branch development—the Group estimates the target amount of own shops signed CCC logo at 300 and franchise at 130. The target number of shops in Czech Republic is estimated at 60 shops, QUAZI–100 and the BOTI should keep the highest rate of growth with its estimated target amount of shops at 900, including 600 own sales points. 3. The continuation of profitability growth in distribution areas. 4. Increasing the goodwill for shareholders.

of the many outdoor bazaars operating in Poland at the time.

Milek put in long hours, often arriving at the bazaar at 5:00 a.m. and closing up shop only late at night. Before long, Milek was able to trade his camp bed for a lockable steel shed, so that he was no longer required to carry his stock home with him each night. Noting the success of a neighbor's footwear sales, Milek decided to specialize in this category as well.

An important part of Milek's early success came when he approached the managers of a struggling footwear factory in nearby Polkowice, offering to buy up a large part of its shoe stock. As Milek told the *Financial Times*: "In the early days, it was more difficult to get the shoes than to sell them." The managers, holdovers from the Communist era, agreed to sell Milek the shoes at a 40 percent discount in exchange for payment in cash. Milek passed this discount to his customers, and his sales grew quickly.

Milek hired a number of employees to sell his shoes for him. He then implemented his next idea, buying up a number of shipping containers that had been converted into rudimentary retail shops. By renting these out to other sellers, Milek was able to focus on building a growing wholesale business. Milek next bought a small warehouse in order to supply this network of retailers.

FIRST RETAIL CHAIN IN 1996

Poland slowly pulled itself out of the chaos that had marked its transition to a free market economy through much of the first half of the 1990s. By the middle of the decade, the country had begun to take its first steps toward developing a full-fledged, Western-style retail sector. Milek recognized the opportunity to take the lead in this development. In 1996 Milek converted his network of sellers into his first true retail format, Żółta Stopa (Golden Feet), providing low-priced discount shoes.

By maintaining a cash-based purchasing policy, Milek was able to persuade the country's cash-strapped footwear manufacturers to supply him with shoes at a strong discount. This allowed him to target Poland's large lower-income population. Milek adapted his shop format to appeal to this consumer segment. For example, instead of displaying shoes in their boxes, Milek placed them in wire bins. As Milek told the *Financial Times*: "The look wasn't as important as the price."

Milek developed a franchise formula in order to develop the chain more quickly. Franchisees, including those working from Milek's original network of shipping containers, were required to purchase their stock exclusively from Milek. He also took steps to ensure franchisee loyalty, including, according to the *Financial Times*, opening competing Golden Feet franchises near an existing but uncooperative franchise.

CCC IN 1999

Western-style shopping centers became more and more commonplace in Poland through the second half of the 1990s. Milek, who by then had assembled a management team around him, saw the opportunity to reformulate his existing retail operations for the more modern accommodations then available. In 1999 Milek created a new company, CCC Sp. Z.o.o., and unveiled a new retail format. Called CCC, the new store chain advertised itself under the slogan "Cena Czyni Cuda" (Price Works Wonders, also translated as Price Makes Miracles).

CCC started out with a network of more than 100 franchises, many of which had formerly operated Golden Feet stores. However, most of the company's growth over the next several years came through the development of a company-owned store network. By the end of the decade, these stores greatly outnumbered the group's franchised stores.

CCC's slogan, along with its low- to mid-price structure, helped attract shoppers, enabling the company

KEY DATES

1991: Dariuz Milek begins selling footwear at the Lubin bazaar.
1996: Milek establishes his first retail footwear format, Żółta Stopa (Golden Feet).
1999: Milek creates a new retail format and company, CCC.
2004: CCC goes public on the Warsaw Stock Exchange.
2007: The company changes its name to NG2 (New Gate Group).
2010: NG2's total retail operations top 700 stores.

to expand the chain quickly. CCC before long established a presence in nearly all of Poland's growing number of shopping centers. The rapid growth of the CCC chain led the company to build a new headquarters and logistics center in Polkowice, in the city's Legnica Special Economic Zone, in April 2001.

CCC then added its own manufacturing component as well, building a factory next to its new headquarters. The new production facilities allowed CCC to gain greater control over the quality of its higher-priced shoe designs. In the meantime, the company also put into place a series of contracting partnerships with manufacturers in China and, to a lesser extent, in India.

PUBLIC OFFERING IN 2004

By 2004 CCC had grown into a chain of 78 stores, more than two-thirds of which operated from Poland's shopping malls. By then, CCC had become one of the largest footwear retailers in Poland. CCC sought further expansion, earmarking some PLN 50 million (approximately $15 million) for that purpose. In keeping with Poland's rising affluence and its growing middle class, the company also eyed a shift in its sales target, from the low end to a stronger emphasis on the mid-priced market.

In order to fund this expansion, Milek announced plans to open the group's capital to outside investment. The company completed a restructuring of its operations, converting CCC into a joint stock company and transferring ownership of the company's factory, previously set up as an affiliate, wholly under the umbrella of CCC. The company then launched a securities offering in November 2004, before completing a listing on the Warsaw Stock Exchange at the beginning of December.

Milek remained as the company CEO and chairman, as well as its majority shareholder.

Flushed by the success of its public offering, CCC announced plans to open more than 35 new stores in Poland through 2005. The company also announced plans to enter the Czech Republic, forming a subsidiary for this effort, CCC Boty Czech s.r.o. The company opened its first stores in that country in Ostrava and Karlove Vary in March 2005, targeting a total of five Czech stores by the end of the year. Milek also acknowledged the company's interest in bringing its discount shoe format into other European markets, including Germany.

NEW BRANDS IN 2006

CCC then made its first attempt to enter the high-end footwear market, adding a new line of Italian-made women's footwear to its store shelves. That effort failed to inspire Polish consumers, who associated the CCC chain more closely with the low- to mid-price footwear segments.

The company returned to the drawing board instead, developing not one but two new retail formats. The first of these, called Quazi, positioned itself at the mid- to high-end range, with a smaller store format featuring the company's own women's footwear designs. Targeting Poland's growing number of high-end shopping malls, the company announced plans to open as many as 45 Quazi stores by 2008.

The company also launched development of a second new retail format. For this, the company sought to fill a gap in its retail offering, targeting Poland's small and medium-sized towns, and the lower-income populations there. In 2007 the company debuted its new Boti retail store format. Boti stores featured a smaller selling space than the CCC shops, 110 square meters compared to the 330-square-meter CCC stores. They also emphasized lower priced footwear designs, with prices starting at $6 and topping off at a maximum of $60 per pair.

BECOMING NG2 IN 2007

In keeping with its new multibrand strategy, CCC decided to change it name, becoming New Gate Group, or NG2, in January 2007. NG2 was Poland's leading footwear retailer by this time, with sales of EUR 154 million ($215 million). Milek, who had joined the ranks of Poland's wealthiest people, had also begun to rack up an impressive list of awards, including Ernst & Young's Polish Entrepreneur of the Year award. NG2 itself won recognition as The Best Managed Company on the Warsaw Stock Market (Najlepiej Zarządzana Spółka Giełdowa) in 2008.

NG2 maintained a steady program of store openings through 2008, topping 575 stores by the end of that year. While most of that growth took place in Poland, the company also continued to expand its Czech network, which soon reached a total of 40 stores. Nevertheless, the company's international expansion remained limited, as the company abandoned earlier announced plans to enter Russia and other neighboring markets.

The company's reluctance to invest in a wider international expansion proved to be shrewd strategy, however, as the economic crisis at the end of the decade caught up with Poland and the other Eastern European markets. As NG2's more aggressively expansive rivals struggled amid the difficult economic climate, NG2's financial position remained stable.

The company's longtime focus on the discount footwear sector also enabled the company to continue its expansion. As Milek told the *Financial Times*: "People are counting their money now. Paradoxically, that helps us." Milek also explained to the *Polish News Bulletin*: "We are selling middle- and low-price goods, so we are looking forward to an increase in the numbers of our customers."

CONTINUED SUCCESS IN 2010

NG2 maintained the pace of its program of store openings, taking advantage of the upsurge in demand for lower-priced footwear. By early 2009 the company had 614 stores. Much of this growth was achieved by the steady expansion of the Boti retail chain, which then numbered 165 company-owned stores and 73 franchised stores.

The company's growth continued even as the deepening recession crippled its rivals. Milek explained the company's success to *Manufacturing Journal Magazine* thusly: "When the economy was seemingly booming, we did not fall for costly acquisitions. We have a mind of our own, hence the idea of sustainable growth and the focus on the domestic market." This focus paid off for NG2, which raised its total store portfolio to 708 stores, including nearly 330 CCC

stores and more than 290 Boti stores by mid-2010. NG2 had succeeded in capturing a 12 percent share of the Polish footwear market. With its record of achievement, NG2 appeared to have laid a solid foundation for future growth.

M. L. Cohen

PRINCIPAL SUBSIDIARIES

CCC Factory Sp. Z.o.o.; CCC Boty Czech s.r.o.

PRINCIPAL DIVISIONS

Manufacturing; Retail.

PRINCIPAL OPERATING UNITS

CCC; Boti; Quazi.

PRINCIPAL COMPETITORS

Donianna Sh.p.k; Godiva-Viktoriya Joint Stock Co.; Leder & Schuh AG; MAGMA d.d.; Marko Footwear Enterprise Ltd.; Sergio Tacchini International S.p.A.

FURTHER READING

Barteczko, Agnieszka. "CCC Set to Splurge on Shoe Shops." *Warsaw Business Journal*, March 21, 2005.

Cienski, Jan. "Big Strides for a Market Trader." *Financial Times*, June 3, 2009, p. 12.

Debek, Katarzyna. "CCC Steps Up with New Brands." *Warsaw Business Journal*, March 6, 2006.

Kalembasiak, Anna. "NG2 Takes Strides towards Profit." *Warsaw Business Journal*, March 3, 2008.

"NG2 Is Poland's Footwear Superstar." *Business Week*, November 12, 2008.

"NG2 Posts Record Monthly Sales, Future Looks Bright." *Polish News Bulletin*, May 5, 2009.

"Polish Shoe Maker CCC May Enter Stock Market." *Polish News Bulletin*, August 20, 2004.

"Retailer Resilient to Economic Slowdown." *World Finance Retailer*, December 17, 2009.

Sowinski, Bartosz. "NG2 S.A." *Manufacturing Journal Magazine*, July 9, 2010.

Nippon Oil Corporation

—■—

3-12, Nishi Shimbashi 1-chome
Minato-ku
Tokyo, 105-8412
Japan
Telephone: (+81 3) 3502 1131
Fax: (+81 3) 3502 9352
Web site: http://www.eneos.co.jp

Public Company
Incorporated: 1931
Employees: 14,144 (2010)
Sales: $75.95 billion (2009)
Stock Exchanges: Tokyo Osaka Nagoya
Ticker Symbol: 5001
NAICS: 324110 Petroleum Refineries; 211111 Crude Petroleum and Natural Gas Extraction; 324121 Asphalt Paving Mixture and Block Manufacturing; 324191 Petroleum Lubricating Oil and Grease Manufacturing; 325110 Petrochemical Manufacturing; 447110 Gasoline Stations with Convenience Stores; 447190 Other Gasoline Stations; 454311 Heating Oil Dealers; 454312 Liquefied Petroleum Gas (Bottled Gas) Dealers

■■■

Nippon Oil Corporation is Japan's largest importer and distributor of petroleum products, controlling 23 percent of the market. The company's main petroleum products include gasoline, naphtha, kerosene, diesel fuel, jet fuel, heavy fuel oil, lubricants, and asphalt. Nippon owns seven crude oil refineries in Japan that have a total daily capacity of about 1.22 million barrels. It operates a network of 9,745 service stations in that country under the ENEOS brand. Nippon Oil also is engaged in a number of related activities, including oil and natural gas exploration and production, natural gas distribution, electric power generation, and the manufacture of petrochemicals. Oil and natural gas production is centered in Vietnam, the U.K. North Sea, the Gulf of Mexico, Canada, Papua New Guinea, and Myanmar. Nippon Oil shares a broad alliance with Cosmo Oil Co., Ltd., involving crude-oil procurement, refining, and distribution, and is also active in several alliances with Idemitsu Kosan Co., Ltd. Additional partnerships have enabled the company to branch out into additional product and energy offerings, including coal mining and optical films, composites, and TU cloth manufacturing. In April 2010, the company merged with Nippon Mining Company to form JX Holdings Inc.

ORIGINS DURING JAPAN'S OIL INDUSTRY'S INFANCY

Nippon Oil Company was founded in 1888 during the Meiji restoration, which lasted from 1867 to 1912. This was a time of extraordinary changes in Japan. The government transformed Japan into a world power and sought to model the country's development on that of the West. Western technology, especially that of the United States, was used to modernize the Japanese economy. A parliamentary system of government was introduced in 1885, modeled on that of Germany.

While the Japanese oil industry was itself in its infancy, many entrepreneurs (*yamashi*) capitalized on the

KEY DATES

1888: Twenty-one entrepreneurs form Nippon Oil Company.

1907: Nippon buys the Japanese assets of International Petroleum.

1937: Nippon Oil comes under control of a state-run monopolistic organization known as Oil Co-operative Sales.

1941: The Japanese government merges Nippon Oil with Ogura Oil.

1999: Nippon Oil and Mitsubishi Oil merge to form Nippon Mitsubishi Oil Corporation, the largest oil company in Japan.

2001: Two majority owned, publicly traded refinery affiliates, Koa Oil Company Ltd. and Tohoku Oil Co., Ltd., are made into wholly owned subsidiaries; conversion of service stations to the new ENEOS brand begins.

2002: Nippon Mitsubishi Oil Corporation changes its name to Nippon Oil Corporation.

growing demand for oil created by Japanese industrialization. In 1888, 21 *yamashi* founded Nippon Oil. All were wealthy landowners at a time when most Japanese were landless peasants. Control of Nippon Oil rested with these shareholders, who owned 66 percent of the stock. However, most decisions were made by two men, Gonzaburo Yamaguchi and the man who became the first company president, Hisahiro Natio. Almost immediately after the company was formed, successful drilling for crude oil began at Amaze, north of Tokyo. Within a year drilling also took place off the Japanese coast, and Nippon became the first Japanese company to drill offshore for oil.

A key to the company's initial success was its willingness to obtain technology from abroad. In particular, Nippon Oil looked to the United States, which had pioneered technological innovations in the oil industry. In 1889 Yamaguchi visited the United States to obtain information on the latest advances in oil drilling. Impressed by the sophistication of U.S. technology, Yamaguchi, on his return, persuaded his colleagues to purchase an advanced drilling machine from the Pierce company of New York. Yamaguchi hired a Texan to instruct Nippon Oil employees in the operation of the new equipment. Profits in the infant oil company were small. The salary of the U.S. drilling equipment expert amounted to 12 percent of total

company expense, yet Nippon Oil was determined to master Western technology. The financial depression of 1897, which led to the collapse of many of Japan's smaller oil companies, left Nippon Oil with an ever-increasing share of Japanese oil production and refining.

KEY ACQUISITIONS IN THE EARLY 20TH CENTURY

In 1900 Nippon Oil experienced stiff competition from the newly arrived International Petroleum. This company had been founded in Japan but was operated by the American Standard Oil Company. In 1907 Nippon Oil overcame this domestic competition by purchasing all the Japanese assets of International Petroleum. By so doing, Nippon Oil became one of the largest oil companies in Japan. Its major competitor was now another Japanese company, Hoden Oil.

From 1908 onward, Nippon Oil's output of oil gradually decreased as wells became exhausted. Nippon Oil, again relying on U.S. technology, introduced a rotary drill that enabled existing wells to be deepened. Other Japanese companies soon followed Nippon Oil's example, leading to increased oil production throughout Japan.

In World War I, Japan concentrated its activities against the German colonial empire in the Far East. Following Germany's defeat, Japan not only acquired former German colonial possessions in the Pacific but also gained important commercial concessions in China. The war, too, led to the rapid development of Japanese industry as well as an increase in the demand for oil. In 1921, three years after the end of the war, Nippon Oil merged with its former competitor, Hoden Oil, and controlled 80 percent of domestic crude oil production.

The interwar period in Japan witnessed not only industrial expansion but also an increase in living standards. As the number of automobiles on Japanese roads grew, Nippon Oil established a network of gasoline-storage depots throughout the country. In 1919 the company set up its first hand-pump gasoline service station with an underground storage tank, in Tokyo. By the late 1920s more than 160 stations were in operation.

By the late 1920s, also, Japan's oil reserves were insufficient to meet the needs of a growing industrialized economy. Imported oil, therefore, became vital for the continued growth of the Japanese economy, and Nippon Oil, like most other Japanese oil refineries, increasingly relied on imported oil. In 1923 Nippon Oil imported only 170,000 kiloliters of oil. The ratio of domestic oil to imported oil was 63 percent to 23 percent. By 1937 only 20 percent of Nippon Oil's crude oil supply came from domestic sources. The remaining 80 percent had to be imported, mainly from the United States. As domestic oil production lessened, importing and refining gradually became Nippon Oil's principal business activity.

LOSS OF INDEPENDENCE DURING WORLD WAR II

During the 1930s, Japan, like other industrialized countries, suffered the effects of the worldwide Great Depression. The Japanese government, under pressure from its army and navy chiefs, sought new markets on the Chinese mainland through military aggression. In 1931 the Japanese military seized Manchuria, forcing Chinese troops to withdraw from the area. In 1937 war had broken out with China. By this time, the military had gained control of the Japanese government and had begun to regulate the Japanese economy to the needs of the war effort. All important industries came under state control. In 1937 Nippon Oil lost all of its independence, coming under the control of a state-run monopolistic organization known as Oil Co-operative Sales.

Japan's role in World War II had a devastating impact on the economy. Japan's reliance on imported oil and other raw materials meant that the country was vulnerable to an Allied blockade. U.S. submarines operating close to the Japanese coast inflicted heavy losses on Japanese oil tankers carrying supplies to the mainland. Slowly the Japanese economy ground to a halt.

Because of the blockade, Nippon Oil's supply of imported oil almost totally dried up. In 1941, in an attempt to encourage domestic production of oil under embargo conditions, the Japanese government merged Nippon Oil with Ogura Oil. However, under the weight of heavy bombing attacks on oil installations, little could be done to remedy Japan's acute oil shortage.

REESTABLISHMENT OF NIPPON OIL IN THE POSTWAR PERIOD

Japanese defeat in 1945 was followed by a lengthy period of reconstruction under the Allied occupation authority, the objective of which was the reestablishment of a peacetime industrial economy. The old state monopolies were broken up and competition between smaller economic units was encouraged. Nippon Oil Company was reestablished as a wholesaler in 1949 and occupied a much smaller role in the Japanese postwar economy than it had had for decades. Its main activity continued to be the importing and refining of mostly imported oil.

The Korean War, which broke out in 1950, transformed Japan into an important ally of the United States in the Far East and led to closer economic ties between the two countries. In 1951, recognizing the importance of the U.S. connection, Nippon Oil established Nippon Petroleum Refining Company Ltd. as a joint venture with Caltex Petroleum Corporation of the United States. Caltex itself was a joint venture of Standard Oil Company of California (later Chevron Corporation) and the Texas Company (later Texaco Inc.). Most of Nippon's crude oil supply was subsequently purchased from Caltex and refined by Nippon Petroleum. Also in 1951, a further subsidiary, Tokyo Tanker Co., Ltd., was established to transport oil to Japan. In 1955 Nippon Oil entered the petrochemical and gas industry through the establishment of two subsidiaries, Nippon Petrochemicals Company, Limited and Nippon Petroleum Gas Company, Limited.

In 1960 Nippon Oil established an overseas office in the United States, incorporated in Delaware. The 1960s witnessed a period of sustained growth at Nippon Oil. In 1961 operating profits for the year stood at ¥2.13 billion. For 1970 Nippon Oil declared a profit of ¥10.76 billion. This trend of increased profitability was interrupted by events in the Middle East early in the 1970s. Since the end of World War II, Japan had increasingly relied on Middle East oil. The Yom Kippur War of 1973 between Israel and its Arab neighbors interrupted the oil supply. The Arab-dominated Organization of Petroleum Exporting Countries (OPEC) cut production and raised prices. Within a year of the war, prices had quadrupled. These increases might have been passed on to the Japanese consumer, but in 1974 the Japanese government froze retail gas prices. After-tax profit fell at Nippon Oil to ¥902 million, less than one-tenth of what it had been in 1970.

MANEUVERING THROUGH AN INDUSTRY IN FLUX IN THE EIGHTIES AND NINETIES

By 1977 Nippon had recovered from the energy crisis through the growing strength of the Japanese economy and the high appreciation of the yen on world money markets. In 1980 profits reached an all-time high of ¥45.67 billion. The early 1980s, however, witnessed a slump in the oil industry because of an abundance of supply and too much refining capacity. The Japanese Ministry of International Trade and Industry sought to rationalize the oil industry by encouraging cooperation among the large companies. In November 1984 Nippon Oil and Mitsubishi Oil Company, Limited, reached an accord on the sharing of marketing and facilities. This pact gave both companies joint command of 25 percent of Japan's oil market. Under the agreement, the two companies cooperated in wholesale and retail operations and use of tanker and storage facilities. Mitsubishi Oil had been 50 percent owned by the U.S. Getty Oil Company until earlier in 1994 when Getty was acquired by Texaco; as part of that buyout, Getty sold its interest to members of the Mitsubishi group and other Japanese buyers for $335 million.

Under the leadership of its chairman, Yasuoki Takeuchi, Nippon Oil during the 1980s took steps to reduce its dependence on Middle East oil. In 1985 alone, Nippon Oil set aside $100 million for the development of oil fields in the United States, and in 1986, Nippon Oil found promising oil fields in North Dakota. The company also reached an agreement with Texaco of the United States for joint development of Alaskan oil fields. Another joint exploration deal with Chevron led to the discovery of two gas fields in the Gulf of Mexico.

This policy of developing alternative sources of supply somewhat reduced dependence on Middle East oil. In 1989 while 56.6 percent of Nippon Oil imports came from the Middle East, 37 percent came from Southeast Asia, and the remaining 6.4 percent from other regions, mainly Mexico.

Japanese oil refiners and distributors were hit hard by the prolonged economic stagnation that afflicted Japan in the wake of the bursting of the bubble economy of the late 1980s. Demand for petroleum products fell sharply in the 1990s, hampering an industry already struggling with overcapacity. Under pressure from the Japanese government, Nippon Oil and two other Japanese refiners in 1991 entered into a joint venture with Saudi Arabian Oil Company and Caltex to build a new export refinery in Saudi Arabia and to turn a mothballed refinery in Japan owned by Nippon Oil into a state-of-the-art plant. The Japanese government hoped to establish a stable procurement route through the venture, but late in 1993, as the economic environment continued to deteriorate, the Japanese refiners pulled out. Meantime, in mid-1992 Hidejiro Osawa was promoted to president, replacing Kentaro Iwamoto, with Takeuchi remaining chairman.

In the fiscal year ending in March 1995, Nippon Oil ceded its number one position in the Japanese oil industry to Idemitsu Kosan Co., Ltd. Competition in the industry, which was already fierce because of refinery overcapacity and the economic travails, was about to intensify as a result of deregulatory moves initiated by the government. In April 1996 a law limiting oil imports to 29 refiners and distributors was repealed, opening the door for supermarkets, trading companies, and even farm cooperatives to begin importing petroleum products for direct distribution in Japan. In anticipation of this sea change, Caltex elected to partially exit from the Japanese refinery industry, having concluded that it could more profitably import into Japan petroleum products that had been refined elsewhere in Asia, where production costs were lower. Caltex, therefore, sold its 50 percent interest in Nippon Petroleum Refining to Nippon Oil for $1.98 billion in April 1996. Caltex held onto a 50 percent interest in Koa Oil Company, Limited, a Japanese oil refiner that supplied almost all of its output to Nippon Oil. In May 1996 Takeuchi stepped down from his post of chairman, which was subsequently made vacant.

The newly competitive environment led to lower prices for petroleum products, sending profits at Nippon Oil and other Japanese refiners on a steadily downward path during the late 1990s. Cost-cutting came to the fore, and Nippon announced in 1996 that it would cut its workforce from 4,200 to 3,600 by decade's end. The company closed 6 of 18 branch offices and also began seeking alliances as an additional way of cutting costs. During 1996 Nippon Oil and Idemitsu Kosan began jointly supplying kerosene and fuel oil, and then the following year the two firms reached an agreement to merge some of their oil tank stations that supplied gasoline to service stations. In November 1997 Nippon announced that it would close its refinery in the city of Niigata in another cost-cutting move. The Niigata refinery was the smallest of Nippon's three wholly owned refineries, with a capacity of just 26,000 barrels per day. A further consequence of lower prices at the gas pump was that many Japanese gas stations were no longer operating profitably. Nippon Oil, along with the other Japanese refiners, began shuttering underperforming outlets. Between March 1997 and September 1998, for example, Nippon reduced the number of stations in its network by nearly 500.

Further roiling the industry was the late 1990s debut in Japan of self-service gasoline stations, after they had long been banned because of an arcane fire regulation. In April 1998 Nippon Oil opened its first self-service station in Kobe through a joint venture with McDonald's Company (Japan) Ltd., an affiliate of McDonald's Corporation. This service station complex included a drive-through McDonald's restaurant and a video rental shop. Additional complexes were subsequently opened in cooperation with McDonald's, the Kentucky Fried Chicken restaurant chain, and other partners. Through these multipurpose outlets, Nippon aimed to reduce labor costs and increase sales of gasoline. Toward similar goals, the company opened its first Dr. Drive service station, also in April 1998. In addition to gasoline, these stations offered a wide range of auto-related products and services, with the latter including vehicle checkups, maintenance and repairs, government-mandated vehicle inspections, and car washing and waxing. By March 2000, Nippon was operating 20 service station complexes incorporating other shops and restaurants and 44 Dr. Drive service stations.

1999 MERGER WITH MITSUBISHI, ALLIANCE WITH COSMO, RESTRUCTURING

In October 1998 Nippon Oil announced that it had agreed to merge with Mitsubishi Oil in a marriage of the second- and sixth-largest Japanese oil companies. The stock-swap deal, completed in April 1999, a difficult environment for Japanese oil companies, ultimately created the biggest oil company in Japan. The new Nippon Mitsubishi Oil Corporation also saved Mitsubishi, which posted a net loss of ¥20.2 billion in 1999, from possible financial trouble.

Nippon Mitsubishi wholly or partially owned nine refineries with a total capacity of 1.35 million barrels per day. It controlled about 25 percent of Japan's market for petroleum products, surpassing the previous market leader, Idemitsu Kosan. Its retail network included some 14,000 stations, which at least initially continued to operate under the Nisseki and Mitsubishi Oil names. The firm also had a much stronger upstream side, having gained Mitsubishi Oil's exploration and production operations in Vietnam and Papua New Guinea, as well as Mitsubishi's interest in a liquefied natural gas venture in Malaysia.

Under the direction of Osawa, formerly of Nippon, Nippon Mitsubishi moved quickly to achieve its stated goal of cutting annual costs by ¥70 billion ($574 million) over a three-year period. During 2000 its refinery operations were streamlined through several strategic measures. The Mizushima refinery, formerly operated by Mitsubishi Oil, was transferred to Nippon Mitsubishi's main refining subsidiary, the newly renamed Nippon Mitsubishi Petroleum Refining Company. Mitsubishi's refinery in Kawasaki, near Tokyo, a smaller facility with a capacity of 75,000 barrels per day, was shut down. Nippon Mitsubishi also spent ¥26.1 billion ($224 million) to buy out Caltex's remaining stake in Koa Oil. Nippon thus gained majority control of the publicly traded Koa Oil, which operated refineries in Marifu and Osaka with a refinery capacity of 252,000 barrels a day.

In October 1999, in its most significant alliance to that time (one that stopped just short of a full merger) Nippon Mitsubishi reached an agreement with Cosmo Oil Company, Limited, the number three Japanese oil firm, to cooperate in a number of areas, including crude

oil procurement, tanker allocation, oil refining, petroleum product distribution, lubricant manufacturing, and distribution. The alliance did not extend into the firms' service station operations. The companies hoped to save at least ¥15 billion ($140 million) from synergies by the third year of the partnership. Yet another alliance was entered into in February 2000 with Teikoku Oil Co., Ltd., a firm that had particular strength on the upstream side of the oil business. Nippon Mitsubishi subsequently became Teikoku's largest shareholder, increasing its stake to 16.5 percent.

For the fiscal year ending in March 2000, Nippon Mitsubishi reported a net loss of ¥4.86 billion ($45.8 million) because of a ¥23.3 billion ($220 million) charge it took to change the way it accounted for retirement benefits. About ¥50 billion ($470 million) in cost savings was achieved that year, representing 60 percent of the three-year target. Revenues for the year totaled ¥3.59 trillion ($33.91 billion). In June 2000 Osawa retired and was replaced as president by Fumiaki Watari, who had been vice president and had joined the former Nippon Oil in 1960.

A main focus for Nippon Mitsubishi over the next two years was the further restructuring of its refinery operations. During 2001 refinery capacity was reduced to 1.23 million barrels per day, increasing the company's capacity utilization from 76 percent to 84 percent. In October 2001 Nippon Mitsubishi bought the minority stakes in two of its majority-owned, publicly traded oil refining affiliates, Koa Oil and Tohoku Oil Co., Ltd.; the latter operated a 145,000-barrel-per-day refinery in the northern Japanese city of Sendai. Then in April 2002 Koa and Tohoku were merged into Nippon Mitsubishi Petroleum Refining Company, which now had refining capacity of 1.17 million barrels per day, or 95 percent of the parent company's total capacity, through the six refineries it operated. Nippon Mitsubishi's seventh refinery, located in Toyama, was operated by the majority-owned Nihonkai Oil Co., Ltd.

At the same time that the integration of the refining operations was nearing completion, integration also was occurring on the retailing side. The company's Nisseki and Mitsubishi Oil service stations were united under a new brand, ENEOS, a process completed in March 2002. The new name was a combination of the words *energy* and *neos*, meaning "new energy." Over the previous three years, Nippon Mitsubishi had gradually trimmed its service station network, so that by the time the name change was effected, it ran about 12,000 stations. Of this total, about 1,300 were Dr. Drive stations.

In June 2002 the company dropped "Mitsubishi" from its name, becoming simply Nippon Oil

Corporation. Likewise, the refining subsidiary was renamed Nippon Petroleum Refining Company, Limited. In December 2002 Nippon Oil entered into an oil refining alliance with Idemitsu Kosan that would enable the latter firm to close its Hyogo refinery. Nippon agreed to supply Idemitsu with 40,000 barrels per day of petroleum products, including gasoline, kerosene, jet fuel, diesel fuel, and fuel oil. Nippon simultaneously cut its refinery capacity by 10,000 barrels per day. Although the Japanese economy remained sluggish during 2003, Nippon Oil managed a 6 percent increase in net sales, to ¥4.19 trillion ($34.89 billion), while net income increased one-third, jumping from ¥24.01 billion to ¥32.28 billion ($269 million).

In August 2003 Nippon Oil temporarily shut down two of its refineries after discovering that they had falsified inspection reports during a four-year period starting in 1998. Nippon issued an apology for this scandal, but that did not preclude Japan's Ministry of Economy, Trade, and Industry from launching an investigation to determine what penalties, if any, should be imposed on the company. Nippon reduced its profit forecast for 2004 because of the shutdowns.

Looking to the future, Nippon was likely to continue to seek opportunities for streamlining its refining and marketing operations and to pursue further alliances and perhaps mergers. The company also wanted to achieve a better balance between its upstream and downstream operations by expanding its capacity to produce oil and gas from the 2003 level of 50,000 barrels of oil equivalent per day (BOED) to 150,000 BOED within a few years. Nippon Oil was also likely to continue another initiative: using its remaining refineries as bases for expanding into related energy fields, such as electric power generation and liquefied natural gas storage and supply. It was making a concerted effort to become a more comprehensive energy enterprise, lessening its dependence on the troubled Japanese oil refining and distribution sector.

MORE ALLIANCES AND A MERGER WITH NIPPON MINING: 2004–10

Contrary to projections, in 2004 Nippon Oil reversed its previous years' losses and earned record profits thanks to high crude oil prices, cost reductions, gains from equity-valued investment, and a cut in interest payments. At the end of the year, the company was back into the black, posting a net profit of ¥131.52 billion. The following year, in 2005, surging crude oil prices pushed up the value of Nippon's oil inventory an additional ¥33 billion. With the influx of extra capital, Nippon Oil made a bid for full-scale entry into the electricity retail business, investing ¥200 billion in natural resources development.

By 2006 Japan's domestic oil demand had reached record highs, and oil prices were skyrocketing. The average retail price of regular gasoline in Japan was ¥143.7 per liter, the highest level since record keeping began in 1987. With 90 percent of the country's crude oil imports originating in the politically volatile Middle East, Japan's government began accelerating a transition from fuel oil to alternative energy sources, such as natural gas and biodiesel. Nippon Oil, which had seven oil refineries in Japan and was refining 1.22 million barrels a day, made an effort to stabilize and diversify its crude oil supply by importing 700,000 barrels of crude oil from an oil development project off the coast off Russia. It also built a biodiesel plant in Indonesia's Jambi Province.

Finding new supply sources and marketing new products were not the company's only foci in 2007. Nippon Oil also looked for ways to expand its alliances. That year, Nippon Oil entered into a strategic partnership with SK Corporation, South Korea's largest oil refiner, with each company buying a 1 percent stake in each other. Nippon Oil also increased its refining relationship with ChinaOil by 10,000 to 50,000 barrels per day. By the end of 2007, high demand for fuel and crude oil combined with surging oil futures prices (at an all-time high of $147 per barrel) led to net profits of ¥148 billion.

However, record profits did not last. As 2008 began, oil prices began to plummet. By March they had dropped to $46 per barrel. As a result, demand for Nippon oil slumped, and the company reported net losses for the year. At the end of 2008, Nippon Oil announced that it planned to reduce its capital spending sharply over the next three years in response to the global economy's slowdown.

Nippon Oil's major tactic for reducing spending and increasing profits was to announce a merger with Nippon Mining Holdings Incorporated, Japan's sixth-ranked refiner. The combined firms planned to reorganize, reduce redundancy at both their facilities, and streamline capacity, consolidating and reducing their combined 10 refineries to six or seven. There were also plans to reduce their network of gas stations and to cut personnel. The merger would create a new holding company, JX Holdings Incorporated, and was expected to be complete by October 2009. The merged entity would comprise JX Nippon Oil & Energy Corporation, JX Nippon Oil & Gas Exploration, and JX Nippon Mining & Metals Corporation.

A year later, in November 2009, Nippon Oil president, Shinji Nishio, and Nippon Mining chief executive officer, Mitsunori Takahagi, announced that JX Holding's launch date would be delayed until April 2010, with a completion of the merger in July 2010. They also announced dramatic plans to further cut their refining capacity to a total of 600,000 barrels per day by March 2015, almost a third of the companies' combined refining capacity of 1.831 million barrels. At the time, Nippon Oil had reduced its service stations under the ENEOS brand from 13,000 to 9,745. In addition. Nippon Mining's refining arm, Japan Energy, had 3,269 service stations under its JOMO brand. Once the merger was complete, JX Group's holdings were projected to total 34 percent of Japan's domestic oil products market. Nishio would be the chairman of the JX Group and Nippon Mining's Takahagi would be president. Both companies planned on delisting from the Tokyo Stock Exchange and relisting as the JX Group. In early 2010 Nippon Oil was looking to secure additional oil sources and was in talks with the Iraqi government to obtain the right to develop an oil field in the southern Iraqi city of Nasiriyah.

Michael Doorley
Updated, David E. Salamie; Christina Stansell Weaver

PRINCIPAL SUBSIDIARIES

Nippon Petroleum Refining Company Ltd.; Nippon Petroleum Processing Company Ltd.; Nihonkai Oil Co., Ltd. (66%); Wakayama Petroleum Refining Co., Ltd. (50%); Nippon Oil Staging Terminal Company, Ltd.; Nippon Oil Tanker Corporation; Okinawa CTS Corporation (65%); Nippon Petroleum Gas Company, Ltd. (95.2%); Nippon Oil Exploration Ltd.; Nippon Oil Exploration U.S.A. Ltd.; Nippon Oil Exploration and Production U.K. Ltd.; Japan Vietnam Petroleum Co., Ltd. (53.1%); Nippon Oil (U.S.) Limited; Nippon Oil (Asia) Pte. Ltd. (Singapore); Nippon Petrochemicals Company, Ltd.; Nippon Oil Engineering and Construction Co., Ltd.; Nippon Hodo Co., Ltd. (56%); Nippon Oil (Australia) Pty. Ltd.; Nippon Oil Finance (Netherlands) B.V.; Nippon Oil Real Estate Company, Ltd.; Nippon Oil Trading Corporation; Nippon Oil Information Systems Company, Ltd.

PRINCIPAL COMPETITORS

Exxon Mobil Corporation; Idemitsu Kosan Co., Ltd.; Showa Shell Sekiyu K.K.

FURTHER READING

Abrahams, Paul. "Oil Groups Reveal Big Merger Deal." *Financial Times*, October 29, 1998, p. 27.

Aoto, Maki. "Nippon Mitsubishi Merges Units." *Asian Wall Street Journal*, February 8, 2002, p. M7.

Kumagai, Takeo. "Japan Merger Partners to Shut More Refining." *Platts Oilgram Price Report*, November 2, 2009, p. 1.

———. "Nippon Oil, Idemitsu to Team in Crude-Refining Operations." *Asian Wall Street Journal*, December 11, 2002, p. M3.

———. "Nippon Oil-Nippon Mining Merged Firm to Push for Resources Development." *Kyodo News International*, January 6, 2009.

———. "Nippon Oil to Process 70,000 b/d for ChinaOil." *Platts Oilgram Price Report*, April 3, 2008, p. 2.

"Nippon-Mitsubishi Merger Speeds Overhaul of Japanese Refining Marketing Industry." *Oil and Gas Journal*, March 1, 1999, pp. 23–26.

"Nippon Oil, Mitsubishi Oil Agree to Merge." *Oil and Gas Journal*, November 2, 1998.

"Refineries Strike Deal to Trim Capacity." *Nikkei Weekly*, December 16, 2002.

Timmermans, Jeffrey. "Chevron, Texaco to Sell Refinery Stake to Nippon Oil for Total of $1.98 Billion." *Wall Street Journal*, December 7, 1995, p. A11.

Uyehara, S. *The Industry and Trade of Japan*. London: P.S. King & Son, 1936.

Watanabe, Mika. "Alliance Should Boost Oil Firms' Profit: Nippon Mitsubishi, Cosmo Will Integrate Most Operations to Cut Cost." *Asian Wall Street Journal*, October 13, 1999, p. 4.

———. "Nippon Mitsubishi to Purchase Caltex's Remaining Koa Oil Shares." *Asian Wall Street Journal*, July 29, 1999, p. 4.

Norseland Inc.

———————— ■ ————————

1290 East Main Street
Stamford, Connecticut 06902-3555
U.S.A.
Telephone: (203) 324-5620
Fax: (203) 325-3189
Web site: http://www.norseland.com

Wholly Owned Subsidiary of Tine BA
Incorporated: 1978
Employees: 27
Sales: $200 million (2008 est.)
NAICS: 424430 Dairy Products (Except Dried or
    Canned) Merchant Wholesalers

■ ■ ■

Norseland Inc. is a wholly owned subsidiary of Tine BA, Norway's largest dairy products cooperative, comprising 24,000 Norwegian dairy farmer members. The company maintains its headquarters in Stamford, Connecticut, and regional sales offices in Baltimore, Boston, Dallas, Los Angeles, New York, and Montreal, Canada. Norseland is best known as the importer of Jarlsberg brand cheese, the top-selling specialty cheese in the United States, but the cheese is also produced under license at a pair of U.S. plants. The all-purpose cheese, good for cooking as well as snacking, is a cow's milk semisoft cheese, sold in 22-pound wheels, 10-pound loaves, and deli-slice packages. Norseland also offers Jarlsberg Lite in loaves and deli slices, featuring 50 percent less fat and 30 percent fewer calories. The company also offers Norwegian specialty cheeses, including Ridder, Ski-

Queen Gjetost, Snofrisk, and Ekte Gjetost.

Norseland represents cheeses from other parts of the world as well. It markets the goat's milk cheeses of Ontario, Canada's Woolrich Dairy. It offers the Spanish cheeses of García Baquero, made from cow's milk, goat's milk, and sheep's milk, including Spain's best known cheese, Gran Maestro D.O., produced from 100 percent sheep's milk. Norseland markets Dutch cheese from Old Amsterdam, makers of Holland's number one brand of mature cheese, Aged Matured Gouda. Gabriella of Italy provides a wide variety of hard and table artisan cheeses as well as grated cheeses, primarily produced in Sicily. Norseland also offers the Suprema brand of Italian grated and shredded Parmesan and Romano cheese used in pasta, pizza, salads, and soups.

JARLSBERG'S ORIGINS: 1956

The date of origin of Jarlsberg cheese is regarded as 1956, but in fact the seeds were planted a year earlier at the Dairy Institute at the Agricultural University of Norway. It was there in the autumn of 1955 that a dairy science graduate student named Per Sakshaug began conducting cheese-making experiments as part of his master's thesis, "Addition of Propionibacteria Culture to Cheese Milk." Sakshaug was investigating why in recent years it had become increasingly difficult to produce large eyes (holes) in Gouda cheese. For the previous 40 years, large-eyed Gouda had been Norway's most important cheese, making the inquiry highly relevant.

Sakshaug believed that propionibacteria, a gut bacteria, was important in the formation of eyes by creating pockets of carbon dioxide. He postulated that because of improvements in milking hygiene the amount of naturally occurring propionibacteria in the milking parlor had been reduced. The result was less propionibacteria in the cheese milk and smaller eyes in the Gouda. His hypothesis was that the addition of a pure culture of propionibacteria to the cheese milk following pasteurization would result in cheese with larger eyes. Because of the small sample size of his experiments, Sakshaug was unable to draw any general conclusions, but his work had shown enough possibilities that the staff at the Dairy Institute decided to pursue further investigations.

Professor Ole Martin Ystgaard, who had overseen Sakshaug's cheese-making experiments, headed the Dairy Institute. Ystgaard had supplied his student with the crucial propionibacteria culture that had been developed at Iowa State University, where Ystgaard had strong ties. A graduate of the Dairy College at the Agricultural University of Norway, Ystgaard had also earned a master of science degree from Iowa State in 1950. A year later he was named head of the Agricultural University's new Dairy Institute, which housed its own research dairy. This unit became fully outfitted in 1956, in time for Ystgaard to make use of it in the development of new cheeses that built upon his student's pioneering work.

JARLSBERG NAME ADOPTED: 1957

Ystgaard's cheese-making experiments led to the development of two cheeses, a small Swiss cheese, and a Gouda with larger eye formations. It soon became apparent that the latter was in fact a new cheese type that held commercial potential. The experimental cheese was sold at the Research Dairy's shop as "research cheese" or "extra cheese," and soon developed a following. The question of a suitable name was then considered. In 1957 the Jarlsberg name was adopted. According to Norseland information, the cheese was named after Count Vadel Jarlsberg, whose estate on the Oslo Fjord was located close to where the cheese was first manufactured.

The Dairy Institute began teaching commercial cheese makers how to produce the new cheese in 1957

and it became available to the public later that year. Development of the cheese continued until 1965. A number of Norwegian dairies would produce Jarlsberg cheese, the largest of which was the Norwegian Dairies Sales Association (Norkse Meieriers), Tine BA's predecessor and Norway's first dairy cooperative, with roots dating back to 1856. In 1928 it began exporting Norwegian dairy products. Thus, it was natural that Norwegian Dairies would also begin exporting Jarlsberg cheese.

A representative from Norwegian Dairies first showed Jarlsberg cheese to buyers in the United Kingdom in 1962. Later in the year a representative shared the product with his largest customer for brown whey cheese, a longtime Norwegian export. The new product was well received and exports to both the United Kingdom and United States began in 1963. Initially the product was distributed in North America by a subsidiary of Nestlé S.A. as part of the Norwegian cheeses offered by the specialty food division of the Swiss food giant. The U.S. market became so important that Norwegian Dairies accommodated a request made in the late 1960s to produce Jarlsberg in larger blocks, making them more suitable for the growing U.S. market for sliced cheese.

NORSELAND INC. FORMED: 1978

Norwegian Dairies placed a high price on Jarlsberg to avoid import quotas in the United States but still found a ready market for the popular cheese. Although a change in U.S. subsidies in 1976 forced a 30 percent price increase, Jarlsberg cheese continued to increase in sales. Only a quota restriction on cheese imports, imposed from 1976 to 1979, hindered the brand's growth. By this time, Nestlé had undergone a reorganization and another party began importing Jarlsberg into North America. According to a 2004 article in the *Stamford (Connecticut) Advocate*, a Greenwich entrepreneur "acquired the Jarlsberg business from Nestlé" and started Norseland Inc. The company, founded in 1978, would later become a Norwegian Dairies subsidiary.

Norseland continued to grow sales of Jarlsberg cheese in the 1980s. In 1988 it made a request of its corporate parent to further accommodate U.S. consumers by developing a low-fat version of the product. A similar demand was emerging in Norway, and steps were taken to produce a reduced-fat Jarlsberg. The initial product with a 16 percent fat content was introduced in Norway but did not fare well and was soon pulled from the shelves. A version made specifically for the U.S. market called Jarlsberg Lite was also introduced in 1989

KEY DATES

1956: Development of Jarlsberg cheese begins.
1963: Jarlsberg cheese is introduced in United States.
1978: Norseland Inc. is established in United States.
1991: David Brohel is named chief executive officer.
2002: Norseland's parent company changes its name to Tine BA.
2006: Brohel retires.

and enjoyed better success. Two years later U.S. regulators insisted that the fat content be reduced further in order for the product to retain "lite" status. Not only did Norwegian Dairies begin producing Jarlsberg cheese with a 13 percent fat content, it also began including vitamin A at the behest of the Americans.

The late 1980s also brought an executive, David Brohel, who would lead Norseland into the next century. Although he joined Norseland in 1989 as a vice president and became president and chief executive officer in 1991, Brohel was no stranger to Jarlsberg cheese. In the 1970s he served as the brand manager of Norwegian cheeses in Nestlé's specialty food division, which included Jarlsberg. Around the same time Jarlsberg was taken over by Norseland, Brohel left Nestlé to start his own food brokerage business, running it for the next decade before taking a position with Norseland.

Under Brohel's leadership, Norseland grew from a niche cheese importer with $45 million in annual sales to a major cheese importer with more than $200 million in annual sales. A key to his success was a quick recognition that the food industry was embarking on a period of consolidation, one in which supermarket chains and other large retailers would demand direct sales and the elimination of distributors. As a result, Brohel developed a long-term strategic plan that included significant investments in technology as well as marketing and advertising. In order to support these initiatives, Norseland would also have to increase sales volumes by adding now products. In 1990 Jarlsberg cheese accounted for 95 percent of Norseland's revenues.

NORSELAND BEGINS SELLING BOURSIN: 1993

To expand its product offerings, Norseland arranged in 1993 to become the exclusive marketing and sales agent

for Boursin, maker of Gournay cheese, which had been sold in the United States for about 30 years. Norseland was able to grow sales to new heights. Also in the mid-1990s, Norseland attempted to diversify beyond cheese when it introduced a Jarlsberg cheese-flavored bagel crisp. Although U.S. consumers did not balk at a premium price for Jarlsberg cheese, they were not willing to pay extra for a Jarlsberg bagel crisp. It was the last time Bohel and Norseland would attempt to sell a non-cheese item.

To expand its slate of imported cheese brands, Norseland formed a series of strategic alliances. In 1996 it reached an agreement to become the exclusive marketing and sales agent for Laura Chenel's Chevre and Laura Chenel's Select Norwegian Chevre, commencing in January 1998. On June 2000 another important alliance went into effect when Norseland began representing the Saga and Blue Castello brands of Tholstrup Cheese USA.

There were other changes as the new century dawned. Jarlsberg cheese began to be produced in the United States under a license agreement. Also of note, Norseland's parent company changed its name to Tine BA in 2002. As he turned 60 Bohel introduced a succession plan to have someone ready to replace him as chief executive when he retired upon turning 65 in the autumn of 2006. Succeeding him was John Sullivan, a longtime Norseland employee who had risen through the ranks and was familiar with all aspects of the business. For his efforts on behalf of Norseland and the Norwegian dairy industry, the American Bohel was named Officer of the Royal Norwegian Order of Merit.

NEW PRODUCTS ADDED

Brohel left behind a company that was poised for further growth. In 2007 it renewed efforts to sell the Norwegian Snofrisk brand of cheese in the U.S. market. In that same year, Norseland forged a strategic alliance with Woolwich Dairy of Canada to carry its brands of goat's milk cheeses. Starting in January 2008 Norseland began selling the Old Amsterdam brand of Dutch cheese in an alliance with Westland Kaasexport B.V. A month later Norseland began representing the Spanish cheeses of García Baquero S.A. In May 2008 another strategic alliance was established with Lotito Foods, Inc., to sell the Gabriella of Italy, Lotito, and Suprema di Avellino brands of Italian grated and shredded cheeses. With a diverse slate of imported specialty cheeses, and more likely to follow, Norseland appeared to be well positioned for ongoing growth.

Ed Dinger

PRINCIPAL COMPETITORS

Atalanta Corporation; DCI Cheese Company; Dominique Delugeau.

FURTHER READING

Abrahamsen, Roger K., et al. *Jarlsberg Cheese History and Development.* Dairy Institute at the Agricultural University of Norway, 2006.

Delia-Loyle, Donna. "More Cheese, Please." *Global Trade*, November 1990, p. 39.

Fishman-Lapin, Julie. "CEO to Hand Over Helm at Stamford, Connecticut, Cheese Importer Norseland Inc." *Stamford Advocate*, December 23, 2005.

Maar, Nancy T. "Jarlsberg's Stamford, Conn., Importer Eyes U.S. Growth." *Stamford Advocate*, June 20, 2004.

"Norseland Incorporated." *News of Norway*, Issue 7, 1995.

OC Oerlikon Corporation AG

———■———

Churerstrasse 120
Pfäffikon, 8808
Switzerland
Telephone: (41 58) 360-9696
Fax: (41 58) 360-9196
Web site: http://www.oerlikon.com

Public Company
Incorporated: 1906 as Schweizerische Werkzeugm-
aschinenfabrik Oerlikon (SWO) AG
Employees: 16,369
Sales: CHF 2.88 billion ($2.65 billion) (2009)
Stock Exchanges: SIX Swiss Exchange
Ticker Symbol: OERL
NAICS: 551112 Holding Companies

■ ■ ■

OC Oerlikon Management AG is the holding company for the Swiss-based Oerlikon Group, a diversified industrial conglomerate with a special focus on innovative high-tech solutions in textile manufacturing, thin-film coating, automotive drive and gear systems, vacuum propulsion, aerospace, solar energy systems, and nanotechnology. Oerlikon is organized in six divisions, including Oerlikon Solar, Oerlikon Coating, Oerlikon Vacuum, Oerlikon Textile, Oerlikon Drive Systems, and Oerlikon Advanced Technologies. With more than 150 subsidiaries in 36 countries, OC Oerlikon generates the majority of its sales in Europe, the United States, and Asia. The Russian investment firm Renova Industries

Ltd. holds roughly 45 percent in the publicly traded company.

1906–24: MACHINE TOOL MAKER CHANGES HANDS

The early roots of OC Oerlikon go back to Daverio, Siewerdt and Giesker, a machine tool building company which in 1872 moved to Oerlikon, a small town north of Zurich. Renamed Maschinenfabrik Oerlikon (MFO) 10 years later, the company extended its business activities to electro-technical products, which over time became MFO's main focus. In 1906 the machine tool division, including about 180 staff, was transferred to the newly established Schweizerische Werkzeugm-aschinenfabrik Oerlikon (SWO) AG, a stock corporation.

With industrialization in full swing, the company manufactured a broad variety of roughly 100 different machine tools, mainly milling and drilling machines, a selection of which was also exported to other countries. In 1910 SWO designed the first Swiss airplane motor, which was also built at the company. Five years later the company began with the mass production of the so-called Oerlikon Lathe, an SWO construction and design.

Despite the high demand for machine tools during World War I, SWO found itself struggling financially during the postwar recession of the early 1920s. In 1923 the German machine tool manufacturer Magdeburger Werkzeugmaschinenfabrik acquired the company, which was renamed Werkzeugmaschinenfabrik Oerlikon AG (WO). One year later the new parent company sent

COMPANY PERSPECTIVES

We make it possible for our customers to be successful in economic terms with new technical solutions that go to the limits of what is feasible. One focus of innovation at Oerlikon is the area of "Clean Technologies," which will allow us to tackle the environmental challenges of the 21st century with clean and forward-looking technologies. *Mission:* To put the concentrated technological knowledge of the entire Group to work so that we can continuously reinvent ourselves, develop new applications and tap new markets: that is the Oerlikon DNA. The tightly knit structure of the individual business units allows us to capitalize on the synergies that exist within the Group. Organization structures and processes are simple and streamlined with clear responsibilities. Our highly-qualified employees put all of their talent and passion into satisfying the individual needs of Oerlikon customers.

Emil Georg Bührle to reorganize WO's business activities and to put the company on a sound footing. Bührle soon realized that machine tool building alone was not sufficient to secure long-term profitability and began to look for additional promising market opportunities.

1924: GUN MANUFACTURING BECOMES MAIN ACTIVITY

The opportunity arose in the following year when WO was offered to take over the financially struggling Maschinenbau AG Seebach (Semag), a Swiss subsidiary of the German steel products manufacturer Edelstahlwerk Becker located in nearby Seebach. One of Edelstahlwerk Becker's products was the so-called Becker Cannon, a gun of a 20-millimeter (mm) caliber designed by the German engineer Reinhold Becker that was developed and used during World War I. After the treaty of Versailles forbade German companies the production of such weapons, Edelstahlwerk Becker transferred these activities to the Swiss Semag. Bührle, a World War I veteran, recognized the commercial potential of the Becker Cannon in a conflict-ridden world. In 1924 WO acquired the patents and manufacturing rights for the Becker Cannon, including ammunition, as well as the production equipment and the employees from Semag. In the following two decades, gun manufacturing became the company's main business.

When WO's parent company Magdeburger Werkzeugmaschinenfabrik experienced a severe crisis in 1927, Bührle, with the support of his father-in-law Ernst Schalk, a banker in Magdeburg, acquired a minority share in WO. Two years later he raised his stake in the company to a majority. In 1936 Bührle took over control of WO when he acquired the remaining company stock, and transformed the business into the limited partnership Werkzeugmaschinenfabrik Oerlikon Bührle & Co. This step gave Bührle the unrestricted power of decision for the company. The original stock corporation continued to exist as a holding company and was renamed Verwaltungsgesellschaft der Werkzeugmaschinenfabrik Oerlikon.

Based on the Becker Cannon's principal design, WO developed a series of significantly improved designs with performance features adjusted to a variety of uses. Aimed by a gunner and fixated on flexible mounts, one of the main advantages of the 20-mm Oerlikon gun was its secure lock mechanism that withstood heavy blow-back and guaranteed its proper functioning even under difficult combat conditions. Newly developed models with different rates of fire were adjusted to be used as antitank and antiaircraft weapons that could be used on the ground or mounted on naval ships.

In the 1920s, the first Oerlikon guns were shipped to Finland, Mexico, Colombia, Bolivia, and Peru. A big breakthrough followed in 1929 when China placed an order for 120 Oerlikon cannons as well as large amounts of ammunition worth about CHF 1 million. All in all, WO exported about 250 guns in the 1920s. By the 1930s armament production had become Oerlikon's main business activity. With few restrictions by the Swiss government, 20-mm Oerlikon cannons were exported to various countries such as the Baltic states, Austria, Czechoslovakia, Greece, Turkey, and the Ethiopian Empire.

WORLD WAR II ERA

As the world's main powers began to spend massively on rearmament in the second half of the 1930s, WO cooperated with or granted production licenses to manufacturers in France, Great Britain, Italy, Germany, and Japan. Two of the most successful models of that period were the 20-mm Oerlikon FF series to be mounted on the wings of fighter aircraft, which was introduced in 1935, and the Oerlikon SS gun launched in 1938, which was widely used as an antiaircraft gun by the Allied forces' navies, including the U.S. Navy, during World War II.

As a result of the success of the 20-mm Oerlikon antiaircraft line of guns, the company evolved during

KEY DATES

1906: Schweizerische Werkzeugmaschinenfabrik Oerlikon is founded in Switzerland.

1924: The company acquires the patents for the Becker Cannon and starts manufacturing guns.

1946: Oerlikon Bührle takes over research company Contraves; thin-film manufacturer Gerätebauanstalt is founded.

1957: The company ventures into vacuum technology.

1973: The new holding Oerlikon-Bührle is listed on the Swiss Stock Exchange.

1976: Balzers AG becomes part of Oerlikon-Bührle.

1994: The company acquires vacuum technology specialist Leybold.

2005: The company returns to profits after restructuring under new management.

2006: The company is renamed OC Oerlikon Corporation.

2008: The Russian Renova Industries becomes Oerlikon's new main shareholder; the company sells its optics division.

the 1930s to become the largest private Swiss armament manufacturer by far, with more than 2,000 employees, according to Swiss historian Daniel Heller in *Zwischen Unternehmertum, Politik und Überleben*. WO's main customers in the late 1930s, including France, England, the Netherlands, and the Swiss army, placed large orders worth an estimated CHF 250 million. In addition to the Oerlikon gun, the company manufactured light machine guns as well as different types of ammunition.

After the capitulation of France in mid-1940, and with permission of the Swiss authorities, WO began to supply Germany, Italy, and Romania with guns and ammunition. According to Heller's research, the company delivered more than 7,000 cannons as well as large amounts of ammunition and spare parts worth approximately CHF 543 million to these countries between 1940 and 1944. Altogether, Oerlikon-Bührle's annual weapons sales increased from roughly CHF 7.4 million in 1937–38 to over CHF 113 million in 1943–44. The number of employees reached its peak with more than 3,700 in 1941. However, after the Swiss authorities issued an export ban on weapons to nations involved in the war in 1944, sales declined rapidly to

CHF 15 million in 1945–46, and the company's workforce shrank to roughly 1,600.

Soon after he had taken over WO in 1936, Bührle started developing a variety of business areas to secure the company's long-term future by diminishing its dependence on the highly competitive and volatile markets for machine tools and guns. WO's machine tool business suffered a severe slump in the early 1930s but was carried on throughout the decade. During World War II, the machine tool division continued to improve its line of lathing machines and launched cutting-edge models of radial drilling machines and machines for manufacturing spiral bevel gear.

In 1938 the company acquired Citogène, a manufacturer of welding rods, which became WO's welding technology division. In December 1939 Bührle founded aircraft and aircraft parts manufacturer Pilatus Flugzeugwerke AG based in Stans. However, the company did not produce profits until after World War II. In the early 1940s WO acquired two Swiss yarn and textile manufacturers, and ventured into hotels, and later insurance and real estate. The company's own line of products was expanded to include brake valves for railway cars, stocking looms, and office machines.

In 1946 the WO holding acquired Contraves, a research company in the area of antiaircraft technology cofounded by Bührle in 1936. In the same year Bührle together with physicist Max Auwärter and Prince Franz Josef II established Gerätebau-Anstalt, a company that developed equipment for the industrial application of the then-evolving thin-film technology. Based in Balzers, Liechtenstein, the company, which was later renamed Balzers, became one of Oerlikon Bührle's main business activities.

Another important strategic step was taken in 1957 when Balzers ventured into vacuum technology, another potential growth market. The company built a manufacturing plant for production systems to be able to offer all the necessary installations and equipment along with the technologies it developed. For example, for Japanese camera manufacturers such as Nikon and Canon, Balzers developed the technologies for generating antireflex layers and built the production equipment as well.

After E. Bührle's death in 1956, his son Dietrich took over the company and continued with WO's diversification strategy. By 1968 when the company was transformed into the stock corporation Werkzeugmaschinenfabrik Oerlikon-Bührle AG, the conglomerate consisted of roughly 100 subsidiaries. Its main areas of business were machine tools, defense, railway brakes, plastics machines, program controls, and other industrial products.

1973: GOING PUBLIC

In 1973 the newly established holding company Oerlikon-Bührle Holding AG (OBH) took over Werkzeugmaschinenfabrik Oerlikon-Bührle AG and its subsidiaries from the Bührle family, and was listed on the Swiss Stock Exchange. In 1975 Contraves was awarded a contract to supply fairings for the European launch vehicle/carrier rocket Ariane, which became another new business area. The company became a regular supplier for the European Space Agency and later also for NASA.

Oerlikon-Bührle's defense division thrived as well in the 1970s, thanks to lucrative contracts with Middle Eastern countries, according to the *Economist* on February 29, 1992. However, the costly development of an advanced antiaircraft and antitank guided missile system called ADATS resulted in huge losses, so the magazine reported. In 1989 Contraves was merged with Oerlikon-Bührle's defense division to form Oerlikon Contraves.

In 1976 Balzers AG was integrated into the Oerlikon-Bührle concern. One year later OBH acquired a majority stake in shoe and fashion accessories manufacturer C.F. Bally AG. In the second half of the 1970s Oerlikon-Bührle evolved as one of Switzerland's largest industrial conglomerates. At the height of its growth in 1980 the company employed a workforce of 37,000. However, in the middle of the decade the broadly diversified company started experiencing serious problems when the profits of its technology divisions were eaten up by the significant losses produced by its defense and consumer goods divisions. By the end of the 1980s Oerlikon-Bührle was deeply in debt.

RESTRUCTURING AFTER CRISIS

After 34 years, Dietrich Bührle resigned from his leading position at Oerlikon-Bührle in 1990. In the following years the company continued to pursue the strategy of a diversified industrial conglomerate, but focused on a number of main areas, including technology with Balzers, Oerlikon, and Contraves; consumer products with Bally and the textiles division; and services, including hotels and real estate management. On the other hand, the company sold its insurance subsidiary, its welding, pressing, and stamping plant divisions, among others, while the defense activities were cut back.

In the mid-1990s SBO continued to sharpen its focus on technology. A major step was the acquisition of the German Leybold Heraeus Group, SBO's main competitor in the area of vacuum technology, in 1994. Leybold was merged with Balzers to form Balzers & Leybold, a worldwide leader in thin-film and vacuum technology. On the other hand, the company disposed of its hotel and textile products subsidiaries and its CD manufacturing machines division. In 1997 SBO's shareholders were paid a dividend for the first time in 10 years. However, sales and profits continued to stagnate in some of the company's major divisions.

Two years later the decision was made to dissolve the conglomerate. Oerlikon-Bührle sold shoe manufacturer Bally as well as its defense subsidiary Oerlikon-Contraves and its real estate subsidiary Oerlikon-Bührle Immobilien. Finally, in 2000 the company sold aircraft manufacturer Pilatus and its Large Area Coating division, followed by the sale of its Leybold Optics division one year later.

The acquisition of the U.S.-based semiconductor products manufacturer Plasma-Therm in 2000 marked the company's entry into another high-tech industry. To communicate the strategic reorientation toward information technology, the company was renamed Unaxis AG. In the same year the company took over Esec, a manufacturer of production equipment for computer chips. However, the new strategy failed to produce the expected growth.

TURNAROUND IN 2005

The turnaround happened in the second half of 2005. After the general shareholder meeting appointed a new top management team to get the company out of the red, Unaxis returned to profits within a year. In addition to strict cost-cutting measures, the company was managed as one unit for the first time in its history, and not as a group of relatively independent companies. In 2006 the company was renamed OC Oerlikon Corporation and, again, started investing in a number of new business activities to get back onto the path to growth.

With a focus on cutting-edge, research-based technologies, Oerlikon established a new business unit for solar energy applications in 2006. The company invested in the development of thin-film solar cells and was the first manufacturer worldwide offering turnkey manufacturing plants to produce them. Oerlikon also developed new generations of high-performance Blue-ray optical storage discs, Biochips for the cost-effective analysis of biomaterial, and highly productive layer application systems for the automotive industry.

MAJOR ACQUISITION, NEW OWNERSHIP, FINANCIAL CRISIS

In 2007 Oerlikon took over Swiss textile machine manufacturer Saurer AG based in Arbon. Founded in 1853 as an iron foundry by mechanic and entrepreneur Franz Saurer, the company emerged as a major manufacturer of commercial trucks in the first half of the 20th century which were exported to many countries, and built under license in Austria, Yugoslavia, France, and the United States. In addition, Saurer was a world leader in the development of diesel engines. However, with the demand for Saurer motor vehicles decreasing significantly in the early 1980s, the company finally abandoned this business branch.

In the 1990s Saurer focused on textile machine manufacturing and became one of the world market leaders with about EUR 1.6 billion in sales, and approximately 9,000 employees in 2007. Roughly one-third of the company's revenues, however, were generated by Graziano Transmissioni, a manufacturer of special gear and transmission systems based in Turin, Italy. After the takeover by Oerlikon, Saurer was integrated into the concern.

After the Russian investment holding Renova Industries Ltd. had acquired a stake of almost 40 percent in OC Oerlikon, Vladimir Kuznetsov became the company's new chairman in 2008. In the wake of the global financial crisis, the company continued to streamline its business activities and sold Balzers optics division as well as Esec. In 2010 Oerlikon raised an estimated CHF 300 million in a series of three capital increases after generating losses of over CHF 1 billion in the two preceding years combined. With a strategic focus on cutting-edge technology solutions for textile manufacturing, thin-film coating, automotive drive systems, vacuum technology, solar energy, transmission components for wind turbines and electric motor vehicles, and advanced nanotechnology, Oerlikon saw itself as a technology leader in key markets of the future.

Evelyn Hauser

PRINCIPAL SUBSIDIARIES

SAC Saurer Automotive Components B.V. (Netherlands); Oerlikon Graziano Group S.p.A. (Italy); OC Oerlikon Balzers AG (Liechtenstein); Oerlikon Balzers Coating India Ltd.; Oerlikon Balzers Coating (Suzhou) Co. Ltd. (China); OC Oerlikon Management AG; Oerlikon SB Holdings Arbon AG; Aktiengesellschaft Adolph Saurer; Oerlikon Deutschland Holding GmbH (Germany); Oerlikon France Holding SAS; Oerlikon IT Solutions AG; Oerlikon Leybold Vacuum Taiwan Ltd.; Oerlikon Nihon Balzers Coating Co. Ltd. (Japan); Oerlikon Solar Holding AG; Oerlikon USA Holding Inc.; Saurer AG; Oerlikon Textile Components Far East Ltd. (Hong Kong); Oerlikon Textile Components Singapore Pte. Ltd.; Oerlikon Textile do Brasil Máquinas Ltda.; Oerlikon Tekstil Middle East Tekstil Makinalari Dis Ticaret A.S. (Turkey); Unaxis IT (UK) Ltd., Barnwood/UK; InnoDisc AG.

PRINCIPAL COMPETITORS

Bosch Solar Energy AG; GETRAG Corporate Group; Magna International Inc.; Rieter Holding Ltd.; Toyota Industries Corporation.

FURTHER READING

Heller, Daniel. *Zwischen Unternehmertum, Politik und Überleben: Emil G. Bührle und die Werkzeugmaschinenfabrik Oerlikon, Bührle & Co. 1924 bis 1945*. Frauenfeld, Switzerland: Huber & Co. AG, 2002.

Murphy, Robert, and Vicki M. Young. "Swiss Firm to Sell Bally to Texas Pacific Group." *WWD*, August 31, 1999, p. 2.

"Neues Saurer-Museum in Arbon TG Arbons Industriegeschichte kommt is Museum." *SDA*, April 23, 2008.

"Oerlikon-Buhrle Sells PBN." *Interavia Business & Technology*, 1998, p. 12.

"Oerlikon Solar and Tokyo Electron Join Thin Film PV Forces." *Asia Business Newsweekly*, March 17, 2009, p. 14.

"Those Who Live by the Sword…: Oerlikon-Buhrle." *Economist*, February 29, 1992, p. 77.

Wicks, John. "Bally to the Fore." *swissBusiness*, September–October 1993, p. 4.

Wipf, Hans Ulrich, et al. *From a Small Eastern Swiss Company to an International Technology Group*. Baden, Germany: hier + jetzt Verlag für Kultur und Geschichte GmbH, 2003.

Odlo Sports Group AG

Bösch 47
Hünenberg, CH-6331
Switzerland
Telephone: (41 41) 785-7070
Fax: (41 41) 785-7077
Web site: http://www.odlo.com

Joint Stock Corporation
Founded: 1946 as Odlo Fabrikker A/S
Incorporated: 1946 as Odlo Fabrikker A/S
Employees: 650
Sales: CHF 159.6 million ($146 million) (2009)
NAICS: 315221 Men's and Boys' Cut and Sew Underwear and Nightwear Manufacturing; 315231 Women's and Girls' Cut and Sew Lingerie, Loungewear, and Nightwear Manufacturing; 315228 Men's and Boys' Cut and Sew Other Outerwear Manufacturing; 315239 Women's and Girls' Cut and Sew Other Outerwear Manufacturing; 315299 All Other Cut and Sew Apparel Manufacturing

■ ■ ■

Odlo Sports Group AG is a leading European manufacturer of functional sportswear based in Hünenberg, Switzerland, and holds the number one market position in sports underwear. Odlo offers a full range of year-round apparel for men, women, and children, which are custom designed for different kinds of sports. The company's product line includes underpants and undershirts, sports bras, shirts and pants, vests and jackets, gloves, and hats that are made of highly sophisticated synthetic materials. Some of the company's most successful collections are Nordic Walking, Running, Bike, Outdoors, and X-Country.

The company's apparel is manufactured mostly in Odlo's production plants in Portugal and Romania, but also in Asia. Sold under the ODLO brand name in more than 20 countries, the lion's share of company's sales is generated in Germany, Switzerland, France, Austria, Belgium, and the Netherlands. In addition to the roughly 3,000 points of sale, mostly sports specialty stores, that carry ODLO, the company runs more than 20 ODLO stores, about half of them franchises, in large cities all across Europe. Norwegian investment firm Herkules Capital owns a majority stake in the company.

SMALL KNITWEAR FACTORY SET UP IN 1946

When Norwegian entrepreneur Odd Lofterød Sr. founded the knitwear company Odlo Fabrikker A/S in 1946, he had no formal training in the industry. However, having worked in a factory for textile machine tools, the 30-year-old sports fanatic had gathered enough technical knowledge to be able to operate such machines. Lofterød Sr. bought a knitting and sewing machine from his former employer and set up his own textile production. In the same year he officially registered the brand name ODLO, a combination of the first two letters of his first and last names. With raw materials in short supply in postwar Norway, Lofterød Sr. started manufacturing women's underwear in 1947.

Lofterød's son, Odd Roar Lofterød Jr., who was born in that year, developed a strong interest in sports and became a member of Norway's national speed skating junior team. When the young sportsman complained about getting cold too easily in the woolen pants worn by speed skaters at the time, his father decided to help. Using, a highly elastic, textured synthetic filament yarn made of Helanca fibers, Lofterød Sr. designed new track pants for his son. During a training camp, Lofterød Jr.'s unique pants were not only admired by his peers, but also by some top athletes who asked Lofterød Jr. to get them a pair for themselves.

COMMERCIAL SUCCESS WITH FUNCTIONAL SPORTSWEAR AFTER 1963

The success of Lofterød's track pants was the cornerstone for his company's sustained growth as a manufacturer of functional sportswear. The next major step in that direction followed in 1963 when the company founder developed the prototype of a sports suit for cross-country skiers and speed skaters. Made of Helanca fibers, the elastic and heat-storing suit became an instant success. During the winter Olympic Games in Innsbruck, Austria, in 1964 the Norwegian national winter sports team was wearing the new ODLO suit.

In the following years Lofterød's company greatly expanded its line of functional sportswear. At the Olympic Games in the winter of 1972 in Sapporo, Japan, not only the Norwegians, but 25 national teams competed for the Olympic medals in ODLO suits. The launch of the first collection of synthetic sports underwear under the label ODLO Thermic in 1973 was another major milestone for the company. The new product line was designed to ideally supplement the company's upper wear. Unlike the usual cotton or wool undershirts and underpants, it kept the body dry by transporting body perspiration away from the skin. In 1979 Odd Lofterød Sr. retired and his son, a passionate

speed skater, cross-country skier, and sailor, took over the company.

THREE-LAYER SYSTEM LAUNCHED IN 1987

Eight years after taking over the business from his father, in 1986, Odd Lofterød Jr. moved company headquarters to Switzerland where Odlo International AG, a joint stock corporation, was established. Just as his father did, Odd Lofterød Jr. continuously worked on improving the company's product lines to stay ahead of the competition. In 1987 Odlo introduced a major innovation, the so-called Athletic Clothing System. The material of the new product line combined three different layers in one suit. The first layer transported moisture away from the skin, the second layer regulated the temperature, and the third, protective layer shielded the body from wind and cold or rain.

Based on this revolutionary principle, the company greatly expanded its product range in the late 1980s and continued on that path in the 1990s. New items were developed for different kinds of sports to meet the needs of hobby athletes as well as for world-class professionals, for men and women as well as for children. Each piece of clothing was developed "from the inside out" with the idea in mind that an athlete should feel good in his skin to really enjoy his sport. In 1994 Odlo launched two completely new collections of functional sportswear, one for running and one for outdoors.

GEOGRAPHIC EXPANSION AND ACQUISITIONS AFTER 1990

In addition to keeping the pipeline of innovations well filled, Odd Lofterød Jr. and his business partners focused on expanding into new geographical markets. In the 1990s Odlo established subsidiaries in Germany, Austria, Switzerland, and France. Sales offices were established in many other Western European countries, such as Italy, Greece, the United Kingdom, Spain, Belgium, the Netherlands, Norway, Denmark, and Finland. In 1992 the company set up an additional production plant in Portugal, followed by a new factory in Romania in 2004. The company also ventured into Eastern Europe, including Poland, the Czech Republic, Slovakia, Slovenia, Russia, and Ukraine, and into Hong Kong and Korea in Asia.

At the end of the 1990s, Odlo Sports Group AG, a new holding company for the expanding group, was founded in Switzerland. Lofterød's business partner Didi Serena's marketing and distribution firm Trisport also became part of the Odlo group. To reenter the

KEY DATES

1946: Odlo Fabrikker A/S is founded in Norway by Odd Lofterød Sr.

1963: The company founder develops a functional sports suit for cross-country skiers and speed skaters.

1973: Synthetic sports underwear collection ODLO Thermic is launched.

1986: Company headquarters are moved to Switzerland; Odlo International AG is established.

1987: The three-layer Athletic Clothing System is introduced.

2002: Odlo launches the first line of synthetic underwear with odor-suppressing silver ions.

2010: The company is acquired by Norwegian investment firm Herkules Capital.

Scandinavian market, Odlo took over Norwegian cross-country skiing and outdoors sports apparel manufacturer Bona Ratio Sport, including the well-known runner's brand Bjørn Dæhlie, in 2000, according to Ursula Pfleger-Edel in *TextilWirtschaft*, on February 17 of that year.

The company also acquired the German alpine sports clothing firm Gentic Mountain Wear, and the Norwegian brand Kjus Systems Skiwear. Both brands, however, as well as Trisport were sold in the second half of the decade, after Serena had left the company. Odlo's plans to expand into the United States and Canada were also put on hold. Instead, the company focused on strengthening its original brand.

FOCUS ON MARKETING AFTER 2000

As more and more competitors, from brand-name lingerie manufacturers to large retail chains, entered the promising growth market of functional sportswear and underwear, Odlo launched a comprehensive re-branding campaign in the early 2000s. With a modernized logo and the new slogan "passion for sports," ODLO was positioned as the brand made by sports enthusiast for sports enthusiast. With a special focus on public relations, the company put together the Odlo Functionality Team, a group of selected top athletes in Odlo's core sports disciplines, such as Norwegian cross-country skier Bjørn Dæhlie, Swiss mountain biking world champion Thomas Frischknecht, and the winner of the Olympic

gold medal in triathlon, Swiss athlete Brigitte McMahon, who tested and helped improve the desired product characteristics.

A second major focus of Odlo's new strategy, the company intensified its marketing and promotion activities at the point of sale. The company's slimmed-down and restructured product range was presented in four basic lines that were named Cool, Light, Warm, and X-Warm for the different temperatures in which the clothes were worn, and enhanced by a color-coded packaging system. Instead of perfectly styled models, the company's posters and ads showed sportsmen in action, such as sweaty joggers or mountain bikers with muddy faces, to communicate authenticity, simplicity, and passion for sports.

At a major trade show in Munich in 2003, Odlo built a winter sports arena right on the exhibition grounds and hosted a live competition between hobby athletes and top professionals in cross-country skiing, Nordic walking, and other disciplines. In addition, Odlo launched *Passion*, a 30-page biannual customer magazine with a print run of 500,000, which was distributed at the points of sale. The company also printed inserts, flyers that were placed in special interest magazines and newspapers. Moreover, Odlo organized seminars for some 5,000 sales clerks from stores carrying the brand, and informed them about the company's latest products.

PRODUCT INNOVATIONS FOR THE 21ST CENTURY

While Odlo refined its marketing and expanded its sales network during the first decade of the 21st century, the company continued to invest heavily in research and development. As a result, the company launched a constant stream of new and innovative products. To tackle the problem of body odor, Odlo introduced the first line of odor-suppressing synthetic underwear in 2002. The new material was made of a new fiber that contained silver ions which had an odor-suppressing effect. Two years later, all of the company's items contained the new fiber called Effect by ODLO.

Two years later the company introduced its first Nordic Walking collection to tap this new growth market. In 2004 Odlo launched Just One, a double-layer T-shirt designed to regulate the athlete's body temperature in a hot summer climate. The company's next innovation was Cubic, a new ultralight synthetic material with a cubical structure that optimized body temperature regulation. Used in Odlo's new underwear collections, it received a number of industry awards. Also in 2006 the company received the MedTech Award for the concept of a revolutionary shirt with in-built sensors that could be used to produce electrocardiograms, which was developed together with an interdisciplinary team of researchers.

In the later years of the decade Odlo continued to expand its product range. In 2007 the company launched its first comprehensive collection for children, including, underwear, upper wear, and outdoors items. In the following year Odlo introduced Evolution Light, a new line of functional sports underwear, and a new range of sports bras. By the end of the decade the company's range of products had grown to a year-round line of functional sports men's, women's, and children's apparel, custom designed to meet the needs of hobby sports enthusiast as well as professional athletes.

OWNERSHIP CHANGES IN 2006

In addition to intensified marketing and new product development, Odlo significantly strengthened its presence at the point of sale. To make the ODLO brand more visible, the company began to set up shop-in-shop systems with a broad variety of items on display in core markets such as Germany, Austria, and Switzerland. Moreover, Odlo decided to set up its own stores. As Dieterich noted in *TextilWirtschaft*, on July 11, 2002, by that year, the company had installed about 35 shop-in-shops as well as a handful of ODLO stores in France, Switzerland, and Germany, all of which were managed by specialty retailers who had worked with the company for many years.

In 2006 Odlo was taken over by TowerBrook Capital Partners, a private-equity firm based in the United States and the United Kingdom, which acquired a majority stake in the company. Two years later TowerBrook secured an $87 million refinancing deal for Odlo to restructure the company's debt, and to finance its further expansion, as reported by *PrivateEquityOnline.com* on September 29, 2008. Having secured the necessary financing, Odlo invested massively in new shop-in-shops, and opened additional ODLO outlets.

In the later years of the decade, Odlo's sales continued to rise, if not at the above 20 percent annual growth rates of the 1990s. Annual sales of the ODLO product line rose from roughly CHF 100 million in 2001 to about CHF 160 million by 2009, while the company's workforce roughly doubled. In April 2009, Odd Lofterød Jr., who had worked at the company for 30 years, retired from the day-to-day business and was succeeded by the company's former head of marketing,

Andreas Kessler. By then, ODLO products were offered at more than 3,000 sales points worldwide, mainly in the specialist sports trade, with roughly 900 of them equipped with shop-in-shop systems.

On May 5, 2010, the company announced that Norwegian investment firm Herkules Capital had acquired a majority share in Odlo, including Tower-Brook's stake in the company. The remaining shares were held by Lofterød Jr. and other Odlo top executives. In the same year ODLO's functional suit by Ole Einar Björndalen, the world's most successful biathlete at the time, won the renowned international Red Dot design award. Optimistic about the future of the company's prospects in a promising growth market, Odlo set its sights on strengthening the company's position as a technology leader, and at conquering new geographic markets.

Evelyn Hauser

PRINCIPAL SUBSIDIARIES

ODLO (Schweiz) AG (Switzerland); ODLO Sports GmbH (Germany); ODLO Österreich GmbH (Austria); ODLO France SAS (Frankreich); ODLO Sportswear NV (Netherlands); ODLO Sportswear NV (Belgium).

PRINCIPAL COMPETITORS

adidas AG; Falke KG; Helly Hansen AS, Haglöfs Scandinavia AB; Jack Wolfskin Ausrüstung für Draussen GmBH & Co. KGaA; Löffler GmbH; Medico sports fashion GmbH; Patagonia, Inc.; Salomon SAS; VF Corporation.

FURTHER READING

Dieterich, Elke. "Odlo: Voellig ungeschminkt; Schweizerischer Sportwäschehersteller mit neuem Markenimage." *Textil-Wirtschaft*, July 11, 2002.

Michaelis, Karin. "Draussen vor der Tür." *Werben und Verkaufen*, November 18, 2004.

"Norway/Switzerland: Herkules Capital Acquires Odlo." *Dagens Næringsliv*, May 5, 2010.

Pfleger-Edel, Ursula. "Odlo uebernimmt Gentic und Bona Ratio; 15% jaehrliches Wachstum angepeilt, Nordamerika im Visier." *TextilWirtschaft*, February 17, 2000.

"TowerBrook Executes CHF87m Odlo Refinancing." *PrivateEquityOnline.com*, September 29, 2008.

Pacific Aerospace &
Electronics, Inc.

434 Olds Station Road
Wenatchee, Washington 98801-5975
U.S.A.
Telephone: (509) 667-9600
Fax: (509) 667-9696
Web site: http://www.pacaero.com

Wholly Owned Subsidiary of Souriau Holding SAS
Incorporated: 1996
Employees: 210
Sales: $30 million (2009 est.)
NAICS: 334419 Other Electronic Component
   Manufacturing

■ ■ ■

Based in Wenatchee, Washington, Pacific Aerospace &
Electronics, Inc. (PA&E), is a onetime high-flying supplier to aviation giant Boeing Company. A prolonged
slump in the aerospace industry that reduced PA&E to
penny stock status and led to its eventual sale to French
company Souriau Holding SAS has resulted in a
broadened approach. Offering engineering design, testing, and manufacturing capabilities, PA&E serves four
sectors: defense, space, medical, and commercial.

The company provides interconnect systems and
hermetic sealing solutions used in combat aircraft and
other applications for the defense market. PA&E serves
the space market with microelectronic packages,
hermetic connectors, and electromagnetic interference
(EMI) filters that are used in communication satellites as
well as in the space shuttle orbiters and International

Space Station. PA&E has also made its hermetic seals
available to the medical market, where they are used in
implantable devices. Additionally, the company produces
other medical implant components. For the commercial
sector, PA&E designs and manufactures EMI filters and
hermetic connectors, housings, and microelectronic
packages for use in a variety of aviation, energy, and
telecommunications applications.

ORIGINS

PA&E grew out of a company founded in Mission
Viejo, California, in 1976 by James Kyle. Known as
Medical Components Corp., it manufactured hermetic
feedthroughs for pacemakers and other implantable
devices using Kyle's patented Kyroflex polycrystalline
ceramic. In 1978 Kyle acquired Petroleum Components
Corp. and began manufacturing harsh-environment
connectors for down-hole well logging instruments.
Medical Components moved to Roseburg, Oregon, in
1982 and changed its name to Kyle Technology Corp.
Four years later it began developing aerospace product
lines. In 1989 Seattle businessman Donald A. Wright
reached an agreement to buy the company for about $3
million. The deal was completed in early 1990.

A Washington native, Wright did not attend
college. Rather, he was drafted into the U.S. Army in
1970 and after his discharge went to work in a sawmill.
A turning point in his life occurred during a vacation in
Hawaii when a chance encounter led to a job offer from
a Los Angeles electronics distributor. Wright took a job
in the stockroom and in a matter of a year worked his
way up to assistant vice president. A short time later he

decided to return to Washington, where in 1977 he used the knowledge he had gained in California to start a company in Everett called Component Concepts, a test laboratory for memory chips and semiconductors and maker of testing equipment. He ran the company for 14 years before selling his interest to acquire Kyle Technology.

When Wright bought the business Kyle Technology employed 15 people and generated revenues of less than $2 million. Although it exhibited no growth, the company possessed excellent technology and valuable patents. Wright renamed the company Pacific Coast Technologies, Inc., invested in new equipment, and added new technology. He would also use it as a platform to build a larger company that would become PA&E.

MOVE TO WENATCHEE: 1993

Wright continued to operate Pacific Coast Technologies out of Roseburg, but in the early 1990s began looking for a new location. After considering several cities in the Pacific Northwest, he settled on Wenatchee, Washington, where the Port of Chelan County agreed to construct a $1.3 million building for the company on a two-acre site in exchange for a 10-year lease with two five-year options. Pacific Coast Technologies moved into its new facility in 1993.

Late in 1993 Wright reached an agreement on his first add-on acquisition. In a transaction that would be completed in 1994, Pacific Coast Technologies acquired Cashmere Manufacturing Company. Founded in 1966, Cashmere was an aerospace machine shop that supplied small aluminum parts to Boeing and inner frames to other customers. To complete the acquisition, Wright formed a holding company under the name PCT Holdings, Inc. In 1995 he then acquired an inactive public company, Varazzana Ventures, Ltd., which he merged with PCT. Varazzana then assumed the PCT name. The end result of these maneuvers was that Wright controlled a public company positioned to act as a consolidator.

The timing of the Cashmere acquisition proved fortuitous. Boeing enjoyed a surge in orders, leading to an increase in production that benefited Cashmere and its parent company. Revenues for PCT increased from $2.94 million in fiscal 1994 (the fiscal year ended May 31) to more than $11 million in fiscal 1995. To take advantage of its momentum, PCT tacked on three further acquisitions in 1995.

KEY ACQUISITIONS

The first of these acquisitions was Ceramics Devices Inc. (CDI). Founded in San Diego, California, in 1982, CDI was a supplier of ceramic EMI filters for high-performance electronics systems for military and other applications that brought $3 million to the balance sheet. Because PCT products used CDI's ceramic filtering devices, the addition of the company helped PCT to pursue a strategy of vertical integration.

Next, PCT acquired Morel Industries Inc., an Entiat, Washington, manufacturer of precision cast aluminum components used in aerospace and transportation applications. In a situation similar to CDI, Morel was already working with PCT, although in this case Cashmere was providing precision machine services for Morel products. As a result, Morel was folded into the Cashmere operations.

Also in late 1995, PCT acquired Seismic Safety Products, Inc., a Florida manufacturer of safety gas shut-off valves for use during seismic activity. Wright considered the company to be a good fit because, like other units, it manufactured a proprietary product that was intended to perform in harsh environments. The operation was subsequently relocated to Wenatchee.

The three 1995 acquisitions helped to drive revenues to more than $20.7 million in fiscal 1996. Three months after the fiscal year came to an end, PCT in September 1996 changed its trade name to Pacific Aerospace & Electronics (PA&E) to emphasize the company's two primary business segments. PA&E reported revenues of $34.2 million in fiscal 1997. A short time before the close of the fiscal year, the company completed another acquisition, using $2 million in stock to add Sequim, Washington-based Northwest Technical Industries Inc., a manufacturer of explosively formed and clad dissimilar metals.

More acquisitions followed in 1998. PA&E added an East Coast presence by purchasing Butler, New Jersey-based Balo Precision Parts, a designer and manufacturer of hermetic enclosures and modules for the military, aerospace, medical, and fiber-optics industries. In April 1998 PA&E acquired Vancouver, Washington-based Electronic Specialty Corporation and its wholly owned subsidiary Displays & Technologies,

KEY DATES

1990: Don Wright acquires Kyle Technology Corp., which is renamed Pacific Coast Technologies.
1993: Company moves to Wenatchee, Washington.
1996: Name is changed to Pacific Aerospace & Electronics, Inc. (PA&E).
2004: Company is taken private.
2006: Company is sold to French company Souriau Holding SAS.

Inc. They formed the nucleus of the company's new Advanced Products group. In the meantime, PA&E had also announced plans to launch an information technology (IT) division and struck tentative deals to acquire several IT companies. Wright soon thought better of the idea and in November 1997 the plans were scrapped. Instead, PA&E began to look overseas.

AEROMET ACQUIRED: 1998

Shortly before posting record revenues of $54 million and net income of $3.6 million in fiscal 1998, PA&E reached an agreement to acquire a U.K.-based company, Aeromet International plc, for $70 million. A supplier to such European aerospace manufacturers as British Aerospace, Airbus, Rolls-Royce, and Lucas Aerospace, Aeromet and its five plants in England brought $49 million in additional sales, effectively allowing PA&E to double in size in one stroke. In addition to serving different parts of the world, the two companies shared little overlap in products, allowing them to open up new markets for one another.

PA&E took on considerable debt to finance the Aeromet deal and create more operating capital. It borrowed $75 million at 11.25 percent, the best rate available at the time, and also issued $17 million worth of preferred stock. It soon became apparent, however, that the acquisition was ill fated. Most investors believed that PA&E paid too much for the property and began to bid down the price of PA&E stock. Furthermore, PA&E was regarded as little more than a Boeing supplier. When Boeing's business began to drop off dramatically as the global aerospace market slumped in response to an Asian economic crisis, the price of PA&E's stock fell even further. Although sales increased to $107.4 million in fiscal 1999, PA&E lost $12.9 million, due in large measure to steep interest payments related to the Aeromet acquisition. Sales continued to climb the following year, reaching $112.7 million, but the loss widened to more than $13 million.

FACING DIFFICULT TIMES

PA&E attempted to cut costs by trimming its workforce and pursuing other belt-tightening measures. The company also took steps to lessen its dependence on Boeing, in part by building its medical technology sales. However, conditions grew worse in fiscal 2001, as sales slipped to $109.3 million while losses ballooned to more than $75 million. The company warned investors that its cash shortage threatened to put it out of business. Although management insisted that it did not expect to go out of business, this pro forma disclosure served only to create a further drag on the price of PA&E stock, which was soon trading at around 25 cents, prompting a delisting notice from the NASDAQ.

As 2000 came to a close, PA&E announced its intention to sell Aeromet. While the company would shrink considerably, the divestiture of the British concern would eliminate all of the debt on the books and return PA&E to profitability. While a buyer was sought for Aeromet, PA&E closed operations that supplied Boeing and worked on a plan to restructure its debt, which was slated to be consummated at the end of September 2001. After six months of effort, a deal was also on the verge of completion for the sale of Aeromet. Both of these arrangements, however, came unraveled in the wake of the terrorist attacks of September 11, 2001, that roiled the global economy and the aerospace industry in particular.

COMPANY REBORN: 2006

While many companies that served the aerospace industry failed during the difficult early years of the 21st century, PA&E managed to survive. In 2002 New York acquisition firm GSC Partners bought 90 percent of PA&E's stock and began preparing it for sale. The company was taken private in 2004 and downsized further. In 2006 the French company Souriau Holding SAS bought the Pacific Coast Technology subsidiary as well as the Pacific Aerospace & Electronics name. In the process, Pacific Coast Technology changed its name to Pacific Aerospace & Electronics and began anew. Souriau did not purchase Aeromet from GSC partners, however. Wright left PA&E in 2006 to launch a consulting firm.

The new PA&E refocused itself on high margin, high-end niche markets. It was a strategy that was soon paying dividends. In order to keep up with orders the company began hiring again, and by the summer of 2008 had a backlog of work worth $14 million. Annual revenues were then in the $25 million range, and the workforce topped 200, still a far cry from the 1,000 employed at the height of PA&E's success. Although smaller than its predecessor, the new, leaner PA&E appeared better prepared to experience long-term, sustained success.

Ed Dinger

PRINCIPAL COMPETITORS

Amphenol Corporation; Precision Castparts Corp.; Schott AG.

FURTHER READING

Bentley, Ryan. "PA&E: Manufacturer Sheds Reliance on Boeing, Revamps Approach." *Wenatchee Business Journal*, June 2008, p. 1.

Boone, Rolf. "A Conversation with Don Wright." *Wenatchee Business Journal*, November 2002, p. A10.

Malott, Kristen. "From Smashing Bricks to Smashing Business Barriers." *Wenatchee Business Journal*, February 1995, p. 1.

"Manufacturing Firms to Merge and Offer Stock." *Wenatchee World*, December 29, 1993, p. 6.

Martinez, Marc. "Tech Firm Growing at Warp Speed." *Wenatchee World*, August 23, 1998, p. 13.

Mehaffey, K. C. "French Company Buying PAE." *Wenatchee World*, December 22, 2006, p. A3.

Wilhelm, Steve. "Pacific Aero Rides Industry Upsurge." *Puget Sound Business Journal*, July 18, 1997, p. 1.

The Parsons Corporation

100 West Walnut Street
Pasadena, California 91124
U.S.A.
Telephone: (626) 440-2000
Fax: (626) 440-2630
Web site: http://www.parsons.com

Private Company
Incorporated: 1944 as Ralph M. Parsons Company
Employees: 12,000
Sales: $2.87 billion (2009 est.)
NAICS: 541330 Engineering Services; 541310 Architectural Services

■ ■ ■

The Parsons Corporation is a leading international planning, engineering, and construction firm with operations in 50 states and 25 countries across the globe. Founded in 1944, the company serves both government and private clients and operates in a wide range of markets, including communications, education, energy, environmental, facilities, health care, infrastructure, life sciences, transportation, vehicle inspection, and water/wastewater. During 2010 Parsons was involved in over 4,500 projects that included the $4.5 billion renovation of the Pentagon, the $3 billion design and construction of the World Trade Center Port Authority Trans-Hudson Transportation Hub, the management and design of the Shchuch'ye Chemical Weapons Destruction Facility in Russia, and the design of the Saadiyat Bridge in Abu Dhabi.

ORIGINS AND EARLY GROWTH

The Parsons Corporation has gone through a number of configurations over the years. Ralph M. Parsons started his namesake company in 1944. Parsons was described in a December 1969 *New York Times* profile as an "outstanding, self-made engineer" as well as a "first-class salesman" and an "accomplished manager of people." According to the profile, Parsons first demonstrated his ability to combine engineering and business at the age of 13, when he and his brother opened a garage and machine shop in Amagansett, New York.

Parsons went on to study steam and machine design at the Pratt Institute, from which he graduated in 1916. After a brief stint in the Navy, he worked as an aeronautical engineer before turning his attention to oil refinery engineering. During World War II Parsons formed an engineering partnership that included Stephen D. Bechtel, who later became one of his chief rivals. Then in 1944 he founded the Ralph M. Parsons Company (RMPCo.) with capital of $100,000.

By 1945 U.S. industry was able to turn to projects that had been delayed by World War II. Within three years, RMPCo., having reaped the benefits of such a business climate, grew to more than 100 employees and expanded its services in architect-engineering, systems engineering, and design. During these first years RMPCo. constructed plants and facilities for a number of companies, including Shell Chemical Corporation and Standard Oil Company of California. In addition, RMPCo. designed the Point Mugu Missile Test Center in California.

In an early major project, RMPCo. designed test facilities for the development of nuclear weapons at Los Alamos, New Mexico, in 1948. The following year, the company began its first overseas project with a water development program that included 125 wells in Taiwan. The company continued these efforts in 1950 with a survey on water resources conducted for the government of India.

FURTHER GROWTH AND EXPANSION

During the early 1950s RMPCo. expanded into the chemical and petroleum industries. The company engineered a sulfur recovery plant, which produced sulfur from hydrogen sulfide, in Baton Rouge, Louisiana, for Consolidated Chemical Industries, Inc., in 1951. During this decade the company also oversaw the construction of a number of refineries for natural gas and petroleum in Turkey and several European nations, including the world's largest to date in Lacq, France.

RMPCo. was also involved in a number of advanced aviation projects during the 1950s, including high energy fuel development, programs to develop nuclear-powered aircraft for the U.S. Air Force and Navy, and the design of facilities at the National Reactor Test Station in Idaho for nuclear engine development. The company designed underground bulk fuel storage facilities for Strategic Air Command bases all around the world.

RMPCo. offered a diverse range of skills to clients, as demonstrated by the high-thrust rocket test station it designed at Edwards Air Force Base during the mid-1950s. The station included control facilities, test stands, instrumentation, and laboratories, as well as systems for storing and handling fuel and disposing of hazardous waste. In 1958 the company began the first of many airport projects in the United States and around the world with the design and development of a large terminal in Saudi Arabia. Other international efforts during the late 1950s and early 1960s included additional petroleum refineries in Europe and several in Latin America. All told, RMPCo. provided architect-engineering services for construction facilities worth more than $2 billion between the late 1940s and the late 1950s.

ACQUISITION ADDS MINING AND METALLURGY

The purchase of Anaconda-Jurden Associates in 1961 brought significant involvement in mining and metallurgy. Renamed Parsons-Jurden Corporation, the new acquisition had experience in mining facilities around the world. A copper concentrator was started in Butte, Montana, within the year. In addition to engineering such facilities, Parsons-Jurden was involved in other aspects of metallurgical projects, including geological and mineral surveys and feasibility and market studies.

RMPCo. continued throughout the 1960s with the types of projects they had successfully completed in earlier years. The company designed several major petroleum refineries in the United States and abroad, including a $100 million facility for Atlantic-Richfield in Cherry Point, Washington. New mining projects included an underground copper mine complex located in the Chilean Andes and designed for Cerro Corporation, and a comprehensive mineral resources exploration and inventory program for India.

RMPCo. also planned an expansion and modernization of Honolulu Airport, designed a terminal for Tunis/Carthage International Airport, and managed the construction of a $110 million airport complex in the Dallas-Fort Worth area. In addition, the company received a contract from the Federal Aviation Administration to expand and modernize air traffic control centers.

By the late 1960s RMPCo. had designed 150 plants that produced sulfur from hydrogen sulfide. A $60 million natural gas processing plant engineered and constructed by the company in Alberta, Canada, for Chevron Standard Limited in 1969 included the world's largest single sulfur recovery unit at that time. RMPCo. also became involved in an even wider range of activities, some of which were experimental.

The company engineered a saline water conversion plant in California and was involved in preliminary ef-

The Parsons Corporation

KEY DATES

■

1944: Ralph M. Parsons establishes the Ralph M.
Parsons Company (RMPCo.)
1949: The company begins its first overseas project.
1961: Anaconda-Jurden Associates is acquired.
1969: RMPCo. goes public.
1977: De Leuw, Cather & Company and S.I.P. are
purchased.
1979: Parsons Corp. is created to act as a holding
company for RMPCo., De Leuw, Cather &
Company, S.I.P., and subsidiary Parsons
Constructors, Inc.
1984: The firm returns to private ownership.
1996: Chairman and CEO Leonard J. Pieroni dies
in a plane crash in Croatia.
2001: Parsons adds H.E. Hennigh Inc. and Finley
McNary Engineers Inc. to its lineup.
2006: The company's reconstruction work in Iraq is
called into question.

forts to enable the countries of North America to collect
unused runoff water in the subarctic. A test site
designed and built by the company demonstrated that
ballistic missiles could be fired from underground silos.
RMPCo. also designed the first "lunar proving ground"
to test flight hardware used in the Apollo moon flights.

EXPANSION AS A PUBLIC COMPANY

RMPCo. was by then one of the nation's largest
engineering and construction firms, with projects totaling $1.2 billion in 1968. The company went public in
July 1969, selling a combination of stock worth about
$7 million. A majority of the stock was sold on behalf
of Parsons, who was serving as chairman of the
company. Much of the remainder was sold to increase
the working capital available for the company.

In addition to the stock sale, RMPCo. began to
explore more aggressively the possibility of acquiring
companies. Parsons noted in a December 1969 *New
York Times* article that these new practices represented
quite a shift in his approach. He remarked that he
would have to move beyond an adage from his child-
hood, "Never tell your friends where you shoot ducks,"
admitting, "We'll have to be more open."

RMPCo. expanded during the early 1970s. The
company acquired a controlling interest in an Australian

engineering firm, adding approximately 500 employees
to its Australian operations. RMPCo. also formed a new
company to aid in the integration of physical distribution services by providing warehousing, transportation
management, and information services. This new
company, called National Distribution Services, Inc.,
was the result of a joint effort between RMPCo.,
Eastern Airlines, and TRW Inc.

RMPCo. also restructured its network of offices for
improved efficiency. Activities in London were
consolidated into one new facility, and a new office was
opened in Australia. Parsons-Jurden moved from New
York to Los Angeles, and RMPCo. consolidated its offices from four separate leased buildings in Los Angeles
to a new headquarters facility in Pasadena.

Increasing concern with energy sources and pollution in the early 1970s provided opportunities for
RMPCo. The company developed several new processes
that helped decrease pollution. The Beavon Sulfur
Removal Process reduced air pollution by increasing the
amount of sulfur recovered from gases in gas processing
plants and petroleum refineries, while the Double
Contact/Double Absorption Process, applied in sulfuric
acid plants, increased productivity as well as reducing
emissions.

NEW FOREIGN AND DOMESTIC PROJECTS

Despite these apparently promising developments,
demand for construction services was down in the early
years of the decade, and RMPCo.'s revenue fell sharply,
from $4.6 million in 1971 to $2.1 million the following
year. The company attributed this development to a
range of factors, including the unsettled condition of the
economy, the lack of a coherent energy policy and
uncertainty regarding energy requirements and supplies,
the lack of government pollution standards, and pressures brought by environmental groups. The slump was
short-lived, and by the mid-1970s revenues had begun a
rapid and consistent rise. New projects, contracts, and
acquisitions contributed to RMPCo.'s growth during
these years.

On the international front, the Middle East was the
main source of new foreign projects. RMPCo. was
involved in the preliminary studies for and the design of
Yanbu, a multibillion-dollar industrial city on the Red
Sea in Saudi Arabia. In 1976 the joint venture company
Saudi Arabian Parsons Limited was founded to help
administer projects and pursue other opportunities in
the Middle East. Along with another firm, Saudi
Arabian Parsons Limited was selected by the government
of Saudi Arabia to manage the construction of the new
international airport in Jeddah.

RMPCo. also began a major domestic undertaking in 1976: the company received a contract from the Federal Railroad Administration to manage the design and construction of a five-year, $1.75 billion program to modernize the Northeast Corridor, the passenger railroad route from Boston to Washington, D.C. RMPCo. was also involved in several projects with the Department of Energy, including an oil storage program, a synthesis gas plant, and the design of facilities and techniques for the handling of nuclear materials during the nuclear fuel cycle.

Parsons also became involved in an increasing number of "mega-projects," large, complex engineering ventures with multibillion-dollar budgets and decades-long schedules. One of the company's first such undertakings was a massive oil and gas production facility at Prudhoe Bay in Alaska. This project, the largest undertaken by private industry to date, required the transportation of hundreds of prefabricated modules to a site 350 miles north of the Arctic Circle.

In 1977 RMPCo. acquired De Leuw, Cather & Company of Chicago and S.I.P., Inc., based in Houston. A leading engineering-design firm specializing in transportation systems, De Leuw, Cather & Company was involved in the Northeast Corridor railroad project as well as other ventures. Robert B. Richards, president and chairman of De Leuw, Cather, which retained its own corporate identity and management, was made a vice president at RMPCo. S.I.P., Inc., provided RMPCo. with a strategic location: the Gulf Coast area, the site of much of the nation's petroleum, chemical, and gas processing industries.

REORGANIZATION: 1978–79

Partly as a result of these acquisitions, and in an attempt to maximize the potential for future growth, RMPCo. management proposed a major reorganization of the company. Approved by shareholders on September 19, 1978, the reorganization divided RMPCo. into two separate corporations, although both were still owned by the same stockholders. In the United States, The Parsons Corporation was incorporated in Delaware as a holding company for RMPCo., De Leuw, Cather & Company, and S.I.P., Inc. Parsons Constructors, Inc. (PCI), a new subsidiary intended to provide increased construction capability, was added to The Parsons Corporation early in 1979. Shares of RMPCo. stock were converted to shares of The Parsons Corporation automatically at a one-to-one ratio. The company's management hoped that this restructuring would increase flexibility, aid growth, and make it easier to add subsidiaries.

On the international side, the plan was designed to improve the company's competitive position and

provide tax savings. As a result of the reorganization, RMP International, Limited, was incorporated in the Cayman Islands. Shareholders of The Parsons Corporation received shares of RMP International, Limited, on a one-for-one basis. The shares of the two new corporations were required to be traded together.

The Parsons Corporation continued to grow and to experience increasing revenue in the years immediately following the reorganization. For example, in 1980 Parsons was involved in almost 270 projects in 31 different countries. Revenue increased 25 percent in 1980 over the 1979 figure, and new records were established again in 1981 and 1982, when revenue reached $1.2 billion. William E. Leonhard, chairman, president, and CEO of The Parsons Corporation, summed up the company's strategy this way in an annual report: "The key to our continuing strength is a basic policy of providing engineering, construction, and related services, a business we fully understand, while diversifying both geographically and in terms of the industries we serve."

RETURNING TO PRIVATE COMPANY STATUS: 1984

In 1984, after 15 years as a public company, Parsons began to explore the possibility of returning to private status. According to *Business Week*, provisions of the 1984 tax law made the purchase of companies by employee stock ownership plans particularly attractive. An additional reason for the move was offered in the *San Francisco Business Journal* by Marion Gordon, a Parsons spokesperson, who stated, "If you're not accountable [to shareholders and the public], it gives you more flexibility and the ability to map out big plans without the whole world looking on. This is a competitive industry and operating as a private company can provide a benefit in forming strategy." Chairman Leonhard similarly stated in a January 1985 *Wall Street Journal* article that he supported the plan "so we could be in control of our own destiny."

In October 1984 The Parsons Corporation returned to private ownership as a result of a $560 million buyout by the Employee Stock Option Plan. Almost immediately questions were raised about the deal, one of the largest such transactions in U.S. history to date. The U.S. Labor Department investigated charges brought by employee groups that executives who designed the plan benefited disproportionately, while employees were saddled with debt. The employees also argued that they had no meaningful input in the decision to go private and that they would be excluded from the process of shaping the company's future.

In addition, some retirement experts expressed concern about the loss of a profit-sharing program of diversified stocks and bonds. Finally, the corporation was the target of several lawsuits. One suit, brought by employees in 1985, claimed that the purchase was a "breach of fiduciary responsibility, misuse of corporate assets, and a termination of predecessor plans," according to the May 21, 1985, *Wall Street Journal*. Five years later, however, a federal court upheld the buyout.

Despite the difficulties resulting from the buyout, Parsons, then the largest 100 percent employee-owned company of its kind in the United States, continued to adapt and prosper. The company benefited from an increasing trend toward privatization, providing services to municipal governments in Chester County, Pennsylvania, for example. In addition, while opportunities in the Middle East decreased in the early 1990s, Parsons increasingly turned its attention to Asian markets.

GLOBAL EXPANSION AND DIVERSIFICATION: 1995–2003

Success continued throughout the mid-1990s. During 1995 Parsons was named the top design firm in the United States based on domestic and international billings by trade publication *Engineering News Record*. The publication also ranked Parsons as the second-largest global design firm in the world. By this time, the company was involved in projects related to the Idaho National Engineering Laboratory, the Amoco Gas Terminal in the United Kingdom, the Kaohsiung Mass Rapid Transit System in Taiwan, and had various other international contracts in Argentina, Oman, Kuwait, Korea, Italy, Russia, and Thailand.

The firm strengthened its holding in 1995 by acquiring Gilbert/Commonwealth Inc., a company involved in power plant design and nuclear facility decommissioning. Parsons, which was headed by Chairman and CEO Leonard J. Pieroni, then launched a restructuring effort in early 1996 that included a reorganization into four business units: Parsons Process Group Inc., Parsons Infrastructure and Technology Group Inc., Parsons Power Group Inc., and Parsons Transportation Group Inc. The strategy also included the creation of a new global business development unit designed to increase the company's international revenue, which by 1996 accounted for just 30 percent of overall revenue.

However, just four months after initiating its new strategy, the company experienced a significant loss. While on a business trip with Commerce Secretary Ronald H. Brown and other business executives, Pieroni was killed when the plane carrying the group went down in Croatia. As the company mourned the loss of their leader, board members scrambled to elect a new CEO. James F. McNulty was given the task and promised to continue the company's current direction. "My plans are to make Parsons into a big player in the global marketplace," McNulty commented in an April 1996 *Business Week* article. The authors of the piece pointed to the importance of McNulty's strategy, observing, "It's a mission that Len Pieroni endorsed with his life."

Parsons grew during the latter half of the 1990s by diversifying into telecommunications, pharmaceuticals, and vehicle inspections. Annual revenue had more than doubled throughout the decade, growing from $1 billion in 1990 to $2.4 billion in 2000. Parsons continued to expand in the early years of the new century. The firm complemented its vehicle inspections business by adding Protect Air Inc. to its arsenal in 2000. The following year it acquired H.E. Hennigh Inc., a telecommunications general contracting firm, and bridge engineering concern Finley McNary Engineers Inc.

By this time, the company had contracts with the Federal Aviation Administration to upgrade U.S. air traffic control facilities and with Denver's Stapleton Airport to redesign its facilities. The firm's other major domestic projects included the construction of the Olivenhain Dam in San Diego County, the expansion of the Seattle-Tacoma International Airport, and the Alameda Corridor rail project in Los Angeles, California. During 2003 the company was involved in the bidding process to repair postwar Iraq.

CONTRACTS AND CRITICISM

While the company's involvement in its Middle East projects would eventually prove to be a source of negative publicity, the company forged ahead with its growth plans by securing lucrative contracts as well as making strategic acquisitions during this period. During 2004 the company purchased MW Consultants and Process Facilities Inc., two companies involved in the pharmaceuticals and life sciences sector. Primus Infrastructure Inc., a water and infrastructure firm, was purchased later that year. Parsons E&C Corp., the company's engineering and construction arm serving the oil and gas, refining, petrochemicals, and power markets, was purchased by joint venture partner Worley Group Ltd. in 2004. The company's Cultural Resources group was sold in 2005.

In 2005 RCI Construction Group was acquired and added to the company's water and wastewater, transportation, and urban infrastructure holdings. Wireless telecommunications site development services firm Alaris Group LLC and project manager META Associates Inc. were also purchased that year. Project management firm 3D/International was acquired in 2006. McMunn Associates Inc., an analytical and management services company serving the U.S. intelligence community, was added to the Parsons portfolio in 2009.

Meanwhile, the company was actively pursuing projects on both domestic and international levels. The involvement of Parsons in Iraq became a source of trouble in 2006 when the company came under fire for what critics were calling "shoddy work." By this time, the company had secured nearly $2 billion in contracts to construct a police training facility in Baghdad, a prison, and medical facilities. Cost overruns and delays forced the U.S. Corps of Engineers to cancel contracts with the company while Parsons maintained it had done the best it could, given the conditions in Iraq. "The security situation made it impossible to do the work the way we would normally do it," CEO McNulty told *Forbes* magazine in 2007.

A 2008 report by the Special Inspector General for Iraq Reconstruction, an independent federal agency, found that many of the Parsons contracts were terminated by the United States before they reached completion. According to a January 2008 *New York Times* article, reasons included poor contract oversight, unrealistic schedules, and poor management by the U.S. Army Corps of Engineers.

NEW LEADERSHIP

Despite the company's Iraq-based setbacks, it continued to post sound financial results. Net operating income increased every year from 2000 through 2009. Parsons was involved in over 4,500 projects during this period, including the $4.5 billion renovation of the Pentagon, the $3 billion design and construction of the World Trade Center Port Authority Trans-Hudson Transportation Hub, the management and design of the Shchuch'ye Chemical Weapons Destruction Facility in Russia, and the design of the Saadiyat Bridge in Abu Dhabi.

The company had also designed and constructed the Improvised Explosive Device (IED) Test and Evaluation Facility in Fort Irwin, California. This mock village, used by the U.S. Army, was created to test and evaluate new sensing equipment used in the detection of IEDs. Parsons was also the construction manager for Northrop Grumman Corp.'s shipyard upgrade. In 2010 the company was awarded a wastewater services contract in Abu Dhabi worth approximately $160 million.

McNulty retired in 2008, leaving Charles Harrington at the helm. Under new leadership, Parsons continued to focus on using its expertise and technological strengths to win contracts. By securing long-term contracts, Parsons managed to remain financially strong during the economic downturn that plagued the United States and most of the world during this period. With a solid strategy in place, Parsons appeared to be well positioned to succeed in the years to come.

Michelle L. McClellan
Updated, Christina M. Stansell

PRINCIPAL OPERATING UNITS

Advanced Technologies; Commercial Technology; Infrastructure and Technology; Transportation.

PRINCIPAL COMPETITORS

AECOM Technology Corp.; Bechtel Group Inc.; URS Corp.

FURTHER READING

"And at Parsons This Week." *Business Week*, October 1, 1984, p. 50.

Armstrong, Larry. "A Death in the Parsons Family." *Business Week*, April 22, 1996, p. 39.

Brown, Heidi. "Rebuilding: Its Iraq Mission Came a Cropper, but This Feisty Private Engineering Company Is Building on a Much Brighter Future." *Forbes*, November 26, 2007.

Downey, Kirsten E. "Vulnerable San Francisco Builder Takes Stock, Goes Public." *San Francisco Business Journal*, September 2, 1985, p. 1.

Glanz, James. "An American Builder's Failures in Iraq Are Found to Have Been More Widespread." *New York Times*, January 29, 2008.

Gottschalk, Earl C., Jr. "Parsons's Acquisition by Employee Stock Plan Raises Some Questions About Who Benefited." *Wall Street Journal*, January 29, 1985, p. 4.

"Parsons Buys RCI to Boost Markets." *Engineering News Record*, April 18, 2005.

"Parsons Employees Sue Firm and Others over Recent Buyout." *Wall Street Journal*, May 21, 1985, p. 24.

Satzman, Darrell. "Staying Alive—Privately." *Los Angeles Business Journal*, October 29, 2001, p. 1.

Smith, Kevin. "Parsons Proves Recession-Proof." *San Bernardino County Sun*, April 18, 2010.

Streitfeld, David, and Nancy Cleeland. "War with Iraq: Finalists for Rebuilding Down to 2 Firms." *Los Angeles Times*, April 3, 2003, p. 1.

Wright, Robert A. "Parsons, a Canny Hunter." *New York Times*, December 5, 1969.

Paychex Inc.

—■—

911 Panorama Trail South
Rochester, New York 14625-0397
U.S.A.
Telephone: (585) 385-6666
Toll Free: (800) 322-7292
Fax: (585) 383-3428
Web site: http://www.paychex.com

Public Company
Incorporated: 1971
Employees: 12,500
Sales: $2.08 billion (2009)
Stock Exchanges: NASDAQ
Ticker Symbol: PAYX
NAICS: 541211 Offices of Certified Public Accountants

■ ■ ■

Rochester, New York-based Paychex Inc. is a leading provider of payroll and human resource services. During the early 2010s the company served more than 500,000 clients from approximately 100 locations nationwide. In addition to payroll and tax filing services, Paychex also administers workers' compensation and retirement plans for its customers. The company serves large organizations with its Paychex Premier Human Resources and Major Market Payroll Services solutions.

ORIGINS

Paychex was founded by B. Thomas Golisano. In 1971 Golisano worked as a sales manager at Electronic Ac-

counting Systems (EAS), a payroll processing company based in Rochester, New York. EAS aimed its services at large companies with at least 50 employees. Its minimum charges were generally too much for smaller companies to afford, and EAS did not pursue the small-company market. However, Golisano, then 29 years old, speculated that small companies had as much need for a payroll accounting service as large companies.

A little research at the library confirmed Golisano's suspicions that the potential market was enormous (in 1971, 95 percent of the nation's 3.5 million businesses had fewer than 50 employees). Golisano's father ran his own small heating contracting firm, and Golisano knew firsthand that making out payroll checks was a big headache for the small businessperson. Golisano decided to market a payroll service that would be cheap enough for small businesses like his father's to afford.

When Golisano first took his idea to EAS, the company was not interested in pursuing small clients. But EAS did agree to rent Golisano an office for his venture, and in 1971 Golisano started his own company, then called PayMaster. His service was offered to companies for only a $5 minimum charge per pay period, and the total fee was proportional to the number of employees.

Not only was the price reasonable, but Golisano made his service extremely convenient. Whereas clients of EAS had to fill out forms each pay period and turn them in to the company, Golisano's clients had only to make one phone call. The client simply called in the hours each employee worked, and any changes, and the company did the rest. The process took only about four minutes.

EARLY GROWTH

It took Golisano a year to attract 42 clients, and Paychex did not break-even for three more years. During that time Golisano kept the business afloat, somewhat precariously, with borrowed money and credit card loans. Because Paychex clients were small, the company needed a lot of accounts to keep going. Golisano marketed to certified public accountants and increasingly got referrals from satisfied customers. After five years Paychex had attracted about 300 clients in Rochester, and the business was relatively stable.

The impetus to expand the company came from two friends of Golisano, who approached him independently in 1974. One suggested opening a branch office in Syracuse, and he and Golisano would be co-owners. The second asked Golisano to sell him a franchise, and he started up a branch in Miami. Then Golisano began to recruit people to open branches in other cities. By 1979 Golisano had 17 partners, including 11 joint ventures and six franchises. These operated in 22 cities spread across the country. Golisano's partners came from various backgrounds, such as teaching, sales, and engineering. Some were high school friends or friends of the family; some were his softball buddies. Golisano gained one partner, the doorman of the Boca Raton Hotel, on a trip to Florida. They were all then trained at the company's Rochester base, after which they received help to set up business elsewhere.

By 1979 it began to be apparent that there were problems with the looseness of the organization. Paychex had 200 employees, 5,700 clients, and 18 principals. Different partners had different skills and different aims. Some locations offered different services from others, so that the Paychex product was not consistent. There was little central planning, and little input from one office to another.

Golisano decided he wanted to consolidate Paychex into one company. For this he needed the acquiescence

of his partners. It was difficult to persuade people who had headed their own branches that they would be better off as part of a more traditional company organization. Golisano came up with an equitable stock distribution formula and presented a five-year plan for the future of the company, which included taking it public. After a tense two-day meeting in the Bahamas, all the principals agreed to the consolidation. In 1979 the company incorporated as Paychex, Inc.

ADJUSTING TO REORGANIZATION

Paychex began to change quickly. People who had been president of their own branches became vice presidents of the new corporation. The company immediately began hiring and training a crew of sales professionals. The branches, which had previously operated more or less independently, were now subjected to management controls such as location-by-location comparisons of productivity.

Paychex also strove to standardize its services. This was extremely important as the company grew. Most of its new business came from referrals from satisfied clients. It was crucial that if one company praised the way its account was handled by, for example, the Syracuse office, a company in New York could also expect the very same service. Golisano himself kept careful track of his growing organization, lugging around a three-ring notebook with hundreds of pages of relevant figures wherever he went.

Paychex initially experienced financial difficulties as a result of the reorganization, and at one point in 1980 cash-flow problems caused the company to suspend salaries. However, this crisis was quickly resolved, and Paychex did grow as expected. With its new professional sales team in place, Paychex began to attract clients in numbers much higher than anticipated. By 1982 the average salesperson was bringing in 100 clients a year. This figure rose steadily. In August 1983 Paychex made its initial public offering (IPO). The company raised $7.7 million, which was used to fuel further expansion.

By 1986 Paychex had close to 60,000 clients. The company had 58 offices in 32 states. Sales doubled to $51 million in the three years since the IPO. The company was far bigger than Golisano's former employer, EAS.

PRODUCT EXPANSION

Revenues close to doubled again in the next three years. In 1989 the company brought in $101 million from its

KEY DATES

1971: B. Thomas Golisano establishes PayMaster.
1979: The firm incorporates as Paychex Inc.
1983: Paychex goes public.
1998: The firm is added to the S&P 500.
2003: Revenues surpass $1 billion.
2004: Golisano retires as CEO and is succeeded by former IBM executive Jonathan J. Judge.

client base of 115,000 accounts. Some of the growth came from acquisitions, such as the 900 clients acquired when Paychex bought a Minneapolis company, Purchase Payroll, in 1987. Paychex also began to expand its services. In 1987 Paychex opened a division of Benefit Services to keep track of clients' employee benefit plans. The next year, the company opened a Personnel Services division. The new services under this rubric included preparation of employee handbooks, providing information on new laws affecting the workplace, and updating clients on equal-employment regulations.

In 1989 Paychex began offering a new service called Taxpay. For clients selecting Taxpay, Paychex prepared payroll tax returns, made the payments, and actually filed the returns with the government. Taxpay provided a real revenue boost to Paychex for two reasons. For each client who selected Taxpay, Paychex gained about a 45 percent increase in revenue on that account due to the fact that this service required only a little additional work.

Paychex also benefited from Taxpay because it accepted money in advance to pay the taxes. Before the taxes came due, Paychex could collect interest on this "float" money. Paychex invested the float money, an average daily balance of $4,000 per customer, in tax-free municipal securities, and earned an average annual return of 3 to 4 percent. In just a few years, almost half of Paychex payroll clients were also using Taxpay, and Paychex experienced a vital boost in revenue.

FOCUS ON TRAINING

Paychex had experienced growth of around 20 percent annually in the 1980s, and the company was consistently featured on lists such as *Forbes'* "Best Small Companies in America" and the *OTC Review* list of "100 Most Profitable NASDAQ Companies." The company's success did not go unnoticed, and Paychex began to face competition from the leading payroll accounting service firm, Automatic Data Processing Inc.

(ADP). ADP began a separate sales division to try to hook small business accounts. By 1989 ADP had 400 sales representatives in this division, versus Paychex's 310. In that year companies with fewer than 50 employees made up 60 percent of ADP's accounts and brought in about twice as much revenue as did Paychex.

Despite this challenge, the small business market was enormous, and there was still room for growth. Best of all, about 80 percent of Paychex's clients renewed every year. Most of the clients the company lost did not turn to another provider. The rate of failure among small businesses is very high, and most lost clients simply went out of business. But to keep up with this turnover, Paychex sales representatives had to bring in an average of 160 new clients a year, or more than three a week.

To train salespeople to keep up with this demanding quota, Paychex opened its own school at its Rochester branch. In 1991 Paychex spent approximately $3,500 per trainee to put its new salespeople through a seven-week course in tax law, accounting principles, and selling skills, and to send them on rounds with experienced sales representatives. The expense of the school, which had 11 full-time instructors, was far less than it cost Paychex to recruit a replacement for sales reps who quit or were fired. In addition, new hires who had come through the training school started making money for the company twice as fast as before. Paychex had started in the 1970s with people who had little or no background in either selling or payroll accounting; in the 1990s the company was operating with a highly professional and well-prepared staff.

SUCCESS WITH NEW SERVICES

By 1990 Paychex had 335 sales representatives and around 125,000 clients. However, a recession in the autumn of that year set back the number of paychecks the company was processing, and sales representatives found it hard to meet their ambitious quotas. Nevertheless, the Taxpay service was increasingly successful. At the end of fiscal 1991 Paychex estimated it had lost several million dollars due to recessionary cutbacks, but it more than made up the difference with revenue from Taxpay. That year saw record sales of $137 million, as well as record earnings of $9.6 million. At this time the company had around 26,000 Taxpay customers, and that number rose to over 50,000 by 1993.

Paychex added other services as well. In 1991 the company formed a Human Resource Services division, offering clients a package of employee evaluation and testing tools, employee handbooks, insurance services, customized job descriptions, and other benefits. Paychex used its expertise to help its Human Resource clients keep abreast of government regulations affecting the workplace and took over time-consuming administrative procedures.

The company then introduced Paylink in 1993. Paylink appealed to businesses that used personal computers, allowing clients to send payroll information in to the Paychex database via computer modem. In 1994 Paychex added a similar service, Reportlink. After a client's payroll was computed, Reportlink sent the figures back to the client's computers for use in internal reports and accounting.

A COMPETITIVE CLIMATE

Paychex continued to roll out new services, although in 1994 over 80 percent of its revenue still came from its basic payroll accounting service. Enrolling new payroll clients was still the key to the company's growth. Paychex aimed to expand its client base by 11 to 12 percent a year in order to keep revenue growing at close to 20 percent annually. This actually meant bringing in even more new clients than it seemed, because Paychex always had to make up the 20 percent of clients it lost each year.

Although there were still more than 4.6 million businesses with fewer than 100 employees in 1994, more than 60 percent of these had only one to four employees, and thus were too small to be likely potential clients. Paychex also had to contend with increasing competition from software manufacturers. Business owners with personal computers had an array of low-cost software packages to choose from that made doing their own payroll relatively cheap and convenient.

However, Golisano was confident the company could meet its goal. He took time off in 1994 to run for governor of New York as an independent party candidate. Golisano had become increasingly interested in trying to solve Rochester's urban problems, working with city youths on running their own businesses and heading a city campaign to lower the rate of teen pregnancies. Golisano also had an in-depth knowledge of government regulations and tax codes that he believed harassed small businesses. Although Paychex had made its living dealing with government red tape for its clients, Golisano claimed he would work for tax reform and simplification if elected.

A long shot at best, Golisano did not win the governorship, but Paychex flourished. In 1995 the company increased its client base by 11.8 percent, exactly as Golisano had wished. Paychex had over 200,000 clients, and half of these were using the lucrative Taxpay service. Earnings were up almost 40 percent,

with net income of $39 million. The company increased its penetration in the California market with two acquisitions: Pay-Fone and Payday. The Human Services division introduced a 401(k) record-keeping service, and other human resources services, as well as Paylink and Taxpay, continued to grow significantly.

CONTINUED GROWTH

Paychex aimed to expand even more through the remainder of the 1990s. Its market penetration was still low enough to leave room for growth. The company also committed to make use of blossoming technologies in computer networking and digital communications to enhance its service and capabilities. In 1996 Paychex acquired California-based Olsen Computer Systems Inc. and National Business Solutions of Florida. The firm celebrated its 25th anniversary that year and was ranked number two on the "Industrial & Commercial Services" segment of the *Wall Street Journal's* Shareholder Scoreboard ranking of 1,000 companies.

By 1997 Paychex had recorded five consecutive years of 30 percent-plus earnings growth. The company continued to expand its product and services offerings, including the addition of the Paychex Access Card. In a partnership with First Chicago NBD Corp., the firm developed the card to allow wages to be deposited into a Paychex Access Card account. These wages could then be withdrawn using a MasterCard-branded debit card, thus eliminating the need for paper paychecks. The firm's success continued to be recognized throughout the industry, and during 1998 the company was added to Standard and Poor's 500 Index (S&P 500).

Paychex looked for continued expansion in the United States, eyeing the domestic market as a lucrative avenue for increased revenues and earnings. When questioned about whether his company could continue to secure such solid results, Golisano replied in a 1999 *Business Week* article that Paychex only had 5 percent of the payroll processing market and the entire industry had just 13 percent overall penetration. "So there is no reason that we shouldn't grow at relatively the same rates, as long as we continue to do our job," Golisano stated firmly.

Paychex did just that as it entered the new millennium. In fiscal 2001 the company posted its 11th consecutive year of record revenues and net income. The firm continued to invest in new technology and develop new services that catered to its small business clientele. Paychex also held strong to its long-standing belief that employee training was essential to its success. In fact, during 2000, approximately 5,000 employees were trained at the University of Paychex, and 750,000 hours were spent on field training and ongoing training programs.

ACQUISITIONS

The firm's focus on its employees led to its first-time ranking in *Fortune*'s 2002 list of "100 Best Companies to Work For" in the United States. That year Golisano parted with $50 million of his own money in another unsuccessful run for New York governor. The company also acquired Advantage Payroll Services, Inc., along with 49,000 new clients, in a $240 million cash deal. Paychex saw its customer base grow to 390,000 clients in 2002, and net income reached a record $274.5 million.

Paychex's growth accelerated in 2003. Offices were established in Wilmington, North Carolina; Lexington, Kentucky; Chattanooga, Tennessee; and Greenville, South Carolina. In addition, the national payroll and human resource administrative services provider InterPay Inc. was acquired from FleetBoston Financial Corp. in a $155 million deal. The addition of InterPay's 33,000 customers pushed Paychex's client base to 490,000, and revenues surpassed the $1 billion mark.

Growth continued in 2004 when Paychex acquired the Lake Mary, Florida-based time and attendance software firm Stromberg. A major development in the company's history unfolded during the latter part of the year when Golisano retired as CEO and was succeeded by former IBM executive Jonathan J. Judge. Golisano remained with the company as chairman. That year, customers totaled 505,000.

CHANGING TIMES

In 2005 Paychex began offering health savings accounts to its customers. In addition, a comprehensive human resource outsourcing solution called Paychex Premier Human Resources was developed. Following the Hurricane Katrina disaster, Paychex processed, printed, and mailed approximately 270,000 disaster relief checks for victims in Louisiana, via a partnership with Hibernia National Bank and the American Red Cross. Paychex ended the year with record earnings of $368 million on sales of $1.4 billion.

Change was the theme at Paychex in 2006. That year Vice President of Human Resources Diane Rambo retired after 25 years with the company and was succeeded by Martin Stowe. In addition, Director of Legal Affairs Stephanie L. Schaeffer was promoted to vice president and chief legal officer. In 2006 Paychex also relaunched its Web site with enhanced features, and moved its $342 million 401(k) plan from INVESCO to Fidelity Institutional Retirement Services Co.

In 2007 Paychex introduced a new Tax Credit Services product for small and medium-sized businesses and announced a $1 billion stock buyback program. In addition, the company increased its quarterly dividend by 43 percent. It also was in 2007 that Paychex obtained the online employee benefits management and administration system BeneTrac, as part of the acquisition of Hawthorne Benefit Technologies Inc.

INDUSTRY LEADER

In 2008 Paychex recorded revenues of $2.1 billion and generated record net income of $576.1 million. The company continued to receive national recognition during the later years of the decade. For example, in 2008 and 2009 it was included on *Fortune* magazine's "100 Best Companies to Work For" listing.

Despite difficult economic times, growth continued. Paychex's customer base reached 572,000 in 2009. That year, the company sold its Stromberg time and attendance business to Kronos Inc. However, the company remained committed to the sector, expanding its Internet-based time and attendance labor management system, Time and Labor Online.

Paychex continued to receive accolades in 2010. That year the company was once again included on *Fortune* magazine's "100 Best Companies to Work For" listing. In addition, for the ninth straight year it was recognized as one of the best training organizations when *Training* magazine ranked the company 32nd in the Training Top 125.

As Paychex forged ahead in the payroll industry, it remained committed to its customers. The company prepared to celebrate its 40th anniversary in 2011. With 572,000 customers and 100 offices, Paychex appeared to be well positioned for continued success during the 21st century's second decade.

A. Woodward
Updated, Christina M. Stansell; Paul R. Greenland

PRINCIPAL SUBSIDIARIES

Advantage Payroll Services, Inc.; Paychex Agency, Inc.; Paychex Benefit Technologies, Inc.; Paychex Business Solutions, Inc.; Paychex Deutschland GmbH (Germany); Paychex Insurance Concepts, Inc.; Paychex Investment Partnership LP; Paychex Management Corp.; Paychex of New York LLC; Paychex North America Inc.; Paychex Recordkeeping Services, Inc.; Paychex Securities Corporation; Paychex Time & Attendance Inc.; PXC Inc.; Rapid Payroll, Inc.

PRINCIPAL COMPETITORS

Administaff, Inc.; Automatic Data Processing, Inc.; Tri-Net Group, Inc.

FURTHER READING

Burlingham, Bo, and Michael S. Hopkins. "How to Build an Inc. 500 Company." *Inc.*, December 1988, pp. 41–56.

Gold, Howard R. "Lofty Paychex." *Barron's*, October 24, 1994, p. 13.

"Golisano Leaves Paychex." *Accounting Technology*, November 2004, p. 14.

Meisler, Andy, and Todd Raphael. "Spare Him the Gurus." *Workforce*, June 2003, p. 34.

"Paychex Announces Acquisition of BeneTrac." *Business Wire*, September 13, 2007.

"Paychex Ranked 32 among Training Magazine's Top 125." *Business Wire*, February 24, 2010.

"Q&A with Paychex's Thomas Golisano." *Business Week*, March 29, 1999.

Welles, Edward O. "Tom Golisano Goes Public." *Inc.*, November 1992, pp. 126–30.

Performance, Inc.

———————————■———————————

1 Performance Way
Chapel Hill, North Carolina 27514
U.S.A.
Telephone: (919) 933-9113
Fax: (919) 942-5431
Web site: http://www.performancebike.com

Private Company
Incorporated: 1982
Employees: 220
Sales: $216 million (2006 est.)
NAICS: 451111 Sporting Goods Stores

■ ■ ■

Performance, Inc., is a major retailer of bicycles, parts, accessories, nutrition and hydration products, and apparel, offering major name brands as well as private-label products. Billing itself as the nation's largest specialty bike shop, the Chapel Hill, North Carolina-based private company operates more than 90 stores in 16 states, scattered from coast to coast, serving both cycling enthusiasts and recreational riders. In addition, the stores offer financing and repair services. Performance also maintains a robust mail-order and online business. The company is majority owned by North Castle Partners of Greenwich, Connecticut.

COMPANY ORIGINS: 1981

Performance, Inc., was founded by Garry Snook and his wife Sharon. Cycling was hardly a passion for them, just a niche opportunity recognized by the aspiring entrepreneurs. Garry Snook earned an MBA degree from Duke University's Fuqua School of Business in 1981. He then began work on a doctorate in finance at the University of North Carolina at Chapel Hill, while also looking for a business opportunity.

During the Christmas holidays of 1981 the Snooks talked seriously about starting their own company. Because they had only $25,000 in savings to draw upon, they knew that the capital requirements had to be meager. The type of business was a secondary consideration. The idea to pursue the cycling industry was inspired by Snook's brother, Richard Snook, an avid cyclist and former manager of a bicycling store who indicated that the typical cycling store offered a limited choice of goods and poor service.

His interest piqued, Snook studied the market further and was pleased to find that not only were cycling products on the expensive side, they could be easily shipped via UPS. Moreover, cycling was gaining in popularity as an interest in fitness swept the country. Furthermore, Snook discovered that the average age of committed cyclists, 32, was much older than he had expected. They were ideal customers because they possessed discretionary income.

As a result of his research, Snook developed an idea for a mail-order cycling company. After reading a book on how to start a mail-order business, he pored over the few existing cycling catalogs and was far from impressed by the potential competition. They were essentially penny-pinching operations, loath to invest in color printing or pay for an 800 number or anything more than small rudimentary ads tucked deep inside cycling magazines. The catalogers simply focused on price, offered no substantial warranties, and paid scant attention to customer service.

FIRST CATALOGS MAILED: 1982

Snook was convinced that he could win a significant market share by combining quality products and fair prices with a four-color catalog, a toll-free number that would be answered at any hour of the day, and a no-questions-asked, 100 percent money-back guarantee. Having worked previously in banking, Snook turned to a former client, a printer, who helped launch the mail-order business by offering generous terms, spreading payments over three months.

The Snooks assembled a 16-page four-color catalog. It was an exercise in spreading risk. Unsure what items would sell, they crammed 10 items on each page. The plan was to then buy small quantities from suppliers as orders came in, and pay COD to conserve cash. Snook printed 35,000 copies, the maximum number his modest budget allowed, and they were mailed in April 1982, marking the launch of Performance, Inc.

Snook hoped for a 2 percent response rate and a $45 average order, just enough business to warrant a second printing of 35,000 catalogs. Response was better than expected and he was able to print an additional 100,000 catalogs. Operating out of their basement, Snook and his wife, who gave birth shortly before the first mailing, took orders at all hours and never left the house together to avoid missing an order. Their dedication paid off, and in its first year the mail-order business generated $700,000 in gross sales. A year later that amount grew to $3.2 million.

SOCK SUCCESS

Performance enjoyed a successful launch, but was not devoid of challenges. The company had gained a toehold in the market through better customer service. However, Snook was well aware that in order to secure his position he also had to find a way to compete on price, which meant he needed to become a manufacturer. Producing hard goods was out of the question, leading Snook to consider soft goods, which his research indicated were not impacted by significant brand loyalty. Performance and price were the key attributes. As a result, Snook decided to develop an apparel line.

Still determined to limit his risk, Snook was able in 1983 to strike another key alliance with a former banking client, Burlington, North Carolina-based Pickett Hosiery Mills, Inc. The mill was producing high-quality socks for a major sporting goods company and agreed to print the Performance logo on the tail end of the run. Snook was able to order just 10 dozen pairs of socks for $1 each. He then sold them at $2.25 a pair, well below the $3.50 the same socks were fetching in stores. Only after he sold out his inventory of socks in a month's time did Snook place a reorder. The success in socks led to the creation of a product-development group at the rising company that sought out niches for products to bear the Performance label.

MANUFACTURING BEGINS: 1984

Annual sales topped $7 million in 1984, prompting Snook to take the next step in the development of Performance: bringing manufacturing in-house. The decision was in large part a reaction to delivery problems Snook was experiencing with an Italian manufacturer of cycling shorts. In the fall of 1984 Snook arranged to rent 1,000 square feet from the Pickett Hosiery Mills on a month-to-month basis for $500 a month, including utilities.

He then paid $600 for three sewing machines from a bankruptcy sale, hired three seamstresses, and ordered enough Lycra to make 500 pairs of shorts. By cutting out the middleman, Snook was able to price his shorts for about $20, which was $5 to $7 less than the Italian-made shorts he sold at less profit. The in-house shorts were a success and not only spawned a subsidiary, Nova Designs, but also set the stage for further manufacturing.

The next step in the evolution of Performance was adding a retail presence to provide some diversity in the event the mail-order business struggled. Further market research reassured Snook that opening retail stores was a sound move. Typical bike shops tended to be operated by cycling enthusiasts rather than businessmen. Their shops often fell short on presentation, selection, and service, hardly an attractive combination for Performance's target customers. Because of his catalog sales, Snook knew that the bulk of his customers could be found in California, Colorado, and the Washington, D.C., area. For the site of his first store he chose

KEY DATES

1982: Garry and Sharon Snook launch cycling mail-order business.
1984: In-house manufacturing operations launched.
1986: First retail store opens in Boulder, Colorado.
2000: Specialty bike cataloger and Internet company Bike Nashbar acquired.
2007: North Castle Partners acquires majority control.

Boulder, Colorado, a town that had seven times the number of cyclists as the average U.S. city.

FIRST STORE OPENS: 1986

The Boulder store opened in August 1986. At 6,000 square feet, it devoted 40 percent of its space to high-margin apparel, instead of the 5 percent of the typical store with a footprint half the size. The presentation was also upscale and the prices more than competitive. This proved to be a winning combination, one that resulted in first year sales of $1.3 million, an excellent performance given that less than 5 percent of bike shops in the country reached the $1 million level. In 1986 a second store opened in Denver and generated comparable numbers, followed by a store in the Denver suburb of Lakewood that also posted first-year sales of more than $1 million.

By the summer of 1991 Performance was operating 14 stores, generating 40 percent of the company's annual sales of $47 million. The retail and mail-order operations also reinforced one another. Catalog sales helped Snook to determine where to open new stores, and the stores helped to create new catalog customers. Snook also looked for new merchandise to sell through catalogs in the belief that avid cyclists were interested in other outdoor activities as well. He tried catalogs featuring ski and golf products but enjoyed better success with scuba gear.

To support the opening of more stores, Snook completed a round of venture capital in the late 1980s. He would not seek further funding until 1999. In the meantime, Performance opened a new catalog telemarketing operation in West Virginia in 1995. At that stage the company had increased the number of stores to 33 and annual sales had grown to the $80 million range. In the second half of the decade 13 more stores were added and sales increased to $102.5 million. By this time,

Snook was eager to build an online business as well. In 1999 he completed a second round of funding, raising $50 million from Patricof & Co. Ventures and three limited partners.

CONTROLLING INTEREST SOLD: 2007

Not only did Snook build Performance's online presence, he used the new funds to acquire the five-store Washington, D.C.-area Bike USA chain in late 1999. Other acquisitions and new stores were opened in the early years of the new century. In addition, in April 2000 Performance acquired specialty bike cataloger and Internet company Bike Nashbar.

The pace of expansion picked up a few years later. Another 25 stores were added in 2007, bringing the total to more than 80 sites. In the middle of 2007, Patricof, then known as Apax Partners, was ready to cash in, and Snook agreed to sell a controlling interest in the company to North Castle Partners of Greenwich, Connecticut, to support even further growth of the company. Thus, both Apax and Snook achieved their goals in the transaction.

North Castle gained control of a company that posted sales of $216 million in 2006. Snook retained a significant interest in the business he founded and stayed on as CEO for a year. In July 2008 he turned over the reins to a new chief executive, although he remained involved as chairman. His successor was Jim Thompson, an executive with 25 years of experience in retailing, much of it related to similar specialty sports businesses.

Thompson was the former CEO of Golfsmith International Holdings Inc., a golf equipment retailer that also started out as a catalog operation. Although Thompson had guided Golfsmith through its initial public offering, he maintained that was not his goal with Performance. Rather, he was quoted in the July 2008 issue of *Sporting Goods Business*, as saying, "My real interest is in the company going from the entrepreneurial phase to the professional phase."

After some groundwork, Thompson implemented what he called a "concept revolution" in 2009. The stores then began to emphasize the cycling lifestyle to enhance the Performance brand. In addition, the Spin Doctor repair and maintenance department was created to develop a secondary brand akin to Best Buy's Geek Squad. It was also an important step in demystifying cycling to appeal to a wider marketplace. The company harbored ambitious plans for the future, and time would tell how well they would succeed.

Ed Dinger

PRINCIPAL SUBSIDIARIES

Bike Nashbar.

PRINCIPAL COMPETITORS

Competitive Cyclist; Recreational Equipment, Inc.; The Sports Authority, Inc.

FURTHER READING

Cox, Jonathan B. "Equity Firm Buys Performance." *News & Observer* (Raleigh, N.C.), July 4, 2007.

Lunan, Charlie. "Golfsmith's Thompson to Steer Performance, Inc." *Sporting Goods Business*, July 2008, p. 10.

Norman, Jason. "Performance Goes After Enthusiast Dollars." *Bicycle Retailer News*, July 30, 2010.

Ranii, David. "Wheels of Fortune Turn in Bike Chain's Favor." *News & Observer*, October 9, 1999, p. D1.

Ryan, Thomas J. "Performance Bicycle Sold to Private Equity Firm." *Sporting Goods Business*, August 2007, p. 10.

Smith, Lisa F. "Performance Poised for Future Growth." *Herald Sun* (Durham, N.C.), November 30, 1999, p. B1.

Welles, Edward O. "A Quantified Success." *Inc.*, August 1991, p. 54.

Pre-Paid Legal Services,
Inc.

One Pre-Paid Way
Ada, Oklahoma 74820
U.S.A.
Telephone: (580) 436-1234
Toll Free: (800) 654-7757
Fax: (580) 421-6305
Web site: http://www.prepaidlegal.com

Public Company
Incorporated: 1976
Employees: 719
Revenues: $458.4 million (2009)
Stock Exchanges: New York
Ticker Symbol: PPD
NAICS: 525190 Other Insurance Funds

■ ■ ■

Pre-Paid Legal Services, Inc., develops, underwrites, and markets various legal expense plans for customers in 48 states, the District of Columbia, and four Canadian provinces. Its offerings include plans for families, for specialized professions and groups, and for businesses, including the self-employed. It also provides products such as Identity Theft Shield and its Internet-based Forms Resource Center with more than 60,000 legal forms. Members pay a monthly premium and have access to a network of independent law firms under contract to Pre-Paid Legal.

The family plans generally cover unlimited, toll-free telephone consultations with provider firms; a call or letter regarding a related matter; review of personal legal documents; and a will with annual reviews and updates. Benefits also include limited representation regarding Internal Revenue Service (IRS) audits and for certain motor vehicle matters, civil cases, and criminal suits. Members also receive a reduced rate at the provider firm for legal services not covered in the plan. One of the pioneers in the United States to provide prepaid legal services, Pre-Paid Legal remains a leader in the industry. It is the nation's first public corporation devoted entirely to developing and marketing prepaid legal services. In 2009 it served over 1.5 million families.

ORIGINS: 1972–79

Backed by the American Bar Association, the first prepaid legal plan in modern America began in 1971 in Shreveport, Louisiana, where the General Contractors Association began providing limited legal services for union members. This set the stage for Harland C. Stonecipher to start Pre-Paid Legal Services. In the June 2, 1986, *Forbes*, he explained one of the reasons for his career choices. "When you grow up a sharecropper's son like I did, you make a list of things you don't want to do for the rest of your life. I didn't want to farm." Stonecipher was the only person in his family to finish high school and attend college. He went to East Central University in Ada, Oklahoma, near his hometown of Tupelo.

After he graduated from college in 1961, Stonecipher began teaching high school English, debate, and drama. He loved teaching but not its low pay, so five years later he quit teaching and began selling life insurance. He did quite well in his new career, and by

COMPANY PERSPECTIVES

We know the wealthiest 10 percent of the population keep their own legal teams on retainer. Conversely, the bottom 10 percent are provided access to the public defender system. It is our goal to make sure the 80 percent in between have a legal voice, and that "Equal Justice Under Law" is a reality for them also!

the early 1970s he was considered starting his own life insurance company rather than work for someone else.

Then in 1972, Stonecipher had a serious car accident that changed his life. He found his insurance covered both his car and medical bills but not his legal expenses of several thousand dollars. He first approached the Oklahoma insurance commissioner to gain approval for his idea for providing legal insurance. Stonecipher and his wife Shirley then established Pre-Paid Legal's predecessor company, Sportsman's Motor Club, an Oklahoma "motor service club" which offered reimbursement for legal expenses.

Stonecipher began his business in Ada, a farming and college community of about 17,000 located a couple hours drive southeast of Oklahoma City. Many at first discounted at his idea, and he had to rely on friends to help finance the new enterprise.

In the November 1987 *Nation's Business*, the founder reflected on the somewhat haphazard origins of Pre-Paid Legal: "If I hadn't had the accident, I probably would have started a life-insurance company. If you wait until you know all the answers, you're not going to start. My theory is simple: ready, fire, aim. I think that's the story of anybody who makes a success. What that means is that you adjust your course as you go along. Looking back, it seems like everything I've done was like jumping off a cliff. But it seems like when I've jumped, things have come out fairly well."

In January 1976 Stonecipher incorporated Pre-Paid Legal Services, which acquired Sportsman's Motor Club through an exchange of stock. Stonecipher became the chairman, president, and CEO of the company. In 1979 Pre-Paid Legal became a public corporation when its stock was traded on the NASDAQ.

NETWORK MARKETING AND FINANCIAL CRISIS: 1983–87

Pre-Paid Legal used typical marketing strategies in the insurance industry to sell its legal insurance. In 1982 sales reached $4 million. At that point, Stonecipher decided to take the advice of an old friend, John Hail, who suggested that multilevel marketing (MLM), also known as network marketing, would be a viable and effective way to sell goods and services. Hail created and independent firm called TVC Marketing Associates to promote Pre-Paid Legal, as an experiment in a few states.

Pre-Paid Legal's use of MLM began well. In just a few years Pre-Paid Legal's sales increased to $8 million. In fact, the results were so favorable that Stonecipher in 1985 purchased TVC and began using network marketing as the sole means of selling its legal services contracts. Pre-Paid Legal also diversified its offerings, using its distributors to market a small radio device called Companion Caller and to sell a package of noninsurance services called TVC Advantage, consisting of a service to help consumers find the best prices on retail merchandise.

By 1986 Pre-Paid Legal had recruited over 110,000 sales associates working as independent contractors. Each paid $55 to sign up and then took a commission. Under network marketing, sales representatives were encouraged to recruit more people to sell the product and to share commissions. Pre-Paid Legal's revenues jumped from $4.5 million and 39,836 policies sold in 1983 to $42 million and 229,632 policies in 1986. In October of that year, the company moved from NASDAQ to the American Stock Exchange. Its AMEX symbol was PPD.

However, some industry analysts were wary of Pre-Paid's structure and practices. An article in the November 2, 1998, issue of *Forbes* explained that to stimulate sales, Pre-Paid "had to pay three years of commissions up front before premiums were collected—yet accounted for them as if they were paid out over three years instead of recording an instant hit to earnings." Several periodicals ran articles questioning the financial stability of Pre-Paid Legal, and the company's stock price dropped to $1. The negative publicity led banks to cut off credit to Pre-Paid Legal.

Owing over $23 million, the company could repay its debt only from internal cash flow. In an interview in the July/August 1997 issue of *Success*, Stonecipher described this most serious crisis in his firm's history: "[We] didn't have the cash to keep growing. So in 1986, we basically shut down our marketing, laid off half our office staff, and just focused on maintaining the accounts we had."

While Pre-Paid Legal was barely surviving in the late 1980s, several other firms had entered the rapidly growing field of legal insurance. The National Resource Center for Consumers of Legal Services estimated that

KEY DATES

■

1972: Harlan Stonecipher establishes The Sportsman's Motor Club offering reimbursement for legal expenses.
1976: Stonecipher incorporates Pre-Paid Legal Services, which acquires Sportsman's.
1979: Pre-Paid Legal Services goes public.
1983: Company initiates sales through network/multilevel marketing.
1993: Pre-Paid Legal markets group legal plans to businesses.
1999: Company expands into Canada.
2003: Opening of new corporate headquarters.

in 1987 about 30 million Americans were enrolled in a prepaid legal plan. In the late 1980s, newcomers to this industry included the Montgomery Ward Signature Group, which sold its plan through direct mail; in just two-and-a-half years it sold 200,000 plans. Other firms using direct mail to promote legal insurance included Hyatt Legal Services and Jacoby & Meyers. Amway used its distributor network to sell 14,000 plans in just eight states within one year of starting its Ultimate Legal Network.

RESTRUCTURING AND CAREFUL GROWTH: 1987–95

Between 1987 and 1991 the company reported losses of $1.1 million, which attributed largely to payments to attorneys. To offset these costs, Pre-Paid Legal made a major change in its legal services when it stopped offering the type of contract called an open plan, whereby members could choose their own attorneys. Experience showed that Pre-Paid had too little control on fees charged by the independent attorneys, which cost the company too much money.

In 1987 the company began selling only closed plans in which clients had to choose from a network of law firms created by Pre-Paid Legal. Usually, the company contracted with one law firm per state. Provider attorneys received a fee for each customer in their area. Of course, Pre-Paid Legal continued to honor the open plans signed before 1987, but those declined as time passed. To raise more money, the company made another stock offering, resulting in several million dollars with which to expand in major ways in the 1990s and reverse its earlier financial woes.

Pre-Paid Legal offered several different prepaid plans. Most individual Pre-Paid Legal customers chose the Family Plan, which allowed the customer to have preventive legal services such as unlimited toll-free phone consultations, correspondence, will preparation, and review of all legal documents. The Family Plan also covered trial defense, IRS audit assistance, and motor vehicle legal services. By 1997 the firm was offering its Family Plan in Spanish in states such as Florida, California, and Texas.

The company also offered its Commercial Driver Legal Plan designed for truck drivers and others who drove commercial vehicles. Underwritten by the Road America Motor Club, this plan's benefits included legal assistance in case of moving and nonmoving violations, arrest and bail bonds, tragic accident defense, car rental discounts, and ambulance services.

In 1991 Pre-Paid Legal began offering its Law Officers Legal Plan, which provided many benefits from the Family Plan, plus 24-hour emergency telephone access to attorneys and also legal assistance for any administrative and post-termination hearings.

The firm's Small Business Legal Plan was first developed and marketed in 1995. It was aimed at small businesses with a maximum of 15 employees and no more than $250,000 in net annual income. The plan covered limited legal correspondence for debt collection or other business disputes, limited document reviews, certain trial defense benefits that increased each year the contract was renewed, and limited other legal consultations and services.

Pre-Paid Legal added two other plans for targeted groups in the 1990s. In 1993 it developed the School Teachers Legal Plan to help teachers facing administrative hearings. Two years later the company worked with a CPA firm to introduce its Tax and Financial Services Plan, designed to help Pre-Paid Legal sales associates receive the legal advice needed to prepare their state and federal income tax forms.

Regardless of the specific legal plan, Pre-Paid Legal customers were entitled to limited benefits. For additional services from a provider attorney, they received a discount, usually 25 percent off standard hourly fees. Average annual prices for new legal plans increased from $165 in 1993 to $215 in 1996.

MARKETING CHANGES 1995–97

Pre-Paid Legal added some new features to its MLM system. Beginning March 1995, it introduced a level commission schedule whereby commissions of about 25 percent were paid during each year customers paid their premiums. Previously, Pre-Paid Legal had paid first-year commissions of around 70 percent, followed by commissions in later years of about 16 percent.

A second innovation to the MLM system was the creation of the regional vice president (RVP) program in July 1996. Pre-Paid Legal Services at that time promoted 14 of its top distributors to become regional vice presidents. This decentralization gave each RVP the responsibility to train sales associates within his or her area.

Third, Pre-Paid Legal began in January 1997 a one-day classroom and field training program for sales associates. Costing $249, which included the regular $65 enrollment fee, this optional program promised new associates enhanced training and the opportunity to advance faster in the firm's MLM program. Current associates paid just $25 for this new Fast Start Program.

By the end of 1996, Pre-Paid Legal had 110,350 active sales associates, an increase from 78,281 in 1995. The company defined active associates as those who sold at least three new contracts per quarter or retained his or her personal contract. As with many other MLM companies, a significant number of sales associates or distributors worked part time.

Another marketing strategy used by Pre-Paid Legal at this time took advantage of the fame of sports celebrities. In 1993 the company entered a marketing agreement to use the services of Roger Staubach, the former Dallas Cowboys quarterback. In 1996 Fran Tarkenton, another former National Football League quarterback, joined the Pre-Paid Legal board of directors. In May 1997 Pre-Paid Legal added membership in the Fran Tarkenton Small Business NETwork as one of the benefits of subscribing to its Small Business Legal Plan. This new benefit allowed small businesses to receive motivational audiotapes, newsletters, advice on setting up a Web site, and various other aids.

CONTINUED GROWTH

By 1997 Pre-Paid Legal had contracts with 35 law firms, ranging in size from 10 to 60 attorneys. Generally there was one contracted firm in each state in which the company operated. For example, the Columbus law firm of Maguire, Vivyan and Schneider was the only firm in Ohio authorized to provide legal services for Pre-Paid Legal customers. Pre-Paid Legal began marketing its individual plans in Ohio in February 1995.

The nation's various plans were represented by a trade organization established by the American Bar Association, Chicago-based American Prepaid Legal Services Institute. In 1996 the institute's executive direc-

tor reported that 90 percent of all prepaid plan subscribers were satisfied with their plans, most state bars had approved prepaid plans, and that they were increasing by 10 percent annually. A 1997 Salomon Brothers report verified that last statistic. It reported that the industry grew 11 percent from 29.5 million consumers 1995 to 33 million in 1996.

Fueling this growth were several general trends in the 1990s. First, increasing litigation over all kinds of issues had increased the need for access to an attorney. The growth of the concept of individual rights unheard of in past years helped create this litigation. Second, attorneys became more aggressive in seeking work for themselves, influenced by a 1977 U.S. Supreme Court decision that lawyers have a right to advertise. With more lawyers graduating from law school, they needed ways to find work, even if it meant working under reduced fees through prepaid legal insurance plans. Third, an increasing number of Americans were starting home-based businesses, including those using MLM.

In 1999 Pre-Paid Legal expanded into Canada. The plans offered there were similar to those in the United States, with slight modifications to address differences between the two judicial systems. Eventually, the company operated in four provinces: Ontario, British Columbia, Alberta, and Manitoba. By 2009 it served about 28,000 families, with about 11,700 sales associates, and collected some $8.2 million in membership fees.

During the 1990s, Pre-Paid developed and implemented a telecommunications monitoring system of the toll-free lines used to contact provider law firms. In an effort to establish and maintain quality control, the system was used to determine, among other benchmarks, the number of calls to participating attorney offices and how quickly the telephone was typically answered. It produced a daily report to the law firms. As part of its customer service efforts, Pre-Paid Legal also randomly surveyed customers each month.

2000 TO THE PRESENT

Over the next decade, the company instituted other changes. It began to repurchase outstanding shares of stock in 1999. In 2000 it introduced the Legal Shield benefit. This rider to a family plan cost $1 and provided immediate access to an attorney should the member be arrested or detained by the police.

During this time, Pre-Paid Legal began using the Internet and direct mail in its marketing plans. This appeared to be an effort to ensure a high renewal rate among members. The company also revised its commission structure and announced it would build a new headquarters in Ada at a cost of $30 million.

The company moved into its new corporate campus in 2003 and introduced a new product, Identify Theft Shield. This was the result of a marketing agreement between Pre-Paid Legal and Kroll Background America Inc. It provided toll-free access to identify theft experts at Kroll, a credit report and credit score along with instructional guides, credit report monitoring and notification, up to $25,000 in credit restoration expense reimbursement insurance, and comprehensive restoration services.

Revenues continued to grow, reaching $361 million in 2003 and $386 million in 2004. Operations generated $61 million and $62 million in cash, respectively. Pre-Paid continued to buy up outstanding shares of stock. 2006 saw the payment of a cash dividend of 30 centers per share. Then, in 2006, the company announced a stock split.

Options for legal services were also growing. In addition to more companies offering legal expense plans, increased amounts of legal information, advice, and documents were now available on the Internet. Legal software packages also began appearing. Pre-Paid Legal offered its own Web-based resource center with over 60,000 legal forms. The company also announced, in 2009, a new Web based marketing process, in a partnership with Blastoff Communications.

In 2010 Stonecipher stepped down as CEO and president. He continued to serve as chairman of the board. Chief Operating Officer Randy Harp was appointed co-CEO and president. Chief Marketing Director and Senior Vice President Mark Brown added co-CEO to his responsibilities.

In its more than three decades of operations, Pre-Paid Legal has faced several challenges. In at least three instances, in 1986, 1997, and 2002, it may have been the target of investors secretly trying to drive down its stock price. Its network marketing structure has been criticized by some as a Ponzi scheme. There have been investigations by the Securities and Exchange Commission and the Federal Trade Commission. Sales associates and customers filed individual and class-action lawsuits about MLM or about inaccurately described benefits.

However, most of the lawsuits were withdrawn, dismissed, or won by Pre-Paid. The company revised its accounting practices and repurchased 14.9 million shares between April 1999 and November 2009. This action made the shares more valuable even as Pre-Paid's once explosive growth leveled off. Furthermore, the company continued to be recognized as among *Forbes's* 200 Best Small Companies.

During the economic recession, Pre-Paid Legal's provider attorneys reported an increased number of calls from customers seeking help with foreclosures and debt collection matters. With some 2.3 million requests for service in 2009, Pre-Paid Legal Services worked to meet the ongoing need for families and businesses to have access to good legal help.

David M. Walden
Updated, Ellen D. Wernick

PRINCIPAL SUBSIDIARIES

Pre-Paid Legal Casualty, Inc.; Pre-Paid Legal Services, Inc., of Florida; Legal Service Plans of Virginia, Inc.; Ohio Access to Justice, Inc.

PRINCIPAL COMPETITORS

ARAG Group; Caldwell Legal, U.S.A.; GE Financial Assurance (Signature Group); Legal Club of America Corporation; MetLife (Hyatt Legal Plans).

FURTHER READING

Anderson, Duncan. "Toughness." *Success*, July/August 1997, pp. 27–28.

Atkinson, William. "Easy Sell?" BenefitsSellingMag.com, July 2010, p. 27.

Bell, Bonnie. "Making America Fairer." *Equities*, January/February 1999, pp. 6–9.

Garland, Susan B. "The H.M.O. Approach to Choosing a Lawyer." *New York Times*, January 11, 2004, p. BU8.

Gubernick, Lisa. "Pyramid Play." *Forbes*, June 2, 1986, p. 125.

Hanania, Joseph. "Who's Minding the Prepaid Legal Service Plans?" *Los Angeles Times*, July 9, 1996, p. E3.

Lubove, Seth. "Fixing the Product." *Forbes*, November 2, 1998, p. 224.

Nuccio, Sal. "Pre-Paid Shadow Boxes with Secret Short Sellers." *Equities*, October/November/December 2002, pp. 28–29.

Palmeri, Christopher. "On the Defense at Pre-Paid Legal Services." *BusinessWeek Online*, April 25, 2002.

"Pre-Paid Legal Services, Inc.—Redefining the Legal Industry." *Salomon Brothers: United States Equity Research*, May 29, 1997.

"Pro's Pick: Legal Care." *USA Today*, August 20, 1996.

Stonecipher, Harland C., and James W. Robinson. *The Pre-Paid Legal Story: The Story of One Man, His Company, and Its Mission to Provide Affordable Legal Protection for Everyone*, New York: Prima Lifestyles, 2000.

Thompson, Roger. "Ready, Fire, Aim." *Nation's Business*, November 1987, p. 77.

Precision Foods, Inc.

———— ■ ————

11457 Olde Cabin Road
St. Louis, Missouri 63141-7139
U.S.A.
Telephone: (314) 567-7400
Fax: (314) 567-7421
Web site: http://www.precisionfoods.com

Wholly Owned Subsidiary of Muscatine Foods Corporation
Incorporated: 1992
Employees: 150
Sales: $85 million (2009 est.)
NAICS: 311000 Food Manufacturing

■ ■ ■

A subsidiary of Muscatine Foods Corporation, Precision Foods, Inc., develops, produces, markets, and distributes a variety of dry blended and packaged foods products. The company serves foodservice, retail, industrial, and international accounts. Notable customers have included such restaurant chains as Cheesecake Factory, Hard Rock Café, Long John Silver's, Ponderosa, Sonic, and Wendy's. Based in St Louis, Missouri, Precision Foods maintains manufacturing operations in Bolingbrook, Illinois; New Sharon, Iowa; and Columbus, Ohio.

The company's branded products include Frostline soft-serve ice cream mix, yogurts, shakes, and smoothies; Mrs. Dash seasoning; Foothill Farms salad dressings and seasoning mixes; Tuf gravies, cheese sauces, soups, and desserts; Thick-It pureed food thickener for dietary care patients; Dole Soft Serve fruit flavored ice cream mix; Land O'Lakes Cocoa Classics hot chocolate mix; Milani Gourmet gravies, salad dressings, cheese sauces, rice and stuffing, desserts, and drink mixes; Smithers beef, chicken, and vegetarian broth; Baker's Joy no-stick spray; and Sugar Twin portion control sweeteners.

ORIGINS IN 1927

Precision Foods was created by Varied Investments, Inc., whose origins date to 1927 when G.A. Kent formed Kent Feeds in Indianola, Iowa. Kent moved the livestock feed manufacturing business to Muscatine, Iowa, in 1936 to take advantage of the town's proximity to the Mississippi River. Seven years later he took on a partner to form Grain Processing Corporation (GPC) to produce grain alcohol for use in the production of synthetic rubber. The Kent family went on to acquire other feed companies and in 1988 formed Varied Investments, Inc., to serve as a holding company for its business interests. Varied Investments took the name Muscatine Foods Corporation in 2005.

In early 1992 the Kent family acquired Precision Pack Foods to form the foundation for Precision Foods. Jerry Fritz and three partners had founded Precision Pack in 1989 as a custom dry seasoning blender. Fritz had previously run the foodservice operations for Pet Incorporated. Fritz stayed on as president of Precision Pack under the new ownership. He took on greater responsibility later in 1992 when Precision Pack was merged with the Frostline Foods division of GPC, a one-product company offering soft-serve ice cream mix. The combined operation took the name of Precision Foods, which was initially a GPC subsidiary and maintained its headquarters in Iowa. Annual sales at the time were in the $16 million range.

DACUS FOODS ACQUIRED: 1995

Precision Foods relied on internal growth until 1995, when it began pursuing acquisitions in earnest. In May of that year it acquired Dacus Foods Group Inc., a Tupelo, Mississippi-based consumer packaging food company that made canning products, gourmet foods, and custom-blended spices and seasonings for the institutional markets. Also in 1995, Precision Foods opened its Bolingbrook, Illinois, manufacturing operation, leasing about 50,000 square feet at a new industrial facility located near Chicago.

In early 1996 Precision Foods relocated its headquarters to St. Louis, Missouri, and became a stand-alone business. The move had been a goal of Fritz, who had lived in St. Louis since 1978 when he joined Pet. In August 1996 Precision Foods acquired Melrose Park, Illinois-based Milani Foods from Albert-Culver Co. Started in 1938, Milani was well established, a provider of shelf stable products in all the major food categories, including food bases, soups, beverages, salad dressings, condiments, desserts, and dietetic food products. Customers included restaurants, hotels, hospitals and clinics, nursing homes, and schools. All told, with the acquisition Precision Foods added more than 300 products, as well as $15 million in combined annual sales, but not Milani's manufacturing operation. Acquired brands included Milani, Smithers, Diafoods, and Thick-It.

The acquisition of Milani helped Precision Foods to increase revenues to $43.5 million in 1997. The company then set a goal of double-digit growth each year on its way to establishing a $100 million sales target. However, for the next few years the company depended on organic growth and failed to enjoy the kind of sales increases it envisioned. In 2001 the company added to its slate of products through a distribution deal with West Chicago, Illinois-based Jel Sert Co. Precision then marketed and distributed the Royal brand of gelatin, pudding, and mousse products, as well as Fleischmann's Baking Powder, to the foodservice sector in the United States.

In the early years of the 21st century the Bolingbrook plant was expanded to 125,000 square feet, and a second shift was then added. To take full advantage of the facility's increased capacity, Precision Foods in 2003 closed its Tupelo plant, which had served as a specialty operation focused on small-batch orders. Precision Foods was experiencing an increase in large-batch orders, and because the Bolingbrook facility was better suited to satisfy the new sales trend, the Tupelo operation became unnecessary and was shuttered.

BENNO FOODS ACQUIRED: 2003

Annual revenues were in the $50 million range in 2003. Precision Foods completed its next significant acquisition a year later. In the spring of that year it purchased Stockton, California-based Benno Food Products Corporation for a price that was reportedly "under $10 million." Benno brought the Foothill Farms brand of sauces, seasoning mixes, and dry salad dressing mixes, which were distributed across the United States and Canada to restaurants, bars, hospitals, schools, and correctional facilities.

Because all of Benno's business was in the foodservice trade, which was also the bulk of the business of Precision Foods, Benno was an excellent fit. For Benno Food and its founder and president, Ed Brink, the time had come to join forces with a larger player like Precision Foods. Manufacture of Foothill Farms products was moved from California to the Bolingbrook plant and Brink stayed on as a consultant to help with the transition in production.

Brink was also instrumental in the next acquisition made by Precision Foods. One of his friends, Arnie D'Angelo, was president of International Marketing Systems, whose Shelton, Connecticut-based subsidiary Alternative Channels LLC manufactured hot cocoa and cappuccino mixes for club stores such as Costco, BJ's Wholesale Club, and Sam's Club. Brink introduced D'Angelo to Jerry Fritz, and the two began negotiating a sale of Alternative Channels to Precision Foods. The deal was completed in October 2006, at a price reportedly "under $20 million."

Not only did Alternative Channels immediately bring $20 million in sales to the balance sheet, it was a good fit for Precision Foods for a number of other reasons. Because so much of the business of Precision Foods was ice cream mixes, sales of which were made mostly during the warmer months, the addition of hot drink mixes helped to balance out sales over the course of the year. Furthermore, Alternative Channels had limited penetration in the foodservice area, providing an

KEY DATES

1992: Company is formed through merger of Precision Pack with Frostline Foods division of GPC.
1995: Dacus Foods Group is acquired.
1996: Headquarters move to St. Louis.
2004: Benno Food Products is acquired.
2007: Total Ultimate Foods is acquired.

opportunity for Precision Foods to use its existing customer base in this area, as well as its deeper pockets, to increase sales.

Although the Alternatives Channels name was retired, Precision Foods retained the customer lists, recipes, and brands, including Cocoa Classic and Cappuccino Classic. A deal was also reached with St. Paul, Minnesota-based Land O'Lakes Inc. to continue to market mixes under the valuable Land O'Lakes label. Moreover, Precision Foods hired D'Angelo and his partner Tom O'Hara to serve as the company's agents with the club stores, thus realizing another valuable benefit from the acquisition.

TOTAL ULTIMATE FOODS ACQUIRED: 2007

With annual sales of $70 million, Precision Foods pursued further external growth, as much by necessity as by choice. The foodservice industry was undergoing a period of consolidation, making it imperative for a midsize company like Precision Foods to continue to expand in order to achieve the kind of scale necessary to remain competitive. In May 2007 Precision Foods acquired Columbus, Ohio-based Total Ultimate Foods Inc. This was a family-owned business and a competitor with which Fritz was very familiar. In recent years he had broached the idea of an acquisition, but only after the death of the founder did officials at Total Ultimate Foods call Fritz about selling the business as part of a succession plan to ensure the future of the employees.

Founded in 1981, Total Ultimate Foods developed premium mixes, working with local, regional, and national foodservice customers, including such notable restaurant chains as Bob Evans, Denny's, Kentucky Fried Chicken, Shoney's, Skyline Chili, and Wendy's. Schools and correctional facilities were also important sectors. Products included sauces, gravies, salad dressings, seasoning mixes, and desserts. Annual sales were estimated by industry sources at $13 million, but Fritz

told the press that sales for Total Ultimate Foods were more than $15 million. The deal moved Precision Foods closer to its $100 million annual sales target.

The benefits of the combination of Precision Foods and Total Ultimate Foods were manifold. Not only did increased scale bring greater buying power, it created deeper research and development capabilities and prepared the ground for further innovation. Unlike with previous acquisitions, Precision Foods also elected to retain the manufacturing operations. The company thus added an 80,000-square-foot plant in Columbus to go with the operations it maintained in Bolingbrook and New Sharon, Iowa, as well as a new distribution hub. Furthermore, this was the first time that Precision Foods acquired a direct competitor. Hence, it added an entirely new slate of customers, ones that could be cross-sold other products of Precision Foods.

SAMS FOOD ADDED: 2008

As industry consolidation continued, Precision Foods added another $5 million in annual sales in the summer of 2008 with the acquisition of Bedford Park, Illinois-based SAMS Food Group Inc. for about $10 million. The business had become available in late 2007 when the company's lease for its production facility was set to expire. Forced to either relocate or sell the company, Alan Levin, the owner of SAMS, opted for the latter course and contacted Fritz about a possible sale.

SAMS produced the Orrington Farms brand of dry blended soup bases, sauces, gravies, and seasonings. In addition to restaurants, schools, and hospitals, SAMS served industrial food processors and retail grocery stores. The retail business, which accounted for about 60 percent of sales for SAMS, was especially important to Precision Foods as the company sought to build up its consumer products division, already enjoying solid growth.

Because of poor economic conditions, consumers were eating out less and cooking at home to save money. As a result, supermarket sales were improving for Precision Foods, offsetting sluggish sales in other sectors. As with previous acquisitions, Precision Foods also benefited from the addition of the research and development efforts of SAMS. With the loss of its manufacturing facility, SAMS was then able to transfer its operations to the Precision Foods plant in nearby Bolingbrook. The proximity of the two plants also allowed some 20 employees of SAMS to keep their jobs and commute to Bolingbrook.

While assimilating the SAMS acquisition, Precision Foods looked for further ways to pursue organic growth during the prevailing poor economic conditions. Catering to consumers' desire for desserts with some health benefits, for example, the company introduced Nutri-Packets in 2009. The mix-in pouches added nutrients to Frostline soft-serve.

Consumers were also keen to save money, and many of them were rediscovering home canning of fruits and vegetables. One of the Precision Foods brands, Mrs. Wages, benefited from this trend. On the market for 40 years, Mrs. Wages was a leading brand of home canning pickling spices, and salsa, chili, and pasta sauce mixes. Given the breadth of its product offerings, there was every reason to believe that Precision Foods would successfully weather lean times and resume strong growth in the years to come.

Ed Dinger

PRINCIPAL DIVISIONS

Food Service; Industrial; International; Retail Consumers.

PRINCIPAL COMPETITORS

ConAgra Foods, Inc.; Heinz Foodservice; Sara Lee North American Foodservice.

FURTHER READING

Duran, Karen M. "Precision Foods Breaks Ground for New Bolingbrook Facility." *Daily Herald*, July 31, 1995, p. 1.

Jackson, Margaret. "Precision Foods Mixes Up $43 Million in Revenue." *St. Louis Business Journal*, May 1, 1998.

Tritto, Christopher. "Deal to Stir Up $70 Million in Sales for Precision Foods." *St. Louis Business Journal*, October 13, 2006.

———. "Precision Adds $5 Million in Sales with SAMS Buy." *St. Louis Business Journal*, August 1, 2008.

———. "Precision Foods Buys Benno, Looks for More Acquisitions." *St. Louis Business Journal*, March 5, 2004.

———. "Precision Foods' Fritz Closes TUF Deal." *St. Louis Business Journal*, May 4, 2007.

Progress Software
Corporation

———————■———————

14 Oak Park Drive
Bedford, Massachusetts 01730-1414
U.S.A.
Telephone: (781) 280-4000
Toll Free: (800) 477-6473
Fax: (781) 280-4095
Web site: http://www.progress.com

Public Company
Incorporated: 1981 as Data Language Corp.
Employees: 1,821
Sales: $494.1 million (2009)
Stock Exchanges: NASDAQ
Ticker Symbol: PRGS
NAICS: 511210 Software Publishers

■ ■ ■

A public company based in Bedford, Massachusetts, Progress Software Corporation is a global enterprise software company that divides its business into three units: Application Development Platforms, Enterprise Business Solutions, and Enterprise Data Solutions. The main product offered by the Application Development Platforms business unit is the OpenEdge line that helps customers to develop, deploy, and manage business applications. Products offered by the Enterprise Business Solutions unit help customers to integrate and manage business applications in real time. The Enterprise Data Solutions unit provides data management, data integration, replication, caching, access, and security capabilities covering multiple data sources.

All told, Progress serves more than 140,000 customers in more than 180 countries. They include corporations in financial services, health care, manufacturing, and technology, as well as government agencies. In addition to its Bedford headquarters, Progress maintains 24 locations in North America and 35 locations in other parts of the world.

COMPANY FOUNDED: 1981

Progress Software Corporation was founded in Bedford, Massachusetts, in 1981 by three veterans of the mainframe computer application development market, Joseph Alsop (nephew of the political columnist Joseph Alsop and older brother of future computer industry commentator Stewart Alsop II), Clyde Kessel, and Charles Ziering. It was incorporated that same year as Data Language Corporation. Alsop went on to become president of the company, while Kessel became director of development and Ziering became chief technical officer.

Data Language Corporation targeted the need for comprehensive and high-level application development products able to enhance information processing productivity in a growing midrange computer systems market. The company was launched after its founders developed the PROGRESS Application Development Environment (ADE), designed to enable development and deployment of software applications that were scalable, portable, and reconfigurable across client/server, host-based, and mixed computer environments.

Opting to avoid head-on competition with established mainframe computer software companies and choosing not to develop software for the then young IBM personal computer (with limited memory), the company's founders initially developed the PROGRESS ADE for only the Unix operating system, closely associated with the third-generation COBOL or language C, a programming language popular only within academic and scientific communities at that time.

PROGRESS SOFTWARE NAME ADOPTED: 1987

Data Language released its first commercial version of the PROGRESS ADE for Unix in 1984, and the following year unveiled a version for MS-DOS. Data Language recorded its first profitable year in 1985, the company's first full year of product shipments. By 1987 the company had released PROGRESS software for computer networks and the VAX/VMS (a Digital Equipment platform) and CTOS/BTOS operating systems and was gaining increasing marketplace attention and brand name recognition. As a result, the company changed its name to Progress Software Corporation to reflect the name of its software.

During the late 1980s about half of Progress's revenues were being generated annually from international business that stemmed from a network of 10 wholly owned subsidiaries in Europe and Australia and a distribution system spanning Europe, Asia, and Latin America. By 1990 company sales had increased sevenfold since 1987, from $6.1 million to $40 million.

Between 1989 and 1990 Progress released PROGRESS Version 5 and Version 6, both enhanced versions of its fourth-generation language (4GL) and Relational Database Management System (RDBMS). New features of Version 5 included support for ANSI-standard Structured Query Language (SQL) and a DOS memory saver. Applications developed with Version 5 could run unaltered on multiple operating systems, diverse networks, and numerous operating systems and network protocols. Version 6 allowed users to access, modify, and integrate data in and among databases made by Progress, Oracle, and Digital Equipment Corp. (DEC), and the updated RDBMS additionally allowed

users to access third-generation language (3GL) and as many as 240 databases simultaneously.

CROSS-PLATFORM REACH EXPANDED: 1991

By 1990 Unix had become a commercially popular operating system because it was not restricted to particular computer brands and functioned on a multiple-user network. As a result Unix was popular with Progress's customers, large corporation computer programmers writing custom-designed software for in-house use, representing about one-third of the company's business, and resellers, typically selling deployment versions to clients in retailing, medical accounting, manufacturing, and trucking.

Entering the 1990s the company's marketing focus was directed toward these "value-added" resellers that used Progress products to develop their own commercially sold software applications. The middleman resellers of PROGRESS products purchased program development software from Progress and then in turn spawned business as their clients purchased dozens of scaled-down program versions, each requiring a deployment license from Progress and thereby generating substantial follow-on revenues (represented by more than 60 percent of the company's 1990 North American revenues).

In 1991 Progress expanded its cross-platform reach after agreeing with Micro Decisionware Inc. to develop and market a link from the PROGRESS 4GL and RDBMS to IBM host environments that could connect to Micro Decisionware's database. That same year the PROGRESS ADE was chosen over competing systems made by Oracle, Ingres, Informix, and Sybase to support the new second-generation library automation system made by CLSI Inc., a leader in the library automation industry.

TAKEN PUBLIC: 1991

Progress went public in July 1991, selling 1.2 million shares of stock (half by the company and half by certain stockholders) at an initial offering price of $25. The company's stock debuted as one of the most active stocks in over-the-counter trading on the New York Stock Exchange. Proceeds were used to cover working capital needs through the 1992 fiscal year. With technology stocks a hot commodity on Wall Street, within a week of the initial public offering Progress's stock had climbed to $28.75 a share and by November of that same year had risen to $44. For its 1991 fiscal year, Progress's earnings rose 58 percent to $6 million

```
┌─────────────────────────────────────────────┐
│  ┌─────────────────────────────────────────┐ │
│  │                                         │ │
│  │            KEY DATES                    │ │
│  │                 ■                       │ │
│  │  ─────────────────────────────────      │ │
│  │  1981:  Company is founded as Data      │ │
│  │         Language Corp.                  │ │
│  │  1987:  Name is changed to Progress     │ │
│  │         Software.                       │ │
│  │  1991:  Company is taken public.        │ │
│  │  2001:  Progress reorganizes operations.│ │
│  │  2008:  Annual revenues top $500 million.│ │
│  │                                         │ │
│  └─────────────────────────────────────────┘ │
└─────────────────────────────────────────────┘
```

on revenues that jumped 46 percent to $58.3 million.

After broadening its focus in 1991 to include IBM platforms, in February 1992 Progress released PROGRESS/400, an updated version of its application development software for the IBM AS/400 operating environment. The new software allowed AS/400 developers and users to create and run client/server applications in the AS/400 environment and for the first time allowed users to access data across a network of MS-Windows, OS/2 and RS/6000-AIX that was linked to IBM AS/400 database servers. The release of PROGRESS/400 not only brought the capabilities of PROGRESS to the IBM AS/400 midrange computer family, it also marked a formalization of a marketing and sales agreement that named Progress an IBM "industry applications specialist" and helped spawn an agreement for Progress to develop cooperative applications for J.D. Edwards & Company, a leading supplier of AS/400 environment software.

In 1992 Progress and Object Design, Inc., agreed to jointly develop and market software linking the PROGRESS 4GL to Object Design's ObjectStore object-oriented (OO) database management system. That same year Progress linked up with Avis Inc. to develop a new transaction-processing system for rental car tracking based on the PROGRESS system. By the close of 1992 Progress's global operations had been expanded to 12 subsidiaries and 34 distributors operating in more than 50 countries. For fiscal 1992 Progress's earnings grew 58 percent to $9.61 million on revenues that increased 46 percent to $85 million.

Progress entered 1993 fifth in the $1.2 billion Unix market for application development tools (controlling about 4 percent of the market), with its shares trading at $57. Progress's business strategy had evolved by this time to include competing with major application development forces such as Oracle in the open database system market by producing application development tools that could run on both PROGRESS and Oracle databases. While larger competitors often targeted a customer base that focused on central corporate offices such as accounting, Progress's products targeted individual lines of business within corporations that tended to require customized applications and thereby offered a marketing niche for Progress.

STRATEGIC ALLIANCES MULTIPLY: 1993

In order to broaden the ability of PROGRESS to support other operating systems, in 1993 Progress expanded its strategic alliances and was named an "independent software vendor" for Unisys, making the PROGRESS ADE the first to be jointly marketed under the Unisys developer relations program. That same year Progress also signed a cooperative software marketing agreement with IBM, becoming one of the first application development tool vendors chosen by IBM to join its market development program designed to increase the number of AS/400 application development tools available.

Also in 1993, Progress signed an agreement to support Novell Inc.'s network operating systems (which in turn could be connected to IBM's AS/400 midrange platform), as well as an agreement with Santa Cruz Operation, an international leader in open systems software, for joint engineering, training, and support.

Delays in the delivery of PROGRESS Version 7 pushed the company's stock to around $35 a share in 1993 before the new operating system was released late that year in Progress's first worldwide marketing initiative and global positioning of its product line. Version 7, a cross-platform ADE featuring new capabilities for client/server environments, expanded Progress's stake in the server and application development market to include Windows and Motif graphical user interface (GUI) platforms, with versions released for Windows, SCO Unix, HP/UX, AIX, and SPARC operating systems. Version 7's cross-platform ADE allowed users to create both character-based and GUI applications and to move applications to Windows or Motif without any code changes, making it easier for developers to create new Windows and Motif applications.

EXPANDED MARKET REACH

In 1993 Progress continued expanding its marketing reach, adding three new wholly owned subsidiaries, in Spain, Mexico, and Singapore, aimed at strengthening the company's position in Asian/Pacific, Latin American, and European markets. By the end of the year Progress had 15 international subsidiaries and the company was ranked 82nd on *Fortune* magazine's list of America's 100 fastest-growing companies and 86th on the *Forbes* 1993 list of the 200 best small publicly traded companies.

Progress also had a network of more than 2,000 resellers using the company's application tools to develop custom applications, with 60 percent of the company's revenues in 1993 coming from these activities and add-on sales of deployment software versions. For 1993 the company's earnings rose 34 percent to $12.8 million on revenues that rose 31 percent to $111.64 million. Despite the company's move into the IBM AS/400, more than two-thirds of the company's revenues came from Unix products in 1993.

By 1994 Progress had a range of products that could work in a variety of development and deployment environments and support graphical, character mode, and block mode application deployment using either the PROGRESS RDBMS or other high-performance data servers to work across networked, client/server designs. In 1994 Progress began focusing on speeding up the process of application development and providing greater access to various operating systems, resulting in the release of PROGRESS Dataserver, a Windows-based program enabling users to access information in databases of two competitors, Oracle and Sybase. That same year Progress entered into a cross-platform support agreement with Novell.

In June 1994 Progress formed a joint venture subsidiary with Nissho Iwai Corporation, one of Japan's largest diversified general trading companies. The new 50 percent owned subsidiary, designed to market PROGRESS products and expand the company's presence in the Pacific Rim, was later incorporated as Progress Software KK.

CRESCENT SOFTWARE ACQUIRED: 1995

With more than 250,000 product licenses worldwide and a network of 18 international subsidiaries and 33 distributors operating in 60 countries, Progress began 1995 by substantially expanding its product line through a significant acquisition. In January 1995 Progress acquired Crescent Software Inc., a Connecticut-based leading developer of add-on components for users of Microsoft's Visual Basic (VB), for $3 million (including about $2.5 million of in-process software development). At the same time Progress created two divisions within the company, the Enterprise Division, to develop and market all PROGRESS products, and the Crescent Division, to market existing Crescent add-on components and develop an integrated suite of high-performance products to enhance and make application development within VB easier.

The acquisition of Crescent targeted Progress's growing interest in serving an estimated one million VB

users and giving those developers of client/server applications more options when working with the Microsoft application development program. With VB growing in popularity as a client/server tool for personal and workgroup market segments, the acquisition resulted in several strategic benefits. It legitimized the market for VB add-ons (which previously were often of low quality and developed by smaller software firms); it expanded Progress's product line into low-end software; and it provided the company with a means to turn around a two-year slide in sales growth by capitalizing on the growing popularity of VB and offering developers tools and components to build more complex applications.

At the time of the acquisition Crescent developed and sold VB tools and components and had its own communications add-on code. In addition, Progress set its new division on a course to create development tools for faster VB applications and announced the planned development of new VB add-ons that could translate VB code into C++ (a modified version of language C). Two months after Progress acquired Crescent, the company unveiled the division's first new product, PowerPak Pro, a suite of VB development tools and components designed to provide users with more efficient development and deployment of workgroup and departmental applications for businesses.

Progress continued expanding its international operations in 1995. In February the company opened its first Central European subsidiary (and its 13th European subsidiary) in Prague, Czech Republic. The new subsidiary, Progress Software SPOL, S.R.O., was formed to market and support the company's PROGRESS ADE in the rapidly growing republic and serve governmental and industrial customers, including those in banking, finance, health care, and manufacturing. In June 1995 Progress opened a centralized technical support facility in Rotterdam, Netherlands, to serve its operations in Europe, the Middle East, and Africa. The new EMEA Technical Service Centre, offering a laboratory, training capabilities, and engineers fluent in local languages, initiated service for the Netherlands with support for other countries to be phased in through 1996.

INTERNET SUPPLIER: 1996

In November 1995 Progress released its PROGRESS Version 8 ADE, making client/server application development easier and faster by capitalizing on the power of OO programming, a component-based visual programming development environment. Features of Version 8 included the new PROGRESS SmartObjects that capitalized on the advanced OO technology and provided reusable application components (or preprogrammed components) that could be assembled into applications.

In late 1995 Progress announced it would support DEC's Alpha systems running on the Microsoft Windows operating system, and the Crescent Division released its new VB4 Jump Start Kit, which could assist corporate developers with their transition to the Microsoft Windows 95 operation system and VB 4.0. Crescent also introduced OLE Custom Controls (OCX) versions of its entire product line, enabling corporate developers to create more sophisticated VB business applications using custom controls.

Progress's sales growth began declining during the early 1990s, falling from 46 percent in 1992 to 25 percent in 1994 as resellers were slow to convert from the company's older character-driven versions of PROGRESS to the more graphical, event-driven programs beginning with Version 7. That conversion was nearly complete by the close of 1995, however. For the year Progress's sales growth climbed to 29 percent, and earnings rose 16 percent to $16.68 million on revenues of $180.13 million (compared to 1994 when the company's stock fluctuated from a high of $56.50 to a low of $27.25 and Progress earned $16.9 million on revenues of $139.2 million).

In early 1996 Progress began initial steps to become a major Internet supplier of products by using the Web to market its products, offering buyers the opportunity to secure and order delivery of products. The company also announced that by midyear its Enterprise Division would sell SmartObjects products through a Web site storefront. In early 1996 the Crescent Division also took initial steps to use the Internet for marketing purposes and launched Code Depot, an online storefront designed to serve the needs of VB application programmers.

OPERATIONS REORGANIZED: 2001

By the close of 1996 Progress's principal competition consisted of larger companies, including Oracle, Sybase (which in 1995 acquired another competitor, PowerSoft Corp.), and Informix. Nevertheless, Progress had a distinct competitive advantage in its RDBMS, which could work on most types of computer hardware, including that made by competitors. The company also expected to profit from the growing VB add-on tools market by introducing new products and capitalizing on the strong relationship Crescent had with Microsoft Corp., allowing Progress to take advantage of the release of new Microsoft desktop standards.

Progress additionally hoped to benefit from two business trends: the growth in corporate client/server-based networks; and the decentralization of large corporations, which increased the importance of the departmental market for application development software. Progress completed another significant acquisition in 1997 when it paid $13 million in cash and stock for Apptivity Corp., adding Java-based client/server development tools to its product line.

Progress closed the 1990s by forming a unit that catered to independent software venders interested in entering the application services provider market. The company then reorganized its operations in 2001 to convert a diverse number of products into three operating subsidiaries: Progress Company, a development software division; Sonic Software Corporation, focusing on messaging software; and NuSphere Corporation, offering open source software and services. The following year the company added a fourth operating unit, Peer-Direct Corporation, a computing applications distributor.

The broadened scope of Progress proved beneficial in the early years of the new century when the technology industry experienced a steep downturn. While most areas were weak, there were enough ascending markets in which the company was involved to make up the difference. Progress was healthy enough to continue to pursue external growth during this period. In 2002 database software company eXcelon was acquired for $24 million, adding XML services and database products.

A year later Progress paid $88 million for data connectivity tools supplier DataDirect Technologies. Progress then grew its ObjectStore unit in 2004 with the $16 million addition of Persistence Software, Inc., a provider of distributed data access and caching software, and the $25 million purchase of Apama Inc., a U.K. provider of event stream processing technology. Apama was also a prized acquisition because it counted among its customers JP Morgan Chase.

ADDITIONAL ACQUISITIONS

More acquisitions followed in 2006. NEON Systems, a provider of mainframe data access and integration software, and Actional Corporation, developer of service-oriented architecture (SOA) management software, were added in early 2006. Later in the year Progress acquired Pantero Corporation, an innovative provider of semantic integration technology to deliver data in business integration projects. Also in 2006, Progress acquired OpenAccess Software, a developer of toolkits and runtime software used to create custom drivers for data sources. These additions helped Progress to increase revenues to $447 million in fiscal 2006 and $493.5 million in fiscal 2007.

More acquisitions followed in 2008. Data integration leader Xcalia was added, along with Mindreef Inc., a developer of software tools for implementing SOAs, and IONA Technologies, a developer of SOA infrastructure software that rounded out Progress's product portfolio. Revenues improved to $514.6 million in fiscal 2008. A downturn in the economy led to a dip in revenues to $494.1 million in fiscal 2009. While Progress took steps to cut costs, reducing its global workforce by 12 to 14 percent, it retained its ability to make strategic acquisitions.

In early 2010 Progress purchased Savvion Inc., a provider of business process management technology. Progress also shuffled its operations, creating three business units, Application Development Platforms, Enterprise Business Solutions, and Enterprise Data Solutions. By this time, Progress had a proven 30-year track record of adapting to changes in the marketplace. There was every reason to believe that the company would continue to succeed in the foreseeable future.

Roger W. Rouland
Updated, Ed Dinger

PRINCIPAL OPERATING UNITS

Application Development Platforms; Enterprise Business Solutions; Enterprise Data Solutions.

PRINCIPAL COMPETITORS

IBM Software; Oracle Corporation; TIBCO Software Inc.

FURTHER READING

Bonasia, J. "Progress Software Helping Firms Think Fast by Crunching Data." *Investor's Business Daily*, June 20, 2005, p. A6.

Churbuck, David. "Speaking the Language." *Forbes*, November 25, 1991, p. 192.

Coleman, Murray. "For Progress Software, Small Databases Bring Solid Earnings Growth." *Investor's Business Daily*, April 26, 2002, p. A4.

Gambon, Jill. "Progress Software Reaps Profits, Wants Visibility." *Boston Business Journal*, January 25, 1993, p. 7.

Holland, Roberta. "One Company Resolves Midlife Woes." *eWeek*, January 29, 2001, p. 34.

Kingoff, Elaine. "Progress Marches On." *VarBusiness*, April 15, 1995.

Leach, Norvin. "Progress Looks to Low End Tools for Higher Growth." *PC Week*, February 6, 1995, p. 116.

PUMA AG Rudolf Dassler Sport

Wurzburger Strasse 13
Herzogenaurach, D-91074
Germany
Telephone: (49 9132) 81-0
Fax: (49 9132) 81-22-46
Web site: http://www.puma.com

Public Company
Incorporated: 1948 as PUMA Schuhfabrik Rudolf Dassler
Employees: 9,503
Sales: EUR 2.46 billion ($3.53 billion) (2009)
Stock Exchanges: Frankfurt Munich
Ticker Symbol: PUM
NAICS: 316211 Rubber and Plastics Footwear Manufacturing; 316219 Other Footwear Manufacturing; 315212 Women's, Girls', and Infants' Cut and Sew Apparel Contractors; 315211 Men's and Boys' Cut and Sew Apparel Contractors

∎∎∎

PUMA AG is among the world's leading sportlifestyle manufacturers of footwear, apparel, and accessories. The company's Sports Performance and Lifestyle labels are worn by footballers across the globe as well as athletes involved in motorsports, golf, and sailing. Soccer stars Pelé and Diego Maradona wore the PUMA logo during their legendary careers. PUMA's fashion products have been created by well-known designers including the late Alexander McQueen, Mihara Yasuhiro, and Sergio Rossi. The company's brands, including PUMA, Cobra, and Tretorn, are distributed in over 120 countries across the globe. French luxury group PPR SA purchased over 60 percent of PUMA in 2007.

SMALL-TOWN ORIGINS

In the small town of Herzogenaurach, not far from the German city of Nuremberg, two brothers laid the foundation for what would become the European capital of sportswear. Adolf and Rudolf Dassler were born into a poor family at the dawn of the 19th century. Their father, Christoph Dassler, was a worker at a shoe factory, while their mother, Pauline Dassler, ran a small laundry business. At age 15 Rudolf Dassler started working at the same shoe factory as his father and soon showed the qualities of an entrepreneur. He was energetic, persistent, and ambitious, and he saved his hard-earned money instead of spending it right away. However, it was not until after World War I that he had an opportunity to prove himself in business. After the war, Rudolf Dassler took his first positions in business management, first at a porcelain factory and later in a leather wholesale business in Nuremberg.

In the early 1920s Rudolf Dassler decided to go back to Herzogenaurach and team up with his brother Adolf in a business partnership. Their company, which was incorporated as the Gebrüder Dassler Schuhfabrik in 1924, produced slippers and outdoor shoes. Rudolf Dassler ran the business, while Adolf took care of the technical operations and production. Soon they realized that there was not a particularly promising market for their shoes and so switched their focus to the manufacture of track shoes and football boots, a market that was just getting started at that time.

At PUMA, we believe that our position as the creative leader in Sportlifestyle gives us the opportunity and the responsibility to contribute to a better world for the generations to come. A better world in our vision—the PUMAVision—would be safer, more peaceful, and more creative than the world we know today. The 4Keys is the tool we have developed to help us stay true to this PUMAVision, and we use it by constantly asking ourselves if we are being Fair, Honest, Positive, and Creative in everything we do. We believe that by staying true to our values, inspiring the passion and talent of our people, working in sustainable, innovative ways, and doing our best to be Fair, Honest, Positive, and Creative, we will keep on making the products our customers love, and at the same time bring that vision of a better world a little closer every day.

With a great deal of luck the company acquired its first major client, the sports club in Herzogenaurach, which ordered no fewer than 10,000 pairs of athletic shoes in 1925. Thus, despite the ongoing worldwide economic depression in the late 1920s, the Dassler company took off and gained a reputation among athletes and sporting goods companies. Half of all athletes at the Olympic Games in Amsterdam in 1928 wore Dassler shoes. In 1936 African-American track star Jesse Owens brought the company into the public eye when he won four gold medals at the Olympic Games in Berlin wearing Dassler shoes.

PARTING WAYS: 1948

Three years later World War II broke out. Although the brothers could have given up for a number of reasons during the war, it was not this world-shattering event that led to the Dassler company's sudden end, but a homemade war of a different kind. In 1948 the two brothers had a serious falling-out, and they stopped talking to each other. Their company was split into two new companies: Adolf Dassler formed his own business named adidas, combining his nickname Adi with the first three letters of his last name; Rudolf Dassler set up his own shop called PUMA Schuhfabrik Rudolf Dassler. The two brothers had become competitors.

A number of world-class athletes, especially runners and soccer players, helped the young PUMA brand gain

acceptance. In 1950, at the first international soccer match after World War II, several German players wore the PUMA "Atom" shoe. The Olympic Games in 1952 in Helsinki were a spectacular success for PUMA and opened the British market to the young company. The American Olympic Committee made PUMA its official shoe supplier in 1952 and again 1956. In 1952 the U.S. women's 400-meter relay team won the Olympic gold medal in PUMA running shoes. PUMA's image was also carried around the world by the rising soccer star Pelé, the Brazilian "king of the stadium" who favored PUMA's "King" shoes.

After some early difficulty, the company's export business began to thrive. PUMA shoes were shipped to 55 countries on five continents. The first licensed production line was opened in Austria. In 1959 Rudolf Dassler's firm was transformed into PUMA Sportschuhfabriken Rudolf Dassler Kommanditgesellschaft, as Dassler's wife and his two sons, Armin and Gerd, became part owners of the firm. By 1962 PUMA shoes were exported to almost 100 countries around the world.

Another PUMA hallmark was product innovation. In 1960 PUMA introduced a new technology for soccer shoes, using a vulcanization process to join the soles to the uppers. Soon 80 percent of all soccer shoes were manufactured with this technology. In the early 1960s PUMA also developed running shoes with a uniquely shaped sole that supported the natural movement of the foot, based on the latest medical research of the time. In the late 1960s PUMA was the first company to offer athletic shoes with a Velcro strap.

A SECOND GENERATION OF FAMILY LEADERSHIP: 1974

Rudolf Dassler died in 1974, and his son Armin A. Dassler, who since the early 1960s had been managing PUMA's first foreign subsidiary in Salzburg, Austria, took his place. Twelve years later PUMA went public and was renamed PUMA AG Rudolf Dassler Sport. The company continued to introduce innovative products. In the mid-1970s PUMA introduced the so-called S.P.A. technology, which were sport shoes with a higher heel that relieved strain on the Achilles tendon. In 1982 Armin A. Dassler invented the PUMA Duoflex sole, with special slots that increased the foot's mobility. In 1989 the company introduced the new Trinomic sport shoe system with hexagonal cells between sole and shoe that cushioned the runner's foot. Other innovations followed in 1990 and 1991. Inspector Shoes were shoes for kids with a "window" in their soles that allowed parents or trainers to observe whether the shoes were still the perfect fit during those years of rapid foot growth. The

KEY DATES

1924: Rudolf and Adolf Dassler incorporate their first shoe company.

1948: Rudolf Dassler sets up his own company PUMA Schuhfabrik Rudolf Dassler.

1959: Rudolf Dassler's wife and two sons become part owners of the PUMA Sportschuhfabriken Rudolf Dassler KG.

1962: PUMA shoes are shipped to almost 100 countries.

1974: Armin A. Dassler takes over as CEO.

1986: PUMA goes public.

1991: Swedish conglomerate Proventus AB becomes majority shareholder.

1993: 30-year-old Jochen Zeitz takes over as CEO.

1999: Monarchy/Regency becomes PUMA's largest single shareholder.

2007: PPR S.A. acquires a 62.1 percent stake in PUMA.

high-tech PUMA Disc System athletic and leisure shoes, which, instead of laces, used a disk that tightened a series of wires.

During the 1970s and 1980s, world famous athletes wore PUMA products on their feet and bodies. High-jumper Dwight Stones broke the world record in PUMA shoes three times in the years 1973 through 1976. In 1977 tennis player Guillermo Vilas won the French and U.S. Open in PUMA shoes. Sprinter Renaldo Nehemia ran three world records in 100-meter hurdles between 1979 and 1981 in PUMA spikes. In the early 1980s U.S. football star Marcus Allen of the Oakland Raiders, as well as baseball greats Jim Rice and Roger Clemens of the Boston Red Sox, and George Brett of the Kansas City Royals, favored PUMA shoes. U.S. sprinter Evelyn Ashford won two gold medals in PUMA shoes at the Olympic Games 1984 in Los Angeles. Tennis stars Martina Navratilova and Boris Becker won their events at the famous Wimbledon tennis competition in the mid-1980s in PUMA shoes.

In 1991 the Swedish conglomerate Proventus AB bought all PUMA common stock traded publicly in Frankfurt and Munich. That same year saw the founding of PUMA International, a holding company for PUMA's divisions in the Far East, Australia, Spain, France, Austria, and Germany, which were organized as independent profit centers. Despite the company's high profile and success, its profits had steadily declined until, in the early 1990s, they were nonexistent. It was not until 1994 that PUMA again turned a profit, and PUMA shareholders received a dividend for the first time in 1996.

FINDING NEW LEADERSHIP: 1993

In 1993 PUMA's prospects looked anything but bright. The company had been in the red for almost a decade. In December 1992 parent company Proventus gave PUMA a badly needed capital boost of DEM 50 million. However, the company was competing in a stagnating market driven increasingly rapid product cycles that resulted in rising research and development and marketing costs, as well as losses through more frequent markdowns of older models. Although PUMA scored high in brand name recognition, the company that in the 1980s had generated half of all sales with shoes in the lower price ranges was now struggling with its cheap image. Much like its competitor adidas, PUMA tried to succeed by leaving low price markets that allowed only low profit margins; breaking into premium price markets, which were the traditional territory of U.S. giants Nike and Reebok, became their new goal. It was perhaps too little, too late. This strategy at first resulted in significant losses in sales and market share.

Adding to the company's problems was the fact that the successful introduction of the innovative PUMA Disc System shoes in 1992 had been an expensive undertaking. By February 1993 it was clear that PUMA needed new leadership, and parent company Proventus replaced PUMA CEO Stefan Jacobsson with Niels Stenboej, who came from Abu Garcia, another Proventus subsidiary that made equipment for sports fishing. However, only three month later Stenboej left amid changes in upper management at the Proventus Helsingborg headquarters.

REVIVAL UNDER JOCHEN ZEITZ: 1993–95

The arrival of 30-year-old Jochen Zeitz hailed better times for PUMA. At the time the youngest CEO of a European publicly traded company, Zeitz had an MBA from the European Business School and had traveled the world from Brazil to the United States, making his first mark as a product manager for Colgate Palmolive in New York and Hamburg. In 1990 he joined PUMA and as a vice president of international marketing and sales, where he was responsible for the company's international communications strategy and contributed significantly to the repositioning of the PUMA brand.

One year after Zeitz became CEO, PUMA reported its first profit since its initial public offering in 1986.

Under Zeitz's leadership the company initiated a fundamental, market-oriented "fitness pro-gram" that included rigorous cost-cutting and reorganization measures. Inflexible structures were replaced, as was the case when the purchasing and product development departments were merged. Several warehouses were replaced by a central distribution center, and all departments became profit centers.

PUMA's restructuring was but one part of its new success story. The other was its innovative marketing plan. At its core was the positioning of the PUMA brand as an international performance sports brand for high-quality athletic shoes, sport textiles, and accessories. The company also based its innovative marketing concepts on the latest trend research, earlier ignorance of which had in part caused PUMA's past downturns.

As a result, PUMA launched the "PUMA-Offensive '95," a marketing program with four key areas of activity. The first was based on the revival of the classic PUMA suede shoes in the trendy clubs of New York, Los Angeles, and San Francisco. PUMA developed a collection of shoe "originals" in various colors and matching textile collections targeting fashion and trend conscious youth. The second element of the marketing offensive was the PUMA "World Team." Top sports figures, such as German soccer star Lothar Matthäus and Jamaican sprinter Merlene Ottey, represented PUMA products in an advertising campaign. The third piece in PUMA's marketing mix was known as "Replica," a line of "fashions for fans" made available through sports retailers and soccer clubs.

MARKETING THE STREET SOCCER CUP: 1994

One of the most successful elements of PUMA's concerted marketing effort was the Street Soccer Cup, a worldwide street soccer competition first organized in 1994. The idea was developed in cooperation with Leonberg-based advertising agency Godenrath, Preiswerk & Partner (GPP). In 1993 the "street ball" wave had become immensely popular, as kids began storming Germany's courtyards, playgrounds, and parking lots to play pickup games of basketball. PUMA and GPP worked together to popularize street soccer, which was characterized by its favoring of technique and finesse over athleticism, its focus on casual fun rather than club regulations, and its preference for free style dress over uniforms. New rules for the game had to be established as well. Street Soccer was played in the street on a concrete or asphalt surface, not on a grass field. The 20-by-14 meter field was bordered by a fence. Four players plus one reserve player stormed two goals. Street Soccer was played in two age groups: 10 to 13 and 14 to 16.

The event campaign was carried out in cooperation with the major German sports magazine *Sport-Bild* and was supported by retail sporting goods stores. Other prominent German companies also joined PUMA as sponsors. Germany's teenagers embraced the idea. Demand far exceeded supply, and thousands of registrations could not be accepted. About 31,000 youngsters between age 10 and 16 kicked the ball in over 6,000 teams with names like "Magic," "Street Attacks," and "Turkish Brothers." Over 250,000 people watched the games at almost 200 events. The finals were played out in front of the Reichstag building in Berlin.

The success of this innovative concept encouraged PUMA to continue it on an international scale in 1995. The Street Soccer Cup '95 was also played in France, Hong Kong, and Tokyo. PUMA introduced a new line of Street Soccer shoes and a collection of colorful clothing for players and spectators. All told, approximately 800,000 people watched 70,000 kids playing soccer at more than 400 events during this PUMA event.

CONQUERING WESTERN EUROPE AND NORTH AMERICA: 1996-99

The year 1996 marked the end of the restructuring period PUMA had been undergoing since 1993. This was followed by a period of new alliances and higher investment in international marketing and new product development. For the first time since the company went public, PUMA shareholders saw a dividend in 1996 after the company achieved a three-year sales record in comparison to previous years. A PUMA stock offering on the Frankfurt and Munich stock exchanges in June 1996 reduced the holdings of parent company Proventus Handels AB to 25 percent. A few months later the U.S. movie production and distribution firm Monarchy/Regency bought a 12.5 percent stake from Proventus; it obtained the other 12.5 percent in 1997.

In 1999 Monarchy/Regency upgraded its shareholdings to 32 percent. The transaction made Monarchy/Regency PUMA's largest single shareholder. The interests of the new partners complemented one another in that Monarchy/Regency was interested in a platform from which it could build relationships in the sports world to diversify into new markets, while PUMA CEO Zeitz believed that the entertainment company could help PUMA with its marketing efforts.

In the second half of the 1990s PUMA intensified its international activities. A new subsidiary named PUMA Italia S.r.l. began operations in 1997. Two years later PUMA opened its new subsidiary PUMA UK.

However, the most important strategic market for PUMA was the United States. In 1997 PUMA generated about 80 percent of its sales outside Germany, and this figure shrank to 10 percent if license income was included. PUMA's position was especially strong in Japan where 10 percent of all license fees were collected.

On the other hand, only a tiny fraction, some 4.5 percent, of PUMA sales of approximately $846 million derived from the United States, representing less than 1 percent market share. A first step toward penetrating the largest sports market was the acquisition of PUMA North America and the PUMA trademark from Proventus AB in January 1996. In 1998 PUMA sealed a long-term contract with the Women's Tennis Association (WTA), making PUMA the official supplier of shoes and textiles for the WTA's tour. In the same year PUMA acquired a 25 percent share in Logo Athletic, one of the leading licensed suppliers for the U.S. professional sports leagues. The deal started paying off in the very next year.

In 1999 PUMA became one of four suppliers of the American National Football League (NFL). Beginning in the 1999/2000 season 13 NFL football teams were wearing PUMA, as well as nine National Basketball Association teams. When the St. Louis Rams and the Tennessee Titans competed for the Super Bowl in January 1999, about 1.3 billion television watchers worldwide were exposed to the PUMA logo. Another novelty was the 1998 contract between PUMA and then 16-year-old U.S. tennis talent Serena Williams. The five-year contract included not only promotion activities for PUMA-wear but also engagements in movie and music projects of PUMA parent Monarchy/Regency. The strategy certainly seemed to be paying off in 1999 when PUMA's U.S. sales increased by 60 percent.

EXPANSION CONTINUES

Under Zeitz's leadership, PUMA continued to grow. Its operating profit doubled in 2001 and 2002. Monarchy Enterprises sold its stake in the company during 2003. While the sell-off came as a surprise to investors, PUMA secured a five-year contract to have its products placed in New Regency films. Investors Gunter and Daniela Herz raised their stake in PUMA to 25 percent in 2005.

The company continued to strengthen its foothold in international markets during this time period, especially in the United States. The popularity of sports-related fashion apparel and accessories was growing, and PUMA was opening new stores to keep up with increasing demand. The company's flagship Manhattan store, which opened its doors in 2006, was used as model for all future stores. By 2010 there were PUMA outlets in nearly 30 states.

At the same time the company's presence at the FIFA World Cup, soccer's premier global event, was growing. The company sponsored 12 teams at the Germany event in 2006 as well as seven in the South African tournament in 2010. Italy, a PUMA-sponsored team, won the event in 2006.

By now, PUMA's success caught the eye of the French luxury group PPR S.A. PPR had ownership stakes in luxury brands including Gucci, Yves Saint Laurent, Balenciaga, and Sergio Rossi and was looking to expand its footprint. It offered approximately $7 billion to purchase a majority stake in PUMA in 2007. As PPR CEO François-Henri Pinault told *Footwear News* in December 2007, "This acquisition represents the intersection of sport, lifestyle, and fashion."

Indeed, the PPR purchase left PUMA well positioned as the world's third-largest sporting goods manufacturer behind Nike and adidas. At this time, PUMA called itself a "sportlifestyle manufacturer" of footwear, apparel, and accessories and looked for ways to bolster is product line. In 2009, it purchased Sweden's Brandon Company AB, a corporate merchandising firm. PUMA and Brandon partnered in 2008 to distribute the official Volvo Ocean Race Merchandising collection. During 2010 it acquired California-based Cobra Golf from Acushnet Co.

PUMA's vision at this time was based on making the world safer, more peaceful, and more creative. The company opened its new headquarters in 2009, claiming it was the first carbon neutrally operated facility in its industry. The headquarters included an administration center, a brand center, and the world's largest PUMA store. Backing up its dedication to peace, the company shook hands with longtime competitor and rival adidas. Employees from both companies played football, or soccer, on United Nations Peace Day in September 2009.

With Zeitz at the helm, PUMA continued to grow well into the new millennium. Annual sales increased for the 14th consecutive year in 2008. The global economic downturn that affected the retail sector eventually caught up with the company in 2009. Sales and profits fell that year as the company worked to control costs and revamp its operating structure to compensate for falling demand. Nevertheless, the company's strategy over the past several years had positioned it to meet these challenges head on.

Evelyn Hauser
Updated, Christina M. Stansell

PRINCIPAL SUBSIDIARIES

Austria PUMA Dassler Ges. m.b.H.; PUMA Vertrieb GmbH; PUMA Sprint GmbH; Premier Flug

GmbH&Co. KG (50%); PUMA Hellas S.A. (Greece); PUMA Cyprus Ltd.; PUMA Benelux B.V. (Netherlands); Dobotex International BV (Netherlands); Brandon Company AB (Sweden); Tretorn AB (Sweden); Mount PUMA AG (Switzerland); Unisol S.A. (Argentina); PUMA CHILE S.A.; PUMA Mexico Sport S.A. de C.V.; PUMA Sports LA S.A. (Uruguay); World Cat Ltd. (Hong Kong); PUMA Asia Pacific Ltd. (Hong Kong); PUMA Korea Ltd.; PUMA Sports Goods Sdn. Bhd. (Malaysia); PUMA Sports Singapore Pte. Ltd.

PRINCIPAL COMPETITORS

adidas AG; ASICS Corporation; Nike, Inc.; Saucony, Inc.

FURTHER READING

Crane, Joyce Pellino. "On Runway, PUMA Roars Back." *Boston Globe*, June 8, 2006.

Diekhof, Rolf. "Eine Katze zeigt die Krallen." *Werben und Verkaufen*, March 24, 1995, p. 102.

Fallon, James. "U.S. Film Producer Buys 12.5% Interest in PUMA." *Daily News Record*, November 8, 1996, p10.

Marsh, Emilie. "PPR Closes PUMA Deal, Begins Work on Expansion Plans." *Women's Wear Daily*, July 23, 2007.

———, "Puma in Deal for Cobra Golf." *Women's Wear Daily*, March 29, 2010.

Michaelis, Karin. "PUMA wetzt die Krallen." *Werben und Verkaufen*, February 4, 2000, p. 106.

Milne, Richard. "PUMA Determined to Make It, One Step at a Time." *Financial Times*, December 22, 2005.

———. "View from the Top: Jochen Zeitz, Puma Chief Executive." *Financial Times*, April 19, 2010.

Popp, Regina. "French Class—With Gucci, Balenciaga and PUMA Now in One House, PPR Hopes to Entice Both the Luxury Shopper and the Mainstream Consumer." *Footwear News*, December 3, 2007.

"PUMA Unveils 2010 African Football Team Kits and Announces Partnership with the Algerian Football Federation." *Canada Newswire*, October 8, 2009.

"Puma's Latest Retail Concept Pounces on Manhattan." *DSN Retailing Today*, October 23, 2006.

Rhymer, Rigby. "The Spat That Begat Two Empires." *Management Today*, July 1998, p. 90.

"Wir sind wie David im Kampf gegen Goliath." *Süddeutsche Zeitung*, December 8, 1997.

Rand McNally and Co.

P.O. Box 7600
Chicago, Illinois 60680-7600
U.S.A.
Telephone: (847) 329-8100
Toll Free: (800) 678-7263
Fax: (800) 934-3479
Web site: http://www.randmcnally.com

Private Company
Incorporated: 1856
Employees: 636
Sales: $173 million (2004 est.)
NAICS: 451210 Book Stores and News Dealers; 451211 Book Stores; 453998 All Other Miscellaneous Store Retailers (Except Tobacco Stores); 511130 Book Publishers; 511190 Other Publishers; 511210 Software Publishers

∎ ∎ ∎

Rand McNally and Co. is the largest commercial mapmaker in the world. It is famous for its top-selling flagship product, the *Rand McNally Road Atlas*. The company sells its products and services to the consumer, business, education, government, and commercial transportation markets. Its print and electronic products and tools include the Thomas Guide map books and educational tools, custom-made wall maps on the Internet, wireless navigation solutions, software for commercial mileage and routing and travel, and free online maps, directions, and trip planning at www.randmcnally. com. Rand McNally has an online travel store at www.

randmcnallystore.com and also sells its products through 50,000 retail outlets.

19TH-CENTURY BEGINNINGS

Rand McNally and Co. began in 1856 as a small printing business established on Chicago's Lake Street by company cofounders William Rand and Andrew McNally. In 1864 Rand and McNally bought the job printing department of the *Chicago Tribune* and began printing railroad tickets and timetables. Nearly 10 years later, the first Rand McNally map appeared in the 1872 *Railway Guide*.

Opting to expand the scope of its printed products, the company began producing globes and maps for schools in 1880. By the end of the century, when Rand retired and sold his share of the company to McNally, the fledgling printing business had grown to employ a workforce of nearly 700. Andrew McNally died in 1904, and cofounder William Rand passed away the following year.

ROAD MAP AND ATLAS PUBLISHING BEGINS: 1907

Rand McNally began publishing road maps and road atlases in 1907 with the first photo-auto guide, which detailed the route of an automobile trip from Chicago to New York. The photo-auto guide consisted of directions for automobile drivers, along with accompanying photos to aid the traveler. During their honeymoon in 1909, Andrew McNally II and his bride took the photos used in the company's subsequent Chicago-to-Milwaukee photo-auto guide.

In 1917 Rand McNally published the first road map to feature numbered highways. The numbering system, invented by a map draftsman named John Brink, eliminated the need for long names, which were difficult to depict on maps. Brink became the head of Rand McNally's new Blazed Trails department. In addition to producing the road maps, Rand McNally was also responsible for erecting many highway signs.

In the first of many partnerships between Rand McNally and the nation's oil companies, Rand McNally was hired in 1918 by the Gulf Oil Company to produce maps for a Gulf Oil promotional campaign. The company also began producing educational materials for students. In 1922 Rand McNally published the first edition of *Goode's World Atlas*, named for its first editor, Dr. J. Paul Goode. The book became the standard geography text for U.S. high schools and colleges and would see its 19th edition published in the mid-1990s.

The first *Rand McNally Road Atlas* was published in 1924. By this time Rand McNally had published a complete set of numbered highway maps covering the United States, Canada, and Mexico. Among company milestones was the fact that in 1927 Charles Lindbergh used Rand McNally railroad maps for navigation over land during his historic flight across the Atlantic Ocean. In 1933 Andrew McNally II became president of the company. Under his leadership an early foray into retail operations was realized when the first Rand McNally Map and Travel Store was opened in New York City in 1937.

WARTIME PRODUCTION

Demand for Rand McNally maps, particularly European maps, escalated during World War II. The company's presses began working 24 hours a day to meet orders, and that schedule continued throughout the war. In addition to products for the war effort, the company also published children's books. During the 1940s Rand McNally published the works of noted children's author Marguerite Henry, whose best-selling children's books included *Misty of Chincoteague* and *King of the Wind*.

In 1947 the company published *Kon-Tiki*, written by a relatively unknown Norwegian scientist, Thor Heyerdahl. The book became an international best seller. Another Rand McNally printing specialty during this time involved tickets used in the transportation industry. In 1945 the company created a new ticket book with carbons that eliminated the previously bulky accordion-fold product used for airline and train tickets.

A third generation of McNallys continued the tradition of family leadership when Andrew McNally III became president of the company in 1948. The following year, Rand McNally entered the book manufacturing business on a full-scale basis with the purchase of the W.B. Conkey Company.

REVOLUTIONS IN MAPMAKING

In 1952 Rand McNally moved its headquarters to a newly constructed facility in the Chicago suburb of Skokie. New product development characterized the era. In 1953 the company's ticket division produced the first pressure-sensitive tickets, which eliminated the need for carbons. Moreover, Rand McNally became the first commercial mapmaker to use the scribing process to draft maps, a process that revolutionized mapmaking during this time.

With the publication of the first full-color *Rand McNally Road Atlas* in 1960, the modestly successful publication became the world's most popular travel guide. Increased title production and demand for Rand McNally products prompted the 1962 construction of an additional book manufacturing plant. Over time this Versailles, Kentucky, plant was expanded to cover more than a million square feet and became one of the largest book manufacturing plants in the country. By the end of the 1980s the Versailles printing plant would be the largest maker of juvenile books in the United States.

In 1969 the Book Manufacturing Company, a subsidiary of the company, automated the process by which thumb indexes were cut and labeled for dictionaries and encyclopedias. Also that year, the company published the first edition of *The New International Atlas* following a two-year, multimillion-dollar investment. The publication marked a new standard for U.S. mapmakers and enabled the company to overcome the traditional dominance of European mapmakers. In 1971 the company acquired a book manufacturing facility in Taunton, Massachusetts.

With the Arab oil embargo and higher oil prices in the early 1970s, the days of the free service station road map came to an end. As a result, Rand McNally began to place more importance on the merchandising of the *Rand McNally Road Atlas*. In 1974 Andrew McNally IV was named company president, becoming CEO as well four years later.

KEY DATES

1856: William Rand and Andrew McNally start Rand McNally and Co. as a small printing business.

1924: The first *Rand McNally Road Atlas* is published.

1949: The company purchases the W.B. Conkey Company.

1952: Rand McNally moves its headquarters to the Chicago suburb of Skokie.

1980: Rand McNally acquires Transportation Data Management (TDM).

1992: Rand McNally acquires Nicholstone Holdings Inc.

1997: AEA Investors, Inc., acquires a controlling share of the company.

1999: The company acquires Thomas Bros. Maps, and King of the Road Map Service.

2003: The company files for Chapter 11 bankruptcy; Leonard Green & Partners becomes the new majority owner.

2007: Private-equity firm Patriarch Partners purchases the company.

ADVANCES IN TECHNOLOGY

In 1980 Rand McNally acquired Transportation Data Management (TDM), a small, technology-oriented company. This enabled Rand McNally to meld its enormous map database with a sophisticated electronic delivery system to provide routing and mileage information to the trucking and shipping industries. Focus on technology continued, as TDM introduced the computerized version of MileMaker, an online mileage and routing system for truckers and shippers that soon became an industry standard.

By 1988 TDM was offering a PC-based Micro-MileMaker version of its MileMaker mileage and routing system that was previously available only as a mainframe or minicomputer package or on a timeshare basis. The PC-based system was aimed at smaller carriers who did not require a mainframe computer and who found timesharing too expensive.

During this time, Rand McNally's DocuSystems unit specialized in supplying airline and ground transportation tickets and baggage tags, along with other technologically complex documents for automated systems. DocuSystems pioneered the application of magnetic stripes onto automated ticket and boarding passes for United Airlines. The unit also developed an electronic ticketing system for airlines that used bar codes to detect ticket fraud, which was costing the airline industry $200 million to $500 million a year internationally. By the end of the 1980s DocuSystems had completed a series of strategic acquisitions to enhance the development of advanced capabilities in magnetic striping and baggage tags.

NICHOLSTONE HOLDINGS ACQUIRED: 1992

In 1992 Rand McNally acquired Nicholstone Holdings Inc. of Nashville, Tennessee. Nicholstone specialized in book manufacturing, packaging, specialty printing, and binding, and produced computer software and documentation. This operation's capabilities in electronic publishing, multimedia printing, and packaging technology comprised the foundation of the Rand McNally Media Services unit, which became a leading provider of digital packaging solutions for the software and entertainment industries.

In addition to the newly created Media Services group, Rand McNally's operations were organized into three other business groups: Book Services, which provided manufacturing services to other book and information publishers; DocuSystems, which specialized in transportation tickets and tags and other complex documents for automated systems; and Publishing, which encompassed the company's core geographic publishing business in travel, reference, education, and entertainment.

In 1993 Andrew McNally IV was named chairman, succeeding his father, Andrew McNally III, who became chairman emeritus. John S. Bakalar was appointed president, becoming the first nonfamily member to hold that position in the company's history. Bakalar also served as the company's COO. Also during this time, a fifth generation of McNallys joined the company, when Andrew McNally V began work in the company's Media Services Group in 1994.

ENTERING THE DIGITAL AGE

Toward the end of 1993 the Versailles printing operation began to move to digital production. Many of the company's customers were equipped to submit digital files instead of the traditional mechanical-and-film materials used to create printing plates. In February 1994 Rand McNally and Eastman Kodak announced plans to install a direct-to-plate system to test the computer-to-plate system for long print runs. After completing a successful test period, Rand McNally purchased a full-time production system for installation in September 1995. A combination test site, production center, and showplace, the Versailles plant had grown from 300,000 square feet and 23 employees in 1962 to more than 1,000 employees and one million square feet.

In 1994 Rand McNally introduced the company's first consumer software product, TripMaker, to allow consumers to plan their trips on their home computers. The product demonstrated that Rand McNally had the ability to leverage its key assets into a new product that provided value to its customers, in spite of entering the market behind more technologically accomplished competitors.

Rand McNally had begun to convert its vast database resources into electronic form in 1989 when it hired Henry Feinberg to head its electronic systems division. Although TripMaker entered the CD-ROM market several years after Microsoft's Automap product, it surpassed Automap in sales in only two months. By 1995 TripMaker accounted for a leading 32 percent market share, while Automap had fallen from more than a 50 percent market share to 14 percent. Complementing TripMaker, which was designed to plan long vacations or business trips, Rand McNally introduced Street-Finder in 1995. StreetFinder focused on navigating in cities and became the market share leader in its category.

During this time, the company also launched its New Media Division to create and market consumer geographic products and services. Among the products to be offered later in the year was a full line of geographic software, including travel, reference, entertainment, and educational programs. The Media Services group acquired the software manufacturing, assembly, packaging, and order fulfillment facilities of DCA Ireland Ltd., based in Shannon, Ireland.

FACING CHALLENGES

By the late 1990s expansion at Rand McNally had come to a halt. The privately held company, about which little financial information was made available, began to divest several of its operations. In January 1997 Rand McNally announced its intentions to sell its Book Services Group, which included the company's Versailles printing plant and another printing plant in Taunton, Massachusetts. A company spokesperson announced that Rand McNally would concentrate on its core map-making business.

The plants were sold to World Color Press, Inc., based in Greenwich, Connecticut, the third-largest provider of print and digital information in the United States with 1995 revenues of $1.3 billion. Prior to the sale, Rand McNally was one of the three largest producers of hardcover books in the United States, and its Book Services Group accounted for $150 million of the company's estimated annual revenue of $500 million. The division had about 1,700 employees.

Also on the block were Rand McNally's Media Services division and DocuSystems. Within several months Media Services was sold to McQueen, a Scottish software company, and DocuSystems was sold to a Chicago investment banking firm. That left Rand McNally with about 1,000 employees, down from 4,000 prior to the sales.

EXPLORING OPTIONS

In April 1997 Rand McNally hired investment banking firm Goldman Sachs to explore its strategic options. By September an announcement was made that controlling interest in the company would be sold to AEA Investors, Inc. In November of that year, the shareholders of AEA Investors, Inc., and the management of Rand McNally acquired a controlling interest in Rand McNally and Co.

AEA was founded in 1969 by leading industrial families and chief executives of major corporations for the purpose of making investments in market-leading companies with attractive growth opportunities. Following the sale, the McNally family retired from active management in the company, with Andrew McNally IV remaining on the board of directors. Henry Feinberg was promoted from president of the company's publishing group to president and chairman of the entire company.

At the end of the 1990s, the newly streamlined Rand McNally was organized into seven divisions: Map and Atlas Publishing, Consumer Software, Educational Publishing, Rand McNally-TDM (Transportation Data Management), Map and Travel Stores, Allmaps (Canada), and Cartographic and Information Services. In December 1997 Rand McNally opened a new Internet travel store at www.randmcnallystore.com. This site offered consumers more than 3,000 products, including maps, travel guides, globes, software, games, and travel accessories.

With cash in hand Rand McNally was prepared to grow through strategic acquisitions. In November 1998 the company executed a letter of intent to acquire Thomas Bros. Maps, a privately held map publisher based in Irvine, California. The deal closed in the first quarter of 1999. Analysts had noted that the mapmaking industry was ripe for consolidation, and Thomas was considered one of the major regional players. Also purchased was King of the Road Map Service of Washington State.

CHANGES IN MANAGEMENT

Later in 1999 Henry Feinberg resigned as chairman and chief executive, replaced by Richard Davis. The company, which then operated 24 retail stores with 6 on the West Coast, introduced a new trucking database called IntelliRoute, which combined traffic routing and satellite communications to facilitate equipment tracking and allowed for address-to-address mapping.

In 2000 the company became the primary North American distributor of National Geographic maps, and Norman Wells replaced Davis as chief executive. Rand McNally also relaunched its Web site with additional trip-planning capabilities, lists of local events, hotel booking options, and map and travel book sales. This feature was expanded in 2001 to include "Best of the Road" information on maps—top stops and "Cool and Unusual Events" along select routes. The 2002 *Motor Carriers' Road Atlas* also included Web addresses and telephone hotlines that provided access to information on road construction and conditions for states, Canadian provinces, and Mexico.

Having joined the digital revolution belatedly, randmcnally.com still had far fewer visitors than MapQuest and MapBlast! In 2001, top heavy with debt and needing cash, Rand McNally named Michael Hehir of McGraw-Hill Ventures its new chief executive. Hehir spearheaded a restructuring and recapitalization effort. Although revenues rebounded, AEA retained Deutsche Banc Alex Brown Brokerage Services to explore a possible sale of the company.

BANKRUPTCY FILING AND NEW OWNERSHIP

In 2003 Rand McNally filed for Chapter 11 bankruptcy protection. The company exited bankruptcy within two months, losing more than $250 million in debt. Buyout firm Leonard Green & Partners became its new majority owner with a 54 percent equity stake. Also in 2003, Hehir left the company, succeeded by Allstate executive Robert Apatoff, and the company closed its 25 retail stores.

After two changes of ownership and bankruptcy reorganization, Rand McNally appeared to have regained its bearings. In 2004 it purchased Perly's Maps, which produced the leading navigation tools for the greater Toronto area. The following year, it introduced a new self-mapping tool online and added "RoadWork Alerts" to IntelliRoute. In fall 2006 it released its Rand McNally GPS Navigator as part of its push into electronic gadgets and mapping software.

Rand McNally then suspended product development to focus on remaining profitable. Late in 2007 private-equity firm Patriarch Partners purchased the company, and Andrzej Wrobel of Patriarch took over as chief executive from 2008 to 2009. Rand McNally sold its Canadian subsidiary to the newly formed Canadian Cartographics Corporation as part of its ongoing efforts to refocus, streamline, and develop.

The company moved into a newer and smaller building, also in Skokie, in January 2009. Still the nation's top seller of road maps and regional atlases, Rand McNally would in the future continue the balance between its digital and paper format maps and mapping tools.

David Bianco
Updated, Carrie Rothburd

PRINCIPAL OPERATING UNITS

Map and Atlas Publishing; Consumer Software; Educational Publishing; Rand McNally-TDM (Transportation Data Management); Cartographic and Information Services.

PRINCIPAL COMPETITORS

American Educational Products, LLC; DeLorme Publishing Company, Inc.; Google, Inc.; MapQuest, Inc.; R.L. Polk & Co.

FURTHER READING

Borden, Jeff. "A Sale? IPO? The Borders Shift on Rand McNally Map." *Crain's Chicago Business*, February 10, 1997, p. 1.

Campbell, Ronald. "Irvine, Calif.-Based Thomas Bros. Technology Attracts Rand McNally." *Knight-Ridder/Tribune Business News*, November 15, 1998.

Milliot, Jim. "Investors to Buy Rand McNally." *Publishers Weekly*, September 8, 1997, p. 12.

———. "Rand McNally Weighing Possible Sale of Company." *Publishers Weekly*, May 5, 1997, p. 11.

Navarrete, Angela. "Rand McNally's Dynamic Trip-Taking Duo." *PC World*, October 1998, p. 80.

Pack, Todd. "Rand McNally to Sell Book Services Group." *Knight-Ridder/Tribune Business News*, January 8, 1997.

"Rand McNally Sells Its Printing Group." *Publishers Weekly*, January 13, 1997, p. 12.

Schifrin, Matthew. "The Message, Not the Medium." *Forbes*, September 11, 1995, p. 86.

Stanton, Elizabeth. "At Rand McNally Is the Future Drawn to Scale?" *New York Times*, March 17, 2002, p. 4.

Weller, Sam. "Rand McNally Buys Thomas Bros." *Publishers Weekly*, December 7, 1998, p. 16.

Wolinsky, Howard. "Rand McNally Positions Itself on the Road Back; Map Retailer Finds Success on the Net." *Chicago Sun-Times*, November 7, 2000, p. 47.

The Worlds of Rand McNally. Skokie, Ill.: Rand McNally, 1994.

Raven Industries, Inc.

———■———

205 East 6th Street
Sioux Falls, South Dakota 57104-5931
U.S.A.
Telephone: (605) 336-2750
Fax: (605) 335-0268
Web site: http://www.ravenind.com

Public Company
Incorporated: 1956
Employees: 955
Sales: $237.8 million (2009)
Stock Exchanges: NASDAQ
Ticker Symbol: RAVN
NAICS: 326113 Unsupported Plastics Film and Sheet
   (Except Packaging) Manufacturing; 334412 Printed
   Circuit Board Manufacturing

■ ■ ■

Based in Sioux Falls, South Dakota, Raven Industries, Inc., is a publicly traded diversified technology company that divides its operations among four business segments. The Applied Technology Division, formerly the Flow Controls unit, manufactures electronic and Global Positioning System (GPS) devices used in such agricultural applications as seed and fertilizer control and automated steering systems. Raven's Engineered Films Division manufactures flexible films and sheeting used to make construction enclosures, temporary walls, greenhouse coverings, and weatherproofing in the energy, industrial, environmental, and agricultural markets.

The Electronic Systems Division provides contract electronic manufacturing services in such segments as avionics, secure communication, and environmental controls. Finally, the Aerostar Division manufactures high-altitude and tethered aerostats, military and scientific parachutes, high-altitude balloons, airships, space inflatables, and interplanetary balloons, as well as protective garments.

THE EARLY YEARS

Raven Industries was launched in 1956 by a group of four General Mills Inc. (GM) employees. Much of the impetus for founding Raven came from Ed Yost, a maverick thinker at GM's High Altitude Research Division. GM had received a contract from the U.S. Navy in the early 1950s to explore the new balloon technologies for defense and scientific purposes, and Yost took charge of the project. While gas balloons were used sporadically at this time, they were expensive and could carry little weight. In 1955 Yost successfully flew a tethered hot air balloon, much to the Navy's satisfaction.

After receiving a $47,000 grant from the Office of Naval Research in 1956, Yost founded Raven Industries to design, build, and launch hot air balloons. Yost and his investors opted to locate the company in Sioux Falls, South Dakota, because of the favorable wind conditions there. With relatively balanced spring and fall winds, balloons tended to ascend and descend straight up and down there, which made retrieving and tracking them an easier task. In addition to earning Yost the title "father of hot air ballooning," Raven quickly won other classified contracts from the Navy.

COMPANY PERSPECTIVES

Raven is a diversified technology company that embraces an integrated approach, where all operations support each other, sharing knowledge and best practices. Our diversity works because it was not imposed by management or created through acquisitions. It developed internally through innovation and cooperation.

Almost from its inception, Raven expanded beyond making balloons, applying the technologies it had mastered in that endeavor to new ventures. David Christensen, who joined the company in 1962, explained to *Barron's* how the seemingly disjointed directions in which Raven's early growth took the company were actually logical: "The balloons were largely made of plastic, so the company got into plastics. It learned about electronics for the research instruments carried up in the air, so we [branched] into electronics. And then, when the balloon flight was over and the recordings had been made, the data ... had to be recovered by parachute. So the company got into sewn goods." To be sure that the company did not drift too far from its original mission, Yost formed Aerostar in 1960. That division was devoted solely to producing balloons.

Even with all of its diversification, Raven continued to rely heavily on government contracts. For example, during the late 1960s the company won a massive five-year $74 million contract to produce electronic equipment, especially radios and modules, for the armed forces. This arrangement accounted for a significant portion of the company's revenues during that period. In 1972 Christensen became president and CEO and guided the company as it continued to seek out new markets.

DIVERSIFICATION PROVIDES PROTECTION

Raven's sales had risen to $31 million by 1983. Although the United States was then mired in a recession, Raven's diversification protected it from the most turbulent vicissitudes of the period. The economic downturn certainly damaged the company's business of producing large plastic containers for agriculture and industry. "People aren't investing yet in large capital improvements," Christensen told the *Dow Jones News Service* on August 20, 1982, by way of explanation.

However, Raven's innovative ballute, a fabric membrane that was a cross between a balloon and a parachute, was in heavy demand from the military because ballutes could be used to drop ammunition from aircraft.

Raven also continued to develop electronic technology. By building on the control devices it had devised for balloons, Raven was able to launch several successful products that controlled various aspects of farms and feed mills. For instance, in 1983 the company released a system that controlled the manufacture of feed pellets for cattle.

Nevertheless, government contracts remained essential to Raven's viability. In 1984 alone defense orders accounted for more than 20 percent of the company's total sales. "The question we have to debate internally is how much defense business do we want in relation to our total business," Christensen explained to the *Dow Jones News Service* on November 25, 1983. This was particularly true because military procurement was not the only potential venue for Raven's diverse products.

As the dominant paradigm of U.S. agriculture shifted from small family farms to agribusinesses that operated on vast scales, Raven found new customers for its productivity-enhancing electronic control systems. For instance, the company's computerized monitoring system for the application of herbicide to fields sold quite briskly in 1985. Another key product in this sector was Raven's grain loss monitor, an electronic device used with combines to measure the amount of grain wasted in planting. To bolster its position in this industry, Raven acquired Beta 11 Inc. in 1984. This St. Louis, Missouri-based producer of electronic feed mill control systems had annual sales exceeding $2 million.

ENTERING NEW MARKETS

The company clearly recognized that opening up new markets would remain crucial to its continued success. As Christensen later explained to *Barron's*, the company's aim during this period was to forge a "diverse, recession-resistant structure." To this end, Raven acquired Glasstite, Inc., of Dunnell, Minnesota, in April 1986. This privately held company manufactured fiberglass truck tops, and the purchase afforded Raven entrance to the automotive market.

Raven solidified its place in that sector in 1987 when it acquired Astoria Fibra-Steel, a utility truck body business. The company continued to develop its original product lines as well. In 1987 Raven's Aerostar was chosen to produce custom-made inflatables for the annual Macy's Thanksgiving Day Parade. Moreover, Aerostar did a brisk business supplying hot air balloons to the growing recreational ballooning market.

KEY DATES

1956: Raven Industries is founded by four former General Mills employees.
1986: Raven acquires Glasstite, Inc., and Poly Plastic & Design Corp.
1995: Raven acquires A.J. Electronics Inc. and certain assets of Winzen International, and sells Astoria.
1999: Company sells Glasstite.
2001: Starlink, Inc., is acquired.

Despite all of the changes the company underwent during the 1980s, Raven adhered to its long-standing organizational structure. Because its operations were so far-flung, the company gave the directors of each division a great deal of autonomy. Raven termed this system "intrapreneurialism," and allowed each division head to maintain his or her own sales, production, and engineering staffs. "They're almost independent entities," a company executive told the *Journal of Business Strategy*. "The idea is that the division manager knows the business best so, to some extent, let him or her run it." Raven did provide a managerial umbrella over the divisions, however, overseeing credit, accounting, data processing, and most personnel functions.

PERSIAN GULF TENSIONS BENEFIT RAVEN

Tensions in the Persian Gulf and the involvement of the United States in the Gulf War were a boon to Raven's short-term sales. After the U.S. Air Force awarded Raven a $6 million contract to produce electronic temperature control devices for the C-130 cargo transplant planes in 1989, the company won a $22 million contract from the U.S. Army in 1991 to manufacture 250,000 suits designed to protect U.S. soldiers from possible chemical and biological warfare attacks in Iraq.

Sales for fiscal year 1992 (which ended January 31, 1992) rose dramatically, to $100.6 million, up from $85.5 million in 1991. The company was named one of the fastest-growing companies in the United States by *Financial World* in 1991. Moreover, immediately after the Gulf War, Raven received orders from different military departments to restock electronic equipment that had been depleted during the campaign. However, despite the revenue garnered by defense orders, Christensen would later rue the large contracts. "In some

ways, working with the military can spoil you, in that a large contract can lull you to sleep," he noted to the *Journal of Business Strategy*.

Christensen's concerns were triggered by the rapid decrease in defense spending that occurred in the aftermath of the Gulf War. With the Cold War over and no significant threats on the horizon, the military's budget was severely curtailed. Nevertheless, despite the fact that 30 percent of its total sales in fiscal year 1991 were connected to defense contracts, Raven remained optimistic. With six years of record sales behind it by 1993, the company set itself the goal of becoming a $200 million company by 2000.

Christensen confidently told *Barron's* that Raven could make up for losses in defense work with orders for the company's automotive products, automation controls, precision farming devices, and outerwear. To this end, the company had formed an alliance with major catalog retailers Lands' End and L.L. Bean to produce Gore-Tex parkas and sportswear.

EXPANDED OPERATIONS

Raven continued to try to reduce its dependence on government contracts throughout the mid-1990s. To strengthen its position in the non-defense-related electronics market, Raven acquired Automatic Coil Corp. from Designatronics in 1993 and A.J. Electronics Inc. from DDL Electronics in January 1995. The company focused on expanding other aspects of its operations as well. Also in 1995, Raven bought several assets of Winzen International that were related to high-altitude balloon manufacturing.

Moreover, in January 1996 Raven acquired a full line of ultrasonic sensor controls from K. Eldredge Electronics of Australia. Intended to strengthen Raven's position in the precision farming sector, the Eldredge purchase added to Raven's product line devices, which included a sensor control that automatically regulated operating depths on air seeders and planters and an ultrasonic head height control system for combines.

It seemed initially that Raven would be able to recover quickly from the loss of defense-related revenue. Sales for fiscal year 1994 rose to $121.5 million from $111.2 million in fiscal year 1993. Raven's sales flattened in fiscal year 1995, however, reaching only $121.7 million, and dropped for the first time in more than a decade in 1996, to $120.4 million. The company also experienced diminishing profits. Net income reached an all-time high of $7 million in fiscal year 1994, but dropped nearly 13 percent, to $6.1 million, in fiscal year 1995, and recovered only marginally, back to $6.2 million, in 1996.

NORCORE PLASTICS ACQUIRED: 1997

Raven resolved to overcome these difficulties. In February 1997 the company made an important acquisition when it added Norcore Plastics, Inc., to its plastics division. Based in Tacoma, Washington, Norcore was a leader in the manufacture of large industrial storage tanks. Norcore had benefited in particular from its application of "dual laminate" technology, which produced tanks capable of handling high-purity chemicals and liquids (of special use to the semiconductor manufacturing industry). This $3 million acquisition not only complemented Raven's existing storage tank operations, but also provided the company with a West Coast manufacturing location.

Through moves such as this one, and buoyed by the soaring U.S. economy, Raven was able to recapture its earlier momentum by the late 1990s. In fiscal year 1997 the company earned a net profit of $7.7 million on sales of $139.4 million. Sales rose to $149.6 million in fiscal 1998, and again to $152.8 million the following year. However, the company's continued success was called into question by the underperformance of certain of its divisions, which threatened to weigh down the entire company. At the close of the decade Christensen declared in a press release that Raven would "refocus" on core operations through a restructuring in which it intended "to redeploy or dispose of non-core assets." At the time of the announcement the company had shed its Astoria unit, and in October 1999 made the decision to sell the flagship enterprise of its automotive business, Glasstite, for $8.5 million. Although Glasstite had returned to profitability in 1998 after two years of losses, analysts had long accused Raven of overextending itself in the automotive sector. Of special concern was the company's investment of $1.5 million to build a new 50,000-square-foot manufacturing plant for Glasstite, an outlay that Raven had not been able to recoup.

By exiting the automotive market Raven demonstrated its commitment to concentrating on sportswear, agriculture, and plastics. Raven also continued to compete in its original niche, ballooning. Aerostar had launched a major international marketing campaign in June 1998, seeking to boost orders for its custom-made inflatable balloons. In 1999 the company received a contract from the National Aeronautics and Space Administration (NASA) to produce a unique high-atmosphere balloon.

ASSETS DIVESTED: 2000

Raven continued to shed noncore assets as the new century dawned. In 2000 it sold the Plastic Tank division to Northwest Equity Partners for $12 million, a deal that included plants in Ohio and Alabama. A facility in Tacoma, Washington, was not part of the deal. Later in the year Raven closed the two plants of its Sportswear Division located in Salem and Beresford, South Dakota, because customers had been increasingly turning to offshore suppliers. Product lines were shifted to the division's three other plants, and a year later Sportswear was folded into the Aerostar Division. Also of note in 2000, Christensen retired and was succeeded as CEO by Ronald Moquist, who had been with Raven since 1975 and over the years had held a number of top posts in the company.

Raven reinforced its commitment to precision agriculture in 2001 when the Flow Controls Divisions acquired Austin, Texas-based Starlink, Inc., maker of GPS technology. Raven had been using Starlink GPS receivers in its precision products for several years, and thus gained control over a crucial aspect of its precision products as well as expanding its market presence.

A year later Raven forged an alliance with Farm Works Software to combine Raven's GPS-based guidance system with Farm Works mapping software to supply a personal digital assistant device with instantaneous guidance, data logging, and coverage map for seed and fertilizer applications in the field. Raven established a similar alliance with Beeline Technologies, a maker of GPS and inertial navigation steering-assist systems for the agricultural market, creating a farm vehicle steering system under the Trueline name to combine steering assistance with precision chemical-application control.

BUILDING THE AGRICULTURAL BUSINESS

In the summer of 2002 Raven sold off another business that was no longer considered to be a core operation. Beta Raven, a St. Louis-area provider of computerized process controls and ingredient precision scaling systems, was sold to an Iowa company, California Pellet Mill. At the same time, Raven was not reluctant to invest in its other businesses. In 2002 it spent $4 million to build a three-layer film extruder.

Raven was especially devoted to building its agricultural business. In 2004 it acquired Madison, Wisconsin-based Fluent Systems, LLC, gaining access to wireless technology that Raven would incorporate into its agriculture applications. A year later Raven bought most of the assets of a Canadian company, Montgomery Industries, Inc., to add to the capabilities of the Flow Controls Division. Montgomery was the developer of the Autoboom automatic boom height control system used in agricultural sprayers. The technology allowed the sprayers to maintain the proper optimum boom height while traversing uneven terrain without sacrificing speed.

In 2009 Raven acquired assets from Ranchview, Inc., a Canadian start-up company that made use of cellular networks instead of the usual radio systems to deliver real-time corrections to GPS enabled equipment. The following year Raven established a relationship with Jacto Inc., a manufacturer of sprayers, coffee and orange harvesters, and fertilizers. Jacto agreed to carry Raven precision agricultural products through its dealer network.

Raven enjoyed success in other divisions as well. For example, in 2005 Aerostar launched and flew the second airship in history to achieve powered flight in the stratosphere. The early years of the new century were an era of strong growth for Raven, which in fiscal 2006 passed the $200 million mark in annual sales. That amount increased to $280 million in fiscal 2009, due especially to the performance of the company's agricultural business, which accounted for more than $100 million, making it Raven's largest division.

Raven had clearly performed well during Moquist's term as chief executive. In August 2010 he retired and was replaced by Daniel A. Rykhus, who had been with the company since 1990 and was well prepared to lead Raven to continued growth.

Rebecca Stanfel
Updated, Ed Dinger

PRINCIPAL DIVISIONS

Applied Technology; Engineered Films; Electronic Systems; Aerostar.

PRINCIPAL COMPETITORS

Graco Inc.; SigMa Plastics Group; Spartech Corporation.

FURTHER READING

"CEO Interview: Raven Industries." *Wall Street Transcript*, October 24, 1994.

Meyer, Harvey. "Underdog: A Military Contractor Spreads Its Wings." *Journal of Business Strategy*, September 19, 1997.

Palmer, Jay. "Raven Industries Enjoys Ballooning Business." *Barron's*, August 17, 1992, p. 14.

"Raven Industries." *Implement and Tractor*, January 11, 1996.

"Raven Industries Acquires Norcore Plastics, Tank & Technology." *Composite News*, February 10, 1997.

"Raven Industries Outlook." *Dow Jones News Service*, August 12, 1983.

"Raven Industries Sees Net Up Strongly in 4th Quarter." *Dow Jones News Service*, November 25, 1983.

"Raven Tied to Beeline Farm Works." *GPS World*, September 2002, p. 63.

Slovak, Julianne. "Raven Industries." *Fortune*, May 21, 1990.

Rennoc Corporation

3501 South East Boulevard
Vineland, New Jersey 08360-7780
U.S.A.
Telephone: (856) 327-5400
Toll Free: (800) 372-7100
Fax: (800) 675-1727
Web site: http://www.rennoc.com

Wholly Owned Subsidiary of Visant Corporation
Incorporated: 1953
Employees: 145
Sales: $19.7 million (2003 est.)
NAICS: 315228 Men's and Boys' Cut and Sew Other
Outerwear Manufacturing

■ ■ ■

Rennoc Corporation is a Vineland, New Jersey-based company that has reinvented itself several times since its founding in 1953. The focus of the company is on the manufacture of men's and women's wool and leather specialty jackets, including varsity jackets and overcoats. They are available with various collar styles, as well as scalloped zipper hoods. Rennoc also sells blankets in major team colors that it will decorate as requested.

Since 2010 Rennoc has discontinued its nylon sportswear product line and elected to focus on wool jackets. Products are mostly sold through a network of sporting goods dealers. After struggling through much of the early years of the 21st century, Rennoc was sold in 2009 to Visant Corporation, a major marketing and publishing service company that owned a Rennoc

competitor. Rennoc's New Jersey manufacturing plant was closed as a result, and production assigned to a plant in the Dominican Republic.

BOARD GAME ORIGINS

Rennoc Corporation was founded in 1953 by Richard Conner. He had planned to become a doctor and was pursuing his goal as a medical student at Temple University in Philadelphia, Pennsylvania. Due to an eye problem, however, he was forced to quit school at the age of 27 and undergo surgery in 1951. While recovering in the hospital he thought about what to give his teenage brother as a Christmas present and developed an elaborate board game. The game proved so popular with family and friends that he decided to make and market it. He called the company Rennoc, his last name spelled backwards, and in 1953 set up shop in a World War II Quonset hut, a prefabricated galvanized steel structure, at the Millville Municipal Airport in the southern New Jersey town of Millville.

Conner did not do particularly well as a toy manufacturer. By 1960 Conner was forced to file for bankruptcy. He managed to save the business, however, when he took the advice of his salesman, Walt Henricks, who urged him to manufacture Christmas decorations. Although he was completely unfamiliar with the field and far from certain about success, Conner had no other ideas about how he could pay off his creditors and decided to give the idea a try. In 1961 he bought a used sewing machine for $75, spent another $65 on a cutting machine, and bought a cutting table and 300 yards of fabric to begin making Christmas stockings of his own design.

Instead of the usual red flannel stockings sold at the time, Conner made his Christmas stockings out of plush. "They looked like something Santa might wear—and everybody wants a relic of Santa by the fireplace," he told the *Philadelphia Inquirer* in 1983. The stockings proved highly popular and the company turned a profit in the first year. Conner built on his success by turning his attention to Santa suits, including beards made from yak hair. The company also sold Santa hats separately and made plush Santa dolls ranging in size from 10 to 45 inches, as well as other plush Christmas decorations, such as Frosty the Snowman purses, holly-shaped bow ties, tree skirts, table covers, tree ornaments, Santa doorknob covers, and "Ho Ho Ho" toilet seat covers.

BECOMING DIVERSIFIED

Rennoc grew to become the world's largest maker of Santa Claus suits and plush Christmas decorations. By the early 1980s his factory in Vineland, New Jersey, and its 250 sewing machines each year produced 50,000 Santa suits that fetched as much as $300 each. The beards, made of 100 percent yak hair, retailed at $160. It was a seasonal business, however, with workers employed from March until late fall and then laid off.

To diversify the business and make further use of his equipment, Conner added such product lines as Hang-N-Stuff animals, puppets, and animated and illuminated Halloween figures. Rennoc also entered the jacket market in 1974. As had been the case with Christmas decorations, he paid attention to detail to produce a high-quality product to earn an excellent reputation in the marketplace. To keep pace with steady growth, the company expanded its operations several times. The headquarters grew to 217,99 square feet and in 1989 an adjacent 172,000-square-foot building was added.

In November 1991 Conner elected to merge Rennoc's Christmas business with Manitowoc, Wisconsin-based National Tinsel Manufacturing Co. and its National Decorations affiliate to form a more competitive one-stop-shopping Christmas-oriented company and the largest non-gift wrapping company in the field.

National Tinsel was established in Manitowoc in 1889 by the city's mayor and had grown into America's largest tinsel manufacturer. National Decorations, on the other hand, was only three years old and was a major importer of Christmas bead garland, tree ornaments, and porcelain villages. The merged company took the name National Rennoc, but was subsequently renamed Santa's Best and its headquarters moved to Northfield, Illinois.

Manufacturing continued to be conducted in Vineland, but the economics of the business were changing. Everything but garland and tinsel production was moved to China in the late 1990s. Because these products were too bulky and costly to ship, they continued to be made in the United States. In 1999 the Wisconsin operation was closed and manufacturing was consolidated in one of the Vineland sewing plants built by Rennoc, but it too eventually fell victim to Chinese production. The Vineland plant was closed in 2005, as was a Millville distribution hub, and all manufacturing was transferred to China.

CLASSIC COLLECTION INTRODUCED: 1996

Rennoc's jacket division was not part of the National Tinsel merger. Conner remained chairman, president, and chief executive officer of this business, as well as chairman of Santa's Best, but in February 1992 he relinquished his day-to-day responsibilities with the Christmas division. Rennoc continued to grow its remaining jacket business. While varsity jackets and warm-up suits remained its core business, Rennoc entered the specialty/corporate identity market in 1995 with the launch of its Classic Collection.

The merger with National Tinsel also afforded Conner the opportunity to devote more time to charitable endeavors. Rennoc partnered with a nonprofit organization, Brother to Brother International, to provide jackets and sweatpants to disadvantaged youths, including Native American and inner-city children. He also helped to raise money and build the board of trustees for a local halfway house to help men recovering from alcoholism. This was an outgrowth of a program he launched in 1984 to help his employees who were engaged in alcohol and drug abuse. The program had enjoyed success, but Conner believed that some of the people who were not able to restore their lives could have been helped if the support of a halfway house had been available in the area.

RIVAL FIRM ACQUIRED: 1999

Rennoc expanded its jacket business further in 1999 with the acquisition of a rival firm, St. Paul, Minnesota-based Butwin Sportswear Company. Butwin was a pioneer in the varsity jacket field. Jack Butwin and his nephew Ray Butwin founded the company in St. Paul in 1938. Athletes wore letter sweaters at the time, but the Butwins began manufacturing what they called Hero Jackets, which featured wool shells and leather sleeves and became a standard for high school and college varsity sports letter winners. The company became an international jacket maker and over the years expanded into other product lines, including jackets for professional and college sports teams, surcoats for professional football players, jackets for Olympians, and nylon softball jackets.

The company remained owned and operated by the Butwin family, but by the 1990s business began to suffer when management failed to invest in the business and adopt new methods, including computers. Quality suffered and the company had trouble filling orders on time. After three consecutive years of losses, Butwin was unable to pay its loans and in the spring of 1995 was put up for sale. The company's bank, Norwest Bank Minnesota, required that interested parties include a $50,000 nonrefundable payment with their bids. When no one proved willing to comply, the bank later in 1995 forced Butwin to close its doors.

The addition of Butwin spurred a sharp increase in sales for Rennoc, but productivity lagged behind. Minnesota's low unemployment rate made it difficult for Rennoc to hire enough people to take full advantage of the Butwin division plants in St. Paul and Litchfield, Minnesota. As a result, Rennoc elected to consolidate its operations and move all production to Vineland, where the company had a larger pool of labor and could take better advantage of its computerized operations.

NEW CENTURY PROBLEMS

Conner was well into his 70s at the start of the new century when he turned over the reins of Rennoc to a new management team. The company was generating about $14 million in annual sales, but in 2001 sales fell off dramatically. Rennoc's sales forecasts were particularly poor, and as a result the company maintained an inadequate supply of jackets. Hence, when orders were received, Rennoc lacked the necessary stock to make good on its promise of 24-hour shipment. Instead, orders in many cases did not arrive for weeks, adversely impacting Rennoc's reputation and leading to further erosion in sales. Sales in 2004 were half the level of 2000.

Short of cash, Rennoc turned to the town of Vineland for help. Because Rennoc had been a major employer for many years, Vineland began lending money to the company in 2002. By the fall of 2005 the total exposure reached $4.6 million, including a $3.5 million loan from the city's Urban Enterprise Zone. By this time, Conner was back in charge, having returned as CEO in January 2005. He took immediate steps to increase inventory levels and improve delivery, and as the company's busy season began in 2004 it was able to increase sales by more than 10 percent over the previous year.

COMPANY SOLD: 2009

Conner was not able to completely turn Rennoc around, however. The company was unable to keep up with its government loan payments and eventually defaulted, putting Vineland in line to assume ownership of Rennoc's building. In July 2009 Rennoc was sold to New York-based Visant Corporation, a marketing and publishing services company that included a Scholastic unit that produced class rings, graduation products, and other school-oriented products for the high school, college, and postgraduate markets. Part of this segment was a Rennoc competitor, Neff Motivation, a manufacturer of varsity jackets, as well as chenille letters, other apparel and sportswear, and custom award programs.

Visant was interested in Rennoc's name, equipment, and clients, but not its Vineland factory, which was closed later in 2009. To save money and consolidate operations, the production of Rennoc's products was transferred to Neff's factory in the Dominican Republic. Rennoc's products would still be marketed by Rennoc and mostly sold through its existing independent sales channel, but the product lines were to be trimmed. In 2010 Rennoc discontinued its nylon sportswear product line and the outstanding stock was made available to the company's dealers at 50 percent off list price. Rennoc then focused all of its attention on its wool product line. The company, adept at changing strategies as necessary, had survived for more than half a century. As part of a much larger enterprise, however, Rennoc's future as an independent company was far from certain.

Ed Dinger

PRINCIPAL COMPETITORS

AAC Group Holding Corp.; Holloway Sportswear; T&M Sportswear.

FURTHER READING

Key, Peter. "Merger Helps Rennoc Make Yule Merrier." *Press of Atlantic City*, November 27, 1991, p. D6.

O'Reilly, David. "'Tis the Season for Vineland, N.J., Company, It's Always Christmas in July." *Philadelphia Inquirer*, July 6, 1983, p. B1.

Prelow, Dessie. "Rennoc Corp. Expands in Vineland." *Press of Atlantic City*, July 20, 1989, p. A1.

"Rennoc Acquires Minnesota Jacket Maker Butwin." *Wearables Business*, November 1999, p. 12.

Sotelo, Gisell. "The Long Road Back to Glory." *Daily Journal* (Vineland, N.J.), October 3, 2005.

"Stocking Fear: From Bankrupt to Bankroll." *Philadelphia Daily News*, December 22, 1986, p. 39.

Resolution, Inc.

—■—

687 Marshall Avenue
Williston, Vermont 05495-7856
U.S.A.
Telephone: (802) 862-8881
Toll Free: (800) 862-8900
Fax: (802) 865-2308
Web site: http://www.resodirect.com

Private Company
Incorporated: 1981 as Resolution Video Audio and Film
Employees: 70
Sales: $568 million (2008 est.)
NAICS: 541614 Process, Physical Distribution, and Logistics Consulting Services

■ ■ ■

Originally a video duplication provider, Williston, Vermont-based Resolution, Inc., bills itself as an e-commerce solutions provider, primarily helping broadcasters, print and electronic publishers, and direct marketers to sell DVDs, books, and media property-related apparel, mugs, and other merchandise. The private company's wide range of services include e-commerce management, logistics and fulfillment, assembly, product development and sourcing, and on-demand manufacturing. In essence, Resolution helps companies to set up and manage Web site shops and complete online orders. Customers have included CBS, NBC, the BBC, the *New York Times*, Discovery Education, The Nature Conservancy, Pepsi, Prairie Home Companion, Sesame Workshop, History Channel, Golf Channel, A&E Television, HGTV, and United Feature Syndicate's Dilbert cartoon character.

ORIGINS

Resolution was cofounded by its longtime chief executive officer, William Schubart, who was born in New York City in 1945. His father, a naval officer, died earlier that year in the Philippines in World War II. He and his widowed mother moved to Stowe, Vermont, two years later. As a youngster Schubart developed a keen interest in radio and electronics. He attended prep school in New Hampshire at the Phillips Exeter Academy, where he benefited from the fact that another of the school's students was the son of RCA founder General David Sarnoff, who donated excellent audio equipment to the school.

After completing a degree in Romance languages from the University of Vermont and teaching French for two years, Schubart decided to pursue his earlier interest. In 1970 he teamed up with his half-brother, Michael Couture, and opened the first multitrack recording studio in northern New England in a former dairy barn in North Ferrisburg, Vermont.

The new business, Earth Audio Techniques, did well enough to allow the brothers to earn a modest living through a full range of commercial work, including film soundtracks, radio spots, and master tapes for record companies. In 1973 the partners decided to start recording music that appealed to them and launched Philo Records, turning out more than 150 albums over the next several years, mostly catering to folk artists.

Schubart and Couture also formed three companion publishing companies.

While Schubart and Couture enjoyed success with their barn operation, and introduced such new artists as Nanci Griffith and Christine Lavin, they were not able to earn enough money to support a comfortable lifestyle for their families. Hence, in 1981 they sold Philo to Boston's Rounder Records and launched a new business to become involved in both audio and video projects. The result was Resolution Video Audio and Film.

However, Schubart and Couture quickly realized they lacked the necessary film and video background. They found some like-minded people in Jim Taylor and Brian Doubleday, who owned Blue Jay Films. The two companies were merged together, although Doubleday was soon bought out. To purchase the necessary equipment, Resolution sold stock in a limited private offering that raised about $120,000 from some 20 minority shareholders. A capital lease of $250,000 was also arranged.

RESOLUTION OPENS DOORS: 1982

With five employees, Resolution became operational in the fall of 1982. Because Taylor was an experienced cinematographer, he served in that capacity at Resolution, while Couture, adept at audio, headed that unit. Essentially by default, Schubart became president of the company. He was also an obvious choice to serve as the public face for the company. In the past decade he had developed a name for himself in Vermont's cultural scene.

Because of Philo Records Schubart organized musical festivals and at the age of 26 was elected chairman of the Vermont Arts Council. A man of varied interests, he joined the board of the Vermont Symphony Orchestra at age 30. He later became chairman of the Vermont Folklife Center and was appointed by the governor to chair the Vermont Statehood Bicentennial Committee. He would also become a prominent industry leader, founding the American Video Duplication Association and serving as chairman of that organization.

In its first year of operation Resolution was able to land the 26-episode *The Joy of Gardening* television series. The series proved popular and ran in national syndication for many years. It was also a key to the company's survival because it provided much-needed cash flow to allow Resolution to establish itself in the marketplace. The video unit would go on to produce programming for A&E, Discovery, and Turner Broadcasting. Another national series was *Pets: Part of the Family*. Other program titles included *Battleship*, *Floating Palaces*, *The Secret World of Air Freight*, and *Dream Seekers*.

Resolution also took advantage of its equipment to offer real-time audio duplication services, turning out high-quality audiocassette products, serving such clients as Time-Life Music, PolyGram, Ford Motor Company, and the General Motors-Delco-Bose partnership. This proved to be a lucrative niche and Resolution soon became the largest such operation in North America. Schubart and his partners were more interested in video, however, and in 1986 sold the audio duplication business to Bose Corporation to invest the money in video duplication equipment and take advantage of the growing market for consumer videocassettes.

VIDEOTAPE DISTRIBUTION BEGINS: 1986

Schubart was also eager to pursue video duplication because he believed he spotted an opportunity to save money and undercut the competition. Rather than outsource loading, as did other duplicators, he planned to do it in-house to save about 7 percent of the $7.50 it cost to duplicate a full-length feature film. Resolution also applied for a line of credit to support the new business, but in the short time it took to secure the funding, consumer demand for VHS tapes exploded so that economies of scale reduced the price of duplicating a cassette to less than $3, eliminating Schubart's perceived advantage.

Nevertheless, Resolution found a way to spend 12 percent less than competitors by acquiring machines that could load the precise amount of tape required in a VHS shell. Videotape loading and duplication operations began in 1986. In 1990 Resolution became one of the first companies to make use of thermomagnetic duplication technology that allowed a high-quality transfer of a two-hour feature film to tape in just 45 seconds.

Unable to compete purely in terms of price, Resolution elected instead to focus on quality and to strive to be the best service provider of its kind. It was by listening to customers and serving their interests that Resolu-

KEY DATES

■

1981: Resolution Video Audio and Film formed.
1982: Operations begin.
1986: Audio duplication unit sold; videotape loading and duplication operations begin.
1997: E-commerce services launched.
2007: Headquarters moved to Williston, Vermont.

tion expanded beyond tape duplication. In 1987 some of the company's customers asked Resolution to help field orders. As a result, Resolution added other services tangential to duplication, but highly valuable to customers, such as fulfillment and inventory management.

Over the years Resolution invested in order management software, call center infrastructure, and electronic data interchange networks. Wholesale distribution logistics were also added, as well as a distribution center. As the business picked up, three additional distribution centers followed, until combined capacity reached 450,000 square feet.

In the early 1990s Resolution began working for clients who did not require video duplication but could make use of the company's order processing and fulfillment capabilities. What had once been an ancillary business gradually became Resolution's core operation. As the Internet emerged as a factor in direct marketing in the mid-1990s, Resolution added e-commerce expertise so that it could work with clients to help make their Web sites transaction-capable. Resolution also processed mail, phone, and online orders for customers. In 1997 the company integrated its e-commerce products and services, so that clients with retail Web sites could integrate their virtual shopping carts with Resolution's system to create a seamless fulfillment of orders.

VIDEO PRODUCTION UNIT SPUN OFF: 2000

The online business grew steadily to become the company's largest component. Resolution increased sales to about $27 million in 1999. The company continued to maintain its video production unit, which in addition to television specials produced sales presentations, infomercials, and advertising campaigns for such major clients as Disney, IBM, and Troy-Bilt. Video production, however, no longer fit in with what had become Resolution's core business, which was managing the productions of other companies. As a result, the video

production unit was spun off and sold to Jim Taylor as Resolution Productions, Inc., in July 2000. Taylor remained a partner of Resolution, Inc., and the independent company continued to serve as a strategic partner.

Following the split, Resolution began doing business as ResoDirect, although its legal name remained unchanged. The ResoDirect brand was intended to better reflect what the company had to offer. The company used the ResoDirect name until the spring of 2002 when it reverted to its legal name. Because the name www.resolutioninc.com was already taken, the company continued to employ "ResoDirect" in its Web address.

As Resolution completed the 1990s, VHS tape duplication remained an important part of the business, because most consumers continued to demand cassettes. Resolution recognized, however, that conditions were changing and that DVDs would soon supplant VHS tapes as the video medium of choice. The VHS business reached its peak in 1999 when Resolution was loading, duplicating, and packaging as many as one million tapes a month. Switching to DVD manufacturing was problematic for Resolution because the DVD patent holders charged 22 cents per disc, an amount that was too high for the company to bear.

VHS tapes had supplied the lion's share of Resolution's revenues, but as the new century dawned Resolution switched its focus to e-commerce fulfillment, incurring losses as it made the transition. In the summer of 2003 the company moved into a new 205,000-square-foot distribution center in Williston, Vermont, to improve its customer fulfillment capabilities. It also added the necessary equipment to offer a Media Just in Time service that allowed clients to produce VHS cassettes, CDs, and DVDs on a demand basis, so that single units could be produced and shipped without additional mastering costs. As a result, customers' entire title catalogs could be made available to consumers. DVD burning on a limited custom basis also became viable as part of the new business model.

With its enhanced capabilities Resolution was able to land significant customers. In 2006 the company worked with CBS to celebrate the 40th anniversary of the original *Star Trek* television series by creating an e-commerce Web site. Resolution would also be responsible for merchandising, customer service, and fulfillment. Later in the year Resolution landed another major client in Sesame Workshop, the nonprofit educational organization that operated *Sesame Street*. Resolution was responsible for the educational products and toys offered by the new online Sesame Store.

SURVIVING THE ECONOMIC SLUMP

Resolution was operating out of two main locations and elected in 2007 to combine all of its operations at its newer distribution center in Williston, which then housed the company's headquarters. The cost savings became especially important the following year when the deteriorating economy made its impact on Resolution. The company had shed a significant number of workers in recent years, but in the summer of 2008 it lost a major client and was forced to lay off 44 workers. Later in the year another 32 workers were laid off as the headcount dipped to 70, far fewer than the 200 people the company had employed at the start of the new decade.

There was a changing of the guard in the top ranks as well. In October 2008 Schubart left the company and a few months later became a principal at White Mountain Consulting to provide help in corporate financing, management consulting, and other services. The company carried on, and in 2009 took steps to refresh its brand and Web site. Late in the year the company landed a major new client in the *Dilbert* comic strip and launched a Dilbert store. The company's future prospects, however, remained uncertain.

Ed Dinger

PRINCIPAL COMPETITORS

ExpressFulfillment.com; Inktel Direct; Karol Media.

FURTHER READING

Daley, Dan. "ResoDirect's Bill Schubart." *Tape-Disc Business,* September 2000, p. 102.

Marcel, Joyce. "ResoDirect Keeps Busy Staying Ahead of the Curve." *Vermont Business Magazine,* January 1, 2001.

McLean, Dan. "Resolution Loses Clients, Lays Off 44." *Burlington Free Press,* August 23, 2008, p. A1.

O'Reilly, Tom. "From Tapes to T-Shirts, Resolution Serving Customers." *Tape-Disc Business,* December 1999, p. 40.

"Resolution: One of the Great Companies in Recording History." *Vermont Business Magazine,* February 1, 2003.

Smith, Robert F. "ResoDirect Is a Leader of the Broadband Revolution." *Vermont Business Magazine,* July 1, 2000.

Turner, Shawn. "Resolution's Evolution." *Burlington Free Press,* April 26, 2004, p. D2.

Woolmington, Rob. "Sound Business from a Barn: Phil/Fretless Recording Co." *Bennington Banner,* April 10, 1976, p. 6.

RioTinto

Rio Tinto PLC

—■—

5 Aldermanbury Square
London, EC2V 7HR
United Kingdom
Telephone: (+44 20) 7781-2000
Fax: (+44 20) 7781-1800
Web site: http://www.riotinto.com

Public Company
Incorporated: 1962
Employees: 102,000
Sales: $43.41 billion (2009)
Stock Exchanges: London New York
Ticker Symbols: RIO (London); RTP (New York)
NAICS: 212234 Copper Ore and Nickel Ore Mining; 212393 Other Chemical and Fertilizer Mineral Mining; 212221 Gold Ore Mining; 212222 Silver Ore Mining; 213113 Support Activities for Coal Mining

■ ■ ■

Rio Tinto PLC is an international dual-listed mining group with headquarters in the United Kingdom. Its counterpart, Rio Tinto Ltd., has offices in Melbourne and trades on the Australian Stock Exchange. The dual company, while trading on separate exchanges, operates as one unit that is involved in the mining, refining, and production of aluminum, copper, diamonds and minerals, and iron ore. It also produces thermal coal, coking coal, and uranium used by energy companies. While nearly 85 percent of its assets are in Australia and North America, the company is also active in South America, Europe, southern Africa, and Asia.

Rio Tinto acquired Canada-based Alcan Inc. in 2007. The $38 billion deal created Rio Tinto Alcan Inc., the world's largest aluminum producer. Rio Tinto divested nearly $10 billion in assets during 2008 and 2009. During 2008 Alcoa Inc. and the Aluminum Corporation of China Limited (Chinalco) made a $14.5 billion investment in Rio Tinto. Competitor BHP Billiton Plc ended its attempts to purchase Rio Tinto later that year. The deal, once estimated at nearly $170 billion, fell through due to falling commodity prices and a downturn in the global economy.

THE ORIGINS OF RIO TINTO PREDECESSORS RTC AND CZ

It had been the policy of the previously named RTZ Corporation PLC, since its formation in 1962 through the merger of the Rio Tinto Company (RTC) and the Consolidated Zinc Corporation (CZ), to invest only in first-class mining properties with large reserves and low-production costs. Both the RTC and CZ were formed during the years between 1870 and 1914, when London rose to prominence as the hub of international mining and metallurgical activities.

The number of overseas metal mining and processing companies listed on the London Stock Exchange climbed from 39 in 1875 to 913 in 1913, with the long-term capital employed in the industry rising at an average annual rate of more than 8 percent over the same period. In the city of London, for every prospective mine or group of mines, a new operating company

COMPANY PERSPECTIVES

Rio Tinto aims to maximize the overall return to its shareholders by sustainably finding, mining and processing mineral resources—areas of expertise in which we have a clear competitive advantage. A fundamental part of this is to deliver value while operating in an ethically and socially responsible manner, and remaining committed to long term sustainable development.

would be created. A syndicate composed of city interests including specialist company promoters, bankers, stockbrokers, merchants, mining engineers, and others would purchase a concession from a foreign vendor or exploration company, and a mining company would be formed to purchase the concession from the syndicate. Syndicates usually profited from the sale of the concession, and from securing contracts for financial or other services.

When launched in 1873, the RTC was by far the largest international mining venture ever brought to market, and it remained the flagship of the British-owned sector of the international industry until well into the 20th century. The Rio Tinto mines, in the province of Huelva in southern Spain, had produced large quantities of copper, on and off, since before Roman times, most recently under the ownership of the government of Spain. In 1872, following a series of financial losses, the mines were offered for sale at a price equivalent to several million pounds sterling. The Spanish government was in a financial crisis and did not have the cash or the expertise needed to exploit the large reserves of cuprous pyrites known to exist at RTC. Substantial investments were needed to introduce opencast mining, and to build workshops, tramways, crushing and metallurgical plants, a railway from the mines to the seaport of Huelva, a shipping pier, and the many other works necessary to operate on a large scale.

THE MATHESON PURCHASE

The availability of the mines was brought to the attention of Matheson & Company, the London-based agent for the Far Eastern merchants Jardine Matheson, by Heinrich Doetsch of Sundheim & Doetsch, a general merchant of Huelva. Doetsch had the foresight to see that if the Rio Tinto mines were developed to their full potential, his business eventually stood to gain from a

large increase in trade. A syndicate to purchase the Rio Tinto concession was organized by Hugh Matheson, senior partner in Matheson & Company, in London. The mines were purchased by the syndicate for £3.7 million, over a period of nine years, and immediately sold to the RTC. The new company was floated on the London Stock Exchange with an issued share capital of £2 million and debentures valued at £600,000. Hugh Matheson was appointed as first chairman of the RTC with Heinrich Doetsch as his deputy.

Matheson remained chairman of the RTC for a quarter of a century until his death in 1898. Matheson was a shrewd dealer in commodities, an outstanding entrepreneur with an ability to think on a scale that few could match, and a natural leader who could win the support needed to build very large enterprises in distant lands. The formation, survival, and ultimate prosperity of the RTC was the crowning achievement of his life. Matheson held together the original German and British banking, trading, and engineering consortium formed to launch the RTC in the crisis that followed the issue of its prospectus.

The claims made in this document, especially the report of the mining engineer David Forbes, were vigorously denounced by the Tharsis Company, a Scottish firm set up in 1866 to work a group of mines not far distant from those at Rio Tinto. It was alleged that Matheson and his associates had falsely inflated potential revenues and grossly underestimated development and operating costs. The new company, it was said, could never earn a positive rate of return on the huge capital it was seeking to raise from investors. Matheson launched a massive press campaign, an early example of skillful public relations, and he won the day.

The Tharsis assault, however, did some damage, and this was further compounded by a three-year price war between the two companies. The pyrites mined in southern Spain and in Portugal were first burned to drive off the sulfur content. The sulfurous gases were used to make sulfuric acid, one of the fundamental products of the chemicals industry. The burnt ore from the chemical works was then treated to remove the copper and other valuable metals it contained. The iron cinders that remained were sent to ironworks for smelting. During these difficult years, revenues were low and development costs were running at more than £100,000 per month. The purchase agreement with the Spanish government was renegotiated on more favorable terms; the company was financially restructured, and additional funds were raised through the issue of mortgage bonds. Eventually, in 1876, a favorable price-fixing

KEY DATES

■

1873: The Rio Tinto Company (RTC) is launched.

1930: RTC forms the Rhokana Corporation with Sir Ernest Oppenheimer of the Anglo American Corporation.

1955: The company purchases a majority interest in the Algom group of uranium mines.

1962: RTZ Corporation PLC is incorporated through the merger of RTC and the London-based Consolidated Zinc Corporation.

1989: The company acquires BP Minerals, including Kennecott Corporation, becoming one of the world's largest producers of gold outside South Africa.

1995: RTZ merges with Australia's CRA Ltd., creating RTZ-CRA Group, the largest mining company in the world.

1997: RTZ-CRA Group changes its name to Rio Tinto PLC, and headquarters are established in London.

2007: Alcan Inc. is acquired.

and market-sharing agreement was made with Tharsis, and the prospects for both companies began to improve.

The RTC was the major beneficiary of the 1876 agreement. Under this, the company gained control of the lucrative and rapidly expanding German market for pyrites, and within a matter of years it had become the dominant firm with a 50 percent market share in an oligopolistic world industry, with some degree of control over prices. At the same time, more of the product of the mines was treated locally to recover the copper contained therein. By the end of the 1880s, RTC was the leading producer of copper in the world. The company had smelters in Spain and a smelter and refinery in south Wales. In 1887, French entrepreneur Hyacinthe Secretan attempted to corner the world copper market to raise prices by attempting to buy all its copper at fixed prices. RTC at first reaped the benefits of its participation in the scheme, and was not severely affected when Secretan's scheme backfired in 1889, resulting in a spectacular collapse in the copper market. The company held a strong market position. Indeed, by 1887 it was responsible for 8 percent of the total world copper supply.

NEW TECHNOLOGY AT THE DAWN OF THE CENTURY

Hugh Matheson laid the foundations for the subsequent prosperity of the RTC, which rose to a high level under the leadership of Sir Charles Fielding. In his first 10 years as chairman, 1898 to 1908, the company paid an average annual dividend of 41 percent on a share capital of £3.5 million. Fielding built solidly on the achievements of the Matheson era, assuming personal responsibility for the introduction of a range of new technologies such as pyritic smelting. He also streamlined management, accounting, and decision-making practices, and, at a time of strong market growth, these innovations helped elevate the company to a higher level of profitability.

The Spanish government, under pressure from nationalists of all descriptions, tried to lay claim to a larger share of company revenues, but these efforts were generally thwarted, nor did the laborers of the mining district have much success in raising the level of wages paid by RTC. The company showed scant regard for the argument that it could afford to pay much more than it did, pointing out that it already paid more in cash and kind than most other large employers in Spain. The real wages per head of the 15,000 workers employed by the RTC in Spain in 1913 were actually less than those paid to 10,000 workers employed 20 years earlier. Low-cost housing; discretionary pensions; and company stores, schools, taverns, and other recreational facilities as substitutes for higher wages began to cause resentment among the workers and their families.

WARTIME TROUBLES

Strikes of varying lengths and bitterness became commonplace at RTC following the outbreak of World War I, exacerbated by ever-rising prices and declining real wages. A violent and acrimonious nine-month strike in 1920 ended with the exhausted unions and resentment toward the company in many sections of Spanish society, across the political spectrum. From this time onward, the fate of the RTC in Spain was bound up with the turbulent course of national politics. There was a period of relative stability between 1923 and 1929 under the dictatorship of Miguel Primo de Rivera, and the company was fortunate to escape lightly when it was discovered to have been evading export taxes through under-recording of the copper content of minerals shipped from Huelva.

After Primo de Rivera left office, however, there followed a long period of disruption and uncertainty that lasted until the mines were sold to Spanish interests in 1954. As left- and right-wing political factions vied for power between 1929 and 1936, the RTC came to be seen as an economic Rock of Gibraltar that must concede more in the interests of Spain. Damaging labor laws and taxation policies were introduced at the very time when the company was suffering from depressed trading conditions around the world, and when the copper content of the ores mined at Rio Tinto was plummeting. The decision was made by the third chairman of the company, Sir Auckland Geddes, who served from 1925 to 1947, to invest only as much money in Spain as was needed to sustain the operation.

The 1936–39 Spanish Civil War brought further problems. From an early date, the Rio Tinto mines were occupied by the insurgent forces led by General Francisco Franco. The mineral wealth of the district was seen by Franco as a means of procuring arms from the Axis powers, and within months the RTC found itself caught up in a complex web of diplomatic intrigue involving London, Berlin, Rome, and the Franco regime. Control over the company's Spanish assets had been lost, and was never effectively regained. During World War II and the period of reconstruction that followed, the RTC had little control over production, prices, or the numbers of workers employed in Spain. The company was held in check by restrictive laws and regulations, causing the real value of its assets to fall with the passage of each frustrating year. It was with great relief that the RTC managed to sell its Spanish operations in 1954. After many years of negotiations, involving Franco himself, the business was sold to a newly formed Spanish company in exchange for a one-third interest in the enterprise plus £7.7 million in seven annual installments.

GLOBAL EXPANSION

Auckland Geddes involved the company in ventures in other parts of the world and brought to the RTC a new style of business leadership. Unlike previous chairmen, he eschewed close involvement in day-to-day administrative matters in favor of major questions of policy and organization. He delegated responsibilities to full-time directors recruited from outside the business, and he initiated a search for major new investment opportunities in mining and related fields. Exploration subsidiaries were formed and research stations opened. A large minority shareholding in the Davison Chemical Corporation, a leading U.S. artificial-fertilizer manufacturer, was purchased. Together with Davison, the RTC set up a series of subsidiaries throughout Europe to manufacture and market the versatile chemical absorbent, silica gel. Substantial minority shareholdings were also acquired in several other companies devoted to exploration and the development of new products.

By far the most significant of the new departures inspired by Geddes was the involvement of the RTC in the development of the Northern Rhodesian (now Zambian) copperbelt. The opportunity to secure a stake in the field came early in 1929 when U.S. interests attempted to take over the promising N'Changa deposits. Along with Sir Ernest Oppenheimer and other members of the British-cum-South African business community, Geddes judged this move to be detrimental to British business interests, and led the resistance to it. By the time the struggle was over, the RTC had acquired sizable copperbelt holdings and valuable information which suggested that the deposits were among the richest and most extensive ever discovered.

Further shares were purchased in major copperbelt development companies in the months following the N'Changa struggle, and by 1930 the RTC had become a major economic force in Northern Rhodesia. In that year Geddes and Oppenheimer, whose Anglo American Corporation was the leading company in copperbelt finance, forced through the merger of three of the largest development companies to form the Rhokana Corporation. Geddes was appointed chairman of the new company. Under his leadership Rhokana emerged during the next 17 years as one of the largest and lowest-cost copper companies in the world.

Not all of Geddes's business initiatives were so successful. The RTC's venture into chemicals proved in the end to be a financial disaster, and the firm's exploration activities never yielded anything of worth. Failure in these fields was largely a consequence of the world economic depression but in part such losses were due to ill-informed and hasty judgments on the part of the RTC board. The returns on the Northern Rhodesian investments, however, more than compensated for these setbacks, enabling the firm to survive the protracted decline of its Spanish business and laying the foundations for its emergence as a modern multinational enterprise.

THE POSTWAR PERIOD

The regeneration of the RTC after World War II was, to a great extent, the work of two men, Mark Turner and Val Duncan, who formed one of the most creative business partnerships of modern times. Turner, the elder of the two and an investment banker by training, was appointed acting managing director of the company in 1948 on a part-time basis. He was charged with finding a full-time replacement, and for the position he groomed Duncan, a younger lawyer he had met during the war. Duncan was appointed managing director of the RTC in January 1951, allowing Turner, who remained a leading member of the RTC board and

Duncan's closest colleague, to devote more of his time to the banking business of Robert Benson, Lonsdale, which would later be named Kleinwort Benson.

Together, Duncan and Turner persuaded their colleagues and leading shareholders that RTC should aim to become a growth-oriented, broadly based natural resource company with operations concentrated in politically stable parts of the world, especially the Commonwealth countries. In the late 1940s and early 1950s, interests in a range of potential mines were secured, from tin and wolfram in Portugal to diamonds in South Africa and copper in Uganda. Between 1952 and 1954, a network of amply funded exploration subsidiaries was established to search for mineral deposits that might be exploited on a large scale in Canada, Africa, and Australia.

The sale of the Spanish mines in 1954 released further human and financial resources for the task of rebuilding and reorienting the RTC. An intense period of exploration followed, which sent Duncan and other executives to all parts of the world to supervise exploration agreements and consider the mine-development deals put to the company from time to time. The first tangible result of this activity came in 1955 with the purchase of a majority interest in the Algom group of uranium mines in the Elliot Lake district of Canada. The authorized capital of the RTC was raised from £8 million to £12 million to accommodate the purchase, and a loan of $200 million was raised against various supply contracts to fund the development of seven major mines.

The company's position in the uranium industry was consolidated by the simultaneous acquisition of a controlling interest in the Mary Kathleen mine in Australia. By the end of the 1950s, RTC was responsible for the production of 15 percent of the world's uranium oxide, and along the way the company had gained control over two highly promising mineral prospects: the vast Hammersley iron ore deposits in Western Australia and the Palabora copper deposit in South Africa.

MERGING RTC AND CONSOLIDATED ZINC

By the early 1960s, Duncan was confident enough to take the decisive step toward realizing his vision of the RTC as a first-rank multinational enterprise. Merging was the obvious means of speeding the process of building up the organization, and he found an ideal prospective partner in the London-based Consolidated Zinc Corporation. This company had steadily expanded its activities since 1905 when it was launched to recover the

large quantities of zinc remaining in the tailings dumps of the legendary silver-lead mines at Broken Hill in New South Wales, Australia. CZ's operations were still concentrated in Australia, but had been progressively extended to include a wide range of mining and metallurgical activities.

The compatibility of CZ and the RTC was both strategic and structural. Strategically, the leading directors of CZ wished to attain major-company status through geographic diversification and the development of important new prospects, particularly the vast Weipa bauxite deposits of northern Queensland. Structurally, the company was about the same size as the RTC with net profits running at a little over £1 million per annum, and its major interests were in complementary rather than competing areas. The merger would, at a stroke, produce a large and broadly based organization with financial and technological resources to undertake a range of promising new ventures. In July 1962 the two companies came together to form RTZ. Duncan was appointed managing director of the new concern, and in 1963, on the retirement of A.M. Baer, he became chairman and chief executive of RTZ. He retained these positions until his death in December 1975.

EXPANSION UNDER DUNCAN: 1963–75

Under Duncan's leadership, RTZ rapidly rose to prominence in the natural resources industries of the world. In partnership with Kaiser Aluminum, the firm established an integrated aluminum business in Australia, Comalco Limited. The Hammersley iron and Palabora copper projects were brought to fruition. Extensive exploration was continued, eventually yielding large-scale mines in Papua New Guinea (Bougainville Copper), Canada (Lornex Copper), and Namibia (Rossing Uranium).

Meanwhile, the scale and the scope of the business was further expanded through the purchase of going concerns: Atlas Steels (high-grade specialty steels) in Canada; Borax Holdings (industrial raw materials) in the United States; and Capper Pass (tin refiners) and Pillar Holdings (aluminum fabricators) in the United Kingdom. By the early 1970s, RTZ had achieved the geographically and geologically diverse pattern of operations long pursued by Val Duncan.

Duncan made an important contribution to advancing the fortunes of the enterprise. He was the principal architect of the strategy of promoting growth through involvement in a stream of large-scale, capital-intensive natural resources projects. Potential financial limits to growth were overcome through the funding of massive projects with a high ratio of loan capital to equity. Multimillion-dollar loans were raised by Duncan and his team throughout the by offering long-term supply contracts as collateral. Potential organizational and managerial limits to growth were overcome by the progressive devolution of responsibilities to a series of nationally based companies, each charged with the goal of involving RTZ in substantial new projects. By the early 1970s, RTZ had emerged as a loosely knit family of companies with the activities of the parent concern limited to the provision of group services, the controlling of major strategic and financial decisions, and the appointment of top personnel.

The strategy, organization, and policies devised by Duncan remained in place in the 1980s. Duncan was succeeded as chief executive by Mark Turner. He continued in office until his death in December 1980. Turner saw no need to change course, nor did Anthony Tuke who replaced him, nor did Alistair Frame, who retired in 1991, or Derek Birkin, who was succeeded by Sir Robert Wilson. The essential integrity of RTZ was maintained while growth continued. New mines and smelters were brought on stream and new processing facilities developed. Some businesses were bought, others sold.

THE BP MINERALS PURCHASE: 1989

The biggest boost to the enterprise came in 1989 with the acquisition of BP Minerals for £2.6 billion. This deal brought to RTZ one of the greatest names in world mining, the Kennecott Corporation, and a portfolio of assets in 15 countries, including the world's largest opencast copper mine and the world's largest producer of titanium dioxide feedstock. RTZ immediately became one of the world's largest producers of gold outside South Africa. The shares of world output accounted for by the much-enlarged company in 1989 were 55 percent of borates, 30 percent of titanium dioxide feedstock, 13 percent of zircon, 15 percent of industrial diamonds, 14 percent of vermiculite, 8 percent of talc, and 5 percent or more of uranium, copper, and molybdenum. RTZ also ranked among the world's largest producers of tin, bauxite, silver, iron ore, gold, lead, and zinc.

Robert Wilson played a vital role in closing the BP Minerals deal. He joined the company in 1970, becoming managing director of its European zinc and lead smelting subsidiary in 1979. He moved to the head office in 1982 and was appointed to the main board in 1987 as executive director responsible for planning and development. It was in this capacity that he led the

significant purchase that brought with it Kennecott Corporation. Wilson would go on to be named chief executive of Rio Tinto in 1991 and be appointed chairman in 1997.

CREATING A DUAL-LISTED COMPANY: 1995–97

When the London-based RTZ Corporation PLC and its Australian subsidiary CRA Limited completed a dual-listed companies merger in December 1995, the largest mining company in the world was created, RTZ-CRA Group. Combined revenues for the next year were $8.4 billion, double the $4.22 billion in sales reported by RTZ alone for 1995. As a result of the unique merger, both companies maintained separate identities and stock market listings.

In March 1997 RTZ-CRA announced a management restructuring into six new global product businesses, with three to be based in London and three in Australia. As a result, operations for copper, gold and other minerals, as well as operations for industrial minerals, were now based in London. In Australia, aluminum operations were headquartered in Brisbane, energy in Melbourne, and iron ore in Perth. These businesses were supported by the worldwide technology and exploration groups that remain headquartered in London. In June 1997 the company changed its name to Rio Tinto PLC.

Kennecott Corporation, the world's leader in copper output throughout most of the 20th century, by 1997 ceased to exist as a separate entity. That year it was divided into a group of wholly owned subsidiaries of Rio Tinto, who continued to operate Kennecott's chief U.S. businesses: Kennecott Utah Copper, Kennecott Minerals, and Kennecott Energy. However, these operations were absorbed into Rio Tinto's copper and energy units.

In the mid-1990s, Rio Tinto's exploration of mines around the world continued, with projects for gold in Papua New Guinea, prospecting in northern Norway's Finnmark region, and expanded coal mining by buying U.S. operators Nerco and Cordero Mining. In 1997 copper and gold exploration looked promising at Famatina in northwestern Argentina.

As the 1990s drew to a close, Rio Tinto was looking at a strong world economy that would demand primary raw materials, such as copper, gold, and coal. Prices were holding, as well, but competition was a possible concern from emerging markets such as Russia and China.

RIO TINTO HANGS TOUGH IN DIFFICULT MARKET

In January 1999 Rio Tinto deferred construction on its Hail Creek Coal Project in Queensland Basin in reaction to an economic recession in Asia. Development eventually resumed in June 2001. In April the company moved to shuffle chief executives in its copper, gold, and technology groups in an attempt to exchange best practices between the business groups. This came just two months after Rio Tinto declared a 10 percent drop in earnings to $1.1 billion and a 2 percent decline in sales to $9.2 billion. In September, Rio Tinto sold its Las Cruces copper deposit in Andalucia, southern Spain, to MK Gold Company for $42 million cash.

In February 2000 Rio put up a for-sale notice on its 40 percent stake in the rich Nevada gold mine, the Cortez Pipeline. Three years previously, Rio had considered spinning off its gold mines, but since a sizable proportion of production was a by-product of copper companies, the idea was shelved. The sale never went through, but this period continued as an era of a fragile global economy.

Despite a tumultuous couple of years, a growth in demand would lead Rio Tinto to declare first-half net earnings in 2000 at $677 million, a 33 percent increase over the previous year. Copper prices were averaging 23 percent above the low levels of first half 1999 and aluminum prices were up 25 percent. Rio Tinto would go on to achieve a record level of earnings, helped by the full ownership of Comalco Limited and the acquisition of North Limited.

Unfavorable economic conditions abounded in the United States, the European Union, and Japan, weakening demand and price for many Rio Tinto products. However, protected by the quality of the company's asset base, strength of its margins, and strong economic growth in China, Rio Tinto's adjusted earnings in 2001 would reach $1.62 billion, up from $1.51 billion in 2000.

By November 2001, Kennecott Utah Copper was taking steps to cut costs and improve productivity to secure its future. Record-low copper prices led to the permanent closing of its North Concentrator. In February 2001 Rio Tinto posted a 23 percent drop in pretax earnings to $1.93 billion in 2001 after taking an exceptional charge of $583 million primarily due to the reduction in value of Kennecott Utah Copper.

In keeping with its reputation for high environmental and community standards, Rio Tinto stopped its incursions into aboriginal land in Queensland, Australia, in early 2002, after increased pressure from the public and several nongovernmental

organizations. The company also abruptly ended a decade-long battle against unions over individual workplace contracts, instead offering collective agreements in line with federal law to 4,000 workers at four mines in Western Australia.

THE ALCAN DEAL: 2007

Rio Tinto spent the next few years unloading noncore assets and investing its Australian businesses. Commodity prices remained high during this period and the industry began to experience a significant wave of consolidation as mining companies looked to bolster their holdings. Rio Tinto made industry headlines with the announcement of its $38.1 billion purchase of Alcan Inc., the third-largest aluminum producer in the world. Rio Tinto outbid competitor Alcoa Inc. in 2007 and was able to significantly diversify its iron ore and copper holdings with the purchase. The combined company, Rio Tinto Alcan, was headquartered in Montreal, Canada, and was positioned as the largest aluminum producer in the world.

Tom Albanese, named CEO of Rio Tinto in May 2007, oversaw the deal and believed it was crucial to the company's future growth. Shortly after the deal, Rio Tinto itself became a target and competitor BHP Billiton made a $125 billion play for the company. The pursuit continued during most of 2008. At the same time, Alcoa Inc. and the Aluminum Corporation of China Limited (Chinalco) made a $14.5 billion investment in Rio Tinto and hoped to cash in on what would become the largest mining company in the world. BHP Billiton ended its attempts to purchase Rio Tinto, however, in late 2008. The deal, which was once estimated at nearly $170 billion, fell through due to sharply falling commodity prices and a downturn in the global economy. Despite the failed purchase attempt, Rio Tinto and BHP Billiton teamed up in June 2009 in an iron ore production joint venture that would combine both companies' Western Australian production assets.

OVERCOMING HARDSHIPS: 2008 AND BEYOND

Faltering economies across the globe, a sudden and steep decline in commodity prices, and an enormous debt load related to the Alcan purchase forced Rio Tinto to launch a divestment program in 2008. During the year the company unloaded its investment in the Kintyre energy project for $495 million, its Greens Creek copper mine for $750 million, and its portion of the Cortez copper joint venture for $1.7 billion. Rio Tinto continued to sell assets in 2009 while it cut jobs and reduced its capital expenditure plan. Its Corumba iron ore mine was sold as well as exploration projects in Argentina and Canada. Various other holdings were divested and the company spun off Cloud Peak Energy Inc., its U.S.-based coal mining company. Overall, Rio Tinto raised nearly $10 billion as a result of its divestment program during 2008 and 2009.

With lower debt levels and a strong balance sheet, Rio Tinto's strategy appeared to pay off. Its financial performance appeared to be back on track, but the company continued to face challenges. Rio Tinto signed a mining convention with the government of Guinea in 2003 to develop a mining concession at Simandou, which was considered to be one of the largest iron ore reserves in the world. The company lost 50 percent of its rights to develop the mine during a period of political unrest in 2008. As of that time, Rio Tinto had invested nearly $600 million in development of Simandou.

At the same time, four Rio Tinto executives were arrested in China on bribery and commercial spying charges. China accounted for nearly a quarter of company revenues in 2009 and future partnerships in the region were considered crucial for Rio Tinto's future growth. The arrests did not appear to damage the company's relationship with Chinalco. Indeed, during early 2010 the two companies announced a joint venture to develop the Simandou mine.

While global economies remained in flux during 2010, Rio Tinto remained optimistic about its future. As one of the largest mining companies with interests in some of the world's largest mineral deposits, Rio Tinto was poised for success as global demand rebounded, especially in China and India.

Charles Edward Harvey
Updated, Dorothy Kroll; Stacee Sledge;
Christina M. Stansell

PRINCIPAL SUBSIDIARIES

Argyle Diamond Mines (Australia); Coal & Allied Industries Limited Coal (Australia; 75.71%) Dampier Salt Limited (Australia; 68.40%); Energy Resources of Australia Limited (68.39%); Hamersley Iron Pty Limited (Australia); Queensland Coal Pty Limited; Rio Tinto Aluminium (Holdings) Limited; Iron Ore Company of Canada Inc. (58.72%); QIT-Fer et Titane Inc. (Canada); Rio Tinto Alcan Inc. (Canada); Talc de Luzenac France SA; P.T. Kelian Equatorial Mining (Indonesia; 90%); QIT Madagascar Minerals SA (80%); Rössing Uranium Limited (Namibia; 65.58); Bougainville Copper Limited Papua New Guinea; 53.58%); Palabora Mining Company Limited (South Africa; 57.67%); Kennecott Holdings Corporation (USA); U.S. Borax Inc.

PRINCIPAL OPERATING UNITS

Iron Ore; Aluminum; Copper; Energy; Diamonds & Minerals.

PRINCIPAL COMPETITORS

Anglo American plc; BHP Billiton Plc; Vale S.A.; WMC Resources Ltd.

FURTHER READING

Avery, David. *Not on Queen Victoria's Birthday: The Story of the Rio Tinto Mines.* London: Collins, 1974.

"China and Rio Tinto; A Big African Deal Signals a Potential Thaw in Relations." *Economist.com,* April 27, 2010.

Green, William. "Lords of Dispassion." *Forbes,* January 12, 1998, p. 45.

Harvey, Charles E. *The Rio Tinto Company: An Economic History of a Leading International Mining Concern 1873–1954.* St. Ives: Alison Hodge, 1981.

Jennemann, Tom. "Alcan in Focus as Rio Slashes Debt, Jobs." *American Metal Market,* December 10, 2008.

Lucas, Alastair. "How CRA and RTZ Went Dutch." *Corporate Finance,* December 1996, pp. 18–20.

Mason, Josephine. "Rio Tinto Brushes Alcoa Aside with $38bn Bid for Alcan." *Metal Bulletin,* July 16, 2007.

Matthews, Robert Guy. "Mining Giants Are Forced to Lessen Global Ambitions." *Wall Street Journal,* July 17, 2009.

Matthews, Robert Guy, Dana Cimilluca, and Patrick Barta. "Death of a Megadeal: BHP Ends Its Pursuit of Rio." *Wall Street Journal,* November 26, 2008.

Webb, Toby. "Interview with Sir Robert Wilson, Chairman, Rio Tinto." *Ethical Corporation Magazine,* December 2001.

RIS Paper Company, Inc.

—■—

50 East RiverCenter Boulevard, Suite 260
Covington, Kentucky 41011-1654
U.S.A.
Telephone: (859) 292-5000
Fax: (859) 291-9777
Web site: http://www.domtardisgroup.com

Wholly Owned Subsidiary of Domtar Corporation
Founded: 1915
Employees: 550
Sales: $600 million (2000 est.)
NAICS: 424110 Printing and Writing Paper Merchant
Wholesalers

■ ■ ■

RIS Paper Company, Inc., is a wholly owned subsidiary of Domtar Corporation, a major Canadian paper concern. Ris Paper is the largest contributor of the Domtar Distribution Group, which comprises four regional paper distributors and a publishing solutions group. Ris Paper serves the eastern, midwestern, and southwestern portions of the United States through 19 business units. The company participates mostly in four market segments: coated and uncoated papers for magazine publishers, catalogers, and direct-mail companies; fine printing paper for commercial and in-plant printers; communication products, including copier, laser, and computer papers; and industrial and packaging products, including corrugated cardboard, films, tapes, and packaging equipment. Ris Paper maintains its main office in Covington, Kentucky.

COMPANY FOUNDED: 1915

Ris Paper was founded in New York City in 1915 as an office products company by the Ris family. Under the leadership of president Charles H. Ris, the business changed its focus to paper distribution and took the name Ris Paper Company, Inc., in 1938. It was not until after his death in 1954 and his son, Howard C. Ris, became president that the firm began growing at a rapid rate. By the early 1960s, Ris Paper was generating $5 million in annual sales, an amount that increased to $400 million over the next 25 years.

A key to the growth of Ris Paper was a steady stream of acquisitions. The first significant deal was the 1965 purchase of John Carter & Company of Boston, which took Ris Paper beyond the metropolitan New York City market for the first time. Two years later Ris Paper expanded to Philadelphia, Pennsylvania, with the acquisition of Quaker City Paper Company. Further external growth followed in the 1970s. The company entered the Washington, D.C., market in 1972 with the addition of R.P. Andrews, which also served other areas, including markets in Pennsylvania and Virginia. In 1975 Ris Paper solidified its standing in New York with the purchase of an old-guard paper house located in Lower Manhattan, John F. Sarle Company. Bradley & Reese of Baltimore was then acquired to fill out Ris Paper's mid-Atlantic business.

As the 1970s came to a close, Ris Paper had long since outgrown its location at West 25th Street in Manhattan, a site that required customers to take a freight elevator if they wanted to avoid the stairs. Thus, in 1979 Ris Paper, like many other companies, fled

Manhattan and its high rents for new offices and a warehouse in Long Island City, a neighborhood in the borough of Queens. Just three years later, the company moved even farther away from the heart of the city, relocating to the suburbs of Garden City, Long Island.

CINCINNATI COMPANY ACQUIRED: 1984

Even as its headquarters was migrating eastward, Ris Paper continued to expand its reach through further acquisitions. Cincinnati, Ohio-based Diem and Wing Company was purchased in 1984, bringing additional operations in Indiana, and Dayton and Columbus, Ohio. Next, Ris Paper acquired Paper Distributors Inc. of Harrisburg, Pennsylvania. A year later, two more paper distributors were brought into the fold: Ft. Wayne, Indiana-based Taylor Martin Paper Company, and Cleveland, Ohio-based Petrequin Paper Company. Ris Paper closed the 1980s with the purchase of Andrews Nelson Whitehead Company of New York.

Even as Howard Ris was overseeing the vast expansion of the company he inherited, he was taking steps to turn over the reins to the next generation. In 1988 he retired as chairman of the board, relinquishing that post to his son-in-law, Thomas Walden, who had been serving as chief financial officer. Ris stayed on as chairman emeritus but had no official authority. Nevertheless, he remained involved, communicating frequently with his successor as chief executive officer, Benjamin W. Krieger, who since 1984 had served as president and chief operating. Prior to that, Krieger had spent a quarter-century in the paper industry, starting out of college with the Chatfield Paper Corporation in 1956.

The early 1990s brought a variety of changes to Ris Paper. A recession forced some of its major's customers out of business, including Pandick Inc., a major financial printer whose business had been in steep decline since the Wall Street crash of 1987. Not only was this firm forced into bankruptcy in 1990, three of the top four printers serving the financial community were now bankrupt or out of business. To avoid a similar fate, Ris Paper reduced the amount of its New York business to about 20 percent, this from a company that had once exclusively served the needs of the city. Many of its old customers had left the confines of New York City as well, and Ris Paper's breadth of operations allowed it to chase the business to new locales.

Ris Paper had not given up on New York. In fact, in 1992 the company decided to move its headquarters back to Long Island City, leaving behind a government sales division and computer operations. Although many of the company's longtime printing customers had moved their headquarters, many of them retained offices in the city, for cachet if nothing else, and Ris Paper elected to move closer to keep closer tabs on them as well as to be closer to paper mill representatives and the company's bankers. The return to Long Island City would be short-lived, however.

MOVE TO CINCINNATI: 1994

In 1994 the company recruited a new chief executive and settled on Mark W. Griffin, an International Paper executive in Kansas City who had 25 years of experience in the paper industry. Because New York accounted for only 20 percent of Ris Paper's $400 million in annual sales, he decided to move the company's corporate headquarters to a more central location. (Howard Ris remained the company's largest stockholder.) Griffin settled on the Cincinnati area, which not only offered the kind of family atmosphere he valued but also possessed a Delta Air lines hub that allowed him to fly to any of the company's locations in no more than 90 minutes.

Ris Paper established temporary quarters in Cincinnati in 1994 and transferred its information management system. Early the next year the company moved to permanent accommodations across the Ohio River in Kentucky. Rather than pursue acquisitions, Griffin for the next few years focused on improving efficiencies and achieving internal growth. Even as it was making the move to the Midwest, the company was expanding its product lines to include magnetic computer storage media. Early in 1995 the company also opened a warehouse in Texas to expand its market reach.

Ris Paper generated sales of $540 million in 1998, the second best year in its history, but in order to maintain growth the company resumed its pursuit of external growth. Moreover, the industry was undergoing a period of intense consolidation, driven in large part by declining paper prices that forced distributors like Ris Paper to seek alliances to become even more cost-efficient and gain more leverage with paper mills. In the spring of 1999 the company completed its first acquisition in more than a decade when it purchased Cincinnati-based Johnston Paper Company, one of the

KEY DATES

1915: Company launched as New York office products company.
1938: Focus switches to paper distribution.
1965: John Carter & Company acquired.
1994: Company moves to Covington, Kentucky.
2000: Domtar Corporation acquires Ris Paper.

city's largest fine-paper distributors. The deal added about $50 million in sales to the balance sheet.

Even as Ris Paper was completing the acquisition for Johnston Paper, it was busy growing its business organically as well. In March 1999 it opened a new unit in Lancaster, Pennsylvania, Ris Converting, which specialized in converting master paper rolls into the kind of press-sized sheets used in book publishing and commercial prints. With paper prices expected to improve soon, however, Griffin expressed an eagerness to pursue further acquisitions. Especially inviting were companies located in Atlanta or Chicago where Ris Paper was not represented. He was also interested in building up markets where the company already possessed operations.

DOMTAR ACQUIRES RIS PAPER: 2000

A little more than a year after acquiring Johnston Paper, Ris Paper became the acquired party instead of the buyer. In July 2000 it agreed to be bought by Domtar Inc., Canada's largest producer of specialty and fine papers and the seventh-largest company in its field in North America with $2.3 billion in annual sales. The $90 million deal included $24 million in stock and cash and $66 million of assumed debt. The two companies were already familiar with one another. For the past six years, Ris Paper had served as a Domtar franchiser in the Midwest.

Domtar's roots were not in paper. Rather, it was launched in Nova Scotia 1903 as the Dominion Tar & Chemical Company Ltd. with the opening of a coal tar distillation plant that in addition to pitch residue produced such chemicals as hydrocarbons, acids, and bases. It was not until 1957 that Domtar became involved in the paper industry with the acquisition of a one-third stake in Howard Smith Paper Mills Ltd. Further paper acquisitions were made in the 1960s and wallboard assets were added in the 1970s and 1980s. The original coal tar products business was then divested in 1989. By the early 1990s Domtar emerged as a leading Canadian producer of fine papers and containerboard.

Later in the decade the company decided to narrow its focus to fine papers. Domtar had developed a paper merchanting business in Canada, but the addition of Ris Paper and its extensive operation in a wide swath of the United States, along with its $600 million in annual sales, was a considered major coup for Domtar. A year later Domtar grew even larger, paying $1.65 billion to Georgia-Pacific Group for four integrated pulp and paper mills in the United States, essentially doubling the company's production capacity.

With the industry continuing to consolidate at a rapid pace, Ris Paper decided that its best chance for ongoing growth was to join forces with a larger concern such as Domtar. The early 2000s proved to be a struggle for Domtar, however. Softening demand for specialty paper led to the closing of a pair of plants in 2002, and a year later the company lost $147 million. In addition, the company had to contend with a struggling economy, increased costs, and intense competition.

DISTRIBUTION GROUP FORMED: 2004

In adapting to business conditions, changes were in order. In 2004 Domtar reorganized its paper merchanting companies, and Ris Paper, the flagship unit, became part of the Domtar Distribution Group (DDG), the fifth-largest paper merchant organization in North America. The recasting of the business created a more consistent brand. Although the local brand names were retained, the phrase "the paper house" was added. Thus, Ris Paper now did business as Ris The Paper House.

Revenues at DDG increased to $9.9 billion in 2008. A year later the unit had to contend with lower selling prices and other factors that resulted in a 12 percent decrease to $873 million. During the year further changes were made to DDG, with the Contract Paper Group folded into Ris Paper. As Ris Paper approached its centennial, it was a small but significant part of a larger concern. Whether it would ever again emerge as an independent company was far from certain.

Ed Dinger

PRINCIPAL DIVISIONS

Eastern Region; Midwest Region.

PRINCIPAL COMPETITORS

Central National-Gottesman Inc.; Gould Paper Corporation; Unisource Worldwide, Inc.

FURTHER READING

Boyer, Mike. "Ris Looks Good on Paper." *Cincinnati Enquirer*, May 30, 1999.

Byczkowski, John J. "Ris Paper Resettling in Cincinnati." *Cincinnati Enquirer*, December 19, 1994, p. D1.

Kamen, Robin. "Paper Firms Puts Its Stock in N.Y." *Crain's New York Business*, January 27, 1992, p. 43.

Miller, Nick. "Ris Paper Acquires Johnston." *Cincinnati Post*, March 13, 1999, p. 10B.

"The Private File: Ris Paper Inc." *Business Record*, January 2, 1995, p. 21.

Sekhri, Rajiv. "Ris Completes Purchase, Looks for More." *Business Courier of Cincinnati*, March 12, 1999.

———. "Ris Paper Looks to Acquire in Chicago, Atlanta." *Business Courier of Cincinnati*, April 16, 1999, p. 19.

Roman, Inc.

———■———

472 Brighton Drive
Bloomingdale, Illinois 60108-3100
U.S.A.
Telephone: (630) 705-4600
Fax: (630) 705-4601
Web site: http://www.roman.com

Private Company
Founded: 1963 as Roman's Religious Goods
Employees: 150
Sales: $40 million (2008 est.)
NAICS: 424990 Other Miscellaneous Nondurable
   Goods Merchant Wholesalers

■ ■ ■

Roman, Inc., is a privately owned wholesaler of more than 4,000 giftware and religious items. The Bloomingdale, Illinois-based company offers Christmas decorations and other seasonal items as well as year-round giftware and inspirational figurines. Collections include Fontanini Heirloom Nativity, The Millenium Collection, The Valencia Collection, Seraphim Classics, and Jingle Buddies. Roman maintains showrooms in Atlanta; Columbus, Ohio; Dallas; Denver; Los Angeles; Minneapolis; and Seattle; as well as a showroom in Canada. Customers include department stores, gift shops, specialty retailers, and catalogers. The company is owned and managed by the Jedlinski family.

COMPANY FOUNDED: 1963

Roman, Inc., was founded in Chicago as Roman's Religious Goods in 1963 by Ronald T. Jedlinski, who named the business after his father, Roman Jedlinski. Born in 1939, the younger Jedlinski often worked as a child in his father's store, Roman's Art & Gift Shop, which mostly served the city's large Polish community. He enrolled at Northwestern University, and helped to pay the bills by peddling religious figurines and other wares to area retail stores. Upon graduation Jedlinski completed a two-year obligation to the U.S. Navy. Stationed in Spain, he remained involved in the business, buying religious figurines that he shipped home to be sold in his father's store. After his discharge in 1963, Jedlinski went into the giftware business full time.

Not a devout man by his own description, Jedlinski viewed religious figurines as more of a business opportunity than a calling. Nevertheless, his timing proved perfect. The early 1960s was a time of significant change in the Catholic Church, which took steps to keep pace with political and societal developments through the Second Ecumenical Council of the Vatican, or Vatican II, which opened in 1962. Among the changes that resulted were the adoption of a more contemporary service and the elimination of many ceremonial trappings. As a result, much of the inventory of longtime religious goods merchants became superfluous and many of them left the business, allowing an ambitious young man like Ronald Jedlinski to fill the void.

Jedlinski started Roman's Religious Goods in the back of his father's store with just $500 in capital and a station wagon. Much of his initial inventory consisted of the figurines he sent home from Spain that his father was unable to sell. He added other inspirational items, which he sold for $1.50 to the gift retailers. An early top-selling product was a flower-adorned, silk-screened ornament that featured a picture of Jesus Christ and the painted words, "God Bless Our Home."

In his first six months in business Jedlinski recorded sales of $10,000, resulting in a profit of $3,000. After three years his annual revenues reached $50,000. A key to his success was tapping into new sales channels. Rather than limit himself to Catholic and religious organizations like the old guard religious goods merchants, Jedlinski sold to secular gift shops and persuaded department stores such as Marshall Field's and Wieboldt's to create religious gift sections that he could supply. Moreover, these large new accounts became a selling point for Jedlinski in reaching out to other large retailers, and prompted him to begin conducting his own overseas buying trips. He spent about two months of each year on the road, mostly visiting suppliers in Europe and the Far East.

MOVE TO NEW SITE: 1971

Growth was so steady that Jedlinski moved his business to a larger site in 1971. He began importing Fontanini products from Italy during this period, prompting a growth spurt that led to a need for even larger accommodations by the mid-1970s. The name of the company also evolved. Jedlinski incorporated the business as Roman Religious Goods, Inc., and then shortened the name to Roman, Inc.

A major development in the evolution of Roman took place in 1979 when Jedlinski persuaded Frances Hook to produce figurines for the company. She was a successful commercial illustrator, best known for her depictions of children that were issued as prints by Northern Tissue in the late 1950s and early 1960s. When the market for illustrations was curtailed by the increasing popularity of television, Hook and her husband Richard turned their attention to the inspirational market, illustrating children's books. Following her husband's death from cancer, Hook, herself a cancer survivor, continued her career alone by

accepting a commission from Jedlinski. One of her most popular prints created for Roman was a simple chalk portrait of Jesus called "The Carpenter." Offering a more human portrayal of Jesus than most illustrations, it became an enduring and iconic work. In addition to inspirational prints, Hook worked for the first time in three dimensions, producing plates and figurines that became very popular collectibles for Roman.

Frances Hook died in 1983 but left a lasting impact on Roman. For many years her work remained a major presence in the company's catalog. A year after her death Jedlinski played an important role in the launch of the Frances Hook Scholarship Fund to aid young art students. The company would also honor the artist and her work by later constructing the Frances Hook Memorial Garden at its new headquarters.

ROSELLE FACILITY OPENS: 1987

A new facility became necessary in the 1980s because of a surge in the sale of religious gifts, books, and other inspirational items. Between 1980 and 1990 the market tripled to $2.7 billion. The decade featured both solid and poor economic conditions, but it mattered little to an industry that enjoyed good business during good times and even better business during lean times. In 1987 Roman moved into a new 160,000-square-foot complex in Roselle, Illinois, that included 115,000 square feet of warehouse space, 20,000 square feet of office space, and a 5,000-square-foot showroom.

Over the years, Roman expanded its product range to appeal to Protestant and Jewish customers as well as Catholics. In 1991 the company looked to general consumers as well when it entered the Christmas decorations market. Unlike Roman's other merchandise whose designs remained constant over the years, Christmas decorations were akin to fashion lines, requiring continual changes to keep pace with consumers' shifting tastes. The new business performed well for Roman, which in a matter of three years grew its Christmas business from $3 million to $15 million. Moreover, the new business helped Roman to double overall sales to $40 million from 1986 to 1992.

With sales continuing to grow, Roman again found itself short of space. In 1996 the company broke ground on a new facility in Addison, Illinois, which opened two years later. It included a new 525,000-square-foot warehouse, which served as the company's national distribution center, as well as a 42,000-square-foot retail store. Roman essentially tripled the size of its warehouse space. The company continued to maintain its headquarters in Roselle.

By the end of the 1990s Roman topped the $100 million mark in annual sales. For its performance, Ro-

KEY DATES

1963: Roman's Religious Goods is founded.
1979: Frances Hook collection is introduced.
1987: Company moves to Roselle, Illinois.
1998: New facility opens in Addison, Illinois.
2007: Company moves to smaller facility in Bloomingdale, Illinois.

man was selected as a 1998 finalist in the Illinois Family Business of the Year Contest. Roman was also gaining an excellent reputation, albeit unsolicited, for its philanthropic endeavors. The company was a major sponsor of the Sunshine Foundation, which granted wishes to disabled and terminally ill children. Roman also began supporting breast cancer research.

After learning that the angels of its Seraphim Classics collection were being given as gifts to people fighting breast cancer, Roman designed a figurine with breast cancer in mind, an angel called "Hope—Light in the Distance," wearing a pink sash and holding a candle. A percentage of the sales was then donated to the Susan G. Komen Foundation, an organization dedicated to the eradication of breast cancer.

In 2000 Roman launched a similar effort to support the American Cancer Society through the sale of a second angel, "Victoria—Embrace Life." The figurine was placed in a field of daffodils and included a daffodil pin that could be removed and worn to reinforce the American Cancer Society's Daffodil Days fundraising program. In addition, Roman supported other fundraising activities to fight cancer.

21ST-CENTURY STRATEGY

Roman made changes to its business to remain competitive as the new century dawned, but nevertheless experienced increasing difficulties. In 2000 the company embarked on a new sales strategy by severing ties with rep groups and dealing directly with retailers. By doing so, Roman hoped to lower costs as well as increase the number of calls paid to retailers to further sales growth. Although annual revenues increased to $130 million by 2004, the company found it difficult to remain profitable. Jedlinski cut staff and then attempted to sell the company. That effort failed at the last minute in 2005, and Jedlinski then attempted to liquidate the business.

At the behest of its lenders, Roman hired Chicago consulting firm Morris Anderson & Associates Ltd. to take stock of the company's situation. The conclusion was that Roman's longtime strategy of achieving profitability through growth had run its course. At the heart of the company's success was a core line of products that sold year in and year out. The problem lay with other lines that came in and out of fashion and were far less predictable.

As a result of the analysis, Roman elected to reduce its size to achieve sustainable profitability. The number of products was cut from a high of about 15,000 to fewer than 5,000, most of which were traditional religiously oriented products. The company continued to offer Christmas lines but the business was cut down from 10 lines offering as many as 50 products to just two or three lines. The marginally profitable line of pre-lit Christmas trees, for example, was divested.

No longer in need of a massive distribution center, Roman in 2006 sold its Addison facility, which it had renovated just two years earlier. Atlanta-based Industrial Developments International Inc., a real estate company with an extensive slate of industrial and distribution space, paid $26.5 million for the property. Roman took a short-term lease on the Addison site but at the same time executed a lease on a smaller and more appropriately sized property in Bloomingdale, Illinois. A move to the Bloomingdale site was completed in 2007.

Other changes were also taking place at Roman. Ronald Jedlinski began taking steps to turn over control of the company to the next generation. His daughter Julie Loughman became a co-owner, and her husband, Dan Loughman, who had served as Roman's vice president of product development, took over as president and CEO. Ronald Jedlinski stayed on as chairman of the board.

MERGER: 2008

The right-sizing strategy succeeded, and after two years of losses, Roman netted $1 million in 2007. Roman was not alone in experiencing tough times in the giftware industry as the new century progressed. Less successful companies went out of business and others were forced to merge in order to remain competitive. Although Roman had returned to health, it continued to take steps to ensure its future. In October 2008 it agreed to merge with Cottage Garden Collections. Based in Bainbridge, Indiana, Cottage Garden was known for its music boxes and musical frames.

Both companies maintained that the merger was not a way to increase efficiencies, nor were there any plans to cut jobs. Dan Loughman told *Gifts and Decorative Accessories* in December 2008, "This isn't a buyout or a bailout of one weaker company by another. No one is buying the assets of another and then trying to salvage something out of it." With the company having passed the baton to a new generation of leadership, Roman appeared well positioned to enjoy ongoing success in its niche market.

Ed Dinger

PRINCIPAL DIVISIONS
Cottage Gardens.

PRINCIPAL COMPETITORS
Swanson Christian Products.

FURTHER READING
Anderson, Veronica. "Business Is Divine for Church Supplier." *Crain's Chicago Business*, August 9, 1993, p. 1.

Lee, Amy. "A Religious Products Company Is Saved." *Medill Reports*, March 14, 2008.

Pohl, Kimberly. "Christmas Ornament Maker Sells Headquarters." *Daily Herald* (Arlington Heights, Ill.), October 21, 2006, p. 1.

Schwartz, Meredith. "A Leaner Gift Industry." *Gifts and Decorative Accessories*, December 1, 2008.

Smith, Jack A. "Meet Ronald T. Jedlinski." *Gifts and Decorative Accessories*, May 1990, p. 74.

Ron Jon Surf Shop

—■—

3850 South Banana River Boulevard
Cocoa Beach, Florida 32931
U.S.A.
Telephone: (321) 799-8888
Toll Free: (888) RJ-SURFS
Fax: (321) 799-8805
Web site: http://www.ronjonsurfshop.com

Private Company
Founded: 1959
Employees: 400
Sales: $50 million (2010 est.)
NAICS: 448140 Family Clothing Stores; 451110 Sporting Goods Stores; 451120 Hobby, Toy, and Game Stores; 453220 Gift, Novelty, and Souvenir Stores

■■■

Ron Jon Surf Shop is a leading retailer of merchandise related to the surfing lifestyle. At 52,000 square feet, the company's flagship store in Cocoa Beach, Florida, is the world's largest surf shop. Open 24 hours a day, it bills itself as a tourist destination in its own right. Other Florida locations include Fort Lauderdale, Orlando, Key West, Fort Myers, and Panama City Beach. The company also operates a pair of stores in Myrtle Beach, South Carolina. Its first location, in Long Island Beach, New Jersey, has been expanded several times. Licensing agreements have led to locations in airports as well as in Mexico, the Caribbean, and Canada. There is also a licensed surf resort in Cape Canaveral and a surfing school in Cocoa Beach. Ron Jon Surf Shop carries dozens of brands of equipment and apparel, but its private-label clothing is its biggest seller.

BORN ON THE JERSEY SHORE

Born in ancient Hawaii and popularized in California, surfing had reached the East Coast by the 1940s thanks to pioneers such as Gary Propper. New Jersey's Long Beach Island, a barrier island, was well positioned to capture what swells the Atlantic had to offer. A host of social factors made it a launching point for the sport and the surfing lifestyle.

The nearby cities of New York and Philadelphia ensured a supply of vacationers eager to surf when they could. Surfing was also popular among local youth working in the clam industry, sources later told the *PressofAtlanticCity.com*. Proper surfboards were rare, although an existing boatbuilding industry would eventually provide skills for their manufacture.

Company founder Ron DiMenna began trading in surfboards in 1959 when, following his father's advice, he had three boards shipped from California and then sold two of them to pay for his own. The company name came from the founder, who reportedly also designed the logo himself.

DiMenna and his neighbor John Spodofora opened the first Ron Jon Surf Shop in 1961. It measured just 1,000 square feet. The business was poised to take off when surfing captured the popular imagination in the 1960s via pop culture such as the *Gidget* movies and the Beach Boys.

Over the years the Long Beach Island store grew to include a sprawling outdoor display of garden ornaments and other kitschy items, at one point including 22,000 hatch covers salvaged from World War II-era Liberty ships. One of several expansions doubled it to 10,000 square feet in 1996.

FLAGSHIP STORE OPENS IN 1963

In 1963 DiMenna opened a second store, in Cocoa Beach, Florida. It moved to a permanent location four years later. Each of these stores was originally 3,000 square feet. In 1986 the Cocoa Beach store, already at 18,000 square feet, was nearly doubled in size with a $1 million, 15,000-square-foot addition. The store then claimed the title of the world's largest surf store.

Located on two acres a block from the beach, the Cocoa Beach location became the flagship of the chain, and a tourist destination in its own right. Sales were growing 25 to 30 percent a year. Annual revenues were $20 million by 1990.

In early 1991 a $2.2 million expansion added another story to the Cocoa Beach store. The redesign, done in Art Deco style, added colorful columns, an indoor waterfall, and a state-of-the-art lighting system, as well as a stage for musical groups. With 52,000

square feet of space, the site then offered more surfing-related merchandise than any other store in the United States. It sold more than 100 types of baseball caps and dozens of different T-shirts, Frisbees, and other beach essentials.

The store hours were also extended around the clock. By the late 1990s, two million people were visiting the store every year, and it was becoming a popular stop for visitors from overseas on bus tours. It was also a favorite of cruise ship passengers and high school students. More than 100 billboards made the logo impossible to miss for tourists driving through Florida, and logo stickers appeared on countless cars.

FURTHER EXPANSION

In 1998 Ron Jon opened its third store, a 25,700-square-foot surf store in Orange County, California, the largest such store on the West Coast at that time. Decorated with a woodie station wagon and massive wave sculptures, the $5 million building featured a stage for surf bands. Ron Jon next opened a store in Sunrise, Florida, and a 50,000-square-foot store in Orlando in 1999. The following year a shop opened in Tampa (Channelside), Ron Jon's first location on Florida's Gulf Coast.

DiMenna had hired new management in April 1997, led by Ed Moriarty, a consultant who was once a vice president at Walt Disney World. The new team was expansion-oriented, both in terms of geography and product range. Annual sales were $42 million in 1999. While the stores carried dozens of brands, the Ron Jon brand was by far the largest by volume, accounting for more than a third of total sales at the original store and 45 percent at Cocoa Beach, according to *Sports Trend*.

The company was expanding Ron Jon's range of merchandise beyond T-shirts into other items of surf-inspired apparel. Embracing the fast fashion ethic, the company changed its shorts supplier from one overseas to a shop in California in order to reduce turnaround time.

LICENSING IN 2000

At the dawn of the new century the company began to extend the brand through licensing agreements. Ron Jon lent its name to a pair of time-share developments by Island One Resorts in Orlando and Ormond Beach that opened in June 2000. The resorts were decorated with graphics similar to those at the stores. Capitalizing on the global allure of surfing, a licensing deal completed in 2000 with Avant Garde Spirit and Takashima USA brought Ron Jon-branded apparel and souvenirs into Japanese surf shops.

KEY DATES

1959: New Jersey resident Ron DiMenna enters the surfboard business by buying three surfboards from California, selling two of them.
1961: First Ron Jon Surf Shop opens in Long Beach Island, New Jersey.
1963: Original Cocoa Beach store opens.
1986: Cocoa Beach store is nearly doubled in size.
1998: Ron Jon opens its third store, in Orange County, California.
2000: Ron Jon lends its name to Orlando-area timeshare developments.
2004: First airport store opens in Orlando.
2005: A licensing agreement leads to Ron Jon stores in the Caribbean.
2008: Ron Jon closes its only West Coast location.

In 2002 Chrysler Corporation made a Ron Jon edition of its PT Cruiser, complete with wood paneling on the sides. It was offered for sale only in Florida. Company founder Ron DiMenna brought the woodie station wagon theme to his new motor home. Built by Eugene, Oregon's Monaco Coach Corp. and customized by local artisans, the vehicle featured faux wood paneling on the sides. DiMenna and his wife Lynne traveled most of the year in it, following the sun to visit friends at various surf spots from coast to coast.

Revenues were $49 million in 2003. There were about 350 employees, 250 of them at the Cocoa Beach store and company headquarters. Ron Jon was a relatively small player in the surfing lifestyle apparel market, which by then extended even to discount department stores such as Target Corp. Ron Jon countered by maintaining exclusive, authentic brands such as O'Neill.

NEW LOCATIONS

The company continued to open new locations in Florida, including a store in the Orlando tourist district in 2003 and a store at the Orlando airport the following year. Susan Stackhouse, CEO of Stellar Partners, who had previous success operating duty-free and toy stores in airport terminals, licensed the airport store. Other airport locations followed in Newark, New Jersey, and Miami, Florida. A 2005 licensing agreement with Jayram Inc. took Ron Jon stores into the Caribbean. The second Caribbean store opened on Grand Turk Island in 2008.

In 2006 Ron Jon joined with Surfparks, LLC, as a partner in a proposed $150 million surf resort at Festival Bay Mall in Orlando, including a 400-room hotel and a surf stadium with artificial waves. Ron Jon backed out of the surf park project two years later, however, after its developers scaled it down.

Ron Jon headed north in 2006, opening the first of a planned half-dozen licensed Canadian stores in Toronto. Florida's popularity with Canadians as a tourist destination was part of the rationale. There was also some cold-water surfing in British Columbia and on the Great Lakes.

LEAVING CALIFORNIA: 2008

In February 2008 the company opened a 12,000-square-foot store at the new Pier Park boardwalk in Panama City Beach in northwest Florida. In 2007 Ron Jon had opened a 9,000-square foot store in Myrtle Beach, South Carolina. Three years later another 7,500-square-foot store opened on the southern end of the Grand Strand, making it the only market with two Ron Jon locations. As the recession dragged on, consumers grew tired of not going anywhere and some turned to Myrtle Beach as an affordable destination.

Ron Jon was unable to agree on lease terms with the landlord of its Orange County, California, store when its lease expired there after 10 years. As a result, it closed its only West Coast location in December 2008.

Fifty years after Ron DiMenna's initial surfboard swap, his empire was selling an estimated 350,000 T-shirts a year. His hometown of Long Beach Island had sprouted 10 smaller rivals to the original Ron Jon store, and was opening a museum dedicated to surfing. In Florida, Ron Jon was sponsoring a program to bring surfing to Special Olympics athletes while its associated nonprofit called Surfing's Evolution and Preservation Corp. was lobbying for a vanity license plate to fund its heritage projects.

Frederick C. Ingram

PRINCIPAL SUBSIDIARIES

California Ron Jon, LLC; Rjss Orlando, LLC; Ron Jon McO Airport, Inc.; Ron Jon Miami Airport, Inc.; Ron Jon Newark Airport, Inc.; Ron Jon Tampa Airport, Inc.; Ron Jon Aruba, Inc. (USA); Ron Jon Canada, Inc. (USA); Ron Jon Cozumel, Inc.; Ron Jon Fort Myers, LLC; Ron Jon Holdings Management, Inc.; Ron Jon Key West, LLC; Ron Jon Licensing, Inc.; Ron Jon Myrtle Beach, LLC; Ron Jon Resorts One, Inc.; Ron

Jon Resorts Orlando, Inc.; Ron Jon Surfparks, Inc.; Ron Jon Worldwide, Inc.; Sawgrass Ron Jon, LLC.

PRINCIPAL OPERATING UNITS

Ship Bottom–New Jersey; Cocoa Beach–Florida; Ft. Lauderdale–Florida; Orlando–Florida; Key West–Florida; Ft. Myers–Florida; Myrtle Beach–South Carolina (Barefoot Landing); Panama City Beach–Florida; Myrtle Beach–South Carolina (Broadway at the Beach); Surf Grill–Florida; Surf School–Florida.

PRINCIPAL COMPETITORS

BC Surf and Sport; Billabong International Limited; Brighton Beach Surf Shop; Huntington Surf and Sport; Hurley International LLC; O'Neill Inc.; Quiksilver, Inc.; Target Corp.

FURTHER READING

Bryant, Dawn. "Surf's Up for Coastal Carolina Shops: Shops Expanding as Summer Wave Season Approaches." *Sun News* (Myrtle Beach), May 16, 2010.

Bumpus-Hooper, Lynne. "Ron Jon Anything but a Wipeout." *Orlando Sentinel*, October 7, 1996.

Caporale, Patricia. "Ron Jon Debuts New Surfing Image; Shop Becoming County Attraction." *Orlando Sentinel*, March 21, 1991.

Carson, Daniel. "Another New Store Rides Wave of Pier Park Openings: Surf's Up for Ron Jon." *News Herald* (Panama City, Florida), February 22, 2008.

Cotroneo, Christian. "Malibu, Bondi Beach and ... the Great Lakes? Surf Scene Active on the Big Lakes; U.S. Surfing-Gear Retailer Heads North." *Toronto Star*, March 11, 2006, p. F3.

Davis, Nancy. "Late-Night Shoppers Roam Store Aisle Long after Dark." *Orlando Sentinel*, June 30, 1991.

Gordon, Cheryl. "Toys at this Turf Always Seem to Surf into Top 10." *Orlando Sentinel*, June 8, 1986.

Lloyd, Brenda. "Ron Jon Riding Expansion Express; Cocoa Beach, Fla.-Based Surf Retailer Plans New Retail Unites, Building Up Its Own Brand." *Daily News Record*, February 2, 2000, p. 24.

Reinhard, Eileen. "Ship Bottom Journal; A Surf Shop Folds Awning after 30 Years." *New York Times*, September 18, 1988.

"Ron Jon Image 'Sticks' with Consumers." *Sports Trend*, October 1, 1999.

Smith, Prior. "Surfin', Surfin', U.S.A.; Waves of Tourists Visit Florida Shop," *Toronto Star*, Travel Sec., December 16, 2000, p. 1.

Spar, Rob. "Documentary, Museum Celebrate New Jersey Surfing Scene as It Comes of Age." *PressofAtlanticCity.com*, July 18, 2010.

———. "Iconic Ron Jon Surf Shop Was Born in Ship Bottom on Long Beach Island." *PressofAtlanticCity.com*, July 17, 2010.

Whalin, George. "Ron Jon Surf Shop." *Retail Superstars: Inside the 25 Best Independent Stores in America*. New York: Portfolio, 2009, pp. 77–84.

Roundy's Supermarkets, Inc.

---

875 East Wisconsin Avenue
P.O. Box 473
Milwaukee, Wisconsin 53201-0473
U.S.A.
Telephone: (414) 231-5000
Toll Free: (866) 742-6728
Web site: http://www.roundys.com

Private Company
Incorporated: 1902 as Roundy, Peckham & Dexter Co.
Employees: 22,000
Sales: $4.15 billion (2008 est.)
NAICS: 424410 General Line Grocery Merchant Wholesalers; 445110 Supermarkets and Other Grocery (Except Convenience) Stores

∎∎∎

Founded in 1872, Roundy's Supermarkets, Inc., is among the oldest and largest grocery wholesalers and retailers in the nation, with annual sales of over $4 billion. The company's three Wisconsin distribution centers supply independent supermarkets in the upper Midwest. Roundy's has built the biggest supermarket chain in Wisconsin. It operates 154 retail stores in Wisconsin and Minnesota under the names Pick 'n Save, Copps Food Centers, and Rainbow Foods.

Roundy's is known for pioneering the warehouse store concept in the 1970s with its successful Milwaukee Pick 'n Save chain. Once structured as a cooperative owned primarily by the retailers it served, Roundy's underwent a major financial restructuring in 2002, when it was acquired by Willis Stein & Partners, a Chicago investment firm. In 2005 it sold off most of its wholesale distribution operations outside Wisconsin in order to focus on retail.

ORIGINS OF A WISCONSIN INSTITUTION: 1872–1939

Roundy's founder, Judson A. Roundy, came to Milwaukee from Rhode Island. In 1872 he and two partners, Sidney Hauxhurst and William A. Smith, founded a wholesale grocery company called Smith, Roundy & Co. Smith went on to become governor of Wisconsin six years later. The company grew out of its first quarters and moved to a larger building at Milwaukee's Broadway and Buffalo Streets in 1885. This building was destroyed by the famous 3rd Ward Fire in 1892. By 1895, the company completed new headquarters at the same location.

The firm took on new partners and reincorporated in 1902 as Roundy, Peckham & Dexter Co. Its president was Charles Dexter, who had been a partner since 1880 and who continued as president and chairman until his death in 1939. Roundy's began to offer its own private Roundy's brand beginning in 1922, when it introduced Roundy's Salt. The company expanded in the first half of the century until its stockholders numbered about 60, most of whom had inherited their holdings.

MOVING FORWARD AS A GROCERY COOPERATIVE: 1953–72

In 1953 the firm reorganized as a grocery cooperative, with only independent retailers allowed to hold

Roundy's stock. Even the president and other top executives were required to sell their stock and assets unless they were themselves retailers. After this change, Roundy's management set out to offer services to independent grocers that would allow them to compete with large chains. Roundy's retailer-stockholders were offered bookkeeping and payroll services at low cost, and the company held seminars on grocery-related business topics, such as store security and job training.

Roundy's opened a grocery distribution center in Wauwatosa, Wisconsin, in 1955, which grew into a 450,000-square-foot complex on 10 acres of land. The company began to expand rapidly around this time, becoming one of the largest grocery distributors in Wisconsin. Sales reached $50 million in 1962 and doubled to $100 million in the next nine years. The huge Wauwatosa warehouse stocked close to 9,700 items, including both Roundy's private-label and national brand foods. Using rail sidings and more than 40 truck loading docks in the early 1970s, the company moved more than 5,000 tons of merchandise a week. The Roundy's private label had grown to include about 800 items, and sales in 1972 were close to $115 million. As early as 1972, ordering was controlled by computer, and the company's processing system also was mechanized. Roundy's believed in using the most modern technology available to run its business and was often at the forefront of grocery innovation, particularly in its landmark warehouse stores.

LAUNCHING THE PICK 'N SAVE CONCEPT IN 1975

During the recession that began in 1974, the warehouse stores became important. Roundy's management detected changing consumer attitudes as the economy worsened and decided to experiment with a new type of store that would appeal to the budget-conscious. Roundy's rented a vacant discount store in Milwaukee on a short-term lease and opened Pick 'n Save Warehouse Foods in March 1975. The store had minimal decoration and very few perishable items,

including no fresh meat and very little produce. The store stood in sharp contrast to the traditional supermarket: packing crates and cases served as the main decor, and untiled floors and plywood walls emphasized the cost-cutting environment.

Unique at the time, Pick 'n Save at first drew customers curious to shop in this innovative establishment. Customers used crayons to mark prices on items because the store saved labor by not price-marking, and customers also did their own bagging. The store catered to people doing large-volume shopping. Pick 'n Save became quite popular, and the store at times had long lines of customers waiting to get in. The warehouse concept proved so successful that Roundy's opened almost 20 more such stores in the next five years, spreading from metropolitan Milwaukee across southern Wisconsin and northern Illinois. Other grocers imitated the warehouse concept as well.

Roundy's sales expanded in the late 1970s even as the economy pulled out of its slump, proving that the warehouse was not just a fad. The company's warehouse stores evolved, however, to include more produce and a more finished decor. They began to have brightly painted walls and tiled floors, bringing the look closer to that of the traditional supermarket. However, low prices remained the essential difference that set the warehouse stores apart. The stores flourished by moving large volumes of stock, most of which was bought at "deal" prices. Low-priced merchandise coupled with the low overhead and inexpensive fixtures of the warehouse kept prices below those of competitors. Labor costs were also kept in check. To avoid running a labor-intensive fresh meat counter, most stores offered smoked meats only, and stock work was simple and fast because much merchandise was displayed on pallets at the ends of aisles.

Sales per employee hour at Pick 'n Save were said to be almost triple the average at traditional supermarkets, and one Roundy's executive claimed Pick 'n Save could sell 100 cases of groceries for the same labor cost a traditional store would take to sell only 10. Use of electronic scanner technology also allowed Roundy's warehouse stores to control costs. Information from scanners was used to determine exactly which brands and sizes sold best, which was crucial for management to know when buying deal merchandise. By keeping costs down, Roundy's warehouse stores offered consumers consistently low prices, and by 1980 a survey of Milwaukee-area stores found all the company's major competitors losing market share, while the Roundy's Pick 'n Save chain gained.

Roundy's had 27 Pick 'n Save stores in Wisconsin by 1983. With four stores in the Chicago area,

KEY DATES

■

1872: Judson A. Roundy and two partners found a wholesale grocery company called Smith, Roundy & Co. in Milwaukee, Wisconsin.

1902: The firm takes on new partners and incorporates as Roundy, Peckham & Dexter Co.

1922: Roundy's private-label products are introduced.

1953: The firm reorganizes as a grocery cooperative, with only independent retailers allowed to hold Roundy's stock.

1975: Roundy's opens its first Pick 'n Save Warehouse Foods.

1991: Roundy's and the Teamsters Union sign a five-year contract, ending a bitter labor dispute.

2002: Roundy's is acquired by Willis Stein & Partners, a Chicago investment firm.

2005: Company is renamed Roundy's Supermarkets, Inc.; it sells off most of its wholesale operations outside Wisconsin.

Roundy's strengthened its position in the Chicago market by purchasing Wayco Foods, a suburban grocery. The Wayco acquisition gained Roundy's a 218,000-square-foot warehouse near Chicago's O'Hare airport. Now with a base from which to service its Chicago stores, Roundy's made plans to open 10 to 15 more Pick 'n Saves in the area. This move put Roundy's in competition with other established warehouse-type chains, such as Cub Foods, owned by Supervalu Inc. of Minnesota.

ACQUISITION DOUBLES SALES IN 1984

Roundy's continued to expand in the 1980s, with somewhat mixed success. Returns on sales began to slip in 1982, and in 1984 and 1985 revenues were stagnant. Profits also fell, and in those two years Roundy's did not pay rebates (equivalent to stockholder dividends) to its member retailers. The company spent $40 million in 1984 to buy Scot Lad Foods, a grocery distributor in Lansing, Illinois. Although this acquisition doubled corporate sales, it also increased debt. Sales by 1986 were $1.8 billion, coming from the Pick 'n Save chain, wholesale distribution, and stores Roundy's operated under the names Roundy's, Shop-Rite, and United

Foods. The four Chicago Pick 'n Save stores were not doing well, however, and Roundy's decided to sell them. Another venture, a gourmet food retailer, also was not doing well. Roundy's had spent between $1 million and $2.5 million to open the gourmet store, called V. Richards, but the store did not quickly turn a profit.

Roundy's chairman and CEO Vincent R. Little took early retirement in 1986 after 12 years at the post. After Little's exit, the new CEO appointed two outside directors to Roundy's board and added two new trustees as well. The new directors and trustees came from outside the grocery business and so brought new perspectives on running a firm as large as Roundy's. After this management shift, Roundy's continued to expand through acquisitions. In 1988, the company bought Cardinal Foods Inc., an Ohio-based food distributor, and another Ohio firm, a health and beauty aid distributor called American Merchandising Associates Inc. A year later, Roundy's spent an undisclosed amount of cash on Viking Foods, Inc. This food distributor, based in Muskegon, Michigan, had 1988 sales of $100 million. That same year, Roundy's reported a significant increase in sales, which were now up to $2.4 billion.

LABOR UNREST IN 1991

As Roundy's grew, it required more warehouse space to service its retailers. The company leased a new warehouse in Mazomanie, Wisconsin, in 1989, as it ran out of space in its old Wauwatosa facility. Roundy's grew by more than 20 percent between 1988 and 1991, and warehouse space continued to be a problem. In January 1991, the company announced plans to replace its 30-year-old Wauwatosa plant with a one-million-square-foot warehouse center it would build in Waterloo, Wisconsin. Roundy's wanted to spend $50 million building a state-of-the-art warehouse facility to service more than 170 stores in Wisconsin and Illinois. This decision, however, set off a storm of protest from the company's Wauwatosa workers, who were represented by the Teamsters Union. The company would not say whether its 900 employees at the Wauwatosa plant would be offered jobs at the new warehouse, which was about an hour's drive away. Because the Waterloo plant would also be in a county different from Wauwatosa, it would be outside the jurisdiction of the existing union contract.

When the Teamster's Union contract expired in July 1991, negotiations on a new contract quickly broke down. Workers objected to Roundy's insistence on its right to relocate its entire warehouse operation at any time. To preempt a strike, Roundy's management decided to lock out its workers. Workers picketed and called for a consumer boycott of stores supplied by Roundy's.

During the bitter contract dispute, another issue surfaced. The Roundy's warehouse, like that of its major competitors in the area, was run by a computer, which filed orders from customer stores electronically and then calculated how long it should take human workers to fill each order. The computer set a productivity standard, and workers were required under the old contract to achieve 85 percent of that standard. In its new contract negotiations, Roundy's demanded that workers achieve 100 percent of the computer's productivity standard. Workers complained that such a goal was impossible and that Roundy's was trying to gain an advantage over its competitors at their expense.

Roundy's ended its lockout after three weeks, then announced that it was changing its plans to build a new warehouse in Waterloo. The company would instead relocate the work done at the Wauwatosa warehouse even farther away, to Westville, Indiana. The company had a warehouse in Westville, a small town between Gary and South Bend. Although drivers would have to go through Chicago to service Wisconsin stores, Roundy's claimed that it had excess capacity in Westville, and the move was reasonable.

Roundy's and the Teamsters Union finally signed a five-year contract in late September 1991. The company abandoned its plans to move either to Westville or to Waterloo, and workers gained a small wage increase and a new productivity standard of 95 percent. Then in April 1992 Roundy's announced plans to add capacity at its Wauwatosa plant and move some work from a Fort Wayne, Indiana, warehouse to its other Wisconsin warehouse in Mazomanie. Without actually adding jobs in Wisconsin, this move did seem to emphasize Roundy's commitment to keeping work in its home state.

By 1994 Roundy's supplied more than 1,800 grocery stores, with distribution centers in Wisconsin, Illinois, Michigan, Indiana, and Ohio. Its Pick 'n Save chain continued to grow in the Milwaukee area. Roundy's had 42 stores in metropolitan Milwaukee in 1994, with a growing market share said to be between 39 and 47 percent. The newest stores were quite different from the original warehouse stores, although Pick 'n Save continued to be distinguished by low prices. Whereas the early stores had no fresh meat and unadorned walls, one newer store boasted an $18,000 imported Italian cappuccino machine in its coffee bar and a reputation as a fine meat market. The stores were tailored to individual neighborhoods and to the owner's tastes, and, except for sheer size, there was little to tie them to the bare-bones warehouses of the 1970s.

Roundy's suggested in 1994 that it might make a public offering in order to fund future expansion. Then in October 1994, the company announced that it would merge with Spartan Stores, another grocery wholesale cooperative based in Grand Rapids, Michigan. The merger of Roundy's, the nation's sixth-largest food wholesaler, and Spartan, the seventh largest, would have made the new combined corporation the third largest in the United States. However, the merger was called off a month later. The companies announced that they would pursue separate growth strategies, and a Roundy's vice president declared that the time was not right for the merger.

RETAIL EXPANSION: 1995–2003

In 1997 Roundy's celebrated its 125th anniversary. Having achieved $2.6 billion in sales the preceding year, the company ranked as the largest food corporation in Wisconsin, and the sixth-largest grocery wholesaler in the country. Jerry Lestina, who had been named CEO in 1993, seemed intent on staying the course. Although Roundy's had purchased five Ron and Lloyd's stores earlier that year, Lestina explained that the purpose of these acquisitions was only to maintain Roundy's supply chain and its customer base, and that the company would be seeking buyers for these stores. Furthermore, at this time Roundy's viewed its corporate stores merely as a means of maintaining knowledge of the industry and conducting research and development, rather than as a significant source of revenue. As Lestina told the *Post-Crescent* on September 29, 1997, "We are primarily wholesalers. It is not our intent to grow our base of corporate stores."

The 1990s, however, was a decade of rapid consolidation in the grocery industry, and it soon became apparent that Roundy's would have to adjust its business strategy in order to remain competitive with such industry giants as Minneapolis-based Supervalu or Oklahoma City-based Fleming Companies. Although roughly 90 percent of the company's revenue came from the wholesale business, the profit margin on these sales was only about 7.5 percent in 1998, and there were few opportunities to substantially increase this percentage. By comparison, the profit margin on retail operations in 1998 was 21 percent.

By 1999 Roundy's was on a mission to compete with Jewel-Osco, Wal-Mart, Target, and others to become one of Wisconsin's leading retail supermarket chains. Key to realizing this goal was a flurry of acquisitions. In November 1999 Roundy's reached an agreement to purchase seven Pick 'n Save stores in eastern Wisconsin (the supermarket assets of Ultra Mart Inc.) whose annual sales topped $150 million. Also that month, Roundy's announced plans to buy Mega Marts, Inc., the operator of 17 Pick 'n Saves in Wisconsin and Illinois. Together, the deals were expected to increase annual revenue from $2.58 billion to about $3.2 billion.

Roundy's made another auspicious acquisition in 2001 when it bought Copps Food Centers, then the largest family-owned supermarket chain in Wisconsin, for $95 million. While the Mega Marts and Ultra Mart acquisitions were located mainly in southeastern Wisconsin, the purchase of Copps Corporation's 21 supermarkets significantly increased Roundy's presence in central Wisconsin and the Upper Peninsula of Michigan. Moreover, as the Copps stores were well-run and enjoyed strong brand recognition, Roundy's was able to take them over, keeping the Copps name, with little additional investment. The acquisition was expected to increase annual sales by more than 20 percent and to bring the retail percentage of the company's overall sales up to 42 percent. Ultimately, according to Lestina, the company's goal was to bring retail sales close to 50 percent of overall earnings.

Roundy's fared very well with these acquisitions, realizing a 15.6 percent increase in sales in 2001, for a total of $3.5 billion. The company's cooperative, grocer-owned business model was not ideal for its ongoing growth strategy, however, as it did not afford access to the funds needed for major capital investments. In order to finance the $95 million Copps purchase in 1999, for example, Roundy's had to assemble a $300 million credit agreement with various lenders. To keep pace with the aggressive expansion strategies of its competitors, Roundy's underwent a major financial restructuring in 2002, whereby the company was acquired by Willis Stein & Partners, a Chicago investment firm.

Under the agreement, which was valued at $750 million, Roundy's retained its independent status as a grocery wholesaler and retailer. With new access to investor capital, growth objectives included ongoing expansion of the retail business through the introduction of new product lines and through further acquisitions. A major example of the latter occurred in May 2003, when Roundy's announced plans to purchase 31 Rainbow Foods stores, all but one located in the Minneapolis-St. Paul metropolitan area, from Fleming Companies, Inc., in a deal worth nearly $120 million. With a proven record of success, Roundy's appeared well positioned to maintain its competitive edge in the industry.

NEW HEADQUARTERS IN 2003

Roundy's added four Pick 'n Save and three Rainbow stores in 2002. In June 2003 the new Copps subsidiary took over a half-dozen Kohl's Food Stores in Milwaukee from Great Atlantic & Pacific Tea Company (A&P).

Soon after, Roundy's bought 31 Minneapolis-area Rainbow stores from bankrupt Fleming Companies, Inc., in a deal worth $121.5 million. A rival bidder, Miner's Inc., was disqualified after Roundy's complained it lacked sufficient resources. The purchase added more than 3,000 employees. It did not include a dozen other Rainbow stores, which were closed.

In October 2003 Roundy's acquired seven more former Kohl's locations for conversion into Pick 'n Save stores, paying $9 million. The company was budgeting $100 million for the year to upgrade its recent acquisitions and revamp its distribution network.

Robert A. Mariano became Roundy's chairman and CEO in 2002 after it was acquired by Willis Stein. He was a 26-year veteran of Dominick's in Chicago and served as its CEO for three years until its 1998 sale to Safeway. Mariano was known for his emphasis on produce departments.

In October 2003 Roundy's corporate offices were consolidated at a new site in downtown Milwaukee, 20 miles east of its old headquarters in Pewaukee, the suburban town that had been its home since 1954. Milwaukee provided $3 million worth of incentives. Roundy's posted earnings of $54.6 million on sales of $4.38 billion in 2003. Earnings reached $60.6 million on sales of $4.82 billion in 2004.

Roundy's had an estimated 70 percent market share in Milwaukee, but it continued to look for ways to stay ahead. Its urban shopping prototype Metro Market opened in downtown Milwaukee in August 2004. It boasted such features such as finger scanning at checkout, updated décor, and a café with Wi-Fi.

SCALING BACK WHOLESALE AFTER 2004

Gradually the company was occupying itself less and less with wholesaling. It closed distribution centers in Eldorado, Illinois, and Evansville, Indiana, in 2004. The Lima, Ohio, and Westville, Indiana, distribution centers, which did $1 billion a year worth of business supplying 500 retailers, was sold to Nash Finch in 2005 for $225 million.

Roundy's wholesale distribution was limited thereafter to independent retailers in parts its home state. The company opened a new 1.1-million-square-foot distribution center in Oconomowoc, Wisconsin, in 2005. That year Roundy's also acquired seven Pick 'n Save stores in the Madison area from an independent; it bought another six stores in 2006.

The company was renamed Roundy's Supermarkets, Inc., in June 2005, underscoring its retail orientation. For fiscal 2005, the company posted revenues of $4.7 billion. With its healthy balance sheet and strong management team, Roundy's became an attractive acquisition target, which some industry analysts speculated might be part of a movement to consolidate the industry in the Great Lakes region.

A 120,000-square-foot food-processing plant opened in Kenosha, Wisconsin, in 2006 to manufacture a wide variety of Roundy's Own Brand products. Roundy's bought five Milwaukee area Jewel-Osco stores from SUPERVALU in January 2007. By the end of the year it had 153 stores in all and more than 22,000 employees.

President and CEO Mariano became a pitchman in 2008, touting a handful of Roundy's 2,500 private-label products in TV commercials and print advertising as "Chairman Bob." Within two years Mariano was leading Roundy's into Chicago, a city notoriously unwelcoming to outside supermarket chains. Mariano had launched his career there, starting as a deli clerk at Dominick's and leaving 30 years later as CEO in 1998.

Roundy's first Illinois store opened in Arlington Heights in July 2010 under the name Mariano's Fresh Market. Others were planned for Chicago and environs within the next few years. Despite the earlier speculation, management at Willis Stein held off on plans to sell Roundy's.

A. Woodward
Updated, Erin Brown; Frederick C. Ingram

PRINCIPAL SUBSIDIARIES

Badger Assurance. Ltd. (Bermuda); The Copps Corporation; Ultra Mart Foods, Inc.; Mega Marts, Inc.; Holt Public Storage, Inc.; Midland Grocery of Michigan, Inc.; I.T.A., Inc.; Ropak, Inc.; Jondex Corp.; Scot Lad Foods, Inc.; Kee Trans, Inc.

PRINCIPAL DIVISIONS

Home Office; Retail; Distribution; Manufacturing.

PRINCIPAL OPERATING UNITS

Pick 'n Save; Copps Food Center; Rainbow Foods; Metro Market; Oconomowoc Distribution Center; Mazomanie Distribution Center; Stephens Point Distribution Center; Commissary / Food Processing Plant; The Roundy's Foundation.

PRINCIPAL COMPETITORS

Aldi Inc.; Costco Wholesale Food Corp.; Fleming Companies, Inc.; Lund Food Holdings, Inc.; Supervalu Inc.; Target Corp.; Wal-Mart Stores Inc.; Whole Foods Market, Inc.

FURTHER READING

Bennett, Stephen. "Good as Gold." *Progressive Grocer*, June 1994, pp. 42–44.

Daniel, Tina. "Growing Pains at Roundy's." *Milwaukee Journal*, July 27, 1986, pp. 1D, 4D.

Daykin, Tom. "Former Milwaukee-Area Supermarkets to Be Converted into Pick 'n Save Stores." *Milwaukee Journal Sentinel*, October 9, 2003.

———. "Grocery Wholesaler Announces Plan to Buy Eastern Wisconsin Supermarkets." *Milwaukee Journal Sentinel*, November 3, 1999.

———. "Grocery Wholesaler to Buy Milwaukee-Based Supermarket Operator." *Milwaukee Journal Sentinel*, November 5, 1999.

———. "Pewaukee, Wis.-Based Supermarket Operator to Buy Grocery Chain." *Milwaukee Journal Sentinel*, February 11, 2001.

Fanelli, Christa. "Willis Stein Checks Out Roundy's." *Buy Outs*, April 29, 2002.

Fauber, John. "Changes at Roundy's Expected to Stabilize Employment Here." *Milwaukee Journal*, April 19, 1992, p. D4.

———. "Jobs Hang in Balance at Roundy's." *Milwaukee Journal*, August 11, 1991.

"Food Stores Scrap Plans to Merge." *Wisconsin State Journal*, November 22, 1994.

Gunn, Erik. "Productivity Is Key to Roundy's Dispute." *Milwaukee Journal*, July 7, 1991.

Hajewski, Doris. "Roundy's Narrows Focus to Retail." *Milwaukee Journal Sentinel*, February 25, 2005.

———. "Roundy's Opens Door to Chicago Market." *Journal Sentinel Online*, July 24, 2010.

Horst, David. "Grocery Industry Pioneer Looks to the Future." *Post-Crescent*, September 29, 1997.

Johnson, Paul. "Roundy's, Spartan Finalize Merger." *Wisconsin State Journal*, October 11, 1994.

Lank, Avrum D. "Roundy's Acquires Firm in Chicago Area." *Milwaukee Sentinel*, May 23, 1983.

Lee, Thomas. "Riley Quits as Head of Rainbow; Roundy's Effort at a Turnaround Is Struggling." *Minneapolis Star Tribune*, June 4, 2004, p. 1D.

Riddle, Jennifer. "Roundy's Makes Mazo Move." *Wisconsin State Journal*, March 9, 1989.

———. "Roundy's Plans Waterloo Move." *Wisconsin State Journal*, January 11, 1991.

Tanner, Ronald. "Roundy's Latest: Barebones with a Difference." *Progressive Grocer*, February 1980, pp. 81–90.

Zwiebach, Elliot. "Dominick's Veteran Takes Roundy's into Chicago." *Supermarket News*, February 19, 2007.

Saker ShopRites, Inc.

---

922 Highway 33
Building 6, Suite 1
Freehold, New Jersey 07728
U.S.A.
Telephone: (732) 462-4700
Fax: (732) 294-2322
Web site: http://www.sakershoprites.com

Private Company
Incorporated: 1958 as Foodarama Supermarkets Inc.
Employees: 6,850
Sales: $1.22 billion (2005 est.)
NAICS: 311812 Commercial Bakeries; 311821 Cookie and Cracker Manufacturing; 311615 Meat Products; 444220 Nursery and Garden Centers; 445110 Supermarkets and Other Grocery Stores; 445310 Beer, Wine, and Liquor Stores

■ ■ ■

Saker ShopRites, Inc., formerly known as Foodarama Supermarkets, Inc., operates approximately 27 grocery stores in central New Jersey under the ShopRite name. The company's stores are at least 50,000 square feet and include in-store premium departments for international foods and kosher products, as well as bakeries, snack bars, and pharmacies. Saker also owns a central meat and food processing facility, two liquor stores, a garden center, and a bakery. The company is a member of Wakefern Food Corporation, the largest retailer-owned food cooperative in the United States and the owner of the ShopRite name. Members of the founding Saker family took Foodarama Supermarkets private in 2006 and changed the company name shortly thereafter.

ORIGINS

The business began as a single grocery store in 1916. It was owned by Joseph Saker's parents when he graduated from high school in 1946. He took an entry-level job at a local Nescafé factory, loading and unloading coffee beans. According to Saker, after two years of hard work he was demoted in favor of a brother-in-law of the supervisor. Saker then joined the family store, which was grossing about $900 a week. He got his parents to spend $3,000 to remodel the store, and in 1950 to lay out $20,000 for a self-service "superette" employing about 12 people. He also helped found Wakefern Food Corporation, which made it possible for its members to compete with the supermarket chains by providing purchasing, warehousing, and distribution services on a cooperative basis.

Saker opened his first supermarket, 10 times the size of the superette, in 1956, and incorporated Foodarama Supermarkets in 1958. By August 1965 the company was operating 14 stores, which included two that it owned, within a 30-mile radius of headquarters in Freehold, New Jersey. These stores operated under the Shop-Rite (later ShopRite) name and carried nonfood items such as housewares and health and beauty aids as well as a full range of groceries. The company also owned seven parcels of land in central New Jersey and one parcel in Farmington, Pennsylvania, and it was leasing office and storage space in Freehold and Manville, New Jersey. Sales came to $43.3 million in fiscal 1963 (the year ended February 2, 1964), and net income was $387,000. These totals rose to $48.4 million and $653,000 in fiscal 1964.

GOING PUBLIC: 1965

Foodarama Supermarkets became a public corporation in 1965, when it collected about $2 million by selling stock at $12.75 a share. Joseph Saker and his brother John, the treasurer, retained almost 56 percent of the shares. The infusion of fresh funds enabled Foodarama to acquire seven Shop-Rite stores in the next two years, one of which was closed, and also to open seven new stores. By October 1967 the company had 22 stores in Pennsylvania, Connecticut, and Maryland, as well as New Jersey. The following year it acquired four more supermarkets in New Jersey and Pennsylvania, plus a fifth under construction, for $3 million in cash and notes. Sales volume increased by more than fourfold between fiscal 1962 and 1968, and earnings rose by 750 percent. In 1968 the company raised over $40 million by selling more stock at $23.50 a share.

During 1969 and 1970 Foodarama Supermarkets acquired Big Apple Supermarkets, a chain of 48 stores mainly on Long Island. With the defection in 1968 of Supermarkets General Corporation, which took the Pathmark name for its stores, Foodarama was then largest member of Wakefern. A number of its units had in-store pharmacies, and it also had successfully opened tobacco and record shops in a few stores. The 78 Food-aramas were large suburban stores in the range of 20,000 to 35,000 square feet. Net income reached $2.5 million in fiscal 1970 (the year ended November 1, 1970) on sales of $302.9 million. There were plans not only for more supermarkets but also for chains of private-brand gas stations and discount drugstores adjacent to the supermarkets.

LEGAL DISPUTES WITH WAKEFERN

Sales volume for Foodarama Supermarkets reached a record $321 million in fiscal 1971, but its profit

dropped by about 50 percent. By 1972 it was clear that the company had swallowed more than it could comfortably digest. Fourteen stores were sold in fiscal 1972 and 11 more during the three months ended January 31, 1973, leaving Foodarama with 41. The company also was operating six Shop-Rite gas stations contiguous or close to its supermarkets. It lost $8.2 million in fiscal 1972, including a charge of $5.3 million for discontinued operations, and then returned to profitability. It acquired two liquor stores and two garden centers adjacent to its stores in 1975 and 1976, respectively, and disposed of the gasoline stations in 1975.

Foodarama Supermarkets also was locked in a bitter dispute with Wakefern in the 1970s, filing lawsuits in 1971 alleging that certain of Wakefern's directors and members had illegally removed stock purchased from Supermarkets General from the cooperative's treasury, an action that led to the ouster of the existing officers, including Saker, who was secretary. Because of the change in control, Saker contended, nonmembers of Wakefern were barred from using the former Big Apple warehouse in New York, and as a result the warehouse lost money and was eventually sold. Saker lost his lawsuit in 1979 but remained the largest shareholder in Wakefern.

OVERCOMING CHALLENGES: 1980–90

Foodarama Supermarkets had 38 supermarkets in four states in fiscal 1980. Sales came to $412.9 million that year, but net income was only $1.3 million. The company's stock dipped as low as $3.25 a share in 1981, the first of three years out of the next four in which its net income fell below $1 million. Foodarama began paring its holdings, disposing of some of its smaller stores. Others were renovated and enlarged, with service centers added for specialties such as salad bars and cheese counters. In December 1982 the company opened the first of what it called "World Class" stores, in Bricktown, New Jersey.

After a strong fiscal 1985 Saker, who with close allies controlled 48 percent of the stock of Foodarama Supermarkets, proposed a leveraged buyout of the company. The offer of $20.50 per share in cash and notes was scorned as inadequate by other shareholders, however, and only passed by a narrow margin. A December 1986 New Jersey court decision voided the proposal. Foodarama disposed of its Connecticut stores in 1987, reducing the number of its units to 24. It acquired a processing facility for prepared foods in

KEY DATES

1956: Joseph Saker opens his first grocery store.
1958: Foodarama Supermarkets is incorporated.
1965: The company is operating 14 stores; Foodarama goes public.
1982: First "World Class" store opens in Bricktown, New Jersey.
1986: A processing facility for prepared foods is acquired.
1993: Company sells its five Long Island stores to Grand Union.
1995: Two Pennsylvania stores are sold to Wakefern.
2003: Richard Saker takes over as CEO; Joseph Saker remains as chairman.
2006: Members of the Saker family take the company private.
2010: Company operates as Saker ShopRites, Inc.

1986, however, and was fielding eight World Class stores in early 1988.

Foodarama Supermarkets had record net income of $3.7 million on sales of $482 million in fiscal 1987 and made almost as much profit the following year. Its stock rose to more than $38 a share in 1989, the year the company purchased four stores from Hilltop Supermarkets Inc., a New Jersey operator, for $24 million. The acquired stores had annual volume of $120 million. In 1990 Foodarama was operating 26 supermarkets, plus the two adjacent liquor stores and two adjacent garden centers. Nineteen of the 26 were in New Jersey, five on Long Island, and two in Pennsylvania. They ranged in size from 26,000 to 75,000 square feet. Eighteen of the 26 had in-store pharmacies. Foodarama also was operating a bakery in Eatontown, New Jersey.

The acquisition of the Hilltop stores enabled sales for Foodarama Supermarkets to reach $673.1 million in fiscal 1990, but net income was only a little more than $1 million. The company's long-term debt reached $71.7 million in early 1991. Although Foodarama's revenues reached a peak of $695.3 million in fiscal 1991, the company lost $553,000 and also lost money for two of the next three years. At the company's annual meeting the following spring, as reported in the annual report, Saker said that the recession had continued to "cast a cloud over shoppers' buying habits last year."

FENDING OFF COMPETITION: 1990–93

In order to increase its profits, Foodarama Supermarkets was counting on its 11 World Class stores, which were placing an emphasis on service and nonfood departments and on upscale goods that would allow higher markups than the chain's everyday grocery items. Among the specialty nonfood items at some of the 11 stores were expensive watches and perfumes and gourmet kitchen utensils. At the same time, Foodarama was discounting such items as greeting cards and paperback books as well as selling high-ticket goods such as television sets at promotional prices to draw in shoppers.

In order to meet competition from the growing number of deep discounters and warehouse club operators, Foodarama also had begun adding warehouse outlet units of 3,000 to 7,000 square feet to some stores. Space for these units was found in the back rooms of 10 stores and stocked with some 1,500 grocery, perishable, and nonfood items at prices matching those of the clubs. In addition, in September 1992, all 182 ShopRite supermarkets in five states cut prices on more than 3,000 health and beauty care items.

The competitive challenge of the warehouse clubs also led Foodarama to establish bigger stores, especially a 113,000-square-foot outlet in Neptune, New Jersey, that replaced an earlier 28,000-square-foot facility. To lure shoppers to this store from beyond the usual two- or three-mile radius, the new superstore began in 1993 to offer a rabbi-supervised "Kosher Experience." Building on Foodarama's 10 years in ultra-Orthodox Lakewood, New Jersey, the Neptune store offered thousands of stock keeping units of fresh, frozen, and shelf-stable kosher items, including a delicatessen island.

Foodarama's Neptune store with its 30,000 square feet of selling space for nonfood products was larger than most conventional supermarkets. It included sections for sporting goods, books and magazines, consumer electronics and camera equipment, automotive needs, flowers, and clothing and accessories. The health and beauty care section included 65 feet for hair care and 43 feet for vitamins. The warehouse store in back "could easily fill a basketball court," wrote Frank Hammel in *Supermarket Business* in 1994. Its stock included stereos, radios, microwave ovens, and television sets. A leased video store was to open in the front of the store. Foodarama officials saw this gigantic unit as an attraction for every consumer in Monmouth County.

RESTRUCTURING: 1993–96

However, in the face of an impending $2 million loss on reduced revenues in fiscal 1993, Foodarama

Supermarkets was forced to sell its five Long Island stores to Grand Union for a total of $18.3 million. In February 1994 the company announced that it had defaulted on $35.2 million of loans and disclosed increasing operating losses. A restructuring of the company was made possible a year later, when it received a credit and loan facility of $38 million in order to pay three bank creditors and certain senior note holders a total of $32.9 million. A year later Foodarama sold its two Pennsylvania stores to Wakefern for $8.3 million.

Two World Class Foodarama ShopRite stores opened in 1996, in Marlboro and Montgomery, New Jersey. Another opened in February 1998 in East Windsor as a replacement for an older, smaller unit in Highstown. A fourth opened in late 1998 in Bound Brook, and three more were expected before the end of 2000. Three leases had been signed by April 1998 for replacement locations, with additional plans to expand one existing store. The expansion of the chain's Long Branch store was also under way.

After putting its finances in order Foodarama Supermarkets returned to the black, but its profit remained thin, with net income of only $1.1 million in fiscal 1997 on sales of $636.7 million. These totals improved to $1.8 million and a record $697.4 million, respectively, in fiscal 1998. Of the 1998 sales, groceries accounted for around 40 percent; dairy and frozen foods, 16.5 percent; meats, poultry, and seafood, 11 percent; nonfoods, 10 percent; produce, 8.5 percent; appetizers and prepared foods, 6 percent; pharmacy, 4 percent; bakery, 2 percent; and liquor, floral, and garden centers, 2 percent. Products under the ShopRite label came to 17 percent of sales in fiscal 1997.

All of the company's 21 stores were being leased in 1998 and ranged in size from 30,000 to 101,000 square feet. The 15 World Class supermarkets were significantly larger than conventional ones and featured such premium services as fresh fish on ice, prime meat departments with butcher service, imported cheese cases, salad and snack bars, bulk foods, and pharmacies. Many of these services were also available in the other stores. Foodarama's bakery was then in Howell, New Jersey. Its facility for meat and prepared foods was in Linden, New Jersey.

Joseph Saker, chairman and president of Foodarama Supermarkets at the time, owned 30 percent of the company's common stock in February 1998. Saker family members collectively owned 43 percent. The company's long-term debt was $50.7 million at the end of fiscal 1998. Foodarama held a one-eighth share of Wakefern.

MOVING INTO THE 21ST CENTURY

Foodarama Supermarkets focused on slow and steady growth during the early years of the new millennium. A new 67,000-square-foot store that the company billed as a one-stop shopping experience opened in Branchburg, New Jersey. Richard Saker, son of the founder, explained the decision to focus on offering products and services that went above and beyond traditional supermarket offerings. "Time is at a premium," he told *Real Estate Weekly* in May 2000. "And customers are looking for a one-stop shopping alternative. All of the features at this new ShopRite will be on a grand scale, including a variety of customer driven services based on focus group responses." Some of these new features included a concierge to help with catering and party planning needs, a full-service florist, a coffee shop, and an in-store dry cleaning service.

Richard Saker was named CEO in 2003 while his father remained chairman. The father and son duo continued to revamp existing stores while opening new World Class locations in its home state. The new Woodbridge store opened its doors in 2003 and included a 99-cent store, as well as premium features including a bakery, a host of fresh food stations including a Caribbean Grill area, a Dunkin' Donuts store, and a space to offer cooking classes. Foodarama shuttered its two existing garden centers in 2004 and also opened a new garden center location that year.

By 2005 sales had surpassed $1 billion and the company was operating 26 ShopRite stores in New Jersey. It was at this time that the Saker family began formulating a plan to take Foodarama private. In December 2005 an investor group consisting of Saker family members made a $52 per share bid for the company. They increased the bid to $53 per share by February of the following year. The investment group, operating under the name Saker Holdings Corp., completed the deal in July 2006.

Under the leadership of the Saker family, Foodarama took on the Saker ShopRites Inc. name in 2010. It remained a member of Wakefern, which was the largest retailer-owned food cooperative in the United States and owner of the ShopRite name. By 2010 the cooperative had 45 members who owned and operated supermarkets under the ShopRite banner.

Competition remained fierce at this time, especially from regional supermarket operator Wegmans Food Markets Inc. and from Wal-Mart Stores Inc. Saker ShopRites continued to rely on its World Class store format to lure new customers. As it looked to the future, Saker ShopRites hoped to expand its 27-store roster. Its existing lineup included locations in Monmouth, Ocean, Middlesex, Somerset, and Mercer counties.

Robert Halasz
Updated, Christina M. Stansell

PRINCIPAL COMPETITORS

Acme Markets, Inc.; The Great Atlantic & Pacific Tea Company, Inc.; Wal-Mart Stores, Inc.; Wegmans Food Markets Inc.

FURTHER READING

Elson, Joel. "Foodarama Develops Format to Fight Clubs." *Supermarket News*, April 20, 1992, p. 42.

———. "Foodarama Sets Growth by Construction." *Supermarket News*, April 13, 1998, p. 4.

"Foodarama Continues Growth." *Supermarket News*, April 17, 2000.

Hammel, Frank. "Now, Here's an Unorthodox Instore Service!" *Supermarket Business*, January 1994.

"New Supermarket Designed as One-Stop Shopping Alternative." *Real Estate Weekly*, May 3, 2000.

Norris, Floyd. "Why Not Shop Around?" *Barron's*, August 4, 1986, p. 30.

Turcsik, Richard. "At the Crossroads: Foodarama's New Flagship World Class ShopRite in Woodbridge, N.J., Merges Upscale Service with Low Prices to Create a Traffic-Stopping Experience." *Progressive Grocer*, August 1, 2003.

Wahlgren, Gary. "Foodarama Supermarkets, Inc." *Wall Street Transcript*, March 8, 1971.

Scott Sports S.A.

Route du Crochet 17
Givisiez, CH-1762
Switzerland
Telephone: (41 026) 460 16 16
Toll Free: (800) 292-5874
Fax: (41 026) 460 16 00
Web site: http://www.scott-sports.com

Private Company
Incorporated: 1969 as Scott USA Inc.
Employees: 450
Sales: $325.7 million (2008 est.)
NAICS: 339920 Sporting and Athletic Good Manufacturing

■ ■ ■

Scott Sports S.A. manufactures and distributes cycling and winter sports equipment and apparel, as well as running shoes. The company's origins date to the 1958 introduction of aluminum ski poles by Idaho-based inventor Edward Scott. The brand has been built on innovation since then. The business has changed hands a few times and in the mid-1990s owned the venerable Schwinn brand of bicycles. Scott's European partners took over the business in 1998.

Scott established a subsidiary in Switzerland in 1978 and became one of Europe's leading bicycle brands thanks to its command of industry trends such as mountain biking. However, it withdrew from the U.S. bike market for several years after selling off Schwinn in 1997. Scott was also at the forefront of the European snowboard industry, at one point making boards at the massive Blizzard factory in Austria. Scott claims industry leadership in carbon bike frames.

SUN VALLEY ORIGINS

Company founder Edward L. Scott was one of the original ski bums. Born in Philadelphia in 1914, he served in the U.S. Army in World War II. Around 1947 he arrived in Idaho, which would be his home for the rest of his life. At the time, there was little industry beyond sheepherding and not much of a permanent population in the area.

In 1950 *Life* magazine found Scott in Ketchum, the "dean" of a group of young adults indulging their passion for the slopes by living frugally and working odd jobs at night. Scott worked as a janitor at a café. At the time of the *Life* visit Scott owned 15 pairs of skis. He had gotten his first pair in 1924, when his father made some using a blueprint in *Boy Mechanic* magazine. In 1949 Scott began repairing and tuning skis in his one-room cabin.

Five years later Scott was making his own ski poles. Using aluminum rather than the traditional bamboo and steel, he crafted a much lighter pole better suited for slalom racing and improved the grip as well. He began marketing these revolutionary ski polies in 1958. The following year, Scott donated poles to the U.S. and Canadian national ski teams, which they used to win Olympic medals at Squaw Valley. This generated a lot of publicity, and Scott's annual sales exceeded $1 million within five years.

COMPANY PERSPECTIVES

Times have changed and Scott has developed into a worldwide powerhouse in wintersports, motorsports and cycling. But the vision has always remained the same from the humble beginnings 50 years ago in Ed Scott's one man ski tuning business: innovation, technology, design. Push the envelope with advanced materials, be creative, and constantly try to improve products.

NEW CORPORATE OWNERSHIP IN 1969

In 1969 Kentucky-based Kingsford Co. acquired the business, presumably to strike a seasonal balance for its summertime sales of charcoal briquettes. Edward Scott stayed on with the company for another two years. Clorox Co. acquired Kingsford in March 1973. By this time the booming Scott U.S.A. Inc. (incorporated in Idaho four years earlier) had 70 full-time employees and another 100 or so temporary workers.

Scott brought out the first goggles specifically designed for motocross racing in 1970. The next year it introduced lightweight plastic ski boots and a line of double-lens thermal ski goggles developed by California orthodontist Robert Smith. These were among the first to use foam, which prevented fogging.

NEW OWNERSHIP IN 1981

In 1978 a European headquarters opened in Switzerland. The company was bankrupt within a few years, however. Charles T. Ferries III, once a world class skier, led a group including Bob Smith and Dr. Richard Sugden that acquired Scott U.S.A. in 1981. Annual sales were just $5 million at the time. Ferries added bicycle accessories to the company's lineup to balance its seasonal dependence on winter sports.

Scott began making mountain bikes in 1986. Road bike racing was changed forever when Scott introduced the first aerodynamic handlebar in 1989, used to good effect by Greg LeMond in winning the Tour de France that year. The company's mountain bike suspension, the Unishock, introduced two years later, helped Ruthie Matthews win the MTB World Championship. Scott became a stronger mountain bike brand in Europe, where it was early to the trend and benefited from strong name recognition among winter sports dealers.

By 1993 Scott was the third-leading European bike brand imported into the United States. Scott began making snowboards in 1993 and added ski gloves the next year. In 1995 a distribution center was added in Londerzeel, Belgium. In 1996 the group acquired a huge ski factory in Austria called Blizzard Marketing GmbH, which Scott steered toward more snowboard manufacture. In 1997 Scott unveiled outerwear for winter sports.

SCHWINN OWNERSHIP: 1993–97

Schwinn, a company that had ignored the mountain biking movement until too late, went bankrupt in 1992 after leading the bicycle industry for most of the century. In January 1993 Scott USA and Zell-Chilmark Fund LP, led by David Schulte and Sam Zell, formed Scott Sports Group Inc. The new group took over most of the assets of Schwinn Bicycle Co., apart from its last U.S. factory in Waterford, Wisconsin, for $43 million, also picking up $17 million in assumed debt. It outbid Dore Enterprises, a Michigan holding company. Ferries and Scott Sports CEO Tom Srendahl were also shareholders. (Zell had met Ferries playing paintball at Sun Valley.)

Scott Sports had sales of about $250 million in 1995. Schwinn made up $120 million of the total. Despite an ambitious attempt to relaunch the venerable brand, Scott did not own the company for long. Soon after the purchase, Scott halved the workforce and moved Schwinn's remaining 130 employees from Chicago to a 24,000-square-foot site in Boulder, Colorado, at the epicenter of the mountain bike and fitness movement. It was renamed Schwinn Cycling & Fitness Inc.

Sales increased after the brand added mountain bikes. By 1995 Schwinn was second only to Trek in sales volume at specialty bike shops. However, it was sold in 1997 to Questor Partners Fund LP of Southfield, Michigan, a turnaround specialist. Schwinn then had annual revenues of $140 million and sales of 350,000 units (including stationary exercise bikes). The next year it merged with GT Bicycles Inc. to form Schwinn/GT Corp., which was bought by mass-market bike manufacturer Huffy Corp. in 2001.

MANAGEMENT BUYOUT IN 1998

In 1998 Scott itself was sold to a management group of 20 people led by Beat Zaugg, company president. Zaugg, formerly a World Cup ski racer, had begun working for Scott USA in 1988. The new owners soon withdrew from the U.S. bike market to regroup.

KEY DATES

1958: Ski bum Edward Scott begins marketing his revolutionary aluminum ski poles from Ketchum, Idaho.

1969: Kingsford Co. acquires company.

1973: Clorox Co. acquires Kingsford.

1978: European headquarters opens in Switzerland.

1981: Partnership led by Chuck Ferries acquires Scott USA brand out of bankruptcy.

1993: Scott Sports takes over assets of Schwinn for $41 million.

1996: Scott buys Austrian ski manufacturer Blizzard Marketing GmbH.

1997: Scott sells Schwinn to turnaround specialist.

1998: Blizzard divested; Beat Zaugg leads management buyout of Scott.

2004: Scott reenters bicycle market in the United States.

2008: Scott USA moves into new headquarters; brand celebrates 50th anniversary.

Scott had begun working with carbon fiber in 1994, and in 1995 introduced the first carbon frame mountain bike, the Endorphin. Weight savings continued to be a focus of innovation, as well as a key selling point. The company's G-Zero full-suspension mountain bike was billed as the world's lightest when introduced in 1998. The even lighter Strike debuted two years later, followed in 2003 by the lighter still CR1, a carbon frame, in 2003. In 2005 Scott introduced the Plasma, the lightest triathlon-specific frame, made of carbon. Entering a new market area, Scott claimed the lightest road bike frame in 2001 with the Team Issue. One of its bikes won a stage at the Tour de France the next year.

SNOWBOARD DEVELOPMENTS: 1995–98

In early 1995 Scott bought Seattle's American Snowboard Manufacturing, maker of Hooger and Pill snowboards. Scott then acquired ski manufacturer Blizzard Marketing GmbH from its bank, Raiffeisenverband Salzburg, in October 1996. Blizzard employed 300 people at one of the world's largest ski factories in Mittersill, Austria. The factory was capable of producing 400,000 units a year, but sales had fallen below the 250,000 or so units needed to break even. Blizzard's revenues were ATS 330 million ($31 million) in 1996.

Scott aimed to devote more of its production capacity to the booming snowboard market. It cut employment at Blizzard nearly in half and streamlined production processes but was unable to turn the plant around. The bank resumed ownership in 1998. Renamed Blizzard Sport GmbH, the company finally broke even in fiscal 1999–2000.

Scott had stopped selling bikes in the United States in 1997. It reentered the market in 2004 at the urging of Scott Montgomery, scion of the family that had founded Cannondale, a pioneer in aluminum bicycles until its collapse and eventual sell-off in 2003. Montgomery was hired to lead the effort after investing his own money in it.

As *Forbes* noted, Montgomery focused the U.S. business on triathlons, a small but highly visible and very competitive specialty niche. It also courted the even smaller time-trial market. In addition to shaving as much weight as possible from the frames and components, Scott used wind tunnel testing to tweak the design of the aerodynamic handlebars. Scott also brought some of the Contessa line of bikes to the United States. Scott had been successfully selling this line, designed specifically for women, in Europe for five years.

BIKES AND MORE

Scott's return to the U.S. bike market was complicated by a patent dispute with Specialized Bicycle Components over a four-bar linkage suspension for mountain bikes. (There was no patent on it in Europe.) After spending a year and a half and a reported $1 million on litigation, in 2006 Scott agreed not to market its Genius model in the United States. Montgomery explained that the suit would have been too expensive to defend at trial, and Scott already had a replacement bike, the Ransom. Specialized refused to license its technology to Scott, as it had to other bike manufacturers. In addition, it all but compelled its retailers to choose between the two brands.

In 2005 sporting goods chain Goldwin Inc. became Scott's exclusive distributor in Japan. Scott signed up Mica Sport Canada, which handled Scott's winter sports lines, as its exclusive bicycle distributor north of the 49th parallel. In 2010 Scott shifted its New Zealand bike business from Colorado Traders to Sheppard Industries, in which it was taking an equity stake. In Australia the brand was distributed by Sheppard and Sola.

Scott continued to develop its other businesses as it was relaunching bikes in the United States. In 2004 Scott bought Finland's Yoko and Reima brands of motorcycle and snowmobile apparel. It began offering running shoes in 2006.

The group had 530 employees and revenues of CHF 270 million ($212 million) in 2005. Bikes accounted for 55 percent or more of total revenues. In 2006 the Swiss Venture Club awarded Scott CEO Beat Zaugg its Expace-Mittelland prize for entrepreneurship.

In 2006 Scott USA moved its warehouse operation from a World War II-era hangar in Salt Lake City to a new 240,000-square-foot facility in Ogden, Utah. This allowed it to easily shift personnel between its bike, winter sports, and motor sports operations depending on seasonal demands.

50TH ANNIVERSARY IN 2008

Group revenues were $300 million per year by 2007. Scott USA accounted for $19 million of the total. The company was selling more than ¥200 million ($1.8 million) worth of bikes a year in Japan. In 2007 Scott USA ended a relationship with Denk Engineering, which had helped it develop its lightweight carbon bikes for 12 years. As its bike business grew, Scott took more of its engineering work in-house.

Company founder Edward Scott died in 2001. He had been inducted into the U.S. National Ski Hall of Fame in 1999 and entered the Intermountain Ski Hall of Fame five years later. Scott celebrated its 50th anniversary in 2008. During the year the U.S. headquarters moved to 33,000 square feet of space in a mixed-use building, just four years after its last move into a 15,000-square-foot office in Sun Valley.

In 2010 Scott USA was promoting its line of running shoes to help balance seasonal business cycles. Known for high-end bikes priced at $3,000 or more, the company was also rolling out a line of lower priced bikes in the United States, in response to a downturn in the market in a dismal economy. It was expanding its apparel offerings at the same time.

Frederick C. Ingram

PRINCIPAL SUBSIDIARIES

SSG (Europe) Distribution Center SA (Belgium); Scott Sports SA (France); Scott Svenska AB (Sweden); Scott Sports Ltd. (UK); Scott USA Inc.

PRINCIPAL COMPETITORS

Amer Sports Corporation; Cervélo Cycles Inc.; Dorel Industries Inc.; Specialized Bicycle Components; Trek Bicycle Corp.

FURTHER READING

Barret, Victoria. "Spinning Wheels; Scott Montgomery Wants to Make Scott Sports' Bikes a Hot Brand in the U.S.; He Also Aims to Reclaim His Family's Iconic Status in Cycling." *Forbes*, May 19, 2008, p. 68.

Ferguson, Tim. "Combat Veterans of Sorts Raise the Schwinn Flag." *Wall Street Journal*, July 27, 1993, p. A19.

Jefferson, Elana Ashanti. "Michigan Firm Buys Schwinn." *Denver Post*, August 14, 1997, p. C1.

"Life Visits Some Ski Bums; At Sun Valley They Live by Their Wits, Work at Night and Eat Horse Meat in Order to Schuss Down the Slopes." *Life*, February 27, 1950, pp. 114–120.

Masia, Seth. "Chuck Ferries: Rail Rider." *Skiing Heritage*, December 2009, pp. 37–38.

Narvaes, Emily. "Schwinn Back in the Pack; Mountain Bikes Boost Company." *Denver Post*, May 15, 1996, p. C1.

"Scotty, Lash Make Ski Shrine." *Mountain Express* (Ketchum, Idaho), September 22, 2004.

Tompkins, Megan. "Scott USA Opens New Warehouse, Expands Outside Rep Force." *Bicycle Retailer and Industry News* 15.15 (2006): 22.

Wiebe, Matt. "Denk to Forge New Partnerships, Launch New Projects Next Year." *Bicycle Retailer and Industry News* 16.15 (2007): 15.

Woody, Robert H. "Great Scott, the Right Ski Pole, Produced and Sold from Idaho." *Salt Lake Tribune*, July 1, 1973, p. B13.

Showa Shell Sekiyu K.K.

Daiba Frontier Building
2-3-2 Daiba
Minato-ku
Tokyo, 135-8074
Japan
Telephone: (81 03) 5531-5591
Fax: (81 03) 5531-5598
Web site: http://www.showa-shell.co.jp

Public Company
Incorporated: 1942 as Showa Oil Co., Ltd.
Employees: 5,439
Sales: ¥2.02 trillion ($21.93 billion) (2009)
Stock Exchanges: Tokyo
Ticker Symbol: 5002
NAICS: 324110 Petroleum Refineries; 324121 Asphalt
Paving Mixture and Block Manufacturing; 324191
Petroleum Lubricating Oil and Grease Manufactur-
ing; 422710 Petroleum Bulk Stations and
Terminals; Petroleum and Petroleum Products
Wholesalers (Except Bulk Stations and Terminals);
447110 Gasoline Stations with Convenience Stores;
447190 Other Gasoline Stations; 454311 Heating
Oil Dealers; 454312 Liquefied Petroleum Gas
(Bottled Gas) Dealers

■■■

Showa Shell Sekiyu K.K. is one of Japan's leading oil refiners and distributors of petroleum products. The company's main petroleum products include gasoline, diesel fuel, fuel oil, liquefied petroleum gas (LPG), liquefied natural gas, and lubricants. It controls three crude oil refineries in Japan through three affiliated companies: Showa Yokkaichi Sekiyu Co., Ltd. (refinery in Yokkaichi), Toa Oil Co., Ltd. (Keihin), and Seibu Oil Co., Ltd. (Yamaguchi). Collectively, these refineries have a daily capacity of about 515,000 barrels.

Two plants manufacture lubricants in Yokohama and Kobe, and the company also maintains a petroleum import terminal in Niigata. Showa Shell operates approximately 4,100 gasoline service stations in Japan, garnering a 16.1 percent share of the domestic gasoline market in 2008. Showa Shell has further interests in the alternative energy sector, principally solar power generation systems. Showa Shell Sekiyu was formed through the 1985 merger of two oil companies, Showa Oil Co., Ltd., and Shell Sekiyu K.K. The two companies had had close ties ever since the close of World War II. The Royal Dutch/Shell Group holds a 35 percent stake in Showa Shell. Saudi Aramco controls nearly 15 percent of the company.

EARLY HISTORY

Petroleum was not commonly used in Japan until after 1868, when Japan opened its commerce to Western markets. Until that time, domestically mined coal was used for heating and energy. Although some oil fields were discovered in Japan, from the 1880s through World War II the Japanese oil market was dominated by two foreign organizations, Standard Oil and Royal Dutch/Shell. These groups, already operating on a global scale, were able to flood the Japanese market with inexpensive imported oil.

COMPANY PERSPECTIVES

Showa Shell Sekiyu K.K. can only achieve a further leap and perpetual growth by constantly making its contribution to society, while securing reasonable profits and constructing a strong management base and sound corporate constitution.

With Japan's military and industrial buildup in the years preceding World War II, petroleum came to be important to the country's economy. Jet fuel in particular was crucial to the success of the Japanese air force. Tokyo-based Showa Oil Co., Ltd., was established during the war, in 1942, from the merger of three smaller oil companies, Hayama Oil, Asahi Oil, and Niitsu Oil. Shell Sekiyu was begun around 1876 in Yokohama by Samuel Samuel & Co., a forerunner of the Shell Group. In 1900 the company was incorporated as the Rising Sun Petroleum Company, to handle escalating petroleum imports.

Prior to World War II, oil production had never really been enough to support the industrializing nation. In addition, bombing during the war had decimated the company's physical plants. After the war occupation forces refused to allow the Japanese refining industry to start up until 1949. At that time joint operation with a foreign company was the most effective way to revive the almost dead petroleum industry, and Showa Oil signed an operating agreement with Royal Dutch/Shell in 1949. Shell Sekiyu did the same a year later. The U.S. occupation forces encouraged these mergers. In 1951 the ties between Showa Oil and Royal Dutch/Shell deepened when the latter began making equity investments in Showa, eventually gaining a 50 percent stake. Shell Sekiyu remained 100 percent owned by Royal Dutch.

BUILDING REFINERY CAPACITY IN THE POSTWAR ERA

In the 1950s Showa Oil and Shell Sekiyu were among several foreign-owned companies that dominated the Japanese petroleum market, focusing on rebuilding and expanding their refineries. Like most Japanese oil companies at that time, the Shell companies were not interested in exploration but in importing crude. The crude was refined, marketed, and distributed in Japan. In 1949 Showa Oil's Kawasaki refinery could handle 6,000 barrels of crude per day but capacity increased to 102,000 barrels per day by 1965. At the same time Shell

Sekiyu had the capacity to refine 180,000 barrels per day. Most of the crude oil was imported from the Persian Gulf countries.

The tremendous buildup of the Shell affiliates' refining capacities was made possible without government loans, and with minimal government regulation. In the early 1960s, however, Japan's Ministry of International Trade and Industry (MITI) took an increasingly large role in the oil industry, in some ways working against Showa and other foreign-owned companies. The Petroleum Industry Law was enacted in 1962, which favored the development of domestically owned oil companies. The law also assigned to MITI a permanent supervisory role over the future development of the petroleum industry.

REGULATION BRINGS CHANGES: 1962–73

The Japanese government wanted to avoid control of the oil industry by international oil companies, as had been the case before the war, and used its regulatory forces to ensure that domestic companies got favorable positions in the booming petroleum market. Around this time, Showa and Shell Sekiyu supplied roughly 12 percent of the Japanese oil market. Foreign-owned companies combined controlled roughly 80 percent of Japan's oil market, of which the Shell group was the third largest. MITI's aim was to approximate an even split between the international and domestic companies' shares of the market. MITI achieved this desired balance over the next 10 years, without adversely affecting Showa Oil or Shell Sekiyu. The new government regulations directly or indirectly shaped the business strategies of the Shell companies in the years to come.

An overall effect of the 1962 regulatory act was to increase competition among all the companies dealing in the Japanese oil market. MITI actively encouraged mergers between smaller domestic companies so they could rival the larger, older, foreign-affiliated firms such as Showa. The major *zaibatsu* established banking and corporate dynasties such as Mitsui, Sumitomo, and Mitsubishi, and plunged into the oil business around the end of the 1950s. With long-standing political and economic power in Japan, these groups did not take long to come to the fore of the petroleum industry. The Japanese oil market became more competitive because the major companies were for the most part caught up to each other technologically. Japanese engineers, sponsored by MITI, were working diligently to master and improve petrochemical technology. As long as the price of imported crude remained stable, the competitive edge in the domestic market would go to the

KEY DATES

1876: Forerunner of Shell Sekiyu is founded in Yokohama by Samuel Samuel & Co. (later Shell Sekiyu).

1900: Yokohama firm is incorporated as Rising Sun Petroleum Company.

1942: Tokyo-based Showa Oil Co., Ltd., is established from the merger of three oil companies, Hayama Oil, Asahi Oil, and Ni-itsu Oil.

1949: Showa Oil signs an operating agreement with Royal Dutch/Shell.

1951: Royal Dutch/Shell begins making equity investments in Showa Oil, eventually gaining a 50 percent stake.

1985: Showa Oil and Shell Sekiyu merge to form Showa Shell Sekiyu K.K., which is 50 percent owned by Royal Dutch/Shell.

1993: Company loses ¥166.3 billion from $6.4 billion worth of speculative foreign-exchange contracts.

1996: Deregulation of Japan's oil industry begins; Showa Shell launches a multiyear restructuring program to adapt to the new environment.

2005: Saudi Aramco increases stake in company to nearly 15 percent; Royal Dutch/Shell's holdings drop to 35 percent.

company with the most efficient, low-cost refining technology.

The powerful backing of Royal Dutch/Shell propelled Showa Oil and Shell Sekiyu through the first decade of MITI's regulation. In addition, Royal Dutch/Shell had sources for crude oil in all parts of the globe. Foreign-affiliated firms still had advantages, particularly in international contract negotiations. The newer Japanese companies had little experience in negotiating drilling and exploration rights. Experts in Japan and abroad agreed that the new Japanese companies were not ready to take a major position in the world oil scene.

In the early 1970s, with rising political tensions in the Middle East, finding new sources of crude became important to the stability of the oil industry. By comparison with the other major international oil firms, Royal Dutch/Shell was considered short on crude oil. Its

historical position as one of the two or three largest international oil companies was based on its efficient refining and marketing and long-range planning. Well before the 1973 OPEC embargo, the Shell companies were looking for oil sources outside the Middle East. Showa Oil began to seek out joint refining ventures abroad at the same time.

ACQUISITIONS, DISCOVERIES, AND JOINT VENTURES: 1975–84

In 1975 Showa made an agreement with Algeria's National Hydrocarbon Corporation to provide technical assistance for the design and operation of two new oil refineries. Royal Dutch/Shell discovered a large natural gas field off Australia's northwest shelf around the same time; that gas was intended for marketing in Japan. Royal Dutch/Shell discovered the gigantic North Sea gas field in 1979, which improved the Shell affiliates' position considerably.

In the same year as the North Sea discovery, Showa Oil acquired a 25 percent interest in another Japanese company, Toa Oil Co., Ltd., which interest was formerly held by C. Itoh, a Japanese holding company. In addition to operating a refinery in Keihin, Toa Oil had valuable contracts to import and wholesale 230,000 barrels of oil daily through direct purchases. Toa could buy this oil directly from the oil field, without any international oil company intermediary. MITI had encouraged the domestic oil companies to make direct purchase contracts.

Although C. Itoh initiated the sale of Toa to Showa, MITI was disturbed by the transaction. The domestic company would lose its direct purchase contracts to the foreign-affiliated Showa, shifting the balance within the Japanese oil industry to foreign affiliates. The market split between the foreign and domestic groups was very nearly 50-50 before the Toa sale, and MITI wanted to maintain this even split or tip it in favor of the domestic companies. In this case, however, the industry went against the regulators' wishes.

Following the acquisition of Toa, Showa strengthened its ties with Kuwait. In 1980 the Kuwaiti government agreed to export 30,000 more barrels of crude oil per day to Showa Oil. Showa's efforts to secure a variety of sources for crude oil were generally successful in the 1970s. In the 1980s Showa found its profits still too closely tied to the fluctuations in the price of crude. In 1981 the company posted a loss of ¥21.2 billion. The next year, Showa showed a profit of ¥1.2 billion. In spite of highly sophisticated refining and marketing techniques, the company could do little to control the swings of the world's crude oil markets.

Showa began to diversify its product line, and in the 1980s built and bought office buildings and apartment houses, to gain rental income. Showa also invested in rental car and travel businesses.

FORMATION OF SHOWA SHELL SEKIYU: 1985

Showa Oil and Shell Sekiyu formally merged in 1985. They had had a close operating relationship through most of their history. The merger made them equal partners in the new corporation, Showa Shell Sekiyu K.K. Royal Dutch/Shell retained a 50 percent interest in the new company. The merger streamlined the Shell affiliates' operations and made management more efficient and cost-effective. Tokio Nagayama was named chairman of Showa Shell, having served for 17 years as president of Showa Oil, earning the nickname the "Emperor."

Despite the company's ventures into non-oil areas, including the 1987 launch of a computer software company, Computer Plaza K.K., Showa Shell Sekiyu's focus remained on oil. Exploration was still very much a part of the company's interests. For example, in 1990 the company bought a 20 percent interest in the development rights to inland oil concessions in Myanmar. Two years later Showa Shell took a stake in exploration blocks off the southwestern coast of Vietnam. By this time, Nagayama had retired, and Kiyoshi Takahashi had taken over as chairman, with Takeshi Henmi serving as president.

The two leaders, however, resigned in August 1993 to take responsibility for a huge loss that Showa Shell had incurred on foreign-exchange futures contracts. The company had revealed in February of that year that it had an unrealized loss of ¥125 billion ($1.05 billion) stemming from $6.4 billion worth of speculative foreign-exchange contracts involving bets on the value of the dollar versus the yen. The loss later ballooned to ¥166.3 billion because of further declines in the U.S. currency's value. As it wrote off these losses over the next couple of years, Showa Shell compensated by raising cash through the sale of securities and property.

RESTRUCTURING FOLLOWING DEREGULATION: 1996–2002

The Japanese oil industry entered a new, more highly competitive era in the late 1990s as a result of deregulatory moves initiated by the government. In April 1996 a law limiting oil imports to 29 refiners and distributors was repealed, opening the door for supermarkets, trading companies, and even farm cooperatives to begin importing petroleum products for direct distribution in Japan. Further roiling the industry was the late 1990s introduction of self-service gasoline stations in the Japanese market for the first time, after they had long been banned because of an arcane fire regulation.

Even before the deregulation began, Showa Shell launched an aggressive, multiyear program of restructuring to retain its competitiveness in the new environment. An ambitious cost-cutting effort gradually reduced the corporation's annual operating costs by ¥111.2 billion ($937 million) by 2002. During this period the workforce was cut in half mainly through attrition and voluntary retirement programs. The new competition resulted in lower gas prices at the pump, leading in turn to many gas stations no longer being profitable. Showa Shell, along with the other Japanese refiners, began shuttering underperforming outlets.

Between 1996 and 2002, Showa Shell reduced the number of stations in its network by nearly 2,000. The company also joined in on the self-service revolution, opening its first such stations in 1999 and operating nearly 200 of the cheaper-to-operate outlets by 2002. In 1999 Showa Shell also closed down one of its four refineries, the one in Niigata, which had a daily capacity of 40,000 barrels. In addition to the cost-containment efforts, Showa Shell also strengthened its balance sheet, reducing its interest-bearing debt from ¥439.8 billion in 1996 to ¥150.5 billion in 2002.

In another key move during this period, Showa Shell began concentrating on the refining and distribution side of the oil business. The company gradually dissolved and liquidated its oil-field development projects, finally shutting down its remaining upstream subsidiaries early in the first decade of the 21st century. Eventually, therefore, the company began relying fully on imports from other firms to supply its refineries, and increasingly it derived its crude oil from companies within the Royal Dutch/Shell Group, which was nearly 50 percent of the total by 2001.

BATTLING COMPETITION IN THE 21ST CENTURY

The new competitive environment, coupled with overcapacity within Japan in both refining and distribution, brought about pressure for consolidation within the oil industry. For instance, Nippon Oil Company, Limited bought Mitsubishi Oil Co., Ltd., in 1999, and Tonen Corporation merged with General Sekiyu K.K. to form TonenGeneral Sekiyu K.K. the following year. For its part, Showa Shell in 1997–98 had discussed a merger of its refinery operations with those of Mitsubishi Oil, but the latter firm called off the talks. In the early

2000s, however, Showa Shell succeeded in creating several alliances and joint ventures with Japan Energy Corporation through which the two firms began cooperating in various areas of refining and distribution.

Showa Shell was simultaneously pursuing a greater focus on more profitable value-added products. In March 2002 the company launched Shell Pura in the Tokyo metropolitan area, touting the new product as a high-octane "environmentally friendly," "engine-cleansing" gasoline; it was formulated to remove deposits from automobile engines, thereby improving performance and reducing the emission of harmful pollutants. Following its successful Tokyo introduction, Shell Pura began to be rolled out to other areas.

Heading up Showa Shell in the first decade of the 21st century was Haruyuki Niimi. In March 2002 John S. Mills was promoted from vice president to president and chief operating officer, with Niimi remaining chairman and CEO. Mills became the first foreign national to occupy the presidency at Showa Shell Sekiyu, and he was expected to promote closer ties with the Royal Dutch/Shell Group. Showa Shell had positioned itself through its thorough post-deregulation restructuring as one of the most financially sound of the major Japanese oil industry players.

The company posted a net profit of $199 million in 2003, up 13 percent over the previous year. The company's recent success caught the eye of Saudi Arabian Oil Company. Known as Saudi Aramco, the state-owned company was looking to increase its Asian footprint and struck a deal to purchase a 10 percent stake of Showa Shell in 2004 and an additional 5 percent in 2005. Upon completion of the deal, Aramco secured the rights to supply Showa Shell 300,000 barrels per day. Royal Dutch/Shell's stake in Showa Shell was reduced to 35 percent as a result of the Aramco purchase.

OVERCOMING CHANGES IN THE OIL INDUSTRY

Mills resigned in 2005 leaving Niimi at the helm as president and chairman. Yasuo Murayama was named president in 2006 and held the title until 2008. Jun Arai was brought in to take over the presidency while Shigeya Kato was named chairman in 2009 to replace retiring Niimi. Amid these management changes, Showa Shell found itself at a crossroads in its history. The global promotion of energy conservation and the need to find alternative energy sources prompted Showa Shell to adopt a new business strategy to overcome falling demand for oil products in Japan as well as overcapacity issues.

In response to the changing business environment, Showa Shell made several strategic moves to strengthen its bottom line while remaining competitive. During 2007 the company transferred its international trading operations of oil products to Royal Dutch/Shell. While the transfer would lower Showa Shell's overall revenues, the company's profits would remain intact given that Royal Dutch/Shell would continue to make lease payments to Showa Shell as part of the transfer agreement. During 2008 Showa Shell and Sumitomo Corp. combined their LPG businesses to create Enessance Holdings Ltd.

The company worked to reposition its oil business amid harsh conditions in 2008. Showa Shell posted its first net loss since its inception that year. The $181.43 million loss was due in part to falling prices of crude oil in the latter half of 2008 and weak demand. Excess capacity forced the company to announce the closure of the Ohgimachi Factory at the Keihin Refinery operated by Toa Oil. Operations would cease by September 2011 and would reduce Showa Shell's refining capacity by 20 percent. Showa Shell posted a net loss of $642 million in 2009.

Meanwhile, the company was bolstering its solar panel business. During 2007 the company completed the construction of its first Miyazaki Plant that produced solar panels. A second facility was built in 2009 and a third was expected to go online during 2011 that would produce thin-film copper-indium-selenium solar modules. The company hoped its focus on solar panels would secure future profits. Indeed, Showa Shell anticipated that it would control 10 percent of the global market for solar panels by 2014 and that nearly half of its pretax profits would stem from solar panel operations.

By positioning the company as a major alternative energy player while streamlining its oil business, president Arai and chairman Kato Showa Shell expected a quick return to profitability. The management team also looked to future partnerships and strategic alliances to bolster the company's bottom line. While only time would tell if Showa Shell's gamble on solar panels would pay off, it appeared as though the company was positioned to meet future challenges head on.

Angela Woodward
Updated, David E. Salamie; Christina M. Stansell

PRINCIPAL SUBSIDIARIES

Showa Yokkaichi Sekiyu Co., Ltd.; Toa Oil Co., Ltd.; Showa Shell Sempaku K.K.; Heiwa Kisen Kaisha, Ltd.; Shoseki Overseas Oil Development Co., Ltd.; Shoseki

Engineering & Construction Co., Ltd.; Nippon Grease Co., Ltd.; Solar Frontier K.K.; Shoseki Kako K.K.; K.K. Rising Sun; On Site Power Co., Ltd.; Wakamatsu Gas K.K.; Genex Co., Ltd.; Kanto Koyu Energy Co., Ltd.; K.K. Sun Road; Jonen Co.; K.K. Shinyo Sekiyu; Chuo Shell Sekiyu Hanbai K.K.; Tokyo Shell Pack K.K.; Nakagawa Oil Co., Ltd.; Petro Star Kansai Co., Ltd.; Petro Star Kanto Co., Ltd.; K.K. Marushin; Nissho Koyu K.K.; Nagase Oil Ltd.; Enessance Holdings Co., Ltd.

PRINCIPAL COMPETITORS

Cosmo Oil Company, Ltd.; Idemitsu Kosan Co., Ltd.; Nippon Oil Corporation.

FURTHER READING

Ando, Mayumi. "Slick Moves Fuel Financial Strength." *Nikkei Weekly*, September 9, 2002.

"Aramco Ups Showa Stake." *International Petroleum Finance*, July 7, 2005.

Harney, Alexandra. "Showa Shell to Cut Costs with Refinery Closure." *Financial Times*, July 16, 1998, p. 41.

Kumagai, Takeo. "Japan's Showa Shell Tips Return to Profit in 2010." *Platts Oilgram News*, February 24, 2010.

Kumagai, Takeo, and Atsuko Kawasaki. "Showa Shell Posts 2009 Loss on Margins." *Platts Oilgram News*, February 17, 2010.

"Showa Shell Maps Out Own Solar Journey." *Nikkei Report*, September 14, 2009.

"Showa Shell to Set Up Biggest Solar Cell Plant in Japan." *Asia Pulse*, September 8, 2009.

Vernon, Raymond. *Two Hungry Giants: The United States and Japan in the Quest for Oil and Ores*. Cambridge, Mass.: Harvard University Press, 1983.

Watanabe, Mika. "Japan Energy and Showa Shell Face Hurdles as New Partners." *Asian Wall Street Journal*, March 20, 2000, p. 22.

Yoshino, M. Y. *Japan's Multinational Enterprises*. Cambridge, Mass.: Harvard University Press, 1976.

Siderúrgica del Orinoco
Alfredo Maneiro

——————— ■ ———————

Avenida La Estancia
Edifico General de Seguros
Caracas, D.C. 1064
Venezuela
Telephone: (58 212) 902-3800
Fax: (58 212) 902-3924
Web site: http://www.sidor.com

State-Owned Company
Incorporated: 1964
Employees: 11,760
Sales: $1.75 billion (2009 est.)
NAICS: 331111 Iron and Steel Mills; 391112 Electro-
    metallurgical Ferroalloy Product Manufacturing;
    331221 Cold-Rolled Steel Shape Manufacturing

■ ■ ■

Siderúrgica del Orinoco Alfredo Maneiro (SIDOR) is
one of the largest steel-producing companies in Latin
America. An enterprise owned principally by the
Venezuelan government, it is located near Ciudad
Guayana, on the banks of the Orinoco River, 175 miles
southwest of the river's termination in the Atlantic
Ocean. Iron ore from the region is converted into pellets
and briquets that are fed into furnaces producing
molten steel. This steel is then transformed into bullion,
billets, and slabs. These semifinished products are
fashioned into long products (bars and rods) and flat
products (hot- and cold-rolled coils and chrome-coated
sheets).

THE START-UP YEARS

Sparsely settled southeastern Venezuela yields many
valuable minerals, including high-grade iron ore first
extracted in 1950. The region's Caroní River, the
easternmost major tributary of the Orinoco, contains
rapids capable when harnessed of providing large
amounts of power cheaply for industry. Plentiful natural
gas is also available nearby for industrial processes. Low
cost, ample natural resources and electricity, plus ease of
transport, were expected to make Ciudad Guayana, at
the confluence of the Caroní and Orinoco, the
Pittsburgh of South America. The Orinoco is deep
enough there to accommodate oceangoing vessels that
can carry products to other Venezuelan ports and to
export markets abroad.

These advantages led in 1957 to the beginnings of a
steel mill where Ciudad Guayana would one day stand.
The Corporación Venezolana de Guayana (CVG) was
established in 1960 as a superagency for the development of the southern half of Venezuela. It began
producing raw steel in 1962 with an initial investment
of $300 million. SIDOR, created in 1964, became one
of CVG's most important companies. CVG Ferrominera
Orinoco provided SIDOR with the iron ore. By 1969
the steelmaking complex occupied about a square mile
and included roads and railroad tracks, as well as a port.

In 1970 SIDOR opened a mill for making seamless
pipes, a sophisticated product. A plant for flat steel
products was added to the complex in 1974. SIDOR
lost $80 million in its first five years. Between 1968 and
1976 it broke even.

CVG appointed representatives to SIDOR's board of directors and had the legal power to decide major issues. In practice, however, because the company's managers were far from the capital and had technical experience not found at the highest levels, they enjoyed considerable autonomy. A project and construction group within SIDOR monitored the building of new facilities. It consisted of civil, electrical, and mechanical inspectors; engineers and draftsmen; and personnel experienced in time and cost control, progress analysis, and facility planning. In all, the group's members numbered about 840, some of them foreigners.

One of SIDOR's problems was a shortage of qualified personnel. Fewer than 15 percent of new workers in 1968 had completed five years of schooling. In its first years the company trained some 10,000 persons, but half moved on to jobs in other industries. Some of these were middle managers who were able to secure better positions and higher pay by going to work for privately owned firms.

COSTLY EXPANSION

At first SIDOR employed the open-hearth blast furnace process to make steel, using imported coke and scrap iron as necessary inputs. However, during the early 1970s a decision was made to increase production fourfold, removing oxygen from iron ore by the direct reduction (DRI) method and feeding the resulting sponge iron, in powdered form, into electric arc furnaces for conversion to raw molten steel. The first such SIDOR DRI plant began operations in 1979. A second one was added later.

In place of costly imported scrap iron, SIDOR established a joint venture with the subsidiary of a Japanese company to produce hot briqueted iron (HBI) from pellets, which were also used in making sponge iron. SIDOR's pellet plant, reported to be the world's largest of its kind at the time, was completed in 1978. The DRI and HBI technologies were not perfected until 1988, but Venezuela eventually became the leading producer in the world of hot briqueted iron.

MOUNTING DEBT

By the time SIDOR's expansion project was completed in 1984, at a cost of some $300 million, a world economic recession that began at the beginning of the decade had reduced demand for SIDOR's annual productive capacity of 4.8 million metric tons of molten steel. In addition to its start-up costs, the company had accumulated operational losses of at least $400 million over its last decade. Most of its production had been earmarked for domestic use, but Venezuela's sagging economy could not absorb such high levels of steel, forcing the company to export it at prices below cost. SIDOR lost $1.19 billion between 1979 and 1983.

By 1987 SIDOR's overseas debt had reached an additional $300 million, much of it in short-term debt. Furthermore, the company began in 1985 to add capacity to the small seamless pipe mill. Not completed because of financial and technical problems, the ill-starred venture cost an additional $350 million. Because of limited demand, the expanded steel complex never ran at more than about 70 percent of its greatly increased capacity.

The oldest production facilities were closed in the early 1990s, reducing overall capacity to 3.6 million metric tons. In 1993 the Venezuelan government assumed 60 percent ($904 million) of SIDOR's debt, plus $166 million in accumulated interest. The company reduced its expenses by dismissing some of its 15,000 employees, and by 1995 it was earning a profit. In 1997, however, its losses reached $440 million.

SIDOR UNDER PRIVATE CONTROL: 1997–2008

At the end of 1997 a controlling stake of 70 percent of SIDOR was sold to a consortium of Latin American steel companies for about $1.2 billion, plus the assumption of about $600 million of its remaining debt. The company, in which the Venezuelan state had invested about $8 billion over the years, was the last major steelmaker to be privatized in Latin America.

SIDOR's fortunes did not change measurably under private ownership. Both supply of and demand for its products fell. The new owners blamed this on a number of factors, including the overvalued Venezuelan currency and high labor costs despite having reduced the workforce by half. Production came to about 3.3 million

KEY DATES

1964: Siderúrgica del Orinoco Alfredo Maneiro (SIDOR) is founded as a subsidiary of the Corporación Venezolana de Guayana.
1997: A majority stake in SIDOR is sold to a consortium of Latin American companies.
2008: SIDOR is nationalized again by the government of Venezuela.

metric tons of raw steel in 2000, of which about 30 percent was made into long products and 70 percent flat products.

The company lost $234 million in 1998. In early 1999 it fell into default on its debt of about $1 billion by failing to make a $40 million payment. A restructuring completed in early 2000 included the refinancing of a $449 million loan from about 30 banks and the renegotiation of around $640 million in debt owed to the Venezuelan government. However, the following year found the world economy mired in a slump, and the appreciation of the Venezuelan bolivar against the dollar boosted the price for SIDOR's steel. The result was that the company was again forced to seek a restructuring of its debt.

The year 2002 was even worse for SIDOR. A general strike aimed at driving President Hugo Chávez Frías from power reduced the company's steel production. In December of that year natural gas supplies were cut off, and production stopped completely for a time.

Grupo Techint, an Argentine-based multinational steelmaker, took a 60 percent stake in SIDOR in 2005 and made it a unit of Ternium S.A. Company workers and retirees and the government owned the rest of the shares. At about the same time, Chávez threatened to renationalize the company unless it paid more for the iron ore it received from Ferrominera.

A new contract almost doubled the price of the ore. Chávez again threatened to take over SIDOR in 2007, saying that in the company's drive to increase exports it was neglecting domestic markets. SIDOR soon after agreed that its prices for steel supplied to the domestic market would not exceed export prices.

Chávez was also siding with company workers who were stopping steel production from time to time in a bid for higher salaries and alleged unpaid retirement benefits owed to them. By this time employment had

dropped to 5,537, as Ternium outsourced as many as 7,500 jobs to at least 200 private contractors.

RETURN TO STATE OWNERSHIP: 2008

In April 2008 Chávez made good on his threat to take over SIDOR. He also warned he would expropriate the company without compensation unless agreement was reached with Ternium on the size of the payment. In 2009 an agreement was reached by which CVG agreed to pay Ternium $1.97 million for its stake in SIDOR.

SIDOR was renamed Siderúrgica del Orinoco Alfred Maneiro in honor of a deceased Communist militant. It was not reintegrated into CVG. Instead, it came under a newly created state-owned steel holding company named Corporación Siderúrgica de Venezuela S.A. The state then owned 80 percent of SIDOR's shares, while its workers and pensioners held the remaining 20 percent. In 2007 the government had also nationalized Matesi Materiales Siderúrgicos S.A., a SIDOR-Ternium joint venture producing hot briqueted iron.

In 2010 SIDOR's semifinished products were bullion (polygonal-section steel for rolling seamless tubes for the oil industry); billets (square cross-sectioned steel used as raw material in the rolling process); and slabs (rectangular-section steel for the production of hot-rolled sheets).

These semifinished products were made into rods and wires, including circular-section long products hot-rolled from billets; and bars, which were similar but with surface ridges for concrete reinforcement. The flat products were hot-rolled products derived from slabs; sheet chrome, cold-rolled low-carbon steel applied by an electrolytic process for use in the packaging industry; tin, cold-rolled low-carbon steel coated with a layer of tin applied by an electrolytic process for use in the manufacture of containers; and hot-rolled sheets subjected to the cold-rolling process.

The SIDOR steel complex included the pellet plant, two DRI facilities, and a steelmaking plant with six electric arc furnaces and three continuous slab-casting machines. There was a hot-rolling and a cold-rolling mill. The facilities for billet production included two electric arc furnaces and two continuous billet-casting machines. The complex also included facilities for the production of wire rod and bars. The port had 11 cranes for loading and unloading. The dock could accommodate six ships of up to 20,000 tons.

STEELMAKERS FACE HARD TIMES

The world's steelmakers experienced hard times with the economic recession that began in late 2007. Steel prices fell by about a half compared to the previous year. SIDOR's production dropped from 4.3 million to 3.5 million metric tons, and the company lost VEB 435 million ($202.5 million).

SIDOR's operations were hard hit in early 2010 by a reduction in power from Guri Dam because a severe drought had reduced water levels. The company was ordered to suspend production for six months in order to conserve electricity, but it was not allowed to lay off workers. Venezuela's central bank granted SIDOR a credit line of VEB 2 billion ($930 million). The loan was earmarked to enable SIDOR to pay suppliers the money it owed them and avoid insolvency.

As the drought dissipated and power supplies again became available, SIDOR's expectations of production of raw steel in 2010 rose from 800,000 metric tons to as high as two million tons. The company was building two thermal power plants at a cost of $400 million. The government in January 2009 had announced a national steel plan. Its goal was to increase Venezuela's steel production from five million metric tons in 2009 to nine million in 2013 and 15 million in 2019. SIDOR's share of the latter total would be eight million.

Robert Halasz

PRINCIPAL COMPETITOR

Siderúrgica Venezolana Sivensa, S.A.

FURTHER READING

Colitt, Raymond. "New Mettle." *Business Latin America*, September 14, 1998, p. 6.

Coronel, Gustavo. *Una perspectiva gerencial de la Corporación Venezolana de Guayana*. Sabana del Media, Carabobo: Editorial Melvin, 1995.

Enright, Michael J., et al. *Venezuela: The Challenge of Competitiveness*. New York: St. Martin's Press, 1996.

Haplich, Frank. "Struggling with Steelmaking." *American Metal Market*, July 8, 1999, pp. 1, 12.

Mendes de Paula, Germano. "Sidor's Renationalisation—The Repetitive Threat that Finally Became a Reality." *Steel Times International*, July/August 2008, p. 16.

———. "Sidor's Renationalisation Transition Phrase." *Steel Times International*, September 2008, p. 18.

———. "Venezuelan Steel Industry Becomes Ever More Nationalised." *Steel Times International*, May/June 2009, p. 12.

"Sidor's Holders Restructuring Debt Again." *American Metal Market*, November 7, 2001, p. 2.

Vogel, Thomas T., Jr. "Latin Consortium Wins Control of Venezuelan Steelmaker Sidor." *Wall Street Journal*, December 19, 1997, p. 19.

Skadden, Arps, Slate, Meagher & Flom LLP

---

4 Times Square
New York, New York 10036
U.S.A.
Telephone: (212) 735-3000
Fax: (212) 735-2000
Web site: http://www.skadden.com

Private Company
Founded: 1948 as Skadden, Arps & Slate
Employees: 4,500
Sales: $2.2 billion (2008 est.)
NAICS: 541110 Offices of Lawyers

■ ■ ■

Skadden, Arps, Slate, Meagher & Flom LLP is one of the largest law firms in the world with over 2,000 lawyers in 24 offices across the globe. The firm is known for its work in mergers and acquisitions, corporate restructuring, and corporate finance. Skadden was the first U.S. law firm to reach $1 billion in revenue in 2000 and has a long-standing history of garnering legal accolades and is recognized as a top law firm by industry rankings and publications. During 2010 Skadden ranked first among law firms in mergers and acquisitions for the 18th consecutive year by the *American Lawyer*.

ORIGIN AND FOUNDERS

According to Lincoln Caplan, in *Skadden: Power, Money, and the Rise of a Legal Empire*, the firm was founded on April Fools' Day in 1948 as an informal partnership with $12,000 of start-up capital. The firm's first fee was a modest $532.50. Joe Flom, a graduate of Harvard Law School, joined the firm as an associate in 1948, and eventually influenced the firm's growth more than any founding partner.

Flom served as the visionary architect of Skadden, Arps's growth. According to an *Institutional Investor* article published in 1994, "Flom built Skadden, Arps, Slate, Meagher & Flom into one of the largest, most profitable law firms in America, while ... redefining the use of the law in M&A. ... Flom was the epitome of the market warrior, and he brought the Darwinian ethos of the marketplace into the world of corporate law." Flom's early expertise centered on shareholder's derivative actions. Such actions were devices for the owners of a company to bring suit against its board of directors and management for failing to uphold their duties in running a company. In a typical corporation, the owners/shareholders elected the board of directors, who in turn selected management to run the company. If the board entered into a buyout in a way that did not give maximum value to the shareholders, a derivative action was likely.

GROWTH: 1960–89

In 1961 the firm adopted the Skadden, Arps, Slate, Meagher & Flom name. Skadden's growth was remarkable. In the mid-1960s, the firm grew to 20 lawyers and had more work than it could handle. According to Caplan, Skadden, Arps started by making $37,660 in revenue and $6,510 in profits its first year, however, "by the late seventies, intense demand allowed

Skadden to raise its hourly billing rates to as high a level as any firm's in New York City." Those rates allowed Skadden to bring in $225 million a year in revenue by the end of 1986.

A decade later, Skadden made $210 million profits on $635 revenues. The firm was not totally peerless in terms of generating revenue. For example, in 1992 Baker & McKenzie surpassed Skadden, Arps in terms of revenue. More than large revenues were required to build a lasting firm. As a reminder that not all mega-firms managed to survive intact, Skadden, Arps was hired by bankruptcy creditors of one of its former competitors, Finley Kumble.

The growth in the firm's revenues was due in part to growth in its physical size and reach. Skadden had over 3,000 employees, including 1,000 attorneys, and hired up to 700 new employees every year. Its first expansion efforts came in 1973, with the opening of an office in Boston. In 1976, Skadden opened a Washington office, and it opened a Chicago office in 1984. Skadden had 13 offices in 1990, with half of its attorneys in its New York office. The firm's nine domestic offices at this time were in New York; Boston; Washington, D.C.; Wilmington, Delaware; Los Angeles; San Francisco; and Newark, New Jersey. The firm made its first international foray in 1987 with the opening of an office in Tokyo. Additional international expansion led to offices in Beijing, Brussels, Budapest, Frankfurt, Hong Kong, London, Moscow, Paris, Prague, Sydney, and Toronto.

LAW FIRM MARKETING

Notably, the ethical canons and codes of the legal profession, in particular rules restricting solicitation of clients, limited the ways in which law firms could attract new business. The last half of the 20th century, however, saw a shift in law firm marketing. Clients became more sophisticated, and law firms operated more like other businesses, trends that corresponded to a lessening of ethical restrictions on law firm marketing. According to a 1982 memorandum, Skadden's goal was to "enhance the reputation of the firm and insure its continued viability and its ability to earn substantial income for its partners." Skadden did this by aggressively developing new business.

According to Caplan's book, Joe Flom described the takeover movement positively: "Merger and acquisition activity has performed a critically important function. Companies have become leaner and meaner." As a key feature of its marketing strategy, Skadden cunningly analyzed the business environment for opportunities that could gain advantages for its clients. Skadden went beyond the services offered by typical firms, aiming to work harder and longer at solutions to their clients' broader problems. Skadden seems to have filled a hole left by the "white shoe" law firms of Wall Street. Many more established firms would not handle takeovers for fear of upsetting their long-standing corporate clientele. Beyond innovations in client development, Skadden pioneered new fee structures. For example, the firm instituted a revenue-generating practice of charging corporate clients retainers. In return for paying a sizable retainer, the client could expect to have Skadden available as counsel in the event of a hostile takeover. This also prevented potential acquiring companies from using Skadden against a client on retainer.

Trends in the U.S. business climate contributed in part to the amazing revenues gathered by the firm. Takeovers, the field in which Skadden gained its greatest dominance, became an increasingly popular option in corporate America for several reasons. Individuals, who represented an increasing segment of post-World War II investors, demanded shorter-term returns on investment than had earlier investors. With such pressures on the annual bottom line, corporate management needed to find ways to sustain growth in the face of increasing global competition. Furthermore, takeovers grew in fiscal size as well as in number in the 1980s as the price of stocks rose.

In the 1980s, companies were offered new vehicles to raise large amounts of capital, such as leveraged buyouts (LBOs) and junk bonds. In an LBO, a buyer could acquire a target by getting a loan secured by the target's assets. If the ratio of secured assets to outstanding debt was high, the bonds used to leverage the takeover were known as junk bonds. In other words, junk bonds basically represented high-risk, unratable debt. Companies attempted to use junk bonds to acquire larger ones, increasing the demand for law firms with significant mergers-and-acquisitions experience.

KEY DATES

1948: The firm is founded; Joe Flom joins the firm as an associate.

1961: Company adopts the Skadden, Arps, Slate, Meagher & Flom name.

1973: Company begins expansion by opening an office in Boston.

1987: International expansion begins with the opening of an office in Tokyo.

1998: Skadden lawyer Robert Bennett successfully defends President Clinton in the Paula Jones trial.

2003: Firm represents State Farm Mutual Insurance Company in a landmark case.

2008: Revenues surpass $2 billion.

LAW FIRM GOVERNANCE

Since its inception as a partnership with no formal agreement, the firm has changed into a limited liability company (LLC), a hybrid juridical form. LLCs were created by state legislatures as ways of infusing partnerships with the corporate feature of limited liability, while allowing them to retain their partnership characteristics. According to Caplan, profits in Skadden, Arps were split between members by an eight-member committee. The committee looked at the members' quality of work, their hours billed, profitability of their respective practice areas, and their contributions to firm management. Since the late 1970s, Skadden's partners (now, members) have been some of the highest-paid attorneys in the country.

Skadden took novel steps in law firm governance. In 1990 the firm changed its management structure to operate less like a partnership and more like a typical U.S. corporation, emulating a board of directors. The firm also developed the Rainy Day Fund, for a law firm a financially ultraconservative measure, which provides a means of leaving the firm with enough money to carry all expenses for six months in case of emergency, as explained by Caplan.

LAWYER COMPENSATION

Traditionally, Skadden hired and promoted based on merit, progressively recognizing employees, including legal secretaries, paralegals, and clerks, from all segments of society. For example, Skadden promoted its first female partner in 1981. For the long hours and stress, employees at the firm were well compensated. At rates competitive with any law firm in the world, first-year Skadden associates made $85,000 per year during the early 1990s and could increase their earnings to $178,000 annually after seven years. Those levels of compensation were earned by long hours. Lawyers at Skadden were known to bill over 2,000 hours per year, as well as doing an average of 42 hours per year on free legal services for the poor.

GAINING A MERGERS-AND-ACQUISITIONS REPUTATION

Skadden, Arps handled its first tender offer in 1964, and Flom worked on a number of deals in the 1970s that defined the firm's reputation as a leader in corporate takeovers. "The firm's turning point occurred in 1974 when Flom represented International Nickel Corporation and successfully won control of a target company, ESB Inc.," according to Caplan. Flom saved Chicago's Marshall Field from a takeover attempt by Carter Hawley Hale in 1975, by delivering a clever piece of advice.

The firm advised takeover target Marshall Field to build stores where Carter Hawley Hale already had outlets. This potential saturation of any particular market could be seen to have anticompetitive effects under the Sherman Act, thereby inviting the possibility of Federal Trade Commission scrutiny of the merger. The antitrust aspects of the takeover overly complicated the deal. As a result of this advice, Marshall Field made itself an extremely unattractive takeover target. Flom's reputation for aggressively defending corporate-takeover clients in ways such as in the Marshall Field deal solidified his firm's reputation in mergers and acquisitions. In the late 1970s and through the 1980s, Skadden was involved in almost every major merger and acquisition in the United States.

Its reputation as the nonpareil law firm in an exciting field brought attention to Skadden. While law firms typically were reserved and press-wary, Skadden regularly garnered the type of media attention previously reserved for the most public of corporations. For example, journalist Steve Brill featured the firm in a major *Esquire* article as well as in the first issue of *American Lawyer*. The firm also attracted its share of glamour in other ways. In the early 1980s, the former president of MGM, Frank Rothman, became a partner in the Los Angeles office of Skadden.

SETBACKS, LESSONS LEARNED

Despite its reputation as a competent and respected corporate firm, Skadden stumbled at times. *Pennzoil v.*

Texaco serves as a textbook example, literally, of a spectacular defeat for the firm on an unprecedented scale. As told by Caplan, the firm's client, Texaco, acquired Getty Oil, a prudent move, according to many legal experts at the time. Unfortunately, in so doing, Texaco was found to have interfered with prior contractual relations for the sale of Getty Oil to Pennzoil. As a result of that tort, Pennzoil was awarded $10.5 billion, the largest judgment in history to that time. A procedural error on the part of Skadden may have contributed to the high award. Skadden passed up the opportunity to have the case tried in Delaware where juries, reportedly, did not favor granting such high awards.

Skadden also failed in preventing a book about the Mossad, the Israeli intelligence agency, from being published. The firm had been engaged by the government of Israel to keep the book off the shelves because it contained information that could threaten the lives of Mossad agents. Although the book was published, the commotion raised by the firm's efforts served as free publicity, piquing interest in the book from the public and multiplying the book's sales.

CHALLENGES, THEN GROWTH: 1990–99

The early 1990s were challenging for Skadden as much of its merger-and-acquisition activity dwindled during an economic recession. The firm cut staff and opted to diversify in order to shore up profits. In 1990 the firm represented Occidental Petroleum Corporation as well as American Express Company. The two firms' public offerings were the largest of the year. In 1994 Skadden worked with both the National Hockey League and the National Basketball Association during labor disputes with their respective players' associations. The firm opened an office in Singapore in 1995 to gain a stronger foothold in the Asian market.

By the mid-to-late 1990s, merger-and-acquisition activity had resumed but Skadden was making headlines for its involvement in representing President Bill Clinton in the infamous Paula Jones sexual harassment suit. Bob Bennett, a partner at Skadden, was Clinton's personal lawyer and won the case in 1998 when it was dismissed. Bennett, known for representing high-profile political clients, left Skadden in 2009 to work for competitor Hogan & Hartson.

By 1999 Skadden was part of some of the largest merger-and-acquisitions deals in the business world. During the year the firm was involved in the $81 billion Exxon Corp. and Mobil Corp. merger that created Exxon Mobil Corp., one of the largest publicly traded companies in the world. By 2000 Skadden's revenues had surpassed $1 billion, securing its position as the first U.S. law firm to reach that achievement.

SKADDEN IN THE 21ST CENTURY

To accommodate its growing workforce, Skadden moved into new headquarters in Times Square in 2000. The firm was on the advising team for the underwriters of MetLife Inc.'s public offering that year as well as representing Warner-Lambert Co. in its merger with Pfizer Inc. The firm enjoyed success during this period. Indeed, during 2001 the company was ranked first in two new *National Law Journal* surveys titled "Who Defends Corporate America" and "Who Defends Financial America." It was also named "Law Firm of 2001: The Americas" by *Global Counsel 3000*.

While the company enjoyed success during this time, it did not remain immune to tragedy. Indeed, Skadden represented Cantor Fitzgerald, a bond brokerage firm with offices on the top floors of One World Trade Center in New York City. During the terrorist attacks that occurred on September 11, 2001, Cantor Fitzgerald lost 658 employees, or nearly two-thirds of its workforce. Skadden continued to represent the company after the attacks during its rebuilding process.

Skadden remained involved in corporate restructurings including struggling retailer Kmart Corp. and was also part of litigation that would set a precedent for future cases. During 2003 the firm successfully represented State Farm Mutual Insurance Company in its case against Curtis Campbell. Campbell had been found guilty in a car accident that killed one person and disabled another. State Farm initially refused to pay the $135,000 judgment against him. Campbell and his wife then sued State Farm for bad faith and a jury awarded the Campbells' $145 million in punitive damages. The U.S. Supreme Court, however, ruled the damages were excessive and set forth future constitutional limits on punitive damages.

In addition to its domestic business, Skadden continued to focus on bolstering its international presence. Skadden represented China Construction Bank in 2005 during its initial public offering (IPO), which was considered to be the largest IPO in the world during that time. The firm continued its global expansion, opening an office in Shanghai and São Paulo in 2008. Skadden's revenues surpassed $2 billion in 2008.

Eric Friedman was named executive partner in 2009. Under his leadership, Skadden worked to overcome hardships that were brought on by the economic downturn plaguing the United States and many of its international markets. The firm cut costs and encouraged lawyers to take part in its Sidebar

Program, which allowed employees to take a year off to pursue other interests and receive one-third of their pay. While harsh economic conditions would doubtlessly bring future challenges, it appeared as though Skadden was well positioned for continued success in the years to come.

Edward C. Ingram
Updated, Christina M. Stansell

PRINCIPAL COMPETITORS

Shearman & Sterling LLP; Sullivan & Cromwell LLP; Wachtell, Lipton, Rosen & Katz.

FURTHER READING

Caplan, Lincoln. *Skadden: Power, Money, and the Rise of a Legal Empire.* New York: Farrar Straus Giroux, 1993.

Eisler, Kim Isaac. *Shark Tank: Greed, Politics, and the Collapse of Finley, Kumble, One of America's Largest Law Firms.* New York: St. Martin's Press, 1990.

"Focus—The Lawyer's Transatlantic Elite: World Beaters." *Lawyer,* February 18, 2008.

"Joseph Flom." *Institutional Investor,* June 1987, pp. 392–94.

"New Skadden Chief Still Thinks Big." *Lawyer,* March 23, 2009.

Skadden, Arps, Slate, Meagher & Flom: An Overview. New York: Skadden, Arps, Slate, Meagher & Flom, 1994.

"Skadden Looks on the Bright Side." *Lawyer,* May 25, 2009.

"Supreme Court Asked to Rule Again on State Farm Punitives." *Employment Litigation Reporter,* August 31, 2004.

Teitelman, Robert. "Flom's Way." *Institutional Investor,* February 1994.

Spir Communication S.A.

———————— ■ ————————

BP 30460, Europarc de Pichaury, Batiment D5
1330 Avenue de Guillibert de la Lauziere
Aix-en-Provence, F-13592 Cedex 3
France
Telephone: (+33 04) 42 33 65 00
Fax: (+33 04) 42 24 90 36
Web site: http://www.spir.fr

Public Company
Incorporated: 1989
Employees: 3,935
Sales: EUR 577.1 million ($785.1 million) (2009)
Stock Exchanges: Paris
Ticker Symbol: SPI
NAICS: 511110 Newspaper Publishers; 541860 Direct
Mail Advertising; 518111 Internet Service Providers

■■■

Spir Communication S.A. is one of France's leading publishers and distributors of free classified advertising newspapers, with 224 titles primarily in France, but also in Belgium, Switzerland, the Netherlands, and the Czech Republic. In France the company's free newspapers are distributed primarily as localized versions under the *Top Annonces* and *Logic-Immo* titles. Other titles in France and abroad include *Demeures & Châteaux*, *HaH*, *Helvetissimmo*, *Properties Côte d'Azur*, and *Starcq*.

Spir has responded to the ongoing shift in the classified advertising market to the Internet, launching its own range of Web sites, including Topannonces.fr and Logic-Immo.com, as well as the automotive-specific site caradisiac.com. The group's press and Internet operations, which constitute its Media division, represented 44 percent of the company's revenues of EUR 577 million ($785 million) in 2009.

Spir's Distribution division, which operates largely through subsidiary Adrexo, encompasses the company's operations in the distribution of advertising circulars, as well as a national parcel delivery service. The former represents the company's largest business, at 48 percent of sales. The parcel delivery business adds approximately 9 percent to the group's revenues. Spir is listed on the Euronext Paris Stock Exchange and is led by Louis Echelard. Newspaper publishing group Ouest-France controls nearly 65 percent of Spir.

FIRST FREE CLASSIFIEDS NEWSPAPER: 1960

France's free classifieds newspaper sector dates back to the early 1960s and the growth of a company called Carillon, founded in 1960 by Marcel Timmers, an advertising executive based in the Sarthe region. Timmers had been in charge of editing the parochial bulletins, called *Les Cloches* (The Bells), for his local parish when he hit upon the idea of selling advertisements, particularly classified advertisements, in order to cover costs.

Timmers quickly spotted the potential for extending the advertising-based format into the commercial sector. In 1960 Timmers launched what is considered to be France's first free advertisement-based newspaper, in support of a new shopping zone established near Le

Mans. Inspired by the parish newsletter, Timmers called the newspaper *Le Carillon*. This was also the name Timmers chose for his company.

This first newspaper, also known as *72 Sud* (the number referred to the department in which Le Mans is located), proved immediately successful, largely because it provided an advertising outlet for the small and local business market neglected by the country's primarily national newspapers. By the end of its first year, Timmers's company had launched its second title, *Le 61*, for the Alençon market.

Other titles followed quickly, and by 1965 the company had added newspapers in Orléans, Caen, Angers, Rennes, and Tours. Timmers continued to develop the company, which formally incorporated as Carillon in 1970. By the end of that decade Carillon had grown to nearly 20 titles.

SPIR FOUNDED: 1971

Timmers's success had by then inspired a number of other entrepreneurs to enter this promising market. These new newspapermen were, for the most part, outside of France's traditional publishing industry, with little or no experience in editing or publishing. Claude Léoni became one of the best known and most successful of this new breed of newspaper publisher. Lacking a formal education, Léoni approached publishing as a purely commercial business. Léoni developed his own free weekly, which featured limited editorial content as a framework for advertisements, and an extensive classifieds section. In 1971 Léoni launched his paper, called *Aix Hebdo*, and founded Spir Communication. Spir soon added two more titles, for the PACA (Provence-Alpes Côte-d'Azur) and Languedoc-Roussillon regions.

Léoni was not alone in the market. The 1970s saw an explosion of free newspapers as the concept quickly spread throughout France. While many of these

newspapers were launched by small, local companies, several regional and national players appeared during this period, including Comareg, founded in 1968, which grew into France's leader; Carillon; and S3G (La Société des Gratuits de Guyenne et Gascogne), founded in 1978 and targeting the southwestern region.

Despite the intense competition, Spir quickly became a major player as well, extending its reach into Normandy and other regions of France. Part of Spir's success came from its early determination to develop a vertically integrated structure. This led the company to acquire its own printing facilities, in 1975 buying a majority stake in Rotosud, based in Avignon. The company added a second printing facility in Rouen in the early 1980s, supporting its extension into France's northern regions.

Spir also founded its own newspaper distribution subsidiary, SDP, in 1979. Soon after, the company became one of the first to spot the potential offered by the new Minitel online system introduced by France's Postal Telephone and Telegraph in the early 1980s. Spir developed its own presence on the Minitel, allowing potential purchasers to look through the classified section at the company's Minitel site.

PUBLIC OFFERING: 1989

France's free press became an industry in its own right during the 1980s. By 1990 the sector counted some 500 newspapers, with a total circulation of more than 45 million, and industry-wide revenues topped FRF 5 billion (approximately $400 million). Part of the growth of the free press sector came as a result of the large-scale distribution sector, as France's supermarkets, hypermarkets, and other increasingly national retail groups rose to prominence. The door-to-door distribution model of many, if not most, of France's free papers made them a natural vehicle for the retail sector's advertising campaigns.

Spir Communication played a major role in the growth of the free press industry, maintaining its own steady expansion through the decade. Spir quickly grew into one of France's leading free press companies, behind perennial leader Comareg, and ahead of Carillon and S3B. Spir's newspaper portfolio in the late 1980s included 40 titles, with a total circulation of more than 3.5 million per week. In 1989 the company crowned its growth with a highly successful listing on the Paris Stock Exchange's Secondary Market. The company reincorporated at that time as Spir Communication S.A.

The public offering provided Spir with the backing for a new expansion of its printing capacity. In 1989 it added a third printing facility, in Reyrieux, in the

KEY DATES

1971: Claude Léoni launches *Aix Hebdo* and founds Spir Communication.

1989: Spir Communication lists on the Paris Stock Exchange.

1991: Léoni sells control of Spir to the Ouest-France newspaper group.

2002: Spir, Schibsted, and Ouest-France partner to launch *20 Minutes* in France.

2006: Spir and Schibsted launch Leboncoin classifieds Web site.

2010: Spir sells its 50 percent stake in Leboncoin to Schibsted.

Rhône-Alpes region. This facility then enabled the company to expand more deeply into the Rhône-Alpes region, as well as into the neighboring Savoy region. Spir also put into place a central advertising sales operation, called Régicom, which took over this function for the company's newspaper network.

SOLD TO OUEST-FRANCE: 1991

Claude Léoni retired from the company in 1991, selling majority control of Spir to Sofiouest–Ouest-France, a major newspaper group based on France's western region. At that time Léoni turned over the operation of Spir to his younger brother, Philippe Léoni, who then led the company through a new period of expansion that continued late into the first decade of the next century.

Soon after joining Ouest-France, Spir completed two important merger-acquisitions. The first included the purchase of 95 percent of Groupe IPS, a major newspaper printer with its own portfolio of 26 free papers in the Paris area. Spir then merged all of its printing operations into IPS, which became France's second-largest newspaper printer.

Next, Spir's SPD subsidiary took control of the Carillon group distribution activities, extending its reach into the west and central regions of France. These acquisitions helped boost Spir's total portfolio to 70 titles, with a circulation of more than six million per week. Spir's total revenues grew to EUR 150 million by the middle of the decade. The company's network by then included eight prepress facilities, four printing presses, and more than 100 distribution centers throughout the country.

The company had launched a new newspaper title by this time, the classifieds-oriented *Top Affaires*. The new format started with an edition for the city of Lyon and quickly reached a circulation of 460,000, becoming the largest in the group. The success of the *Top* format led the company to roll it out as a national brand, called *Top Annonces*.

Spir's strong growth enabled the company to move its listing to the Paris Bourse's main board in 1995. The company then put its increased capital base to work on a fresh expansion drive. Spir acquired Carillon outright during this time, adding that company's 40 titles and raising its total circulation to more than nine million per week. In 1997 the company acquired a 66 percent stake of northern France-based Le Galibot, adding another 22 free press titles and 18 distribution centers to its list.

These were followed by the takeover of Concept Multimedia in 1998. The purchase of this company gave Spir its second national title, *Logic-Immo*, a free magazine specializing in real estate advertisements. Created in 1995, *Logic-Immo* had grown to include five titles by this time. Concept Multimedia grew rapidly under Spir, reaching 75 titles in the next decade.

20 MINUTES IN 2002

These acquisitions enabled Spir to double its annual sales, which topped EUR 300 million by 2000. The company took a step in a new strategic direction that year when it decided to expand its SPD distribution operations beyond the distribution of free newspapers and advertising circulars. With one of the most extensive door-to-door distribution operations in France already in place, Spir hoped to extend into the recently deregulated market for parcel and courier deliveries as well. SPD changed its name as part of this effort, becoming Adrexo in 2000.

Both Adrexo and Concept Multimedia grew strongly, helping to raise the company's total revenues past EUR 378 million in 2001. This figure allowed the company to pass longtime rival Comareg, which had slipped for the first time amid a change in ownership. Spir's portfolio by this time included 175 free newspapers, distributed through Régicom, and the 75 *Logic-Immo* magazines distributed by Concept Multimedia.

Spir sought to broaden its operations in the new decade, notably into the rising new market for free daily newspapers. This market, which had been growing steadily in Europe at the dawn of the 21st century, was dominated by two major players, Metro, the leader, based in Sweden, and Schibsted, its main rival, based in

Norway and publisher of the *20 Minutes* format. Spir spotted an opportunity to get in on the ground floor of this promising market, and in 2002 the company agreed to join with Schibsted and Ouest-France in the creation of a French edition of *20 Minutes*.

Spir paid EUR 9.5 million for its 25 percent stake in the new company, 20 Minutes France SAS, and parent company Ouest-France acquired an additional 25 percent. The free news sheet launched later that year and by September 2002 claimed a readership of nearly one million. *20 Minutes* struggled to turn a profit, however, dragging down Spir's own balance sheet.

CATCHING UP: 2005

Despite the struggles at *20 Minutes*, Spir's own fortunes remained bright. The company's revenues had grown past EUR 505 million in 2005. Much of this growth was driven by Adrexo, which took advantage of changes in French legislation that allowed it to begin door-to-door deliveries of targeted advertising (that is, addressed to the home) packets. Adrexo was also preparing for the promised deregulation of the French (and European) postal delivery market. This was expected to occur at the beginning of 2006, allowing private companies to deliver mail. To this end, Adrexo acquired its own postal license.

By the middle of the decade, however, the company was forced to recognize that it had neglected another fast-growing trend. The growth of broadband Internet access in France in the early years of the decade had transformed this sector. With faster and, especially, unlimited access (users had previously paid by the minute with older dial-up connections), the market for Internet-based classified advertising had taken off strongly. More and more people began to migrate to new Internet-based sites offering free classified ads. Auction sites such as eBay were also growing strongly, further draining Spir's customer base.

Spir had not overlooked the Internet entirely. The company had launched its own classified Web site, petites-annonces.fr, in 1998. The growth of the free classifieds sites quickly outpaced Spir's efforts to keep up with the market, however. In 2005 Spir made a new attempt to shore up its dwindling classifieds base, announcing its decision to roll out the *Top Annonces* title across its entire portfolio of 175 free newspapers. The company also launched an accompanying Web site for the brand. Also in 2005, Spir acquired its first Internet-only classifieds operations, the automotive-specific caradisiac.com.

NEW LEADERSHIP: 2009

Spir's plans to enter the postal delivery market faced a major setback in 2006, when the European Union postponed the full deregulation of the market. Only the corporate market became deregulated, forcing Adrexo to revise its strategy. However, the company formed a new 50/50 partnership with Schibsted in 2006 in order to launch a new free classifieds Web site, called Leboncoin.fr. This Web site became one of the stars of the French Internet-based classifieds market, growing rapidly to become the market leader by the end of the decade.

Also in 2006, the company acquired a 25 percent stake in S3G, strengthening the two companies' existing relationship. Spir and Schibsted continued to explore new joint projects as well. This led to the creation of Carboatmédia Holding, which took over Spir's Caradisiac and Schibsted's La Centrale in 2007. Together, these efforts allowed Spir to post new revenue gains, of EUR 588 million in 2007 and EUR 650 million in 2008. Amid the real estate boom of the middle of the decade, the company had also posted several years of strong profits.

This growth came to a halt at the end of the decade, however. The economic crisis, provoking the collapse of the housing market, cut deeply into the group's real estate advertising business. The company was also forced to shut down its Adrexo postal service. Spir's classifieds business continued to suffer from the ongoing migration toward Internet sites, including its own. Finally, the company suffered from new legislation allowing supermarkets and other retailers to launch television advertisements. This resulted in a major drop-off for Spir's advertising delivery business as well.

Spir was forced to restructure its operations, including cutting a number of jobs. At the beginning of 2009 the company also experienced the loss of longtime head Philippe Léoni, who announced his decision to leave the company in January 2009. Patrick Leleu, former head of cable television and Internet group Noos, was named Léoni's replacement, but left the company just six months later amid a dispute over strategy with Spir's majority shareholder, Ouest-France. That company's Louis Echelard then took over as Spir's CEO. In the meantime, Spir's revenues had fallen back to EUR 577 million ($785 million) for the year. The company's losses reached EUR 93 million for the year.

LEBONCOIN SOLD: 2010

Faced with these difficulties, Spir began searching for new expansion opportunities. In August 2010 the company announced an agreement to establish an online insurance brokerage firm in partnership with a group of investors. The new company was expected to contribute to Spir's other operations by placing advertisements on the company's motor vehicle and real estate sites. Spir expected the brokerage firm to be operational by early 2011.

Spir also took steps to reduce its debt load. This led the company to agree to sell its 50 percent stake in Leboncoin to Schibsted in September 2010. As part of that transaction, Schibsted agreed to transfer its stake in Carboatmédia Holding to Spir, together with a payment of EUR 140 million. This sale was well received by the investment community, boosting the company's share price. Nevertheless, Spir itself still needed to find a convincing strategy for success in the face of its falling classifieds revenues and the other challenges facing France's free press industry.

M. L. Cohen

PRINCIPAL SUBSIDIARIES

20 Minutes France SAS (25%); Adrexo SAS; Carboatmédia Holding SAS (50%); CIP SAS (33.94%); Concept Multimédia SA (97.91%); Editions Aixoises Multimédia SAS (50%); Imprimeries IPS SAS; Inter Hebdo SAS (25%); Les Oiseaux SCI (90%); Régicom SAS; S3G Com SA (25%).

PRINCIPAL DIVISIONS

Media (Press, Internet); Distribution (Advertising, Parcels).

PRINCIPAL OPERATING UNITS

Adrexo; Imprimeries IPS; Top Annonces; Logic-Immo; Caradisiac.

PRINCIPAL COMPETITORS

Artemis S.A.; Bollore S.A.; Comareg S.A.S.; Financiere de l'Odet S.A.; La Voix du Nord S.A.; Le Dauphine Libere S.A.; Le Monde et Partenaires Associes S.A.S.; Les Editions P Amaury S.A.; Media Participations Paris S.A.; Mondadori France S.A.S.

FURTHER READING

Beuth, Marie-Catherine. "Spir Communication Plonge dans le Rouge en 2009." *Le Figaro*, February 26, 2010.

Boucaud, Pierre. "Spir, le Groupe de Communication Aixois, Malmené Ce Matin à la Bourse." *Marsactu*, February 26, 2010.

Brun, Caroline, and Joël Morio. "Un Nouveau Business: La Presse Gratuite." *Communication et Langages*, Number 93, Third Trimester, 1992, p. 6.

"Départ Surprise du PDG de Spir." *La Tribune*, January 22, 2009.

Laurent, Alexandre. "Spir Communication se Sépare de Leboncoin.fr." *Clubic*, September 22, 2010.

"Leboncoin.fr Valorisé 400 Millions d'Euros." *L'Expansion*, September 22, 2010.

Poussielgue, Grégoire. "Petites Annonces: le Modèle Economique de Spir Communication en Question." *Les Echos*, October 30, 2006, p. 30.

"Spir Communication Announces Reorganisation of Free Press Business." *ADP News France*, October 22, 2009.

"Spir Stabilise Sa Marge Malgré une Nouvelle Chute du CA." *Reuters*, July 27, 2010.

The Sports Authority, Inc.

1050 West Hampden Avenue
Englewood, Colorado 80110
U.S.A.
Telephone: (303) 200-5050
Web site: http://www.sportsauthority.com

Private Company
Incorporated: 1987
Employees: 15,825
Sales: $2.98 billion (2008)
NAICS: 451110 Sporting Goods Stores; 454110
Electronic Shopping and Mail-Order Houses

■ ■ ■

The Sports Authority, Inc. (TSA), is the largest full-line
sporting goods retailer in the United States. The
company sells a wide range of sports and fitness equipment, bikes, and athletic shoes and apparel in over 460
stores located in 45 states. TSA stores offer a host of
services including ski and snowboard rentals, skate
sharpening, racquet restringing, and a golf club trade-in
program. TSA stores are also found in Japan through a
partnership with AEON Co. Ltd. The company merged
with Gart Sports Co. in 2003 and went private in 2006.

EARLY HISTORY

The idea behind the company that would grow to
become the nation's largest sporting goods chain in just
five years came from Jack Smith, a former CEO of Herman's World of Sports, who opened the first TSA store
in Fort Lauderdale, Florida, in 1987. While at Herman's, Smith tried unsuccessfully to bring the same
comprehensive megastore concept that had fueled the
tremendous growth of Toys "R" Us and Home Depot to
the sporting goods industry. With the backing of a
group of venture capitalists, he got another chance and
set out to build his own sporting goods giant. By 1990,
he was running eight megastores, mainly in Florida, and
while his company had yet to turn a profit, the then 55-
year-old fitness enthusiast was convinced he could make
the idea work if he could obtain the capital to fund full-
scale expansion.

Joseph Antonini, then chairman of Kmart Corporation, shared Smith's confidence and acquired the sporting goods minichain for $75 million in March of that
same year. With the financial backing of the
multibillion-dollar retail giant, Smith now had the
resources he needed to implement his plans fully and
begin an expansion program that would see TSA grow
to 100 stores four years later. In 1990 the company
more than doubled its size to 19 stores. While such
rapid growth was accompanied by proportional gains in
total revenue, it did not translate well onto the balance
sheet. At the end of the fiscal year, the company
reported a loss of $3.3 million, its fourth consecutive
year in the red.

Although the company was unable to realize a
profit during these developmental years, it succeeded in
building the technological infrastructure needed to support more important long-term growth. At the expense
of short-term profits, the experienced sporting goods
executive had the foresight to invest heavily in state-of-
the-art computer systems that closely monitored

inventory. Not only would this give TSA an early technological edge on the competition; it would enable the company to keep its shelves stocked without the use of a distribution facility. The accuracy and availability of information housed in the company's extensive computer system would allow vendors to ship directly to individual stores.

GROWTH: 1991–93

In 1991, as revenues rose to $240 million, the company enjoyed its first profitable year of operation, reporting an operating income of $3.3 million. With financial support from Kmart, it was also able to again more than double the size of its operations, building 11 new stores and taking over six existing stores. The company's 36 stores now occupied a total of more than 1.5 million square feet. Although the company at this time had not won over many of the major brand names in the industry, such as Nike, its strong growth suggested that Smith's version of the sporting goods superstore was quickly gaining in popularity.

One of the key factors to its success was its ability to combine the best features of the small specialty sporting goods store and the large discount store. While other companies preceded TSA in introducing the public to the idea of a sporting goods megastore, their stores quickly gained a reputation for being warehouse type operations that offered poor service and an unpleasant shopping environment. What Smith contributed to the field were significant improvements on both counts. He made merchandise displays more attractive, investing in high-quality displays that added to the shopping experience, and staffed his stores with enough well-trained employees to give customers the type of service they might receive at a specialty store. In short, he was able to make the "big box" of the superstore workable.

The company's rapid expansion program unfolded at an even faster rate over the next two years. In 1992 sales climbed more than 70 percent while income more than tripled as 20 new stores were opened. The following year, sales increased 50 percent as earnings doubled and 24 new stores entered the fold. Again, TSA followed its simple, time-honored retailing philosophy, which included keeping shelves stocked, keeping stores clean, and providing good service. Patterned after category killers such as Home Depot and Toys "R" Us, the company did not attempt to beat the competition by undercutting their prices. Instead it tried to win customers over with shelves so densely stocked that virtually anyone would have a difficult time leaving the store empty-handed.

The company's receipts at the cash register, in keeping with its policy of "consistent everyday fair pricing," would likely fall somewhere between those of specialty sporting goods retailers and mass merchandisers. Nonetheless, while the company tried to keep its prices comparable to other sporting goods superstores, it did not take temporary price reductions to promote product sales. It simply relied on the product quality strength of its ever-increasing stable of brand names.

By the start of 1993, TSA had become less dependent on Kmart and had gained enough financial strength to fund the opening of 10 new stores on its own during the first six months of the year. As intense competition from Wal-Mart threatened Kmart's future ability to support the expansion of its top subsidiaries, TSA's increasing sense of autonomy became an even more important factor. At this time, the company also stepped up its bid to increase its share and presence by opening up multiple stores in major markets.

This growth strategy, known as "cannibalizing" because new stores sometimes "eat up" sales from existing stores in an attempt to capture a dominant overall market share, enabled the company to take advantage of economies of scale in advertising and promotion in Florida locations such as Dade and Broward counties, where it had 10 stores by the end of the year. The company also attempted to make a strong entrance in major markets such as Seattle and New York City, where it opened 15 stores.

INITIAL PUBLIC OFFERING: 1994

Just as TSA was fast becoming the largest sporting goods store in the nation, its parent company, Kmart, the second-largest retail company in the United States, struggled in the face of increasing competition from Wal-Mart, Target, and other top retailers. In August 1994, following a record $974 million loss the previous

KEY DATES

1928: Nathan Gart opens his first store.
1987: Founder Jack Smith opens first store in Fort Lauderdale, Florida.
1990: Company is acquired by Kmart Corporation.
1994: Company is spun off from Kmart and goes public; 100th store is opened.
1995: Company sales top $1 billion.
2001: New CEO Martin Hanaka refinances and refocuses company amid tumultuous times.
2003: Company merges with Gart Sports Co.
2006: The Sports Authority is taken private.
2008: Approximately 40 new stores open.

year, Kmart made the decision to take its three most successful specialty shops public to fund the renovation of its older stores and the introduction of Super Kmart Centers. TSA, along with OfficeMax and Borders-Walden bookstores, were subsequently approved for initial public offerings with the hope of raising more than $1 billion. Kmart's loss, however, proved to be a boon for Smith and TSA. On November 18, 71 percent of the company was sold to the public for around $270 million. Although TSA had always essentially run its own business, its growth would no longer be hindered by the retail giant.

That same year, TSA opened its 100th store as it recorded another record-breaking performance. Sales increased to $838 million, up 38 percent from the previous year, and earnings rose to $16.9 million, a 33 percent jump. While growing at such a rapid rate, the company managed to maintain a strong balance sheet and cash flow. With equity in excess of $250 million, cash and cash equivalents of around $37 million, and no long-term debt, the company placed itself in a favorable position to continue its aggressive national expansion program, focusing its growth on the New York metropolitan area, where it opened six stores, and Chicago, where it opened four. In addition to opening 12 stores in existing markets, the company entered several new markets, including Anchorage, Sacramento, and Tucson.

INTERNATIONAL EXPANSION, NEW VENDORS

TSA complemented its efforts toward dominating the domestic sporting goods market by also launching an international program in 1994. Its first movement

outside of U.S. borders consisted of a plan to open five new stores in Toronto. Not only did Canada offer the company a market with characteristics and dynamics similar to those in the United States, but it also featured an easily accessible supply line from existing vendors, most of whom already had Canadian operations.

That same year, the company also laid the groundwork for overseas expansion, signing a joint venture agreement with JUSCO Co., Ltd., to operate TSA stores in Japan. The country's third-largest retailer, JUSCO brought to the table a wealth of experience in property management and retail site selection as well as broad experience in working with other Western-based retailers. With an estimated size of $16 billion, the Japanese sporting goods market presented the opportunity to tap a densely populated market with high disposable income, a strong attraction to branded products, and a commitment to sports and leisure activities.

Perhaps the most visible sign of the company's arrival, however, was the addition of one of the most popular vendors in the industry, Nike. After seven years of refusing to sell to TSA, the footwear and apparel giant began selling to the fast-growing chain, paving the way for a number of upscale brands to enter the fold. Timberland and Teva quickly followed suit, adding significantly to the company's bid to offer its customers the most comprehensive array of products in the industry.

BREAKING THE BILLION-DOLLAR BARRIER IN 1995

In 1995, its first full year of operation as a publicly traded company, TSA became the first full-line sporting goods retailer to top $1 billion in sales. The now 136-store chain also proved to its investors that such unprecedented growth did not come without a concomitant boost in earnings, which increased 32 percent. A number of strategic moves contributed to the record-breaking success of the company and provided a foundation for continued growth over the long run.

Although the company had long earned high marks for its extensive product line, its reputation for customer service had not been as strong. In an effort to set itself apart from other large-format sporting goods retailers and other mass merchandisers, TSA launched a company-wide initiative to enhance customer service in each one of its stores. Known as TSA 2000, the new standard tried to address the most common complaint against the company, that employees were too busy stocking shelves to devote full attention to the needs of customers.

TSA 2000 attempted to eliminate this problem by moving receiving and stocking duties, as well as other non-selling functions, to the hours immediately prior to opening or shortly after closing, enabling associates to place a greater emphasis on listening to customers and providing information about products.

In keeping with the year's focus on improving the environment of its stores, the company also invested $4 million in new ladder-style apparel fixtures designed to display and coordinate merchandise in a more user-friendly manner. Installed to replace conventional gondolas, the in-house designed ladder fixtures enabled stores to combine graphics and coordinate presentations on the same fixture to make a more powerful impression on the customer and save store space at the same time.

Another significant merchandising presentation innovation implemented that year was the use of "statement shops," which were designated areas located near the front of the store that featured specialized footwear and related apparel from top manufactures. A New Jersey store, for instance, created a Rugged Apparel shop complete with a wooden sign with carved letters outlined in green that featured hiking boots as well as shirts, shorts, and winter flannel apparel from upscale vendors such as Woolrich, Columbia, and Jansport.

ON THE COMEBACK TRAIL

The latter half of the 1990s brought tumultuous times to the company. By 1998, when Martin Hanaka replaced the spirited, longtime CEO Jack Smith, the company was in dire need of a turnaround. Hanaka, with formidable experience at retailers Staples and Sears Roebuck & Co., inherited a litany of woes, including weakening sales of athletic shoes and clothing, burgeoning debt from years of overexpansion, and nonproducing stores, all of which had placed the company in distressed territory. For a successful turnaround, stabilizing the company and stopping losses resulting from the overexpansion, and restoring a modest level of profitability were paramount and no small tasks. One of the first steps Hanaka took was to refinance the company, fortifying the capital structure and speeding vendor payments.

The ambitious new store program was scrapped and money-losing stores were closed, including all Canadian locations. By 2000 the company had completely exited the Canadian market and reduced its ownership interest in JUSCO, later known as AEON Co. Ltd., the joint venture in Japan. Competitors as well struggled against mounting difficulties such as relentless promotional pressure, increasing markdowns, and oversaturation in the sporting goods sector. Industry insiders speculated about potential mergers, and sure enough, merger proposals were announced by both Gart Sports and Venator Group, neither of which succeeded at the time.

The next step for Hanaka's newly assembled management team was to revive the productivity of existing stores. A store-by-store edit of merchandise categories culminated in a new, variable merchandising plan by market, which increased margin rates and sales while reducing advertising costs. To encourage cross-shopping and higher average tickets, a new floor plan was designed to showcase apparel in four specialty quadrants, which created a more appealing ambience than the previous warehouse look and feel. A $30 million investment in new point-of-purchase and merchandising technology systems helped reduce inventories and increase sales; a $9.7 million refurbishing plan gave badly needed facelifts to several existing stores.

Sales in fiscal years ending 2000 and 2001 were relatively flat but the company continued to narrow its losses. In 2001, the company was scheduled to pay its first bonus in five years. According to CEO Hanaka in *Daily News Record* dated March 19, 2001, "We didn't hit a grand slam homer, but we scored some runs and we returned to a moderate level of profitability." There were no plans to open new stores in 2001, but the company was considering modest expansion for 2002 and 2003.

TSA's sales strategy, signified by the slogan "Get out and play," was designed to inspire consumers to participate or attend any type of sports, leisure, or recreational activity, and make it a meaningful part of their lifestyle. As Hanaka described to *Daily News Record*, "Our job is not just to sell product. Our job is to have fun and make sure [shoppers] have fun. We want TSA to be their place for fun." The company also embarked on a grassroots effort to promote youth physical fitness. Partnering with the Boys & Girls Clubs of America, it helped educate children on fitness and nutrition, and offered instructional clinics and fitness programs. More than 100,000 children participated in the inaugural year, culminating in championships in Fort Lauderdale with Kickball Olympics and Basketball Biathlon.

MERGING WITH GART SPORTS: 2003

By early 2003 it was apparent that a merger would be the best means for growth in the retail sporting goods industry. Sure enough, TSA forged a merger agreement with Gart Sports, a Denver-based sporting goods firm that had been established by Nathan Gart in 1928. Gart

Sports had grown steadily throughout its history. It established a superstore called the Sports Castle in 1971, which remained one of the largest retail sporting goods stores in the world until the 1980s. Thrifty Corp. purchased the company in 1986. Thrifty was then purchased by Leonard Green & Partners, LP in 1992.

Under new ownership, Gart Sports expanded during the remainder of the 1990s. In 1998 it purchased the Sportmart chain of stores. The deal secured its position as the second-largest sports retailer in the United States with 120 stores in 16 states. By the time of its merger with TSA, Gart Sports operated 180 stores in 25 states under the Gart Sports, Sportmart, and Oshman's names.

The Sports Authority and Gart Sports combination secured the retailer's position as largest sporting goods chain in the United States with 385 stores in 45 states and sales of nearly $2.5 billion. Upon completion of the deal in August 2003, company headquarters were moved to Englewood, Colorado. Hanaka assumed the chairman position of the merged company while Gart Sport's John Douglas Morton became CEO. The new management team oversaw TSA's emergence as the only national sports retail chain at the time.

TSA focused heavily on growth in 2004. As it opened new stores it worked to integrate both companies. As Morton told *Footwear News* in August 2004, "I think what the merger has done is enabled us to examine business practices on both sides of the company and focus internally on what the best practices between the two companies are." He went on to claim, "It was a very unique opportunity to put two companies together and help come up with a model to improve the performance."

GOING PRIVATE: 2006

At this time TSA faced stiff competition from regional sports retailer Dick's Sporting Goods, Inc., as well as from Wal-Mart Stores Inc. and Target Corp. By now, Morton was heading up TSA as chairman and CEO, and David Campisi had been named president. The company, suffering from lackluster same-store sales and under much scrutiny as a public entity, opted to accept a $1.3 billion buyout offer made by private-equity group Leonard Green & Partners. The transaction returned TSA to private ownership, allowing it to expand and make decisions without reaction by Wall Street investors.

Under new ownership, TSA embarked on an aggressive expansion plan. The company opened 28 new stores

in 2007 and nearly 40 in 2008. Store growth slowed in 2009 however, and as the economy in the United States weakened TSA looked for ways to remain competitive. During late 2009, the company partnered with Nintendo of America Inc. to sell the Wii interactive gaming system in its stores. It also created a new store concept called S.A. Elite, which catered to high-end sports enthusiasts. The first S.A. Elite opened in Denver in August 2010 and a second was slated to open in Highlands Ranch, Colorado, in November of that year. Morton retired from the CEO post in 2009, while remaining chairman of the company. Campisi was named CEO in 2010.

Jason Gallman
Updated, Suzanne Selvaggi; Christina M. Stansell

PRINCIPAL SUBSIDIARIES

TSA Stores, Inc.; The Sports Authority Michigan, Inc.; TSA Corporate Services, Inc.; TSA Gift Card, Inc.

PRINCIPAL COMPETITORS

Academy Sports & Outdoors, Ltd.; Dick's Sporting Goods, Inc.; Wal-Mart Stores, Inc.

FURTHER READING

Edelson, Sharon. "Smith Leaves Sports Authority." *WWD*, April 19, 1999, p. 14.

Fickes, Michael. "Fighting Back." *Sporting Goods Business*, January 19, 2001, p. 72.

"Gart & TSA: Built on Pioneering Traditions." *Retailing Today*, October 22, 2007.

Halverson, Richard. "Sports Authority Aims for $5B in Sales, 500 Stores by Year 2000." *Discount Store News*, July 17, 1995, pp. 15–16.

"Image, Presentation Key to Merchandising." *Discount Store News*, July 17, 1995, pp. 19–20.

Lloyd, Brenda. "At Sports Authority, the Fix Is In." *Daily News Record*, March 19, 2001, p. 2.

"Sports Authority Creates New Small Store Concept 'S.A. Elite.'" *Health & Beauty Close-Up*, May 17, 2010.

"The Sports Authority to Go Private." *Sporting Goods Business*, March 1, 2006.

Troy, Mike. "TSA Turnaround Inches from Endzone." *DSN Retailing Today*, April 16, 2001, p. 3.

Zmuda, Natalie. "Questioning Authority—One Year after His Company Became the Only National Sporting Goods Retailer, Sports Authority CEO Doug Morton Speaks Out on How the Chain Is Revitalizing Its Footwear Business." *Footwear News*, August 2, 2004.

Suning Appliance Chain Store Company Ltd.

68 Huaihai Road
Nanjing, 210005
China
Telephone: (+86 025) 8441 8888
Fax: (+86 025) 8446 7008
Web site: http://www.cnsuning.com

Public Company
Founded: 1990 as Suning Electrical Appliance
Employees: 120,000
Sales: CNY 58.3 billion ($8.69 billion) (2009)
Stock Exchanges: Shenzhen
Ticker Symbol: 002024
NAICS: 443112 Radio, Television, and Other Electronics Stores; 443111 Household Appliance Stores

■ ■ ■

Suning Appliance Chain Store Company Ltd. has risen to the top of China's highly competitive home appliance market, claiming the number one position in 2010. The Nanjing-based company, founded in 1990, employs over 120,000 people at more than 1,000 retail stores in 300 cities in 30 provinces. The company maintains an aggressive expansion strategy, with plans to open over 200 new stores per year, reaching more than 3,000 stores by 2020.

Suning's stores operate across four different categories: Flagship Stores, Neighborhood Stores, Specialized Stores, and Boutique Stores. The company's largest flagship stores reach 110,000 square feet of selling space, and stock as many as 300,000 different items from 300 Chinese and international brands. The company covers the full range of the home appliance sector, including air conditioning, computers, telephones and other communications products, audio-video and television, white goods including refrigerators and washing machines among others, and small appliances. Suning has also launched a discount retail format, selling demonstration models, remaindered, and B-stock items.

Other retail initiatives by the company include a move into the Internet-based B2C (business to consumer) market with the launch of the marketplace Web site Suning.cn in February 2010. Suning has also expanded outside the Chinese mainland, in 2009 buying up Hong Kong's Citicall and Japan's video game and toy retailer Laox, which also operates the MusicVox musical instruments chain. In 2010 Suning opened the first of a proposed 10 MusicVox shops in China, in Pudong, Shanghai.

Suning supports its distribution operations with an extensive network of logistics and distribution centers, with plans to have 60 centers in operation by 2015, including a new generation of large-scale modern logistics facilities. Founder and Chairman Zhang Jindong and CEO Wang Zhiquan lead Suning. The company listed on the Shenzhen Stock Exchange in 2004. Suning posted total sales of CNY 58.3 billion ($8.69 billion) in 2009.

AIR CONDITIONING NANJING IN 1990

Zhang Jindong started his career working for one of the Chinese government's state-owned enterprises (SOEs) in

KEY DATES

1990: Zhang Jindong and brother Zhang Guiping found Suning Electrical Appliance to sell air conditioners in Nanjing.

1999: Suning expands its range to become a full-scale home appliance retailer.

2004: The company goes public on the Shenzhen Stock Exchange as Suning Appliance Chain Store Company Ltd.

2009: Suning acquires retailers Laox in Japan and Citicall in Hong Kong.

2010: Suning announces plans to enter China's rural market; the company opens its first MusicVox retail store.

the 1980s. The SOEs, a product of China's centrally planned economy, dominated the country's notoriously primitive distribution sector. Retailing remained a largely undeveloped industry during the decades following the founding of the People's Republic of China. The scarcity of goods, especially home appliances, the lack of a middle class to buy them, and the reluctance of the SOEs to adopt modern retailing methods, further hampered the development of the retail appliance sector.

Nevertheless, the economic reform policies put in place by the government in the late 1970s had begun to stimulate the first stirrings of a privately owned retail sector by the end of the 1980s. A new class of entrepreneurs emerged, eager to venture beyond the restrictive atmosphere of the state-run companies.

Born in 1963, Zhang Jindong studied literature at Nanjing Normal University before taking a position with Industry Company of Gulou in Nanjing in 1984. From there Zhang moved to the Haowei clothing factory, becoming a manager by 1989. In 1990 Zhang gathered together CNY 100,000 (about $12,000) in savings to found his business with his older brother, Zhang Guiping.

The pair opened a small 200-square-meter shop called Suning Electrical Appliance on Nanjing's Ninghai Road, and began selling air conditioners, a promising product given the often-sweltering heat of the Nanjing region. Goods were scarce, however, and air conditioners remained high priced, out of the reach of the majority of people. The Zhangs recognized that the key to their growth lay in offering a strong service component, a direct break from the SOEs, which were known to be service-unfriendly.

Suning also moved to secure its supply of air conditioners, becoming one of the first companies in China to approach manufacturers directly, instead of negotiating through wholesalers and other middlemen. Suning began working with manufacturers in order to develop new air conditioner models that would appeal more directly, both in features and in price, to the country's nascent middle class. In another bold move the company agreed to pay for its goods in advance, ensuring a full inventory before the peak purchasing season in late spring and early summer. By paying cash in advance, Suning was also able to negotiate lower prices, which the company passed on to its customers, undercutting the larger state-controlled enterprises.

FULL-SCALE APPLIANCE RETAILER IN 1999

These policies helped Suning grow strongly, and the company soon began preparing to open new stores in Nanjing, before expanding into other Chinese markets. However, this effort was hampered by the company's difficulties in hiring enough college graduates to manage its new stores. In the early 1990s the SOEs still represented a more stable employment base than China's growing and volatile ranks of entrepreneurs.

Suning also came into direct conflict with the state-controlled appliance retailers, which increasingly found themselves outflanked by Suning and other fast-growing private retailers, such as Gome Electrical Appliances and others. This conflict came to a head in 1993, when appliance manufacturer Sanyo extended invitations to Suning and other private sector retailers to attend a meeting for its air conditioning agents. Zhang Jindong was chosen to address the meeting. In protest, the representatives from the eight major state-owned appliance retailers staged a walkout during Zhang's speech.

The protest backfired, and Zhang, who continued calmly delivering his speech, established his reputation as one of China's up-and-coming appliance retailers. The company's fortunes soared further that year when a heat wave struck Nanjing, sparking a run on air conditioners. Suning's lower prices and ready supply of air conditioners enabled the company easily to outpace the state-run companies. In the meantime, the growing reputation of Suning, and Zhang, enabled the company to compete more successfully for the country's college graduates, strengthening its efforts to expand into a full-fledged appliance chain.

The company hired its first college graduate in 1993. The company then set out to distinguish itself from competitors, which often staffed their counters with sales employees sent by manufacturers. Suning in contrast developed its own sales staff, allowing them to provide independent advice and assistance to customers.

The 1990s represented a major period in China's transition to a free market economy. This transition was characterized by the sudden rise of a huge middle class population, to more than 300 million by the dawn of the 21st century, along with a surge in interest for consumer goods. Suning moved to take advantage of the new market, and in 1999 redeveloped itself as a full-scale appliance retailer.

The company opened its first large-scale new format store on Huaihai Road in Nanjing that year, becoming one of China's first full-range appliance retailers. The company then announced plans to open as many as 1,500 chain stores over the next three years. While this program proved somewhat ambitious, with the company's chain reaching just 400 stores by the middle of the next decade, Suning claimed the number two position in home appliance retail, behind longtime rival Gome.

PUBLIC OFFERING IN 2004

Suning's expansion plans had been bogged down by two important obstacles. The first of these was the need to find qualified staff for its proposed new stores. In 2003 the company launched a recruiting effort, called the 1200 Project, in which it set out to hire 1,200 new college graduates per year. By 2010 this project had enabled the company to expand its payroll by more than 10,000 employees.

Financing the company's expansion remained the second obstacle to Suning's growth plans through the early years of the decade. Despite China's strong economic growth, institutional investors remained hesitant to enter the market, particularly in order to back privately held companies. While a number of companies managed to obtain listings on the Hong Kong Stock Exchange, government restrictions put listing on the mainland's Shenzhen Stock Exchange out of reach.

New government reforms eased these restrictions, however, and in July 2004 Suning became the first of China's private sector appliance companies to list its shares on the Shenzhen exchange. The offering, which reduced Zhang's stake in the company to just one-third of its shares, placed Zhang among China's wealthiest entrepreneurs. Significantly, Suning distributed shares in the company to many of its employees, and at the time of the offering, four other executives at Suning joined the country's Rich List. The company expected to create many more billionaires among its employees. Following the offering, the company changed its name to Suning Appliance Chain Store Company Ltd.

Backed by the offering, Suning launched new efforts both to add new stores and to strengthen its logistics component. The company began setting up a new series of large-scale, modern logistics facilities, starting with centers in Beijing and Hangzhou. The company also boosted its after-sales service component, launching a plan in 2005 to open up 500 new service centers.

Suning's public offering also helped to raise Suning's profile among appliance manufacturers. This led the company to reach an agreement with Chinese appliance leader Haier to form a marketing and sales joint venture in November 2004. The partnership helped strengthen the position of both companies ahead of the approaching deregulation of the Chinese appliance market, wherein China lowered its import and trade barriers to foreign companies as part of its entry into the World Trade Organization.

BEYOND CHINA IN 2009

Suning opened its largest store to date in Shanghai in 2005, in a bid to go head-to-head with Gome on its rival's home turf. The new Shanghai flagship featured a selling space of 18,000 square meters, stocking 300,000 items from more than 300 brands. Suning opened more than 200 stores through that year, allowing it to establish a presence in all of China's first-tier cities.

The company's store opening program continued strongly through the decade, topping more than 200 stores per year. The company's total neared 800 stores by the end of 2008, and topped 1,000 by mid-2010. The company then targeted China's midsized city markets, as well as expanding its operations in the first-tier markets. Suning's expansion was all the more noteworthy given the difficulties faced by its major rivals, such as Best Buy, Tamada, and Gome. That company had stumbled following fraud charges leveled against its founder Wong Kwong Yu. As a result, Suning claimed the position as China's leading home appliance retailer in 2010.

Suning had also been developing new areas of expansion. In 2008 the company launched a new discount store format, allowing it to sell off its demonstration models, B-stock (items presenting largely cosmetic damage), and remaindered and other unsold stock, at lowered prices. The following year Suning targeted its first moves outside of the Chinese mainland. The company's first move outside of China was to Japan, where Suning acquired majority control of toy and video game retailer Laox in 2009. Laox also operated a chain of musical instrument stores, called MusicVox. Soon after the Laox purchase, Suning moved into Hong Kong, acquiring Citicall Retail Management Ltd., the third-largest electronics and appliance retailer in that market.

The purchase of Laox provided Suning with an opportunity to enter new retail categories in China, including multimedia and comic books. The company made a start in this direction with the opening of the first of 10 proposed MusicVox stores in Pudong, Shanghai, in July 2010. By this time Suning had established a presence in the booming Internet-based B2C (business-to-consumer) marketplace sector. In February 2010 the company established its own Internet marketplace, Suning.cn.

With 2009 sales of CNY 58.3 billion ($8.69 billion), Suning had become China's leading home appliance company, and its largest commercial retail company. Suning then announced plans to extend its reach into China's vast retail market. The company's 2010 plans included the opening of 300 rural stores, a further 200 city-based stores, and eight foreign stores. From a tiny Nanjing storefront, Suning had grown to become China's retail giant, with no plans to slow down.

M. L. Cohen

PRINCIPAL SUBSIDIARIES

Beijing Suning Appliance Co. Ltd.; Citicall Retail Management Ltd. (Hong Kong); Hangzhou Suning Appliance Co. Ltd.; Laox (Japan).

PRINCIPAL DIVISIONS

Flagship Stores; Neighborhood Stores; Specialized Stores; Boutique Stores; MusicVox; Suning.cn.

PRINCIPAL COMPETITORS

Bailian Group; China 3C Group; Dashang Group Co., Ltd.; Gome Electrical Appliances Holding Ltd.; Shenzhen Sed Electronics Corp.; Telling Telecom Holding Company Ltd.

FURTHER READING

"Eight Chinese Retailers Vault into World's Top 250." *SinoCast Daily Business Beat*, January 21, 2010.

Flannery, Russell. "The Rivers Flows West." *Forbes Global*, November 13, 2006, p. 57.

Moore, Malcolm. "Suning Appliance King Zhang Jindong Set to Plug into Foreign Markets." *Daily Telegraph*, August 25, 2009.

"Samsung Signs $1.46 Bln Sales Agreement with Chinese Retailer." *Philippines News Agency*, March 29, 2010.

"Suning Flips the Switch on Rural Expansion Plan." *Shanghai Daily*, January 29, 2010.

"Suning Home Appliance: 2009 Net Profit Increased over 30%." *China Chain Store Franchise Association*, March 2010.

"Suning Plans Beachheads in B2C Sector." *SinoCast Daily Business Beat*, January 26, 2010.

"Suning Tightens Laox Control." *Shanghai Daily*, August 19, 2010.

"Suning to Purchase HK's Retailer Citicall." *Xinhua*, December 31, 2009.

Swagelok Company

29500 Solon Road
Solon, Ohio 44139
U.S.A.
Telephone: (440) 248-4600
Fax: (440) 349-5970
Web site: http://www.swagelok.com

Private Company
Incorporated: 1947 as Crawford Fitting Co.
Employees: 4,000
Sales: $1.3 billion (2010 est.)
NAICS: 332912 Fluid Power Valve and Hose Fitting Manufacturing; Machine Tool (Metal Cutting Types) Manufacturing; 332919 Other Metal Valve and Pipe Fitting Manufacturing; 332811 Metal Heat Treating

■ ■ ■

Swagelok Company is a leading manufacturer of fluid system components for the oil and gas, power, chemical, semiconductor, pharmaceutical, and biotechnology industries. In addition to making pipes, fittings, valves, and instruments, the firm has also developed a patented process for hardening stainless steel that is used in military, aviation, and industrial applications. Swagelok has nearly two-dozen manufacturing operations in North America, Europe, and the Far East, and its products are sold through a network of more than 200 independently owned sales and service centers in 57 countries.

BEGINNINGS

Swagelok traces its roots to 1947, when 42-year-old salesman Fred A. Lennon and engineer Cullen Crawford founded the Crawford Fitting Company in Cleveland, Ohio. The firm was created to produce Crawford's innovative design for a high-pressure pipe fitting that sealed as it was "swaged" (seated into place), which was branded the Swagelok. Lennon borrowed $500 from his wife's uncle to fund the fledgling company, which was initially run out of his apartment. Within a year he had bought Crawford's stake in the business for $2,000, and in 1950 moved its operations to a larger manufacturing facility in Cleveland. In addition to overseeing manufacturing, Lennon made sales calls and took orders, while his wife Alice typed invoices and mailed out ad circulars.

Crawford's swage design was simple but highly reliable, eliminating the need for welding to get a leak-proof seal, and it functioned well under heat and extreme pressure. It could be used in a wide range of applications, from pipelines to hydraulic fittings, and demand soon began to grow.

Crawford Fitting was managed with Lennon's "pride of perfection" philosophy, which strove for the best possible product quality, respectful treatment of employees (referred to as "associates"), a high level of job safety, a clean workplace, and sales through a network of independent distributors that handled only the Swagelok brand. Employees were provided with life insurance and tuition reimbursement programs before such benefits were common.

During the 1950s a network of regional warehouses was established to keep the firm's growing distributor ranks supplied. The company also expanded its product line to offer a wide range of tube fittings and quick-connect couplings. Developers of new technologies such as gas chromatography and other industrial researchers used the firm's products, and, as work in these areas grew, Swagelok did as well.

CAJON FOUNDED IN 1955

In 1955 Crawford Fitting established a subsidiary called Cajon Company which offered precision pipe fittings, while also enabling the parent firm to boost its production capacity. The company had by now launched a manufacturing operation in Canada, and two years later another new subsidiary called Nuclear Products Company (later known as Nupro) was created, whose products included precision metering valves. In 1958 Crawford Fitting also bought a firm called Whitey Tool and Die. Sales now stood at $2.5 million, and by decade's end the firm's distribution network had grown to serve 43 cities in 28 states, plus Canada.

Growth was now such that a new plant was needed, and in 1965 one opened in the Cleveland suburb of Solon, which would also serve as Crawford Fitting's headquarters. Two years later, the company acquired high-pressure component manufacturer Sno-Trik, as well. Swagelok brand products were now used in a wide range of applications that included diving submersibles and the breathing apparatus worn by astronauts.

In 1972 the company began selling its products to Japan, where four sales and service centers were established that would be supported by a regional warehouse. New products of this period included vacuum fittings, flexible tubing, regular and miniature quick-connect fittings, and needle and ball valves. Crawford Fitting was now seeing great interest from the oil industry, which used its products in exploration and refining operations.

SWAGELOK COMPANIES FORMED IN 1986

In 1986 the firm's operations were consolidated under the name the Swagelok Companies. The following year Swagelok strengthened its ability to produce ultrahigh-purity fittings with polished internal finishes for semiconductor applications, and sales in this category grew rapidly. New manufacturing processes, including a microprocessor-controlled welding system, were developed, as well, which led to the creation of new products and larger tubing sizes. Other new offerings of the decade included hoses, plug valves, diaphragm valves, and instrument manifolds.

Over the years both Swagelok and founder Fred Lennon had gained a reputation for secretiveness. The firm's public relations director told *Crain's Cleveland Business* in 1986 that his job was to keep Swagelok out of the papers, and *Forbes*, which began to include Lennon on its list of the 400 wealthiest Americans in 1990, could not find a photo of him taken more recently than 1957. To avoid crowds the devout Catholic attended church services at a nearby college chapel on Saturday, rather than Sunday. Swagelok was divided into several dozen subsidiaries, whose manufacturing was typically conducted in small, unmarked facilities so that production volume could be concealed. The company's unofficial motto was reportedly "Secrecy is success. Success is secrecy."

In the 1980s Swagelok products had become available nearly worldwide, reaching such places as China, South Africa, and Finland, and this reach was extended the following decade to include most of Europe. In 1992 the firm opened a new 110,000-square-foot distribution center in Solon with automated material handling capabilities, and in 1994 its first global distributor meeting was convened. Employment now stood at more than 3,000.

In 1997 the firm was officially renamed Swagelok Co., and the following year it bought MarcValve Corp. of New Hampshire, a start-up that had developed a valve for biotechnology applications, whose operations were relocated to Solon. The company now had six warehouses around the world that stocked some 8,500 different products, which could be delivered within two business days. There were more than 200 sales and service centers worldwide, which extended to Israel, Vietnam, and South America. The firm's many customers included du Pont and the U.S. Navy.

FRED LENNON DIES IN 1998

In July 1998 Fred Lennon died at the age of 92. Although he left an estate worth more than $1 billion,

---

KEY DATES

1947: Crawford Fitting is founded in Cleveland to make Swagelok brand fittings.

1965: Company moves into new headquarters/manufacturing plant in Solon, Ohio.

1986: Swagelok Companies is formed to consolidate firm's subsidiaries.

1998: Fred Lennon dies at 92; his 70 percent stake is left in trust to daughter.

2001: The SAT-12 stainless steel hardening process is introduced.

Lennon had worn suits purchased off the rack, drove a Honda Acura, and lived for 40 years in the same un-air-conditioned house. Lennon's 70 percent stake in Swagelok was left to his daughter in the form of a trust, while his son received $25 million and a nephew $1 million. The Fred A. Lennon Charitable Trust was also set up to continue his long history of giving, with up to $100 million pledged to its endowment.

Over the years Lennon's contributions to charitable causes such as the Cleveland Clinic, Gilmour Academy, and the Catholic Church had totaled an estimated $57 million, and he had also been a strong supporter of the Republican Party. During Bill Clinton's first term Lennon was ranked the largest political contributor in the United States by *Mother Jones*, giving more than a half-million dollars to the GOP and its candidates during a 30-month period.

Outside observers loudly criticized the estate planning of the fiscally conservative Lennon, which resulted in a $500 million tax liability and caused the publicity-shy billionaire's financial information to be publicly revealed in Probate Court. Some of his nine grandchildren were also reportedly unhappy with their omission from the will. In the fall of 2002 grandson William Lennon sued the estate, seeking an independent panel to run the trust that controlled Swagelok. The case was later settled out of court, with the grandchildren each reportedly receiving $1.25 million and giving up all future claims to the trust that oversaw the firm.

JENSEN FITTINGS ACQUIRED IN 2001

In January 2001 Swagelok acquired the Jensen Fittings Corp. of New York, which was renamed Swagelok Biopharm Services Co. Its product line was soon expanded to include items for the biopharmaceutical, sanitary, and food/beverage industries. The firm now had some 3,000 employees, and its annual revenues were estimated at $1 billion.

In the mid-1990s the company had launched a Web site, and as the number of online orders grew it was reconstituted as the Swagelok Products eStore, which coordinated sales and service requests with the company's local distributors, and also offered extensive information resources. The revision was an immediate success, with page views spiking into the millions over the next few months. The company now had more than 30 manufacturing, research, or distribution facilities, most in northeast Ohio, and 240 independent sales and service centers on six continents.

Swagelok's distribution partners were not employees but independent entrepreneurs. Before they could open for business, the firm required that they and their families spend two months in the United States touring manufacturing facilities and absorbing its culture. They also could not carry any other products besides Swagelok's.

SAT-12 PROCESS ANNOUNCED IN 2001

The firm had always worked to develop innovative new products and technologies, and in 2001 it announced the SAT-12 process, which enabled a dramatic hardening of stainless steel without loss of corrosion resistance. Over the years the company's engineers had received or were seeking patents on more than 500 ideas in 23 countries, and Swagelok was now filing applications for about 75 new ones each year.

In 2002 the company formed the field engineers group, a specially trained unit that worked directly with customers as well as assisting sales and service centers to solve problems and develop new products. The Swagelok Capital Products Company was also created to manage global projects that stretched beyond the range of a single region.

Acquisitions continued in 2003 with the purchase of Kenmac Ltd. of the United Kingdom, a maker of pressure regulators and piping control products. During the year the firm created the Silicon Valley-based Swagelok Semiconductor Services Co. to support the needs of the semiconductor industry, and introduced the Modular Platform Components product line, which helped system designers streamline their work.

In January 2004 company president Arthur F. Anton was named CEO, with CEO William R. Cosgrove staying on as chairman. During the year the company introduced the ALD valve series, which was designed to offer long life and rapid actuation for the atomic layer deposition field in semiconductor processing. Swagelok also received a $1.5 million U.S. Department of Energy grant to partner with Case Western Reserve University and Oak Ridge National Laboratory to find uses for the patented SAT-12 process. An additional $5.5 million was later awarded by the state of Ohio.

In 1998 the company had begun consolidating its manufacturing operations by shutting down plants such as one started in 1954 in Niagara Falls, Canada, and moving their work to Ohio. In 2005 this process continued with the relocation of Swagelok Biopharm Services Co. from North Tonawanda, New York, to Solon. The firm was also working to increase training opportunities, and had created an online learning service called Swagelok University that offered more than 350 training programs in six languages.

NEW DISTRIBUTION CENTER OPENS IN 2006

In 2006 a new $29 million, 360,000-square-foot order fulfillment/assembly center was completed adjacent to the firm's headquarters in Solon. Facilitated by tax abatements and the declaration of the area as a state Foreign Trade Zone, it enabled the firm to consolidate several Ohio operations. Swagelok was also expanding the services offered by its sales centers to include assembly of some products, and added a "make-to-stock" capability for low-volume specialty items.

In 2007 the company bought Hy-Level Industries, an Ohio-based manufacturer of automotive, electronic, and fluid power components. The firm also set up Swagelok Technology Services Co. to further develop and market the SAT-12 process, which was now being tested by the U.S. Navy for use on ship hulls.

In 2008 the company purchased Florida-based Plant Support and Evaluations, Inc., which was renamed Swagelok Energy Advisors, Inc., and relocated to Solon. The firm also acquired hose-maker Coreflex LLC of Bowie, Maryland, during the year, and sales hit a record $1.3 billion.

With the United States now entering a severe economic downturn, many manufacturers began to cut staff as orders fell, but Swagelok kept its full workforce on duty. The firm reasoned that it was more difficult to find skilled machinists than it was to keep people working, even when revenues had dropped some 20 percent from their record 2008 levels. The recent purchase of Hy-Level had in fact primarily been made to get that firm's 250 workers, many of them machinists. Swagelok's staff was kept busy building up inventory for the future and receiving extra training, with some also transferred to research and development assignments.

In 2009 plans to expand the firm's U.K. operations were announced, and in 2010 Swagelok purchased RHPS B.V. of the Netherlands, a maker of high-quality industrial pressure regulators. The company also set up a technology center in Pune, India, that would perform assembly, training, and customer service, in support of the two sales and service centers in that country. The firm now had five technology centers, with the others located in the United States, Japan, Switzerland, and China.

More than six decades after its founding in a Cleveland apartment, Swagelok Company had become a world leader in the development, manufacture, and service of high-quality fluid system components. The firm had developed a strong portfolio of products, and was also increasing its service offerings while branching out into new areas with its SAT-12 steel hardening process. It appeared well-positioned for future success.

Frank Uhle

PRINCIPAL SUBSIDIARIES

Cajon Co.; Crawford Fitting Co.; Kenmac Ltd.; Nuclear Products Co.; Sno-Trik Co.; Swagelok Biopharm Services Co.; Swagelok Capital Products Co.; Swagelok Energy Advisors, Inc.; Swagelok Marketing Co.; Swagelok Scotland (UK); Swagelok Semiconductor Services Co.; Swagelok Technology Services Co.; Whitey Tool and Die Co.

PRINCIPAL COMPETITORS

CIRCOR International, Inc.; Curtiss-Wright Corp.; ITT Corp.; Tyco Flow Control.

FURTHER READING

Ashyk, Loretta. "Success, Secrecy Fit Together at Crawford." *Crain's Cleveland Business*, February 17, 1986, p. F1.

Baranick, Alana. "Fred A. Lennon, 92, Shared His Riches." *Cleveland Plain Dealer*, July 26, 1998, p. 6B.

Bennett, David. "Swagelok, Navy Set Sail Together." *Crain's Cleveland Business*, August 13, 2007, p. 4.

Gup, Ted. "Fred Who?" *Mother Jones*, March/April 1996, pp. 39–42.

"Happy 60th!" *Machine Design*, July 12, 2007.

Hiaasen, Scott, and James F. McCarty. "Swagelok Estate Hauled into Court." *Cleveland Plain Dealer*, October 19, 2002, p. B1.

Krishnadas, K. C. "It's No Cakewalk for Swagelok Sales Partners." *Economic Times*, September 10, 1999.

———. "Swagelok Thinks Big in Solon." *Crain's Cleveland Business*, September 22, 2003, p. 1.

Shingler, Dan. "Swagelok Boss: Lean Operations Not for Us." *Crain's Cleveland Business*, June 29, 2009.

Stundza, Tom. "Swagelok Develops Its Own Process to Harden Stainless Steel." *Purchasing*, April 9, 2009, p. 26.

Tabio Corporation

———————————■———————————

2-10-70 Nanba-Naka
Naniwa-ku
Osaka, 556-0011
Japan
Telephone: (+81 06) 6632-1200
Web site: http://www.tabio.com

Public Company
Incorporated: 1977 as Dan Co. Ltd.
Employees: 215
Sales: ¥14.73 billion ($159.3 million) (2009)
Stock Exchanges: Osaka
Ticker Symbol: 2668
NAICS: 315111 Sheer Hosiery Mills; 424330 Women's, Children's, and Infants' Clothing and Accessories Merchant Wholesalers

■ ■ ■

Tabio Corporation is a specialist designer, manufacturer, distributor, and retailer of socks and hosiery. Formerly known as Dan Co. Ltd., and also as Dansox, Tabio focuses exclusively on the higher-end, high-quality socks and hosiery segment, and produces a wide range of hosiery for the women's, men's, and children's market segments. Tabio operates on a national basis in Japan, where it is one of the major hosiery producers and brands. The company distributes its products through third-party retailers as well as through its own chains of franchised and company-owned shops.

As of 2010 the company operated nearly 1,375 stores under the Sock Shop, Chaussettes, Mighty Soxer, and Tabio Homme brands, as well as the Kutsushitaya franchise format. Tabio opened its first international store in London in 2002, and has since opened three freestanding stores in that city, as well as boutiques in several department stores, including Harrods, Harvey Nichols, and Selfridges. Tabio also opened its first store in Paris in 2009. Headquartered in Osaka, the company is listed on the Tokyo Stock Exchange and is led by founder and chairman, Naomasa Ochi, and his son and company president, Katushiro Ochi. The Ochi family controls nearly 58 percent of the company. In 2009 Tabio posted total sales of ¥14.73 billion ($159.3 million).

SOCKS SELLER IN 1968

Naomasa Ochi and three partners founded the future Tabio Corporation with just ¥130,000 (approximately $10,000) in capital in Osaka in 1968. Ochi's idea was to create a wholesale distribution company specializing in socks and hosiery. With little money available for purchases, the young company found it difficult to convince Japan's socks manufacturers to supply it. Ochi's friendship with Haruhiko Yamashita, then head of another hosiery wholesaler, BS Socks, allowed the company to make a start. Yamashita agreed to supply Ochi with merchandise, collecting cash for his purchases only at the end of each month.

With a stock of goods in hand, Ochi had to decide on a name for his new company. Ochi's original inclination was to name the company *Ij*, the Japanese word for "man." When others suggested that the character for the word in Chinese might not translate appropriately as a company's symbol, Ochi turned to another word, *IjeO*.

This word, which in Japanese signified a man of good standing, was translated as "dandy" in Ochi's Japanese-English dictionary. Ochi's limited command of English led him to believe that the first syllable, *dan* was the English word for "man." As a result, Ochi named his company Dan, and launched wholesale sales under the trade name Dansox.

Dansox originally focused on the wholesale market, purchasing socks from BS Socks and other wholesalers. The company also began to build up a small network of retail clients, primarily women's clothing shops. The company struggled to turn a profit, however. Ochi recognized that in order to survive, the company would have to develop its own socks designs and contract directly with manufacturers to supply them.

Ochi's inspiration came from an order of knee socks received from BS Socks. These socks used the linking method to seam the toes, producing a smoother, more comfortable fit. Ochi went to visit the manufacturer of the knee socks, Masahiro Horiuchi, and the pair struck up a lifelong friendship. Horiuchi soon joined Ochi's company, overseeing the production of the first Dansox branded socks.

UNIT CONTROL SYSTEM INTRODUCED

Dan quickly expanded its range of socks, focusing on producing high-quality products. This quality helped attract new retail clients in the Osaka area, and the company's client base grew steadily. Developing its own product line proved costly for the company, however, and Dan soon ran up more than ¥70 million in debt. In 1973 the company came close to bankruptcy when one of its loans, for ¥5.3 million, came due. The company managed to gather together ¥3.3 million in cash, and then went to a credit bank for help. The bank agreed to extend new credit to the company, allowing Dan to stay afloat.

With demand growing, Dan expanded its network of manufacturers, allowing the company to increase its range of socks and hosiery products. On the other hand, this expansion presented the company with a new problem to solve. Manufacturers at the time required

the company to place minimum production orders of 3,000 pairs of socks for each new design. The company's client base, composed primarily of small shops, was not large enough to absorb this increase in production.

Attempts to place its products with high-volume discount department stores met with resistance. These stores complained that while Dansox represented good quality, they were too expensive to be sold in the discount channel. Dan decided instead to focus its attention on developing a retail base among the area's upscale clothing shops. The wealthier clientele in this segment provided a stronger outlet for the company's sales. The upscale sales channel also helped reinforce the company's reputation for high quality.

This reputation soon brought the company its first orders from outside of Osaka. The company had until then tracked its sales by sending sales staff to the shops to check inventory and take new orders. The company was thus able to recognize its strongest selling hosiery designs and ensure that customers could find them in the stores. However, sending sales staff to stores outside of the Osaka area would have been economically unfeasible for the still-fragile company.

Dan instead developed what it called its Unit Control System. Rather than visiting stores, the company called its retail customers at the end of the day. Store clerks then checked their inventory and were able to place new orders accordingly. The new system was quite innovative for the time, enabling the company to attract a new customer base from across Japan.

RETAILING

Dan continued to refine its tracking system as its client base grew. The Unit Control System, which enabled the company to extend its range beyond the Osaka region, nevertheless represented something of a burden for retailers, who were required to devote more and more time and energy to maintaining their inventory. The solution for this problem arose from one of Japan's bookstores, based on cards that were taken from books as they were sold. Dan developed its own card system, attaching a card to each pair of socks. When the socks were sold the salesclerks could remove the card, which was then sent back to the company. Dan thus took over the burden of overseeing its clients' inventory.

Dan's sales continued to build strongly through the decade. The company was on solid financial footing by 1977, officially incorporating as Dan Co. Ltd. that year. The company's capital by that time had grown to ¥6

```
┌─────────────────────────────────────────────┐
│                                               │
│              KEY DATES                        │
│                   ▪                           │
│                                               │
│  1968: Naomasa Ochi and partners found a      │
│        wholesale company distributing socks in│
│        Osaka, Japan.                          │
│  1977: The company incorporates as Dan Co. Ltd.│
│  1982: Dan Co. opens its first in-store retail│
│        boutique, called DOS, in Kobe.         │
│  1984: The company introduces its franchise   │
│        format, Kutsushitaya.                  │
│  1992: Dan Co. founds the CSM cooperative with│
│        its manufacturing subcontractors.      │
│  2000: The company goes public on the Osaka   │
│        Stock Exchange.                         │
│  2002: Dan Co. opens its first Tabio store, in│
│        London.                                │
│  2006: The company changes its name to Tabio  │
│        Corporation.                           │
│  2009: Tabio opens its first store in Paris.  │
│                                               │
└─────────────────────────────────────────────┘
```

million. The company continued to expand its reach, leading it to establish an office in Tokyo in 1981.

Japan's retail clothing market had also been evolving during this period. At the beginning of the 1980s more and more stores were developing into regional and national chains. As part of this movement, stores were beginning to adapt their selling practices. One change that affected Dansox especially was the decision by many chains to abandon the practice of hiring trained sales staff dedicated solely to hosiery sales.

Dansox had introduced a new line of high-quality alpaca socks during this time. This material required a higher level of care than other fabrics. The company soon found itself receiving complaints, as well as returns from customers. This underscored for Dan Co. its conviction that its retail clients needed to maintain a trained and knowledgeable sales staff. However, retailers, already hard hit by the gloomy economic climate of the time, balked at the extra expense.

Dan Co. instead took matters into its own hands. In 1982 one of the company's clients, San-ai, approached the company with the request that Dan Co. take over the socks department in its store in San-nomiya, Kobe. Dan Co. agreed, taking the opportunity to train the hosiery department's staff in its product line. The company then developed its own in-store boutique format, which it called DOS, for Dan Operation System.

CSM IN 1992

Dan Co. quickly began rolling out the DOS boutiques to other clothing and department stores in Japan. Meanwhile, Dan Co. began developing an idea to create a new retail format, dedicated solely to hosiery sales. The opportunity to pursue this idea came when the company was approached by a couple who operated a number of small tea shops in the city of Kurume in Fukuoka Prefecture. The couple hoped to convert one of their tea shops into a store specializing in the sale of socks. Dan Co. agreed, developing its own franchise concept for the store, which it called Kutsushitaya. The first of this new type of store opened in 1984. The Kutsushitaya format became hugely successful, and by the end of 1988 had expanded to more than 60 stores.

The rapid growth of the Kutsushitaya chain put a new strain on the company's inventory and distribution system. In order to provide a foundation for the chain's further growth, Dan Co. made the decision to invest in a new computerized point-of-sale (POS) system. The company's initial POS system provided a link between its retail network and its dyeing facility. The company then began preparations to extend the system to include the full range of its operations, including its manufacturing, distribution, and inspection and testing departments.

In order to carry out this extension, the company turned to its network of subcontractor factories, proposing the creation of a cooperative to back the expansion of the Kutsushitaya franchise network. That cooperative, called CSM, for Cooperative Society Kutsushitaya Mutual Prosperity, was formally created in November 1992. The new cooperative established its own headquarters and testing facility, located nearby the group's main factory suppliers.

KNITTING MACHINERY IN 1997

While Kutsushitaya grew strongly in the 1990s, Dan also achieved new success with a second company-owned store concept, called Chaussettia (later Chaussettes). This store opened its first branch in Daikanyama, Tokyo, in 1989. The following year the company established a dedicated office for the Chaussettia chain, also in Daikanyama.

Amid the recession that devastated the Japanese economy through much of the 1990s, Dan Co. faced a new challenge to its business. The world's textiles industry had undergone a major transformation during the 1980s and 1990s, with the emergence of new low-cost manufacturing markets. The economic reforms in Communist China in particular had helped to transform the global manufacturing sector, as the low wages in that country permitted manufacturers to produce clothing and other goods at lower prices than ever before.

Manufacturers around the world soon found themselves unable to compete with the flood of inexpensive goods coming from China and other low-cost markets, such as Vietnam and Indonesia, among others. Manufacturers throughout the world abandoned their own factories, turning instead to suppliers in Asia.

Dan Co. joined in on this trend, in 1994 establishing a manufacturing joint venture in Shanghai, called Shanghai Tsu-Dan-Koh Knitting Factory Corp. Dan Co.'s insistence on high quality ran counter to the low quality standards of much of the Chinese manufacturing sector during this period. However, maintaining production in Japan, and particularly incorporating the labor-intensive linking method, threatened to price the company out of business as it was forced to compete with the lower priced brands then flooding the market.

Technology provided the way forward for Dan Co. The company launched its own research and development program in cooperation with Ritsumeikan University, in order to develop the first fully automated production system using the linking method of manufacturing socks. This effort resulted in the introduction of a prototype machine in 1997.

INTERNATIONAL EXPANSION IN 2002

The introduction of this new machine was only a first step in Dan Co.'s technology drive. While the linking machine enabled the company to automate the production process, the company was still forced to carry out the post-processing of its production, including pairing, packing, folding, tagging, printing and labeling, and inspection, using traditionally labor-intensive methods. In order to compete against the flood of low-cost foreign socks and hosiery, the company needed to automate the post-processing steps as well. The company once again began developing its own machinery, starting in 2001. This effort soon resulted in the successful launch of a fully automated post-processing system.

Dan Co. had by then become a public company, listing its shares on the Osaka Stock Exchange's Second Section in 2000. Founder Naomasa Ochi, then joined by son Katushiro Ochi, remained in control of more than 58 percent of the group's shares. The public offering helped raise Dan Co.'s profile as it prepared to introduce its high-quality socks to the international market.

London became the company's first target, and in 2001 the company established a U.K. subsidiary there.

The following year Dan Co. opened its first international retail shop, on King's Road in London. The company decided to create a new brand for this store, which it called Tabio. According to the company the name stood for "The Trend and the Basics in Order." The name also evoked *tabi*, an older type of socks once worn in Japan.

The London market quickly embraced the Tabio store and the company's brightly colored and playful socks and hosiery designs. The company had opened four stores in the London area by the end of the decade. The company also placed its own in-store boutiques in a number of prominent London department stores, including Harrods and Selfridges.

BECOMING TABIO IN 2006

Meanwhile, back at home the company in 2004 launched a new retail format called Dan, specializing in men's socks. In 2006 the company changed its name to Tabio Corporation. The company then rebranded its stores under this name as well, creating the Tabio and Tabio Homme chains. The cooperative CSM also changed its name soon after, becoming Tabio Nara Corporation in 2007.

In 2008 Naomasa Ochi stepped down as the company's president after 40 years, taking up the position of chairman. Katushiro Ochi then took over as the company's head. The change in leadership corresponded with the next step in the company's international expansion. The company formed a French subsidiary in 2008, and opened a first store in Paris in 2009. Tabio also began preparing to launch its brand on a wider international scale. As one of Japan's best known and most well-respected hosiery specialists, Tabio hoped to become a good fit for the rest of the world as well.

M. L. Cohen

PRINCIPAL SUBSIDIARIES

Tabio Europe Ltd. (UK); Tabio France SARL; Tabio Nara Co. Ltd.

PRINCIPAL DIVISIONS

Kutsushitaya; Chaussettes; Others; Machinery Manufacturing.

PRINCIPAL OPERATING UNITS

Tabio; Kutsushitaya; Mighty Soxer; Tabio Homme; Chaussettes; Sock Shop.

PRINCIPAL COMPETITORS

Dim S.A.S.; Facalca Hiltex S.A. de C.V.; Faiz Joint Stock Co.; Fruit of the Loom Inc.; Golden Lady Company S.p.A.; Gunze Ltd.; Industrias Cannon S.A. de C.V.; Jockey International Inc.; Kim Vitebsk Joint Stock Co.; Nisshinbo Holdings Inc.; Ruey Tay Fibre Industrial Company Ltd.

FURTHER READING

"Architect MCA Designs London Store." *Nottingham Evening Post*, December 2, 2008.

"Denim Leggings—the Latest Sensation from Japan." *PRWeb*, March 25, 2009.

Gaudoin, Tina. "Tabio Socks." *Times*, April 2, 2005, p. 17.

"Sock Specialist Tabio Launches First Paris Store." *PRWeb*, April 24, 2009.

The TJX Companies, Inc.

770 Cochituate Road
Framingham, Massachusetts 01701-4672
U.S.A.
Telephone: (508) 390-1000
Fax: (508) 390-2828
Web site: http://www.tjx.com

Public Company
Incorporated: 1962 as Zayre Corp.
Employees: 154,000
Sales: $20.29 billion (2010)
Stock Exchanges: New York
Ticker Symbol: TJX
NAICS: 448140 Family Clothing Stores; 442299 All Other Home Furnishings Stores; 454111 Electronic Shopping; 551112 Offices of Other Holding Companies

■ ■ ■

The TJX Companies, Inc., is the largest off-price apparel and home fashions retailer in the United States and in the world, with over 2,700 stores worldwide at the end of fiscal 2009. The company operates eight retail chains that target fashion and value conscious shoppers. All of its concepts aim to offer quality brand-name merchandise at prices 20 to 60 percent below department store and specialty store regular prices. T.J. Maxx and Marshalls, the nation's first and second-largest off-price retailers respectively, operate over 1,700 stores in the United States and offer brand-name family apparel, accessories, fine jewelry, home fashions,

women's shoes, and lingerie. Marshalls, acquired by TJX in 1995, also offers a full line of family footwear and a wider assortment of menswear.

HomeGoods, a chain of off-price home fashion stores, operates some 323 stores offering giftware, accent furnishings, rugs, lamps, and seasonal merchandise. A.J. Wright, a 150-unit chain launched in 1998, offers family apparel and footwear, lingerie, accessories, home fashions, and costume jewelry. Launched in 2001 and expanded to 79 stores by 2009, HomeSense is a Canadian version of the HomeGoods chain. HomeSense was launched in the United Kingdom in 2008. The company's other international chains include Winners in Canada and T.K. Maxx in Europe.

COMPANY ORIGINS

The TJX Companies, Inc., traces its origins to Zayre Corp., parent of the Zayre Store chain of discount department stores incorporated in 1962. The first Zayre (Yiddish for "very good") store opened in Hyannis, Massachusetts, in 1956. Its founders were two cousins, Stanley and Sumner Feldberg. With sales doubling every second or third year, the Feldbergs were quick to establish new Zayre stores, which numbered more than 200 by the early 1970s. By then, the company had diversified into specialty retailing.

Among Zayre's early acquisitions was the Hit or Miss chain, an off-price chain specializing in upscale women's clothing. The first store, which opened in Natick, Massachusetts, in 1965, flourished and grew into a chain so quickly that within four years it had attracted the attention of a giant by comparison, Zayre. In 1969

COMPANY PERSPECTIVES

Since our inception, delivering value to our customers has been our mission, valuing our Associates has been at our core, returning value to our shareholders has been a constant priority and adding value to our communities has been a central pursuit. Above all else, our corporate value has always been to act with integrity which impacts everything we do.

Zayre bought the Hit or Miss chain and began its exploration of the upscale off-price fashion market. During the recession of the 1970s, Hit or Miss's results climbed so rapidly that Zayre began to think of expanding its off-price upscale apparel merchandising.

Zayre first attempted to buy the Marshalls chain, which had established itself as a retailer of off-price apparel for the whole family. When that effort failed, the company hired Bernard Cammarata, who had been top buyer for Marshalls, to essentially create a Marshalls clone. In March 1977 he opened the first T.J. Maxx in Auburn, Massachusetts.

FOCUS ON OFF-PRICE PAYS OFF: 1980–86

Within six years of that opening, Zayre had found another avenue to the off-price fashion market. In 1983 Chadwick's of Boston began to sell selected Hit or Miss items through mail-order catalogs. Hit or Miss and Chadwick's crossover operations allowed customers to handle products before ordering, and brought the frequent buyer the convenience of home shopping.

By the mid-1980s off-price specialty retailing was becoming more important to Zayre. Hit or Miss and T.J. Maxx had brought in 14 percent of the company's operating income in 1980. By the first half of 1983 these operations were producing nearly 45 percent of income. At the same time, however, Zayre was renovating its discount department stores and expanding its product mix. In 1984 Zayre entered the membership warehouse club market, launching B.J.'s Wholesale Club. Home Club, Inc., a chain of home improvement stores, was acquired the following year. While neither of these ventures was immediately profitable, Hit or Miss and T.J. Maxx continued to thrive.

By 1986 the number of Hit or Miss stores in the United States had reached 420, and sales had climbed to $300 million. Some 70 percent of its inventory was made up of nationally known brands. The remaining 30 percent consisted of standard apparel, such as turtlenecks and corduroy pants, which were produced by Hit or Miss under its own private label. With such a merchandise mix, Hit or Miss was able to sell current fashion at 20 to 50 percent less than most specialty stores.

In 1986 profits for the Zayre chain, targeting low to middle-income customers, dropped, although T.J. Maxx, Hit or Miss, and Chadwick's of Boston, targeting mid to higher-income customers, continued to grow. That year Zayre Corp. opened 35 more T.J. Maxx stores and 31 new Hit or Miss stores. Zayre Corp.'s off-price retailing chains were so successful that by 1987 Zayre organized them under one name and granted them autonomy from the decreasingly prosperous parent company.

ESTABLISHMENT OF TJX COMPANIES AND DIVESTMENT OF ZAYRE

In June 1987, just 10 years after its flagship chain, T.J. Maxx, opened its first store, The TJX Companies, Inc., was established as a subsidiary of Zayre, with Cammarata serving as president and CEO. It sold 9.35 million shares of common stock in its initial public offering; Zayre owned 83 percent of the subsidiary.

Zayre was facing several challenges during this time. In the first half of 1988, Zayre had operating losses of $69 million on sales of $1.4 billion. Observers blamed technological inferiority, poor maintenance, inappropriate pricing, and inventory pileups, and speculated that Zayre was ripe for takeover. Throughout all this, subsidiary TJX continued to yield a profit.

In October 1988 the company decided to focus on TJX. It sold the entire chain of over 400 Zayre stores to Ames Department Stores, Inc. In exchange, the company received $431.4 million in cash, a receivable note, and what was then valued at $140 million of Ames cumulative senior convertible preferred stock.

The company continued to hone in on its profitable new core business, selling unrelated operations. In June 1989 it spun off its warehouse club division, Waban, Inc., which owned B.J.'s and Home Club. Zayre gave shareholders one share of Waban for each two shares of Zayre they owned, as well as a $3.50 per share cash payment. The same month, the company acquired an outstanding minority interest in TJX. On the day it acquired the minority interest, the company merged with TJX. Later that month, the company changed its name from Zayre Corp. to The TJX Companies, Inc.

KEY DATES

■

1956: Cousins Stanley and Sumner Feldberg open their first Zayre discount department store in Hyannis, Massachusetts.

1962: The company is incorporated as Zayre Corp.

1977: The first T.J. Maxx opens in Auburn, Massachusetts.

1987: The TJX Companies, Inc., is established as a subsidiary of Zayre; TJX is taken public through an initial public offering, with Zayre retaining an 83 percent stake.

1989: Warehouse club division, including B.J.'s and Home Club, is spun off; outstanding minority interest in TJX is acquired and company merges with TJX; company name is changed from Zayre Corp. to The TJX Companies.

1992: The HomeGoods home fashions chain is launched.

1994: T.K. Maxx, modeled after T.J. Maxx, is launched in the United Kingdom.

1995: The Hit or Miss chain is divested; Marshalls is acquired from Melville Corporation for $606 million in cash and preferred stock.

2001: HomeSense, modeled after HomeGoods, begins operations in Canada.

2009: Sales surpass $20 billion for the first time.

The newly named company, headed by Cammarata, began trading on the New York Stock Exchange.

The company's transition into an off-price fashion business was relatively smooth, but the Ames preferred stock it received in the Zayre transaction proved to be a problem. This preferred stock was not registered and had no active market. While the stock was entitled to 6 percent annual dividends, Ames had the option of paying the first four semiannual dividends with more Ames preferred stock rather than cash, an option that Ames exercised for each of the payments it had met. The value of Ames preferred stock was dubious, however, since Ames had been closing stores and experiencing losses.

In April 1990 TJX established a $185 million reserve against its Ames preferred stock and contingent lease liabilities on former Zayre stores as a result of Ames's announcement of continued poor performance. That same month, Ames filed for protection from creditors under Chapter 11 of the U.S. Bankruptcy Code.

MARSHALLS PURCHASED: 1995

TJX's operations nevertheless remained solid. In 1991 T.J. Maxx, by far the company's largest division, posted record results for the 15th consecutive year since it opened. At the end of 1991 T.J. Maxx had 437 stores in 46 states. It planned to open many more stores, focusing primarily on the still sparsely penetrated southwestern United States, as well as expanding several existing stores. T.J. Maxx also planned to follow its success in jewelry and shoes by adding these departments to locations that did not already carry the items.

T.J. Maxx also planned to expand high-performance non-apparel categories, such as giftware and domestic items. In addition, T.J. Maxx embarked on an effort to enlarge a number of stores to a larger format ranging from 30,000 to 40,000 square feet. This change facilitated expansion of all departments, especially giftware and housewares, as well as other non-apparel categories. T.J. Maxx opened 21 stores during 1996 and closed 30. The chain recorded excellent sales in 1996, with an increase of 5 percent over the previous year.

The November 1995 purchase of Marshalls from the Melville Corporation for $606 million in cash and preferred stock brought TJX a prize to complement T.J. Maxx. The immediate plan called for closing certain underperforming T.J. Maxx and Marshalls stores. Marshalls opened 11 stores in 1996 and closed 53. Sales at Marshalls rose 10 percent in 1996.

Planned for 1997 were 15 openings and 50 closings. More were not expected, because many of the existing stores had performed so well. TJX credited this success with its back-to-basics approach. The prior Marshalls ownership had strayed from off-price strategies. TJX refocused the business, emphasizing non-promotional marketing, quality brand names at low prices, and timely markdowns in order to draw customers back and strongly.

Success at T.J. Maxx and Marshalls hinged on execution of the off-price concept, which demanded rapid inventory turnover at the store level. Buying was done close to customer need. Merchandise moved into warehouses and out to stores through state-of-the-art distribution centers and sophisticated inventory tracking systems. Markdowns also played a major role, adding value for customers and clearing shelves. Despite the similarities in operations, TJX was determined that T.J. Maxx and Marshalls retain distinct identities.

INTERNATIONAL EXPANSION

TJX ventured into Canada in 1990 to acquire the five-store Winners Apparel Ltd. chain. Building on the off-price concept, similar to that of T.J. Maxx, Winners opened 13 stores in 1996, bringing its total to 65. Moreover, Winners planned on opening about 13 more stores in 1997. TJX viewed Winners as a meaningful way to expand over the next several years, at the rate of about 12 new stores per year. Store sales posted an increase of 13 percent in 1996, plus an increase in operating income of 114 percent.

T.K. Maxx, launched in the United Kingdom in 1994 and inspired by the T.J. Maxx concept, caught on in 1996. Comparable store sales increased by 30 percent, outperforming any predicted sales figures. This move abroad signaled that further expansion would be key to TJX's growth strategy.

Not all the news among TJX holdings was good. Despite concerted efforts to bolster merchandise assortment and value, sales flagged at TJX's HomeGoods chain, which had been launched in 1992 as an off-price home fashions retailer. Moreover, Hit or Miss had a difficult time in the early 1990s, transitioning its business in a recessionary economy. After closing many nonperforming stores and renovating others, TJX sold this women's specialty division in September 1995 to the division's management and outside investors.

In late 1996 the company also sold its Chadwick's of Boston catalog division to Brylane L.P., owner of the Lane Bryant women's fashion chain. Proceeds from the sale totaled about $300 million in cash, a note, and certain receivables. The after-tax gain enabled TJX to repay about $500 million of debt, including the debt incurred in relation to the 1995 acquisition of Marshalls. The transaction left TJX with a stronger cash position and in a position of greater flexibility. Overall, 1996 was a banner year for The TJX Companies. Sales from continuing operations hit $6.69 billion, up from $3.98 billion in 1995, fueled largely by the Marshalls acquisition and the economies of scale it allowed TJX to achieve.

A GROWING OFF-PRICE EMPIRE

The late 1990s saw TJX leveraging the strong performance of its main chains into the launching of experimental new hybrid formats as well as brand-new chains. Having improved the performance of Home-Goods, in part through tweaking the merchandise mix by eliminating appliances and emphasizing home decorating items, the company began testing superstore concepts that combined HomeGoods with the T.J. Maxx and Marshalls formats. By the end of 1998 there were 14 of these larger, 50,000-square-foot superstores, known as T.J. Maxx 'N More and Marshalls Mega-Stores, respectively, and these units were performing well.

Also in 1998, TJX opened two T.K. Maxx stores in the Netherlands as a first tentative step onto continental Europe. These stores got off to a slower than anticipated start. The company also launched A.J. Wright in 1998, opening six stores in New England. This marked the firm's first attempt to create an off-price family clothing store for the moderate-income consumer.

As T.J. Maxx, Marshalls, and Winners continued their consistently profitable performance in the late 1990s, the HomeGoods and T.K. Maxx operations finally turned the corner into profitability in 1999. Nine more A.J. Wright outlets opened their doors in 1999, although that division remained in the red. Overall, net sales reached $8.8 billion, with more than 88 percent attributable to T.J. Maxx and Marshalls.

Cammarata took on the additional post of chairman in 1999, while Ted English was named president and COO. The following year, English was promoted to president and CEO, with Cammarata remaining chairman. English had joined TJX in 1983 as a buyer for T.J. Maxx, having previously worked for several years at Filene's Basement, the Boston-based off-price pioneer.

CONTINUED GROWTH IN THE 21ST CENTURY

TJX maintained its growth path into the new century. During 2000 alone, the T.J. Maxx store count increased by 29, both Marshalls and HomeGoods by 30, A.J. Wright by 10, Winners by 17, and T.K. Maxx by 20. Another 172 stores were added to the overall store count during 2001, although TJX did take one step backward that year, closing its three T.K. Maxx stores in the Netherlands because of their disappointing results. Also that year, TJX rolled out its latest new concept: a Canadian chain called HomeSense, which was modeled after HomeGoods.

Seven HomeSense stores began operating in 2001, all located in Ontario, and company officials were very pleased with their initial performance. Even with the poor economic environment of 2001 and the effects on consumer spending of the terrorist attacks against the United States on September 11, 2001, TJX still managed to increase revenues 12 percent, to $10.71 billion, surpassing the $10 billion mark for the first time. Net income fell slightly, however, dropping to $500.4 million from $538.1 million. TJX was also directly affected by the events of September 11, 2001. Seven company employees, traveling on business, died when their jetliner crashed into the World Trade Center.

During another year of economic uncertainty and worldwide geopolitical disturbance, TJX once again managed to achieve a 12 percent jump in revenues during 2002. All seven of the company's formats were expanded. Overall, the firm added 178 stores, bringing the total count to 1,843. The only unprofitable operation was A.J. Wright, but the company expressed high hopes for the young chain, which was already 75 units strong.

NEW LEADERSHIP TEAM BRINGS SUCCESS

During 2003 TJX acquired Bob's Stores, a chain of 31 stores based in the Northeast. The company planned to expand this chain, which catered to value-conscious male customers, and looked to the concept to aid in future growth. CEO English left in 2005 at a time when Bob's, A.J. Wright, and HomeGoods were experiencing lackluster financial results. Cammarata temporarily took over until Carol Meyrowitz, TJX president, was named CEO in 2006. TJX opted to pare back growth at those chains while shuttering its unprofitable e-commerce sites. TJX sold the Bob's chain in 2008.

Meanwhile, under the guidance of CEO Meyrowitz and Chairman Cammarata, TJX continued its international expansion efforts. T.K. Maxx opened its first store in Germany in 2007, while HomeSense made its debut in the United Kingdom in 2008. The StyleSense chain made its debut in Canada that year. Four T.K. Maxx stores opened their doors in Poland in 2009.

While TJX continued to strengthen its business, it hit an obstacle in 2007 after revealing that a hacker had stolen consumer data from its network in 2005. While the company suffered from bad press during this episode, TJX ensured both consumers and shareholders that it had taken necessary precautions to strengthen its network security. The company also set aside approximately $107 million to cover any litigation that resulted from the security breach.

THRIVING DURING TOUGH ECONOMIC TIMES

By this time, the retailing sector in the United States had been hit hard by a weakening U.S. economy and waning consumer confidence. TJX, however, stood uniquely positioned in the retail industry as many shoppers turned to off-price venues. While many retail companies pared back expansion efforts, TJX took the opposite approach. The company opened 120 new stores during 2008, followed by nearly 90 new store openings in 2009. By mid-2010 TJX was operating 903 T.J. Maxx, 819 Marshalls, 328 HomeGoods, and 154 A.J. Wright stores in the United States. In Canada there

were 208 Winners, 79 HomeSense, and 3 StyleSense stores. There were 281 T.K. Maxx and 19 HomeSense stores in Europe.

With sales surpassing the $20 billion mark in 2009, TJX planned to open an additional 130 stores during 2010. Net profits for 2009 grew by 37.8 percent over the previous year to $1.21 billion. Buoyed by strong sales and profits, TJX planned for significant international expansion in Europe as well, hoping to open an additional 500 stores by 2014. The company also announced in 2010 that it would bring the Marshalls chain into Canada the following year. Overall, the company's capital budget for 2010 was $750 million. TJX also hinted at the launch of a new off-price retail concept by the spring of 2011.

The company's customer base grew during 2009 as it began to attract more customers from the middle and high-income demographics. The company believed it had strong potential to gain additional market share as new customers came through its doors. A quote from Meyrowitz in a June 2010 *Women's Wear Daily* demonstrated the CEO's optimism. "We have seen positive business trends accelerate during the recession, underscoring our belief that there has been a fundamental shift in the consumer psyche toward value." With both sales and profits rising and more customers shopping at TJX chains than ever before, the company appeared well positioned for growth in the years to come.

Maya Sahafi
Updated, Catherine Hamrick; David E. Salamie;
Christina M. Stansell

PRINCIPAL SUBSIDIARIES

NBC Attire Inc.; Newton Buying Corp.; NBC Distributors Inc.; NBC Merchants, Inc.; TJX Incentive Sales, Inc.; Marmaxx Operating Corp.; New York Department Stores de Puerto Rico, Inc.; Newton Buying Company of CA, Inc.; Strathmex Corp.; HomeGoods, Inc.; H.G. Indiana Distributors, Inc.; H.G. Conn. Merchants, Inc.; H.G. Beverage, LLC; HomeGoods of Puerto Rico, Inc.; HomeGoods Imports Corp.; NBC Apparel, Inc.; Concord Buying Group, Inc.; AJW Merchants Inc.; NBC Manager, LLC; NBC Trust; NBC Operating, LP; NBC GP, LLC; Newton Buying Imports, Inc.; NBC Trading, Inc.; TJX Europe Limited; TJX UK TK Maxx Limited; TJX Europe Buying Group Limited; T.K. Maxx Holding GmbH; T.K. Maxx Management GmbH; T.K. Maxx GmbH & Co. KG; TJX Ireland; WMI-1 Holding Company; WMI-99 Holding Company; Winners Merchants International, L.P.; NBC

Holding, Inc.; NBC Hong Kong Merchants Limited; NBC Fashion India Private Limited; Jusy Meazza Buying Company S.r.l.; TJX Poland sp. z o.o; TJX European Distribution sp. z o.o.

PRINCIPAL COMPETITORS

Kohl's Corporation; Macy's, Inc.; Target Corporation.

FURTHER READING

Bowers, Katherine. "TJX to Launch New Off-Price Concept." *Women's Wear Daily*, June 3, 2010.

Corral, Cecile B. "TJX Companies Look to Expand Home." *Home Textiles Today*, August 20, 2007.

Duff, Mike. "Resilient Record Bodes Well for Off-Price Leader." *DSN Retailing Today*, December 10, 2001, pp. 31, 32.

Lillo, Andrea. "TJX Maps out Expansion Plans." *Home Textiles Today*, June 10, 2002, pp. 1, 27.

Pereira, Joseph. "TJX Tailor-Makes a Marshalls Plan to Revitalize Retailer." *Wall Street Journal*, October 8, 1996, p. B4.

Talley, Karen. "Marshalls Is Taking Its Off-Price Retail Approach to Canada." *Dow Jones Business News*, July 20, 2010.

Thompson, James. "Taking It to the Maxx." *Independent*, August 19, 2009.

Williams, Christopher C. "Cheap Skates Ahead." *Barron's*, October 26, 2009.

U.S. Foodservice, Inc.

———■———

9399 West Higgins Road
Rosemont, Illinois 60018
U.S.A.
Telephone: (847) 720-8000
Fax: (847) 720-8099
Web site: http://www.usfoodservice.com

Private Company
Incorporated: 1989 as JPF Holdings, Inc.
Employees: 26,000
Sales: $19.81 billion (2008 est.)
NAICS: 423850 Service Establishment Equipment and
    Supplies Merchant Wholesalers; 424410 General
    Line Grocery Merchant Wholesalers; 424490 Other
    Grocery and Related Products Merchant
    Wholesalers

■ ■ ■

U.S. Foodservice, Inc., is the second-largest distributor of food and related products in the United States, serving over 250,000 customers across the country. The company markets more than 300,000 items to restaurants, hospitals, schools, colleges and universities, hotels, government entities, and other eating establishments. The company was purchased by Royal Ahold N.V. in 2000 and became involved in an accounting scandal shortly thereafter. The overstatement of earnings led to investigations, criminal charges, and a $1.1 billion shareholder class-action lawsuit. Royal Ahold opted to sell U.S. Foodservice for $7.1 billion to private-equity firms Kohlberg Kravis Roberts & Co. and Clayton, Dubilier & Rice in 2007.

EARLY HISTORY

Several of the entities that constituted what became U.S. Foodservice started in the 19th century. Monarch Foods, for example, traces its roots to Reid-Murdock Co., a Dubuque, Iowa, company founded in 1853 to provision wagon trains heading west. John Sexton & Co. began as a tea and coffee merchant in Chicago in 1883. Sexton soon discovered hotels and restaurants were his biggest customers and he dropped his retail business altogether. Before the dawn of the 20th century, Sexton began manufacturing pickles, salad dressings, preserves, and jellies to guarantee a uniform high level of quality for his institutional customers.

Los Angeles-based S.E. Rykoff & Co. was established in 1911, and the Mazo and Lerch families started their business, Mazo-Lerch Company, in northern Virginia in 1927. Most of these wholesalers tended to specialize, selling items to local grocery stores. In the early 1930s distributors, including Mazo-Lerch Company, began offering frozen foods, primarily frozen french fries and orange juice.

SOWING THE SEEDS OF AN INDUSTRY: 1940–70

Foodservice distributors served institutional clients that provided food away from home, unlike retail distributors, who sold to grocery stores. The first distinction between the two groups came about in 1951, with the

COMPANY PERSPECTIVES

The promise that our 26,000 employees make every day—to be "Your partner beyond the plate"—is based on a set of principles that define our company, guide our business and drive our success. U.S. Foodservice: demands the highest levels of integrity; helps customers win; provides unmatched food safety and quality; is a great place to work; and invests for the long-term.

formation of the Association of Institutional Distributors. With fighting going on in Korea, the federal government reinstituted price controls, including a 16 percent ceiling on food distributors' gross profits. About a dozen companies met in Chicago to respond to that action. Because it cost more to distribute to their institutional customers than to grocery stores, the distributors wanted to be considered separately from grocery wholesalers and to have their ceiling raised to at least 21 percent. They were successful in their lobbying efforts.

The federal government also helped open up foodservice markets. Five years earlier, in 1946, the U.S. Congress passed the National School Lunch Act. Suddenly, large numbers of schoolchildren were eating cooked meals away from home, and school cafeterias became the first institutional mass market. One of the few distributors to focus on schools was the Pearce-Young-Angel Company (PYA) in the Carolinas. That same year, Consolidated Foods Corp., the precursor of Sara Lee Corporation, acquired Monarch Foods.

By the late 1950s most distributors had added frozen foods to their product lines. In 1958 Mazo-Lerch held the first food show, and was one of the first distributors to offer both custom cut meats and beverage dispenser programs. The diversification trend continued over the years, as foodservice distributors provided disposable items such as napkins and tablecloths, followed by china and glassware, then light and heavy equipment.

In 1965 Americans spent just 20 cents of every food dollar for food away from home. Total distributor sales that year were an estimated $9 billion, and the average institutional distributor had an annual volume of $1.5 billion to $2 billion. *Institutional Distributor*, in its first survey of the foodservice distribution industry, found that the average order size of respondents was $80.40, and the average number of customers was 572. The survey also found that nearly half of the

respondents sold to both grocery and institutional customers.

NATIONAL DISTRIBUTORS: 1971–82

The 1970s saw the move to broadline, multibranch organizations. Consolidated Foods bought the old PYA distribution network in 1971 and merged it with its Monarch Foods subsidiary to form PYA/Monarch, which would eventually become the foundation of U.S. Foodservice. Within a few years, PYA/Monarch had linked data-processing operations in its branches with the computer in its headquarters. S.E. Rykoff went public in 1972, one of the few foodservice distributors to do so.

The distribution industry went through a difficult period during the early 1980s, with companies under pressure as a result of inflation and economic slowdown. However, people still needed to eat, and much of the pressure was from competition. Speakers at national conferences focused on customer service, productivity, and professional development. Computers were playing a greater role in the business, enabling a distributor to provide customers with information to help control inventory, determine menu costs, and analyze profitability. As distributors became more professional, restaurant chains such as Marriott and Howard Johnson folded or reduced their self-distribution activities and focused on their restaurant operations.

By 1982 foodservice distribution was a $69 billion industry. Five companies were considered "national distributors," with a total of 168 distribution centers covering major portions of the country. PYA/Monarch and John Sexton & Co. were two of the five, joined by SYSCO Corporation of Houston, CFS Continental, Inc., and Kraft Foodservice. Despite their geographic dominance, these multibranch distributors reported combined sales in 1982 of $4.8 billion, which was 7 percent of the industry.

MAJOR ACQUISITIONS: 1983–84

Over the next several years, the big distributors made major acquisitions. S.E. Rykoff bought Sexton & Co. in 1983, in what was then the largest acquisition in the industry. The renamed Rykoff-Sexton took fourth place among foodservice distributors with $800 million in sales. CFS Continental's purchase of Publix Fruit and Produce moved it into third place, with sales in the $1.1 billion range. Number one SYSCO acquired B.A. Railton, along with Pegler, increasing its volume to over $2 billion. Meanwhile, in Greenville, South Carolina,

KEY DATES

1971: Consolidated Foods buys Pearce-Young-Angel distribution network, merges it with its Monarch Foods subsidiary to form PYA/Monarch.

1989: JPF Holdings is incorporated, acquires all the capital stock of Sara Lee subsidiary JP Foodservice Distributors, Inc.

1990: Sales surpass $1 billion.

1994: The company adopts the name JP Foodservice, Inc., and goes public.

1996: JP holds a public offering involving the sale of all the common stock held by Sara Lee.

1997: Rival Rykoff-Sexton Inc. is acquired.

1998: The company changes its name to U.S. Foodservice.

2000: Royal Ahold N.V. acquires U.S. Foodservice.

2005: Ahold agrees to pay $1.1 billion to settle a shareholder class-action suit.

2007: Kohlberg Kravis Roberts & Co. and Clayton, Dubilier & Rice purchase U.S. Foodservice for $7.1 billion.

number two PYA/Monarch bought Fleming Foodservice of Austin, Texas, raising its 1984 sales volume to an estimated $1.3 billion. By the end of its fiscal year in June 1984, PYA/Monarch was serving some 70,000 foodservice operators, and its 22 distribution centers blanketed 60 percent of the United States.

PYA/Monarch was one of the first distributors to compete as a provider of services as well as products, as well as to embrace new technology. Using the largest computer in the industry at that time, PYA/Monarch phased in a new state-of-the-art data-processing system. Totally centralized, the system made it possible for headquarters to carry out data processing for each of the 22 branches.

The 1980s saw a tremendous change in eating habits in the United States. By 1986 Americans were spending one-third of every food dollar outside the supermarket, and foodservice distribution had grown to a $78 billion industry.

CREATION OF JP FOODSERVICE: 1989

By April 1989 Sara Lee Corporation had decided to sell off the northern division of PYA/Monarch, citing dis-

satisfaction with its performance. Although the southeast division was the top food distributor in its region, overall PYA/Monarch ranked third behind SYSCO and Kraft, and Sara Lee was committed to being first or second in each of its businesses.

In June 1989 members of PYA/Monarch management incorporated a new entity, JPF Holdings, Inc. Two weeks later, on July 3, 1989, JPF Holdings acquired all the capital stock of the Sara Lee subsidiary, JP Foodservice Distributors, Inc., including the mid-Atlantic and northeastern operations of PYA/Monarch Inc. Under the terms of the leveraged buyout, Sara Lee retained ownership of PYA/Monarch, then operating in the southeast, as well as 47 percent of the shares in JP Foodservice.

Headed by James L. Miller, who had been executive vice president of PYA/Monarch's northern division, the new company immediately sold three of its branches, including Los Angeles, Little Rock, and Paducah, to Kraft Foodservice. The result was a major regional operation with nine distribution centers serving a territory stretching from Virginia north to Maine and west to Nebraska.

GROWING A NEW COMPANY

JP Foodservice Distributors passed the $1 billion mark in its first year, with sales for fiscal 1990 of $1.02 billion. That was a jump of more than 12 percent from the division's sales in fiscal 1989, and made the new company number five among the top 50 distributors selected by *Institutional Distributor*. However, Miller and the other managers had borrowed over 95 percent of the $317 million they paid for the company. With that amount of debt, and with a soft economy, JP concentrated on building the lowest cost structure in the industry.

The company invested primarily in improving facilities, adding a new $15 million replacement center between Washington, D.C., and Baltimore, and building an addition at its Allentown, Pennsylvania, warehouse that doubled freezer and cooler capacity. It also used technology to cut costs and provide greater service to its customers. For example, a handheld electronic device allowed JP customers to monitor their inventory and send information to the company.

In November 1994, five years after it was created, the company adopted the name JP Foodservice, Inc., and went public in November, listed on the NASDAQ under the symbol JPFS. Sara Lee Corporation then held 37 percent of JP common stock. The public offering raised $86 million, and JP restructured and paid off much of its debt.

JP Foodservice had more than 21,000 customers in 25 states in the mid-Atlantic, Midwest, and northeast regions of the country and was the sixth-largest food distributor. It provided customers with a broad line of products, including canned, dry, frozen, and fresh foods, paper products, detergents, and light restaurant equipment. With its debt problems resolved, the company set a new growth strategy, which, in addition to increasing internal growth, included acquiring smaller distributors. Its first purchases were Tri River Foods, Inc., and Rotelle Inc., two Pennsylvania distributors. JP's strategy also called for increasing its line of private-label products, which included Hilltop Hearth breads, Cattleman's Choice meats, and Roseli Italian foods.

INDUSTRY TRENDS

Mergers and acquisitions were also continuing in the industry as a whole. Early in 1995, Rykoff-Sexton merged with U.S. Foodservice and acquired Continental Foods of Baltimore. Foodservice distribution had grown to become a $124 billion industry, and the 10 largest distributors accounted for 18 percent of the business. JP's business, which for fiscal 1995 reached $1.12 billion, was about 55 percent independent (hospital cafeterias and family-owned restaurants) and 45 percent chains. The increasing product demands and bigger menus of the chains and large restaurants were important factors fueling consolidation among distributors.

Toward the end of 1995, the company and its former parent, Sara Lee Corporation, began talks about exchanging PYA/Monarch, Sara Lee's southeastern foodservice subsidiary, for JP stock worth about $946 million. However, the two companies failed to reach agreement on several factors, including valuation (JP's stock price had gone up in expectation of the merger), structure, and dilution of earnings to existing shareholders, and the deal fell through in February 1996.

The experience left both sides bitter, and JP was expected to find a way to reduce Sara Lee's presence or end its investment in the company altogether. That separation occurred before the end of 1996, when JP held a public offering involving the sale of all the common stock held by Sara Lee. On December 31, 1996, JP Foodservice moved to the New York Stock Exchange, trading under the symbol JPF.

EXPANSION CONTINUES: 1997–99

JP continued buying smaller companies, paying for them with $66 million raised by another stock offering. Acquisitions included Valley Industries of Las Vegas, Ar-

row Paper and Supply Company, based in Connecticut, Squeri Food Service of Cincinnati, and Mazo-Lerch Company, Inc., the 70-year-old food distributor based in northern Virginia that had held the first food fair in 1958 By the end of the fiscal year in June, net sales were up 17 percent to $1.7 billion, with acquisitions accounting for about 6 percent of the increase and the remaining 11 percent from internal growth. JP's growth was significantly higher than the 3 percent for the foodservice distribution industry as a whole.

The company credited its internal growth to sales training and promotions and to the expansion of its private and signature brands. During 1997 JP introduced Harbor Banks, a seafood line. In December 1997 the company jumped into second place among foodservice distributors with the purchase of rival Rykoff-Sexton Inc. for $1.4 billion. Unlike its previous acquisitions, Rykoff-Sexton was much larger than JP. Sales expanded significantly and the number of JP customers ballooned from 35,000 to 130,000. As a result, Standard & Poor's added JP to the S&P MidCap 400 Index. The merger also changed JP from a major distributor in the East and Midwest to one operating coast-to-coast. New territories included the Southeast, the Sun Belt, and the West Coast.

Acquisitions continued even as JP worked to assimilate the Rykoff-Sexton operations, adding Sorrento Food Service, Inc., of Buffalo, and Westlund, a Minnesota custom cut meat specialist. In February 1998 the company changed its corporate name to U.S. Foodservice and its trading symbol to UFS, and introduced a new logo.

Sales for the 1998 fiscal year that ended in June were better than expected, totaling $5.5 billion, an increase of 7 percent from 1997. Chairman and CEO Jim Miller was justifiably proud of the accomplishments, telling the *Baltimore Sun*, "We not only successfully completed the largest merger ever in our industry, tripling the size of our company, we did so achieving record earnings and meeting or exceeding virtually every goal set out in our merger plan." A few days later, the company announced it was selling the assets of its Rykoff-Sexton manufacturing division as part of its plan to shed its noncore operations.

In the $141 billion foodservice distribution industry the top 50 companies accounted for only 28 percent of sales, and most of those sales, 23.7 percent, were by the 10-largest companies. The successful integration of the larger Rykoff-Sexton made U.S. Foodservice a favorite among analysts, and the company itself indicated it was still on the lookout for purchases in the highly fragmented industry.

OVERCOMING SCANDAL: 2000–05

The company continued to make key acquisitions in the new century. Its success and industry position made it an attractive suitor. U.S. Foodservice became a target itself in 2000 when the Dutch food and supermarket conglomerate Royal Ahold N.V. made a successful $3.6 billion play for the company. Royal Ahold, with nearly $35 billion in sales during 1999, positioned U.S. Foodservice among its Ahold USA division and planned to expand the company at an even greater pace than it had experienced during the late 1990s.

During the transition phase of the acquisition, U.S. Foodservice continued to grow its business, acquiring GFG Foodservice Inc. in 2000. Alliant Exchange Inc. was purchased for $2.2 billion in 2001 and gave the company access to Alliant's health care and lodging customers in 21 geographic regions. Parkway Food Service and Mutual Wholesale Co. were also acquired that year.

The company's expansion came to an abrupt halt during 2003 when it came under fire for its accounting practices. Royal Ahold posted a $1.4 billion loss in 2002 and admitted it had overstated profits at its new U.S. Foodservice subsidiary. In fact, both companies had used fake rebates from suppliers to inflate earnings by as much as $1 billion. The Securities and Exchange Commission and the U.S. Department of Justice brought civil and criminal charges against U.S. Foodservice executives as a result.

A shareholder class-action lawsuit brought against the company ended in a $1.1 billion settlement in 2005 and was estimated to be the fifth-largest securities class-action settlement in U.S. history at the time. Michael Resnick, U.S. Foodservice's chief financial officer at the time of the scandal, was sentenced to six months of home detention and three years of probation in 2006 for his involvement.

SALE TO PRIVATE-EQUITY FIRMS: 2007

By 2007 both Royal Ahold and U.S. Foodservice looked to put scandal behind them. As U.S. Foodservice worked to restore profitability and restructure operations, Royal Ahold announced that it planned to sell the company. Private-equity firms Kohlberg Kravis Roberts & Co. and Clayton, Dubilier & Rice purchased U.S. Foodservice for $7.1 billion later that year.

With its ties to Royal Ahold in its past, the company focused once again on growing its business. By this time, U.S. Foodservice was headed by CEO Robert Aiken and was organized into three main divisions, including Broadline, which served independent restaurants and small chains, and North Star, which served multi-unit businesses. The company's Monarch Foods Group was its third division and oversaw the company's exclusive brands. Some of these brands were Beyond butter alternatives, Devonshire desserts, Bluewater frozen seafood, el Pasado Mexican entrees, Cattleman's Selection steak and ground beef, Glenview Farms dairy products, Hilltop Hearth bakery products, and Roseli pastas and Italian products.

Since its ownership transition in 2007, the company had spent $160 million in upgrading its facilities in order to improve its customer service capabilities. During 2008 the company bolstered its Broadline division with the purchase of Clark National Inc., an Indiana-based broadline foodservice distributor. With sales reaching nearly $20 billion in 2008, it appeared as though U.S. Foodservice had emerged from its troubled past and was focused on retaining its position as one of the largest foodservice distributors in the United States.

Ellen D. Wernick
Updated, Christina M. Stansell

PRINCIPAL DIVISIONS

Monarch Foods Group; Broadline; North Star.

PRINCIPAL COMPETITORS

McLane Foodservice, Inc.; Performance Food Group Company; SYSCO Corporation.

FURTHER READING

"Ahold Sheds Foodservice Company." *Gourmet Retailer*, May 4, 2007.

DeMarco, Donna. "Price Nabs Foodservice Stock." *Baltimore Business Journal*, July 24, 1998, p. 1.

Hamstra, Mark. "Ahold Takes Steps Toward Recovery." *Supermarket News*, December 22, 2003.

Hyman, Julie. "Big Merger Goes Well for U.S. Foodservice." *Washington Times*, September 14, 1998, p. D28.

"JP Foodservice, Inc., the Top 50." *Institutional Distributor*, December 1989, p. 102.

Lanchner, David. "Shopping for a Turnaround." *Institutional Investor*, November 12, 2004.

Martin, Ellen James. "JP Buys Sizable Part of Rotelle." *Baltimore Sun*, November 28, 1995, p. 1C.

Mirabella, Lorraine. "Restaurant Supplier's Profit Soars." *Baltimore Sun*, August 14, 1998, p. 3C.

Mullaney, Timothy J. "JP Foodservice Has Appetite for Rivals." *Baltimore Sun*, January 30, 1995, p. 13C.

U.S. Foodservice, Inc.

Perkins, Caroline. "U.S. Foodservice's Aiken: We're Building a Proud Legacy." *Nation's Restaurant News*, August 11, 2008.

"Royal Ahold Acquires U.S. Foodservice for $3.6B." *Nation's Restaurant News*, March 20, 2000.

"Sara Lee to Spin Off PYA-Monarch Northern Division in Executive Buyout." *Institutional Distributor*, May 1, 1989, p. 40.

Tanyeri, Dana. "The Lerch Tradition: Mazo-Lerch Is Independent, Family-Run, Built to Stay that Way." *Institutional Distributor*, July 1989, p. 8.

"The Top 50." *Institutional Distributor*, December 1990, p. 86.

Zwiebach, Elliot. "Ahold's $1.1 Billion Suit Settlement Ranks as Fifth Largest." *Supermarket News*, December 5, 2005.

Ulster Bank Ltd.

11-16 Donegall Square East
Belfast, BT1 5UB
United Kingdom
Telephone: (+44 028) 9027 6000
Fax: (+44 028) 9027 6525
Web site: http://www.ulsterbank.com

Wholly Owned Subsidiary of Royal Bank of Scotland
Founded: 1836 as Ulster Banking Company
Employees: 6,164
Total Assets: £61.751 billion ($98.8 billion)
NAICS: 522110 Commercial Banking; 523120 Securities Brokerage

■ ■ ■

Ulster Bank Ltd. is one of the oldest and largest Irish banks, operating both in Northern Ireland, where it is the largest bank, and in the Republic of Ireland, where it is the third-largest bank. The company provides a full range of commercial banking services through two divisions, Retail Markets and Corporate Markets. The Retail Markets division oversees the bank's consumer-oriented banking services, including savings, checking, lending, and debit and credit card services. The Corporate Markets division provides investment banking, foreign exchange, money market services, and lending services for the corporate and institutional sectors.

Ulster Bank's branch network includes 236 locations, with 146 in the Republic of Ireland and 90 in Northern Ireland. The bank also operates nearly 60 business banking offices, and a network of more than 1,200 automated teller machines (ATMs) throughout both Northern Ireland and the Republic of Ireland. Altogether, the company boasts a customer base of more than 1.9 million, and total assets of £61.751 billion ($98.8 billion). Ulster Bank is a wholly owned subsidiary of the Royal Bank of Scotland.

A BANK FOR ULSTER IN 1836

Ulster, the region at the north of Ireland, enjoyed strong economic growth in the first decades of the 19th century. Centered around Belfast, the region became well known for its prosperous linen industry, as well as for its prominent shipbuilding industry. The region was also a major agricultural center of Ireland. The region nevertheless remained underserved for banking services, which remained centered in Dublin in the 1830s.

However, by this time Belfast's population had grown to more than 60,000, creating a need for a strong local bank. In 1836 a group of Belfast businessmen joined together to create the Ulster Banking Company. The new bank's first branch opened in July of that year, on Belfast's Waring Street. Ulster Banking Company also issued its first series of banknotes at the same time.

The new bank sought to establish itself from the outset as a bank for the entire Ulster region. By the end of its first year the bank had opened branch offices in most of the region's major population centers, including Antrim, Armagh, Ballymoney, Cootehill, Downpatrick, Lurgan, Portadown, and Enniskillen. Ulster Banking Company also established relationships with banks in other markets, including in Dublin, London, and other cities in England, and in the United States.

COMPANY PERSPECTIVES

Our commitment to the community. Ulster Bank is one of Ireland's leading banks. But banking isn't all that matters to us. We believe in giving back to the communities we serve. We do this in two ways: By helping our staff play an active role in voluntary work, fundraising and community projects. By giving financial support through our community investment programmes and sponsorship. Ulster Bank has been at the heart of Irish life now for nearly 175 years. We're proud of our long and distinguished history. The journey we've made over the last two centuries is an important part of who we are today.

Ulster grew in prominence, despite the devastation wrought by the potato famine. By 1860 the bank prepared to establish itself as a leading Irish bank, opening its first branch office outside of Ulster, in Sligo. Two years later the bank opened a branch in Dublin. The company's strongest market remained in Ulster, however, and by the early 1880s the bank operated more than 32 branches in the region. The bank's growth prompted it to incorporate as a limited liability company in 1883. The bank then changed its name, becoming Ulster Bank Ltd.

ACQUIRED IN 1917

Ulster Bank continued to grow strongly. The company had added several more branches in Dublin by the 1890s, including a branch on Camden Street in 1888 and a branch in a landmark building on College Green in 1891. The bank added a number of branches in the future Republic of Ireland through the dawn of the 20th century, including Mullingar and Tullamore in 1892; Dundalk in 1895; Waterford, Wexford, and Cork in 1902; Limerick and Dun Laoghaire (formerly Kingstown) in 1903; and Kilkenny in 1904.

Ulster Bank's expansion continued through the years leading up to World War I, as the company continued to expand its branch network both in the Ulster region and throughout the midlands and southern regions of Ireland. Ulster Bank was one of Ireland's largest banks by the outbreak of the war, and the only Ulster-based bank with a truly national network of operations.

Despite the hardships brought on by World War I, Ulster Bank's expansion continued. New branches appeared in Clogher in 1914, Edgeworthstown in 1915, and Killyleagh in 1916. This period represented a time of change for the British banking sector, which had entered a consolidation phase creating a number of large-scale, dominant banks. Ulster Bank faced difficult trading conditions in Ireland at the same time, especially following the Easter Rising of 1916.

As a result, a number of Ulster Bank's rivals joined up with larger partners in England. For example, in 1917 Belfast Banking Company became part of the London City and Midland Bank. In order to preserve its leadership position, Ulster Bank also sought out a larger British partner. By October 1917 Ulster Bank had agreed to be acquired by London County & Westminster Bank (later Westminster Bank). The merger allowed Ulster Bank to consolidate its leadership position in Ireland, adding a number of new branches, including in Ballycastle, Ballyclare, Ballymena, Ballynahinch, Bangor, Draperstown, Dromore, Kircubbin, Newtownhamilton, and Rathfriland. Despite becoming part of the larger group, Ulster Bank continued to operate as an independent business.

PART OF NATWEST IN 1968

Following the establishment of the Republic of Ireland and the split off of Northern Ireland under British control in 1922, Ulster Bank's new branch openings slowed for a time. The company stopped printing its own banknotes after the creation of the Irish Currency Commission in 1927. Ulster Bank continued to print consolidated banknotes for the commission, and later for the Central Bank of Ireland, until 1954.

Ulster Bank began adding new services and operations in the 1920s and 1930s, including a foreign department, thrift deposit accounts, and trustee services. Hard hit by the Great Depression, the expansion of the bank's branch network remained largely on hold, with just two Belfast branches added during the decade, in 1930 and 1932. During World War II, Ulster Bank's operations faced wartime restrictions, as well as substantial bombing damage.

The postwar period brought fresh growth for the bank. Ulster Bank became one of the first in Ireland to offer personal loans, starting in 1958. The bank also experimented with modernized banking services, introducing drive-in banking to the Irish market in 1961. In the mid-1960s the bank began once again adding to its branch network. The company added several new branches in Belfast, including in Finaghy in 1960, Antrim Road and Woodstock Road in 1961, University Road in 1962, Dunmurry in 1963, Andersonstown in 1965, and Dundonald and Ormeau Road in 1966.

KEY DATES

1836: Ulster Banking Company is founded in Belfast, Ireland.

1883: The bank incorporates as a limited liability company, becoming Ulster Bank Ltd.

1917: Ulster Bank is acquired by London County & Westminster Bank (later Westminster Bank).

1968: Ulster Bank becomes part of the newly merged NatWest.

1990s: Ulster Bank adds stockbroking operations through subsidiary Ulster Bank Investment Services.

2000: Ulster Bank becomes part of the Royal Bank of Scotland Group.

2003: Ulster Bank acquires First Active in Ireland.

2010: All First Active branches are rebranded under Ulster Bank name.

Ulster Bank benefited from its position as part of NatWest. By 1974 the bank's branch network had grown to 230 locations. The bank also posted profits that year of nearly £6 million, compared to just £1 million at the start of the decade. The bank grew still stronger through the decade, particularly following NatWest's decision to transfer the Irish operations of two of its other subsidiaries, Lombard Bank and North Central Finance, to Ulster Bank. Further expansion of the company's branch network added a number of new locations, including Holywood in 1976; Claremorrie and Tandragee in 1977; Ennis, Newbridge, Maynooth, and Belfast's Kings Road in 1978; and Raphoe in 1979.

Ulster Bank became one of the first in Ireland to take advantage of new online data transfer technologies, and by 1983 had connected all of its branches to its information technology network. The company rolled out ATMs to its branch network through the decade, and then began installing ATMs in non-branch locations. By the middle of the 1990s the company operated the largest ATM network in Ireland.

The company had also added its own Visa card in 1989, followed by the launch of the Switch debit card in the 1990s. Ulster Bank also added stockbroking services during the 1990s, called Ulster Bank Investment Services, which developed total assets of some $20 billion by the dawn of the new century. The company sold off this unit to Northern Trust in 2000.

Elsewhere in Ireland, the group added a branch in Dublin Airport in 1961, Dalkey in 1962, Dublin's Dorset Street and Walkinstown Cross in 1963, Londonderry Waterside in 1963, three branches in Galway in 1964, Glengormley in 1965, and Drogheda and Newcastle in 1967, among others. Ulster Bank in this way expanded beyond the Irish town centers to serve the growing suburban population.

Ulster Bank found itself under new ownership in 1968, when parent company Westminster Bank merged with National Provincial Bank in a deal that created one of the world's top five banks. Ulster Bank became the Irish spearhead for NatWest, as the new entity was called.

EXPANSION AND STRONG GROWTH

Ulster Bank became the first in Ireland to introduce cash dispenser machines, an early form of the ATM, in 1968. The company also expanded its range of services, including the launch of a check guarantee card. In the 1970s the bank introduced its first credit cards, called Access cards, as well as adding a fleet of mobile banks to provide services to Ireland's rural areas. The company also moved into new headquarters on Donegall Place in Belfast during this decade. The outbreak of the Troubles in Northern Ireland dampened the bank's growth as its branch network became a prime target for Irish Republican Army (IRA) bombings.

PART OF ROYAL BANK OF SCOTLAND IN 2000

Ulster Bank launched a new string of branch openings through the middle of the 1990s, targeting especially the Republic of Ireland. During this period the company added operations in the towns of Bray, Celbridge, Clane, Clondalkin, Croom, Doradoyle, Donnybrook, Castleblayney, and Blanchardstown in 1994; Castletroy, Buncrana, and Ballybofey in 1995; and Athy and Belmullet in 1996. New branches added toward the end of the decade included Dungarvan and Londonderry in 1998 and Monkstown in 1999. The company also opened new head offices for its Republic of Ireland and Northern Ireland operations during this time, in Dublin in 1997 and in Belfast in 2000.

Ulster Bank found itself under a new parent company in 2000, following the takeover of NatWest by the Royal Bank of Scotland (RBS) that year. Despite the change in ownership, Ulster Bank remained an independently operating business, operating as a direct subsidiary of NatWest while providing RBS with its presence in the Irish markets. Ulster Bank then restructured its operations, spinning off its Republic of

Ireland operation into a subsidiary unit, Ulster Bank Ireland Ltd. in 2001. The new structure permitted Ulster Bank to maintain its pound-denominated operations in Northern Ireland, while its Republic of Ireland operations converted to the euro.

Ulster Bank made a rare acquisition in 2003, when it bought up First Active plc, the oldest active building society in Ireland. This gave the company a second strong brand in Ireland, as First Active's branch network continued to operate alongside the group's main Ulster Bank network.

MOBILE TELEPHONE BANKING SERVICES IN 2010

Ulster Bank remained on top of the growing new technologies available to the banking market at the dawn of the 21st century. The company acquired a stake in Mondex International, a developer of smart cards, in 1997, in order to roll out smart cards to the Irish market. In 2000 the company became the first bank in the United Kingdom to offer mobile telephone access to customer accounts. Ulster Bank had also developed online banking services by then, with the system receiving a major overhaul in 2004.

The enormous growth of mobile telephone usage in the United Kingdom and Ireland during the first decade of the new century led Ulster Bank to boost its range of services. In 1998 the company, in partnership with NatWest, had rolled out a range of short message services (SMS) for its customers. In the meantime, Ulster continued its branch opening drive, opening more than 35 new branches through the decade.

RBS placed Ulster Bank's operations under review in 2008, as the beginnings of a new economic recession began to be felt. As a result, Ulster Bank in 2009 announced its plans to end the mortgage and investment operations of First Active, cutting 750 jobs in the process. Ulster Bank completed this restructuring in 2010, rebranding the First Active branch network under the Ulster Bank name that year.

Like most of the banks in the United Kingdom, Ulster Bank struggled to overcome the worst effects of the global economic recession, particularly its exposure to the crisis-laden home mortgage sector. By 2010 the company was forced to set aside £499 million in order to cover its bad loan portfolio, driving the group into a net loss of £314 million for the year. Amid this turmoil, the group also faced the decision by its CEO, Cormac McCarthy, to step down from this position in 2011.

Ulster Bank nevertheless continued to seek out new profit centers, as well as new services for its customers.

In April 2010 the company announced plans to begin offering automobile insurance through its bank network, as well as through the Internet and telephone. The company also announced plans to extend its branch opening hours on Saturdays in 2010 in response to customer demand. Ulster also expanded its range of mobile telephone services the following month, becoming the first in the United Kingdom to launch a free application for the Apple iPhone to provide customers easier online account access. With a history reaching back nearly 175 years, Ulster Bank looked forward to the future as one of the leading Irish banks.

M. L. Cohen

PRINCIPAL SUBSIDIARIES

Easycash (Ireland) Ltd.; First Active plc; Ulster Bank (Ireland) Holdings; Ulster Bank Commercial Services Ltd.; Ulster Bank Holdings (ROI) Ltd.; Ulster Bank Ireland Ltd.; Ulster Bank Wealth.

PRINCIPAL DIVISIONS

Retail Markets; Corporate Markets.

PRINCIPAL COMPETITORS

Barclays Bank plc; DEPFA Bank plc; HBOS plc; Lloyds Banking Group; Prudential plc; Standard Chartered plc.

FURTHER READING

Carswell, Simon. "First Active Clients Switch to Ulster Bank as Name Expunged." *Irish Times*, February 13, 2010.

Noonan, Laura. "McCarthy to Step Down from Ulster Bank Top Job." *Irish Independent*, July 3, 2010.

"RBS to Review Future of Ulster Bank, First Active." *Global Banking News*, October 20, 2008.

"Royal Bank of Scotland Buys Irish Lender." *National Mortgage News*, November 10, 2003, p. 25.

"Ulster Bank Announces EUR1bn Fund for Small Companies." *Global Banking News*, March 5, 2009.

"Ulster Bank Reports £314m Loss." *BBC News*, August 6, 2010.

"Ulster Bank Reports Loss." *Global Banking News*, February 25, 2010.

"Ulster Bank to Expand Working Hours." *Global Banking News*, September 6, 2010.

"Ulster Bank to Offer Motor Insurance." *Reactions*, April 2010.

"Ulster Bank to Offer Protected Mortgage." *Global Banking News*, February 12, 2009.

United Surgical Partners International Inc.

———————— ■ ————————

15305 Dallas Parkway, Suite 1600
Addison, Texas 75001
U.S.A.
Telephone: (972) 713-3500
Fax: (972) 713-3550
Web site: http://www.unitedsurgical.com

Private Company
Incorporated: 1998
Employees: 5,500
Sales: $622.4 million (2009 est.)
NAICS: 622100 General Medical and Surgical Hospitals

■ ■ ■

Based in Addison, Texas, United Surgical Partners International Inc. (USPI) develops and acquires ambulatory surgery centers and short-stay hospitals. The company's operations are located in the United States, and also in London, England. USPI has partnered with more than 2,800 physician-owners, and each year approximately 6,500 surgeons use the company's facilities.

ORIGINS

USPI traces its roots to February 1998, when the company was established by Donald E. Steen and the New York-based equity firm Welsh, Carson, Anderson & Stowe. Steen had served as CEO of Medical Care America, a company that had become the nation's largest day surgery chain by the time it was sold to Columbia/HCA in 1994. With Steen serving as CEO,

the company embarked on a strategy of acquiring or developing surgery centers through partnerships with physicians and existing health-care systems.

USPI recorded a net loss of $6.8 million on revenues of $70.4 million in 1999. The company's revenues climbed to $135 million in 2000. However, USPI recorded a net loss of $8.3 million. USPI made its initial public offering on June 8, 2001, offering nine million shares at $14 apiece and generating $126 million. The company's shares began trading under the symbol USPI on the NASDAQ. By this time USPI either owned or managed 34 surgery centers and a private hospital. USPI's shares quickly soared in value, increasing 45.8 percent by mid-October.

By the latter part of the year USPI operated 46 surgical facilities. In addition to the United States, the company had made international inroads, with facilities in the United Kingdom and Spain. USPI was in the process of planning or establishing clinics with some of the nation's leading health-care systems, including New York-based Mount Sinai Health System and Dallas, Texas-based Baylor Health Care System.

EARLY GROWTH

A significant acquisition took place in October 2001. At that time USPI secured majority ownership in a surgery center in Sarasota, Florida, furthering its expansion in the southern United States. The state-of-the-art facility offered capabilities ranging from general surgery to orthopedics and urology. In addition, the company announced that it had signed a number of letters of intent with other hospitals, paving the way for further expansion in existing markets.

In November 2001 USPI agreed to acquire the San Gabriel Valley Surgical Center near Los Angeles, as well as the Fredericksburg, Virginia-based Surgi-Center of Central Virginia Inc. The following month an agreement was signed to acquire a 35 percent stake in the Torrance, California-based Coast Surgery Center of South Bay Inc. Additionally, plans were made to acquire the San Carlos Hospital in Murcia, Spain, bringing to 11 the number of its European facilities.

USPI ended 2001 with revenues of $244.37 million, up from $138.41 million in 2000. The company began 2002 at a strong pace, on the heels of greater than expected surgical volumes. Specifically, in 2001 USPI had experienced same-facility surgical growth of approximately 15 percent. In January the company completed its acquisition of the Coast Surgery Center of South Bay Inc. Plans were made to acquire an additional 7 to 10 facilities by the year's end.

JOINT VENTURES INTENSIFY

A number of significant joint ventures were established in 2002. Early in the year the company announced a 50-50 joint venture with Memorial Hermann Healthcare System, calling for the establishment of Sugar Land, Texas-based Sugar Land Surgical Hospital. Around the same time, USPI announced a joint venture with Northside Hospital-Cherokee and Northside Hospital to establish a network of ambulatory surgery centers and surgical specialty hospitals in the Atlanta, Georgia, area.

In August 2002 USPI announced a joint venture with Robert Wood Johnson University Hospital. The venture called for the formation of the 10,500-square-foot Robert Wood Johnson Surgery Center in East Brunswick, New Jersey. The company also acquired a majority stake in the Middleburg Heights, Ohio-based Surgery Center.

USPI began 2003 by announcing a joint venture with San Francisco-based Catholic Healthcare West, calling for the development of surgical hospitals and

surgery centers in Maricopa County, Arizona. In addition, the company completed the acquisition of Europa Hospital in Marbella, Spain. Midway through the year USPI acquired three additional surgery centers in Texas, two of which were affiliated with Baylor Health Care System. By the latter part of the year USPI either owned or had a stake in 70 surgical facilities throughout the world. USPI ended 2003 with net revenues of $446.3 million. This represented an increase from $342.4 million the previous year. The company began 2004 on a strong note. For eight consecutive quarters profits had grown at a rate of 21 percent or more.

VIABILITY OF SPANISH OPERATIONS QUESTIONED

It was around this time that some industry analysts questioned USPI's long-term strategy in Spain, noting that other markets held more significant growth potential. This was especially the case during the summer months. Because many Spaniards vacationed during the entire month of August, the company was forced to temporarily close some of its facilities during that time.

An important leadership change took place in April 2004 when William H. Wilcox, who had joined the company in 1998 as president, became CEO. Prior to that time Wilcox served as CEO of United Dental Care, president of HCA's Surgery Group, and president and CEO of HCA's Ambulatory Surgery Division. In addition, his career included a stint as president and chief operating officer of Medical Care International. After Wilcox was named CEO, Donald Steen remained with the organization as chairman.

It was also in April 2004 that USPI entered the Michigan market, via a joint venture with McLaren Health Care Corporation. Around the same time the company announced a joint venture agreement with Adventist Health System, which called for the establishment of a surgery center with Huguley Memorial Medical Center in Fort Worth, Texas. In July the company's Spanish operation, United Surgical Partners Europe, was divested via a joint venture arrangement with a private Spanish investment firm, resulting in $145 million cash to USPI.

CONTINUED EXPANSION

Growth continued during the latter part of 2004. In August USPI established a partnership with Integris Health, the largest nonprofit health system in Oklahoma. The deal resulted in the acquisition of ownership stakes in two facilities in Oklahoma City.

In September USPI announced plans to develop new ambulatory surgery centers in partnership with

```
┌─────────────────────────────────────────────┐
│                                             │
│              KEY DATES                      │
│                   ■                         │
│                                             │
│  1998:  United Surgical Partners International Inc.
│         (USPI) is established by Donald E. Steen and
│         the equity firm Welsh, Carson, Anderson &
│         Stowe.
│  2001:  USPI makes its initial public offering on June
│         8.
│  2004:  William H. Wilcox is named CEO; USPI
│         divests United Surgical Partners Europe, its
│         Spanish operation.
│  2007:  The company is acquired by Welsh, Carson,
│         Anderson & Stowe and becomes privately
│         held.
│                                             │
└─────────────────────────────────────────────┘
```

Ascension Health, which was both the nation's largest nonprofit health system and its largest Catholic health system. The following month, the company expanded in the Midwest via the acquisition of Same Day Surgery LLC. The deal resulted in the addition of five Chicago-area surgery centers. By this time USPI operated 80 facilities worldwide, 77 of which were located in the United States.

USPI finished 2004 on a high note. The company acquired 13 facilities during the fourth quarter alone. In addition, USPI saw its quarterly net income increase 49 percent. For the year, net revenues climbed 25 percent, reaching $408.2 million.

USPI continued expanding during the middle of the decade. In early 2005 the company acquired a majority ownership stake in San Antonio, Texas-based Alamo Heights Surgery Center. Midway through the year, USPI acquired a stake in the six-room Lewisville Surgery Center, which was located in the Dallas/Fort Worth area. In addition, it was during the same period that USPI added the San Antonio Endoscopic Surgery Center to its lineup.

MIDWESTERN EXPANSION

Building on the company's acquisition of several Chicago-area surgery centers in 2004, USPI cemented a joint venture agreement with Evanston Northwestern Healthcare (ENH) in mid-2005. As part of the deal, ENH secured an ownership interest in four of USPI's surgery centers. In addition, the two organizations planned to either develop or acquire new surgery centers together. Finally, through a joint venture with North Kansas City Hospital, USPI laid the groundwork to develop and operate freestanding ambulatory surgery centers in the Kansas City market.

By mid-2005 USPI either operated or had ownership stakes in 92 surgical facilities worldwide. Of these, 89 were located in the United States and 58 were owned in partnership with nonprofit health-care systems. In June the company announced a three-for-two stock split. Subsequently, the number of its outstanding shares increased from 29 million to 43.5 million.

USPI made major inroads in the St. Louis market in early 2006. At that time the company secured ownership of nine surgical centers in a deal with local physicians and the national surgery center development firm, SurgCenter. During the fourth quarter new surgery centers were established in Manitowoc, Wisconsin, and Richmond, Virginia. In addition, two facilities were acquired in Lansing, Michigan, via a deal with McLaren Health Care.

GOING PRIVATE

USPI saw its revenues reach $578.8 million in 2006, up from $469.6 million the previous year. A number of significant changes unfolded at the company in 2007. Early in the year Mark Kopser was named executive vice president and chief financial officer. Around the same time USPI agreed to be acquired by Welsh, Carson, Anderson & Stowe in a $1.8 billion deal. As part of the merger USPI's shareholders received $31.05 for each share of their common stock.

USPI's board of directors approved Welsh, Carson, Anderson & Stowe's takeover offer in January. The company's shareholders granted their approval in April. The conclusion of the deal on April 19 marked USPI's transition back to private ownership. By this time the company's operations had grown to include 150 surgery centers, 147 of which were located in the United States.

Expansion continued at USPI in 2008. That year the company celebrated its 10th anniversary and either opened or acquired ownership stakes in 14 surgery centers. Geographically, new operations were established in markets such as Portland, Oregon, and Denver, Colorado. The company ended the year with consolidated net revenue of $642.2 million, down slightly from $643.8 million in 2007.

SUCCEEDING IN DIFFICULT TIMES

USPI maintained strong momentum in 2009. That year the company added 11 new facilities to its roster, divested its interest in six others, and was in the process of developing an additional eight surgery centers. System-wide, USPI's revenue increased 10 percent and the company's domestic operations achieved same-facility revenue growth of 8 percent.

By 2010 USPI was operating in a difficult economic climate. The company faced a market characterized by high levels of unemployment, insurance plan changes, and a growing number of uninsured individuals. Although these factors definitely had an impact on USPI's surgical volumes, CEO William Wilcox was confident that the company had a strong strategy in place to weather the storm.

USPI's surgical volumes were relatively flat through the second quarter of 2010. However, the company saw its net patient services revenue grow 7 percent, reaching $462.8 million. This marked an increase from $433.9 million during the same period in 2009. The company continued to add new facilities to its operational base.

USPI had achieved remarkable growth to this point. Compared to the beginning of the decade, when the company owned or managed approximately 35 surgery centers, its operations had grown to include 172 facilities. USPI appeared to have excellent prospects for continued success during the second decade of the 21st century.

Paul R. Greenland

PRINCIPAL COMPETITORS

AmSurg Corp.; HCA Inc.; Universal Health Services, Inc.

FURTHER READING

"Initial Public Offering for Dallas-Based Surgical Group Turns Healthy Profit." *Knight-Ridder/Tribune Business News*, October 15, 2001.

"United Surgical Partners International Announces Creation of Spanish Joint Venture." *Business Wire*, July 29, 2004.

"United Surgical Partners International Announces Three-for-Two Stock Split." *Business Wire*, June 16, 2005.

"United Surgical Partners International Continues Expansion in Both Domestic and International Markets." *Business Wire*, March 24, 2003.

"United Surgical Partners International Names William H. Wilcox Chief Executive Officer." *Business Wire*, February 26, 2004.

"United Surgical Partners International Stockholders Approve Merger." *Business Wire*, April 18, 2007.

"United Surgical Partners International to Be Acquired by Welsh Carson for $31.05 Cash per Share." *Business Wire*, January 8, 2007.

Universal Electronics Inc.

6101 Gateway Drive
Cypress, California 90630-4841
U.S.A.
Telephone: (714) 820-1000
Fax: (714) 820-1010
Web site: http://www.uei.com

Public Company
Incorporated: 1986
Employees: 565
Sales: $317.5 million (2009)
Stock Exchanges: NASDAQ
Ticker Symbol: UEIC
NAICS: 334310 Audio and Video Equipment Manufacturing

■ ■ ■

Universal Electronics Inc. (UEI) develops and markets a variety of preprogrammed universal control devices, including remote controls and wireless keyboards. The company has a library of 400,000 infrared codes, allowing its products to control virtually all entertainment devices, digital media, and home systems. Under the One For All brand, UEI sells and licenses its wireless control products to distributors and retailers across North America.

The company's major customers include consumer electronics original equipment manufacturers (OEMs), the cable and satellite market, and private-label clients. UEI's major customers include Bose Corp., Denon Electronics USA LLC, Hitachi Ltd., Microsoft Corp., Sony Corp., Vizio Inc., Yamaha Corp., Comcast Communications Inc., Cox Communications Inc., DIRECTV Inc., Best Buy Co. Inc., Costco Wholesale Corp., and Wal-Mart Stores Inc. According to UEI, over 250 million people touch its technology each week.

ORIGINS

Incorporated in 1986, Universal began producing its signature and sole product the following year, the One For All television set remote control device. For founders Frank Doherty, Paul Darbee, and Frank O'Donnell, the debut of the One For All marked the introduction of a pioneering product, one that they hoped would spark explosive growth for their entrepreneurial creation. Before Universal's remote was released, those who purchased televisions were forced to purchase remotes from the manufacturer of their television. As its name implied, the One For All operated virtually any remote-controlled television, representing a major evolutionary step beyond the capabilities of existing remotes.

The distinction proved to be a marketable one, fueling remarkable growth for the Twinsburg, Ohio-based company. Profit margins were high, enabling the company to finance further advancements in technology. After being developed at the company's research and development center in Anaheim, California, later models of the One For All allowed customers to operate their audio systems and televisions with the same remote.

Under the stewardship of Thomas Tyler, Universal's first president and CEO, the company grew quickly,

COMPANY PERSPECTIVES

At UEI, we are obsessed with a certain kind of technology; the kind that makes people's lives infinitely simpler.

drawing the attention of the national business press. From $166,000 in 1988, annual revenue swelled to $50 million by 1992 and reached $89 million in 1993, the year *Business Week* listed Universal as the seventh-fastest growing company in the country.

GOING PUBLIC IN 1993

According to research sponsored by Universal, Tyler and his management team could look forward to further substantial growth. In 1993, the year Universal filed with the Securities and Exchange Commission for an initial public offering, the company sold 11.76 million remotes. The retail market was expected to expand significantly by 1997, with forecasts calling for the sale of 46 million units.

The projected growth, according to Universal's estimates, would lift retail sales from the $347 million generated within the market in 1993 to $751 million by 1997. Such prognostications caused a stir of excitement, both at Universal's headquarters and among investors. Company executives signed long-term production contracts, while investors flocked toward Universal's stock, lifting its per share price from $13 to a high of $30.

The enthusiasm swirling around Universal in 1993 was underpinned by the company's technology and the database of information the company had collected to use its technology. Universal maintained a database, or "library," of infrared codes that gave the company's products their ability to communicate with a range of electronic products. The digital codes were obtained by purchasing the original remotes sold with consumer electronics manufacturers' equipment, analyzing the codes in a lab, and then storing the codes on Universal's database, which contained nearly 40,000 individual codes.

The wealth of the company's library, which was augmented daily, enabled Universal to compete on an international basis. The remotes were manufactured overseas, primarily in Korea by a company named Kimex Electronics, and distributed in 15 other

countries. Universal sold its products to retailers such as Kmart, Wal-Mart, Montgomery Ward, Sears, and Circuit City, and to other manufacturers such as Bose, Goldstar, JVC, and Samsung. The company also supplied remotes to cable operators, including Comcast, TCI, Time Warner, and Continental. Although nearly all of Universal's sales were derived from the sale of remotes, the company also sold a line of home safety and automation products under the Eversafe brand name, which it had acquired in 1991 from Eversafe Battery for $1.6 million.

PROFOUND PROBLEMS SURFACE IN 1994

Universal's broad market reach coupled with its extensive library of digital codes pointed toward robust growth during the 1990s, particularly in light of the growth projections for the retail remote market, where the company collected more than half of its sales. The frenetic growth of the Tyler-led era came to a halt in 1994, however, just months after the company was hailed as one of the country's fastest-growing enterprises. The high profit margins enjoyed by Universal during its first years in business were gone, stripped away by the emergence of a host of competitors who drove retail prices downward.

During a six-month period ending January 1993, for instance, the retail price of remotes had plunged 40 percent. Universal was also crippled by excess inventory, a result of long-term production contracts that saddled the company with large, slow-moving supplies of merchandise. In addition, Universal suffered from what it termed "production difficulties," according to a statement filed with the Securities and Exchange Commission. By December 1994 the company was hobbled by $14.7 million in backlog orders, including $2.4 million worth of orders from cable operators that it could not ship because of Universal's production difficulties.

After Universal posted a staggering loss of $12.8 million in 1994, Tyler left the company, vacating his posts as president and CEO in January 1995. His replacement had joined the company one month earlier, having spent the previous five years at Mr. Coffee. At Mr. Coffee, David M. Gabrielsen had risen to the offices of executive vice president and COO, the same posts he occupied when he was hired by Universal in December 1994. When Tyler left the company in January, Gabrielsen was promoted to president and CEO, inheriting control over a company that had spent the previous 12 months losing money.

KEY DATES

1987: The One For All universal television remote control device debuts.
1991: The company acquires the Eversafe brand.
1995: Universal restructures under new leadership.
1997: Management announces plans to exit the domestic retail market for universal remotes.
1998: Camille Jayne assumes leadership of Universal.
2001: Paul Arling is named chairman.
2004: The company signs deals to provide remote controls to Sky Italia and La Television Par Satellite; SimpleDevices Inc. is acquired.
2005: UEI secures a supply partnership with Multichoice Africa Pty Ltd.
2008: UEI and Audiovox Accessories Corp. form a partnership.
2009: Revenues surpass $300 million; Zilog Inc.'s remote control business is acquired.

OVERCOMING HARDSHIPS

Gabrielsen faced a daunting task when he took over early in 1995. The company's relationship with banks that issued lines of credit had deteriorated, as had the company's reputation among creditors, vendors, and customers. The prices of its shares had toppled from a high of $30 to $4, further eroding any confidence in the company. In an interview with the trade publication *HFN* on January 1, 1996, Gabrielsen shared his recollection of Universal's condition at the beginning of 1995: "We had issues with inventory. We had far too much. We had issues with our information systems. We had issues with turnaround time with our vendors. We had product development issues; not getting product to the marketplace. Our market share was declining."

Although Gabrielsen faced numerous problems, perhaps the most threatening challenge was presented by the complexion of the retail market. Retail sales were crucial to Universal's financial well-being, but since it had introduced the One For All, other companies had followed suit and had begun producing similar products. The existence of a variety of universal remotes induced competitive pricing, making it harder to make a profit. During Gabrielsen's first three months at the helm, Universal posted another loss of $2.5 million, but he nevertheless did make progress.

Gabrielsen reduced the company's direct sales force, turning instead to independent representatives, and

brought in senior and middle-level executives who had worked at Mr. Coffee. Gradually, Universal's reputation among its business associates began to improve, and the company, with revamped retail lines, narrowed its losses as it slowly reduced its bloated inventories. By the end of 1995, the value of the company's stock had doubled, reinvigorated by three consecutive profitable quarters. For the year, the company posted a profit, albeit meager, of $320,000.

Although the company was far from reclaiming the vitality that characterized its growth during its first five years in business, Gabrielsen was convinced full recovery was near. In a January 1996 interview with *HFN*, he noted: "Phase 1 [of the restructuring in 1995] is getting the business stabilized, which I think we did a good job of ... 1996 should be a good year. 1997 should be a great year."

HOME SECURITY EXPANSION

In mid-1996 the company announced its decision to expand its home security electronics business, which accounted for 15 percent of sales. Management was keen to strike a more even balance between its two business segments, thereby reducing its reliance on the troublesome retail market for universal remotes. The home safety and security products, which were used to operate lighting, temperature, and thermostat control, used radio frequency and infrared technologies. "We've been perceived as a one-product company," explained Universal's senior vice president of marketing and product development to *HFN* on June 10, 1996. He added: "We're looking to expand our business. Our thrust going forward is on home control. We're going to move into the wireless area." Universal planned to market its line of home security systems under the One For All and Eversafe brands, hoping to derive 35 percent of its revenues from the sale of such products by 1998.

As the company attempted to move beyond the troubles of 1994, the harsh condition of the retail market delayed its recovery. Several months after it announced the plans for a greater involvement in home control products, founders Doherty, Darbee, and O'Donnell resigned from Universal. Their departure ceded greater authority to Gabrielsen, who added the title of chairman to his posts as president and CEO. Concurrent with his promotion, Gabrielsen had the task of informing analysts that Universal was failing to perform as expected. "It's going to take us a little longer to make this business profitable than we originally thought," he conceded in the September 2, 1996, issue of *Television Digest*.

Net income for 1996, Gabrielsen told analysts, was expected to be half the per-share price projected by the company earlier in the year. The news delivered a crushing blow to the hope that the restructuring of 1995 had cured the company's ills. Universal continued to wade through excess inventories of outdated products and memory chips. Furthermore, profit margins continued to shrink because of price pressures, forcing Gabrielsen to submit new, much lower, earnings projections to analysts. By the end of 1996, the news was grim. Universal lost $2.3 million during the year, reverting to the money-losing enterprise that had stumbled profoundly in 1994.

EXITING NORTH AMERICAN RETAIL MARKET: 1997

Hounded by the losses incurred from its retail operations, Universal entered its second decade of business backpedaling. In January 1997 a deal to sell the company's One For All retail remote business collapsed. In the wake of the failed divestiture, the company announced it was not actively seeking another buyer for its beleaguered retail operations. However, in late 1997 the company announced it was abandoning the North American retail business for universal remotes, which accounted for 29 percent, or $26 million, of its overall business.

The company also decided to relocate its headquarters from Twinsburg to Cypress City, California, 25 miles north of Los Angeles, completing the move in 1998. Universal officially exited the North American retail market in 1998, licensing the One For All brand name and certain proprietary technology to third parties, who assumed Universal's former role of selling to domestic retailers.

Amid the drastic changes that occurred in 1998, Universal gained new leadership, marking the end of the Gabrielsen era. Camille Jayne joined Universal in February 1998 as president and COO, before being named CEO in August 1998 and chairwoman four months later. Formerly the senior vice president in charge of the digital television business unit at TCI, Jayne took control of Universal in the company's new guise. Although the company had abandoned the North American retail market, it continued to participate in retail sales in Europe, where profit margins remained sufficiently high to warrant further investment. The company was also supported by sales to OEMs, cable and satellite television operators, and by private-label sales.

RENEWED GROWTH

Analysts were encouraged by the composition of the restructured Universal, at last free of the domestic retail

business that had halted the company's remarkable growth during its first five years of business. Universal's proprietary technology and its library of digital codes, which exceeded 80,000 individual codes by the late 1990s, were valuable assets in a digital age replete with consumer electronics products.

No longer forced to compete as a low-cost producer of what had become a commodity product, Universal stood in a better position to reap the rewards of its technological advantages over competitors. The company's financial performance during the last two years of the 1990s demonstrated as much, ending the pattern of debilitating annual losses. After posting a $6.5 million loss in 1997, Universal recorded a $5.6 million profit in 1998, followed by a $7.7 million gain in 1999.

The difficulties of the mid-1990s appeared to have disappeared as Universal entered the 21st century. The company derived one-third of its sales from OEM customers, another third from cable and satellite operators, and the remainder from private-label and international retail sales. Expansion continued on all fronts, and the company was particularly interested in increasing its cable and satellite business. Universal's new management team explored new distribution relationships and was intent on expanding the company's presence in Europe, Asia, South America, and Canada.

NEW LEADERSHIP FOR A NEW CENTURY

Universal, which by this time was referred to as UEI, experienced success and growth during the early years of the new millennium. Jayne handed over chairmanship of the company to CEO Paul Arling in 2001. Under his leadership, the company continued to take advantage of new technologies, including digital video recorders (DVRs). By the end of 2001 UEI had posted profits for the previous 15 quarters, provided remote controls to 70 percent of the digital cable boxes for six out of seven major cable companies, and had added digital satellite provider DIRECTV to its growing list of clients. Overall, nearly 20 percent of universal remote controls sold across the globe were based on UEI technology.

With the popularity of DVDs and DVRs growing significantly and the eventual June 2009 switch from analog to digital signals in broadcast television, UEI found itself well positioned for additional growth. During 2002 the company launched Nevo, technology that allowed users to control and interact with a wide variety of consumer electronic devices in the home or office. Along with new product development, the company continued to eye international expansion as crucial to its future success.

In 2004 the company signed a deal to provide remote controls to Sky Italia, the largest subscription television provider in Italy. At the same time, it began to provide its Focus remote control technology to La Television Par Satellite (TPS), the leading satellite television provider in France. SimpleDevices Inc., a wireless software manufacturer, was acquired in October of that same year.

Sales climbed to $158.4 million while net income grew to $9.1 million in 2004. UEI's financial success continued into 2005 with revenues increasing to $181.3 million. During the year the company formed a supply partnership with Multichoice Africa Pty Ltd., the leading provider of digital satellite services in Africa. UEI inked a deal with Mitsubishi Electric Corp. in early 2006 to provide a custom line of universal remote controls for its high-definition Diamond series television screens.

CONTINUED GROWTH: 2007 AND BEYOND

By 2007 UEI was the leading supplier of remote control technology and held 168 remote-related patents. Revenue had more than doubled in four years, climbing from $104 million in 2002 to $236 million in 2006. DIRECTV and Comcast were the company's largest customers, accounting for 19 percent and 11 percent of total revenues, respectively. During 2007 the company began supplying universal remote controls for Vizio's large format plasma televisions. It also signed a deal with PCCW Media Ltd., the largest communications provider in Hong Kong.

UEI and Audiovox Accessories Corp. formed a partnership in 2008. As part of the deal, Audiovox secured distribution rights for remote controls sold in North America and various Latin American and Asian markets under the UEI One For All brand. In addition, UEI became the exclusive supplier of microcontrollers and software for universal remote controls sold under the RCA brand. UEI purchased the universal remote control business from Zilog Inc. in 2009. It also secured EchoStar Corp. as a customer that year. EchoStar, one the world's largest providers of satellite technology and set-top box equipment providers, was spun off from DISH Network L.L.C. in 2008.

Revenues surpassed $300 million in 2009 and the company secured its 12th consecutive year of profitability. The company was ranked 116 on the *Forbes* 200 Best Small Companies in America list based on its financial performance that year. While many companies suffered during this period due to an overall downturn in global economies, UEI had prospered. Indeed, with demand for UEI's technologies and products expected to continue its upward climb, the company appeared to be well positioned for additional growth in the years to come.

Jeffrey L. Covell
Updated, Christina M. Stansell

PRINCIPAL SUBSIDIARIES

Universal Electronics B.V. (Netherlands); One For All GmbH (Germany); One For All Iberia S.L. (Spain); One For All UK Ltd.; One For All Argentina S.R.L.; One For All France S.A.S.; Universal Electronics Italia S.R.L.; UE Singapore Pte. Ltd.; UEI Hong Kong Pte. Ltd.; UEI Electronics Pte. Ltd. (India); UEI Cayman Inc.; Ultra Control Consumer Electronics GmbH (Germany); Hong Kong Holdings Co. Pte. Ltd.

PRINCIPAL COMPETITORS

AMX Corporation; Interlink Electronics, Inc.; Philips Electronics North America Corporation.

FURTHER READING

Bloomfield, Judy. "Universal Locks into Security." *HFN—The Weekly Newspaper for the Home Furnishing Network*, June 10, 1996, p. 63.

"CEO Interview: P. Arling." *Wall Street Transcript*, March 10, 2005.

Clark, Don. "The New Remote—Changing Channels with Your PDA." *Wall Street Journal*, June 18, 2002.

"Inside Universal Electronics." *Television Digest*, March 8, 1993, p. 17.

Laposky, John. "Audiovox, Universal Ink Remotes Deal." *TWICE*, May 19, 2008.

Martin, Neil A. "Here's the Remote!" *Barron's*, February 26, 2007.

Ryan, Ken. "Universal Electronics' Comeback." *HFN—The Weekly Newspaper for the Home Furnishing Network*, January 1, 1996, p. 66.

"Sizing up Remote Market." *Television Digest*, June 7, 1993, p. 17.

Stump, Matt. "UEI Picks up SimpleDevices." *Multichannel News*, October 4, 2004.

"UEI Develops Control Solutions for New Vizio Line of HD Televisions." *Wireless News*, February 21, 2007.

"Universal Electronics Acquires Zilog's Universal Remote Control Software Technology and Related Assets." *Wireless News*, February 26, 2009.

"Universal Electronics Honored by *Forbes*." *Electronics News-weekly*, December 2, 2009.

"Universal Founders Quit." *Television Digest*, September 2, 1996, p. 15.

"Universal Restructuring." *Television Digest*, May 22, 1995, p. 14.

"Universal Weighs Strategy." *Television Digest*, April 21, 1997, p. 18.

VAILRESORTS®

EXPERIENCE OF A LIFETIME™

Vail Resorts, Inc.

---

390 Interlocken Crescent, Suite 1000
Broomfield, Colorado 80021
U.S.A.
Telephone: (303) 404-1800
Fax: (303) 404-6415
Web site: http://www.vailresorts.com

Public Company
Incorporated: 1997
Employees: 14,960
Sales: $977 million (2009)
Stock Exchanges: New York
Ticker Symbol: MTN
NAICS: 713990 Amusement and Recreation; 531390 Real Estate Agents and Managers; 721110 Hotels and Motels; 722110 Eating Places; 722410 Drinking Places

■ ■ ■

Vail Resorts, Inc., is one of the largest ski resort owners and operators in North America. The company's Mountain division includes the Colorado resorts of Vail, Beaver Creek, Breckenridge, and Keystone, as well as Heavenly, which is located on the California and Nevada border. Vail Resort's Lodging division manages the RockResorts brand, as well as condominiums, three resorts in Grand Teton National Park, and six golf courses. The company's Real Estate Development arm buys, sells, and develops real estate near its resort communities. During the 2008–09 season, the five mountain destinations of Vail Resorts had over 5.8 million visitors.

THE MAKING OF A MOUNTAIN

The Vail Valley, also known as Gore Creek Valley, lies in west-central Colorado near the Continental Divide. Cut off at one end by a pass of 10,600 feet, and at the other end by a canyon about the width of a horse, the valley long maintained an obscure presence in Colorado. For generations it was a place where Native American Utes would come to escape the summer heat. After the Civil War, white settlers pushed into the valley, among the first of whom were miners searching for gold and silver, as well as map surveyors, who charted its canyons, cliffs, and other features. The land was settled by a small number of ranchers, but the steep terrain and cold climate eventually drove most of them away, leaving the area to sheepherders, who used the valley as pastureland during the spring and summer.

During World War II, the U.S. Army set up a training center, Camp Hale, in another isolated valley about 23 miles from Vail. There, the army trained ski troopers of the Tenth Mountain Division, who were later sent to fight in the Apennine mountains of northern Italy. Pete Seibert, one of these troopers, was lucky to have made it through the war alive. Hit by small-arms fire and two mortar shells, Seibert was badly wounded, and one of the shells blew off his right kneecap. Doctors told him he would never again be able to ski. A few years later, however, Seibert was working as a ski instructor at Aspen, the famous Colorado resort, and in 1950 he made the U.S. Ski Team, although torn

COMPANY PERSPECTIVES

Our values are based on our mission and align the needs of our five constituents—our guests, our employees, our communities, our environment and our shareholders: provide an exceptional experience to each of our guests and employees; bring passion, safety and integrity to everything we do; partner with our communities; protect our spectacular natural environment; and drive growth in shareholder value.

ligaments kept him from competing. During the next few years he studied at a hotel school in Lausanne, Switzerland.

Like many others in Colorado during the 1950s, Seibert dreamed of a way to establish his own resort, though perhaps with a bit more zeal than the others. "I had first started thinking of running a resort when I was 12 years old," Seibert explained in *Vail: Triumph of a Dream* noting, "there was nothing I wanted more in my life than to start a ski area." In this endeavor, Seibert would have considerable help from Earl Eaton, another Camp Hale veteran. Born not far from the present Vail resort, Eaton had become a uranium prospector. One day, while searching for uranium in Gore Creek Valley, he arrived at the ridge of an unnamed mountain. Looking south his eyes fell upon a vast expanse of treeless slopes, later called the "back bowls," some of the most famous ski terrain in the United States. In March 1957 Eaton took Seibert to the mountain, and they both trudged seven hours through deep snow up to the ridge. When they arrived, Seibert, too, was stunned by the back bowls, as well as by the view of the towering peaks of the Gore Range.

Their first step was buying land. Although unable to purchase the mountain itself, which was owned by the U.S. Forest Service, they were able to purchase a 500-acre ranch at the base for $55,000 in 1957. Funded by six partners (mostly from Denver), Seibert and Eaton bought the land under the guise of a new company, Transmontane Rod and Gun Club, a name they used to keep their plans a secret from the local residents. During this time, they also searched for a name for their new resort. One suggestion was Shining Mountains, the Ute phrase for the western Colorado region. However, "when mountains shine," Seibert pointed out, "it means they're icy." They settled on Vail, the name of the pass at the eastern end of the valley, named for Charles D.

Vail, a former chief engineer of the Colorado Highway Department.

BEGINNINGS OF A SKI SLOPE

Next, Seibert and Eaton applied for a "Conditional Special Use Permit." The U.S. Forest Service, however, turned them down, claiming there were already enough ski resorts in the White River National Forest. Undeterred, the group appealed the decision and, a year later, they received the permit, allowing them to attract 21 new investors, some from as far away as Texas and New York, and to found a new company, Vail Corp., which was used to raise additional funds. In 1960, again through Transmontane Rod and Gun Club, the group purchased an adjacent property, also of 500 acres. Finally, in 1961, after the group brought in 100 limited partners (each putting up $10,000), Vail Associates, Inc., was born.

Vail Associates got the go-ahead from the U.S. Forest Service in December 1961, and the company wasted no time in developing the foundations of the resort. Ski lifts were ordered, bulldozers pushed the snow out of the way to make room for construction, and trails on the mountain were cut. The mountain's front side was ideal for the kind of gentle, tree-lined, slopes appropriate for beginners and intermediates, while the back bowls were the draw for advanced and expert skiers. Some of the trail names emerged from the early ski experiences of the Vail Associates group. The "Forever" trail in the back bowls, for example, was named one spring day when snow conditions were so perfect that a number of people skied down the back of the mountain. Without a ski lift, the walk back up the mountain seemed to last forever.

With about $2 million slated for development, the group was able to cut the necessary trails and construct a nearly two-mile gondola (including a building at its base), two double-chair lifts (holding two persons per chair), a beginners surface lift, a lodge at mid-mountain ("Mid-Vail"), a ski patrol shack at the top, and a bridge across Gore Creek. Bob Parker, also from the Tenth Mountain Division and a former editor of *Skiing Magazine*, became the marketing director of Vail Associates, and his contributions included organizing numerous crowd-gathering events. Especially important was an agreement by the U.S. Ski Team to hold an Olympic training camp at Vail, an event that began on December 23, 1961, just eight days after the resort opened.

ESTABLISHING A SKI RESORT: 1963–66

Opening day was hardly indicative of the resort's future greatness. With no snow at the base and snow only

KEY DATES

1962: Vail Mountain opens for skiing with two chairlifts, one gondola, and a $5 lift ticket.

1972: Vail Associates purchases 2,200 acres of Beaver Creek property.

1980: Beaver Creek ski area officially opens with 4 chairlifts, 28 runs, and 425 skiable acres.

1985: Vail Associates becomes a subsidiary of Gillett Holdings, Inc.

1992: Apollo Ski Partners of New York acquires Vail Associates.

1997: Ralcorp Holdings and resort operations merge with Vail Associates, creating Vail Resorts, Inc.; Vail Resorts goes public.

1999: Company acquires the Grand Teton Lodge Company in Grand Teton National Park, Wyoming.

2002: Heavenly Ski Resort in Lake Tahoe on the California and Nevada border is acquired.

about ankle deep at the top, the resort sold a small number of $5 lift tickets, only a few of which actually went to skiers. Most of the tickets were purchased by area residents who wanted to experience the novelty of riding the lifts up and down the mountain. Three weeks later, on January 10, 1963, the resort managed to draw just 12 skiers, bringing in a total of $60 from lift tickets.

Nevertheless, the resort's fortunes soon improved. Its large amount of gentle terrain attracted families, and its more fearsome back bowls became legendary among experienced skiers. Vail, closer to Denver than its soon-to-be archrival Aspen, began to draw tourists. More importantly, however, Vail also benefited from a tremendous increase in the popularity of skiing during the 1960s and 1970s. The 1960 Winter Olympics, held at Squaw Valley, California, encouraged many Americans to try skiing, as did the new Head metal skis, which made the sport easier. Other important developments included safer ski bindings; "stretch" ski pants, which were more fashionable than the traditional bulky skiwear; heavy promotions by airlines, which saw in skiing a new market for their services; and legal changes that made condominium ownership more practical and appealing.

As a result, Vail took off, growing faster than even the most optimistic hopes of its founders. By 1964 the company had developed enough new terrain to triple skier capacity, and trails and lifts continued to spread east and west across the mountain. Its Golden Peak and Lionshead ski areas opened in 1967 and 1969, respectively. For the base area, the company followed its master plan, which called for an Austrian-style village, complete with winding lanes, footbridges, arcades, and a clock tower, while avoiding such distractions as neon lights. Each building in the town offered unique features, while conforming to the general style. In 1966, however, the town of Vail was incorporated and the company was no longer able to control the town's development.

EXPANSION AND DEVELOPMENT: 1969–74

During the late 1960s, Vail continued new resort development projects on both sides of the valley. To help pay for the development, costing some $13 million by 1969, the company sold part of its land in the valley as commercial and residential lots. In 1966 it began to offer its stock over the counter, a move that left Seibert as chairperson while effectively reducing his power. In 1971 the company also spent $4.4 million to purchase 2,200 acres of land 10 miles down the road, which would later become the site of its Beaver Creek resort. By 1973 Vail Mountain had some 800 acres of skiable terrain, two gondolas, nine chairlifts, and four restaurants (two on the top of the mountain and two at the bottom). Total revenues were about $7 million.

Even more attention was focused on Vail in 1974, when Gerald Ford took over the U.S. presidency from the resigning Richard Nixon. Ford, in addition to being the first "skiing president," frequently took vacations at Vail and owned a three-bedroom condominium in the center of town. His first Vail ski vacation while president took place in December 1974, but for security reasons he rented out the home of Harry W. Bass, a Texas multimillionaire and Vail board member. Some began to dub this rented home the "Western White House."

TRAGEDY STRIKES: 1976

Vail's next major source of publicity was the result of a tragic accident. On March 26, 1976, a frayed cable on the Lionshead gondola got caught in one of the lift towers, causing the passing cars to bounce and shake. Two cars then fell off, plummeting 125 feet to the ground, while the rest of the lift came to a halt. Although the ski patrol was able to rescue those trapped in the stalled lift, four people died and eight others were injured. At the time, this was the worst accident at a U.S. ski resort.

The tragedy was bad publicity for Vail and, worse, prompted a wave of lawsuits totaling more than $50 million. Fearing its liability in the accident, the board decided to sell the company, and, in late 1976, Harry Bass was able to gain controlling interest in Vail Associates for $13 million. Soon afterward, Seibert was forced out of the company, reportedly because of a personality clash with Bass. Ironically, Vail Associates eventually settled all the lawsuits out of court for only a fraction of the total claim.

NEW SITE IMPROVES IMAGE: 1976–85

During this time, the company's Beaver Creek site was chosen to host the downhill event for the Winter Olympics, scheduled to take place in Colorado in 1976. The Olympic offer, however, was turned down by Colorado voters and, instead, the games were held at Innsbruck, Austria. Initially seen as a setback, the loss of the Olympic Games gave the company more time to plan Beaver Creek. In fact, the planning alone would take seven years and cost $50 million.

Ultimately, Beaver Creek became not merely a ski resort but an elegant, truly luxurious, all-season resort area, which included facilities for conventions and conferences. Opened on December 14, 1980, Beaver Creek initially offered 450 acres of skiable terrain, boosted to some 1,000 acres by the decade's end. During this period, Vail Associates was also marketing the valley as a summer vacation area, where people could hike, raft, ride the gondola, shop at the more than 200 stores, or golf at one of the four 18-hole courses.

By 1982 Vail Associates had assets of nearly $100 million and revenues of $43.7 million. Ski resorts accounted for $31 million and real estate operations accrued $12 million. Vail Mountain was without a doubt one of the country's premier ski resorts, and Beaver Creek, although small, had built a reputation for opulence. All boded well for the company save two developments. First, the popularity of skiing in the United States had declined dramatically, and secondly, sales of the Beaver Creek properties were dismal. By the mid-1980s, real estate prices in the valley had collapsed, causing the near failure of Vail Associates. Problems for the company were further complicated in 1984 by a confrontation between Bass and his children, whose trust, established by Bass, owned enough Vail stock to oust him from the chairmanship.

NEW OWNER, IMPROVEMENTS, AND EXPANSION: 1985–90

In the summer of 1985, Vail Associates was purchased for $115 million by George Gillett, head of Gillett

Holdings Inc., which at the time owned nine television stations, 21 newspapers, two radio stations, and a meat-packing plant. George Gillett had been a customer at Vail since 1963 and was an enthusiastic skier prepared to make large capital investments. Nevertheless, his appraisal of the resort's recent past was harsh. He noted that Vail was not making money and that it had over six years of condominium inventory in Beaver Creek. Gillett also criticized the company for maintaining an entire department devoted to real estate development when there was no demand. Employee attitudes toward the customers were cited as poor, and the people who owned many of the businesses in town viewed skiers as intruders on their peaceful lifestyle.

Gillett set out to change this environment, emphasizing the simple principle that "the customer is king." One of the first areas he focused on was training. Gillett personally led every employee-training program at the Vail resort, as well as additional training programs for city employees, restaurant workers, bus drivers, and cab companies. He arranged to have television crews follow several families on a Vail vacation, which included from the moment they made their reservations until they left the resort for home, and then showed a film of these trips to Vail's management. Among the problems they discovered was the lack of a central reservations system, the high incidence of lost baggage at the airport, long lines at ticket windows and lifts, and the lack of children's activities after skiing.

From 1985 to 1989, the company invested $60 million in capital improvements. Part of this sum went to the China Bowl expansion, which opened up an immense new area of advanced terrain on the back side of the mountain, in the process doubling the resort's skiable terrain to 3,787 acres. With the addition of China Bowl, Vail became the country's largest ski resort, surpassing the former leader, Mammoth Mountain in California. By 1989 it had also installed six high-speed quad lifts (with four-person chairs), which, although costing several million dollars each, considerably reduced lift lines. For children, the company opened a kids-only hill, which included Ft. Whippersnapper, an adventure park with mock hunting camps, and an Indian village. Remarkably, by 1989 all the condominiums in Beaver Creek were occupied.

The readers' poll of *SKI Magazine* rated Vail Mountain the top resort in North America three years in a row during 1989, 1990, and 1991 and the company also set attendance records, with over 1.5 million "skier visits" each year at Vail Mountain and more than 400,000 at Beaver Creek. Capital improvements continued as Vail constructed a public bobsled course in 1990 and installed its 10th high-speed quad in 1992. By

1993 it had 4,020 acres of skiable terrain and a total of 25 lifts. Vail was also the host of the 1989 World Alpine Ski Championships, an event that had not been held in the United States since 1950. The event gave Vail extensive international press coverage, which Vail Associates hoped would encourage skiers from other countries to visit the resort.

While Vail thrived, however, its parent, Gillett Holdings, was collapsing under the weight of failed junk bonds (high-risk, high-yielding debt certificates), issued in the 1980s to finance its acquisitions. The holding company filed for bankruptcy on June 25, 1991, and its eventual reorganization transferred the ownership of Vail Associates to Apollo Advisors, L.P. of New York, a company headed by Leon Black, a former Drexel Burnham banker. Nevertheless, George Gillett continued to serve as chairman of Vail Associates.

CONTROVERSY AND IPO: 1993–97

Despite the financial complications of its parent company, the day-to-day operations of Vail Associates remained profitable, and the company continued to make ambitious expansion plans. In 1993 Vail sought approval from the U.S. Forest Service to develop a giant, north-facing bowl, which would again almost double the resort's already huge amount of skiable terrain. Further west, the company had purchased Arrowhead, a new, small ski resort next to Beaver Creek, and plans were underway to connect the two resorts with a chair lift. Nevertheless, the many projects taken on by Vail Associates were also reflected in the price of Vail Mountain's daily lift ticket, which increased from $30 in 1986 to $46 in 1994.

Vail Associates was not alone in its plans for expanding terrain and upgrading facilities, nor in its raising of lift ticket prices. Many other resort owners, who noted that Americans were increasingly going to the biggest and best-equipped ski areas, were also investing in expansion projects, while small ski areas, unable to compete, were failing at a rapid rate. Vail Mountain had managed to remain at the top of North American ski resorts, though not without competition. Nearby Aspen, for example, with its four separate ski mountains, continued to benefit from its reputation as a more "authentic," culturally sophisticated town. Moreover, several Utah resorts offered drier snow and steeper terrain. Farther north, Whistler and Blackcomb, contiguous resorts in British Columbia, Canada, both had a much larger vertical drop (the difference in elevation between the base and the summit) and, when viewed as a single ski area, a greater amount of skiable terrain.

In 1996 Vail Associates signed a deal with Ralcorp Holdings, Inc., purchasing nearby Breckenridge and Keystone resorts and establishing Vail Resorts, Inc. Now skiers had access to four ski resorts and the Arapaho Basin. That year, the company also invested $30 million in improvements at Vail, including more ski lifts, a 12-passenger gondola, and a new base lodge that catered to a variety of customers.

The popularity of snowboarding meant Vail had to expand not only in a geographic sense but also in a business sense. Snowboarders were typically a different demographic than the affluent skiers of Vail's majority. The company also recognized the need to establish Vail as not just a place to ski but also a place to vacation. Adventure Ridge, a winter-amusement park, soon opened at the top of the Lionshead gondola. The park included four new restaurants, bars featuring live music, extreme snowboarding movies, and an upscale restaurant, primarily geared toward a younger crowd. By 1997 new CEO Adam M. Aron had tripled sales of season passes and planned to spend another $74 million in added improvements and expansion efforts.

In February 1997 Vail Resorts became the first North American ski resort to go public. The initial public offering (IPO) raised $213 million, a welcome contribution to Vail's expansion efforts. Investor Ronald Baron, Ralcorp Holdings, and Apollo Advisors together controlled about 75 percent of the company's stock.

OVERCOMING CHALLENGES

Continued expansion, however, proved to be challenging. Vail Resorts' plans for an 885-acre Category III project in the Vail Mountain back bowls met with opposition from the townspeople and from environmental groups. Locals and animal rights activists protested vehemently in March 1998, objecting to what they viewed as the project's reckless encroachment on the habitats of elk and the Canada lynx. Although lawsuits were filed against the development, the project was ultimately approved by the U.S. Forest Service and by the Eagle County Commission. In October, on the day construction was to commence, fire broke out, damaging four chair lifts and destroying the $5 million Two Elk Lodge and ski patrol headquarters. Damage totaled $12 million. Members of the activist group Earth Liberation Front claimed responsibility.

Ironically, the fire invoked local sympathy for Vail and the expansion continued as planned. By 1999 Vail Mountain had repaired the fire damage and, along with Beaver Creek, hosted the 1999 World Alpine Skiing Championships, making them the only North American venues to twice host the event. In 2000 the Category III expansion, now named Blue Sky Basin, was completed and opened for business.

Also in 1999, Vail Resorts finalized acquisition of the Grand Teton Lodge Company in Grand Teton National Park, Wyoming, its first resort property outside of Colorado. In 2000 the company acquired a 51 percent stake in, and assumed management of, the Renaissance Resort and Spa in Jackson Hole, Wyoming, near Grand Teton National Park. The property was renovated and renamed Snake River Lodge and Spa. Also in 2000, Vail Mountain was voted the number one ski resort in North America by readers of *SKI Magazine* for the third time since 1996 and for the 10th time since the poll began in 1987. Vail Resorts' other Colorado ski properties, including Breckenridge, Keystone, and Beaver Creek, all earned high ratings in the poll.

MOVING INTO THE 21ST CENTURY

The 2000–01 season set a new attendance record of 4.9 million skiers at Vail Resorts' four Colorado properties, and the company entered the new millennium employing handheld computers to register ski students, check in rental equipment, and verify ski passes at the lift. Moving forward, the company's goals were to maintain the "best resort" rating, continue improving the resort experiences of a broad base of clientele, sustain strategic expansions and acquisitions, leverage new Internet technologies to provide areas of growth and benefit core business, and increase profits and stock prices for investors.

Indeed, Vail Resorts continued to diversify its portfolio in order to secure future profits. In 2001 the company acquired a majority interest in RockResorts International LLC, a luxury resort hotel company with 11 properties throughout the United States. At the same time, Vail Marriott Mountain Resort and the Inn at Beaver Creek were purchased and added to the company's growing lodging division. During 2002 the company purchased the Heavenly Ski Resort in Lake Tahoe on the California and Nevada border, making it the fifth Vail Resorts-owned destination. The Red Sky Ranch golf community opened that year near Beaver Creek.

The 2001–02 ski season saw a decline in skier visits due in part to the travel slowdown that occurred after the terrorist attacks against the United States on September 11, 2001. The company issued a series of cost-cutting measures that saved nearly $10 million but the effects of the industry downturn had an impact on the company's bottom line. Vail Resorts posted its first net loss in over 10 years during fiscal 2003.

DIVERSIFICATION, EXPANSION, AND CONSERVATION: 2006 AND BEYOND

The company's financial woes proved short-lived. By fiscal 2005, Vail Resorts was selling a record number of lift tickets and had secured revenues of $810 million and net income of $23.1 million. Adam Aron, chairman and CEO of Vail Resorts since 1996, left the company in 2006. Robert A. Katz was named his replacement and continued to explore new areas of growth for Vail Resorts. The company's RockResorts subsidiary was expanding its holdings, with plans to manage Rum Cay Resort Marina in the Bahamas, The Chateau at Heavenly Village, the Eleven Biscayne Hotel & Spa in Miami, The Landings St. Lucia, and the Hotel Jerome in Aspen. It also added a new resort in the Dominican Republic to its holdings in 2009. Vail Resorts acquired resort ground transportation firm Colorado Mountain Express in 2008 and Mountain News Corporation, operator of the snow sports Web site OnTheSnow.com, in 2010.

While expansion was at the forefront of the company's strategy, Vail Resorts was also focused on energy conservation. During 2006 the company became the second-largest corporate wind power purchaser in the United States behind Whole Foods Market, Inc. It also partnered with the National Forest Foundation to raise funds and awareness for conservation projects aimed at bolstering and preserving the National Forest system. During 2007 the company announced plans for the $1 billion Ever Vail project, which was the largest Leadership in Energy & Environmental Design (LEED)-certified village in North America. Ever Vail continued to be in the planning stages in 2010.

Meanwhile, Vail Resorts worked to remain competitive while an economic downturn in 2008 and 2009 wreaked havoc on the travel and leisure industry. In March 2008 the company launched its Epic Pass, which cut the price of a Vail Resorts season pass from $1,849 to $579 and offered unrestricted access to all of its five resorts. Nevertheless, the company saw an overall 3.5 percent decline in skier visits to its Colorado locations during the 2008–09 season. While revenue hit $1.15 billion in fiscal 2008, it dropped to $977 million in fiscal 2009. Net income also fell by 59 percent over the previous year to $48.95 million. With sales and profits tumbling and skier visits continuing to fall, the company announced wage cuts in lieu of layoffs in 2009. Katz also announced that he would forgo his salary for one year.

By 2010 the company began to see small improvements in its bottom line. While the U.S. economy was slow to recover, Katz and his management team were optimistic that the company's growth and diversification during the first decade of the 21st century had positioned Vail Resorts for success in the years to come. While only time would tell if the company's strategy would pay off, skiers and snow sport enthusiasts would no doubt continue to enjoy Vail, Beaver Creek, Breckenridge, Keystone, and Heavenly for years to come.

Thomas Riggs
Updated, Kerri DeVault; Christina M. Stansell

PRINCIPAL SUBSIDIARIES

RockResorts International LLC; Vail Holdings Inc.; Vail Resorts Development Company; Vail Hotel Management Company, LLC; Vail Resorts Development Company; Vail Resorts Lodging Company; Vail RR, Inc.; Vail Summit Resorts, Inc.; Vail Trademarks, Inc.; Vail/Arrowhead, Inc.; Vail/Beaver Creek Resort Properties, Inc.; Vamhc, Inc.; VR Heavenly Concessions, Inc.; VR Holdings, Inc.; Zion Lodge Company.

PRINCIPAL DIVISIONS

Mountain; Lodging; Real Estate Development.

PRINCIPAL COMPETITORS

Aspen Skiing Company; Booth Creek Ski Holdings, Inc.; Intrawest ULC.

FURTHER READING

Blevins, Jason. "Vail, Colo. Resort Company's Ski Season Gets Big Lift." *Denver Post,* June 7, 2001.

Boyd, Tom. "Price War Escalates on Heels of Vail Resorts' 'Epic Pass.'" *Rocky Mountain News*, November 15, 2008.

Glick, Daniel. *Powder Burn: Arson, Money and Mystery on Vail Mountain.* New York: Public Affairs, 2001.

Gorrell, Mike. "Vail Resort's Numbers Show Recession's Impact." *Salt Lake Tribune*, March 13, 2009.

Markels, Alex. "Backfire." *Mother Jones,* March 1999, p. 60.

Olsen, Patricia R. "Concerns about the Climate that Go beyond Snow." *New York Times*, March 1, 2008.

Raabe, Steve. "Flexing Its Muscle." *Denver Post*, April 11, 2010.

———. "Vail Resorts' Income Slides 52%." *Denver Post*, September 25, 2009.

Seibert, Pete. *Vail: Triumph of a Dream.* Berkeley, Calif.: Publisher's Group West, 2000.

Simonton, June. *Vail: Story of a Colorado Mountain Valley.* Dallas: Taylor Publishing Co., 1987.

Vall Companys S.A.

Polígono Industrial El Segre
Parc. 410
Lleida, E-25191
Spain
Telephone: (+34 973) 20 11 54
Fax: (+34 973) 20 62 87
Web site: http://www.vallcompanys.es

Private Company
Founded: 1956 as Harinera La Meta
Employees: 2,500
Sales: EUR 993 million ($1.39 billion) (2009 est.)
NAICS: 311119 Other Animal Food Manufacturing;
    112340 Poultry Hatcheries; 112990 All Other
    Animal Production

■ ■ ■

Vall Companys S.A. is a leading European producer of pork, chicken, and other meats. The company operates businesses producing bread flour, animal feed, processed and cured meats, and veterinary pharmaceuticals. Vall Companys also operates its own slaughterhouses. The meat production of Vall Companys operates through an integrated model whereby the company supplies animals, feed, veterinary care, logistics, and other services to a network of 1,900 independent farmers. Each year the company sells more than 189 million kilos of pork, 85 million kilos of chicken, and 18 million kilos of beef, as well as 10 million kilos of processed meat products. The company's livestock operations encompass 3.6 million pigs and 59 million chickens.

This production is destined both for the Spanish and other European markets, as well as for markets in Asia and elsewhere. In addition, Vall Companys produces more than 1.5 million tons of feed and 250 million tons of bread flour each year. Together these operations generated revenues of EUR 993 million ($1.39 billion) in 2009, making the company the second-largest pork and chicken producer in Spain. Vall Companys is a privately held company controlled by the founding Vall family. José Vall Palou, son of the founder, is the company's president.

FLOUR MILLING ORIGINS

Brothers Josep Maria and Antonio Vall Companys, who were both still teenagers at the end of the Spanish civil war, founded Vall Companys. The Vall brothers launched a career buying and selling wheat flour. By 1956 they had generated enough funds to purchase a flour mill, known as Harinera La Meta, located in Lleida.

The move into flour milling inspired the entrepreneurial spirit of the Vall brothers. In the 1960s the brothers began seeking ways to extend their business. The large quantities of waste by-products generated by the flour milling process provided the brothers with their next opportunity, and by the early 1960s the company had developed its first animal feed production facility.

Integration became a hallmark of the growing business empire of the Vall Companys family. The production of feed encouraged the Vall brothers to add pork production as well. The company added its first pig

KEY DATES

1956: Brothers Josep Maria and Antonio Vall Companys acquire a flour mill in Lleida, Spain.

1960s: The brothers expand into pig and poultry production, incorporating as Vall Companys.

1989: Vall Companys forms a veterinary pharmaceuticals subsidiary, Mevet.

1994: Vall Companys launches pig production in the United States.

2001: José Vall Palou acquires control of the company.

2008: Vall Companys acquires the Doux Iberia poultry operations.

2010: Vall Companys posts total revenues of nearly EUR 1 billion.

farming business during the 1960s. Buoyed by the success of its entry into pork production, Vall Companys also began raising poultry.

The Vall brothers incorporated these new businesses as Vall Companys in 1970. The company at the same time moved to larger facilities in Lleida's El Segre industrial zone. The new headquarters provided the company with space to ramp up production volume.

INTEGRATED BUSINESS MODEL

In the 1970s Vall Companys shifted its pork and poultry production to a new integrated business model. Under this structure Vall Companys no longer operated its own farms, instead developing a network of partner farms. Vall Companys supplied the animals, feed, and a growing range of associated services to farmers, who provided the facilities and the labor.

The integrated model allowed Vall Companys to build its production volumes far more rapidly, while also stimulating the growth of its feed operations. The company initially supplied its feed in sacks. As its volumes grew, and as a growing number of partner farms established large-scale operations, the company ramped up its feed production and began supplying feed in bulk.

In order to achieve this Vall Companys continued to deepen its integrated model, developing its own logistics wing during the early 1970s, called Transegre. Vall Companys also began providing veterinary control services for its farmer-partners during the decade. Soon after rolling out the integrated model for its pork

production, Vall converted its poultry production as well.

Vall Companys sought new expansion as its network of partner farms grew. In 1977 Vall made its first expansion beyond its home Lleida region, buying up Gepesa, operator of a pig and poultry feed production unit in Vic, near Barcelona. Vall also continued its organic growth, setting up a new flour mill with a capacity of 300,000 metric tons per year.

Meanwhile, the growth of the company's pork production enabled the company to build up its livestock supply. This effort focused especially on developing a large pool of breeding sows. A single sow was capable of producing up to 18 piglets per year. With control of its supply of sows, Vall also gained greater control of the health of its herds and the quality of the meat produced. This became especially important following a series of health scandals that rocked the meat sector in the 1990s.

PHARMACEUTICALS AND SLAUGHTERING

Health issues remained at the center of Vall's business in the early 1980s. The operation of large-scale, intensive animal farms brought a whole range of health-related and ethical issues. Animals in intensive farms were often closely packed together, with little room to move about, and often never allowed outdoors. As a result, animals tended to become far more vulnerable to diseases and other maladies. In order to minimize the impact of the intensive farming conditions, Vall began developing its own veterinary pharmaceuticals division, starting in 1981. In 1989 these operations were formalized into the creation of a new subsidiary, Mevet.

Vall Companys in the meantime also continued to deepen its vertical integration model. In 1984 Vall Companys entered animal slaughtering, opening its first abattoir in Tarragona that year. Spain's entry into the European market in the 1990s provided the company with new export possibilities. The country's entry into the European Union (EU) also brought Vall Companys in contact with the EU's increasingly rigid array of legislation and regulations governing the food industry in general, and the meat production sector in particular. Vall Companys completed a series of upgrades and investments in the 1990s in order to ensure the safety of its operations and products.

U.S. VENTURE IN 1994

The geographic expansion of Vall Companys continued in the 1990s as the company extended its network of feed production facilities to reach farmers throughout Spain. In 1993 the group moved into the Valencia region, buying up Producción Agropecuarias del Turia, S.A.U., or Agroturia. Like Vall, Agroturia operated as an integrated meat producer, expanding the group's pork and poultry production, while also providing the company with its first exposure to beef production.

Vall also continued to build up its sow herd through the 1990s, allowing the company to become self-sufficient in piglet supply for the first time. As part of this effort the company built its own artificial insemination center in Lleida. The new center also provided the company with tighter control over the genetic makeup of its pig herds.

The second generation of the Vall family had taken over running the business by this time. The operations of Vall Companys were divided up among José Vall Palou, son of Josep Maria Vall Companys, and his cousins, Ramon Pla Vall and Josep Pla Vall. Each family owned 50 percent of the group. Vall Palou took charge of the group's flour milling businesses and part of its feed operations. The Pla Vall branch took charge of the rest, including Agroturia.

In 1994 the Pla Vall branch initiated a still more ambitious expansion of the group's operations. The company entered the United States that year, launching its own livestock production unit in Texhoma, Oklahoma. Departing from Vall's integrated model in Spain, the U.S. unit moved into livestock farming directly, acquiring an initial herd of 2,500 sows from Pig Improvement Co. The company also planned to invest up to $100 million, expanding the herd to 10,000 sows.

The Vall operation in fact more than doubled that capacity, ultimately overseeing a herd of more than 20,000 sows in Oklahoma, Kentucky, and Texas, and selling more than 350,000 hogs per year. Most of these were sold by Seaboard Corp., an early partner in the venture. Vall had begun supplying Seaboard by 1995.

SIMPLIFYING OWNERSHIP IN 2001

The decision to move into the United States exposed a rift between the two branches of the Vall family, as José Vall Palou clashed with his cousins over strategy. Losses at the U.S. facility and at home further exacerbated tension in the family. While the U.S. business finally managed to turn a profit in 1999, Vall Companys overall had slipped into losses during the late 1990s.

The conflict between the two family branches cut sharply into further expansion of Vall Companys at the dawn of the new century. As a result of continued disputes, the company found it impossible to push through a number of its planned investments, such as the opening of a new EUR 110 million meat production complex in Aragon.

One of the few projects to move ahead during this period was the acquisition of Patel, based in Vic, near Barcelona. Patel not only expanded the company's network of slaughtering facilities, it also allowed the company to deepen its vertical integration with a move into the processed and cured packaged meat segments. Patel also brought the company a brand name that was well recognized both in Spain and in export markets.

The purchase of Patel provided a new lift to the group's revenues. Vall Companys also benefited from the bovine spongiform encephalopathy (BSE, also known as mad cow disease) crisis in Europe at that time. As consumers turned away from beef, Vall's sales of pork and chicken soared. By the end of 2000 Vall recorded a revenue increase of 32 percent, to EUR 380.3 million. The company also posted its first profit since 1997 that year, of nearly EUR 33 million. By then, total production volumes for Vall Companys included more than 300,000 metric tons of pork, nearly 82,000 metric tons of chicken, and one million metric tons of feed.

These strong results helped the two branches of the Vall family to resolve their ongoing conflict. In July 2001, after nearly two years of negotiations, José Vall Palou persuaded his cousins to sell him their half of the company. Vall Palou agreed to pay nearly EUR 140 million to buy out his cousins' 50 percent of the company.

REFOCUSING IN 2002

Vall Palou quickly moved to reorient the company's strategy in line with his own ambitions. Vall Companys then focused its future expansion more firmly on the Spanish and other European markets, leading to the November 2002 sale of the company's U.S. operations to Smithfield Foods for $60.7 million.

The sale followed Vall's latest expansion efforts back home. In January 2002 the company agreed to pay EUR 4.1 million to acquire 20 percent of Frimancha Industrias Carnicas, based in Valdepenas, Ciudad Real, and majority controlled by Queseria Manchega. The Frimancha stake allowed Vall to boost its operations in beef production, as well as to expand its range of processed meat products to include hams and sausages.

Soon after Vall purchased its stake in Frimancha, the two companies agreed to establish a beef slaughtering and processing joint venture, called Frivall, based in Cuenca and controlled at 75 percent by Vall, with Frimancha holding the rest. In 2004 Frivall expanded its slaughtering operation to include pork and poultry as well. When Frivall closed its Cuenca slaughterhouse in 2006, Frimancha added its own slaughterhouse in 2007. At the beginning of 2008 Vall Companys increased its stake in Frimancha to 75 percent. Vall at the same time acquired 100 percent control of Frivall.

INCREASED EXPORTS TO ASIA

By 2008 Vall Companys was Europe's leading pork producer. The company was also one of Spain's two leading pork processors, slaughtering 1.8 million hogs per year for total meat volumes of nearly 150,000 metric tons. Vall Companys then set out to expand its poultry production to a similar level.

The group found its opportunity in October 2008 when it reached an agreement with France's Doux S.A. to acquire its Spanish poultry operations, Doux Iberia. The purchase included two slaughtering facilities, and a total annual production of more than 60,000 metric tons of poultry meat. The addition of the Doux Iberia operation propelled Vall Companys into second place among Spain's poultry producers, trailing only Nutreco-owned Sada.

The increase in production enabled Vall Companys to pursue the continued growth of its exports, notably those of frozen poultry products for the Asian region. The company continued to invest in expanding these and other operations through the end of the decade, adding a new subsidiary, Agrocesa, which operated a feed factory and artificial insemination facility in Valladolid.

In 2010 the company began building a new feed factory in Ejea de los Caballeros, and also invested in the modernization of two poultry plants, as well as the installation of a ham production unit. Vall Companys had raised its total revenues to nearly EUR 1 billion ($1.38 billion) by then, confirming its status as one of Spain's, and Europe's, leading meat producers at the beginning of the 21st century.

M. L. Cohen

PRINCIPAL SUBSIDIARIES

Cárnicas Frivall, S.L.; Comercial Grup Vall, S.A.; Escorxador D'aus Torrent I Fills S.A.; Especialitats Costa, S.L.U.; Frimancha Industrias Cárnicas S.A.; General Pecuaria, S.A.; Harinera La Meta S.A.; Mevet, S.A.U.; Nutrivall S.L.; Patel, S.A.U.; Pondex, S.A.U.; Producción Agropecuarias Del Turia, S.A.U; Producción Agropecuarias Del Turia, S.A.U.; Transegre S.L.

PRINCIPAL DIVISIONS

Animal Nutrition; Livestock Production; Logistics and Purchasing; Meat Industry; Processed and Cured Products; Veterinary Pharmacy.

PRINCIPAL OPERATING UNITS

Frivall; Frimancha; La Meta; Patel; Pondex.

PRINCIPAL COMPETITORS

Casa Tarradellas S.A.; Cooperativa del Camp d'Ivars d'Urgell SCCL; Copaga Sociedad Cooperativa; Grupo Sada P.A. S.A.; Hibramer S.A.; Nutreco Espana S.A; Piensos del Segre S.A.; Productos Florida S.A.; Sada P.A. Andalucia S.A.; Sada P.A. Valencia S.A.

FURTHER READING

Bonnardel, Xavier. "Doux sur le Point de Vendre Sa filale Espagnole." *Ouest France,* September 13, 2008.

"Frimancha Opens to Vall Companys." *Expansion*, January 12, 2002.

"La Facturació de Vall Companys Creix un 11%, Fins als 606 Milions." *ADN.es*, September 24, 2007.

Rodriguez, David. "Vall Companys Estudia Comprar el Matadero de Pollos de Milsa en Lleida." *Le Manana*, July 17, 2008.

"Smithfield Foods Purchases Texhoma, Okla., Hog Producer from Spanish Company." *Virginian-Pilot*, November 14, 2002.

"Smithfield to Buy Hog Producer Vall." *Feedstuffs*, November 25, 2002, p. 6.

Torrado, Damaris. "Vall Companys Compra las Plantas de Doux en España." *El Pais*, July 31, 2008.

"Vall Companys Completa el 75% en Frimancha y el 100% en Frivall." *Alimarket*, February 25, 2008.

"Vall Companys Compra el Negocio Del Francés Doux en España." *El Periodico d'Aragon*, July 31, 2008.

Vêt'Affaires S.A.

112 Avenue Kleber
Paris, F-75016
France
Telephone: (+33 02) 40 13 08 10
Fax: (+33 02) 40 31 28 60
Web site: http://www.vetaffaires.fr

Public Company
Incorporated: 1999
Employees: 799
Sales: EUR 92.7 million ($126.2 million) (2009)
Stock Exchanges: Paris
Ticker Symbol: VET
NAICS: 448130 Children's and Infants' Clothing Stores; 448110 Men's Clothing Stores; 448120 Women's Clothing Stores

■ ■ ■

Vêt'Affaires S.A. is one of France's leading retailers specializing in the deep discount clothing market. Founded in 1987 near Nantes, the company had built a national network of 115 stores by 2010, with a target of 206 stores by 2013. Vêt'Affaires stores focus especially on a selection of undergarments, pajamas, and other "hidden" clothing items, as well as a full range of other clothing, including jeans, jackets and coats, footwear, and accessories. The average price of clothing featured in Vêt'Affaires stores is EUR 4 ($6). The company ensures its low prices by sourcing approximately 80 percent of its stock from low-wage markets in Asia and elsewhere.

Vêt'Affaires stores, typically located in out-of-town shopping zones, are open seven days a week, despite French restrictions on Sunday store operations. Vêt'Affaires is listed on the Euronext Paris Stock Exchange's Secondary Market, and generated sales of nearly EUR 93 million ($126 million) in 2009. The company is led by Rémy Lesguer, president and cofounder.

ORIGINS

Although their father was a worker in the shipyards in the Nantes region, brothers Rémy and Patrice Lesguer decided to follow their older brother into the retail sector in the early 1970s. The older Lesguer brother operated a small chain of discount clothing stores in the center of Nantes called Au Vrac. Rémy and Patrice Lesguer started working in the three Au Vrac stores in 1970, and remained with their brother's company for the next six years.

By 1976 the younger Lesguer brothers were determined to set out on their own. As they explained to *L'Entreprise*, their career path was highly influenced by their elder brother's success: "He was free, obeyed no one and earned a lot of money. He taught us to gather as much information as possible by listening to everyone around us: customers, employees, suppliers and other entrepreneurs ... and to follow our intuition."

The region's markets provided the framework for the two younger brothers' first foray into business. In 1976 they each acquired a van in order to travel from market to market, where they sold surplus and remaindered clothing. In 1982 the Lesguers brought two of

We continually adapt to consumer expectations and evolutions by offering a large, accessible, quality selection while respecting the entirety of existing legislation and enforcing their application.

their nephews, Frédéric Peraudeau and Xavier Gallois, into their business.

With the increasing quantity of stock required to supply the team of four sellers, the four partners bought a 500-square-meter warehouse along a main truck route in Rezé. They then in 1987 converted part of the warehouse into a retail shop, which they called Vêt'Affaires. From the start, the store focused on basic clothing items, especially undergarments, lingerie, and other hidden clothing items, at extremely low prices. The store adopted the bazaar formula made popular by Parisian retail legend Tati and others, selling the clothing from large bins.

BUILDING A NETWORK

With sales growing briskly, the company expanded the warehouse, which doubled in size in 1989. The Vêt'Affaires shop then featured 500 square meters of selling space. This quickly proved insufficient, and two years later the retail section of the warehouse was expanded to 1,000 square meters.

This success encouraged the Lesguer family's ambitions to expand the Vêt'Affaires concept into a full-fledged retail brand. The company opened its second store in 1992, in Nantes. By 1994 the company had added stores in St. Nazaire, Angers, and La Roche sur Yon as well. By then, the company's total sales had grown to the equivalent of EUR 10 million.

In order to supply its growing chain, and to prepare for future expansion, in 1994 the company created a new subsidiary, Central'Vet, which took over as the central purchasing operation for the chain. Central'Vet opened its own 3,000-square-meter warehouse, as well as its own offices. The creation of a dedicated purchasing body allowed the company to extend this part of its business farther afield, taking advantage of the low-wage markets in North Africa and Asia, as well as in parts of Europe.

The new purchasing division permitted the company to step up its store opening program. By 1999 the company had opened 20 stores, primarily in

France's northwestern corner. The company's sales had also grown strongly, topping $42 million.

SUNDAY OPENING LOOPHOLE

In 1999 Vêt'Affaires also put into place an important feature of its business plan. The company converted all of its stores to a new franchise model based on the status of a *Société en Nom Collectif* (General Partnership). Under this system the company recruited two husband-and-wife teams, which together owned 24 percent of the store, with the remainder held by Vêt'Affaires. The company supplied the store fittings and furnishings, as well as all of the clothing stock, and provided marketing and other support services.

The General Partnership model held a number of distinct advantages for the company. A store's status as a General Partnership meant that its owner-managers were treated administratively not as employees of Vêt'Affaires, but rather as independent workers. In this capacity, the Vêt'Affaires store owners were able to circumvent the French restrictions on Sunday store openings. These laws, which also included most holidays, were originally enacted in order to protect workers and to provide a guaranteed day of leisure.

The legislation served at the same time to limit the growing dominance of large-scale supermarkets over the retail sector, allowing the survival of small retailers by providing an important exception: stores were permitted to open on Sunday provided they were staffed by the owners or members of the owners' families. By opening its stores on Sundays and on most legal holidays, Vêt'Affaires attracted a growing client base. Because the stores were staffed by their owner-partners, the company also avoided additional payroll costs, making the Sunday openings even more profitable.

The Lesguers then prepared to accelerate the company's expansion. In 2000 the company announced plans to open five new stores each year, and to boost its revenue growth to 20 percent per year (as compared to an average of 12 percent per year since the mid-1990s). By expanding the retail network, and therefore the volume of its sales, Vêt'Affaires expected to lower its own purchasing prices. The company then passed these savings along to its stores, reducing the average per-item price from EUR 5 to EUR 4.

In order to finance its expansion, Vêt'Affaires announced its plans to go public. In 2000 the company took a step in this direction when it launched an offering of nearly 5 percent of its shares on the Paris Exchange's Marché Libre, equivalent to the over-the-counter (OTC) market in the United States. At the same time, the company announced its intention to

KEY DATES

1987: Brothers Rémy and Patrice Lesguer establish the first Vêt'Affaires store in Rezé, near Nantes, France.

1994: Vêt'Affaires creates a central purchasing division as it expands its retail network.

2000: Vêt'Affaires sells shares on the Paris Bourse's Marché Libre.

2003: Vêt'Affaires lists its stock on the Secondary Market of the Euronext Paris exchange.

2010: Vêt'Affaires announces plans to extend its retail network to more than 200 stores by 2013.

shift its listing to the Bourse's Secondary Market early in the new decade.

FILLING THE GAP

The public offering helped raise the company's profile, and its sales soared in 2001, gaining 36 percent over the previous year. The company's firm focus on the hard discount segment of the clothing market played a major part in its success. At the dawn of the 21st century the large-scale distribution sector, once the leading source of low-priced clothing, had shifted its own textile sales model to more upscale clothing. As Rémy Lesguer explained to *Les Echos*: "There left a gap to be filled."

The demand for low-cost clothing continued to soar at the beginning of the new century. In response, Vêt'Affaires decided to launch a still more ambitious store opening program, with plans to open 10 stores per year. The company's new expansion program also targeted wider growth beyond its core northwestern region, in order to build Vêt'Affaires into a national retail player. As part of this effort, the company added a new 4,000-square-meter warehouse and logistics platform.

Vêt'Affaires made good on its promise to join the Secondary Market in June 2003. By then the company's retail network neared 50 stores, topping that milestone before the end of the year. However, a shadow fell over the company's success when the company's Sunday store opening schedule brought it under investigation by the Nantes Fraud Commission. The company and the Lesguers defended themselves against charges of violating the commercial code, while affirming their desire to see the restrictions on Sunday store openings lifted. The

Lesguers also responded to accusations that the company violated the rights of the store managers by pointing out that, unlike other franchise models, Vêt'Affaires also enabled their store managers to become owners of the stores and shareholders in the company.

In the meantime, the company's revenues continued to build strongly. By the end of 2004 the company's total sales had topped EUR 115 million, generating net profits of EUR 16.4 million. Part of this increase came through the ongoing expansion of the company's store network, which topped 60 stores by the end of 2004. At the same time, the company also succeeded in increasing its per-client purchases. This was accomplished in part by redeveloping the company's existing textiles lines with updated fashions. The company also expanded its range of products, adding shoes and accessories.

REVENUES TUMBLE

Vêt'Affaires had good reason to be optimistic at the middle of the decade. Trade barriers that had blocked the massive entry of low-cost textiles from China and other Asian markets into the European Union were lowered in 2005. While this spelled disaster for the remnants of the European textiles industry, discount retailers such as Vêt'Affaires rejoiced in the new availability of larger quantities of even lower cost goods. Vêt'Affaires shifted still more of its sourcing to the Far East. By the end of the decade, more than 80 percent of the goods sold in the company's stores came from China and other Asian markets.

Vêt'Affaires also moved to gain greater control of its purchasing program. To this end, the company created a new subsidiary in Hong Kong that instead of buying clothing directly, purchased the basic fabrics, which were then supplied to a network of partner manufacturers chosen by Vêt'Affaires. This move helped to drive down the company's costs still further, while also raising the quality of its garments.

The influx of inexpensive Asian clothing caused prices to drop across the retail sector, a development that benefited especially more upscale, branded retail networks, such as Zara, H&M, and C&A, as well as the large-scale hypermarket groups. The company also faced competition from a growing number of hard discount clothing chains, including Tati and Babou. As a result, Vêt'Affaires saw its revenues tumble, despite the further extension of its retail network to 75 stores by the end of 2005.

By the end of 2006 the company saw its network of stores shrink for the first time, dropping back to just 73 stores. At the same time, its sales tumbled to EUR 90.4

million while its net profits dropped to EUR 1.6 million. Furthermore, a dispute over strategy broke out between the founding Lesguer brothers. As a result, Patrice Lesguer resigned as the company president, replaced by Rémy Lesguer.

EXPANSION DRIVE CONTINUES

Vêt'Affaires faced new troubles from the law when two of its former managers filed a lawsuit against the company in the Nantes court in 2005. The pair claimed in the suit that they had been de facto employees of Vêt'Affaires, and not independent workers, and sought to be recognized as such. The lawsuit, which reached a final decision in 2008, provided another distraction for the company as it sought to regain its momentum in the second half of the decade.

Vêt'Affaires nevertheless forged ahead with its expansion drive, topping 85 stores by the end of 2008. Rémy and Patrice Lesguer suffered a personal setback that year when they lost the lawsuit against them. The brothers each received a sentence of eight months' probation and a fine of EUR 30,000. Despite the loss, Vêt'Affaires refused to abandon its commitment to its owner-manager model and the Sunday store opening schedule. Instead, the company developed a new model for its store operations. The new model created a series of 35 limited liability companies, entirely owned by the store managers. Each company in turn operated three Vêt'Affaires stores. In this way, Vêt'Affaires could more successfully claim that its store managers remained independent of the company.

While Vêt'Affaires remained under pressure, it nevertheless benefited from the economic crisis at the end of the decade. As the difficult economic conditions extended into the beginning of the next decade, the company's hard discount formula became all the more attractive to shoppers. The company also continued to pursue its retail expansion strategy, opening its 100th store in March 2010. By September of that year, the company's network counted 115 stores. Vêt'Affaires also announced plans to expand its total retail network to more than 200 stores by 2013. Vêt'Affaires thus hoped to remain one of France's leaders in the discount clothing sector through the new decade.

M. L. Cohen

PRINCIPAL SUBSIDIARIES

Alens SNC; Central'Vet SARL; Format Vet SARL; Moda Tanio sp zoo (Poland); Pm Dis SARL; Roll (Hong Kong); Yvet SAS.

PRINCIPAL DIVISIONS

Retail; Wholesale; Internet.

PRINCIPAL COMPETITORS

Camaieu International S.A.S.; C&A France SCS; Financiere Zannier S.A.S.; La Halle S.A.; H & M Hennes & Mauritz S.A.R.L.; Kiabi Europe S.A.S.; Phildar S.A.; Poloco S.A.S.; Tati S.A.; Vetir S.A.S.

FURTHER READING

Cousseau, Christine. "Règlement de Compte au Sein de la Famille Lesguer." *Investir*, October 10, 2005.

"French Discount Clothing Retail Chain Vêt'Affaires (EPA:VET) Wishes to Double Its Sales Points Network in the Next 10 Years." *ADPNews*, January 9, 2010.

Guimard, Emmanuel. "Vêt'Affaires Renforce Ses Structures pour Doubler de Taille." *Les Echos*, April 15, 2004, p. 18.

La Casiniere, Nicolas de. "Vêt'Affaires, l'Art du Déguisement." *Liberation*, September 29, 2003.

Le Masson, Thomas. "Le Bourse s'Inquiète des Difficultés du Hard-discounter Vêt'Affaires." *Les Echos*, April 5, 2006, p. 19.

———. "L'Enseigne de Hard-discount Vêt'Affaires Cherche à Redresser la Barre." *Les Echos*, November 16, 2005, p. 22.

Mourlot, Nathalie. "L'École de la Vie." *L'Entreprise*, April 22, 2002.

"Vêt'Affaires Bénéficie des Nouvelles Conditions d'Achat en Chine." *Les Echos*, April 8, 2005, p. 19.

"Vêt'Affaires dans de Sales Draps." *20 Minutes*, December 19, 2008.

"Vêt'Affaires Plunges on '09 Results." *ADP News France*, April 9, 2010.

"Vêt'Affaires Taille un Costard à la Concurrence." *Points de Vente*, April 19, 2010.

"Vêt'Affaires Veut S'Etendre au-delà du Grand Ouest." *Les Echos*, April 20, 2001, p. 19.

Weinbrenner Shoe
Company, Inc.

108 South Polk Street
Merrill, Wisconsin 54452-2348
U.S.A.
Telephone: (715) 536-5521
Fax: (715) 536-1172
Web site: http://www.weinbrennerusa.com

Private Company
Incorporated: 1892 as Weinbrenner-Peffer Co.
Employees: 300
NAICS: 316200 Footwear Manufacturing

■ ■ ■

Weinbrenner Shoe Company, Inc., is one of the few U.S. shoe manufacturers to survive global competition by focusing on niche categories. The Merrill, Wisconsin-based private company offers work and safety shoes under the Thorogood brand, as well as shoes made specifically for postal carriers and police officers, and boots for firefighters under the Thorogood Hellfire name. Weinbrenner also manufactures military boots, motorcycle boots, hiking boots, and wading boots for fishing. In addition to a plant in Merrill, Weinbrenner operates a manufacturing facility in Marshfield, Wisconsin. The company is owned by its employees through a stock ownership plan.

SHOE JOBBER ORIGINS: 1892

The person behind the Weinbrenner name was Albert H. Weinbrenner. Born in 1865, he was the son of one of Milwaukee's earliest shoemakers, Peter Weinbrenner,

described by the *Milwaukee Sentinel*, on November 12, 1942, as a "fashionable bootier." He advertised himself as "P. Weinbrenner, Premium Boot and Shoe Maker." The younger Weinbrenner learned the trade at the age of 13 from his father, who passed away in 1881 at the age of 55.

Albert Weinbrenner continued to work as a shoemaker and in 1892 was able to take on a partner, Joseph Peffer. The partners established a business as a shoe jobber, buying large quantities of shoes and reselling them. The business, known as Weinbrenner-Peffer Co., started out with just $340 in capital and was located on Lake Street in Milwaukee.

Weinbrenner-Peffer enjoyed success providing boots to the logging industry, allowing Weinbrenner after seven years to begin manufacturing shoes as a side venture. Starting out with $500 in capital, Weinbrenner was able to increase that amount to $10,000 by the dawn of the 20th century. In 1903 the partners went their separate ways. Peffer preferred to remain a jobber and Weinbrenner elected to dedicate himself to manufacturing, operating as the Albert H. Weinbrenner Shoe Company. Weinbrenner prospered in his line of business, and in 1909 built a plant on Juneau Avenue in Milwaukee.

Focusing on dress and work shoes for boys and men, Weinbrenner ran his business until 1927. Then in his early 60s, he decided to sell a controlling interest in the company and go into semi-retirement, although he remained chairman of the board. New management soon had to contend with the impact of the Great Depression that lingered until the early 1940s when the

COMPANY PERSPECTIVES

Weinbrenner Shoe Company has been both a leading manufacturer and a pioneering force in the American footwear industry since beginning operations in 1892, initiating many of the safety and job-fitted design elements that are common today.

economy finally recovered. In the meantime, efforts were made to stimulate the economy at both national and local levels.

In 1933 the city of Marshfield, Wisconsin, persuaded Weinbrenner Shoe to operate a factory on the site of a former furniture factory to create jobs for its residents. The city paid for the land, and funds from the Federal Emergency Relief Administration paid for the construction of the factory, which opened in 1935. The city leased back the factory to Weinbrenner Shoe at a nominal fee. By the end of the year, the factory was employing 200 people.

COMPANY SOLD: 1960

Other Wisconsin communities followed Marshfield's lead, and in 1936 Weinbrenner Shoe added a factory in Merrill, followed two years later by a plant in Antigo. Another plant later opened in Rib Lake, Wisconsin. As a result, the Milwaukee plant, which at its peak employed more than 1,000, was closed. The company elected to retain its Milwaukee headquarters and warehouse, however.

A death in Weinbrenner's management in 1940 forced Albert Weinbrenner to come out of retirement to take a more direct role in running the business. The company enjoyed a surge in business, due in large measure to orders for boots from the Army and Navy that resulted from increased military spending for World War II. Weinbrenner remained active in the company through the war years. He retired again in 1946, due to illness. Weinbrenner died in 1949 at the age of 84.

Then known as the Weinbrenner Shoe Manufacturing Co., the company operated plants in Antigo, Marshfield, and Merrill. In 1960 the Weinbrenner family sold the company to Textron, Inc., a diversified industrial company based in Providence, Rhode Island, that many considered to be the world's first conglomerate.

Founded by Royal Little in 1928 as a specialty yarn manufacturer, Textron branched out in a number of directions in the 1950s in an effort to achieve diversity.

In the same year it acquired Weinbrenner, for example, Textron also entered the aerospace industry with the purchase of Bell Aircraft. The company was soon involved in such areas as tools, industrial machines, appliances, consumer goods, and plastics.

COMPANY ACQUIRED BY BATA LIMITED: 1966

Textron, although it soon acquired a second shoe company, Beloit, Illinois-based Freeman Shoe Corp., was not committed to the shoe business. In 1966 Textron sold Weinbrenner, which was then making its headquarters in Merrill. The buyer was Bata Limited, a family business with ties to shoemaking that stretched back more than 20 generations to 1580 and a small Czech village.

Three hundred years later the Bata family opened its first factory, comprising two sewing machines in a pair of rented rooms. In 1900 the operation was moved to a larger facility where steam-driven machines were installed. The Bata operation became a true factory following a visit to the United States to learn the ways of mass production from a New England shoe company.

Military sales from World War I took Bata to another level, and intelligent management during a recession in the early 1920s helped Bata to become the largest shoemaker in the world a decade later. In many developing countries where there was no word for shoe, "bata" entered the vocabulary in that capacity. World War II then interrupted the company's growth.

In 1939, when Nazi Germany was on the verge of invading Czechoslovakia, a member of the Bata family fled to Canada to establish a factory. The operations in Czechoslovakia were lost to the Germans and after the war were nationalized by the Communist government installed by the Soviet Union. The Canadian outpost was left to rebuild the shoe business, which the family did with great success. By the mid-1950s Bata maintained 56 factories in 46 countries.

CONSOLIDATION LEADS TO SALE

Weinbrenner was just a small part of the Bata empire. The company focused on service, duty, and safety-toe footwear, although it also launched a line of women's work shoes in the late 1970s and produced outdoor footwear. James V. Greenlee served as president starting in 1971. He held the post until 1982, when he suffered a stroke and lost his ability to speak. After recovering and working as a consultant for several years, he emerged as a suitor for Weinbrenner.

By this time, the manufacture of shoes had shifted increasingly to Pacific Rim countries, where lower labor

KEY DATES

1892: Weinbrenner-Peffer Co. is founded as a shoe jobber business.
1903: Albert Weinbrenner splits with partner to focus on shoe manufacturing.
1960: Company sold to Textron Inc.
1966: Bata Limited acquires company.
1987: Company sold to management group.
2003: Company secures procurement contract for boots from U.S. Department of Defense.

costs provided manufacturers with a competitive edge that drove shoe companies elsewhere in the world out of business. Because of its far-flung operations, Bata was better able to compete than most, but it too suffered and was forced to make changes.

In the United States the company elected to focus on retailing rather than manufacturing, and in the process closed Weinbrenner's Antigo plant in 1986, consolidating the operations with the Merrill plant. Bata was thus open to a possible sale of Weinbrenner to Greenlee and a group of investors he led that included members of Weinbrenner's management team as well as local investors.

MANAGEMENT BUYOUT: 1987

After nine months of negotiations, Greenlee acquired Weinbrenner in December 1987 for an undisclosed sum. Furthermore, Weinbrenner had made the transition from dress shoes to safety, work, and uniform shoes, a niche that still allowed a U.S. manufacturer to remain competitive. Well established in its market, Weinbrenner was a major supplier of service shoes to police forces and postal workers, selling its products under its own Thorogood brand as well as private labels. The company also produced electrostatic dissipating footwear for workers assembling computer circuit boards.

Greenlee once again served as Weinbrenner's president. Although the company's focus remained work shoes, Greenlee was also interested in expanding the women's line of safety shoes and rebuilding the Wood 'N Stream line of outdoor footwear, including hunting, fishing, hiking, and walking boots, many of which were sold to such catalogers as L.L. Bean, Eddie Bauer, and Lands' End. The business had been neglected in favor of the core work shoe business.

A new chief executive, Lance Niewnow, who had been with the company since 1959, took charge in 1992. Weinbrenner added a new raw materials warehouse to the Merrill plant in 1993 and later acquired a warehouse in the area. Although work shoes remained the heart of Weinbrenner's business in the 1990s, the company could not rely on the same models year after year. Although hardly as mercurial as the dress and athletic shoe business, dependent on constantly shifting fashions, work shoes still had to change with the needs of the customers.

For the important law enforcement market, Weinbrenner had to keep tabs on what younger police officers wanted. Because market research indicated that they wanted duty shoes that were lightweight and offered more athletic styling, Weinbrenner introduced a new line of Thorogood uniform shoes that met those goals. The shoes also featured deep tread patterns for better traction and a wedge-designed heel to distribute body weight evenly to alleviate tired feet.

Weinbrenner also made advances in safety shoes in the early 1990s. It introduced a nonmetallic toe cap, the ULTEC 2000, which the company claimed was the first major advancement in protective footwear in nearly 70 years. Instead of metal, the toe cap was molded from a new polymer composite specifically designed to dissipate impact and compression. The cap also weighed one-third less than a comparable metal version.

21ST-CENTURY OPPORTUNITIES

Weinbrenner remained competitive in the United States by focusing on job-specific shoes, while also developing customers around the world. By the start of the new century about 10 percent of its sales came from outside North America. World events then presented the company with new and unexpected opportunities. The terrorist attacks against the United States on September 11, 2001, heightened the need for domestic security and led to increased federal funding for police officers, SWAT teams, sky marshals, and airport security personnel. For Weinbrenner that meant increased demand for the kind of footwear in which the company specialized.

Weinbrenner also continued to introduce new features to cater to this growing market, incorporating athletic technology to create footwear that could bear the 20 to 30 pounds of gear worn by law enforcement officers, including weapons, ammunition, and radios. For example, in 2002 Weinbrenner introduced a new dual air-bag system that placed a cushioned air bag in the heel reinforced with PVC molded springs. The result was a lightweight comfortable shoe with improved load-bearing capabilities.

In addition to security concerns at home, the United States was soon fighting wars in Afghanistan and Iraq. Although Weinbrenner had not provided boots to the military for many years, it was prepared to meet the footwear needs created by the overseas conflicts. In 2003 the company secured a procurement contract from the U.S. Department of Defense for a Safety Toe Desert Boot. In 2008 Weinbrenner won a contract to supply hot weather boots for all branches of the military, as well as the Coast Guard. In business for well over a century, Weinbrenner appeared to be well positioned to enjoy continued growth for many years to come.

Ed Dinger

PRINCIPAL COMPETITORS

Justin Brands, Inc.; Red Wing Shoe Company Inc.; Wolverine World Wide, Inc.

FURTHER READING

"Albert H. Weinbrenner in Business 50 Years." *Milwaukee Sentinel*, November 12, 1942.

Goldenberg, Jane. "Weinbrenner Ex-President to Buy Concern from Bata." *Footwear News*, January 4, 1988, p. 2.

——. "Weinbrenner Goals Undergoing Change." *Footwear News*, March 28, 1988, p. 17.

Marquardt, Joy. "Shoe Maker Outfits World's Workers." *Wausau Daily Herald*, May 15, 2007, p. A6.

Schneider-Levy, Barbara. "Securing a Market." *Footwear News*, November 11, 2002, p. 14.

Wirtgen Beteiligungsgesellschaft mbh

Reinhard-Wirtgen-Strasse 2
Windhagen, D-53578
Germany
Telephone: (+49 2645) 131-0
Fax: (+49 2645) 131-813
Web site: http://www.wirtgen-group.com

Private Company
Incorporated: 1961 as Wirtgen GmbH
Employees: 4,500
Sales: EUR 1.2 billion ($1.6 billion) (2009)
NAICS: 333120 Construction Machinery Manufacturing; 333516 Rolling Mill Machinery and Equipment Manufacturing; 333131 Mining Machinery and Equipment Manufacturing

■ ■ ■

Wirtgen Beteiligungsgesellschaft mbh is the holding company of the German Wirtgen Group, a leading manufacturer of heavy machinery for road construction and mining. The company is represented by four major brands, all headquartered in Germany. Wirtgen GmbH, located in Windhagen, produces machinery used to build new roads and to rehabilitate older roads. The company is the world's leading manufacturer of cold-milling equipment.

Another subsidiary, Joseph Vögele AG of Mannheim, makes pavers and other equipment for paving processes. Vögele is also the global leader in its sector. A third subsidiary, Hamm AG, with production facilities in Tirschenreuth, Bavaria, is the third-largest maker of rollers used in the compaction of soils and asphalt. Wirtgen's fourth subsidiary, Kleemann GmbH of Göppingen, manufactures mobile and stationary crushers and screeners in the mining and stone and earth industries.

In addition, the Wirtgen Group has three foreign production sites: Vögele America Inc. of Chambersburg, Pennsylvania; Ciber Ltda. in Brazil; and Wirtgen Machinery Langfang in China. Wirtgen is represented throughout the world by another 55 subsidiaries that specialize in sales and service. Over 100 additional licensed dealers round out the company's global network. The Wirtgen Group is owned and managed by the Wirtgen family.

FROM TRANSPORTATION TO MACHINE BUILDING AFTER 1961

When company founder Reinhard Wirtgen started his own transportation business in 1961, he was only eighteen years old. As a subcontractor for road construction companies, the one-man operation hauled materials to and from construction sites in a truck in and around Windhagen, a small city southeast of Bonn in the German Westerwald region. After a day's work was done, Wirtgen rolled up his sleeves for a second shift, working on the modest building that was soon to become the headquarters of his company. Reinhard Wirtgen, however, was not only a driven and hardworking man. The passionate entrepreneur was also a skilled electronic technician, and had an exceptional talent for developing technical solutions for an industry in which much work was still being done by hand.

COMPANY PERSPECTIVES

Innovator—market leader—pacesetter—pioneer—trailblazer. There are many names for the strong position of the four German brands united under the umbrella of the Wirtgen Group. For Wirtgen, Vögele, Hamm and Kleemann have shaped numerous tried-and-tested technologies for the construction industry and opencast mining industry worldwide. This strength will continue to be a hallmark of the Wirtgen Group. For innovative construction, mining and processing methods—made in Germany—are more in demand than ever before, and are appreciated by investors and users around the globe.

One of Wirtgen's first inventions was a concrete crushing machine for the building rubble his company removed from old torn-down structures. With road construction booming in West Germany in the 1960s, the company founder set his sights on this major growth market. It was in the late 1960s when Wirtgen built his first hot-milling machine that removed the defective asphalt pavement before a road was repaved. Used in practice for the first time in 1970, Wirtgen's machine proved to be a success, which led the company on to a different path—the construction of machinery.

By the mid-1970s the company had built more than 100 machines that were rented out to customers in Germany as well as in many other European countries. In the late 1970s Wirtgen pioneered the cold-milling technology by developing the first cold planer. Until then the old pavement had to be reheated before it could be removed. Wirtgen's cold-milling machine made this energy-intensive process obsolete. The end of the decade marked the beginning of Wirtgen's success as a machine manufacturer when the company sold its first machines to customers in the construction industry.

In 1980 Wirtgen developed the first surface miner, a machine used for open-cast mining. Shortly after, Wirtgen decided to give up his transportation services branch and to focus solely on machine building. In 1986 the company launched a cold recycler for road repairs. Three years later Wirtgen established a new division for the development and manufacturing of slipform pavers for concrete road coverings. In the late 1980s and early 1990s Wirtgen's enterprise grew by leaps and bounds. The company established sales offices in many countries in Europe and around the world.

FROM COOPERATION WITH VÖGELE TO ACQUISITION IN 1996

The acquisition of Germany's leading manufacturer of asphalt pavers, Joseph Vögele AG, marked the beginning of a new era in the company's history. In order to offer his customers a full range of road construction machines and equipment, Reinhard Wirtgen began to complement his own product line by acquiring other German manufacturers. Established in 1836 by Joseph Vögele as a forge, the company started out as a manufacturer of railroad equipment. Vögele built switches, sliding and turning platforms, and shunting installations. However, as motorized vehicles evolved as a new means of transport in the first half of the 20th century, the company changed its main focus to road construction.

In 1929 the company launched a towed spreader for placing crushed stone and asphalt on the prepared road surface. In the decades that followed Vögele continued to develop highly innovative road-paving technologies. The company introduced a self-propelled spreader that not only spread but also smoothed out the bituminous pavement mix in 1938. After road construction had come to a halt in Germany during World War II, Vögele launched the first road paver that transported the mix to the applicator via a conveyor in 1950. Six years later the company's new Super 100 Asphalt Paver with its electrically heated floating screed set a milestone in modern asphalt paving methods.

Over the next 30 years Vögele continued to pioneer road-paving technologies. The company's diesel-hydraulic drive systems allowed regulation of the compacting pressure of the screed, and a new automated grade and slope control corrected the applied pavement profile to uneven surfaces. Vögele introduced paving equipment with varying widths, from half-road width that allowed the continuation of traffic in the lane next to the one that was being worked on, to heavy-duty pavers up to 16 meters wide. Other Vögele innovations were special pressure bars for high compaction that greatly increased pavement density, and an environmentally friendly paver with a combined diesel-electric drive system.

The early 1990s saw Vögele and Wirtgen cooperate in selected export markets. Since the two companies targeted the same clientele while their product lines complemented each other, Wirtgen which had established an extensive sales network in many parts of the world, started selling Vögele products as well, for example in Eastern Europe. By that time Vögele was leading the world market for pavers and exported roughly two-thirds of its annual output. In 1994 Wirtgen acquired a 12 percent stake in the publicly traded

KEY DATES

1961: Reinhard Wirtgen starts a transportation business for construction materials.

1970: Wirtgen's first hot-milling machine is used in road construction.

1979: The company pioneers cold-milling technology.

1996: Wirtgen acquires a majority stake in asphalt paver manufacturer Joseph Vögele.

1997: Reinhard Wirtgen's sons Jürgen and Stefan take over company management.

2006: Wirtgen takes over rock-crushing equipment firm Kleemann.

2009: Wirtgen and Kleemann open new production facilities in Windhagen and Göppingen.

company, according to *Börsen-Zeitung,* on May 11, 1995. In the following two years Wirtgen GmbH raised its share in Vögele to a majority stake of roughly 70 percent by acquiring stakes in the company from other major shareholders.

CONTINUED GROWTH THROUGH ACQUISITIONS IN LATE 20TH CENTURY

In addition to Vögele, Wirtgen acquired the milling machine division from the U.S.-manufacturer Ingersoll-Rand in late 1995. In 1997, however, only one year after the Vögele acquisition that made his company the leading supplier of mobile asphalt processing machines, Reinhard Wirtgen died in a car accident. Literally over night, his two sons Jürgen, in his early 30s, and Stefan, in his mid-20s, jointly took on the company's management. One of their first tasks was the integration of Vögele into the company. In 1999 Wirtgen took over complete control over Vögele when the company bought out the Vögele family and acquired the remaining shares from small shareholders.

Only two years later the two Wirtgen brothers continued their father's strategy of growth by acquisitions when the company took over Hamm AG, a Bavarian manufacturer of compaction machines and equipment based in Tirschenreuth in the Upper Palatinate. Founded in 1878 by the two brothers and gunsmiths Franz and Anton Hamm as Maschinenfabrik Gebr. Hamm, the company built threshing machines at first. After the turn of the 19th century, however, the Hamm brothers changed their focus from agricultural machines

to road construction when they presented the world's first diesel-powered road roller in 1911. Hamm's three-wheeled motor roller became an instant success in the market and the company enjoyed rapid growth until World War I.

In the early 1920s Anton Hamm's two sons Alois and Anton Jr. took over the company. They decided to focus solely on road rollers and continued to pioneer the field. In 1932 the company launched its patented tandem roller with all-wheel drive and steering, another world-first. With road reconstruction in full swing after World War II, Hamm continued to thrive. In 1963 the company introduced the first roller with rubber wheels, and all-wheel drive and steering. In the following years Hamm established its own worldwide network of independent dealers and distributors. During the 1970s and 1980s the company continued to update and broaden its range of tandem, rubber-wheeled, and static three-wheel rollers and compactors.

After a series of reorganizations and an owner change in the early 1980s the company was renamed Hamm Walzenfabrik GmbH in 1984. In the middle of the decade Hamm built a brand-new factory at a larger site, and established a subsidiary in the United States. In the 1990s the company worked intensively on the development of new machines for soil stabilization and bitumen recycling, which were launched later in the decade. In 1997 the company was transformed into a stock corporation and renamed Hamm AG. After the Wirtgen takeover two years later, Hamm was able to significantly increase its sales due to the new parent company's extensive sales and distribution network.

KLEEMANN ACQUISITION FOLLOWS IN 2006

With the acquisition of Kleemann GmbH, a manufacturer of mobile and stationary crushing and screening equipment for the quarry, construction, demolition, and recycling industries in 2006, Wirtgen further expanded its product portfolio to the market for construction raw materials processing equipment. Kleemann's history began in 1857 when Ferdinand Kleemann set up a workshop in Obertürkheim near Stuttgart where he started making rasps. By the time the company founder's four sons took over the business in 1878, it had grown into an industrial enterprise that manufactured agricultural equipment and machines which were sold all over Germany. Heinrich Kleemann, one of the sons, married the daughter of entrepreneur J. G. Hildebrand and became partner and in 1902 owner of the machine tool and equipment firm Hildebrand & Söhne based in Faurndau near Göppingen.

In 1902 the two companies were merged as Kleemann's Vereinigte Fabriken Obertürkheim und Faurndau, which manufactured a broad variety of products, from wine presses and pumps to electrical lifts and elevators to brick machines and diggers. By 1920 the company's workforce had grown to roughly 300. It was around that time when Kleemann started manufacturing equipment for processing natural rock and stone, which evolved as the company's main business activity after World War II. After a prosperous period in the 1950s and 1960s the company found itself struggling financially a decade later.

In 1980 the company was taken over by conveyor producer Reiner, and the two companies were merged as Kleemann-Reiner Maschinen- und Anlagenbau GmbH. With the development of the first tracked crushing and screening equipment for hard rock in the late 1980s, the company returned to healthy growth. Within a decade, Kleemann's sales tripled and the company began to export its continuously expanding range of rock crushers, which were used in mining as well as in construction materials recycling. In 2005 the company was renamed Kleemann GmbH. One year later the Wirtgen group acquired an 80 percent stake in the company.

RISING DEMAND AND GROWING COMPETITION AFTER 2005

For many years Wirtgen had enjoyed annual two-digit growth rates, often of over 20 percent. By the middle of the first decade of the 2000s the Wirtgen Group had become one of the world's leading manufacturers of road-building equipment, grossing more than $1 billion annually. The company positioned itself as the all-round supplier of machinery and equipment to road-building contractors and rental companies around the world with additional production and assembly plants in the United States, Brazil, and China. In 2005 the American Road & Transportation Builders Association named Reinhard Wirtgen one of the Top 100 private sector transportation construction professionals of the 20th century.

An unprecedented global road construction boom in the second half of the decade brought the Wirtgen companies to the limits of their production capacity. In 2009 a newly built plant for the manufacturing of special machinery commenced production on the greatly extended premises of Wirtgen GmbH in Windhagen. In the same year Kleemann moved production to a brand-new and much larger plant in Göppingen. In 2010 construction activities had begun for Vögele's new and much larger production site in Ludwigshafen-Rheingöttingen, to which the company was planning to move its headquarters from Mannheim.

One of the main challenges Wirtgen was facing late in the decade was the rising competition from Chinese manufacturers, who offered road-building equipment at much lower prices. However, company owners and managers Stefan and Jürgen Wirtgen were optimistic that, because of numerous infrastructure projects in emerging economies and in industrialized as well as in developing countries around the world, the demand for high-quality road construction machines and rock processing equipment made in Germany would remain on a high level in the foreseeable future.

In 2009 the company announced that new Wirtgen subsidiaries had been established in Ankara, Turkey; Poznań, Poland; and Pune, India, where an assembly plant for Hamm single-drum compactors was set up in addition to a large sales and service center. The company also reported that 70 machines made by the Wirtgen Group were being used in the construction of the Autoroute Transmaghrébine, the world's largest highway construction project connecting Morocco, Algeria, and Tunisia. In 2010 Wirtgen appointed Construmac as the company's new dealer in Mexico.

Evelyn Hauser

PRINCIPAL SUBSIDIARIES

Joseph Vögele AG (98%); Wirtgen GmbH; Kleemann GmbH; Hamm AG; Vögele America Inc. (USA); Ciber Ltda. (Brazil); Wirtgen Machinery Langfang (China); baukema Handel GmbH; Wirtgen International GmbH.

PRINCIPAL COMPETITORS

BOMAG GmbH; Caterpillar; Deutag GmbH & Co KG; Dynapac; Ed. Züblin AG; Herbert Preissler Baumaschinen GmbH & Co.; Sany Group; Shantui Construction Machinery Co., Ltd.; Zoomlion.

FURTHER READING

Cooper, Martin. "Hamm Heads to Number One: With a New Owner, Hamm Is Competing Strongly in the Compaction Market." *Plant Manager's Journal,* February 1, 2005, p. 18.

Dierig, Carsten. "So einen Aufschwung haben wir noch nie erlebt." *Welt,* May 14, 2007, p. 13.

Fasse, Markus. "Wirtgen: Die Asphaltbrüder." *Handelsblatt,* May 4, 2007.

"Gründerfamilie nicht mehr bei Vögele." *Börsen-Zeitung,* January 13, 1999, p. 10.

Kern, Felix, and Michaela Mayländer. *Faszination Strassenbau.* Stuttgart, Germany: Motorbuch Verlag, 2005.

"Kleemann Inc., USA." *Pit & Quarry,* December 1, 2008, p. 52.

"Q & A with Evan Clarke." *Rock Products,* January 1, 2008.

Retrospective. Tirschenreuth, Germany: Hamm AG, 2002.

Sachsenroeder, Delphine. "Wirtgen will 100 Stellen in Windhagen schaffen." *General-Anzeiger* (Bonn), August 13, 2005, p. 4.

Sleight, Chris. "Family Values." *International Construction,* June 1, 2006, p. 12.

"Wirtgen Group." *Equipment Today Magazine,* January 1, 2005, p. 80.

"Wirtgen haelt 12 Prozent an Vögele." *Börsen-Zeitung,* May 11, 1995, p. 11.

"Wirtgen haelt nun 26 Prozent an Vögele." *Börsen-Zeitung,* December 13, 1995, p. 6.

"Wirtgen uebernimmt Vögele-Mehrheit." *Börsen-Zeitung,* September 10, 1996, p. 9.

Zimmer Holdings, Inc.

345 East Main Street
Warsaw, Indiana 46580
U.S.A.
Telephone: (574) 267-6131
Toll Free: (800) 613-6131
Fax: (574) 372-4988
Web site: http://www.zimmer.com

Public Company
Incorporated: 1927 as Zimmer Manufacturing Company
Employees: 8,200
Sales: $4.1 billion (2009)
Stock Exchanges: New York
Ticker Symbol: ZMH
NAICS: 339113 Surgical Appliance and Supplies Manufacturing; 339114 Dental Equipment and Supplies Manufacturing

∎ ∎ ∎

Zimmer Holdings, Inc., is a global leader in orthopedic products including knee and hip implants. The company's other products are used in shoulder and elbow surgeries, dental reconstruction, the treatment of injured and broken bones, and in spinal procedures. Its customers are orthopedic surgeons, neurosurgeons, oral surgeons, dentists, hospitals, stocking distributors, and health-care dealers. Zimmer has operations in more than 25 countries and its products are marketed in over 100 countries across the globe. Approximately 40 percent of its sales originate outside the United States. In 2001 Zimmer was spun off as an independent company from Bristol-Myers Squibb. Since that time, the company has grown by making acquisitions and launching new products.

ORIGINS: 1920-29

Justin Zimmer was a national sales manager for DePuy, a splint company located in Warsaw, Indiana. He sold splints for the DePuy Company for 20 years and knew the market and the product. When he came up with a new product idea for aluminum splints in 1926, his employer was not interested in pursuing the idea or Zimmer's request to purchase an interest in the company.

Justin Zimmer decided to start his own company, and in 1927 Zimmer Manufacturing Company was born. He found two investors, William Felkner and William Rogers, and recruited two of his coworkers to join him in the new venture. J. J. Ettinger was the factory manager, and Donna Belle Harmon Cox, who had been his secretary at DePuy, was secretary and bookkeeper at the new company. Zimmer's basement provided the first manufacturing site for the company, and by May 1927 the company had products available for display.

Within one year, Zimmer Manufacturing was outselling DePuy and the new aluminum splints were in high demand. The company soon moved to a building on North Detroit Street in Warsaw, Indiana. In the first seven months, Zimmer had sales of $160,000. During the boom years of the 1920s, Zimmer grew quickly. In 1928 the company developed a fracture bed with a system to support patients while hospital sheets were

COMPANY PERSPECTIVES
■

Our vision is to be the global leader in enhanced quality of life for orthopaedic patients. To place confidence in the surgeons' skilled hands. To reaffirm our traditions, inspire our future and ensure our success through each patient's new freedom.

changed. The company also embraced the international market early in its history with the first order coming from a surgeon in Scotland.

STEADY GROWTH

While most of the businesses in the United States were experiencing major problems and downturns due to the Depression in the 1930s, Zimmer's sales and business continued to grow. Despite a high unemployment rate and mass layoffs across other industries, Zimmer had no layoffs during the difficult decade. In fact, during the Bank Holiday in 1933, the employees at Zimmer worked overtime to finish manufacturing a large shipment of splints for hospitals in New York City.

In 1930 sales topped $200,000. Zimmer was a key player during the polio epidemic in the late 1930s and developed custom fabricating braces that could be fitted to each patient's specific measurements. In that same period the company also introduced Dr. Vernon Luck's bone saw, complete with a motor and cord that could be sterilized. By 1942 Zimmer's sales exceeded $1 million.

In 1951 Justin Zimmer died while on vacation in Florida, leaving behind a successful company that would continue to bear his name. Zimmer's sales topped $2 million, and the company made several significant developments. Zimmer marketed the first hip prosthesis, developed with Dr. Palmer Eicher, in the 1950s, and the company released the Harrington Spinal Instrument, used to treat scoliosis, in 1958. The company worked closely with the American Medical Association to develop products that would benefit medicine and health.

By 1960 Zimmer's annual sales were $4 million, and its foreign sales increased with the opening of an Export Department within the company. The company continued to grow and in 1968 an expansion was planned for the manufacturing facility in Warsaw. In 1969 Zimmer purchased Little Manufacturing Company in North Carolina.

PART OF BRISTOL-MYERS

In 1970 total employment at Zimmer reached 522 people and sales were $27.2 million. The company's growth had been steady throughout the years and thus attracted the attention of an interested buyer. Zimmer became a subsidiary of Bristol-Myers, a New York-based medical company, in 1972. While operating as a subsidiary, Zimmer continued to grow and develop new products. The development of new tools with the availability of CAD/CAM systems allowed innovation to accelerate by the end of the 1970s. The new technology helped Zimmer with the development of such products as a hip prosthesis and the total knee system, a fully integrated modular system to replace artificial knees, in the 1980s.

The company helped fuel progress within the industry as well. Zimmer sponsored the first arthroscopy telesession that allowed 1,000 surgeons in 27 cities to view an arthroscopy surgery in real time. Zimmer's parent company, Bristol-Myers, began offering research grants under the Orthopedic Research and Education Foundation in 1983.

In 1990 the company built a new corporate headquarters in Warsaw, Indiana, and in 1997 Ray Elliott joined the Zimmer team as its president. Elliott had previously been vice president of Bristol-Myers Squibb and had 20 years of experience in the orthopedic industry. He had formerly worked for Baxter International, Southam, Inc., and Cablecom, Inc.

The company experienced rapid sales growth in the 1990s due to new developments and the aging of the baby boom population. In the 1990s this generation began turning 50 and reaching the age when they might need the orthopedic products and services of Zimmer. In 1998 sales were $861 million, and by 1999 that number had increased to $939 million. With more than 3,200 employees and $1 billion in sales, Zimmer's results for 2000 showed continued growth for the company and its products.

A NEW FUTURE AS ZIMMER
HOLDINGS, INC.: 2001

On August 7, 2001, the company spun off from its parent company, Bristol-Myers Squibb, and began trading on the New York Stock Exchange as an independent company. For nearly 30 years Zimmer had operated as a subsidiary, and it was once again its own entity. "We are excited about the opportunity to operate Zimmer as an independent public company and to continue to strengthen Zimmer's position as a global leader in orthopedics," said President and CEO Ray Elliott in a company press release. "Zimmer's recent financial

KEY DATES

1927: Company is founded by Justin Zimmer.
1928: Zimmer lands its first international customer.
1942: Sales exceed $1 million.
1951: Founder Justin Zimmer dies.
1972: Zimmer becomes a subsidiary of Bristol-Myers.
1997: Ray Elliott joins Zimmer as president and CEO.
2001: Zimmer spins off to become Zimmer Holdings, Inc.
2003: Swiss-based Centerpulse AG is purchased.
2007: Company pays the government $169.5 million to settle kickback charges; David Dvorak is named president and CEO.
2008: Abbott Spine is acquired.

performance has been excellent, and we plan to continue to pursue opportunities to leverage our brand and sales force in high-growth adjacent orthopedic product categories."

The company was selected by Standard & Poor's to be a part of the S&P 500 Index. In an interview with CNNfn on August 7, 2001, Elliott commented that he heard about the S&P 500 selection while on the road at a trade show. "We were hopeful of that, but it's an opportunity. We're actually the—I'm told, at least—we're the largest health care spinoff or IPO in the history of the business. So at a market cap of ... more than $5 billion, it's pretty exciting times," he said.

The company received Frost & Sullivan's Market Engineering Award for Sales Strategy Leadership in September 2001. Zimmer's sales force received the award due to the company's unique strategy of technical expertise and cooperation with the physician community. The company continued its close relationship within the medical community and announced the formation of a business team to further develop minimally invasive surgery options for hip surgery replacement.

FACING CHALLENGES

The newly spun off company also experienced challenges in 2001. The Japanese Fair Trade Commission brought unfair pricing practice allegations against Zimmer and three other orthopedic companies. A major share of Zimmer's international business was located in Japan, and the company announced that its pricing

practices did comply with the Japanese government regulations and that it was in full cooperation during the investigation. The commission alleged that Zimmer and the other companies had formed a cartel to fix prices in Japan.

In the third quarter of 2001, Zimmer's first quarter as an independent publicly traded company, the company increased sales by 14 percent worldwide and 22 percent in North and South America. As other segments of the economy were sluggish during a late 2001 recession, Zimmer's sales continued to increase and the company was on track to achieve its 13 percent sales increase for the year. By 2001 the company's products included knee implants, hip implants, and fracture management products, as well as other surgical products, including tourniquets, blood management systems, and orthopedic soft goods.

EMBRACING NEW TECHNOLOGY IN THE 21ST CENTURY

Just as Zimmer embraced CAD/CAM technology in the 1970s, it embraced the technology of the new millennium by working in conjunction with Alteer Office to market Internet-based management systems to orthopedic surgeons. The software provided a solution to paperwork and administration challenges, giving surgeons more time to focus on medical advances. The company's close relationship with the surgical community allowed it to provide the surgeons with tools to increase productivity both in and out of the operating room.

With aggressive product development and a history of growth, Zimmer Holdings, Inc., looked ahead to even greater goals. An aging population was one positive indicator for the company's future. By 2008 the U.S. Census Bureau reported that 12.8 percent of all Americans were 65 and over. People 65 and over were expected to make up 21 percent of the U.S. population by 2050. Better alternatives for orthopedic surgery and less-invasive options were also expected to increase the number of patients who participated in the surgeries. Population and technological advances were just two of the many factors that indicated continued success for the company.

ACQUISITIONS FUEL GROWTH

To take advantage of the growing orthopedic market, Zimmer made key acquisitions. During 2003 the company purchased Swiss-based Centerpulse AG, which gave the company a foothold in the spinal implant market as well as the reconstructive dental market. The $3.2 billion deal secured Zimmer's position as one of the world's largest orthopedic implant companies with leading market share in Europe, Japan, and the United States. By this time, the global orthopedic market was estimated at $14 billion and was growing at nearly 12 percent per year.

The company acquired Implex Corporation in 2004. The New Jersey-based metal technology developer had created Hedrocel, a biomaterial that was similar to human bone. Zimmer had marketed Hedrocel as Trabecular Metal since 2000.

Along with acquisitions, Zimmer continued to expand its arsenal by developing new products. During 2004 the company launched its Minimally Invasive Solutions Quad-Sparing product that allowed surgeons to perform total knee replacement without cutting muscles or tendons. It also developed new computer navigation technology used in knee replacement surgery. The company partnered with Medtronic Inc. in 2005 to launch the iNav Portable Electromagnetic Navigation System, which was also used in knee surgeries. The Gender Solutions Knee Implant, designed for female patients, was launched in 2006.

OVERCOMING KICKBACK ALLEGATIONS

While Zimmer enjoyed the leading spot in the industry based on sales during this period, the company fell victim to bad press in March 2005 when it received its first subpoena from the U.S. Attorney's Office in New Jersey related to a kickback investigation. A U.S. Department of Justice investigation ensued that claimed Zimmer and other competing orthopedic firms gave money and gifts to surgeons in exchange for using their products. Zimmer agreed to pay the government $169.5 million to settle the charges in 2007. The company admitted no wrongdoing and agreed to be monitored through 2009. It also set a strict compliance program in place.

Meanwhile, Chairman, President, and CEO Elliott retired in 2007, leaving David C. Dvorak at the helm as president and CEO. The company made two acquisitions that year, including Endius Inc. and Orthosoft Inc. Massachusetts-based Endius developed minimally invasive spine surgery products while Montreal's Orthosoft developed orthopedic surgery computer navigation systems. Abbott Spine was acquired in 2008 for nearly $380 million. The deal expanded Zimmer's spine offerings and gave it a stronger foothold in this growing segment of the surgical market. Sales in 2008 surpassed $4 billion for the first time in company history.

During this period, the United States entered a recession that began to affect Zimmer's bottom line. Sales and net income both fell in 2009 as patients began putting off knee and hip replacement surgeries. Furthermore, the company was still feeling the effects of the kickback investigation it had been a part of. As surgeons continued to leave the company, Zimmer found itself battling for market share.

Despite these problems, Zimmer management was optimistic that conditions would improve and that new product development would bolster sales. While the company continued to invest in new technologies and looked for opportunities to secure its market position, it stood firm in its commitment to develop, produce, and market high-quality orthopedic products.

Melissa Rigney Baxter
Updated, Christina M. Stansell

PRINCIPAL SUBSIDIARIES

Zimmer, Inc.; Zimmer US, Inc.; Zimmer CEP USA Holding Co.; Zimmer Production, Inc.; Zimmer Spine, Inc.; Zimmer Manufacturing B.V.; Zimmer Investment Luxembourg SARL; Zimmer Switzerland Holdings Ltd.; Zimmer GmbH (Switzerland); Zimmer Germany GmbH; Zimmer K.K. (Japan).

PRINCIPAL COMPETITORS

Biomet, Inc.; DePuy Orthopaedics, Inc.; Smith & Nephew plc; Stryker Corporation; Synthes, Inc.; Tornier, Inc.; Wright Medical Group, Inc.

FURTHER READING

Burton, Thomas M., "Zimmer Taps Dvorak as CEO." *Wall Street Journal*, May 1, 2007.

Kamp, Jon. "Zimmer to Buy Abbott's Spinal Business for $360M." *Dow Jones Newswires*, September 5, 2008.

Nicklaus, David. "Shares in Spinoffs Can Clutter Up a Small Investor's Portfolio." *St. Louis Post-Dispatch*, September 1, 2001, p. 1.

"Orthopedics; David C. Dvorak Named President and CEO of Zimmer Holdings, Inc." *Biotech Week*, May 16, 2007.

Roniger, Lori Rochelle. "Zimmer Readies to Buy Orthosoft." *Biomechanics*, November 1, 2007.

Sherman, Debra. "Indiana City Thrives on Artificial Joints." *Reuters Business Report*, December 9, 2001.

"A Spinoff at Bristol-Myers." *New York Times*, August 7, 2001, p. C7.

"Warsaw, Ind.-Based Orthopedics Implant Maker Reports Financial Results." *News Sentinel*, July 26, 2001.

"Warsaw, Ind.-Based Orthopedics Implant Maker Zimmer Joins a Stock Index." *News Sentinel*, August 20, 2001.

"Zimmer Completes Its Exchange Offer for Centerpulse to Create Worldwide #1 Pure-Play in Orthopedics." *PR Newswire Europe*, October 2, 2003.

"Zimmer Seen Bleeding More Market Share in 2009." *Reuters News*, February 25, 2009.

Cumulative Index to Companies

*Listings in this index are arranged in alphabetical order under the company name. Company names beginning with a letter or proper name such as Eli Lilly & Co. will be found under the first letter of the company name. Definite articles (The, Le, La) are ignored for alphabetical purposes as are forms of incorporation that precede the company name (AB, NV). Company names printed in **bold** type have full, historical essays on the page numbers appearing in bold. Updates to entries that appeared in earlier volumes are signified by the notation (**upd.**). This index is cumulative with volume numbers printed in bold type.*

1–999

1-800-FLOWERS.COM, Inc., 26 344–46; 102 315–20 (upd.)
1-800-GOT-JUNK? LLC, 74 225–27
3Com Corporation, 11 518–21; 34 441–45 (upd.); 106 465–72 (upd.)
The 3DO Company, 43 426–30
3i Group PLC, 73 338–40
3M Company, 61 365–70 (upd.)
4imprint Group PLC, 105 187–91
4Kids Entertainment Inc., 59 187–89
5 & Diner Franchise Corporation, 72 135–37
7-Eleven, Inc., 32 414–18 (upd.); 112 364–71 (upd.)
8x8, Inc., 94 189–92
19 Entertainment Limited, 112 295–98
24/7 Real Media, Inc., 49 421–24
24 Hour Fitness Worldwide, Inc., 71 363–65

84 Lumber Company, 9 196–97; 39 134–36 (upd.); 120 1–5 (upd.)
99¢ Only Stores, 25 353–55; 100 301–05 (upd.)
180s, L.L.C., 64 299–301
365 Media Group plc, 89 441–44
800-JR Cigar, Inc., 27 139–41

A

A&E Television Networks, 32 3–7
A&P *see* The Great Atlantic & Pacific Tea Company, Inc.
A & W Brands, Inc., 25 3–5 *see also* Cadbury Schweppes PLC.
A-dec, Inc., 53 3–5
A-Mark Financial Corporation, 71 3–6
A. Smith Bowman Distillery, Inc., 104 1–4
A.B. Chance Industries Co., Inc. *see* Hubbell Inc.
A.B.Dick Company, 28 6–8
A.B. Watley Group Inc., 45 3–5
A.C. Moore Arts & Crafts, Inc., 30 3–5
A.C. Nielsen Company, 13 3–5 *see also* ACNielsen Corp.
A. Duda & Sons, Inc., 88 1–4
A. F. Blakemore & Son Ltd., 90 1–4
A.G. Edwards, Inc., 8 3–5; 32 17–21 (upd.)
A.G. Spanos Companies, 115 1–4
A.H. Belo Corporation, 10 3–5; 30 13–17 (upd.) *see also* Belo Corp.
A.L. Pharma Inc., 12 3–5 *see also* Alpharma Inc.
A.M. Castle & Co., 25 6–8
A. Moksel AG, 59 3–6
A.N. Deringer, Inc., 113 1–4
A. Nelson & Co. Ltd., 75 3–6

A. O. Smith Corporation, 11 3–6; 40 3–8 (upd.); 93 1–9 (upd.)
A.P. Møller-Mærsk A/S, 57 3–6; 119 1–6 (upd.)
A.S. Eesti Mobiltelefon, 117 1–4
A.S. Watson & Company Ltd., 84 1–4
A.S. Yakovlev Design Bureau, 15 3–6
A. Schulman, Inc., 8 6–8; 49 3–7 (upd.)
A.T. Cross Company, 17 3–5; 49 8–12 (upd.)
A.W. Faber-Castell Unternehmensverwaltung GmbH & Co., 51 3–6
A/S Air Baltic Corporation, 71 35–37
Aachener Printen- und Schokoladenfabrik Henry Lambertz GmbH & Co. KG, 110 1–5
AAF-McQuay Incorporated, 26 3–5
Aalborg Industries A/S, 90 5–8
AAON, Inc., 22 3–6
AAR Corp., 28 3–5
Aardman Animations Ltd., 61 3–5
Aarhus United A/S, 68 3–5
Aaron Brothers Holdings, Inc. *see* Michaels Stores, Inc.
Aaron's, Inc., 14 3–5; 35 3–6 (upd.); 114 1–6 (upd.)
AARP, 27 3–5
Aavid Thermal Technologies, Inc., 29 3–6
AB Volvo, I 209–11; 7 565–68 (upd.); 26 9–12 (upd.); 67 378–83 (upd.)
Abar Corporation *see* Ipsen International Inc.
ABARTA, Inc., 100 1–4
Abatix Corp., 57 7–9
Abaxis, Inc., 83 1–4
ABB Ltd., II 1–4; 22 7–12 (upd.); 65 3–10 (upd.)

CEMEX S.A. de C.V., 20 123–26; 59 111–16 (upd.)

CEMIG *see* Companhia Energética De Minas Gerais S.A.

Cencosud S.A., 69 92–94

Cendant Corporation, 44 78–84 (upd.) *see also* Wyndham Worldwide Corp.

Centamin Egypt Limited, 119 97–100

Centel Corporation, 6 312–15 *see also* EMBARQ Corp.

Centennial Communications Corporation, 39 74–76

Centerior Energy Corporation, V 567–68 *see also* FirstEnergy Corp.

Centerplate, Inc., 79 96–100

CenterPoint Energy, Inc., 116 96–99

Centex Corporation, 8 87–89; 29 93–96 (upd.); 106 100–04 (upd.)

Centocor Inc., 14 98–100

Central and South West Corporation, V 569–70

Central European Distribution Corporation, 75 90–92

Central European Media Enterprises Ltd., 61 56–59

Central Florida Investments, Inc., 93 137–40

Central Garden & Pet Company, 23 108–10; 58 57–60 (upd.)

Central Hudson Gas And Electricity Corporation, 6 458–60

Central Independent Television, 7 78–80; 23 111–14 (upd.)

Central Japan Railway Company, 43 103–06

Central Maine Power, 6 461–64

Central National-Gottesman Inc., 95 87–90

Central Newspapers, Inc., 10 207–09 *see also* Gannett Company, Inc.

Central Parking System, 18 103–05; 104 74–78 (upd.)

Central Retail Corporation, 110 77–81

Central Soya Company, Inc., 7 81–83

Central Sprinkler Corporation, 29 97–99

Central Vermont Public Service Corporation, 54 53–56

Centrica plc, 29 100–05 (upd.); 107 65–73 (upd.)

Centuri Corporation, 54 57–59

Century Aluminum Company, 52 71–74

Century Business Services, Inc., 52 75–78

Century Casinos, Inc., 53 90–93

Century Communications Corp., 10 210–12

Century Telephone Enterprises, Inc., 9 105–07; 54 60–63 (upd.)

Century Theatres, Inc., 31 99–101

Cenveo Inc., 71 100–04 (upd.)

CEPCO *see* Chugoku Electric Power Company Inc.

Cephalon, Inc., 45 93–96; 115 116–21 (upd.)

Cepheid, 77 93–96

Ceradyne, Inc., 65 100–02

Cerebos Gregg's Ltd., 100 96–99

Cerner Corporation, 16 92–94; 94 111–16 (upd.)

CertainTeed Corporation, 35 86–89

Certegy, Inc., 63 100–03

Cerveceria Polar, I 230–31 *see also* Empresas Polar SA.

České aerolinie, a.s., 66 49–51

Cesky Telecom, a.s., 64 70–73

Cessna Aircraft Company, 8 90–93; 27 97–101 (upd.)

Cetelem S.A., 21 99–102

CeWe Color Holding AG, 76 85–88

ČEZ a. s., 97 112–15

CF Industries Holdings, Inc., 99 89–93

CG&E *see* Cincinnati Gas & Electric Co.

CGM *see* Compagnie Générale Maritime.

CH2M HILL Companies Ltd., 22 136–38; 96 72–77 (upd.)

Chadbourne & Parke, 36 109–12

Chadwick's of Boston, Ltd., 29 106–08 *see also* Boston Apparel Group.

Chalk's Ocean Airways *see* Flying Boat, Inc.

The Chalone Wine Group, Ltd., 36 113–16

Champagne Bollinger S.A., 114 125–28

Champion Enterprises, Inc., 17 81–84

Champion Industries, Inc., 28 74–76

Champion International Corporation, IV 263–65; 20 127–30 (upd.) *see also* International Paper Co.

Championship Auto Racing Teams, Inc., 37 73–75

Chancellor Beacon Academies, Inc., 53 94–97

Chancellor Media Corporation, 24 106–10

Chanel SA, 12 57–59; 49 83–86 (upd.)

Channel Four Television Corporation, 93 141–44

Chantiers Jeanneau S.A., 96 78–81

Chaoda Modern Agriculture (Holdings) Ltd., 87 96–99

Chaparral Steel Co., 13 142–44

Charal S.A., 90 117–20

Chargeurs International, 6 373–75; 21 103–06 (upd.)

Charisma Brands LLC, 74 75–78

Charles M. Schulz Creative Associates, 114 129–33

The Charles Machine Works, Inc., 64 74–76

Charles River Laboratories International, Inc., 42 66–69

The Charles Schwab Corporation, 8 94–96; 26 64–67 (upd.); 81 62–68 (upd.)

The Charles Stark Draper Laboratory, Inc., 35 90–92

Charles Vögele Holding AG, 82 63–66

Charlotte Russe Holding, Inc., 35 93–96; 90 121–25 (upd.)

The Charmer Sunbelt Group, 95 91–94

Charming Shoppes, Inc., 8 97–98; 38 127–29 (upd.)

Charoen Pokphand Group, 62 60–63

Chart House Enterprises, Inc., 17 85–88; 96 82–86 (upd.)

Chart Industries, Inc., 21 107–09

Charter Communications, Inc., 33 91–94; 116 100–05 (upd.)

Charter Financial Corporation, 103 96–99

Charter Manufacturing Company, Inc., 103 100–03

ChartHouse International Learning Corporation, 49 87–89

Chas. Levy Company LLC, 60 83–85

Chase General Corporation, 91 102–05

The Chase Manhattan Corporation, II 247–49; 13 145–48 (upd.) *see also* JPMorgan Chase & Co.

Chateau Communities, Inc., 37 76–79

Chattanooga Bakery, Inc., 86 75–78

Chattem, Inc., 17 89–92; 88 47–52 (upd.)

Chautauqua Airlines, Inc., 38 130–32

CHC Helicopter Corporation, 67 101–03

Check Into Cash, Inc., 105 90–93

Check Point Software Technologies Ltd., 119 101–05

Checker Motors Corp., 89 144–48

Checkers Drive-In Restaurants, Inc., 16 95–98; 74 79–83 (upd.)

CheckFree Corporation, 81 69–72

Checkpoint Systems, Inc., 39 77–80

Chedraui *see* Grupo Comercial Chedraui S.A. de C.V.

The Cheesecake Factory Inc., 17 93–96; 100 100–05 (upd.)

Chef Solutions, Inc., 89 149–52

Chello Zone Ltd., 93 145–48

Chelsea Ltd., 102 74–79

Chelsea Milling Company, 29 109–11

Chelsea Piers Management Inc., 86 79–82

Chelsfield PLC, 67 104–06

Cheltenham & Gloucester PLC, 61 60–62

Chemcentral Corporation, 8 99–101

Chemed Corporation, 13 149–50; 118 88–91 (upd.)

Chemfab Corporation, 35 97–101

Chemi-Trol Chemical Co., 16 99–101

Chemical Banking Corporation, II 250–52; 14 101–04 (upd.)

Chemical Waste Management, Inc., 9 108–10

Chemring Group plc, 113 75–79

Chemtura Corporation, 91 106–20 (upd.)

CHEP Pty. Ltd., 80 63–66

Cherokee Inc., 18 106–09

Cherry Brothers LLC, 105 94–97

Cherry Lane Music Publishing Company, Inc., 62 64–67

Chesapeake Corporation, 8 102–04; 30 117–20 (upd.); 93 149–55 (upd.)

Chesapeake Utilities Corporation, 56 60–62

Chesebrough-Pond's USA, Inc., 8 105–07

Cheshire Building Society, 74 84–87

Cogentrix Energy, Inc., 10 229–31
Cognex Corporation, 76 102–06
Cognizant Technology Solutions
Corporation, 59 128–30
Cognos Inc., 44 108–11
Cohen & Steers, Inc., 119 110–13
Coherent, Inc., 31 122–25
Cohu, Inc., 32 117–19
Coinmach Laundry Corporation, 20
152–54
Coinstar, Inc., 44 112–14
Colas S.A., 31 126–29
Cold Spring Granite Company, 16
111–14; 67 118–22 (upd.)
Cold Stone Creamery, 69 98–100
Coldwater Creek Inc., 21 129–31; 74
88–91 (upd.)
Coldwell Banker Real Estate LLC, 109
132–37
Cole National Corporation, 13 165–67;
76 107–10 (upd.)
Cole Taylor Bank, 107 74–77
The Coleman Company, Inc., 9 127–29;
30 136–39 (upd.); 108 171–77 (upd.)
Coleman Natural Products, Inc., 68
89–91
Coles Express Inc., 15 109–11
Coles Group Limited, V 33–35; 20
155–58 (upd.); 85 49–56 (upd.)
Cole's Quality Foods, Inc., 68 92–94
Colfax Corporation, 58 65–67
Colgate-Palmolive Company, III 23–26;
14 120–23 (upd.); 35 110–15 (upd.);
71 105–10 (upd.)
Colle+McVoy, 110 93–96
Collectors Universe, Inc., 48 98–100
College Hunks Hauling Junk *see* CHHJ
Franchising LLC.
Colliers International Property
Consultants Inc., 92 56–59
Collins & Aikman Corporation, 13
168–70; 41 91–95 (upd.)
The Collins Companies Inc., 102 88–92
Collins Industries, Inc., 33 105–07
Colonial Properties Trust, 65 115–17
Colonial Williamsburg Foundation, 53
105–07
Color Kinetics Incorporated, 85 57–60
Colorado Baseball Management, Inc.,
72 75–78
Colorado Boxed Beef Company, 100
117–20
Colorado Group Ltd., 107 78–81
Colorado MEDtech, Inc., 48 101–05
Colt Industries Inc., I 434–36
COLT Telecom Group plc, 41 96–99
Colt's Manufacturing Company, Inc.,
12 70–72
Columbia Forest Products Inc., 78
74–77
The Columbia Gas System, Inc., V
580–82; 16 115–18 (upd.)
Columbia House Company, 69 101–03
Columbia Manufacturing, Inc., 114
138–41
Columbia Sportswear Company, 19
94–96; 41 100–03 (upd.)

Columbia TriStar Motion Pictures
Companies, II 135–37; 12 73–76
(upd.)
Columbia/HCA Healthcare
Corporation, 15 112–14
Columbus McKinnon Corporation, 37
95–98
Com Ed *see* Commonwealth Edison.
Comair Holdings Inc., 13 171–73; 34
116–20 (upd.)
Combe Inc., 72 79–82
Comcast Corporation, 7 90–92; 24
120–24 (upd.); 112 96–101 (upd.)
Comdial Corporation, 21 132–35
Comdisco, Inc., 9 130–32
Comerci *see* Controladora Comercial
Mexicana, S.A. de C.V.
Comerica Incorporated, 40 115–17; 101
120–25 (upd.)
Comex Group *see* Grupo Comex.
COMFORCE Corporation, 40 118–20
Comfort Systems USA, Inc., 101
126–29
Cominco Ltd., 37 99–102
Comisión Federal de Electricidad, 108
178–81
Command Security Corporation, 57
71–73
Commerce Bancshares, Inc., 116
140–43
Commerce Clearing House, Inc., 7
93–94 *see also* CCH Inc.
Commercial Credit Company, 8 117–19
see also Citigroup Inc.
Commercial Federal Corporation, 12
77–79; 62 76–80 (upd.)
Commercial Financial Services, Inc., 26
85–89
Commercial Metals Company, 15
115–17; 42 81–84(upd.)
Commercial Union plc, III 233–35 *see
also* Aviva PLC.
Commercial Vehicle Group, Inc., 81
91–94
Commerzbank A.G., II 256–58; 47
81–84 (upd.)
Commodore International, Ltd., 7
95–97
Commonwealth Bank of Australia Ltd.,
109 138–42
Commonwealth Edison, V 583–85
Commonwealth Energy System, 14
124–26 *see also* NSTAR.
Commonwealth Telephone Enterprises,
Inc., 25 106–08
CommScope, Inc., 77 112–15
Community Coffee Co. L.L.C., 53
108–10
Community Health Systems, Inc., 71
111–13
Community Newspaper Holdings, Inc.,
91 128–31
Community Psychiatric Centers, 15
118–20
Compagnia Italiana dei Jolly Hotels
S.p.A., 71 114–16

Compagnie de Saint-Gobain, III
675–78; 16 119–23 (upd.); 64 80–84
(upd.)
Compagnie des Alpes, 48 106–08
Compagnie des Cristalleries de Baccarat
see Baccarat.
Compagnie des Machines Bull S.A., III
122–23 *see also* Bull S.A.; Groupe Bull.
Compagnie Financière de Paribas, II
259–60 *see also* BNP Paribas Group.
Compagnie Financière Richemont AG,
50 144–47
Compagnie Financière Sucres et
Denrées S.A., 60 94–96
Compagnie Générale d'Électricité, II
12–13
Compagnie Générale des Établissements
Michelin, V 236–39; 42 85–89
(upd.); 117 52–57 (upd.)
Compagnie Générale Maritime et
Financière, 6 379–81
Compagnie Maritime Belge S.A., 95
110–13
Compagnie Nationale à Portefeuille, 84
55–58
Compal Electronics Inc., 117 58–61
Companhia Brasileira de Distribuiçao,
76 111–13
Companhia de Bebidas das Américas,
57 74–77
Companhia de Tecidos Norte de Minas
- Coteminas, 77 116–19
Companhia Energética de Minas Gerais
S.A., 65 118–20
Companhia Siderúrgica Nacional, 76
114–17
Companhia Suzano de Papel e Celulose
S.A., 94 130–33
Companhia Vale do Rio Doce, IV
54–57; 43 111–14 (upd.) *see also* Vale
S.A.
Compania Cervecerias Unidas S.A., 70
61–63
Compañia de Minas
BuenaventuraS.A.A., 92160–63
Compañía Española de Petróleos S.A.
(Cepsa), IV 396–98; 56 63–66 (upd.)
Compañia Industrial de Parras, S.A. de
C.V. (CIPSA), 84 59–62
Compañia Sud Americana de Vapores
S.A., 100 121–24
Compaq Computer Corporation, III
124–25; 6 221–23 (upd.); 26 90–93
(upd.) *see also* Hewlett-Packard Co.
Compass Bancshares, Inc., 73 92–94
Compass Diversified Holdings, 108
182–85
Compass Group plc, 34 121–24; 110
97–102 (upd.)
Compass Minerals International, Inc.,
79 109–12
CompDent Corporation, 22 149–51
Compellent Technologies, Inc., 119
114–18
CompHealth Inc., 25 109–12
Complete Business Solutions, Inc., 31
130–33

The Grocers Supply Co., Inc., 103
201–04
Grohe *see* Friedrich Grohe AG & Co. KG.
Grolier Inc., 16 251–54; 43 207–11
(upd.)
Grolsch *see* Royal Grolsch NV.
Grontmij N.V., 110 190–94
Grossman's Inc., 13 248–50
Ground Round, Inc., 21 248–51
Group 1 Automotive, Inc., 52 144–46
Group 4 Falck A/S, 42 165–68
Group Health Cooperative, 41 181–84
Groupama S.A., 76 167–70
Groupe Air France, 6 92–94 *see also*
Societe Air France.
Groupe Alain Manoukian, 55 173–75
Groupe André, 17 210–12 *see also*
Vivarte SA.
ARES *see* Groupe Ares S.A.
Groupe Bigard S.A., 96 151–54
Groupe Bolloré, 67 196–99
Groupe Bourbon S.A., 60 147–49
Groupe Bull *see* Compagnie des Machines
Bull.
Groupe Caisse d'Epargne, 100 200–04
Groupe Casino *see* Casino
Guichard-Perrachon S.A.
Groupe Castorama-Dubois
Invesrissemenrs, 23 230–32 *see also*
Castorama-Dubois Investissements SCA
Groupe CECAB S.C.A., 88 131–34
Groupe Crit S.A., 74 134–36
Groupe Danone, 32 232–36 (upd.); 93
233–40 (upd.)
Groupe Dassault Aviation SA, 26
179–82 (upd.) *see also* Dassault
Aviation S.A.
Groupe de la Cité, IV 614–16
Groupe DMC (Dollfus Mieg & Cie), 27
186–88
Groupe Dubreuil S.A., 102 162–65
Groupe Euralis, 86 169–72
Groupe Flo S.A., 98 172–75
Groupe Fournier SA, 44 187–89
Groupe Genoyer, 96 155–58
Groupe Glon, 84 155–158
Groupe Go Sport S.A., 39 183–85
Groupe Guillin SA, 40 214–16
Groupe Henri Heuliez S.A., 100 205–09
Groupe Herstal S.A., 58 145–48
Groupe Jean-Claude Darmon, 44
190–92
Groupe Lactalis, 78 128–32 (upd.)
Groupe Lapeyre S.A., 33 175–77
Groupe LDC *see* L.D.C. S.A.
Groupe Le Duff S.A., 84 159–162
Groupe Léa Nature, 88 135–38
Groupe Legris Industries, 23 233–35
Groupe Les Echos, 25 283–85
Groupe Limagrain, 74 137–40
Groupe Louis Dreyfus S.A., 60 150–53
Groupe Lucien Barrière S.A.S., 110
195–99
Groupe Monnoyeur, 72 157–59
Groupe Open, 74 141–43
Groupe Partouche SA, 48 196–99
Groupe Pinault-Printemps-Redoute *see*
Pinault-Printemps-Redoute S.A.

Groupe Promodès S.A., 19 326–28
Groupe Rougier SA, 21 438–40
Groupe SEB, 35 201–03
Groupe Sidel S.A., 21 252–55
Groupe Soufflet SA, 55 176–78
Groupe Stalaven S.A., 117 126–29
Groupe Vidéotron Ltée., 20 271–73
Groupe Yves Saint Laurent, 23 236–39
see also Gucci Group N.V.
Groupe Zannier S.A., 35 204–07
Grow Biz International, Inc., 18 207–10
see also Winmark Corp.
Grow Group Inc., 12 217–19
GROWMARK, Inc., 88 139–42
Groz-Beckert Group, 68 184–86
Grubb & Ellis Company, 21 256–58;
98 176–80 (upd.)
Gruma, S.A.B. de C.V., 31 234–36; 103
205–10 (upd.)
Grumman Corp., I 61–63; 11 164–67
(upd.) *see aslo* Northrop Grumman
Corp.
Grunau Company Inc., 90 209–12
Grundfos Group, 83 171–174
Grundig AG, 27 189–92
Gruntal & Co., L.L.C., 20 274–76
Grupo Aeroportuario del Centro Norte,
S.A.B. de C.V., 97 186–89
Grupo Aeroportuario del Pacífico, S.A.
de C.V., 85 160–63
Grupo Aeropuerto del Sureste, S.A. de
C.V., 48 200–02
Grupo Algar *see* Algar S/A
Emprendimentos e Participações
Grupo Ángeles Servicios de Salud, S.A.
de C.V., 84 163–166
Grupo Brescia, 99 194–197
Grupo Bufete *see* Bufete Industrial, S.A.
de C.V.
Grupo Carso, S.A. de C.V., 21 259–61;
107 163–67 (upd.)
Grupo Casa Saba, S.A. de C.V., 39
186–89
Grupo Clarín S.A., 67 200–03
Grupo Comercial Chedraui S.A. de
C.V., 86 173–76
Grupo Comex, 115 224–26
Grupo Corvi S.A. de C.V., 86 177–80
Grupo Cydsa, S.A. de C.V., 39 190–93
Grupo Dina *see* Consorcio G Grupo
Dina, S.A. de C.V.
Grupo Dragados SA, 55 179–82
Grupo Elektra, S.A. de C.V., 39 194–97
Grupo Eroski, 64 167–70
Grupo Ferrovial S.A., 40 217–19; 118
166–70 (upd.)
Grupo Ficosa International, 90 213–16
Grupo Financiero Banamex S.A., 54
143–46
Grupo Financiero Banorte, S.A. de C.V.,
51 149–51
Grupo Financiero BBVA Bancomer S.A.,
54 147–50
Grupo Financiero Galicia S.A., 63
178–81
Grupo Financiero Serfin, S.A., 19
188–90
Grupo Gigante, S.A. de C.V., 34 197–99

Grupo Herdez, S.A. de C.V., 35 208–10
Grupo IMSA, S.A. de C.V., 44 193–96
Grupo Industrial Bimbo, 19 191–93
Grupo Industrial Durango, S.A. de C.V.,
37 176–78
Grupo Industrial Herradura, S.A. de
C.V., 83 175–178
Grupo Industrial Lala, S.A. de C.V., 82
154–57
Grupo Industrial Saltillo, S.A. de C.V.,
54 151–54
Grupo Leche Pascual S.A., 59 212–14
Grupo Lladró S.A., 52 147–49
Grupo Martins, 104 175–78
Grupo Mexico, S.A. de C.V., 40 220–23
Grupo Modelo, S.A. de C.V., 29 218–20
Grupo Omnilife S.A. de C.V., 88
143–46
Grupo Planeta, 94 218–22
Grupo Portucel Soporcel, 60 154–56
Grupo Posadas, S.A. de C.V., 57 168–70
Grupo Positivo, 105 196–99
Grupo Sanborns, S.A. de C.V., 107
168–72 (upd.)
Grupo SLC *see* SLC Participaçoes S.A.
Grupo TACA, 38 218–20
Grupo Televisa, S.A., 18 211–14; 54
155–58 (upd.)
Grupo TMM, S.A. de C.V., 50 208–11
Grupo Transportación Ferroviaria
Mexicana, S.A. de C.V., 47 162–64
Grupo Viz, S.A. de C.V., 84 167–170
Gruppo Coin S.p.A., 41 185–87
Gruppo Italiano Vini, 111 173–76
Gruppo Riva Fire SpA, 88 147–50
Gryphon Holdings, Inc., 21 262–64
GSC Enterprises, Inc., 86 181 84
GSD&M Advertising, 44 197–200
GSD&M's Idea City, 90 217–21
GSG&T, Inc. *see* Gulf States Utilities Co.
GSI Commerce, Inc., 67 204–06
GSU *see* Gulf States Utilities Co.
GT Bicycles, 26 183–85
GT Interactive Software, 31 237–41 *see
also* Infogrames Entertainment S.A.
GT Solar International, Inc., 101
224–28
GTE Corporation, V 294–98; 15
192–97 (upd.) *see also* British
Columbia Telephone Company; Verizon
Communications.
GTSI Corp., 57 171–73
Guangzhou Pearl River Piano Group
Ltd., 49 177–79
Guangzhou R&F Properties Co., Ltd.,
95 167–69
Guararapes Confecçöes S.A., 118
171–74
Guardian Financial Services, 11 168–70;
64 171–74 (upd.)
Guardian Holdings Limited, 111
177–80
Guardian Industries Corp., 87 197–204
Guardian Life Insurance Company of
America, 116 262–66
Guardian Media Group plc, 53 152–55
Guardsmark, L.L.C., 77 171–74

Hokkaido Electric Power Company Inc. (HEPCO), V 635–37; 58 160–63 (upd.)

Hokuriku Electric Power Company, V 638–40

Holberg Industries, Inc., 36 266–69

Holden Ltd., 62 180–83

Holderbank Financière Glaris Ltd., III 701–02 *see also* Holnam Inc

N.V. Holdingmaatschappij De Telegraaf, 23 271–73 *see also* Telegraaf Media Groep N.V.

Holiday Companies, 120 168–71

Holiday Inns, Inc., III 94–95 *see also* Promus Companies, Inc.

Holiday Retirement Corp., 87 221–223

Holiday RV Superstores, Incorporated, 26 192–95

Holidaybreak plc, 96 182–86

Holland & Barrett Retail Limited, 118 188–91

Holland & Knight LLP, 60 171–74

Holland America Line Inc., 108 262–65

Holland Burgerville USA, 44 224–26

Holland Casino, 107 191–94

The Holland Group, Inc., 82 174–77

Hollander Home Fashions Corp., 67 207–09

Holley Performance Products Inc., 52 157–60

Hollinger International Inc., 24 222–25; 62 184–88 (upd.)

Holly Corporation, 12 240–42; 111 205–10 (upd.)

Hollywood Casino Corporation, 21 275–77

Hollywood Entertainment Corporation, 25 208–10

Hollywood Media Corporation, 58 164–68

Hollywood Park, Inc., 20 297–300

Holme Roberts & Owen LLP, 28 196–99

Holmen AB, 52 161–65 (upd.); 111 211–17 (upd.)

Holnam Inc., 8 258–60; 39 217–20 (upd.)

Hologic, Inc., 106 233–36

Holophane Corporation, 19 209–12

Holson Burnes Group, Inc., 14 244–45

Holt and Bugbee Company, 66 189–91

Holt's Cigar Holdings, Inc., 42 176–78

Holtzbrinck *see* Verlagsgruppe Georg von Holtzbrinck.

Homasote Company, 72 178–81

Home Box Office Inc., 7 222–24; 23 274–77 (upd.); 76 178–82 (upd.)

Home City Ice Company, Inc., 111 218–22

The Home Depot, Inc., V 75–76; 18 238–40 (upd.); 97 208–13 (upd.)

Home Hardware Stores Ltd., 62 189–91

Home Inns & Hotels Management Inc., 95 195–95

Home Insurance Company, III 262–64

Home Interiors & Gifts, Inc., 55 202–04

Home Market Foods, Inc., 110 213–16

Home Product Center plc, 104 205–08

Home Products International, Inc., 55 205–07

Home Properties of New York, Inc., 42 179–81

Home Retail Group plc, 91 242–46

Home Shopping Network, Inc., V 77–78; 25 211–15 (upd.) *see also* HSN.

HomeAway, Inc., 116 291–94

HomeBase, Inc., 33 198–201 (upd.)

Homestake Mining Company, 12 243–45; 38 229–32 (upd.)

Hometown Auto Retailers, Inc., 44 227–29

HomeVestors of America, Inc., 77 195–98

Homex *see* Desarrolladora Homex, S.A. de C.V.

Hon Hai Precision Industry Company, Ltd., 59 234–36; 117 139–43 (upd.)

HON Industries Inc., 13 266–69 *see* HNI Corp.

Honda Motor Company Ltd., I 174–76; 10 352–54 (upd.); 29 239–42 (upd.); 96 187–93 (upd.)

Honeywell International Inc., II 40–43; 12 246–49 (upd.); 50 231–35 (upd.)109 300–07 (upd.)

Hong Kong and China Gas Company Ltd., 73 177–79

Hong Kong Dragon Airlines Ltd., 66 192–94

Hong Kong Telecommunications Ltd., 6 319–21 *see also* Cable & Wireless HKT.

Hongkong and Shanghai Banking Corporation Limited, II 296–99 *see also* HSBC Holdings plc.

Hongkong Electric Holdings Ltd., 6 498–500; 23 278–81 (upd.); 107 195–200 (upd.)

Hongkong Land Holdings Ltd., IV 699–701; 47 175–78 (upd.)

Honshu Paper Co., Ltd., IV 284–85 *see also* Oji Paper Co., Ltd.

Hood *see* H.P. Hood L.L.C.

Hoogovens *see* Koninklijke Nederlandsche Hoogovens en Staalfabrieken NV.

Hooker Furniture Corporation, 80 143–46

Hooper Holmes, Inc., 22 264–67

Hooters of America, Inc., 18 241–43; 69 211–14 (upd.)

The Hoover Company, 12 250–52; 40 258–62 (upd.)

Hoover's, Inc., 108 266–69

HOP, LLC, 80 147–50

Hops Restaurant Bar and Brewery, 46 233–36

Hopson Development Holdings Ltd., 87 224–227

Horace Mann Educators Corporation, 22 268–70; 90 237–40 (upd.)

Horizon Food Group, Inc., 100 225–28

Horizon Lines, Inc., 98 197–200

Horizon Organic Holding Corporation, 37 195–99

Hormel Foods Corporation, 18 244–47 (upd.); 54 164–69 (upd.); 114 227–34 (upd.)

Hornbach Holding AG, 98 201–07

Hornbeck Offshore Services, Inc., 101 246–49

Hornby PLC, 105 221–25

Horry Telephone Cooperative, Inc., 120 172–75

Horsehead Industries, Inc., 51 165–67

Horserace Totalisator Board (The Tote), 107 201–05

Horseshoe Gaming Holding Corporation, 62 192–95

Horton Homes, Inc., 25 216–18

Horween Leather Company, 83 183–186

Hoshino Gakki Co. Ltd., 55 208–11

Hospira, Inc., 71 172–74

Hospital Central Services, Inc., 56 166–68

Hospital Corporation of America, III 78–80 *see also* HCA, Inc.

Hospital for Special Surgery, 115 243–46

Hospitality Franchise Systems, Inc., 11 177–79 *see also* Cendant Corp.

Hospitality Worldwide Services, Inc., 26 196–98

Hoss's Steak and Sea House Inc., 68 196–98

Host America Corporation, 79 202–06

Host Hotels & Resorts, Inc., 112 211–13

Hot Dog on a Stick *see* HDOS Enterprises.

Hot Stuff Foods, 85 171–74

Hot Topic Inc., 33 202–04; 86 190–94 (upd.)

Hotel Properties Ltd., 71 175–77

Hotel Shilla Company Ltd., 110 217–20

Houchens Industries, Inc., 51 168–70; 117 144–48 (upd.)

Houghton Mifflin Company, 10 355–57; 36 270–74 (upd.)

House of Fabrics, Inc., 21 278–80 *see also* Jo-Ann Stores, Inc.

House of Fraser PLC, 45 188–91 *see also* Harrods Holdings.

House of Prince A/S, 80 151–54

Household International, Inc., II 417–20; 21 281–86 (upd.) *see also* HSBC Holdings plc.

Houston Industries Incorporated, V 641–44 *see also* Reliant Energy Inc.

Houston Wire & Cable Company, 97 214–17

Hovnanian Enterprises, Inc., 29 243–45; 89 254–59 (upd.)

Howard Hughes Medical Institute, 39 221–24

Howard Johnson International, Inc., 17 236–39; 72 182–86 (upd.)

Howden Group Limited, 111 223–26

Howmet Corporation, 12 253–55 *see also* Alcoa Inc.

HP *see* Hewlett-Packard Co.

J. & W. Seligman & Co. Inc., 61
141–43

J.A. Jones, Inc., 16 284–86

J. Alexander's Corporation, 65 177–79

J.B. Hunt Transport Services, Inc., 12
277–79; 119 267–71 (upd.)

J. Baker, Inc., 31 270–73

J C Bamford Excavators Ltd., 83
216–222

J. C. Penney Company, Inc., V 90–92;
18 269–73 (upd.); 43 245–50 (upd.);
91 263–72 (upd.)

J. Crew Group, Inc., 12 280–82; 34
231–34 (upd.); 88 203–08

J.D. Edwards & Company, 14 268–70
see also Oracle Corp.

J.D. Heiskell & Company, 117 176–79

J. D. Irving, Limited, 118 205–08

J.D. Power and Associates, 32 297–301

J. D'Addario & Company, Inc., 48
230–33

J.F. Shea Co., Inc., 55 234–36; 120
187–92 (upd.)

J.H. Findorff and Son, Inc., 60 175–78

J.I. Case Company, 10 377–81 *see also*
CNH Global N.V.

J.J. Darboven GmbH & Co. KG, 96
208–12

J.J. Keller & Associates, Inc., 81
2180–21

The J. Jill Group, Inc., 35 239–41; 90
249–53 (upd.)

J.L. Hammett Company, 72 196–99

J Lauritzen A/S, 90 254–57

J. Lohr Winery Corporation, 99
229–232

The J. M. Smucker Company, 11
210–12; 87 258–265 (upd.)

J.M. Voith AG, 33 222–25

J.P. Morgan Chase & Co., II 329–32;
30 261–65 (upd.); 38 253–59 (upd.)

The J. Paul Getty Trust, 105 255–59

J.R. Simplot Company, 16 287–89; 60
179–82 (upd.)

J Sainsbury plc, II 657–59; 13 282–84
(upd.); 38 260–65 (upd.); 95 212–20
(upd.)

J. W. Pepper and Son Inc., 86 220–23

J. Walter Thompson Co. *see* JWT Group
Inc.

j2 Global Communications, Inc., 75
219–21

Jabil Circuit, Inc., 36 298–301; 88
209–14

Jack B. Kelley, Inc., 102 184–87

Jack Henry and Associates, Inc., 17
262–65; 94 258–63 (upd.)

Jack in the Box Inc., 89 265–71 (upd.)

Jack Morton Worldwide, 88 215–18

Jack Schwartz Shoes, Inc., 18 266–68

Jackpot Enterprises Inc., 21 298–300

Jackson Hewitt, Inc., 48 234–36

Jackson National Life Insurance
Company, 8 276–77

Jacmar Companies, 87 266–269

Jaco Electronics, Inc., 30 255–57

Jacob Leinenkugel Brewing Company,
28 209–11

Jacobs Engineering Group Inc., 6
148–50; 26 220–23 (upd.); 106
248–54 (upd.)

Jacobs Suchard (AG), II 520–22 *see also*
Kraft Jacobs Suchard AG.

Jacobson Stores Inc., 21 301–03

Jacor Communications, Inc., 23 292–95

Jacques Torres Chocolate *see*
Mrchocolate.com LLC.

Jacques Vert Plc, 118 209–12

Jacques Whitford, 92 184–87

Jacquot *see* Établissements Jacquot and Cie
S.A.S.

Jacuzzi Brands Inc., 23 296–98; 76
204–07 (upd.)

JAFCO Co. Ltd., 79 221–24

Jaguar Cars, Ltd., 13 285–87

Jaiprakash Associates Limited, 101
269–72

JAKKS Pacific, Inc., 52 191–94

JAL *see* Japan Airlines Company, Ltd.

Jalate Inc., 25 245–47

Jamba Juice Company, 47 199–202

James Avery Craftsman, Inc., 76 208–10

James Beattie plc, 43 242–44

James Fisher and Sons Public Limited
Company, 118 213–18

James Hardie Industries N.V., 56
174–76

James Original Coney Island Inc., 84
197–200

James Purdey & Sons Limited, 87
270–275

James River Corporation of Virginia, IV
289–91 *see also* Fort James Corp.

Jani-King International, Inc., 85
191–94

JanSport, Inc., 70 134–36

Janssen Pharmaceutica N.V., 80 164–67

Janus Capital Group Inc., 57 192–94

Japan Airlines Corporation, I 104–06;
32 288–92 (upd.); 110 242–49 (upd.)

Japan Broadcasting Corporation, 7
248–50

Japan Leasing Corporation, 8 278–80

Japan Post Holdings Company Ltd.,
108 281–85

Japan Pulp and Paper Company
Limited, IV 292–93

Japan Tobacco Inc., V 403–04; 46
257–60 (upd.); 113 184–88 (upd.)

Jarden Corporation, 93 255–61 (upd.)

Jardine Cycle & Carriage Ltd., 73
193–95

Jardine Matheson Holdings Limited, I
468–71; 20 309–14 (upd.); 93
262–71 (upd.)

Jarvis plc, 39 237–39

Jason Incorporated, 23 299–301

Jay Jacobs, Inc., 15 243–45

Jayco Inc., 13 288–90

Jaypee Group *see* Jaiprakash Associates
Ltd.

Jays Foods, Inc., 90 258–61

Jazz Basketball Investors, Inc., 55
237–39

Jazzercise, Inc., 45 212–14

JB Oxford Holdings, Inc., 32 293–96

JBS S.A., 100 233–36

JCDecaux S.A., 76 211–13

JD Group Ltd., 110 250–54

JD Wetherspoon plc, 30 258–60

JDA Software Group, Inc., 101 273–76

JDS Uniphase Corporation, 34 235–37

JE Dunn Construction Group, Inc., 85
195–98

The Jean Coutu Group (PJC) Inc., 46
261–65

Jean-Georges Enterprises L.L.C., 75
209–11

Jeanneau *see* Chantiers Jeanneau S.A.

Jefferies Group, Inc., 25 248–51

Jefferson-Pilot Corporation, 11 213–15;
29 253–56 (upd.)

Jefferson Properties, Inc. *see* JPI.

Jefferson Smurfit Group plc, IV 294–96;
19 224–27 (upd.); 49 224–29 (upd.)
see also Smurfit Kappa Group plc

Jel Sert Company, 90 262–65

Jeld-Wen, Inc., 45 215–17

Jelly Belly Candy Company, 76 214–16

Jenkens & Gilchrist, P.C., 65 180–82

Jennie-O Turkey Store, Inc., 76 217–19

Jennifer Convertibles, Inc., 31 274–76

Jenny Craig, Inc., 10 382–84; 29
257–60 (upd.); 92 188–93 (upd.)

Jenoptik AG, 33 218–21

Jeppesen Sanderson, Inc., 92 194–97

Jerónimo Martins SGPS S.A., 96
213–16

Jerry's Famous Deli Inc., 24 243–45

Jersey European Airways (UK) Ltd., 61
144–46

Jersey Mike's Franchise Systems, Inc.,
83 223–226

Jervis B. Webb Company, 24 246–49

Jet Airways (India) Private Limited, 65
183–85

JetBlue Airways Corporation, 44
248–50

Jetro Cash & Carry Enterprises Inc., 38
266–68

Jewett-Cameron Trading Company, Ltd.,
89 272–76

JFE Shoji Holdings Inc., 88 219–22

JG Industries, Inc., 15 240–42

Jiangsu Shagang Group Company Ltd.,
117 180–83

Jillian's Entertainment Holdings, Inc.,
40 273–75

Jim Beam Brands Worldwide, Inc., 14
271–73; 58 194–96 (upd.)

The Jim Henson Company, 23 302–04;
106 255–59 (upd.)

The Jim Pattison Group, 37 219–22

Jimmy Carter Work Project *see* Habitat
for Humanity International.

Jimmy John's Enterprises, Inc., 103
227–30

Jitney-Jungle Stores of America, Inc., 27
245–48

JJB Sports plc, 32 302–04

JKH Holding Co. LLC, 105 260–63

JLA Credit *see* Japan Leasing Corp.

JLG Industries, Inc., 52 195–97

JLL *see* Jones Lang LaSalle Inc.

Kruger Inc., 17 280–82; 103 239–45 (upd.)
Krung Thai Bank Public Company Ltd., 69 225–27
Krupp AG see Fried. Krupp GmbH; ThyssenKrupp AG.
Kruse International, 88 227–30
The Krystal Company, 33 239–42
KSB AG, 62 214–18
KT&G Corporation, 62 219–21
KTM Power Sports AG, 100 256–59
K12 Inc., 118 242–46
KU Energy Corporation, 11 236–38 see also LG&E Energy Corp.
Kubota Corporation, III 551–53
Kudelski Group SA, 44 263–66
Kuehne & Nagel International AG, V 466–69; 53 199–203 (upd.)
Kuhlman Corporation, 20 333–35
Kühne see Carl Kühne KG (GmbH & Co.).
Kühne & Nagel International AG, V 466–69
Kulicke and Soffa Industries, Inc., 33 246–48; 76 229–31 (upd.)
Kum & Go, L.C., 112 248–52
Kumagai Gumi Company, Ltd., I 579–80
Kumho Tire Company Ltd., 105 276–79
Kumon Institute of Education Co., Ltd., 72 211–14
Kumpulan Fima Bhd., 117 220–23
Kuoni Travel Holding Ltd., 40 284–86
Kurzweil Technologies, Inc., 51 200–04
The Kushner-Locke Company, 25 269–71
Kuwait Airways Corporation, 68 226–28
Kuwait Flour Mills & Bakeries Company, 84 232–234
Kuwait Petroleum Corporation, IV 450–52; 55 240–43 (upd.)
Kvaerner ASA, 36 321–23
Kwang Yang Motor Company Ltd., 80 193–96
Kwik-Fit Holdings plc, 54 205–07
Kwik Save Group plc, 11 239–41
Kwik Trip Inc., 113 196–99
Kwizda Holding GmbH, 102 209–12
Kymmene Corporation, IV 299–303 see also UPM-Kymmene Corp.
Kyocera Corporation, II 50–52; 21 329–32 (upd.); 79 231–36 (upd.)
Kyokuyo Company Ltd., 75 228–30
Kyowa Hakko Kogyo Co., Ltd., III 42–43; 48 248–50 (upd.)
Kyphon Inc., 87 292–295
Kyushu Electric Power Company Inc., V 649–51; 107 229–33 (upd.)

L

L-3 Communications Holdings, Inc., 48 251–53; 111 263–67 (upd.)
L. and J.G. Stickley, Inc., 50 303–05
L.A. Darling Company, 92 203–06
L.A. Gear, Inc., 8 303–06; 32 313–17 (upd.)

L.A. T Sportswear, Inc., 26 257–59
L.B. Foster Company, 33 255–58
L.D.C. SA, 61 155–57
L. Foppiano Wine Co., 101 290–93
L.L. Bean, Inc., 10 388–90; 38 280–83 (upd.); 91 307–13 (upd.)
The L.L. Knickerbocker Co., Inc., 25 272–75
L. Luria & Son, Inc., 19 242–44
L. M. Berry and Company, 80 197–200
L.S. Starrett Company, 13 301–03; 64 227–30 (upd.)
La Choy Food Products Inc., 25 276–78
La Doria SpA, 101 294–97
La Madeleine French Bakery & Café, 33 249–51
La Poste, V 270–72; 47 213–16 (upd.); 109 355–61 (upd.)
The La Quinta Companies, 11 242–44; 42 213–16 (upd.)
La Reina Inc., 96 252–55
La Seda de Barcelona S.A., 100 260–63
La Senza Corporation, 66 205–07
La Serenísima see Mastellone Hermanos S.A.
La-Z-Boy Incorporated, 14 302–04; 50 309–13 (upd.)
LAB see Lloyd Aéreo Boliviano S.A
Lab Safety Supply, Inc., 102 213–16
LaBarge Inc., 41 224–26
Labatt Brewing Company Limited, I 267–68; 25 279–82 (upd.)
Labeyrie SAS, 80 201–04
LabOne, Inc., 48 254–57
Labor Ready, Inc., 29 273–75; 88 231–36 (upd.)
Laboratoires Arkopharma S.A., 75 231–34
Laboratoires de Biologie Végétale Yves Rocher, 35 262–65
Laboratoires Pierre Fabre S.A., 100 353–57
Laboratory Corporation of America Holdings, 42 217–20 (upd.); 119 291–97 (upd.)
LaBranche & Co. Inc., 37 223–25
LaCie Group S.A., 76 232–34
Lacks Enterprises Inc., 61 158–60
Laclede Steel Company, 15 271–73
Lacoste S.A., 108 318–21
LaCrosse Footwear, Inc., 18 298–301; 61 161–65 (upd.)
Ladbroke Group PLC, II 141–42; 21 333–36 (upd.) see also Hilton Group plc.
LADD Furniture, Inc., 12 299–301 see also La-Z-Boy Inc.
Ladish Company Inc., 30 282–84; 107 234–38 (upd.)
Lafarge Cement UK, 54 208–11 (upd.)
Lafarge Coppée S.A., III 703–05
Lafarge Corporation, 28 228–31
Lafuma S.A., 39 248–50
Lagardère SCA, 112 253–61
Laidlaw International, Inc., 80 205–08
Laing O'Rourke PLC, 93 282–85 (upd.)
L'Air Liquide SA, I 357–59; 47 217–20 (upd.)

Laïta S.A.S., 113 200–04
Lakeland Industries, Inc., 45 245–48
Lakes Entertainment, Inc., 51 205–07
Lakeside Foods, Inc., 89 297–301
Lala see Grupo Industrial Lala, S.A. de C.V.
Lam Research Corporation, 11 245–47; 31 299–302 (upd.)
Lam Son Sugar Joint Stock Corporation (Lasuco), 60 195–97
Lamar Advertising Company, 27 278–80; 70 150–53 (upd.)
The Lamaur Corporation, 41 227–29
Lamb Weston, Inc., 23 319–21
Lambda Legal Defense and Education Fund, Inc., 106 276–80
Lambertz see Aachener Printen- und Schokoladenfabrik Henry Lambertz GmbH & Co. KG.
Lamborghini see Automobili Lamborghini S.p.A.
Lamonts Apparel, Inc., 15 274–76
The Lamson & Sessions Co., 13 304–06; 61 166–70 (upd.)
Lan Chile S.A., 31 303–06
Lancair International, Inc., 67 224–26
Lancaster Colony Corporation, 8 307–09; 61 171–74 (upd.)
Lance Armstrong Foundation, Inc., 111 268–71
Lance, Inc., 14 305–07; 41 230–33 (upd.)
Lancer Corporation, 21 337–39
Land and Houses PCL, 104 257–61
Land O'Lakes, Inc., II 535–37; 21 340–43 (upd.); 81 222–27 (upd.)
Land Securities PLC, IV 704–06; 49 246–50 (upd.)
LandAmerica Financial Group, Inc., 85 213–16
Landauer, Inc., 51 208–10; 117 224–27 (upd.)
Landec Corporation, 95 235–38
Landmark Communications, Inc., 12 302–05; 55 244–49 (upd.)
Landmark Theatre Corporation, 70 154–56
Landor Associates, 81 228–31
Landry's Restaurants, Inc., 15 277–79; 65 203–07 (upd.)
Lands' End, Inc., 9 314–16; 29 276–79 (upd.); 82 195–200 (upd.)
Landsbanki Islands hf, 81 232–35
Landstar System, Inc., 63 236–38
Lane Bryant, Inc., 64 231–33
The Lane Co., Inc., 12 306–08
Langer Juice Company, Inc., 107 239–42
Lanier Worldwide, Inc., 75 235–38
Lanoga Corporation, 62 222–24 see also Pro-Build Holdings Inc.
Lapeyre S.A. see Groupe Lapeyre S.A.
Larry Flynt Publishing Inc., 31 307–10
Larry H. Miller Group of Companies, 29 280–83; 104 262–67 (upd.)
Larsen and Toubro Ltd., 117 228–32
LarsonAllen, LLP, 118 247–50

The Major Automotive Companies, Inc.,
45 260–62

Make-A-Wish Foundation of America,
97 262–65

Makedonski Telekom AD Skopje, 113
242–46

Makhteshim-Agan Industries Ltd., 85
230–34

Makita Corporation, 22 333–35; 59
270–73 (upd.)

Malayan Banking Berhad, 72 215–18

Malaysian Airline System Berhad, 6
100–02; 29 300–03 (upd.); 97
266–71 (upd.)

Malcolm Pirnie, Inc., 42 242–44

Malden Mills Industries, Inc., 16
351–53 see also Polartec LLC.

Malév Plc, 24 310–12

Mallinckrodt Group Inc., 19 251–53

Malt-O-Meal Company, 22 336–38; 63
249–53 (upd.)

Mammoet Transport B.V., 26 278–80

Mammoth Mountain Ski Area, 101
322–25

Man Aktiengesellschaft, III 561–63

Man Group PLC, 106 290–94

MAN Roland Druckmaschinen AG, 94
294–98

Management and Training Corporation,
28 253–56

Manatron, Inc., 86 260–63

Manchester United Football Club plc,
30 296–98

Mandalay Resort Group, 32 322–26
(upd.)

Mandom Corporation, 82 205–08

Manhattan Associates, Inc., 67 243–45

Manhattan Beer Distributors LLC, 114
284–87

Manhattan Group, LLC, 80 228–31

Manheim, 88 244–48

Manila Electric Company (Meralco), 56
214–16

Manischewitz Company see B.
Manischewitz Co.

Manitoba Telecom Services, Inc., 61
184–87

Manitou BF S.A., 27 294–96

The Manitowoc Company, Inc., 18
318–21; 59 274–79 (upd.); 118
269–76 (upd.)

Manna Pro Products, LLC, 107 256–59

Mannatech Inc., 33 282–85

Mannesmann AG, III 564–67; 14
326–29 (upd.); 38 296–301 (upd.) see
also Vodafone Group PLC.

Mannheim Steamroller see American
Gramophone LLC.

Manning Selvage & Lee (MS&L), 76
252–54

MannKind Corporation, 87 300–303

Manor Care, Inc., 6 187–90; 25 306–10
(upd.)

Manpower Inc., 9 326–27; 30 299–302
(upd.); 73 215–18 (upd.)

Mansfield Oil Company, 117 247–50

ManTech International Corporation, 97
272–75

Manufacture Prelle & Cie, 118 277–80

Manufactured Home Communities,
Inc., 22 339–41

Manufacturers Hanover Corporation, II
312–14 see also Chemical Bank.

Manulife Financial Corporation, 85
235–38

Manutan International S.A., 72 219–21

Manville Corporation, III 706–09; 7
291–95 (upd.) see also Johns Manville
Corp.

MAPCO Inc., IV 458–59

Mapfre S.A., 109 394–98

MAPICS, Inc., 55 256–58

Maple Grove Farms of Vermont, 88
249–52

Maple Leaf Foods Inc., 41 249–53; 108
327–33 (upd.)

Maple Leaf Sports & Entertainment
Ltd., 61 188–90

Maples Industries, Inc., 83 260–263

Marathon Oil Corporation, 109
399–403

Marble Slab Creamery, Inc., 87
304–307

Marc Ecko Enterprises, Inc., 105
288–91

Marc Glassman, Inc., 117 251–54

March of Dimes, 31 322–25

Marchesi Antinori SRL, 42 245–48

Marchex, Inc., 72 222–24

marchFIRST, Inc., 34 261 64

Marco Business Products, Inc., 75
244–46

Marcolin S.p.A., 61 191 94

Marconi plc, 33 286–90 (upd.)

Marcopolo S.A., 79 247–50

Marco's Franchising LLC, 86 264–67

The Marcus Corporation, 21 359–63

Marelli see Magneti Marelli Holding SpA.

Marfin Popular Bank plc, 92 222–26

Margarete Steiff GmbH, 23 334–37

Marie Brizard et Roger International
S.A.S., 22 342–44; 97 276–80 (upd.)

Marie Callender's Restaurant & Bakery,
Inc., 28 257–59 see also Perkins &
Marie Callender's Inc.

Mariella Burani Fashion Group, 92
227–30

Marine Products Corporation, 75
247–49

MarineMax, Inc., 30 303–05

Mariner Energy, Inc., 101 326–29

Marion Laboratories Inc., I 648–49

Marion Merrell Dow, Inc., 9 328–29
(upd.)

Marionnaud Parfumeries SA, 51 233–35

Marisa Christina, Inc., 15 290–92

Marisol S.A., 107 260–64

Maritz Holdings Inc., 38 302–05; 110
305–09 (upd.)

Mark IV Industries, Inc., 7 296–98; 28
260–64 (upd.)

Mark T. Wendell Tea Company, 94
299–302

The Mark Travel Corporation, 80
232–35

Markel Corporation, 116 331–34

Märklin Holding GmbH, 70 163–66

Marks and Spencer p.l.c., V 124–26; 24
313–17 (upd.); 85 239–47 (upd.)

Marks Brothers Jewelers, Inc., 24
318–20 see also Whitehall Jewellers,
Inc.

Marlin Business Services Corp., 89
317–19

The Marmon Group, Inc., IV 135–38;
16 354–57 (upd.); 70 167–72 (upd.)

Marquette Electronics, Inc., 13 326–28

Marriott International, Inc., III 102–03;
21 364–67 (upd.); 83 264–270 (upd.)

Mars, Incorporated, 7 299–301; 40
302–05 (upd.); 114 288–93 (upd.)

Mars Petcare US Inc., 96 269–72

Marsh & McLennan Companies, Inc.,
III 282–84; 45 263–67 (upd.)

Marsh Supermarkets, Inc., 17 300–02;
76 255–58 (upd.)

Marshall & Ilsley Corporation, 56
217–20

Marshall Amplification plc, 62 239–42

Marshall Field's, 63 254–63 see also
Target Corp.

Marshalls Incorporated, 13 329–31

Martek Biosciences Corporation, 65
218–20

Martell and Company S.A., 82 213–16

Marten Transport, Ltd., 84 243–246

Martha Stewart Living Omnimedia,
Inc., 24 321–23; 73 219–22 (upd.)

Martha White Foods Inc., 104 284–87

Martignetti Companies, 84 247–250

Martin Baker Aircraft Company
Limited, 61 195–97

Martin Franchises, Inc., 80 236–39

Martin Guitar Company see C.F. Martin
& Co., Inc.

Martin Industries, Inc., 44 274–77

Martin Marietta Corporation, I 67–69
see also Lockheed Martin Corp.

Martini & Rossi SpA, 63 264–66

MartinLogan, Ltd., 85 248–51

Martins see Grupo Martins.

Martin's Super Markets, Inc., 101
330–33

Martz Group, 56 221–23

Marubeni Corporation, I 492–95; 24
324–27 (upd.); 104 288–93 (upd.)

Maruha Group Inc., 75 250–53 (upd.)

Marui Company Ltd., V 127; 62
243–45 (upd.)

Maruzen Company Ltd., 18 322–24;
104 294–97 (upd.)

Marvel Entertainment, Inc., 10 400–02;
78 212–19 (upd.)

Marvell Technology Group Ltd., 112
268–71

Marvelous Market Inc., 104 298–301

Marvin Lumber & Cedar Company, 22
345–47

Mary Kay Inc., 9 330–32; 30 306–09
(upd.); 84 251–256 (upd.)

Maryland & Virginia Milk Producers
Cooperative Association, Inc., 80
240–43

Maryville Data Systems Inc., 96 273–76

Mitsubishi Oil Co., Ltd., IV 460–62 *see also* Nippon Mitsubishi Oil Corp.

Mitsubishi Rayon Co. Ltd., V 369–71

Mitsubishi Trust & Banking Corporation, II 323–24

Mitsubishi UFJ Financial Group, Inc., 99 291–296 (upd.)

Mitsui & Co., Ltd., I 505–08; 28 280–85 (upd.); 110 320–27 (upd.)

Mitsui Bank, Ltd., II 325–27 *see also* Sumitomo Mitsui Banking Corp.

Mitsui Marine and Fire Insurance Company, Limited, III 295–96

Mitsui Mining & Smelting Co., Ltd., IV 145–46; 102 274–78 (upd.)

Mitsui Mining Company, Limited, IV 147–49

Mitsui Mutual Life Insurance Company, III 297–98; 39 284–86 (upd.)

Mitsui O.S.K. Lines Ltd., V 473–76; 96 282–87 (upd.)

Mitsui Petrochemical Industries, Ltd., 9 352–54

Mitsui Real Estate Development Co., Ltd., IV 715–16

Mitsui Trust & Banking Company, Ltd., II 328

Mitsukoshi Ltd., V 142–44; 56 239–42 (upd.)

Mity Enterprises, Inc., 38 310–12

MIVA, Inc., 83 271–275

Mizuho Financial Group Inc., 25 344–46; 58 229–36 (upd.)

MN Airlines LLC, 104 321–27

MNS, Ltd., 65 236–38

Mo och Domsjö AB, IV 317–19 *see also* Holmen AB

Mobil Corporation, IV 463–65; 7 351–54 (upd.); 21 376–80 (upd.) *see also* Exxon Mobil Corp.

Mobile Mini, Inc., 58 237–39

Mobile Telecommunications Technologies Corp., 18 347–49

Mobile TeleSystems OJSC, 59 300–03

Mocon, Inc., 76 275–77

Modell's Sporting Goods *see* Henry Modell & Company Inc.

Modern Times Group AB, 36 335–38

Modern Woodmen of America, 66 227–29

Modine Manufacturing Company, 8 372–75; 56 243–47 (upd.)

MoDo *see* Mo och Domsjö AB.

Modtech Holdings, Inc., 77 284–87

Moelven Industrier ASA, 110 328–32

Moen Incorporated, 12 344–45; 106 295–98 (upd.)

Moe's Southwest Grill *see* MSWG, LLC.

Moët-Hennessy, I 271–72 *see also* LVMH Moët Hennessy Louis Vuitton SA.

Mohawk Fine Papers, Inc., 108 353–57

Mohawk Industries, Inc., 19 274–76; 63 298–301 (upd.)

Mohegan Tribal Gaming Authority, 37 254–57

Moksel *see* A. Moksel AG.

MOL *see* Mitsui O.S.K. Lines, Ltd.

MOL Rt, 70 192–95

Moldflow Corporation, 73 227–30

Molex Incorporated, 11 317–19; 14 27; 54 236–41 (upd.)

Moliflor Loisirs, 80 252–55

Molina Healthcare, Inc., 116 353–56

Molinos Río de la Plata S.A., 61 219–21

Molins plc, 51 249–51

The Molson Companies Limited, I 273–75; 26 303–07 (upd.)

Molson Coors Brewing Company, 77 288–300 (upd.)

Monaco Coach Corporation, 31 336–38

Monadnock Paper Mills, Inc., 21 381–84

Monarch Casino & Resort, Inc., 65 239–41

The Monarch Cement Company, 72 231–33

Mondadori *see* Arnoldo Mondadori Editore S.p.A.

Mondragón Corporación Cooperativa, 101 347–51

MoneyGram International, Inc., 94 315–18

Monfort, Inc., 13 350–52

Monnaie de Paris, 62 246–48

Monnoyeur Group *see* Groupe Monnoyeur.

Monoprix S.A., 86 282–85

Monro Muffler Brake, Inc., 24 337–40

Monrovia Nursery Company, 70 196–98

Monsanto Company, I 365–67, 9 355–57 (upd.); 29 327–31 (upd.); 77 301–07 (upd.)

Monsoon plc, 39 287–89

Monster Cable Products, Inc., 69 256–58

Monster Worldwide Inc., 74 194–97 (upd.)

Montana Coffee Traders, Inc., 60 208–10

The Montana Power Company, 11 320–22; 44 288–92 (upd.)

Montblanc International GmbH, 82 240–44

Montedison S.p.A., I 368–69; 24 341–44 (upd.)

Monterey Pasta Company, 58 240–43

Montgomery Ward & Co., Incorporated, V 145–48; 20 374–79 (upd.)

Montres Rolex S.A., 13 353–55; 34 292–95 (upd.)

Montupet S.A., 63 302–04

Moody's Corporation, 65 242–44

Moog Inc., 13 356–58

Moog Music, Inc., 75 261–64

Mooney Aerospace Group Ltd., 52 252–55

Moore Corporation Limited, IV 644–46 *see also* R.R. Donnelley & Sons Co.

Moore-Handley, Inc., 39 290–92

Moore Medical Corp., 17 331–33

Moran Towing Corporation, Inc., 15 301–03

The Morgan Crucible Company plc, 82 245–50

Morgan Grenfell Group PLC, II 427–29 *see also* Deutsche Bank AG.

The Morgan Group, Inc., 46 300–02

Morgan, Lewis & Bockius LLP, 29 332–34

Morgan Motor Company, 105 304–08

Morgan Stanley Dean Witter & Company, II 430–32; 16 374–78 (upd.); 33 311–14 (upd.)

Morgan's Foods, Inc., 101 352–55

Morgans Hotel Group Company, 80 256–59

Morguard Corporation, 85 287–90

Morinaga & Co. Ltd., 61 222–25

Morinda Holdings, Inc., 82 251–54

Morningstar Inc., 68 259–62

Morris Communications Corporation, 36 339–42

Morris Travel Services L.L.C., 26 308–11

Morrison & Foerster LLP, 78 220–23

Morrison Knudsen Corporation, 7 355–58; 28 286–90 (upd.) *see also* The Washington Companies.

Morrison Restaurants Inc., 11 323–25

Morrow Equipment Co. L.L.C., 87 325–327

Morse Shoe Inc., 13 359–61

Morton International, Inc., 9 358–59 (upd.); 80 260–64 (upd.)

Morton Thiokol Inc., I 370–72 *see also* Thiokol Corp.

Morton's Restaurant Group, Inc., 30 329–31; 88 262–66 (upd.)

The Mosaic Company, 91 330–33

Mosinee Paper Corporation, 15 304–06 *see also* Wausau-Mosinee Paper Corp.

Moss Bros Group plc, 51 252–54

Mossimo, 27 328–30; 96 288–92 (upd.)

Mota-Engil, SGPS, S.A., 97 290–93

Motel 6, 13 362–64; 56 248–51 (upd.) *see also* Accor SA

Mothercare plc, 17 334–36; 78 224–27 (upd.)

Mothers Against Drunk Driving (MADD), 51 255–58

Mothers Work, Inc., 18 350–52

Motiva Enterprises LLC, 111 311–14

The Motley Fool, Inc., 40 329–31

Moto Photo, Inc., 45 282–84

Motor Cargo Industries, Inc., 35 296–99

Motorcar Parts & Accessories, Inc., 47 253–55

Motorola, Inc., II 60–62; 11 326–29 (upd.); 34 296–302 (upd.); 93 313–23 (upd.)

Motown Records Company L.P., 26 312–14

Mott's Inc., 57 250–53

Moulinex S.A., 22 362–65 *see also* Groupe SEB.

Mount *see also* Mt.

Mount Sinai Medical Center, 112 281–84

NII *see* National Intergroup, Inc.
NIKE, Inc., V 372–74; 8 391–94 (upd.);
 36 343–48 (upd.); 75 279–85 (upd.)
Nikken Global Inc., 32 364–67
The Nikko Securities Company
 Limited, II 433–35; 9 377–79 (upd.)
Nikon Corporation, III 583–85; 48
 292–95 (upd.)
Nilson Group AB, 113 273–76
Niman Ranch, Inc., 67 267–69
Nimbus CD International, Inc., 20
 386–90
Nine West Group Inc., 11 348–49; 39
 301–03 (upd.)
Nintendo Co., Ltd., III 586–88; 7
 394–96 (upd.); 28 317–21 (upd.); 67
 270–76 (upd.)
NIOC *see* National Iranian Oil Co.
Nippon Credit Bank, II 338–39
Nippon Electric Glass Co. Ltd., 95
 301–05
Nippon Express Company, Ltd., V
 477–80; 64 286–90 (upd.)
Nippon Life Insurance Company, III
 318–20; 60 218–21 (upd.)
Nippon Light Metal Company, Ltd., IV
 153–55
Nippon Meat Packers, Inc., II 550–51;
 78 255–57 (upd.)
Nippon Mining Holdings Inc., IV
 475–77; 102 306–10 (upd.)
Nippon Oil Corporation, IV 478–79;
 63 308–13 (upd.); 120 281–87 (upd.)
Nippon Paint Company Ltd., 115
 366–68
Nippon Seiko K.K., III 589–90
Nippon Sheet Glass Company, Limited,
 III 714–16
Nippon Shinpan Co., Ltd., II 436–37;
 61 248–50 (upd.)
Nippon Soda Co., Ltd., 85 303–06
Nippon Steel Corporation, IV 156–58;
 17 348–51 (upd.); 96 317–23 (upd.)
Nippon Suisan Kaisha, Limited, II
 552–53; 92 269–72 (upd.)
Nippon Telegraph and Telephone
 Corporation, V 305–07; 51 271–75
 (upd.); 117 279–85 (upd.)
Nippon Yusen Kabushiki Kaisha (NYK),
 V 481–83; 72 244–48 (upd.)
Nippondenso Co., Ltd., III 591–94 *see
 also* DENSO Corp.
NIPSCO Industries, Inc., 6 532–33
NiSource Inc., 109 416–20 (upd.)
Nissan Motor Company Ltd., I 183–84;
 11 350–52 (upd.); 34 303–07 (upd.);
 92 273–79 (upd.)
Nisshin Seifun Group Inc., II 554; 66
 246–48 (upd.)
Nisshin Steel Co., Ltd., IV 159–60
Nissho Iwai K.K., I 509–11
Nissin Food Products Company Ltd.,
 75 286–88
Nitches, Inc., 53 245–47
Nixdorf Computer AG, III 154–55 *see
 also* Wincor Nixdorf Holding GmbH.
NKK Corporation, IV 161–63; 28
 322–26 (upd.)

NL Industries, Inc., 10 434–36
Noah Education Holdings Ltd., 97
 303–06
Noah's New York Bagels *see*
 Einstein/Noah Bagel Corp.
Nobel Biocare Holding AG, 119 339–42
Nobel Industries AB, 9 380–82 *see also*
 Akzo Nobel N.V.
Nobel Learning Communities, Inc., 37
 276–79; 76 281–85 (upd.)
Nobia AB, 103 304–07
Noble Affiliates, Inc., 11 353–55
Noble Group Ltd., 111 338–42
Noble Roman's Inc., 14 351–53; 99
 297–302 (upd.)
Nobleza Piccardo SAICF, 64 291–93
Noboa *see also* Exportadora Bananera
 Noboa, S.A.
Nocibé SA, 54 265–68
NOF Corporation, 72 249–51
Nokia Corporation, II 69–71; 17
 352–54 (upd.); 38 328–31 (upd.); 77
 308–13 (upd.)
NOL Group *see* Neptune Orient Lines
 Ltd.
Noland Company, 35 311–14; 107
 295–99 (upd.)
Nolo.com, Inc., 49 288–91
Nomura Securities Company, Limited,
 II 438–41; 9 383–86 (upd.)
Noodle Kidoodle, 16 388–91
Noodles & Company, Inc., 55 277–79
Nooter Corporation, 61 251–53
Noranda Inc., IV 164–66; 7 397–99
 (upd.); 64 294–98 (upd.)
Norcal Waste Systems, Inc., 60 222–24
Norddeutsche Affinerie AG, 62 249–53
Nordea Bank AB, 40 336–39; 117
 286–90 (upd.)
Nordex AG, 101 362–65
NordicTrack, 22 382–84 *see also* Icon
 Health & Fitness, Inc.
Nordisk Film A/S, 80 269–73
Nordson Corporation, 11 356–58; 48
 296–99 (upd.)
Nordstrom, Inc., V 156–58; 18 371–74
 (upd.); 67 277–81 (upd.)
Norelco Consumer Products Co., 26
 334–36
Norfolk Southern Corporation, V
 484–86; 29 358–61 (upd.); 75
 289–93 (upd.)
Norinchukin Bank, II 340–41
Norm Thompson Outfitters, Inc., 47
 275–77
Norrell Corporation, 25 356–59
Norseland Inc., 120 288–91
Norsk Hydro ASA, 10 437–40; 35
 315–19 (upd.); 109 421–27 (upd.)
Norske Skogindustrier ASA, 63 314–16
Norstan, Inc., 16 392–94
Nortek, Inc., 34 308–12 *see also* NTK
 Holdings Inc.
Nortel Networks Corporation, 36
 349–54 (upd.)
North American Galvanizing &
 Coatings, Inc., 99 303–306

North Atlantic Trading Company Inc.,
 65 266–68
North Carolina National Bank
 Corporation *see* NCNB Corp.
The North Face, Inc., 18 375–77; 78
 258–61 (upd.)
North Fork Bancorporation, Inc., 46
 314–17
North Pacific Group, Inc., 61 254–57
North Star Steel Company, 18 378–81
The North West Company, Inc., 12
 361–63
North West Water Group plc, 11
 359–62 *see also* United Utilities PLC.
Northeast Utilities, V 668–69; 48
 303–06 (upd.)
Northern and Shell Network plc, 87
 341–344
Northern Foods plc, 10 441–43; 61
 258–62 (upd.)
Northern Rock plc, 33 318–21
Northern States Power Company, V
 670–72; 20 391–95 (upd.) *see also*
 Xcel Energy Inc.
Northern Telecom Limited, V 308–10
 see also Nortel Networks Corp.
Northern Trust Corporation, 9 387–89;
 101 366–72 (upd.)
Northland Cranberries, Inc., 38 332–34
Northrop Grumman Corporation, I
 76–77; 11 363–65 (upd.); 45 304–12
 (upd.); 111 343–53 (upd.)
Northwest Airlines Corporation, I
 112–14; 6 103–05 (upd.); 26 337–40
 (upd.); 74 204–08 (upd.)
Northwest Natural Gas Company, 45
 313–15
NorthWestern Corporation, 37 280–83
Northwestern Mutual Life Insurance
 Company, III 321–24; 45 316–21
 (upd.); 118 312–18 (upd.)
Norton Company, 8 395–97
Norton McNaughton, Inc., 27 346–49
 see also Jones Apparel Group, Inc.
Norwegian Cruise Lines *see* NCL
 Corporation
Norwich & Peterborough Building
 Society, 55 280–82
Norwood Promotional Products, Inc.,
 26 341–43
Notations, Inc., 110 342–45
Nova Corporation of Alberta, V 673–75
NovaCare, Inc., 11 366–68
Novacor Chemicals Ltd., 12 364–66
Novar plc, 49 292–96 (upd.)
Novartis AG, 39 304–10 (upd.); 105
 323–35 (upd.)
NovaStar Financial, Inc., 91 354–58
Novell, Inc., 6 269–71; 23 359–62
 (upd.)
Novellus Systems, Inc., 18 382–85
Noven Pharmaceuticals, Inc., 55 283–85
Novo Nordisk A/S, I 658–60; 61
 263–66 (upd.)
Novozymes A/S, 118 319–22
NOW *see* National Organization for
 Women, Inc.
NPC International, Inc., 40 340–42

Universal Electronics Inc., 39 405–08; 120 455–60 (upd.)

Universal Foods Corporation, 7 546–48 *see also* Sensient Technologies Corp.

Universal Forest Products, Inc., 10 539–40; 59 405–09 (upd.)

Universal Health Services, Inc., 6 191–93

Universal International, Inc., 25 510–11

Universal Manufacturing Company, 88 423–26

Universal Security Instruments, Inc., 96 434–37

Universal Stainless & Alloy Products, Inc., 75 386–88

Universal Studios, Inc., 33 429–33; 100 423–29 (upd.)

Universal Technical Institute, Inc., 81 396–99

Universal Truckload Services, Inc., 111 511–14

The University of Chicago Press, 79 451–55

University of Phoenix *see* Apollo Group, Inc.

Univision Communications Inc., 24 515–18; 83 434–439 (upd.)

UNM *see* United News & Media plc.

Uno Restaurant Holdings Corporation, 18 538–40; 70 334–37 (upd.)

Unocal Corporation, IV 569–71; 24 519–23 (upd.); 71 378–84 (upd.)

UNUM Corp., 13 538–40

UnumProvident Corporation, 52 376–83 (upd.)

Uny Co., Ltd., V 209–10; 49 425–28 (upd.)

UOB *see* United Overseas Bank Ltd.

UPC *see* United Pan-Europe Communications NV.

UPI *see* United Press International.

Upjohn Company, I 707–09; 8 547–49 (upd.) *see also* Pharmacia & Upjohn Inc.; Pfizer Inc.

UPM-Kymmene Corporation, 19 461–65; 50 505–11 (upd.)

The Upper Deck Company, LLC, 105 462–66

UPS *see* United Parcel Service, Inc.

Uralita S.A., 96 438–41

Uranium One Inc., 111 515–18

Urban Engineers, Inc., 102 435–38

Urban Outfitters, Inc., 14 524–26; 74 367–70 (upd.)

Urbi Desarrollos Urbanos, S.A. de C.V., 81 400–03

Urbium PLC, 75 389–91

URS Corporation, 45 420–23; 80 397–400 (upd.)

URSI *see* United Road Services, Inc.

US *see also* U.S.

US 1 Industries, Inc., 89 475–78

US Airways Group, Inc., I 131–32; 6 131–32 (upd.); 28 506–09 (upd.); 52 384–88 (upd.); 110 472–78 (upd.)

USA Interactive, Inc., 47 418–22 (upd.)

USA Mobility Inc., 97 437–40 (upd.)

USA Truck, Inc., 42 410–13

USAA, 10 541–43; 62 385–88 (upd.) *see also* United Services Automobile Association.

USANA, Inc., 29 491–93

USCC *see* United States Cellular Corp.

USF&G Corporation, III 395–98 *see also* The St. Paul Companies.

USG Corporation, III 762–64; 26 507–10 (upd.); 81 404–10 (upd.)

Ushio Inc., 91 496–99

Usinas Siderúrgicas de Minas Gerais S.A., 77 454–57

Usinger's Famous Sausage *see* Fred Usinger Inc.

Usinor SA, IV 226–28; 42 414–17 (upd.)

USO *see* United Service Organizations.

USPS *see* United States Postal Service.

USSC *see* United States Surgical Corp.

UST Inc., 9 533–35; 50 512–17 (upd.)

USTA *see* United States Tennis Association

USX Corporation, IV 572–74; 7 549–52 (upd.) *see also* United States Steel Corp.

Utah Medical Products, Inc., 36 496–99

Utah Power and Light Company, 27 483–86 *see also* PacifiCorp.

UTG Inc., 100 430–33

Utilicorp United Inc., 6 592–94 *see also* Aquilla, Inc.

UTStarcom, Inc., 77 458–61

UTV *see* Ulster Television PLC.

Utz Quality Foods, Inc., 72 358–60

UUNET, 38 468–72

Uwajimaya, Inc., 60 312–14

Uzbekistan Airways National Air Company, 99 470–473

V

V&S Vin & Sprit AB, 91 504–11 (upd.)

VA TECH ELIN EBG GmbH, 49 429–31

Vail Resorts, Inc., 11 543–46; 43 435–39 (upd.); 120 461–67 (upd.)

Vaillant GmbH, 44 436–39

Vaisala Oyj, 104 459–63

Valassis Communications, Inc., 8 550–51; 37 407–10 (upd.); 76 364–67 (upd.)

Vale S.A., 117 437–42 (upd.)

Valeo, 23 492–94; 66 350–53 (upd.)

Valero Energy Corporation, 7 553–55; 71 385–90 (upd.)

Valhi, Inc., 19 466–68; 94 431–35 (upd.)

Valio Oy, 117 443–47

Vall Companys S.A., 120 468–71

Vallen Corporation, 45 424–26

Valley Media Inc., 35 430–33

Valley National Gases, Inc., 85 434–37

Valley Proteins, Inc., 91 500–03

ValleyCrest Companies, 81 411–14 (upd.)

Vallourec SA, 54 391–94

Valmet Oy, III 647–49 *see also* Metso Corp.

Valmont Industries, Inc., 19 469–72

Valora Holding AG, 98 425–28

Valorem S.A., 88 427–30

Valores Industriales S.A., 19 473–75

The Valspar Corporation, 8 552–54; 32 483–86 (upd.); 77 462–68 (upd.)

Value City Department Stores, Inc., 38 473–75 *see also* Retail Ventures, Inc.

Value Line, Inc., 16 506–08; 73 358–61 (upd.)

Value Merchants Inc., 13 541–43

ValueClick, Inc., 49 432–34

ValueVision International, Inc., 22 534–36

Valve Corporation, 101 483–86

Van Camp Seafood Company, Inc., 7 556–57 *see also* Chicken of the Sea International.

Van de Velde S.A./NV, 102 439–43

Van Hool S.A./NV, 96 442–45

Van Houtte Inc., 39 409–11

Van Lanschot NV, 79 456–59

Van Leer N.V. *see* Royal Packaging Industries Van Leer N.V.; Greif Inc.

Vance Publishing Corporation, 64 398–401

Vandemoortele S.A./NV, 113 443–46

Vanderbilt *see* R.T. Vanderbilt Company, Inc.

Vanderbilt University Medical Center, 99 474–477

The Vanguard Group, Inc., 14 530–32; 34 486–89 (upd.)

Vanguard Health Systems Inc., 70 338–40

Vann's Inc., 105 467–70

Van's Aircraft, Inc., 65 349–51

Vans, Inc., 16 509–11; 47 423–26 (upd.)

Vapores *see* Compañia Sud Americana de Vapores S.A.

Varco International, Inc., 42 418–20

Vari-Lite International, Inc., 35 434–36

Varian Associates Inc., 12 504–06

Varian, Inc., 48 407–11 (upd.)

Variety Wholesalers, Inc., 73 362–64

Variflex, Inc., 51 391–93

VARIG S.A. (Viação Aérea Rio-Grandense), 6 133–35; 29 494–97 (upd.)

Varity Corporation, III 650–52 *see also* AGCO Corp.

Varlen Corporation, 16 512–14

Varsity Brands, Inc., 15 516–18; 94 436–40 (upd.)

Varta AG, 23 495–99

VASCO Data Security International, Inc., 79 460–63

Vastar Resources, Inc., 24 524–26

Vattenfall AB, 57 395–98

Vaughan Foods, Inc., 105 471–74

Vauxhall Motors Limited, 73 365–69

VBA - Bloemenveiling Aalsmeer, 88 431–34

VCA Antech, Inc., 58 353–55

VDL Groep B.V., 113 447–50

Veba A.G., I 542–43; 15 519–21 (upd.) *see also* E.On AG.

Vebego International BV, 49 435–37

Vecellio Group, Inc., 113 451–54

Index to Industries

Carmichael Lynch Inc., 28
Cash Systems, Inc., 93
Cazenove Group plc, 72
CCC Information Services Group Inc., 74
CDI Corporation, 6; 54 (upd.)
Cegedim S.A., 104
Central Parking System, 18; 104 (upd.)
Century Business Services, Inc., 52
Chancellor Beacon Academies, Inc., 53
Chiat/Day Inc. Advertising, 11
Chicago Board of Trade, 41
Chisholm-Mingo Group, Inc., 41
Christie's International plc, 15; 39 (upd.)
Cintas Corporation, 21
CMG Worldwide, Inc., 89
Coalition America Inc., 113
Colle+McVoy, 110
COMFORCE Corporation, 40
Command Security Corporation, 57
comScore, Inc., 119
Concentra Inc., 71
Convergys Corporation, 119
CoolSavings, Inc., 77
The Corporate Executive Board Company, 89
Corporate Express, Inc., 22; 47 (upd.)
CORT Business Services Corporation, 26
Cox Enterprises, Inc., IV; 22 (upd.); 67 (upd.)
CRA International, Inc., 93
craigslist, inc., 89
Creative Artists Agency LLC, 38
Crispin Porter + Bogusky, 83
CSG Systems International, Inc., 75
Cyrk Inc., 19
Daiko Advertising Inc., 79
Dale Carnegie & Associates Inc. 28; 78 (upd.)
D'Arcy Masius Benton & Bowles, Inc., 6; 32 (upd.)
Dawson Holdings PLC, 43
DDB Needham Worldwide, 14
Deluxe Corporation, 22 (upd.); 73 (upd.)
Dentsu Inc., I; 16 (upd.); 40 (upd.)
Deutsch, Inc., 42
Deutsche Messe AG, 104
Deutsche Post AG, 29
DeVito/Verdi, 85
Dewberry, 78
DG FastChannel, Inc., 111
DHL Worldwide Network S.A./N.V., 69 (upd.)
Digitas Inc., 81
DoubleClick Inc., 46
Draftfcb, 94
Drake Beam Morin, Inc., 44
Earl Scheib, Inc., 32
eBay Inc., 67 (upd.)
EBSCO Industries, Inc., 17
Ecolab Inc., I; 13 (upd.); 34 (upd.); 85 (upd.)
Ecology and Environment, Inc., 39
Edelman, 62
Electro Rent Corporation, 58
EMAK Worldwide, Inc., 105
Employee Solutions, Inc., 18
Ennis, Inc., 21; 97 (upd.)
Equifax Inc., 6; 28 (upd.); 90 (upd.)

Equity Marketing, Inc., 26
ERLY Industries Inc., 17
Euro RSCG Worldwide S.A., 13
Expedia, Inc., 58
Fallon Worldwide, 22; 71 (upd.)
Farmers Cooperative Society, 118
FedEx Office and Print Services, Inc., 109 (upd.)
FileNet Corporation, 62
Finarte Casa d'Aste S.p.A., 93
First Advantage Corporation, 119
First Artist Corporation PLC, 105
Fiserv, Inc., 11; 33 (upd.); 106 (upd.)
FlightSafety International, Inc., 29 (upd.)
Florists' Transworld Delivery, Inc., 28
Foote, Cone & Belding Worldwide, I; 66 (upd.)
Forrester Research, Inc., 54
Frankel & Co., 39
Franklin Covey Company, 37 (upd.)
Freeze.com LLC, 77
frog design inc., 115
Frost & Sullivan, Inc., 53
FTI Consulting, Inc., 77
Gage Marketing Group, 26
Gallup, Inc., 37; 104 (upd.)
Gartner, Inc., 21; 94 (upd.)
GEMA (Gesellschaft für musikalische Aufführungs- und mechanische Vervielfältigungsrechte), 70
General Employment Enterprises, Inc., 87
George P. Johnson Company, 60
George S. May International Company, 55
Gevity HR, Inc., 63
GfK Aktiengesellschaft, 49
Glotel plc, 53
Golin/Harris International, Inc., 88
Goodby Silverstein & Partners, Inc., 75
Grace & Wild, Inc., 115
Grey Global Group Inc., 6; 66 (upd.)
Group 4 Falck A/S, 42
Groupe Crit S.A., 74
Groupe Jean-Claude Darmon, 44
GSD&M Advertising, 44
GSD&M's Idea City, 90
GSI Commerce, Inc., 67
Guardsmark, L.L.C., 77
Gwathmey Siegel & Associates Architects LLC, 26
Hakuhodo, Inc., 6; 42 (upd.)
Hall, Kinion & Associates, Inc., 52
Ha-Lo Industries, Inc., 27
Handleman Company, 15; 86 (upd.)
Harris Interactive Inc., 41; 92 (upd.)
Harte-Hanks, Inc., 63
Havas SA, 33 (upd.)
Hay Group Holdings, Inc., 100
Hays plc, 27; 78 (upd.)
Headway Corporate Resources, Inc., 40
Heidrick & Struggles International, Inc., 28
Henry Dreyfuss Associates LLC, 88
Hewitt Associates, Inc., 77
Hildebrandt International, 29
Hogg Robinson Group PLC, 105
IAP Worldwide Services, Inc., 119
Idearc Inc., 90

IKON Office Solutions, Inc., 50
IMS Health, Inc., 57
Interbrand Corporation, 70
Interep National Radio Sales Inc., 35
International Management Group, 18
International Profit Associates, Inc., 87
International Total Services, Inc., 37
The Interpublic Group of Companies, Inc., I; 22 (upd.); 75 (upd.)
Intertek Group plc, 95
inVentiv Health, Inc., 81
Ipsos SA, 48
Iron Mountain, Inc., 33; 104 (upd.)
J.D. Power and Associates, 32
Jack Morton Worldwide, 88
Jackson Hewitt, Inc., 48
Jani-King International, Inc., 85
Japan Leasing Corporation, 8
JCDecaux S.A., 76
Jostens, Inc., 25 (upd.)
JOULÉ Inc., 58
JTH Tax Inc., 103
JWT Group Inc., I
Kantar Group, 119
Katz Communications, Inc., 6
Katz Media Group, Inc., 35
Keane, Inc., 56
Kelly Services, Inc., 6; 26 (upd.); 109 (upd.)
Ketchum Communications Inc., 6
Kforce Inc., 71
Kinko's Inc., 16; 43 (upd.)
Kirshenbaum Bond + Partners, Inc., 57
Kohn Pedersen Fox Associates P.C., 57
Korn/Ferry International, 34; 102 (upd.)
Kratos Defense & Security Solutions, Inc., 108
Kroll Inc., 57
L. M. Berry and Company, 80
Labor Ready, Inc., 29; 88 (upd.)
Lamar Advertising Company, 27; 70 (upd.)
Landor Associates, 81
Le Cordon Bleu S.A., 67
LECG Corporation, 93
Lender Processing Services, Inc., 110
Leo Burnett Company Inc., I; 20 (upd.)
The Leona Group LLC, 84
The Lewin Group Inc., 104
LinkedIn Corporation, 103
Lintas: Worldwide, 14
LivePerson, Inc., 91
MacDonald, Dettwiler, and Associates Ltd., 119
Mail Boxes Etc., 18; 41 (upd.)
Manhattan Associates, Inc., 67
Manning Selvage & Lee (MS&L), 76
Manpower Inc., 30 (upd.); 73 (upd.)
Marchex, Inc., 72
marchFIRST, Inc., 34
Marco Business Products, Inc., 75
Maritz Holdings Inc., 38; 110 (upd.)
Marlin Business Services Corp., 89
MAXIMUS, Inc., 43
McMurry, Inc., 105
MDC Partners Inc., 63
Mediaset SpA, 50
Merkle Inc., 114

Aerospace

Agribusiness & Farming

Airlines

Automotive

Bio-Technology

Chemicals

International Flavors & Fragrances Inc., 9; 38 (upd.)
Israel Chemicals Ltd., 55
KBR Inc., 106 (upd.)
Kemira Oyj, 70
KMG Chemicals, Inc., 101
Koppers Industries, Inc., I; 26 (upd.)
Kwizda Holding GmbH, 102 (upd.)
L'Air Liquide SA, I; 47 (upd.)
Lawter International Inc., 14
LeaRonal, Inc., 23
Loctite Corporation, 30 (upd.)
Lonza Group Ltd., 73
Loos & Dilworth, Inc., 100
Lubrizol Corporation, The, I; 30 (upd.); 83 (upd.)
LyondellBasell Industries Holdings N.V., 45 (upd.); 109 (upd.)
M.A. Hanna Company, 8
MacDermid Incorporated, 32
Makhteshim-Agan Industries Ltd., 85
Mallinckrodt Group Inc., 19
MBC Holding Company, 40
Melamine Chemicals, Inc., 27
Methanex Corporation, 40
Mexichem, S.A.B. de C.V., 99
Minerals Technologies Inc., 52 (upd.)
Mississippi Chemical Corporation, 39
Mitsubishi Chemical Corporation, I; 56 (upd.)
Mitsui Petrochemical Industries, Ltd., 9
Monsanto Company, I; 9 (upd.); 29 (upd.)
Montedison SpA, I
Morton International Inc., I; 9 (upd.); 80 (upd.)
Mosaic Company, The, 91
Nagase & Company, Ltd., 8
Nalco Holding Company, I; 12 (upd.); 89 (upd.)
National Distillers and Chemical Corporation, I
National Sanitary Supply Co., 16
National Starch and Chemical Company, 49
NCH Corporation, 8
NewMarket Corporation, 116
Nippon Soda Co., Ltd., 85
Nisshin Seifun Group Inc., 66 (upd.)
NL Industries, Inc., 10
Nobel Industries AB, 9
NOF Corporation, 72
North American Galvanizing & Coatings, Inc., 99
Novacor Chemicals Ltd., 12
Nufarm Ltd., 87
OAO Gazprom, 42; 107 (upd.)
Occidental Petroleum Corporation, 71 (upd.)
Olin Corporation, I; 13 (upd.); 78 (upd.)
OM Group, Inc., 17; 78 (upd.)
OMNOVA Solutions Inc., 59
Orica Ltd., 112
Penford Corporation, 55
Pennwalt Corporation, I
Perstorp AB, I; 51 (upd.)
Petrolite Corporation, 15
Pfizer Inc., 79 (upd.)

Pioneer Hi-Bred International, Inc., 41 (upd.)
PolyOne Corporation, 87 (upd.)
Praxair, Inc., 11; 48 (upd.); 113 (upd.)
Quaker Chemical Corp., 91
Quantum Chemical Corporation, 8
Red Spot Paint & Varnish Company, Inc., 112 (upd.)
Reichhold, Inc., 10; 112 (upd.)
Renner Herrmann S.A., 79
Rentech, Inc., 110
Rhodia S.A., 38; 115 (upd.)
Rhône-Poulenc S.A., I; 10 (upd.)
Robertet SA, 39
Rockwood Holdings, Inc., 117
Rohm and Haas Company, I; 26 (upd.); 77 (upd.)
Roussel Uclaf, I; 8 (upd.)
RPM International Inc., 8; 36 (upd.); 91 (upd.)
RWE AG, 50 (upd.); 119 (upd.)
S.C. Johnson & Son, Inc., III; 28 (upd.); 89 (upd.)
Scotts Company, The, 22
SCP Pool Corporation, 39
Sequa Corporation, 13; 54 (upd.)
Shanghai Petrochemical Co., Ltd., 18
Sigma-Aldrich Corporation, I; 36 (upd.); 93 (upd.)
Sociedad Química y Minera de Chile S.A., 103
Solutia Inc., 52
Solvay S.A., I; 21 (upd.); 61 (upd.)
Stepan Company, 30; 105 (upd.)
Sterling Chemicals, Inc., 16; 78 (upd.)
Sumitomo Chemical Company Ltd., I; 98 (upd.)
Syral S.A.S., 113
Takeda Chemical Industries, Ltd., 46 (upd.)
Teknor Apex Company, 97
Terra Industries, Inc., 13
Tessenderlo Group, 76
Teva Pharmaceutical Industries Ltd., 22
Tosoh Corporation, 70
Transammonia Group, 95
Ube Industries, Ltd., III; 38 (upd.); 111 (upd.)
Union Carbide Corporation, I; 9 (upd.); 74 (upd.)
UNIPAR – União de Indústrias Petroquímicas S.A., 108
United Industries Corporation, 68
Univar Corporation, 9
Valspar Corporation, The, 8; 32 (upd.); 77 (upd.)
VeraSun Energy Corporation, 87
Vista Chemical Company, I
Wacker-Chemie AG, 112 (upd.)
WD-40 Company, 18; 87 (upd.)
Witco Corporation, I; 16 (upd.)
Woodstream Corporation, 115
Yule Catto & Company plc, 54
Zakłady Azotowe Puławy S.A., 100
Zeneca Group PLC, 21
3M Company, I; 8 (upd.); 26 (upd.); 61 (upd.)

Conglomerates

ABARTA, Inc., 100
Abengoa S.A., 73
Accor SA, 10; 27 (upd.)
Ackermans & van Haaren N.V., 97
Adani Enterprises Ltd., 97
Aditya Birla Group, 79
Administración Nacional de Combustibles, Alcohol y Pórtland, 93
AEG A.G., I
Agrofert Holding A.S., 117
Al Habtoor Group L.L.C., 87
Alcatel Alsthom Compagnie Générale d'Electricité, 9
Alco Standard Corporation, I
Alexander & Baldwin, Inc., 10, 40 (upd.); 118 (upd.)
Alfa, S.A. de C.V., 19
Alfa Group, 99
Algar S/A Emprendimentos e Participações, 103
Alleghany Corporation, 60 (upd.)
Allied Domecq PLC, 29
Allied-Signal Inc., I
AMFAC Inc., I
Andrade Gutierrez S.A., 102
Anschutz Company, The, 36 (upd.); 73 (upd.)
Antofagasta plc, 65
Apax Partners Worldwide LLP, 89
APi Group, Inc., 64
Aramark Corporation, 13
ARAMARK Corporation, 41
Archer Daniels Midland Company, I; 11 (upd.); 75 (upd.)
Arkansas Best Corporation, 16
Associated British Ports Holdings Plc, 45 (upd.)
BAA plc, 33 (upd.)
Barlow Rand Ltd., I
Barloworld Ltd., 109 (upd.)
Barratt Developments plc, 56 (upd.)
Bat Industries PLC, I
Baugur Group hf, 81
Bayer Hispania S.L., 120
BB Holdings Limited, 77
Berjaya Group Bhd., 67
Berkshire Hathaway Inc., III; 18 (upd.); 42 (upd.); 89 (upd.)
Block Communications, Inc., 81
Bond Corporation Holdings Limited, 10
Brascan Corporation, 67
BTR PLC, I
Bunzl plc, 31 (upd.)
Burlington Northern Santa Fe Corporation, 27 (upd.)
Business Post Group plc, 46
C.I. Traders Limited, 61
C. Itoh & Company Ltd., I
Camargo Corrêa S.A., 93
Cargill, Incorporated, II; 13 (upd.); 40 (upd.); 89 (upd.)
CBI Industries, Inc., 7
Charoen Pokphand Group, 62
Chesebrough-Pond's USA, Inc., 8
China Merchants International Holdings Co., Ltd., 52
Cisneros Group of Companies, 54
CITIC Pacific Ltd., 18; 116 (upd.)

Construction

Containers

Inland Container Corporation, 8
Interpool, Inc., 92
Kerr Group Inc., 24
Keyes Fibre Company, 9
Libbey Inc., 49
Liqui-Box Corporation, 16
Longaberger Company, The, 12
Longview Fibre Company, 8
Mead Corporation, The, 19 (upd.)
Metal Box PLC, I
Mobile Mini, Inc., 58
Molins plc, 51
National Can Corporation, I
Owens-Illinois, Inc., I; 26 (upd.); 85
   (upd.)
Packaging Corporation of America, 51
   (upd.)
Pochet SA, 55
Primerica Corporation, I
Printpack, Inc., 68
PVC Container Corporation, 67
Rexam PLC, 32 (upd.); 85 (upd.)
Reynolds Metals Company, 19 (upd.)
Royal Packaging Industries Van Leer N.V.,
   30
RPC Group PLC, 81
Sealright Co., Inc., 17
Shurgard Storage Centers, Inc., 52
Smurfit Kappa Group plc, 112 (upd.)
Smurfit-Stone Container Corporation, 26
   (upd.); 83 (upd.)
Sonoco Products Company, 8; 89 (upd.)
Thermos Company, 16
Tim-Bar Corporation, 110
Toyo Seikan Kaisha, Ltd., I
U.S. Can Corporation, 30
Ultra Pac, Inc., 24
Viatech Continental Can Company, Inc.,
   25 (upd.)
Vidrala S.A., 67
Vitro Corporativo S.A. de C.V., 34

Drugs & Pharmaceuticals

A.L. Pharma Inc., 12
A. Nelson & Co. Ltd., 75
Abbott Laboratories, I; 11 (upd.); 40
   (upd.); 93 (upd.)
Aché Laboratórios Farmacéuticas S.A., 105
Actavis Group hf., 103
Actelion Ltd., 83
Adolor Corporation, 101
Akorn, Inc., 32
Albany Molecular Research, Inc., 77
Alfresa Holdings Corporation, 108
Allergan, Inc., 77 (upd.)
Alpharma Inc., 35 (upd.)
ALZA Corporation, 10; 36 (upd.)
American Home Products, I; 10 (upd.)
American Oriental Bioengineering Inc., 93
American Pharmaceutical Partners, Inc.,
   69
AmerisourceBergen Corporation, 64
   (upd.)
Amersham PLC, 50
Amgen, Inc., 10; 89 (upd.)
Amylin Pharmaceuticals, Inc., 67
Andrx Corporation, 55
Angelini SpA, 100

Aspen Pharmacare Holdings Limited, 112
Astellas Pharma Inc., 97 (upd.)
AstraZeneca PLC, I; 20 (upd.); 50 (upd.)
AtheroGenics Inc., 101
Axcan Pharma Inc., 85
Barr Pharmaceuticals, Inc., 26; 68 (upd.)
Bayer AG, I; 13 (upd.); 41 (upd.); 118
   (upd.)
Berlex Laboratories, Inc., 66
Biovail Corporation, 47
Block Drug Company, Inc., 8
Boiron S.A., 73
Bristol-Myers Squibb Company, III; 9
   (upd.); 37 (upd.); 111 (upd.)
BTG Plc, 87
C.H. Boehringer Sohn, 39
Cahill May Roberts Group Ltd., 112
Caremark Rx, Inc., 10; 54 (upd.)
Carter-Wallace, Inc., 8; 38 (upd.)
Celgene Corporation, 67
Cephalon Technology, Inc, 45; 115 (upd.)
Chiron Corporation, 10
Chugai Pharmaceutical Co., Ltd., 50
Ciba-Geigy Ltd., I; 8 (upd.)
CSL Limited, 112
D&K Wholesale Drug, Inc., 14
Discovery Partners International, Inc., 58
Dr. Reddy's Laboratories Ltd., 59
Egis Gyogyszergyar Nyrt, 104
Eisai Co., Ltd., 101
Elan Corporation PLC, 63
Eli Lilly and Company, I; 11 (upd.); 47
   (upd.); 109 (upd.)
Endo Pharmaceuticals Holdings Inc., 71
Eon Labs, Inc., 67
Express Scripts Inc., 44 (upd.)
F. Hoffmann-La Roche Ltd., I; 50 (upd.)
Ferring Pharmaceuticals S.A., 119
Fisons plc, 9; 23 (upd.)
Forest Laboratories, Inc., 52 (upd.); 114
   (upd.)
FoxMeyer Health Corporation, 16
Fujisawa Pharmaceutical Company, Ltd.,
   I; 58 (upd.)
G.D. Searle & Co., I; 12 (upd.); 34
   (upd.)
Galenica AG, 84
GEHE AG, 27
Genentech, Inc., I; 8 (upd.); 75 (upd.)
Genetics Institute, Inc., 8
Genzyme Corporation, 13, 77 (upd.)
Glaxo Holdings PLC, I; 9 (upd.)
GlaxoSmithKline plc, 46 (upd.); 119
   (upd.)
Groupe Fournier SA, 44
Groupe Léa Nature, 88
H. Lundbeck A/S, 44
Hauser, Inc., 46
Heska Corporation, 39
Hexal AG, 69
Hikma Pharmaceuticals Ltd., 102
Hospira, Inc., 71
Huntingdon Life Sciences Group plc, 42
ICN Pharmaceuticals, Inc., 52
ICU Medical, Inc., 106
Immucor, Inc., 81
Integrated BioPharma, Inc., 83
IVAX Corporation, 55 (upd.)

Janssen Pharmaceutica N.V., 80
Johnson & Johnson, III; 8 (upd.)
Jones Medical Industries, Inc., 24
Judge Group, Inc., The, 51
King Pharmaceuticals, Inc., 54
Kinray Inc., 85
Kos Pharmaceuticals, Inc., 63
Kyowa Hakko Kogyo Co., Ltd., 48 (upd.)
Laboratoires Arkopharma S.A., 75
Laboratoires Pierre Fabre S.A., 100
Leiner Health Products Inc., 34
Ligand Pharmaceuticals Incorporated, 47
MannKind Corporation, 87
Marion Merrell Dow, Inc., I; 9 (upd.)
Matrixx Initiatives, Inc., 74
McKesson Corporation, 12; 47 (upd.)
Medco Health Solutions, Inc., 116
Medicis Pharmaceutical Corporation, 59
MedImmune, Inc., 35
Merck & Co., Inc., I; 11 (upd.); 34
   (upd.); 95 (upd.)
Merck KGaA, 111
Merial Ltd., 102
Merz Group, 81
Miles Laboratories, I
Millennium Pharmaceuticals, Inc., 47
Monsanto Company, 29 (upd.), 77 (upd.)
Moore Medical Corp., 17
Murdock Madaus Schwabe, 26
Mylan Laboratories Inc., I; 20 (upd.); 59
   (upd.)
Myriad Genetics, Inc., 95
Nadro S.A. de C.V., 86
Nastech Pharmaceutical Company Inc., 79
National Patent Development
   Corporation, 13
Natrol, Inc., 49
Natural Alternatives International, Inc., 49
Nektar Therapeutics, 91
Novartis AG, 39 (upd.); 105 (upd.)
Noven Pharmaceuticals, Inc., 55
Novo Nordisk A/S, I; 61 (upd.)
Obagi Medical Products, Inc., 95
Omnicare, Inc., 49
Omrix Biopharmaceuticals, Inc., 95
Onyx Pharmaceuticals, Inc., 110
Par Pharmaceutical Companies, Inc., 65
PDL BioPharma, Inc., 90
Perrigo Company, 12; 59 (upd.); 118
   (upd.)
Pfizer Inc., I; 9 (upd.); 38 (upd.); 79
   (upd.)
Pharmacia & Upjohn Inc., I; 25 (upd.)
Pharmion Corporation, 91
PLIVA d.d., 70
PolyMedica Corporation, 77
POZEN Inc., 81
QLT Inc., 71
Quigley Corporation, The, 62
Quintiles Transnational Corporation, 21
R.P. Scherer, I
Ranbaxy Laboratories Ltd., 70
ratiopharm Group, 84
Reckitt Benckiser plc, II; 42 (upd.); 91
   (upd.)
Recordati Industria Chimica e
   Farmaceutica S.p.A., 105
Roberts Pharmaceutical Corporation, 16

Roche Bioscience, 14 (upd.)
Roche Holding AG, 109
Rorer Group, I
Roussel Uclaf, I; 8 (upd.)
Salix Pharmaceuticals, Ltd., 93
Sandoz Ltd., I
Sankyo Company, Ltd., I; 56 (upd.)
Sanofi-Synthélabo Group, The, I; 49 (upd.)
Santarus, Inc., 105
Schering AG, I; 50 (upd.)
Schering-Plough Corporation, I; 14 (upd.); 49 (upd.); 99 (upd.)
Sepracor Inc., 45; 117 (upd.)
Serono S.A., 47
Shionogi & Co., Ltd., III; 17 (upd.); 98 (upd.)
Shire PLC, 109
Sigma-Aldrich Corporation, I; 36 (upd.); 93 (upd.)
SmithKline Beecham plc, I; 32 (upd.)
Solvay S.A., 61 (upd.)
Squibb Corporation, I
Sterling Drug, Inc., I
Stiefel Laboratories, Inc., 90
Sun Pharmaceutical Industries Ltd., 57
Sunrider Corporation, The, 26
Syntex Corporation, I
Takeda Pharmaceutical Company Limited, I; 115 (upd.)
Taro Pharmaceutical Industries Ltd., 65
Teva Pharmaceutical Industries Ltd., 22; 54 (upd.); 112 (upd.)
UCB Pharma SA, 98
Upjohn Company, The, I; 8 (upd.)
Vertex Pharmaceuticals Incorporated, 83
Virbac Corporation, 74
Vitacost.com Inc., 116
Vitalink Pharmacy Services, Inc., 15
Warner Chilcott Limited, 85
Warner-Lambert Co., I; 10 (upd.)
Watson Pharmaceuticals Inc., 16; 56 (upd.)
Wellcome Foundation Ltd., The, I
WonderWorks, Inc., 103
Wyeth, Inc., 50 (upd.); 118 (upd.)
XOMA Ltd., 117
Zentiva N.V./Zentiva, a.s., 99
Zila, Inc., 46

Education & Training
ABC Learning Centres Ltd., 93
ACT, Inc., 114
American Management Association, 76
American Public Education, Inc., 108
Apollo Group, Inc., 24; 119 (upd.)
Archipelago Learning, Inc., 116
Benesse Corporation, 76
Berlitz International, Inc., 13; 39 (upd.)
Bridgepoint Education, Inc., 108
Capella Education Company, 109
Career Education Corporation, 45
ChartHouse International Learning Corporation, 49
Childtime Learning Centers, Inc., 34
Computer Learning Centers, Inc., 26
Corinthian Colleges, Inc., 39; 92 (upd.)
Cornell Companies, Inc., 112

Council on International Educational Exchange Inc., 81
DeVry Inc., 29; 82 (upd.)
ECC International Corp., 42
Edison Schools Inc., 37
Educate Inc., 86 (upd.)
Education Management Corporation, 35; 120 (upd.)
Educational Testing Service, 12; 62 (upd.)
GP Strategies Corporation, 64 (upd.)
Green Dot Public Schools, 99
Grupo Positivo, 105
Huntington Learning Centers, Inc., 55
ITT Educational Services, Inc., 39; 76 (upd.)
Jones Knowledge Group, Inc., 97
Kaplan, Inc., 42; 90 (upd.)
KinderCare Learning Centers, Inc., 13
Knowledge Learning Corporation, 51; 115 (upd.)
K12 Inc., 118
Kumon Institute of Education Co., Ltd., 72
LeapFrog Enterprises, Inc., 54
Learning Care Group, Inc., 76 (upd.)
Learning Company Inc., The, 24
Learning Tree International Inc., 24
Lincoln Educational Services Corporation, 111
LPA Holding Corporation, 81
Management and Training Corporation, 28
Mount Sinai Medical Center, 112
National Heritage Academies, Inc., 60
New Horizons Worldwide, Inc., 120
The New School, 103
Noah Education Holdings Ltd., 97
Nobel Learning Communities, Inc., 37; 76 (upd.)
Plato Learning, Inc., 44
Renaissance Learning, Inc., 39; 100 (upd.)
Rosetta Stone Inc., 93
Scientific Learning Corporation, 95
Strayer Education, Inc., 53
Sylvan Learning Systems, Inc., 35
Whitman Education Group, Inc., 41
Youth Services International, Inc., 21

Electrical & Electronics
ABB ASEA Brown Boveri Ltd., II; 22 (upd.)
ABB Ltd., 65 (upd.)
Acer Incorporated, 16; 73 (upd.)
Acuson Corporation, 10; 36 (upd.)
ADC Telecommunications, Inc., 30 (upd.)
Adtran Inc., 22
Advanced Circuits Inc., 67
Advanced Energy Industries, Inc., 118
Advanced Micro Devices, Inc., 6; 30 (upd.); 99 (upd.)
Advanced Technology Laboratories, Inc., 9
Agere Systems Inc., 61
Agilent Technologies Inc., 38; 93 (upd.)
Agilysys Inc., 76 (upd.)
Aiwa Co., Ltd., 30
AIXTRON AG, 118
AKG Acoustics GmbH, 62
Akzo Nobel N.V., 13; 41 (upd.)

Alienware Corporation, 81
Alliant Techsystems Inc., 30 (upd.); 77 (upd.)
AlliedSignal Inc., 9; 22 (upd.)
Alpine Electronics, Inc., 13
Alps Electric Co., Ltd., II; 44 (upd.)
Altera Corporation, 18; 43 (upd.); 115 (upd.)
Altron Incorporated, 20
Amdahl Corporation, 40 (upd.)
American Power Conversion Corporation, 24; 67 (upd.)
American Superconductor Corporation, 97
American Technical Ceramics Corp., 67
American Technology Corporation, 103
Amerigon Incorporated, 97
Amkor Technology, Inc., 69
AMP Incorporated, II; 14 (upd.)
Amphenol Corporation, 40
Amstrad plc, 48 (upd.)
Analog Devices, Inc., 10
Analogic Corporation, 23
Anam Group, 23
Anaren Microwave, Inc., 33
Andrew Corporation, 10; 32 (upd.)
Anixter International, 88
Anritsu Corporation, 68
Anthem Electronics, Inc., 13
Apex Digital, Inc., 63
Apple Computer, Inc., 36 (upd.); 77 (upd.)
Applied Materials, Inc., 114 (upd.)
Applied Micro Circuits Corporation, 38
Applied Power Inc., 9; 32 (upd.)
Applied Signal Technology, Inc., 87
Argon ST, Inc., 81
Arotech Corporation, 93
ARRIS Group, Inc., 89
Arrow Electronics, Inc., 10; 50 (upd.); 110 (upd.)
Artesyn Technologies Inc., 46 (upd.)
Ascend Communications, Inc., 24
Astronics Corporation, 35
ASUSTeK Computer Inc., 107
Atari Corporation, 9; 23 (upd.); 66 (upd.)
ATI Technologies Inc., 79
Atmel Corporation, 17
ATMI, Inc., 93
AU Optronics Corporation, 67
Audiovox Corporation, 34; 90 (upd.)
Ault Incorporated, 34
Autodesk, Inc., 10; 89 (upd.)
Avnet Inc., 9; 111 (upd.)
AVX Corporation, 67
Axcelis Technologies, Inc., 95
Axsys Technologies, Inc., 93
Ballard Power Systems Inc., 73
Bang & Olufsen Holding A/S, 37; 86 (upd.)
Barco NV, 44
Bel Fuse, Inc., 53
Belden CDT Inc., 19; 76 (upd.)
Bell Microproducts Inc., 69
Benchmark Electronics, Inc., 40
Bharat Electronics Limited, 113
Bharat Heavy Electricals Limited, 119
Bicoastal Corporation, II

Black Box Corporation, 20; 96 (upd.)
Blonder Tongue Laboratories, Inc., 48
Blue Coat Systems, Inc., 83
BMC Industries, Inc., 17; 59 (upd.)
Bogen Communications International, Inc., 62
Borrego Solar Systems, Inc., 111
Bose Corporation, 13; 36 (upd.); 118 (upd.)
Boston Acoustics, Inc., 22
Bowthorpe plc, 33
Braun GmbH, 51; 109 (upd.)
Bridgelux, Inc., 112
Brightpoint Inc., 18; 106 (upd.)
Brightstar Corp., 114
Broadcom Corporation, 34; 90 (upd.)
Bull S.A., 43 (upd.)
Burr-Brown Corporation, 19
BVR Systems (1998) Ltd., 93
Cabletron Systems, Inc., 10
Cadence Design Systems, Inc., 48 (upd.)
Cambridge SoundWorks, Inc., 48
Campbell Hausfeld, 115
Canadian Solar Inc., 105
Canon Inc., III; 18 (upd.); 79 (upd.)
Carbone Lorraine S.A., 33
Cardtronics, Inc., 93
Carl Zeiss AG, III; 34 (upd.); 91 (upd.)
Cash Systems, Inc., 93
CASIO Computer Co., Ltd., III; 16 (upd.); 40 (upd.)
C-COR.net Corp., 38
CDW Computer Centers, Inc., 52 (upd.)
Celestica Inc., 80
Checkpoint Systems, Inc., 39
Chi Mei Optoelectronics Corporation, 75
Christie Digital Systems, Inc., 103
Chubb, PLC, 50
Chunghwa Picture Tubes, Ltd., 75
Cirrus Logic, Inc., 48 (upd.)
Cisco Systems, Inc., 34 (upd.); 77 (upd.)
Citizen Watch Co., Ltd., III; 21 (upd.); 81 (upd.)
Clarion Company Ltd., 64
Cobham plc, 30
Cobra Electronics Corporation, 14
Coherent, Inc., 31
Cohu, Inc., 32
Color Kinetics Incorporated, 85
Comfort Systems USA, Inc., 101
Compagnie Générale d'Électricité, II
Compal Electronics Inc., 117
Concurrent Computer Corporation, 75
Conexant Systems Inc., 36; 106 (upd.)
Continental Graphics Corporation, 110
Cooper Industries, Inc., II; 44 (upd.)
Cray Inc., 75 (upd.)
Cray Research, Inc., 16 (upd.)
Creative Technology Ltd., 57
Cree Inc., 53
CTS Corporation, 39
Cubic Corporation, 19; 98 (upd.)
Cypress Semiconductor Corporation, 20; 48 (upd.)
D&H Distributing Co., 95
Dai Nippon Printing Co., Ltd., 57 (upd.)
Daiichikosho Company Ltd., 86
Daktronics, Inc., 32; 107 (upd.)

Dallas Semiconductor Corporation, 13; 31 (upd.)
DDi Corp., 97
De La Rue plc, 34 (upd.)
Dell Inc., 9; 31 (upd.); 63 (upd.)
DH Technology, Inc., 18
Dictaphone Healthcare Solutions, 78
Diehl Stiftung & Co. KG, 79
Digi International Inc., 9
Digi-Key Corporation, 109
Diodes Incorporated, 81
Directed Electronics, Inc., 87
Discreet Logic Inc., 20
Dixons Group plc, 19 (upd.)
D-Link Corporation, 83
Dolby Laboratories Inc., 20
Dot Hill Systems Corp., 93
DRS Technologies, Inc., 58
DTS, Inc., 80
DXP Enterprises, Inc., 101
Dynatech Corporation, 13
E-Systems, Inc., 9
Electronics for Imaging, Inc., 15; 43 (upd.)
Elma Electronic AG, 83
Elpida Memory, Inc., 83
EMCORE Corporation, 97
Emerson, II; 46 (upd.)
Emerson Radio Corp., 30
Eminence Speaker LLC, 111
EMS Technologies, Inc., 114
ENCAD, Incorporated, 25
Equant N.V., 52
Equus Computer Systems, Inc., 49
ESS Technology, Inc., 22
Essex Corporation, 85
Everex Systems, Inc., 16
Evergreen Solar, Inc., 101
Exabyte Corporation, 40 (upd.)
Exar Corp., 14
Exide Electronics Group, Inc., 20
Finisar Corporation, 92
First International Computer, Inc., 56
First Solar, Inc., 95
Fisk Corporation, 72
Flextronics International Ltd., 38; 116 (upd.)
Fluke Corporation, 15
FormFactor, Inc., 85
Foxboro Company, 13
Freescale Semiconductor, Inc., 83
Frequency Electronics, Inc., 61
FuelCell Energy, Inc., 75
Fuji Electric Co., Ltd., II; 48 (upd.)
Fuji Photo Film Co., Ltd., 79 (upd.)
Fujitsu Limited, III; 16 (upd.); 42 (upd.); 103 (upd.)
Funai Electric Company Ltd., 62
Galtronics Ltd., 100
Gateway, Inc., 63 (upd.)
Gemini Sound Products Corporation, 58
General Atomics, 57; 112 (upd.)
General Dynamics Corporation, I; 10 (upd.); 40 (upd.); 88 (upd.
General Electric Company, II; 12 (upd.)
General Electric Company, PLC, II
General Instrument Corporation, 10
General Signal Corporation, 9

Genesis Microchip Inc., 82
GenRad, Inc., 24
GM Hughes Electronics Corporation, II
Goldstar Co., Ltd., 12
Gould Electronics, Inc., 14
GPS Industries, Inc., 81
Grundig AG, 27
Guillemot Corporation, 41
Hadco Corporation, 24
Hamilton Beach/Proctor-Silex Inc., 17
Harman International Industries, Incorporated, 15; 101 (upd.)
Harmonic Inc., 109 (upd.)
Harris Corporation, II; 20 (upd.); 78 (upd.)
Hayes Corporation, 24
Hemisphere GPS Inc., 99
Herley Industries, Inc., 33
Hewlett-Packard Company, 28 (upd.); 50 (upd.); 111 (upd.)'
High Tech Computer Corporation, 81
Hitachi, Ltd., I; 12 (upd.); 40 (upd.); 108 (upd.)
Hittite Microwave Corporation, 106
Holophane Corporation, 19
Hon Hai Precision Industry Company, Ltd., 59; 117 (upd.)
HON INDUSTRIES Inc., 13
Honeywell International Inc., II; 12 (upd.); 50 (upd.); 109 (upd.)
Hubbell Inc., 9; 31 (upd.); 76 (upd.)
Hughes Supply, Inc., 14
Hutchinson Technology Incorporated, 18; 63 (upd.)
Hynix Semiconductor Company Ltd., 111
Hypercom Corporation, 27
IDEO Inc., 65
IEC Electronics Corp., 42
Illumina, Inc., 93
Imax Corporation, 28
In Focus Systems, Inc., 22
Indigo NV, 26
InFocus Corporation, 92
Ingram Micro Inc., 52
Innovative Solutions & Support, Inc., 85
Integrated Defense Technologies, Inc., 54
Intel Corporation, II; 10 (upd.); 75 (upd.)
Intermec Technologies Corporation, 72
International Business Machines Corporation, III; 6 (upd.); 30 (upd.); 63 (upd.)
International Electric Supply Corp., 113
International Rectifier Corporation, 31; 71 (upd.)
Intersil Corporation, 93
Ionatron, Inc., 85
Itel Corporation, 9
Jabil Circuit, Inc., 36; 88 (upd.)
Jaco Electronics, Inc., 30
JDS Uniphase Corporation, 34
Johnson Controls, Inc., III; 26 (upd.); 59 (upd.); 110 (upd.)
Juno Lighting, Inc., 30
Katy Industries, Inc., I; 51 (upd.)
Keithley Instruments Inc., 16
Kemet Corp., 14
Kent Electronics Corporation, 17
Kenwood Corporation, 31

Kesa Electricals plc, 91
Kimball International, Inc., 12; 48 (upd.)
Kingston Technology Company, Inc., 20; 112 (upd.)
KitchenAid, 8
KLA-Tencor Corporation, 45 (upd.)
KnowledgeWare Inc., 9
Kollmorgen Corporation, 18
Konami Corporation, 96
Konica Corporation, III; 30 (upd.)
Koninklijke Philips Electronics N.V., 50 (upd.); 119 (upd.)
Koor Industries Ltd., II
Kopin Corporation, 80
Koss Corporation, 38
Kudelski Group SA, 44
Kulicke and Soffa Industries, Inc., 33; 76 (upd.)
Kyocera Corporation, II; 21 (upd.); 79 (upd.)
L-3 Communications Holdings, Inc., 111 (upd.)
LaBarge Inc., 41
Lamson & Sessions Co., The, 13; 61 (upd.)
Lattice Semiconductor Corp., 16
LDK Solar Co., Ltd., 101
LeCroy Corporation, 41
Legrand SA, 21
Lenovo Group Ltd., 80
Leoni AG, 98
Lexmark International, Inc., 18; 79 (upd.)
Linear Technology Corporation, 16; 99 (upd.)
Littelfuse, Inc., 26
Loewe AG, 90
Loral Corporation, 9
LOUD Technologies, Inc., 95 (upd.)
Lowrance Electronics, Inc., 18
LSI Logic Corporation, 13; 64
Lucent Technologies Inc., 34
Lucky-Goldstar, II
Lunar Corporation, 29
Lynch Corporation, 43
Mackie Designs Inc., 33
MagneTek, Inc., 15; 41 (upd.)
Magneti Marelli Holding SpA, 90
Marconi plc, 33 (upd.)
Marquette Electronics, Inc., 13
Marshall Amplification plc, 62
Marvell Technology Group Ltd., 112
Matsushita Electric Industrial Co., Ltd., II; 64 (upd.)
Maxim Integrated Products, Inc., 16
McDATA Corporation, 75
Measurement Specialties, Inc., 71
Medis Technologies Ltd., 77
MEMC Electronic Materials, Inc., 81
Merix Corporation, 36; 75 (upd.)
Methode Electronics, Inc., 13
Micrel, Incorporated, 77
Midway Games, Inc., 25; 102 (upd.)
Mitel Corporation, 18
MITRE Corporation, 26
Mitsubishi Electric Corporation, II; 44 (upd.); 117 (upd.)
Molex Incorporated, 11; 54 (upd.)
Monster Cable Products, Inc., 69

Motorola, Inc., II; 11 (upd.); 34 (upd.); 93 (upd.)
N.F. Smith & Associates LP, 70
Nam Tai Electronics, Inc., 61
National Instruments Corporation, 22
National Presto Industries, Inc., 16; 43 (upd.)
National Semiconductor Corporation, II; 26 (upd.); 69 (upd.)
NEC Corporation, II; 21 (upd.); 57 (upd.)
Network Equipment Technologies Inc., 92
Nexans SA, 54
Nintendo Company, Ltd., III; 7 (upd.); 28 (upd.); 67 (upd.)
Nokia Corporation, II; 17 (upd.); 38 (upd.); 77 (upd.)
Nortel Networks Corporation, 36 (upd.)
Northrop Grumman Corporation, 45 (upd.); 111 (upd.)
Oak Technology, Inc., 22
Océ N.V., 24; 91 (upd.)
Oki Electric Industry Company, Limited, II
Omnicell, Inc., 89
OMRON Corporation, II; 28 (upd.); 115 (upd.)
Onvest Oy, 117
Oplink Communications, Inc., 106
OPTEK Technology Inc., 98
Orbit International Corp., 105
Orbotech Ltd., 75
Otari Inc., 89
Otter Tail Power Company, 18
Pacific Aerospace & Electronics, Inc., 120
Palm, Inc., 36; 75 (upd.)
Palomar Medical Technologies, Inc., 22
Parlex Corporation, 61
Peak Technologies Group, Inc., The, 14
Peavey Electronics Corporation, 16
Philips Electronics N.V., II; 13 (upd.)
Philips Electronics North America Corp., 13
Pioneer Electronic Corporation, III; 28 (upd.)
Pioneer-Standard Electronics Inc., 19
Pitney Bowes Inc., III; 19 (upd.); 47 (upd.)
Pittway Corporation, 9; 33 (upd.)
Pixelworks, Inc., 69
Planar Systems, Inc., 61
Plantronics, Inc., 106
Plessey Company, PLC, The, II
Plexus Corporation, 35; 80 (upd.)
Polaroid Corporation, III; 7 (upd.); 28 (upd.); 93 (upd.)
Polk Audio, Inc., 34
Potter & Brumfield Inc., 11
Premier Industrial Corporation, 9
Protection One, Inc., 32
QUALCOMM Incorporated, 114 (upd.)
Quanta Computer Inc., 47; 79 (upd.); 110 (upd.)
Racal Electronics PLC, II
RadioShack Corporation, 36 (upd.); 101 (upd.)
Radius Inc., 16
RAE Systems Inc., 83

Ramtron International Corporation, 89
Raychem Corporation, 8
Raymarine plc, 104
Rayovac Corporation, 13; 39 (upd.)
Raytheon Company, II; 11 (upd.); 38 (upd.); 105 (upd.)
RCA Corporation, II
Read-Rite Corp., 10
Redback Networks, Inc., 92
Reliance Electric Company, 9
Research in Motion Ltd., 54
Rexel, Inc., 15
Richardson Electronics, Ltd., 17
Ricoh Company, Ltd., III; 36 (upd.); 108 (upd.)
Rimage Corp., 89
Rival Company, The, 19
Rockford Corporation, 43
Rogers Corporation, 61; 80 (upd.)
S&C Electric Company, 15
SAGEM S.A., 37
St. Louis Music, Inc., 48
Sam Ash Music Corporation, 30
Samsung Electronics Co., Ltd., 14; 41 (upd.); 108 (upd.)
Sanmina-SCI Corporation, 109 (upd.)
SANYO Electric Co., Ltd., II; 36 (upd.); 95 (upd.)
Sarnoff Corporation, 57
ScanSource, Inc., 29; 74 (upd.)
Schneider Electric SA, II; 18 (upd.); 108 (upd.)
SCI Systems, Inc., 9
Scientific-Atlanta, Inc., 45 (upd.)
Scitex Corporation Ltd., 24
Seagate Technology, 8; 34 (upd.); 105 (upd.)
SEGA Corporation, 73
Semitool, Inc., 79 (upd.)
Semtech Corporation, 32
Sennheiser Electronic GmbH & Co. KG, 66
Sensormatic Electronics Corp., 11
Sensory Science Corporation, 37
SGI, 29 (upd.)
Sharp Corporation, II; 12 (upd.); 40 (upd.); 114 (upd.)
Sheldahl Inc., 23
Shure Inc., 60
Siemens AG, II; 14 (upd.); 57 (upd.)
Sierra Nevada Corporation, 108
Silicon Graphics Incorporated, 9
Siltronic AG, 90
SL Industries, Inc., 77
Sling Media, Inc., 112
SMA Solar Technology AG, 118
SMART Modular Technologies, Inc., 86
Smiths Industries PLC, 25
Solectron Corporation, 12; 48 (upd.)
Sony Corporation, II; 12 (upd.); 40 (upd.); 108 (upd.)
Spansion Inc., 80
Spectrum Control, Inc., 67
SPX Corporation, 10; 47 (upd.); 103 (upd.)
Square D, 90
Sterling Electronics Corp., 18
STMicroelectronics NV, 52

Engineering & Management Services

Food Products

Uniq plc, 83 (upd.)
United Biscuits (Holdings) plc, II; 42 (upd.)
United Brands Company, II
United Farm Workers of America, 88
United Foods, Inc., 21
United Plantations Bhd., 117
United States Sugar Corporation, 115
Universal Foods Corporation, 7
Utz Quality Foods, Inc., 72
Valio Oy, 117
Vall Companys S.A., 120
Van Camp Seafood Company, Inc., 7
Vandemoortele S.A./NV, 113
Vaughan Foods, Inc., 105
Ventura Foods LLC, 90
Vestey Group Ltd., 95
Vienna Sausage Manufacturing Co., 14
Vilmorin Clause et Cie, 70
Vion Food Group NV, 85
Vista Bakery, Inc., 56
Vita Food Products Inc., 99
Vlasic Foods International Inc., 25
Voortman Cookies Limited, 103
W Jordan (Cereals) Ltd., 74
Wagers Inc. (Idaho Candy Company), 86
Walkers Shortbread Ltd., 79
Walkers Snack Foods Ltd., 70
Warburtons Ltd., 89
Warrell Corporation, 68
Warrnambool Cheese and Butter Factory Company Holdings Limited, 118
Wattie's Ltd., 7
Weaver Popcorn Company, Inc., 89
Weetabix Limited, 61
Weis Markets, Inc., 84 (upd.)
Welch Foods Inc., 104
Wells' Dairy, Inc., 36
Wenner Bread Products Inc., 80
White Lily Foods Company, 88
White Wave, 43
Wilbur Chocolate Company, 66
William Jackson & Son Ltd., 101
Wimm-Bill-Dann Foods, 48
Wisconsin Dairies, 7
Wise Foods, Inc., 79
WLR Foods, Inc., 21
Wm. B. Reily & Company Inc., 58
Wm. Wrigley Jr. Company, 7; 58 (upd.)
World's Finest Chocolate Inc., 39
Worthington Foods, Inc., 14
Yamazaki Baking Co., Ltd., 58
Yarnell Ice Cream Company, Inc., 92
Yeo Hiap Seng Malaysia Bhd., 75
YOCREAM International, Inc., 47
Young's Bluecrest Seafood Holdings Ltd., 81
Zachary Confections, Inc., 108
Zacky Farms LLC, 74
Zaro Bake Shop Inc., 107
Zatarain's, Inc., 64
Zweigle's Inc., 111
5 & Diner Franchise Corporation, 72
7-Eleven, Inc., 32 (upd.); 112 (upd.)

Food Services, Retailers, & Restaurants

A. F. Blakemore & Son Ltd., 90

ABP Corporation, 108
Advantica Restaurant Group, Inc., 27 (upd.)
AFC Enterprises, Inc., 32 (upd.); 83 (upd.)
Affiliated Foods Inc., 53
Albertson's, Inc., II; 7 (upd.); 30 (upd.); 65 (upd.)
Aldi Einkauf GmbH & Co. OHG, 13; 86 (upd.)
Alex Lee Inc., 18; 44 (upd.)
Allen Foods, Inc., 60
Almacenes Exito S.A., 89
Alpha Airports Group PLC, 77
American Restaurant Partners, L.P., 93
American Stores Company, II; 22 (upd.)
America's Favorite Chicken Company, Inc., 7
Andronico's Market, 70
Applebee's International, Inc., 14; 35 (upd.)
ARA Services, II
Arby's Inc., 14
Arden Group, Inc., 29
Áreas S.A., 104
Arena Leisure Plc, 99
Argyll Group PLC, II
Ark Restaurants Corp., 20
Arthur Lundgren Tecidos S.A., 102
Aryzta AG, 112 (upd.)
ASDA Group Ltd., II; 28 (upd.); 64 (upd.)
Associated Grocers, Incorporated, 9; 31 (upd.)
Association des Centres Distributeurs E. Leclerc, 37
Atlanta Bread Company International, Inc., 70
Au Bon Pain Co., Inc., 18
Auchan Group, 37; 116 (upd.)
Auntie Anne's, Inc., 35; 102 (upd.)
Autogrill SpA, 49
Avado Brands, Inc., 31
B.R. Guest Inc., 87
Back Bay Restaurant Group, Inc., 20; 102 (upd.)
Back Yard Burgers, Inc., 45
Balducci's, 108
Bashas' Inc., 33; 80 (upd.)
Bear Creek Corporation, 38
Ben E. Keith Company, 76
Benihana, Inc., 18; 76 (upd.)
Bertucci's Corporation, 64 (upd.)
Bettys & Taylors of Harrogate Ltd., 72
Big Bear Stores Co., 13
Big Food Group plc, The, 68 (upd.)
Big V Supermarkets, Inc., 25
Big Y Foods, Inc., 53
Blimpie, 15; 49 (upd.); 105 (upd.)
Bob Evans Farms, Inc., 9; 63 (upd.)
Bob's Red Mill Natural Foods, Inc., 63
Boddie-Noell Enterprises, Inc., 68
Bojangles Restaurants Inc., 97
Bon Appetit Holding AG, 48
Boston Market Corporation, 12; 48 (upd.)
Boston Pizza International Inc., 88
Bozzuto's, Inc., 13

Brazil Fast Food Corporation, 74
Briazz, Inc., 53
Brinker International, Inc., 10; 38 (upd.); 75 (upd.)
Bristol Farms, 101
Brookshire Grocery Company, 16; 74 (upd.)
Bruegger's Corporation, 63
Bruno's Supermarkets, Inc., 7; 26 (upd.); 68 (upd.)
Bubba Gump Shrimp Co. Restaurants, Inc., 108
Buca, Inc., 38
Buckhead Life Restaurant Group, Inc., 100
Buddy Squirrel, LLC, 120
Budgens Ltd., 59
Buffalo Wild Wings, Inc., 56
Buffets Holdings, Inc., 10; 32 (upd.); 93 (upd.)
Burger King Corporation, II, 17 (upd.), 56 (upd.); 115 (upd.)
Busch Entertainment Corporation, 73
C&K Market, Inc., 81
C & S Wholesale Grocers, Inc., 55
C.H. Robinson, Inc., 11
Café Britt Coffee Corporation Holdings NV, 119
Caffè Nero Group PLC, 63
Cains Beer Company PLC, 99
California Pizza Kitchen Inc., 15; 74 (upd.)
Captain D's, LLC, 59
Cargill, Incorporated, II; 13 (upd.); 40 (upd.); 89 (upd.)
Caribou Coffee Company, Inc., 28; 97 (upd.)
Carlson Companies, Inc., 6; 22 (upd.); 87 (upd.)
Carlson Restaurants Worldwide, 69
Carr-Gottstein Foods Co., 17
Carrols Restaurant Group, Inc., 92
Casey's General Stores, Inc., 19; 83 (upd.)
Casino Guichard-Perrachon S.A., 59 (upd.)
CBRL Group, Inc., 35 (upd.); 86 (upd.)
CEC Entertainment, Inc., 31 (upd.)
Centerplate, Inc., 79
Chart House Enterprises, Inc., 17
Checkers Drive-In Restaurants, Inc., 16; 74 (upd.)
Cheesecake Factory Inc., The, 17; 100 (upd.)
Chicago Pizza & Brewery, Inc., 44
Chi-Chi's Inc., 13; 51 (upd.)
Chick-fil-A Inc., 23; 90 (upd.)
Chipotle Mexican Grill, Inc., 67
Church's Chicken, 66
CiCi Enterprises, L.P., 99
Cinnabon Inc., 23; 90 (upd.)
Circle K Corporation, The, II
CKE Restaurants, Inc., 19; 46 (upd.)
Coborn's, Inc., 30
Coffee Beanery, Ltd., The, 95
Coffee Holding Co., Inc., 95
Cold Stone Creamery, 69
Coles Group Limited, V; 20 (upd.); 85 (upd.)

Health Care Services

Health Care & Retirement Corporation, 22
Health Management Associates, Inc., 56
Health Net, Inc., 109 (upd.)
Health Risk Management, Inc., 24
Health Systems International, Inc., 11
HealthSouth Corporation, 14; 33 (upd.)
Henry Ford Health System, 84
Highmark Inc., 27
Hillhaven Corporation, The, 14
Holiday Retirement Corp., 87
Hologic, Inc., 106
Hooper Holmes, Inc., 22
Hospital Central Services, Inc., 56
Hospital Corporation of America, III
Hospital for Special Surgery, 115
Howard Hughes Medical Institute, 39
Humana Inc., III; 24 (upd.); 101 (upd.)
IASIS Healthcare Corporation, 112
Intermountain Health Care, Inc., 27
Jenny Craig, Inc., 10; 29 (upd.); 92 (upd.)
Kaiser Foundation Health Plan, Inc., 53; 119 (upd.)
Kinetic Concepts, Inc. (KCI), 20
LabOne, Inc., 48
Laboratory Corporation of America Holdings, 42 (upd.); 119 (upd.)
LCA-Vision, Inc., 85
Legacy Health System, 114
Life Care Centers of America Inc., 76
Lifeline Systems, Inc., 53
LifePoint Hospitals, Inc., 69
Lincare Holdings Inc., 43
Manor Care, Inc., 6; 25 (upd.)
Marshfield Clinic Inc., 82
Matria Healthcare, Inc., 17
Maxicare Health Plans, Inc., III; 25 (upd.)
Mayo Foundation for Medical Education and Research, 9; 34 (upd.); 115 (upd.)
McBride plc, 82
McKesson Corporation, 108 (upd.)
MDVIP, Inc., 118
Medical Management International, Inc., 65
Medical Staffing Network Holdings, Inc., 89
Memorial Sloan-Kettering Cancer Center, 57
Merge Healthcare, 85
Merit Medical Systems, Inc., 29
MeritCare Health System, 88
Molina Healthcare, Inc., 116
Mount Sinai Medical Center, 112
Myriad Genetics, Inc., 95
National Health Laboratories Incorporated, 11
National Jewish Health, 101
National Medical Enterprises, Inc., III
National Research Corporation, 87
Natus Medical Incorporated, 119
Navarro Discount Pharmacies, 119
New York City Health and Hospitals Corporation, 60
New York Health Care, Inc., 72
NewYork-Presbyterian Hospital, 59
NovaCare, Inc., 11
NSF International, 72

Omnicare, Inc., 111 (upd.)
Option Care Inc., 48
OrthoSynetics Inc., 35; 107 (upd.)
Oxford Health Plans, Inc., 16
PacifiCare Health Systems, Inc., 11
Palomar Medical Technologies, Inc., 22
Pediatric Services of America, Inc., 31
Pediatrix Medical Group, Inc., 61
PHP Healthcare Corporation, 22
PhyCor, Inc., 36
PolyMedica Corporation, 77
Primedex Health Systems, Inc., 25
Providence Health System, 90
Providence Service Corporation, The, 64
Psychemedics Corporation, 89
Psychiatric Solutions, Inc., 68
Quest Diagnostics Inc., 26; 106 (upd.)
Radiation Therapy Services, Inc., 85
Ramsay Youth Services, Inc., 41
RehabCare Group, Inc., 114
Renal Care Group, Inc., 72
Res-Care, Inc., 29
Response Oncology, Inc., 27
Rural/Metro Corporation, 28
Sabratek Corporation, 29
St. Jude Children's Research Hospital, Inc., 114
St. Jude Medical, Inc., 11; 43 (upd.); 97 (upd.)
Salick Health Care, Inc., 53
Scripps Research Institute, The, 76
Select Medical Corporation, 65
Shriners Hospitals for Children, 69
Sierra Health Services, Inc., 15
Sisters of Charity of Leavenworth Health System, 105
Smith & Nephew plc, 41 (upd.)
Sports Club Company, The, 25
SSL International plc, 49
Stericycle Inc., 33
Sun Healthcare Group Inc., 25
Sunrise Senior Living, Inc., 81
SwedishAmerican Health System, 51
Tenet Healthcare Corporation, 55 (upd.); 112 (upd.)
The Cleveland Clinic Foundation, 112
Twinlab Corporation, 34
U.S. Healthcare, Inc., 6
U.S. Physical Therapy, Inc., 65
Unison HealthCare Corporation, 25
United HealthCare Corporation, 9
United Surgical Partners International Inc., 120
UnitedHealth Group Incorporated, 9; 103 (upd.)
Universal Health Services, Inc., 6
Vanderbilt University Medical Center, 99
Vanguard Health Systems Inc., 70
VCA Antech, Inc., 58
Vencor, Inc., 16
VISX, Incorporated, 30
Vivra, Inc., 18
WellPoint, Inc., 25; 103 (upd.)

Health, Personal & Medical Care Products

A-dec, Inc., 53
Abaxis, Inc., 83

Abbott Laboratories, I; 11 (upd.); 40 (upd.); 93 (upd.)
Abiomed, Inc., 47
Accuray Incorporated, 95
Acuson Corporation, 10; 36 (upd.)
Advanced Medical Optics, Inc., 79
Advanced Neuromodulation Systems, Inc., 73
Akorn, Inc., 32
ALARIS Medical Systems, Inc., 65
Alberto-Culver Company, 8; 36 (upd.); 91 (upd.)
Alco Health Services Corporation, III
Alès Groupe, 81
Allergan, Inc., 10; 30 (upd.); 77 (upd.)
American Medical Alert Corporation, 103
American Oriental Bioengineering Inc., 93
American Safety Razor Company, 20
American Stores Company, II; 22 (upd.)
Amway Corporation, III; 13 (upd.)
Andis Company, Inc., 85
AngioDynamics, Inc., 81
Ansell Ltd., 60 (upd.)
ArthroCare Corporation, 73
Artsana SpA, 92
Ascendia Brands, Inc., 97
Atkins Nutritionals, Inc., 58
Aveda Corporation, 24
Avon Products, Inc., III; 19 (upd.); 46 (upd.); 109 (upd.)
Ballard Medical Products, 21
Bally Total Fitness Holding Corp., 25
Bare Escentuals, Inc., 91
Bausch & Lomb Inc., 7; 25 (upd.); 96 (upd.)
Baxter International Inc., I; 10 (upd.); 116 (upd.)
BeautiControl Cosmetics, Inc., 21
Becton, Dickinson and Company, I; 11 (upd.); 36 (upd.); 101 (upd.)
Beiersdorf AG, 29
Big B, Inc., 17
Bindley Western Industries, Inc., 9
Biolase Technology, Inc., 87
Biomet, Inc., 10; 93 (upd.)
BioScrip Inc., 98
Biosite Incorporated, 73
Block Drug Company, Inc., 8; 27 (upd.)
Body Shop International plc, The, 11; 53 (upd.)
Boiron S.A., 73
Bolton Group B.V., 86
Borghese Inc., 107
Bristol-Myers Squibb Company, III; 9 (upd.)
Bronner Brothers Inc., 92
Burt's Bees, Inc., 58
C.O. Bigelow Chemists, Inc., 114
C.R. Bard Inc., 9; 65 (upd.)
Candela Corporation, 48
Cantel Medical Corporation, 80
Cardinal Health, Inc., 18; 50 (upd.); 115 (upd.)
Carl Zeiss AG, III; 34 (upd.); 91 (upd.)
Carma Laboratories, Inc., 60
Carson, Inc., 31
Carter-Wallace, Inc., 8
Caswell-Massey Co. Ltd., 51

Reckitt Benckiser plc, II; 42 (upd.); 91 (upd.)

Redken Laboratories Inc., 84

Reliv International, Inc., 58

Remington Products Company, L.L.C., 42

Retractable Technologies, Inc., 99

Revlon Inc., III; 17 (upd.); 64 (upd.)

Roche Biomedical Laboratories, Inc., 11

Rockwell Medical Technologies, Inc., 88

S.C. Johnson & Son, Inc., III; 28 (upd.); 89 (upd.)

Safety 1st, Inc., 24

Sage Products Inc., 105

St. Jude Medical, Inc., 11; 43 (upd.); 97 (upd.)

Schering-Plough Corporation, I; 14 (upd.); 49 (upd.); 99 (upd.)

Sephora Holdings S.A., 82

Shaklee Corporation, 39 (upd.)

Shionogi & Co., Ltd., III; 17 (upd.); 98 (upd.)

Shiseido Company, Limited, III; 22 (upd.); 81 (upd.)

Slim-Fast Foods Company, 18; 66 (upd.)

Smith & Nephew plc, 17

SmithKline Beecham PLC, III

Soft Sheen Products, Inc., 31

Sola International Inc., 71

Sonic Innovations Inc., 56

SonoSite, Inc., 56

Spacelabs Medical, Inc., 71

STAAR Surgical Company, 57

Stephan Company, The, 60

Straumann Holding AG, 79

Stryker Corporation, 11; 29 (upd.); 79 (upd.)

Sunrise Medical Inc., 11

Sybron International Corp., 14

Syneron Medical Ltd., 91

Synthes, Inc., 93

Tambrands Inc., 8

Terumo Corporation, 48

Thane International, Inc., 84

Thermo Fisher Scientific Inc., 105 (upd.)

Tom's of Maine, Inc., 45

Transitions Optical, Inc., 83

Tranzonic Companies, The, 37

Turtle Wax, Inc., 15; 93 (upd.)

Tutogen Medical, Inc., 68

Unicharm Corporation, 84

United States Surgical Corporation, 10; 34 (upd.)

USANA, Inc., 29

Utah Medical Products, Inc., 36

Ventana Medical Systems, Inc., 75

VHA Inc., 53

VIASYS Healthcare, Inc., 52

Vion Food Group NV, 85

VISX, Incorporated, 30

Vitacost.com Inc., 116

Vitamin Shoppe Industries, Inc., 60

VNUS Medical Technologies, Inc., 103

Wahl Clipper Corporation, 86

Water Pik Technologies, Inc., 34; 83 (upd.)

Weider Nutrition International, Inc., 29

Weleda AG, 78

Wella AG, III; 48 (upd.)

West Pharmaceutical Services, Inc., 42

Wright Medical Group, Inc., 61

Wyeth, Inc., 50 (upd.); 118 (upd.)

Zila, Inc., 46

Zimmer Holdings, Inc., 45; 120 (upd.)

Hotels

Accor S.A., 69 (upd.)

Amerihost Properties, Inc., 30

Ameristar Casinos, Inc., 69 (upd.)

Archon Corporation, 74 (upd.)

Arena Leisure Plc, 99

Aztar Corporation, 13; 71 (upd.)

Bass PLC, 38 (upd.)

The Biltmore Company, 118

Boca Resorts, Inc., 37

Boyd Gaming Corporation, 43

Boyne USA Resorts, 71

Bristol Hotel Company, 23

Broadmoor Hotel, The, 30

Caesars World, Inc., 6

Candlewood Hotel Company, Inc., 41

Carlson Companies, Inc., 6; 22 (upd.); 87 (upd.)

Castle & Cooke, Inc., 20 (upd.)

Cedar Fair Entertainment Company, 22; 98 (upd.)

Cendant Corporation, 44 (upd.)

Choice Hotels International, Inc., 14; 83 (upd.)

Circus Circus Enterprises, Inc., 6

City Developments Limited, 89

City Lodge Hotels Limited, 114

Club Méditerranée S.A., 6; 21 (upd.); 91 (upd.)

Compagnia Italiana dei Jolly Hotels S.p.A., 71

Daniel Thwaites Plc, 95

Doubletree Corporation, 21

EIH Ltd., 103

Extended Stay America, Inc., 41

Fairmont Hotels & Resorts Inc., 69

Fibreboard Corporation, 16

Four Seasons Hotels Limited, 9; 29 (upd.); 106 (upd.)

Fuller Smith & Turner P.L.C., 38

Gables Residential Trust, 49

Gaylord Entertainment Company, 11; 36 (upd.)

Gianni Versace S.p.A., 22; 106 (upd.)

Global Hyatt Corporation, 75 (upd.)

Granada Group PLC, 24 (upd.)

Grand Casinos, Inc., 20

Grand Hotel Krasnapolsky N.V., 23

Great Wolf Resorts, Inc., 91

Grupo Posadas, S.A. de C.V., 57

Helmsley Enterprises, Inc., 9

Hilton Hotels Corporation, III; 19 (upd.); 49 (upd.); 62 (upd.)

Holiday Inns, Inc., III

Home Inns & Hotels Management Inc., 95

Hospitality Franchise Systems, Inc., 11

Host Hotels & Resorts, Inc., 112

Hotel Properties Ltd., 71

Hotel Shilla Company Ltd., 110

Howard Johnson International, Inc., 17; 72 (upd.)

Hyatt Corporation, III; 16 (upd.)

ILX Resorts Incorporated, 65

InterContinental Hotels Group, PLC, 109 (upd.)

Interstate Hotels & Resorts Inc., 58

ITT Sheraton Corporation, III

JD Wetherspoon plc, 30

John Q. Hammons Hotels, Inc., 24

Jumeirah Group, 83

Kerzner International Limited, 69 (upd.)

Kimpton Hotel & Restaurant Group, Inc., 105

La Quinta Companies, The, 11; 42 (upd.)

Ladbroke Group PLC, 21 (upd.)

Landry's Restaurants, Inc., 65 (upd.)

Las Vegas Sands Corp., 50; 106 (upd.)

Madden's on Gull Lake, 52

Mammoth Mountain Ski Area, 101

Mandalay Resort Group, 32 (upd.)

Manor Care, Inc., 25 (upd.)

Marcus Corporation, The, 21

Marriott International, Inc., III; 21 (upd.); 83 (upd.)

McMenamins Pubs and Breweries, 65

Melco Crown Entertainment Limited, 103

MGM MIRAGE, 98 (upd.)

Millennium & Copthorne Hotels plc, 71

Mirage Resorts, Incorporated, 6; 28 (upd.)

Monarch Casino & Resort, Inc., 65

Morgans Hotel Group Company, 80

Motel 6, 13; 56 (upd.)

Mövenpick Holding, 104

MTR Gaming Group, Inc., 75

MWH Preservation Limited Partnership, 65

NETGEAR, Inc., 81

NH Hoteles S.A., 79

Olympic Entertainment Group A.S., 117

Omni Hotels Corp., 12

Paradores de Turismo de España S.A., 73

Park Corp., 22

Players International, Inc., 22

Preferred Hotel Group, 103

Preussag AG, 42 (upd.)

Prime Hospitality Corporation, 52

Promus Companies, Inc., 9

Real Turismo, S.A. de C.V., 50

Red Roof Inns, Inc., 18

Regent Inns plc, 95

Resorts International, Inc., 12

Rezidor Hotel Group AB, 118

Ritz-Carlton Hotel Company, L.L.C., The, 9; 29 (upd.); 71 (upd.)

Riviera Holdings Corporation, 75

Rotana Hotel Management Corporation LTD., 114

Sandals Resorts International, 65

Santa Fe Gaming Corporation, 19

SAS Group, The, 34 (upd.)

SFI Group plc, 51

Shangri-La Asia Ltd., 71

Showboat, Inc., 19

Sinclair Oil Corporation, 111

Sol Meliá S.A., 71

Sonesta International Hotels Corporation, 44

Southern Sun Hotel Interest (Pty) Ltd., 106

Information Technology

Insurance

Legal Services

Materials

Mining & Metals

Personal Services

UAW (International Union, United Automobile, Aerospace and Agricultural Implement Workers of America), 72
Weight Watchers International Inc., 12; 33 (upd.); 73 (upd.)
Yak Pak, 108
York Group, Inc., The, 50
YTB International, Inc., 108

Petroleum

Abraxas Petroleum Corporation, 89
Abu Dhabi National Oil Company, IV; 45 (upd.); 114 (upd.)
Adani Enterprises Ltd., 97
Aegean Marine Petroleum Network Inc., 89
Agland, Inc., 110
Agway, Inc., 21 (upd.)
Alberta Energy Company Ltd., 16; 43 (upd.)
Alon Israel Oil Company Ltd., 104
Amerada Hess Corporation, IV; 21 (upd.); 55 (upd.)
Amoco Corporation, IV; 14 (upd.)
Anadarko Petroleum Corporation, 10; 52 (upd.); 106 (upd.)
ANR Pipeline Co., 17
Anschutz Corp., 12
Apache Corporation, 10; 32 (upd.); 89 (upd.)
Aral AG, 62
Arctic Slope Regional Corporation, 38
Arena Resources, Inc., 97
Ashland Inc., 19; 50 (upd.); 115 (upd.)
Ashland Oil, Inc., IV
Atlantic Richfield Company, IV; 31 (upd.)
Atwood Oceanics, Inc., 100
Aventine Renewable Energy Holdings, Inc., 89
Badger State Ethanol, LLC, 83
Baker Hughes Incorporated, 22 (upd.); 57 (upd.); 118 (upd.)
Basic Earth Science Systems, Inc., 101
Belco Oil & Gas Corp., 40
Benton Oil and Gas Company, 47
Berry Petroleum Company, 47
BG Products Inc., 96
Bharat Petroleum Corporation Limited, 109
BHP Billiton, 67 (upd.)
Bill Barrett Corporation, 71
BJ Services Company, 25
Blue Rhino Corporation, 56
Blue Sun Energy, Inc., 108
Boardwalk Pipeline Partners, LP, 87
Bolt Technology Corporation, 99
Boots & Coots International Well Control, Inc., 79
BP p.l.c., 45 (upd.); 103 (upd.)
Brigham Exploration Company, 75
British Petroleum Company plc, The, IV; 7 (upd.); 21 (upd.)
British-Borneo Oil & Gas PLC, 34
Broken Hill Proprietary Company Ltd., 22 (upd.)
Bronco Drilling Company, Inc., 89
Burlington Resources Inc., 10
Burmah Castrol PLC, IV; 30 (upd.)

Callon Petroleum Company, 47
Caltex Petroleum Corporation, 19
Calumet Specialty Products Partners, L.P., 106
CAMAC International Corporation, 106
Cano Petroleum Inc., 97
Carrizo Oil & Gas, Inc., 97
Chevron Corporation, IV; 19 (upd.); 47 (upd.); 103 (upd.)
Chiles Offshore Corporation, 9
The China National Offshore Oil Corp., 118
China National Petroleum Corporation, 46; 108 (upd.)
China Petroleum & Chemical Corporation (Sinopec Corp.), 109
Chinese Petroleum Corporation, IV; 31 (upd.)
Cimarex Energy Co., 81
CITGO Petroleum Corporation, IV; 31 (upd.)
Clayton Williams Energy, Inc., 87
Coastal Corporation, The, IV; 31 (upd.)
Compañia Española de Petróleos S.A. (Cepsa), IV; 56 (upd.)
Complete Production Services, Inc., 118
Compton Petroleum Corporation, 103
Comstock Resources, Inc., 47
Conoco Inc., IV; 16 (upd.)
ConocoPhillips, 63 (upd.)
CONSOL Energy Inc., 59
Continental Resources, Inc., 89
Cooper Cameron Corporation, 20 (upd.); 58 (upd.)
Cosmo Oil Co., Ltd., IV; 53 (upd.)
CPC Corporation, Taiwan, 116
Crimson Exploration Inc., 116
Crown Central Petroleum Corporation, 7
Daniel Measurement and Control, Inc., 16; 74 (upd.)
Dead River Company, 117
DeepTech International Inc., 21
Den Norske Stats Oljeselskap AS, IV
Denbury Resources, Inc., 67
Deutsche BP Aktiengesellschaft, 7
Devon Energy Corporation, 61
Diamond Shamrock, Inc., IV
Distrigaz S.A., 82
DOF ASA, 110
Double Eagle Petroleum Co., 114
Dril-Quip, Inc., 81
Duvernay Oil Corp., 83
Dyneff S.A., 98
Dynegy Inc., 49 (upd.)
E.On AG, 50 (upd.)
Edge Petroleum Corporation, 67
Egyptian General Petroleum Corporation, IV; 51 (upd.)
El Paso Corporation, 66 (upd.)
Elf Aquitaine SA, 21 (upd.)
Empresa Colombiana de Petróleos, IV
Enbridge Inc., 43
EnCana Corporation, 109
Encore Acquisition Company, 73
Energen Corporation, 21; 97 (upd.)
ENI S.p.A., 69 (upd.)
Enron Corporation, 19
ENSCO International Incorporated, 57

Ente Nazionale Idrocarburi, IV
Enterprise GP Holdings L.P., 109
Enterprise Oil PLC, 11; 50 (upd.)
Entreprise Nationale Sonatrach, IV
EOG Resources, 106
Equitable Resources, Inc., 54 (upd.)
Ergon, Inc., 95
Etablissements Maurel & Prom S.A., 115
Exxon Mobil Corporation, IV; 7 (upd.); 32 (upd.); 67 (upd.)
F.L. Roberts & Company, Inc., 113
Ferrellgas Partners, L.P., 35; 107 (upd.)
FINA, Inc., 7
Flotek Industries Inc., 93
Fluxys SA, 101
Flying J Inc., 19
Forest Oil Corporation, 19; 91 (upd.)
Frontier Oil Corporation, 116
Galp Energia SGPS S.A., 98
GDF SUEZ, 109 (upd.)
General Sekiyu K.K., IV
GeoResources, Inc., 101
Giant Industries, Inc., 19; 61 (upd.)
Global Industries, Ltd., 37
Global Marine Inc., 9
Global Partners L.P., 116
GlobalSantaFe Corporation, 48 (upd.)
Grant Prideco, Inc., 57
Grey Wolf, Inc., 43
Gulf Island Fabrication, Inc., 44
Gulfport Energy Corporation, 119
Halliburton Company, III; 25 (upd.); 55 (upd.)
Hanover Compressor Company, 59
Hawkeye Holdings LLC, 89
Helix Energy Solutions Group, Inc., 81
Hellenic Petroleum SA, 64
Helmerich & Payne, Inc., 18; 115 (upd.)
Hindustan Petroleum Corporation Ltd., 116
Holly Corporation, 12; 111 (upd.)
Hunt Consolidated, Inc., 7; 27 (upd.)
Hunting plc, 78
Hurricane Hydrocarbons Ltd., 54
Husky Energy Inc., 47; 118 (upd.)
Idemitsu Kosan Co., Ltd., 49 (upd.)
Idemitsu Kosan K.K., IV
Imperial Oil Limited, IV; 25 (upd.)
Indian Oil Corporation Ltd., IV; 48 (upd.); 95 (upd.); 113 (upd.)
INPEX Holdings Inc., 97
Input/Output, Inc., 73
Iogen Corporation, 81
Ipiranga S.A., 67
Irving Oil Limited, 118
Kanematsu Corporation, IV; 24 (upd.); 102 (upd.)
KBR Inc., 106 (upd.)
Kerr-McGee Corporation, IV; 22 (upd.); 68 (upd.)
Kinder Morgan, Inc., 45; 111 (upd.)
King Ranch, Inc., 14
Knot, Inc., The, 74
Koch Industries, Inc., IV; 20 (upd.), 77 (upd.)
Koppers Industries, Inc., 26 (upd.)
Korea Gas Corporation, 114

Softbank Corp., 13
Source Enterprises, Inc., The, 65
Southam Inc., 7
Southern Progress Corporation, 102
SPIEGEL-Verlag Rudolf Augstein GmbH
  & Co. KG, 44
Spir Communication S.A., 120
Standard Register Company, The, 15; 93
  (upd.)
Stephens Media, LLC, 91
Strine Printing Company Inc., 88
Sunrise Greetings, 88
Tamedia AG, 53
Taschen GmbH, 101
Taylor & Francis Group plc, 44
Taylor Corporation, 36
Taylor Publishing Company, 12; 36 (upd.)
TechBooks Inc., 84
TechTarget, Inc., 99
Telegraaf Media Groep N.V., 98 (upd.)
Thomas Crosbie Holdings Limited, 81
Thomas Nelson, Inc., 14; 38 (upd.)
Thomas Publishing Company, 26
Thomson Corporation, The, 8; 34 (upd.);
  77 (upd.)
Time Out Group Ltd., 68
Time Warner Inc., IV; 7 (upd.); 109
  (upd.)
Times Mirror Company, The, IV; 17
  (upd.)
Tohan Corporation, 84
TOKYOPOP Inc., 79
Tom Doherty Associates Inc., 25
Toppan Printing Co., Ltd., IV; 58 (upd.)
Topps Company, Inc., The, 13; 34 (upd.);
  83 (upd.)
Torstar Corporation, 29
Trader Classified Media N.V., 57
Tribune Company, IV, 22 (upd.); 63
  (upd.)
Trinity Mirror plc, 49 (upd.)
Tuttle Publishing, 86
Tyndale House Publishers, Inc., 57
U.S. News & World Report Inc., 30; 89
  (upd.)
United Business Media Limited, 52
  (upd.); 114 (upd.)
United News & Media plc, IV; 28 (upd.)
United Press International, Inc., 25; 73
  (upd.)
University of Chicago Press, The, 79
Valassis Communications, Inc., 8
Value Line, Inc., 16; 73 (upd.)
Vance Publishing Corporation, 64
Verlagsgruppe Georg von Holtzbrinck
  GmbH, 35
Verlagsgruppe Weltbild GmbH, 98
Village Voice Media, Inc., 38
VistaPrint Limited, 87
VNU N.V., 27
Volt Information Sciences Inc., 26
W.W. Norton & Company, Inc., 28
Wallace Computer Services, Inc., 36
Walsworth Publishing Co., 78
Washington Post Company, The, IV; 20
  (upd.); 109 (upd.)
Waverly, Inc., 16
WAZ Media Group, 82

Wegener NV, 53
Wenner Media, Inc., 32
West Group, 7; 34 (upd.)
Western Publishing Group, Inc., 13
WH Smith PLC, V; 42 (upd.)
William Reed Publishing Ltd., 78
Wizards of the Coast LLC, 112 (upd.)
Wolters Kluwer NV, 14; 33 (upd.)
Workman Publishing Company, Inc., 70
World Book, Inc., 12
World Color Press Inc., 12
World Publications, LLC, 65
Xeikon NV, 26
Yell Group PLC, 79
Zebra Technologies Corporation, 14; (53
  (upd.)
Ziff Davis Media Inc., 12; 36 (upd.); 73
  (upd.)
Zondervan Corporation, 24; 71 (upd.)

Real Estate

Acadia Realty Trust, 106
Akerys S.A., 90
Alexander's, Inc., 45
Alexandria Real Estate Equities, Inc., 101
Alico, Inc., 63
AMB Property Corporation, 57
American Campus Communities, Inc., 85
Amfac/JMB Hawaii L.L.C., 24 (upd.)
Apartment Investment and Management
  Company, 49
Archstone-Smith Trust, 49
Associated Estates Realty Corporation, 25
AvalonBay Communities, Inc., 58
Baird & Warner Holding Company, 87
Berkshire Realty Holdings, L.P., 49
Bluegreen Corporation, 80
Boston Properties, Inc., 22
Bouygues S.A., I; 24 (upd.); 97 (upd.)
Bramalea Ltd., 9
British Land Plc, 54
Brookfield Properties Corporation, 89
Burroughs & Chapin Company, Inc., 86
Camden Property Trust, 77
Canary Wharf Group Plc, 30
CapStar Hotel Company, 21
CarrAmerica Realty Corporation, 56
Castle & Cooke, Inc., 20 (upd.)
Catellus Development Corporation, 24
CB Commercial Real Estate Services
  Group, Inc., 21
CB Richard Ellis Group, Inc., 70 (upd.)
Central Florida Investments, Inc., 93
Chateau Communities, Inc., 37
Chelsfield PLC, 67
Cheung Kong (Holdings) Limited, IV; 20
  (upd.)
CITIC Pacific Ltd., 116 (upd.)
City Developments Limited, 89
Clayton Homes Incorporated, 13; 54
  (upd.)
Cohen & Steers, Inc., 119
Coldwell Banker Real Estate LLC, 109
Colliers International Property
  Consultants Inc., 92
Colonial Properties Trust, 65
Corcoran Group, Inc., The, 58
Corky McMillin Companies, The, 98

CoStar Group, Inc., 73
Cousins Properties Incorporated, 65
CSX Corporation 79 (upd.)
Cushman & Wakefield, Inc., 86
Cyrela Brazil Realty S.A.
  Empreendimentos e Participações, 110
Del Webb Corporation, 14
Desarrolladora Homex, S.A. de C.V., 87
Developers Diversified Realty
  Corporation, 69
Douglas Emmett, Inc., 105
Draper and Kramer Inc., 96
Ducks Unlimited, Inc., 87
Duke Realty Corporation, 57
Durst Organization Inc., The, 108
EastGroup Properties, Inc., 67
Edward J. DeBartolo Corporation, The, 8
Enterprise Inns plc, 59
Equity Office Properties Trust, 54
Equity Residential, 49
Erickson Retirement Communities, 57
Fairfield Communities, Inc., 36
First Industrial Realty Trust, Inc., 65
Forest City Enterprises, Inc., 16; 52
  (upd.); 112 (upd.)
Gale International Llc, 93
Gecina SA, 42
General Growth Properties, Inc., 57
GMH Communities Trust, 87
Great White Shark Enterprises, Inc., 89
Griffin Land & Nurseries, Inc., 43
Grubb & Ellis Company, 21; 98 (upd.)
Guangzhou R&F Properties Co., Ltd., 95
Habitat Company LLC, The, 106
Haminerson Property Investment and
  Development Corporation plc, The, IV
Hammerson plc, 40
Hang Lung Group Ltd., 104
Harbert Corporation, 14
Helmsley Enterprises, Inc., 39 (upd.)
Henderson Land Development Company
  Ltd., 70
Holiday Retirement Corp., 87
Home Properties of New York, Inc., 42
HomeAway, Inc., 116
HomeVestors of America, Inc., 77
Hongkong Land Holdings Limited, IV;
  47 (upd.)
Hopson Development Holdings Ltd., 87
Hovnanian Enterprises, Inc., 29; 89 (upd.)
Hyatt Corporation, 16 (upd.)
Icahn Enterprises L.P., 110
ILX Resorts Incorporated, 65
IRSA Inversiones y Representaciones S.A.,
  63
J.F. Shea Co., Inc., 55
Jardine Cycle & Carriage Ltd., 73
JMB Realty Corporation, IV
Jones Lang LaSalle Incorporated, 49
JPI, 49
Kaufman and Broad Home Corporation,
  8
Kennedy-Wilson, Inc., 60
Kerry Properties Limited, 22
Kimco Realty Corporation, 11
Koll Company, The, 8
Land Securities PLC, IV; 49 (upd.)
Lefrak Organization Inc., 26

Retail & Wholesale

Textiles & Apparel

Tobacco

Transport Services

Utilities

Black Hills Corporation, 20
Bonneville Power Administration, 50
Boston Edison Company, 12
Bouygues S.A., I; 24 (upd.); 97 (upd.)
British Energy Plc, 49
British Gas plc, V
British Nuclear Fuels plc, 6
Brooklyn Union Gas, 6
BW Group Ltd., 107
California Water Service Group, 79
Calpine Corporation, 36
Canadian Utilities Limited, 13; 56 (upd.)
Cap Rock Energy Corporation, 46
Carolina Power & Light Company, V; 23
    (upd.)
Cascade Natural Gas Corporation, 9
Cascal N.V., 103
Centerior Energy Corporation, V
CenterPoint Energy, Inc., 116
Central and South West Corporation, V
Central Hudson Gas and Electricity
    Corporation, 6
Central Maine Power, 6
Central Vermont Public Service
    Corporation, 54
Centrica plc, 29 (upd.); 107 (upd.)
ČEZ a. s., 97
Chesapeake Utilities Corporation, 56
China Shenhua Energy Company
    Limited, 83
China Southern Power Grid Company
    Ltd., 116
Chubu Electric Power Company, Inc., V;
    46 (upd.); 118 (upd.)
Chugoku Electric Power Company Inc.,
    V; 53 (upd.)
Cincinnati Gas & Electric Company, 6
CIPSCO Inc., 6
Citizens Utilities Company, 7
City Public Service, 6
Cleco Corporation, 37
CMS Energy Corporation, V; 14 (upd.);
    100 (upd.)
Coastal Corporation, The, 31 (upd.)
Cogentrix Energy, Inc., 10
Columbia Gas System, Inc., The, V; 16
    (upd.)
Comisión Federal de Electricidad, 108
Commonwealth Edison Company, V
Commonwealth Energy System, 14
Companhia Energética de Minas Gerais
    S.A. CEMIG, 65
Compañia de Minas Buenaventura S.A.A.,
    93
Connecticut Light and Power Co., 13
Consolidated Edison, Inc., V; 45 (upd.);
    112 (upd.)
Consolidated Natural Gas Company, V;
    19 (upd.)
Constellation Energy Group, Inc., 116
    (upd.)
Consumers' Gas Company Ltd., 6
Consumers Power Co., 14
Consumers Water Company, 14
Copperbelt Energy Corporation PLC, 116
Covanta Energy Corporation, 64 (upd.)
Crosstex Energy Inc., 107
Dalkia Holding, 66

Delmarva Power & Light Company, 118
Destec Energy, Inc., 12
Detroit Edison Company, The, V
Dominion Resources, Inc., V; 54 (upd.)
DPL Inc., 6; 96 (upd.)
DQE, Inc., 6
Drax Group PLC, 119
DTE Energy Company, 20 (upd.)
Duke Energy Corporation, V; 27 (upd.);
    110 (upd.)
E.On AG, 50 (upd.)
Eastern Enterprises, 6
Edison International, 56 (upd.)
EDP - Energias de Portugal, S.A., 111
    (upd.)
El Paso Electric Company, 21
El Paso Natural Gas Company, 12
Electrabel N.V., 67
Electricidade de Portugal, S.A., 47
Electricité de France S.A., V; 41 (upd.);
    114 (upd.)
Electricity Generating Authority of
    Thailand (EGAT), 56
Elektrowatt AG, 6
Empire District Electric Company, The,
    77
Empresas Públicas de Medellín S.A.E.S.P.,
    91
Enbridge Inc., 43
EnBW Energie Baden-Württemberg AG,
    109
ENDESA S.A., V; 46 (upd.)
Enel S.p.A., 108 (upd.)
Enersis S.A., 73
ENMAX Corporation, 83
Enron Corporation, V; 46 (upd.)
Enserch Corporation, V
Ente Nazionale per L'Energia Elettrica, V
Entergy Corp., V; 45 (upd.); 117 (upd.)
Environmental Power Corporation, 68
EPCOR Utilities Inc., 81
Equitable Resources, Inc., 6; 54 (upd.)
EVN AG, 115
Exelon Corporation, 48 (upd.)
FirstEnergy Corp., 112 (upd.)
Florida Progress Corporation, V; 23 (upd.)
Florida Public Utilities Company, 69
Fortis, Inc., 15; 47 (upd.)
Fortum Corporation, 30 (upd.)
FPL Group, Inc., V; 49 (upd.)
Gas Natural SDG S.A., 69
Gaz de France, V; 40 (upd.)
GDF SUEZ, 109 (upd.)
General Public Utilities Corporation, V
Générale des Eaux Group, V
Golden Valley Electric Association, 110
GPU, Inc., 27 (upd.)
Great Plains Energy Incorporated, 65
    (upd.)
Gulf States Utilities Company, 6
Hawaiian Electric Industries, Inc., 9; 120
    (upd.)
Hokkaido Electric Power Company Inc.
    (HEPCO), V; 58 (upd.)
Hokuriku Electric Power Company, V
Hong Kong and China Gas Company
    Ltd., 73

Hongkong Electric Holdings Ltd., 6; 23
    (upd.); 107 (upd.)
Houston Industries Incorporated, V
Hyder plc, 34
Hydro-Québec, 6; 32 (upd.)
Iberdrola, S.A., 49
Idaho Power Company, 12
Illinois Bell Telephone Company, 14
Illinois Power Company, 6
Indiana Energy, Inc., 27
Integrys Energy Group, Inc., 109
International Power PLC, 50 (upd.)
IPALCO Enterprises, Inc., 6
ITC Holdings Corp., 75
Kansai Electric Power Company, Inc.,
    The, V; 62 (upd.)
Kansas City Power & Light Company, 6
Kelda Group plc, 45
Kenetech Corporation, 11
Kentucky Utilities Company, 6
KeySpan Energy Co., 27
Korea Electric Power Corporation, 56;
    117 (upd.)
KU Energy Corporation, 11
Kyushu Electric Power Company Inc., V;
    107 (upd.)
LG&E Energy Corporation, 6; 51 (upd.)
Long Island Power Authority, V; 102
    (upd.)
Lyonnaise des Eaux Dumez, V
Madison Gas and Electric Company, 39
Magma Power Company, 11
Maine & Maritimes Corporation, 56
Manila Electric Company (Meralco), 56
MCN Corporation, 6
MDU Resources Group, Inc., 7; 42 (upd.)
Middlesex Water Company, 45
Midwest Resources Inc., 6
Minnesota Power, Inc., 11, 34 (upd.)
Mirant Corporation, 98
Mississippi Power Company, 110
Montana Power Company, The, 11; 44
    (upd.)
National Fuel Gas Company, 6; 95 (upd.)
National Grid USA, 51 (upd.)
National Power PLC, 12
Nebraska Public Power District, 29
Nevada Power Company, 11
New England Electric System, V
New Jersey Resources Corporation, 54
New York State Electric and Gas, 6
Neyveli Lignite Corporation Ltd., 65
Niagara Mohawk Holdings Inc., V; 45
    (upd.)
Nicor Inc., 6; 86 (upd.)
NIPSCO Industries, Inc., 6
NiSource Inc., 109 (upd.)
Norsk Hydro ASA, 10; 35 (upd.); 109
    (upd.)
North West Water Group plc, 11
Northeast Utilities, V; 48 (upd.)
Northern States Power Company, V; 20
    (upd.)
Northwest Natural Gas Company, 45
NorthWestern Corporation, 37
Nova Corporation of Alberta, V
NRG Energy, Inc., 79
NSTAR, 106 (upd.)

Geographic Index

Brazil Fast Food Corporation, 74
Bunge Brasil S.A., 78
Camargo Corrêa S.A., 93
Casas Bahia Comercial Ltda., 75
Cia Hering, 72
Companhia Brasileira de Distribuiçao, 76
Companhia de Bebidas das Américas, 57
Companhia de Tecidos Norte de Minas - Coteminas, 77
Companhia Energética de Minas Gerais S.A. CEMIG, 65
Companhia Siderúrgica Nacional, 76
Companhia Suzano de Papel e Celulose S.A., 94
Cosan Ltd., 102
Cyrela Brazil Realty S.A. Empreendimentos e Participações, 110
EBX Investimentos, 104
Embratel Participações S.A., 119
Empresa Brasileira de Aeronáutica S.A. (Embraer), 36
G&K Holding S.A., 95
Gerdau S.A., 59
Globex Utilidades S.A., 103
Globo Comunicação e Participações S.A., 80
Gol Linhas Aéreas Inteligentes S.A., 73
Grendene S.A., 102
Grupo Martins, 104
Grupo Positivo, 105
Guararapes Confecções S.A., 118
Hypermarcas S.A., 117
Ipiranga S.A., 67
JBS S.A., 100
Klabin S.A., 73
Localiza Rent a Car S.A., 111
Lojas Americanas S.A., 77
Lojas Arapua S.A., 22; 61 (upd.)
Lojas Renner S.A., 107
Magazine Luiza S.A., 101
Marcopolo S.A. 79
Meridian Industries Inc., 107
Natura Cosméticos S.A., 75
Odebrecht S.A., 73
Perdigao SA, 52
Petróleo Brasileiro S.A., IV
Randon S.A. 79
Renner Herrmann S.A. 79
Sadia S.A., 59
Sao Paulo Alpargatas S.A., 75
Schincariol Participações e Representações S.A., 102
SLC Participações S.A., 111
Souza Cruz S.A., 65
TAM Linhas Aéreas S.A., 68
Tele Norte Leste Participações S.A., 80
Tigre S.A. Tubos e Conexões, 104
TransBrasil S/A Linhas Aéreas, 31
Tupy S.A., 111
Unibanco Holdings S.A., 73
UNIPAR – União de Indústrias Petroquímicas S.A., 108
Usinas Siderúrgicas de Minas Gerais S.A., 77
Vale S.A., IV; 43 (upd.); 117 (upd.)
VARIG S.A. (Viaçâo Aérea Rio-Grandense), 6; 29 (upd.)
Vicunha Têxtil S.A., 78

Votorantim Participaçoes S.A., 76
Vulcabras S.A., 103
Weg S.A., 78
White Martins Gases Industriais Ltda., 111

Brunei
Royal Brunei Airlines Sdn Bhd, 99
1-800-GOT-JUNK? LLC, 74

Canada
AbitibiBowater Inc., V; 25 (upd.); 99 (upd.)
Abitibi-Price Inc., IV
Agnico-Eagle Mines Limited, 71
Agrium Inc., 73
Ainsworth Lumber Co. Ltd., 99
Air Canada, 6; 23 (upd.); 59 (upd.)
AirBoss of America Corporation, 108
Alberta Energy Company Ltd., 16; 43 (upd.)
Alcan Aluminium Limited, IV; 31 (upd.)
Alderwoods Group, Inc., 68 (upd.)
Algo Group Inc., 24
Alimentation Couche-Tard Inc., 77
Alliance Atlantis Communications Inc., 39
Andrew Peller Ltd., 101
ATI Technologies Inc. 79
Axcan Pharma Inc., 85
Ballard Power Systems Inc., 73
Bank of Montreal, II; 46 (upd.)
Bank of Nova Scotia, The, II; 59 (upd.)
Barrick Gold Corporation, 34, 112 (upd.)
Bata Ltd., 62
BCE Inc., V; 44 (upd.)
Bell Canada, 6
BFC Construction Corporation, 25
Biovail Corporation, 47
BioWare Corporation, 81
Birks & Mayors Inc., 112
Bombardier Inc., 42 (upd.); 87 (upd.)
Boston Pizza International Inc., 88
Bradley Air Services Ltd., 56
Bramalea Ltd., 9
Brascan Corporation, 67
British Columbia Telephone Company, 6
Brookfield Properties Corporation, 89
Cameco Corporation, 77
Campeau Corporation, V
Canada Bread Company, Limited, 99
Canada Council for the Arts, 112
Canada Packers Inc., II
Canadair, Inc., 16
Canadian Broadcasting Corporation, 37; 109 (upd.)
Canadian Imperial Bank of Commerce, II; 61 (upd.)
Canadian National Railway Company, 6, 71 (upd.)
Canadian Pacific Railway Limited, V; 45 (upd.); 95 (upd.)
Canadian Solar Inc., 105
Canadian Tire Corporation, Limited, 71 (upd.)
Canadian Utilities Limited, 13; 56 (upd.)
Canam Group Inc., 114
Canfor Corporation, 42

Canlan Ice Sports Corp., 105
Canstar Sports Inc., 16
CanWest Global Communications Corporation, 35
Cascades Inc., 71
Catalyst Paper Corporation, 105
Celestica Inc., 80
CHC Helicopter Corporation, 67
Cinar Corporation, 40
Cineplex Odeon Corporation, 6; 23 (upd.)
Cinram International, Inc., 43
Cirque du Soleil Inc., 29; 98 (upd.)
Clearly Canadian Beverage Corporation, 48
Cloverdale Paint Inc., 115
Cognos Inc., 44
Cominco Ltd., 37
Compton Petroleum Corporation, 103
Consumers' Gas Company Ltd., 6
CoolBrands International Inc., 35
Corby Distilleries Limited, 14
Corel Corporation, 15; 33 (upd.); 76 (upd.)
Cott Corporation, 52
Creo Inc., 48
Dare Foods Limited, 103
Diavik Diamond Mines Inc., 85
Discreet Logic Inc., 20
Dofasco Inc., IV; 24 (upd.)
Doman Industries Limited, 59
Dominion Textile Inc., 12
Domtar Corporation, IV; 89 (upd.)
Dorel Industries Inc., 59
Duvernay Oil Corp., 83
Dylex Limited, 29
Dynatec Corporation, 87
easyhome Ltd., 105
Echo Bay Mines Ltd., IV; 38 (upd.)
Empire Industries Ltd., 114
Enbridge Inc., 43
EnCana Corporation, 109
ENMAX Corporation, 83
E1 Entertainment Ltd., 111
EPCOR Utilities Inc., 81
Extendicare Health Services, Inc., 6
Fairfax Financial Holdings Limited, 57
Fairmont Hotels & Resorts Inc., 69
Falconbridge Limited, 49
Finning International Inc., 69
Fortis, Inc., 15; 47 (upd.)
Forzani Group Ltd., The, 79
Four Seasons Hotels Limited, 9; 29 (upd.); 106 (upd.)
Future Shop Ltd., 62
Ganz, 98
GEAC Computer Corporation Ltd., 43
George Weston Ltd, II; 36 (upd.); 88 (upd.)
Gildan Activewear, Inc., 81
Goldcorp Inc., 87
GPS Industries, Inc., 81
Great Canadian Gaming Corporation, 114
Great-West Lifeco Inc., III
Groupe Vidéotron Ltée., 20
Hammond Manufacturing Company Limited, 83
Harlequin Enterprises Limited, 52

Cayman Islands

Chile

Sabaté Diosos SA, 48
SAFRAN, 102 (upd.)
Saft Groupe S.A., 113
SAGEM S.A., 37
Salomon Worldwide, 20
Sanofi-Synthélabo Group, The, I; 49
    (upd.)
Saur S.A.S., 92
Schneider Electric SA, II; 18 (upd.); 108
    (upd.)
SCOR S.A., 20
Seita, 23
Selectour SA, 53
Sephora Holdings S.A., 82
Simco S.A., 37
Skalli Group, 67
Skis Rossignol S.A., 15; 43 (upd.)
Smoby International SA, 56
Snecma Group, 46
Société Air France, 27 (upd.)
Société BIC S.A., 73
Societe des Produits Marnier-Lapostolle
    S.A., 88
Société d'Exploitation AOM Air Liberté
    SA (AirLib), 53
Société du Figaro S.A., 60
Société du Louvre, 27
Société Générale, II; 42 (upd.)
Société Industrielle Lesaffre, 84
Société Nationale des Chemins de Fer
    Français, V; 57 (upd.)
Société Nationale Elf Aquitaine, IV; 7
    (upd.)
Société Norbert Dentressangle S.A., 67
Sodexho SA, 29; 91 (upd.)
Sodiaal S.A., 36 (upd.)
SODIMA, II
Sommer-Allibert S.A., 19
Sperian Protection S.A., 104
Spir Communication S.A., 120
SR Teleperformance S.A., 86
Steria SA, 49
Suez Lyonnaise des Eaux, 36 (upd.)
Syral S.A.S., 113
Taittinger S.A., 43
Tati SA, 25
Technip, 78
Télévision Française 1, 23
Tergal Industries S.A.S., 102
Terrena L'Union CANA CAVAL, 70
Thales S.A., 42
THOMSON multimedia S.A., II; 42
    (upd.)
Tipiak S.A., 113
Total S.A., IV; 24 (upd.); 50 (upd.); 118
    (upd.)
Toupargel-Agrigel S.A., 76
Touton S.A., 92
Transiciel SA, 48
Trigano S.A., 102
Turbomeca S.A., 102
Ubisoft Entertainment S.A., 41; 106
    (upd.)
Ugine S.A., 20
Unibail SA, 40
Unilog SA, 42
Union des Assurances de Pans, III

Union Financière de France Banque SA,
    52
Usinor SA, IV; 42 (upd.)
Valeo, 23; 66 (upd.)
Vallourec SA, 54
Veolia Environnement, SA, 109
Vêt'Affaires S.A., 120
Veuve Clicquot Ponsardin SCS, 98
Vicat S.A., 70
Viel & Cie, 76
Vilmorin Clause et Cie, 70
Vinci S.A., 43; 113 (upd.)
Vivarte SA, 54 (upd.)
Vivendi, 46 (upd.); 112 (upd.)
Vranken Pommery Monopole S.A., 114
Wanadoo S.A., 75
Weber et Broutin France, 66
Worms et Cie, 27
Zodiac S.A., 36

Germany

A. Moksel AG, 59
A.W. Faber-Castell
    Unternehmensverwaltung GmbH &
    Co., 51
Aachener Printen- und Schokoladenfabrik
    Henry Lambertz GmbH & Co. KG,
    110
Adam Opel AG, 7; 21 (upd.); 61 (upd.)
adidas Group AG, 14; 33 (upd.); 75
    (upd.)
Adolf Würth GmbH & Co. KG, 49
AEG A.G., I
Air Berlin GmbH & Co. Luftverkehrs
    KG, 71
AIXTRON AG, 118
Aldi Einkauf GmbH & Co. OHG 13; 86
    (upd.)
Alfred Kärcher GmbH & Co KG, 94
Alfred Ritter GmbH & Co. KG, 58
Allgemeiner Deutscher Automobil-Club
    e.V., 100
Allianz SE, III; 15 (upd.); 57 (upd.); 119
    (upd.)
ALTANA AG, 87
AMB Generali Holding AG, 51
Andreas Stihl AG & Co. KG, 16; 59
    (upd.)
Anton Schlecker, 102
AOK–Bundesverband (Federation of the
    AOK), 78
Aral AG, 62
ARD, 41
August Storck KG, 66
AVA AG (Allgemeine Handelsgesellschaft
    der Verbraucher AG), 33
AXA Colonia Konzern AG, 27; 49 (upd.)
Axel Springer Verlag AG, IV; 20 (upd.)
Bahlsen GmbH & Co. KG, 44
Barmag AG, 39
BASF SE, I; 18 (upd.); 50 (upd.); 108
    (upd.)
Bauer Publishing Group, 7
Bayer A.G., I; 13 (upd.); 41 (upd.); 118
    (upd.)
Bayerische Hypotheken- und
    Wechsel-Bank AG, II
Bayerische Landesbank, 116

Bayerische Motoren Werke AG, I; 11
    (upd.); 38 (upd.); 108 (upd.)
Bayerische Vereinsbank A.G., II
Bayernwerk AG, V; 23 (upd.)
BayWa AG, 112
Beate Uhse AG, 96
Behr GmbH & Co. KG, 72
Beiersdorf AG, 29
Berentzen-Gruppe AG, 113
Berliner Stadtreinigungsbetriebe, 58
Berliner Verkehrsbetriebe (BVG), 58
Berlinwasser Holding AG, 90
Bertelsmann A.G., IV; 15 (upd.); 43
    (upd.); 91 (upd.)
Bewag AG, 39
Bibliographisches Institut & F.A.
    Brockhaus AG, 74
Bilfinger & Berger AG, I; 55 (upd.)
Bitburger Braugruppe GmbH, 110
Brauerei Beck & Co., 9; 33 (upd.)
Brauerei C. & A. Veltins GmbH & Co.
    KG, 120
Braun GmbH, 51; 109 (upd.)
Brenntag Holding GmbH & Co. KG, 8;
    23 (upd.); 101 (upd.)
BRITA GmbH, 112
Brose Fahrzeugteile GmbH & Company
    KG, 84
BSH Bosch und Siemens Hausgeräte
    GmbH, 67
Buderus AG, 37
Burda Holding GmbH. & Co., 23
C&A Brenninkmeyer KG, V
C. Bechstein Pianofortefabrik AG, 96
C.H. Boehringer Sohn, 39
Carl Kühne KG (GmbH & Co.), 94
Carl Zeiss AG, III; 34 (upd.); 91 (upd.)
CeWe Color Holding AG, 76
Commerzbank A.G., II; 47 (upd.)
Continental AG, V; 56 (upd.)
Cornelsen Verlagsholding GmbH & Co.,
    90
Dachser GmbH & Co. KG, 88
Daimler-Benz Aerospace AG, 16
DaimlerChrysler AG, I; 15 (upd.); 34
    (upd.); 64 (upd.)
Dalli-Werke GmbH & Co. KG, 86
dba Luftfahrtgesellschaft mbH, 76
Debeka Krankenversicherungsverein auf
    Gegenseitigkeit, 72
Degussa Group, IV
Degussa-Huls AG, 32 (upd.)
Deutsche Babcock A.G., III
Deutsche Bahn AG, 46 (upd.)
Deutsche Bank AG, II; 14 (upd.); 40
    (upd.); 114 (upd.)
Deutsche Börse AG, 59
Deutsche BP Aktiengesellschaft, 7
Deutsche Bundesbahn, V
Deutsche Bundespost TELEKOM, V
Deutsche Fussball Bund e.V., 98
Deutsche Lufthansa AG, I; 26 (upd.); 68
    (upd.)
Deutsche Messe AG, 104
Deutsche Post AG, 29; 108 (upd.)
Deutsche Steinzeug Cremer & Breuer
    Aktiengesellschaft, 91

United States